ALMANAC OF
BUSINESS
AND
INDUSTRIAL
FINANCIAL
RATIOS

2006 EDITION

LEO TROY, Ph.D.

CCH
a Wolters Kluwer business

Editorial Staff

Production...Christopher Zwirek
Design ....Craig Arritola

This publication is designed to provide accurate and authoritative information in regard to the subject matter covered. It is sold with the understanding
that the publisher is not engaged in rendering legal, accounting, or other
professional service and that the author is not offering such advice in this
publication. If legal advice or other professional assistance is required, the
services of a competent professional person should be sought.

ISBN: 0-8080-8989-7

© 2005, CCH INCORPORATED
4025 W. Peterson Avenue
Chicago, IL 60646-6085
1 800 248 3248
http://tax.cchgroup.com

Dedicated

**To Alexander, Suzannah, Dale, Ariel Sarah Troy, Abigayle Hannah Troy,
and Rachel Ilana Troy**

Preface

Now in its 37th Edition, the *Almanac of Business and Industrial Financial Ratios* provides a precise benchmark for evaluating an individual company's financial performance. The performance data is derived from the latest available IRS figures on U.S. and international companies, and tracks 50 operating and financial factors in 195 industries. The *Almanac* provides competitive norms in actual dollar amounts for revenue and capital factors, as well as important average operating costs in percent of net sales. It also provides other critical financial factors in percentage, including debt ratio, return on assets, return on equity, profit margin, and more. Beyond its reliable insights into corporate behavior, the *Almanac* can be used by other countries looking to model their economies on American performance.

Also included with the text, in a special pocket provided in the inside cover of the book, is a CD-ROM that contains all the materials found in the book including the explanatory discussion, the data tables, and the supporting index. Also included on the CD, but not in the book itself, is a special template that allows the reader to add individual company data of interest to compare and contrast with data from the book.

2006 Edition Highlights

The 2006 Edition of the *Almanac of Business and Industrial Financial Ratios* has been updated to include the following:

- **Broad scope:** *2006 Almanac* features the North American Industry Classification System (NAICS), so you can benchmark or analyze results consistently with corporations in the United States, Canada, and Mexico.

- **Most industry types:** *2006 Almanac* highlights most industry types, including industries with advanced technologies and newly emerging industries such as paging and wireless communications.

- **A truer picture** of corporate financial performance, since the data isn't based on a mixed bag of averages that might include partnerships or sole proprietors. *2006 Almanac* features a homogeneous universe of American corporate financial performance.

- **Many classifications:** *2006 Almanac* analyzes 195 industries with 50 financial performance items.

- **Benchmarks:** *2006 Almanac* provides 13 benchmarks, including such critical measures as Receipts to Cash Flow, Debt to Total Assets, and Return on Equity both before and after taxes.

- **Analytical tables:** *Table I, Corporations with and without Net Income (All Corporations), and Table II, Corporations with Net Income.*

- **Easier apples-to-apples comparisons:** Each table is divided into 13 asset sizes.

- **More comprehensive:** Total receipts of all corporations covered by *2006 Almanac* is $19.7 trillion, making the *Almanac* the Anatomy of American Corporate Capitalism.

Leo Troy, Ph. D.

November 2005

About the Author

Dr. Leo Troy is Professor of Economics at Rutgers University. He has been a faculty member of Rutgers for more than 40 years. In addition to authoring the widely praised *Almanac*, he has written many other books and articles published in leading journals. Professor Troy has been the recipient of numerous awards including two from the National Science Foundation, and two Fulbright grants. In addition, he has received numerous awards from private foundations. Dr. Troy received his Ph.D. from Columbia University and is a member of Phi Beta Kappa. He is a veteran of World War II with three battle stars and the combat infantry badge. He is the father of two children and is also a grandfather of three girls, including twins.

Acknowledgments

I wish to acknowledge the contributions of five people in particular for the development of the 37th Edition of the *Almanac*: Phil Wilson, Alan Kovar of Brighton Best, Lawrence R. Chodor, CPA, CVA, Wiss & Company, Marvin Sunshine, and Karen Kane.

Philip is responsible for the programming, which dealt with a very large amount of data, covering both the current and trend information. Alan, drawing upon his knowledge and experience as a CPA and Partner of Wiss and Company of Livingston, N.J., contributed significantly to the new content of the book. To Marvin Sunshine, Esq, my appreciation for actions and support that helped make the *Almanac* a continuing publication. Karen Kane is acknowledged for her contributions to the graphics of this issue.

Special acknowledgement is due my late friend and colleague, Stan Katz, CPA, and to Professor Emeritus of Accounting, Rutgers University, John Gilmour. I thank, too, Professor David Zaumeyer, Ph.D., CPA, and Director of Accounting at Rutgers, for recommending several ratios that continue to be included in the *Almanac*. I thank Mr. Ka-Neng Au, Business Librarian, Rutgers University, for significant contributions to the *Almanac*.

I wish to recognize, too, the cooperation of members of the Statistics of Income Division of the Internal Revenue Service—in particular, Ken Szeflinksi, Martha A. Harris, and Phylliss J. Whiles of the Corporation Returns Analysis Section. Without their data and its reliability, the Almanac would not be possible. Responsibility for the use of their facts and figures is, of course, solely my own. In this regard, I recall the valuable assistance I received from Barry Rosenstein, MBA, CPA, in checking procedures, in earlier editions, and which have continued into the current one. Finally, I wish to recognize the help of Suzannah B. Troy in bringing about the 37th annual edition of the *Almanac*. I anticipate continuation of her valuable assistance in subsequent editions.

INTRODUCTION

WHAT'S NEW IN THIS EDITION

Beginning with the year 2002, the *Almanac of Business and Industrial Financial Ratios* began using the North American Industry Classification System (NAICS). NAICS replaces the Internal Revenue Service's own system, which it had used for many years, an adaptation of Standard Industrial Classification (SIC); all previous *Almanacs* had used that adaptation.

The new industrial classification system is the product of the North American Free Trade Agreement (NAFTA), and it replaces the existing classification systems not only of the United States but also of Canada and Mexico. Hence, the new system applies uniformly to the three countries, and users of the *Almanac 2006*, utilizing the new international industrial classification system, can now compare their results with corporations in all three nations.

In the United States, the new manual was created by the Office of Management and Budget (OMB). The NAICS system gives special attention to industries producing and furnishing advanced technologies, new and emerging industries, as well as service industries in general. NAICS divides the economy into 21 sectors, five in the predominantly goods-producing area, and 16 in the service producing area.

INDUSTRY SECTORS

Particularly noteworthy is NAICS's introduction of an Information sector. This sector assembles the industries from Newspaper Publishers (511110) to Internet Service Providers, Web Portals, and Data Processing Services (518115). Within this span, NAICS and therefore the *Almanac* include such important industries as software publishing, database and directory publishing, satellite telecommunications, paging and cellular, and other wireless communications. NAICS and the *Almanac* also provide a category of industries on Professional, Scientific, and Technical Services, industries in which human capital is the major input. The sector includes Legal Services (541115) and Scientific Research and Development Services (541700), as well as Management, Scientific, and Technical Services (541600) and Computer Systems Design and Related Services (541515).

Other important sectors are the Arts, Entertainment, and Recreation including Amusement, Gambling, and Recreation (713105), and the Health Care and Social Assistance including Offices of Physicians (621115), Hospitals, Nursing, and Residential Care Facilities (622005). Within Manufacturing, the key goods sector industry, there is now a category embracing Computer and Electronic Product Manufacturing. It spans industries such as Computer and Peripheral Equipment (334110) to Navigational, Measuring, Electromedical, and Control Instruments (334500).

The source of the IRS's data are the tax returns of all *active* public and private corporations. Because the *Almanac's* data are derived only from corporate tax returns, there is a mixture of corporate with the financial performance of partnerships and individual proprietorships; the *Almanac's* information constitutes a **homogeneous universe**. The tax returns are classified by the IRS on the basis of the business activity which accounts for a corporation's largest percentage of total receipts. Large corporations with dissimilar business activities are included in only one industry, despite operations that are unrelated to the industry in which they are grouped.

The data developed by the IRS are derived from a stratified probability sample of corporation income tax returns. Where the sample data from the sample are small and should those numbers be used in a denominator, the result is reported as a hyphen (-) in the *Almanac*. Returns of the largest corporations are generally in the sample from year to year, but comparability can be affected by consolidations and mergers, changes in the law and the tax forms, and changes in the industrial classification system used over the years.

REPRESENTATIVE INDUSTRIES

The *Almanac* reports on 195 industries. Minor industries are denoted by a six-digit code; major industries are designated by a three-digit industry code; industrial sectors by a two-digit code; and industrial divisions by a two-digit code. When the data are the same for minor, major, sector, and industrial division, the IRS reports only the industrial division, and similarly for other identities applicable to the major and sectoral industries; the *Almanac* follows this procedure.

Almanac 2006 continues the previous coverage of reporting information: for all industries, **Table I, Corporations with and without Net Income** (that is, the entire universe of active reporting corporations), and **Table II, Corporations with Net Income**, a subset of the universe. In the *Almanac 2006*, Table I covers over 5.2 million enterprises (corporations), and Table II covers 2.8 million corporations with net income. This implies that 2.4 million corporations reported deficits. The IRS defines net income (or deficit) as the companies' net profit or loss from taxable sources of income reduced by allowable deductions. Total receipts of the 5 million corporations reported in *Almanac 2006* was $19.7 trillion, down by $500 million.

The *Almanac* continues to report performance results not only by the total for each industry, but by 12 other asset size groups (a total of 13 asset size groups), providing 50 items of data and/or ratios on corporate performance:

Total

Zero
$1 to $500,000
$500,001 to $1,000,000
$1,000,001 to $5,000,000
$5,000,001 to $10,000,000
$10,000,001 to $25,000,000
$25,000,001 to $50,000,000
$50,000,001 to $100,000,000
$100,000,001 to $250,000,000
$250,000,001 to $500,000,000
$500,000,001 to $2,500,000,000
$2,500,000,001 or more

All data in Tables I and II cover an accounting period identified on all tables and are the most recent information available from the IRS. For the *Almanac 2006*, the accounting period is July 2002 through June 2003. The dating of the data is counterbalanced by the most extensive industrial coverage available in any report on financial performance, the number of items of corporate performance, and their availability in thirteen asset size groups. Moreover, the timing of the data are also counterbalanced by the stability of the *Almanac's* values as past trends have indicated. Therefore, the *Almanac's* financial results are reliable in assessing current corporate performance.

Beyond its reliable insights into corporate behavior on a micro basis, its comprehensive and detailed coverage make the *Almanac* the **Anatomy of American Corporate Capitalism**. In this macro sense, it constitutes **the** example to those countries desirous of modeling their economies on the American performance.

HOW TO USE THE ALMANAC

On the micro level, the *Almanac* multiplies manyfold the power of financial analysis to evaluate an individual company's financial performance: In contrast to many standard reports, the *Almanac* gives management, and analysts independent of any company, more of the fundamental analytical tools needed to compare their company with companies in the same industry and of the same asset size. The *Almanac* can enhance the value of any company's annual report because it affords the analyst and the stockholder detailed background of financial information for comparison.

All items and ratios are listed in Both Table I and Table II. No figures are reported in the *Almanac* when the IRS has either suppressed the underlying data, or the sample size, or other reasons affecting a calculated result, and where the ratio/item was not applicable to an industry. The 50 tax-based items that provide that financial analysis are as follows:

1. Number of Enterprises

These are the count of corporate tax returns filed by active corporations on one of the Form 1120-series returns.

SPECIAL NOTE: Net Sales is used to compute the percentage of items 3 to 7 to Net Sales for all industries, except Finance, Insurance, and Real Estate (FIRE). For the FIRE industries, Total Receipts are used to compute the percentage of items 3 to 7.

REVENUES ($ IN THOUSANDS), ITEMS 2 TO 9

2. Operating Income (Net Sales)

This is the IRS item Business Receipts, the gross operating receipts reduced by the cost of returned goods and allowances.

3. Interest

Taxable interest includes interest on U.S. Government obligations, loans, notes, mortgages, arbitrage bonds, nonexempt private activity bonds, corporate bonds, bank deposits, and tax refunds; interest received from tax-exempt state or local municipal bonds and ESOP loans are not included in this item.

4. Rents

These are the gross amounts received from the use or occupancy of property by corporations whose principal activities did not involve operating rental properties.

5. Royalties

These are gross payments received for the use of property rights before taking deductions.

6. Other Portfolio Income

These consist of cash, notes, and accounts receivable, less allowance for bad debts and inventories.

7. Other Receipts

These receipts include such items as income from minor operations, cash discounts, claims, license rights, judgments, and joint ventures.

8. Total Receipts

Total receipts are the sum of ten items: 1. Business receipts; 2. Interest; 3. Interest on government obligations: state and local; 4. Rents; 5. Royalties; 6. Net capital gains (excluding long-term gains from regulated investment companies); 7. Net gain, noncapital assets; 8. Dividends received from domestic corporations; 9. Dividends received from foreign corporations; 10. Other receipts.

9. Average Total Receipts

Total receipts divided by the number of enterprises.

OPERATING COSTS/OPERATING INCOME, ITEMS 10 TO 22

10. Cost of Operations

This is the IRS's Costs of Goods Sold; it consists of the costs incurred in producing the goods or furnishing the services that generated the corporations' business receipts.

11. Salaries and Wages

These include the amount of salaries and wages paid as well as bonuses and director's fees, but no contributions to pension plans (see item 16) nor compensation of officers (see item 20).

12. Taxes Paid

Excludes Federal Income Taxes; they are the amounts paid for ordinary state and local taxes, social security, payroll taxes, unemployment insurance taxes, excise taxes, import and tariff duties, and business license and privilege taxes.

13. Interest Paid

These amounts consist of interest paid on all business indebtedness.

14. Depreciation

The charges allowed are governed principally by the IRS rules in effect in 1997, basically enacted in 1986, but also include other modifications. Hence, depreciation could represent amounts computed by different sets of rules.

15. Amortization and Depletion

Most amortization is calculated on a straight-line basis. Depletion is allowed for the exhaustion of natural deposits and timber.

16. Pensions, Profit-Sharing, Stock Bonus, and Annuity Plans

These are amounts deducted during the current year for qualified pension, profit-sharing, or other funded deferred compensation plans.

17. Employee Benefits

These are employer contributions to death benefit, insurance, health, accident, and sickness, and other welfare plans.

18. Advertising

Amounts include promotion and publicity expenses.

19. Other Expenses

These include expenses for repairs, bad debts, rent paid on business property, contributions and gifts, and expenses not allocable to specific deductible items.

20. Officers' Compensation

Salaries, wages, stock bonuses, bonds, and other forms of compensation are included in this item.

21. Operating Margin

This is the net income after all operating costs have been deducted.

22. Operating Margin Before Officers' Compensation

This measure takes into account the effect of Officers' Compensation on the operating margin.

SELECTED AVERAGE BALANCE SHEET ITEMS ($ IN THOUSANDS) ITEMS 23 TO 29

23. Average Net Receivables

The total of Notes and Accounts Receivable, less Allowance for Bad Debts, divided by the number of enterprises. Notes and Accounts Receivable are the gross amounts arising from business sales or services to customers on credit in the course of ordinary trade or business. This includes commercial paper, charge accounts, current intercompany receivables, property investment loans, and trade acceptances.

24. Average Inventories

Total inventories are divided by the number of enterprises. Inventories include finished goods, partially finished goods, new materials and supplies acquired for sale, merchandise on hand or in transit, and growing crops reported as assets by agricultural enterprises.

25. Average Net Property, Plant and Equipment

This includes depreciable assets less accumulated depreciation, depletable assets less accumulated depletion, and land; the sum is divided by the number of enterprises. Depreciable assets consist of end-of-year balance sheet tangible property, such as buildings and equipment used in trade or business, or held for the production of income, and that has a useful life of one year or more. The amount of accumulated depreciation represents the portion written off in the current year, as well as in prior years. Depletable assets represent the end-of-year value of mineral property, oil and gas wells, and other natural resources; standing timber; intangible development and drilling costs capitalized; and leases and leaseholds, subject to depletion. Accumulated depletion represents the cumulative adjustment of these assets.

26. Average Total Assets

Total Assets (and Total Liabilities) are amounts reported in the end-of-year balance sheet. Total Assets are net amounts after reduction from accumulated depreciation, accumulated amortization, accumulated depletion, and the reserve for bad debts. Total Liabilities include the claims of creditors and stockholders' equity, and were net after reduction by the cost of treasury stock. The average of total assets was obtained by dividing it by the number of enterprises.

27. Average of Notes and Loans Payable, and Mortgages

These liabilities were separated on the balance sheet according to the time to maturity of the obligations. Time to maturity was based on the date of the balance sheet, rather than the date of issue of the obligations. The total was divided by the number of enterprises.

28. Average of All Other Liabilities

These included accounts payable, and other liabilities including other current liabilities. The total was divided by the number of enterprises.

29. Average Net Worth

Net Worth represents the stockholders' equity in the corporation (total assets minus the claims of creditors). It consists of Capital Stock, Paid-In Capital Surplus, Retained Earnings Appropriated, Retained Earnings Unappropriated, less cost of treasury stock.

SELECTED FINANCIAL RATIOS, NUMBER OF TIMES TO ONE, RATIOS 30 TO 44

30. Current Ratio

The items that used Current Assets for this ratio are Cash; Notes and Accounts Receivable, Less: Allowance for Bad Debts; Inventories; Government Obligations; Tax-Exempt Securities; and Other Current Assets. For Current Liabilities, the following items were included: Accounts Payable; Mortgages and Notes Maturing in Less than 1 Year; and Other Current Liabilities.

This ratio, rated highest by CPAs as a measure of liquidity, gauges the ability of a company to meet its short-term financial obligations should it be compelled to liquidate its assets. However, it is not an absolute measure of the company's ability to meet its obligations. It is obtained by dividing current assets by current liabilities. The standard guideline has been a ratio of 2 to 1; however, some companies have found that in their experience, a ratio less than 2 to 1 is adequate, while others consider a larger one to be necessary. The ratio is affected by the method of valuation of inventory (LIFO or FIFO) and by inflation. The Almanac provides measures that can be treated as standards by size of asset.

31. Quick Ratio

This ratio is also known as the "Acid Test Ratio" because it is often used to estimate a company's general liquidity. There is some disagreement about the inclusion of inventory in the numerator because it may be slow moving, obsolete, or pledged to specific creditors, and, therefore, not be readily convertible into cash. The *Almanac* adopts a conservative approach and does not include the item in calculating the ratio. Excluding inventories and other current assets, the numerator is the same as that used in determining current assets. The denominator, current liabilities, is unchanged. The ratio of 1 to 1 has been considered a reasonable standard, but it is jeopardized because accounts and notes receivable may not be convertible into cash at face value and at short notice. The *Almanac* provides measures that can be treated as standards by size of asset.

32. Net Sales to Working Capital

This is an efficiency, or turnover, ratio that measures the rate at which current assets less current liabilities (Working Capital) is used in making sales. (In industries in Finance, Insurance, and Real Estate, total receipts rather than net sales is used.) A low ratio indicates a less efficient (profitable) use of working capital in making sales. The *Almanac* provides measures that can be treated as standards by size of asset. Working Capital is the difference between current assets and current liabilities.

33. *Coverage Ratio*

This ratio measures the number of times all interest paid by the company is covered by earnings before interest charges and taxes (EBIT). For that reason, the ratio is also known as the "times interest earned ratio." The ratio indicates the company's ability to service its debt based on its income.

34. *Total Asset Turnover*

The ratio is an efficiency ratio because it indicates the effectiveness of the company's use of its total assets in generating sales. It is measured by dividing total assets by sales.

35. *Inventory Turnover*

Inventory turnover measures the liquidity of the inventory. It is computed by dividing the cost of goods sold by the average inventory. The result shows the number of times that the average inventory can be converted into receivables or cash. The ratio reflects both on the quality of the inventory and the efficiency of management. Typically, the higher the turnover rate, the more likely profits will be higher.

SPECIAL NOTE: Inventory turnover is not computed for industries in Finance, Insurance, and Real Estate.

36. *Receivables Turnover*

This ratio measures the liquidity of accounts receivable. It indicates the average collection period throughout the year. It is obtained by dividing sales average by net receivables. It is not computed in the Finance, Insurance, and Real Estate industries (although it is calculated for all other industries even though conventional analysis typically omits it) for many of the industries in the *Almanac*.

37. *Total Liabilities to Net Worth*

This ratio indicates the extent to which the company's funds are supplied by short- and long-term creditors compared to its owners. It is an indicator of the company's long-term debt paying ability. The ratio is one of the most important bearing on the company's capital structure. Net worth is defined in ratio 29.

38. *Current Assets to Working Capital*

The dependence of Working Capital in part on current assets is important to understanding this part of the source of Working Capital. Current Assets are defined in ratio 30 and Working Capital is defined in ratio 32.

39. *Current Liabilities to Working Capital*

The dependence of Working Capital in part on current liabilities is important to understanding this part of the source of Working Capital. Current Liabilities are defined in ratio 30 and Working Capital is defined in ratio 32.

40. *Working Capital to Net Sales or Total Receipts*

The purpose of this ratio is to determine the working capital needed in relation to projected sales or receipts. Working Capital is defined in ratio 32.

41. *Inventory to Working Capital*

This ratio, by showing the proportion of Working Capital invested in Inventory, indicates the part of Current Assets that are least liquid. Inventories which exceed working capital indicate that current liabilities exceed liquid current assets. Working Capital is defined in ratio 32.

42. Total Receipts to Cash Flow

Cash Flow is the difference between cash receipts and cash disbursements. The ratio of total receipts to cash flow could suggest steps which management might take to improve the company's cash position.

43. Cost of Goods to Cash Flow

This ratio can be the basis for projections of cash requirements needed to fund projected costs of production. Cash flow is defined in ratio 42.

44. Cash Flow to Total Debt

This ratio indicates the extent to which a company could service its total debt from cash flow. It is analogous to the coverage ratio; refer to ratio 33. Cash flow is defined in ratio 42.

SELECTED FINANCIAL FACTORS (IN PERCENTAGES), ITEMS 45 TO 50

45. Debt Ratio (Total Liabilities to Total Assets)

This ratio indicates the company's ability to pay all its debts. It measures the creditors' and owners' of the company's ability to withstand losses. It is an indicator of the long-run solvency of the firm.

46. Return on Total Assets

The ratio combines the turnover and profit ratios (Sales/Total Assets x [times] Profit/Sales) and yields the return on investment (Total Assets). The result is the end product of the DuPont System of financial analysis. The system takes into account both operating income and operating assets. In Table I of each industry, the Return on Investment (ROI) is net income less deficit before income taxes divided by total assets. In Table II of each industry, the ROI is net income before income taxes divided by Total Assets. Total Assets are used because management has discretion in the investment of the resources provided by both the creditors and owners.

47. Return on Equity Before Income Taxes

This ratio measures the profitability of the company's operations to owners, before income taxes. For Table I this is net income, less deficit before income taxes and before credits. For Table II this is net income minus income tax before credits.

48. Return on Equity After Income Taxes

This ratio measures the profitability of the company's operations to owners, after income taxes. For Table I this is net income, less deficit and minus income tax before credits. For Table II this is net income minus income tax and before credits.

49. Profit Margin (Before Income Tax)

This is net income before income tax divided by net sales (or total receipts) and indicates the contribution of sales to the profitability of the company. Competition, capital structure, and operating characteristics cause the margin to vary within and among industries. For Table I, net income less deficit and before income taxes is the numerator; for Table II it is net income before tax.

50. Profit Margin (After Income Tax)

This ratio is the same as ratio 49 except that income taxes are taken into account.

SPECIAL NOTE: The NAICS (North American Industrial Classification System) was revised in 2002 with substantial changes in the construction (23) and information (51) sectors. Both the wholesale trade (42) and retail trade (44) sectors also saw reclassifications and re-numbering. New categories of business activity include Wholesale electronic markets (425115), Internet publishing and broadcasting (516100), and Internet service providers and web portals (518115).

Table of Contents

Page references to tables for industries with net income are in italic

PRINCIPAL BUSINESS ACTIVITY (BASED ON NAICS)

ALMANAC
of Business and Industrial
FINANCIAL RATIOS

37th ANNUAL EDITION
2006

Table I

Corporations with and without Net Income

AGRICULTURAL PRODUCTION

MONEY AMOUNTS AND SIZE OF ASSETS IN THOUSANDS OF DOLLARS

Item Description for Accounting Period 7/02 Through 6/03	Total	Zero Assets	Under 500	500 to 1,000	1,000 to 5,000	5,000 to 10,000	10,000 to 25,000	25,000 to 50,000	50,000 to 100,000	100,000 to 250,000	250,000 to 500,000	500,000 to 2,500,000	2,500,000 and over
Number of Enterprises **1**	101066	7983	64105	14349	13020	953	401	128	70	42	8	7	0
Revenues ($ in Thousands)													
Net Sales **2**	76825908	599480	10551831	9487354	17154337	7544363	6030989	5013092	5048922	6384331	2185408	6825802	0
Interest **3**	302630	6513	36928	30233	81543	31864	25008	13100	17812	24616	11942	23071	0
Rents **4**	717010	29136	169523	131263	229527	48659	25861	15661	44161	8460	3870	10889	0
Royalties **5**	126123	2903	6262	3811	8803	533	7870	229	12425	2694	985	79607	0
Other Portfolio Income **6**	1390560	104904	203104	140502	402766	69068	180614	50636	73698	93287	12833	59145	0
Other Receipts **7**	7296266	153013	2331244	837929	2590048	398261	250660	142342	194469	138515	55576	204211	0
Total Receipts **8**	86665497	895949	13298892	10631092	20467024	8092748	6521002	5235060	5391487	6651903	2270614	7202725	0
Average Total Receipts **9**	857	112	207	741	1572	8492	16262	40899	77021	158379	283827	1028961	•
Operating Costs/Operating Income (%)													
Cost of Operations **10**	53.5	43.9	26.7	44.9	42.3	61.1	63.3	64.5	67.7	75.3	82.8	69.9	•
Salaries and Wages **11**	9.5	10.2	13.6	10.2	12.2	8.1	8.1	7.1	5.9	5.4	2.1	9.1	•
Taxes Paid **12**	2.5	4.3	3.8	3.5	3.2	1.8	2.0	1.6	1.2	1.9	1.9	1.1	•
Interest Paid **13**	3.1	3.9	3.8	2.8	4.4	2.7	2.3	2.1	1.9	2.3	1.5	3.1	•
Depreciation **14**	6.8	8.9	10.7	7.2	8.9	5.9	5.2	4.5	4.7	4.9	4.7	3.1	•
Amortization and Depletion **15**	0.2	0.6	0.0	0.1	0.1	0.1	0.1	0.3	0.4	0.9	0.2	0.6	•
Pensions and Other Deferred Comp. **16**	0.2	0.1	0.1	0.2	0.2	0.2	0.2	0.2	0.1	0.2	0.3	0.4	•
Employee Benefits **17**	1.1	0.6	1.4	1.4	1.0	0.7	0.8	0.9	0.6	0.9	0.9	2.6	•
Advertising **18**	0.4	0.9	0.4	0.4	0.4	0.2	0.3	0.4	0.2	0.3	0.1	0.7	•
Other Expenses **19**	34.6	54.4	68.4	39.0	45.3	27.9	24.4	21.3	22.0	10.1	6.7	14.4	•
Officers' Compensation **20**	2.1	2.8	4.0	3.0	3.1	1.1	1.4	1.2	0.7	0.8	0.6	0.4	•
Operating Margin **21**	•	•	•	•	•	•	•	•	•	•	•	•	•
Operating Margin Before Officers' Comp. **22**	•	•	•	•	•	•	•	•	•	•	•	•	•

Selected Average Balance Sheet ($ in Thousands)

	•	•	•	•	•	•	•	•	•	•	•	•
Net Receivables 23	68	0	4	20	82	378	1763	4923	8628	22584	15474	271346
Inventories 24	83	0	10	41	169	836	1984	4764	11418	15328	53334	128248
Net Property, Plant and Equipment 25	420	0	95	433	1099	3624	7027	15054	30902	62446	136404	250178
Total Assets 26	847	0	163	704	1825	6931	14983	34490	70612	151189	322434	1479302
Notes and Loans Payable 27	452	0	136	407	1080	4136	7396	16784	29347	53583	91335	418989
All Other Liabilities 28	116	0	12	47	139	880	2206	5529	12913	34064	91035	424364
Net Worth 29	279	0	15	250	606	1915	5382	12177	28353	63543	140063	635949

Selected Financial Ratios (Times to 1)

	•	•	•	•	•	•	•	•	•	•	•	•
Current Ratio 30	1.2	•	1.2	1.2	1.0	1.3	1.3	1.5	1.4	1.0	1.3	
Quick Ratio 31	0.6	•	0.8	0.6	0.3	0.7	0.7	0.8	0.7	0.3	0.7	
Net Sales to Working Capital 32	16.7	•	26.0	20.9	220.5	11.4	12.9	7.4	10.6	102.6	8.5	
Coverage Ratio 33	0.6	5.7	•	0.8	0.6	0.0	0.9	1.2	1.7	1.4	2.3	1.3
Total Asset Turnover 34	0.9	•	1.0	0.9	0.7	1.0	1.1	1.0	1.0	0.8	0.7	
Inventory Turnover 35	4.9	•	4.6	7.2	3.3	5.8	4.8	5.3	4.3	7.5	4.2	5.3
Receivables Turnover 36	11.2	•	34.5	31.8	17.4	15.7	8.2	7.9	8.2	7.7	6.2	4.3
Total Liabilities to Net Worth 37	2.0	•	10.0	1.8	2.6	1.8	1.8	1.5	1.4	1.3	1.3	
Current Assets to Working Capital 38	5.3	•	6.0	6.8	54.4	4.1	4.4	3.0	3.6	30.8	4.4	
Current Liabilities to Working Capital 39	4.3	•	5.0	5.8	53.4	3.1	3.4	2.0	2.6	29.8	3.4	
Working Capital to Net Sales 40	0.1	•	0.0	0.0	0.0	0.1	0.1	0.1	0.1	0.0	0.1	
Inventory to Working Capital 41	1.8	•	1.4	2.1	25.8	1.4	1.4	1.2	1.1	17.3	1.2	
Total Receipts to Cash Flow 42	4.4	2.1	2.9	3.9	5.4	5.9	5.2	5.0	12.1	18.2	8.7	
Cost of Goods to Cash Flow 43	2.4	0.9	0.8	1.8	3.3	3.7	3.4	3.4	9.2	15.1	6.1	
Cash Flow to Total Debt 44	0.3	•	0.4	0.3	0.3	0.3	0.3	0.3	0.1	0.1	0.1	

Selected Financial Factors (in Percentages)

	•	•	•	•	•	•	•	•	•	•	•	•
Debt Ratio 45	67.0	•	90.9	64.4	66.8	72.4	64.1	64.7	59.8	58.0	56.6	57.0
Return on Total Assets 46	1.7	•	•	2.0	1.8	0.1	2.2	2.9	3.3	3.4	3.0	2.7
Return on Equity Before Income Taxes 47	•	•	•	•	•	•	•	1.7	3.5	2.4	4.0	1.5
Return on Equity After Income Taxes 48	•	•	•	•	•	•	•	0.4	2.2	1.6	1.5	0.8
Profit Margin (Before Income Tax) 49	•	18.7	•	•	•	•	•	0.5	1.4	1.0	2.1	1.0
Profit Margin (After Income Tax) 50	•	16.0	•	•	•	0.1	0.1	0.1	0.9	0.7	0.8	0.5

1

Table II

Corporations with Net Income

AGRICULTURAL PRODUCTION

MONEY AMOUNTS AND SIZE OF ASSETS IN THOUSANDS OF DOLLARS

Item Description for Accounting Period 7/02 Through 6/03	Total	Zero Assets	Under 100	100 to 250	251 to 500	501 to 1,000	1,001 to 5,000	5,001 to 10,000	10,001 to 25,000	25,001 to 50,000	50,001 to 100,000	100,001 to 250,000	250,001 and over
Number of Enterprises **1**	46213	2484	27226	8817	6974	384	188	67	41	24	4	4	0
Revenues ($ in Thousands)													
Net Sales **2**	45083958	350289	5952643	7238867	10518819	3844438	3206523	3079747	3307160	4170849	1263350	2154274	0
Interest **3**	192406	4257	26548	22436	60851	19234	17395	7780	12256	13590	2294	5765	0
Rents **4**	493895	457	107926	110884	161094	43837	14744	5638	35566	3889	1328	8531	0
Royalties **5**	49902	2893	5678	25	4257	85	7186	194	12274	1852	925	14532	0
Other Portfolio Income **6**	1006393	93559	143934	95641	274015	41586	154748	42478	50677	87088	4241	18430	0
Other Receipts **7**	4397912	85752	1221818	632621	1643913	190692	116264	63855	172291	99613	42047	129044	0
Total Receipts **8**	51224466	537207	7458547	8100474	12662949	4136872	3516860	3199692	3590224	4376881	1314185	2330576	0
Average Total Receipts **9**	1108	216	274	919	1816	10773	18707	47757	87566	182370	328546	582644	•
Operating Costs/Operating Income (%)													
Cost of Operations **10**	52.6	34.9	35.1	47.5	42.9	64.2	62.3	68.6	59.8	70.3	76.0	50.7	•
Salaries and Wages **11**	9.2	4.5	10.7	9.5	11.4	5.8	8.4	6.1	7.2	6.6	2.4	18.1	•
Taxes Paid **12**	2.5	4.2	3.5	3.3	3.1	1.6	2.1	1.7	1.3	2.0	2.0	0.7	•
Interest Paid **13**	2.3	3.0	2.3	1.8	3.2	1.4	1.7	1.5	1.8	2.6	1.0	2.9	•
Depreciation **14**	5.4	4.1	6.4	5.7	7.2	4.0	4.0	3.6	4.8	4.4	4.2	4.4	•
Amortization and Depletion **15**	0.2	0.1	0.0	0.0	0.1	0.1	0.1	0.1	0.3	0.9	0.1	1.0	•
Pensions and Other Deferred Comp. **16**	0.2	0.1	0.2	0.2	0.2	0.1	0.3	0.2	0.2	0.2	0.4	0.1	•
Employee Benefits **17**	1.3	0.2	1.2	1.3	0.9	0.6	0.9	1.0	0.6	1.3	1.3	6.2	•
Advertising **18**	0.4	0.1	0.4	0.5	0.3	0.2	0.3	0.5	0.2	0.3	0.1	1.5	•
Other Expenses **19**	29.6	42.2	50.3	33.1	39.6	23.3	19.0	13.5	25.5	11.0	8.8	15.1	•
Officers' Compensation **20**	2.2	2.4	4.3	2.6	3.2	1.1	1.6	1.1	0.6	0.9	0.9	0.9	•
Operating Margin **21**	•	4.3	•	•	•	•	•	2.0	•	2.8	•	•	•
Operating Margin Before Officers' Comp. **22**	•	6.7	•	•	•	•	0.9	3.1	•	3.7	0.5	•	•

Selected Average Balance Sheet ($ in Thousands)

Net Receivables 23	67	0	5	25	70	285	1973	6212	10389	27972	14052	52693
Inventories 24	96	0	7	42	173	809	2060	5003	9777	13840	86042	87851
Net Property, Plant and Equipment 25	440	0	87	402	983	3347	5783	13170	29992	74251	106754	211795
Total Assets 26	905	0	165	700	1732	6678	15004	35013	71416	162268	303370	826653
Notes and Loans Payable 27	350	0	81	248	716	2688	5620	13321	28187	61893	89949	202928
All Other Liabilities 28	124	0	15	45	130	721	2646	5717	13367	42447	59840	261438
Net Worth 29	431	0	69	407	886	3269	6738	15975	29863	57929	153582	362286

Selected Financial Ratios (Times to 1)

Current Ratio 30	1.4	•	1.3	1.4	1.6	1.2	1.5	1.7	1.5	1.3	3.8	1.1
Quick Ratio 31	0.8	•	0.9	0.8	0.8	0.4	0.8	0.9	0.9	0.7	1.0	0.4
Net Sales to Working Capital 32	11.8	•	20.4	16.6	9.8	41.0	8.6	7.3	8.5	14.1	3.4	31.3
Coverage Ratio 33	4.4	20.5	5.7	4.4	3.6	4.6	6.2	4.9	4.4	2.7	7.7	3.2
Total Asset Turnover 34	1.1	•	1.3	1.2	0.9	1.5	1.1	1.3	1.1	1.1	1.0	0.7
Inventory Turnover 35	5.3	•	10.4	9.2	3.7	7.9	5.2	6.3	4.9	8.8	2.8	3.1
Receivables Turnover 36	12.4	•	38.7	44.2	20.9	22.4	7.7	8.3	7.4	8.6	45.0	20.4
Total Liabilities to Net Worth 37	1.1	•	1.4	0.7	1.0	1.0	1.2	1.2	1.4	1.8	1.0	1.3
Current Assets to Working Capital 38	3.3	•	4.0	3.5	2.8	7.6	3.1	2.5	3.1	4.7	1.4	11.8
Current Liabilities to Working Capital 39	2.3	•	3.0	2.5	1.8	6.6	2.1	1.5	2.1	3.7	0.4	10.8
Working Capital to Net Sales 40	0.1	•	0.0	0.1	0.1	0.0	0.1	0.1	0.1	0.1	0.3	0.0
Inventory to Working Capital 41	1.1	•	0.5	1.0	1.0	2.9	0.9	0.8	1.0	1.3	0.9	5.1
Total Receipts to Cash Flow 42	3.7	1.3	2.5	3.7	2.9	4.3	5.2	5.9	3.5	8.4	9.1	5.6
Cost of Goods to Cash Flow 43	1.9	0.5	0.9	1.8	1.2	2.8	3.2	4.0	2.1	5.9	6.9	2.9
Cash Flow to Total Debt 44	0.6	•	0.9	0.8	0.6	0.7	0.4	0.4	0.6	0.2	0.2	0.2

Selected Financial Factors (in Percentages)

Debt Ratio 45	52.4	•	58.2	41.9	48.8	51.1	55.1	54.4	58.2	64.3	49.4	56.2
Return on Total Assets 46	10.7	•	17.5	9.5	9.9	10.0	12.1	9.7	9.1	7.5	8.1	6.1
Return on Equity Before Income Taxes 47	17.4	•	34.5	12.7	14.0	16.1	22.7	17.0	16.9	13.3	14.0	9.7
Return on Equity After Income Taxes 48	15.7	•	32.8	11.9	12.9	14.8	18.8	15.2	14.9	11.7	9.3	7.6
Profit Margin (Before Income Tax) 49	7.7	57.6	10.9	6.3	8.2	5.2	9.0	5.9	6.2	4.4	6.8	6.5
Profit Margin (After Income Tax) 50	6.9	53.1	10.4	5.9	7.6	4.9	7.4	5.3	5.5	3.9	4.5	5.1

Table I

Corporations with and without Net Income

FORESTRY AND LOGGING

MONEY AMOUNTS AND SIZE OF ASSETS IN THOUSANDS OF DOLLARS

Item Description for Accounting Period 7/02 Through 6/03	Total	Zero Assets	Under 500	500 to 1,000	1,000 to 5,000	5,000 to 10,000	10,000 to 25,000	25,000 to 50,000	50,000 to 100,000	100,000 to 250,000	250,000 to 500,000	500,000 to 2,500,000	2,500,000 and over
Number of Enterprises **1**	11527	647	8656	1190	918	23	55	24	6	4	0	3	0
Revenues ($ in Thousands)													
Net Sales **2**	10488380	68687	2773356	2323768	2857389	92902	661932	565768	242120	394222	0	508236	0
Interest **3**	41396	219	4856	736	7794	175	2205	2468	2017	4925	0	16002	0
Rents **4**	38945	367	6449	1348	4788	281	1649	7112	722	727	0	15503	0
Royalties **5**	2578	0	0	1812	0	0	66	0	424	0	0	277	0
Other Portfolio Income **6**	214627	8633	33770	11389	17923	646	13843	10694	9401	27710	0	80618	0
Other Receipts **7**	142238	-19116	36934	11609	51094	-9133	9703	10978	5408	9292	0	35466	0
Total Receipts **8**	10928164	58790	2855365	2350662	2938988	84871	689398	597020	260092	436876	0	656102	0
Average Total Receipts **9**	948	91	330	1975	3202	3690	12535	24876	43349	109219	·	218701	·
Operating Costs/Operating Income (%)													
Cost of Operations **10**	63.8	14.3	52.6	56.6	64.5	82.5	76.6	90.6	81.3	80.3	·	89.4	·
Salaries and Wages **11**	7.4	16.9	8.0	8.0	9.1	6.5	4.5	4.5	4.9	2.4	·	3.6	·
Taxes Paid **12**	2.0	1.1	2.0	1.8	2.5	1.7	2.4	2.1	1.9	1.6	·	0.8	·
Interest Paid **13**	3.0	3.5	2.2	1.2	1.6	1.1	1.9	1.8	0.7	4.1	·	26.3	·
Depreciation **14**	7.7	12.2	10.0	8.0	7.7	1.5	3.8	2.8	1.9	10.2	·	5.1	·
Amortization and Depletion **15**	0.8	0.6	0.0	0.0	0.0	0.0	1.8	0.6	1.7	10.9	·	2.9	·
Pensions and Other Deferred Comp. **16**	0.2	·	0.2	0.3	0.3	·	0.4	0.3	0.1	0.3	·	0.0	·
Employee Benefits **17**	0.8	0.0	0.9	0.6	1.2	1.0	1.2	0.3	0.9	0.3	·	0.2	·
Advertising **18**	0.1	0.0	0.1	0.1	0.1	0.0	0.1	0.0	0.1	0.1	·	0.4	·
Other Expenses **19**	18.3	126.3	21.6	19.5	15.6	9.6	9.9	5.6	10.0	24.3	·	20.3	·
Officers' Compensation **20**	3.2	0.3	5.7	2.8	3.0	1.2	1.8	1.1	1.0	0.4	·	0.7	·
Operating Margin **21**	·	·	·	1.0	·	·	·	·	·	·	·	·	·
Operating Margin Before Officers' Comp. **22**	·	·	2.4	3.8	·	·	·	·	·	·	·	·	·

Selected Average Balance Sheet ($ in Thousands)

Net Receivables 23	45	0	5	36	107	166	1314	1530	4938	7787	54003	•
Inventories 24	38	0	4	4	156	455	1869	1404	3766	7036	19515	•
Net Property, Plant and Equipment 25	447	0	74	477	1094	650	6415	18280	20424	113374	518807	•
Total Assets 26	774	0	111	688	2062	6218	14999	34478	66458	203706	747606	•
Notes and Loans Payable 27	430	0	95	381	982	1249	4902	10764	8972	72322	625618	•
All Other Liabilities 28	78	0	7	45	193	242	1284	2703	3950	50654	80311	•
Net Worth 29	266	0	9	262	887	4727	8813	21011	53537	80730	41677	•

Selected Financial Ratios (Times to 1)

Current Ratio 30	1.4	•	1.1	1.0	1.4	4.3	1.8	1.9	4.2	1.7	1.1	•
Quick Ratio 31	0.8	•	0.8	0.8	0.9	0.8	0.9	0.9	1.8	0.5	0.5	•
Net Sales to Working Capital 32	16.6	•	122.7	•	16.4	3.2	6.2	6.1	2.3	6.7	10.1	•
Coverage Ratio 33	•	•	0.8	2.8	•	•	0.9	•	4.6	•	0.2	•
Total Asset Turnover 34	1.2	•	2.9	2.8	1.5	0.6	0.8	0.7	0.6	0.5	0.2	•
Inventory Turnover 35	15.4	•	45.6	309.8	12.9	7.3	4.9	15.2	8.7	11.2	7.8	•
Receivables Turnover 36	18.8	•	44.9	69.2	26.6	18.5	8.2	18.4	9.1	7.1	3.2	•
Total Liabilities to Net Worth 37	1.9	•	11.9	1.6	1.3	0.3	0.7	0.6	0.2	1.5	16.9	•
Current Assets to Working Capital 38	3.4	•	9.8	•	3.3	1.3	2.3	2.1	1.3	2.4	8.2	•
Current Liabilities to Working Capital 39	2.4	•	8.8	•	2.3	0.3	1.3	1.1	0.3	1.4	7.2	•
Working Capital to Net Sales 40	0.1	•	0.0	•	0.1	0.3	0.2	0.2	0.4	0.1	0.1	•
Inventory to Working Capital 41	0.7	•	1.8	•	1.0	0.4	0.8	0.5	0.2	0.5	1.0	•
Total Receipts to Cash Flow 42	10.2	4.9	6.3	5.8	12.3	•	15.3	•	10.7	•	•	•
Cost of Goods to Cash Flow 43	6.5	0.7	3.3	3.3	7.9	•	11.7	•	8.7	•	•	•
Cash Flow to Total Debt 44	0.2	•	0.5	0.8	0.2	0.1	0.7	0.6	0.3	•	•	•

Selected Financial Factors (in Percentages)

Debt Ratio 45	65.6	•	92.3	62.0	57.0	24.0	41.2	39.1	19.4	60.4	94.4	•
Return on Total Assets 46	•	•	5.2	9.4	•	•	1.4	•	2.0	•	1.3	•
Return on Equity Before Income Taxes 47	•	•	•	16.0	•	•	•	•	1.9	•	•	•
Return on Equity After Income Taxes 48	•	•	•	15.6	•	•	•	•	0.9	•	•	•
Profit Margin (Before Income Tax) 49	•	•	•	2.1	•	•	•	•	2.6	•	•	•
Profit Margin (After Income Tax) 50	•	•	•	2.1	•	•	•	•	1.2	•	•	•

3

Table II

Corporations with Net Income

FORESTRY AND LOGGING

MONEY AMOUNTS AND SIZE OF ASSETS IN THOUSANDS OF DOLLARS

Item Description for Accounting Period 7/02 Through 6/03	Total	Zero Assets	Under 500	500 to 1,000	1,000 to 5,000	5,000 to 10,000	10,000 to 25,000	25,000 to 50,000	50,000 to 100,000	100,000 to 250,000	250,000 to 500,000	500,000 to 2,500,000	2,500,000 and over
Number of Enterprises **1**	5281	503	3647	750	344	3	25	6	3	0	0	0	0
Revenues ($ in Thousands)													
Net Sales **2**	5722791	58427	1484467	1915081	1293797	27549	488563	282915	171993	0	0	0	0
Interest **3**	11263	19	3924	689	3489	170	1684	783	505	0	0	0	0
Rents **4**	19054	213	6449	677	2770	7	1620	6788	529	0	0	0	0
Royalties **5**	2301	0	0	1812	0	0	66	0	424	0	0	0	0
Other Portfolio Income **6**	66735	8633	18929	1253	12114	17	12271	4859	8661	0	0	0	0
Other Receipts **7**	62187	8	35475	9067	4787	86	4850	6599	1312	0	0	0	0
Total Receipts **8**	5884331	67300	1549244	1928579	1316957	27829	509054	301944	183424	0	0	0	0
Average Total Receipts **9**	1114	134	425	2571	3828	9276	20362	50324	61141	•	•	•	•
Operating Costs/Operating Income (%)													
Cost of Operations **10**	63.0	1.6	54.2	64.1	62.4	70.7	75.3	86.5	78.3	•	•	•	•
Salaries and Wages **11**	6.8	19.4	7.8	6.7	7.3	5.8	3.5	5.0	5.1	•	•	•	•
Taxes Paid **12**	1.8	0.6	1.9	1.4	2.3	2.4	2.2	1.5	1.6	•	•	•	•
Interest Paid **13**	1.3	0.5	1.6	0.8	1.5	0.8	1.7	0.8	0.6	•	•	•	•
Depreciation **14**	6.3	12.5	9.5	5.3	6.8	1.3	3.2	1.6	1.6	•	•	•	•
Amortization and Depletion **15**	0.0	0.6	0.0	0.0	0.0	•	0.1	0.2	0.1	•	•	•	•
Pensions and Other Deferred Comp. **16**	0.3	•	0.3	0.3	0.2	•	0.4	0.1	0.0	•	•	•	•
Employee Benefits **17**	0.9	•	1.5	0.3	1.1	0.9	1.2	0.4	1.0	•	•	•	•
Advertising **18**	0.1	0.0	0.1	0.1	0.3	0.1	0.1	0.0	0.1	•	•	•	•
Other Expenses **19**	14.8	62.8	15.6	16.4	14.8	3.6	9.3	5.2	7.8	•	•	•	•
Officers' Compensation **20**	2.9	0.3	5.8	2.0	2.2	3.6	1.5	1.2	0.5	•	•	•	•
Operating Margin **21**	1.8	1.7	1.7	2.6	1.2	10.7	1.5	•	3.2	•	•	•	•
Operating Margin Before Officers' Comp. **22**	4.6	2.0	7.5	4.6	3.3	14.3	3.0	•	3.8	•	•	•	•

Selected Average Balance Sheet ($ in Thousands)

Net Receivables 23	35	0	8	55	144	756	1688	1708	2831
Inventories 24	43	0	6	6	279	2908	2535	1315	7649
Net Property, Plant and Equipment 25	226	0	86	458	690	943	6419	13318	19110
Total Assets 26	484	0	146	738	1899	9358	15724	33295	65235
Notes and Loans Payable 27	228	0	98	404	859	3884	6352	10851	3758
All Other Liabilities 28	34	0	13	53	79	420	1463	2180	5248
Net Worth 29	222	0	35	281	962	5055	7909	20264	56229

Selected Financial Ratios (Times to 1)

Current Ratio 30	1.6	•	1.5	0.9	1.9	3.0	2.0	2.3	8.1
Quick Ratio 31	0.9	•	1.1	0.7	0.8	0.9	0.9	1.1	2.4
Net Sales to Working Capital 32	15.9	•	31.1	•	10.3	2.8	6.5	7.4	1.9
Coverage Ratio 33	4.6	34.8	4.7	5.0	2.9	15.7	4.4	6.0	17.3
Total Asset Turnover 34	2.2	•	2.8	3.5	2.0	1.0	1.2	1.4	0.9
Inventory Turnover 35	15.9	•	34.6	289.2	8.4	2.2	5.8	31.0	5.9
Receivables Turnover 36	29.7	•	29.9	68.1	30.4	9.0	9.3	49.4	15.6
Total Liabilities to Net Worth 37	1.2	•	3.2	1.6	1.0	0.9	1.0	0.6	0.2
Current Assets to Working Capital 38	2.5	•	3.1	•	2.1	1.5	2.0	1.8	1.1
Current Liabilities to Working Capital 39	1.5	•	2.1	•	1.1	0.5	1.0	0.8	0.1
Working Capital to Net Sales 40	0.1	•	0.0	•	0.1	0.4	0.2	0.1	0.5
Inventory to Working Capital 41	0.8	•	0.7	•	1.1	1.0	0.9	0.4	0.2
Total Receipts to Cash Flow 42	6.4	1.3	5.6	6.1	7.9	6.8	8.6	15.7	7.6
Cost of Goods to Cash Flow 43	4.1	0.0	3.0	3.9	4.9	4.8	6.5	13.6	5.9
Cash Flow to Total Debt 44	0.6	•	0.7	0.9	0.5	0.3	0.3	0.2	0.8

Selected Financial Factors (in Percentages)

Debt Ratio 45	54.1	•	76.0	61.9	49.4	46.0	49.7	39.1	13.8
Return on Total Assets 46	13.0	•	21.6	14.4	8.9	12.3	9.2	6.9	8.6
Return on Equity Before Income Taxes 47	22.2	•	70.7	30.2	11.5	21.3	14.1	9.5	9.4
Return on Equity After Income Taxes 48	20.8	•	69.5	29.7	10.9	14.1	11.4	8.4	7.5
Profit Margin (Before Income Tax) 49	4.6	16.9	6.1	3.3	2.9	11.7	5.7	4.1	9.3
Profit Margin (After Income Tax) 50	4.3	16.0	6.0	3.3	2.8	7.8	4.6	3.6	7.4

Table I

Corporations with and without Net Income

SUPPORT ACTIVITIES AND FISHING, HUNTING AND TRAPPING

MONEY AMOUNTS AND SIZE OF ASSETS IN THOUSANDS OF DOLLARS

Item Description for Accounting Period 7/02 Through 6/03	Total	Zero Assets	Under 500	500 to 1,000	1,000 to 5,000	5,000 to 10,000	10,000 to 25,000	25,000 to 50,000	50,000 to 100,000	100,000 to 250,000	250,000 to 500,000	500,000 to 2,500,000	2,500,000 and over
Number of Enterprises **1**	27631	3706	20185	2033	1325	272	81	20	6	3	0	0	0
Revenues ($ in Thousands)													
Net Sales **2**	20617105	348883	7719743	2181702	4345435	2320293	1624453	846662	370872	859061	0	0	0
Interest **3**	30741	636	3885	5181	6576	3934	3986	4219	1373	952	0	0	0
Rents **4**	17774	0	2043	4275	1925	6819	2387	324	0	0	0	0	0
Royalties **5**	1688	0	0	0	0	1688	0	0	0	0	0	0	0
Other Portfolio Income **6**	161155	14620	80414	12009	10779	18492	8355	3016	1732	11743	0	0	0
Other Receipts **7**	736119	6604	254022	158430	155208	75006	45261	25998	5932	9655	0	0	0
Total Receipts **8**	21564582	370743	8060107	2361597	4519923	2426232	1684442	880219	379909	881411	0	0	0
Average Total Receipts **9**	780	100	399	1162	3411	8920	20796	44011	63318	293804	•	•	•
Operating Costs/Operating Income (%)													
Cost of Operations **10**	60.0	45.1	52.1	49.6	63.1	69.0	75.9	83.3	48.3	74.5	•	•	•
Salaries and Wages **11**	8.5	18.2	6.8	9.3	12.2	9.0	5.5	3.9	18.1	4.4	•	•	•
Taxes Paid **12**	2.2	2.3	2.1	2.2	3.1	1.7	1.5	1.1	2.9	3.2	•	•	•
Interest Paid **13**	1.1	0.2	1.0	1.5	1.0	0.8	1.2	1.2	1.0	1.9	•	•	•
Depreciation **14**	3.9	2.7	3.0	7.3	3.8	4.7	2.9	2.4	5.7	4.1	•	•	•
Amortization and Depletion **15**	0.1	0.1	0.0	0.2	0.0	0.1	0.1	0.1	0.5	0.3	•	•	•
Pensions and Other Deferred Comp. **16**	0.2	•	0.1	0.1	0.2	0.6	0.3	0.1	0.3	0.1	•	•	•
Employee Benefits **17**	0.8	0.4	0.6	0.9	0.9	1.0	0.6	0.4	1.9	0.4	•	•	•
Advertising **18**	0.4	0.3	0.5	0.1	0.2	0.5	0.2	0.3	1.2	0.3	•	•	•
Other Expenses **19**	21.0	30.2	29.2	31.9	13.2	12.9	11.7	8.0	16.8	8.9	•	•	•
Officers' Compensation **20**	3.1	1.0	4.9	2.0	3.2	2.0	1.1	0.6	1.5	0.5	•	•	•
Operating Margin **21**	•	•	•	•	•	•	•	•	2.0	1.5	•	•	•
Operating Margin Before Officers' Comp. **22**	1.9	0.5	4.6	•	2.2	•	0.1	•	3.5	2.0	•	•	•

Selected Average Balance Sheet ($ in Thousands)

Net Receivables 23	58	0	12	79	288	1070	3468	6358	9434	23715
Inventories 24	42	0	6	42	174	628	1931	7581	2852	74916
Net Property, Plant and Equipment 25	146	0	37	274	767	2980	4928	7064	12392	90908
Total Assets 26	398	0	109	673	1847	7176	15119	35372	61874	237055
Notes and Loans Payable 27	162	0	61	338	837	1648	5506	10123	17456	86621
All Other Liabilities 28	73	0	21	62	255	1225	4095	10690	12477	58411
Net Worth 29	163	0	28	272	755	4303	5518	14560	31941	92023

Selected Financial Ratios (Times to 1)

Current Ratio 30	1.8	•	1.8	2.0	1.7	2.0	1.5	1.4	2.2	1.8
Quick Ratio 31	1.2	•	1.3	1.4	1.2	1.5	0.9	0.7	1.8	0.6
Net Sales to Working Capital 32	9.7	•	17.1	9.6	10.7	5.3	7.9	7.1	3.1	5.3
Coverage Ratio 33	4.2	37.9	5.2	3.0	3.9	4.0	3.2	3.1	5.5	3.2
Total Asset Turnover 34	1.9	•	3.5	1.6	1.8	1.2	1.3	1.2	1.0	1.2
Inventory Turnover 35	10.8	•	35.8	12.6	11.9	9.4	7.9	4.6	10.5	2.8
Receivables Turnover 36	13.6	•	34.3	15.0	13.0	7.5	6.5	6.5	9.3	11.5
Total Liabilities to Net Worth 37	1.4	•	2.9	1.5	1.4	0.7	1.7	1.4	0.9	1.6
Current Assets to Working Capital 38	2.3	•	2.3	2.0	2.3	2.0	3.1	3.4	1.9	2.3
Current Liabilities to Working Capital 39	1.3	•	1.3	1.0	1.3	1.0	2.1	2.4	0.9	1.3
Working Capital to Net Sales 40	0.1	•	0.1	0.1	0.1	0.2	0.1	0.1	0.3	0.2
Inventory to Working Capital 41	0.6	•	0.3	0.6	0.6	0.4	0.8	1.5	0.2	1.5
Total Receipts to Cash Flow 42	5.9	3.8	4.8	4.0	8.0	8.7	8.4	10.9	5.6	9.8
Cost of Goods to Cash Flow 43	3.5	1.7	2.5	2.0	5.1	6.0	6.3	9.0	2.7	7.3
Cash Flow to Total Debt 44	0.5	•	1.0	0.7	0.4	0.3	0.3	0.2	0.4	0.2

Selected Financial Factors (in Percentages)

Debt Ratio 45	59.1	•	74.2	59.6	59.1	40.0	63.5	58.8	48.4	61.2
Return on Total Assets 46	8.4	•	17.7	7.3	7.1	3.6	5.1	4.5	5.3	7.3
Return on Equity Before Income Taxes 47	15.6	•	55.4	12.0	13.0	4.5	9.6	7.4	8.4	12.9
Return on Equity After Income Taxes 48	14.3	•	53.8	11.2	11.8	3.8	8.7	5.5	6.5	10.6
Profit Margin (Before Income Tax) 49	3.4	5.7	4.1	3.0	3.0	2.3	2.6	2.6	4.3	4.1
Profit Margin (After Income Tax) 50	3.1	4.3	4.0	2.8	2.7	1.9	2.4	1.9	3.3	3.4

5

Table II

Corporations with Net Income

SUPPORT ACTIVITIES AND FISHING, HUNTING AND TRAPPING

MONEY AMOUNTS AND SIZE OF ASSETS IN THOUSANDS OF DOLLARS

Item Description for Accounting Period 7/02 Through 6/03		Total	Zero Assets	Under 500	500 to 1,000	1,000 to 5,000	5,000 to 10,000	10,000 to 25,000	25,000 to 50,000	50,000 to 100,000	100,000 to 250,000	250,000 to 500,000	500,000 to 2,500,000	2,500,000 and over
Number of Enterprises	1	14005	1422	10165	1159	997	182	59	16	6	0	0	0	0
Revenues ($ in Thousands)														
Net Sales	2	16640734	214425	5851854	1533471	3784904	2047241	1439147	769511	1000181	0	0	0	0
Interest	3	21270	617	630	1811	6326	3006	3470	4043	1367	0	0	0	0
Rents	4	10720	0	1054	4275	1834	1274	1958	324	0	0	0	0	0
Royalties	5	0	0	0	0	0	0	0	0	0	0	0	0	0
Other Portfolio Income	6	148364	14620	74175	9432	10403	16693	6968	2957	13116	0	0	0	0
Other Receipts	7	617194	9640	214293	152970	107849	58698	35390	23272	15083	0	0	0	0
Total Receipts	8	17438282	239302	6142006	1701959	3911316	2126912	1486933	800107	1029747	0	0	0	0
Average Total Receipts	9	1245	168	604	1468	3923	11686	25202	50007	171624	•	•	•	•
Operating Costs/Operating Income (%)														
Cost of Operations	10	64.5	63.0	62.7	52.8	60.8	68.1	78.0	84.0	65.9	•	•	•	•
Salaries and Wages	11	7.8	3.1	5.1	10.8	12.9	8.5	4.6	3.7	7.5	•	•	•	•
Taxes Paid	12	2.1	0.8	1.8	1.6	3.3	1.4	1.4	0.9	3.5	•	•	•	•
Interest Paid	13	0.8	0.3	0.7	1.3	0.8	0.5	0.9	0.9	1.7	•	•	•	•
Depreciation	14	3.3	1.9	2.2	5.7	3.8	3.9	2.3	2.1	4.5	•	•	•	•
Amortization and Depletion	15	0.1	0.2	0.0	0.1	0.0	0.1	0.1	0.1	0.2	•	•	•	•
Pensions and Other Deferred Comp.	16	0.2	•	0.0	0.1	0.2	0.7	0.3	0.1	0.2	•	•	•	•
Employee Benefits	17	0.6	0.6	0.3	0.8	1.0	0.8	0.5	0.4	0.8	•	•	•	•
Advertising	18	0.4	0.4	0.5	0.1	0.3	0.5	0.2	0.4	0.4	•	•	•	•
Other Expenses	19	15.1	24.9	18.4	25.9	12.5	11.0	9.4	7.3	10.1	•	•	•	•
Officers' Compensation	20	3.1	1.6	4.7	2.0	3.5	2.0	1.0	0.6	0.5	•	•	•	•
Operating Margin	21	2.0	3.2	3.5	•	0.9	2.5	1.3	•	4.7	•	•	•	•
Operating Margin Before Officers' Comp.	22	5.1	4.8	8.2	0.7	4.4	4.4	2.4	0.1	5.2	•	•	•	•

Selected Average Balance Sheet ($ in Thousands)

Net Receivables 23	88	0	17	102	332	960	3803	7431	14826
Inventories 24	65	0	9	30	163	787	2266	7123	37471
Net Property, Plant and Equipment 25	172	0	35	256	694	2224	4334	6910	49458
Total Assets 26	544	0	133	637	1903	7239	15340	34958	142493
Notes and Loans Payable 27	185	0	47	346	769	1014	4721	9819	53437
All Other Liabilities 28	106	0	32	38	223	1258	4416	12179	33325
Net Worth 29	254	0	53	253	911	4966	6203	12960	55731

Selected Financial Ratios (Times to 1)

Current Ratio 30	1.9	•	2.1	2.2	2.0	2.6	1.4	1.3	2.0
Quick Ratio 31	1.3	•	1.5	2.0	1.3	1.9	0.9	0.6	0.9
Net Sales to Working Capital 32	9.0	•	14.2	10.4	9.6	4.9	9.1	9.7	4.1
Coverage Ratio 33	9.0	59.3	12.9	8.2	6.1	13.2	6.2	4.7	5.6
Total Asset Turnover 34	2.2	•	4.3	2.1	2.0	1.6	1.6	1.4	1.2
Inventory Turnover 35	11.8	•	38.6	23.1	14.2	9.7	8.4	5.7	2.9
Receivables Turnover 36	14.8	•	42.8	13.9	14.7	8.2	7.4	8.0	12.2
Total Liabilities to Net Worth 37	1.1	•	1.5	1.5	1.1	0.5	1.5	1.7	1.6
Current Assets to Working Capital 38	2.1	•	1.9	1.8	2.0	1.6	3.2	4.4	2.0
Current Liabilities to Working Capital 39	1.1	•	0.9	0.8	1.0	0.6	2.2	3.4	1.0
Working Capital to Net Sales 40	0.1	•	0.1	0.1	0.1	0.2	0.1	0.1	0.2
Inventory to Working Capital 41	0.6	•	0.3	0.2	0.5	0.3	0.9	2.0	1.1
Total Receipts to Cash Flow 42	5.7	3.3	4.6	3.6	7.6	7.1	8.0	10.6	6.7
Cost of Goods to Cash Flow 43	3.6	2.1	2.9	1.9	4.6	4.9	6.3	8.9	4.4
Cash Flow to Total Debt 44	0.7	•	1.6	1.0	0.5	0.7	0.3	0.2	0.3

Selected Financial Factors (in Percentages)

Debt Ratio 45	53.4	•	59.9	60.3	52.1	31.4	59.6	62.9	60.9
Return on Total Assets 46	16.7	•	39.7	22.7	10.0	10.7	8.8	6.1	10.9
Return on Equity Before Income Taxes 47	31.9	•	91.2	50.3	17.5	14.4	18.2	12.9	22.8
Return on Equity After Income Taxes 48	30.2	•	89.5	48.8	16.3	13.4	17.1	10.2	19.8
Profit Margin (Before Income Tax) 49	6.8	14.8	8.5	9.6	4.2	6.3	4.6	3.5	7.6
Profit Margin (After Income Tax) 50	6.5	12.4	8.3	9.3	3.9	5.9	4.4	2.7	6.6

Table I

Corporations with and without Net Income

OIL AND GAS EXTRACTION

MONEY AMOUNTS AND SIZE OF ASSETS IN THOUSANDS OF DOLLARS

Item Description for Accounting Period 7/02 Through 6/03	Total	Zero Assets	Under 500	500 to 1,000	1,000 to 5,000	5,000 to 10,000	10,000 to 25,000	25,000 to 50,000	50,000 to 100,000	100,000 to 250,000	250,000 to 500,000	500,000 to 2,500,000	2,500,000 and over
Number of Enterprises **1**	16068	1375	10826	1018	1933	352	223	122	73	66	28	36	14
Revenues ($ in Thousands)													
Net Sales **2**	58673838	534428	2633941	601732	2235186	996755	1427390	1929292	1330836	3303902	6274156	8702013	28704207
Interest **3**	2011561	31015	3501	2651	12201	16196	15295	16509	19941	29807	74621	208907	1580918
Rents **4**	130228	2388	2814	1574	14787	1351	4535	13614	3287	13578	3813	26034	42454
Royalties **5**	395647	1072	5776	151	18571	49179	23411	38691	9326	102446	11270	66626	69127
Other Portfolio Income **6**	2062788	46969	28656	15872	143967	58041	45724	106737	108813	135296	195394	191947	985370
Other Receipts **7**	4205174	47509	183821	5652	160982	124360	144572	239446	303715	316363	206601	583286	1888867
Total Receipts **8**	67479236	663381	2858509	627632	2585694	1245882	1660927	2344289	1775918	3901392	6765855	9778813	33270943
Average Total Receipts **9**	4200	482	264	617	1338	3539	7448	19215	24328	59112	241638	271634	2376496
Operating Costs/Operating Income (%)													
Cost of Operations **10**	48.3	11.5	24.7	8.4	47.2	21.2	42.1	39.3	23.9	31.1	66.9	26.5	59.5
Salaries and Wages **11**	5.6	16.9	8.3	12.3	9.7	10.0	8.9	8.3	12.6	8.9	2.4	5.8	4.2
Taxes Paid **12**	3.1	3.7	3.6	6.1	3.8	5.4	4.1	4.2	4.9	4.1	1.7	3.3	2.8
Interest Paid **13**	8.9	6.3	0.8	1.2	3.2	1.7	3.1	4.3	7.8	8.4	4.4	8.4	12.4
Depreciation **14**	7.3	14.1	3.8	5.4	7.9	8.9	7.9	8.0	11.6	10.4	3.7	11.1	6.4
Amortization and Depletion **15**	7.6	22.2	1.3	0.2	3.7	7.2	6.7	8.8	13.9	11.1	7.1	15.5	5.4
Pensions and Other Deferred Comp. **16**	0.5	0.0	0.5	0.5	0.7	0.5	0.4	0.3	1.7	0.3	0.1	0.4	0.5
Employee Benefits **17**	0.8	1.9	1.0	2.0	0.7	1.6	1.0	0.9	2.1	1.1	0.4	0.9	0.7
Advertising **18**	0.0	0.0	0.1	0.1	0.2	0.3	0.2	0.1	0.0	0.0	0.0	0.0	0.0
Other Expenses **19**	28.8	77.3	45.6	39.6	34.6	47.8	33.8	41.9	60.3	35.9	17.9	39.3	20.7
Officers' Compensation **20**	1.6	2.9	6.6	6.5	5.3	7.2	3.9	2.7	3.5	2.2	0.6	1.1	0.6
Operating Margin **21**	•	•	3.6	17.8	•	•	•	•	•	•	•	•	•
Operating Margin Before Officers' Comp. **22**	•	•	10.2	24.3	•	•	•	•	•	•	•	•	•

Selected Average Balance Sheet ($ in Thousands)

Net Receivables 23	1138	0	25	73	280	1261	1590	4174	6226	17679	31982	71306	786323
Inventories 24	93	0	0	4	16	46	188	636	559	1247	6247	3618	64105
Net Property, Plant and Equipment 25	4709	0	45	111	698	1972	5838	14315	36194	81854	203796	612400	2441529
Total Assets 26	14488	0	143	668	2053	7410	15648	35309	69690	159767	349281	1046232	10936847
Notes and Loans Payable 27	4243	0	54	312	1254	775	4605	9101	25222	51343	108781	310140	3071222
All Other Liabilities 28	2659	0	58	207	428	1829	3269	7319	14044	33043	87120	170985	1928229
Net Worth 29	7586	0	30	149	370	4806	7775	18890	30424	75381	153380	565107	5937396

Selected Financial Ratios (Times to 1)

Current Ratio 30	1.6	•	1.0	0.6	1.2	1.8	1.2	1.4	1.1	1.5	1.0	1.7	1.8
Quick Ratio 31	1.1	•	0.9	0.5	1.0	1.5	1.0	1.1	0.8	1.1	0.8	0.9	1.4
Net Sales to Working Capital 32	4.8	•	131.0	•	8.3	1.7	6.3	5.1	14.3	3.7	82.4	3.3	3.9
Coverage Ratio 33	1.3	•	15.8	19.6	0.5	8.7	2.3	1.6	•	1.6	1.6	1.0	1.3
Total Asset Turnover 34	0.3	•	1.7	0.9	0.6	0.4	0.4	0.4	0.3	0.3	0.6	0.2	0.2
Inventory Turnover 35	18.9	•	168.3	11.2	34.7	12.9	14.3	9.8	7.8	12.5	24.0	17.7	19.0
Receivables Turnover 36	3.5	•	10.1	6.9	4.3	2.7	3.5	4.4	3.0	2.9	6.0	2.8	3.1
Total Liabilities to Net Worth 37	0.9	•	3.7	3.5	4.5	0.5	1.0	0.9	1.3	1.1	1.3	0.9	0.8
Current Assets to Working Capital 38	2.8	•	44.3	•	5.7	2.2	5.2	3.7	12.2	3.1	22.4	2.4	2.2
Current Liabilities to Working Capital 39	1.8	•	43.3	•	4.7	1.2	4.2	2.7	11.2	2.1	21.4	1.4	1.2
Working Capital to Net Sales 40	0.2	•	0.0	•	0.1	0.6	0.2	0.2	0.1	0.3	0.0	0.3	0.3
Inventory to Working Capital 41	0.1	•	0.2	•	0.1	0.0	0.1	0.2	0.2	0.1	2.6	0.0	0.1
Total Receipts to Cash Flow 42	4.0	3.7	2.3	1.8	4.0	2.1	3.2	3.2	2.3	3.2	6.5	3.3	5.0
Cost of Goods to Cash Flow 43	1.9	0.4	0.6	0.1	1.9	0.4	1.3	1.3	0.5	1.0	4.4	0.9	2.9
Cash Flow to Total Debt 44	0.1	•	0.9	0.6	0.2	0.5	0.3	0.3	0.2	0.2	0.2	0.2	0.1

Selected Financial Factors (in Percentages)

Debt Ratio 45	47.6	•	78.7	77.7	82.0	35.1	50.3	46.5	56.3	52.8	56.1	46.0	45.7
Return on Total Assets 46	2.9	•	22.0	20.5	1.0	5.5	2.9	3.1	•	4.2	4.6	2.0	2.9
Return on Equity Before Income Taxes 47	1.3	•	96.9	87.3	•	7.6	3.3	2.2	•	3.3	4.0	0.1	1.1
Return on Equity After Income Taxes 48	0.4	•	95.3	86.9	•	6.6	2.0	•	•	2.1	0.3	•	0.5
Profit Margin (Before Income Tax) 49	2.7	•	12.1	22.0	•	12.8	4.0	2.6	•	5.0	2.7	0.2	3.1
Profit Margin (After Income Tax) 50	0.9	•	11.9	21.9	•	11.3	2.4	•	•	3.1	•	•	1.4

Table II

Corporations with Net Income

OIL AND GAS EXTRACTION

MONEY AMOUNTS AND SIZE OF ASSETS IN THOUSANDS OF DOLLARS

Item Description for Accounting Period 7/02 Through 6/03		Total	Zero Assets	Under 500	500 to 1,000	1,000 to 5,000	5,000 to 10,000	10,000 to 25,000	25,000 to 50,000	50,000 to 100,000	100,000 to 250,000	250,000 to 500,000	500,000 to 2,500,000	2,500,000 and over
Number of Enterprises	1	8447	36	6041	751	1002	315	116	74	35	35	15	19	8
Revenues ($ in Thousands)														
Net Sales	2	43598931	206187	2132698	490699	1679121	945548	1085585	1438948	795601	1917065	5144528	4612370	23150580
Interest	3	1834071	12712	2375	2409	10615	14217	8735	12043	12461	19039	46971	158838	1533656
Rents	4	113060	33	2803	1035	14648	1079	3558	9937	2455	12422	1129	23972	39989
Royalties	5	330595	487	356	22	14626	49179	17902	37402	9198	101407	3923	51840	44253
Other Portfolio Income	6	1667631	46589	28065	15666	135207	54842	24052	80593	58994	90665	136244	130623	866092
Other Receipts	7	3421220	24981	131532	1053	104215	125604	100075	202871	251784	205701	99166	507488	1666749
Total Receipts	8	50965508	290989	2297829	510884	1958432	1190469	1239907	1781794	1130493	2346299	5431961	5485131	27301319
Average Total Receipts	9	6034	8083	380	680	1955	3779	10689	24078	32300	67037	362131	288691	3412665
Operating Costs/Operating Income (%)														
Cost of Operations	10	53.8	5.2	22.6	5.8	54.8	20.1	46.4	40.1	12.3	37.6	74.3	21.6	65.2
Salaries and Wages	11	4.5	2.0	7.1	8.7	4.0	9.1	6.1	7.7	15.8	6.0	1.1	5.6	3.8
Taxes Paid	12	2.8	2.0	3.7	5.4	2.7	5.3	3.8	4.0	5.5	3.8	0.8	3.0	2.6
Interest Paid	13	8.4	0.5	0.7	0.8	1.5	1.4	2.0	2.3	4.3	3.8	1.8	6.9	13.0
Depreciation	14	5.5	2.8	3.6	5.9	4.5	8.0	5.8	7.5	9.7	8.8	2.2	8.7	5.1
Amortization and Depletion	15	5.3	7.6	1.6	0.2	1.2	7.2	4.8	5.8	8.0	5.3	3.6	15.6	4.1
Pensions and Other Deferred Comp.	16	0.5	0.0	0.6	0.4	0.9	0.5	0.4	0.3	2.7	0.3	0.1	0.5	0.6
Employee Benefits	17	0.8	0.0	0.8	2.4	0.3	1.6	0.9	0.9	0.4	0.9	0.2	1.0	0.8
Advertising	18	0.0	0.0	0.1	0.1	0.1	0.3	0.1	0.1	0.0	0.0	0.0	0.0	0.0
Other Expenses	19	21.1	61.3	38.6	34.9	21.5	35.5	19.8	26.8	45.0	23.8	9.3	39.7	15.8
Officers' Compensation	20	1.3	0.6	5.7	3.3	3.7	7.3	2.7	2.3	3.3	0.4	0.4	1.3	0.4
Operating Margin	21	•	18.0	14.9	32.2	4.8	3.7	7.3	2.1	•	7.4	6.3	•	•
Operating Margin Before Officers' Comp.	22	•	18.7	20.6	35.4	8.5	11.0	10.0	4.5	•	9.7	6.6	•	•

Selected Average Balance Sheet ($ in Thousands)

Net Receivables 23	1636	0	39	17	366	1226	1819	4721	7615	16110	33064	91736	1149029
Inventories 24	123	0	0	6	13	34	262	587	596	1265	8052	5002	81936
Net Property, Plant and Equipment 25	4789	0	42	129	510	1775	5435	13282	30349	69472	169321	602409	2492368
Total Assets 26	20356	0	178	622	1934	7380	15708	35377	69839	153887	335657	1152026	15868197
Notes and Loans Payable 27	5156	0	65	126	584	655	3494	6730	22096	32723	63822	279804	4147658
All Other Liabilities 28	3639	0	69	23	480	1449	2818	7682	13782	31762	92565	181508	2754651
Net Worth 29	11561	0	45	473	869	5276	9397	20965	33961	89402	179270	690715	8965888

Selected Financial Ratios (Times to 1)

Current Ratio 30	2.0	•	1.1	3.8	1.4	2.3	2.0	1.6	1.5	2.0	1.2	2.3	2.2
Quick Ratio 31	1.4	•	1.0	3.5	1.1	1.9	1.6	1.4	1.0	1.5	0.9	1.1	1.7
Net Sales to Working Capital 32	3.3	•	24.1	5.9	7.0	1.4	3.1	4.0	2.8	2.4	30.1	1.7	3.2
Coverage Ratio 33	2.6	112.9	34.2	45.1	15.5	22.2	11.8	12.2	9.2	9.0	7.6	3.2	1.5
Total Asset Turnover 34	0.3	•	2.0	1.0	0.9	0.4	0.6	0.5	0.3	0.4	1.0	0.2	0.2
Inventory Turnover 35	22.5	•	203.0	6.4	70.3	17.6	16.5	13.3	4.7	16.3	31.7	10.5	23.0
Receivables Turnover 36	3.5	•	10.7	18.9	4.3	3.3	3.9	4.5	3.0	2.7	7.3	2.2	3.2
Total Liabilities to Net Worth 37	0.8	3.0	0.3	1.2	0.4	0.7	0.7	0.7	1.1	0.7	0.9	0.7	0.8
Current Assets to Working Capital 38	2.0	8.4	1.4	3.8	1.7	2.0	2.7	2.8	2.0	2.0	5.9	1.8	1.8
Current Liabilities to Working Capital 39	1.0	7.4	0.4	2.8	0.7	1.0	1.0	1.7	1.8	1.0	4.9	0.8	0.8
Working Capital to Net Sales 40	0.3	0.0	0.2	0.1	0.7	0.3	0.3	0.2	0.4	0.4	0.0	0.6	0.3
Inventory to Working Capital 41	0.1	•	0.0	0.0	0.0	0.1	0.1	0.1	0.1	0.0	0.6	0.0	0.1
Total Receipts to Cash Flow 42	3.5	2.1	1.4	2.8	1.7	2.7	2.7	2.2	1.4	2.1	5.6	2.2	5.3
Cost of Goods to Cash Flow 43	1.9	0.5	0.1	1.5	0.3	1.2	1.2	0.9	0.2	0.8	4.1	0.5	3.5
Cash Flow to Total Debt 44	0.2	1.2	3.0	0.6	0.8	0.6	0.6	0.6	0.5	0.4	0.4	0.2	0.1

Selected Financial Factors (in Percentages)

Debt Ratio 45	43.2	•	74.9	23.9	55.0	28.5	40.2	40.7	51.4	41.9	46.6	40.0	43.5
Return on Total Assets 46	5.5	•	46.2	38.8	19.5	12.4	13.9	15.5	12.7	12.2	14.2	4.6	3.7
Return on Equity Before Income Taxes 47	6.0	•	178.5	49.9	40.7	16.6	21.3	24.0	23.3	18.7	23.0	5.3	2.3
Return on Equity After Income Taxes 48	4.9	•	176.6	49.7	37.7	15.7	19.8	20.6	20.4	16.7	17.1	4.0	1.6
Profit Margin (Before Income Tax) 49	13.3	59.2	22.7	36.2	21.1	29.2	21.4	25.9	34.8	30.5	12.0	15.0	7.0
Profit Margin (After Income Tax) 50	10.9	41.0	22.4	36.0	19.6	27.5	19.9	22.2	30.5	27.3	8.9	11.4	4.9

Table I

Corporations with and without Net Income

COAL MINING

MONEY AMOUNTS AND SIZE OF ASSETS IN THOUSANDS OF DOLLARS

Item Description for Accounting Period 7/02 Through 6/03	Total	Zero Assets	Under 500	500 to 1,000	1,000 to 5,000	5,000 to 10,000	10,000 to 25,000	25,000 to 50,000	50,000 to 100,000	100,000 to 250,000	250,000 to 500,000	500,000 to 2,500,000	2,500,000 and over
Number of Enterprises **1**	1447	0	0	246	117	69	43	15	7	7	0	6	3
Revenues ($ in Thousands)													
Net Sales **2**	16231579	0	0	297318	773938	2149710	1045459	627479	750521	858752	0	4944826	4337809
Interest **3**	93966	0	0	411	2086	818	2394	1060	2061	9806	0	34771	40372
Rents **4**	33162	0	0	25	23	4541	2810	1143	9660	3575	0	6996	3478
Royalties **5**	92345	0	0	1838	137	19	791	308	6131	12441	0	63707	3465
Other Portfolio Income **6**	210392	0	0	29289	292	8108	6960	20362	2665	1915	0	37873	102923
Other Receipts **7**	634215	0	0	656	9251	8445	12866	11327	17541	75685	0	319277	127857
Total Receipts **8**	17295659	0	0	329537	785727	2171641	1071280	661679	788579	962174	0	5407450	4615904
Average Total Receipts **9**	11953	•	•	1340	6716	31473	24913	44112	112654	137453	•	901242	1538635
Operating Costs/Operating Income (%)													
Cost of Operations **10**	65.3	•	•	52.1	30.2	84.2	62.1	42.5	76.8	78.1		70.6	57.9
Salaries and Wages **11**	3.6	•	•	13.9	1.7	2.7	6.3	8.2	1.5	2.1		1.9	4.2
Taxes Paid **12**	7.3	•	•	8.3	6.2	1.2	5.1	5.5	5.7	5.2		7.3	11.6
Interest Paid **13**	3.4	•	•	0.6	0.7	0.5	1.5	0.9	3.4	2.5		6.7	3.0
Depreciation **14**	6.3	•	•	5.0	2.2	2.0	6.1	8.0	7.8	4.3		7.9	7.4
Amortization and Depletion **15**	4.3	•	•	•	0.2	1.0	2.1	4.1	3.5	3.7		5.3	7.0
Pensions and Other Deferred Comp. **16**	0.9	•	•	6.6	0.0	0.0	0.5	0.3	0.5	0.6		1.6	0.9
Employee Benefits **17**	3.6	•	•	4.0	0.6	0.2	1.9	3.3	3.2	1.8		5.2	5.1
Advertising **18**	0.1	•	•	0.2	0.1	0.0	0.0	0.0	0.0	0.0		0.1	0.1
Other Expenses **19**	14.1	•	•	25.8	62.6	8.1	17.7	29.3	11.6	11.6		8.5	10.3
Officers' Compensation **20**	0.6	•	•	1.3	1.1	0.1	1.2	1.2	0.5	0.7		0.7	0.7
Operating Margin **21**	•	•	•	•	•	0.0	•	•	•	•		•	•
Operating Margin Before Officers' Comp. **22**	•	•	•	•	•	0.2	•	•	•	•		•	•

Selected Average Balance Sheet ($ in Thousands)

Item										
Net Receivables **23**	2795	29	681	977	2253	3754	8185	14015	105518	981023
Inventories **24**	594	1	157	153	518	891	3668	7461	59770	114333
Net Property, Plant and Equipment **25**	7467	171	600	3270	7045	13721	32410	108769	655923	1663761
Total Assets **26**	18770	579	2354	7949	16404	34075	72331	229550	1374140	4836713
Notes and Loans Payable **27**	5039	87	1731	2348	6257	9171	59018	98107	496269	786526
All Other Liabilities **28**	8604	81	652	1278	4758	6205	39731	101130	704254	2237194
Net Worth **29**	5127	411	-29	4322	5389	18700	-26418	30312	173617	1812992

Selected Financial Ratios (Times to 1)

Item										
Current Ratio **30**	1.0	•	3.8	2.3	1.1	1.2	0.4	1.1	0.7	1.1
Quick Ratio **31**	0.7	•	3.8	2.0	0.8	0.9	0.2	0.7	0.4	1.0
Net Sales to Working Capital **32**	4.3	•	35.9	14.1	85.6	28.1	•	17.8	•	10.2
Coverage Ratio **33**	0.1	•	3.1	•	3.1	•	1.6	0.0	•	0.7
Total Asset Turnover **34**	0.6	2.1	2.8	3.9	1.5	1.2	1.5	0.5	0.6	0.3
Inventory Turnover **35**	12.3	1018.8	12.7	171.8	29.2	20.0	22.5	12.8	9.7	7.3
Receivables Turnover **36**	3.1	33.6	11.0	43.8	11.4	8.9	15.6	5.9	6.6	1.1
Total Liabilities to Net Worth **37**	2.7	•	0.4	0.8	2.0	0.8	•	6.6	6.9	1.7
Current Assets to Working Capital **38**	1.4	•	8.3	1.8	20.6	6.2	•	7.7	•	8.2
Current Liabilities to Working Capital **39**	0.4	•	7.3	0.8	19.6	5.2	•	6.7	•	7.2
Working Capital to Net Sales **40**	0.2	•	0.0	0.1	0.0	0.0	•	0.0	0.1	0.1
Inventory to Working Capital **41**	0.0	•	0.9	0.1	2.1	0.5	•	1.0	•	0.9
Total Receipts to Cash Flow **42**	15.7	8.3	1.7	14.5	10.3	4.6	•	1.5	9.6	28.0
Cost of Goods to Cash Flow **43**	10.2	4.3	0.5	12.2	6.4	2.0	•	7.5	•	16.2
Cash Flow to Total Debt **44**	0.1	0.9	1.6	0.6	0.2	0.6	•	0.1	•	0.0

Selected Financial Factors (in Percentages)

Item										
Debt Ratio **45**	72.7	29.0	101.2	45.6	67.1	45.1	136.5	86.8	87.4	62.5
Return on Total Assets **46**	0.3	•	5.6	•	3.5	•	2.1	•	0.1	0.6
Return on Equity Before Income Taxes **47**	•	•	915.2	7.0	•	4.3	•	38.8	•	6.0
Return on Equity After Income Taxes **48**	•	•	937.8	6.6	•	3.5	•	38.8	•	1.9
Profit Margin (Before Income Tax) **49**	•	•	1.0	•	1.9	•	•	1.5	•	•
Profit Margin (After Income Tax) **50**	•	•	0.9	•	1.6	•	•	0.5	•	•

Table II

Corporations with Net Income

COAL MINING

MONEY AMOUNTS AND SIZE OF ASSETS IN THOUSANDS OF DOLLARS

Item Description for Accounting Period 7/02 Through 6/03	Total	Zero Assets	Under 500	500 to 1,000	1,000 to 5,000	5,000 to 10,000	10,000 to 25,000	25,000 to 50,000	50,000 to 100,000	100,000 to 250,000	250,000 to 500,000	500,000 to 2,500,000	2,500,000 and over
Number of Enterprises 1	499	0	229	147	51	0	21	10	0	4	0	0	0
Revenues ($ in Thousands)													
Net Sales 2	6697035	0	124188	175365	210773	0	459902	465714	0	345481	0	0	0
Interest 3	44600	0	149	0	1952	0	2084	1056	0	5049	0	0	0
Rents 4	11562	0	0	0	0	0	2174	1143	0	1855	0	0	0
Royalties 5	17915	0	0	0	0	0	436	308	0	12382	0	0	0
Other Portfolio Income 6	146393	0	5	29006	185	0	4133	20211	0	1480	0	0	0
Other Receipts 7	308236	0	3793	1	6438	0	5627	10979	0	61780	0	0	0
Total Receipts 8	7225741	0	128135	204372	219348	0	474356	499411	0	428027	0	0	0
Average Total Receipts 9	14480	·	560	1390	4301	·	22588	49941	·	107007	·	·	·
Operating Costs/Operating Income (%)													
Cost of Operations 10	68.2	·	·	77.6	67.9	·	68.5	41.6	·	59.3	·	·	·
Salaries and Wages 11	5.6	·	29.6	3.3	3.4	·	4.5	8.1	·	2.9	·	·	·
Taxes Paid 12	7.0	·	5.5	5.3	2.6	·	4.1	5.0	·	10.5	·	·	·
Interest Paid 13	2.8	·	2.4	·	1.4	·	1.1	0.6	·	4.6	·	·	·
Depreciation 14	4.7	·	16.1	6.5	4.6	·	5.6	6.9	·	6.6	·	·	·
Amortization and Depletion 15	4.4	·	·	0.5	0.5	·	3.4	4.3	·	8.5	·	·	·
Pensions and Other Deferred Comp. 16	0.4	·	·	11.1	0.0	·	0.5	0.4	·	0.3	·	·	·
Employee Benefits 17	0.8	·	0.2	·	2.2	·	1.1	3.6	·	1.8	·	·	·
Advertising 18	0.1	·	0.1	0.3	0.4	·	0.1	0.0	·	0.0	·	·	·
Other Expenses 19	9.4	·	27.9	7.0	13.2	·	8.8	30.4	·	19.2	·	·	·
Officers' Compensation 20	0.8	·	16.1	2.2	3.4	·	1.9	1.0	·	1.5	·	·	·
Operating Margin 21	·	·	2.1	·	0.3	·	0.6	·	·	·	·	·	·
Operating Margin Before Officers' Comp. 22	·	·	18.2	·	3.8	·	2.5	·	·	·	·	·	·

Selected Average Balance Sheet ($ in Thousands)

Net Receivables 23	5923	1	0	738	2768	4574	16224
Inventories 24	602	0	0	264	432	1142	6477
Net Property, Plant and Equipment 25	8983	114	199	1003	6458	12643	128028
Total Assets 26	28552	171	612	2521	17163	35896	302547
Notes and Loans Payable 27	3620	151	22	1382	4508	9860	98902
All Other Liabilities 28	10413	8	0	809	2756	4991	154588
Net Worth 29	14518	13	590	330	9899	21046	49057

Selected Financial Ratios (Times to 1)

Current Ratio 30	1.3	0.9	30.3	1.2	1.8	1.8	1.4
Quick Ratio 31	1.1	0.5	30.3	0.8	1.5	1.3	0.9
Net Sales to Working Capital 32	7.4	•	3.3	26.3	7.0	9.5	4.5
Coverage Ratio 33	2.3	3.2	•	4.0	4.3	9.8	2.9
Total Asset Turnover 34	0.5	3.2	1.9	1.6	1.3	1.3	0.3
Inventory Turnover 35	15.2	•	•	10.6	34.7	17.0	7.9
Receivables Turnover 36	1.8	7.8	40.1	7.2	9.1	7.9	10.6
Total Liabilities to Net Worth 37	1.0	12.6	0.0	6.6	0.7	0.7	5.2
Current Assets to Working Capital 38	4.4	•	1.0	7.2	2.2	2.3	3.5
Current Liabilities to Working Capital 39	3.4	•	0.0	6.2	1.2	1.3	2.5
Working Capital to Net Sales 40	0.1	•	0.3	0.0	0.1	0.1	0.2
Inventory to Working Capital 41	0.4	•	•	1.6	0.1	0.2	0.3
Total Receipts to Cash Flow 42	12.0	4.4	23.5	6.0	10.7	4.1	3.9
Cost of Goods to Cash Flow 43	8.2	•	18.2	4.1	7.3	1.7	2.3
Cash Flow to Total Debt 44	0.1	0.8	2.3	0.3	0.3	0.8	0.1

Selected Financial Factors (in Percentages)

Debt Ratio 45	49.2	92.7	3.6	86.9	42.3	41.4	83.8
Return on Total Assets 46	3.1	24.2	6.4	9.6	6.2	7.3	3.8
Return on Equity Before Income Taxes 47	3.5	226.3	6.6	55.0	8.2	11.2	15.4
Return on Equity After Income Taxes 48	3.2	215.7	6.6	50.5	7.7	10.2	11.0
Profit Margin (Before Income Tax) 49	3.8	5.2	3.3	4.4	3.7	5.1	8.8
Profit Margin (After Income Tax) 50	3.5	5.0	3.3	4.0	3.5	4.6	6.2

Table I

Corporations with and without Net Income

METAL ORE MINING

MONEY AMOUNTS AND SIZE OF ASSETS IN THOUSANDS OF DOLLARS

Item Description for Accounting Period 7/02 Through 6/03	Total	Zero Assets	Under 500	500 to 1,000	1,000 to 5,000	5,000 to 10,000	10,000 to 25,000	25,000 to 50,000	50,000 to 100,000	100,000 to 250,000	250,000 to 500,000	500,000 to 2,500,000	2,500,000 and over
Number of Enterprises 1	2280	0	0	203	71	21	24	12	8	6	5	8	6
Revenues ($ in Thousands)													
Net Sales 2	14298362	0	0	1173	618	66170	43528	108424	180379	576963	820461	3284386	9176529
Interest 3	329334	0	0	221	293	360	1256	3090	3010	4493	10787	55671	249423
Rents 4	22438	0	0	4669	2	0	28	661	0	0	203	2004	14851
Royalties 5	114385	0	0	0	0	0	1801	323	14651	2437	2416	32235	60210
Other Portfolio Income 6	270939	0	0	28864	4286	3849	2570	3648	2811	6270	1152	54886	151821
Other Receipts 7	387739	0	0	-4520	47414	2953	5863	14271	984	19353	30549	121880	127097
Total Receipts 8	15423197	0	0	30407	52613	73332	55046	130417	201835	609516	865568	3551062	9779931
Average Total Receipts 9	6765	•	•	150	741	3492	2294	10868	25229	101586	173114	443883	1629988
Operating Costs/Operating Income (%)													
Cost of Operations 10	56.8	•	•	•	279.1	54.6	61.6	74.0	83.3	78.3	52.6	83.4	45.7
Salaries and Wages 11	3.6	•	•	17.6	1792.4	6.2	12.3	33.6	2.8	2.8	1.2	0.8	4.3
Taxes Paid 12	2.2	•	•	157.5	151.5	5.6	2.3	3.5	1.8	0.8	1.4	1.8	2.4
Interest Paid 13	6.8	•	•	•	956.3	1.7	8.6	2.0	4.7	2.6	2.6	6.8	7.5
Depreciation 14	11.5	•	•	18.7	2464.1	16.4	14.0	9.2	10.1	8.8	7.6	11.3	11.9
Amortization and Depletion 15	10.0	•	•	•	270.7	6.3	11.4	4.5	13.2	5.9	17.6	5.1	11.3
Pensions and Other Deferred Comp. 16	0.1	•	•	•	0.8	1.9	0.1	0.2	0.1	•	0.0	0.1	0.1
Employee Benefits 17	2.3	•	•	71.8	99.4	0.5	0.3	10.2	3.6	2.4	2.3	1.7	2.4
Advertising 18	0.0	•	•	•	120.7	0.1	0.2	0.1	0.0	0.0	•	0.0	0.1
Other Expenses 19	19.3	•	•	717.1	6226.5	29.5	64.2	8.0	10.7	16.3	10.6	9.3	22.4
Officers' Compensation 20	0.5	•	•	202.9	79.8	12.8	2.6	1.4	6.2	0.7	0.2	0.3	0.4
Operating Margin 21	•	•	•	•	•	•	•	•	•	•	3.9	•	•
Operating Margin Before Officers' Comp. 22	•	•	•	•	•	•	•	•	•	•	4.0	•	•

Selected Average Balance Sheet ($ in Thousands)

Net Receivables 23	2250	•	13	14	351	1269	5578	638	11822	6050	138379	634667
Inventories 24	975	•	0	14	45	1393	2556	1927	20519	24980	71663	220229
Net Property, Plant and Equipment 25	7920	•	179	1050	2134	6050	12075	32284	68412	141039	561564	1957513
Total Assets 26	29627	•	559	2255	6034	16275	34227	72786	155706	313219	1340277	8740782
Notes and Loans Payable 27	4918	•	0	366	1064	9351	8884	10199	38095	55807	351168	1236255
All Other Liabilities 28	7483	•	121	1025	989	5254	17722	16272	48964	139197	435133	1981939
Net Worth 29	17227	•	438	864	3982	1670	7621	46315	68647	118214	553976	5522588

Selected Financial Ratios (Times to 1)

Current Ratio 30	1.0	•	10.7	0.6	1.7	1.1	1.6	3.8	0.5	1.2	0.9	1.1
Quick Ratio 31	0.7	•	10.4	0.3	1.5	0.7	0.9	2.6	0.3	0.6	0.6	0.8
Net Sales to Working Capital 32	49.2	•	0.0	•	3.0	3.5	1.6	1.7	•	15.8	•	16.2
Coverage Ratio 33	0.4	•	•	•	•	•	•	•	•	4.6	•	1.0
Total Asset Turnover 34	0.2	•	0.0	0.5	0.1	0.3	0.3	0.6	0.5	0.3	•	0.2
Inventory Turnover 35	3.7	•	•	1.8	38.4	0.8	2.6	9.7	3.7	3.5	4.8	3.2
Receivables Turnover 36	2.4	•	0.6	7.2	1.7	1.7	3.7	6.1	28.2	1.6	3.4	2.0
Total Liabilities to Net Worth 37	0.7	•	0.3	0.5	8.7	3.5	0.6	0.6	1.3	1.6	1.4	0.6
Current Assets to Working Capital 38	33.5	•	1.1	2.4	8.6	2.7	1.4	6.4	5.4	•	•	11.3
Current Liabilities to Working Capital 39	32.5	•	0.1	1.4	7.6	1.7	0.4	5.4	•	•	•	10.3
Working Capital to Net Sales 40	0.0	•	56.9	0.3	0.3	0.6	0.6	•	•	0.1	•	0.1
Inventory to Working Capital 41	7.6	•	•	0.1	2.9	0.3	0.1	3.1	•	•	•	2.2
Total Receipts to Cash Flow 42	10.3	•	0.1	•	25.7	•	•	•	86.0	5.6	•	6.4
Cost of Goods to Cash Flow 43	5.9	•	0.2	•	15.8	•	•	•	67.3	2.9	•	2.9
Cash Flow to Total Debt 44	0.0	•	0.1	•	0.0	•	•	•	0.0	0.2	•	0.1

Selected Financial Factors (in Percentages)

Debt Ratio 45	41.9	•	21.6	61.7	34.0	89.7	77.7	36.4	55.9	62.3	58.7	36.8
Return on Total Assets 46	0.5	•	14.0	•	•	•	•	•	•	6.2	•	1.3
Return on Equity Before Income Taxes 47	•	•	17.8	•	•	•	•	•	•	13.0	•	•
Return on Equity After Income Taxes 48	•	•	12.3	•	•	•	•	•	•	10.6	•	•
Profit Margin (Before Income Tax) 49	•	•	1353.3	•	•	•	•	•	•	9.4	•	•
Profit Margin (After Income Tax) 50	•	•	936.1	•	•	•	•	•	•	7.6	•	•

Table II

Corporations with Net Income

METAL ORE MINING

MONEY AMOUNTS AND SIZE OF ASSETS IN THOUSANDS OF DOLLARS

Item Description for Accounting Period 7/02 Through 6/03	Total	Zero Assets	Under 500	500 to 1,000	1,000 to 5,000	5,000 to 10,000	10,000 to 25,000	25,000 to 50,000	50,000 to 100,000	100,000 to 250,000	250,000 to 500,000	500,000 to 2,500,000	2,500,000 and over
Number of Enterprises 1	661	0	440	139	48	0	7	0	0	•	0	0	3

Revenues ($ in Thousands)

Item	Total	Zero Assets	Under 500	500 to 1,000	1,000 to 5,000	5,000 to 10,000	10,000 to 25,000	25,000 to 50,000	50,000 to 100,000	100,000 to 250,000	250,000 to 500,000	500,000 to 2,500,000	2,500,000 and over
Net Sales 2	4752849	0	18462	1173	420	0	5475	0	0	•	0	0	3935473
Interest 3	114434	0	0	0	183	0	1795	0	0	•	0	0	89934
Rents 4	4733	0	0	0	0	0	0	0	0	•	0	0	4527
Royalties 5	65249	0	0	0	0	0	16452	0	0	•	0	0	37538
Other Portfolio Income 6	131166	0	0	28118	4281	0	2250	0	0	•	0	0	90673
Other Receipts 7	145179	0	13348	0	47195	0	6795	0	0	•	0	0	58465
Total Receipts 8	5213610	0	31810	29291	52079	0	32767	0	0	•	0	0	4216610
Average Total Receipts 9	7887	•	72	211	1085	•	4681	•	•	•	•	•	1405537

Operating Costs/Operating Income (%)

Item	Total	Zero Assets	Under 500	500 to 1,000	1,000 to 5,000	5,000 to 10,000	10,000 to 25,000	25,000 to 50,000	50,000 to 100,000	100,000 to 250,000	250,000 to 500,000	500,000 to 2,500,000	2,500,000 and over
Cost of Operations 10	40.4	•	•	•	341.4	•	3.0	•	•	•	•	•	38.7
Salaries and Wages 11	6.4	•	•	•	973.6	•	17.1	•	•	•	•	•	7.6
Taxes Paid 12	0.9	•	0.8	64.5	81.0	•	26.9	•	•	•	•	•	0.7
Interest Paid 13	6.3	•	9.3	•	0.2	•	5.5	•	•	•	•	•	7.2
Depreciation 14	11.7	•	2.1	13.2	3292.1	•	1.2	•	•	•	•	•	12.1
Amortization and Depletion 15	15.9	•	7.7	•	•	•	106.8	•	•	•	•	•	15.8
Pensions and Other Deferred Comp. 16	0.1	•	•	•	•	•	1.4	•	•	•	•	•	0.1
Employee Benefits 17	0.7	•	•	71.8	133.8	•	•	•	•	•	•	•	0.3
Advertising 18	0.1	•	•	•	•	•	0.6	•	•	•	•	•	0.1
Other Expenses 19	15.0	•	66.7	550.7	6682.4	•	101.8	•	•	•	•	•	14.5
Officers' Compensation 20	0.7	•	10.3	•	•	•	17.3	•	•	•	•	•	0.5
Operating Margin 21	1.8	•	3.1	•	•	•	•	•	•	•	•	•	2.5
Operating Margin Before Officers' Comp. 22	2.5	•	13.4	•	•	•	•	•	•	•	•	•	3.1

Selected Average Balance Sheet ($ in Thousands)

	Col 1	Col 2	Col 3	Col 4	Col 5	Col 6	Col 7
Net Receivables 23	3301	•	0	10	•	2324	710725
Inventories 24	979	•	0	0	•	2233	159948
Net Property, Plant and Equipment 25	9692	•	1	236	77	10436	1834064
Total Assets 26	47786	•	121	571	1678	27280	9906046
Notes and Loans Payable 27	4861	•	20	0	13	1919	1027304
All Other Liabilities 28	11393	•	0	59	635	7867	2371662
Net Worth 29	31532	•	101	512	1030	17493	6507080

Selected Financial Ratios (Times to 1)

	Col 1	Col 2	Col 3	Col 4	Col 5	Col 6	Col 7
Current Ratio 30	0.8	•	1023.6	6.5	0.8	•	1.9
Quick Ratio 31	0.6	•	1023.6	6.4	0.3	•	1.6
Net Sales to Working Capital 32	•	•	0.7	0.0	•	•	0.1
Coverage Ratio 33	3.3	•	9.1	•	3763.0	•	58.6
Total Asset Turnover 34	0.2	•	0.3	0.0	0.0	•	0.1
Inventory Turnover 35	3.0	•	•	•	•	•	3.2
Receivables Turnover 36	1.5	•	•	1.7	1.7	•	3.7
Total Liabilities to Net Worth 37	0.5	•	0.2	0.1	0.6	•	0.5
Current Assets to Working Capital 38	•	•	1.0	1.2	•	•	2.1
Current Liabilities to Working Capital 39	•	•	0.0	0.2	•	•	1.1
Working Capital to Net Sales 40	•	•	1.5	27.2	•	•	7.3
Inventory to Working Capital 41	•	•	•	•	•	•	0.4
Total Receipts to Cash Flow 42	5.0	•	0.9	0.0	0.0	•	0.3
Cost of Goods to Cash Flow 43	2.0	•	•	0.1	0.1	•	0.0
Cash Flow to Total Debt 44	0.1	•	2.2	0.9	•	•	0.3

Selected Financial Factors (in Percentages)

	Col 1	Col 2	Col 3	Col 4	Col 5	Col 6	Col 7
Debt Ratio 45	34.0	•	16.8	10.3	38.6	•	35.9
Return on Total Assets 46	3.1	•	29.4	26.6	4.7	•	2.7
Return on Equity Before Income Taxes 47	3.3	•	31.4	29.6	7.6	•	2.7
Return on Equity After Income Taxes 48	2.3	•	31.4	22.7	7.6	•	1.7
Profit Margin (Before Income Tax) 49	14.4	75.4	1796.9	895.7	895.7	•	13.3
Profit Margin (After Income Tax) 50	10.1	75.4	1379.8	895.7	895.7	•	8.6

Table I
Corporations with and without Net Income

NONMETALLIC MINERAL MINING AND QUARRYING

MONEY AMOUNTS AND SIZE OF ASSETS IN THOUSANDS OF DOLLARS

Item Description for Accounting Period 7/02 Through 6/03	Total	Zero Assets	Under 500	500 to 1,000	1,000 to 5,000	5,000 to 10,000	10,000 to 25,000	25,000 to 50,000	50,000 to 100,000	100,000 to 250,000	250,000 to 500,000	500,000 to 2,500,000	2,500,000 and over
Number of Enterprises **1**	5299	838	2619	1072	430	106	143	50	13	15	6	8	0
Revenues ($ in Thousands)													
Net Sales **2**	19892537	578769	535943	822241	892380	850936	1898363	1391317	828233	1618179	1555256	8920922	0
Interest **3**	111614	7332	254	802	1108	1198	4655	6215	4143	6722	11420	67766	0
Rents **4**	40190	0	32	7	1074	501	5180	4413	2350	5165	1298	20170	0
Royalties **5**	28115	0	0	0	0	3782	57	2540	191	1306	4816	15423	0
Other Portfolio Income **6**	407924	7777	24845	7257	7653	1679	22998	12701	10560	8027	21029	283398	0
Other Receipts **7**	351220	9342	526	14600	12008	14664	41490	29451	9776	12978	18519	187862	0
Total Receipts **8**	20831600	603220	561600	844907	914223	872760	1972743	1446637	855253	1652377	1612338	9495541	0
Average Total Receipts **9**	3931	720	214	788	2126	8234	13795	28933	65789	110158	268723	1186943	·
Operating Costs/Operating Income (%)													
Cost of Operations **10**	62.5	63.6	59.9	52.1	56.3	56.2	62.6	65.3	66.6	65.2	53.6	65.1	·
Salaries and Wages **11**	4.8	9.0	7.9	6.7	1.8	3.4	4.7	4.0	4.7	5.0	4.0	4.8	·
Taxes Paid **12**	2.7	2.0	1.4	4.5	4.2	2.7	2.8	3.0	2.5	1.8	5.2	2.2	·
Interest Paid **13**	3.2	1.3	1.9	3.6	0.9	1.4	1.7	1.4	1.6	1.3	4.6	4.6	·
Depreciation **14**	7.7	0.5	4.0	4.3	13.0	6.2	9.3	8.8	9.3	7.2	8.8	7.6	·
Amortization and Depletion **15**	2.5	0.8	0.3	0.6	0.9	2.3	2.2	2.9	1.7	3.0	5.5	2.6	·
Pensions and Other Deferred Comp. **16**	0.7	0.0	·	0.3	1.0	0.4	0.6	0.7	0.9	1.2	0.7	0.8	·
Employee Benefits **17**	2.1	0.0	0.4	2.6	0.6	2.9	1.6	1.2	2.4	1.8	4.1	2.2	·
Advertising **18**	0.2	0.0	0.2	0.9	0.1	0.1	0.2	0.1	0.1	0.2	0.1	0.1	·
Other Expenses **19**	13.6	20.4	15.6	20.2	21.2	15.7	11.2	11.0	9.9	8.2	15.8	13.4	·
Officers' Compensation **20**	1.3	2.2	0.0	4.1	5.2	2.7	2.3	2.3	1.3	1.5	0.7	0.3	·
Operating Margin **21**	·	0.1	8.5	0.0	·	6.0	0.7	·	·	3.4	·	·	·
Operating Margin Before Officers' Comp. **22**	·	2.3	8.5	4.2	0.0	8.7	3.0	1.5	0.2	5.0	·	·	·

Selected Average Balance Sheet ($ in Thousands)

Net Receivables 23	518	0	11	69	461	1147	1798	3907	9069	17707	30642	162531	•
Inventories 24	362	0	13	72	74	556	1321	2381	6670	15060	22761	122218	•
Net Property, Plant and Equipment 25	2156	0	23	444	985	3584	6583	15204	39704	56857	190581	733738	•
Total Assets 26	7267	0	94	775	1957	7622	14944	34657	73234	150701	374730	3306654	•
Notes and Loans Payable 27	1608	0	39	404	799	2688	4076	10173	20738	27151	166128	573916	•
All Other Liabilities 28	1015	0	22	197	545	776	1911	7498	11146	27480	86991	383426	•
Net Worth 29	4644	0	32	174	613	4157	8957	16986	41351	96070	121610	2349311	•

Selected Financial Ratios (Times to 1)

Current Ratio 30	2.0	•	1.9	0.8	1.3	2.7	2.4	1.7	2.0	2.3	1.4	2.3
Quick Ratio 31	1.2	•	1.4	0.5	1.2	1.7	1.5	1.1	1.3	1.2	0.7	1.3
Net Sales to Working Capital 32	5.1	•	7.9	•	9.6	3.6	3.9	5.1	5.1	3.8	13.7	4.2
Coverage Ratio 33	2.1	4.2	7.8	1.8	•	7.2	3.6	3.2	2.4	5.3	1.2	1.6
Total Asset Turnover 34	0.5	•	2.2	1.0	1.1	1.1	0.9	0.8	0.9	0.7	0.7	0.3
Inventory Turnover 35	6.5	•	9.6	5.5	15.9	8.1	6.3	7.6	6.4	4.7	6.1	5.9
Receivables Turnover 36	7.0	•	34.0	9.6	4.7	5.7	7.0	8.2	7.2	5.6	9.7	6.3
Total Liabilities to Net Worth 37	0.6	•	1.9	3.5	2.2	0.8	0.7	1.0	0.8	0.6	2.1	0.4
Current Assets to Working Capital 38	2.0	•	2.1	•	3.9	1.6	1.7	2.4	2.0	1.8	3.8	1.8
Current Liabilities to Working Capital 39	1.0	•	1.1	•	2.9	0.6	0.7	1.4	1.0	0.8	2.8	0.8
Working Capital to Net Sales 40	0.2	•	0.1	•	0.1	0.3	0.3	0.2	0.2	0.3	0.1	0.2
Inventory to Working Capital 41	0.5	•	0.5	•	0.4	0.2	0.4	0.6	0.5	0.5	1.4	0.5
Total Receipts to Cash Flow 42	9.2	7.7	4.0	6.0	12.9	5.4	8.7	9.6	12.6	8.4	8.3	11.6
Cost of Goods to Cash Flow 43	5.8	4.9	2.4	3.1	7.3	3.0	5.5	6.3	8.4	5.5	4.5	7.5
Cash Flow to Total Debt 44	0.2	0.8	0.8	0.2	0.1	0.4	0.3	0.2	0.2	0.1	0.1	0.1

Selected Financial Factors (in Percentages)

Debt Ratio 45	36.1	•	65.7	77.6	68.7	45.5	40.1	51.0	43.5	36.3	67.5	29.0
Return on Total Assets 46	3.4	•	33.2	6.3	•	10.5	5.5	3.7	3.3	4.9	3.8	2.5
Return on Equity Before Income Taxes 47	2.7	•	84.5	12.3	•	16.5	6.7	5.2	3.4	6.3	1.9	1.4
Return on Equity After Income Taxes 48	1.9	•	83.9	10.7	•	15.2	5.8	3.9	2.0	4.9	•	0.7
Profit Margin (Before Income Tax) 49	3.4	4.3	13.3	2.8	•	8.5	4.5	3.2	2.2	5.6	0.9	2.9
Profit Margin (After Income Tax) 50	2.4	2.6	13.2	2.4	•	7.9	3.9	2.4	1.3	4.4	•	1.6

Table II
Corporations with Net Income

NONMETALLIC MINERAL MINING AND QUARRYING

MONEY AMOUNTS AND SIZE OF ASSETS IN THOUSANDS OF DOLLARS

Item Description for Accounting Period 7/02 Through 6/03	Total	Zero Assets	Under 500	500 to 1,000	1,000 to 5,000	5,000 to 10,000	10,000 to 25,000	25,000 to 50,000	50,000 to 100,000	100,000 to 250,000	250,000 to 500,000	500,000 to 2,500,000	2,500,000 and over
Number of Enterprises 1	2489	5	1332	640	265	93	93	34	7	0	0	0	0
Revenues ($ in Thousands)													
Net Sales 2	15143389	345511	477562	528374	627791	844792	1240225	907160	478353	0	0	0	0
Interest 3	90242	7327	86	802	1100	1178	2689	2299	3447	0	0	0	0
Rents 4	29410	0	32	7	254	501	3768	1269	2265	0	0	0	0
Royalties 5	21181	0	0	0	0	0	34	2494	191	0	0	0	0
Other Portfolio Income 6	377035	7777	24057	7257	3279	1671	20665	8584	8375	0	0	0	0
Other Receipts 7	241238	8696	527	10881	11964	14628	38612	20740	6375	0	0	0	0
Total Receipts 8	15902495	369311	502264	547321	644388	862770	1305993	942546	499006	0	0	0	0
Average Total Receipts 9	6389	73862	377	855	2432	9277	14043	27722	71287	•	•	•	•
Operating Costs/Operating Income (%)													
Cost of Operations 10	62.7	88.8	64.5	57.9	56.3	56.1	58.9	59.7	66.5	•	•	•	•
Salaries and Wages 11	4.5	0.8	6.8	7.7	1.3	3.3	4.3	4.1	3.7	•	•	•	•
Taxes Paid 12	2.5	0.3	1.0	4.1	4.1	2.7	3.1	2.7	2.5	•	•	•	•
Interest Paid 13	3.0	2.2	1.6	2.1	1.0	1.3	1.4	1.1	1.2	•	•	•	•
Depreciation 14	7.1	0.7	2.6	4.7	8.8	6.1	8.9	9.3	6.8	•	•	•	•
Amortization and Depletion 15	2.5	1.3	0.1	1.0	0.9	2.3	2.8	3.4	1.8	•	•	•	•
Pensions and Other Deferred Comp. 16	0.8	0.0	•	0.3	1.3	0.4	0.8	0.7	0.8	•	•	•	•
Employee Benefits 17	1.7	0.1	0.4	1.6	0.9	2.9	1.6	0.8	1.9	•	•	•	•
Advertising 18	0.2	0.0	0.2	1.3	0.1	0.1	0.2	0.1	0.1	•	•	•	•
Other Expenses 19	12.4	2.9	10.3	11.2	19.2	14.4	9.6	9.7	12.0	•	•	•	•
Officers' Compensation 20	1.2	0.1	0.0	2.9	4.7	2.7	2.7	2.6	1.3	•	•	•	•
Operating Margin 21	1.5	2.8	12.4	5.4	1.4	7.6	5.5	5.6	1.4	•	•	•	•
Operating Margin Before Officers' Comp. 22	2.6	2.9	12.4	8.3	6.1	10.3	8.3	8.2	2.7	•	•	•	•

Selected Average Balance Sheet ($ in Thousands)

Net Receivables 23	818	0	22	59	422	1300	1687	3495	8812
Inventories 24	552	0	25	25	80	547	1429	2364	7447
Net Property, Plant and Equipment 25	3371	0	21	447	1039	3912	6381	15721	41363
Total Assets 26	12555	0	124	715	2082	7585	14833	34068	75986
Notes and Loans Payable 27	2236	0	45	267	770	1759	3159	5411	18098
All Other Liabilities 28	1510	0	44	212	817	830	1792	4868	11293
Net Worth 29	8809	0	36	236	496	4996	9881	23789	46596

Selected Financial Ratios (Times to 1)

Current Ratio 30	2.5	•	2.3	1.1	1.1	2.1	2.9	2.8	2.3
Quick Ratio 31	1.6	•	1.7	0.9	1.0	1.7	1.8	1.9	1.6
Net Sales to Working Capital 32	4.0	•	6.3	52.0	22.0	5.6	3.3	3.4	4.1
Coverage Ratio 33	3.2	5.4	12.2	5.3	5.2	8.4	8.7	9.6	5.9
Total Asset Turnover 34	0.5	•	2.9	1.2	1.1	1.2	0.9	0.8	0.9
Inventory Turnover 35	6.9	•	9.2	19.1	16.7	9.3	5.5	6.7	6.1
Receivables Turnover 36	7.2	•	32.1	10.1	6.4	7.5	6.9	7.6	15.5
Total Liabilities to Net Worth 37	0.4	•	2.4	2.0	3.2	0.5	0.5	0.4	0.6
Current Assets to Working Capital 38	1.7	•	1.8	13.0	8.7	1.9	1.5	1.6	1.8
Current Liabilities to Working Capital 39	0.7	•	0.8	12.0	7.7	0.9	0.5	0.6	0.8
Working Capital to Net Sales 40	0.2	•	0.2	0.0	0.0	0.2	0.3	0.3	0.2
Inventory to Working Capital 41	0.4	•	0.4	1.4	1.1	0.3	0.4	0.3	0.4
Total Receipts to Cash Flow 42	7.8	8.3	4.1	6.2	7.7	5.4	6.0	6.1	7.9
Cost of Goods to Cash Flow 43	4.9	7.4	2.7	3.6	4.4	3.0	3.5	3.6	5.3
Cash Flow to Total Debt 44	0.2	•	1.0	0.3	0.2	0.7	0.4	0.4	0.3

Selected Financial Factors (in Percentages)

Debt Ratio 45	29.8	•	70.9	67.0	76.2	34.1	33.4	30.2	38.7
Return on Total Assets 46	4.7	•	55.2	12.8	5.7	13.2	10.9	8.3	6.2
Return on Equity Before Income Taxes 47	4.6	•	173.8	31.4	19.3	17.6	14.5	10.7	8.4
Return on Equity After Income Taxes 48	3.7	•	172.7	29.4	18.6	16.4	13.3	9.3	6.2
Profit Margin (Before Income Tax) 49	6.7	9.7	17.6	9.0	4.0	9.7	10.8	9.5	5.7
Profit Margin (After Income Tax) 50	5.3	7.0	17.5	8.4	3.9	9.0	9.9	8.3	4.2

Table I

Corporations with and without Net Income

SUPPORT ACTIVITIES FOR MINING

MONEY AMOUNTS AND SIZE OF ASSETS IN THOUSANDS OF DOLLARS

Item Description for Accounting Period 7/02 Through 6/03	Total	Zero Assets	Under 500	500 to 1,000	1,000 to 5,000	5,000 to 10,000	10,000 to 25,000	25,000 to 50,000	50,000 to 100,000	100,000 to 250,000	250,000 to 500,000	500,000 to 2,500,000	2,500,000 and over
Number of Enterprises 1	5193	450	3340	504	736	66	37	12	6	7	9	19	7
Revenues ($ in Thousands)													
Net Sales 2	33151168	382595	1756532	622678	1762790	411632	669681	494478	247514	806256	1586574	8795339	15615099
Interest 3	678810	5154	857	144	9109	2107	1259	1467	199	2490	47066	146010	462949
Rents 4	94642	0	0	0	213	0	2674	532	6	11795	4323	58859	16240
Royalties 5	292502	0	0	3621	28908	15	1	118	0	189	640	89179	169830
Other Portfolio Income 6	1225447	7722	124	15943	6137	4450	2116	1948	3654	15855	97709	258985	810804
Other Receipts 7	826583	970	9613	2943	172085	258	6638	4005	5095	7030	-14309	266579	365676
Total Receipts 8	36269152	396441	1767126	645329	1979242	418462	682369	502548	256468	843615	1722003	9614951	17440598
Average Total Receipts 9	6984	881	529	1280	2689	6340	18442	41879	42745	120516	191334	506050	2491514
Operating Costs/Operating Income (%)													
Cost of Operations 10	56.2	18.3	4.5	35.1	44.4	52.2	55.7	61.6	63.0	65.3	63.5	57.1	63.2
Salaries and Wages 11	11.7	20.8	14.8	12.3	13.2	10.6	12.6	11.0	12.6	9.8	6.3	9.8	12.7
Taxes Paid 12	2.6	1.2	2.9	3.5	3.8	2.9	3.0	2.7	1.4	3.0	3.6	1.8	2.6
Interest Paid 13	5.0	7.4	0.4	2.3	2.3	1.5	1.0	2.3	1.4	3.1	4.6	5.2	6.2
Depreciation 14	12.1	42.9	2.6	10.1	9.6	8.0	7.3	11.6	6.3	11.2	8.0	15.1	12.1
Amortization and Depletion 15	1.1	0.2	0.1	0.6	0.3	0.0	0.2	0.3	0.3	0.2	3.7	2.7	0.3
Pensions and Other Deferred Comp. 16	0.5	0.9	0.1	0.1	0.2	0.1	0.3	0.7	0.1	0.2	0.5	0.4	0.7
Employee Benefits 17	2.9	3.9	1.0	2.7	1.1	4.5	2.7	0.6	0.2	0.5	2.2	2.2	4.0
Advertising 18	0.2	0.1	0.2	0.1	0.2	0.1	0.3	0.1	0.1	0.2	0.1	0.2	0.2
Other Expenses 19	17.1	29.4	59.1	23.3	34.7	15.3	16.8	11.2	16.7	11.7	15.1	18.8	9.6
Officers' Compensation 20	1.5	5.1	5.9	10.8	3.3	1.7	2.5	1.1	0.6	1.0	0.9	1.0	0.7
Operating Margin 21	•	•	8.4	•	•	3.0	•	•	•	•	•	•	•
Operating Margin Before Officers' Comp. 22	•	•	14.3	10.0	•	4.7	0.1	•	•	•	•	•	•

Selected Average Balance Sheet ($ in Thousands)

Net Receivables 23	1451	0	17	138	340	1093	4444	8206	15303	18927	64695	125854	517516
Inventories 24	379	0	0	87	95	697	2141	7409	7133	12476	30787	149996	
Net Property, Plant and Equipment 25	4539	0	33	350	846	2452	4248	17912	14201	56219	81417	566424	1450860
Total Assets 26	16063	0	119	715	1941	6552	15762	35701	68161	139531	320488	1143846	7683286
Notes and Loans Payable 27	5984	0	41	406	1535	2117	4155	14139	44433	91555	384802	2948025	
All Other Liabilities 28	2365	0	16	192	623	3764	9404	18008	48714	161734	1117596		
Net Worth 29	7714	0	62	257	213	3812	7843	12158	40747	46383	182169	597310	3617665

Selected Financial Ratios (Times to 1)

Current Ratio 30	2.1	•	2.3	1.5	2.3	2.7	1.6	1.7	1.4	1.6	2.0	2.3	2.0
Quick Ratio 31	1.5	•	1.7	1.4	1.8	2.5	1.4	1.3	1.0	1.1	1.5	1.8	1.5
Net Sales to Working Capital 32	3.7	•	14.6	15.0	4.8	4.0	6.3	6.7	5.0	6.8	3.4	3.3	3.2
Coverage Ratio 33	1.1	•	22.3	2.2	0.6	4.2	0.4	0.3	1.6	0.5	1.1	0.4	1.4
Total Asset Turnover 34	0.4	•	4.4	1.7	1.2	1.0	1.1	1.2	0.6	0.8	0.6	0.4	0.3
Inventory Turnover 35	9.5	•	85.2	108.2	12.2	34.2	14.5	11.9	3.6	10.2	9.0	8.6	9.4
Receivables Turnover 36	3.5	•	31.0	6.8	6.2	3.3	4.3	4.5	3.3	3.9	2.3	4.1	2.8
Total Liabilities to Net Worth 37	1.1	•	0.9	1.8	8.1	0.7	1.0	1.9	0.7	2.0	0.8	0.9	1.1
Current Assets to Working Capital 38	1.9	•	1.7	3.0	1.7	1.6	2.8	2.4	3.3	2.6	2.1	1.7	2.0
Current Liabilities to Working Capital 39	0.9	•	0.7	2.0	0.7	0.6	1.8	1.4	2.3	1.6	1.1	0.7	1.0
Working Capital to Net Sales 40	0.3	•	0.1	0.1	0.2	0.2	0.2	0.1	0.2	0.1	0.3	0.3	0.3
Inventory to Working Capital 41	0.2	•	•	0.1	0.2	0.0	0.2	0.3	0.9	0.5	0.2	0.2	0.2
Total Receipts to Cash Flow 42	10.4	•	1.5	5.1	4.4	7.1	9.1	13.5	6.2	29.7	18.5	10.2	46.4
Cost of Goods to Cash Flow 43	5.8	•	0.1	1.8	1.9	3.7	5.0	8.3	3.9	19.4	11.7	5.8	29.3
Cash Flow to Total Debt 44	0.1	•	6.0	0.5	0.3	0.3	0.3	0.1	0.2	0.0	0.1	0.1	0.0

Selected Financial Factors (in Percentages)

Debt Ratio 45	52.0	•	48.4	64.0	89.0	41.8	50.2	65.9	40.2	66.8	43.2	47.8	52.9
Return on Total Assets 46	2.2	•	41.4	9.0	1.8	5.8	0.4	0.8	1.3	1.3	2.9	0.9	2.4
Return on Equity Before Income Taxes 47	0.4	•	76.7	13.8	7.6	•	•	•	0.8	•	0.7	•	1.4
Return on Equity After Income Taxes 48	•	•	76.3	5.2	6.0	•	•	•	•	•	•	•	•
Profit Margin (Before Income Tax) 49	0.5	•	9.0	2.9	4.7	0.8	•	0.8	•	0.5	•	0.7	2.2
Profit Margin (After Income Tax) 50	•	•	8.9	1.1	3.6	•	•	•	•	•	•	•	•

Table II
Corporations with Net Income

SUPPORT ACTIVITIES FOR MINING

MONEY AMOUNTS AND SIZE OF ASSETS IN THOUSANDS OF DOLLARS

Item Description for Accounting Period 7/02 Through 6/03	Total	Zero Assets	Under 500	500 to 1,000	1,000 to 5,000	5,000 to 10,000	10,000 to 25,000	25,000 to 50,000	50,000 to 100,000	100,000 to 250,000	250,000 to 500,000	500,000 to 2,500,000	2,500,000 and over
Number of Enterprises **1**	3000	0	2396	311	212	28	19	7	0	0	0	7	0
Revenues ($ in Thousands)													
Net Sales **2**	21920483	0	1583762	406146	824912	340365	398875	345080	0	0	0	16243349	0
Interest **3**	389201	0	686	133	1031	22	777	954	0	0	0	335360	0
Rents **4**	41020	0	0	0	0	0	581	532	0	0	0	23815	0
Royalties **5**	287850	0	0	0	28898	0	0	118	0	0	0	258634	0
Other Portfolio Income **6**	999223	0	124	1337	5671	4288	1074	1195	0	0	0	869653	0
Other Receipts **7**	461691	0	3586	2088	137059	3996	5181	1638	0	0	0	282556	0
Total Receipts **8**	24409468	0	1588158	409704	997571	348671	406488	349517	0	0	0	18013367	0
Average Total Receipts **9**	8033	.	663	1317	4706	12453	21394	49931	.	.	.	2573338	.
Operating Costs/Operating Income (%)													
Cost of Operations **10**	56.2	.	0.6	13.7	39.1	49.3	54.1	70.8	.	.	.	63.8	.
Salaries and Wages **11**	12.9	.	13.8	17.5	18.7	10.5	12.8	5.6	.	.	.	12.4	.
Taxes Paid **12**	2.6	.	2.7	4.6	2.8	3.1	3.2	2.4	.	.	.	2.5	.
Interest Paid **13**	3.0	.	0.4	0.6	0.9	1.2	0.8	1.1	.	.	.	3.5	.
Depreciation **14**	6.8	.	2.2	6.7	3.5	5.8	4.0	7.7	.	.	.	7.2	.
Amortization and Depletion **15**	0.2	.	0.1	0.9	0.5	0.0	0.1	0.1	.	.	.	0.2	.
Pensions and Other Deferred Comp. **16**	0.5	.	0.1	0.1	0.2	0.1	0.4	0.3	.	.	.	0.6	.
Employee Benefits **17**	3.3	.	0.3	0.7	0.6	5.4	2.3	0.3	.	.	.	4.0	.
Advertising **18**	0.2	.	0.2	0.0	0.3	0.1	0.2	0.1	.	.	.	0.3	.
Other Expenses **19**	15.8	.	62.8	30.0	36.6	13.2	13.1	7.7	.	.	.	9.9	.
Officers' Compensation **20**	1.5	.	6.3	14.1	2.7	1.4	2.2	1.1	.	.	.	0.6	.
Operating Margin **21**	.	.	10.5	11.0	.	9.8	6.7	2.8	.	.	.	.	.
Operating Margin Before Officers' Comp. **22**	.	.	16.9	25.1	.	11.2	9.0	3.9	.	.	.	.	.

Selected Average Balance Sheet ($ in Thousands)

Net Receivables 23	1697	24	135	594	1770	6369	10015	556667
Inventories 24	547	•	0	179	170	803	2295	121358
Net Property, Plant and Equipment 25	2252	33	302	433	2699	3371	16203	788776
Total Assets 26	12390	128	664	2012	7593	16123	34817	4646705
Notes and Loans Payable 27	3624	32	202	329	1371	4995	10983	1395482
All Other Liabilities 28	2705	23	21	251	992	5576	8366	1032940
Net Worth 29	6062	73	441	1432	5230	5552	15468	2218283

Selected Financial Ratios (Times to 1)

Current Ratio 30	2.4	2.2	9.4	3.7	3.3	1.3	2.1	2.4
Quick Ratio 31	1.8	1.5	9.3	2.8	3.1	1.1	1.7	1.7
Net Sales to Working Capital 32	3.4	16.1	5.3	4.0	4.0	8.9	5.4	3.3
Coverage Ratio 33	4.2	27.2	20.5	17.3	10.8	12.0	4.7	3.7
Total Asset Turnover 34	0.6	5.2	2.0	1.9	1.6	1.3	1.4	0.5
Inventory Turnover 35	7.5	9.7	958.0	8.5	35.3	14.2	15.2	12.2
Receivables Turnover 36	3.4	28.2	6.7	4.7	3.3	3.7	4.0	6.0
Total Liabilities to Net Worth 37	1.0	0.8	0.5	0.4	0.5	1.9	1.3	1.1
Current Assets to Working Capital 38	1.7	1.9	1.1	1.4	1.4	4.3	1.9	1.7
Current Liabilities to Working Capital 39	0.7	0.9	0.1	0.4	0.4	3.3	0.9	0.7
Working Capital to Net Sales 40	0.3	0.1	0.2	0.3	0.3	0.1	0.2	0.3
Inventory to Working Capital 41	0.2	0.2	•	0.3	0.0	0.3	0.3	0.3
Total Receipts to Cash Flow 42	5.7	1.4	3.1	2.4	5.3	6.1	9.7	8.9
Cost of Goods to Cash Flow 43	3.2	0.0	0.4	0.9	2.6	3.3	6.9	5.7
Cash Flow to Total Debt 44	0.2	8.6	1.9	2.8	1.0	0.3	0.3	0.1

Selected Financial Factors (in Percentages)

Debt Ratio 45	51.1	43.0	33.5	28.8	31.1	65.6	55.6	52.3
Return on Total Assets 46	7.4	57.8	24.6	30.8	21.5	12.3	7.4	6.4
Return on Equity Before Income Taxes 47	11.5	97.7	35.3	40.8	28.4	32.6	13.2	9.7
Return on Equity After Income Taxes 48	8.4	97.2	27.1	34.5	25.5	31.4	10.5	6.6
Profit Margin (Before Income Tax) 49	9.5	10.8	11.9	15.0	12.2	8.6	4.1	9.3
Profit Margin (After Income Tax) 50	7.0	10.7	9.2	12.7	11.0	8.3	3.3	6.3

Table I
Corporations with and without Net Income

ELECTRIC POWER GENERATION, TRANSMISSION AND DISTRIBUTION

MONEY AMOUNTS AND SIZE OF ASSETS IN THOUSANDS OF DOLLARS

Item Description for Accounting Period 7/02 Through 6/03		Total	Zero Assets	Under 500	500 to 1,000	1,000 to 5,000	5,000 to 10,000	10,000 to 25,000	25,000 to 50,000	50,000 to 100,000	100,000 to 250,000	250,000 to 500,000	500,000 to 2,500,000	2,500,000 and over
Number of Enterprises	1	891	294	315	27	43	41	35	25	13	24	14	25	35
Revenues ($ in Thousands)														
Net Sales	2	234007722	2090097	89978	57077	15113	319218	273517	669345	2709570	1447453	1449262	12109153	212777939
Interest	3	6324697	36482	195	1096	238	1776	9063	18088	2270	44035	87106	614126	5510222
Rents	4	2152785	1298	0	0	0	0	1175	1118	116	850	7339	29159	2111730
Royalties	5	47317	0	0	0	0	0	0	229	74	502	0	16550	29962
Other Portfolio Income	6	2627573	133166	0	0	24203	4129	8919	54087	2	280558	228952	286659	1606898
Other Receipts	7	7753645	54808	-3109	0	39047	-7385	26116	72958	7995	49691	322970	426027	6764527
Total Receipts	8	252913739	2315851	87064	58173	78601	317738	318790	815825	2720027	1823089	2095629	13481674	228801278
Average Total Receipts	9	283854	7877	276	2155	1828	7750	9108	32633	209233	75962	149688	539267	6537179
Operating Costs/Operating Income (%)														
Cost of Operations	10	63.9	62.4	*	3.1	*	13.5	29.1	77.0	92.4	49.4	49.1	65.6	63.8
Salaries and Wages	11	4.3	7.4	29.9	13.0	28.2	24.3	22.0	2.3	1.3	4.6	4.1	3.9	4.3
Taxes Paid	12	3.4	3.2	5.1	2.8	5.8	1.7	4.9	1.8	0.3	3.6	2.6	2.9	3.5
Interest Paid	13	7.8	5.6	1.7	*	65.7	1.3	5.7	6.0	0.8	9.0	14.6	7.7	7.9
Depreciation	14	7.1	6.2	1.3	17.9	191.8	3.7	6.2	3.0	1.5	7.7	7.0	7.7	7.2
Amortization and Depletion	15	0.7	0.8	*	*	1.0	1.9	1.2	0.9	0.1	1.6	2.8	0.9	0.7
Pensions and Other Deferred Comp.	16	0.7	0.0	*	0.4	*	0.2	0.1	0.7	0.1	0.1	0.9	0.7	0.7
Employee Benefits	17	1.1	1.9	5.5	*	1.7	0.4	1.9	0.3	0.1	1.4	0.4	0.9	1.2
Advertising	18	0.1	0.1	0.0	0.2	0.0	0.0	0.3	0.4	0.3	0.0	0.9	0.1	0.1
Other Expenses	19	16.0	17.9	63.4	20.0	107.8	49.6	32.0	16.7	6.8	61.3	74.5	28.0	14.6
Officers' Compensation	20	0.3	0.2	*	34.5	1.5	2.3	3.3	0.7	0.3	1.7	1.4	0.4	0.3
Operating Margin	21	*	*	*	8.3	*	1.1	*	*	*	*	*	*	*
Operating Margin Before Officers' Comp.	22	*	*	*	42.9	*	3.4	*	*	*	*	*	*	*

Selected Average Balance Sheet ($ in Thousands)

Item													
Net Receivables 23	45273	0	0	0	86	280	1949	4519	10889	13455	11732	88678	1065597
Inventories 24	8121	0	0	0	0	24	123	337	540	976	5374	21913	187688
Net Property, Plant and Equipment 25	306209		84	449	1546	3810	4972	15869	21941	59554	165717	690257	7163117
Total Assets 26	671385		336	864	2469	7314	17174	35636	71231	148720	348979	1224802	15890743
Notes and Loans Payable 27	288092	0	218		1005	5802	90805	14957	37218	82634	198910	664517	6597798
All Other Liabilities 28	226758	0	169	415	1851	944	6260	21375	30504	33018	94248	283714	5471550
Net Worth 29	156535	0	-51		-387	568	-79891	-696	3509	33068	55822	276572	3821395

Selected Financial Ratios (Times to 1)

Ratio													
Current Ratio 30	0.8		0.7	0.9	0.3	2.4	0.1	0.9	0.8	1.8	1.1	1.3	0.8
Quick Ratio 31	0.4		0.7	0.7	0.2	1.6	0.1	0.7	0.7	1.5	0.8	0.9	0.4
Net Sales to Working Capital 32						6.4				3.4	25.1	12.1	
Coverage Ratio 33	1.4	1.9			2.8	1.5	2.7	3.0			0.1	0.0	1.5
Total Asset Turnover 34	0.4		0.9	2.4	0.1	1.1	0.5	0.8	2.9	0.4	0.3	0.4	0.4
Inventory Turnover 35	20.7					44.5	18.6	61.2	356.5	30.5	9.4	14.5	20.7
Receivables Turnover 36	5.6	6427.0	6.7		3.6	42.4	4.6	8.0	14.0	5.2	8.0	6.8	5.4
Total Liabilities to Net Worth 37	3.3			0.9		11.9			19.3	3.5	5.3	3.4	3.2
Current Assets to Working Capital 38						1.7				2.3	9.2	4.7	
Current Liabilities to Working Capital 39						0.7				1.3	8.2	3.7	
Working Capital to Net Sales 40						0.2				0.3	0.0	0.1	
Inventory to Working Capital 41						0.0				0.1	0.8	0.6	
Total Receipts to Cash Flow 42	7.2	3.0	4.6	0.5	2.1	2.9	7.4		6.2	2.1	12.7	7.1	
Cost of Goods to Cash Flow 43	4.6	4.3	0.1		0.3	0.8	5.7		3.1	1.0	8.3	4.6	
Cash Flow to Total Debt 44	0.1	0.2	1.1	0.3	0.6	0.0	0.1		0.1	0.2	0.0	0.1	

Selected Financial Factors (in Percentages)

Factor													
Debt Ratio 45	76.7		115.3	48.1	115.7	92.2	565.2	102.0	95.1	77.8	84.0	77.4	76.0
Return on Total Assets 46	4.1			25.1	25.9	2.1	7.0	13.6		2.1	0.3	0.1	4.4
Return on Equity Before Income Taxes 47	4.6		56.6	48.3	9.2								5.7
Return on Equity After Income Taxes 48	2.5		56.6	48.3									3.7
Profit Margin (Before Income Tax) 49	2.7	5.2	10.2	116.3	0.7	9.8	12.1						3.6
Profit Margin (After Income Tax) 50	1.5	2.5	10.2	116.3	6.1	7.7							2.3

Table II

Corporations with Net Income

ELECTRIC POWER GENERATION, TRANSMISSION AND DISTRIBUTION

MONEY AMOUNTS AND SIZE OF ASSETS IN THOUSANDS OF DOLLARS

Item Description for Accounting Period 7/02 Through 6/03	Total	Zero Assets	Under 500	500 to 1,000	1,000 to 5,000	5,000 to 10,000	10,000 to 25,000	25,000 to 50,000	50,000 to 100,000	100,000 to 250,000	250,000 to 500,000	500,000 to 2,500,000	2,500,000 and over
Number of Enterprises 1	405	12	247	27	4	24	19	14	6	12	8	8	24
Revenues ($ in Thousands)													
Net Sales 2	197791584	2061703	89978	57077	15113	253660	186398	371212	2251691	698272	747854	3437964	187620660
Interest 3	2945556	36085	0	1096	133	1529	6643	13809	748	12060	23870	81282	2768302
Rents 4	1934088	1298	0	0	0	0	914	696	0	473	7187	14508	1909013
Royalties 5	45884	0	0	0	0	0	0	229	74	0	0	16513	29069
Other Portfolio Income 6	1976153	132962	0	0	23173	4078	8910	37823	2	81972	228916	24764	1433555
Other Receipts 7	5551226	44251	1692	0	39038	1496	22112	99662	-2974	10290	8063	129779	519815
Total Receipts 8	210244491	2276299	91670	58173	77457	260763	224977	523431	2249541	803067	1015890	3704810	198958414
Average Total Receipts 9	519122	189692	371	2155	19364	10865	11841	37388	374924	66922	126986	463101	8289934
Operating Costs/Operating Income (%)													
Cost of Operations 10	64.1	63.2	•	3.1	•	4.6	30.5	78.7	92.6	45.8	59.2	55.9	64.2
Salaries and Wages 11	4.0	7.5	29.5	13.0	23.5	29.0	21.6	2.2	0.7	1.1	0.7	4.6	4.0
Taxes Paid 12	3.5	2.8	5.1	2.8	5.8	1.0	5.1	2.4	0.2	4.6	2.6	4.3	3.5
Interest Paid 13	6.2	5.2	1.7	•	29.4	0.2	3.8	7.5	0.4	5.1	11.2	5.9	6.3
Depreciation 14	6.6	5.7	0.7	17.9	104.3	0.6	5.7	2.4	0.3	8.0	7.1	9.1	6.6
Amortization and Depletion 15	0.6	0.8	•	•	•	2.1	0.3	1.3	0.0	0.2	0.7	1.0	0.6
Pensions and Other Deferred Comp. 16	0.7	•	•	0.4	•	0.0	0.2	0.3	0.1	0.2	1.0	2.0	0.7
Employee Benefits 17	1.2	1.9	5.5	•	1.7	0.0	1.1	0.3	0.1	1.5	0.4	1.3	1.2
Advertising 18	0.1	0.1	0.0	•	0.2	0.0	0.1	0.0	0.0	0.0	0.0	0.1	0.1
Other Expenses 19	13.2	15.3	55.5	20.0	86.2	52.5	24.2	13.0	3.9	26.0	35.4	15.7	13.0
Officers' Compensation 20	0.3	0.1	•	34.5	1.5	2.4	3.0	0.6	0.1	0.9	0.4	0.6	0.3
Operating Margin 21	•	•	2.1	8.3	•	7.7	4.3	•	1.6	6.5	•	•	•
Operating Margin Before Officers' Comp. 22	•	•	2.1	42.9	•	10.0	7.4	•	1.7	7.4	•	•	0.0

	1	2	3	4	5	6	7	8	9	10	11	12	13
Net Receivables 23	73796	0	0	0	900	181	2491	2193	13496	7631	9650	48871	1215026
Inventories 24	13379	0	0	0	0	11	220	438	773	1337	2077	28346	214029
Net Property, Plant and Equipment 25	498400		0	4	179	4141	3876	17104	26648	76637	134263	631900	8092373
Total Assets 26	1107745		327	864	3012	7922	17193	35213	71075	151810	339552	1058660	18086543
Notes and Loans Payable 27	417522		238	.0	0	5243	3313	14365	41142	79469	176022	540929	6737978
All Other Liabilities 28	400285		3	415	629	736	5464	27261	29792	38495	121236	283790	6571535
Net Worth 29	289939	0	85	448	2383	1943	8415	-6412	140	33847	42293	233941	4777030

	1	2	3	4	5	6	7	8	9	10	11	12	13
Current Ratio 30	0.9	•	1.3	0.9	5.3	2.8	1.2	1.4	1.1	1.7	1.0	1.4	0.9
Quick Ratio 31	0.4	•	1.3	0.7	5.1	1.9	0.9	1.0	0.9	1.5	0.8	0.8	0.4
Net Sales to Working Capital 32	•	•	4.5	•	1.4	7.7	8.2	14.3	161.8	4.7	387.1	11.0	•
Coverage Ratio 33	2.0	2.5	3.3	•	9.8	45.0	7.5	5.3	4.9	5.2	2.5	2.2	1.9
Total Asset Turnover 34	0.4	•	1.1	2.4	1.3	1.3	0.6	0.8	5.3	0.4	0.3	0.4	0.4
Inventory Turnover 35	23.4	•	•	•	•	45.6	13.6	47.7	449.7	20.0	26.6	8.5	23.4
Receivables Turnover 36	6.5	6427.0	•	•	8.4	65.8	7.9	11.4	55.6	8.6	19.4	5.3	6.3
Total Liabilities to Net Worth 37	2.8	•	2.8	0.9	0.3	3.1	1.0	•	504.9	3.5	7.0	3.5	2.8
Current Assets to Working Capital 38	•	•	4.0	•	1.2	1.6	5.0	3.4	11.6	2.4	83.2	3.5	•
Current Liabilities to Working Capital 39	•	•	3.0	•	0.2	0.6	4.0	2.4	10.6	1.4	82.2	2.5	•
Working Capital to Net Sales 40	•	•	0.2	•	0.7	0.1	0.1	0.1	0.0	0.2	0.0	0.1	•
Inventory to Working Capital 41	•	•	•	•	0.0	0.0	0.2	0.3	0.3	0.1	8.6	0.4	•
Total Receipts to Cash Flow 42	6.7	6.7	2.1	4.6	0.3	1.6	2.5	3.4	36.6	2.8	2.0	5.6	6.8
Cost of Goods to Cash Flow 43	4.3	4.2	•	•	•	0.1	0.8	2.7	33.9	1.3	1.2	3.1	4.4
Cash Flow to Total Debt 44	0.1	•	0.7	1.1	20.5	1.1	0.4	0.2	0.1	0.2	0.2	0.1	0.1

	1	2	3	4	5	6	7	8	9	10	11	12	13
Debt Ratio 45	73.8	•	73.8	48.1	20.9	75.5	51.1	118.2	99.8	77.7	87.5	77.9	73.6
Return on Total Assets 46	5.3	•	6.3	25.1	362.9	14.2	16.5	30.0	10.1	10.2	7.8	5.3	5.2
Return on Equity Before Income Taxes 47	10.0	•	16.7	48.3	412.0	56.8	29.2	•	4058.2	36.9	37.9	13.2	9.4
Return on Equity After Income Taxes 48	7.5	•	16.7	48.3	412.0	43.1	23.0	•	3913.4	28.9	33.4	9.9	7.1
Profit Margin (Before Income Tax) 49	5.9	8.0	3.9	10.2	259.8	10.4	25.0	32.3	1.5	21.5	17.1	7.2	5.7
Profit Margin (After Income Tax) 50	4.5	5.2	3.9	10.2	259.8	7.9	19.7	24.4	1.5	16.8	15.1	5.4	4.3

Table I

Corporations with and without Net Income

NATURAL GAS DISTRIBUTION

MONEY AMOUNTS AND SIZE OF ASSETS IN THOUSANDS OF DOLLARS

Item Description for Accounting Period 7/02 Through 6/03		Total	Zero Assets	Under 500	500 to 1,000	1,000 to 5,000	5,000 to 10,000	10,000 to 25,000	25,000 to 50,000	50,000 to 100,000	100,000 to 250,000	250,000 to 500,000	500,000 to 2,500,000	2,500,000 and over
Number of Enterprises	1	972	0	741	0	116	0	0	9	10	12	3	13	13
Revenues ($ in Thousands)														
Net Sales	2	80260597	0	110100	0	178330	0	0	178747	1112854	1915503	669384	13900532	61453759
Interest	3	1916687	0	0	0	0	0	0	323	3145	6528	1382	24826	1878732
Rents	4	127142	0	0	0	0	0	0	965	2305	13	89	7183	116523
Royalties	5	27323	0	0	0	0	0	0	0	5	246	0	65	27007
Other Portfolio Income	6	2960357	0	76	0	0	0	0	257	708	12120	1525	54606	2888563
Other Receipts	7	2665317	0	0	0	0	0	0	578	6151	26727	20227	129890	2480571
Total Receipts	8	87957423	0	110176	0	178330	0	0	180870	1125168	1961137	692607	14117102	68845155
Average Total Receipts	9	90491	•	149	•	1537	•	•	20097	112517	163428	230869	1085931	5295781
Operating Costs/Operating Income (%)														
Cost of Operations	10	78.3	•	80.3	•	47.8	•	•	73.2	89.8	82.1	62.7	71.8	79.8
Salaries and Wages	11	3.4	•	3.3	•	9.5	•	•	1.9	1.3	2.6	5.1	2.6	3.7
Taxes Paid	12	2.0	•	2.9	•	2.1	•	•	2.9	0.8	1.5	5.0	3.0	1.8
Interest Paid	13	7.1	•	0.0	•	3.1	•	•	5.0	0.9	1.7	2.7	3.6	8.3
Depreciation	14	6.1	•	0.8	•	10.1	•	•	8.9	2.4	3.4	6.9	8.2	5.8
Amortization and Depletion	15	0.7	•	•	•	•	•	•	1.4	0.0	0.4	0.9	0.6	0.8
Pensions and Other Deferred Comp.	16	0.3	•	•	•	0.3	•	•	0.3	0.1	0.2	0.2	0.5	0.3
Employee Benefits	17	1.1	•	•	•	1.0	•	•	1.1	0.5	0.4	1.5	1.0	1.2
Advertising	18	0.1	•	0.1	•	0.8	•	•	0.1	0.0	0.2	0.0	0.1	0.1
Other Expenses	19	16.7	•	14.7	•	11.3	•	•	7.1	4.2	5.1	12.6	8.3	19.4
Officers' Compensation	20	0.4	•	3.8	•	3.2	•	•	1.5	0.3	0.4	0.8	0.4	0.4
Operating Margin	21	•	•	•	•	10.8	•	•	•	•	2.1	1.5	0.0	•
Operating Margin Before Officers' Comp.	22	•	•	•	•	14.0	•	•	•	•	2.5	2.3	0.4	•

Selected Average Balance Sheet ($ in Thousands)

Net Receivables 23	54797	0	151	·	5572	17858	22606	13327	115374	3930051
Inventories 24	3212	0	59	·	1010	3336	7782	5539	52935	174093
Net Property, Plant and Equipment 25	71263	3	1027	·	20141	27472	66742	213023	993045	4164971
Total Assets 26	258612	34	1766	·	36195	67825	146914	311820	1414672	17583237
Notes and Loans Payable 27	101405	0	876	·	14405	11044	39495	114653	574846	6911407
All Other Liabilities 28	102708	33	195	·	8870	27208	50361	50823	379372	7200081
Net Worth 29	54498	0	694	·	12920	29573	57058	146344	460454	3471749

Selected Financial Ratios (Times to 1)

Current Ratio 30	0.9	·	2.8	·	3.2	1.2	1.2	1.0	0.8	0.9
Quick Ratio 31	0.6	·	2.8	·	2.3	1.0	0.8	0.5	0.4	0.6
Net Sales to Working Capital 32	·	·	8.7	·	3.1	22.0	25.6	·	1.4	·
Coverage Ratio 33	0.1	·	4.4	·	4.4	1.8	3.6	2.8	·	·
Total Asset Turnover 34	0.3	·	0.9	·	0.5	1.6	1.1	0.7	0.8	0.3
Inventory Turnover 35	20.1	·	12.4	·	14.4	30.0	16.8	25.3	14.5	21.7
Receivables Turnover 36	1.5	·	7.4	·	2.7	7.9	10.3	15.4	8.5	1.2
Total Liabilities to Net Worth 37	3.7	·	111.8	·	1.8	1.3	1.6	1.1	2.1	4.1
Current Assets to Working Capital 38	·	·	1.6	·	6.7	5.9	7.6	·	·	·
Current Liabilities to Working Capital 39	·	·	0.6	·	5.7	4.9	6.6	·	·	·
Working Capital to Net Sales 40	·	·	0.1	·	0.1	0.0	0.0	·	·	·
Inventory to Working Capital 41	·	·	0.1	·	0.5	0.6	1.8	·	·	·
Total Receipts to Cash Flow 42	12.0	·	19.2	·	31.0	22.7	11.9	6.0	13.5	11.8
Cost of Goods to Cash Flow 43	9.4	·	15.4	·	22.7	20.4	9.8	3.8	9.7	9.4
Cash Flow to Total Debt 44	0.0	·	0.2	·	0.0	0.1	0.0	0.2	0.1	0.0

Selected Financial Factors (in Percentages)

Debt Ratio 45	78.9	·	99.1	·	64.3	56.4	61.2	53.1	67.5	80.3
Return on Total Assets 46	0.2	·	12.1	·	1.5	2.5	6.8	5.5	3.9	·
Return on Equity Before Income Taxes 47	·	·	23.8	·	2.6	12.6	7.6	3.6	·
Return on Equity After Income Taxes 48	·	·	23.8	·	1.3	10.9	5.4	2.2	·
Profit Margin (Before Income Tax) 49	·	·	10.8	·	0.7	4.5	5.0	1.6	·
Profit Margin (After Income Tax) 50	·	·	10.8	·	0.3	3.9	3.6	0.9	·

Table II

Corporations with Net Income

NATURAL GAS DISTRIBUTION

MONEY AMOUNTS AND SIZE OF ASSETS IN THOUSANDS OF DOLLARS

Item Description for Accounting Period 7/02 Through 6/03	Total	Zero Assets	Under 500	500 to 1,000	1,000 to 5,000	5,000 to 10,000	10,000 to 25,000	25,000 to 50,000	50,000 to 100,000	100,000 to 250,000	250,000 to 500,000	500,000 to 2,500,000	2,500,000 and over
Number of Enterprises **1**	130	0	•	•	51	21	15	3	0	0	0	10	6
Revenues ($ in Thousands)													
Net Sales **2**	28015652	0	•	•	70087	78870	414808	79247	0	0	0	11131734	13147746
Interest **3**	421149	0	•	•	0	381	843	9	0	0	0	19394	395526
Rents **4**	42631	0	•	•	0	0	62	8	0	0	0	3823	36685
Royalties **5**	1964	0	•	•	0	0	0	0	0	0	0	65	1653
Other Portfolio Income **6**	270811	0	•	•	0	849	1632	188	0	0	0	35527	231673
Other Receipts **7**	1755895	0	•	•	0	789	2515	321	0	0	0	156612	1554523
Total Receipts **8**	30508102	0	•	•	70087	80889	419860	79773	0	0	0	11347155	15367806
Average Total Receipts **9**	234678	•	•	•	1374	3852	27991	26591	•	•	•	1134716	2561301
Operating Costs/Operating Income (%)													
Cost of Operations **10**	61.2	•	•	•	38.2	44.2	81.9	76.8	•	•	•	73.6	45.5
Salaries and Wages **11**	4.6	•	•	•	10.6	7.5	2.6	3.8	•	•	•	2.2	7.1
Taxes Paid **12**	3.1	•	•	•	1.6	4.0	0.9	1.4	•	•	•	3.0	3.6
Interest Paid **13**	5.3	•	•	•	•	0.6	0.6	0.8	•	•	•	3.2	8.2
Depreciation **14**	7.5	•	•	•	0.0	10.9	1.4	4.7	•	•	•	7.3	9.0
Amortization and Depletion **15**	0.7	•	•	•	•	0.2	0.3	0.1	•	•	•	0.6	0.9
Pensions and Other Deferred Comp. **16**	0.6	•	•	•	0.2	1.4	0.2	0.7	•	•	•	0.5	0.8
Employee Benefits **17**	1.8	•	•	•	0.1	1.8	0.6	0.7	•	•	•	0.9	3.0
Advertising **18**	0.1	•	•	•	0.0	1.0	0.1	0.1	•	•	•	0.1	0.1
Other Expenses **19**	16.1	•	•	•	8.7	16.2	6.5	6.9	•	•	•	7.4	26.5
Officers' Compensation **20**	0.8	•	•	•	3.0	2.6	0.6	1.0	•	•	•	0.3	1.3
Operating Margin **21**	•	•	•	•	37.5	9.6	4.2	3.0	•	•	•	0.9	•
Operating Margin Before Officers' Comp. **22**	•	•	•	•	40.5	12.2	4.9	3.9	•	•	•	1.2	•

Selected Average Balance Sheet ($ in Thousands)

Net Receivables 23	41852	115	177	5784	7447	122620	615701
Inventories 24	16433	92	36	444	1806	60541	233488
Net Property, Plant and Equipment 25	250181	10	3568	3968	16072	971769	3562194
Total Assets 26	415483	1295	5781	15701	36769	1420549	6177437
Notes and Loans Payable 27	161004	0	445	2909	2985	514887	2520059
All Other Liabilities 28	122674	100	868	6886	5759	412970	1816370
Net Worth 29	131805	1195	4467	5905	28025	492692	1841008

Selected Financial Ratios (Times to 1)

Current Ratio 30	1.2	12.8	1.7	1.5	3.2	0.8	1.4
Quick Ratio 31	0.7	9.2	1.3	1.4	1.5	0.4	0.8
Net Sales to Working Capital 32	12.8	1.2	14.5	8.2	2.3		5.4
Coverage Ratio 33	2.3		20.7	9.9	5.4	1.9	2.3
Total Asset Turnover 34	0.5	1.1	0.6	1.8	0.7	0.8	0.4
Inventory Turnover 35	8.0	5.7	45.7	51.0	11.2	13.5	4.3
Receivables Turnover 36	3.3	8.2	11.3	4.8	1.6	18.2	2.0
Total Liabilities to Net Worth 37	2.2	0.1	0.3	1.7	0.3	1.9	2.4
Current Assets to Working Capital 38	5.2	1.1	2.4	2.8	1.5		3.2
Current Liabilities to Working Capital 39	4.2	0.1	1.4	1.8	0.5		2.2
Working Capital to Net Sales 40	0.1	0.9	0.1	0.1	0.4		0.2
Inventory to Working Capital 41	0.8	0.1	0.0	0.0	0.0		0.4
Total Receipts to Cash Flow 42	4.9	2.2	4.4	9.1	10.1	12.6	3.0
Cost of Goods to Cash Flow 43	3.0	0.8	2.0	7.5	7.8	9.3	1.3
Cash Flow to Total Debt 44	0.2	6.2	0.6	0.3	0.3	0.1	0.2

Selected Financial Factors (in Percentages)

Debt Ratio 45	68.3	7.8	22.7	62.4	23.8	65.3	70.2
Return on Total Assets 46	6.4	39.8	8.1	10.7	3.2	4.7	6.7
Return on Equity Before Income Taxes 47	11.4	43.1	10.0	25.6	3.4	6.5	12.8
Return on Equity After Income Taxes 48	8.1	43.1	6.8	24.0	3.1	4.7	8.8
Profit Margin (Before Income Tax) 49	7.0	37.5	11.9	5.5	3.6	2.9	10.8
Profit Margin (After Income Tax) 50	5.0	37.5	8.0	5.1	3.3	2.1	7.4

20

Table I

Corporations with and without Net Income

WATER, SEWAGE AND OTHER SYSTEMS

MONEY AMOUNTS AND SIZE OF ASSETS IN THOUSANDS OF DOLLARS

Item Description for Accounting Period 7/02 Through 6/03		Total	Zero Assets	Under 500	500 to 1,000	1,000 to 5,000	5,000 to 10,000	10,000 to 25,000	25,000 to 50,000	50,000 to 100,000	100,000 to 250,000	250,000 to 500,000	500,000 to 2,500,000	2,500,000 and over
Number of Enterprises	1	5961	280	4818	124	619	38	39	17	5	9	4	7	0
Revenues ($ in Thousands)														
Net Sales	2	6174618	6446	627570	39155	805497	454548	287148	138842	65582	317557	422741	3009532	0
Interest	3	33040	42	1544	34	6288	40	965	2702	336	5358	1116	14615	0
Rents	4	16208	30	0	0	1193	0	420	509	60	1145	2641	10210	0
Royalties	5	3477	0	0	0	7	0	479	0	0	2979	0	11	0
Other Portfolio Income	6	244998	2699	13489	246	519	3	9519	1324	367	338	1479	215015	0
Other Receipts	7	127654	4113	19133	3025	8610	73	2267	1746	348	53367	6626	28349	0
Total Receipts	8	6599995	13330	661736	42460	822114	454664	300798	145123	66693	380744	434603	3277732	0
Average Total Receipts	9	1107	48	137	342	1328	11965	7713	8537	13339	42305	108651	468247	•
Operating Costs/Operating Income (%)														
Cost of Operations	10	30.4	10.5	11.9	31.7	35.1	0.1	50.6	30.9	36.9	37.8	41.7	33.1	•
Salaries and Wages	11	10.9	15.1	8.9	7.6	10.2	63.4	11.5	5.9	4.0	10.3	6.0	4.7	•
Taxes Paid	12	7.6	7.0	5.3	7.3	7.0	5.2	4.2	9.3	7.7	7.5	10.3	8.5	•
Interest Paid	13	8.6	21.4	1.1	2.1	4.5	0.4	6.1	7.3	10.2	22.5	5.2	11.9	•
Depreciation	14	13.0	25.2	6.5	14.8	12.0	0.8	12.5	17.0	19.2	17.5	15.0	15.5	•
Amortization and Depletion	15	1.4	0.3	0.0	0.0	0.4	•	0.7	0.4	1.3	3.4	0.3	2.3	•
Pensions and Other Deferred Comp.	16	0.9	0.9	0.6	0.1	1.1	•	0.3	0.7	1.4	0.6	1.0	1.1	•
Employee Benefits	17	4.0	3.4	1.3	0.9	1.3	23.4	2.0	2.1	3.8	4.3	2.3	2.9	•
Advertising	18	0.4	0.0	1.2	•	0.5	0.0	0.2	0.0	0.1	1.9	0.0	0.1	•
Other Expenses	19	36.8	95.0	49.4	28.8	30.3	6.8	18.6	29.2	10.5	328.6	11.7	15.8	•
Officers' Compensation	20	2.6	2.6	10.1	13.2	4.4	0.1	3.3	1.8	2.2	2.4	1.0	1.0	•
Operating Margin	21	•	3.6	•	•	•	•	•	•	2.7	•	5.4	3.1	•
Operating Margin Before Officers' Comp.	22	•	13.7	6.7	•	•	•	•	•	4.9	•	6.5	4.0	•

Selected Average Balance Sheet ($ in Thousands)

Line Item													
Net Receivables 23	132	0	13	54	153	62	1541	1402	1129	3683	14573	63424	•
Inventories 24	32	0	5	87	2	231	129	60	282	13481	834	3683	•
Net Property, Plant and Equipment 25	2561	0	52	654	1457	4318	11203	24323	53423	106114	290191	1519152	•
Total Assets 26	3550	0	103	903	2265	7071	16696	33388	71967	166860	349693	2057351	•
Notes and Loans Payable 27	1560	0	34	95	1232	4059	6508	9450	24664	72645	85449	953578	•
All Other Liabilities 28	996	0	22	158	571	3134	5771	10600	20563	38249	151238	554585	•
Net Worth 29	993	0	46	651	462	-123	4418	13338	26740	55966	113006	549189	•

Selected Financial Ratios (Times to 1)

Line Item													
Current Ratio 30	1.0	•	2.1	7.1	1.2	0.9	1.4	1.8	1.7	2.2	0.8	0.7	•
Quick Ratio 31	0.6	•	1.8	6.6	0.9	0.1	1.1	1.3	1.3	1.2	0.7	0.4	•
Net Sales to Working Capital 32	•	•	5.6	1.5	17.5	•	6.8	3.5	5.9	1.7	•	•	•
Coverage Ratio 33	•	2.2	9.1	1.9	•	0.9	0.3	0.9	1.4	•	2.6	2.0	•
Total Asset Turnover 34	0.3	•	1.3	0.3	0.6	1.7	0.4	0.2	0.2	0.2	0.3	0.2	•
Inventory Turnover 35	9.8	•	2.8	1.2	193.3	0.1	29.0	42.3	17.2	1.0	52.9	38.7	•
Receivables Turnover 36	7.3	•	11.6	3.8	7.5	10.6	4.7	7.0	8.0	6.9	6.1	7.0	•
Total Liabilities to Net Worth 37	2.6	•	1.2	0.4	3.9	•	2.8	1.5	1.7	2.0	2.1	2.7	•
Current Assets to Working Capital 38	•	•	1.9	1.2	7.2	•	3.4	2.2	2.5	1.8	•	•	•
Current Liabilities to Working Capital 39	•	•	0.9	0.2	6.2	•	2.4	1.2	1.5	0.8	•	•	•
Working Capital to Net Sales 40	•	•	0.2	0.7	0.1	•	0.1	0.3	0.2	0.6	•	•	•
Inventory to Working Capital 41	•	•	0.2	0.0	0.0	•	0.1	0.0	0.2	0.7	•	•	•
Total Receipts to Cash Flow 42	5.4	1.9	2.1	3.8	5.7	15.2	10.9	3.7	9.1	•	6.0	5.4	•
Cost of Goods to Cash Flow 43	1.6	0.2	0.3	1.2	2.0	0.0	5.5	1.1	3.3	•	2.5	1.8	•
Cash Flow to Total Debt 44	0.1	•	1.1	0.3	0.1	0.1	0.1	0.1	0.0	•	0.1	0.1	•

Selected Financial Factors (in Percentages)

Line Item													
Debt Ratio 45	72.0	•	54.9	28.0	79.6	101.7	73.5	60.1	62.8	66.5	67.7	73.3	•
Return on Total Assets 46	•	•	12.8	1.4	0.6	0.6	0.8	1.7	2.7	•	4.1	5.0	•
Return on Equity Before Income Taxes 47	•	•	25.4	0.9	5.4	•	2.2	•	2.2	•	7.7	9.4	•
Return on Equity After Income Taxes 48	•	•	24.5	0.8	5.4	•	1.1	•	1.1	•	5.1	6.1	•
Profit Margin (Before Income Tax) 49	•	25.4	9.0	1.9	•	•	4.4	•	4.4	•	8.3	12.0	•
Profit Margin (After Income Tax) 50	•	25.0	8.7	1.6	•	•	2.3	•	2.3	•	5.5	7.8	•

Table II
Corporations with Net Income

WATER, SEWAGE AND OTHER SYSTEMS

MONEY AMOUNTS AND SIZE OF ASSETS IN THOUSANDS OF DOLLARS

Item Description for Accounting Period 7/02 Through 6/03	Total	Zero Assets	Under 500	500 to 1,000	1,000 to 5,000	5,000 to 10,000	10,000 to 25,000	25,000 to 50,000	50,000 to 100,000	100,000 to 250,000	250,000 to 500,000	500,000 to 2,500,000	2,500,000 and over
Number of Enterprises **1**	3374	3	2953	95	270	0	0	11	0	0	4	7	0
Revenues ($ in Thousands)													
Net Sales **2**	4909474	2637	408264	36143	573052	0	0	79369	0	0	422741	3009532	0
Interest **3**	21521	5	812	31	771	0	0	602	0	0	1116	14615	0
Rents **4**	15571	26	0	0	1155	0	0	345	0	0	2641	10210	0
Royalties **5**	29	0	0	0	7	0	0	0	0	0	0	11	0
Other Portfolio Income **6**	241138	2696	13489	246	337	0	0	317	0	0	1479	215015	0
Other Receipts **7**	47610	636	760	3025	2145	0	0	693	0	0	6626	28349	0
Total Receipts **8**	5235343	6000	423325	39445	577467	0	0	81326	0	0	434603	3277732	0
Average Total Receipts **9**	1552	2000	143	415	2139	•	•	7393	•	•	108651	468247	•
Operating Costs/Operating Income (%)													
Cost of Operations **10**	33.1	3.1	12.1	34.3	39.9	•	•	23.2	•	•	41.7	33.1	•
Salaries and Wages **11**	5.4	12.0	7.7	6.4	6.8	•	•	4.8	•	•	6.0	4.7	•
Taxes Paid **12**	8.0	15.1	5.8	6.8	5.6	•	•	11.6	•	•	10.3	8.5	•
Interest Paid **13**	8.6	8.3	0.9	2.3	1.6	•	•	4.4	•	•	5.2	11.9	•
Depreciation **14**	13.5	21.9	6.9	13.8	6.6	•	•	15.9	•	•	15.0	15.5	•
Amortization and Depletion **15**	1.5	•	0.0	0.0	0.0	•	•	0.3	•	•	0.3	2.3	•
Pensions and Other Deferred Comp. **16**	1.0	1.5	0.3	0.1	1.5	•	•	0.7	•	•	1.0	1.1	•
Employee Benefits **17**	2.4	8.0	0.8	0.9	1.6	•	•	1.7	•	•	2.3	2.9	•
Advertising **18**	0.3	0.0	1.8	•	0.6	•	•	0.0	•	•	0.0	0.1	•
Other Expenses **19**	18.8	44.0	41.2	27.9	25.5	•	•	31.4	•	•	11.7	15.8	•
Officers' Compensation **20**	2.4	6.3	10.1	14.3	4.7	•	•	0.3	•	•	1.0	1.0	•
Operating Margin **21**	4.9	•	12.3	•	5.6	•	•	5.6	•	•	5.4	3.1	•
Operating Margin Before Officers' Comp. **22**	7.2	•	22.3	7.4	10.3	•	•	5.9	•	•	6.5	4.0	•

Selected Average Balance Sheet ($ in Thousands)

Net Receivables 23	198	0	15	47	248	•	627	•	14573	63424
Inventories 24	15	0	0	12	2	•	80	•	1222	1989
Net Property, Plant and Equipment 25	4053	0	43	598	1416	•	24401	•	290191	1519152
Total Assets 26	5466	0	95	884	2383	•	31546	•	349693	2057351
Notes and Loans Payable 27	2309	0	21	122	740	•	8126	•	85449	953578
All Other Liabilities 28	1531	0	20	30	435	•	10101	•	151238	554585
Net Worth 29	1627	0	53	732	1208	•	13320	•	113006	549189

Selected Financial Ratios (Times to 1)

Current Ratio 30	0.9	•	3.1	6.7	1.7	•	2.0	•	0.8	0.7
Quick Ratio 31	0.6	•	2.9	6.1	1.3	•	1.5	•	0.7	0.4
Net Sales to Working Capital 32	•	•	4.8	1.6	6.7	•	4.4	•	•	2.0
Coverage Ratio 33	2.3	13.9	18.0	2.0	4.9	•	2.8	•	2.6	2.0
Total Asset Turnover 34	0.3	•	1.5	0.4	0.9	•	0.2	•	0.3	0.2
Inventory Turnover 35	32.3	•	37.2	10.7	456.3	•	21.0	•	36.0	71.6
Receivables Turnover 36	7.0	•	9.9	9.1	6.6	•	9.5	•	14.5	13.6
Total Liabilities to Net Worth 37	2.4	•	0.8	0.2	1.0	•	1.4	•	2.1	2.7
Current Assets to Working Capital 38	•	•	1.5	1.2	2.5	•	2.0	•	•	•
Current Liabilities to Working Capital 39	•	•	0.5	0.2	1.5	•	1.0	•	•	•
Working Capital to Net Sales 40	•	•	0.2	0.6	0.1	•	0.2	•	•	•
Inventory to Working Capital 41	•	•	0.0	0.1	0.0	•	0.0	•	•	•
Total Receipts to Cash Flow 42	4.6	0.8	2.3	3.8	4.2	•	2.7	•	6.0	5.4
Cost of Goods to Cash Flow 43	1.5	0.0	0.3	1.3	1.7	•	0.6	•	2.5	1.8
Cash Flow to Total Debt 44	0.1	•	1.4	0.7	0.4	•	0.1	•	0.1	0.1

Selected Financial Factors (in Percentages)

Debt Ratio 45	70.2	•	43.6	17.2	49.3	•	57.8	•	67.7	73.3
Return on Total Assets 46	5.4	•	24.6	2.0	7.1	•	2.8	•	4.1	5.0
Return on Equity Before Income Taxes 47	10.3	•	41.2	1.2	11.2	•	4.3	•	7.7	9.4
Return on Equity After Income Taxes 48	7.5	•	40.0	1.0	11.0	•	3.2	•	5.1	6.1
Profit Margin (Before Income Tax) 49	11.5	107.3	15.9	2.2	6.4	•	7.9	•	8.3	12.0
Profit Margin (After Income Tax) 50	8.4	106.3	15.5	1.9	6.3	•	5.9	•	5.5	7.8

Table I

Corporations with and without Net Income

COMBINATION GAS AND ELECTRIC

MONEY AMOUNTS AND SIZE OF ASSETS IN THOUSANDS OF DOLLARS

Item Description for Accounting Period 7/02 Through 6/03	Total	Zero Assets	Under 500	500 to 1,000	1,000 to 5,000	5,000 to 10,000	10,000 to 25,000	25,000 to 50,000	50,000 to 100,000	100,000 to 250,000	250,000 to 500,000	500,000 to 2,500,000	2,500,000 and over
Number of Enterprises **1**	40	0	•	•	•	0	0	•	•	0	3	0	32

Revenues ($ in Thousands)

	Total	Zero Assets	Under 500	500 to 1,000	1,000 to 5,000	5,000 to 10,000	10,000 to 25,000	25,000 to 50,000	50,000 to 100,000	100,000 to 250,000	250,000 to 500,000	500,000 to 2,500,000	2,500,000 and over
Net Sales **2**	217440798	0	•	•	•	0	0	•	•	0	801356	0	215818744
Interest **3**	4276095	0	•	•	•	0	0	•	•	0	4868	0	4263253
Rents **4**	1228665	0	•	•	•	0	0	•	•	0	2578	0	1226072
Royalties **5**	11189	0	•	•	•	0	0	•	•	0	0	0	11189
Other Portfolio Income **6**	2778299	0	•	•	•	0	0	•	•	0	846	0	2776648
Other Receipts **7**	5136489	0	•	•	•	0	0	•	•	0	15262	0	5116466
Total Receipts **8**	230871535	0	•	•	•	0	0	•	•	0	824910	0	229212372
Average Total Receipts **9**	5771788	•	•	•	•	•	•	•	•	•	274970	•	7162887

Operating Costs/Operating Income (%)

	Total	Zero Assets	Under 500	500 to 1,000	1,000 to 5,000	5,000 to 10,000	10,000 to 25,000	25,000 to 50,000	50,000 to 100,000	100,000 to 250,000	250,000 to 500,000	500,000 to 2,500,000	2,500,000 and over
Cost of Operations **10**	57.9	•	•	•	•	•	•	•	•	•	44.9	•	58.1
Salaries and Wages **11**	4.8	•	•	•	•	•	•	•	•	•	4.7	•	4.8
Taxes Paid **12**	3.9	•	•	•	•	•	•	•	•	•	3.4	•	3.9
Interest Paid **13**	7.7	•	•	•	•	•	•	•	•	•	3.9	•	7.8
Depreciation **14**	7.7	•	•	•	•	•	•	•	•	•	9.7	•	7.7
Amortization and Depletion **15**	0.7	•	•	•	•	•	•	•	•	•	0.8	•	0.7
Pensions and Other Deferred Comp. **16**	0.8	•	•	•	•	•	•	•	•	•	1.4	•	0.8
Employee Benefits **17**	1.2	•	•	•	•	•	•	•	•	•	1.6	•	1.2
Advertising **18**	0.1	•	•	•	•	•	•	•	•	•	0.2	•	0.1
Other Expenses **19**	22.0	•	•	•	•	•	•	•	•	•	29.9	•	21.9
Officers' Compensation **20**	0.2	•	•	•	•	•	•	•	•	•	0.7	•	0.2
Operating Margin **21**	•										•		•
Operating Margin Before Officers' Comp. **22**	•										•		•

Selected Average Balance Sheet ($ in Thousands)

Net Receivables 23	1842252	40510	2298363
Inventories 24	235906	10281	293785
Net Property, Plant and Equipment 25	5597243	316401	6963082
Total Assets 26	14697721	608363	18309390
Notes and Loans Payable 27	5403947	268757	6726525
All Other Liabilities 28	4723211	145055	5888733
Net Worth 29	4570563	194550	5694132

Selected Financial Ratios (Times to 1)

Current Ratio 30	0.8	0.9	0.8
Quick Ratio 31	0.5	0.6	0.5
Net Sales to Working Capital 32			
Coverage Ratio 33	0.9	1.4	0.9
Total Asset Turnover 34	0.4	0.4	0.4
Inventory Turnover 35	13.3	11.7	13.3
Receivables Turnover 36	2.8	6.6	2.8
Total Liabilities to Net Worth 37	2.2	2.1	2.2
Current Assets to Working Capital 38			
Current Liabilities to Working Capital 39			
Working Capital to Net Sales 40			
Inventory to Working Capital 41			
Total Receipts to Cash Flow 42	5.8	3.7	5.9
Cost of Goods to Cash Flow 43	3.4	1.7	3.4
Cash Flow to Total Debt 44	0.1	0.2	0.1

Selected Financial Factors (in Percentages)

Debt Ratio 45	68.9	68.0	68.9
Return on Total Assets 46	2.6	2.4	2.6
Return on Equity Before Income Taxes 47		2.3	
Return on Equity After Income Taxes 48		0.1	
Profit Margin (Before Income Tax) 49		1.6	
Profit Margin (After Income Tax) 50		0.1	

23

Table II
Corporations with Net Income

COMBINATION GAS AND ELECTRIC

MONEY AMOUNTS AND SIZE OF ASSETS IN THOUSANDS OF DOLLARS

Item Description for Accounting Period 7/02 Through 6/03	Total	Zero Assets	Under 500	500 to 1,000	1,000 to 5,000	5,000 to 10,000	10,000 to 25,000	25,000 to 50,000	50,000 to 100,000	100,000 to 250,000	250,000 to 500,000	500,000 to 2,500,000	2,500,000 and over
Number of Enterprises 1	25	0	·	·	·	·	0	·	·	0	0	0	21

Revenues ($ in Thousands)

	Total	Zero Assets	Under 500	500 to 1,000	1,000 to 5,000	5,000 to 10,000	10,000 to 25,000	25,000 to 50,000	50,000 to 100,000	100,000 to 250,000	250,000 to 500,000	500,000 to 2,500,000	2,500,000 and over
Net Sales 2	119672036	0	·	·	·	·	0	·	·	0	0	0	118441720
Interest 3	3385046	0	·	·	·	·	0	·	·	0	0	0	3375312
Rents 4	1127978	0	·	·	·	·	0	·	·	0	0	0	1125386
Royalties 5	10798	0	·	·	·	·	0	·	·	0	0	0	10798
Other Portfolio Income 6	1772222	0	·	·	·	·	0	·	·	0	0	0	1770907
Other Receipts 7	3859339	0	·	·	·	·	0	·	·	0	0	0	3847467
Total Receipts 8	129827419	0	·	·	·	·	0	·	·	0	0	0	128571590
Average Total Receipts 9	5193097	·	·	·	·	·	·	·	·	·	·	·	6122457

Operating Costs/Operating Income (%)

	Total	Zero Assets	Under 500	500 to 1,000	1,000 to 5,000	5,000 to 10,000	10,000 to 25,000	25,000 to 50,000	50,000 to 100,000	100,000 to 250,000	250,000 to 500,000	500,000 to 2,500,000	2,500,000 and over
Cost of Operations 10	47.5	·	·	·	·	·	·	·	·	·	·	·	47.6
Salaries and Wages 11	6.1	·	·	·	·	·	·	·	·	·	·	·	6.1
Taxes Paid 12	4.1	·	·	·	·	·	·	·	·	·	·	·	4.1
Interest Paid 13	9.6	·	·	·	·	·	·	·	·	·	·	·	9.6
Depreciation 14	9.8	·	·	·	·	·	·	·	·	·	·	·	9.9
Amortization and Depletion 15	0.7	·	·	·	·	·	·	·	·	·	·	·	0.7
Pensions and Other Deferred Comp. 16	0.9	·	·	·	·	·	·	·	·	·	·	·	0.9
Employee Benefits 17	1.4	·	·	·	·	·	·	·	·	·	·	·	1.4
Advertising 18	0.1	·	·	·	·	·	·	·	·	·	·	·	0.1
Other Expenses 19	21.2	·	·	·	·	·	·	·	·	·	·	·	21.0
Officers' Compensation 20	0.1	·	·	·	·	·	·	·	·	·	·	·	0.1
Operating Margin 21	·	·	·	·	·	·	·	·	·	·	·	·	·
Operating Margin Before Officers' Comp. 22	·	·	·	·	·	·	·	·	·	·	·	·	·

Selected Average Balance Sheet ($ in Thousands)

Net Receivables 23	2528651	3007545
Inventories 24	282138	334707
Net Property, Plant and Equipment 25	5939146	7039499
Total Assets 26	17027085	20216472
Notes and Loans Payable 27	6098772	7242537
All Other Liabilities 28	5418796	6430318
Net Worth 29	5509517	6543618

Selected Financial Ratios (Times to 1)

Current Ratio 30	0.9	0.9
Quick Ratio 31	0.6	0.6
Net Sales to Working Capital 32	*	*
Coverage Ratio 33	1.7	1.7
Total Asset Turnover 34	0.3	0.3
Inventory Turnover 35	8.1	8.0
Receivables Turnover 36	1.7	1.7
Total Liabilities to Net Worth 37	2.1	2.1
Current Assets to Working Capital 38	*	*
Current Liabilities to Working Capital 39	*	*
Working Capital to Net Sales 40	*	*
Inventory to Working Capital 41	*	*
Total Receipts to Cash Flow 42	4.2	4.3
Cost of Goods to Cash Flow 43	2.0	2.0
Cash Flow to Total Debt 44	0.1	0.1

Selected Financial Factors (in Percentages)

Debt Ratio 45	67.6	67.6
Return on Total Assets 46	4.7	4.6
Return on Equity Before Income Taxes 47	6.0	6.0
Return on Equity After Income Taxes 48	4.0	3.9
Profit Margin (Before Income Tax) 49	7.0	7.0
Profit Margin (After Income Tax) 50	4.6	4.6

Table I

Corporations with and without Net Income

CONSTRUCTION OF BUILDINGS

MONEY AMOUNTS AND SIZE OF ASSETS IN THOUSANDS OF DOLLARS

Item Description for Accounting Period 7/02 Through 6/03	Total	Zero Assets	Under 500	500 to 1,000	1,000 to 5,000	5,000 to 10,000	10,000 to 25,000	25,000 to 50,000	50,000 to 100,000	100,000 to 250,000	250,000 to 500,000	500,000 to 2,500,000	2,500,000 and over
Number of Enterprises **1**	191551	21025	128201	15995	20995	3054	1576	388	177	70	34	30	6
Revenues ($ in Thousands)													
Net Sales **2**	458876455	4643464	67094693	27497576	94947164	45271061	48438624	27323607	23936584	17764441	21016898	46576145	34366198
Interest **3**	1130199	2837	24840	34811	96812	40407	40642	22465	21292	15303	47235	372636	410919
Rents **4**	621096	775	37936	32010	83569	28477	49552	40582	68479	55038	93097	90586	40994
Royalties **5**	188625	0	1019	0	0	0	480	0	130	37	9855	164931	12174
Other Portfolio Income **6**	738125	26434	59893	53686	107682	48929	48503	30043	31990	61509	58343	158309	52805
Other Receipts **7**	5763650	71323	590001	289961	419589	404417	374578	243969	158624	187735	232430	1037981	1753043
Total Receipts **8**	467318150	4744833	67808382	27908044	95654816	45793291	48952379	27660666	24217099	18084063	21457858	48400588	36636133
Average Total Receipts **9**	2440	226	529	1745	4556	14995	31061	71290	136820	258344	631113	1613353	6106022
Operating Costs/Operating Income (%)													
Cost of Operations **10**	81.7	70.6	71.3	79.7	84.5	87.4	88.2	88.9	88.6	88.4	87.2	85.3	58.3
Salaries and Wages **11**	3.5	4.4	4.6	4.1	2.8	2.7	2.7	2.7	2.9	3.1	3.0	3.9	5.9
Taxes Paid **12**	1.1	1.8	1.8	1.8	1.0	0.9	0.7	0.7	0.6	0.6	0.8	0.8	1.6
Interest Paid **13**	0.7	1.2	0.6	0.7	0.6	0.4	0.4	0.4	0.5	0.7	0.8	1.3	1.8
Depreciation **14**	0.8	1.5	1.3	1.3	0.8	0.7	0.6	0.6	0.7	0.6	1.0	0.6	0.5
Amortization and Depletion **15**	0.1	0.1	0.0	0.0	0.0	0.0	0.0	0.0	0.0	0.1	0.1	0.3	0.2
Pensions and Other Deferred Comp. **16**	0.2	0.1	0.3	0.4	0.3	0.3	0.2	0.2	0.3	0.2	0.3	0.2	0.1
Employee Benefits **17**	0.5	0.3	0.7	0.7	0.5	0.6	0.4	0.5	0.5	0.3	0.3	0.5	0.3
Advertising **18**	0.3	0.4	0.4	0.2	0.2	0.2	0.2	0.2	0.2	0.3	0.4	0.6	0.6
Other Expenses **19**	7.3	16.0	12.2	7.7	5.3	3.4	3.1	2.7	3.2	3.1	3.9	4.3	27.6
Officers' Compensation **20**	2.3	2.8	5.6	3.7	2.6	1.9	1.7	1.3	1.1	0.7	0.7	0.9	0.4
Operating Margin **21**	1.5	0.8	1.1	•	1.4	1.6	1.7	1.8	1.3	2.0	1.7	1.3	2.8
Operating Margin Before Officers' Comp. **22**	3.8	3.6	6.7	3.5	4.1	3.6	3.3	3.1	2.4	2.7	2.4	2.2	3.1

Selected Average Balance Sheet ($ in Thousands)

Net Receivables **23**	252	0	15	108	398	1951	4380	10773	21277	34217	98235	208017	569668
Inventories **24**	295	0	18	163	549	1531	3090	6509	12508	42132	49261	283750	2108796
Net Property, Plant and Equipment **25**	144	0	27	113	293	805	1506	3069	8258	20289	63781	135879	160821
Total Assets **26**	1225	0	112	701	2119	7066	14933	34433	68612	150002	352831	1131326	6270564
Notes and Loans Payable **27**	470	0	63	290	874	2321	4349	9816	21537	42462	88370	352780	3481007
All Other Liabilities **28**	437	0	34	242	786	3173	6857	16299	32282	62858	154326	405351	787137
Net Worth **29**	318	0	15	169	460	1571	3728	8318	14792	44682	110135	373195	2002420

Selected Financial Ratios (Times to 1)

Current Ratio **30**	1.5	•	1.4	1.5	1.4	1.4	1.4	1.4	1.3	1.5	1.5	1.7	2.2
Quick Ratio **31**	0.7	•	0.8	0.6	0.6	0.7	0.7	0.8	0.8	0.7	0.9	0.8	0.6
Net Sales to Working Capital **32**	8.4	•	24.1	10.6	9.4	8.9	9.7	9.6	10.5	7.0	8.8	5.8	3.2
Coverage Ratio **33**	5.5	3.4	4.8	2.9	4.8	7.2	7.6	7.7	6.3	6.7	5.8	4.9	6.3
Total Asset Turnover **34**	2.0	•	4.7	2.5	2.1	2.1	2.1	2.0	2.0	1.7	1.8	1.4	0.9
Inventory Turnover **35**	6.6	•	20.3	8.4	7.0	8.5	8.8	9.6	9.6	5.3	10.9	4.7	1.6
Receivables Turnover **36**	•	•	•	•	•	•	•	•	•	•	•	•	•
Total Liabilities to Net Worth **37**	2.9	•	6.7	3.1	3.6	3.5	3.0	3.1	3.6	2.4	2.2	2.0	2.1
Current Assets to Working Capital **38**	3.0	•	3.3	3.1	3.4	3.4	3.7	3.7	4.0	2.9	3.2	2.5	1.8
Current Liabilities to Working Capital **39**	2.0	•	2.3	2.1	2.4	2.4	2.7	2.7	3.0	1.9	2.2	1.5	0.8
Working Capital to Net Sales **40**	0.1	•	0.0	0.1	0.1	0.1	0.1	0.1	0.1	0.1	0.1	0.2	0.3
Inventory to Working Capital **41**	1.0	•	0.8	1.0	1.1	0.9	1.0	0.9	1.0	1.2	0.7	1.1	1.2
Total Receipts to Cash Flow **42**	10.6	5.8	8.0	13.8	15.5	19.2	20.5	20.3	20.1	16.4	15.4	12.0	2.8
Cost of Goods to Cash Flow **43**	8.7	4.1	5.7	11.0	13.1	16.7	18.0	18.0	17.9	14.5	13.4	10.2	1.6
Cash Flow to Total Debt **44**	0.2	•	0.7	0.2	0.2	0.1	0.1	0.1	0.1	0.1	0.2	0.2	0.5

Selected Financial Factors (in Percentages)

Debt Ratio **45**	74.1	•	87.0	75.9	78.3	77.8	75.0	75.8	78.4	70.2	68.8	67.0	68.1
Return on Total Assets **46**	7.8	•	12.9	4.7	5.8	6.8	6.5	7.0	5.8	7.6	7.9	8.9	10.2
Return on Equity Before Income Taxes **47**	24.8	•	78.5	12.7	21.2	26.3	22.6	25.1	22.5	21.6	20.9	21.5	26.8
Return on Equity After Income Taxes **48**	20.7	•	76.7	11.5	19.4	25.2	21.2	23.3	20.7	20.7	17.7	14.3	18.1
Profit Margin (Before Income Tax) **49**	3.3	3.0	2.2	1.2	2.2	2.8	2.7	3.0	2.5	3.8	3.7	5.2	9.4
Profit Margin (After Income Tax) **50**	2.7	2.9	2.1	1.1	2.0	2.7	2.6	2.7	2.3	3.7	3.2	3.4	6.3

Table II
Corporations with Net Income

CONSTRUCTION OF BUILDINGS

MONEY AMOUNTS AND SIZE OF ASSETS IN THOUSANDS OF DOLLARS

Item Description for Accounting Period 7/02 Through 6/03	Total	Zero Assets	Under 500	500 to 1,000	1,000 to 5,000	5,000 to 10,000	10,000 to 25,000	25,000 to 50,000	50,000 to 100,000	100,000 to 250,000	250,000 to 500,000	500,000 to 2,500,000	2,500,000 and over
Number of Enterprises **1**	109586	9081	72974	9561	13883	0	1233	313	137	57	28	23	0
Revenues ($ in Thousands)													
Net Sales **2**	369873672	3213948	45556766	18716637	71899818	0	41460655	23134439	21248911	15589922	18479516	40164373	0
Interest **3**	921267	1361	15092	19933	66989	0	31438	17921	19197	10482	36711	261701	0
Rents **4**	454875	706	19663	29321	40432	0	37487	34084	42629	36462	89783	62138	0
Royalties **5**	187186	0	115	0	0	0	2	0	72	37	9855	164931	0
Other Portfolio Income **6**	449742	19690	27996	45202	69149	0	37548	23480	20793	41009	47632	26305	0
Other Receipts **7**	5225281	111764	505136	276225	361498	0	317155	211883	151113	171585	189038	848006	0
Total Receipts **8**	377112023	3347469	46124768	19087318	72437886	0	41884285	23421807	21482715	15849497	18852535	41527454	0
Average Total Receipts **9**	3441	369	632	1996	5218	•	33969	74830	156808	278061	673305	1805541	•
Operating Costs/Operating Income (%)													
Cost of Operations **10**	80.9	71.9	69.6	78.8	83.3	•	87.7	88.2	88.5	87.3	87.2	84.8	•
Salaries and Wages **11**	3.3	2.9	4.3	4.1	2.7	•	2.5	2.6	2.8	3.1	2.7	3.7	•
Taxes Paid **12**	1.0	1.2	1.7	1.9	1.0	•	0.7	0.7	0.6	0.6	0.7	0.8	•
Interest Paid **13**	0.6	1.5	0.5	0.5	0.5	•	0.3	0.4	0.4	0.5	0.7	1.0	•
Depreciation **14**	0.7	1.3	1.1	1.0	0.6	•	0.6	0.5	0.5	0.5	0.9	0.3	•
Amortization and Depletion **15**	0.1	0.0	0.0	0.0	0.0	•	0.0	0.0	0.0	0.0	0.1	0.2	•
Pensions and Other Deferred Comp. **16**	0.2	0.0	0.3	0.5	0.3	•	0.2	0.2	0.3	0.2	0.3	0.2	•
Employee Benefits **17**	0.5	0.1	0.7	0.5	0.5	•	0.4	0.5	0.5	0.3	0.3	0.5	•
Advertising **18**	0.3	0.4	0.4	0.2	0.2	•	0.2	0.3	0.2	0.3	0.4	0.6	•
Other Expenses **19**	6.9	9.2	11.1	6.8	4.8	•	2.8	2.5	3.1	2.8	3.3	3.6	•
Officers' Compensation **20**	2.1	1.9	5.4	3.5	2.6	•	1.6	1.3	1.0	0.6	0.7	0.9	•
Operating Margin **21**	3.3	9.6	4.8	2.2	3.4	•	2.8	2.8	2.1	3.7	2.7	3.3	•
Operating Margin Before Officers' Comp. **22**	5.3	11.5	10.2	5.8	6.1	•	4.5	4.2	3.1	4.3	3.4	4.2	•

Selected Average Balance Sheet ($ in Thousands)

Net Receivables 23	337	0	15	96	405	•	4542	10918	23423	35338	93874	203762	•
Inventories 24	440	0	19	194	598	•	3316	7299	13764	46069	56458	337343	•
Net Property, Plant and Equipment 25	157	0	25	95	263	•	1267	2837	6822	18401	64441	86159	•
Total Assets 26	1640	0	110	689	2158	•	15001	34804	67906	149830	353444	1050362	•
Notes and Loans Payable 27	589	0	53	281	811	•	4016	9095	18479	39516	81311	267637	•
All Other Liabilities 28	574	0	30	224	791	•	6893	16272	33865	63101	156801	409716	•
Net Worth 29	476	0	27	184	556	•	4092	9436	15562	47213	115332	373008	•

Selected Financial Ratios (Times to 1)

Current Ratio 30	1.6	•	1.7	1.6	1.5	•	1.4	1.3	1.5	1.5	1.7		•
Quick Ratio 31	0.7	•	1.0	0.7	0.6	•	0.8	0.8	0.7	0.9	0.7		•
Net Sales to Working Capital 32	7.9	•	21.5	10.0	8.9	•	9.7	11.2	6.9	8.0	6.1		•
Coverage Ratio 33	9.1	10.1	14.2	8.9	9.7	•	12.1	9.6	12.3	7.5	7.5		•
Total Asset Turnover 34	2.1	•	5.7	2.8	2.4	•	2.2	2.3	1.8	1.9	1.7		•
Inventory Turnover 35	6.2	•	22.9	8.0	7.2	•	8.9	10.0	5.2	10.2	4.4		•
Receivables Turnover 36	•	•	•	•	•	•	•	•	•	•	•		•
Total Liabilities to Net Worth 37	2.4	•	3.1	2.7	2.9	•	2.7	3.4	2.2	2.1	1.8		•
Current Assets to Working Capital 38	2.7	•	2.5	2.7	3.0	•	3.6	4.0	2.9	2.8	2.4		•
Current Liabilities to Working Capital 39	1.7	•	1.5	1.7	2.0	•	2.6	3.0	1.9	1.8	1.4		•
Working Capital to Net Sales 40	0.1	•	0.0	0.1	0.1	•	0.1	0.1	0.1	0.1	0.2		•
Inventory to Working Capital 41	1.0	•	0.7	1.0	1.0	•	1.0	0.9	1.2	0.7	1.2		•
Total Receipts to Cash Flow 42	9.0	4.7	6.5	10.3	12.5	•	17.1	17.7	13.7	14.4	10.5		•
Cost of Goods to Cash Flow 43	7.3	3.3	4.5	8.1	10.4	•	15.0	15.7	11.9	12.6	8.9		•
Cash Flow to Total Debt 44	0.3	1.2	0.4	0.3	0.3	•	0.2	0.2	0.2	0.2	0.2		•

Selected Financial Factors (in Percentages)

Debt Ratio 45	71.0	•	75.4	73.3	74.2	•	72.7	72.9	77.1	68.5	67.4	64.5	•
Return on Total Assets 46	12.1	•	37.2	13.5	11.2	•	9.4	9.5	8.2	10.6	10.0	12.7	•
Return on Equity Before Income Taxes 47	37.0	•	140.4	44.7	39.0	•	31.5	31.6	32.1	30.8	26.5	31.1	•
Return on Equity After Income Taxes 48	32.2	•	138.7	42.9	36.8	•	29.9	30.0	29.8	29.8	22.9	21.7	•
Profit Margin (Before Income Tax) 49	5.2	13.7	6.1	4.2	4.2	•	3.8	3.2	3.2	5.3	4.6	6.6	•
Profit Margin (After Income Tax) 50	4.5	13.5	6.0	4.0	4.0	•	3.6	3.0	3.0	5.1	4.0	4.6	•

Table I

Corporations with and without Net Income

HEAVY AND CIVIL ENGINEERING CONSTRUCTION

MONEY AMOUNTS AND SIZE OF ASSETS IN THOUSANDS OF DOLLARS

Item Description for Accounting Period 7/02 Through 6/03	Total	Zero Assets	Under 500	500 to 1,000	1,000 to 5,000	5,000 to 10,000	10,000 to 25,000	25,000 to 50,000	50,000 to 100,000	100,000 to 250,000	250,000 to 500,000	500,000 to 2,500,000	2,500,000 and over
Number of Enterprises **1**	29579	985	18195	2814	5362	1143	734	189	91	42	7	12	5
Revenues ($ in Thousands)													
Net Sales **2**	154644741	599238	11618750	6488239	25591098	16887999	22211588	11779052	11350007	10027200	4364873	16052343	17674355
Interest **3**	398939	1922	6980	6822	25589	15068	45771	12683	10629	13935	46631	99976	112933
Rents **4**	209716	812	0	12279	19177	3593	47441	19892	5518	9360	207	43755	47682
Royalties **5**	94883	0	0	0	0	0	1703	1391	0	1895	0	37308	52583
Other Portfolio Income **6**	542837	11885	35020	28556	115064	64734	79536	43719	40342	64700	5259	28940	25086
Other Receipts **7**	1619782	20500	12718	27518	68914	73194	106806	81525	67689	77966	-16187	181871	917262
Total Receipts **8**	157510898	634357	11673468	6563414	25819845	17044588	22492845	11938262	11474185	10195056	4400783	16444193	18829901
Average Total Receipts **9**	5325	644	642	2332	4815	14912	30644	63165	126090	242739	628683	1370349	3765980
Operating Costs/Operating Income (%)													
Cost of Operations **10**	75.3	75.5	47.5	44.9	71.2	76.4	79.5	80.7	82.7	82.6	88.8	84.2	80.1
Salaries and Wages **11**	4.8	5.7	9.8	9.2	4.9	3.7	2.9	3.0	2.9	3.2	2.8	4.8	6.8
Taxes Paid **12**	1.8	2.0	2.7	2.5	2.4	1.9	1.7	1.7	1.4	1.2	0.9	2.0	1.0
Interest Paid **13**	1.1	0.7	1.0	0.8	0.8	0.6	0.6	0.7	0.7	0.7	0.8	1.3	3.1
Depreciation **14**	3.9	5.2	5.4	5.4	4.6	4.4	4.0	3.6	3.7	4.6	1.6	2.5	2.3
Amortization and Depletion **15**	0.2	0.1	0.0	0.0	0.0	0.0	0.1	0.1	0.2	0.2	0.3	0.7	0.4
Pensions and Other Deferred Comp. **16**	0.4	0.1	0.3	0.3	0.4	0.3	0.4	0.4	0.3	0.3	0.2	0.2	1.3
Employee Benefits **17**	1.1	0.4	0.9	0.8	1.1	1.3	1.2	1.3	1.1	0.9	1.0	1.0	1.3
Advertising **18**	0.1	0.3	0.5	0.3	0.2	0.1	0.1	0.1	0.1	0.1	0.1	0.1	0.1
Other Expenses **19**	10.6	16.2	25.0	35.6	10.9	8.3	6.7	6.7	5.7	4.6	4.6	8.8	10.5
Officers' Compensation **20**	2.2	1.5	6.6	3.8	3.8	2.2	1.9	1.3	1.1	1.0	0.5	0.6	0.8
Operating Margin **21**	•	•	0.3	•	•	0.7	1.0	0.5	0.2	0.5	•	•	•
Operating Margin Before Officers' Comp. **22**	0.8	•	7.0	0.3	3.6	2.9	2.9	1.8	1.3	1.5	•	•	•

Selected Average Balance Sheet ($ in Thousands)

Item	1	2	3	4	5	6	7	8	9	10	11	12	13
Net Receivables 23	801	0	18	130	572	2375	4868	11349	20414	38278	155272	236414	818707
Inventories 24	91	0	3	5	88	380	481	786	2273	5520	5879	16358	105623
Net Property, Plant and Equipment 25	771	0	86	372	705	1944	4330	8318	18951	47534	60959	136785	728491
Total Assets 26	3227	0	162	733	2039	6910	15254	34251	69841	142393	344098	785060	5958552
Notes and Loans Payable 27	751	0	109	340	592	1754	3451	8434	17390	37857	147677	215324	637687
All Other Liabilities 28	1098	0	38	103	596	2483	5469	12669	22849	40280	162392	312899	2078474
Net Worth 29	1378	0	14	290	850	2673	6333	13148	29602	64256	34029	256837	3242392

Selected Financial Ratios (Times to 1)

Item	1	2	3	4	5	6	7	8	9	10	11	12	13
Current Ratio 30	1.3	*	1.1	1.4	1.7	1.5	1.5	1.5	1.5	1.5	1.1	1.2	0.9
Quick Ratio 31	1.0	*	0.9	1.2	1.3	1.2	1.2	1.2	1.1	1.1	0.8	0.8	0.7
Net Sales to Working Capital 32	14.1	*	158.9	24.1	10.4	9.5	9.4	8.8	9.8	9.6	26.6	16.6	*
Coverage Ratio 33	1.4	*	1.8	*	2.0	3.5	4.6	3.6	2.8	4.0	*	*	0.6
Total Asset Turnover 34	1.6	*	4.0	3.1	2.3	2.1	2.0	1.8	1.8	1.7	1.8	1.7	0.6
Inventory Turnover 35	43.4	*	98.4	189.4	38.7	29.7	50.0	64.0	45.3	35.7	94.2	68.9	26.8
Receivables Turnover 36	*	*	*	*	*	*	*	*	*	*	*	*	*
Total Liabilities to Net Worth 37	1.3	*	10.3	1.5	1.4	1.6	1.4	1.6	1.4	1.2	9.1	2.1	0.8
Current Assets to Working Capital 38	4.3	*	14.8	3.3	2.5	2.9	2.9	3.0	3.1	2.8	11.2	5.7	*
Current Liabilities to Working Capital 39	3.3	*	13.8	2.3	1.5	1.9	1.9	2.0	2.1	1.8	10.2	4.7	*
Working Capital to Net Sales 40	0.1	*	0.0	0.0	0.1	0.1	0.1	0.1	0.1	0.1	0.0	0.1	0.1
Inventory to Working Capital 41	0.2	*	0.8	0.1	0.2	0.2	0.1	0.1	0.2	0.2	0.3	0.2	*
Total Receipts to Cash Flow 42	13.9	11.9	5.4	4.0	14.1	15.1	18.9	19.3	31.2	22.3	40.4	69.9	12.7
Cost of Goods to Cash Flow 43	10.5	9.0	2.6	1.8	10.1	11.6	15.0	15.6	25.8	18.4	35.9	58.9	10.1
Cash Flow to Total Debt 44	0.2	*	0.8	1.3	0.3	0.2	0.2	0.2	0.1	0.1	0.0	0.0	0.1

Selected Financial Factors (in Percentages)

Item	1	2	3	4	5	6	7	8	9	10	11	12	13
Debt Ratio 45	57.3	*	91.1	60.5	58.3	61.3	58.5	61.6	57.6	54.9	90.1	67.3	45.6
Return on Total Assets 46	2.4	*	7.0	*	3.6	4.7	5.6	4.6	3.3	4.9	*	*	1.2
Return on Equity Before Income Taxes 47	1.5	*	36.1	*	4.3	8.8	10.5	8.6	5.1	8.2	*	*	*
Return on Equity After Income Taxes 48	0.5	*	33.4	*	3.3	7.5	9.1	7.6	4.1	7.4	*	*	*
Profit Margin (Before Income Tax) 49	0.4	*	0.8	*	0.8	1.6	2.2	1.8	1.2	2.2	*	*	*
Profit Margin (After Income Tax) 50	0.1	*	0.7	*	0.6	1.4	1.9	1.6	1.0	2.0	*	*	*

Table II

Corporations with Net Income

HEAVY AND CIVIL ENGINEERING CONSTRUCTION

MONEY AMOUNTS AND SIZE OF ASSETS IN THOUSANDS OF DOLLARS

Item Description for Accounting Period 7/02 Through 6/03	Total	Zero Assets	Under 500	500 to 1,000	1,000 to 5,000	5,000 to 10,000	10,000 to 25,000	25,000 to 50,000	50,000 to 100,000	100,000 to 250,000	250,000 to 500,000	500,000 to 2,500,000	2,500,000 and over
Number of Enterprises 1	15414	443	9216	964	3258	0	521	129	63	35	3	0	0
Revenues ($ in Thousands)													
Net Sales 2	102073969	357053	7592979	3171588	16698814	0	16510717	8811953	8354123	8933227	2778715	0	0
Interest 3	155810	796	2919	1529	19662	0	17560	6596	8394	9787	9060	0	0
Rents 4	90857	660	0	5550	10755	0	23352	14758	483	9360	207	0	0
Royalties 5	86678	0	0	0	3	0	792	1385	0	488	0	0	0
Other Portfolio Income 6	365086	8140	20259	20071	70002	0	54793	27171	23838	53779	5082	0	0
Other Receipts 7	1285234	989	9361	7843	60299	0	89271	59827	81551	40473	14897	0	0
Total Receipts 8	104057634	367638	7625518	3206581	16859535	0	16696485	8921690	8468389	9047114	2807961	0	0
Average Total Receipts 9	6751	830	827	3326	5175	•	32047	69160	134419	258489	935987	•	•
Operating Costs/Operating Income (%)													
Cost of Operations 10	75.0	72.2	49.5	27.4	70.5	•	78.1	81.7	81.7	83.0	89.7	•	•
Salaries and Wages 11	4.1	3.4	9.0	8.7	4.6	•	2.9	2.3	3.0	3.0	2.5	•	•
Taxes Paid 12	1.6	1.2	2.7	2.0	2.2	•	1.7	1.7	1.2	1.2	0.5	•	•
Interest Paid 13	0.6	0.6	0.9	0.6	0.5	•	0.5	0.5	0.4	0.7	0.3	•	•
Depreciation 14	3.6	2.8	4.8	4.8	4.0	•	3.6	3.3	3.4	4.3	0.5	•	•
Amortization and Depletion 15	0.1	0.0	0.0	0.0	0.0	•	0.0	0.1	0.1	0.3	0.0	•	•
Pensions and Other Deferred Comp. 16	0.4	0.1	0.3	0.3	0.4	•	0.4	0.5	0.3	0.3	0.3	•	•
Employee Benefits 17	1.0	0.3	0.8	0.3	1.0	•	1.2	1.2	1.0	0.8	0.6	•	•
Advertising 18	0.1	0.2	0.4	0.1	0.1	•	0.1	0.1	0.1	0.1	0.0	•	•
Other Expenses 19	9.0	8.3	18.7	51.4	9.4	•	6.3	4.8	4.9	3.5	2.0	•	•
Officers' Compensation 20	2.3	1.4	7.9	2.3	3.7	•	2.0	1.3	1.2	1.0	0.7	•	•
Operating Margin 21	2.2	9.6	4.9	2.0	3.5	•	3.3	2.5	2.7	1.9	2.8	•	•
Operating Margin Before Officers' Comp. 22	4.5	10.9	12.8	4.4	7.2	•	5.3	3.8	3.8	2.9	3.5	•	•

Selected Average Balance Sheet ($ in Thousands)

Net Receivables 23	982	0	27	21	622	•	4991	11701	19897	39778	132155
Inventories 24	81	0	2	6	45	•	445	676	1884	6067	8090
Net Property, Plant and Equipment 25	906	0	101	476	628	•	3982	8032	18546	46403	44844
Total Assets 26	3401	0	193	735	2018	•	15092	34146	69542	142467	308098
Notes and Loans Payable 27	678	0	98	399	445	•	2813	6602	12752	36349	14876
All Other Liabilities 28	1258	0	40	50	593	•	5303	12870	23202	40731	130299
Net Worth 29	1465	0	55	286	981	•	6976	14675	33588	65386	162922

Selected Financial Ratios (Times to 1)

Current Ratio 30	1.5	•	1.2	1.4	1.8	•	1.6	1.6	1.6	1.6	1.6
Quick Ratio 31	1.2	•	1.1	1.0	1.6	•	1.3	1.3	1.3	1.2	1.5
Net Sales to Working Capital 32	10.6	23.0	52.2	54.1	9.1	•	8.4	8.7	8.5	9.4	10.6
Coverage Ratio 33	7.5	•	6.9	6.0	9.4	•	10.1	7.8	10.1	5.7	12.7
Total Asset Turnover 34	1.9	•	4.3	4.5	2.5	•	2.1	2.0	1.9	1.8	3.0
Inventory Turnover 35	61.0	•	206.8	142.7	80.9	•	55.5	82.5	57.5	34.9	102.7
Receivables Turnover 36	•	•	•	•	•	•	•	•	•	•	•
Total Liabilities to Net Worth 37	1.3	•	2.5	1.6	1.1	•	1.2	1.3	1.1	1.2	0.9
Current Assets to Working Capital 38	3.1	•	5.1	3.6	2.2	•	2.6	2.8	2.6	2.7	2.6
Current Liabilities to Working Capital 39	2.1	•	4.1	2.6	1.2	•	1.6	1.8	1.6	1.7	1.6
Working Capital to Net Sales 40	0.1	•	0.0	0.0	0.1	•	0.1	0.1	0.1	0.1	0.1
Inventory to Working Capital 41	0.1	•	0.1	0.1	0.1	•	0.1	0.1	0.1	0.2	0.1
Total Receipts to Cash Flow 42	10.1	5.6	5.3	2.3	10.1	•	14.0	17.9	18.1	20.4	18.8
Cost of Goods to Cash Flow 43	7.6	4.1	2.6	0.6	7.1	•	10.9	14.6	14.8	16.9	16.8
Cash Flow to Total Debt 44	0.3	•	1.1	3.2	0.5	•	0.3	0.2	0.2	0.2	0.3

Selected Financial Factors (in Percentages)

Debt Ratio 45	56.9	•	71.3	61.1	51.4	•	53.8	57.0	51.7	54.1	47.1
Return on Total Assets 46	9.3	•	26.6	16.7	12.7	•	10.3	8.5	8.4	6.9	12.2
Return on Equity Before Income Taxes 47	18.6	•	79.4	35.8	23.3	•	20.1	17.3	15.7	12.4	21.2
Return on Equity After Income Taxes 48	16.8	•	78.0	35.0	21.9	•	18.3	16.1	14.6	11.5	15.8
Profit Margin (Before Income Tax) 49	4.1	12.5	5.3	3.1	4.5	•	4.4	3.7	4.0	3.2	3.7
Profit Margin (After Income Tax) 50	3.7	11.6	3.0	3.0	4.2	•	4.0	3.5	3.7	2.9	2.8

Table I

Corporations with and without Net Income

LAND SUBDIVISION

MONEY AMOUNTS AND SIZE OF ASSETS IN THOUSANDS OF DOLLARS

Item Description for Accounting Period 7/02 Through 6/03	Total	Zero Assets	Under 500	500 to 1,000	1,000 to 5,000	5,000 to 10,000	10,000 to 25,000	25,000 to 50,000	50,000 to 100,000	100,000 to 250,000	250,000 to 500,000	500,000 to 2,500,000	2,500,000 and over
Number of Enterprises **1**	44477	4455	24438	6033	7617	1146	514	151	71	29	15	8	*

Revenues ($ in Thousands)

Item Description for Accounting Period 7/02 Through 6/03	Total	Zero Assets	Under 500	500 to 1,000	1,000 to 5,000	5,000 to 10,000	10,000 to 25,000	25,000 to 50,000	50,000 to 100,000	100,000 to 250,000	250,000 to 500,000	500,000 to 2,500,000	2,500,000 and over
Net Sales **2**	33264634	1859167	2261089	2604984	7831297	3444883	3728337	2313599	2062388	1772393	2118550	3267947	*
Interest **3**	385784	5130	11539	13343	54148	19348	41307	32384	32546	49233	32478	94328	*
Rents **4**	521384	4217	20821	5669	43045	13816	69565	32261	78199	42037	78910	132843	*
Royalties **5**	27573	0	2242	2	583	758	549	5546	0	28	0	17866	*
Other Portfolio Income **6**	685238	44960	16520	33949	61427	40094	135142	49565	49520	152552	14885	86624	*
Other Receipts **7**	1998200	35209	179053	13025	402721	218477	223160	111069	212516	191405	181427	230137	*
Total Receipts **8**	36882813	1948683	2491264	2670972	8393221	3737376	4198060	2544424	2435169	2207648	2426250	3829745	*
Average Total Receipts **9**	829	437	102	443	1102	3261	8167	16850	34298	76126	161750	478718	*

Operating Costs/Operating Income (%)

Item Description for Accounting Period 7/02 Through 6/03	Total	Zero Assets	Under 500	500 to 1,000	1,000 to 5,000	5,000 to 10,000	10,000 to 25,000	25,000 to 50,000	50,000 to 100,000	100,000 to 250,000	250,000 to 500,000	500,000 to 2,500,000	2,500,000 and over
Cost of Operations **10**	69.6	91.7	36.6	75.1	72.7	72.5	77.0	76.9	77.1	66.8	70.5	47.1	*
Salaries and Wages **11**	6.2	0.5	13.1	1.6	5.9	4.7	5.1	5.6	5.4	11.0	8.8	8.1	*
Taxes Paid **12**	2.4	0.5	3.6	2.9	2.3	1.9	1.8	1.8	1.5	2.2	4.8	3.8	*
Interest Paid **13**	3.9	0.6	2.8	3.1	3.4	3.9	3.6	3.7	9.7	3.8	5.7	4.0	*
Depreciation **14**	1.8	0.3	4.0	2.2	1.3	1.1	1.9	1.9	1.5	3.0	2.4	1.9	*
Amortization and Depletion **15**	0.2	0.1	0.0	0.0	0.1	0.1	0.2	0.2	0.2	0.5	0.3	0.6	*
Pensions and Other Deferred Comp. **16**	0.3	0.0	0.1	0.5	0.8	0.1	0.2	0.1	0.1	0.7	0.2	0.0	*
Employee Benefits **17**	0.5	0.0	0.4	0.4	0.3	0.4	0.3	0.4	0.4	0.9	1.0	0.8	*
Advertising **18**	0.7	0.1	0.2	0.4	0.4	0.9	0.9	0.8	0.8	0.7	1.6	1.1	*
Other Expenses **19**	14.2	21.3	31.9	10.4	9.7	11.1	9.5	8.9	14.5	26.1	14.1	17.8	*
Officers' Compensation **20**	2.7	0.1	9.9	3.6	3.0	2.4	2.7	2.0	1.5	2.5	1.2	0.5	*
Operating Margin **21**	*	*	*	*	0.3	0.8	*	*	*	*	*	14.2	*
Operating Margin Before Officers' Comp. **22**	0.3	*	7.2	3.3	3.3	3.2	*	*	*	*	*	14.8	*

Selected Average Balance Sheet ($ in Thousands)

Net Receivables **23**	114	0	7	72	141	300	1174	2728	6813	11954	18598	117891
Inventories **24**	343	0	20	154	594	1726	3330	9450	11571	25559	79299	182979
Net Property, Plant and Equipment **25**	407	0	39	232	524	1894	4042	8735	13638	48691	103900	279195
Total Assets **26**	1512	0	130	707	2033	6930	15338	34082	69554	150812	346479	1104149
Notes and Loans Payable **27**	874	0	145	497	1272	4332	8984	19015	31310	61288	186894	424427
All Other Liabilities **28**	305	0	71	98	352	1061	2677	7375	14453	40167	66434	206494
Net Worth **29**	333	0	-86	112	410	1537	3677	7691	23791	49356	93151	473228

Selected Financial Ratios (Times to 1)

Current Ratio **30**	1.8	•	0.9	2.3	2.1	1.8	2.0	2.1	2.2	2.0	1.4	1.5
Quick Ratio **31**	0.6	•	0.5	0.8	0.5	0.4	0.6	0.6	0.8	0.7	0.4	0.7
Net Sales to Working Capital **32**	2.4	•	•	2.2	1.7	2.0	2.0	1.6	1.9	2.2	3.8	3.4
Coverage Ratio **33**	3.2	3.7	3.7	1.7	3.2	3.4	3.6	3.0	1.6	2.7	1.7	8.9
Total Asset Turnover **34**	0.5	0.7	0.7	0.6	0.5	0.4	0.5	0.4	0.4	0.4	0.4	0.4
Inventory Turnover **35**	1.5	1.7	1.7	2.1	1.3	1.3	1.7	1.2	1.9	1.6	1.3	1.1
Receivables Turnover **36**	•	•	•	•	•	•	•	•	•	•	•	•
Total Liabilities to Net Worth **37**	3.5	•	5.3	4.0	3.5	3.2	3.4	1.9	1.9	2.1	2.7	1.3
Current Assets to Working Capital **38**	2.2	•	1.8	1.9	2.2	2.0	1.9	1.8	2.0	2.0	3.4	2.9
Current Liabilities to Working Capital **39**	1.2	•	0.8	0.9	1.2	1.0	0.9	0.8	0.8	1.0	2.4	1.9
Working Capital to Net Sales **40**	0.4	•	0.5	0.6	0.5	0.5	0.6	0.6	0.5	0.4	0.3	0.3
Inventory to Working Capital **41**	1.1	•	0.8	1.0	1.2	0.9	1.0	0.8	0.8	0.9	2.1	1.5
Total Receipts to Cash Flow **42**	5.2	11.9	9.9	6.7	5.7	6.8	7.2	6.6	6.6	4.1	6.3	2.2
Cost of Goods to Cash Flow **43**	3.6	10.9	7.4	4.9	4.2	5.3	5.6	5.1	5.1	2.7	4.5	1.0
Cash Flow to Total Debt **44**	0.1	0.2	0.1	0.1	0.1	0.1	0.1	0.1	0.1	0.1	0.1	0.3

Selected Financial Factors (in Percentages)

Debt Ratio **45**	78.0	•	166.6	84.1	77.8	79.9	76.0	77.4	65.8	67.3	73.1	57.1
Return on Total Assets **46**	6.1	•	7.3	3.2	5.5	5.7	6.1	5.1	6.3	4.1	3.9	13.1
Return on Equity Before Income Taxes **47**	18.9	•	•	8.5	18.8	18.2	18.5	15.0	6.6	7.8	5.8	27.1
Return on Equity After Income Taxes **48**	15.2	•	•	7.2	17.9	17.0	17.9	12.7	5.4	6.0	3.6	17.6
Profit Margin (Before Income Tax) **49**	8.4	•	7.5	2.2	7.5	9.3	7.5	5.4	5.4	6.3	3.8	31.4
Profit Margin (After Income Tax) **50**	6.8	7.3	1.9	8.7	7.1	9.1	8.7	6.4	4.4	4.9	2.4	20.4

29

Table II
Corporations with Net Income

LAND SUBDIVISION

MONEY AMOUNTS AND SIZE OF ASSETS IN THOUSANDS OF DOLLARS

Item Description for Accounting Period 7/02 Through 6/03	Total	Zero Assets	Under 500	500 to 1,000	1,000 to 5,000	5,000 to 10,000	10,000 to 25,000	25,000 to 50,000	50,000 to 100,000	100,000 to 250,000	250,000 to 500,000	500,000 to 2,500,000	2,500,000 and over
Number of Enterprises **1**	18613	1539	9656	2606	3719	0	287	82	44	16	9	0	•
Revenues ($ in Thousands)													
Net Sales **2**	25567380	1771133	1725372	2022272	5678073	0	2789898	1730182	1752892	1310261	1385565	0	•
Interest **3**	254836	5009	8208	11107	34869	0	30789	20879	25478	46284	10951	0	•
Rents **4**	363824	3867	14799	5669	33378	0	49540	21198	63999	15090	50546	0	•
Royalties **5**	8596	0	2242	2	10	0	549	5035	0	0	0	0	•
Other Portfolio Income **6**	616711	44884	16520	27725	59267	0	124868	27419	33793	150083	11212	0	•
Other Receipts **7**	1830856	58100	163565	9784	340437	0	182867	102330	193335	189343	136021	0	•
Total Receipts **8**	28742203	1882993	1930706	2076559	6146034	0	3178511	1907043	2069497	1711061	1594295	0	•
Average Total Receipts **9**	1544	1224	200	797	1653	•	11075	23257	47034	106941	177144	•	
Operating Costs/Operating Income (%)													
Cost of Operations **10**	69.3	91.1	37.8	76.7	69.7	•	75.9	74.8	77.6	67.8	61.4	•	•
Salaries and Wages **11**	4.7	0.4	8.2	0.5	4.1	•	4.1	4.8	4.2	10.8	10.2	•	•
Taxes Paid **12**	2.1	0.4	2.6	1.8	1.8	•	1.5	1.4	1.2	1.8	6.3	•	•
Interest Paid **13**	2.5	0.3	2.0	1.2	2.3	•	2.2	2.5	3.3	2.5	6.7	•	•
Depreciation **14**	1.4	0.1	3.3	1.1	1.2	•	1.4	1.3	1.0	2.7	2.5	•	•
Amortization and Depletion **15**	0.1	0.0	0.0	0.0	0.0	•	0.1	0.1	0.2	0.3	0.4	•	•
Pensions and Other Deferred Comp. **16**	0.3	0.0	0.0	0.6	0.6	•	0.2	0.1	0.1	0.7	0.4	•	•
Employee Benefits **17**	0.4	0.0	0.4	0.4	0.2	•	0.2	0.3	0.4	0.6	1.2	•	•
Advertising **18**	0.6	0.0	0.1	0.4	0.4	•	0.7	0.7	0.7	0.8	2.3	•	•
Other Expenses **19**	9.3	2.7	19.1	7.5	7.5	•	7.0	6.6	10.1	26.5	14.1	•	•
Officers' Compensation **20**	2.4	0.0	8.5	2.6	3.2	•	2.3	2.0	1.3	1.5	1.1	•	•
Operating Margin **21**	6.8	5.0	18.0	7.0	9.0	•	4.2	5.5	•	•	•	•	•
Operating Margin Before Officers' Comp. **22**	9.2	5.1	26.5	9.6	12.2	•	6.5	7.5	1.3	•	•	•	•

Selected Average Balance Sheet ($ in Thousands)

Net Receivables 23	179	0	6	78	201	•	1234	3342	6794	15136	12812
Inventories 24	501	0	21	165	580	•	3857	11767	15919	34137	76103
Net Property, Plant and Equipment 25	442	0	30	175	379	•	3225	5361	11510	45725	121503
Total Assets 26	2050	0	142	722	2057	•	15381	34545	69305	151889	342580
Notes and Loans Payable 27	936	0	70	344	1014	•	8021	16000	27667	43831	214723
All Other Liabilities 28	386	0	20	134	357	•	2822	6597	13415	38405	63879
Net Worth 29	728	0	52	243	686	•	4538	11947	28223	69653	63977

Selected Financial Ratios (Times to 1)

Current Ratio 30	2.0	•	2.4	2.0	2.3	•	2.0	2.4	2.7	2.3	1.4
Quick Ratio 31	0.6	•	1.3	0.6	0.7	•	0.5	0.8	0.9	0.8	0.3
Net Sales to Working Capital 32	2.7	•	5.5	3.8	2.1	•	2.2	1.6	2.0	2.2	4.7
Coverage Ratio 33	8.6	34.4	16.2	8.7	8.6	•	9.0	7.3	6.5	6.8	2.3
Total Asset Turnover 34	0.7	•	1.3	1.1	0.7	•	0.6	0.6	0.6	0.5	0.4
Inventory Turnover 35	1.9	•	3.3	3.6	1.8	•	1.9	1.3	1.9	1.6	1.2
Receivables Turnover 36	•	•	•	•	•	•	•	•	•	•	•
Total Liabilities to Net Worth 37	1.8	•	1.8	2.0	2.0	•	2.4	1.9	1.5	1.2	4.4
Current Assets to Working Capital 38	2.0	•	1.7	2.0	1.8	•	2.0	1.7	1.6	1.8	3.6
Current Liabilities to Working Capital 39	1.0	•	0.7	1.0	0.8	•	1.0	0.7	0.6	0.8	2.6
Working Capital to Net Sales 40	0.4	•	0.2	0.3	0.5	•	0.5	0.6	0.5	0.4	0.2
Inventory to Working Capital 41	1.0	•	0.6	0.8	0.8	•	0.9	0.9	0.8	0.9	2.3
Total Receipts to Cash Flow 42	4.0	8.6	2.2	6.8	4.4	•	4.9	4.9	4.1	3.2	5.0
Cost of Goods to Cash Flow 43	2.8	7.8	0.8	5.2	3.1	•	3.7	3.7	3.2	2.2	3.1
Cash Flow to Total Debt 44	0.3	•	0.9	0.2	0.3	•	0.2	0.2	0.2	0.3	0.1

Selected Financial Factors (in Percentages)

Debt Ratio 45	64.5	•	63.7	66.3	66.6	•	70.5	65.4	59.3	54.1	81.3
Return on Total Assets 46	14.3	•	40.1	11.7	14.5	•	12.8	11.2	12.2	9.2	6.8
Return on Equity Before Income Taxes 47	35.6	•	103.4	30.7	38.4	•	38.7	27.8	25.4	17.1	20.3
Return on Equity After Income Taxes 48	31.6	•	102.5	29.4	37.4	•	37.8	25.2	23.7	14.9	15.0
Profit Margin (Before Income Tax) 49	18.8	11.3	29.9	9.6	17.3	•	18.1	15.8	18.0	14.6	8.5
Profit Margin (After Income Tax) 50	16.7	10.7	29.6	9.2	16.8	•	17.6	14.2	16.8	12.6	6.2

ELECTRICAL CONTRACTORS

Table I

Corporations with and without Net Income

MONEY AMOUNTS AND SIZE OF ASSETS IN THOUSANDS OF DOLLARS

Item Description for Accounting Period 7/02 Through 6/03	Total	Zero Assets	Under 500	500 to 1,000	1,000 to 5,000	5,000 to 10,000	10,000 to 25,000	25,000 to 50,000	50,000 to 100,000	100,000 to 250,000	250,000 to 500,000	500,000 to 2,500,000	2,500,000 and over
Number of Enterprises 1	40615	5054	29052	2638	3109	510	186	45	12	5	·	3	·
Revenues ($ in Thousands)													
Net Sales 2	62400545	529564	12440157	4996481	16888299	8535465	6536097	2984008	1853310	1195717	·	6441447	·
Interest 3	89968	0	6144	3622	21290	5299	2840	1030	1644	3269	·	44829	·
Rents 4	15202	0	4960	1111	3909	3441	863	176	726	0	·	16	·
Royalties 5	36499	0	0	0	0	1254	48	20	0	0	·	35177	·
Other Portfolio Income 6	69787	8236	25677	3559	12086	6295	5779	4781	939	780	·	1658	·
Other Receipts 7	477726	36	31137	15474	275255	76620	21437	19410	9346	17578	·	11431	·
Total Receipts 8	63089727	537836	12508075	5020247	17200839	8628374	6567064	3009425	1865965	1217344	·	6554558	·
Average Total Receipts 9	1553	106	431	1903	5533	16918	35307	66876	155497	243469	·	2178186	·
Operating Costs/Operating Income (%)													
Cost of Operations 10	69.6	46.1	48.7	65.1	73.8	75.7	77.8	76.3	78.2	78.1	·	81.0	·
Salaries and Wages 11	6.7	14.2	11.6	8.3	5.4	4.0	4.9	4.9	4.4	9.0	·	4.8	·
Taxes Paid 12	2.7	2.8	3.8	3.2	2.8	2.4	2.3	2.0	1.9	1.5	·	1.6	·
Interest Paid 13	0.7	1.4	0.9	0.5	0.4	0.4	0.3	0.5	0.7	1.7	·	1.8	·
Depreciation 14	1.8	2.5	2.7	2.0	1.6	1.3	1.0	1.5	2.1	3.4	·	1.7	·
Amortization and Depletion 15	0.1	0.0	0.0	0.1	0.0	0.0	0.0	0.1	0.3	0.1	·	1.0	·
Pensions and Other Deferred Comp. 16	0.5	0.0	0.5	0.4	0.6	0.8	0.8	0.4	0.5	0.1	·	0.1	·
Employee Benefits 17	2.4	3.7	1.2	2.4	2.9	3.1	3.0	3.8	2.8	0.4	·	0.7	·
Advertising 18	0.2	1.0	0.4	0.4	0.2	0.1	0.2	0.1	0.1	0.1	·	0.1	·
Other Expenses 19	9.1	23.1	16.1	11.9	7.9	5.4	4.5	5.2	4.5	10.2	·	8.3	·
Officers' Compensation 20	4.8	5.5	9.7	5.5	4.4	4.2	2.6	2.1	2.1	0.9	·	1.4	·
Operating Margin 21	1.3	·	4.4	0.2	·	2.5	2.5	3.1	2.5	·	·	·	·
Operating Margin Before Officers' Comp. 22	6.1	5.2	14.1	5.7	4.3	6.7	5.0	5.2	4.6	·	·	·	·

Selected Average Balance Sheet ($ in Thousands)

Net Receivables 23	247	0	20	246	917	3163	7809	16411	35773	49060	495794
Inventories 24	29	0	10	45	102	464	562	613	542	1253	20523
Net Property, Plant and Equipment 25	89	0	37	114	265	680	1346	3320	5080	24335	166965
Total Assets 26	609	0	117	683	2031	6960	14473	33336	71745	152854	1279963
Notes and Loans Payable 27	145	0	51	166	410	1676	1949	6391	9165	36731	296133
All Other Liabilities 28	235	0	22	211	819	3066	6682	15326	38606	57886	508796
Net Worth 29	229	0	44	306	803	2218	5842	11619	23974	58237	475035

Selected Financial Ratios (Times to 1)

Current Ratio 30	1.6	•	1.8	2.1	1.5	1.6	1.6	1.6	1.6	1.6	1.4
Quick Ratio 31	1.3	•	1.4	1.7	1.3	1.2	1.3	1.3	1.3	1.3	1.0
Net Sales to Working Capital 32	9.2	•	15.1	6.7	10.1	8.1	7.4	6.2	7.0	8.3	9.4
Coverage Ratio 33	4.4	1.5	6.4	2.3	5.0	9.9	11.0	8.4	5.8	•	0.3
Total Asset Turnover 34	2.5	•	3.7	2.8	2.7	2.4	2.4	2.0	2.2	1.6	1.7
Inventory Turnover 35	37.3	•	21.1	27.7	39.3	27.3	48.7	82.6	222.5	149.0	84.8
Receivables Turnover 36	•	•	•	•	•	•	•	•	•	•	•
Total Liabilities to Net Worth 37	1.7	•	1.7	1.2	1.5	2.1	1.5	1.9	2.0	1.6	1.7
Current Assets to Working Capital 38	2.6	•	2.2	1.9	2.9	2.8	2.6	2.6	2.7	2.8	3.3
Current Liabilities to Working Capital 39	1.6	•	1.2	0.9	1.9	1.8	1.6	1.6	1.7	1.8	2.3
Working Capital to Net Sales 40	0.1	•	0.1	0.1	0.1	0.1	0.1	0.2	0.1	0.1	0.1
Inventory to Working Capital 41	0.2	•	0.3	0.2	0.2	0.2	0.1	0.1	0.0	0.0	0.1
Total Receipts to Cash Flow 42	10.5	4.7	5.5	10.0	13.0	13.7	17.0	13.6	17.1	22.3	17.6
Cost of Goods to Cash Flow 43	7.3	2.1	2.7	6.5	9.6	10.4	13.2	10.4	13.3	17.4	14.2
Cash Flow to Total Debt 44	0.4	•	1.1	0.5	0.3	0.3	0.2	0.2	0.2	0.1	0.2

Selected Financial Factors (in Percentages)

Debt Ratio 45	62.3	•	62.8	55.2	60.5	68.1	59.6	65.1	66.6	61.9	62.9
Return on Total Assets 46	7.8	•	21.3	3.4	5.9	9.7	7.8	8.9	8.1	•	1.0
Return on Equity Before Income Taxes 47	16.1	•	48.4	4.3	11.9	27.3	17.6	22.5	20.0	•	•
Return on Equity After Income Taxes 48	14.3	•	47.9	3.0	9.9	24.3	15.6	20.5	16.5	•	•
Profit Margin (Before Income Tax) 49	2.4	0.7	4.9	0.7	1.8	3.6	2.9	3.9	3.1	•	•
Profit Margin (After Income Tax) 50	2.1	0.7	4.9	0.5	1.5	3.2	2.6	3.6	2.6	•	•

Table II

Corporations with Net Income

ELECTRICAL CONTRACTORS

MONEY AMOUNTS AND SIZE OF ASSETS IN THOUSANDS OF DOLLARS

Item Description for Accounting Period 7/02 Through 6/03	Total	Zero Assets	Under 500	500 to 1,000	1,000 to 5,000	5,000 to 10,000	10,000 to 25,000	25,000 to 50,000	50,000 to 100,000	100,000 to 250,000	250,000 to 500,000	500,000 to 2,500,000	2,500,000 and over
Number of Enterprises **1**	26595	2408	19371	1971	2182	0	149	35	9	0	•	0	•

Revenues ($ in Thousands)

	Total	Zero Assets	Under 500	500 to 1,000	1,000 to 5,000	5,000 to 10,000	10,000 to 25,000	25,000 to 50,000	50,000 to 100,000	100,000 to 250,000	250,000 to 500,000	500,000 to 2,500,000	2,500,000 and over
Net Sales **2**	45999902	323101	8429263	3952355	12734485	0	5347029	2436981	1361310	0	•	0	•
Interest **3**	32860	0	2318	2543	18277	0	2405	376	501	0	•	0	•
Rents **4**	7859	0	0	30	3890	0	333	127	81	0	•	0	•
Royalties **5**	1301	0	0	0	0	0	48	0	0	0	•	0	•
Other Portfolio Income **6**	40442	4698	9456	3548	5507	0	4642	4255	939	0	•	0	•
Other Receipts **7**	356350	36	27477	7048	183943	0	17161	18330	7601	0	•	0	•
Total Receipts **8**	46438714	327835	8468514	3965524	12946102	0	5371618	2460069	1370432	0	•	0	•
Average Total Receipts **9**	1746	136	437	2012	5933	•	36051	70288	152270	•	•	•	•

Operating Costs/Operating Income (%)

	Total	Zero Assets	Under 500	500 to 1,000	1,000 to 5,000	5,000 to 10,000	10,000 to 25,000	25,000 to 50,000	50,000 to 100,000	100,000 to 250,000	250,000 to 500,000	500,000 to 2,500,000	2,500,000 and over
Cost of Operations **10**	68.4	43.7	44.3	60.2	73.7	•	77.2	76.7	75.7	•	•	•	•
Salaries and Wages **11**	6.3	14.6	11.1	8.9	5.1	•	4.7	4.8	5.0	•	•	•	•
Taxes Paid **12**	2.6	1.3	3.5	3.1	2.5	•	2.2	1.9	1.7	•	•	•	•
Interest Paid **13**	0.5	1.2	1.0	0.4	0.3	•	0.2	0.4	0.2	•	•	•	•
Depreciation **14**	1.6	1.6	2.7	2.0	1.4	•	1.0	1.2	2.7	•	•	•	•
Amortization and Depletion **15**	0.0	0.0	0.0	0.1	0.0	•	0.0	0.0	0.0	•	•	•	•
Pensions and Other Deferred Comp. **16**	0.6	•	0.3	0.5	0.6	•	0.9	0.4	0.7	•	•	•	•
Employee Benefits **17**	2.2	2.4	1.4	1.9	2.3	•	2.6	3.4	2.5	•	•	•	•
Advertising **18**	0.2	0.6	0.3	0.5	0.3	•	0.2	0.1	0.1	•	•	•	•
Other Expenses **19**	8.1	20.3	15.6	11.2	7.2	•	4.4	4.5	4.6	•	•	•	•
Officers' Compensation **20**	4.9	0.2	9.7	6.1	4.1	•	2.8	2.2	2.4	•	•	•	•
Operating Margin **21**	4.5	14.1	10.1	5.1	2.4	•	3.8	4.5	4.4	•	•	•	•
Operating Margin Before Officers' Comp. **22**	9.4	14.3	19.8	11.2	6.5	•	6.5	6.6	6.8	•	•	•	•

Selected Average Balance Sheet ($ in Thousands)

Net Receivables 23	282	0	17	234	948	7876	18055	33860
Inventories 24	28	0	7	46	94	488	516	660
Net Property, Plant and Equipment 25	90	0	39	120	267	1309	2610	5561
Total Assets 26	648	0	117	653	2041	14555	33786	68287
Notes and Loans Payable 27	126	0	48	114	332	1565	5758	3958
All Other Liabilities 28	263	0	21	170	830	6760	16337	37557
Net Worth 29	259	0	48	368	879	6230	11691	26772

Selected Financial Ratios (Times to 1)

Current Ratio 30	1.7	•	1.8	2.6	1.7	1.8	1.7	1.8
Quick Ratio 31	1.4	•	1.4	2.2	1.5	1.4	1.3	1.5
Net Sales to Working Capital 32	8.8	•	16.8	6.7	8.8	6.7	6.1	5.7
Coverage Ratio 33	12.9	14.1	11.8	15.3	12.6	18.8	15.4	25.7
Total Asset Turnover 34	2.7	•	3.7	3.1	2.9	2.5	2.1	2.2
Inventory Turnover 35	41.9	•	29.1	26.1	46.0	56.8	103.6	173.5
Receivables Turnover 36	•	•	•	•	•	•	•	•
Total Liabilities to Net Worth 37	1.5	•	1.4	0.8	1.3	1.3	1.9	1.6
Current Assets to Working Capital 38	2.5	•	2.2	1.6	2.4	2.3	2.5	2.2
Current Liabilities to Working Capital 39	1.5	•	1.2	0.6	1.4	1.3	1.5	1.2
Working Capital to Net Sales 40	0.1	•	0.1	0.1	0.1	0.1	0.2	0.2
Inventory to Working Capital 41	0.1	•	0.3	0.2	0.1	0.1	0.0	0.0
Total Receipts to Cash Flow 42	8.6	3.0	4.3	6.9	10.4	14.3	11.8	12.9
Cost of Goods to Cash Flow 43	5.9	1.3	1.9	4.1	7.7	11.1	9.1	9.7
Cash Flow to Total Debt 44	0.5	•	1.5	1.0	0.5	0.3	0.3	0.3

Selected Financial Factors (in Percentages)

Debt Ratio 45	60.0	•	59.1	43.6	56.9	57.2	65.4	60.8
Return on Total Assets 46	15.8	•	42.9	17.8	12.6	11.0	12.0	11.6
Return on Equity Before Income Taxes 47	36.5	•	96.2	29.5	26.9	24.3	32.3	28.5
Return on Equity After Income Taxes 48	34.2	•	95.4	28.1	24.3	22.0	29.7	24.3
Profit Margin (Before Income Tax) 49	5.5	15.6	10.6	5.4	4.1	4.2	5.4	5.0
Profit Margin (After Income Tax) 50	5.1	15.6	10.5	5.2	3.7	3.8	5.0	4.3

Table I

Corporations with and without Net Income

PLUMBING, HEATING, AND AIR-CONDITIONING CONTRACTORS

MONEY AMOUNTS AND SIZE OF ASSETS IN THOUSANDS OF DOLLARS

Item Description for Accounting Period 7/02 Through 6/03	Total	Zero Assets	Under 500	500 to 1,000	1,000 to 5,000	5,000 to 10,000	10,000 to 25,000	25,000 to 50,000	50,000 to 100,000	100,000 to 250,000	250,000 to 500,000	500,000 to 2,500,000	2,500,000 and over
Number of Enterprises **1**	62515	7327	46719	4181	3634	440	168	29	14	0	3	0	•
Revenues ($ in Thousands)													
Net Sales **2**	84059570	931307	26098430	10870873	22435418	8348197	5911875	2344293	2759259	0	4359918	0	•
Interest **3**	234718	125	18829	7018	16096	4263	2130	568	1112	0	184576	0	•
Rents **4**	20413	916	1695	6084	5945	327	1647	1131	2629	0	38	0	•
Royalties **5**	97732	0	0	0	0	0	61	0	71	0	97600	0	•
Other Portfolio Income **6**	120871	10714	17212	7602	15440	3168	4601	353	3061	0	58720	0	•
Other Receipts **7**	225062	1720	22054	48620	48264	27894	21313	9974	46983	0	-1760	0	•
Total Receipts **8**	84758366	944782	26158220	10940197	22521163	8383849	5941627	2356319	2813115	0	4699092	0	•
Average Total Receipts **9**	1356	129	560	2617	6197	19054	35367	81252	200937	•	1566364	•	•
Operating Costs/Operating Income (%)													
Cost of Operations **10**	67.6	47.2	54.5	62.5	73.9	79.2	80.8	81.8	77.4	•	77.4	•	•
Salaries and Wages **11**	7.9	7.4	11.1	8.6	6.0	4.7	4.6	4.9	8.3	•	7.6	•	•
Taxes Paid **12**	2.8	2.2	3.3	3.1	2.5	1.9	2.1	1.5	1.2	•	5.6	•	•
Interest Paid **13**	0.8	0.9	0.6	0.3	0.4	0.3	0.3	0.4	1.0	•	6.3	•	•
Depreciation **14**	1.6	2.9	2.2	1.6	1.5	1.1	0.8	0.9	0.9	•	1.1	•	•
Amortization and Depletion **15**	0.0	0.2	0.0	0.0	0.0	0.0	0.0	0.0	0.0	•	0.4	•	•
Pensions and Other Deferred Comp. **16**	0.5	0.0	0.4	0.7	0.6	0.6	0.6	0.4	0.5	•	0.2	•	•
Employee Benefits **17**	1.8	1.2	1.4	1.8	1.9	2.4	2.1	1.9	2.1	•	1.4	•	•
Advertising **18**	0.7	0.5	1.2	1.0	0.5	0.2	0.1	0.2	0.1	•	0.2	•	•
Other Expenses **19**	10.4	31.5	14.8	11.1	7.7	4.2	3.9	4.5	8.6	•	16.8	•	•
Officers' Compensation **20**	5.0	6.1	7.9	6.5	4.1	3.1	2.3	1.4	1.1	•	0.1	•	•
Operating Margin **21**	0.8	•	2.5	2.7	0.6	2.3	2.3	2.1	•	•	•	•	•
Operating Margin Before Officers' Comp. **22**	5.8	6.0	10.4	9.2	4.7	5.4	4.5	3.5	•	•	•	•	•

Selected Average Balance Sheet ($ in Thousands)

Net Receivables 23	170	0	23	252	967	3784	7604	19427	37371	323083
Inventories 24	25	0	8	60	148	384	593	2615	1906	8712
Net Property, Plant and Equipment 25	63	0	31	132	286	765	1107	3705	13115	21952
Total Assets 26	394	0	104	683	2012	7243	14056	34189	74825	676047
Notes and Loans Payable 27	99	0	47	124	423	956	1713	7014	22740	239141
All Other Liabilities 28	172	0	28	210	876	3517	7719	17918	41830	473006
Net Worth 29	124	0	30	349	713	2769	4625	9256	10255	-36100

Selected Financial Ratios (Times to 1)

Current Ratio 30	1.7	•	1.7	1.6	1.6	1.6	1.5	1.3	1.6	3.5
Quick Ratio 31	1.4	•	1.3	1.3	1.3	1.3	1.2	1.0	1.3	2.6
Net Sales to Working Capital 32	10.9	•	21.5	10.5	9.3	8.7	8.9	11.9	8.8	4.0
Coverage Ratio 33	3.1	2.5	5.4	3.2	12.0	11.6	10.9	7.4	1.8	•
Total Asset Turnover 34	3.4	•	5.4	3.1	3.8	2.6	2.5	2.4	2.6	2.1
Inventory Turnover 35	36.6	•	39.0	30.8	26.9	39.2	48.0	25.3	80.1	129.1
Receivables Turnover 36	•	•	•	•	•	•	•	•	•	•
Total Liabilities to Net Worth 37	2.2	•	2.5	1.8	1.0	1.6	2.0	2.7	6.3	•
Current Assets to Working Capital 38	2.4	•	2.4	2.7	1.9	2.8	3.0	4.1	2.6	1.4
Current Liabilities to Working Capital 39	1.4	•	1.4	1.7	0.9	1.8	2.0	3.1	1.6	0.4
Working Capital to Net Sales 40	0.1	•	0.0	0.1	0.1	0.1	0.1	0.1	0.1	0.3
Inventory to Working Capital 41	0.2	•	0.3	0.3	0.2	0.2	0.2	0.4	0.1	0.0
Total Receipts to Cash Flow 42	10.6	3.9	6.7	16.0	8.2	17.6	18.5	16.8	13.0	0.0
Cost of Goods to Cash Flow 43	7.2	1.8	3.7	11.8	5.1	13.9	15.0	13.7	10.1	•
Cash Flow to Total Debt 44	0.5	•	1.1	1.0	0.3	0.2	0.2	0.2	0.2	•

Selected Financial Factors (in Percentages)

Debt Ratio 45	68.6	•	71.4	48.9	64.6	61.8	67.1	72.9	86.3	105.3
Return on Total Assets 46	8.2	•	17.9	14.1	4.3	7.7	7.5	7.2	4.7	•
Return on Equity Before Income Taxes 47	17.7	•	51.2	25.2	8.4	18.4	20.8	23.1	15.5	377.2
Return on Equity After Income Taxes 48	16.2	•	49.9	24.5	7.3	16.5	19.1	21.4	11.6	386.6
Profit Margin (Before Income Tax) 49	1.6	1.4	2.7	3.4	1.0	2.7	2.7	2.6	0.8	•
Profit Margin (After Income Tax) 50	1.5	1.0	2.7	3.3	0.8	2.4	2.5	2.5	0.6	•

Table II

Corporations with Net Income

PLUMBING, HEATING, AND AIR-CONDITIONING CONTRACTORS

MONEY AMOUNTS AND SIZE OF ASSETS IN THOUSANDS OF DOLLARS

Item Description for Accounting Period 7/02 Through 6/03	Total	Zero Assets	Under 500	500 to 1,000	1,000 to 5,000	5,000 to 10,000	10,000 to 25,000	25,000 to 50,000	50,000 to 100,000	100,000 to 250,000	250,000 to 500,000	500,000 to 2,500,000	2,500,000 and over
Number of Enterprises **1**	36567	4115	26327	3194	2404	0	135	25	7	0	0	0	•
Revenues ($ in Thousands)													
Net Sales **2**	58371956	656758	16450995	9011110	15468023	0	4986365	2177835	1046340	0	0	0	•
Interest **3**	27076	118	4818	5352	8830	0	1526	276	174	0	0	0	•
Rents **4**	10851	0	1684	1170	4143	0	1420	1131	976	0	0	0	•
Royalties **5**	61	0	0	0	0	0	61	0	0	0	0	0	•
Other Portfolio Income **6**	65471	5083	14261	5187	3928	0	3138	348	88	0	0	0	•
Other Receipts **7**	155521	1719	9139	42575	35605	0	19099	5237	4231	0	0	0	•
Total Receipts **8**	58630936	663678	16480897	9065394	15520529	0	5011609	2184827	1051809	0	0	0	•
Average Total Receipts **9**	1603	161	626	2838	6456	•	37123	87393	150258	•	•	•	•
Operating Costs/Operating Income (%)													
Cost of Operations **10**	67.0	39.2	53.2	61.8	72.5	•	79.9	83.7	72.8	•	•	•	•
Salaries and Wages **11**	7.5	5.9	10.9	8.7	6.0	•	4.5	4.5	7.8	•	•	•	•
Taxes Paid **12**	2.6	1.8	3.2	3.1	2.5	•	2.1	1.4	1.9	•	•	•	•
Interest Paid **13**	0.4	0.7	0.5	0.3	0.3	•	0.2	0.3	0.3	•	•	•	•
Depreciation **14**	1.5	2.2	2.2	1.5	1.4	•	0.7	0.9	1.2	•	•	•	•
Amortization and Depletion **15**	0.0	0.2	0.0	0.0	0.0	•	0.0	0.0	0.0	•	•	•	•
Pensions and Other Deferred Comp. **16**	0.6	•	0.5	0.8	0.6	•	0.5	0.4	0.9	•	•	•	•
Employee Benefits **17**	1.8	1.1	1.0	1.7	2.1	•	2.3	1.7	2.4	•	•	•	•
Advertising **18**	0.7	0.5	1.2	1.0	0.4	•	0.2	0.1	0.1	•	•	•	•
Other Expenses **19**	8.5	33.5	12.9	10.6	6.5	•	3.5	2.5	8.3	•	•	•	•
Officers' Compensation **20**	5.1	8.4	7.7	6.4	4.5	•	2.4	1.4	1.2	•	•	•	•
Operating Margin **21**	4.3	6.4	6.7	4.1	3.0	•	3.6	3.0	3.0	•	•	•	•
Operating Margin Before Officers' Comp. **22**	9.4	14.8	14.4	10.5	7.5	•	6.0	4.5	4.2	•	•	•	•

Selected Average Balance Sheet ($ in Thousands)

Net Receivables 23	194	0	19	257	963	•	7866	21054	25708
Inventories 24	27	0	8	62	136	•	412	1845	974
Net Property, Plant and Equipment 25	70	0	34	118	268	•	1013	3653	14383
Total Assets 26	450	0	116	684	2004	•	13936	34460	66629
Notes and Loans Payable 27	86	0	44	120	345	•	1163	5516	10575
All Other Liabilities 28	175	0	21	196	824	•	7770	18372	27613
Net Worth 29	189	0	51	368	835	•	5003	10573	28440

Selected Financial Ratios (Times to 1)

Current Ratio 30	1.8	•	2.6	2.4	1.8	•	1.5	1.4	1.8
Quick Ratio 31	1.5	•	2.0	2.0	1.4	•	1.3	1.2	1.4
Net Sales to Working Capital 32	10.3	•	15.2	8.9	9.4	•	8.7	10.0	6.9
Coverage Ratio 33	14.1	11.1	13.9	18.4	11.4	•	22.7	10.8	12.8
Total Asset Turnover 34	3.5	•	5.4	4.1	3.2	•	2.7	2.5	2.2
Inventory Turnover 35	39.4	•	41.0	28.1	34.4	•	71.6	39.5	111.8
Receivables Turnover 36	•	•	•	•	•	•	•	•	•
Total Liabilities to Net Worth 37	1.4	•	1.3	0.9	1.4	•	1.8	2.3	1.3
Current Assets to Working Capital 38	2.2	•	1.6	1.7	2.3	•	2.9	3.3	2.2
Current Liabilities to Working Capital 39	1.2	•	0.6	0.7	1.3	•	1.9	2.3	1.2
Working Capital to Net Sales 40	0.1	•	0.1	0.1	0.1	•	0.1	0.1	0.1
Inventory to Working Capital 41	0.2	•	0.2	0.2	0.2	•	0.1	0.2	0.0
Total Receipts to Cash Flow 42	8.8	2.9	5.7	7.6	12.7	•	15.4	21.5	9.2
Cost of Goods to Cash Flow 43	5.9	1.1	3.0	4.7	9.2	•	12.3	18.0	6.7
Cash Flow to Total Debt 44	0.7	•	1.7	1.2	0.4	•	0.3	0.2	0.4

Selected Financial Factors (in Percentages)

Debt Ratio 45	57.9	•	56.1	46.2	58.3	•	64.1	69.3	57.3
Return on Total Assets 46	18.1	•	39.9	20.4	11.7	•	11.4	9.3	8.5
Return on Equity Before Income Taxes 47	40.0	•	84.3	35.8	25.7	•	30.3	27.6	18.3
Return on Equity After Income Taxes 48	38.3	•	83.0	34.9	24.3	•	28.4	25.9	18.1
Profit Margin (Before Income Tax) 49	4.7	7.5	6.9	4.7	3.3	•	4.1	3.3	3.5
Profit Margin (After Income Tax) 50	4.5	7.0	6.8	4.6	3.2	•	3.8	3.1	3.4

Table I

Corporations with and without Net Income

OTHER SPECIALTY TRADE CONTRACTORS

MONEY AMOUNTS AND SIZE OF ASSETS IN THOUSANDS OF DOLLARS

Item Description for Accounting Period 7/02 Through 6/03	Total	Zero Assets	Under 500	500 to 1,000	1,000 to 5,000	5,000 to 10,000	10,000 to 25,000	25,000 to 50,000	50,000 to 100,000	100,000 to 250,000	250,000 to 500,000	500,000 to 2,500,000	2,500,000 and over
Number of Enterprises **1**	279799	29191	220467	14345	13406	1462	698	138	55	25	8	3	•
Revenues ($ in Thousands)													
Net Sales **2**	287309172	3560867	104427479	35336340	72261740	21876964	23244958	9721335	6819765	5089220	2912711	2057794	•
Interest **3**	234691	1940	27735	23540	82085	19717	16134	11184	8529	8423	30969	4437	•
Rents **4**	183204	10	35399	21345	33500	6642	14532	26816	2966	12413	29534	46	•
Royalties **5**	44060	0	38001	0	9	252	105	1990	256	3347	18	80	•
Other Portfolio Income **6**	582360	6177	189238	66936	176491	28541	44933	20097	17085	8335	18685	5840	•
Other Receipts **7**	905429	38642	250541	105977	238176	165423	148312	63516	45958	-409	-151016	310	•
Total Receipts **8**	289258916	3607636	104968393	35554138	72792001	22097539	23468974	9844938	6894559	5121329	2840901	2068507	•
Average Total Receipts **9**	1034	124	476	2479	5430	15115	33623	71340	125356	204853	355113	689502	•
Operating Costs/Operating Income (%)													
Cost of Operations **10**	64.3	39.5	53.4	62.1	68.8	75.2	78.8	79.3	78.7	77.8	75.4	88.4	•
Salaries and Wages **11**	7.8	13.8	10.5	8.2	6.5	4.6	4.5	5.4	5.5	6.0	5.3	5.5	•
Taxes Paid **12**	2.5	2.0	2.9	2.7	2.5	2.0	1.9	1.5	1.8	1.1	1.4	0.2	•
Interest Paid **13**	0.7	0.7	0.6	0.7	0.6	0.6	0.5	0.7	0.9	1.6	2.4	3.8	•
Depreciation **14**	2.6	2.7	2.7	3.0	2.7	2.4	2.0	2.2	2.3	3.3	2.0	4.1	•
Amortization and Depletion **15**	0.1	0.1	0.0	0.0	0.1	0.0	0.0	0.1	0.3	0.6	1.0	0.8	•
Pensions and Other Deferred Comp. **16**	0.4	0.2	0.3	0.6	0.5	0.6	0.5	0.4	0.4	0.2	0.1	0.2	•
Employee Benefits **17**	1.4	0.6	1.2	1.4	1.7	1.9	1.5	1.4	1.8	0.9	0.9	0.1	•
Advertising **18**	0.5	1.5	0.6	0.8	0.3	0.2	0.3	0.2	0.2	0.2	0.2	0.1	•
Other Expenses **19**	12.9	29.1	17.9	13.5	10.3	7.4	6.4	6.6	7.1	5.8	17.0	8.1	•
Officers' Compensation **20**	5.0	8.3	7.4	5.4	4.1	3.0	2.2	1.4	1.4	0.9	0.8	0.6	•
Operating Margin **21**	1.8	1.7	2.5	1.5	1.9	2.1	1.4	0.8	•	1.5	•	•	•
Operating Margin Before Officers' Comp. **22**	6.8	10.0	9.9	6.9	6.0	5.1	3.5	2.2	1.0	2.5	•	•	•

Selected Average Balance Sheet ($ in Thousands)

Item													
Net Receivables 23	117	0	16	213	789	2969	6629	13653	24434	39659	106137	444288	•
Inventories 24	15	0	4	41	100	343	639	1752	2494	3612	9053	12213	•
Net Property, Plant and Equipment 25	83	0	34	225	444	1116	2539	6031	13346	27966	41429	145529	•
Total Assets 26	335	0	84	711	2041	6857	14741	34111	63628	131487	342601	990565	•
Notes and Loans Payable 27	111	0	47	269	579	1424	3165	7500	14280	41628	152758	231603	•
All Other Liabilities 28	118	0	19	186	690	3157	6667	14834	31446	45437	132852	561525	•
Net Worth 29	106	0	18	257	772	2276	4908	11776	17901	44422	56991	197438	•

Selected Financial Ratios (Times to 1)

Item													
Current Ratio 30	1.5	•	1.4	1.6	1.5	1.5	1.4	1.5	1.4	0.9	•	•	•
Quick Ratio 31	1.2	•	1.2	1.3	1.1	1.1	1.1	1.2	1.1	1.0	0.8	•	•
Net Sales to Working Capital 32	14.5	•	37.1	15.0	9.4	9.7	10.7	8.8	9.2	7.3	•	•	•
Coverage Ratio 33	4.6	5.3	6.0	4.2	5.2	6.1	5.5	4.2	1.7	2.4	•	•	•
Total Asset Turnover 34	3.1	•	5.6	3.5	2.2	2.3	2.1	1.9	1.5	1.1	0.7	•	•
Inventory Turnover 35	43.2	•	67.5	37.6	32.8	41.1	31.9	39.1	43.9	30.3	49.6	•	•
Receivables Turnover 36	•	•	•	•	•	•	•	•	•	•	•	•	•
Total Liabilities to Net Worth 37	2.2	•	3.6	1.8	2.0	2.0	1.9	2.6	2.0	5.0	4.0	•	•
Current Assets to Working Capital 38	3.0	•	3.2	2.6	3.2	3.2	3.5	2.9	3.1	3.8	•	•	•
Current Liabilities to Working Capital 39	2.0	•	2.2	1.6	2.2	2.2	2.5	1.9	2.1	2.8	•	•	•
Working Capital to Net Sales 40	0.1	•	0.0	0.1	0.1	0.1	0.1	0.1	0.1	0.1	•	•	•
Inventory to Working Capital 41	0.2	•	0.3	0.2	0.2	0.2	0.3	0.2	0.2	0.2	•	•	•
Total Receipts to Cash Flow 42	8.3	3.7	5.8	8.0	13.3	15.8	16.7	19.3	16.8	23.6	•	•	•
Cost of Goods to Cash Flow 43	5.3	1.5	5.0	7.2	10.0	12.4	13.3	15.2	13.1	17.8	•	•	•
Cash Flow to Total Debt 44	0.5	•	0.7	0.4	0.2	0.2	0.2	0.1	0.1	0.1	•	•	•

Selected Financial Factors (in Percentages)

Item													
Debt Ratio 45	68.4	•	78.4	63.9	62.2	66.8	66.7	65.5	71.9	66.2	83.4	80.1	•
Return on Total Assets 46	9.6	•	20.3	9.7	8.7	8.0	6.3	5.7	2.9	5.8	•	•	•
Return on Equity Before Income Taxes 47	23.7	•	78.0	20.6	18.6	20.3	15.6	12.6	4.4	9.9	•	•	•
Return on Equity After Income Taxes 48	22.0	•	76.1	19.4	17.2	17.7	13.8	10.8	2.6	8.7	•	•	•
Profit Margin (Before Income Tax) 49	2.4	3.0	3.0	2.1	2.7	3.1	2.3	2.1	0.6	2.2	•	•	•
Profit Margin (After Income Tax) 50	2.3	2.6	2.9	2.0	2.5	2.7	2.0	1.8	0.4	1.9	•	•	•

Table II

Corporations with Net Income

OTHER SPECIALTY TRADE CONTRACTORS

MONEY AMOUNTS AND SIZE OF ASSETS IN THOUSANDS OF DOLLARS

Item Description for Accounting Period 7/02 Through 6/03	Total	Zero Assets	Under 500	500 to 1,000	1,000 to 5,000	5,000 to 10,000	10,000 to 25,000	25,000 to 50,000	50,000 to 100,000	100,000 to 250,000	250,000 to 500,000	500,000 to 2,500,000	2,500,000 and over
Number of Enterprises **1**	175573	15145	139615	9662	9455	1037	506	100	36	14	3	·	·	·
Revenues ($ in Thousands)													
Net Sales **2**	208946288	2446513	71647316	25937306	55856705	17127661	18085114	7730378	4562325	3680277	1872693	·	·
Interest **3**	142203	1913	15183	16668	68598	10346	10418	8064	5494	4250	1269	·	·
Rents **4**	104534	0	27175	5768	26889	2670	8195	21412	680	10347	1397	·	·
Royalties **5**	43627	0	38001	0	9	252	0	1990	243	3131	0	·	·
Other Portfolio Income **6**	413327	5543	132924	40541	153237	22614	30423	15855	8759	2444	990	·	·
Other Receipts **7**	801971	32383	223172	82668	137528	131352	115022	42230	19245	12573	5797	·	·
Total Receipts **8**	210451950	2486352	72083771	26082951	56242966	17294895	18249172	7819929	4596746	3713022	1882146	·	·
Average Total Receipts **9**	1199	164	516	2700	5948	16678	36066	78199	127687	265216	627382	·	·
Operating Costs/Operating Income (%)													
Cost of Operations **10**	63.5	42.2	52.0	61.9	67.4	73.5	78.0	79.3	78.5	77.8	82.0	·	·
Salaries and Wages **11**	7.4	11.8	9.9	7.7	6.3	4.7	4.3	4.5	5.3	5.9	4.2	·	·
Taxes Paid **12**	2.4	1.9	2.7	2.5	2.5	2.0	1.9	1.5	1.4	1.0	1.0	·	·
Interest Paid **13**	0.5	0.4	0.5	0.5	0.5	0.4	0.4	0.4	0.4	0.6	1.6	·	·
Depreciation **14**	2.3	2.1	2.4	2.5	2.4	2.3	1.8	2.1	1.5	2.5	1.9	·	·
Amortization and Depletion **15**	0.1	0.1	0.0	0.0	0.1	0.0	0.0	0.0	0.1	0.5	0.3	·	·
Pensions and Other Deferred Comp. **16**	0.4	0.2	0.3	0.4	0.5	0.6	0.6	0.3	0.4	0.2	0.2	·	·
Employee Benefits **17**	1.3	0.4	1.1	1.1	1.7	1.7	1.5	1.3	1.5	1.0	0.7	·	·
Advertising **18**	0.5	0.6	0.6	0.9	0.4	0.2	0.3	0.2	0.1	0.1	0.1	·	·
Other Expenses **19**	12.1	22.2	17.2	13.3	10.0	7.2	5.7	5.8	5.5	5.9	5.6	·	·
Officers' Compensation **20**	4.8	6.9	6.9	5.0	4.2	3.2	2.2	1.5	1.7	0.8	0.8	·	·
Operating Margin **21**	4.9	11.1	6.5	4.1	4.3	4.1	3.3	3.0	3.5	3.6	1.6	·	·
Operating Margin Before Officers' Comp. **22**	9.7	18.0	13.4	9.1	8.5	7.3	5.5	4.5	5.2	4.4	2.4	·	·

Selected Average Balance Sheet ($ in Thousands)

Net Receivables 23	126	0	15	200	841	3088	6983	14327	25004	46621	111676	•
Inventories 24	17	0	4	46	109	300	586	1647	3109	4986	16534	•
Net Property, Plant and Equipment 25	80	0	33	206	397	1056	2292	6259	8518	28615	67132	•
Total Assets 26	348	0	84	701	2077	6807	14688	33853	60489	138912	332083	•
Notes and Loans Payable 27	93	0	36	240	487	1249	2609	6164	8703	31122	126555	•
All Other Liabilities 28	114	0	16	159	661	3001	6475	14622	26248	53961	133229	•
Net Worth 29	141	0	32	302	929	2557	5604	13068	25537	53829	72299	•

Selected Financial Ratios (Times to 1)

Current Ratio 30	1.7	•	1.8	1.9	1.6	1.5	1.5	1.5	1.7	1.4	1.3	•
Quick Ratio 31	1.4	•	1.5	1.6	1.2	1.2	1.2	1.2	1.3	1.0	1.0	•
Net Sales to Working Capital 32	12.4	33.4	28.9	13.2	8.8	9.0	9.9	6.8	11.2		16.3	•
Coverage Ratio 33	12.5	15.7	10.1	10.8	12.7	11.4	10.4	10.8	8.7		2.3	•
Total Asset Turnover 34	3.4	•	6.1	3.8	2.8	2.4	2.4	2.3	2.1	1.9	1.9	•
Inventory Turnover 35	43.5	•	64.5	36.3	36.7	40.5	47.5	37.2	32.0	41.0	30.9	•
Receivables Turnover 36	•	•	•	•	•	•	•	•	•	•	•	•
Total Liabilities to Net Worth 37	1.5	•	1.6	1.3	1.2	1.7	1.6	1.6	1.4	1.6	3.6	•
Current Assets to Working Capital 38	2.4	•	2.3	2.1	2.2	2.8	2.9	3.1	2.4	3.4	4.7	•
Current Liabilities to Working Capital 39	1.4	•	1.3	1.1	1.2	1.8	1.9	2.1	1.4	2.4	3.7	•
Working Capital to Net Sales 40	0.1	•	0.0	0.1	0.1	0.1	0.1	0.1	0.1	0.1	0.1	•
Inventory to Working Capital 41	0.2	•	0.2	0.2	0.2	0.2	0.2	0.2	0.2	0.2	0.4	•
Total Receipts to Cash Flow 42	6.9	3.2	4.8	6.6	8.6	10.5	13.0	13.5	13.3	11.8	18.0	•
Cost of Goods to Cash Flow 43	4.4	1.3	2.5	4.1	5.8	7.7	10.1	10.7	10.5	9.2	14.8	•
Cash Flow to Total Debt 44	0.8	•	2.0	1.0	0.6	0.4	0.3	0.3	0.3	0.3	0.1	•

Selected Financial Factors (in Percentages)

Debt Ratio 45	59.4	•	62.2	56.9	55.3	62.4	61.8	61.4	57.8	61.2	78.2	•
Return on Total Assets 46	20.9	•	46.4	19.6	15.6	13.3	11.2	10.6	9.8	9.7	6.9	•
Return on Equity Before Income Taxes 47	47.3	•	115.0	41.0	31.7	32.7	26.7	24.8	21.2	22.1	17.9	•
Return on Equity After Income Taxes 48	45.3	•	113.2	39.5	30.0	29.6	24.5	22.5	19.3	20.3	13.2	•
Profit Margin (Before Income Tax) 49	5.6	12.7	7.1	4.6	5.0	5.1	4.2	4.2	4.3	4.5	2.1	•
Profit Margin (After Income Tax) 50	5.4	12.1	7.0	4.4	4.7	4.6	3.8	3.8	3.9	4.1	1.5	•

36

Table I

Corporations with and without Net Income

ANIMAL FOOD AND GRAIN AND OILSEED MILLING

MONEY AMOUNTS AND SIZE OF ASSETS IN THOUSANDS OF DOLLARS

Item Description for Accounting Period 7/02 Through 6/03	Total	Zero Assets	Under 500	500 to 1,000	1,000 to 5,000	5,000 to 10,000	10,000 to 25,000	25,000 to 50,000	50,000 to 100,000	100,000 to 250,000	250,000 to 500,000	500,000 to 2,500,000	2,500,000 and over
Number of Enterprises **1**	1652	52	271	452	611	114	85	20	20	14	5	4	4
Revenues ($ in Thousands)													
Net Sales **2**	64561703	312841	38232	1120469	3112192	1697695	2981562	1561871	2556385	3028466	1529402	3243866	43378721
Interest **3**	352789	3179	136	3252	1876	521	5392	1615	4644	3498	9398	19297	299980
Rents **4**	178622	162	0	337	341	5	2619	916	544	223	256	998	172220
Royalties **5**	637650	40	0	0	0	0	279	0	12	29	1666	28191	607433
Other Portfolio Income **6**	715334	253	25566	0	12148	4036	2505	1847	1391	2605	2791	54295	607900
Other Receipts **7**	2042612	1820	3888	3833	17598	13182	30402	37227	26603	52104	15026	42784	1798145
Total Receipts **8**	68488710	318295	67822	1127891	3144155	1715439	3022759	1603476	2589579	3086925	1558539	3389431	46864399
Average Total Receipts **9**	41458	6121	250	2495	5146	15048	35562	80174	129479	220495	311708	847358	11716100
Operating Costs/Operating Income (%)													
Cost of Operations **10**	73.4	74.3	85.8	77.8	81.1	71.4	76.2	77.1	77.9	72.8	58.9	83.2	72.1
Salaries and Wages **11**	4.6	4.4	5.5	6.2	4.0	6.8	5.2	4.6	4.7	5.3	5.8	2.2	4.5
Taxes Paid **12**	1.0	0.8	8.3	1.6	1.2	1.6	1.1	1.0	1.1	1.2	1.7	1.1	0.9
Interest Paid **13**	3.2	1.0	3.4	0.3	0.9	1.0	0.9	0.7	0.9	1.4	3.6	7.4	3.8
Depreciation **14**	2.6	2.6	11.2	1.0	3.3	3.3	2.7	2.7	2.5	2.8	4.0	4.4	2.4
Amortization and Depletion **15**	0.3	0.5	22.0	0.1	0.0	0.0	0.1	0.1	0.2	1.0	1.5	0.6	0.2
Pensions and Other Deferred Comp. **16**	0.8	0.3	0.1	0.5	0.4	0.1	0.2	0.4	0.2	0.4	2.4	0.3	1.0
Employee Benefits **17**	1.0	1.5	•	0.2	0.7	0.4	0.7	0.8	0.6	1.5	1.1	1.6	1.0
Advertising **18**	7.0	7.6	0.1	0.2	0.3	1.2	0.6	0.9	2.0	2.1	4.1	0.2	9.8
Other Expenses **19**	9.1	7.8	183.6	9.8	6.0	10.3	9.0	9.2	7.5	7.6	10.9	4.5	9.6
Officers' Compensation **20**	0.6	0.7	1.5	5.5	2.2	1.3	1.1	1.2	0.6	0.8	0.7	0.6	0.2
Operating Margin **21**	•	•	•	•	•	2.7	2.0	1.2	1.8	3.0	5.2	•	•
Operating Margin Before Officers' Comp. **22**	•	•	•	2.3	2.0	4.0	3.2	2.4	2.4	3.9	6.0	•	•

Selected Average Balance Sheet ($ in Thousands)

Net Receivables 23	2463	0	9	111	503	1180	3145	7585	20056	19097	34460	72902	505802
Inventories 24	3506	0	0	128	453	1066	2633	8319	9437	15392	33994	118552	974659
Net Property, Plant and Equipment 25	7643	0	107	129	653	2999	6281	11629	18393	49309	110435	308999	2046466
Total Assets 26	37888		272	678	2189	6771	15987	33012	68652	146771	300155	989576	12299024
Notes and Loans Payable 27	17541	0	0	272	922	2180	5265	8931	19139	50989	103210	423514	6027544
All Other Liabilities 28	9740		15	162	719	968	4423	9521	14143	28820	53063	222975	3263190
Net Worth 29	10608	0	257	244	547	3623	6299	14560	35370	66962	143882	343088	3008290

Selected Financial Ratios (Times to 1)

Current Ratio 30	1.0	•	18.0	2.7	1.4	1.6	1.6	1.8	1.9	1.7	2.1	0.8	0.8
Quick Ratio 31	0.4	•	10.8	2.0	0.9	1.1	0.9	1.0	1.3	1.0	1.1	0.4	0.3
Net Sales to Working Capital 32	•	•	4.2	7.3	14.3	12.0	11.7	9.6	7.1	10.9	6.2	•	•
Coverage Ratio 33	2.2	1.2	•	•	2.0	4.9	4.7	6.7	4.2	4.4	3.0	0.8	2.2
Total Asset Turnover 34	1.0	•	0.5	3.7	2.3	2.2	2.2	2.4	1.9	1.5	1.0	0.8	0.9
Inventory Turnover 35	8.2	•	•	15.1	9.1	10.0	10.2	7.2	10.6	10.2	5.3	5.7	8.0
Receivables Turnover 36	13.8	•	33.1	44.7	11.2	12.8	11.8	8.7	7.5	13.0	12.0	4.7	18.3
Total Liabilities to Net Worth 37	2.6	0.1	1.8	3.0	3.0	0.9	1.5	1.3	0.9	1.2	1.1	1.9	3.1
Current Assets to Working Capital 38	•	•	1.1	1.6	3.3	2.6	2.7	2.2	2.1	2.3	1.9	•	•
Current Liabilities to Working Capital 39	•	•	0.1	0.6	2.3	1.6	1.7	1.2	1.1	1.3	0.9	•	•
Working Capital to Net Sales 40	•	•	0.2	0.1	0.1	0.1	0.1	0.1	0.1	0.1	0.2	•	•
Inventory to Working Capital 41	•	•	•	0.4	1.2	0.7	1.0	0.8	0.5	0.9	0.7	•	•
Total Receipts to Cash Flow 42	10.7	•	15.1	17.3	20.9	8.7	9.9	9.3	11.2	8.7	6.0	88.2	10.1
Cost of Goods to Cash Flow 43	7.9	•	11.2	13.5	17.0	6.2	7.5	7.2	8.7	6.4	3.6	73.4	7.3
Cash Flow to Total Debt 44	0.1	•	•	0.3	0.1	0.5	0.4	0.5	0.3	0.3	0.3	0.0	0.1

Selected Financial Factors (in Percentages)

Debt Ratio 45	72.0	•	5.5	64.1	75.0	46.5	60.6	55.9	48.5	54.4	52.1	65.3	75.5
Return on Total Assets 46	7.2	•	•	4.1	10.4	9.4	10.8	10.8	7.4	9.3	11.1	5.1	7.3
Return on Equity Before Income Taxes 47	13.8	•	•	8.0	15.5	18.8	20.9	16.9	11.0	15.7	15.4	•	16.2
Return on Equity After Income Taxes 48	9.5	•	•	7.6	12.8	17.0	16.9	16.9	9.5	12.4	11.4	•	11.1
Profit Margin (Before Income Tax) 49	3.7	0.2	•	0.9	3.8	3.4	3.9	3.9	3.0	4.9	7.3	•	4.5
Profit Margin (After Income Tax) 50	2.6	•	0.8	3.1	3.1	3.0	3.1	3.1	2.6	3.8	5.4	•	3.1

Table II
Corporations with Net Income

ANIMAL FOOD AND GRAIN AND OILSEED MILLING

MONEY AMOUNTS AND SIZE OF ASSETS IN THOUSANDS OF DOLLARS

Item Description for Accounting Period 7/02 Through 6/03	Total	Zero Assets	Under 500	500 to 1,000	1,000 to 5,000	5,000 to 10,000	10,000 to 25,000	25,000 to 50,000	50,000 to 100,000	100,000 to 250,000	250,000 to 500,000	500,000 to 2,500,000	2,500,000 and over
Number of Enterprises **1**	1041	4	190	315	339	85	58	15	13	14	5	0	4
Revenues ($ in Thousands)													
Net Sales **2**	57955357	116217	0	973253	2205829	1083728	2184059	1239354	1879269	3028466	1866459	0	43378721
Interest **3**	340701	3179	136	3249	1316	421	3114	1525	2820	3498	21463	0	299980
Rents **4**	175036	0	0	0	40	5	763	901	342	223	542	0	172220
Royalties **5**	636594	40	0	0	0	0	199	0	12	29	28881	0	607433
Other Portfolio Income **6**	687766	234	847	0	11226	4031	1672	1706	972	2605	56573	0	607900
Other Receipts **7**	1979819	925	3887	1121	10847	11333	24131	36776	17917	52104	22636	0	1798145
Total Receipts **8**	61775273	120595	4870	977623	2229258	1099518	2213938	1280262	1901332	3086925	1996554	0	46684399
Average Total Receipts **9**	59342	30149	26	3104	6576	12936	38171	85351	146256	220495	399311	•	11716100
Operating Costs/Operating Income (%)													
Cost of Operations **10**	72.7	81.5	•	79.4	81.7	67.1	75.5	76.2	77.0	72.8	66.7	•	72.1
Salaries and Wages **11**	4.5	1.6	•	4.0	2.4	5.6	4.6	5.1	4.5	5.3	3.2	•	4.5
Taxes Paid **12**	1.0	0.5	•	1.3	1.1	1.6	1.1	1.1	1.1	1.2	1.7	•	0.9
Interest Paid **13**	3.1	2.0	•	0.1	0.5	0.6	0.7	0.6	0.8	1.4	3.2	•	3.8
Depreciation **14**	2.5	4.4	•	0.9	3.1	3.1	2.5	2.6	1.9	2.8	4.9	•	2.4
Amortization and Depletion **15**	0.2	0.4	•	•	0.0	0.0	0.1	0.1	0.2	1.0	0.6	•	0.2
Pensions and Other Deferred Comp. **16**	0.9	0.1	•	0.6	0.6	0.2	0.3	0.4	0.2	0.4	2.0	•	1.0
Employee Benefits **17**	1.0	0.6	•	0.0	0.8	0.4	0.8	0.8	0.7	1.5	1.5	•	1.0
Advertising **18**	7.7	0.4	•	0.0	0.2	1.2	0.6	1.0	2.6	2.1	3.1	•	9.8
Other Expenses **19**	9.0	6.7	•	6.3	3.6	13.6	6.6	8.9	6.2	7.6	8.3	•	9.6
Officers' Compensation **20**	0.5	0.4	•	5.2	2.2	1.7	1.2	1.2	0.7	0.8	0.7	•	0.2
Operating Margin **21**	•	1.3	•	2.0	3.9	4.9	6.1	2.0	4.2	3.0	4.1	•	•
Operating Margin Before Officers' Comp. **22**	•	1.7	•	7.3	6.1	6.6	7.3	3.2	4.9	3.9	4.8	•	•

Selected Average Balance Sheet ($ in Thousands)

Net Receivables 23	3208	0	107	553	995	3291	7761	17872	19097	40342	•	505802
Inventories 24	4962	0	110	535	1134	2795	7995	10473	17136	36212	•	974659
Net Property, Plant and Equipment 25	10591	149	144	732	2485	6059	12084	16529	49309	173675	•	2046466
Total Assets 26	55539	352	729	2342	6438	15828	33575	72637	146771	512204	•	12299024
Notes and Loans Payable 27	25439	0	49	358	886	4345	8640	18331	50989	165244	•	6027544
All Other Liabilities 28	14181	19	134	718	889	3496	8355	13618	28820	87271	•	3263190
Net Worth 29	15918	332	547	1266	4663	7986	16581	40688	66962	259690	•	3008290

Selected Financial Ratios (Times to 1)

Current Ratio 30	1.0	•	32.8	3.8	2.0	1.8	1.9	2.0	1.7	1.5	•	0.8
Quick Ratio 31	0.4	•	15.5	3.0	1.3	1.0	1.0	1.3	1.0	0.7	•	0.3
Net Sales to Working Capital 32	•	•	•	9.5	5.4	10.3	9.9	7.1	10.9	9.6	•	•
Coverage Ratio 33	2.6	3.5	•	21.3	11.9	11.4	9.7	7.5	4.4	4.6	•	2.2
Total Asset Turnover 34	1.0	•	•	4.2	2.8	2.4	2.5	2.0	1.5	0.7	•	0.9
Inventory Turnover 35	8.2	•	•	22.4	9.9	10.2	7.9	10.6	9.2	6.9	•	8.0
Receivables Turnover 36	14.5	•	•	28.0	11.5	11.5	10.1	10.4	22.7	18.5	•	18.3
Total Liabilities to Net Worth 37	2.5	0.1	0.3	0.9	1.0	1.0	0.8	1.2	1.0	•	•	3.1
Current Assets to Working Capital 38	•	1.0	1.4	2.0	2.2	2.2	2.0	2.3	2.9	•	•	•
Current Liabilities to Working Capital 39	•	0.0	0.4	1.0	1.2	1.2	1.0	1.3	1.9	•	•	•
Working Capital to Net Sales 40	•	•	0.1	0.1	0.1	0.1	0.1	0.1	0.1	•	•	•
Inventory to Working Capital 41	•	•	0.2	0.7	0.8	0.8	0.6	0.9	0.9	•	•	•
Total Receipts to Cash Flow 42	9.6	8.7	13.8	14.0	6.2	8.0	7.9	9.7	8.7	5.6	•	10.1
Cost of Goods to Cash Flow 43	7.0	7.1	11.0	11.5	4.2	6.0	6.0	7.4	6.4	3.7	•	7.3
Cash Flow to Total Debt 44	0.1	•	0.1	1.2	0.4	1.2	0.6	0.5	0.3	0.3	•	0.1

Selected Financial Factors (in Percentages)

Debt Ratio 45	71.3	•	5.5	25.0	46.0	27.6	49.5	50.6	44.0	54.4	49.3	75.5
Return on Total Assets 46	8.0	•	1.3	11.0	15.0	13.8	19.3	14.6	12.3	9.3	10.9	7.3
Return on Equity Before Income Taxes 47	17.2	•	1.4	14.0	25.4	17.5	34.9	26.5	19.0	15.7	16.9	16.2
Return on Equity After Income Taxes 48	12.7	•	1.2	12.2	25.1	14.8	32.8	21.8	17.0	12.4	12.4	11.1
Profit Margin (Before Income Tax) 49	4.9	5.0	•	2.5	4.9	6.4	7.4	5.3	5.3	4.9	11.8	4.5
Profit Margin (After Income Tax) 50	3.6	4.2	•	2.2	4.9	5.4	7.0	4.4	4.8	3.8	8.6	3.1

Table I

Corporations with and without Net Income

SUGAR AND CONFECTIONERY PRODUCT

MONEY AMOUNTS AND SIZE OF ASSETS IN THOUSANDS OF DOLLARS

Item Description for Accounting Period 7/02 Through 6/03	Total	Zero Assets	Under 500	500 to 1,000	1,000 to 5,000	5,000 to 10,000	10,000 to 25,000	25,000 to 50,000	50,000 to 100,000	100,000 to 250,000	250,000 to 500,000	500,000 to 2,500,000	2,500,000 and over
Number of Enterprises 1	1455	24	1035	92	197	35	29	14	12	5	3	7	3
Revenues ($ in Thousands)													
Net Sales 2	33751530	2964	1158945	120886	830062	517659	904862	604921	1403423	1392780	753258	3482731	22579040
Interest 3	501185	446	7	12	334	510	735	435	1056	491	7043	55532	434584
Rents 4	50600	0	0	0	2	330	332	2192	1462	10	0	37291	8981
Royalties 5	305983	0	0	0	0	0	132	486	6	1656	399	84514	218791
Other Portfolio Income 6	2130386	0	0	0	293	738	322	1135	581	19	680	282369	1844249
Other Receipts 7	274963	-1170	273	0	282	1590	2381	3263	3293	328	61	48894	215765
Total Receipts 8	37014647	2240	1159225	120898	830973	520827	908764	612432	1409821	1395284	761441	3991331	25301410
Average Total Receipts 9	25440	93	1120	1314	4218	14881	31337	43745	117485	279057	253814	570190	8433803
Operating Costs/Operating Income (%)													
Cost of Operations 10	51.3	80.0	61.5	81.8	63.8	69.8	73.7	75.5	67.5	82.9	50.8	56.9	44.4
Salaries and Wages 11	7.6	6.8	9.6	2.9	6.6	7.3	5.0	5.8	5.4	4.0	11.1	5.3	8.3
Taxes Paid 12	1.4	2.8	4.0	0.3	2.4	2.3	1.5	1.6	1.6	0.6	2.3	1.8	1.1
Interest Paid 13	2.9	0.1	0.3	0.5	1.5	1.7	1.0	0.9	0.7	1.1	2.9	2.7	3.6
Depreciation 14	3.0	3.7	0.6	2.2	5.7	1.3	2.8	3.4	3.2	3.0	6.2	4.1	2.7
Amortization and Depletion 15	0.8	4.5	0.0	0.0	0.2	0.2	0.5	0.3	0.0	0.1	0.6	2.2	0.8
Pensions and Other Deferred Comp. 16	2.1	•	1.5	9.0	0.5	1.1	0.3	0.3	0.9	0.3	1.3	2.0	2.5
Employee Benefits 17	2.2	•	•		1.1	2.3	0.8	1.0	2.4	0.9	2.1	2.7	2.5
Advertising 18	4.9	•	1.0	0.2	0.8	3.3	0.8	1.5	3.0	1.5	6.4	5.1	5.8
Other Expenses 19	23.2	34.1	13.0	8.3	13.9	6.5	9.3	7.3	9.3	5.3	17.9	15.8	28.8
Officers' Compensation 20	0.8	5.1	5.4	7.8	3.6	4.3	2.2	0.9	1.5	0.6	0.8	0.8	0.3
Operating Margin 21	•	•	2.9	•	•	•	2.2	1.5	4.3	•	•	0.5	•
Operating Margin Before Officers' Comp. 22	0.5	•	8.4	•	3.5	4.1	4.4	2.4	5.8	0.3	•	1.3	•

Selected Average Balance Sheet ($ in Thousands)

	1	2	3	4	5	6	7	8	9	10	11	12	13
Net Receivables 23	2473	0	42	553	250	1283	2905	4638	11010	25496	44835	49231	840698
Inventories 24	2244	0	17	176	508	1201	4335	9122	17841	42715	35199	71839	600011
Net Property, Plant and Equipment 25	5367	0	55	46	556	4418	5684	11566	23638	78644	99219	228060	1528767
Total Assets 26	29237	0	189	803	1923	8152	16881	32180	69799	172561	347867	1019351	10261935
Notes and Loans Payable 27	11782	0	32	306	921	5039	5696	11236	13048	84595	151713	149875	4772137
All Other Liabilities 28	8613	0	52	132	400	1386	3253	6462	13177	54559	74429	129108	3532082
Net Worth 29	8842	0	105	365	602	1727	7932	14483	43575	33407	121725	740368	1957716

Selected Financial Ratios (Times to 1)

	1	2	3	4	5	6	7	8	9	10	11	12	13
Current Ratio 30	0.6	•	2.6	4.1	1.5	1.8	1.6	1.8	2.3	1.7	2.2	1.8	0.4
Quick Ratio 31	0.3	•	2.2	3.2	0.6	1.2	0.7	0.7	1.1	0.6	1.1	0.6	0.3
Net Sales to Working Capital 32	•	•	13.7	2.4	10.5	10.5	10.0	5.5	5.2	8.4	4.1	5.2	•
Coverage Ratio 33	4.5	•	9.8	•	1.0	1.2	3.6	3.9	7.3	0.9	0.5	7.9	4.3
Total Asset Turnover 34	0.8	•	5.9	1.6	2.2	1.8	1.8	1.3	1.7	1.6	0.7	0.5	0.7
Inventory Turnover 35	5.3	•	41.7	6.1	5.3	8.6	5.3	3.6	4.4	5.4	3.6	3.9	5.6
Receivables Turnover 36	6.4	•	27.9	2.2	19.9	9.5	10.3	9.6	10.2	12.1	5.2	10.9	5.4
Total Liabilities to Net Worth 37	2.3	•	0.8	1.2	2.2	3.7	1.1	1.2	0.6	4.2	1.9	0.4	4.2
Current Assets to Working Capital 38	•	•	1.6	1.3	2.9	2.2	2.8	2.3	1.8	2.5	1.9	2.3	•
Current Liabilities to Working Capital 39	•	•	0.6	0.3	1.9	1.2	1.8	1.3	0.8	1.5	0.9	1.3	•
Working Capital to Net Sales 40	•	•	0.1	0.4	0.1	0.1	0.1	0.2	0.2	0.1	0.2	0.2	•
Inventory to Working Capital 41	•	•	0.2	0.3	1.5	0.8	1.3	1.3	0.8	1.4	0.6	0.8	•
Total Receipts to Cash Flow 42	3.9	•	9.7	•	8.8	16.6	9.6	12.5	7.8	24.5	6.7	3.4	3.3
Cost of Goods to Cash Flow 43	2.0	•	6.0	•	5.6	11.6	7.1	9.4	5.2	20.3	3.4	1.9	1.5
Cash Flow to Total Debt 44	0.3	•	1.4	•	0.4	0.1	0.4	0.2	0.6	0.1	0.2	0.5	0.3

Selected Financial Factors (in Percentages)

	1	2	3	4	5	6	7	8	9	10	11	12	13
Debt Ratio 45	69.8	•	44.8	54.6	68.7	78.8	53.0	55.0	37.6	80.6	65.0	27.4	80.9
Return on Total Assets 46	10.5	•	19.5	•	3.2	3.8	6.6	4.9	9.2	1.6	1.0	10.5	11.4
Return on Equity Before Income Taxes 47	27.0	•	31.7	•	•	3.5	10.2	8.2	12.7	•	•	12.6	46.0
Return on Equity After Income Taxes 48	17.7	•	31.7	•	•	0.4	9.8	8.1	10.1	•	•	8.2	30.0
Profit Margin (Before Income Tax) 49	10.3	•	3.0	•	•	0.4	2.6	2.7	4.7	•	•	18.7	12.0
Profit Margin (After Income Tax) 50	6.7	•	3.0	•	0.0	0.0	2.5	2.7	3.8	•	•	12.1	7.8

Table II

Corporations with Net Income

SUGAR AND CONFECTIONERY PRODUCT

MONEY AMOUNTS AND SIZE OF ASSETS IN THOUSANDS OF DOLLARS

Item Description for Accounting Period 7/02 Through 6/03	Total	Zero Assets	Under 500	500 to 1,000	1,000 to 5,000	5,000 to 10,000	10,000 to 25,000	25,000 to 50,000	50,000 to 100,000	100,000 to 250,000	250,000 to 500,000	500,000 to 2,500,000	2,500,000 and over
Number of Enterprises **1**	800	16	561	0	76	15	19	9	12	0	0	0	0
Revenues ($ in Thousands)													
Net Sales **2**	31095635	2964	1151189	0	512228	283470	688126	398217	1403423	0	0	0	0
Interest **3**	485604	419	7	0	190	509	419	281	1056	0	0	0	0
Rents **4**	50065	0	0	0	0	330	256	1744	1462	0	0	0	0
Royalties **5**	303991	0	0	0	0	0	128	486	6	0	0	0	0
Other Portfolio Income **6**	2128761	0	0	0	293	736	237	296	581	0	0	0	0
Other Receipts **7**	269739	0	256	0	234	254	950	636	3293	0	0	0	0
Total Receipts **8**	34333795	3383	1151452	0	512945	285299	690116	401660	1409821	0	0	0	0
Average Total Receipts **9**	42917	211	2052	•	6749	19020	36322	44629	117485	•	•	•	•
Operating Costs/Operating Income (%)													
Cost of Operations **10**	50.2	80.0	61.8	•	65.4	73.5	75.2	70.6	67.5	•	•	•	•
Salaries and Wages **11**	7.6	2.3	9.7	•	7.1	4.8	4.4	6.5	5.4	•	•	•	•
Taxes Paid **12**	1.4	1.1	4.1	•	2.1	2.1	1.4	1.7	1.6	•	•	•	•
Interest Paid **13**	2.9	0.1	0.2	•	0.9	2.1	0.9	0.8	0.7	•	•	•	•
Depreciation **14**	2.8	2.4	0.6	•	2.8	1.1	2.5	3.9	3.2	•	•	•	•
Amortization and Depletion **15**	0.6	4.5	•	•	•	0.0	0.1	0.3	0.0	•	•	•	•
Pensions and Other Deferred Comp. **16**	2.2	•	1.5	•	0.4	1.0	0.3	0.4	0.9	•	•	•	•
Employee Benefits **17**	2.3	•	•	•	0.5	0.6	0.7	1.3	2.4	•	•	•	•
Advertising **18**	5.1	•	1.0	•	1.1	3.2	0.6	1.7	3.0	•	•	•	•
Other Expenses **19**	24.2	10.1	12.8	•	14.4	5.5	8.3	7.7	9.3	•	•	•	•
Officers' Compensation **20**	0.7	5.1	5.5	•	2.0	3.8	1.7	1.1	1.5	•	•	•	•
Operating Margin **21**	0.1	•	3.0	•	3.4	2.2	3.8	4.1	4.3	•	•	•	•
Operating Margin Before Officers' Comp. **22**	0.8	•	8.4	•	5.4	6.0	5.5	5.2	5.8	•	•	•	•

Selected Average Balance Sheet ($ in Thousands)

Net Receivables 23	4103	0	78	•	449	1810	2921	4237	11010
Inventories 24	3590	0	30	•	683	1510	5117	9991	19565
Net Property, Plant and Equipment 25	8784	0	101	•	1065	2999	6114	13310	23638
Total Assets 26	50173	0	347	•	2928	8438	16984	33582	69799
Notes and Loans Payable 27	19855	0	49	•	1073	4187	5034	11090	13048
All Other Liabilities 28	15015	0	92	•	485	2093	3573	6032	13177
Net Worth 29	15303	0	206	•	1370	2159	8377	16459	43575

Selected Financial Ratios (Times to 1)

Current Ratio 30	0.6	•	2.7	•	1.6	2.8	1.8	1.8	2.3
Quick Ratio 31	0.3	•	2.3	•	0.8	2.0	0.9	0.8	1.1
Net Sales to Working Capital 32	•	•	13.4	•	11.4	6.3	9.1	5.2	5.2
Coverage Ratio 33	4.9	84.3	16.5	•	5.0	2.4	5.4	7.2	7.3
Total Asset Turnover 34	0.8	•	5.9	•	2.3	2.2	2.1	1.3	1.7
Inventory Turnover 35	5.4	•	41.6	•	6.4	9.2	5.3	3.1	4.0
Receivables Turnover 36	6.3	•	52.5	•	18.1	7.9	10.6	9.8	8.3
Total Liabilities to Net Worth 37	2.3	•	0.7	•	1.1	2.9	1.0	1.0	0.6
Current Assets to Working Capital 38	•	•	1.6	•	2.5	1.6	2.3	2.2	1.8
Current Liabilities to Working Capital 39	•	•	0.6	•	1.5	0.6	1.3	1.2	0.8
Working Capital to Net Sales 40	•	•	0.1	•	0.1	0.2	0.1	0.2	0.2
Inventory to Working Capital 41	•	•	0.2	•	1.2	0.4	1.0	1.2	0.8
Total Receipts to Cash Flow 42	3.7	5.5	9.9	•	6.5	14.2	8.9	9.7	7.8
Cost of Goods to Cash Flow 43	1.8	4.4	6.1	•	4.3	10.5	6.7	6.9	5.2
Cash Flow to Total Debt 44	0.3	•	1.5	•	0.7	0.2	0.5	0.3	0.6

Selected Financial Factors (in Percentages)

Debt Ratio 45	69.5	•	40.5	•	53.2	74.4	50.7	51.0	37.6
Return on Total Assets 46	11.1	•	18.8	•	10.1	11.1	10.6	7.6	9.2
Return on Equity Before Income Taxes 47	29.1	•	29.8	•	17.3	25.2	17.6	13.4	12.7
Return on Equity After Income Taxes 48	19.3	•	29.8	•	12.5	19.5	17.0	13.3	10.1
Profit Margin (Before Income Tax) 49	11.4	8.4	3.0	•	3.5	2.9	4.1	5.0	4.7
Profit Margin (After Income Tax) 50	7.6	8.1	3.0	•	2.5	2.2	3.9	4.9	3.8

Table I

Corporations with and without Net Income

FRUIT AND VEGETABLE PRESERVING AND SPECIALTY FOOD

MONEY AMOUNTS AND SIZE OF ASSETS IN THOUSANDS OF DOLLARS

Item Description for Accounting Period 7/02 Through 6/03	Total	Zero Assets	Under 500	500 to 1,000	1,000 to 5,000	5,000 to 10,000	10,000 to 25,000	25,000 to 50,000	50,000 to 100,000	100,000 to 250,000	250,000 to 500,000	500,000 to 2,500,000	2,500,000 and over
Number of Enterprises **1**	479	0	0	33	208	77	68	37	22	14	4	8	0
Revenues ($ in Thousands)													
Net Sales **2**	35776037	0	0	64768	1418173	1327232	1814940	1967959	2607582	3300278	1863611	19745202	0
Interest **3**	545390	0	0	90	330	389	2020	1936	1295	7445	2628	526465	0
Rents **4**	45309	0	0	0	336	507	665	1358	211	10325	3619	28091	0
Royalties **5**	406980	0	0	0	0	296	0	1613	0	31820	4819	368307	0
Other Portfolio Income **6**	737937	0	0	7	196	3957	3771	801	2683	3634	146	717192	0
Other Receipts **7**	603513	0	0	22	3200	6250	9830	21401	20788	60647	29165	449710	0
Total Receipts **8**	38115166	0	0	64887	1422235	1338631	1831226	1995068	2632559	3414149	1903988	21834967	0
Average Total Receipts **9**	79572	•	•	1966	6838	17385	26930	53921	119662	243868	475997	2729371	•
Operating Costs/Operating Income (%)													
Cost of Operations **10**	67.7	•	•	61.3	77.2	60.2	77.3	74.6	70.7	70.4	76.1	63.5	•
Salaries and Wages **11**	5.8	•	•	0.6	3.3	10.1	4.2	3.9	4.6	6.1	3.3	6.4	•
Taxes Paid **12**	1.3	•	•	5.5	2.5	1.2	1.4	1.3	1.7	1.3	1.3	1.2	•
Interest Paid **13**	3.5	•	•	0.2	0.7	0.9	1.5	2.0	1.3	1.8	3.0	4.8	•
Depreciation **14**	3.0	•	•	1.1	1.1	2.6	2.9	3.7	3.1	3.6	4.7	2.9	•
Amortization and Depletion **15**	0.8	•	•	0.0	0.1	0.8	0.1	0.2	0.1	0.3	0.8	1.0	•
Pensions and Other Deferred Comp. **16**	0.5	•	•	1.7	0.5	0.0	0.3	0.2	0.4	0.3	0.3	0.7	•
Employee Benefits **17**	1.4	•	•	0.3	1.2	1.5	0.9	0.8	1.8	1.2	0.9	1.6	•
Advertising **18**	3.4	•	•	0.1	0.1	4.7	1.0	1.2	1.7	3.0	1.1	4.7	•
Other Expenses **19**	13.7	•	•	5.7	8.4	13.6	7.8	10.6	9.3	14.1	7.3	16.3	•
Officers' Compensation **20**	0.8	•	•	23.2	3.9	1.8	1.5	1.0	1.1	0.6	0.5	0.4	•
Operating Margin **21**	•	•	•	0.3	0.9	2.6	1.2	0.5	4.3	•	0.5	1.0	•
Operating Margin Before Officers' Comp. **22**	•	•	•	23.5	4.8	4.4	2.7	1.5	5.4	•	1.0	•	•

Selected Average Balance Sheet ($ in Thousands)

Net Receivables 23	17286	•	134	507	1219	2961	6251	10401	18588	31974	878300
Inventories 24	9304	•	18	985	2198	4727	10969	26151	55032	84574	173211
Net Property, Plant and Equipment 25	12202	•	373	554	1915	4861	12195	21304	58871	113587	380108
Total Assets 26	75386	•	957	2410	7657	16150	36593	69599	161311	403807	3391257
Notes and Loans Payable 27	31237	•	32	688	2139	6609	16897	22572	67276	154524	1439725
All Other Liabilities 28	14724	•	75	990	1631	3821	8261	16038	44695	97401	598128
Net Worth 29	29425	•	850	733	3887	5720	11435	30989	49340	151882	1353404

Selected Financial Ratios (Times to 1)

Current Ratio 30	1.2	•	5.9	1.4	1.5	1.5	1.5	1.6	1.6	2.4	1.1
Quick Ratio 31	0.8	•	5.6	0.5	0.8	0.6	0.6	0.5	0.5	1.2	0.8
Net Sales to Working Capital 32	12.9	•	4.1	14.2	14.8	9.0	8.6	7.6	7.0	4.8	21.2
Coverage Ratio 33	2.8	•	3.1	2.5	4.9	2.4	2.0	5.2	1.4	1.9	3.0
Total Asset Turnover 34	1.0	•	2.1	2.8	2.3	1.7	1.5	1.7	1.5	1.2	0.7
Inventory Turnover 35	5.4	•	66.0	5.3	4.7	4.4	3.6	3.2	3.0	4.2	9.0
Receivables Turnover 36	4.2	•	29.3	12.3	13.4	9.4	9.0	10.5	11.1	14.9	5.3
Total Liabilities to Net Worth 37	1.6	•	0.1	2.3	1.0	1.8	2.2	1.2	2.3	1.7	1.5
Current Assets to Working Capital 38	5.4	•	1.2	3.4	3.1	3.2	3.1	2.6	2.7	1.7	10.8
Current Liabilities to Working Capital 39	4.4	•	0.2	2.4	2.1	2.2	2.1	1.6	1.7	0.7	9.8
Working Capital to Net Sales 40	0.1	•	0.2	0.1	0.1	0.1	0.1	0.1	0.1	0.2	0.0
Inventory to Working Capital 41	1.7	•	0.0	2.2	1.4	1.7	1.8	1.7	1.6	0.8	2.0
Total Receipts to Cash Flow 42	6.2	•	17.5	15.2	6.6	12.1	9.6	7.7	7.7	13.3	4.9
Cost of Goods to Cash Flow 43	4.2	•	10.7	11.7	4.0	9.4	7.2	5.4	5.4	10.1	3.1
Cash Flow to Total Debt 44	0.3	•	1.0	0.3	0.7	0.2	0.2	0.4	0.3	0.1	0.2

Selected Financial Factors (in Percentages)

Debt Ratio 45	61.0	•	11.2	69.6	49.2	64.6	68.8	55.5	69.4	62.4	60.1
Return on Total Assets 46	9.6	•	1.4	5.3	9.8	5.9	5.7	11.2	3.5	6.5	10.5
Return on Equity Before Income Taxes 47	15.8	•	1.1	10.7	15.3	9.7	8.9	20.3	3.1	8.2	17.6
Return on Equity After Income Taxes 48	10.2	•	•	7.2	15.0	8.4	6.4	17.5	•	6.0	11.0
Profit Margin (Before Income Tax) 49	6.2	•	0.5	1.1	3.5	2.1	1.9	5.3	0.6	2.7	9.6
Profit Margin (After Income Tax) 50	4.0	•	•	0.8	3.4	1.8	1.4	4.6	•	2.0	6.1

41

Table II

Corporations with Net Income

FRUIT AND VEGETABLE PRESERVING AND SPECIALTY FOOD

MONEY AMOUNTS AND SIZE OF ASSETS IN THOUSANDS OF DOLLARS

Item Description for Accounting Period 7/02 Through 6/03	Total	Zero Assets	Under 500	500 to 1,000	1,000 to 5,000	5,000 to 10,000	10,000 to 25,000	25,000 to 50,000	50,000 to 100,000	100,000 to 250,000	250,000 to 500,000	500,000 to 2,500,000	2,500,000 and over
Number of Enterprises **1**	380	0	0	0	183	55	47	22	22	7	4	0	0
Revenues ($ in Thousands)													
Net Sales **2**	27489207	0	0	0	1215401	1000279	1399570	1193900	2607582	1850906	1863611	0	0
Interest **3**	518346	0	0	0	277	278	1517	539	1295	3982	2628	0	0
Rents **4**	28446	0	0	0	154	12	476	387	211	1020	3619	0	0
Royalties **5**	359978	0	0	0	0	296	0	1613	0	31820	4819	0	0
Other Portfolio Income **6**	722233	0	0	0	196	3951	3442	316	2683	1552	146	0	0
Other Receipts **7**	506085	0	0	0	918	4538	5675	11851	20788	11263	29165	0	0
Total Receipts **8**	29624295	0	0	0	1216946	1009354	1410680	1208606	2632559	1900543	1903988	0	0
Average Total Receipts **9**	77959	•	•	•	6650	18352	30014	54937	119662	271506	475997	•	•
Operating Costs/Operating Income (%)													
Cost of Operations **10**	64.7	•	•	•	76.9	61.0	75.5	74.8	70.7	64.6	76.1	•	•
Salaries and Wages **11**	6.1	•	•	•	3.5	10.9	3.9	3.6	4.6	5.7	3.3	•	•
Taxes Paid **12**	1.3	•	•	•	2.4	1.5	1.3	1.2	1.7	1.7	1.3	•	•
Interest Paid **13**	3.6	•	•	•	0.7	0.6	1.1	1.6	1.3	1.2	3.0	•	•
Depreciation **14**	2.7	•	•	•	1.0	3.0	2.5	3.3	3.1	2.9	4.7	•	•
Amortization and Depletion **15**	0.7	•	•	•	0.1	0.0	0.1	0.1	0.1	0.1	0.8	•	•
Pensions and Other Deferred Comp. **16**	0.5	•	•	•	0.2	0.0	0.3	0.2	0.4	0.3	0.3	•	•
Employee Benefits **17**	1.4	•	•	•	0.5	1.9	0.8	0.7	1.8	1.2	0.9	•	•
Advertising **18**	4.0	•	•	•	0.2	5.1	1.1	1.0	1.7	4.3	1.1	•	•
Other Expenses **19**	14.5	•	•	•	9.7	9.1	8.0	8.2	9.3	14.6	7.3	•	•
Officers' Compensation **20**	0.8	•	•	•	3.0	1.8	1.6	0.9	1.1	0.6	0.5	•	•
Operating Margin **21**	•	•	•	•	1.9	5.2	3.8	4.6	4.3	2.7	0.5	•	•
Operating Margin Before Officers' Comp. **22**	0.5	•	•	•	4.8	7.0	5.4	5.4	5.4	3.3	1.0	•	•

Selected Average Balance Sheet ($ in Thousands)

Net Receivables 23	20069	549	1288	3231	6810	10401	15318	31974
Inventories 24	8164	767	2872	4508	13005	24400	61749	87423
Net Property, Plant and Equipment 25	10700	573	2311	4469	10762	21304	51972	113587
Total Assets 26	79438	2431	7008	16269	37831	69599	154097	403807
Notes and Loans Payable 27	33289	727	1145	5266	15389	22572	45519	154524
All Other Liabilities 28	13949	1075	1557	4046	8238	16038	46039	97401
Net Worth 29	32201	628	4306	6956	14204	30989	62539	151882

Selected Financial Ratios (Times to 1)

Current Ratio 30	1.1	1.3	2.0	1.5	1.5	1.6	1.3	2.4
Quick Ratio 31	0.8	0.5	0.9	0.6	0.5	0.5	0.3	1.2
Net Sales to Working Capital 32	17.3	16.1	8.5	8.8	6.9	7.6	12.3	4.8
Coverage Ratio 33	3.5	3.9	11.6	5.1	4.7	5.2	5.4	1.9
Total Asset Turnover 34	0.9	2.7	2.6	1.8	1.4	1.7	1.7	1.2
Inventory Turnover 35	5.7	6.7	3.9	5.0	3.1	3.4	2.8	4.1
Receivables Turnover 36	3.4	15.1	12.7	10.6	8.6	11.1	34.5	8.2
Total Liabilities to Net Worth 37	1.5	2.9	0.6	1.3	1.7	1.2	1.5	1.7
Current Assets to Working Capital 38	7.8	4.0	2.0	2.9	2.9	2.6	4.2	1.7
Current Liabilities to Working Capital 39	6.8	3.0	1.0	1.9	1.9	1.6	3.2	0.7
Working Capital to Net Sales 40	0.1	0.1	0.1	0.1	0.1	0.1	0.1	0.2
Inventory to Working Capital 41	2.2	2.5	1.0	1.6	1.7	1.7	2.9	0.8
Total Receipts to Cash Flow 42	5.1	11.4	7.6	9.2	8.5	7.7	5.4	13.3
Cost of Goods to Cash Flow 43	3.3	8.8	4.7	6.9	6.4	5.4	3.5	10.1
Cash Flow to Total Debt 44	0.3	0.3	0.9	0.3	0.3	0.4	0.5	0.1

Selected Financial Factors (in Percentages)

Debt Ratio 45	59.5	74.1	38.6	57.2	62.5	55.5	59.4	62.4
Return on Total Assets 46	11.8	7.3	17.2	10.3	10.5	11.2	11.4	6.5
Return on Equity Before Income Taxes 47	20.9	21.0	25.6	19.4	22.1	20.3	22.9	8.2
Return on Equity After Income Taxes 48	14.4	16.4	25.2	17.8	18.8	17.5	17.1	6.0
Profit Margin (Before Income Tax) 49	9.3	2.0	6.1	4.5	5.8	5.3	5.4	2.7
Profit Margin (After Income Tax) 50	6.4	1.6	6.0	4.2	4.9	4.6	4.0	2.0

Table I

Corporations with and without Net Income

DAIRY PRODUCT

MONEY AMOUNTS AND SIZE OF ASSETS IN THOUSANDS OF DOLLARS

Item Description for Accounting Period 7/02 Through 6/03	Total	Zero Assets	Under 500	500 to 1,000	1,000 to 5,000	5,000 to 10,000	10,000 to 25,000	25,000 to 50,000	50,000 to 100,000	100,000 to 250,000	250,000 to 500,000	500,000 to 2,500,000	2,500,000 and over
Number of Enterprises 1	584	0	0	60	200	81	56	31	14	9	4	6	0

Revenues ($ in Thousands)

	Total	Zero Assets	Under 500	500 to 1,000	1,000 to 5,000	5,000 to 10,000	10,000 to 25,000	25,000 to 50,000	50,000 to 100,000	100,000 to 250,000	250,000 to 500,000	500,000 to 2,500,000	2,500,000 and over
Net Sales 2	28742434	0	0	226751	1810731	2427935	2591156	2647485	2088841	2729761	2691850	11390067	0
Interest 3	121678	0	0	374	2886	942	1016	4056	2237	3472	733	105688	0
Rents 4	62874	0	0	0	913	1854	3346	2594	2346	357	244	51220	0
Royalties 5	84039	0	0	0	0	0	100	1951	0	64	0	81924	0
Other Portfolio Income 6	29984	0	0	0	7	1062	4223	4612	2015	72	984	16306	0
Other Receipts 7	392130	0	0	10975	7643	1618	8337	9001	3999	34384	27487	287374	0
Total Receipts 8	29433139	0	0	238100	1822180	2433411	2608178	2669699	2099438	2768110	2721298	11932579	0
Average Total Receipts 9	50399	•	•	3968	9111	30042	46575	86119	149960	307568	680324	1988763	•

Operating Costs/Operating Income (%)

	Total	Zero Assets	Under 500	500 to 1,000	1,000 to 5,000	5,000 to 10,000	10,000 to 25,000	25,000 to 50,000	50,000 to 100,000	100,000 to 250,000	250,000 to 500,000	500,000 to 2,500,000	2,500,000 and over
Cost of Operations 10	77.7	•	•	88.1	83.5	84.7	78.6	75.2	79.2	80.8	80.7	74.0	•
Salaries and Wages 11	5.0	•	•	1.8	4.4	3.8	5.5	7.1	5.3	2.2	3.7	5.6	•
Taxes Paid 12	1.2	•	•	1.9	1.7	1.0	1.2	1.3	1.1	0.9	1.1	1.2	•
Interest Paid 13	1.8	•	•	0.2	0.3	0.5	0.5	0.9	0.5	1.9	0.8	3.3	•
Depreciation 14	3.1	•	•	2.4	1.9	1.2	2.3	3.0	3.7	3.0	3.2	3.8	•
Amortization and Depletion 15	0.6	•	•	•	0.0	0.0	0.1	0.1	0.1	0.7	0.4	1.2	•
Pensions and Other Deferred Comp. 16	0.4	•	•	•	0.3	0.1	0.3	0.6	0.5	0.3	0.4	0.4	•
Employee Benefits 17	1.2	•	•	•	1.0	0.5	1.1	1.4	1.0	0.8	2.0	1.3	•
Advertising 18	1.5	•	•	0.5	0.5	0.5	1.1	1.3	1.3	2.3	1.5	1.9	•
Other Expenses 19	7.4	•	•	7.3	5.4	5.7	6.4	5.9	5.4	4.9	3.1	10.3	•
Officers' Compensation 20	0.7	•	•	4.1	1.4	1.2	1.2	1.1	0.5	0.3	0.2	0.5	•
Operating Margin 21	•	•	•	•	•	0.7	1.8	2.1	1.4	1.9	2.9	•	•
Operating Margin Before Officers' Comp. 22	0.2	•	•	•	0.9	1.9	2.9	3.2	1.9	2.2	3.0	•	•

Selected Average Balance Sheet ($ in Thousands)

Net Receivables 23	4153	145	563	2384	3717	7246	10789	23643	41775	191044
Inventories 24	3306	58	566	2277	2681	6348	10551	22809	32781	132949
Net Property, Plant and Equipment 25	9956	341	814	1861	6307	13700	31007	61517	176998	500584
Total Assets 26	36375	785	2540	6971	16055	34438	67632	153940	357444	2393850
Notes and Loans Payable 27	13879	139	486	1968	4773	10618	13361	72809	105402	996031
All Other Liabilities 28	12344	179	1175	2724	4079	9453	13260	35839	152487	848180
Net Worth 29	10152	467	879	2278	7203	14367	41010	45292	99556	549639

Selected Financial Ratios (Times to 1)

Current Ratio 30	0.9	•	1.8	1.1	1.4	1.7	1.5	1.8	2.1	1.1	0.6
Quick Ratio 31	0.5	1.5	0.8	0.8	1.1	0.8	1.0	1.3	0.5	0.3
Net Sales to Working Capital 32	•	21.7	52.9	23.5	13.5	15.0	11.3	8.6	99.2	•
Coverage Ratio 33	2.1	•	1.3	3.0	5.7	4.5	5.0	2.8	5.8	1.4
Total Asset Turnover 34	1.4	4.8	3.6	4.3	2.9	2.5	2.2	2.0	1.9	0.8
Inventory Turnover 35	11.6	57.8	13.4	11.1	13.6	10.1	11.2	10.7	16.6	10.6
Receivables Turnover 36	11.9	•	14.0	11.4	11.1	11.2	13.4	12.0	19.0	10.6
Total Liabilities to Net Worth 37	2.6	0.7	1.9	2.1	1.2	1.4	0.6	2.4	2.6	3.4
Current Assets to Working Capital 38	•	2.3	8.4	3.7	2.4	3.1	2.2	1.9	13.5	•
Current Liabilities to Working Capital 39	•	1.3	7.4	2.7	1.4	2.1	1.2	0.9	12.5	•
Working Capital to Net Sales 40	•	0.0	0.0	0.0	0.1	0.1	0.1	0.1	0.0	•
Inventory to Working Capital 41	•	0.3	2.5	1.3	0.7	1.1	0.9	0.6	6.1	•
Total Receipts to Cash Flow 42	12.8	26.1	23.1	19.2	13.8	14.0	16.1	13.9	21.9	9.8
Cost of Goods to Cash Flow 43	10.0	23.0	19.3	16.3	10.8	10.5	12.8	11.2	17.7	7.2
Cash Flow to Total Debt 44	0.1	0.5	0.2	0.3	0.4	0.3	0.3	0.2	0.1	0.1

Selected Financial Factors (in Percentages)

Debt Ratio 45	72.1	40.5	65.4	67.3	55.1	58.3	39.4	70.6	72.1	77.0
Return on Total Assets 46	5.0	•	1.4	5.9	8.5	9.6	5.3	10.2	9.1	3.6
Return on Equity Before Income Taxes 47	9.4	•	1.0	12.0	15.6	17.9	7.0	22.2	26.9	4.6
Return on Equity After Income Taxes 48	7.6	•	•	11.0	14.0	14.5	4.3	20.2	26.9	3.1
Profit Margin (Before Income Tax) 49	1.9	0.1	•	0.9	2.4	3.0	1.9	3.3	4.0	1.3
Profit Margin (After Income Tax) 50	1.6	•	•	0.8	2.2	2.4	1.2	3.0	4.0	0.9

Table II

Corporations with Net Income

DAIRY PRODUCT

MONEY AMOUNTS AND SIZE OF ASSETS IN THOUSANDS OF DOLLARS

Item Description for Accounting Period 7/02 Through 6/03	Total	Zero Assets	Under 500	500 to 1,000	1,000 to 5,000	5,000 to 10,000	10,000 to 25,000	25,000 to 50,000	50,000 to 100,000	100,000 to 250,000	250,000 to 500,000	500,000 to 2,500,000	2,500,000 and over
Number of Enterprises 1	405	·	0	·	126	69	45	21	9	0	0	0	0
Revenues ($ in Thousands)													
Net Sales 2	23249303	·	0	·	1474024	2243798	2278096	1912355	1353104	0	0	0	0
Interest 3	93872	·	0	·	503	749	825	2739	1305	0	0	0	0
Rents 4	8680	·	0	·	913	1854	3332	1032	391	0	0	0	0
Royalties 5	82852	·	0	·	0	0	0	1951	0	0	0	0	0
Other Portfolio Income 6	28175	·	0	·	7	486	4117	4464	1756	0	0	0	0
Other Receipts 7	376319	·	0	·	5404	1430	6038	6915	3147	0	0	0	0
Total Receipts 8	23839201	·	0	·	1480851	2248317	2292408	1929456	1359703	0	0	0	0
Average Total Receipts 9	58862	·	·	·	11753	32584	50942	91879	151078	·	·	·	·
Operating Costs/Operating Income (%)													
Cost of Operations 10	78.4	·	·	·	84.1	84.0	78.5	73.3	78.4	·	·	·	·
Salaries and Wages 11	4.7	·	·	·	4.0	4.0	5.4	7.0	5.1	·	·	·	·
Taxes Paid 12	1.1	·	·	·	1.2	1.0	1.1	1.2	1.2	·	·	·	·
Interest Paid 13	1.5	·	·	·	0.2	0.4	0.5	0.6	0.2	·	·	·	·
Depreciation 14	2.9	·	·	·	1.5	1.2	2.2	3.1	3.3	·	·	·	·
Amortization and Depletion 15	0.4	·	·	·	0.0	0.0	0.1	0.1	0.1	·	·	·	·
Pensions and Other Deferred Comp. 16	0.4	·	·	·	0.3	0.1	0.4	0.6	0.6	·	·	·	·
Employee Benefits 17	1.2	·	·	·	1.0	0.5	0.9	1.3	0.8	·	·	·	·
Advertising 18	1.1	·	·	·	0.5	0.5	1.2	1.5	1.9	·	·	·	·
Other Expenses 19	6.9	·	·	·	4.1	5.9	5.9	6.1	3.8	·	·	·	·
Officers' Compensation 20	0.7	·	·	·	1.5	1.3	1.1	1.2	0.5	·	·	·	·
Operating Margin 21	0.7	·	·	·	1.5	0.9	2.8	3.8	4.0	·	·	·	·
Operating Margin Before Officers' Comp. 22	1.4	·	·	·	3.0	2.2	3.9	5.0	4.5	·	·	·	·

Selected Average Balance Sheet ($ in Thousands)

Net Receivables 23	4726	672	2591	4017	7710	9707
Inventories 24	3778	710	1812	2440	6743	11013
Net Property, Plant and Equipment 25	11152	845	1931	6264	13339	30484
Total Assets 26	43062	2371	7188	16061	35173	70308
Notes and Loans Payable 27	15573	351	1884	4480	8045	5051
All Other Liabilities 28	15422	969	2940	4204	9812	13943
Net Worth 29	12067	1051	2365	7377	17316	51314

Selected Financial Ratios (Times to 1)

Current Ratio 30	0.8	2.0	1.4	1.8	1.6	2.3
Quick Ratio 31	0.5	1.3	0.8	1.2	0.9	1.3
Net Sales to Working Capital 32		15.6	23.1	13.2	12.8	8.4
Coverage Ratio 33	3.1	10.7	3.6	8.3	8.6	23.6
Total Asset Turnover 34	1.3	4.9	4.5	3.2	2.6	2.1
Inventory Turnover 35	11.9	13.9	15.1	16.3	9.9	10.7
Receivables Turnover 36	12.0	14.8	12.0	12.3	10.6	13.1
Total Liabilities to Net Worth 37	2.6	1.3	2.0	1.2	1.0	0.4
Current Assets to Working Capital 38		2.0	3.6	2.2	2.6	1.8
Current Liabilities to Working Capital 39		1.0	2.6	1.2	1.6	0.8
Working Capital to Net Sales 40		0.1	0.0	0.1	0.1	0.1
Inventory to Working Capital 41		0.6	1.2	0.6	0.9	0.7
Total Receipts to Cash Flow 42	11.7	19.3	17.9	12.9	11.0	13.7
Cost of Goods to Cash Flow 43	9.1	16.2	15.1	10.2	8.1	10.7
Cash Flow to Total Debt 44	0.2	0.5	0.4	0.5	0.5	0.6

Selected Financial Factors (in Percentages)

Debt Ratio 45	72.0	55.7	67.1	54.1	50.8	27.0
Return on Total Assets 46	6.3	10.7	6.9	12.1	14.1	9.8
Return on Equity Before Income Taxes 47	15.3	21.8	15.3	23.2	25.3	12.9
Return on Equity After Income Taxes 48	13.2	17.1	14.1	21.2	21.2	9.6
Profit Margin (Before Income Tax) 49	3.2	2.0	1.1	3.4	4.8	4.4
Profit Margin (After Income Tax) 50	2.8	1.5	1.0	3.1	4.0	3.3

Table I

Corporations with and without Net Income

MEAT AND SEAFOOD PROCESSING

MONEY AMOUNTS AND SIZE OF ASSETS IN THOUSANDS OF DOLLARS

Item Description for Accounting Period 7/02 Through 6/03	Total	Zero Assets	Under 500	500 to 1,000	1,000 to 5,000	5,000 to 10,000	10,000 to 25,000	25,000 to 50,000	50,000 to 100,000	100,000 to 250,000	250,000 to 500,000	500,000 to 2,500,000	2,500,000 and over
Number of Enterprises 1	1659	13	583	272	338	214	112	55	34	27	0	6	4
Revenues ($ in Thousands)													
Net Sales 2	115137945	149002	471440	474499	2382533	5057775	5494537	5135763	6691871	9039207	0	14170321	66070996
Interest 3	351095	123	1400	2062	1624	3194	2719	3096	1886	6935	0	67843	260212
Rents 4	26999	0	0	337	2336	3198	2073	2129	1233	841	0	3794	11058
Royalties 5	75657	0	0	0	0	0	5	0	40	9525	0	20092	45995
Other Portfolio Income 6	319579	47	20134	824	35632	34991	4037	3666	3445	22444	0	15287	179070
Other Receipts 7	1250174	4572	9192	114	37139	14513	32564	17880	33994	62769	0	173794	863648
Total Receipts 8	117161449	153744	502166	477836	2459264	5113671	5535935	5162534	6732469	9141721	0	14451131	67430979
Average Total Receipts 9	70622	11826	861	1757	7276	23896	49428	93864	198014	338582	•	2408522	16857745
Operating Costs/Operating Income (%)													
Cost of Operations 10	81.3	83.0	63.9	67.6	82.1	82.6	81.1	82.0	82.4	81.0	•	79.9	81.7
Salaries and Wages 11	4.7	3.6	5.8	6.5	4.2	5.9	3.8	3.6	2.7	2.6	•	7.5	4.7
Taxes Paid 12	0.9	0.7	3.6	2.6	1.6	1.4	1.2	1.1	0.9	1.1	•	1.0	0.7
Interest Paid 13	1.2	2.1	2.4	0.4	0.5	0.7	0.6	0.8	0.8	1.1	•	1.6	1.4
Depreciation 14	2.0	1.5	3.2	1.2	1.9	1.7	1.8	2.0	1.9	2.9	•	2.4	1.8
Amortization and Depletion 15	0.2	1.5	0.1	0.0	0.0	0.0	0.1	0.1	0.3	0.3	•	0.1	0.2
Pensions and Other Deferred Comp. 16	0.1	0.1	•	0.1	0.4	0.1	0.2	0.3	0.2	0.1	•	0.1	0.0
Employee Benefits 17	1.5	0.7	0.0	1.0	0.6	1.1	0.8	0.9	0.8	1.6	•	1.2	1.8
Advertising 18	1.0	0.4	0.6	1.5	0.7	0.1	0.8	0.7	1.8	0.9	•	0.5	1.1
Other Expenses 19	6.8	7.3	16.6	15.8	7.1	5.3	6.2	5.7	5.8	6.1	•	8.9	6.7
Officers' Compensation 20	0.4	0.5	5.3	7.1	2.5	1.7	1.5	1.0	0.6	0.3	•	0.2	0.1
Operating Margin 21	•	•	•	•	•	•	1.7	1.8	1.7	2.0	•	•	•
Operating Margin Before Officers' Comp. 22	0.3	•	3.7	3.2	0.8	1.0	3.1	2.8	2.4	2.3	•	•	•

Selected Average Balance Sheet ($ in Thousands)

Net Receivables 23	7136	0	66	163	466	1319	3287	6161	13421	23887	•	260205	1986626
Inventories 24	5735	0	19	84	339	1214	3451	7257	14750	36134	•	273339	1300879
Net Property, Plant and Equipment 25	9248	0	117	80	892	2536	5778	12061	23323	62821	•	377841	2085288
Total Assets 26	38665	0	217	675	2406	6758	16115	35206	68795	158576	•	1297268	10857626
Notes and Loans Payable 27	12841	0	105	136	1224	3644	5563	12894	22384	65005	•	345774	3522057
All Other Liabilities 28	12912	0	28	76	652	1387	3521	9271	14370	33058	•	633597	3695044
Net Worth 29	12912	0	85	463	530	1728	7031	13041	32042	60513	•	317898	3640525

Selected Financial Ratios (Times to 1)

Current Ratio 30	1.6	•	2.0	2.0	1.4	1.5	1.7	1.2	1.6	1.6	•	1.3	1.6
Quick Ratio 31	0.6	•	1.9	1.4	1.1	0.6	0.9	0.6	0.8	0.7	•	0.6	0.6
Net Sales to Working Capital 32	9.7	•	17.0	10.2	18.9	20.5	13.2	31.3	14.3	12.8	•	14.7	7.6
Coverage Ratio 33	2.4	1.9	3.0	•	4.0	1.6	4.7	3.8	4.0	3.8	•	0.3	2.5
Total Asset Turnover 34	1.8	•	3.7	2.6	2.9	3.5	3.0	2.7	2.9	2.1	•	1.8	1.5
Inventory Turnover 35	9.8	•	26.7	14.1	17.1	16.1	11.5	10.5	11.0	7.5	•	6.9	10.4
Receivables Turnover 36	12.5	•	15.7	11.6	13.2	17.6	15.0	13.8	14.8	12.9	•	12.1	11.7
Total Liabilities to Net Worth 37	2.0	•	1.6	0.5	3.5	2.9	1.3	1.7	1.1	1.6	•	3.1	2.0
Current Assets to Working Capital 38	2.8	•	2.0	2.0	3.3	3.2	2.4	5.8	2.6	2.8	•	4.0	2.6
Current Liabilities to Working Capital 39	1.8	•	1.0	1.0	2.3	2.2	1.4	4.8	1.6	1.8	•	3.0	1.6
Working Capital to Net Sales 40	0.1	•	0.1	0.1	0.1	0.0	0.1	0.0	0.1	0.1	•	0.1	0.1
Inventory to Working Capital 41	0.9	•	0.0	0.5	0.8	1.2	0.9	2.4	1.1	1.3	•	1.9	0.7
Total Receipts to Cash Flow 42	14.1	16.4	7.7	10.6	16.6	23.2	13.7	14.0	13.9	12.7	•	16.7	13.5
Cost of Goods to Cash Flow 43	11.4	13.6	4.9	7.2	13.7	19.1	11.1	11.5	11.4	10.3	•	13.3	11.0
Cash Flow to Total Debt 44	0.2	•	0.8	0.8	0.2	0.2	0.4	0.3	0.4	0.3	•	0.1	0.2

Selected Financial Factors (in Percentages)

Debt Ratio 45	66.6	•	61.0	31.4	78.0	74.4	56.4	63.0	53.4	61.8	•	75.5	66.5
Return on Total Assets 46	5.3	•	27.5	•	5.9	3.9	9.3	8.4	9.0	8.9	•	0.8	5.3
Return on Equity Before Income Taxes 47	9.3	•	47.1	•	20.2	6.0	16.8	16.7	14.4	17.2	•	9.5	
Return on Equity After Income Taxes 48	6.4	•	46.5	•	18.3	4.9	14.8	14.2	12.9	13.9	•	6.2	
Profit Margin (Before Income Tax) 49	1.7	1.9	4.9	•	1.5	0.4	2.4	2.3	2.4	3.1	•	2.1	
Profit Margin (After Income Tax) 50	1.2	1.6	4.9	•	1.4	0.4	2.1	2.0	2.1	2.5	•	1.4	

Table II

Corporations with Net Income

MEAT AND SEAFOOD PROCESSING

MONEY AMOUNTS AND SIZE OF ASSETS IN THOUSANDS OF DOLLARS

Item Description for Accounting Period 7/02 Through 6/03	Total	Zero Assets	Under 500	500 to 1,000	1,000 to 5,000	5,000 to 10,000	10,000 to 25,000	25,000 to 50,000	50,000 to 100,000	100,000 to 250,000	250,000 to 500,000	500,000 to 2,500,000	2,500,000 and over
Number of Enterprises **1**	1290	0	0	161	237	125	81	41	25	20	3	0	0
Revenues ($ in Thousands)													
Net Sales **2**	88740621	0	0	273627	1482079	3497851	4122391	3994803	5316316	6395232	3785065	0	0
Interest **3**	238445	0	0	1979	803	3106	2418	1409	1301	5768	2430	0	0
Rents **4**	19653	0	0	337	1398	3136	1264	1368	1162	716	1781	0	0
Royalties **5**	19095	0	0	0	0	0	5	0	0	0	9569	0	0
Other Portfolio Income **6**	264932	0	0	778	28331	34196	1555	3298	1835	6706	2596	0	0
Other Receipts **7**	1078739	0	0	113	33534	5755	18760	16151	20688	35495	106009	0	0
Total Receipts **8**	90361485	0	0	276834	1546145	3544044	4146393	4017029	5341302	6443917	3907450	0	0
Average Total Receipts **9**	70048	·	·	1719	6524	28352	51190	97976	213652	322196	1302483	·	·
Operating Costs/Operating Income (%)													
Cost of Operations **10**	81.0	·	·	61.4	79.6	80.2	78.9	80.6	80.5	80.8	85.5	·	·
Salaries and Wages **11**	4.5	·	·	5.6	5.3	5.1	4.0	3.7	3.0	2.5	2.7	·	·
Taxes Paid **12**	0.8	·	·	3.2	1.6	1.1	1.2	1.1	0.8	1.0	1.2	·	·
Interest Paid **13**	1.1	·	·	·	0.5	0.8	0.5	0.6	0.5	1.1	0.8	·	·
Depreciation **14**	1.8	·	·	1.5	1.8	1.8	1.8	1.8	1.8	2.6	2.0	·	·
Amortization and Depletion **15**	0.2	·	·	·	0.0	0.0	0.1	0.1	0.1	0.3	0.3	·	·
Pensions and Other Deferred Comp. **16**	0.1	·	·	·	0.5	0.1	0.3	0.3	0.2	0.1	0.3	·	·
Employee Benefits **17**	1.6	·	·	1.5	0.7	0.9	1.0	0.7	0.8	0.8	2.3	·	·
Advertising **18**	1.1	·	·	2.6	0.5	0.2	1.0	0.8	2.2	0.9	0.2	·	·
Other Expenses **19**	6.6	·	·	17.9	5.8	7.0	6.0	5.7	5.8	5.8	5.1	·	·
Officers' Compensation **20**	0.4	·	·	6.4	3.1	2.0	1.7	1.1	0.8	0.3	0.5	·	·
Operating Margin **21**	0.9	·	·	·	0.5	0.7	3.5	3.4	3.5	3.7	·	·	·
Operating Margin Before Officers' Comp. **22**	1.3	·	·	6.2	3.6	2.7	5.2	4.5	4.2	4.0	·	·	·

Selected Average Balance Sheet ($ in Thousands)

Net Receivables 23	7391	41	483	1546	3299	7010	14710	23510	58205
Inventories 24	5719	53	363	1190	3314	7920	14308	26691	169275
Net Property, Plant and Equipment 25	8321	102	743	2746	5725	11706	23644	57433	145648
Total Assets 26	39267	731	2108	6868	15887	34960	70856	150522	592584
Notes and Loans Payable 27	12709	0	1336	4405	4920	8097	19877	60916	149984
All Other Liabilities 28	12568	29	748	1218	3232	9502	15131	30037	155608
Net Worth 29	13990	701	25	1245	7735	17360	35848	59568	286992

Selected Financial Ratios (Times to 1)

Current Ratio 30	1.6	7.7	1.2	1.4	2.0	1.7	1.8	1.7	2.2
Quick Ratio 31	0.7	4.2	1.0	0.8	1.1	0.9	0.9	0.8	0.6
Net Sales to Working Capital 32	9.0	8.7	28.5	29.7	11.9	12.6	13.4	10.6	9.3
Coverage Ratio 33	3.5		10.7	3.4	9.1	8.0	8.7	5.0	4.0
Total Asset Turnover 34	1.8	2.3	3.0	4.1	3.2	2.8	3.0	2.1	2.1
Inventory Turnover 35	9.7	19.6	13.7	18.9	12.1	9.9	12.0	9.7	6.4
Receivables Turnover 36	11.6	83.2	9.4	19.6	15.0	12.7	14.1	13.9	43.4
Total Liabilities to Net Worth 37	1.8	0.0	83.7	4.5	1.1	1.0	1.0	1.5	1.1
Current Assets to Working Capital 38	2.7	1.1	5.4	3.6	2.0	2.5	2.3	2.4	1.8
Current Liabilities to Working Capital 39	1.7	0.1	4.4	2.6	1.0	1.5	1.3	1.4	0.8
Working Capital to Net Sales 40	0.1	0.1	0.0	0.0	0.1	0.1	0.1	0.1	0.1
Inventory to Working Capital 41	0.7	0.5	0.8	1.2	0.8	1.0	1.0	1.0	1.2
Total Receipts to Cash Flow 42	12.6	7.0	13.0	13.4	11.2	11.4	11.4	11.1	16.7
Cost of Goods to Cash Flow 43	10.2	4.3	10.3	10.7	8.9	9.2	9.2	9.0	14.3
Cash Flow to Total Debt 44	0.2	8.3	0.2	0.4	0.6	0.5	0.5	0.3	0.2

Selected Financial Factors (in Percentages)

Debt Ratio 45	64.4	4.0	98.8	81.9	51.3	50.3	49.4	60.4	51.6
Return on Total Assets 46	6.9	1.8	15.6	11.4	14.6	12.6	13.4	11.9	7.2
Return on Equity Before Income Taxes 47	13.9	1.8	1200.2	44.3	26.7	22.2	23.4	24.1	11.1
Return on Equity After Income Taxes 48	10.5	1.6	1141.7	41.7	24.2	19.7	21.4	21.0	7.2
Profit Margin (Before Income Tax) 49	2.8	0.8	4.8	2.0	4.1	3.9	3.9	4.5	2.5
Profit Margin (After Income Tax) 50	2.1	0.7	4.5	1.9	3.7	3.5	3.6	3.9	1.6

Table I

Corporations with and without Net Income

BAKERIES AND TORTILLA

MONEY AMOUNTS AND SIZE OF ASSETS IN THOUSANDS OF DOLLARS

Item Description for Accounting Period 7/02 Through 6/03	Total	Zero Assets	Under 500	500 to 1,000	1,000 to 5,000	5,000 to 10,000	10,000 to 25,000	25,000 to 50,000	50,000 to 100,000	100,000 to 250,000	250,000 to 500,000	500,000 to 2,500,000	2,500,000 and over
Number of Enterprises 1	4295	260	3260	81	419	131	64	29	22	14	4	10	0
Revenues ($ in Thousands)													
Net Sales 2	41352056	95037	930630	102441	1732130	1773350	1848353	2103451	2595887	3326589	2053635	24790553	0
Interest 3	377280	48	1545	14	1298	1023	1274	1738	3169	6094	2278	358800	0
Rents 4	32545	10	0	0	496	5798	325	3104	11214	659	4042	6897	0
Royalties 5	309374	0	0	0	0	0	0	558	236	38733	22023	247824	0
Other Portfolio Income 6	249863	105	11181	0	676	959	11431	553	2734	71979	9114	141133	0
Other Receipts 7	518461	763	30250	0	2438	52941	11097	6841	11505	39084	13818	349719	0
Total Receipts 8	42839579	95963	973606	102455	1737038	1834071	1872480	2116245	2624745	3483138	2104910	25894926	0
Average Total Receipts 9	9974	369	299	1265	4146	14001	29258	72974	119307	248796	526228	2589493	•
Operating Costs/Operating Income (%)													
Cost of Operations 10	63.0	61.8	46.3	53.9	62.5	64.0	59.9	67.7	57.3	65.4	67.0	63.5	•
Salaries and Wages 11	9.2	58.2	13.7	0.0	9.0	10.5	8.1	7.7	13.9	10.4	9.2	8.3	•
Taxes Paid 12	2.1	6.1	4.4	0.8	2.7	2.7	2.0	1.7	2.1	2.0	1.4	2.1	•
Interest Paid 13	2.7	0.0	0.6	0.2	1.3	1.0	1.0	0.9	1.9	2.1	0.9	3.6	•
Depreciation 14	3.8	4.7	4.5	16.5	3.5	5.1	4.1	4.2	4.4	4.8	3.4	3.5	•
Amortization and Depletion 15	0.6	0.0	0.1	•	0.4	0.3	0.1	0.2	0.3	0.9	0.2	0.8	•
Pensions and Other Deferred Comp. 16	1.3	0.6	0.0	•	0.2	0.6	0.6	0.8	1.9	0.3	0.2	1.8	•
Employee Benefits 17	2.6	1.1	0.1	0.1	1.6	2.2	2.4	1.7	3.6	1.7	1.9	3.0	•
Advertising 18	2.5	0.5	2.2	1.1	0.4	1.0	1.3	0.9	1.1	1.7	3.3	3.2	•
Other Expenses 19	13.4	32.9	24.8	20.5	13.4	13.1	11.6	10.5	12.9	10.3	10.9	14.0	•
Officers' Compensation 20	1.0	9.2	8.0	10.7	2.5	2.6	2.2	1.8	1.2	0.5	1.9	0.3	•
Operating Margin 21	•	•	•	•	2.5	•	6.8	1.9	•	1.9	•	•	•
Operating Margin Before Officers' Comp. 22	•	•	3.2	6.9	5.0	•	8.9	3.7	0.5	0.3	•	•	•

Selected Average Balance Sheet ($ in Thousands)

Net Receivables 23	757	0	14	134	434	1029	2930	5213	10382	20673	38976	186609	•
Inventories 24	586	0	8	102	194	414	1297	3182	5448	13986	29904	173569	•
Net Property, Plant and Equipment 25	2111	0	31	322	723	3167	6927	17434	30162	59406	124228	528202	•
Total Assets 26	12570	0	97	647	2590	6843	14554	34383	69833	176532	395572	4411808	•
Notes and Loans Payable 27	2736	0	63	466	885	2776	4857	12769	23929	45381	95590	854524	•
All Other Liabilities 28	4643	0	21	126	256	1634	2310	8974	20685	46869	92916	1765293	•
Net Worth 29	5190	0	12	55	1450	2433	7387	12640	25219	84282	207066	1791992	•

Selected Financial Ratios (Times to 1)

Current Ratio 30	0.8	•	1.2	2.3	2.9	1.7	2.0	1.4	1.0	1.6	1.8	0.6	•
Quick Ratio 31	0.5	•	0.9	1.0	2.3	1.3	1.5	0.8	0.6	1.1	0.8	0.3	•
Net Sales to Working Capital 32	•	•	44.0	7.0	5.4	11.9	8.8	19.8	•	11.5	9.5	•	•
Coverage Ratio 33	1.7	•	0.7	•	3.2	1.4	9.4	3.7	1.2	3.1	3.3	1.5	•
Total Asset Turnover 34	0.8	•	3.0	2.0	1.6	2.0	2.0	2.1	1.7	1.3	1.3	0.6	•
Inventory Turnover 35	10.4	•	15.8	6.6	13.3	20.9	13.3	15.4	12.4	11.1	11.5	9.1	•
Receivables Turnover 36	13.5	•	19.2	8.0	10.0	14.0	11.2	15.3	11.0	10.2	13.8	14.6	•
Total Liabilities to Net Worth 37	1.4	•	6.9	10.7	0.8	1.8	1.0	1.7	1.8	1.1	0.9	1.5	•
Current Assets to Working Capital 38	•	•	6.3	1.8	1.5	2.4	2.0	3.4	•	2.6	2.3	•	•
Current Liabilities to Working Capital 39	•	•	5.3	0.8	0.5	1.4	1.0	2.4	•	1.6	1.3	•	•
Working Capital to Net Sales 40	•	•	0.0	0.1	0.2	0.1	0.1	0.1	•	0.1	0.1	•	•
Inventory to Working Capital 41	•	•	1.4	0.9	0.2	0.4	0.4	0.9	•	0.7	0.8	•	•
Total Receipts to Cash Flow 42	8.7	•	7.3	11.3	7.9	9.2	5.7	9.5	9.8	8.7	10.9	8.6	•
Cost of Goods to Cash Flow 43	5.5	•	3.4	6.1	4.9	5.9	3.4	6.5	5.6	5.7	7.3	5.5	•
Cash Flow to Total Debt 44	0.1	•	0.5	0.2	0.5	0.3	0.7	0.4	0.3	0.3	0.2	0.1	•

Selected Financial Factors (in Percentages)

Debt Ratio 45	58.7	•	87.3	91.5	44.0	64.4	49.2	63.2	63.9	52.3	47.7	59.4	•
Return on Total Assets 46	3.5	1.3	•	•	6.4	2.7	17.9	7.2	3.9	8.9	4.0	2.9	•
Return on Equity Before Income Taxes 47	3.5	•	•	•	7.9	2.1	31.6	14.3	1.8	12.5	5.3	2.3	•
Return on Equity After Income Taxes 48	2.4	•	•	•	5.4	0.5	30.0	11.9	0.9	9.3	3.3	1.4	•
Profit Margin (Before Income Tax) 49	1.9	•	•	•	2.8	0.4	8.1	2.5	0.4	4.4	2.2	1.6	•
Profit Margin (After Income Tax) 50	1.3	•	•	•	1.9	0.1	7.7	2.1	0.2	3.3	1.3	1.0	•

Table II

Corporations with Net Income

BAKERIES AND TORTILLA

MONEY AMOUNTS AND SIZE OF ASSETS IN THOUSANDS OF DOLLARS

Item Description for Accounting Period 7/02 Through 6/03	Total	Zero Assets	Under 500	500 to 1,000	1,000 to 5,000	5,000 to 10,000	10,000 to 25,000	25,000 to 50,000	50,000 to 100,000	100,000 to 250,000	250,000 to 500,000	500,000 to 2,500,000	2,500,000 and over
Number of Enterprises **1**	2122	9	0	•	322	83	39	20	14	8	0	6	0
Revenues ($ in Thousands)													
Net Sales **2**	32673887	27271	0	•	1490683	1358678	1233744	1208485	1541959	2585122	0	20812875	0
Interest **3**	306557	0	0	•	1047	977	452	951	2505	1297	0	295544	0
Rents **4**	26119	8	0	•	12	987	325	2967	11196	478	0	6105	0
Royalties **5**	307449	0	0	•	0	0	0	558	0	37618	0	247427	0
Other Portfolio Income **6**	215969	0	0	•	455	167	11347	164	1655	71893	0	109994	0
Other Receipts **7**	440024	45	0	•	2412	5585	8086	2153	8294	37030	0	336035	0
Total Receipts **8**	33970005	27324	0	•	1494609	1366394	1253954	1215278	1565609	2733438	0	21807980	0
Average Total Receipts **9**	16008	3036	•	•	4642	16463	32153	60764	111829	341680	•	3634663	•
Operating Costs/Operating Income (%)													
Cost of Operations **10**	64.3	72.8	•	•	61.2	63.3	60.2	60.8	54.6	65.3	•	65.5	•
Salaries and Wages **11**	7.9	1.3	•	•	8.5	10.5	6.0	7.8	14.6	11.3	•	6.9	•
Taxes Paid **12**	2.1	3.2	•	•	2.6	2.9	1.9	1.9	2.1	2.0	•	2.1	•
Interest Paid **13**	2.7	0.1	•	•	1.1	0.8	0.9	1.1	1.2	1.3	•	3.6	•
Depreciation **14**	3.3	4.2	•	•	3.1	3.7	3.7	4.6	4.8	4.3	•	3.0	•
Amortization and Depletion **15**	0.4	•	•	•	0.4	0.1	0.1	0.2	0.2	0.6	•	0.5	•
Pensions and Other Deferred Comp. **16**	1.1	•	•	•	0.3	0.8	0.3	1.2	2.2	0.3	•	1.4	•
Employee Benefits **17**	2.5	0.3	•	•	1.8	2.4	1.3	2.0	3.5	1.6	•	2.8	•
Advertising **18**	2.8	0.3	•	•	0.4	1.2	1.6	1.1	1.1	2.1	•	3.4	•
Other Expenses **19**	13.2	10.1	•	•	12.1	9.7	9.2	12.2	13.3	9.0	•	14.3	•
Officers' Compensation **20**	1.0	1.3	•	•	2.4	2.5	2.3	2.5	1.3	0.5	•	0.3	•
Operating Margin **21**	•	6.4	•	•	6.1	2.2	12.5	4.7	1.0	1.7	•	•	•
Operating Margin Before Officers' Comp. **22**	•	7.7	•	•	8.5	4.8	14.8	7.2	2.3	2.2	•	•	•

Selected Average Balance Sheet ($ in Thousands)

Net Receivables 23	1102	0	•	511	1176	3561	4780	8450	25110	•	229946
Inventories 24	1022	0	•	230	440	1497	3124	5098	18674	•	268992
Net Property, Plant and Equipment 25	3124	0	•	693	2781	6753	16865	30508	60099	•	696583
Total Assets 26	21932	0	•	2890	6625	14760	34238	72736	181990	•	6661298
Notes and Loans Payable 27	4157	0	•	819	2162	4573	11823	16472	36540	•	1199606
All Other Liabilities 28	8197	0	•	232	1146	2504	7299	19641	37552	•	2677569
Net Worth 29	9578	0	•	1839	3317	7683	15116	36623	107898	•	2784122

Selected Financial Ratios (Times to 1)

Current Ratio 30	0.8	•	•	4.2	2.2	2.4	1.6	1.1	1.8	•	0.6
Quick Ratio 31	0.4	•	•	3.2	1.8	1.8	0.9	0.7	1.2	•	0.3
Net Sales to Working Capital 32	•	•	•	4.6	8.3	7.5	13.7	77.0	10.4	•	•
Coverage Ratio 33	2.4	63.4	•	6.9	4.5	16.3	5.7	3.0	6.5	•	1.7
Total Asset Turnover 34	0.7	•	•	1.6	2.5	2.1	1.8	1.5	1.8	•	0.5
Inventory Turnover 35	9.7	•	•	12.3	23.6	12.7	11.8	11.8	11.3	•	8.4
Receivables Turnover 36	13.8	•	•	9.2	15.1	9.8	13.4	11.4	25.7	•	15.0
Total Liabilities to Net Worth 37	1.3	•	•	0.6	1.0	0.9	1.3	1.0	0.7	•	1.4
Current Assets to Working Capital 38	•	•	•	1.3	1.8	1.7	2.7	15.1	2.2	•	•
Current Liabilities to Working Capital 39	•	•	•	0.3	0.8	0.7	1.7	14.1	1.2	•	•
Working Capital to Net Sales 40	•	•	•	0.2	0.1	0.1	0.1	0.0	0.1	•	•
Inventory to Working Capital 41	•	•	•	0.2	0.3	0.3	0.8	2.9	0.6	•	•
Total Receipts to Cash Flow 42	7.8	7.6	•	6.8	10.2	4.7	6.9	7.5	7.9	•	8.0
Cost of Goods to Cash Flow 43	5.0	5.5	•	4.2	6.5	2.8	4.2	4.1	5.2	•	5.2
Cash Flow to Total Debt 44	0.2	•	•	0.6	0.5	1.0	0.5	0.4	0.6	•	0.1

Selected Financial Factors (in Percentages)

Debt Ratio 45	56.3	•	•	36.4	49.9	48.0	55.9	49.6	40.7	•	58.2
Return on Total Assets 46	4.4	•	•	11.9	8.8	32.2	11.1	5.6	15.5	•	3.2
Return on Equity Before Income Taxes 47	5.9	•	•	16.0	13.7	58.0	20.8	7.4	22.2	•	3.1
Return on Equity After Income Taxes 48	4.6	•	•	13.4	11.9	55.5	17.9	6.4	17.8	•	2.2
Profit Margin (Before Income Tax) 49	3.6	6.6	•	6.3	2.8	14.1	5.2	2.5	7.4	•	2.5
Profit Margin (After Income Tax) 50	2.9	6.6	•	5.3	2.4	13.5	4.5	2.1	5.9	•	1.8

Table I

Corporations with and without Net Income

OTHER FOOD

MONEY AMOUNTS AND SIZE OF ASSETS IN THOUSANDS OF DOLLARS

Item Description for Accounting Period 7/02 Through 6/03	Total	Zero Assets	Under 500	500 to 1,000	1,000 to 5,000	5,000 to 10,000	10,000 to 25,000	25,000 to 50,000	50,000 to 100,000	100,000 to 250,000	250,000 to 500,000	500,000 to 2,500,000	2,500,000 and over
Number of Enterprises 1	2841	132	1528	275	419	200	136	77	33	28	5	•	9

Revenues ($ in Thousands)

	Total	Zero Assets	Under 500	500 to 1,000	1,000 to 5,000	5,000 to 10,000	10,000 to 25,000	25,000 to 50,000	50,000 to 100,000	100,000 to 250,000	250,000 to 500,000	500,000 to 2,500,000	2,500,000 and over
Net Sales 2	37363715	61762	162626	291975	3039014	3254994	4424594	5167948	3741686	7088983	1841252	•	8288880
Interest 3	78057	3406	7	51	888	2611	3111	4918	11625	8676	16389	•	26373
Rents 4	22061	0	0	157	566	1925	1830	1303	3103	5706	7346	•	123
Royalties 5	44026	0	0	0	0	406	76	8174	1624	6687	1047	•	26011
Other Portfolio Income 6	168257	0	32415	0	998	4496	4129	11730	40440	8835	36501	•	28713
Other Receipts 7	251609	1720	2	3	8753	31269	12919	19419	36919	29193	1842	•	109576
Total Receipts 8	37927725	66888	195050	292186	3050219	3295701	4446659	5213492	3835397	7148080	1904377	•	8479676
Average Total Receipts 9	13350	507	128	1062	7280	16479	32696	67708	116224	255289	380875	•	942186

Operating Costs/Operating Income (%)

	Total	Zero Assets	Under 500	500 to 1,000	1,000 to 5,000	5,000 to 10,000	10,000 to 25,000	25,000 to 50,000	50,000 to 100,000	100,000 to 250,000	250,000 to 500,000	500,000 to 2,500,000	2,500,000 and over
Cost of Operations 10	68.7	49.4	47.1	69.4	75.0	68.7	71.9	66.5	68.4	70.5	67.0	•	65.7
Salaries and Wages 11	6.4	6.5	2.1	7.7	5.7	9.4	5.9	7.1	7.3	5.2	8.7	•	5.6
Taxes Paid 12	1.5	1.7	2.7	3.0	1.2	1.5	1.5	1.5	1.6	1.2	2.6	•	1.6
Interest Paid 13	1.9	31.4	7.9	1.6	0.7	0.6	0.9	1.4	1.9	1.4	3.4	•	3.6
Depreciation 14	3.1	2.9	17.6	4.3	2.7	2.5	2.7	2.6	3.8	3.3	3.0	•	3.2
Amortization and Depletion 15	0.8	3.4	0.2	•	0.1	0.0	0.2	0.5	0.9	0.4	0.8	•	2.2
Pensions and Other Deferred Comp. 16	0.5	0.7	0.0	•	0.3	0.7	0.3	0.4	0.5	0.2	0.8	•	0.9
Employee Benefits 17	1.2	1.9	0.0	0.5	0.4	0.7	1.0	1.5	1.5	1.1	0.9	•	1.6
Advertising 18	1.8	0.6	3.9	2.2	1.2	0.6	1.3	3.2	2.5	2.9	0.4	•	1.1
Other Expenses 19	11.6	117.2	59.0	15.9	8.5	10.7	10.2	11.6	11.1	9.9	13.2	•	13.5
Officers' Compensation 20	1.4	5.7	3.7	5.5	2.9	2.2	1.9	2.1	1.5	0.6	0.7	•	0.5
Operating Margin 21	0.9	•	•	•	1.3	2.3	2.3	1.5	•	3.1	•	•	0.6
Operating Margin Before Officers' Comp. 22	2.3	•	•	•	4.2	4.6	4.2	3.6	0.6	3.7	1.1	•	1.1

Selected Average Balance Sheet ($ in Thousands)

Net Receivables 23	1355	0	9	17	495	1693	2952	5672	12303	23902	51480	123677
Inventories 24	1470	0	10	41	682	1586	3443	7133	12112	28231	79971	105174
Net Property, Plant and Equipment 25	2559	0	61	274	726	2287	5169	10440	26368	61584	74012	207478
Total Assets 26	9301	0	95	656	2108	6895	15552	33892	70961	159193	362504	1166765
Notes and Loans Payable 27	3973	0	105	301	690	2138	5087	12122	26643	48236	270368	569056
All Other Liabilities 28	1993	0	6	107	614	1783	4240	7578	17301	41302	49622	208227
Net Worth 29	3335	0	-16	248	805	2973	6225	14192	27017	69656	42515	389482

Selected Financial Ratios (Times to 1)

Current Ratio 30	1.6	•	0.5	2.8	1.8	1.7	1.4	1.8	1.5	1.6	5.5	1.2
Quick Ratio 31	0.7	•	0.3	2.4	0.9	1.0	0.8	0.9	0.7	0.8	1.4	0.5
Net Sales to Working Capital 32	8.9	•	•	4.3	13.7	10.0	12.5	8.8	9.3	9.6	1.9	15.2
Coverage Ratio 33	2.3	•	•	•	3.2	6.7	3.9	2.7	1.9	3.7	1.6	1.9
Total Asset Turnover 34	1.4	•	1.1	1.6	3.4	2.4	2.1	2.0	1.6	1.6	1.0	0.8
Inventory Turnover 35	6.1	•	4.8	18.0	8.0	7.0	6.8	6.3	6.4	6.3	3.1	5.8
Receivables Turnover 36	10.0	•	23.9	27.3	11.5	9.2	11.5	11.7	10.2	10.9	5.5	9.1
Total Liabilities to Net Worth 37	1.8	•	•	•	1.6	1.3	1.5	1.4	1.6	1.3	7.5	2.0
Current Assets to Working Capital 38	2.7	•	•	1.5	2.3	2.4	3.3	2.3	2.8	2.6	1.2	5.9
Current Liabilities to Working Capital 39	1.7	•	•	0.5	1.3	1.4	2.3	1.3	1.8	1.6	0.2	4.9
Working Capital to Net Sales 40	0.1	•	•	0.2	0.1	0.1	0.1	0.1	0.1	0.1	0.5	0.1
Inventory to Working Capital 41	1.0	•	•	0.2	1.0	0.9	1.3	0.9	1.2	1.1	0.2	2.0
Total Receipts to Cash Flow 42	8.4	•	9.8	•	12.2	8.3	9.0	8.3	10.1	8.2	7.7	6.6
Cost of Goods to Cash Flow 43	5.8	•	4.6	•	9.1	5.7	6.5	5.5	6.9	5.8	5.2	4.3
Cash Flow to Total Debt 44	0.3	•	0.1	•	0.5	0.5	0.4	0.4	0.3	0.3	0.1	0.2

Selected Financial Factors (in Percentages)

Debt Ratio 45	64.1	117.1	•	62.2	61.8	56.9	60.0	58.1	61.9	56.2	88.3	66.6
Return on Total Assets 46	6.2	•	•	•	8.3	10.0	7.7	7.7	5.8	8.5	5.4	5.3
Return on Equity Before Income Taxes 47	9.7	159.4	•	•	15.0	19.7	14.4	11.6	7.1	14.3	16.6	7.5
Return on Equity After Income Taxes 48	6.0	162.8	•	•	11.8	16.2	11.6	8.8	2.4	11.0	11.5	3.2
Profit Margin (Before Income Tax) 49	2.5	•	•	•	1.7	3.6	2.8	2.5	1.7	3.9	1.9	3.2
Profit Margin (After Income Tax) 50	1.5	•	•	•	1.3	3.0	2.2	1.9	0.6	3.0	1.3	1.4

49

Table II
Corporations with Net Income

OTHER FOOD

MONEY AMOUNTS AND SIZE OF ASSETS IN THOUSANDS OF DOLLARS

Item Description for Accounting Period 7/02 Through 6/03	Total	Zero Assets	Under 500	500 to 1,000	1,000 to 5,000	5,000 to 10,000	10,000 to 25,000	25,000 to 50,000	50,000 to 100,000	100,000 to 250,000	250,000 to 500,000	500,000 to 2,500,000	2,500,000 and over
Number of Enterprises **1**	1177	0	299	137	356	165	99	55	24	22	0	0	·
Revenues ($ in Thousands)													
Net Sales **2**	31013950	0	49456	123362	2690726	2720067	3484496	4105234	2739192	6131949	0	0	·
Interest **3**	58333	0	7	0	819	2541	2747	3400	9586	8422	0	0	·
Rents **4**	13671	0	0	0	566	1675	1622	1003	2752	5571	0	0	·
Royalties **5**	41969	0	0	0	0	406	20	6629	1624	6673	0	0	·
Other Portfolio Income **6**	130277	0	0	0	998	4047	3309	10118	40337	8831	0	0	·
Other Receipts **7**	214425	0	2	3	8665	25597	7522	7647	29010	24667	0	0	·
Total Receipts **8**	31472625	0	49465	123365	2701774	2754333	3499716	4134031	2822501	6186113	0	0	·
Average Total Receipts **9**	26740	·	165	900	7589	16693	35351	75164	117604	281187	·	·	·
Operating Costs/Operating Income (%)													
Cost of Operations **10**	69.0	·	15.3	48.7	78.0	66.7	69.7	67.2	65.7	72.1	·	·	·
Salaries and Wages **11**	6.1	·	·	0.0	4.4	9.8	5.9	6.3	7.3	4.4	·	·	·
Taxes Paid **12**	1.5	·	1.4	2.6	1.2	1.6	1.4	1.5	1.6	1.1	·	·	·
Interest Paid **13**	1.5	·	·	0.4	0.8	0.6	0.8	1.0	1.5	1.1	·	·	·
Depreciation **14**	2.9	·	10.1	2.7	2.1	2.6	2.2	2.4	3.4	3.2	·	·	·
Amortization and Depletion **15**	0.5	·	0.1	0.0	0.0	0.0	0.2	0.3	0.3	0.3	·	·	·
Pensions and Other Deferred Comp. **16**	0.6	·	·	0.3	0.3	0.7	0.3	0.4	0.6	0.3	·	·	·
Employee Benefits **17**	1.2	·	·	·	0.4	0.8	1.0	1.3	1.6	1.0	·	·	·
Advertising **18**	1.7	·	8.6	4.7	0.5	0.7	1.3	2.9	2.4	2.9	·	·	·
Other Expenses **19**	10.0	·	44.1	17.2	6.8	10.7	9.7	11.0	10.2	9.0	·	·	·
Officers' Compensation **20**	1.4	·	9.0	7.8	2.8	2.3	2.2	2.1	1.7	0.6	·	·	·
Operating Margin **21**	3.6	·	11.4	15.7	2.6	3.6	5.2	3.7	3.6	4.1	·	·	·
Operating Margin Before Officers' Comp. **22**	5.0	·	20.4	23.6	5.4	5.9	7.3	5.8	5.2	4.6	·	·	·

Selected Average Balance Sheet ($ in Thousands)

Net Receivables 23	2671	·	0	0	501	1553	3078	5657	13537	24542
Inventories 24	2743	·	0	26	672	1473	3176	7929	12606	27270
Net Property, Plant and Equipment 25	4707	·	61	88	723	2450	4688	10264	24239	59518
Total Assets 26	17851	·	74	708	2180	7039	15873	34077	66902	160903
Notes and Loans Payable 27	7028	·	0	56	762	2260	4544	9458	18519	41029
All Other Liabilities 28	3877	·	2	19	680	1683	4094	7374	19546	35694
Net Worth 29	6946	·	72	633	738	3095	7236	17245	28836	84180

Selected Financial Ratios (Times to 1)

Current Ratio 30	1.7	·	6.3	32.3	1.7	1.8	1.7	1.9	1.7	1.7
Quick Ratio 31	0.8	·	4.8	31.6	0.9	1.1	0.9	0.9	0.9	0.9
Net Sales to Working Capital 32	8.4	·	15.8	1.5	14.4	9.8	9.2	8.4	7.8	9.4
Coverage Ratio 33	4.4	·	•	36.6	4.8	8.7	8.1	5.4	5.3	5.5
Total Asset Turnover 34	1.5	·	2.2	1.3	3.5	2.3	2.2	2.2	1.7	1.7
Inventory Turnover 35	6.6	·	502.9	17.1	8.8	7.5	7.7	6.3	6.0	7.4
Receivables Turnover 36	10.9	·	19782.4	14.9	11.5	9.7	13.2	12.8	9.1	12.9
Total Liabilities to Net Worth 37	1.6	·	0.0	0.1	2.0	1.3	1.2	1.0	1.3	0.9
Current Assets to Working Capital 38	2.5	·	1.2	1.0	2.4	2.2	2.4	2.1	2.3	2.4
Current Liabilities to Working Capital 39	1.5	·	0.2	0.0	1.4	1.2	1.4	1.1	1.3	1.4
Working Capital to Net Sales 40	0.1	·	0.1	0.7	0.1	0.1	0.1	0.1	0.1	0.1
Inventory to Working Capital 41	0.9	·	0.0	0.0	1.1	0.8	1.0	0.9	0.9	1.1
Total Receipts to Cash Flow 42	7.6	·	2.6	3.7	12.9	7.5	7.4	7.4	7.3	8.0
Cost of Goods to Cash Flow 43	5.3	·	0.4	1.8	10.0	5.0	5.1	5.0	4.8	5.8
Cash Flow to Total Debt 44	0.3	·	31.8	3.2	0.4	0.6	0.6	0.6	0.4	0.5

Selected Financial Factors (in Percentages)

Debt Ratio 45	61.1	·	2.7	10.6	66.1	56.0	54.4	49.4	56.9	47.7
Return on Total Assets 46	9.8	·	25.5	20.6	13.2	12.8	14.2	12.0	13.9	10.5
Return on Equity Before Income Taxes 47	19.4	·	26.2	22.4	31.0	25.8	27.2	19.4	26.2	16.5
Return on Equity After Income Taxes 48	15.1	·	22.3	22.4	26.8	21.7	24.0	16.4	20.2	13.0
Profit Margin (Before Income Tax) 49	5.1	·	11.4	15.7	3.0	4.8	5.6	4.5	6.6	5.0
Profit Margin (After Income Tax) 50	4.0	·	9.7	15.7	2.6	4.1	4.9	3.8	5.1	3.9

Table I

Corporations with and without Net Income

SOFT DRINK AND ICE

Money Amounts and Size of Assets in Thousands of Dollars

Item Description for Accounting Period 7/02 Through 6/03	Total	Zero Assets	Under 500	500 to 1,000	1,000 to 5,000	5,000 to 10,000	10,000 to 25,000	25,000 to 50,000	50,000 to 100,000	100,000 to 250,000	250,000 to 500,000	500,000 to 2,500,000	2,500,000 and over
Number of Enterprises 1	516	0	0	221	0	27	56	27	11	15	4	6	7

Revenues ($ in Thousands)

Net Sales 2	80605004	0	0	130147	0	810280	2184449	2138127	1010990	3669499	1634458	7084044	61152888
Interest 3	2700727	0	0	31	0	212	845	1631	1306	19780	4021	94617	2576766
Rents 4	205601	0	0	483	0	40	4878	1058	842	701	11693	1712	181968
Royalties 5	1537832	0	0	0	0	0	79	187	0	0	29426	67699	1440441
Other Portfolio Income 6	1366188	0	0	15	0	1947	11358	11935	19551	5186	2935	11416	1296655
Other Receipts 7	4198940	0	0	544	0	8678	8099	28810	38109	44270	72554	256242	3740720
Total Receipts 8	90614292	0	0	131220	0	821157	2209708	2181748	1070798	3739436	1755087	7515730	70389438
Average Total Receipts 9	175609	•	•	594	•	30413	39459	80805	97345	249296	438772	1252622	10055634

Operating Costs/Operating Income (%)

Cost of Operations 10	54.4	•	•	16.7	•	72.3	70.3	68.1	68.1	65.9	58.0	48.4	52.7
Salaries and Wages 11	9.0	•	•	26.6	•	4.6	7.8	11.5	9.4	9.5	13.7	13.4	8.3
Taxes Paid 12	1.6	•	•	4.3	•	1.9	1.5	1.9	2.3	1.5	2.7	1.8	1.5
Interest Paid 13	5.4	•	•	5.9	•	0.8	0.6	0.7	1.6	1.2	4.0	3.9	6.4
Depreciation 14	4.0	•	•	10.4	•	3.3	3.5	4.1	4.3	5.0	5.9	5.3	3.8
Amortization and Depletion 15	0.6	•	•	0.0	•	0.2	0.2	•	0.6	0.5	1.3	0.9	0.6
Pensions and Other Deferred Comp. 16	1.4	•	•	•	•	0.5	0.3	0.6	0.3	0.3	0.0	0.2	1.7
Employee Benefits 17	1.6	•	•	1.0	•	2.8	0.9	1.4	1.9	2.5	0.9	2.3	1.5
Advertising 18	5.5	•	•	0.3	•	1.6	4.6	2.7	0.8	2.1	4.1	1.4	6.5
Other Expenses 19	21.0	•	•	30.6	•	8.9	7.3	7.7	14.7	7.9	14.7	17.9	23.7
Officers' Compensation 20	0.4	•	•	5.4	•	1.7	1.0	1.1	0.5	0.6	0.6	0.4	0.2
Operating Margin 21	•	•	•	•	•	1.4	2.2	0.4	•	2.9	•	4.1	•
Operating Margin Before Officers' Comp. 22	•	•	•	4.3	•	3.0	3.2	1.5	•	3.5	•	4.5	•

Selected Average Balance Sheet ($ in Thousands)

Item													
Net Receivables 23	167137	·	·	2080	58	·	2484	6596	7536	20527	58351	140109	12045388
Inventories 24	6408	·	·	778	15	·	1886	4484	3689	10820	13734	47634	351699
Net Property, Plant and Equipment 25	34042	·	·	4393	439	·	5962	13479	19841	53803	129188	355194	1838623
Total Assets 26	420008	·	·	8966	732	·	15254	36064	70305	147462	358652	1361427	28793546
Notes and Loans Payable 27	75747	·	·	4596	515	·	4467	10267	27657	30745	197560	629981	4663836
All Other Liabilities 28	213932	·	·	1974	12	·	3732	8105	11574	34519	75163	272876	15319168
Net Worth 29	130329	·	·	2396	205	·	7056	17692	31073	82198	85928	458570	8790542

Selected Financial Ratios (Times to 1)

Item													
Current Ratio 30	0.9	·	·	1.1	5.7	·	1.4	1.7	1.8	1.5	0.8	1.4	0.9
Quick Ratio 31	0.8	·	·	0.8	5.2	·	0.8	1.1	1.4	1.0	0.6	1.1	0.8
Net Sales to Working Capital 32	·	·	·	71.0	4.3	·	21.5	11.5	9.4	15.3	·	12.1	·
Coverage Ratio 33	2.6	·	·	4.4	1.0	·	6.5	4.4	1.6	4.9	1.4	3.6	2.5
Total Asset Turnover 34	0.4	·	·	3.3	0.8	·	2.6	2.2	1.3	1.7	1.1	0.9	0.3
Inventory Turnover 35	13.3	·	·	27.9	6.6	·	14.5	12.0	17.0	14.9	17.3	12.0	13.1
Receivables Turnover 36	1.1	·	·	14.6	13.9	·	14.3	11.3	13.4	11.7	8.6	8.4	0.8
Total Liabilities to Net Worth 37	2.2	·	·	2.7	2.6	·	1.2	1.0	1.3	0.8	3.2	2.0	2.3
Current Assets to Working Capital 38	·	·	·	8.3	1.2	·	3.7	2.4	2.3	3.0	·	3.4	·
Current Liabilities to Working Capital 39	·	·	·	7.3	0.2	·	2.7	1.4	1.3	2.0	·	2.4	·
Working Capital to Net Sales 40	0.2	·	·	0.0	0.2	·	0.0	0.1	0.1	0.1	·	0.1	·
Inventory to Working Capital 41	·	·	·	1.6	0.1	·	1.1	0.6	0.4	0.7	·	0.5	·
Total Receipts to Cash Flow 42	3.8	·	·	11.0	5.2	·	11.4	13.8	12.6	9.1	8.2	4.0	3.3
Cost of Goods to Cash Flow 43	2.0	·	·	8.0	0.9	·	8.0	9.4	8.6	6.0	4.8	1.9	1.7
Cash Flow to Total Debt 44	0.1	·	·	0.4	0.2	·	0.4	0.3	0.2	0.4	0.2	0.3	0.1

Selected Financial Factors (in Percentages)

Item													
Debt Ratio 45	69.0	·	·	73.3	72.0	·	53.7	50.9	55.8	44.3	76.0	66.3	69.5
Return on Total Assets 46	5.2	·	·	11.8	4.6	·	10.0	6.8	3.3	10.0	6.2	12.2	4.8
Return on Equity Before Income Taxes 47	10.2	·	·	34.2	·	·	18.3	10.7	2.8	14.3	7.0	26.3	9.4
Return on Equity After Income Taxes 48	6.6	·	·	34.2	·	·	16.3	8.7	0.5	11.7	3.7	17.5	6.0
Profit Margin (Before Income Tax) 49	8.5	·	·	2.7	·	·	3.3	2.4	1.0	4.8	1.5	10.2	9.5
Profit Margin (After Income Tax) 50	5.5	·	·	2.7	·	·	3.0	1.9	0.2	3.9	0.8	6.8	6.0

Table II

Corporations with Net Income

SOFT DRINK AND ICE

MONEY AMOUNTS AND SIZE OF ASSETS IN THOUSANDS OF DOLLARS

Item Description for Accounting Period 7/02 Through 6/03	Total	Zero Assets	Under 500	500 to 1000	251 to 500	501 to 1,000	1,001 to 5,000	5,001 to 10,000	10,001 to 25,000	25,001 to 50,000	50,001 to 100,000	100,001 to 250,000	250,001 and over
Number of Enterprises **1**	380	0	0	141	108	0	47	21	8	0	0	6	0

Revenues ($ in Thousands)

Item Description for Accounting Period 7/02 Through 6/03	Total	Zero Assets	Under 500	500 to 1000	251 to 500	501 to 1,000	1,001 to 5,000	5,001 to 10,000	10,001 to 25,000	25,001 to 50,000	50,001 to 100,000	100,001 to 250,000	250,001 and over
Net Sales **2**	66376007	0	0	86719	642032	0	1848791	1712657	623559	0	0	7084044	0
Interest **3**	2641269	0	0	26	1353	0	842	1403	1300	0	0	94617	0
Rents **4**	156329	0	0	483	0	0	4838	305	696	0	0	1712	0
Royalties **5**	1537640	0	0	0	0	0	79	0	0	0	0	67699	0
Other Portfolio Income **6**	1342773	0	0	15	1996	0	10935	11922	3767	0	0	11416	0
Other Receipts **7**	4149409	0	0	0	554	0	7015	24299	23235	0	0	256242	0
Total Receipts **8**	76203427	0	0	87243	645935	0	1872500	1750586	652557	0	0	7515730	0
Average Total Receipts **9**	200535	•	•	619	5981	•	39840	83361	81570	•	•	1252622	•

Operating Costs/Operating Income (%)

Item Description for Accounting Period 7/02 Through 6/03	Total	Zero Assets	Under 500	500 to 1000	251 to 500	501 to 1,000	1,001 to 5,000	5,001 to 10,000	10,001 to 25,000	25,001 to 50,000	50,001 to 100,000	100,001 to 250,000	250,001 and over
Cost of Operations **10**	53.9	•	•	18.3	75.5	•	73.1	67.4	71.3	•	•	48.4	•
Salaries and Wages **11**	7.2	•	•	25.9	7.7	•	6.8	11.2	6.6	•	•	13.4	•
Taxes Paid **12**	1.5	•	•	3.2	1.5	•	1.4	1.9	2.7	•	•	1.8	•
Interest Paid **13**	5.6	•	•	6.9	0.3	•	0.5	0.6	1.3	•	•	3.9	•
Depreciation **14**	3.3	•	•	11.1	2.1	•	3.4	3.8	4.8	•	•	5.3	•
Amortization and Depletion **15**	0.4	•	•	0.1	•	•	0.2	•	0.4	•	•	0.9	•
Pensions and Other Deferred Comp. **16**	1.4	•	•	•	0.4	•	0.4	0.6	0.3	•	•	0.2	•
Employee Benefits **17**	1.3	•	•	1.4	1.2	•	0.7	1.3	1.6	•	•	2.3	•
Advertising **18**	6.3	•	•	0.3	1.3	•	2.5	2.8	0.7	•	•	1.4	•
Other Expenses **19**	23.8	•	•	27.5	2.7	•	6.8	7.9	7.1	•	•	17.9	•
Officers' Compensation **20**	0.4	•	•	1.3	5.0	•	1.0	1.2	0.8	•	•	0.4	•
Operating Margin **21**	•	•	•	4.0	2.2	•	3.1	1.7	2.4	•	•	4.1	•
Operating Margin Before Officers' Comp. **22**	•	•	•	5.3	7.2	•	4.1	2.9	3.2	•	•	4.5	•

Selected Average Balance Sheet ($ in Thousands)

Net Receivables 23	224160	86	541	2378	6417	6066	140109
Inventories 24	7000	5	249	1846	3862	3204	47634
Net Property, Plant and Equipment 25	32706	354	514	5965	12731	19414	355194
Total Assets 26	516725	790	2034	15355	35597	68646	1361427
Notes and Loans Payable 27	73936	496	611	3690	9109	18110	629981
All Other Liabilities 28	274809	18	518	3393	7859	8513	272876
Net Worth 29	167979	276	904	8272	18629	42022	458570

Selected Financial Ratios (Times to 1)

Current Ratio 30	0.9	8.0	1.0	1.5	1.9	2.4	1.4
Quick Ratio 31	0.8	7.8	0.8	0.9	1.2	1.9	1.1
Net Sales to Working Capital 32	•	3.0	•	17.0	10.3	5.7	12.1
Coverage Ratio 33	2.9	1.7	9.1	9.1	8.0	6.1	3.6
Total Asset Turnover 34	0.3	0.8	2.9	2.6	2.3	1.1	0.9
Inventory Turnover 35	13.5	20.7	18.0	15.6	14.2	17.4	12.0
Receivables Turnover 36	0.9	14.3	7.9	16.6	13.1	25.7	8.4
Total Liabilities to Net Worth 37	2.1	1.9	1.2	0.9	0.9	0.6	2.0
Current Assets to Working Capital 38	•	1.1	•	3.0	2.1	1.7	3.4
Current Liabilities to Working Capital 39	•	0.1	•	2.0	1.1	0.7	2.4
Working Capital to Net Sales 40	•	0.3	•	0.1	0.1	0.2	0.1
Inventory to Working Capital 41	•	0.0	•	0.9	0.5	0.2	0.5
Total Receipts to Cash Flow 42	3.2	4.6	20.5	10.3	11.4	8.0	4.0
Cost of Goods to Cash Flow 43	1.7	0.8	15.5	7.6	7.7	5.7	1.9
Cash Flow to Total Debt 44	0.2	0.3	0.3	0.5	0.4	0.4	0.3

Selected Financial Factors (in Percentages)

Debt Ratio 45	67.5	65.0	55.5	46.1	47.7	38.8	66.3
Return on Total Assets 46	5.6	8.9	9.3	12.7	10.2	8.8	12.2
Return on Equity Before Income Taxes 47	11.3	10.3	18.7	20.9	17.0	12.1	26.3
Return on Equity After Income Taxes 48	7.5	8.5	17.5	18.9	14.6	9.8	17.5
Profit Margin (Before Income Tax) 49	10.8	4.6	2.8	4.4	3.9	6.5	10.2
Profit Margin (After Income Tax) 50	7.2	3.8	2.7	4.0	3.3	5.3	6.8

Table I

Corporations with and without Net Income

BREWERIES

MONEY AMOUNTS AND SIZE OF ASSETS IN THOUSANDS OF DOLLARS

Item Description for Accounting Period 7/02 Through 6/03	Total	Zero Assets	Under 500	500 to 1,000	1,000 to 5,000	5,000 to 10,000	10,000 to 25,000	25,000 to 50,000	50,000 to 100,000	100,000 to 250,000	250,000 to 500,000	500,000 to 2,500,000	2,500,000 and over
Number of Enterprises **1**	182	0	0	.	0	0	10	6	6	0	.	3	0
Revenues ($ in Thousands)													
Net Sales **2**	22027011	0	0	.	0	0	270745	228889	556460	0	.	18223778	0
Interest **3**	38953	0	0	.	0	0	253	411	6121	0	.	30409	0
Rents **4**	36162	0	0	.	0	0	0	224	0	0	.	35556	0
Royalties **5**	200243	0	0	.	0	0	0	2	0	0	.	181755	0
Other Portfolio Income **6**	74841	0	0	.	0	0	79	52	1880	0	.	72825	0
Other Receipts **7**	270664	0	0	.	0	0	767	1092	5599	0	.	272006	0
Total Receipts **8**	22647874	0	0	.	0	0	271844	230670	570060	0	.	18816329	0
Average Total Receipts **9**	124439	.	.	.	.	.	27184	38445	95010	.	.	6272110	.
Operating Costs/Operating Income (%)													
Cost of Operations **10**	41.4	.	.	.	.	.	74.2	64.3	48.4	.	.	38.2	.
Salaries and Wages **11**	8.3	.	.	.	.	.	3.0	4.3	5.1	.	.	9.3	.
Taxes Paid **12**	13.7	.	.	.	.	.	4.8	5.0	8.2	.	.	14.0	.
Interest Paid **13**	2.2	.	.	.	.	.	1.5	0.8	1.2	.	.	2.4	.
Depreciation **14**	5.8	.	.	.	.	.	3.5	5.3	3.4	.	.	6.2	.
Amortization and Depletion **15**	0.2	.	.	.	.	.	0.3	0.3	0.3	.	.	0.2	.
Pensions and Other Deferred Comp. **16**	1.7	.	.	.	.	.	0.7	0.4	0.3	.	.	1.9	.
Employee Benefits **17**	1.1	.	.	.	.	.	0.7	0.9	0.6	.	.	1.3	.
Advertising **18**	8.0	.	.	.	.	.	3.3	1.9	6.4	.	.	7.6	.
Other Expenses **19**	9.9	.	.	.	.	.	6.0	11.4	15.1	.	.	10.5	.
Officers' Compensation **20**	0.7	.	.	.	.	.	0.7	0.9	0.7	.	.	0.8	.
Operating Margin **21**	7.0	.	.	.	.	.	1.3	4.7	10.1	.	.	7.5	.
Operating Margin Before Officers' Comp. **22**	7.7	.	.	.	.	.	2.0	5.5	10.8	.	.	8.3	.

Selected Average Balance Sheet ($ in Thousands)

Net Receivables 23	8262	1488	5632	4976	462675
Inventories 24	4927	2839	2516	3206	286705
Net Property, Plant and Equipment 25	56780	7429	18289	28675	3322609
Total Assets 26	163935	17558	35457	80911	9620128
Notes and Loans Payable 27	68590	5169	20233	9622	4079658
All Other Liabilities 28	41533	5087	3868	11138	2450849
Net Worth 29	53812	7302	11356	60151	3089621

Selected Financial Ratios (Times to 1)

Current Ratio 30	0.6	1.2	2.8	2.5	0.6
Quick Ratio 31	0.4	0.6	2.0	2.0	0.4
Net Sales to Working Capital 32	•	22.3	5.8	5.8	•
Coverage Ratio 33	5.4	2.2	7.8	11.0	5.5
Total Asset Turnover 34	0.7	1.5	1.1	1.1	0.6
Inventory Turnover 35	10.2	7.1	9.7	14.0	8.1
Receivables Turnover 36	20.4	15.5	7.5	18.5	26.3
Total Liabilities to Net Worth 37	2.0	1.4	2.1	0.3	2.1
Current Assets to Working Capital 38	•	5.7	1.5	1.7	•
Current Liabilities to Working Capital 39	•	4.7	0.5	0.7	•
Working Capital to Net Sales 40	•	0.0	0.2	0.2	•
Inventory to Working Capital 41	•	1.9	0.4	0.2	•
Total Receipts to Cash Flow 42	5.7	16.4	6.4	3.8	5.2
Cost of Goods to Cash Flow 43	2.3	12.1	4.1	1.8	2.0
Cash Flow to Total Debt 44	0.2	0.2	0.2	1.2	0.2

Selected Financial Factors (in Percentages)

Debt Ratio 45	67.2	58.4	68.0	25.7	67.9
Return on Total Assets 46	8.9	5.0	6.7	15.6	8.4
Return on Equity Before Income Taxes 47	22.2	6.4	18.3	19.1	21.4
Return on Equity After Income Taxes 48	14.7	5.4	15.9	17.8	13.9
Profit Margin (Before Income Tax) 49	9.9	1.7	5.4	12.4	10.9
Profit Margin (After Income Tax) 50	6.5	1.5	4.7	11.5	7.1

Table II

Corporations with Net Income

BREWERIES

MONEY AMOUNTS AND SIZE OF ASSETS IN THOUSANDS OF DOLLARS

Item Description for Accounting Period 7/02 Through 6/03	Total	Zero Assets	Under 500	500 to 1,000	1,000 to 5,000	5,000 to 10,000	10,000 to 25,000	25,000 to 50,000	50,000 to 100,000	100,000 to 250,000	250,000 to 500,000	500,000 to 2,500,000	2,500,000 and over
Number of Enterprises **1**	171	0	0	•	31	•	0	6	3	0	•	•	0
Revenues ($ in Thousands)													
Net Sales **2**	21819192	0	0	•	193779	•	0	228889	496931	0	•	•	0
Interest **3**	37638	0	0	•	0	•	0	411	4824	0	•	•	0
Rents **4**	36134	0	0	•	0	•	0	224	0	0	•	•	0
Royalties **5**	200243	0	0	•	0	•	0	2	0	0	•	•	0
Other Portfolio Income **6**	74780	0	0	•	0	•	0	52	1880	0	•	•	0
Other Receipts **7**	268083	0	0	•	0	•	0	1092	4307	0	•	•	0
Total Receipts **8**	22436070	0	0	•	193779	•	0	230670	507942	0	•	•	0
Average Total Receipts **9**	131205	•	0	•	6251	•	•	38445	169314	•	•	•	•
Operating Costs/Operating Income (%)													
Cost of Operations **10**	41.0	•	•	•	87.5	•	•	64.3	46.6	•	•	•	•
Salaries and Wages **11**	8.4	•	•	•	4.9	•	•	4.3	5.2	•	•	•	•
Taxes Paid **12**	13.8	•	•	•	•	•	•	5.0	8.2	•	•	•	•
Interest Paid **13**	2.2	•	•	•	0.0	•	•	0.8	1.1	•	•	•	•
Depreciation **14**	5.8	•	•	•	•	•	•	5.3	2.6	•	•	•	•
Amortization and Depletion **15**	0.2	•	•	•	0.0	•	•	0.3	0.3	•	•	•	•
Pensions and Other Deferred Comp. **16**	1.7	•	•	•	•	•	•	0.4	0.3	•	•	•	•
Employee Benefits **17**	1.1	•	•	•	•	•	•	0.9	0.6	•	•	•	•
Advertising **18**	8.1	•	•	•	1.8	•	•	1.9	7.0	•	•	•	•
Other Expenses **19**	9.9	•	•	•	4.0	•	•	11.4	15.2	•	•	•	•
Officers' Compensation **20**	0.7	•	•	•	•	•	•	0.9	0.4	•	•	•	•
Operating Margin **21**	7.1	•	•	•	1.8	•	•	4.7	12.4	•	•	•	•
Operating Margin Before Officers' Comp. **22**	7.8	•	•	•	1.8	•	•	5.5	12.8	•	•	•	•

Selected Average Balance Sheet ($ in Thousands)

Net Receivables 23	8749	95	5632	9455
Inventories 24	5098	268	2390	5167
Net Property, Plant and Equipment 25	59576	0	18289	22960
Total Assets 26	172800	1559	35457	100694
Notes and Loans Payable 27	72447	236	20233	33
All Other Liabilities 28	43835	1269	3868	14419
Net Worth 29	56519	54	11356	86242

Selected Financial Ratios (Times to 1)

Current Ratio 30	0.6	0.2	2.8	3.7
Quick Ratio 31	0.4	0.1	2.0	3.1
Net Sales to Working Capital 32			5.8	5.3
Coverage Ratio 33	5.5	76.6	7.8	14.2
Total Asset Turnover 34	0.7	4.0	1.1	1.6
Inventory Turnover 35	10.3	20.4	10.3	14.9
Receivables Turnover 36	20.6	131.4	13.5	35.0
Total Liabilities to Net Worth 37	2.1	28.0	2.1	0.2
Current Assets to Working Capital 38			1.5	1.4
Current Liabilities to Working Capital 39			0.5	0.4
Working Capital to Net Sales 40			0.2	0.2
Inventory to Working Capital 41			0.4	0.2
Total Receipts to Cash Flow 42	5.6	17.4	6.4	3.5
Cost of Goods to Cash Flow 43	2.3	15.2	4.1	1.6
Cash Flow to Total Debt 44	0.2	0.2	0.2	3.3

Selected Financial Factors (in Percentages)

Debt Ratio 45	67.3	96.6	68.0	14.4
Return on Total Assets 46	9.1	7.1	6.7	25.7
Return on Equity Before Income Taxes 47	22.6	204.3	18.3	27.8
Return on Equity After Income Taxes 48	15.0	160.2	15.9	26.0
Profit Margin (Before Income Tax) 49	10.0	1.8	5.4	14.5
Profit Margin (After Income Tax) 50	6.7	1.4	4.7	13.5

Table I

Corporations with and without Net Income

WINERIES AND DISTILLERIES

MONEY AMOUNTS AND SIZE OF ASSETS IN THOUSANDS OF DOLLARS

Item Description for Accounting Period 7/02 Through 6/03	Total	Zero Assets	Under 500	500 to 1,000	1,000 to 5,000	5,000 to 10,000	10,000 to 25,000	25,000 to 50,000	50,000 to 100,000	100,000 to 250,000	250,000 to 500,000	500,000 to 2,500,000	2,500,000 and over
Number of Enterprises **1**	970	0	0	340	279	108	60	23	16	11	3	7	0
Revenues ($ in Thousands)													
Net Sales **2**	18323860	0	0	208606	234595	306301	496134	636151	727869	1137499	888094	13631194	0
Interest **3**	349514	0	0	201	722	488	593	1543	1432	2573	2989	338930	0
Rents **4**	54784	0	0	0	0	0	2941	208	244	1284	6	50101	0
Royalties **5**	492050	0	0	0	0	0	1132	0	0	0	188	490730	0
Other Portfolio Income **6**	76284	0	0	25814	386	290	1849	1340	1909	3584	138	39529	0
Other Receipts **7**	417514	0	0	9585	14606	7466	2971	10706	21402	31751	2349	315411	0
Total Receipts **8**	19714006	0	0	244206	250309	314545	505620	649948	752856	1176691	893764	14865895	0
Average Total Receipts **9**	20324	•	•	718	897	2912	8427	28259	47054	106972	297921	2123699	•
Operating Costs/Operating Income (%)													
Cost of Operations **10**	57.0	•	•	39.9	29.7	46.1	55.2	56.0	59.5	68.6	50.1	57.5	•
Salaries and Wages **11**	7.6	•	•	5.0	17.8	17.6	9.8	8.6	6.3	4.9	4.4	7.6	•
Taxes Paid **12**	6.5	•	•	6.7	5.6	5.1	9.6	7.4	7.5	4.3	21.6	5.5	•
Interest Paid **13**	5.8	•	•	7.2	4.3	4.0	4.0	1.7	2.5	3.8	2.1	6.8	•
Depreciation **14**	3.7	•	•	6.7	7.4	8.3	8.0	5.1	5.2	5.5	3.1	3.0	•
Amortization and Depletion **15**	1.7	•	•	0.1	0.3	0.4	0.3	0.3	1.6	0.7	0.6	2.0	•
Pensions and Other Deferred Comp. **16**	0.4	•	•	0.1	1.5	0.2	0.3	0.4	0.5	0.4	0.5	0.3	•
Employee Benefits **17**	1.2	•	•	1.6	1.5	1.6	1.0	1.1	0.8	1.0	0.9	1.3	•
Advertising **18**	6.7	•	•	3.0	1.5	2.6	1.8	1.8	2.2	1.3	6.1	8.1	•
Other Expenses **19**	11.9	•	•	18.4	30.2	11.6	13.4	10.7	7.5	8.5	4.0	12.4	•
Officers' Compensation **20**	1.0	•	•	10.5	6.4	2.1	2.8	2.2	1.4	1.5	0.4	0.6	•
Operating Margin **21**	•	•	•	0.8	•	0.4	•	4.8	5.0	•	6.1	•	•
Operating Margin Before Officers' Comp. **22**	•	•	•	11.3	0.3	2.4	•	6.9	6.5	1.0	6.6	•	•

Selected Average Balance Sheet ($ in Thousands)

Item											
Net Receivables 23	2109	•	•	8	263	249	1269	3334	7492	18508	57150	184925
Inventories 24	6306	•	•	334	714	2601	5668	11008	21397	39224	125534	398720
Net Property, Plant and Equipment 25	5649	•	•	242	566	2783	6394	13799	22389	52823	64220	442606
Total Assets 26	39531	•	•	674	2235	6410	15962	34322	65770	153941	299394	4478675
Notes and Loans Payable 27	10727	•	•	474	542	4220	5747	10190	23200	56888	77226	1106318
All Other Liabilities 28	6438	•	•	73	273	521	2749	5817	11802	34292	53842	721812
Net Worth 29	22366	•	•	128	1420	1669	7466	18315	30768	62760	168325	2650545

Selected Financial Ratios (Times to 1)

Item											
Current Ratio 30	1.6	•	•	3.7	7.3	4.7	1.6	2.0	1.8	2.1	2.5	1.4
Quick Ratio 31	0.3	•	•	0.5	2.2	0.8	0.4	0.7	0.5	0.7	0.8	0.3
Net Sales to Working Capital 32	4.5	•	•	2.3	0.9	1.3	2.8	3.4	3.1	2.7	2.6	6.6
Coverage Ratio 33	1.8	•	•	3.5	1.1	1.8	•	5.1	4.4	1.8	4.3	1.6
Total Asset Turnover 34	0.5	•	•	0.9	0.4	0.4	0.5	0.8	0.7	0.7	1.0	0.4
Inventory Turnover 35	1.7	•	•	0.7	0.3	0.5	0.8	1.4	1.3	1.8	1.2	2.8
Receivables Turnover 36	7.8	•	•	43.3	3.0	8.2	5.8	6.5	7.0	5.1	6.6	13.9
Total Liabilities to Net Worth 37	0.8	•	•	4.3	0.6	2.8	1.1	0.9	1.1	1.5	0.8	0.7
Current Assets to Working Capital 38	2.8	•	•	1.4	1.2	1.3	2.5	2.0	2.3	1.9	1.7	3.8
Current Liabilities to Working Capital 39	1.8	•	•	0.4	0.2	0.3	1.5	1.0	1.3	0.9	0.7	2.8
Working Capital to Net Sales 40	0.2	•	•	0.4	1.2	0.7	0.4	0.3	0.3	0.4	0.4	0.2
Inventory to Working Capital 41	1.5	•	•	1.2	0.7	1.0	1.8	1.2	1.5	1.2	1.1	1.8
Total Receipts to Cash Flow 42	7.2	•	•	4.8	4.7	8.2	15.9	6.6	7.0	9.7	10.0	7.0
Cost of Goods to Cash Flow 43	4.1	•	•	1.9	1.4	3.8	8.7	3.7	4.1	6.7	5.0	4.0
Cash Flow to Total Debt 44	0.2	•	•	0.2	0.2	0.1	0.1	0.3	0.2	0.1	0.2	0.2

Selected Financial Factors (in Percentages)

Item											
Debt Ratio 45	43.4	•	•	81.1	36.5	74.0	53.2	46.6	53.2	59.2	43.8	40.8
Return on Total Assets 46	4.9	•	•	22.8	1.8	3.1	•	6.9	7.6	4.5	8.8	4.8
Return on Equity Before Income Taxes 47	3.8	•	•	86.0	0.3	5.2	•	10.3	12.5	4.9	11.9	3.2
Return on Equity After Income Taxes 48	2.5	•	•	78.4		4.0	•	8.8	10.5	3.8	7.5	2.1
Profit Margin (Before Income Tax) 49	4.5	•	•	17.9	0.5	3.0	•	6.8	8.5	3.0	6.8	4.3
Profit Margin (After Income Tax) 50	3.0	•	•	16.3		2.3	•	5.8	7.1	2.3	4.3	2.8

55

Table II

Corporations with Net Income

WINERIES AND DISTILLERIES

MONEY AMOUNTS AND SIZE OF ASSETS IN THOUSANDS OF DOLLARS

Item Description for Accounting Period 7/02 Through 6/03	Total	Zero Assets	Under 500	500 to 1,000	1,000 to 5,000	5,000 to 10,000	10,000 to 25,000	25,000 to 50,000	50,000 to 100,000	100,000 to 250,000	250,000 to 500,000	500,000 to 2,500,000	2,500,000 and over
Number of Enterprises **1**	583	0	0	340	112	0	29	16	11	0	0	0	0
Revenues ($ in Thousands)													
Net Sales **2**	16875526	0	0	208606	129492	0	297621	578209	589722	0	0	0	0
Interest **3**	345444	0	0	201	722	0	444	457	670	0	0	0	0
Rents **4**	51533	0	0	0	0	0	25	118	0	0	0	0	0
Royalties **5**	492050	0	0	0	0	0	1132	0	0	0	0	0	0
Other Portfolio Income **6**	74384	0	0	25814	293	0	561	1079	1878	0	0	0	0
Other Receipts **7**	418332	0	0	9585	14017	0	12402	10720	17862	0	0	0	0
Total Receipts **8**	18257269	0	0	244206	144524	0	312185	590583	610132	0	0	0	0
Average Total Receipts **9**	31316	•	•	718	1290	•	10765	36911	55467	•	•	•	•
Operating Costs/Operating Income (%)													
Cost of Operations **10**	57.3	•	•	39.9	32.2	•	45.9	56.9	54.5	•	•	•	•
Salaries and Wages **11**	7.2	•	•	5.0	13.1	•	8.1	7.5	6.7	•	•	•	•
Taxes Paid **12**	6.5	•	•	6.7	4.2	•	11.8	7.4	8.5	•	•	•	•
Interest Paid **13**	5.9	•	•	7.2	2.3	•	2.4	1.2	2.5	•	•	•	•
Depreciation **14**	3.3	•	•	6.7	6.2	•	6.9	3.7	4.6	•	•	•	•
Amortization and Depletion **15**	1.8	•	•	0.1	0.5	•	0.2	0.2	1.6	•	•	•	•
Pensions and Other Deferred Comp. **16**	0.4	•	•	0.1	2.8	•	0.3	0.4	0.4	•	•	•	•
Employee Benefits **17**	1.2	•	•	1.6	2.2	•	0.9	0.9	0.8	•	•	•	•
Advertising **18**	7.0	•	•	3.0	0.9	•	1.6	1.8	2.6	•	•	•	•
Other Expenses **19**	11.3	•	•	18.4	28.8	•	11.1	9.1	7.2	•	•	•	•
Officers' Compensation **20**	0.9	•	•	10.5	7.9	•	2.8	2.0	1.5	•	•	•	•
Operating Margin **21**	•	•	•	0.8	•	•	8.0	8.8	8.9	•	•	•	•
Operating Margin Before Officers' Comp. **22**	•	•	•	11.3	6.8	•	10.8	10.8	10.4	•	•	•	•

Selected Average Balance Sheet ($ in Thousands)

Net Receivables 23	3090	8	96	1343	4088	8650
Inventories 24	8790	317	893	5778	10568	23106
Net Property, Plant and Equipment 25	7390	242	809	5705	11291	18487
Total Assets 26	60616	674	3092	16596	35022	64582
Notes and Loans Payable 27	15402	474	302	4829	8984	23133
All Other Liabilities 28	9902	73	570	2685	5744	11947
Net Worth 29	35311	128	2219	9082	20294	29502

Selected Financial Ratios (Times to 1)

Current Ratio 30	1.5	3.7	3.8	2.1	2.2	1.4
Quick Ratio 31	0.3	0.5	0.9	0.5	0.8	0.4
Net Sales to Working Capital 32	5.4	2.3	1.6	2.4	3.5	5.5
Coverage Ratio 33	2.0	3.5	5.6	6.3	10.2	5.9
Total Asset Turnover 34	0.5	0.9	0.4	0.6	1.0	0.8
Inventory Turnover 35	1.9	0.8	0.4	0.8	1.9	1.3
Receivables Turnover 36	8.2	151.4	11.2	6.1	17.7	7.4
Total Liabilities to Net Worth 37	0.7	4.3	0.4	0.8	0.7	1.2
Current Assets to Working Capital 38	3.1	1.4	1.4	2.0	1.9	3.5
Current Liabilities to Working Capital 39	2.1	0.4	0.4	1.0	0.9	2.5
Working Capital to Net Sales 40	0.2	0.4	0.6	0.4	0.3	0.2
Inventory to Working Capital 41	1.6	1.2	1.0	1.3	1.0	2.3
Total Receipts to Cash Flow 42	6.8	4.8	3.9	4.6	5.6	5.6
Cost of Goods to Cash Flow 43	3.9	1.9	1.2	2.1	3.2	3.1
Cash Flow to Total Debt 44	0.2	0.2	0.3	0.3	0.4	0.3

Selected Financial Factors (in Percentages)

Debt Ratio 45	41.7	81.1	28.2	45.3	42.1	54.3
Return on Total Assets 46	5.5	22.8	4.8	9.5	12.5	12.3
Return on Equity Before Income Taxes 47	4.6	86.0	5.5	14.6	19.4	22.4
Return on Equity After Income Taxes 48	3.3	78.4	4.8	12.7	17.3	19.3
Profit Margin (Before Income Tax) 49	5.7	17.9	10.5	12.9	10.9	12.3
Profit Margin (After Income Tax) 50	4.1	16.3	9.2	11.2	9.7	10.6

Table I

Corporations with and without Net Income

TOBACCO MANUFACTURING

MONEY AMOUNTS AND SIZE OF ASSETS IN THOUSANDS OF DOLLARS

Item Description for Accounting Period 7/02 Through 6/03	Total	Zero Assets	Under 500	500 to 1,000	1,000 to 5,000	5,000 to 10,000	10,000 to 25,000	25,000 to 50,000	50,000 to 100,000	100,000 to 250,000	250,000 to 500,000	500,000 to 2,500,000	2,500,000 and over
Number of Enterprises 1	96	39	•	•	39	0	5	0	3	0	6	0	4
Revenues ($ in Thousands)													
Net Sales 2	67538277	136369	•	•	371920	0	234636	0	341012	0	2102629	0	64351710
Interest 3	1625127	0	•	•	0	0	0	0	552	0	85682	0	1538893
Rents 4	2140115	0	•	•	0	0	0	0	0	0	1812	0	2138303
Royalties 5	2074961	0	•	•	0	0	0	0	1527	0	38642	0	2034793
Other Portfolio Income 6	1880533	0	•	•	1723	0	6	0	180	0	4928	0	1873696
Other Receipts 7	2916118	163	•	•	1	0	272	0	8811	0	5378	0	2901493
Total Receipts 8	78175131	136532	•	•	373644	0	234914	0	352082	0	2239071	0	74838888
Average Total Receipts 9	814324	3501	•	•	9581	•	46983	•	117361	•	373178	•	18709722
Operating Costs/Operating Income (%)													
Cost of Operations 10	41.6	94.8	•	•	53.6	•	54.7	•	55.5	•	46.1	•	41.2
Salaries and Wages 11	4.8	3.1	•	•	1.9	•	3.6	•	3.1	•	6.4	•	4.7
Taxes Paid 12	14.6	0.1	•	•	38.0	•	20.4	•	16.4	•	14.5	•	14.5
Interest Paid 13	5.8	0.1	•	•	0.1	•	0.7	•	0.5	•	6.6	•	5.9
Depreciation 14	4.2	•	•	•	1.2	•	2.9	•	1.4	•	3.2	•	4.3
Amortization and Depletion 15	0.4	•	•	•	•	•	0.0	•	0.0	•	1.4	•	0.4
Pensions and Other Deferred Comp. 16	1.8	•	•	•	•	•	0.2	•	1.1	•	0.5	•	1.9
Employee Benefits 17	1.9	0.0	•	•	1.0	•	0.1	•	2.3	•	0.8	•	2.0
Advertising 18	3.9	0.0	•	•	0.0	•	1.6	•	1.3	•	1.5	•	4.1
Other Expenses 19	21.7	1.2	•	•	3.8	•	4.0	•	10.9	•	15.1	•	22.2
Officers' Compensation 20	0.6	1.9	•	•	0.1	•	2.8	•	0.8	•	1.8	•	0.6
Operating Margin 21	•	•	•	•	0.3	•	9.0	•	6.8	•	2.3	•	•
Operating Margin Before Officers' Comp. 22	0.8	•	•	•	0.4	•	11.8	•	7.6	•	4.1	•	•

Selected Average Balance Sheet ($ in Thousands)

Net Receivables 23	41008	0		32	2589		57775	123881	751495
Inventories 24	42755	0		1501	4637		25406	60800	895429
Net Property, Plant and Equipment 25	44765	0		323	5463		16295	64563	955320
Total Assets 26	1120704	0		2864	25021		184401	656035	25715331
Notes and Loans Payable 27	299869	0		192	7711		6544	165472	6932220
All Other Liabilities 28	391887	0		2069	3519		21514	238733	9006491
Net Worth 29	428948	0		603	13791		156343	251831	9776620

Selected Financial Ratios (Times to 1)

Current Ratio 30	0.5			1.2	1.8		6.6	3.1	0.4
Quick Ratio 31	0.2			0.0	0.7		4.6	2.0	0.2
Net Sales to Working Capital 32				28.3	7.3		1.6	1.9	
Coverage Ratio 33	4.0			7.5	14.4		22.2	2.4	4.1
Total Asset Turnover 34	0.6			3.3	1.9		0.6	0.5	0.6
Inventory Turnover 35	6.8			3.4	5.5		2.5	2.7	7.4
Receivables Turnover 36	12.6			149.5	16.3		3.1	2.5	14.6
Total Liabilities to Net Worth 37	1.6			3.8	0.8		0.2	1.6	1.6
Current Assets to Working Capital 38				7.5	2.2		1.2	1.5	
Current Liabilities to Working Capital 39				6.5	1.2		0.2	0.5	
Working Capital to Net Sales 40				0.0	0.1		0.6	0.5	
Inventory to Working Capital 41				4.7			1.0	0.3	
Total Receipts to Cash Flow 42	3.0	1002.7		48.6	8.0		5.1	4.8	2.9
Cost of Goods to Cash Flow 43	1.2	950.1		26.0	4.4		2.8	2.2	1.2
Cash Flow to Total Debt 44	0.3			0.1	0.5		0.8	0.2	0.3

Selected Financial Factors (in Percentages)

Debt Ratio 45	61.7			78.9	44.9		15.2	61.6	62.0
Return on Total Assets 46	14.7			3.0	18.4		6.5	8.3	15.0
Return on Equity Before Income Taxes 47	28.8			12.5	31.0		7.3	12.4	29.7
Return on Equity After Income Taxes 48	18.8			12.5	31.0		3.3	9.1	19.4
Profit Margin (Before Income Tax) 49	17.6			0.8	9.1		10.0	8.9	18.1
Profit Margin (After Income Tax) 50	11.5			0.8	9.1		4.5	6.5	11.8

Table II
Corporations with Net Income

TOBACCO MANUFACTURING

MONEY AMOUNTS AND SIZE OF ASSETS IN THOUSANDS OF DOLLARS

Item Description for Accounting Period 7/02 Through 6/03	Total	Zero Assets	Under 500	500 to 1,000	1,000 to 5,000	5,000 to 10,000	10,000 to 25,000	25,000 to 50,000	50,000 to 100,000	100,000 to 250,000	250,000 to 500,000	500,000 to 2,500,000	2,500,000 and over
Number of Enterprises **1**	92	0	•	•	39	0	0	4	•	0	0	0	4
Revenues ($ in Thousands)													
Net Sales **2**	66674147	0	•	•	371920	0	0	310869	•	0	0	0	64351710
Interest **3**	1551569	0	•	•	0	0	0	0	•	0	0	0	1538893
Rents **4**	2138717	0	•	•	0	0	0	0	•	0	0	0	2138303
Royalties **5**	2060500	0	•	•	0	0	0	0	•	0	0	0	2034793
Other Portfolio Income **6**	1879796	0	•	•	1723	0	0	0	•	0	0	0	1873696
Other Receipts **7**	2902565	0	•	•	1	0	0	8893	•	0	0	0	2901493
Total Receipts **8**	77207294	0	•	•	373644	0	0	319762	•	0	0	0	74838888
Average Total Receipts **9**	839210	•	•	•	9581	•	•	79940	•	•	•	•	18709722
Operating Costs/Operating Income (%)													
Cost of Operations **10**	41.7	•	•	•	53.6	•	•	67.5	•	•	•	•	41.2
Salaries and Wages **11**	4.7	•	•	•	1.9	•	•	3.5	•	•	•	•	4.7
Taxes Paid **12**	14.4	•	•	•	38.0	•	•	0.5	•	•	•	•	14.5
Interest Paid **13**	5.7	•	•	•	0.1	•	•	0.4	•	•	•	•	5.9
Depreciation **14**	4.2	•	•	•	1.2	•	•	1.9	•	•	•	•	4.3
Amortization and Depletion **15**	0.4	•	•	•	•	•	•	•	•	•	•	•	0.4
Pensions and Other Deferred Comp. **16**	1.9	•	•	•	•	•	•	1.2	•	•	•	•	1.9
Employee Benefits **17**	1.9	•	•	•	1.0	•	•	2.3	•	•	•	•	2.0
Advertising **18**	3.9	•	•	•	0.0	•	•	1.3	•	•	•	•	4.1
Other Expenses **19**	21.7	•	•	•	3.8	•	•	3.9	•	•	•	•	22.2
Officers' Compensation **20**	0.6	•	•	•	0.1	•	•	1.3	•	•	•	•	0.6
Operating Margin **21**	•	•	•	•	0.3	•	•	16.2	•	•	•	•	•
Operating Margin Before Officers' Comp. **22**	•	•	•	•	0.4	•	•	17.6	•	•	•	•	•

Selected Average Balance Sheet ($ in Thousands)

Net Receivables 23	42267	·	·	32	·	·	42154	·	·	751495
Inventories 24	42835	·	·	1501	·	·	19914	·	·	895429
Net Property, Plant and Equipment 25	44928	·	·	323	·	·	10521	·	·	955320
Total Assets 26	1159053	·	·	2864	·	·	134135	·	·	25715331
Notes and Loans Payable 27	309317	·	·	192	·	·	6943	·	·	6932220
All Other Liabilities 28	403956	·	·	2069	·	·	6611	·	·	9006491
Net Worth 29	445780	·	·	603	·	·	120582	·	·	9776620

Selected Financial Ratios (Times to 1)

Current Ratio 30	0.5	·	·	1.2	·	·	6.5	·	·	0.4
Quick Ratio 31	0.2	·	·	0.0	·	·	4.3	·	·	0.2
Net Sales to Working Capital 32	·	·	·	28.3	·	·	1.4	·	·	·
Coverage Ratio 33	4.1	·	·	7.5	·	·	47.1	·	·	4.1
Total Asset Turnover 34	0.6	·	·	3.3	·	·	0.6	·	·	0.6
Inventory Turnover 35	7.0	·	·	3.4	·	·	2.6	·	·	7.4
Receivables Turnover 36	12.6	·	·	149.5	·	·	3.7	·	·	14.6
Total Liabilities to Net Worth 37	1.6	·	·	3.8	·	·	0.1	·	·	1.6
Current Assets to Working Capital 38	·	·	·	7.5	·	·	1.2	·	·	·
Current Liabilities to Working Capital 39	·	·	·	6.5	·	·	0.2	·	·	·
Working Capital to Net Sales 40	·	·	·	0.0	·	·	0.7	·	·	·
Inventory to Working Capital 41	·	·	·	4.7	·	·	0.4	·	·	·
Total Receipts to Cash Flow 42	3.0	·	·	48.6	·	·	4.4	·	·	2.9
Cost of Goods to Cash Flow 43	1.2	·	·	26.0	·	·	3.0	·	·	1.2
Cash Flow to Total Debt 44	0.3	·	·	0.1	·	·	1.3	·	·	0.3

Selected Financial Factors (in Percentages)

Debt Ratio 45	61.5	·	·	78.9	·	·	10.1	·	·	62.0
Return on Total Assets 46	14.8	·	·	3.0	·	·	11.3	·	·	15.0
Return on Equity Before Income Taxes 47	29.1	·	·	12.5	·	·	12.3	·	·	29.7
Return on Equity After Income Taxes 48	19.1	·	·	12.5	·	·	8.4	·	·	19.4
Profit Margin (Before Income Tax) 49	17.9	·	·	0.8	·	·	19.1	·	·	18.1
Profit Margin (After Income Tax) 50	11.7	·	·	0.8	·	·	13.0	·	·	11.8

Table I

Corporations with and without Net Income

TEXTILE MILLS

MONEY AMOUNTS AND SIZE OF ASSETS IN THOUSANDS OF DOLLARS

Item Description for Accounting Period 7/02 Through 6/03	Total	Zero Assets	Under 500	500 to 1,000	1,000 to 5,000	5,000 to 10,000	10,000 to 25,000	25,000 to 50,000	50,000 to 100,000	100,000 to 250,000	250,000 to 500,000	500,000 to 2,500,000	2,500,000 and over
Number of Enterprises **1**	1925	6	1092	202	392	62	93	28	21	14	9	6	•

Revenues ($ in Thousands)

	Total	Zero Assets	Under 500	500 to 1,000	1,000 to 5,000	5,000 to 10,000	10,000 to 25,000	25,000 to 50,000	50,000 to 100,000	100,000 to 250,000	250,000 to 500,000	500,000 to 2,500,000	2,500,000 and over
Net Sales **2**	18720387	121762	442329	331029	1566999	943677	2407035	1261601	1991128	2239895	2697800	4717133	•
Interest **3**	186911	96	3	426	3875	330	2126	1318	6512	4972	14551	152704	•
Rents **4**	9505	0	0	0	1041	154	1988	369	563	1318	2758	1315	•
Royalties **5**	88217	0	0	0	0	0	19	0	92	753	10518	76835	•
Other Portfolio Income **6**	124860	4674	0	6475	8591	268	6578	816	8178	2099	29440	57742	•
Other Receipts **7**	185933	127	-1	117	5649	2302	9691	5463	14336	52221	58042	37981	•
Total Receipts **8**	19315813	126659	442331	338047	1586155	946731	2427437	1269567	2020809	2301258	2813109	5043710	•
Average Total Receipts **9**	10034	21110	405	1674	4046	15270	26101	45342	96229	164376	312568	840618	•

Operating Costs/Operating Income (%)

	Total	Zero Assets	Under 500	500 to 1,000	1,000 to 5,000	5,000 to 10,000	10,000 to 25,000	25,000 to 50,000	50,000 to 100,000	100,000 to 250,000	250,000 to 500,000	500,000 to 2,500,000	2,500,000 and over
Cost of Operations **10**	74.1	94.5	71.7	72.7	69.2	75.0	79.3	77.8	79.0	72.1	68.6	73.9	•
Salaries and Wages **11**	6.5	6.9	7.0	4.9	5.4	4.0	5.7	3.9	5.3	6.7	7.9	8.0	•
Taxes Paid **12**	1.8	2.0	2.1	2.7	2.0	1.4	1.8	2.2	1.9	1.8	2.3	1.4	•
Interest Paid **13**	2.7	1.5	0.4	0.3	2.0	1.5	1.2	2.1	1.0	3.3	2.9	5.0	•
Depreciation **14**	4.5	1.7	0.5	0.6	3.6	2.4	3.7	4.8	4.4	5.4	6.0	4.9	•
Amortization and Depletion **15**	0.5	0.1	0.0	0.0	0.1	0.2	0.3	0.3	0.5	0.6	1.4	0.4	•
Pensions and Other Deferred Comp. **16**	0.7	0.1	0.1	•	0.3	1.4	0.1	0.2	0.3	0.5	1.0	1.3	•
Employee Benefits **17**	1.2	0.8	0.0	0.1	1.4	0.9	1.4	1.8	0.9	1.8	1.3	0.8	•
Advertising **18**	0.7	0.2	0.2	0.0	0.5	0.6	0.2	0.3	0.4	0.4	0.4	1.6	•
Other Expenses **19**	10.6	41.1	15.5	15.4	12.8	8.1	7.3	7.8	5.8	11.5	15.8	10.0	•
Officers' Compensation **20**	1.6	1.5	6.6	5.5	5.2	1.5	2.2	1.4	1.1	0.8	0.8	0.7	•
Operating Margin **21**	•	•	•	•	•	3.0	•	•	•	•	•	•	•
Operating Margin Before Officers' Comp. **22**	•	•	2.5	3.3	2.7	4.5	•	•	0.6	•	•	•	•

Selected Average Balance Sheet ($ in Thousands)

Net Receivables 23	1398	0	71	219	608	1953	2970	6696	10626	25039	41324	133590
Inventories 24	1420	0	9	91	534	2398	4002	8162	16758	23545	60897	86612
Net Property, Plant and Equipment 25	2687	0	6	164	530	1832	5147	14203	24037	61883	106909	266990
Total Assets 26	10028	0	211	719	2352	7228	15817	34344	73147	153256	333967	1406511
Notes and Loans Payable 27	3496	0	57	158	627	2730	5403	14226	17849	76056	125739	458210
All Other Liabilities 28	2714	0	44	285	672	2474	3826	6624	17047	39382	88099	409913
Net Worth 29	3818	0	110	276	1052	2024	6588	13493	38251	37818	120129	538388

Selected Financial Ratios (Times to 1)

Current Ratio 30	1.7	•	3.0	1.3	1.7	1.7	1.8	1.4	1.9	1.1	1.2	2.3
Quick Ratio 31	0.9	•	1.3	1.0	1.0	0.9	0.9	0.8	1.0	0.6	0.6	1.4
Net Sales to Working Capital 32	6.0	•	3.3	19.8	6.2	7.7	6.5	8.8	5.3	24.1	19.1	3.2
Coverage Ratio 33	0.4	•	•	0.8	0.4	3.2	•	0.0	1.9	0.4	•	0.8
Total Asset Turnover 34	1.0	•	1.9	2.3	1.7	2.1	1.6	1.3	1.3	1.0	0.9	0.6
Inventory Turnover 35	5.1	•	32.2	13.1	5.2	4.8	5.1	4.3	4.5	4.9	3.4	6.7
Receivables Turnover 36	7.0	•	11.5	8.7	6.3	8.1	7.8	6.0	8.5	6.6	6.5	6.4
Total Liabilities to Net Worth 37	1.6	•	0.9	1.6	1.2	2.6	1.4	1.5	0.9	3.1	1.8	1.6
Current Assets to Working Capital 38	2.4	•	1.5	5.0	2.4	2.5	2.2	3.3	2.1	9.3	6.3	1.8
Current Liabilities to Working Capital 39	1.4	•	0.5	4.0	1.4	1.5	1.2	2.3	1.1	8.3	5.3	0.8
Working Capital to Net Sales 40	0.2	•	0.3	0.1	0.2	0.1	0.2	0.1	0.2	0.0	0.1	0.3
Inventory to Working Capital 41	0.8	•	0.1	1.1	0.8	1.1	0.9	1.3	0.9	3.6	2.8	0.4
Total Receipts to Cash Flow 42	16.6	•	10.6	11.7	17.5	10.9	34.4	24.9	19.3	16.8	11.1	13.8
Cost of Goods to Cash Flow 43	12.3	•	7.6	8.5	12.1	8.2	27.2	19.4	15.2	12.1	7.6	10.2
Cash Flow to Total Debt 44	0.1	•	0.4	0.3	0.2	0.3	0.1	0.1	0.1	0.1	0.1	0.1

Selected Financial Factors (in Percentages)

Debt Ratio 45	61.9	•	47.8	61.6	55.3	72.0	58.3	60.7	47.7	75.3	64.0	61.7
Return on Total Assets 46	1.0	•	•	0.5	1.3	9.9	•	0.1	2.5	1.2	•	2.4
Return on Equity Before Income Taxes 47	•	•	•	•	•	24.5	•	•	2.3	•	•	•
Return on Equity After Income Taxes 48	•	•	•	•	•	19.5	•	•	1.4	•	•	•
Profit Margin (Before Income Tax) 49	•	•	•	•	•	3.3	•	•	0.9	•	•	•
Profit Margin (After Income Tax) 50	•	•	•	•	•	2.6	•	•	0.6	•	•	•

Table II

Corporations with Net Income

TEXTILE MILLS

MONEY AMOUNTS AND SIZE OF ASSETS IN THOUSANDS OF DOLLARS

Item Description for Accounting Period 7/02 Through 6/03	Total	Zero Assets	Under 500	500 to 1,000	1,000 to 5,000	5,000 to 10,000	10,000 to 25,000	25,000 to 50,000	50,000 to 100,000	100,000 to 250,000	250,000 to 500,000	500,000 to 2,500,000	2,500,000 and over
Number of Enterprises **1**	1137	0	598	0	269	56	50	14	14	9	0	0	•
Revenues ($ in Thousands)													
Net Sales **2**	11527460	0	331757	0	1106927	878681	1300889	669735	1432612	1351858	0	0	•
Interest **3**	62056	0	0	0	1693	253	1097	920	6209	2122	0	0	•
Rents **4**	5563	0	0	0	699	154	31	100	21	868	0	0	•
Royalties **5**	21870	0	0	0	0	0	0	0	9	102	0	0	•
Other Portfolio Income **6**	95390	0	0	0	7927	12	1582	714	7825	877	0	0	•
Other Receipts **7**	101982	0	0	0	3645	2295	3610	2531	8378	28221	0	0	•
Total Receipts **8**	11814321	0	331757	0	1120891	881395	1307209	674000	1455054	1384048	0	0	•
Average Total Receipts **9**	10391	•	555	•	4167	15739	26144	48143	103932	153783	•	•	•
Operating Costs/Operating Income (%)													
Cost of Operations **10**	70.7	•	78.0	•	68.0	73.2	74.1	75.4	76.9	67.8	•	•	•
Salaries and Wages **11**	6.8	•	1.3	•	4.8	3.7	5.5	3.7	5.8	6.4	•	•	•
Taxes Paid **12**	1.9	•	0.5	•	1.9	1.3	2.1	1.9	2.1	1.4	•	•	•
Interest Paid **13**	1.2	•	0.1	•	0.8	1.3	1.0	1.6	0.5	2.3	•	•	•
Depreciation **14**	3.5	•	0.1	•	2.0	2.2	3.4	3.0	3.4	5.8	•	•	•
Amortization and Depletion **15**	0.2	•	0.0	•	0.1	0.2	0.1	0.1	0.0	0.2	•	•	•
Pensions and Other Deferred Comp. **16**	0.8	•	0.1	•	0.3	1.5	0.2	0.2	0.4	0.5	•	•	•
Employee Benefits **17**	1.2	•	0.0	•	1.4	1.0	1.4	1.6	0.6	1.6	•	•	•
Advertising **18**	0.8	•	0.0	•	0.7	0.7	0.3	0.2	0.5	0.4	•	•	•
Other Expenses **19**	8.7	•	10.2	•	9.6	7.4	6.0	7.6	4.4	10.9	•	•	•
Officers' Compensation **20**	1.9	•	7.8	•	5.5	1.6	2.6	1.6	1.1	0.7	•	•	•
Operating Margin **21**	2.2	•	1.8	•	5.0	6.1	3.3	3.1	4.4	2.0	•	•	•
Operating Margin Before Officers' Comp. **22**	4.1	•	9.7	•	10.5	7.6	5.9	4.6	5.5	2.7	•	•	•

Selected Average Balance Sheet ($ in Thousands)

Net Receivables 23	1320	121	689	2123	2997	6304	10837	29664
Inventories 24	1165	9	435	2059	3964	6612	17151	18542
Net Property, Plant and Equipment 25	2470	8	477	1594	4452	10940	20039	62939
Total Assets 26	8625	152	2231	7137	15540	32693	71613	145067
Notes and Loans Payable 27	1391	43	425	2840	3748	10783	8321	33380
All Other Liabilities 28	1624	80	464	1502	3245	5797	13431	36245
Net Worth 29	5610	29	1341	2795	8547	16113	49862	75443

Selected Financial Ratios (Times to 1)

Current Ratio 30	2.4	1.3	2.7	1.8	2.4	1.9	2.8	2.1
Quick Ratio 31	1.4	1.2	1.8	0.9	1.2	1.1	1.4	1.3
Net Sales to Working Capital 32	4.2	16.0	3.9	7.0	4.7	5.6	3.8	4.5
Coverage Ratio 33	5.0	29.0	8.5	6.0	4.6	3.2	12.6	2.9
Total Asset Turnover 34	1.2	3.7	1.8	2.2	1.7	1.5	1.4	1.0
Inventory Turnover 35	6.2	49.5	6.4	5.6	4.9	5.5	4.6	5.5
Receivables Turnover 36	8.5	9.2	6.1	9.0	7.6	8.5	9.0	6.6
Total Liabilities to Net Worth 37	0.5	4.2	0.7	1.6	0.8	1.0	0.4	0.9
Current Assets to Working Capital 38	1.7	4.0	1.6	2.3	1.7	2.1	1.5	1.9
Current Liabilities to Working Capital 39	0.7	3.0	0.6	1.3	0.7	1.1	0.5	0.9
Working Capital to Net Sales 40	0.2	0.1	0.3	0.1	0.2	0.2	0.3	0.2
Inventory to Working Capital 41	0.5	0.4	0.5	1.0	0.7	0.9	0.6	0.7
Total Receipts to Cash Flow 42	9.0	9.2	7.4	8.6	12.4	10.9	11.6	8.2
Cost of Goods to Cash Flow 43	6.3	7.2	5.0	6.3	9.2	8.2	8.9	5.6
Cash Flow to Total Debt 44	0.4	0.5	0.6	0.4	0.3	0.3	0.4	0.3

Selected Financial Factors (in Percentages)

Debt Ratio 45	35.0	80.9	39.9	60.8	45.0	50.7	30.4	48.0
Return on Total Assets 46	7.0	6.9	13.1	16.8	8.0	7.8	9.1	6.9
Return on Equity Before Income Taxes 47	8.7	35.1	19.2	35.8	11.3	10.9	12.1	8.7
Return on Equity After Income Taxes 48	7.3	29.8	17.5	31.8	10.4	7.9	11.0	8.3
Profit Margin (Before Income Tax) 49	4.8	1.8	6.3	6.4	3.7	3.7	5.9	4.4
Profit Margin (After Income Tax) 50	4.0	1.6	5.7	5.7	3.4	2.7	5.4	4.2

Table I

Corporations with and without Net Income

TEXTILE PRODUCT MILLS

MONEY AMOUNTS AND SIZE OF ASSETS IN THOUSANDS OF DOLLARS

Item Description for Accounting Period 7/02 Through 6/03		Total	Zero Assets	Under 500	500 to 1,000	1,000 to 5,000	5,000 to 10,000	10,000 to 25,000	25,000 to 50,000	50,000 to 100,000	100,000 to 250,000	250,000 to 500,000	500,000 to 2,500,000	2,500,000 and over
Number of Enterprises	1	2676	3	1688	264	467	76	91	46	17	13	0	11	0
Revenues ($ in Thousands)														
Net Sales	2	29244436	103372	1063447	545363	1669157	1018881	2491435	2228235	1549262	2917352	0	15657931	0
Interest	3	78918	1177	11	30	619	401	1663	1288	2466	13870	0	57393	0
Rents	4	10006	0	34	0	29	120	1033	1804	67	1588	0	5331	0
Royalties	5	99726	0	0	0	0	0	0	1231	65	1237	0	97192	0
Other Portfolio Income	6	91075	3	3570	0	2091	529	3253	8612	2328	27190	0	43499	0
Other Receipts	7	456202	170	37250	6150	6301	2192	8954	18360	19602	19108	0	338117	0
Total Receipts	8	29980363	104722	1104312	551543	1678197	1022123	2506338	2259530	1573790	2980345	0	16199463	0
Average Total Receipts	9	11203	34907	654	2089	3594	13449	27542	49120	92576	229257	•	1472678	•
Operating Costs/Operating Income (%)														
Cost of Operations	10	70.7	86.2	74.6	72.0	67.6	72.8	74.9	71.5	76.5	67.0	•	69.8	•
Salaries and Wages	11	7.7	3.4	5.6	8.1	10.1	5.0	6.2	6.8	4.5	7.2	•	8.5	•
Taxes Paid	12	2.4	1.4	4.5	2.0	2.3	2.1	1.8	2.1	1.8	1.6	•	2.6	•
Interest Paid	13	2.9	0.9	0.6	1.3	1.3	0.9	1.0	1.6	1.5	3.3	•	3.9	•
Depreciation	14	3.3	1.9	1.0	0.6	3.0	3.9	2.4	3.2	4.7	3.5	•	3.6	•
Amortization and Depletion	15	0.3	3.1	0.0	0.1	0.1	0.0	0.1	0.3	0.2	0.5	•	0.4	•
Pensions and Other Deferred Comp.	16	0.5	0.3	0.3	•	0.5	0.4	0.3	0.3	0.7	0.2	•	0.6	•
Employee Benefits	17	2.3	0.4	0.7	0.8	1.9	1.0	1.2	1.9	2.2	3.2	•	2.6	•
Advertising	18	0.7	2.6	0.1	0.3	0.4	0.3	0.6	0.5	0.3	1.6	•	0.8	•
Other Expenses	19	11.2	46.9	18.9	14.8	11.1	6.3	7.0	8.1	6.4	11.5	•	12.2	•
Officers' Compensation	20	1.5	0.5	9.1	4.5	4.1	4.8	2.1	1.8	1.1	1.0	•	0.4	•
Operating Margin	21	•	•	•	•	•	2.4	2.5	1.8	•	•	•	•	•
Operating Margin Before Officers' Comp.	22	•	•	•	0.0	1.7	7.2	4.6	3.6	1.0	0.6	•	•	•

Selected Average Balance Sheet ($ in Thousands)

Net Receivables 23	1426	0	73	266	353	1402	3319	6606	14000	28961	193780	•
Inventories 24	1644	0	36	205	498	1656	4461	8737	16840	39807	211043	•
Net Property, Plant and Equipment 25	2167	0	27	32	512	2763	3604	9464	24356	45802	320316	•
Total Assets 26	8880	0	172	672	1897	6430	15620	34152	71689	173808	1404620	•
Notes and Loans Payable 27	3871	0	195	321	811	2187	4260	12347	22542	81751	636205	•
All Other Liabilities 28	2387	0	69	322	390	982	3701	8177	15028	39067	404760	•
Net Worth 29	2622	0	-93	29	696	3261	7659	13628	34119	52990	363655	•

Selected Financial Ratios (Times to 1)

Current Ratio 30	1.1	•	1.1	1.4	1.8	2.0	2.0	1.6	1.9	1.6	0.9	•
Quick Ratio 31	0.5	•	0.7	0.9	0.6	1.2	1.0	0.7	0.9	0.7	0.4	•
Net Sales to Working Capital 32	24.8	•	83.2	10.9	6.8	7.9	5.7	6.6	5.6	7.9	•	•
Coverage Ratio 33	0.7	•	•	•	•	4.0	4.2	3.0	2.0	1.5	0.5	•
Total Asset Turnover 34	1.2	•	3.7	3.1	1.9	2.1	1.8	1.4	1.3	1.3	1.0	•
Inventory Turnover 35	4.7	•	13.1	7.3	4.8	5.9	4.6	4.0	4.1	3.8	4.7	•
Receivables Turnover 36	7.8	•	17.3	10.2	11.0	9.3	7.4	8.2	6.9	7.0	7.6	•
Total Liabilities to Net Worth 37	2.4	•	•	21.8	1.7	1.0	1.0	1.5	1.1	2.3	2.9	•
Current Assets to Working Capital 38	8.3	•	16.4	3.3	2.3	2.0	2.0	2.6	2.1	2.7	•	•
Current Liabilities to Working Capital 39	7.3	•	15.4	2.3	1.3	1.0	1.0	1.6	1.1	1.7	•	•
Working Capital to Net Sales 40	0.0	•	0.0	0.1	0.1	0.1	0.2	0.2	0.2	0.1	•	•
Inventory to Working Capital 41	3.8	•	4.7	1.3	1.1	0.7	0.9	1.2	1.0	1.3	•	•
Total Receipts to Cash Flow 42	13.0	•	13.3	16.4	14.1	12.3	10.6	15.6	8.9	13.0	•	•
Cost of Goods to Cash Flow 43	9.2	•	9.6	11.1	10.3	9.2	7.6	11.9	6.0	9.1	•	•
Cash Flow to Total Debt 44	0.1	•	•	0.2	0.3	0.3	0.2	0.2	0.2	0.1	•	•

Selected Financial Factors (in Percentages)

Debt Ratio 45	70.5	•	154.1	95.6	63.3	49.3	51.0	60.1	52.4	69.5	74.1	•
Return on Total Assets 46	2.5	•	•	•	7.5	7.2	6.8	3.8	6.5	2.1	•	•
Return on Equity Before Income Taxes 47	•	•	77.5	•	11.1	11.1	11.3	4.0	7.3	•	•	•
Return on Equity After Income Taxes 48	•	•	77.5	•	•	10.9	9.2	8.9	3.7	4.7	•	•
Profit Margin (Before Income Tax) 49	•	•	•	•	•	2.7	3.1	3.2	1.5	1.7	•	•
Profit Margin (After Income Tax) 50	•	•	•	•	•	2.7	2.6	2.5	1.4	1.1	•	•

Table II

Corporations with Net Income

TEXTILE PRODUCT MILLS

MONEY AMOUNTS AND SIZE OF ASSETS IN THOUSANDS OF DOLLARS

Item Description for Accounting Period 7/02 Through 6/03	Total	Zero Assets	Under 500	500 to 1,000	1,000 to 5,000	5,000 to 10,000	10,000 to 25,000	25,000 to 50,000	50,000 to 100,000	100,000 to 250,000	250,000 to 500,000	500,000 to 2,500,000	2,500,000 and over
Number of Enterprises **1**	1204	•	502	0	353	48	64	30	10	0	0	6	0
Revenues ($ in Thousands)													
Net Sales **2**	20058014	•	209439	0	1344918	670021	1950550	1543735	975785	0	0	10081066	0
Interest **3**	41469	•	6	0	540	306	479	1171	1409	0	0	28480	0
Rents **4**	4420	•	34	0	0	0	467	1396	0	0	0	2122	0
Royalties **5**	79779	•	0	0	0	0	0	36	20	0	0	79151	0
Other Portfolio Income **6**	61508	•	0	0	1015	527	2100	4986	544	0	0	33777	0
Other Receipts **7**	293840	•	23	0	5218	707	7669	11917	11384	0	0	247716	0
Total Receipts **8**	20539030	•	209502	0	1351691	671561	1961265	1563241	989142	0	0	11272312	0
Average Total Receipts **9**	17059	•	417	0	3829	13991	30645	52108	98914	•	•	1878719	•
Operating Costs/Operating Income (%)													
Cost of Operations **10**	70.2	•	58.0	•	64.0	66.7	74.3	69.3	76.2	•	•	71.7	•
Salaries and Wages **11**	6.1	•	0.9	•	8.4	4.8	6.2	6.4	5.2	•	•	6.0	•
Taxes Paid **12**	2.3	•	4.1	•	2.2	2.0	1.7	2.3	1.8	•	•	2.7	•
Interest Paid **13**	2.2	•	•	•	0.9	0.7	0.8	1.1	1.0	•	•	3.1	•
Depreciation **14**	2.9	•	0.4	•	2.2	2.7	1.9	2.7	4.0	•	•	3.1	•
Amortization and Depletion **15**	0.4	•	•	•	0.1	0.0	0.2	0.3	0.2	•	•	0.5	•
Pensions and Other Deferred Comp. **16**	0.5	•	1.3	•	0.3	0.4	0.3	0.4	0.5	•	•	0.6	•
Employee Benefits **17**	2.4	•	0.1	•	0.9	1.1	1.2	2.3	2.1	•	•	2.8	•
Advertising **18**	0.8	•	0.0	•	0.4	0.4	0.7	0.6	0.4	•	•	0.7	•
Other Expenses **19**	9.0	•	9.3	•	13.6	6.6	6.1	7.1	4.6	•	•	9.3	•
Officers' Compensation **20**	1.5	•	20.0	•	4.3	6.4	2.0	2.1	1.1	•	•	0.4	•
Operating Margin **21**	1.6	•	6.0	•	2.8	8.0	4.8	5.4	2.9	•	•	•	•
Operating Margin Before Officers' Comp. **22**	3.2	•	25.9	•	7.0	14.5	6.8	7.5	4.1	•	•	•	•

Selected Average Balance Sheet ($ in Thousands)

Net Receivables 23	1914	66	390	1509	3736	6371	15023	193588
Inventories 24	1997	17	491	1174	4093	8882	18650	257378
Net Property, Plant and Equipment 25	2938	13	428	2058	3152	8851	23964	360876
Total Assets 26	13456	126	1848	6135	15476	34025	73835	1788318
Notes and Loans Payable 27	4599	348	786	1237	3610	8661	24517	611423
All Other Liabilities 28	3398	20	313	763	3573	7022	11554	495750
Net Worth 29	5459	-242	749	4135	8292	13342	37763	678146

Selected Financial Ratios (Times to 1)

Current Ratio 30	1.1	5.6	2.0	4.3	2.2	2.4	2.0	0.7
Quick Ratio 31	0.5	4.7	0.7	2.7	1.1	1.1	1.0	0.3
Net Sales to Working Capital 32	31.4	4.5	5.4	4.9	5.2	4.4	5.6	•
Coverage Ratio 33	2.9	•	4.5	12.8	7.9	7.1	5.3	2.0
Total Asset Turnover 34	1.2	3.3	2.1	2.3	2.0	1.5	1.3	1.0
Inventory Turnover 35	5.9	14.5	5.0	7.9	5.5	4.0	4.0	5.1
Receivables Turnover 36	12.2	12.6	11.8	9.7	8.6	9.1	6.4	18.7
Total Liabilities to Net Worth 37	1.5	•	1.5	0.5	0.9	0.9	1.0	1.6
Current Assets to Working Capital 38	9.9	1.2	2.0	1.3	1.8	1.7	2.0	•
Current Liabilities to Working Capital 39	8.9	0.2	1.0	0.3	0.8	0.7	1.0	•
Working Capital to Net Sales 40	0.0	0.2	0.2	0.2	0.2	0.2	0.2	•
Inventory to Working Capital 41	4.7	0.2	0.9	0.4	0.8	0.8	0.9	•
Total Receipts to Cash Flow 42	9.3	7.6	7.5	7.6	10.4	8.4	12.8	10.3
Cost of Goods to Cash Flow 43	6.5	4.4	4.8	5.1	7.7	5.8	9.8	7.4
Cash Flow to Total Debt 44	0.2	0.1	0.5	0.9	0.4	0.4	0.2	0.2

Selected Financial Factors (in Percentages)

Debt Ratio 45	59.4	291.3	59.5	32.6	46.4	46.1	48.9	62.1
Return on Total Assets 46	7.9	19.8	8.6	20.4	12.1	11.7	6.9	6.2
Return on Equity Before Income Taxes 47	12.7	•	16.6	27.9	19.7	18.6	11.0	8.1
Return on Equity After Income Taxes 48	10.5	•	15.6	27.7	17.1	15.8	10.6	5.8
Profit Margin (Before Income Tax) 49	4.2	6.0	3.3	8.3	5.3	6.6	4.3	3.0
Profit Margin (After Income Tax) 50	3.4	6.0	3.1	8.2	4.7	5.6	4.1	2.2

Table I

Corporations with and without Net Income

APPAREL KNITTING MILLS

MONEY AMOUNTS AND SIZE OF ASSETS IN THOUSANDS OF DOLLARS

Item Description for Accounting Period 7/02 Through 6/03	Total	Zero Assets	Under 500	500 to 1,000	1,000 to 5,000	5,000 to 10,000	10,000 to 25,000	25,000 to 50,000	50,000 to 100,000	100,000 to 250,000	250,000 to 500,000	500,000 to 2,500,000	2,500,000 and over
Number of Enterprises 1	459	0	240	•	0	44	31	13	3	5	•	•	0
Revenues ($ in Thousands)													
Net Sales 2	5949641	0	137037	•	0	793813	1029042	811473	270730	1910202	•	•	0
Interest 3	57067	0	0	•	0	462	526	527	304	54958	•	•	0
Rents 4	1152	0	0	•	0	0	1	17	8	1117	•	•	0
Royalties 5	15464	0	0	•	0	0	0	0	3583	11881	•	•	0
Other Portfolio Income 6	9415	0	0	•	0	503	188	823	1809	5648	•	•	0
Other Receipts 7	38226	0	4	•	0	230	3548	3393	861	29272	•	•	0
Total Receipts 8	6070965	0	137041	•	0	795008	1033305	816233	277295	2013078	•	•	0
Average Total Receipts 9	13227	•	571	•	•	18068	33332	62787	92432	402616	•	•	•
Operating Costs/Operating Income (%)													
Cost of Operations 10	72.1	•	59.2	•	•	81.3	73.0	75.7	75.8	67.5	•	•	•
Salaries and Wages 11	5.3	•	18.1	•	•	2.8	5.8	4.9	6.3	6.3	•	•	•
Taxes Paid 12	1.9	•	1.3	•	•	1.9	1.7	2.7	1.4	1.8	•	•	•
Interest Paid 13	2.7	•	2.6	•	•	1.6	1.0	1.1	0.9	5.9	•	•	•
Depreciation 14	3.2	•	14.6	•	•	1.8	2.1	3.2	2.3	4.0	•	•	•
Amortization and Depletion 15	0.3	•	•	•	•	0.1	0.2	0.2	0.1	0.8	•	•	•
Pensions and Other Deferred Comp. 16	0.3	•	0.0	•	•	0.1	0.4	0.2	0.1	0.6	•	•	•
Employee Benefits 17	0.8	•	0.0	•	•	1.4	1.3	1.1	0.5	0.5	•	•	•
Advertising 18	1.5	•	•	•	•	0.1	1.3	0.3	1.5	3.4	•	•	•
Other Expenses 19	11.1	•	18.2	•	•	5.2	8.2	5.3	10.0	12.4	•	•	•
Officers' Compensation 20	1.5	•	14.0	•	•	1.1	1.9	1.7	1.2	0.4	•	•	•
Operating Margin 21	•	•	•	•	•	2.8	3.3	3.7	0.1	•	•	•	•
Operating Margin Before Officers' Comp. 22	0.8	•	•	•	•	3.9	5.2	5.4	1.3	•	•	•	•

Selected Average Balance Sheet ($ in Thousands)

Net Receivables 23	1572	0		1992	3366	7833	13182	56599
Inventories 24	2033	0		1582	5498	7590	20802	90846
Net Property, Plant and Equipment 25	1919	128		1437	3663	8064	14586	90359
Total Assets 26	7116	143		6635	16064	30842	70646	305526
Notes and Loans Payable 27	3084	372		3118	4313	10547	12033	153975
All Other Liabilities 28	1411	38		1928	3461	6412	10479	49873
Net Worth 29	2621	-267		1589	8290	13884	48134	101677

Selected Financial Ratios (Times to 1)

Current Ratio 30	1.6	0.0		1.9	2.2	2.6	2.5	1.3
Quick Ratio 31	0.7	0.0		0.9	0.9	1.4	1.2	0.5
Net Sales to Working Capital 32	8.0			8.7	6.2	4.9	3.9	8.9
Coverage Ratio 33	1.5			2.9	4.7	5.0	3.9	1.3
Total Asset Turnover 34	1.8	4.0		2.7	2.1	2.0	1.3	1.3
Inventory Turnover 35	4.6			9.3	4.4	6.2	3.3	2.8
Receivables Turnover 36	8.2			9.2	8.8	8.7	4.2	6.7
Total Liabilities to Net Worth 37	1.7			3.2	0.9	1.2	0.5	2.0
Current Assets to Working Capital 38	2.7			2.1	1.9	1.6	1.7	4.1
Current Liabilities to Working Capital 39	1.7			1.1	0.9	0.6	0.7	3.1
Working Capital to Net Sales 40	0.1			0.1	0.2	0.2	0.3	0.1
Inventory to Working Capital 41	1.2			0.9	0.9	0.6	0.8	2.0
Total Receipts to Cash Flow 42	9.7			14.4	9.6	12.2	10.6	8.0
Cost of Goods to Cash Flow 43	7.0			11.7	7.0	9.3	8.0	5.4
Cash Flow to Total Debt 44	0.3			0.2	0.4	0.3	0.4	0.2

Selected Financial Factors (in Percentages)

Debt Ratio 45	63.2	286.6		76.0	48.4	55.0	31.9	66.7
Return on Total Assets 46	7.4			12.2	9.6	10.9	4.2	9.4
Return on Equity Before Income Taxes 47	6.9	59.7		33.2	14.7	19.3	4.6	6.4
Return on Equity After Income Taxes 48	4.4	59.7		33.2	12.9	17.1	4.1	3.0
Profit Margin (Before Income Tax) 49	1.4			2.9	3.7	4.3	2.5	1.7
Profit Margin (After Income Tax) 50	0.9			2.9	3.2	3.8	2.2	0.8

Table II

Corporations with Net Income

APPAREL KNITTING MILLS

MONEY AMOUNTS AND SIZE OF ASSETS IN THOUSANDS OF DOLLARS

Item Description for Accounting Period 7/02 Through 6/03	Total	Zero Assets	Under 500	500 to 1,000	1,000 to 5,000	5,000 to 10,000	10,000 to 25,000	25,000 to 50,000	50,000 to 100,000	100,000 to 250,000	250,000 to 500,000	500,000 to 2,500,000	2,500,000 and over
Number of Enterprises **1**	118	•	•	•	54	21	26	0	0	0	•	•	•
Revenues ($ in Thousands)													
Net Sales **2**	3108873	•	•	•	301879	443022	825410	0	0	0	•	•	•
Interest **3**	2052	•	•	•	259	458	424	0	0	0	•	•	•
Rents **4**	25	•	•	•	0	0	1	0	0	0	•	•	•
Royalties **5**	3690	•	•	•	0	0	0	0	0	0	•	•	•
Other Portfolio Income **6**	2124	•	•	•	0	0	129	0	0	0	•	•	•
Other Receipts **7**	17683	•	•	•	2	111	4507	0	0	0	•	•	•
Total Receipts **8**	3134447	•	•	•	302140	443591	830471	0	0	0	•	•	•
Average Total Receipts **9**	26563	•	•	•	5595	21123	31941						
Operating Costs/Operating Income (%)													
Cost of Operations **10**	73.8	•	•	•	77.3	84.0	70.5	•	•	•	•	•	•
Salaries and Wages **11**	4.1	•	•	•	3.1	1.1	5.6	•	•	•	•	•	•
Taxes Paid **12**	1.9	•	•	•	1.7	1.2	1.9	•	•	•	•	•	•
Interest Paid **13**	0.9	•	•	•	0.5	0.9	1.1	•	•	•	•	•	•
Depreciation **14**	2.5	•	•	•	1.8	0.7	2.3	•	•	•	•	•	•
Amortization and Depletion **15**	0.4	•	•	•	0.0	•	0.2	•	•	•	•	•	•
Pensions and Other Deferred Comp. **16**	0.2	•	•	•	•	0.0	0.3	•	•	•	•	•	•
Employee Benefits **17**	1.0	•	•	•	0.1	1.7	1.5	•	•	•	•	•	•
Advertising **18**	1.4	•	•	•	0.1	0.1	1.4	•	•	•	•	•	•
Other Expenses **19**	7.2	•	•	•	10.7	1.2	8.1	•	•	•	•	•	•
Officers' Compensation **20**	1.2	•	•	•	1.1	0.6	2.0	•	•	•	•	•	•
Operating Margin **21**	5.3	•	•	•	3.8	8.5	5.0	•	•	•	•	•	•
Operating Margin Before Officers' Comp. **22**	6.5	•	•	•	4.9	9.1	7.0	•	•	•	•	•	•

Selected Average Balance Sheet ($ in Thousands)

Net Receivables 23	3655	165	3122	3565
Inventories 24	2980	427	1192	5181
Net Property, Plant and Equipment 25	3383	284	887	3543
Total Assets 26	14078	1428	7178	15952
Notes and Loans Payable 27	3312	264	1738	4031
All Other Liabilities 28	3307	461	1729	3076
Net Worth 29	7459	703	3712	8845

Selected Financial Ratios (Times to 1)

Current Ratio 30	2.4	1.4	2.9	2.4
Quick Ratio 31	1.3	0.8	1.9	1.1
Net Sales to Working Capital 32	5.1	31.3	6.5	5.4
Coverage Ratio 33	7.5	9.5	11.0	6.0
Total Asset Turnover 34	1.9	3.9	2.9	2.0
Inventory Turnover 35	6.5	10.1	14.9	4.3
Receivables Turnover 36	8.8	17.5	13.5	8.2
Total Liabilities to Net Worth 37	0.9	1.0	0.9	0.8
Current Assets to Working Capital 38	1.7	3.6	1.5	1.7
Current Liabilities to Working Capital 39	0.7	2.6	0.5	0.7
Working Capital to Net Sales 40	0.2	0.0	0.2	0.2
Inventory to Working Capital 41	0.6	1.4	0.4	0.8
Total Receipts to Cash Flow 42	8.8	9.7	10.7	8.2
Cost of Goods to Cash Flow 43	6.5	7.5	9.0	5.8
Cash Flow to Total Debt 44	0.5	0.8	0.6	0.5

Selected Financial Factors (in Percentages)

Debt Ratio 45	47.0	50.8	48.3	44.6
Return on Total Assets 46	13.2	17.1	27.9	13.4
Return on Equity Before Income Taxes 47	21.5	31.2	49.1	20.2
Return on Equity After Income Taxes 48	18.1	22.0	49.1	18.1
Profit Margin (Before Income Tax) 49	6.1	3.9	8.6	5.6
Profit Margin (After Income Tax) 50	5.1	2.8	8.6	5.0

Table I

Corporations with and without Net Income

CUT AND SEW APPAREL CONTRACTORS AND MFRS.

MONEY AMOUNTS AND SIZE OF ASSETS IN THOUSANDS OF DOLLARS

Item Description for Accounting Period 7/02 Through 6/03	Total	Zero Assets	Under 500	500 to 1,000	1,000 to 5,000	5,000 to 10,000	10,000 to 25,000	25,000 to 50,000	50,000 to 100,000	100,000 to 250,000	250,000 to 500,000	500,000 to 2,500,000	2,500,000 and over
Number of Enterprises **1**	7811	952	5293	518	649	189	114	40	28	12	9	3	4
Revenues ($ in Thousands)													
Net Sales **2**	48631990	726403	2559370	848807	4606642	4204282	4825957	2836487	3238562	2664450	4342024	3419687	14359319
Interest **3**	142866	204	104	81	416	137	1753	907	953	3973	8322	41689	84327
Rents **4**	23791	14	12	0	0	68	1706	453	66	869	94	47	20463
Royalties **5**	624810	9837	0	345	127	0	1053	2967	1506	20309	75603	108568	404495
Other Portfolio Income **6**	345502	9115	4236	722	4801	912	4270	1720	16150	3340	4336	80852	215049
Other Receipts **7**	1999822	1285848	23188	61977	8571	5612	66685	14424	175086	23160	78140	3920	253211
Total Receipts **8**	51768781	2031421	2586910	911932	4620557	4211011	4901424	2856958	3432323	2716101	4508519	3654763	15336864
Average Total Receipts **9**	6628	2134	489	1760	7120	22280	42995	71424	122583	226342	500947	1218254	3834216
Operating Costs/Operating Income (%)													
Cost of Operations **10**	67.1	80.5	52.1	76.0	69.2	69.5	73.4	73.9	73.9	65.0	64.3	74.6	61.7
Salaries and Wages **11**	9.3	11.9	17.9	6.6	7.4	8.8	8.4	7.3	7.9	12.3	8.7	7.4	9.7
Taxes Paid **12**	1.9	3.2	2.7	2.1	1.5	2.9	1.8	1.7	1.9	2.3	1.9	1.6	1.5
Interest Paid **13**	1.6	3.6	0.4	0.8	0.8	1.0	0.9	1.3	0.9	2.5	1.4	2.0	2.6
Depreciation **14**	1.2	1.7	1.4	1.3	0.4	1.0	0.8	0.7	1.4	2.0	1.9	1.5	1.3
Amortization and Depletion **15**	0.5	1.9	0.0	0.0	0.1	0.1	0.1	0.1	0.4	0.5	0.7	1.6	0.9
Pensions and Other Deferred Comp. **16**	0.4	4.7	0.0	0.0	0.2	0.2	0.1	0.1	0.3	0.4	0.5	0.4	0.6
Employee Benefits **17**	1.1	0.4	0.4	0.8	0.8	1.0	0.6	0.8	1.2	1.7	1.9	0.3	1.6
Advertising **18**	2.2	2.8	0.5	0.3	1.0	1.6	0.6	0.9	1.2	1.2	3.0	1.8	4.2
Other Expenses **19**	14.9	214.3	21.9	19.0	10.8	7.7	8.2	8.6	8.0	5.6	12.6	15.0	14.3
Officers' Compensation **20**	2.2	2.3	3.1	2.8	4.5	3.2	3.1	2.5	4.6	1.5	1.6	0.4	0.8
Operating Margin **21**	•	•	•	•	3.2	3.2	2.0	2.0	•	5.0	1.7	•	0.8
Operating Margin Before Officers' Comp. **22**	•	•	2.6	•	7.8	6.4	5.2	4.5	2.8	6.5	3.2	•	1.6

Selected Average Balance Sheet ($ in Thousands)

Net Receivables 23	779	0	19	188	524	1904	3782	7191	14811	28852	122871	140754	545152
Inventories 24	920	0	29	79	692	3115	6080	15101	19850	53721	75689	328161	448221
Net Property, Plant and Equipment 25	431	0	21	196	203	1333	1819	2593	7904	25654	44268	76712	325363
Total Assets 26	4198	0	94	611	2252	8207	15872	32015	70283	154588	368421	880740	4021817
Notes and Loans Payable 27	1195	0	43	130	612	1515	4263	11161	12707	68585	75923	735005	838542
All Other Liabilities 28	1397	0	44	298	743	2746	5134	8437	14372	31733	92775	363776	1471836
Net Worth 29	1606	0	7	183	897	3945	6475	12418	43203	54270	199724	-218041	1711440

Selected Financial Ratios (Times to 1)

Current Ratio 30	1.8	•	2.1	1.1	2.1	1.5	1.7	2.1	2.6	2.0	2.8	1.8	1.5
Quick Ratio 31	0.9	•	1.1	0.8	1.1	0.6	0.7	0.8	1.2	1.0	1.7	1.2	0.7
Net Sales to Working Capital 32	6.1	•	14.8	41.6	7.4	10.6	8.5	5.3	4.0	5.0	3.0	4.2	7.0
Coverage Ratio 33	3.6	•	2.5	•	5.4	4.4	5.1	3.2	5.4	3.9	5.0	1.2	4.5
Total Asset Turnover 34	1.5	•	5.1	2.7	3.2	2.7	2.7	2.2	1.6	1.4	1.3	1.3	0.9
Inventory Turnover 35	4.5	•	8.7	15.8	7.1	5.0	5.1	3.5	4.3	2.7	4.1	2.6	4.9
Receivables Turnover 36	7.4	•	26.4	8.4	13.7	11.8	11.0	9.0	9.4	4.6	4.8	2.6	8.1
Total Liabilities to Net Worth 37	1.6	•	11.9	2.3	1.5	1.1	1.5	1.6	0.6	1.8	0.8	•	1.3
Current Assets to Working Capital 38	2.2	•	1.9	9.8	1.9	2.9	2.5	1.9	1.6	2.0	1.5	2.2	2.9
Current Liabilities to Working Capital 39	1.2	•	0.9	8.8	0.9	1.9	1.5	0.9	0.6	1.0	0.5	1.2	1.9
Working Capital to Net Sales 40	0.2	•	0.1	0.0	0.1	0.1	0.1	0.2	0.3	0.2	0.3	0.2	0.1
Inventory to Working Capital 41	0.8	•	0.9	2.4	0.8	1.6	1.1	1.1	0.8	0.8	0.5	0.7	0.9
Total Receipts to Cash Flow 42	6.5	•	6.8	7.9	8.2	11.2	9.9	10.4	9.6	10.0	6.8	8.0	5.5
Cost of Goods to Cash Flow 43	4.3	0.7	3.5	6.0	5.7	7.8	7.3	7.7	7.1	6.5	4.4	6.0	3.4
Cash Flow to Total Debt 44	0.4	0.6	0.8	0.5	0.6	0.5	0.5	0.3	0.4	0.2	0.4	0.1	0.3

Selected Financial Factors (in Percentages)

Debt Ratio 45	61.7	•	92.2	70.1	60.2	51.9	59.2	61.2	38.5	64.9	45.8	124.8	57.4
Return on Total Assets 46	8.7	•	4.9	•	13.3	11.7	12.0	8.9	8.4	13.9	9.1	3.1	10.3
Return on Equity Before Income Taxes 47	16.5	•	38.3	•	27.2	18.8	23.6	15.7	11.1	29.4	13.5	•	18.8
Return on Equity After Income Taxes 48	11.5	•	33.3	•	26.8	18.0	22.1	13.5	9.8	22.7	10.6	2.3	12.3
Profit Margin (Before Income Tax) 49	4.2	•	0.6	•	3.4	3.3	3.6	2.7	4.1	7.2	5.6	0.4	8.9
Profit Margin (After Income Tax) 50	3.0	•	0.5	•	3.4	3.2	3.4	2.4	3.7	5.6	4.4	•	5.8

Table II

Corporations with Net Income

CUT AND SEW APPAREL CONTRACTORS AND MFRS.

MONEY AMOUNTS AND SIZE OF ASSETS IN THOUSANDS OF DOLLARS

Item Description for Accounting Period 7/02 Through 6/03	Total	Zero Assets	Under 500	500 to 1,000	1,000 to 5,000	5,000 to 10,000	10,000 to 25,000	25,000 to 50,000	50,000 to 100,000	100,000 to 250,000	250,000 to 500,000	500,000 to 2,500,000	2,500,000 and over
Number of Enterprises **1**	3297	0	1760	0	484	181	83	31	20	9	0	0	4
Revenues ($ in Thousands)													
Net Sales **2**	40107170	0	978883	0	3906604	4113971	3877032	2174830	2571365	2132020	0	0	14359319
Interest **3**	101006	0	93	0	325	35	873	506	736	3373	0	0	84327
Rents **4**	23441	0	0	0	0	0	1703	418	66	779	0	0	20463
Royalties **5**	453575	0	0	0	0	0	4	130	0	19330	0	0	404495
Other Portfolio Income **6**	257200	0	3861	0	469	603	3516	1018	15810	3340	0	0	215049
Other Receipts **7**	602078	0	16	0	7828	5335	61481	6440	148726	19133	0	0	253211
Total Receipts **8**	41544470	0	982553	0	3915226	4119944	3944609	2183342	2736703	2177975	0	0	15336864
Average Total Receipts **9**	12601	•	558	•	8089	22762	47525	70430	136835	241997	•	•	3834216
Operating Costs/Operating Income (%)													
Cost of Operations **10**	65.7	•	16.0	•	68.8	69.3	72.8	71.7	73.1	60.8	•	•	61.7
Salaries and Wages **11**	9.3	•	34.0	•	7.1	8.7	8.2	6.4	7.2	13.0	•	•	9.7
Taxes Paid **12**	1.8	•	4.6	•	1.6	2.9	1.6	1.7	1.8	2.8	•	•	1.5
Interest Paid **13**	1.5	•	0.4	•	0.4	1.0	0.7	1.1	0.4	2.5	•	•	2.6
Depreciation **14**	1.1	•	2.7	•	0.3	0.9	0.7	0.7	1.2	2.1	•	•	1.3
Amortization and Depletion **15**	0.4	•	0.0	•	0.0	0.1	0.0	0.1	0.1	0.5	•	•	0.9
Pensions and Other Deferred Comp. **16**	0.4	•	0.0	•	0.2	0.2	0.1	0.2	0.4	0.5	•	•	0.6
Employee Benefits **17**	1.1	•	0.2	•	0.9	0.9	0.6	0.6	0.9	2.1	•	•	1.6
Advertising **18**	2.2	•	0.0	•	0.9	1.6	0.6	0.8	1.0	1.3	•	•	4.2
Other Expenses **19**	11.0	•	32.4	•	9.4	7.4	7.3	8.3	7.4	5.5	•	•	14.3
Officers' Compensation **20**	2.3	•	4.0	•	4.9	3.2	3.4	2.7	5.2	1.6	•	•	0.8
Operating Margin **21**	3.0	•	5.8	•	5.4	3.7	4.0	5.9	1.3	7.2	•	•	0.8
Operating Margin Before Officers' Comp. **22**	5.3	•	9.7	•	10.3	7.0	7.4	8.6	6.5	8.8	•	•	1.6

Selected Average Balance Sheet ($ in Thousands)

Net Receivables 23	1536	18	589	1913	4061	7245	16587	30207	545152
Inventories 24	1678	31	701	3360	6261	14942	19757	52611	448221
Net Property, Plant and Equipment 25	809	40	245	1311	1538	2408	7804	29896	325363
Total Assets 26	8442	96	2341	8195	15905	30953	69830	162441	4021817
Notes and Loans Payable 27	1809	42	587	1292	3553	7639	7080	75211	838542
All Other Liabilities 28	2692	12	747	2721	4945	8491	14961	23909	1471836
Net Worth 29	3941	43	1007	4182	7407	14823	47789	63320	1711440

Selected Financial Ratios (Times to 1)

Current Ratio 30	2.0	2.0	2.4	1.6	1.8	2.2	2.8	2.5	1.5
Quick Ratio 31	1.0	1.4	1.3	0.6	0.7	0.8	1.4	1.4	0.7
Net Sales to Working Capital 32	5.7	25.2	7.1	10.3	8.0	4.9	3.9	4.1	7.0
Coverage Ratio 33	5.8	18.5	13.8	5.1	9.4	6.8	21.2	4.8	4.5
Total Asset Turnover 34	1.4	5.8	3.4	2.8	2.9	2.3	1.8	1.5	0.9
Inventory Turnover 35	4.8	2.9	7.9	4.7	5.4	3.4	4.8	2.7	4.9
Receivables Turnover 36	7.3	25.1	15.2	23.8	11.8	9.1	10.8	4.3	8.1
Total Liabilities to Net Worth 37	1.1	1.3	1.3	1.0	1.1	1.1	0.5	1.6	1.3
Current Assets to Working Capital 38	2.1	2.0	1.7	2.8	2.2	1.8	1.6	1.6	2.9
Current Liabilities to Working Capital 39	1.1	1.0	0.7	1.8	1.2	0.8	0.6	0.6	1.9
Working Capital to Net Sales 40	0.2	0.0	0.1	0.1	0.1	0.2	0.3	0.2	0.1
Inventory to Working Capital 41	0.8	0.6	0.7	1.5	1.0	1.1	0.7	0.6	0.9
Total Receipts to Cash Flow 42	6.7	3.5	7.7	10.8	8.8	7.5	7.4	8.4	5.5
Cost of Goods to Cash Flow 43	4.4	0.6	5.3	7.5	6.4	5.4	5.4	5.1	3.4
Cash Flow to Total Debt 44	0.4	3.0	0.8	0.5	0.6	0.6	0.8	0.3	0.3

Selected Financial Factors (in Percentages)

Debt Ratio 45	53.3	55.6	57.0	49.0	53.4	52.1	31.6	61.0	57.4
Return on Total Assets 46	12.4	37.7	20.9	13.4	18.9	16.6	14.9	17.5	10.3
Return on Equity Before Income Taxes 47	22.0	80.1	45.0	21.1	36.2	29.6	20.7	35.6	18.8
Return on Equity After Income Taxes 48	17.2	77.6	44.4	20.4	34.5	27.3	19.1	27.9	12.3
Profit Margin (Before Income Tax) 49	7.1	6.2	5.6	3.9	5.7	6.3	7.7	9.5	8.9
Profit Margin (After Income Tax) 50	5.6	6.0	5.5	3.8	5.5	5.8	7.1	7.5	5.8

Table I

Corporations with and without Net Income

APPAREL ACCESSORIES AND OTHER APPAREL

MONEY AMOUNTS AND SIZE OF ASSETS IN THOUSANDS OF DOLLARS

Item Description for Accounting Period 7/02 Through 6/03	Total	Zero Assets	Under 500	500 to 1,000	1,000 to 5,000	5,000 to 10,000	10,000 to 25,000	25,000 to 50,000	50,000 to 100,000	100,000 to 250,000	250,000 to 500,000	500,000 to 2,500,000	2,500,000 and over
Number of Enterprises 1	4353	0	3223	519	0	75	53	15	14	4	•	•	•
Revenues ($ in Thousands)													
Net Sales 2	11942657	0	1762584	1352990	0	1348915	1522908	965803	1867400	708741	•	•	•
Interest 3	11333	0	0	91	0	1112	656	467	3111	2953	•	•	•
Rents 4	5385	0	122	0	0	0	374	61	124	2227	•	•	•
Royalties 5	1043	0	0	0	0	0	249	0	0	794	•	•	•
Other Portfolio Income 6	9426	0	0	0	0	32	1134	74	1201	3153	•	•	•
Other Receipts 7	94756	0	5128	237	0	1428	32478	7329	9092	17023	•	•	•
Total Receipts 8	12064600	0	1767834	1353318	0	1351487	1557799	973734	1880928	734891	•	•	•
Average Total Receipts 9	2772	•	549	2608	•	18020	29392	64916	134352	183723	•	•	•
Operating Costs/Operating Income (%)													
Cost of Operations 10	67.5	•	60.1	61.1	•	70.6	69.6	72.1	69.4	63.5	•	•	•
Salaries and Wages 11	7.5	•	7.9	10.8	•	6.3	8.7	5.4	7.0	10.2	•	•	•
Taxes Paid 12	2.5	•	2.0	2.2	•	4.6	2.8	2.7	2.5	2.0	•	•	•
Interest Paid 13	1.3	•	0.6	0.8	•	0.5	1.3	1.5	2.2	2.2	•	•	•
Depreciation 14	1.3	•	1.1	0.3	•	0.5	1.4	2.5	1.6	2.5	•	•	•
Amortization and Depletion 15	0.1	•	0.0	0.0	•	0.1	0.2	0.1	0.3	0.8	•	•	•
Pensions and Other Deferred Comp. 16	0.3	•	0.1	0.8	•	0.4	0.2	0.2	0.2	0.6	•	•	•
Employee Benefits 17	0.9	•	0.4	1.2	•	0.5	1.1	0.9	1.0	1.6	•	•	•
Advertising 18	1.1	•	1.2	1.1	•	0.2	1.1	0.6	2.0	1.6	•	•	•
Other Expenses 19	12.6	•	23.5	9.4	•	9.9	9.7	9.6	9.5	12.8	•	•	•
Officers' Compensation 20	2.9	•	2.1	6.4	•	2.4	3.0	2.1	3.0	1.6	•	•	•
Operating Margin 21	2.0	•	1.1	5.8	•	4.0	0.7	2.4	1.4	0.5	•	•	•
Operating Margin Before Officers' Comp. 22	4.9	•	3.2	12.2	•	6.4	3.8	4.5	4.3	2.1	•	•	•

Selected Average Balance Sheet ($ in Thousands)

Net Receivables 23	275	34	191	2286	5288	8058	14956	17940
Inventories 24	364	51	198	1677	5294	14944	22769	45928
Net Property, Plant and Equipment 25	169	12	42	1170	2139	6771	11496	19769
Total Assets 26	1174	131	744	7593	16331	36545	68804	131130
Notes and Loans Payable 27	722	91	274	1981	5826	11895	35432	32768
All Other Liabilities 28	371	41	219	2384	3818	6987	19087	45575
Net Worth 29	80	-0	252	3229	6687	17663	14285	52787

Selected Financial Ratios (Times to 1)

Current Ratio 30	2.0	1.9	3.1	1.8	1.9	2.0	1.7	2.2
Quick Ratio 31	0.9	1.0	1.7	1.1	1.0	0.8	0.6	1.2
Net Sales to Working Capital 32	6.2	10.0	5.5	6.8	4.7	4.9	6.7	3.6
Coverage Ratio 33	3.3	3.4	8.1	8.6	3.2	3.2	1.9	2.9
Total Asset Turnover 34	2.3	4.2	3.5	2.4	1.8	1.8	1.9	1.4
Inventory Turnover 35	5.1	6.5	8.0	7.6	3.8	3.1	4.1	2.5
Receivables Turnover 36	10.1	32.4	21.2	9.7	5.6	6.4	10.0	6.9
Total Liabilities to Net Worth 37	13.7	·	2.0	1.4	1.4	1.1	3.8	1.5
Current Assets to Working Capital 38	2.0	2.2	1.5	2.2	2.1	2.0	2.4	1.8
Current Liabilities to Working Capital 39	1.0	1.2	0.5	1.2	1.1	1.0	1.4	0.8
Working Capital to Net Sales 40	0.2	0.1	0.2	0.1	0.2	0.2	0.1	0.3
Inventory to Working Capital 41	0.9	0.9	0.7	0.7	0.8	0.9	1.3	0.7
Total Receipts to Cash Flow 42	8.0	5.1	8.1	7.9	9.1	9.2	10.3	8.6
Cost of Goods to Cash Flow 43	5.4	3.0	5.0	5.6	6.3	6.6	7.1	5.4
Cash Flow to Total Debt 44	0.3	0.8	0.7	0.5	0.3	0.4	0.2	0.3

Selected Financial Factors (in Percentages)

Debt Ratio 45	93.2	100.2	66.2	57.5	59.1	51.7	79.2	59.7
Return on Total Assets 46	10.0	8.4	23.2	11.2	7.7	8.3	8.4	8.7
Return on Equity Before Income Taxes 47	103.3	·	60.2	23.3	13.0	11.8	19.4	14.1
Return on Equity After Income Taxes 48	94.3	·	58.7	22.0	12.1	10.1	15.9	9.4
Profit Margin (Before Income Tax) 49	3.0	1.4	5.8	4.2	3.0	3.2	2.1	4.2
Profit Margin (After Income Tax) 50	2.7	1.4	5.7	3.9	2.8	2.8	1.7	2.8

Table II

Corporations with Net Income

APPAREL ACCESSORIES AND OTHER APPAREL

MONEY AMOUNTS AND SIZE OF ASSETS IN THOUSANDS OF DOLLARS

Item Description for Accounting Period 7/02 Through 6/03	Total	Zero Assets	Under 500	500 to 1,000	1,000 to 5,000	5,000 to 10,000	10,000 to 25,000	25,000 to 50,000	50,000 to 100,000	100,000 to 250,000	250,000 to 500,000	500,000 to 2,500,000	2,500,000 and over
Number of Enterprises 1	3044	0	2057	0	349	56	36	0	0	0	•	•	•
Revenues ($ in Thousands)													
Net Sales 2	9846674	0	1242927	0	1993254	1013629	1227014	0	0	0	•	•	•
Interest 3	7159	0	0	0	1237	953	270	0	0	0	•	•	•
Rents 4	5169	0	122	0	2457	0	240	0	0	0	•	•	•
Royalties 5	831	0	0	0	0	0	37	0	0	0	•	•	•
Other Portfolio Income 6	7964	0	0	0	2534	32	997	0	0	0	•	•	•
Other Receipts 7	77918	0	5129	0	21363	1007	31594	0	0	0	•	•	•
Total Receipts 8	9945715	0	1248178	0	2020845	1015621	1260152	0	0	0	•	•	•
Average Total Receipts 9	3267	•	607	•	5790	18136	35004	•	•	•	•	•	•
Operating Costs/Operating Income (%)													
Cost of Operations 10	66.4	•	55.7	•	72.4	64.4	69.3	•	•	•	•	•	•
Salaries and Wages 11	7.5	•	10.0	•	5.1	7.1	8.3	•	•	•	•	•	•
Taxes Paid 12	2.5	•	1.5	•	1.4	6.0	2.6	•	•	•	•	•	•
Interest Paid 13	1.0	•	0.4	•	1.1	0.6	1.1	•	•	•	•	•	•
Depreciation 14	1.0	•	0.5	•	0.8	0.5	1.0	•	•	•	•	•	•
Amortization and Depletion 15	0.1	•	•	•	0.0	0.2	0.2	•	•	•	•	•	•
Pensions and Other Deferred Comp. 16	0.3	•	0.1	•	0.1	0.5	0.2	•	•	•	•	•	•
Employee Benefits 17	0.8	•	0.6	•	0.3	0.5	1.0	•	•	•	•	•	•
Advertising 18	1.0	•	1.0	•	0.8	0.2	0.8	•	•	•	•	•	•
Other Expenses 19	11.7	•	23.8	•	11.4	11.5	9.0	•	•	•	•	•	•
Officers' Compensation 20	3.1	•	1.6	•	2.7	2.2	3.3	•	•	•	•	•	•
Operating Margin 21	4.5	•	4.8	•	3.9	6.3	3.2	•	•	•	•	•	•
Operating Margin Before Officers' Comp. 22	7.6	•	6.4	•	6.6	8.5	6.6	•	•	•	•	•	•

Selected Average Balance Sheet ($ in Thousands)

Net Receivables 23	300	27	284	1752	5151
Inventories 24	361	47	395	1619	5424
Net Property, Plant and Equipment 25	165	7	164	1514	1780
Total Assets 26	1282	118	1679	8019	16361
Notes and Loans Payable 27	400	84	330	2261	4998
All Other Liabilities 28	320	31	516	1126	4297
Net Worth 29	562	3	832	4632	7066

Selected Financial Ratios (Times to 1)

Current Ratio 30	2.4	3.1	2.2	2.6	1.9
Quick Ratio 31	1.1	1.9	0.8	1.6	1.0
Net Sales to Working Capital 32	5.5	8.0	7.7	4.9	5.4
Coverage Ratio 33	6.4	13.2	5.7	11.5	6.5
Total Asset Turnover 34	2.5	5.1	3.4	2.3	2.1
Inventory Turnover 35	5.9	7.2	10.5	7.2	4.4
Receivables Turnover 36	12.1	14.8	21.1	13.4	7.1
Total Liabilities to Net Worth 37	1.3	36.1	1.0	0.7	1.3
Current Assets to Working Capital 38	1.7	1.5	1.8	1.6	2.1
Current Liabilities to Working Capital 39	0.7	0.5	0.8	0.6	1.1
Working Capital to Net Sales 40	0.2	0.1	0.1	0.2	0.2
Inventory to Working Capital 41	0.7	0.5	0.7	0.5	0.9
Total Receipts to Cash Flow 42	6.8	4.2	7.0	6.1	7.5
Cost of Goods to Cash Flow 43	4.5	2.4	5.1	3.9	5.2
Cash Flow to Total Debt 44	0.7	1.2	1.0	0.9	0.5

Selected Financial Factors (in Percentages)

Debt Ratio 45	56.2	97.3	50.4	42.2	56.8
Return on Total Assets 46	16.4	28.7	21.6	16.1	14.6
Return on Equity Before Income Taxes 47	31.6	983.8	35.9	25.5	28.7
Return on Equity After Income Taxes 48	29.8	981.1	35.3	24.3	27.5
Profit Margin (Before Income Tax) 49	5.5	5.2	5.2	6.5	5.9
Profit Margin (After Income Tax) 50	5.2	5.2	5.2	6.2	5.7

Table I

Corporations with and without Net Income

LEATHER AND ALLIED PRODUCT MANUFACTURING

MONEY AMOUNTS AND SIZE OF ASSETS IN THOUSANDS OF DOLLARS

Item Description for Accounting Period 7/02 Through 6/03	Total	Zero Assets	Under 500	500 to 1,000	1,000 to 5,000	5,000 to 10,000	10,000 to 25,000	25,000 to 50,000	50,000 to 100,000	100,000 to 250,000	250,000 to 500,000	500,000 to 2,500,000	2,500,000 and over
Number of Enterprises 1	1685	878	415	62	200	64	35	11	8	6	7	0	0
Revenues ($ in Thousands)													
Net Sales 2	9525989	35972	102235	39397	752877	863651	904117	815707	1135320	1151398	3725314	0	0
Interest 3	32859	8081	0	139	114	130	2177	802	202	2711	18503	0	0
Rents 4	6380	0	0	2275	1099	0	331	251	764	155	1504	0	0
Royalties 5	68139	0	0	0	0	0	501	230	808	12743	53856	0	0
Other Portfolio Income 6	20086	9	0	420	1103	21	1094	606	1163	584	15087	0	0
Other Receipts 7	105183	6489	30	26	6770	4340	3967	4011	22534	9620	47399	0	0
Total Receipts 8	9758636	50551	102265	42257	761963	868142	912187	821607	1160791	1177211	3861663	0	0
Average Total Receipts 9	5791	58	246	682	3810	13565	26062	74692	145099	196202	551666	•	•
Operating Costs/Operating Income (%)													
Cost of Operations 10	65.0	76.9	46.8	63.7	66.6	66.9	69.6	68.3	70.1	59.8	62.9	•	•
Salaries and Wages 11	9.5	2.0	10.7	13.6	11.2	8.2	7.6	8.9	9.1	10.8	9.7	•	•
Taxes Paid 12	1.7	1.2	1.9	4.6	2.6	1.5	1.9	1.5	2.0	2.2	1.4	•	•
Interest Paid 13	1.6	1.5	0.0	1.8	0.1	1.2	1.3	0.8	0.9	1.9	2.3	•	•
Depreciation 14	1.8	2.7	0.8	0.9	1.1	1.9	1.7	1.2	1.6	2.1	1.9	•	•
Amortization and Depletion 15	0.2	•	•	•	0.0	0.3	0.2	0.1	0.1	0.3	0.3	•	•
Pensions and Other Deferred Comp. 16	0.4	0.1	•	•	0.3	0.5	0.3	0.2	0.7	0.5	0.5	•	•
Employee Benefits 17	1.1	•	0.1	•	1.5	0.1	1.9	1.3	1.5	0.7	1.1	•	•
Advertising 18	2.5	1.8	0.6	0.4	1.0	1.9	1.3	4.0	1.9	3.8	2.8	•	•
Other Expenses 19	12.4	29.7	33.1	15.2	10.7	12.3	10.5	10.4	11.2	16.3	12.0	•	•
Officers' Compensation 20	1.9	•	6.2	9.4	3.2	3.4	2.9	3.4	1.3	0.9	1.0	•	•
Operating Margin 21	1.8	•	•	•	1.8	1.7	0.9	•	•	0.6	4.0	•	•
Operating Margin Before Officers' Comp. 22	3.7	•	5.9	•	4.9	5.1	3.8	3.3	0.7	1.5	4.9	•	•

Selected Average Balance Sheet ($ in Thousands)

Net Receivables 23	931	0	26	81	294	1890	4638	11359	22976	53453	82941	•
Inventories 24	1015	0	78	166	658	2838	5076	12227	24374	34642	91316	•
Net Property, Plant and Equipment 25	534	0	3	206	201	841	2497	4049	12081	18616	64360	•
Total Assets 26	3968	0	147	665	2445	7193	15907	34385	72962	159829	450968	•
Notes and Loans Payable 27	1019	0	7	160	137	3309	7612	10888	10941	35409	111251	•
All Other Liabilities 28	1232	0	1	65	576	1757	5363	7491	22944	32388	170763	•
Net Worth 29	1717	0	139	440	1731	2127	2932	16006	39077	92033	168954	•

Selected Financial Ratios (Times to 1)

Current Ratio 30	1.9	•	101.3	6.3	2.9	1.8	1.2	1.9	2.4	3.2	1.7	•
Quick Ratio 31	0.9	•	39.3	3.9	1.1	0.8	0.6	1.0	1.2	2.0	0.7	•
Net Sales to Working Capital 32	4.6	•	1.8	1.9	4.3	5.3	14.2	5.8	4.8	2.6	4.8	•
Coverage Ratio 33	3.7	17.2	•	•	24.2	2.8	2.5	1.9	2.7	2.5	4.3	•
Total Asset Turnover 34	1.4	•	1.7	1.0	1.5	1.9	1.6	2.2	1.9	1.2	1.2	•
Inventory Turnover 35	3.6	•	1.5	2.4	3.8	3.2	3.5	4.1	4.1	3.3	3.7	•
Receivables Turnover 36	6.3	•	5.8	6.1	8.1	8.1	5.2	6.7	6.2	3.7	7.3	•
Total Liabilities to Net Worth 37	1.3	•	0.1	0.5	0.4	2.4	4.4	1.1	0.9	0.7	1.7	•
Current Assets to Working Capital 38	2.1	•	1.0	1.2	1.5	2.3	6.2	2.1	1.7	1.5	2.4	•
Current Liabilities to Working Capital 39	1.1	•	0.0	0.2	0.5	1.3	5.2	1.1	0.7	0.5	1.4	•
Working Capital to Net Sales 40	0.2	•	0.5	0.5	0.2	0.2	0.1	0.2	0.2	0.4	0.2	•
Inventory to Working Capital 41	0.8	•	0.6	0.4	0.7	1.2	2.6	0.9	0.8	0.5	0.8	•
Total Receipts to Cash Flow 42	7.5	1.8	4.1	10.8	9.4	7.8	9.9	11.5	9.1	6.7	6.4	•
Cost of Goods to Cash Flow 43	4.8	1.4	1.9	6.9	6.3	5.2	6.9	7.8	6.4	4.0	4.0	•
Cash Flow to Total Debt 44	0.3	•	7.6	0.3	0.6	0.3	0.2	0.4	0.5	0.4	0.3	•

Selected Financial Factors (in Percentages)

Debt Ratio 45	56.7	•	5.4	33.8	29.2	70.4	81.6	53.4	46.4	42.4	62.5	•
Return on Total Assets 46	8.3	•	•	•	4.7	6.4	5.0	3.3	5.1	5.7	11.7	•
Return on Equity Before Income Taxes 47	14.1	•	•	•	6.4	14.0	16.2	3.3	6.0	5.9	24.1	•
Return on Equity After Income Taxes 48	11.9	•	•	•	6.3	14.0	12.6	2.3	5.5	3.9	20.3	•
Profit Margin (Before Income Tax) 49	4.3	24.5	•	•	2.9	2.2	1.8	0.7	1.7	2.8	7.7	•
Profit Margin (After Income Tax) 50	3.6	24.5	•	•	2.9	2.2	1.4	0.5	1.5	1.9	6.5	•

Table II

Corporations with Net Income

LEATHER AND ALLIED PRODUCT MANUFACTURING

MONEY AMOUNTS AND SIZE OF ASSETS IN THOUSANDS OF DOLLARS

Item Description for Accounting Period 7/02 Through 6/03	Total	Zero Assets	Under 500	500 to 1,000	1,000 to 5,000	5,000 to 10,000	10,000 to 25,000	25,000 to 50,000	50,000 to 100,000	100,000 to 250,000	250,000 to 500,000	500,000 to 2,500,000	2,500,000 and over
Number of Enterprises **1**	526	101	207	0	114	61	22	6	4	0	0	0	0
Revenues ($ in Thousands)													
Net Sales **2**	7509939	0	84703	0	560434	843427	670643	507769	645365	0	0	0	0
Interest **3**	21573	8081	0	0	69	0	1063	64	26	0	0	0	0
Rents **4**	1884	0	0	0	0	0	319	197	764	0	0	0	0
Royalties **5**	22081	0	0	0	0	0	501	162	0	0	0	0	0
Other Portfolio Income **6**	9552	0	0	0	563	21	974	598	1103	0	0	0	0
Other Receipts **7**	88063	6489	7	0	2418	4244	1154	2733	18528	0	0	0	0
Total Receipts **8**	7653092	14570	84710	0	563484	847692	674654	511523	665786	0	0	0	0
Average Total Receipts **9**	14550	144	409	•	4943	13897	30666	85254	166446	•	•	•	•
Operating Costs/Operating Income (%)													
Cost of Operations **10**	63.9	•	49.3	•	66.9	66.7	67.3	66.4	66.9	•	•	•	•
Salaries and Wages **11**	9.2	•	10.4	•	8.1	8.2	7.5	9.0	9.4	•	•	•	•
Taxes Paid **12**	1.7	•	1.7	•	2.1	1.5	1.8	1.4	2.3	•	•	•	•
Interest Paid **13**	1.1	•	0.0	•	0.1	1.1	0.6	0.8	0.9	•	•	•	•
Depreciation **14**	1.7	•	1.0	•	1.0	1.9	1.2	1.3	1.6	•	•	•	•
Amortization and Depletion **15**	0.3	•	•	•	0.0	0.3	0.1	0.1	0.0	•	•	•	•
Pensions and Other Deferred Comp. **16**	0.4	•	•	•	0.1	0.5	0.3	0.2	0.5	•	•	•	•
Employee Benefits **17**	1.0	•	•	•	1.2	0.1	1.9	0.7	2.0	•	•	•	•
Advertising **18**	2.4	•	0.2	•	0.8	2.0	1.3	3.8	1.2	•	•	•	•
Other Expenses **19**	10.9	•	24.5	•	9.5	11.8	8.7	9.5	9.2	•	•	•	•
Officers' Compensation **20**	1.9	•	7.4	•	1.9	3.4	3.4	4.6	1.9	•	•	•	•
Operating Margin **21**	5.7	•	5.4	•	8.4	2.5	6.0	2.3	4.2	•	•	•	•
Operating Margin Before Officers' Comp. **22**	7.6	•	12.8	•	10.3	5.9	9.3	6.9	6.1	•	•	•	•

Selected Average Balance Sheet ($ in Thousands)

Item									
Net Receivables 23	2502	0	51	•	331	1916	4814	11582	29146
Inventories 24	2296	0	19	•	531	2380	5421	12349	24674
Net Property, Plant and Equipment 25	1271	0	7	•	223	789	2015	4062	14028
Total Assets 26	9152	0	145	•	2076	7211	15939	35557	77152
Notes and Loans Payable 27	1839	0	0	•	143	3160	3631	12561	11730
All Other Liabilities 28	1989	0	1	•	545	1649	3200	8625	29495
Net Worth 29	5324	0	143	•	1388	2401	9108	14371	35926

Selected Financial Ratios (Times to 1)

Item									
Current Ratio 30	2.7	86.9		•	2.5	1.9	2.6	1.5	2.0
Quick Ratio 31	1.4	73.1		•	1.1	0.8	1.3	0.7	1.1
Net Sales to Working Capital 32	3.8	3.4		•	5.3	4.9	4.3	9.6	5.6
Coverage Ratio 33	8.2	24.1	109.5	•	146.8	3.7	11.3	5.0	9.5
Total Asset Turnover 34	1.6	2.8		•	2.4	1.9	1.9	2.4	2.1
Inventory Turnover 35	4.0	10.5		•	6.2	3.9	3.8	4.5	4.4
Receivables Turnover 36	6.5	16.0		•	14.5	10.1	5.6	8.0	6.0
Total Liabilities to Net Worth 37	0.7	0.0		•	0.5	2.0	0.7	1.5	1.1
Current Assets to Working Capital 38	1.6	1.0		•	1.7	2.1	1.6	3.1	2.0
Current Liabilities to Working Capital 39	0.6	0.0		•	0.7	1.1	0.6	2.1	1.0
Working Capital to Net Sales 40	0.3	0.3		•	0.2	0.2	0.2	0.1	0.2
Inventory to Working Capital 41	0.7	0.2		•	0.6	1.1	0.7	1.6	0.8
Total Receipts to Cash Flow 42	6.3	3.5		•	6.2	7.4	7.3	9.3	6.4
Cost of Goods to Cash Flow 43	4.0	1.7		•	4.2	4.9	4.9	6.2	4.3
Cash Flow to Total Debt 44	0.6	77.9		•	1.1	0.4	0.6	0.4	0.6

Selected Financial Factors (in Percentages)

Item									
Debt Ratio 45	41.8	1.0		•	33.1	66.7	42.9	59.6	53.4
Return on Total Assets 46	13.5	15.4		•	21.2	7.8	13.9	9.2	17.2
Return on Equity Before Income Taxes 47	20.4	15.4		•	31.5	17.1	22.2	18.2	33.0
Return on Equity After Income Taxes 48	18.2	15.3		•	31.5	17.1	20.4	16.2	32.0
Profit Margin (Before Income Tax) 49	7.6	5.4		•	8.9	3.0	6.6	3.1	7.4
Profit Margin (After Income Tax) 50	6.8	5.4		•	8.9	3.0	6.1	2.8	7.1

Table I

Corporations with and without Net Income

WOOD PRODUCT MANUFACTURING

MONEY AMOUNTS AND SIZE OF ASSETS IN THOUSANDS OF DOLLARS

Item Description for Accounting Period 7/02 Through 6/03	Total	Zero Assets	Under 500	500 to 1,000	1,000 to 5,000	5,000 to 10,000	10,000 to 25,000	25,000 to 50,000	50,000 to 100,000	100,000 to 250,000	250,000 to 500,000	500,000 to 2,500,000	2,500,000 and over
Number of Enterprises **1**	13950	378	8380	1392	2862	479	270	92	53	23	8	10	3
Revenues ($ in Thousands)													
Net Sales **2**	91734027	273989	5088892	2848032	12851527	7904774	8231528	5150218	5546390	4437943	3385050	10100037	25915647
Interest **3**	780721	4113	1706	2067	7973	7607	5518	4920	9429	16634	3811	26384	690560
Rents **4**	86156	79	403	0	11664	6553	6375	989	1912	1171	1402	319	55289
Royalties **5**	33659	0	0	162	0	1	50	417	1573	4064	2909	6081	18402
Other Portfolio Income **6**	308561	73431	29110	3235	63345	4100	23927	10291	18553	8168	24035	4070	46296
Other Receipts **7**	992236	3435	8640	2417	55761	103161	57913	36931	53821	88826	41542	113912	425877
Total Receipts **8**	93935360	355047	5128751	2855913	12990270	8026196	8325311	5203766	5631678	4556806	3458749	10250803	27152071
Average Total Receipts **9**	6734	939	612	2052	4539	16756	30834	56563	106258	198122	432344	1025080	9050690
Operating Costs/Operating Income (%)													
Cost of Operations **10**	75.5	84.4	57.6	62.0	72.8	78.6	80.0	80.3	79.2	73.4	76.3	75.2	78.0
Salaries and Wages **11**	5.8	4.2	11.3	9.0	6.4	5.4	4.4	4.1	4.5	6.9	7.6	5.6	4.9
Taxes Paid **12**	1.6	2.0	2.9	2.0	2.2	2.0	1.7	1.6	1.7	1.8	1.4	1.3	0.9
Interest Paid **13**	2.8	3.6	0.7	0.6	1.0	0.9	1.1	1.2	2.5	1.7	1.2	2.3	6.5
Depreciation **14**	3.3	2.8	3.2	3.7	2.5	2.7	2.9	3.4	3.3	4.2	3.0	2.5	4.1
Amortization and Depletion **15**	0.6	0.1	0.1	0.0	0.0	0.0	0.2	0.3	0.4	0.3	0.2	1.1	1.3
Pensions and Other Deferred Comp. **16**	0.4	0.1	0.8	0.3	0.3	0.3	0.3	0.3	0.2	0.6	0.1	0.6	0.4
Employee Benefits **17**	1.0	0.7	1.2	1.4	1.2	1.0	1.2	1.0	1.0	1.2	2.1	1.3	0.3
Advertising **18**	0.6	0.0	0.2	0.2	0.4	0.3	0.3	0.6	0.7	0.9	0.5	1.1	0.8
Other Expenses **19**	8.6	20.7	14.1	12.6	9.0	6.9	5.7	5.2	7.1	10.6	9.2	8.6	8.8
Officers' Compensation **20**	1.6	1.9	7.6	3.2	3.3	2.3	1.4	1.2	0.9	0.6	0.3	0.5	0.2
Operating Margin **21**	•	•	0.3	4.9	0.9	•	0.9	0.8	•	•	•	•	•
Operating Margin Before Officers' Comp. **22**	•	•	7.9	8.1	4.2	1.9	2.2	2.0	•	•	0.4	•	•

Selected Average Balance Sheet ($ in Thousands)

Net Receivables 23	594	0	29	149	377	1685	2282	4764	8536	16931	30398	82121	999255
Inventories 24	679	0	18	124	476	1798	4140	9800	12540	24086	36549	103616	786931
Net Property, Plant and Equipment 25	1613	0	64	242	596	2318	5404	12731	26507	56005	113575	324473	3113147
Total Assets 26	6340	0	161	702	1992	7646	15382	34544	70008	144228	306396	703968	17636810
Notes and Loans Payable 27	1808	0	81	250	773	2584	5881	12306	32705	49239	82242	237419	4039713
All Other Liabilities 28	2611	0	30	130	416	1561	2693	5396	12398	27280	60279	212715	9645654
Net Worth 29	1921	0	50	322	802	3501	6808	16843	24905	67710	163874	253834	3951443

Selected Financial Ratios (Times to 1)

Current Ratio 30	1.0	•	2.0	2.1	1.8	2.0	1.9	1.9	1.5	2.2	1.0	1.5	0.7
Quick Ratio 31	0.3	•	1.3	1.4	0.9	1.1	0.8	0.6	0.7	1.2	0.4	0.7	0.1
Net Sales to Working Capital 32	•	•	17.2	9.7	8.7	7.2	7.6	7.2	10.9	5.1	145.7	13.3	•
Coverage Ratio 33	1.2	3.5	2.5	9.2	3.0	2.3	2.8	2.5	0.9	1.3	1.1	1.6	0.8
Total Asset Turnover 34	1.0	•	3.8	2.9	2.3	2.2	2.0	1.6	1.5	1.3	1.4	1.4	0.5
Inventory Turnover 35	7.3	•	19.0	10.2	6.9	7.2	5.9	4.6	6.6	5.9	8.8	7.3	8.6
Receivables Turnover 36	10.3	•	18.4	13.4	13.2	10.6	13.7	10.8	13.5	9.2	14.6	12.3	7.1
Total Liabilities to Net Worth 37	2.3	•	2.2	1.2	1.5	1.2	1.3	1.1	1.8	1.1	0.9	1.8	3.5
Current Assets to Working Capital 38	•	•	2.0	1.9	2.3	2.0	2.1	2.2	3.1	1.8	32.1	3.0	•
Current Liabilities to Working Capital 39	•	•	1.0	0.9	1.3	1.0	1.1	1.2	2.1	0.8	31.1	2.0	•
Working Capital to Net Sales 40	•	•	0.1	0.1	0.1	0.1	0.1	0.1	0.1	0.2	0.0	0.1	•
Inventory to Working Capital 41	•	•	0.5	0.5	0.9	0.8	1.1	1.1	1.3	0.6	14.5	1.3	•
Total Receipts to Cash Flow 42	13.6	466.8	9.5	7.4	12.0	16.8	16.2	17.0	18.1	10.6	12.9	11.3	16.2
Cost of Goods to Cash Flow 43	10.3	393.9	5.5	4.6	8.7	13.2	12.9	13.6	14.3	7.8	9.9	8.5	12.7
Cash Flow to Total Debt 44	0.1	•	0.6	0.7	0.3	0.2	0.2	0.2	0.1	0.2	0.2	0.2	0.0

Selected Financial Factors (in Percentages)

Debt Ratio 45	69.7	•	69.2	54.1	59.7	54.2	55.7	51.2	64.4	53.1	46.5	63.9	77.6
Return on Total Assets 46	3.6	•	6.6	17.1	6.6	4.6	6.1	5.0	3.4	2.9	1.9	5.3	2.5
Return on Equity Before Income Taxes 47	2.3	•	12.9	33.2	11.0	5.7	8.9	6.1	•	1.4	0.3	5.5	•
Return on Equity After Income Taxes 48	1.1	•	12.1	30.5	10.1	4.5	7.3	4.7	•	•	•	2.3	•
Profit Margin (Before Income Tax) 49	0.7	9.1	1.1	5.2	2.0	1.2	2.0	1.8	0.5	0.5	0.1	1.4	•
Profit Margin (After Income Tax) 50	0.3	8.6	1.0	4.8	1.8	1.0	1.6	1.4	•	•	•	0.6	•

71

Table II
Corporations with Net Income

WOOD PRODUCT MANUFACTURING

MONEY AMOUNTS AND SIZE OF ASSETS IN THOUSANDS OF DOLLARS

Item Description for Accounting Period 7/02 Through 6/03	Total	Zero Assets	Under 500	500 to 1,000	1,000 to 5,000	5,000 to 10,000	10,000 to 25,000	25,000 to 50,000	50,000 to 100,000	100,000 to 250,000	250,000 to 500,000	500,000 to 2,500,000	2,500,000 and over
Number of Enterprises **1**	8510	40	5095	0	1832	266	177	55	26	13	5	0	0
Revenues ($ in Thousands)													
Net Sales **2**	46107464	182851	3663274	0	9158732	4472956	5878883	3481557	3097457	2880847	2411527	0	0
Interest **3**	165949	4092	1333	0	5990	3764	4520	2830	5628	9601	2059	0	0
Rents **4**	68822	60	403	0	10402	5777	5011	489	1667	591	917	0	0
Royalties **5**	5920	0	0	0	0	1	43	396	1	0	0	0	0
Other Portfolio Income **6**	222703	73382	27454	0	55955	2605	13483	3415	5492	2844	10402	0	0
Other Receipts **7**	542224	3570	1055	0	32583	43025	42864	17518	29807	56102	17703	0	0
Total Receipts **8**	47113082	263955	3693519	0	9263662	4528128	5942804	3506205	3140052	2949985	2442608	0	0
Average Total Receipts **9**	5536	6599	725	•	5057	17023	33575	63749	120771	226922	488522	•	•
Operating Costs/Operating Income (%)													
Cost of Operations **10**	71.2	88.7	52.9	•	71.3	75.3	77.0	77.9	78.1	69.2	69.1	•	•
Salaries and Wages **11**	6.6	3.8	11.1	•	6.7	5.6	4.8	3.9	5.0	7.8	9.3	•	•
Taxes Paid **12**	1.9	0.9	3.0	•	2.0	1.9	1.8	1.6	1.9	1.7	1.8	•	•
Interest Paid **13**	1.0	3.6	0.4	•	0.8	0.7	0.8	0.9	1.1	0.9	1.0	•	•
Depreciation **14**	2.7	2.5	2.6	•	2.1	2.7	2.4	2.8	2.5	3.1	3.7	•	•
Amortization and Depletion **15**	0.3	•	0.1	•	0.0	0.0	0.1	0.3	0.1	0.2	0.1	•	•
Pensions and Other Deferred Comp. **16**	0.5	0.1	1.1	•	0.3	0.3	0.3	0.4	0.2	0.8	0.1	•	•
Employee Benefits **17**	1.3	0.8	1.0	•	1.1	1.1	1.2	1.0	0.9	1.4	2.8	•	•
Advertising **18**	0.6	0.0	0.2	•	0.4	0.3	0.3	0.8	0.6	1.4	0.6	•	•
Other Expenses **19**	8.5	10.7	13.3	•	8.8	6.1	5.8	5.1	5.7	10.6	8.5	•	•
Officers' Compensation **20**	2.1	1.0	9.1	•	2.9	1.6	1.4	1.2	1.0	0.6	0.3	•	•
Operating Margin **21**	3.4	•	5.1	•	3.4	4.4	4.1	4.2	2.9	2.3	2.7	•	•
Operating Margin Before Officers' Comp. **22**	5.5	•	14.3	•	6.3	6.0	5.5	5.5	3.8	2.9	3.0	•	•

Selected Average Balance Sheet ($ in Thousands)

Net Receivables 23	596	0	24	·	401	·	1584	2471	5340	9597	22989	39189
Inventories 24	659	0	17	·	512	·	1633	4151	9443	13841	26914	54942
Net Property, Plant and Equipment 25	883	0	60	·	482	·	2300	4935	11321	20393	44517	131166
Total Assets 26	2973	0	168	·	2020	·	7441	15313	34990	65535	149497	311235
Notes and Loans Payable 27	863	0	47	·	739	·	2268	4529	9998	21350	30032	83490
All Other Liabilities 28	658	0	30	·	397	·	1044	2556	5884	13085	32746	55044
Net Worth 29	1451	0	91	·	885	·	4130	8228	19108	31100	86719	172701

Selected Financial Ratios (Times to 1)

Current Ratio 30	2.1	·	2.6	·	2.1	·	2.1	2.4	2.1	1.9	2.5	1.3
Quick Ratio 31	1.1	·	1.7	·	1.1	·	0.7	1.4	0.9	0.9	1.5	0.6
Net Sales to Working Capital 32	6.3	·	15.1	·	7.6	·	6.7	6.6	6.9	7.2	4.1	16.7
Coverage Ratio 33	6.5	10.0	17.4	·	6.4	·	6.3	8.5	7.7	4.9	5.9	5.0
Total Asset Turnover 34	1.8	·	4.3	·	2.5	·	1.8	2.3	2.2	1.8	1.5	1.5
Inventory Turnover 35	5.9	·	22.3	·	7.0	·	5.2	7.8	6.2	6.7	5.7	6.1
Receivables Turnover 36	7.8	·	61.1	·	13.3	·	12.1	10.2	13.8	13.2	8.3	24.6
Total Liabilities to Net Worth 37	1.0	·	0.9	·	1.3	·	0.8	0.8	0.9	1.1	0.7	0.8
Current Assets to Working Capital 38	1.9	·	1.6	·	1.9	·	1.9	1.7	1.9	2.2	1.7	4.1
Current Liabilities to Working Capital 39	0.9	·	0.6	·	0.9	·	0.9	0.7	0.9	1.2	0.7	3.1
Working Capital to Net Sales 40	0.2	·	0.1	·	0.1	·	0.2	0.2	0.1	0.1	0.2	0.1
Inventory to Working Capital 41	0.6	·	0.4	·	0.8	·	1.0	0.6	0.9	0.9	0.5	1.9
Total Receipts to Cash Flow 42	8.4	6.3	6.8	·	9.2	·	11.2	9.9	10.5	11.4	7.5	9.1
Cost of Goods to Cash Flow 43	6.0	5.6	3.6	·	6.6	·	8.7	7.4	8.1	8.9	5.2	6.3
Cash Flow to Total Debt 44	0.4	·	1.4	·	0.5	·	0.4	0.5	0.4	0.3	0.5	0.4

Selected Financial Factors (in Percentages)

Debt Ratio 45	51.2	·	46.1	·	56.2	·	45.4	44.5	46.3	52.5	42.0	44.5
Return on Total Assets 46	11.9	·	27.0	·	13.4	·	10.7	14.4	12.9	9.7	8.4	7.6
Return on Equity Before Income Taxes 47	20.7	·	47.3	·	25.8	·	16.4	22.9	20.8	16.2	12.0	10.9
Return on Equity After Income Taxes 48	18.2	·	46.5	·	24.6	·	14.3	21.1	18.8	13.4	9.7	10.3
Profit Margin (Before Income Tax) 49	5.5	32.2	6.0	·	4.6	·	4.9	5.6	5.2	4.2	4.7	3.9
Profit Margin (After Income Tax) 50	4.9	31.4	5.9	·	4.4	·	4.3	5.2	4.7	3.5	3.8	3.7

72

Table I
Corporations with and without Net Income

PULP, PAPER, AND PAPERBOARD MILLS

MONEY AMOUNTS AND SIZE OF ASSETS IN THOUSANDS OF DOLLARS

Item Description for Accounting Period 7/02 Through 6/03	Total	Zero Assets	Under 500	500 to 1,000	1,000 to 5,000	5,000 to 10,000	10,000 to 25,000	25,000 to 50,000	50,000 to 100,000	100,000 to 250,000	250,000 to 500,000	500,000 to 2,500,000	2,500,000 and over
Number of Enterprises **1**	160	•	0	•	16	0	20	17	13	15	8	24	10
Revenues ($ in Thousands)													
Net Sales **2**	99161827	•	0	•	269101	0	744855	881837	1153820	1997722	2043913	23963825	67827974
Interest **3**	1569456	•	•	•	0	0	814	577	446	14293	9933	115260	1428128
Rents **4**	141850	•	0	•	0	0	201	269	19	335	1818	17881	121327
Royalties **5**	248032	•	0	•	0	0	0	0	0	0	2220	70896	174917
Other Portfolio Income **6**	1926217	•	0	•	0	0	62	1717	8403	182252	768	359035	1373169
Other Receipts **7**	1323306	•	0	•	0	0	2386	2319	14276	42871	16538	240775	1001681
Total Receipts **8**	104370688	•	0	•	269101	0	748318	886719	1176964	2237473	2075190	24767672	71927196
Average Total Receipts **9**	652317	•	•	•	16819	•	37416	52160	90536	149165	259399	1031986	7192720
Operating Costs/Operating Income (%)													
Cost of Operations **10**	77.4	•	•	•	85.0	•	81.1	83.0	83.8	86.6	70.6	80.7	75.9
Salaries and Wages **11**	5.9	•	•	•	7.9	•	4.6	3.7	4.5	3.1	7.2	3.9	6.7
Taxes Paid **12**	1.3	•	•	•	3.7	•	1.5	1.5	0.9	1.5	1.5	1.1	1.4
Interest Paid **13**	5.0	•	•	•	1.3	•	2.1	1.0	2.1	5.4	3.1	3.6	5.6
Depreciation **14**	6.6	•	•	•	1.4	•	3.7	4.6	4.9	7.8	10.2	8.4	5.9
Amortization and Depletion **15**	0.3	•	•	•	•	•	0.2	0.2	0.6	0.3	0.4	0.4	0.3
Pensions and Other Deferred Comp. **16**	0.6	•	•	•	0.1	•	0.7	0.3	0.3	0.9	1.9	0.5	0.6
Employee Benefits **17**	1.9	•	•	•	0.1	•	1.2	1.2	1.7	2.5	3.9	1.2	2.0
Advertising **18**	0.3	•	•	•	•	•	0.2	0.3	0.5	0.1	0.2	0.3	0.4
Other Expenses **19**	8.6	•	•	•	14.6	•	6.4	6.6	4.4	9.0	10.4	7.6	9.0
Officers' Compensation **20**	0.3	•	•	•	•	•	1.0	1.3	1.1	0.9	0.5	0.4	0.2
Operating Margin **21**	•	•	•	•	•	•	•	•	•	•	•	•	•
Operating Margin Before Officers' Comp. **22**	•	•	•	•	•	•	•	•	•	•	•	•	•

Selected Average Balance Sheet ($ in Thousands)

Net Receivables 23	81212	1046	4464	6003	9799	12841	48405	158307	825576
Inventories 24	59711	1058	2801	6498	9139	15383	37044	90520	647860
Net Property, Plant and Equipment 25	440920	2806	8166	16019	30873	84303	172019	654003	5129536
Total Assets 26	1189845	4753	17558	35160	62892	180025	342472	1193222	15421577
Notes and Loans Payable 27	449889	2918	9755	12524	23146	96576	142440	402758	5896768
All Other Liabilities 28	348930	4945	6768	8934	20588	36874	82572	406380	4420191
Net Worth 29	391026	-3110	1035	13702	19158	46575	117460	384083	5104618

Selected Financial Ratios (Times to 1)

Current Ratio 30	0.6	1.0	1.1	1.4	1.1	1.1	1.8	1.3	0.5
Quick Ratio 31	0.3	0.5	0.6	0.7	0.6	0.4	1.0	0.8	0.2
Net Sales to Working Capital 32	•	•	72.4	11.7	36.2	61.7	6.0	15.8	•
Coverage Ratio 33	0.4	•	•	•	•	•	•	•	0.7
Total Asset Turnover 34	0.5	3.5	2.1	1.5	1.4	0.7	0.7	0.8	0.4
Inventory Turnover 35	8.0	13.5	10.8	6.6	8.1	7.5	4.9	8.9	8.0
Receivables Turnover 36	8.2	32.2	8.5	6.3	9.5	6.0	7.0	7.0	8.9
Total Liabilities to Net Worth 37	2.0	•	16.0	1.6	2.3	2.9	1.9	2.1	2.0
Current Assets to Working Capital 38	•	•	16.1	3.2	10.1	18.5	2.3	4.8	•
Current Liabilities to Working Capital 39	•	•	15.1	2.2	9.1	17.5	1.3	3.8	•
Working Capital to Net Sales 40	•	•	0.0	0.1	0.0	0.0	0.2	0.1	•
Inventory to Working Capital 41	•	•	5.3	1.4	3.5	5.9	0.8	1.5	•
Total Receipts to Cash Flow 42	47.4	31.3	47.4	•	•	•	•	149.1	33.2
Cost of Goods to Cash Flow 43	36.7	25.4	39.4	•	•	•	•	120.4	25.2
Cash Flow to Total Debt 44	0.0	0.1	0.1	0.0	0.0	0.0	0.1	0.0	0.0

Selected Financial Factors (in Percentages)

Debt Ratio 45	67.1	165.4	94.1	61.0	69.5	74.1	65.7	67.8	66.9
Return on Total Assets 46	1.1	•	•	•	•	•	•	•	1.6
Return on Equity Before Income Taxes 47	•	76.9	•	•	•	•	•	•	•
Return on Equity After Income Taxes 48	•	76.9	•	•	•	•	•	•	•
Profit Margin (Before Income Tax) 49	•	•	•	•	•	•	•	•	•
Profit Margin (After Income Tax) 50	•	•	•	•	•	•	•	•	•

Table II
Corporations with Net Income

PULP, PAPER, AND PAPERBOARD MILLS

MONEY AMOUNTS AND SIZE OF ASSETS IN THOUSANDS OF DOLLARS

Item Description for Accounting Period 7/02 Through 6/03	Total	Zero Assets	Under 500	500 to 1,000	1,000 to 5,000	5,000 to 10,000	10,000 to 25,000	25,000 to 50,000	50,000 to 100,000	100,000 to 250,000	250,000 to 500,000	500,000 to 2,500,000	2,500,000 and over
Number of Enterprises **1**	56	•	•	•	•	18	11	5	4	5	3	6	4

Revenues ($ in Thousands)

	Total	Zero Assets	Under 500	500 to 1,000	1,000 to 5,000	5,000 to 10,000	10,000 to 25,000	25,000 to 50,000	50,000 to 100,000	100,000 to 250,000	250,000 to 500,000	500,000 to 2,500,000	2,500,000 and over
Net Sales **2**	30132842	•	•	•	•	137067	399030	410497	494069	773075	818961	4255674	22844468
Interest **3**	1101421	•	•	•	•	0	715	78	55	7003	7265	19101	1067204
Rents **4**	117477	•	•	•	•	0	90	224	14	226	921	4178	111825
Royalties **5**	49757	•	•	•	•	0	0	0	0	0	2218	4436	43104
Other Portfolio Income **6**	818785	•	•	•	•	809	52	1342	8385	175583	31	315971	316611
Other Receipts **7**	610225	•	•	•	•	185	1716	1086	4771	17237	9601	84107	491523
Total Receipts **8**	3283 0507	•	•	•	•	138061	401603	413227	507294	973124	838997	4683467	24874735
Average Total Receipts **9**	586259	•	•	•	•	7670	36509	82645	126824	194625	279666	780578	6218684

Operating Costs/Operating Income (%)

	Total	Zero Assets	Under 500	500 to 1,000	1,000 to 5,000	5,000 to 10,000	10,000 to 25,000	25,000 to 50,000	50,000 to 100,000	100,000 to 250,000	250,000 to 500,000	500,000 to 2,500,000	2,500,000 and over
Cost of Operations **10**	77.5	•	•	•	•	66.9	79.1	80.6	77.1	80.8	56.3	81.0	77.5
Salaries and Wages **11**	6.2	•	•	•	•	4.8	4.0	3.2	4.9	2.0	11.9	3.7	6.8
Taxes Paid **12**	1.2	•	•	•	•	1.2	1.1	1.7	0.9	1.6	2.1	1.0	1.2
Interest Paid **13**	6.3	•	•	•	•	0.1	1.2	0.6	1.5	3.3	0.8	2.9	7.6
Depreciation **14**	6.1	•	•	•	•	0.7	2.6	2.5	3.1	9.3	6.9	6.8	6.1
Amortization and Depletion **15**	0.5	•	•	•	•	0.0	0.2	0.1	0.5	0.3	0.3	0.8	0.5
Pensions and Other Deferred Comp. **16**	0.3	•	•	•	•	0.7	0.4	0.5	0.6	1.9	1.3	0.9	0.1
Employee Benefits **17**	0.8	•	•	•	•	0.8	0.7	0.9	2.2	4.2	3.0	1.8	0.4
Advertising **18**	0.5	•	•	•	•	0.1	0.3	0.3	1.0	0.2	0.0	0.1	0.5
Other Expenses **19**	6.9	•	•	•	•	5.5	6.9	5.5	5.1	7.1	16.6	6.8	6.6
Officers' Compensation **20**	0.3	•	•	•	•	1.2	1.0	1.5	2.1	0.4	0.7	0.7	0.2
Operating Margin **21**	•	•	•	•	•	17.9	2.6	2.6	1.1	•	0.2	•	•
Operating Margin Before Officers' Comp. **22**	•	•	•	•	•	19.1	3.6	4.1	3.1	•	0.9	•	•

Selected Average Balance Sheet ($ in Thousands)

Line Item										
Net Receivables 23	75827	462	•	5113	11414	12342	16878	88475	91595	793990
Inventories 24	59739	628	•	3406	10643	14889	26052	25703	78713	640209
Net Property, Plant and Equipment 25	480392	448	•	5905	15061	33085	98584	125044	512024	5670269
Total Assets 26	1263719	6742	•	16563	41475	67349	184929	345839	1039006	15447942
Notes and Loans Payable 27	466267	33	•	6115	11738	22349	60453	82984	303659	5880459
All Other Liabilities 28	440549	495	•	5193	15599	27800	62945	88643	265292	5560771
Net Worth 29	356904	6213	•	5254	14139	17200	61530	174213	470055	4006713

Selected Financial Ratios (Times to 1)

Line Item										
Current Ratio 30	0.4	5.1	•	1.3	1.5	1.1	1.2	2.1	1.2	0.3
Quick Ratio 31	0.2	3.5	•	0.8	0.7	0.6	0.5	1.5	0.6	0.2
Net Sales to Working Capital 32	•	4.3	•	17.8	9.9	41.3	17.8	3.9	21.2	•
Coverage Ratio 33	1.4	321.5	•	3.8	6.2	3.5	5.5	5.6	2.1	1.2
Total Asset Turnover 34	0.4	1.1	•	2.2	2.0	1.8	0.8	0.8	0.7	0.4
Inventory Turnover 35	7.0	8.1	•	8.4	6.2	6.4	4.8	6.0	7.3	6.9
Receivables Turnover 36	6.8	33.0	•	7.0	7.6	7.7	4.0	6.2	5.9	14.4
Total Liabilities to Net Worth 37	2.5	0.1	•	2.2	1.9	2.9	2.0	1.0	1.2	2.9
Current Assets to Working Capital 38	•	1.2	•	4.5	2.9	8.7	5.0	1.9	6.3	•
Current Liabilities to Working Capital 39	•	0.2	•	3.5	1.9	7.7	4.0	0.9	5.3	•
Working Capital to Net Sales 40	•	0.2	•	0.1	0.1	0.0	0.1	0.3	0.0	•
Inventory to Working Capital 41	•	0.4	•	1.7	1.3	3.5	2.0	0.4	2.2	•
Total Receipts to Cash Flow 42	17.5	4.6	•	11.5	13.4	14.8	912.7	6.4	13.8	19.7
Cost of Goods to Cash Flow 43	13.5	3.1	•	9.1	10.8	11.4	737.9	3.6	11.2	15.3
Cash Flow to Total Debt 44	0.0	3.1	•	0.3	0.2	0.2	0.0	0.2	0.1	0.0

Selected Financial Factors (in Percentages)

Line Item										
Debt Ratio 45	71.8	7.8	•	68.3	65.9	74.5	66.7	49.6	54.8	74.1
Return on Total Assets 46	3.7	20.4	•	9.6	7.6	9.6	15.2	3.3	4.3	3.3
Return on Equity Before Income Taxes 47	3.4	22.1	•	22.2	18.8	26.8	37.4	5.5	5.0	2.1
Return on Equity After Income Taxes 48	2.8	21.6	•	20.4	13.3	24.6	29.1	4.2	4.3	1.7
Profit Margin (Before Income Tax) 49	2.3	18.0	•	3.2	3.2	3.7	14.9	3.5	3.3	1.5
Profit Margin (After Income Tax) 50	1.9	17.7	•	3.0	2.3	3.4	11.6	2.7	2.8	1.2

Table I

Corporations with and without Net Income

CONVERTED PAPER PRODUCT

MONEY AMOUNTS AND SIZE OF ASSETS IN THOUSANDS OF DOLLARS

Item Description for Accounting Period 7/02 Through 6/03	Total	Zero Assets	Under 500	500 to 1,000	1,000 to 5,000	5,000 to 10,000	10,000 to 25,000	25,000 to 50,000	50,000 to 100,000	100,000 to 250,000	250,000 to 500,000	500,000 to 2,500,000	2,500,000 and over
Number of Enterprises **1**	2838	134	0	547	958	0	177	62	31	19	5	7	3
Revenues ($ in Thousands)													
Net Sales **2**	58628283	816433	0	1001162	5541149	0	5282399	3241413	3015691	4927545	2244933	8060178	21527152
Interest **3**	623178	136	0	8	1805	0	4896	4788	5353	9418	5785	71466	518879
Rents **4**	21949	1	0	0	3553	0	2523	2677	2185	2896	1807	2239	3844
Royalties **5**	675378	0	0	0	0	0	1036	3135	194	1203	182	40600	629028
Other Portfolio Income **6**	1124480	23810	0	4183	1551	0	21844	19416	4832	7735	7830	59121	953155
Other Receipts **7**	925994	10811	0	396	34857	0	20292	31956	26579	41597	2223	419133	334367
Total Receipts **8**	61999262	851191	0	1005749	5582915	0	5332990	3303385	3054834	4990394	2262760	8652737	23966425
Average Total Receipts **9**	21846	6352	•	1839	5828	•	30130	53280	98543	262652	452552	1236105	7988808
Operating Costs/Operating Income (%)													
Cost of Operations **10**	64.9	89.5	•	78.3	65.3	•	71.7	72.0	71.9	72.8	70.0	75.2	53.1
Salaries and Wages **11**	9.7	3.1	•	5.3	8.1	•	6.4	6.3	7.5	5.5	8.3	6.2	14.5
Taxes Paid **12**	1.6	0.6	•	1.8	2.5	•	1.9	1.9	1.8	1.6	1.8	1.3	1.2
Interest Paid **13**	2.5	2.5	•	1.1	1.2	•	1.4	1.5	1.4	2.0	1.3	4.5	3.0
Depreciation **14**	5.6	2.8	•	2.7	3.7	•	4.0	3.9	4.4	4.5	3.9	6.0	7.7
Amortization and Depletion **15**	0.6	0.6	•	0.2	0.1	•	0.3	0.3	0.2	0.2	0.3	0.9	1.0
Pensions and Other Deferred Comp. **16**	1.6	0.0	•	0.1	0.4	•	0.5	0.7	0.6	0.7	0.9	0.6	3.4
Employee Benefits **17**	3.0	1.4	•	1.6	1.6	•	1.2	1.7	1.4	1.5	1.7	3.1	5.1
Advertising **18**	0.9	1.2	•	0.4	0.2	•	0.3	0.2	1.0	0.4	1.0	0.2	1.9
Other Expenses **19**	9.6	10.0	•	6.1	10.1	•	8.5	7.6	8.1	8.8	9.7	7.6	11.0
Officers' Compensation **20**	1.3	0.6	•	3.5	4.2	•	2.4	1.7	1.3	0.7	0.8	0.3	0.3
Operating Margin **21**	•	•	•	•	2.6	•	1.5	2.2	0.5	1.3	0.2	•	•
Operating Margin Before Officers' Comp. **22**	•	•	•	2.4	6.8	•	3.9	3.9	1.7	2.0	1.0	•	•

Selected Average Balance Sheet ($ in Thousands)

Net Receivables 23	2807	0	•	308	549	•	3324	7286	12311	29521	57289	114161	1310261
Inventories 24	2043	0	•	77	365	•	2905	6278	12919	26668	54886	129280	733027
Net Property, Plant and Equipment 25	6574	0	•	128	1057	•	5879	11325	27300	65650	129552	484403	3045973
Total Assets 26	25788	0	•	620	2527	•	15347	35390	70829	170296	397234	1221447	16105878
Notes and Loans Payable 27	10104	0	•	283	1074	•	7473	11629	25560	58147	100170	514905	6096260
All Other Liabilities 28	7449	0	•	179	462	•	4061	7371	16165	43920	150654	271892	5031869
Net Worth 29	8235	0	•	159	992	•	3813	16390	29104	68229	146410	434650	4977750

Selected Financial Ratios (Times to 1)

Current Ratio 30	1.1	•	•	1.6	2.0	•	1.2	1.9	1.8	1.7	0.9	1.5	0.9
Quick Ratio 31	0.4	•	•	1.2	1.3	•	0.7	1.1	0.9	1.0	0.4	0.7	0.3
Net Sales to Working Capital 32	31.6	•	•	10.7	8.9	•	22.3	6.5	6.3	8.4	•	13.0	•
Coverage Ratio 33	3.3	•	•	0.4	3.8	•	2.9	3.8	2.1	2.3	2.2	1.4	5.1
Total Asset Turnover 34	0.8	•	•	3.0	2.3	•	1.9	1.5	1.4	1.5	1.1	0.9	0.4
Inventory Turnover 35	6.6	•	•	18.6	10.3	•	7.4	6.0	5.4	7.1	5.7	6.7	5.2
Receivables Turnover 36	6.5	•	•	6.1	11.1	•	8.9	6.3	8.0	8.5	8.6	6.7	4.8
Total Liabilities to Net Worth 37	2.1	•	•	2.9	1.5	•	3.0	1.2	1.4	1.5	1.7	1.8	2.2
Current Assets to Working Capital 38	12.4	•	•	2.7	2.0	•	5.8	2.1	2.2	2.4	•	3.0	•
Current Liabilities to Working Capital 39	11.4	•	•	1.7	1.0	•	4.8	1.1	1.2	1.4	•	2.0	•
Working Capital to Net Sales 40	0.0	•	•	0.1	0.1	•	0.0	0.2	0.2	0.1	•	0.1	•
Inventory to Working Capital 41	2.9	•	•	0.5	0.6	•	2.2	0.7	0.9	0.9	•	1.1	•
Total Receipts to Cash Flow 42	8.7	•	•	153.0	10.4	•	12.5	10.8	14.0	10.3	11.3	13.2	5.6
Cost of Goods to Cash Flow 43	5.7	•	•	119.8	6.8	•	8.9	7.8	10.0	7.5	7.9	9.9	3.0
Cash Flow to Total Debt 44	0.1	•	•	0.0	0.4	•	0.2	0.3	0.2	0.2	0.2	0.1	0.1

Selected Financial Factors (in Percentages)

Debt Ratio 45	68.1	•	•	74.3	60.8	•	75.2	53.7	58.9	59.9	63.1	64.4	69.1
Return on Total Assets 46	6.5	•	•	1.3	10.4	•	7.6	8.1	4.2	7.0	3.2	5.8	6.8
Return on Equity Before Income Taxes 47	14.1	•	•	•	19.6	•	19.9	12.9	5.5	9.9	4.7	4.5	17.7
Return on Equity After Income Taxes 48	9.3	•	•	16.8	18.5	•	16.8	10.1	3.5	7.3	2.9	2.2	11.6
Profit Margin (Before Income Tax) 49	5.6	•	•	2.5	3.4	•	2.5	4.0	1.6	2.6	1.5	1.7	12.3
Profit Margin (After Income Tax) 50	3.7	•	•	3.2	•	•	2.1	3.2	1.0	1.9	0.9	0.8	8.1

Table II
Corporations with Net Income

CONVERTED PAPER PRODUCT

MONEY AMOUNTS AND SIZE OF ASSETS IN THOUSANDS OF DOLLARS

Item Description for Accounting Period 7/02 Through 6/03	Total	Zero Assets	Under 500	500 to 1,000	1,000 to 5,000	5,000 to 10,000	10,000 to 25,000	25,000 to 50,000	50,000 to 100,000	100,000 to 250,000	250,000 to 500,000	500,000 to 2,500,000	2,500,000 and over
Number of Enterprises 1	1543	3	255	316	695	74	117	41	18	16	5	0	3
Revenues ($ in Thousands)													
Net Sales 2	44043360	58234	429143	450562	4582287	1147186	3739779	2158751	1902674	3882997	4164596	0	21527152
Interest 3	545821	0	222	8	1301	117	3580	3604	3833	9389	4887	0	518879
Rents 4	13469	1	0	0	677	200	2037	1655	693	2697	1665	0	3844
Royalties 5	641310	0	0	0	0	0	136	3135	194	1203	7613	0	629028
Other Portfolio Income 6	1057004	10500	18390	4183	1082	2212	19276	15169	4135	7707	21193	0	953155
Other Receipts 7	452015	2399	268	396	25316	863	12450	22463	14178	29689	9630	0	334367
Total Receipts 8	46752979	71134	448023	455149	4610663	1150578	3777258	2204777	1925707	3933682	4209584	0	23966425
Average Total Receipts 9	30300	23711	1757	1440	6634	15548	32284	53775	106984	245855	841917	•	7988808
Operating Costs/Operating Income (%)													
Cost of Operations 10	61.1	71.8	70.6	69.5	64.4	68.0	70.2	68.8	70.5	73.6	66.3	•	53.1
Salaries and Wages 11	10.4	8.7	3.4	5.1	7.8	8.3	6.5	6.2	5.9	6.0	6.5	•	14.5
Taxes Paid 12	1.5	3.6	1.7	2.6	2.6	1.9	1.8	2.0	1.6	1.6	1.5	•	1.2
Interest Paid 13	2.2	1.6	0.3	0.5	1.0	1.2	1.2	1.2	1.3	1.3	2.6	•	3.0
Depreciation 14	5.7	2.3	0.4	1.3	3.6	3.1	3.5	3.8	4.2	4.0	4.9	•	7.7
Amortization and Depletion 15	0.6	0.0	•	0.1	0.1	0.1	0.1	0.2	0.1	0.3	0.6	•	1.0
Pensions and Other Deferred Comp. 16	1.9	0.3	0.0	0.0	0.5	0.4	0.5	0.7	0.5	0.7	0.6	•	3.4
Employee Benefits 17	3.4	3.2	2.0	0.7	1.7	0.6	1.2	1.7	1.7	1.6	2.8	•	5.1
Advertising 18	1.2	0.2	0.0	0.8	0.2	0.3	0.3	0.2	1.2	0.4	0.7	•	1.9
Other Expenses 19	9.5	7.3	7.8	11.9	9.0	9.1	8.1	7.9	7.7	7.3	6.8	•	11.0
Officers' Compensation 20	1.3	2.8	6.8	4.6	4.0	4.4	2.3	1.9	1.3	0.9	0.6	•	0.3
Operating Margin 21	1.3	•	7.1	2.9	5.2	2.5	4.4	5.5	4.0	2.3	6.0	•	•
Operating Margin Before Officers' Comp. 22	2.5	0.9	13.9	7.6	9.2	6.9	6.7	7.4	5.3	3.2	6.6	•	•

Selected Average Balance Sheet ($ in Thousands)

Net Receivables 23	4120	0	16	335	582	1623	3514	6928	11607	27298	90243	•	1310261
Inventories 24	2769	0	11	72	349	1516	2794	5952	14325	23628	103755	•	649077
Net Property, Plant and Equipment 25	9166	0	29	58	1159	2641	5619	11964	26501	54865	295187	•	3045973
Total Assets 26	40243	0	61	583	2545	7155	15363	35413	70868	162630	830269	•	16105878
Notes and Loans Payable 27	14759	0	25	140	984	3114	5031	9288	20120	41915	303338	•	6096260
All Other Liabilities 28	11902	0	18	162	393	1473	3225	6846	17054	42203	238244	•	5031869
Net Worth 29	13582	0	17	281	1169	2569	7107	19280	33694	78513	288687	•	4977750

Selected Financial Ratios (Times to 1)

Current Ratio 30	1.1	•	1.7	2.5	2.2	1.8	2.0	1.8	1.8	1.1	•	0.9
Quick Ratio 31	0.4	•	1.2	2.0	1.4	1.1	1.2	1.0	1.0	0.4	•	0.3
Net Sales to Working Capital 32	38.3	•	127.5	4.7	9.7	8.7	6.0	6.7	7.7	33.5	•	5.1
Coverage Ratio 33	5.1	13.5	44.0	8.9	7.0	5.6	7.5	5.0	3.8	3.8	•	5.1
Total Asset Turnover 34	0.7	•	27.8	2.4	2.6	2.1	1.5	1.5	1.5	1.0	•	0.4
Inventory Turnover 35	6.3	•	103.7	13.8	12.2	8.0	6.1	5.2	7.6	5.3	•	5.9
Receivables Turnover 36	6.2	•	205.6	4.3	11.8	9.3	6.1	8.7	9.4	18.5	•	11.0
Total Liabilities to Net Worth 37	2.0	2.6	1.1	1.2	1.8	1.2	0.8	1.1	1.1	1.9	•	2.2
Current Assets to Working Capital 38	16.8	2.4	1.7	1.9	2.3	2.2	2.0	2.2	2.3	10.6	•	•
Current Liabilities to Working Capital 39	15.8	1.4	0.7	0.9	1.3	1.2	1.0	1.2	1.3	9.6	•	•
Working Capital to Net Sales 40	0.0	0.0	0.2	0.1	0.1	0.1	0.2	0.1	0.1	0.0	•	•
Inventory to Working Capital 41	3.5	0.7	0.2	0.5	0.7	0.8	0.7	0.9	0.8	4.2	•	•
Total Receipts to Cash Flow 42	6.9	7.5	11.1	8.8	10.6	9.6	7.6	9.3	10.7	8.1	•	5.6
Cost of Goods to Cash Flow 43	4.2	5.3	7.7	5.6	7.2	6.7	5.3	6.5	7.9	5.4	•	3.0
Cash Flow to Total Debt 44	0.2	5.1	0.4	0.5	0.3	0.4	0.4	0.3	0.3	0.2	•	0.1

Selected Financial Factors (in Percentages)

Debt Ratio 45	66.3	•	72.1	51.9	54.1	64.1	53.7	45.6	52.5	51.7	65.2	•	69.1
Return on Total Assets 46	7.9	•	327.9	10.9	17.6	8.7	13.1	9.4	7.3	10.2	•	•	6.8
Return on Equity Before Income Taxes 47	18.8	•	1148.8	20.1	32.9	17.0	24.4	20.9	15.7	11.2	21.6	•	17.7
Return on Equity After Income Taxes 48	13.5	•	1144.5	19.6	31.6	14.0	21.9	17.3	12.7	8.5	15.9	•	11.6
Profit Margin (Before Income Tax) 49	8.9	20.3	11.5	4.0	5.8	2.8	5.4	7.6	5.0	3.6	7.5	•	12.3
Profit Margin (After Income Tax) 50	6.4	20.2	11.5	3.9	5.6	2.3	4.9	6.3	4.1	2.7	5.5	•	8.1

Table I
Corporations with and without Net Income

PRINTING AND RELATED SUPPORT ACTIVITIES

MONEY AMOUNTS AND SIZE OF ASSETS IN THOUSANDS OF DOLLARS

Item Description for Accounting Period 7/02 Through 6/03	Total	Zero Assets	Under 500	500 to 1,000	1,000 to 5,000	5,000 to 10,000	10,000 to 25,000	25,000 to 50,000	50,000 to 100,000	100,000 to 250,000	250,000 to 500,000	500,000 to 2,500,000	2,500,000 and over
Number of Enterprises **1**	32282	3160	22301	2377	3288	653	318	103	35	19	10	18	0
Revenues ($ in Thousands)													
Net Sales **2**	88034087	1855387	8570659	4450541	14489568	7488718	8131305	5600499	3351962	3020320	4800940	26274188	0
Interest **3**	284871	1670	3674	3585	7987	6495	4686	3614	3133	19296	38482	192251	0
Rents **4**	35166	250	58	2670	5366	5696	2906	1109	10	1795	337	14967	0
Royalties **5**	480625	8593	0	261	870	178	11498	2952	1723	829	18205	435518	0
Other Portfolio Income **6**	338765	68774	37973	11076	61212	23683	38005	9170	7055	6088	34520	41207	0
Other Receipts **7**	1439457	55179	43023	68735	118590	68663	73172	36654	16661	40491	55341	862946	0
Total Receipts **8**	90612971	1989853	8655387	4536868	14683593	7593433	8261572	5653998	3380544	3088819	4947825	27821077	0
Average Total Receipts **9**	2807	630	388	1909	4466	11629	25980	54893	96587	162569	494782	1545615	•
Operating Costs/Operating Income (%)													
Cost of Operations **10**	60.8	65.3	48.5	49.0	58.3	67.5	65.9	66.6	65.8	57.8	62.6	62.6	•
Salaries and Wages **11**	10.3	9.0	8.3	16.6	11.4	9.0	9.8	9.7	9.2	8.8	10.7	10.1	•
Taxes Paid **12**	2.6	4.3	3.3	2.8	2.7	2.5	2.4	2.3	2.0	2.2	1.6	2.5	•
Interest Paid **13**	2.3	1.2	1.1	0.9	1.7	1.7	1.4	1.6	1.6	4.4	4.7	3.2	•
Depreciation **14**	4.7	3.1	3.2	3.6	5.0	5.0	5.0	4.9	4.6	4.5	3.4	5.4	•
Amortization and Depletion **15**	0.4	0.7	0.3	0.1	0.3	0.1	0.2	0.3	0.4	1.1	0.9	0.5	•
Pensions and Other Deferred Comp. **16**	0.5	0.4	0.2	0.8	0.4	0.3	0.4	0.6	0.7	0.7	0.7	0.6	•
Employee Benefits **17**	2.2	1.7	1.1	1.3	1.3	1.3	1.7	2.2	1.7	2.7	3.0	3.6	•
Advertising **18**	0.7	0.3	1.1	0.4	0.4	0.4	0.7	1.1	2.3	1.3	0.8	0.6	•
Other Expenses **19**	13.4	17.2	23.3	15.7	13.7	11.9	9.1	7.9	8.8	12.7	9.7	13.6	•
Officers' Compensation **20**	3.1	3.5	9.1	7.3	5.6	2.7	2.5	1.8	1.1	1.2	1.0	0.5	•
Operating Margin **21**	•	•	0.5	1.9	•	•	0.9	0.9	1.9	2.6	1.0	•	•
Operating Margin Before Officers' Comp. **22**	2.2	9.7	9.7	9.2	4.7	0.4	3.4	2.8	3.0	3.8	1.9	1.9	•

Selected Average Balance Sheet ($ in Thousands)

Line item													
Net Receivables 23	348	0	28	171	527	1592	3733	8453	12711	21457	60067	217853	•
Inventories 24	128	0	6	54	145	717	1674	3721	7782	12381	26390	68270	•
Net Property, Plant and Equipment 25	595	0	39	209	873	2762	6023	13548	22969	38868	78089	418174	•
Total Assets 26	1877		115	685	2035	6942	15040	35191	69371	146719	340719	1563075	•
Notes and Loans Payable 27	708		83	241	950	3275	5777	13026	25854	72618	183717	437892	•
All Other Liabilities 28	587		38	143	454	1505	3760	8529	19195	33612	118779	594125	•
Net Worth 29	582	-6	301	631	2162	5503	13635	24322	40489	38224		531058	•

Selected Financial Ratios (Times to 1)

Line item													
Current Ratio 30	1.4	•	1.4	2.0	1.5	1.4	1.5	1.5	1.5	1.4	1.2	1.3	•
Quick Ratio 31	1.0	•	1.1	1.7	1.2	1.0	1.0	1.0	1.0	0.9	0.8	0.9	•
Net Sales to Working Capital 32	14.6	•	24.8	9.8	14.2	11.7	10.4	9.5	13.1	22.7	17.1	1.9	•
Coverage Ratio 33	1.9	1.5	2.4	5.1	1.2	0.5	2.2	2.7	2.1	1.9	1.9	1.9	•
Total Asset Turnover 34	1.5	•	3.3	2.7	2.2	1.7	1.5	1.4	1.1	1.4	1.4	0.9	•
Inventory Turnover 35	13.0	•	30.6	17.0	17.7	10.8	10.1	9.7	8.1	7.4	11.4	13.4	•
Receivables Turnover 36	7.2	•	12.6	8.7	8.8	7.0	6.8	7.0	6.8	6.1	8.0	5.5	•
Total Liabilities to Net Worth 37	2.2	•	1.3	2.0	2.2	2.2	1.7	1.6	1.9	2.6	7.9	1.9	•
Current Assets to Working Capital 38	3.6	•	3.8	2.0	3.1	3.3	3.4	3.1	2.9	3.5	5.4	4.6	•
Current Liabilities to Working Capital 39	2.6	•	2.8	1.0	2.1	2.3	2.4	2.1	1.9	2.5	4.4	3.6	•
Working Capital to Net Sales 40	0.1	•	0.0	0.1	0.1	0.1	0.1	0.1	0.1	0.1	0.0	0.1	•
Inventory to Working Capital 41	0.7	•	0.4	0.2	0.5	0.7	0.8	0.8	0.7	1.0	1.1	0.8	•
Total Receipts to Cash Flow 42	8.6	7.6	6.2	7.1	9.8	16.4	11.8	13.5	11.1	10.9	7.0	7.0	•
Cost of Goods to Cash Flow 43	5.2	4.9	3.0	3.5	5.7	11.1	7.8	9.0	7.2	4.0	5.8	4.4	•
Cash Flow to Total Debt 44	0.2	•	0.5	0.7	0.3	0.1	0.2	0.2	0.2	0.2	0.2	0.2	•

Selected Financial Factors (in Percentages)

Line item													
Debt Ratio 45	69.0	•	105.4	56.1	69.0	68.8	63.4	61.3	64.9	72.4	88.8	66.0	•
Return on Total Assets 46	6.2	•	8.8	13.1	4.6	1.3	6.6	5.4	6.0	10.0	12.4	5.6	•
Return on Equity Before Income Taxes 47	9.4	•	•	24.0	2.9	•	11.5	7.6	10.8	19.1	51.4	7.6	•
Return on Equity After Income Taxes 48	6.8	•	•	23.2	1.5	•	10.0	6.6	9.6	15.9	29.8	4.7	•
Profit Margin (Before Income Tax) 49	2.0	0.6	1.5	3.9	0.4	•	2.5	1.9	2.7	4.9	4.1	2.8	•
Profit Margin (After Income Tax) 50	1.4	0.5	1.5	3.7	0.2	•	2.1	1.6	2.4	4.1	2.4	1.7	•

Table II

Corporations with Net Income

PRINTING AND RELATED SUPPORT ACTIVITIES

MONEY AMOUNTS AND SIZE OF ASSETS IN THOUSANDS OF DOLLARS

Item Description for Accounting Period 7/02 Through 6/03	Total	Zero Assets	Under 500	500 to 1,000	1,000 to 5,000	5,000 to 10,000	10,000 to 25,000	25,000 to 50,000	50,000 to 100,000	100,000 to 250,000	250,000 to 500,000	500,000 to 2,500,000	2,500,000 and over
Number of Enterprises **1**	18065	1704	12040	1784	1833	379	209	67	21	10	4	13	0
Revenues ($ in Thousands)													
Net Sales **2**	55336157	462652	5085982	3810762	8874372	4940167	5544306	3785812	2437071	1891388	2257863	16245783	0
Interest **3**	147835	234	1460	2828	4054	2331	3082	1650	686	17870	13134	100506	0
Rents **4**	15248	202	0	2	1112	665	1985	821	10	1789	168	8495	0
Royalties **5**	276358	0	0	261	2	178	11354	245	1711	707	4726	257174	0
Other Portfolio Income **6**	221148	68013	24928	9509	17243	19517	30120	4426	3089	5487	16491	22326	0
Other Receipts **7**	956519	54576	13641	41009	92129	27758	52515	24323	13527	11445	55219	570374	0
Total Receipts **8**	56953265	585677	5126011	3864371	8998912	4990616	5643362	3817277	2456094	1928686	2347601	17204658	0
Average Total Receipts **9**	3153	344	426	2166	4904	13168	27002	56974	116957	192869	586900	1323435	•
Operating Costs/Operating Income (%)													
Cost of Operations **10**	58.4	50.6	49.3	46.9	56.8	66.4	63.2	64.3	64.6	54.7	57.7	59.3	•
Salaries and Wages **11**	10.3	6.6	6.5	17.1	10.3	8.8	9.9	9.4	8.7	7.8	10.9	11.3	•
Taxes Paid **12**	2.3	5.6	2.7	2.5	2.4	2.3	2.4	2.2	1.9	2.1	1.1	2.3	•
Interest Paid **13**	1.6	0.5	0.9	0.9	1.2	1.6	1.2	1.1	1.2	3.0	3.9	2.1	•
Depreciation **14**	4.3	1.7	2.7	3.6	3.9	4.6	4.5	4.1	4.2	4.2	3.3	5.2	•
Amortization and Depletion **15**	0.3	0.8	0.1	0.1	0.4	0.1	0.2	0.2	0.3	1.1	0.8	0.4	•
Pensions and Other Deferred Comp. **16**	0.6	1.3	0.2	0.9	0.5	0.4	0.5	0.6	0.8	0.9	1.0	0.7	•
Employee Benefits **17**	2.1	0.8	0.7	0.7	1.1	1.0	1.6	2.1	1.3	2.5	3.3	3.8	•
Advertising **18**	0.9	0.2	0.8	0.4	0.5	0.4	0.8	1.5	2.6	1.8	1.6	1.0	•
Other Expenses **19**	12.8	24.0	20.0	15.9	14.7	8.3	9.0	7.8	9.0	13.1	8.9	13.4	•
Officers' Compensation **20**	3.0	9.0	7.5	7.2	5.1	2.7	2.7	1.8	1.1	1.3	1.0	0.6	•
Operating Margin **21**	3.2	•	8.5	3.7	3.0	3.5	4.0	4.9	4.3	7.4	6.5	•	•
Operating Margin Before Officers' Comp. **22**	6.3	8.0	16.0	10.8	8.1	6.2	6.7	6.8	5.5	8.7	7.5	0.5	•

Selected Average Balance Sheet ($ in Thousands)

	•	•	•	•	•	•	•	•	•	•	•	•	•
Net Receivables 23	408	0	23	181	597	1758	3725	9045	13680	20992	77789	216430	
Inventories 24	147	0	6	41	178	708	1721	4213	8605	16678	46314	56687	
Net Property, Plant and Equipment 25	624	0	40	239	738	2916	5603	11985	24095	39763	86611	360174	
Total Assets 26	1873	•	110	691	2027	7049	15010	35048	70065	141992	407248	1145511	
Notes and Loans Payable 27	610	0	40	265	765	3087	4987	9792	17652	67829	235882	292503	
All Other Liabilities 28	538	0	24	126	490	1407	3513	8087	16469	28536	99598	420537	
Net Worth 29	725	0	46	300	773	2554	6510	17169	35944	45627	71769	432472	

Selected Financial Ratios (Times to 1)

	•	•	•	•	•	•	•	•	•	•	•	•	•
Current Ratio 30	1.6	•	2.0	2.2	1.7	1.5	1.7	1.7	1.7	1.7	1.5	1.7	1.4
Quick Ratio 31	1.1	•	1.7	1.9	1.4	1.1	1.1	1.1	1.1	1.1	1.0	1.1	0.9
Net Sales to Working Capital 32	10.8	•	14.1	9.9	10.6	13.1	8.9	8.0	8.0	11.9	9.4	12.0	
Coverage Ratio 33	4.9	54.4	11.2	6.6	4.6	3.8	5.9	6.3	5.4	4.1	3.7	3.8	
Total Asset Turnover 34	1.6	•	3.8	3.1	2.4	1.8	1.8	1.7	1.6	1.7	1.3	1.4	1.1
Inventory Turnover 35	12.2	•	35.3	24.6	15.5	12.2	9.7	8.6	8.7	6.2	7.0	13.1	
Receivables Turnover 36	6.7	•	16.1	10.0	8.8	6.9	7.4	6.6	8.7	6.0	6.0	4.6	
Total Liabilities to Net Worth 37	1.6	1.4	1.3	1.6	1.8	1.3	1.0	0.9	2.1	4.7	1.6		
Current Assets to Working Capital 38	2.8	•	2.0	1.8	2.4	3.2	2.5	2.5	2.4	2.8	2.5	3.7	
Current Liabilities to Working Capital 39	1.8	•	1.0	0.8	1.4	2.2	1.5	1.5	1.4	1.8	1.5	2.7	
Working Capital to Net Sales 40	0.1	•	0.1	0.1	0.1	0.1	0.1	0.1	0.1	0.1	0.1	0.1	
Inventory to Working Capital 41	0.5	•	0.3	0.2	0.4	0.7	0.6	0.6	0.7	0.9	0.6	0.5	
Total Receipts to Cash Flow 42	6.4	2.3	4.6	6.3	6.4	9.6	8.7	8.9	8.4	5.2	6.0	5.9	
Cost of Goods to Cash Flow 43	3.7	1.2	2.3	3.0	3.6	6.4	5.5	5.7	5.4	2.8	3.4	3.5	
Cash Flow to Total Debt 44	0.4	•	1.4	0.9	0.6	0.3	0.4	0.4	0.4	0.4	0.3	0.3	

Selected Financial Factors (in Percentages)

	•	•	•	•	•	•	•	•	•	•	•	•	•
Debt Ratio 45	61.3	58.7	56.6	61.9	63.8	56.6	51.0	48.7	67.9	82.4	62.2		
Return on Total Assets 46	12.7	38.9	18.6	13.2	11.4	12.4	11.0	10.3	16.5	20.0	8.7		
Return on Equity Before Income Taxes 47	26.2	85.8	36.3	27.1	23.2	23.7	18.9	16.4	38.9	83.2	17.0		
Return on Equity After Income Taxes 48	22.4	84.9	35.3	25.1	21.0	21.6	17.7	15.1	33.5	54.4	12.1		
Profit Margin (Before Income Tax) 49	6.2	25.6	9.2	5.1	4.3	4.5	5.8	5.7	5.1	9.4	10.6	5.9	
Profit Margin (After Income Tax) 50	5.3	25.3	9.1	5.0	4.0	4.1	5.3	5.4	4.7	8.1	6.9	4.2	

Table I

Corporations with and without Net Income

PETROLEUM REFINERIES (INCLUDING INTEGRATED)

MONEY AMOUNTS AND SIZE OF ASSETS IN THOUSANDS OF DOLLARS

Item Description for Accounting Period 7/02 Through 6/03	Total	Zero Assets	Under 500	500 to 1,000	1,000 to 5,000	5,000 to 10,000	10,000 to 25,000	25,000 to 50,000	50,000 to 100,000	100,000 to 250,000	250,000 to 500,000	500,000 to 2,500,000	2,500,000 and over
Number of Enterprises **1**	524	0	398	0	0	•	6	7	8	4	3	10	15

Revenues ($ in Thousands)

	Total	Zero Assets	Under 500	500 to 1,000	1,000 to 5,000	5,000 to 10,000	10,000 to 25,000	25,000 to 50,000	50,000 to 100,000	100,000 to 250,000	250,000 to 500,000	500,000 to 2,500,000	2,500,000 and over
Net Sales **2**	633137196	0	55270	0	0	•	247668	557544	1496139	1938275	3304528	19920963	603107262
Interest **3**	10185422	0	0	0	0	•	490	761	1348	2420	1619	48129	10129064
Rents **4**	1801466	0	0	0	0	•	0	90	1750	181	8410	41825	1749210
Royalties **5**	625626	0	0	0	0	•	0	0	3316	0	19	0	622291
Other Portfolio Income **6**	8190872	0	0	0	0	•	122	0	260	12412	29207	292932	7855938
Other Receipts **7**	16018156	0	1232	0	0	•	839	3484	14952	649	2504	332244	15649940
Total Receipts **8**	669958738	0	56502	0	0	•	249119	561879	1517765	1953937	3346287	20636093	639113705
Average Total Receipts **9**	1278547	•	142	•	•	•	41520	80268	189721	488484	1115429	2063609	42607580

Operating Costs/Operating Income (%)

	Total	Zero Assets	Under 500	500 to 1,000	1,000 to 5,000	5,000 to 10,000	10,000 to 25,000	25,000 to 50,000	50,000 to 100,000	100,000 to 250,000	250,000 to 500,000	500,000 to 2,500,000	2,500,000 and over
Cost of Operations **10**	83.1	•	4.8	•	•	•	85.9	87.6	91.4	94.1	91.6	92.0	82.7
Salaries and Wages **11**	1.9	•	31.3	•	•	•	2.2	2.6	1.3	1.1	2.4	1.6	1.9
Taxes Paid **12**	3.7	•	2.4	•	•	•	0.2	0.9	1.0	0.2	0.5	1.3	3.9
Interest Paid **13**	2.1	•	2.2	•	•	•	1.2	0.8	0.5	0.3	0.6	1.7	2.2
Depreciation **14**	2.3	•	30.4	•	•	•	3.8	3.4	1.4	2.7	1.1	1.6	2.4
Amortization and Depletion **15**	0.6	•	•	•	•	•	0.9	0.5	0.1	0.0	0.2	0.2	0.6
Pensions and Other Deferred Comp. **16**	0.7	•	•	•	•	•	•	0.1	0.3	0.1	0.1	0.2	0.7
Employee Benefits **17**	0.5	•	0.6	•	•	•	0.5	0.4	0.3	0.1	0.5	0.3	0.5
Advertising **18**	0.1	•	0.0	•	•	•	0.0	0.4	0.2	0.0	0.0	0.0	0.1
Other Expenses **19**	7.6	•	19.2	•	•	•	9.4	4.2	2.2	1.5	5.1	5.3	7.8
Officers' Compensation **20**	0.1	•	•	•	•	•	0.3	0.7	0.8	0.2	0.4	0.2	0.1
Operating Margin **21**	•	•	9.0	•	•	•	•	•	0.6	•	•	•	•
Operating Margin Before Officers' Comp. **22**	•	•	9.0	•	•	•	•	•	1.4	•	•	•	•

Selected Average Balance Sheet ($ in Thousands)

Net Receivables 23	150325	64	•	•	•	•	4880	8302	18269	25684	60133	135545	5124801
Inventories 24	36497	0	•	•	•	•	1058	7088	5577	26926	66845	99326	1181275
Net Property, Plant and Equipment 25	281811	32	•	•	•	•	7346	14392	25094	81654	101551	395943	9514602
Total Assets 26	2352259	190	•	•	•	•	17992	36712	71310	197806	370620	1078566	81255663
Notes and Loans Payable 27	422004	88	•	•	•	•	10019	11157	11345	25336	87195	365937	14456260
All Other Liabilities 28	745788	90	•	•	•	•	7228	12628	29318	67236	145478	335829	25755085
Net Worth 29	1184467	13	•	•	•	•	745	12926	30648	105234	137947	376799	41044318

Selected Financial Ratios (Times to 1)

Current Ratio 30	0.4	5.4	•	•	•	•	1.7	1.1	1.2	1.2	0.9	1.1	0.4
Quick Ratio 31	0.2	5.4	•	•	•	•	1.4	0.6	0.9	0.6	0.6	0.6	0.2
Net Sales to Working Capital 32	•	1.6	•	•	•	•	12.0	43.9	30.3	42.3	•	43.9	•
Coverage Ratio 33	2.9	6.1	•	•	•	•	•	•	5.0	2.1	•	1.0	3.0
Total Asset Turnover 34	0.5	0.7	•	•	•	•	2.3	2.2	2.6	2.4	3.0	1.8	0.5
Inventory Turnover 35	27.5	•	•	•	•	•	33.5	9.8	30.6	16.9	15.1	18.5	28.1
Receivables Turnover 36	6.1	4.3	•	•	•	•	10.0	8.8	11.6	19.4	14.8	18.2	5.9
Total Liabilities to Net Worth 37	1.0	14.0	•	•	•	•	23.2	1.8	1.3	0.9	1.7	1.9	1.0
Current Assets to Working Capital 38	•	1.2	•	•	•	•	2.4	9.6	5.5	6.4	•	7.8	•
Current Liabilities to Working Capital 39	•	0.2	•	•	•	•	1.4	8.6	4.5	5.4	•	6.8	•
Working Capital to Net Sales 40	•	0.6	•	•	•	•	0.1	0.0	0.0	0.0	•	0.0	•
Inventory to Working Capital 41	•	•	•	•	•	•	0.3	3.8	1.0	2.2	•	2.4	•
Total Receipts to Cash Flow 42	10.6	4.8	•	•	•	•	19.0	45.8	28.3	88.5	81.6	27.4	10.2
Cost of Goods to Cash Flow 43	8.8	0.2	•	•	•	•	16.3	40.1	25.9	83.3	74.7	25.2	8.5
Cash Flow to Total Debt 44	0.1	0.2	•	•	•	•	0.1	0.1	0.2	0.1	0.1	0.1	0.1

Selected Financial Factors (in Percentages)

Debt Ratio 45	49.6	93.3	•	•	•	•	95.9	64.8	57.0	46.8	62.8	65.1	49.5
Return on Total Assets 46	3.2	9.8	•	•	•	•	•	•	6.6	1.8	•	2.9	3.2
Return on Equity Before Income Taxes 47	4.1	122.6	•	•	•	•	•	•	12.3	1.8	•	•	4.2
Return on Equity After Income Taxes 48	2.5	102.0	•	•	•	•	•	•	9.9	•	•	•	2.6
Profit Margin (Before Income Tax) 49	4.1	11.2	•	•	•	•	•	2.0	0.4	•	•	•	4.3
Profit Margin (After Income Tax) 50	2.5	9.3	•	•	•	•	•	1.6	•	•	•	•	2.7

Table II
Corporations with Net Income

PETROLEUM REFINERIES (INCLUDING INTEGRATED)

MONEY AMOUNTS AND SIZE OF ASSETS IN THOUSANDS OF DOLLARS

Item Description for Accounting Period 7/02 Through 6/03	Total	Zero Assets	Under 500	500 to 1,000	1,000 to 5,000	5,000 to 10,000	10,000 to 25,000	25,000 to 50,000	50,000 to 100,000	100,000 to 250,000	250,000 to 500,000	500,000 to 2,500,000	2,500,000 and over
Number of Enterprises **1**	210	·	113	0	3	·	0	3	0	4	0	3	8
Revenues ($ in Thousands)													
Net Sales **2**	513842330	·	55270	0	161399	·	0	332390	0	286141	0	1807697	507492316
Interest **3**	9494671	·	0	0	341	·	0	566	0	3271	0	4412	9484371
Rents **4**	1636845	·	0	0	0	·	0	6	0	181	0	2038	1632870
Royalties **5**	503800	·	0	0	0	·	0	0	0	19	0	0	500466
Other Portfolio Income **6**	7675096	·	0	0	1	·	0	0	0	39176	0	276778	7359132
Other Receipts **7**	14673969	·	12	0	505	·	0	2886	0	2675	0	276239	14366448
Total Receipts **8**	547826711	·	55282	0	162246	·	0	335848	0	2906563	0	2367164	540835603
Average Total Receipts **9**	2608699	·	489	·	54082	·	·	111949	·	726641	·	789055	67604450
Operating Costs/Operating Income (%)													
Cost of Operations **10**	81.2	·	4.8	·	90.0	·	·	89.6	·	94.7	·	71.4	81.2
Salaries and Wages **11**	1.9	·	31.3	·	1.9	·	·	2.8	·	0.4	·	4.6	1.9
Taxes Paid **12**	4.0	·	2.4	·	0.3	·	·	0.6	·	0.2	·	1.1	4.1
Interest Paid **13**	2.2	·	·	·	0.3	·	·	0.4	·	0.2	·	1.2	2.3
Depreciation **14**	2.3	·	30.4	·	0.7	·	·	1.3	·	0.9	·	4.2	2.3
Amortization and Depletion **15**	0.6	·	·	·	0.0	·	·	0.1	·	0.2	·	0.7	0.6
Pensions and Other Deferred Comp. **16**	0.8	·	·	·	0.0	·	·	0.2	·	0.1	·	0.5	0.8
Employee Benefits **17**	0.6	·	0.6	·	0.8	·	·	0.7	·	0.0	·	0.4	0.6
Advertising **18**	0.1	·	0.0	·	0.1	·	·	0.1	·	0.0	·	0.0	0.1
Other Expenses **19**	8.4	·	18.8	·	3.3	·	·	2.0	·	1.5	·	10.8	8.5
Officers' Compensation **20**	0.1	·	·	·	0.6	·	·	0.5	·	0.3	·	1.0	0.1
Operating Margin **21**	·	·	11.6	·	2.1	·	·	1.8	·	1.4	·	4.1	·
Operating Margin Before Officers' Comp. **22**	·	·	11.6	·	2.6	·	·	2.3	·	1.7	·	5.1	·

Selected Average Balance Sheet ($ in Thousands)

Net Receivables 23	329294	227	4135	8817	26513	118308	8563742
Inventories 24	74530	0	1304	14261	44808	60375	1859141
Net Property, Plant and Equipment 25	572714	114	3590	8369	53723	376081	14844116
Total Assets 26	5387039	466	13527	38606	284856	1081227	14077454
Notes and Loans Payable 27	929808	100	7290	6467	24248	189783	24310027
All Other Liabilities 28	1752184	317	5627	13914	74132	185570	45859079
Net Worth 29	2705047	49	611	18225	186477	705874	70608347

Selected Financial Ratios (Times to 1)

Current Ratio 30	0.4	7.1	1.5	1.4	1.3	2.3	0.4
Quick Ratio 31	0.2	7.1	1.2	0.7	0.7	1.0	0.2
Net Sales to Working Capital 32		1.6	18.4	16.8	24.2	2.8	
Coverage Ratio 33	3.5		9.2	8.6	17.5	34.9	3.4
Total Asset Turnover 34	0.5	1.1	4.0	2.9	2.5	0.6	0.5
Inventory Turnover 35	26.7		37.1	7.0	15.1	7.1	27.7
Receivables Turnover 36	5.3		26.0	7.0	54.0	10.2	5.3
Total Liabilities to Net Worth 37	1.0	8.5	21.1	1.1	0.5	0.5	1.0
Current Assets to Working Capital 38		1.2	3.2	3.7	4.2	1.7	
Current Liabilities to Working Capital 39		0.2	2.2	2.7	3.2	0.7	
Working Capital to Net Sales 40		0.6	0.1	0.1	0.0	0.4	
Inventory to Working Capital 41			0.4	1.7	1.5	0.3	
Total Receipts to Cash Flow 42	8.7	4.8	18.4	23.7	32.1	2.3	8.7
Cost of Goods to Cash Flow 43	7.1	0.2	16.6	21.2	30.4	1.7	7.1
Cash Flow to Total Debt 44	0.1	0.2	0.2	0.2	0.2	0.7	0.1

Selected Financial Factors (in Percentages)

Debt Ratio 45	49.8	89.5	95.5	52.8	34.5	34.7	49.8
Return on Total Assets 46	3.5	12.2	11.5	9.3	7.9	24.1	3.5
Return on Equity Before Income Taxes 47	5.0	116.9	227.0	17.4	11.4	35.8	4.9
Return on Equity After Income Taxes 48	3.2	97.9	178.5	13.3	10.4	22.7	3.1
Profit Margin (Before Income Tax) 49	5.5	11.7	2.6	2.9	3.0	42.0	5.4
Profit Margin (After Income Tax) 50	3.6	9.8	2.0	2.2	2.7	26.6	3.5

Table I

Corporations with and without Net Income

ASPHALT PAVING, ROOFING, OTHER PETROLEUM AND COAL PRODUCTS

MONEY AMOUNTS AND SIZE OF ASSETS IN THOUSANDS OF DOLLARS

Item Description for Accounting Period 7/02 Through 6/03	Total	Zero Assets	Under 500	500 to 1,000	1,000 to 5,000	5,000 to 10,000	10,000 to 25,000	25,000 to 50,000	50,000 to 100,000	100,000 to 250,000	250,000 to 500,000	500,000 to 2,500,000	2,500,000 and over
Number of Enterprises 1	2369	0	1718	0	305	100	62	15	12	4	6	0	•
Revenues ($ in Thousands)													
Net Sales 2	12786319	0	632876	0	1665255	1078632	1626282	722233	1566368	740277	4432038	0	•
Interest 3	31842	0	0	0	1456	1511	2179	254	2340	6852	17116	0	•
Rents 4	7171	0	0	0	619	248	4007	29	17	16	1529	0	•
Royalties 5	40205	0	0	0	0	3	26	0	170	2439	36603	0	•
Other Portfolio Income 6	36426	0	0	0	1333	1508	4283	3892	997	2031	20633	0	•
Other Receipts 7	111373	0	-15084	0	1215	9200	9942	15881	21256	8409	49405	0	•
Total Receipts 8	13013336	0	617792	0	1669878	1091102	1646719	742289	1591148	760024	4557324	0	•
Average Total Receipts 9	5493	•	360	•	5475	10911	26560	49486	132596	190006	759554	•	
Operating Costs/Operating Income (%)													
Cost of Operations 10	72.8	•	49.6	•	73.6	71.6	70.6	73.7	83.1	76.1	73.8	•	•
Salaries and Wages 11	6.0	•	10.4	•	6.8	5.4	5.6	4.2	4.2	7.0	5.4	•	•
Taxes Paid 12	1.3	•	1.9	•	1.4	2.2	1.6	1.7	0.8	1.5	0.7	•	•
Interest Paid 13	1.5	•	1.9	•	0.6	1.0	0.9	1.1	0.4	1.8	2.6	•	•
Depreciation 14	3.4	•	4.0	•	2.5	4.3	4.0	4.4	2.5	3.4	3.3	•	•
Amortization and Depletion 15	0.2	•	•	•	0.0	0.1	0.1	0.5	0.3	0.9	0.3	•	•
Pensions and Other Deferred Comp. 16	0.5	•	0.0	•	0.7	0.6	0.4	0.4	0.1	0.4	0.6	•	•
Employee Benefits 17	0.8	•	0.6	•	0.2	1.3	0.9	1.0	1.1	0.3	0.8	•	•
Advertising 18	0.4	•	0.5	•	0.1	0.7	0.4	0.6	0.1	0.2	0.5	•	•
Other Expenses 19	9.9	•	20.9	•	6.8	7.8	9.5	9.4	7.8	7.9	10.9	•	•
Officers' Compensation 20	1.7	•	0.1	•	3.5	3.8	2.5	1.8	1.0	0.4	0.5	•	•
Operating Margin 21	1.5	•	10.2	•	3.8	1.2	3.5	1.1	•	0.1	0.5	•	•
Operating Margin Before Officers' Comp. 22	3.3	•	10.3	•	7.3	5.0	6.0	2.9	•	0.5	1.0	•	•

Selected Average Balance Sheet ($ in Thousands)

Net Receivables 23	587	•	14	•	322	•	1632	3654	7456	15081	24812	74423
Inventories 24	304	•	4	•	136	•	755	1680	3896	6095	15219	50079
Net Property, Plant and Equipment 25	1088	•	41	•	597	•	2720	5474	13056	18070	46312	181954
Total Assets 26	3310	•	80	•	2073	•	6500	15548	34295	68333	167390	558777
Notes and Loans Payable 27	1208	•	187	•	878	•	1854	4156	12288	9146	33176	231476
All Other Liabilities 28	923	•	199	•	497	•	1568	3244	7347	27401	35516	118339
Net Worth 29	1178	•	-306	•	698	•	3078	8148	14660	31786	98698	208962

Selected Financial Ratios (Times to 1)

Current Ratio 30	1.6	•	0.1	•	2.1	1.8	2.0	1.5	1.7	1.5	2.6	
Quick Ratio 31	1.1	•	0.1	•	1.9	1.4	1.0	1.1	1.1	0.7	1.9	
Net Sales to Working Capital 32	9.4	•	•	8.3	7.6	6.4	9.7	8.3	9.2	5.0		
Coverage Ratio 33	3.3	•	5.1	•	7.5	3.2	6.1	4.5	1.3	2.5	2.5	
Total Asset Turnover 34	1.6	•	4.6	•	2.6	1.7	1.7	1.4	1.9	1.1	1.3	
Inventory Turnover 35	12.9	•	44.3	•	29.5	10.2	11.0	9.1	17.8	9.3	10.9	
Receivables Turnover 36	10.0	•	23.2	•	17.9	8.8	7.2	6.4	10.5	8.8	10.3	
Total Liabilities to Net Worth 37	1.8	•	•	2.0	1.1	0.9	1.3	1.1	0.7	1.7		
Current Assets to Working Capital 38	2.7	•	•	1.9	2.2	2.0	2.8	2.5	3.0	1.6		
Current Liabilities to Working Capital 39	1.7	•	•	0.9	1.2	1.0	1.8	1.5	2.0	0.6		
Working Capital to Net Sales 40	0.1	•	•	0.1	0.1	0.2	0.1	0.1	0.1	0.2		
Inventory to Working Capital 41	0.6	•	•	0.1	0.4	0.5	0.8	0.5	0.9	0.4		
Total Receipts to Cash Flow 42	9.1	•	3.9	•	11.4	15.4	8.6	9.4	13.8	11.1	8.2	
Cost of Goods to Cash Flow 43	6.6	•	1.9	•	8.4	11.0	6.1	6.9	11.5	8.4	6.1	
Cash Flow to Total Debt 44	0.3	•	0.2	•	0.3	0.2	0.4	0.3	0.2	0.3		

Selected Financial Factors (in Percentages)

Debt Ratio 45	64.4	•	483.9	•	66.3	52.6	47.6	57.3	53.5	41.0	62.6	
Return on Total Assets 46	8.2	•	45.0	•	12.5	5.6	9.5	6.9	1.1	5.0	8.6	
Return on Equity Before Income Taxes 47	15.9	•	•	32.2	8.1	15.1	12.7	0.5	5.1	13.6		
Return on Equity After Income Taxes 48	13.2	•	•	30.6	6.1	12.5	10.6	•	2.6	11.0		
Profit Margin (Before Income Tax) 49	3.5	•	7.8	•	4.1	2.3	4.7	3.9	0.1	2.7	3.9	
Profit Margin (After Income Tax) 50	2.9	•	7.8	•	3.9	1.8	3.9	3.2	•	1.4	3.1	

Table II
Corporations with Net Income

ASPHALT PAVING, ROOFING, OTHER PETROLEUM AND COAL PRODUCTS

MONEY AMOUNTS AND SIZE OF ASSETS IN THOUSANDS OF DOLLARS

Item Description for Accounting Period 7/02 Through 6/03	Total	Zero Assets	Under 500	500 to 1,000	1,000 to 5,000	5,000 to 10,000	10,000 to 25,000	25,000 to 50,000	50,000 to 100,000	100,000 to 250,000	250,000 to 500,000	500,000 to 2,500,000	2,500,000 and over
Number of Enterprises 1	1502	0	960	0	269	56	42	11	0	0	0	0	•
Revenues ($ in Thousands)													
Net Sales 2	10707277	0	361322	0	1546113	647317	1166022	590680	0	0	0	0	•
Interest 3	13333	0	0	0	1438	1494	1475	254	0	0	0	0	•
Rents 4	6553	0	0	0	619	248	3670	29	0	0	0	0	•
Royalties 5	37763	0	0	0	0	3	24	0	0	0	0	0	•
Other Portfolio Income 6	28506	0	0	0	98	106	2999	3623	0	0	0	0	•
Other Receipts 7	92343	0	-15083	0	1181	8254	5571	15539	0	0	0	0	•
Total Receipts 8	10885775	0	346239	0	1549449	657422	1179761	610125	0	0	0	0	•
Average Total Receipts 9	7248	•	361	•	5760	11740	28090	55466	•	•	•	•	•
Operating Costs/Operating Income (%)													
Cost of Operations 10	72.1	•	33.8	•	73.2	71.2	69.2	71.9	•	•	•	•	•
Salaries and Wages 11	5.9	•	16.5	•	5.7	4.5	6.1	4.8	•	•	•	•	•
Taxes Paid 12	1.2	•	1.8	•	1.4	1.9	1.7	1.7	•	•	•	•	•
Interest Paid 13	1.5	•	1.2	•	0.3	1.0	0.7	1.0	•	•	•	•	•
Depreciation 14	2.9	•	3.0	•	1.9	3.0	3.1	3.5	•	•	•	•	•
Amortization and Depletion 15	0.2	•	•	•	•	0.2	0.1	0.6	•	•	•	•	•
Pensions and Other Deferred Comp. 16	0.4	•	0.1	•	0.7	0.6	0.4	0.5	•	•	•	•	•
Employee Benefits 17	0.7	•	0.4	•	0.2	0.3	0.4	1.0	•	•	•	•	•
Advertising 18	0.4	•	0.5	•	0.1	0.9	0.4	0.7	•	•	•	•	•
Other Expenses 19	9.0	•	21.2	•	5.8	6.0	8.2	10.0	•	•	•	•	•
Officers' Compensation 20	1.8	•	•	•	3.5	4.0	2.7	2.1	•	•	•	•	•
Operating Margin 21	3.9	•	21.5	•	7.3	6.5	6.5	2.3	•	•	•	•	•
Operating Margin Before Officers' Comp. 22	5.7	•	21.5	•	10.8	10.5	9.2	4.4	•	•	•	•	•

Selected Average Balance Sheet ($ in Thousands)

Net Receivables 23	734	7	303	1832	3629	8096
Inventories 24	383	0	90	740	1757	4495
Net Property, Plant and Equipment 25	1322	48	432	2475	5036	12184
Total Assets 26	3929	79	2002	6682	15629	34715
Notes and Loans Payable 27	1459	233	188	1966	3103	11115
All Other Liabilities 28	962	61	340	2099	3167	8960
Net Worth 29	1509	-215	1474	2617	9359	14640

Selected Financial Ratios (Times to 1)

Current Ratio 30	1.8	0.1	3.4	1.6	2.3	1.4
Quick Ratio 31	1.2	0.1	3.1	1.4	1.6	0.9
Net Sales to Working Capital 32	9.4	•	6.2	9.0	5.7	11.1
Coverage Ratio 33	5.0	15.4	29.0	8.9	11.4	6.8
Total Asset Turnover 34	1.8	4.7	2.9	1.7	1.8	1.5
Inventory Turnover 35	13.4	•	46.6	11.1	10.9	8.6
Receivables Turnover 36	10.3	102.4	38.0	9.3	6.8	6.4
Total Liabilities to Net Worth 37	1.6	•	0.4	1.6	0.7	1.4
Current Assets to Working Capital 38	2.3	•	1.4	2.7	1.8	3.2
Current Liabilities to Working Capital 39	1.3	•	0.4	1.7	0.8	2.2
Working Capital to Net Sales 40	0.1	•	0.2	0.1	0.2	0.1
Inventory to Working Capital 41	0.5	•	0.1	0.3	0.4	0.9
Total Receipts to Cash Flow 42	8.0	2.9	8.6	8.9	7.3	7.8
Cost of Goods to Cash Flow 43	5.7	1.0	6.3	6.3	5.0	5.6
Cash Flow to Total Debt 44	0.4	0.4	1.3	0.3	0.6	0.3

Selected Financial Factors (in Percentages)

Debt Ratio 45	61.6	371.1	26.4	60.8	40.1	57.8
Return on Total Assets 46	13.1	88.1	22.5	15.6	14.9	10.1
Return on Equity Before Income Taxes 47	27.3	•	29.4	35.5	22.6	20.5
Return on Equity After Income Taxes 48	23.9	•	28.6	31.4	19.3	17.7
Profit Margin (Before Income Tax) 49	5.8	17.4	7.6	8.0	7.6	5.6
Profit Margin (After Income Tax) 50	5.0	17.4	7.3	7.1	6.5	4.8

Table I

Corporations with and without Net Income

BASIC CHEMICAL

MONEY AMOUNTS AND SIZE OF ASSETS IN THOUSANDS OF DOLLARS

Item Description for Accounting Period 7/02 Through 6/03	Total	Zero Assets	Under 500	500 to 1,000	1,000 to 5,000	5,000 to 10,000	10,000 to 25,000	25,000 to 50,000	50,000 to 100,000	100,000 to 250,000	250,000 to 500,000	500,000 to 2,500,000	2,500,000 and over
Number of Enterprises 1	1335	0	642	0	267	117	71	29	27	14	12	28	18
Revenues ($ in Thousands)													
Net Sales 2	97234617	0	409982	0	1211655	1351300	1432182	1186953	2152242	2376891	3275519	21189041	61921686
Interest 3	260826	0	0	0	587	2373	3994	1720	6285	9294	26758	157005	2412264
Rents 4	203870	0	0	0	0	59	432	1737	40	28185	3674	26121	143621
Royalties 5	2480075	0	23503	0	0	0	347	1080	5468	5769	47556	275570	2120782
Other Portfolio Income 6	1919388	0	0	0	502	703	3091	2457	413	7492	32361	699817	1150777
Other Receipts 7	2998249	0	1437	0	8870	529	9038	6984	64526	23009	85339	336436	2442211
Total Receipts 8	107457025	0	434922	0	1221614	1354964	1449084	1200931	2228974	2450640	3471207	22683990	70191341
Average Total Receipts 9	80492	•	677	•	4575	11581	20410	41411	82555	175046	289267	810142	3899519
Operating Costs/Operating Income (%)													
Cost of Operations 10	72.0	•	66.5	•	62.9	55.9	68.8	58.8	71.3	65.9	67.8	66.7	75.2
Salaries and Wages 11	6.9	•	0.7	•	5.7	9.7	8.4	10.0	6.7	8.3	6.2	8.1	6.4
Taxes Paid 12	1.6	•	0.9	•	3.1	2.2	1.7	2.0	1.4	1.4	1.5	1.5	1.6
Interest Paid 13	6.6	•	0.4	•	1.1	1.7	1.3	1.8	2.0	1.9	5.1	4.1	8.4
Depreciation 14	7.1	•	0.4	•	4.1	2.1	4.5	9.9	5.4	6.7	7.5	6.0	7.7
Amortization and Depletion 15	1.1	•	0.6	•	0.6	0.2	0.2	0.5	1.1	0.2	1.8	1.2	1.2
Pensions and Other Deferred Comp. 16	1.5	•	•	•	0.7	0.6	0.6	0.7	0.4	0.8	0.7	1.8	1.6
Employee Benefits 17	2.5	•	1.0	•	1.0	1.2	1.7	1.7	1.5	1.6	1.3	2.2	2.8
Advertising 18	0.8	•	0.1	•	0.3	0.6	0.3	0.2	0.3	0.1	0.2	2.2	0.5
Other Expenses 19	11.5	•	25.1	•	11.2	15.2	9.5	15.7	12.8	14.0	12.0	12.7	10.7
Officers' Compensation 20	0.7	•	5.0	•	8.6	6.9	2.3	1.8	1.1	0.7	0.8	0.6	0.3
Operating Margin 21	•	•	•	•	0.7	3.8	0.5	•	•	•	•	•	•
Operating Margin Before Officers' Comp. 22	•	•	4.3	•	9.3	10.7	2.8	•	•	•	•	•	•

Selected Average Balance Sheet ($ in Thousands)

Item											
Net Receivables 23	41156	127	623	1701	3018	6409	12235	29929	49367	137443	2714947
Inventories 24	9160	28	349	1178	2536	4893	11258	21929	37866	136584	374416
Net Property, Plant and Equipment 25	34439	10	1182	1124	5075	16308	30196	58512	121364	349938	1766078
Total Assets 26	198282	234	2972	7107	15706	35784	73804	162791	350027	1184545	12169784
Notes and Loans Payable 27	79016	155	1625	3211	4809	12238	29220	49756	208108	384095	4949981
All Other Liabilities 28	55085	88	839	1696	3389	8966	20055	41089	77599	411896	3275205
Net Worth 29	64180	-9	509	2200	7508	14580	24529	71946	64320	388554	3944598

Selected Financial Ratios (Times to 1)

Item											
Current Ratio 30	0.9	0.9	1.5	2.8	2.0	1.6	1.5	1.3	1.9	1.6	0.9
Quick Ratio 31	0.7	0.7	1.1	1.5	1.2	1.0	0.8	0.8	1.1	0.7	0.7
Net Sales to Working Capital 32	•	8.8	4.2	4.9	7.8	8.1	11.6	5.3	5.9	5.3	•
Coverage Ratio 33	0.8	14.7	3.4	2.3	•	1.3	1.1	1.9	1.1	0.6	0.8
Total Asset Turnover 34	0.4	2.7	1.6	1.3	•	1.1	1.1	1.0	0.8	0.6	0.3
Inventory Turnover 35	5.7	15.0	5.5	5.5	•	4.9	5.0	5.1	4.9	3.7	6.9
Receivables Turnover 36	1.9	10.1	7.9	6.4	•	6.9	7.4	5.3	5.9	5.4	1.4
Total Liabilities to Net Worth 37	2.1	•	2.2	1.1	•	1.5	2.0	1.3	4.4	2.0	2.1
Current Assets to Working Capital 38	•	•	1.6	2.0	•	2.7	3.0	4.4	2.1	2.8	•
Current Liabilities to Working Capital 39	•	•	0.6	1.0	•	1.7	2.0	3.4	1.1	1.8	•
Working Capital to Net Sales 40	•	•	0.2	0.2	•	0.1	0.1	0.1	0.2	0.2	•
Inventory to Working Capital 41	•	•	0.4	0.6	•	0.9	1.2	1.4	0.8	1.0	•
Total Receipts to Cash Flow 42	15.7	3.8	6.3	10.3	•	8.9	11.1	7.3	10.6	12.3	21.4
Cost of Goods to Cash Flow 43	11.3	2.5	3.5	7.1	•	5.2	7.9	4.8	7.2	8.2	16.1
Cash Flow to Total Debt 44	0.0	0.7	0.4	0.2	•	0.2	0.1	0.3	0.1	0.1	0.0

Selected Financial Factors (in Percentages)

Item											
Debt Ratio 45	67.6	103.7	82.9	69.0	52.2	59.3	66.8	55.8	81.6	67.2	67.6
Return on Total Assets 46	2.1	15.8	4.0	9.2	3.9	•	1.4	3.8	5.6	2.9	1.8
Return on Equity Before Income Taxes 47	•	•	13.4	21.1	4.6	•	•	4.0	8.6	1.0	•
Return on Equity After Income Taxes 48	•	•	12.0	19.9	2.7	•	•	1.7	3.3	•	•
Profit Margin (Before Income Tax) 49	•	5.4	1.5	4.0	1.7	•	1.7	1.7	2.0	0.5	•
Profit Margin (After Income Tax) 50	5.4	5.4	1.3	3.8	1.0	•	0.7	0.7	0.8	•	•

Table II

Corporations with Net Income

BASIC CHEMICAL

MONEY AMOUNTS AND SIZE OF ASSETS IN THOUSANDS OF DOLLARS

Item Description for Accounting Period 7/02 Through 6/03	Total	Zero Assets	Under 500	500 to 1,000	1,000 to 5,000	5,000 to 10,000	10,000 to 25,000	25,000 to 50,000	50,000 to 100,000	100,000 to 250,000	250,000 to 500,000	500,000 to 2,500,000	2,500,000 and over
Number of Enterprises **1**	805	13	376	69	163	74	45	12	13	9	8	13	10
Revenues ($ in Thousands)													
Net Sales **2**	42160534	370807	114575	254875	808372	1023605	1068257	538198	1281841	1562377	2325538	10442370	22369719
Interest **3**	1222176	474	0	14	438	1428	3146	697	2898	5840	24982	66465	1115793
Rents **4**	95280	0	0	0	0	59	275	1732	40	28139	3472	19122	42440
Royalties **5**	994868	0	23503	0	0	0	329	1080	5021	4818	30693	255939	673486
Other Portfolio Income **6**	1483133	18718	0	0	248	64	2586	706	179	6754	31558	557682	864635
Other Receipts **7**	1591580	17849	1437	6012	223	957	4995	5132	6342	18640	73989	145462	1310545
Total Receipts **8**	47547571	407848	139515	260901	809281	1026113	1079588	547545	1296321	1626568	2490232	11487040	26376618
Average Total Receipts **9**	59065	31373	371	3781	4965	13866	23991	45629	99717	180730	311279	883618	2637662
Operating Costs/Operating Income (%)													
Cost of Operations **10**	61.0	79.0	72.2	59.3	59.3	61.4	65.6	49.3	67.9	61.6	67.8	58.3	61.0
Salaries and Wages **11**	9.3	0.8	2.7	7.3	4.9	7.5	8.4	10.2	7.1	10.1	6.3	10.0	9.9
Taxes Paid **12**	1.7	0.8	2.8	1.7	1.9	1.8	1.6	2.1	1.5	1.3	1.6	1.8	1.6
Interest Paid **13**	6.5	2.2	1.4	0.7	0.6	0.9	0.8	1.0	1.5	1.4	3.6	3.6	9.8
Depreciation **14**	7.2	12.4	1.0	1.5	2.6	1.6	3.2	4.4	4.0	5.6	7.0	6.3	8.7
Amortization and Depletion **15**	0.9	0.5	2.1	•	0.0	0.2	0.1	0.1	0.7	0.1	1.5	1.5	0.8
Pensions and Other Deferred Comp. **16**	0.9	•	•	•	0.6	0.3	0.7	0.3	0.3	0.7	1.0	1.8	0.7
Employee Benefits **17**	1.9	0.0	2.9	1.8	1.0	1.2	1.5	1.6	1.9	1.5	1.5	2.0	2.1
Advertising **18**	1.2	0.0	0.3	0.1	0.3	0.4	0.3	0.1	0.3	0.1	0.2	4.1	0.2
Other Expenses **19**	14.4	5.3	5.2	9.9	12.4	9.8	9.1	18.1	8.8	15.7	10.1	13.7	16.0
Officers' Compensation **20**	1.1	0.4	11.0	18.9	10.5	6.0	2.3	2.6	1.2	0.7	0.8	0.7	0.4
Operating Margin **21**	•	•	•	•	5.9	8.8	6.4	10.0	4.7	1.3	1.8	•	•
Operating Margin Before Officers' Comp. **22**	•	•	9.5	17.8	16.5	14.8	8.7	12.6	5.9	2.0	•	•	•

Selected Average Balance Sheet ($ in Thousands)

Net Receivables 23	32118	0	61	398	603	1599	3697	7920	14987	32686	48474	116765	2293159
Inventories 24	5656	0	59	280	371	1288	2812	4025	12774	19331	44646	124252	186554
Net Property, Plant and Equipment 25	25432	0	7	81	499	1055	4720	11897	25365	48381	119605	352612	1364384
Total Assets 26	165884	0	164	883	2583	7307	16123	32311	74009	160253	344498	1257007	10983728
Notes and Loans Payable 27	46517	0	264	484	379	2724	3840	6003	22365	32523	108746	292608	3154801
All Other Liabilities 28	46863	0	16	181	411	1212	2944	9569	17068	46244	58493	460528	3020961
Net Worth 29	72503	0	-116	218	1793	3371	9339	16739	34576	81486	177259	503371	4807966

Selected Financial Ratios (Times to 1)

Current Ratio 30	1.0	•	0.5	1.6	2.9	2.9	2.4	2.0	2.0	1.5	1.7	1.2	0.9
Quick Ratio 31	0.8	•	0.3	1.0	2.2	1.5	1.5	1.4	1.0	0.9	0.9	0.6	0.8
Net Sales to Working Capital 32	•	•	•	12.3	4.4	4.3	4.2	5.8	5.9	7.3	5.8	15.3	•
Coverage Ratio 33	2.2	4.9	15.3	2.8	10.6	10.6	10.2	12.6	5.0	5.0	2.8	3.0	1.8
Total Asset Turnover 34	0.3	•	1.9	4.2	1.9	1.9	1.5	1.4	1.3	1.1	0.8	0.6	0.2
Inventory Turnover 35	5.7	•	3.7	7.8	7.9	6.6	5.5	5.5	5.2	5.5	4.4	3.8	7.3
Receivables Turnover 36	2.2	•	2.1	18.6	7.5	9.4	6.3	5.3	7.9	5.1	7.1	7.4	1.3
Total Liabilities to Net Worth 37	1.3	•	•	3.0	0.4	1.2	0.7	0.9	1.1	1.0	0.9	1.5	1.3
Current Assets to Working Capital 38	•	•	•	2.6	1.5	1.5	1.7	2.0	2.0	3.0	2.4	5.9	•
Current Liabilities to Working Capital 39	•	•	•	1.6	0.5	0.5	0.7	1.0	1.0	2.0	1.4	4.9	•
Working Capital to Net Sales 40	•	•	•	0.1	0.2	0.2	0.2	0.2	0.2	0.1	0.2	0.1	•
Inventory to Working Capital 41	•	•	•	0.9	0.3	0.4	0.5	0.5	0.8	0.8	1.0	1.9	•
Total Receipts to Cash Flow 42	5.9	11.5	4.4	10.5	6.7	5.8	6.5	3.6	8.0	5.2	7.6	7.3	5.2
Cost of Goods to Cash Flow 43	3.6	9.1	3.2	6.2	4.0	3.6	4.3	1.8	5.4	3.2	5.2	4.2	3.2
Cash Flow to Total Debt 44	0.1	•	0.2	0.5	0.9	0.6	0.5	0.8	0.3	0.4	0.2	0.1	0.1

Selected Financial Factors (in Percentages)

Debt Ratio 45	56.3	•	170.9	75.3	30.6	53.9	42.1	48.2	53.3	49.2	48.5	59.9	56.2
Return on Total Assets 46	4.4	•	40.1	8.0	12.8	18.9	12.2	17.7	9.8	7.6	8.6	6.9	3.6
Return on Equity Before Income Taxes 47	5.4	•	•	20.9	16.7	37.1	18.9	31.4	16.7	12.0	10.9	11.5	3.7
Return on Equity After Income Taxes 48	4.1	•	•	17.8	16.0	35.9	16.6	26.0	14.2	8.8	8.0	8.7	2.6
Profit Margin (Before Income Tax) 49	7.5	8.4	20.2	1.2	6.0	9.0	7.5	11.7	5.9	5.6	6.6	7.2	7.9
Profit Margin (After Income Tax) 50	5.7	7.3	20.1	1.0	5.8	8.7	6.5	9.7	5.0	4.1	4.9	5.5	5.6

Table I

Corporations with and without Net Income

RESIN, SYNTHETIC RUBBER AND FIBERS AND FILAMENTS

MONEY AMOUNTS AND SIZE OF ASSETS IN THOUSANDS OF DOLLARS

Item Description for Accounting Period 7/02 Through 6/03		Total	Zero Assets	Under 500	500 to 1,000	1,000 to 5,000	5,000 to 10,000	10,000 to 25,000	25,000 to 50,000	50,000 to 100,000	100,000 to 250,000	250,000 to 500,000	500,000 to 2,500,000	2,500,000 and over
Number of Enterprises	1	606	0	263	0	210	36	27	14	8	7	4	5	4
Revenues ($ in Thousands)														
Net Sales	2	33624310	0	20981	0	1002244	184095	632470	846748	847965	777844	1322980	5399519	22546523
Interest	3	1984285	0	8	0	360	758	848	2753	1225	11406	6161	45422	1914986
Rents	4	85565	0	0	0	30	0	138	707	432	793	499	4250	78652
Royalties	5	552483	0	0	0	0	0	2712	0	231	0	1644	12300	535515
Other Portfolio Income	6	343299	0	3724	0	0	447	81	62	1481	802	57182	52352	227113
Other Receipts	7	855017	0	204	0	442	9303	2307	623	2998	29246	8350	49504	752036
Total Receipts	8	37444959	0	24917	0	1003076	194603	638556	850893	854332	820091	1396816	5563347	26054825
Average Total Receipts	9	61790	•	95	•	4777	5406	23650	60778	106792	117156	349204	1112669	6513706
Operating Costs/Operating Income (%)														
Cost of Operations	10	66.6	•	22.3	•	58.1	54.4	69.5	75.8	79.5	76.7	81.3	74.0	63.2
Salaries and Wages	11	3.1	•	0.2	•	11.7	13.3	6.7	5.0	3.6	4.8	4.3	1.9	2.6
Taxes Paid	12	0.9	•	2.9	•	1.9	1.5	1.7	1.5	1.0	1.1	1.3	0.6	0.8
Interest Paid	13	8.0	•	0.3	•	1.2	2.1	1.2	1.2	1.7	4.9	2.5	3.7	10.5
Depreciation	14	4.9	•	0.6	•	3.6	5.5	3.4	4.1	4.4	11.2	1.9	5.7	4.8
Amortization and Depletion	15	0.5	•	0.1	•	0.0	4.0	0.5	0.2	0.7	2.3	1.2	1.0	0.3
Pensions and Other Deferred Comp.	16	0.3	•	•	•	0.2	0.0	0.2	1.1	0.1	0.3	0.4	0.5	0.2
Employee Benefits	17	2.6	•	0.3	•	0.7	4.0	0.8	1.3	2.1	0.8	1.9	1.0	3.3
Advertising	18	0.4	•	•	•	0.3	1.7	0.4	0.2	0.2	0.1	0.1	0.2	0.5
Other Expenses	19	23.8	•	5.3	•	14.7	15.4	11.6	6.4	4.9	10.7	6.6	13.6	30.0
Officers' Compensation	20	0.3	•	2.9	•	1.7	0.6	2.7	1.2	0.9	1.4	0.7	0.2	0.1
Operating Margin	21	•	•	65.2	•	5.8	•	1.3	1.9	0.9	•	1.0	•	•
Operating Margin Before Officers' Comp.	22	•	•	68.1	•	7.5	•	3.9	3.1	1.8	•	1.0	•	•

Selected Average Balance Sheet ($ in Thousands)

Net Receivables 23	8458	•	3	•	499	569	3318	8649	11775	23553	48265	154547	890472
Inventories 24	7304	•	0	•	491	600	2874	5310	14806	11198	34176	128085	793806
Net Property, Plant and Equipment 25	26572	•	0	•	783	1325	4990	14064	30267	69735	145610	607913	2800938
Total Assets 26	171508	•	8	•	2193	6457	15070	35714	79764	176001	366523	1440561	22941807
Notes and Loans Payable 27	30706	•	4	•	833	1859	5287	10166	25474	107110	73500	538977	3534181
All Other Liabilities 28	63609	•	12	•	727	629	3362	9804	22790	25212	110881	415010	8810286
Net Worth 29	77194	•	-8	•	632	3969	6421	15743	31500	43679	182142	486574	10597340

Selected Financial Ratios (Times to 1)

Current Ratio 30	1.2	•	0.6	•	1.2	1.6	1.6	1.8	1.3	1.2	2.0	1.5	1.1
Quick Ratio 31	0.6	•	0.6	•	0.8	1.0	0.9	1.2	0.6	0.8	1.3	0.8	0.6
Net Sales to Working Capital 32	15.9	•	•	•	20.3	4.8	8.0	7.4	13.7	16.6	6.1	5.8	38.1
Coverage Ratio 33	1.1	•	333.3	•	5.7	2.5	2.8	3.1	2.0	•	3.1	1.3	1.1
Total Asset Turnover 34	0.3	•	10.4	•	2.2	0.8	1.6	1.7	1.3	0.6	0.9	0.7	0.2
Inventory Turnover 35	5.1	•	•	•	5.6	4.6	5.7	8.6	5.7	7.6	7.9	6.2	4.5
Receivables Turnover 36	6.6	•	47.4	•	7.9	6.6	7.7	8.8	6.0	5.6	6.1	7.1	6.5
Total Liabilities to Net Worth 37	1.2	•	•	•	2.5	0.6	1.3	1.3	1.5	3.0	1.0	2.0	1.2
Current Assets to Working Capital 38	5.9	•	•	•	5.5	2.6	2.7	2.2	4.6	6.7	2.0	2.9	13.3
Current Liabilities to Working Capital 39	4.9	•	•	•	4.5	1.6	1.7	1.2	3.6	5.7	1.0	1.9	12.3
Working Capital to Net Sales 40	0.1	•	•	•	0.0	0.2	0.1	0.1	0.1	0.1	0.2	0.2	0.0
Inventory to Working Capital 41	2.0	•	•	•	1.9	0.4	1.0	0.7	1.7	1.5	0.7	0.7	5.3
Total Receipts to Cash Flow 42	4.9	•	1.4	•	5.8	6.1	8.2	13.0	17.7	169.2	11.0	8.2	4.0
Cost of Goods to Cash Flow 43	3.3	•	0.3	•	3.3	3.3	5.7	9.9	14.1	129.8	8.9	6.0	2.5
Cash Flow to Total Debt 44	0.1	•	3.5	•	0.5	0.3	0.3	0.2	0.1	0.0	0.2	0.1	0.1

Selected Financial Factors (in Percentages)

Debt Ratio 45	55.0	•	209.8	•	71.2	38.5	57.4	55.9	60.5	75.2	50.3	66.2	53.8
Return on Total Assets 46	2.9	•	877.9	•	15.4	4.1	5.4	6.1	4.4	•	6.9	3.5	2.7
Return on Equity Before Income Taxes 47	0.7	•	•	•	44.1	3.9	8.1	9.3	5.5	•	9.4	2.2	0.4
Return on Equity After Income Taxes 48	0.2	•	•	•	41.2	2.6	6.8	7.7	5.3	•	4.6	•	0.1
Profit Margin (Before Income Tax) 49	1.0	•	83.9	•	5.8	3.0	2.2	2.4	1.6	•	5.2	1.0	0.7
Profit Margin (After Income Tax) 50	0.3	•	82.1	•	5.5	2.0	1.9	2.0	1.6	•	2.5	•	0.2

Table II
Corporations with Net Income

RESIN, SYNTHETIC RUBBER AND FIBERS AND FILAMENTS

MONEY AMOUNTS AND SIZE OF ASSETS IN THOUSANDS OF DOLLARS

Item Description for Accounting Period 7/02 Through 6/03	Total	Zero Assets	Under 500	500 to 1,000	1,000 to 5,000	5,000 to 10,000	10,000 to 25,000	25,000 to 50,000	50,000 to 100,000	100,000 to 250,000	250,000 to 500,000	500,000 to 2,500,000	2,500,000 and over
Number of Enterprises **1**	259	0	30	27	152	0	18	8	4	0	0	0	0
Revenues ($ in Thousands)													
Net Sales **2**	24098964	0	20981	19112	865245	0	463954	582573	654293	0	0	0	0
Interest **3**	1921988	0	8	310	196	0	742	516	612	0	0	0	0
Rents **4**	43619	0	0	0	0	0	138	292	739	0	0	0	0
Royalties **5**	539870	0	0	0	0	0	2712	0	0	0	0	0	0
Other Portfolio Income **6**	211319	0	3724	56	0	0	47	54	834	0	0	0	0
Other Receipts **7**	740311	0	204	0	160	0	1547	366	1765	0	0	0	0
Total Receipts **8**	27556071	0	24917	19478	865601	0	469140	583801	658243	0	0	0	0
Average Total Receipts **9**	106394	•	831	721	5695	•	26063	72975	164561	•	•	•	•
Operating Costs/Operating Income (%)													
Cost of Operations **10**	61.0	•	22.3	56.3	58.6	•	65.9	74.4	74.9	•	•	•	•
Salaries and Wages **11**	2.4	•	0.2	0.8	11.2	•	7.3	5.9	5.2	•	•	•	•
Taxes Paid **12**	0.9	•	2.9	3.9	1.7	•	1.8	1.3	1.3	•	•	•	•
Interest Paid **13**	9.5	•	0.3	0.0	0.9	•	1.0	0.6	2.5	•	•	•	•
Depreciation **14**	4.8	•	0.6	3.3	1.8	•	2.8	3.4	3.8	•	•	•	•
Amortization and Depletion **15**	0.3	•	0.1	0.0	•	•	0.6	0.1	1.3	•	•	•	•
Pensions and Other Deferred Comp. **16**	0.2	•	•	•	0.2	•	0.3	0.3	0.2	•	•	•	•
Employee Benefits **17**	3.3	•	0.3	•	0.5	•	1.0	1.0	1.0	•	•	•	•
Advertising **18**	0.5	•	•	0.1	0.3	•	0.5	0.2	0.2	•	•	•	•
Other Expenses **19**	28.5	•	5.3	16.1	13.5	•	12.2	5.8	5.6	•	•	•	•
Officers' Compensation **20**	0.3	•	2.9	20.0	1.6	•	3.2	1.0	1.4	•	•	•	•
Operating Margin **21**	•	•	65.2	•	9.5	•	3.4	6.0	2.5	•	•	•	•
Operating Margin Before Officers' Comp. **22**	•	•	68.1	19.4	11.2	•	6.6	7.0	3.9	•	•	•	•

Selected Average Balance Sheet ($ in Thousands)

Net Receivables 23	15868	30	65	634	3443	8868	39788
Inventories 24	12535	0	10	483	2768	5693	15546
Net Property, Plant and Equipment 25	38530	4	107	523	3790	13406	37013
Total Assets 26	349082	67	967	2177	15010	36898	128290
Notes and Loans Payable 27	47332	32	20	548	4128	8694	57865
All Other Liabilities 28	131557	109	809	754	3398	7342	26044
Net Worth 29	170192	-74	137	875	7484	20862	44381

Selected Financial Ratios (Times to 1)

Current Ratio 30	1.6	0.6	1.0	1.3	1.7	2.2	2.8
Quick Ratio 31	0.9	0.6	1.0	0.8	1.0	1.5	2.2
Net Sales to Working Capital 32	6.9			15.7	7.5	6.4	3.9
Coverage Ratio 33	1.4	333.5	244.0	11.9	5.5	11.2	2.9
Total Asset Turnover 34	0.3	10.4	0.7	2.6	1.7	2.0	1.3
Inventory Turnover 35	4.5		39.4	6.9	6.1	9.5	7.9
Receivables Turnover 36	6.0			9.4	8.7	9.2	4.6
Total Liabilities to Net Worth 37	1.1		6.0	1.5	1.0	0.8	1.9
Current Assets to Working Capital 38	2.7			4.3	2.4	1.8	1.5
Current Liabilities to Working Capital 39	1.7			3.3	1.4	0.8	0.5
Working Capital to Net Sales 40	0.1			0.1	0.1	0.2	0.3
Inventory to Working Capital 41	0.9			1.4	0.9	0.5	0.3
Total Receipts to Cash Flow 42	3.7	1.4	6.2	4.9	6.6	9.5	12.4
Cost of Goods to Cash Flow 43	2.3	0.3	3.5	2.9	4.3	7.1	9.3
Cash Flow to Total Debt 44	0.1	3.5	0.1	0.9	0.5	0.5	0.2

Selected Financial Factors (in Percentages)

Debt Ratio 45	51.2	209.8	85.8	59.8	50.1	43.5	65.4
Return on Total Assets 46	3.6	878.9	0.9	27.3	9.5	13.5	9.3
Return on Equity Before Income Taxes 47	2.1		6.5	62.3	15.6	21.7	17.7
Return on Equity After Income Taxes 48	1.6		5.7	59.3	14.0	19.5	16.2
Profit Margin (Before Income Tax) 49	3.9	84.0	1.3	9.6	4.5	6.2	4.8
Profit Margin (After Income Tax) 50	2.9	82.2	1.1	9.1	4.1	5.6	4.4

Table I

Corporations with and without Net Income

PHARMACEUTICAL AND MEDICINE

MONEY AMOUNTS AND SIZE OF ASSETS IN THOUSANDS OF DOLLARS

Item Description for Accounting Period 7/02 Through 6/03	Total	Zero Assets	Under 500	500 to 1,000	1,000 to 5,000	5,000 to 10,000	10,000 to 25,000	25,000 to 50,000	50,000 to 100,000	100,000 to 250,000	250,000 to 500,000	500,000 to 2,500,000	2,500,000 and over
Number of Enterprises 1	1381	39	529	79	328	112	87	61	48	33	15	25	25
Revenues ($ in Thousands)													
Net Sales 2	249096548	334803	32088	196080	1348554	858325	1588649	1815645	2420817	3282725	4071379	19616159	213531325
Interest 3	5418708	41094	159	329	2193	5442	10683	19306	27248	58774	28843	334699	4889940
Rents 4	180561	5151	0	0	3455	20	220	350	1155	2690	603	10638	156280
Royalties 5	13415678	34711	0	0	1612	866	6131	14359	13247	20120	132988	480683	12710961
Other Portfolio Income 6	11795692	14654	0	35	2259	70588	11629	13282	3601	15940	7855	676361	10979489
Other Receipts 7	15356978	848776	230	1	16556	10614	49748	39657	67676	125010	229292	679206	13290206
Total Receipts 8	295264165	1279189	32477	196445	1374629	945855	1667060	1902599	2553744	3505259	4470960	21797746	255558201
Average Total Receipts 9	213805	32800	61	2487	4191	8445	19162	31190	52786	106220	298064	871910	10222328
Operating Costs/Operating Income (%)													
Cost of Operations 10	52.3	41.6	36.6	62.6	53.4	47.4	65.0	45.6	43.1	41.4	41.3	38.9	54.0
Salaries and Wages 11	13.6	14.1	36.1	16.5	17.6	15.8	12.7	16.2	18.1	13.5	8.6	12.3	13.8
Taxes Paid 12	1.6	9.7	3.4	3.8	3.3	3.4	2.6	2.6	2.8	2.0	1.6	2.1	1.5
Interest Paid 13	4.0	1.1	1.8	0.8	1.5	1.7	1.2	1.1	1.7	2.1	2.9	3.0	4.3
Depreciation 14	2.9	2.5	10.2	2.3	4.8	4.4	3.4	5.0	4.0	3.9	1.7	2.3	2.9
Amortization and Depletion 15	1.1	0.6	0.2	1.1	0.4	0.8	2.0	1.6	1.5	0.2	1.1	1.1	1.1
Pensions and Other Deferred Comp. 16	2.2	0.6	0.4	*	0.5	0.6	0.2	0.5	0.7	0.4	0.2	1.0	2.4
Employee Benefits 17	1.6	1.3	1.0	1.7	1.1	2.8	1.7	1.9	2.5	2.8	1.7	1.6	1.6
Advertising 18	4.0	6.2	0.1	0.0	3.1	0.6	1.9	4.4	3.1	2.3	0.9	3.8	4.2
Other Expenses 19	24.5	191.7	85.8	22.9	20.2	32.7	27.4	30.2	32.9	33.4	28.6	27.6	23.5
Officers' Compensation 20	0.4	1.9	3.9	2.4	5.3	4.0	3.5	3.6	3.4	2.0	1.5	1.0	0.2
Operating Margin 21	*	*	*	*	*	*	*	*	*	*	*	10.0	5.2
Operating Margin Before Officers' Comp. 22	*	*	*	*	*	*	*	*	*	*	*	11.5	6.2

Selected Average Balance Sheet ($ in Thousands)

Net Receivables 23	68056	0	3	126	631	1084	2431	5373	10976	29625	58374	164384	3464648
Inventories 24	19435	0	6	243	554	569	2317	4383	10064	12927	41018	119185	863952
Net Property, Plant and Equipment 25	44296	0	47	139	922	2009	3334	8249	15152	30307	41460	133592	2165099
Total Assets 26	371208	0	125	623	2644	6707	16355	35064	72739	168293	331240	1202441	18530688
Notes and Loans Payable 27	144229	0	470	291	2436	1458	3917	7671	16528	33026	79757	268841	7493479
All Other Liabilities 28	124318	0	77	390	652	1411	4411	7608	19333	35733	91486	230025	6446460
Net Worth 29	102661	0	-422	-58	-444	3839	8028	19786	36877	99534	159997	703575	4590749

Selected Financial Ratios (Times to 1)

Current Ratio 30	1.0	•	0.9	1.2	1.7	2.3	2.1	2.3	2.4	2.4	1.6	2.3	0.9
Quick Ratio 31	0.6	•	0.3	0.5	1.1	1.7	1.5	1.4	1.6	1.5	0.7	1.2	0.6
Net Sales to Working Capital 32	•	•	•	26.8	6.1	3.5	3.2	2.7	2.1	2.0	3.8	2.4	•
Coverage Ratio 33	4.3	97.5	•	•	•	•	•	•	•	2.8	8.0	6.7	4.2
Total Asset Turnover 34	0.5	•	0.5	4.0	1.6	1.1	1.1	0.8	0.7	0.6	0.8	0.7	0.5
Inventory Turnover 35	4.9	•	3.6	6.4	4.0	6.4	5.1	3.1	2.2	3.2	2.7	2.6	5.3
Receivables Turnover 36	3.0	•	16.8	11.9	6.6	4.8	7.8	5.3	4.4	4.3	4.9	4.6	2.8
Total Liabilities to Net Worth 37	2.6	•	•	•	•	0.7	1.0	0.8	1.0	0.7	1.1	0.7	3.0
Current Assets to Working Capital 38	•	•	•	5.0	2.4	1.7	1.9	1.8	1.7	1.7	2.8	1.8	•
Current Liabilities to Working Capital 39	•	•	•	4.0	1.4	0.7	0.9	0.8	0.7	0.7	1.8	0.8	•
Working Capital to Net Sales 40	•	•	•	0.0	0.2	0.3	0.3	0.4	0.5	0.5	0.3	0.4	•
Inventory to Working Capital 41	•	•	•	2.8	0.8	0.3	0.4	0.4	0.4	0.3	0.7	0.4	•
Total Receipts to Cash Flow 42	3.3	0.4	•	70.5	15.9	7.4	16.8	5.2	5.0	3.0	2.1	2.6	3.5
Cost of Goods to Cash Flow 43	1.8	0.1	•	44.1	8.5	3.5	10.9	2.4	2.2	1.2	0.9	1.0	1.9
Cash Flow to Total Debt 44	0.2	•	•	0.1	0.1	0.4	0.1	0.4	0.3	0.5	0.7	0.6	0.2

Selected Financial Factors (in Percentages)

Debt Ratio 45	72.3	•	436.9	109.3	116.8	42.8	50.9	43.6	49.3	40.9	51.7	41.5	75.2
Return on Total Assets 46	8.5	•	•	•	•	•	•	•	•	3.5	18.8	13.1	8.4
Return on Equity Before Income Taxes 47	23.6	•	11.3	597.5	85.4	•	•	•	3.8	3.8	34.1	19.0	25.8
Return on Equity After Income Taxes 48	15.8	•	11.3	597.5	85.4	•	•	•	•	•	20.6	13.0	17.8
Profit Margin (Before Income Tax) 49	13.4	110.5	•	•	•	•	•	•	•	3.8	20.1	17.1	13.9
Profit Margin (After Income Tax) 50	9.0	66.0	•	•	•	•	•	•	•	•	12.2	11.6	9.6

Table II

Corporations with Net Income

PHARMACEUTICAL AND MEDICINE

MONEY AMOUNTS AND SIZE OF ASSETS IN THOUSANDS OF DOLLARS

Item Description for Accounting Period 7/02 Through 6/03	Total	Zero Assets	Under 500	500 to 1,000	1,000 to 5,000	5,000 to 10,000	10,000 to 25,000	25,000 to 50,000	50,000 to 100,000	100,000 to 250,000	250,000 to 500,000	500,000 to 2,500,000	2,500,000 and over
Number of Enterprises 1	467	14	0	59	150	0	36	30	23	20	10	22	21
Revenues ($ in Thousands)													
Net Sales 2	221671160	275272	0	186216	809402	0	1218020	1334832	1989749	2412515	3674406	19392497	189551910
Interest 3	4207273	40564	0	0	141	0	1071	4442	2131	27164	22637	283112	3823704
Rents 4	147733	5151	0	0	3286	0	3	202	190	48	580	10636	127617
Royalties 5	11366167	34638	0	0	0	0	0	7041	9899	16216	132888	432075	10732545
Other Portfolio Income 6	9854318	14651	0	0	153	0	1014	11291	3494	11458	7854	674556	9059268
Other Receipts 7	14413281	847831	0	0	12958	0	19379	14015	27095	73659	218738	635191	12557276
Total Receipts 8	261659932	1218107	0	186216	825940	0	1239487	1371823	2032558	2541060	4057103	21428067	225852320
Average Total Receipts 9	560300	87008	•	3156	5506	•	34430	45727	88372	127053	405710	974003	10754872
Operating Costs/Operating Income (%)													
Cost of Operations 10	51.8	38.1	•	65.8	50.8	•	66.7	41.4	43.0	38.8	36.5	39.1	53.6
Salaries and Wages 11	13.1	6.3	•	8.6	17.3	•	5.2	11.6	12.1	7.8	8.0	11.8	13.5
Taxes Paid 12	1.6	10.7	•	3.1	2.1	•	1.2	2.2	2.3	1.8	1.7	2.0	1.5
Interest Paid 13	3.5	0.3	•	0.8	0.8	•	0.6	1.0	1.0	0.9	3.0	2.6	3.7
Depreciation 14	2.6	1.4	•	1.4	3.0	•	1.9	3.2	2.8	2.6	1.3	2.2	2.7
Amortization and Depletion 15	0.9	0.6	•	•	0.1	•	0.2	1.1	0.7	0.4	1.1	1.0	0.9
Pensions and Other Deferred Comp. 16	2.1	0.7	•	•	0.7	•	0.1	0.6	0.6	0.3	0.2	1.0	2.3
Employee Benefits 17	1.5	1.2	•	1.2	1.1	•	0.8	1.5	1.6	2.0	1.7	1.6	1.5
Advertising 18	4.2	7.4	•	•	0.4	•	1.4	4.5	3.2	2.0	1.0	3.7	4.4
Other Expenses 19	22.5	216.2	•	14.9	13.4	•	10.8	20.1	18.8	23.7	28.3	26.3	21.9
Officers' Compensation 20	0.3	1.7	•	2.2	4.5	•	1.8	2.7	2.1	1.1	1.4	1.0	0.2
Operating Margin 21	•	•	•	2.0	5.7	•	9.4	10.3	11.9	18.8	15.9	7.9	•
Operating Margin Before Officers' Comp. 22	•	•	•	4.2	10.2	•	11.2	13.0	14.0	19.9	17.4	8.8	•

Selected Average Balance Sheet ($ in Thousands)

Net Receivables 23	188801	0	169	706	3731	6835	15794	40277	78901	183715	3885794
Inventories 24	48674	0	326	638	3502	5906	13062	16231	35113	124133	883226
Net Property, Plant and Equipment 25	106669	0	56	908	3417	8503	17616	26598	36673	134038	2135845
Total Assets 26	952920	0	617	2489	16051	34884	72440	173055	340044	1268581	19333818
Notes and Loans Payable 27	363674	0	297	1083	4173	7193	20043	20058	76305	243731	7722707
All Other Liabilities 28	330943	0	306	533	4502	7633	25578	41858	115820	252467	6945263
Net Worth 29	258302	0	14	872	7376	20058	26820	111139	147918	772383	4665848

Selected Financial Ratios (Times to 1)

Current Ratio 30	1.0	•	1.8	1.8	2.0	2.4	1.8	2.1	1.3	2.1	0.9
Quick Ratio 31	0.6	•	0.7	1.0	1.1	1.4	1.1	1.4	0.8	1.1	0.6
Net Sales to Working Capital 32	•	461.3	12.4	7.9	6.3	3.7	4.9	2.6	8.5	2.8	•
Coverage Ratio 33	6.0	•	3.6	10.6	20.0	14.2	15.4	28.9	10.0	8.3	5.5
Total Asset Turnover 34	0.5	•	5.1	2.2	2.1	1.3	1.2	0.7	1.1	0.7	0.5
Inventory Turnover 35	5.0	•	6.4	4.3	6.4	3.1	2.8	2.9	3.8	2.8	5.5
Receivables Turnover 36	3.1	•	16.9	7.1	9.9	6.4	5.5	4.0	5.3	4.9	2.9
Total Liabilities to Net Worth 37	2.7	•	44.5	1.9	1.2	0.7	1.7	0.6	1.3	0.6	3.1
Current Assets to Working Capital 38	•	•	2.2	2.3	2.0	1.7	2.3	1.9	4.5	1.9	•
Current Liabilities to Working Capital 39	•	•	1.2	1.3	1.0	0.7	1.3	0.9	3.5	0.9	•
Working Capital to Net Sales 40	•	•	0.1	0.1	0.2	0.3	0.2	0.4	0.1	0.4	•
Inventory to Working Capital 41	•	•	1.3	0.9	0.7	0.5	0.7	0.5	1.1	0.4	•
Total Receipts to Cash Flow 42	3.1	0.3	9.9	5.6	5.0	3.2	3.3	2.2	1.9	2.6	3.3
Cost of Goods to Cash Flow 43	1.6	0.1	6.5	2.8	3.3	1.3	1.4	0.8	0.7	1.0	1.8
Cash Flow to Total Debt 44	0.2	•	0.5	0.6	0.8	0.9	0.6	0.9	1.0	0.7	0.2

Selected Financial Factors (in Percentages)

Debt Ratio 45	72.9	•	97.8	65.0	54.0	42.5	63.0	35.8	56.5	39.1	75.9
Return on Total Assets 46	10.3	•	14.3	18.5	24.7	17.9	18.2	18.4	32.0	15.1	9.5
Return on Equity Before Income Taxes 47	31.6	•	471.6	47.8	51.0	28.9	45.9	27.7	66.2	21.8	32.2
Return on Equity After Income Taxes 48	22.5	•	471.6	47.8	47.0	22.7	39.2	19.1	44.3	15.5	22.9
Profit Margin (Before Income Tax) 49	17.2	158.0	2.0	7.7	11.1	13.0	14.2	25.5	26.7	19.1	16.6
Profit Margin (After Income Tax) 50	12.2	103.8	2.0	7.7	10.2	10.3	12.2	17.6	17.8	13.6	11.8

Table I

Corporations with and without Net Income

PAINT, COATING, AND ADHESIVE

MONEY AMOUNTS AND SIZE OF ASSETS IN THOUSANDS OF DOLLARS

Item Description for Accounting Period 7/02 Through 6/03		Total	Zero Assets	Under 500	500 to 1,000	1,000 to 5,000	5,000 to 10,000	10,000 to 25,000	25,000 to 50,000	50,000 to 100,000	100,000 to 250,000	250,000 to 500,000	500,000 to 2,500,000	2,500,000 and over
Number of Enterprises	1	1198	148	117	238	481	92	62	28	10	8	5	6	3
Revenues ($ in Thousands)														
Net Sales	2	32829347	174205	102677	603807	1901052	1589958	1930589	1507164	957109	1686737	1729664	6092974	14553411
Interest	3	206270	176	0	16	1621	726	2274	1201	1600	15792	3537	43346	135979
Rents	4	10633	190	0	0	31	316	1562	819	107	406	1584	703	4914
Royalties	5	353070	142	0	0	0	4907	615	489	695	10044	13065	95835	227279
Other Portfolio Income	6	277294	2	0	32	2148	383	1877	128	29	13864	5043	172923	80868
Other Receipts	7	204465	974	6909	107	34071	5882	13303	-12851	9152	10188	1969	6302	128457
Total Receipts	8	33881079	175689	109586	603962	1938923	1602172	1950220	1496950	968692	1737031	1754862	6412083	15130908
Average Total Receipts	9	28281	1187	937	2538	4031	17415	31455	53462	96869	217129	350972	1068680	5043636
Operating Costs/Operating Income (%)														
Cost of Operations	10	58.5	57.4	69.1	68.0	59.0	59.4	64.4	60.0	65.3	63.4	63.2	63.5	53.4
Salaries and Wages	11	11.3	16.8	5.1	3.4	6.6	8.6	10.8	9.0	8.7	10.6	13.3	9.8	13.3
Taxes Paid	12	2.1	3.3	1.5	1.9	2.3	2.5	1.7	1.7	2.2	1.8	1.6	1.7	2.4
Interest Paid	13	2.7	1.7	0.0	0.8	1.1	1.0	0.8	0.7	1.1	1.5	4.1	4.0	3.3
Depreciation	14	3.1	1.7	0.6	0.9	2.0	2.3	2.3	2.7	3.6	2.5	3.9	3.4	3.3
Amortization and Depletion	15	0.7	0.2	0.0	0.0	0.1	0.0	0.2	0.2	0.4	0.9	0.9	1.0	0.8
Pensions and Other Deferred Comp.	16	1.3	0.2	0.3	0.9	0.3	0.6	0.5	0.6	1.0	2.5	0.9	1.0	1.8
Employee Benefits	17	2.2	0.3	2.6	1.3	1.5	1.6	1.2	1.2	1.5	1.8	2.0	1.9	2.9
Advertising	18	1.6	0.6	0.0	0.3	1.4	3.4	1.2	0.9	0.7	1.3	0.7	0.5	2.3
Other Expenses	19	14.6	29.9	16.2	15.1	17.2	11.9	12.3	14.6	10.2	11.2	11.6	14.1	16.0
Officers' Compensation	20	1.5	1.2	3.9	8.4	8.3	5.5	2.1	2.0	1.6	1.0	0.6	0.4	0.3
Operating Margin	21	0.4	•	0.7	•	0.3	3.0	2.5	6.3	3.8	1.5	•	•	0.3
Operating Margin Before Officers' Comp.	22	1.9	•	4.6	7.4	8.6	8.5	4.6	8.3	5.4	2.6	•	•	0.6

Selected Average Balance Sheet ($ in Thousands)

Net Receivables 23	4708	97	262	541	1976	3820	7957	14752	32424	38052	256242	843574
Inventories 24	2665	113	309	453	1186	4314	6048	9814	26359	30892	87879	450602
Net Property, Plant and Equipment 25	5676	3	94	555	2002	3894	10190	21056	32774	83058	251723	1133769
Total Assets 26	27311	284	709	1945	6653	15916	34120	71148	148240	344558	1495969	5476807
Notes and Loans Payable 27	7965	3	337	686	2190	3989	7555	20671	31147	164572	767546	862169
All Other Liabilities 28	11462	193	232	498	2234	4497	8509	13375	42651	69000	493832	2969596
Net Worth 29	7884	88	140	761	2229	7430	18056	37101	74442	110987	234591	1645042

Selected Financial Ratios (Times to 1)

Current Ratio 30	1.3	•	2.0	1.7	1.2	1.9	2.3	1.8	2.0	2.3	1.0	1.1
Quick Ratio 31	0.7	•	1.0	1.0	0.7	1.0	1.4	1.1	1.0	1.0	0.6	0.6
Net Sales to Working Capital 32	14.2	10.3	8.4	8.2	27.3	6.5	5.2	6.7	5.7	5.9	126.6	24.9
Coverage Ratio 33	2.4	295.3	•	3.1	4.9	5.3	8.7	5.7	3.9	0.7	2.2	2.4
Total Asset Turnover 34	1.0	•	3.6	2.0	2.6	2.0	1.6	1.3	1.4	1.0	0.7	0.9
Inventory Turnover 35	6.0	5.4	5.6	5.1	8.7	4.6	5.3	6.4	5.1	7.1	7.3	5.7
Receivables Turnover 36	6.3	8.9	7.7	6.3	8.6	7.0	7.2	7.2	5.6	10.3	4.7	6.5
Total Liabilities to Net Worth 37	2.5	2.2	4.1	1.6	2.0	1.1	0.9	0.9	1.0	2.1	5.4	2.3
Current Assets to Working Capital 38	4.8	3.3	2.0	2.4	6.0	2.1	1.8	2.3	2.0	1.8	55.4	8.2
Current Liabilities to Working Capital 39	3.8	2.3	1.0	1.4	5.0	1.1	0.8	1.3	1.0	0.8	54.4	7.2
Working Capital to Net Sales 40	0.1	0.1	0.1	0.1	0.0	0.2	0.2	0.1	0.2	0.2	0.0	0.0
Inventory to Working Capital 41	1.4	1.3	0.9	0.9	2.0	0.9	0.6	0.7	0.6	0.6	10.8	2.3
Total Receipts to Cash Flow 42	6.9	4.9	8.3	5.8	8.9	7.7	5.4	6.9	7.9	13.1	6.7	6.5
Cost of Goods to Cash Flow 43	4.0	3.4	5.7	3.4	5.3	5.0	3.2	4.5	5.0	8.3	4.2	3.5
Cash Flow to Total Debt 44	0.2	•	0.5	0.6	0.4	0.5	0.6	0.4	0.4	0.1	0.1	0.2

Selected Financial Factors (in Percentages)

Debt Ratio 45	71.1	•	80.3	60.9	66.5	53.3	47.1	47.9	49.8	67.8	84.3	70.0
Return on Total Assets 46	6.7	23.1	•	6.8	12.3	8.5	10.2	8.3	8.6	2.9	5.9	6.9
Return on Equity Before Income Taxes 47	13.6	74.2	•	11.8	29.2	14.7	17.1	13.1	12.8	•	20.1	13.3
Return on Equity After Income Taxes 48	9.0	74.2	•	11.0	24.0	11.5	14.1	9.3	11.5	•	12.1	8.2
Profit Margin (Before Income Tax) 49	3.9	7.5	•	2.3	3.8	3.5	5.7	5.1	4.5	•	4.6	4.5
Profit Margin (After Income Tax) 50	2.6	7.5	2.1	2.1	3.1	2.7	4.7	3.6	4.1	•	2.8	2.8

89

Table II

Corporations with Net Income

PAINT, COATING, AND ADHESIVE

MONEY AMOUNTS AND SIZE OF ASSETS IN THOUSANDS OF DOLLARS

Item Description for Accounting Period 7/02 Through 6/03	Total	Zero Assets	Under 500	500 to 1,000	1,000 to 5,000	5,000 to 10,000	10,000 to 25,000	25,000 to 50,000	50,000 to 100,000	100,000 to 250,000	250,000 to 500,000	500,000 to 2,500,000	2,500,000 and over
Number of Enterprises **1**	656	0	0	140	334	0	48	20	0	5	0	6	0
Revenues ($ in Thousands)													
Net Sales **2**	25953252	0	0	403359	1493998	0	1562568	1122055	0	1355844	0	16327920	0
Interest **3**	174956	0	0	4	691	0	1849	805	0	10113	0	155987	0
Rents **4**	8902	0	0	0	31	0	1346	575	0	401	0	4542	0
Royalties **5**	301711	0	0	0	0	0	600	362	0	10044	0	272038	0
Other Portfolio Income **6**	167403	0	0	0	816	0	1774	36	0	12456	0	146864	0
Other Receipts **7**	167906	0	0	4	32834	0	10422	-14387	0	8425	0	116244	0
Total Receipts **8**	26774130	0	0	403367	1528370	0	1578559	1109446	0	1401283	0	17023595	0
Average Total Receipts **9**	40814	·	·	2881	4576	·	32887	55472	·	280257	·	2837266	·
Operating Costs/Operating Income (%)													
Cost of Operations **10**	57.6	·	·	66.5	57.1	·	62.4	55.8	·	60.3	·	55.8	·
Salaries and Wages **11**	11.1	·	·	3.2	5.0	·	10.9	7.9	·	11.4	·	12.2	·
Taxes Paid **12**	2.2	·	·	1.5	2.3	·	1.7	1.7	·	1.8	·	2.3	·
Interest Paid **13**	2.1	·	·	0.7	0.8	·	0.7	0.4	·	1.3	·	2.6	·
Depreciation **14**	2.9	·	·	0.3	1.8	·	2.2	2.3	·	2.6	·	3.2	·
Amortization and Depletion **15**	0.6	·	·	0.0	0.0	·	0.2	0.2	·	0.6	·	0.8	·
Pensions and Other Deferred Comp. **16**	1.4	·	·	1.4	0.3	·	0.6	0.6	·	3.0	·	1.6	·
Employee Benefits **17**	2.1	·	·	0.0	1.7	·	1.1	1.1	·	1.4	·	2.4	·
Advertising **18**	1.5	·	·	0.2	1.5	·	1.3	0.9	·	1.4	·	1.6	·
Other Expenses **19**	14.2	·	·	16.0	15.6	·	12.0	16.3	·	11.4	·	15.3	·
Officers' Compensation **20**	1.6	·	·	9.9	10.0	·	2.3	2.2	·	1.0	·	0.3	·
Operating Margin **21**	2.8	·	·	0.2	3.9	·	4.6	10.6	·	3.7	·	1.9	·
Operating Margin Before Officers' Comp. **22**	4.4	·	·	10.1	13.8	·	6.9	12.8	·	4.7	·	2.2	·

Selected Average Balance Sheet ($ in Thousands)

Net Receivables 23	7117	307	620	4026	7774	41343	571949
Inventories 24	3686	366	431	4161	5830	26404	242423
Net Property, Plant and Equipment 25	7271	11	569	3771	9289	36958	566952
Total Assets 26	36525	701	2058	16093	33444	160219	3105543
Notes and Loans Payable 27	9534	347	569	3829	4864	39776	793668
All Other Liabilities 28	12468	247	487	3752	6432	43335	1153715
Net Worth 29	14524	107	1002	8512	22148	77107	1158160

Selected Financial Ratios (Times to 1)

Current Ratio 30	1.4	2.8	1.8	2.3	2.6	2.3	1.2
Quick Ratio 31	0.8	1.3	1.1	1.2	1.7	1.3	0.7
Net Sales to Working Capital 32	10.1	6.4	7.7	5.4	4.8	5.5	14.2
Coverage Ratio 33	4.0	1.3	8.5	8.6	23.4	6.4	3.5
Total Asset Turnover 34	1.1	4.1	2.2	2.0	1.7	1.7	0.9
Inventory Turnover 35	6.2	5.2	5.9	4.9	5.4	6.2	6.3
Receivables Turnover 36	6.3	6.5	7.7	7.8	7.7	13.2	9.5
Total Liabilities to Net Worth 37	1.5	5.5	1.1	0.9	0.5	1.1	1.7
Current Assets to Working Capital 38	3.5	1.5	2.2	1.8	1.6	1.8	5.3
Current Liabilities to Working Capital 39	2.5	0.5	1.2	0.8	0.6	0.8	4.3
Working Capital to Net Sales 40	0.1	0.2	0.1	0.2	0.2	0.2	0.1
Inventory to Working Capital 41	1.0	0.8	0.8	0.7	0.5	0.5	1.3
Total Receipts to Cash Flow 42	6.0	7.2	5.0	6.7	4.1	6.8	5.8
Cost of Goods to Cash Flow 43	3.5	4.8	2.9	4.2	2.3	4.1	3.2
Cash Flow to Total Debt 44	0.3	0.7	0.8	0.6	1.2	0.5	0.2

Selected Financial Factors (in Percentages)

Debt Ratio 45	60.2	84.7	51.3	47.1	33.8	51.9	62.7
Return on Total Assets 46	8.9	3.6	15.1	12.8	16.8	13.6	8.0
Return on Equity Before Income Taxes 47	16.7	4.9	27.4	21.5	24.3	23.9	15.2
Return on Equity After Income Taxes 48	12.1	4.4	26.5	17.8	20.8	21.9	9.9
Profit Margin (Before Income Tax) 49	6.1	0.2	6.1	5.6	9.6	6.8	6.5
Profit Margin (After Income Tax) 50	4.4	0.2	5.9	4.6	8.2	6.2	4.2

Table I

Corporations with and without Net Income

SOAP, CLEANING COMPOUND, AND TOILET PREPARATION

MONEY AMOUNTS AND SIZE OF ASSETS IN THOUSANDS OF DOLLARS

Item Description for Accounting Period 7/02 Through 6/03		Total	Zero Assets	Under 500	500 to 1,000	1,000 to 5,000	5,000 to 10,000	10,000 to 25,000	25,000 to 50,000	50,000 to 100,000	100,000 to 250,000	250,000 to 500,000	500,000 to 2,500,000	2,500,000 and over
Number of Enterprises	1	2093	243	983	361	296	89	52	22	17	6	7	8	9
Revenues ($ in Thousands)														
Net Sales	2	101727469	88034	556441	552420	2236446	1387424	1620621	1094259	1811548	1130862	2564180	9347788	79337447
Interest	3	636221	416	620	245	779	4042	2187	1573	3377	1821	3572	92518	525071
Rents	4	100931	0	0	112	3152	221	558	455	42	0	1582	49278	45532
Royalties	5	2574699	864	0	0	5857	3681	373	804	1488	2674	17282	235848	2305828
Other Portfolio Income	6	2604677	1644	0	531	2327	390	5815	4100	2529	8173	22384	343908	2212881
Other Receipts	7	1798942	89	7531	2347	20050	18013	6465	11548	36387	-50780	5253	198377	1543656
Total Receipts	8	109442939	91047	564592	555655	2268611	1413771	1636019	1112739	1855371	1092750	2614253	10267717	85970415
Average Total Receipts	9	52290	375	574	1539	7664	15885	31462	50579	109139	182125	373465	1283465	9552268
Operating Costs/Operating Income (%)														
Cost of Operations	10	61.7	43.0	45.8	51.5	57.2	60.1	61.0	53.4	56.6	49.0	55.7	43.5	64.9
Salaries and Wages	11	6.9	19.8	14.3	13.4	9.8	9.2	9.7	10.2	8.0	4.6	9.4	15.6	5.5
Taxes Paid	12	1.1	1.7	2.8	3.1	1.5	1.7	1.8	1.7	1.5	0.9	1.3	1.7	1.0
Interest Paid	13	2.9	2.0	1.7	1.0	0.4	1.1	1.1	1.3	1.3	1.1	2.0	2.2	3.3
Depreciation	14	2.4	0.8	2.0	2.1	1.1	1.8	2.2	1.5	1.8	2.8	4.2	2.0	2.4
Amortization and Depletion	15	1.1	4.4	0.1	0.0	0.0	0.1	0.3	0.6	0.5	0.2	0.4	0.8	1.3
Pensions and Other Deferred Comp.	16	1.2	0.1	•	0.2	1.1	0.4	0.5	0.3	0.4	0.6	0.8	1.2	1.4
Employee Benefits	17	1.4	0.3	0.9	2.3	1.3	0.6	1.3	1.5	1.0	1.1	1.0	2.9	1.3
Advertising	18	5.2	8.0	0.6	0.3	3.6	1.3	2.3	6.2	7.4	4.1	7.2	4.8	5.3
Other Expenses	19	14.5	29.9	26.4	15.5	16.8	15.7	13.5	15.5	13.6	20.5	16.1	25.9	12.9
Officers' Compensation	20	0.9	3.2	8.1	11.4	4.4	3.4	2.8	4.6	1.6	0.7	0.8	1.8	0.4
Operating Margin	21	0.6	•	•	•	2.9	4.8	3.5	3.2	6.3	14.4	1.2	•	0.5
Operating Margin Before Officers' Comp.	22	1.5	•	•	5.4	10.6	7.3	8.1	6.4	7.8	7.9	15.1	2.0	0.9

Selected Average Balance Sheet ($ in Thousands)

Net Receivables 23	9163	0	63	180	800	2501	4467	6890	17564	24480	45247	112536	1838343
Inventories 24	3219	0	68	109	633	2305	3539	7293	10199	21050	39441	167292	442242
Net Property, Plant and Equipment 25	7101	0	41	124	469	842	3640	6509	13198	43103	74807	158420	1328652
Total Assets 26	62986	0	214	687	2675	7582	16272	36556	67216	144135	348574	1373687	12535211
Notes and Loans Payable 27	24071	0	609	202	444	1488	5284	11385	21089	38169	131365	526439	4800179
All Other Liabilities 28	15764	0	101	78	719	1823	4293	6797	17873	39892	109126	449200	3024169
Net Worth 29	23151	0	-496	407	1512	4271	6694	18373	28253	66074	108083	398048	4710863

Selected Financial Ratios (Times to 1)

Current Ratio 30	1.1	•	1.7	5.8	2.3	2.2	1.7	2.2	2.0	1.8	1.1	1.2	1.0
Quick Ratio 31	0.7	•	0.9	2.9	1.4	1.2	1.0	1.3	1.3	0.9	0.4	0.4	0.7
Net Sales to Working Capital 32	47.7	•	8.8	3.4	7.0	5.0	7.5	4.1	5.6	6.3	48.2	17.5	•
Coverage Ratio 33	4.6	•	0.3	0.8	12.5	7.3	5.1	4.8	7.7	11.1	2.7	6.4	4.4
Total Asset Turnover 34	0.8	•	2.7	2.2	2.8	2.1	1.9	1.4	1.6	1.3	1.1	0.9	0.7
Inventory Turnover 35	9.3	•	3.8	7.2	6.8	4.1	5.4	3.6	5.9	4.4	5.2	3.0	12.9
Receivables Turnover 36	7.1	•	7.0	8.1	9.5	5.9	6.8	6.4	7.5	6.8	8.1	9.4	6.9
Total Liabilities to Net Worth 37	1.7	•	•	0.7	0.8	0.8	1.4	1.0	1.4	1.2	2.2	2.5	1.7
Current Assets to Working Capital 38	15.1	•	2.4	1.2	1.8	1.9	2.4	1.8	2.0	2.3	18.1	7.3	•
Current Liabilities to Working Capital 39	14.1	•	1.4	0.2	0.8	0.9	1.4	0.8	1.0	1.3	17.1	6.3	•
Working Capital to Net Sales 40	0.0	•	0.1	0.3	0.1	0.2	0.1	0.2	0.2	0.2	0.0	0.1	•
Inventory to Working Capital 41	3.3	•	1.1	0.3	0.5	0.8	0.8	0.6	0.6	0.7	5.3	2.5	•
Total Receipts to Cash Flow 42	5.0	8.0	4.7	7.9	5.5	5.3	6.5	5.3	4.7	3.3	5.7	3.4	5.2
Cost of Goods to Cash Flow 43	3.1	3.4	2.2	4.1	3.1	3.2	4.0	2.9	2.7	1.6	3.2	1.5	3.4
Cash Flow to Total Debt 44	0.2	•	0.2	0.7	1.2	0.9	0.5	0.5	0.6	0.7	0.3	0.3	0.2

Selected Financial Factors (in Percentages)

Debt Ratio 45	63.2	•	332.3	40.8	43.5	43.7	58.9	49.7	58.0	54.2	69.0	71.0	62.4
Return on Total Assets 46	10.2	•	1.3	1.7	13.3	15.9	10.7	8.3	15.9	15.9	5.6	12.0	10.0
Return on Equity Before Income Taxes 47	21.7	•	1.4	•	21.6	24.4	20.9	13.0	33.0	31.5	11.4	35.0	20.6
Return on Equity After Income Taxes 48	14.4	•	1.4	•	20.9	21.1	18.3	10.6	27.3	20.9	6.0	22.1	13.5
Profit Margin (Before Income Tax) 49	10.3	•	•	•	4.3	6.7	4.5	4.8	8.7	11.0	3.4	11.9	11.0
Profit Margin (After Income Tax) 50	6.8	•	•	•	4.2	5.8	3.9	3.9	7.2	7.3	1.8	7.5	7.2

Table II

Corporations with Net Income

SOAP, CLEANING COMPOUND, AND TOILET PREPARATION

MONEY AMOUNTS AND SIZE OF ASSETS IN THOUSANDS OF DOLLARS

Item Description for Accounting Period 7/02 Through 6/03	Total	Zero Assets	Under 500	500 to 1,000	1,000 to 5,000	5,000 to 10,000	10,000 to 25,000	25,000 to 50,000	50,000 to 100,000	100,000 to 250,000	250,000 to 500,000	500,000 to 2,500,000	2,500,000 and over
Number of Enterprises **1**	1279	240	514	139	206	0	36	18	0	6	0	5	0
Revenues ($ in Thousands)													
Net Sales **2**	97207284	77491	507803	200094	1795663	0	1193112	973818	0	1130862	0	7154329	0
Interest **3**	563941	409	0	19	553	0	1929	1275	0	1821	0	67762	0
Rents **4**	97467	0	0	0	1258	0	370	455	0	0	0	49241	0
Royalties **5**	2520608	864	0	0	5857	0	373	655	0	2674	0	235516	0
Other Portfolio Income **6**	2586349	1638	0	0	2320	0	5421	3890	0	8173	0	343332	0
Other Receipts **7**	1762335	89	0	356	19386	0	5090	7300	0	-50780	0	185108	0
Total Receipts **8**	104737984	80491	507803	200469	1825037	0	1206295	987393	0	1092750	0	8035288	0
Average Total Receipts **9**	81891	335	988	1442	8859	*	33508	54855	*	182125	*	1607058	*
Operating Costs/Operating Income (%)													
Cost of Operations **10**	62.1	40.9	44.3	60.3	54.0	*	57.8	53.6	*	49.0	*	41.8	*
Salaries and Wages **11**	6.6	14.5	14.1	9.3	10.1	*	9.7	9.7	*	4.6	*	16.9	*
Taxes Paid **12**	1.1	1.6	2.7	2.5	1.4	*	1.7	1.4	*	0.9	*	2.0	*
Interest Paid **13**	2.8	2.0	0.1	1.2	0.3	*	1.0	1.4	*	1.1	*	2.1	*
Depreciation **14**	2.4	0.4	0.7	2.1	1.2	*	2.0	1.6	*	2.8	*	1.7	*
Amortization and Depletion **15**	1.1	5.0	*	*	0.0	*	0.3	0.5	*	0.2	*	0.5	*
Pensions and Other Deferred Comp. **16**	1.3	*	*	0.6	1.0	*	0.5	0.3	*	0.6	*	1.4	*
Employee Benefits **17**	1.4	0.4	0.9	1.8	1.1	*	1.1	1.6	*	1.1	*	2.9	*
Advertising **18**	5.1	8.8	0.5	0.2	4.3	*	2.6	5.9	*	4.1	*	2.8	*
Other Expenses **19**	14.3	18.0	18.3	11.8	18.0	*	13.5	16.1	*	20.5	*	28.1	*
Officers' Compensation **20**	0.7	3.6	7.7	8.4	2.8	*	3.2	3.0	*	0.7	*	1.9	*
Operating Margin **21**	1.1	4.7	10.7	1.8	5.8	*	6.6	4.8	*	14.4	*	*	*
Operating Margin Before Officers' Comp. **22**	1.9	8.3	18.4	10.2	8.6	*	9.7	7.8	*	15.1	*	*	*

Selected Average Balance Sheet ($ in Thousands)

Net Receivables 23	14621	0	110	178	955	4781	6739	•	24480	•	151290
Inventories 24	4688	0	60	139	617	3462	6149	•	21855	•	197241
Net Property, Plant and Equipment 25	10910	0	9	112	565	3619	5376	•	43103	•	177906
Total Assets 26	95648	0	263	686	2946	16128	36212	•	144135	•	1423654
Notes and Loans Payable 27	36630	0	927	230	362	4974	11360	•	38169	•	665307
All Other Liabilities 28	23999	0	52	49	878	4191	7141	•	39892	•	451269
Net Worth 29	35019	0	-716	407	1706	6964	17711	•	66074	•	307078

Selected Financial Ratios (Times to 1)

Current Ratio 30	1.1	•	4.7	9.8	2.5	1.8	2.5	•	1.8	•	1.2
Quick Ratio 31	0.7	•	2.7	5.4	1.6	1.1	1.3	•	0.9	•	0.4
Net Sales to Working Capital 32	51.6	•	5.2	3.0	6.8	7.1	4.1	•	6.3	•	18.3
Coverage Ratio 33	4.9	5.3	124.5	2.6	24.4	8.9	5.6	•	11.1	•	8.7
Total Asset Turnover 34	0.8	•	3.8	2.1	3.0	2.1	1.5	•	1.3	•	1.0
Inventory Turnover 35	10.1	•	7.3	6.2	7.6	5.5	4.7	•	4.2	•	3.0
Receivables Turnover 36	7.3	•	16.2	5.0	9.4	6.9	8.6	•	15.4	•	18.9
Total Liabilities to Net Worth 37	1.7	•	•	0.7	0.7	1.3	1.0	•	1.2	•	3.6
Current Assets to Working Capital 38	15.8	•	1.3	1.1	1.7	2.3	1.7	•	2.3	•	7.3
Current Liabilities to Working Capital 39	14.8	•	0.3	0.1	0.7	1.3	0.7	•	1.3	•	6.3
Working Capital to Net Sales 40	0.0	•	0.2	0.3	0.1	0.1	0.2	•	0.2	•	0.1
Inventory to Working Capital 41	3.4	•	0.5	0.2	0.4	0.7	0.6	•	0.7	•	2.5
Total Receipts to Cash Flow 42	4.9	5.2	3.8	9.2	4.4	5.3	4.8	•	3.3	•	2.9
Cost of Goods to Cash Flow 43	3.0	2.1	1.7	5.5	2.4	3.1	2.6	•	1.6	•	1.2
Cash Flow to Total Debt 44	0.3	•	0.3	0.6	1.6	0.7	0.6	•	0.7	•	0.4

Selected Financial Factors (in Percentages)

Debt Ratio 45	63.4	•	372.8	40.6	42.1	56.8	51.1	•	54.2	•	78.4
Return on Total Assets 46	11.0	•	40.6	6.8	22.8	17.8	11.2	•	15.9	•	18.3
Return on Equity Before Income Taxes 47	24.0	•	•	7.1	37.7	36.6	18.9	•	31.5	•	74.9
Return on Equity After Income Taxes 48	16.1	•	•	6.0	36.8	33.0	15.7	•	20.9	•	48.2
Profit Margin (Before Income Tax) 49	11.1	8.6	10.7	2.0	7.4	7.7	6.2	•	11.0	•	16.1
Profit Margin (After Income Tax) 50	7.4	6.4	10.7	1.7	7.2	6.9	5.1	•	7.3	•	10.3

Table I

Corporations with and without Net Income

CHEMICAL PRODUCT AND PREPARATION

MONEY AMOUNTS AND SIZE OF ASSETS IN THOUSANDS OF DOLLARS

Item Description for Accounting Period 7/02 Through 6/03	Total	Zero Assets	Under 500	500 to 1,000	1,000 to 5,000	5,000 to 10,000	10,000 to 25,000	25,000 to 50,000	50,000 to 100,000	100,000 to 250,000	250,000 to 500,000	500,000 to 2,500,000	2,500,000 and over
Number of Enterprises 1	4637	48	3370	351	401	188	129	47	34	30	15	19	5
Revenues ($ in Thousands)													
Net Sales 2	67365614	536758	1579001	380693	1701738	2304189	3040265	2223732	2695827	5090825	3961744	13357780	30493062
Interest 3	479232	2598	1906	561	3969	3113	4127	4464	10677	37188	27478	268622	114528
Rents 4	57991	350	0	806	12	3277	2782	69	1112	470	5339	24002	19773
Royalties 5	1105608	2573	0	0	292	209	4120	7384	5700	20863	112018	208349	744100
Other Portfolio Income 6	1706604	274282	6239	7675	8328	1238	24269	4501	9736	89340	32017	132644	1116339
Other Receipts 7	1131823	27016	6127	18366	20900	20122	30052	21046	55689	65837	63697	503609	299359
Total Receipts 8	71846872	843577	1593273	408101	1735239	2332148	3105615	2261196	2778741	5304523	4202293	14495006	32787161
Average Total Receipts 9	15494	17575	473	1163	4327	12405	24075	48111	81728	176817	280153	762895	6557432
Operating Costs/Operating Income (%)													
Cost of Operations 10	67.7	70.0	59.6	58.1	49.7	63.1	68.6	66.8	64.1	68.1	69.1	62.8	71.9
Salaries and Wages 11	8.4	10.5	8.5	7.2	10.5	10.7	8.4	8.7	9.4	9.1	6.5	8.7	7.9
Taxes Paid 12	1.4	1.1	2.5	7.0	2.5	2.0	1.6	1.6	2.1	1.8	1.2	1.8	0.8
Interest Paid 13	2.8	3.8	1.4	1.3	0.8	1.3	1.1	1.1	2.0	2.7	4.3	6.3	1.6
Depreciation 14	3.8	2.4	2.6	5.3	2.5	3.9	3.4	3.4	4.0	3.7	6.7	5.7	2.9
Amortization and Depletion 15	0.9	0.9	0.0	0.0	0.2	0.2	0.3	0.6	0.7	0.8	2.3	1.3	0.8
Pensions and Other Deferred Comp. 16	1.2	0.4	0.4	1.5	0.4	0.6	0.4	0.8	0.9	0.5	0.3	0.5	1.9
Employee Benefits 17	1.5	1.2	0.2	2.6	1.6	1.0	1.3	1.7	2.1	1.3	1.9	2.5	1.0
Advertising 18	2.2	0.1	0.6	0.8	0.8	0.4	0.8	0.7	0.8	1.2	0.6	2.7	3.0
Other Expenses 19	14.4	16.0	17.8	22.1	22.4	14.9	12.2	11.7	11.8	11.6	12.8	17.1	13.7
Officers' Compensation 20	1.1	1.0	7.8	6.1	6.0	3.4	2.1	2.3	1.4	0.7	0.8	0.9	0.2
Operating Margin 21	•	•	•	•	2.7	•	•	0.5	0.8	•	•	•	•
Operating Margin Before Officers' Comp. 22	•	•	6.4	8.7	1.7	1.9	2.8	2.1	•	•	•	•	•

Selected Average Balance Sheet ($ in Thousands)

Net Receivables 23	1618505	100716	38586	32831	11240	6865	3047	1965	367	115	34	0	2877
Inventories 24	728220	98671	27604	22072	12815	6583	2727	1278	398	97	20	0	1766
Net Property, Plant and Equipment 25	959050	263124	113538	37808	20449	8824	4650	2663	455	116	30	0	3271
Total Assets 26	7180445	1097114	357535	164093	70820	35573	15369	7673	1937	805	121	0	16391
Notes and Loans Payable 27	1787143	475787	153239	49575	19097	10182	4557	2438	739	275	77	0	5302
All Other Liabilities 28	3291202	321831	95930	52225	19652	8258	3542	2255	417	144	35	0	6006
Net Worth 29	2102101	299495	108367	62293	32071	17133	7270	2979	781	386	9	0	5083

Selected Financial Ratios (Times to 1)

Current Ratio 30	1.1	1.2	1.4	1.4	1.6	1.9	1.7	1.6	1.9	2.0	1.6	•	1.2
Quick Ratio 31	0.7	0.5	0.7	0.8	0.8	1.0	0.9	1.0	1.1	1.2	1.0	•	0.7
Net Sales to Working Capital 32	24.0	13.8	7.9	7.3	7.2	5.6	6.8	7.7	7.4	5.8	17.1	•	12.6
Coverage Ratio 33	5.2	0.8	0.9	2.2	3.0	2.9	2.8	0.7	7.3	•	0.7	13.9	2.4
Total Asset Turnover 34	0.8	0.6	0.7	1.0	1.1	1.3	1.5	1.6	2.2	1.3	3.9	•	0.9
Inventory Turnover 35	6.0	4.5	6.6	5.2	4.0	4.8	5.9	6.1	5.3	6.5	14.1	•	5.6
Receivables Turnover 36	2.5	5.7	8.2	5.3	6.9	6.4	7.9	6.1	9.5	9.5	11.9	•	3.8
Total Liabilities to Net Worth 37	2.4	2.7	2.3	1.6	1.2	1.1	1.1	1.6	1.5	1.1	12.3	•	2.2
Current Assets to Working Capital 38	10.2	6.2	3.4	3.3	2.8	2.1	2.5	2.7	2.1	2.0	2.7	•	5.2
Current Liabilities to Working Capital 39	9.2	5.2	2.4	2.3	1.8	1.1	1.5	1.7	1.1	1.0	1.7	•	4.2
Working Capital to Net Sales 40	0.0	0.1	0.1	0.1	0.1	0.2	0.1	0.1	0.1	0.2	0.1	•	0.1
Inventory to Working Capital 41	2.7	1.8	1.0	0.9	1.0	0.8	0.8	0.9	0.6	0.6	0.7	•	1.5
Total Receipts to Cash Flow 42	8.8	8.4	11.0	8.3	7.2	8.1	8.9	8.6	4.3	20.8	8.0	6.1	8.4
Cost of Goods to Cash Flow 43	6.3	5.2	7.6	5.6	4.6	5.4	6.1	5.4	2.2	12.1	4.7	4.3	5.7
Cash Flow to Total Debt 44	0.1	0.1	0.1	0.2	0.3	0.3	0.3	0.3	0.8	0.1	0.5	•	0.2

Selected Financial Factors (in Percentages)

Debt Ratio 45	70.7	72.7	69.7	62.0	54.7	51.8	52.7	61.2	59.7	52.0	92.5	•	69.0
Return on Total Assets 46	7.2	3.1	2.9	6.2	6.5	4.4	4.9	1.4	12.2	•	3.6	•	5.8
Return on Equity Before Income Taxes 47	19.9	•	•	8.9	9.5	6.1	6.6	•	26.2	•	•	•	10.9
Return on Equity After Income Taxes 48	12.3	•	•	5.5	5.9	2.9	4.0	•	23.5	•	•	•	6.1
Profit Margin (Before Income Tax) 49	6.9	•	•	3.3	3.8	2.2	2.0	•	4.8	•	•	49.7	3.8
Profit Margin (After Income Tax) 50	4.2	•	•	2.0	2.4	1.1	1.2	•	4.3	•	•	49.2	2.1

Table II

Corporations with Net Income

CHEMICAL PRODUCT AND PREPARATION

MONEY AMOUNTS AND SIZE OF ASSETS IN THOUSANDS OF DOLLARS

Item Description for Accounting Period 7/02 Through 6/03	Total	Zero Assets	Under 500	500 to 1,000	1,000 to 5,000	5,000 to 10,000	10,000 to 25,000	25,000 to 50,000	50,000 to 100,000	100,000 to 250,000	250,000 to 500,000	500,000 to 2,500,000	2,500,000 and over
Number of Enterprises **1**	2527	0	1616	272	321	128	85	31	24	19	6	0	0
Revenues ($ in Thousands)													
Net Sales **2**	46972680	0	700438	213238	1458885	1641941	2456104	1519449	1996243	3299418	1267286	0	0
Interest **3**	234104	0	1783	549	2607	1724	2014	2361	6424	21247	14383	0	0
Rents **4**	34145	0	0	806	12	3261	1912	4	1111	99	4224	0	0
Royalties **5**	948531	0	0	0	292	150	4120	7366	4295	17011	61526	0	0
Other Portfolio Income **6**	1620343	0	6239	7675	8303	1222	22964	2255	9612	88753	17564	0	0
Other Receipts **7**	844021	0	4079	17611	19975	18817	25359	12315	49423	31058	13986	0	0
Total Receipts **8**	50653824	0	712539	239879	1490074	1667115	2512473	1543750	2067108	3457586	1378969	0	0
Average Total Receipts **9**	20045	•	441	882	4642	13024	29559	49798	86130	181978	229828	•	•
Operating Costs/Operating Income (%)													
Cost of Operations **10**	64.5	•	49.0	49.3	49.7	59.5	67.2	63.7	61.0	64.9	67.4	•	•
Salaries and Wages **11**	9.0	•	4.3	2.2	9.6	10.7	7.7	8.8	10.2	8.8	5.5	•	•
Taxes Paid **12**	1.3	•	2.4	8.8	2.3	1.9	1.4	1.8	2.3	1.9	1.6	•	•
Interest Paid **13**	1.7	•	1.9	1.5	0.6	1.0	0.9	0.8	1.6	2.5	2.1	•	•
Depreciation **14**	3.2	•	4.8	7.1	2.0	3.5	2.5	2.8	3.3	3.4	5.8	•	•
Amortization and Depletion **15**	0.9	•	0.0	•	0.1	0.2	0.1	0.6	0.7	0.6	0.3	•	•
Pensions and Other Deferred Comp. **16**	1.5	•	0.9	2.7	0.4	0.5	0.4	1.0	1.0	0.5	0.5	•	•
Employee Benefits **17**	1.5	•	0.4	3.9	1.9	1.2	1.1	1.9	1.7	1.4	2.3	•	•
Advertising **18**	2.9	•	1.1	0.6	0.6	0.5	0.8	0.8	1.0	1.6	0.1	•	•
Other Expenses **19**	14.6	•	17.7	22.5	20.9	13.6	10.9	9.4	11.9	10.5	10.4	•	•
Officers' Compensation **20**	1.0	•	11.1	7.0	5.4	3.5	1.9	2.6	1.4	0.7	1.3	•	•
Operating Margin **21**	•	•	6.4	•	6.4	4.0	5.0	5.9	4.0	3.4	2.5	•	•
Operating Margin Before Officers' Comp. **22**	•	•	17.5	1.4	11.8	7.5	6.9	8.5	5.3	4.0	3.9	•	•

Selected Average Balance Sheet ($ in Thousands)

Net Receivables 23	3980	•	27	106	440	1987	3403	7041	11534	34975	35837
Inventories 24	2022	•	7	14	366	1257	2913	6856	11989	17510	15853
Net Property, Plant and Equipment 25	3318	•	50	125	389	2234	3887	7685	17016	39237	78891
Total Assets 26	19235	•	137	784	1910	7367	15154	35403	68066	161041	322892
Notes and Loans Payable 27	4953	•	90	229	562	2355	3626	8090	14012	34593	94986
All Other Liabilities 28	6779	•	35	135	417	1541	3611	6857	18769	51351	60283
Net Worth 29	7503	•	13	420	931	3470	7917	20456	35285	75097	167624

Selected Financial Ratios (Times to 1)

Current Ratio 30	1.4	•	0.8	1.3	1.9	1.8	2.0	2.1	2.2	1.7	2.2
Quick Ratio 31	0.8	•	0.5	1.2	1.2	1.1	1.1	1.2	1.2	1.0	1.1
Net Sales to Working Capital 32	9.7	•	•	12.4	7.0	6.4	6.3	5.1	4.7	5.4	3.9
Coverage Ratio 33	6.1	•	5.1	5.7	16.4	6.8	8.9	9.8	5.6	4.6	6.6
Total Asset Turnover 34	1.0	•	3.2	1.0	2.4	1.7	1.9	1.4	1.2	1.1	0.7
Inventory Turnover 35	5.9	•	29.5	26.9	6.2	6.1	6.7	4.6	4.2	6.4	9.0
Receivables Turnover 36	3.7	•	19.3	14.8	9.6	5.9	8.8	6.1	8.1	5.2	7.2
Total Liabilities to Net Worth 37	1.6	•	10.0	0.9	1.1	1.1	0.9	0.7	0.9	1.1	0.9
Current Assets to Working Capital 38	3.8	•	•	4.0	2.1	2.2	2.0	1.9	1.9	2.4	1.9
Current Liabilities to Working Capital 39	2.8	•	•	3.0	1.1	1.2	1.0	0.9	0.9	1.4	0.9
Working Capital to Net Sales 40	0.1	•	•	0.1	0.1	0.2	0.2	0.2	0.2	0.2	0.3
Inventory to Working Capital 41	1.1	•	•	0.2	0.6	0.7	0.7	0.6	0.6	0.6	0.4
Total Receipts to Cash Flow 42	6.4	•	4.9	5.6	3.9	6.1	6.3	6.4	5.7	6.0	5.2
Cost of Goods to Cash Flow 43	4.1	•	2.4	2.8	1.9	3.6	4.2	4.1	3.5	3.9	3.5
Cash Flow to Total Debt 44	0.2	•	0.7	0.4	1.2	0.5	0.6	0.5	0.4	0.3	0.3

Selected Financial Factors (in Percentages)

Debt Ratio 45	61.0	•	90.9	46.3	51.3	52.9	47.8	42.2	48.2	53.4	48.1
Return on Total Assets 46	10.3	•	31.7	8.2	22.2	11.3	15.7	11.5	11.1	12.3	9.1
Return on Equity Before Income Taxes 47	22.0	•	279.6	12.6	42.7	20.5	26.6	17.9	17.7	20.6	14.8
Return on Equity After Income Taxes 48	16.1	•	273.3	10.9	39.8	18.3	23.0	14.0	13.1	16.1	10.2
Profit Margin (Before Income Tax) 49	8.9	•	8.1	6.8	8.8	5.5	7.3	7.5	7.5	8.9	11.8
Profit Margin (After Income Tax) 50	6.5	•	7.9	5.8	8.2	5.0	6.3	5.8	5.6	7.0	8.1

Table I

Corporations with and without Net Income

PLASTICS PRODUCT

MONEY AMOUNTS AND SIZE OF ASSETS IN THOUSANDS OF DOLLARS

Item Description for Accounting Period 7/02 Through 6/03	Total	Zero Assets	Under 500	500 to 1,000	1,000 to 5,000	5,000 to 10,000	10,000 to 25,000	25,000 to 50,000	50,000 to 100,000	100,000 to 250,000	250,000 to 500,000	500,000 to 2,500,000	2,500,000 and over
Number of Enterprises **1**	12618	1645	0	0	2232	480	445	154	105	74	19	22	3
0 Revenues ($ in Thousands)													
Net Sales **2**	91662037	2901043	0	0	10733654	5006937	11731027	7727058	10503362	13069773	5279686	13405227	6288095
Interest **3**	290777	3757	0	0	4098	3867	10839	9112	14877	52745	53816	71382	60848
Rents **4**	54562	68	0	0	2917	400	3916	2914	3891	15381	5126	8983	8590
Royalties **5**	160832	2561	0	0	43	22	1630	2880	7393	53244	10162	28873	43336
Other Portfolio Income **6**	657768	14571	0	0	15516	12878	18701	8489	27476	29238	47471	222766	208929
Other Receipts **7**	1087995	15769	0	0	27024	25127	43159	11582	98237	98117	51426	150272	527784
Total Receipts **8**	93913971	2937769	0	0	10783252	5049231	11809272	7762035	10655236	13318498	5447687	13887503	7137582
Average Total Receipts **9**	7443	1786	•	•	4831	10519	26538	50403	101478	179980	286720	631250	2379194
Operating Costs/Operating Income (%)													
Cost of Operations **10**	70.0	84.6	•	•	70.5	68.9	70.7	69.3	69.4	69.2	69.4	72.0	65.3
Salaries and Wages **11**	6.1	1.9	•	•	5.7	7.0	6.0	6.9	5.5	6.1	6.8	6.1	6.3
Taxes Paid **12**	1.9	1.2	•	•	2.6	2.3	2.0	2.1	1.9	1.8	1.9	1.5	1.5
Interest Paid **13**	3.2	2.4	•	•	1.4	1.2	1.3	2.0	2.1	3.0	4.1	3.9	15.1
Depreciation **14**	4.5	2.6	•	•	3.5	5.5	4.4	5.3	5.0	5.0	5.5	5.5	3.3
Amortization and Depletion **15**	0.5	1.1	•	•	0.1	0.2	0.2	0.4	0.4	0.8	1.1	0.9	0.4
Pensions and Other Deferred Comp. **16**	0.5	0.1	•	•	0.3	0.4	0.4	0.5	0.5	0.5	0.5	0.8	1.1
Employee Benefits **17**	1.8	0.5	•	•	1.6	1.7	1.6	1.7	1.8	2.0	2.2	2.0	1.8
Advertising **18**	0.5	0.6	•	•	0.6	0.8	0.5	0.4	0.7	0.7	0.2	0.2	1.1
Other Expenses **19**	10.0	5.0	•	•	9.7	8.9	8.5	8.0	10.5	9.7	10.8	9.1	14.4
Officers' Compensation **20**	1.8	0.9	•	•	3.9	3.3	1.9	1.4	1.0	0.7	0.7	0.5	0.3
Operating Margin **21**	•	•	•	•	0.2	•	2.5	2.0	1.0	0.4	•	•	•
Operating Margin Before Officers' Comp. **22**	0.9	•	•	•	4.1	3.1	4.5	3.4	2.0	1.1	•	•	•

Selected Average Balance Sheet ($ in Thousands)

Net Receivables 23	1104	0	•	579	1341	3574	6993	14027	23595	58058	115613	679064
Inventories 24	747	0	•	456	1106	2849	5506	11277	18586	39283	61251	244281
Net Property, Plant and Equipment 25	1804	0	•	706	2521	5522	13818	25203	48833	99184	230230	579043
Total Assets 26	9698	0	•	2247	6811	15556	35266	70317	147460	352999	848231	18738633
Notes and Loans Payable 27	2745	0	•	983	2220	5724	12828	27308	61216	144265	389428	2300278
All Other Liabilities 28	1543	0	•	644	1659	3704	9406	19000	34546	81354	202139	1007435
Net Worth 29	5410	0	•	620	2932	6128	13032	24008	51698	127379	256663	15430920

Selected Financial Ratios (Times to 1)

Current Ratio 30	1.4	•	•	1.7	1.5	1.6	1.5	1.4	1.4	1.3	1.1	1.1
Quick Ratio 31	0.8	•	•	1.1	0.9	0.9	0.8	0.8	0.8	0.8	0.7	0.7
Net Sales to Working Capital 32	11.6	•	•	8.3	9.0	8.4	9.8	10.3	10.4	10.0	27.6	36.1
Coverage Ratio 33	1.5	1.2	•	1.5	1.4	3.5	2.2	2.2	1.8	1.1	1.3	1.2
Total Asset Turnover 34	0.7	•	•	2.1	1.5	1.7	1.4	1.4	1.2	0.8	0.7	0.1
Inventory Turnover 35	6.8	•	•	7.4	6.5	6.5	6.3	6.2	6.6	4.9	7.2	5.6
Receivables Turnover 36	7.1	•	•	8.1	7.5	7.5	7.1	6.8	7.6	4.5	6.4	4.7
Total Liabilities to Net Worth 37	0.8	•	•	2.6	1.3	1.5	1.7	1.9	1.9	1.8	2.3	0.2
Current Assets to Working Capital 38	3.8	•	•	2.4	2.9	2.7	3.1	3.2	3.2	4.3	10.5	19.6
Current Liabilities to Working Capital 39	2.8	•	•	1.4	1.9	1.7	2.1	2.2	2.2	3.3	9.5	18.6
Working Capital to Net Sales 40	0.1	•	•	0.1	0.1	0.1	0.1	0.1	0.1	0.1	0.0	0.0
Inventory to Working Capital 41	1.2	•	•	0.8	0.9	0.9	1.1	1.1	1.2	1.1	2.9	3.9
Total Receipts to Cash Flow 42	11.7	23.3	•	16.0	14.2	10.3	12.1	9.2	9.9	12.5	14.8	7.8
Cost of Goods to Cash Flow 43	8.2	19.7	•	11.3	9.8	7.3	8.4	6.4	6.9	8.7	10.7	5.1
Cash Flow to Total Debt 44	0.1	•	•	0.2	0.2	0.3	0.2	0.2	0.2	0.1	0.1	0.1

Selected Financial Factors (in Percentages)

Debt Ratio 45	44.2	•	•	72.4	57.0	60.6	63.0	65.9	64.9	63.9	69.7	17.7
Return on Total Assets 46	3.6	•	•	4.3	2.7	7.6	6.3	6.6	6.3	3.5	3.7	2.1
Return on Equity Before Income Taxes 47	2.2	•	•	4.8	1.8	13.8	9.4	10.3	7.9	0.8	3.1	0.5
Return on Equity After Income Taxes 48	1.4	•	•	3.4	0.5	12.0	7.0	7.8	5.9	•	2.2	0.1
Profit Margin (Before Income Tax) 49	1.6	0.4	•	0.6	0.5	3.2	2.4	2.5	2.3	0.4	1.3	3.4
Profit Margin (After Income Tax) 50	1.0	0.3	•	0.4	•	2.8	1.8	1.9	1.7	•	0.9	0.9

Table II
Corporations with Net Income

PLASTICS PRODUCT

MONEY AMOUNTS AND SIZE OF ASSETS IN THOUSANDS OF DOLLARS

Item Description for Accounting Period 7/02 Through 6/03	Total	Zero Assets	Under 500	500 to 1,000	1,000 to 5,000	5,000 to 10,000	10,000 to 25,000	25,000 to 50,000	50,000 to 100,000	100,000 to 250,000	250,000 to 500,000	500,000 to 2,500,000	2,500,000 and over
Number of Enterprises **1**	5408	0	0	0	1386	270	323	101	76	51	9	0	0
Revenues ($ in Thousands)													
Net Sales **2**	61226488	0	0	0	8230536	3216741	8861205	5268804	8173442	9656606	2816531	0	0
Interest **3**	155453	0	0	0	2827	2980	8491	4228	10783	37048	5968	0	0
Rents **4**	39792	0	0	0	375	25	3694	2579	3018	14670	4200	0	0
Royalties **5**	100684	0	0	0	0	0	664	1552	6414	30952	6158	0	0
Other Portfolio Income **6**	383863	0	0	0	15197	7591	13594	5281	22903	21023	42505	0	0
Other Receipts **7**	413794	0	0	0	17949	15853	36140	13500	80674	76873	22297	0	0
Total Receipts **8**	62320074	0	0	0	8266884	3243190	8923788	5295944	8297234	9837172	2897659	0	0
Average Total Receipts **9**	11524	·	·	·	5965	12012	27628	52435	109174	192886	321962	·	·
Operating Costs/Operating Income (%)													
Cost of Operations **10**	68.1	·	·	·	68.3	64.5	69.2	66.9	70.0	68.5	66.9	·	·
Salaries and Wages **11**	5.9	·	·	·	5.7	6.4	5.9	6.2	5.0	5.4	5.8	·	·
Taxes Paid **12**	2.0	·	·	·	2.5	2.4	1.9	2.1	1.9	1.9	2.0	·	·
Interest Paid **13**	1.6	·	·	·	0.9	1.0	1.0	1.3	1.4	2.4	2.4	·	·
Depreciation **14**	4.3	·	·	·	2.6	5.4	4.1	4.7	4.8	4.8	5.2	·	·
Amortization and Depletion **15**	0.4	·	·	·	0.1	0.1	0.2	0.2	0.2	0.6	0.1	·	·
Pensions and Other Deferred Comp. **16**	0.6	·	·	·	0.3	0.6	0.4	0.5	0.6	0.4	0.5	·	·
Employee Benefits **17**	1.8	·	·	·	1.5	1.7	1.5	1.7	1.9	2.0	1.9	·	·
Advertising **18**	0.6	·	·	·	0.6	0.6	0.4	0.4	0.7	0.7	0.2	·	·
Other Expenses **19**	8.7	·	·	·	8.6	7.2	7.9	8.0	8.8	9.3	10.5	·	·
Officers' Compensation **20**	1.8	·	·	·	3.9	4.2	2.0	1.5	1.0	0.8	0.9	·	·
Operating Margin **21**	4.2	·	·	·	4.9	5.9	5.4	6.6	3.8	3.2	3.6	·	·
Operating Margin Before Officers' Comp. **22**	6.0	·	·	·	8.8	10.2	7.4	8.1	4.7	3.9	4.5	·	·

Selected Average Balance Sheet ($ in Thousands)

Net Receivables 23	1718	688	1535	3600	7189	14663	25946	52341
Inventories 24	1111	512	1069	2721	5487	11027	17276	47332
Net Property, Plant and Equipment 25	2608	696	2456	5331	13090	25923	49966	100613
Total Assets 26	9117	2538	7012	15480	35316	70642	143906	327938
Notes and Loans Payable 27	3079	697	1710	4729	10774	22018	61301	114807
All Other Liabilities 28	2149	690	1289	3476	7314	16973	29796	63849
Net Worth 29	3889	1151	4013	7275	17227	31651	52810	149281

Selected Financial Ratios (Times to 1)

Current Ratio 30	1.5	2.0	2.2	1.8	1.8	1.7	1.5	1.6
Quick Ratio 31	0.9	1.2	1.5	1.1	1.0	0.9	0.9	0.8
Net Sales to Working Capital 32	9.0	7.4	5.5	7.2	6.9	8.0	9.8	7.1
Coverage Ratio 33	4.7	6.7	7.7	7.1	6.5	4.8	3.0	3.9
Total Asset Turnover 34	1.2	2.3	1.7	1.8	1.5	1.5	1.3	1.0
Inventory Turnover 35	6.9	7.9	7.2	7.0	6.4	6.8	7.5	4.4
Receivables Turnover 36	7.4	8.6	7.9	8.1	7.4	7.6	8.6	5.6
Total Liabilities to Net Worth 37	1.3	1.2	0.7	1.1	1.0	1.2	1.7	1.2
Current Assets to Working Capital 38	3.0	2.0	1.8	2.3	2.2	2.5	3.0	2.7
Current Liabilities to Working Capital 39	2.0	1.0	0.8	1.3	1.2	1.5	2.0	1.7
Working Capital to Net Sales 40	0.1	0.1	0.2	0.1	0.1	0.1	0.1	0.1
Inventory to Working Capital 41	0.9	0.7	0.5	0.8	0.8	0.9	1.1	0.8
Total Receipts to Cash Flow 42	8.2	9.2	8.4	8.2	7.7	8.3	8.2	7.5
Cost of Goods to Cash Flow 43	5.6	6.3	5.4	5.7	5.2	5.8	5.6	5.0
Cash Flow to Total Debt 44	0.3	0.5	0.5	0.4	0.4	0.3	0.3	0.2

Selected Financial Factors (in Percentages)

Debt Ratio 45	57.3	54.7	42.8	53.0	51.2	55.2	63.3	54.5
Return on Total Assets 46	9.6	14.8	12.8	12.6	12.3	10.2	9.8	8.8
Return on Equity Before Income Taxes 47	17.8	27.7	19.4	23.0	21.3	18.0	17.9	14.3
Return on Equity After Income Taxes 48	15.2	26.5	17.7	20.9	18.6	15.4	15.2	9.7
Profit Margin (Before Income Tax) 49	6.1	5.4	6.5	6.1	7.0	5.3	5.0	6.8
Profit Margin (After Income Tax) 50	5.2	5.1	6.0	5.5	6.1	4.5	4.2	4.6

Table I

Corporations with and without Net Income

RUBBER PRODUCT

MONEY AMOUNTS AND SIZE OF ASSETS IN THOUSANDS OF DOLLARS

Item Description for Accounting Period 7/02 Through 6/03	Total	Zero Assets	Under 500	500 to 1,000	1,000 to 5,000	5,000 to 10,000	10,000 to 25,000	25,000 to 50,000	50,000 to 100,000	100,000 to 250,000	250,000 to 500,000	500,000 to 2,500,000	2,500,000 and over
Number of Enterprises **1**	858	11	0	0	493	77	76	27	18	6	8	6	4
Revenues ($ in Thousands)													
Net Sales **2**	43644591	20956	0	0	3120186	939851	2233353	1413903	1786225	835165	2567034	7330717	23196848
Interest **3**	238143	4	0	0	748	122	5261	837	2465	7505	26562	15003	179458
Rents **4**	25078	162	0	0	21	0	493	2525	451	0	801	2941	17619
Royalties **5**	307367	0	0	0	0	0	4922	139	1937	2808	1219	25173	271169
Other Portfolio Income **6**	447885	0	0	0	3199	1318	9009	24309	9075	1380	30927	57478	311192
Other Receipts **7**	353705	7026	0	0	8465	18414	10204	6701	10680	48327	64684	52718	125781
Total Receipts **8**	45016769	28148	0	0	3132619	959705	2263242	1448414	1810833	895185	2691227	7484030	24102067
Average Total Receipts **9**	52467	2559	•	•	6354	12464	29780	53645	100602	149198	336403	1247338	6025517
Operating Costs/Operating Income (%)													
Cost of Operations **10**	66.1	85.9	•	•	61.4	70.7	70.6	68.8	73.2	70.7	70.4	73.8	62.2
Salaries and Wages **11**	8.0	3.6	•	•	10.1	7.9	7.1	7.0	5.4	9.7	6.7	6.5	8.7
Taxes Paid **12**	1.6	1.2	•	•	2.5	1.8	2.4	2.1	2.8	1.8	1.7	1.0	1.4
Interest Paid **13**	2.0	0.7	•	•	0.9	0.6	1.7	2.8	2.9	6.1	2.9	1.3	2.0
Depreciation **14**	3.6	6.1	•	•	2.8	4.1	4.0	4.0	4.1	3.7	2.7	4.0	3.5
Amortization and Depletion **15**	0.4	0.2	•	•	0.1	0.0	0.4	0.4	0.7	2.5	1.0	0.7	0.1
Pensions and Other Deferred Comp. **16**	0.9	•	•	•	0.6	0.8	0.5	0.4	0.6	0.6	0.7	2.1	0.7
Employee Benefits **17**	3.4	1.0	•	•	1.8	1.7	2.1	3.1	2.4	4.3	2.8	2.7	4.2
Advertising **18**	1.3	0.5	•	•	1.1	0.5	0.3	0.5	0.6	0.7	1.5	0.6	1.8
Other Expenses **19**	15.2	86.7	•	•	9.7	6.3	8.5	9.1	7.3	12.9	15.7	9.1	19.9
Officers' Compensation **20**	0.9	•	•	•	7.3	3.1	1.5	1.3	0.8	0.8	0.8	0.2	0.1
Operating Margin **21**	•	•	•	•	1.7	2.4	0.9	0.5	0.8	•	•	•	•
Operating Margin Before Officers' Comp. **22**	•	•	•	•	9.0	5.5	2.4	1.9	0.1	•	•	•	•

Selected Average Balance Sheet ($ in Thousands)

Net Receivables 23	7199	0	•	715	1647	3753	6969	12741	13131	39941	164415	897918
Inventories 24	6879	0	•	484	1455	3413	6194	12011	28496	48817	145624	855893
Net Property, Plant and Equipment 25	12738	0	•	886	2697	6447	10649	22412	47748	69947	318956	1582824
Total Assets 26	45896	0	•	2728	7403	16688	34699	69336	162709	342342	1170421	5799571
Notes and Loans Payable 27	15247	0	•	584	810	6577	14339	34505	106205	112851	373832	1853634
All Other Liabilities 28	18978	0	•	636	1836	2975	8162	20232	47256	108918	350010	2936160
Net Worth 29	11671	0	•	1507	4757	7136	12198	14599	9249	120572	446580	1009776

Selected Financial Ratios (Times to 1)

Current Ratio 30	1.3	•	•	2.0	2.1	1.6	1.7	1.1	1.3	0.9	1.4	1.2
Quick Ratio 31	0.7	•	•	1.1	1.4	0.9	1.0	0.6	0.4	0.4	0.7	0.7
Net Sales to Working Capital 32	13.7	•	•	7.8	5.2	8.9	7.1	67.4	12.8	•	11.8	15.0
Coverage Ratio 33	1.0	•	•	3.4	8.2	2.3	2.1	1.2	•	0.3	1.2	0.8
Total Asset Turnover 34	1.1	•	•	2.3	1.6	1.8	1.5	1.4	0.9	0.9	1.0	1.0
Inventory Turnover 35	4.9	•	•	8.0	5.9	6.1	5.8	6.0	3.5	4.6	6.2	4.2
Receivables Turnover 36	7.0	•	•	9.6	7.6	7.7	7.7	7.4	8.3	7.6	7.3	6.4
Total Liabilities to Net Worth 37	2.9	•	•	0.8	0.6	1.3	1.8	3.7	16.6	1.8	1.6	4.7
Current Assets to Working Capital 38	4.5	•	•	2.0	1.9	2.7	2.4	19.7	4.4	•	3.6	5.1
Current Liabilities to Working Capital 39	3.5	•	•	1.0	0.9	1.7	1.4	18.7	3.4	•	2.6	4.1
Working Capital to Net Sales 40	0.1	•	•	0.1	0.2	0.1	0.1	0.0	0.1	0.1	0.1	0.1
Inventory to Working Capital 41	1.8	•	•	0.8	0.6	1.0	0.9	6.9	2.6	•	1.4	2.2
Total Receipts to Cash Flow 42	8.3	2.9	•	10.8	10.2	11.6	11.7	16.1	30.8	11.9	13.4	6.4
Cost of Goods to Cash Flow 43	5.5	2.5	•	6.6	7.2	8.2	8.0	11.7	21.8	8.4	9.9	4.0
Cash Flow to Total Debt 44	0.2	•	•	0.5	0.5	0.3	0.2	0.1	0.0	0.1	0.1	0.2

Selected Financial Factors (in Percentages)

Debt Ratio 45	74.6	•	•	44.8	35.7	57.2	64.8	78.9	94.3	64.8	61.8	82.6
Return on Total Assets 46	2.2	•	•	6.8	8.6	7.1	8.6	5.0	•	0.8	1.7	1.6
Return on Equity Before Income Taxes 47	0.1	•	•	8.8	11.7	9.5	12.7	4.3	•	•	0.8	•
Return on Equity After Income Taxes 48	•	•	•	8.0	11.2	8.0	10.0	2.6	•	•	•	•
Profit Margin (Before Income Tax) 49	0.0	•	•	2.1	4.6	2.3	3.0	0.6	•	•	0.3	•
Profit Margin (After Income Tax) 50	•	•	•	1.9	4.3	1.9	2.3	0.4	•	•	•	•

Table II

Corporations with Net Income

RUBBER PRODUCT

MONEY AMOUNTS AND SIZE OF ASSETS IN THOUSANDS OF DOLLARS

Item Description for Accounting Period 7/02 Through 6/03	Total	Zero Assets	Under 500	500 to 1,000	1,000 to 5,000	5,000 to 10,000	10,000 to 25,000	25,000 to 50,000	50,000 to 100,000	100,000 to 250,000	250,000 to 500,000	500,000 to 2,500,000	2,500,000 and over
Number of Enterprises **1**	545	0	0	0	319	65	53	21	8	•	5	0	0
Revenues ($ in Thousands)													
Net Sales **2**	20018613	0	0	0	2150888	911989	1680862	1138073	757447	•	1257987	0	0
Interest **3**	62549	0	0	0	693	63	3980	610	981	•	4609	0	0
Rents **4**	4289	0	0	0	0	0	123	773	159	•	636	0	0
Royalties **5**	136604	0	0	0	0	0	4902	53	957	•	590	0	0
Other Portfolio Income **6**	146289	0	0	0	587	1160	8210	24216	4062	•	30677	0	0
Other Receipts **7**	164307	0	0	0	7707	11358	7171	9017	6718	•	46344	0	0
Total Receipts **8**	20532651	0	0	0	2159875	924570	1705248	1172742	770324	•	1340843	0	0
Average Total Receipts **9**	37675	•	•	•	6771	14224	32174	55845	96290	•	268169	•	•
Operating Costs/Operating Income (%)													
Cost of Operations **10**	65.9	•	•	•	57.7	69.7	68.6	67.8	68.9	•	67.4	•	•
Salaries and Wages **11**	6.5	•	•	•	9.6	7.8	7.2	6.9	6.4	•	6.3	•	•
Taxes Paid **12**	1.8	•	•	•	2.3	1.7	2.4	2.1	4.2	•	1.6	•	•
Interest Paid **13**	1.6	•	•	•	0.8	0.5	1.5	2.8	1.3	•	2.7	•	•
Depreciation **14**	3.7	•	•	•	2.7	3.3	3.4	3.4	4.7	•	2.3	•	•
Amortization and Depletion **15**	0.4	•	•	•	0.0	0.0	0.4	0.4	0.3	•	1.6	•	•
Pensions and Other Deferred Comp. **16**	0.7	•	•	•	0.8	0.8	0.4	0.5	0.6	•	0.5	•	•
Employee Benefits **17**	4.4	•	•	•	1.2	1.6	2.0	3.2	2.6	•	1.7	•	•
Advertising **18**	1.1	•	•	•	1.0	0.5	0.3	0.5	1.0	•	2.6	•	•
Other Expenses **19**	10.7	•	•	•	10.2	5.8	8.8	7.3	7.5	•	13.7	•	•
Officers' Compensation **20**	1.4	•	•	•	8.0	3.1	1.4	1.3	0.8	•	1.0	•	•
Operating Margin **21**	1.8	•	•	•	5.7	5.2	3.5	3.8	1.5	•	•	•	•
Operating Margin Before Officers' Comp. **22**	3.2	•	•	•	13.7	8.3	4.9	5.1	2.4	•	•	•	•

Selected Average Balance Sheet ($ in Thousands)

Net Receivables 23	6067	693	1662	4152	6941	11166	35765
Inventories 24	4321	462	1509	3206	5948	9687	47155
Net Property, Plant and Equipment 25	8931	1031	2724	5808	9675	20628	44519
Total Assets 26	29430	2954	7599	16243	33341	65377	321505
Notes and Loans Payable 27	8947	524	840	5452	12014	21470	100162
All Other Liabilities 28	9343	514	1114	2296	8904	19462	69262
Net Worth 29	11140	1917	5645	8496	12423	24444	152081

Selected Financial Ratios (Times to 1)

Current Ratio 30	1.4	2.3	3.4	1.7	1.9	1.4	1.2
Quick Ratio 31	0.8	1.4	2.1	1.0	1.1	0.8	0.5
Net Sales to Working Capital 32	10.4	7.1	4.2	8.1	6.5	12.6	12.9
Coverage Ratio 33	3.8	8.2	15.3	4.4	3.5	3.6	2.9
Total Asset Turnover 34	1.2	2.3	1.8	2.0	1.6	1.4	0.8
Inventory Turnover 35	5.6	8.4	6.5	6.8	6.2	6.7	3.6
Receivables Turnover 36	7.4	9.8	9.3	8.3	8.5	9.0	14.1
Total Liabilities to Net Worth 37	1.6	0.5	0.3	0.9	1.7	1.7	1.1
Current Assets to Working Capital 38	3.6	1.8	1.4	2.4	2.2	3.6	5.8
Current Liabilities to Working Capital 39	2.6	0.8	0.4	1.4	1.2	2.6	4.8
Working Capital to Net Sales 40	0.1	0.1	0.2	0.1	0.2	0.1	0.1
Inventory to Working Capital 41	1.3	0.6	0.5	0.9	0.8	1.5	2.4
Total Receipts to Cash Flow 42	7.7	7.3	8.9	8.6	9.5	10.9	7.8
Cost of Goods to Cash Flow 43	5.1	4.2	6.2	5.9	6.5	7.5	5.2
Cash Flow to Total Debt 44	0.3	0.9	0.8	0.5	0.3	0.2	0.2

Selected Financial Factors (in Percentages)

Debt Ratio 45	62.1	35.1	25.7	47.7	62.7	62.6	52.7
Return on Total Assets 46	7.5	15.9	13.0	12.8	15.6	6.5	6.2
Return on Equity Before Income Taxes 47	14.6	21.5	16.3	18.9	30.0	12.6	8.6
Return on Equity After Income Taxes 48	12.9	20.5	15.8	17.0	26.6	10.3	6.0
Profit Margin (Before Income Tax) 49	4.4	6.1	6.6	5.1	6.9	3.2	5.2
Profit Margin (After Income Tax) 50	3.9	5.8	6.3	4.6	6.1	2.7	3.6

Table I

Corporations with and without Net Income

CLAY, REFRACTORY AND OTHER NONMETALLIC MINERAL PRODUCT

MONEY AMOUNTS AND SIZE OF ASSETS IN THOUSANDS OF DOLLARS

Item Description for Accounting Period 7/02 Through 6/03	Total	Zero Assets	Under 500	500 to 1,000	1,000 to 5,000	5,000 to 10,000	10,000 to 25,000	25,000 to 50,000	50,000 to 100,000	100,000 to 250,000	250,000 to 500,000	500,000 to 2,500,000	2,500,000 and over
Number of Enterprises 1	1410	13	608	221	373	64	77	24	13	9	•	8	0
Revenues ($ in Thousands)													
Net Sales 2	15811591	319478	326529	558353	1240787	794561	1546837	1021253	889848	1016326	•	8105619	0
Interest 3	288893	5183	792	416	959	129	1536	929	2690	3275	•	272984	0
Rents 4	29729	0	0	0	0	131	485	174	1827	492	•	26620	0
Royalties 5	223982	0	0	0	2891	0	651	195	448	768	•	219030	0
Other Portfolio Income 6	124978	3	466	0	369	503	4166	3941	1849	6996	•	106687	0
Other Receipts 7	202011	-136	208	1148	2199	4745	11650	4813	4626	11186	•	161569	0
Total Receipts 8	16689184	324528	327995	559917	1247205	800069	1565325	1031305	901288	1039043	•	8892509	0
Average Total Receipts 9	11836	24964	539	2534	3344	12501	20329	42971	69330	115449	•	1111564	•
Operating Costs/Operating Income (%)													
Cost of Operations 10	68.2	71.6	53.1	47.6	63.6	67.1	67.8	69.3	70.2	64.1	•	71.1	•
Salaries and Wages 11	7.8	4.2	18.7	5.9	8.0	7.0	7.1	6.3	7.0	9.5	•	7.9	•
Taxes Paid 12	1.9	2.8	3.2	3.3	2.6	2.0	2.5	2.1	1.5	2.3	•	1.4	•
Interest Paid 13	2.7	2.3	1.1	0.3	1.3	0.9	1.7	1.7	1.3	1.2	•	4.0	•
Depreciation 14	4.8	13.6	5.6	1.1	4.1	3.7	5.1	6.2	5.0	5.8	•	4.6	•
Amortization and Depletion 15	0.8	0.3	0.0	0.1	0.1	0.9	0.3	0.4	0.4	0.5	•	1.2	•
Pensions and Other Deferred Comp. 16	1.6	1.0	0.4	1.0	0.6	0.4	0.5	1.3	0.6	0.9	•	2.4	•
Employee Benefits 17	1.8	0.4	2.3	0.8	1.8	0.7	2.0	2.6	1.4	2.5	•	1.8	•
Advertising 18	0.8	0.9	0.2	0.7	0.5	1.0	0.9	0.8	0.4	0.5	•	0.8	•
Other Expenses 19	13.7	5.7	12.7	20.0	12.6	8.1	9.6	8.5	8.7	9.8	•	16.8	•
Officers' Compensation 20	2.1	1.0	3.4	19.4	4.7	3.1	2.3	1.6	1.5	1.0	•	0.7	•
Operating Margin 21	•	•	•	•	0.0	5.0	0.2	•	2.0	1.9	•	•	•
Operating Margin Before Officers' Comp. 22	•	•	2.7	19.1	4.7	8.1	2.5	0.9	3.5	3.0	•	•	•

Selected Average Balance Sheet ($ in Thousands)

Net Receivables 23	5255	0	51	203	318	1435	2915	5261	9148	31267	796486	•
Inventories 24	1473	0	34	59	454	1998	3576	8040	13074	24772	110183	•
Net Property, Plant and Equipment 25	3302	0	66	65	852	2675	5583	15110	25858	53459	312791	•
Total Assets 26	25028	0	186	631	1947	8067	16326	34907	63346	151937	3668540	•
Notes and Loans Payable 27	8588	0	106	174	796	1924	5346	10467	13664	33296	1305667	•
All Other Liabilities 28	10104	0	31	406	403	1026	3692	8604	10490	31084	1626912	•
Net Worth 29	6336	0	49	51	748	5117	7288	15837	39191	87556	755960	•

Selected Financial Ratios (Times to 1)

Current Ratio 30	1.2	•	4.0	1.1	1.5	1.9	1.8	1.7	2.6	2.0	1.1
Quick Ratio 31	0.7	•	2.2	0.9	0.8	0.9	1.0	0.8	1.3	1.2	0.7
Net Sales to Working Capital 32	6.8	•	6.0	84.2	10.9	6.8	5.2	6.0	3.9	3.3	7.9
Coverage Ratio 33	0.9	0.1	0.8	1.0	1.4	7.4	2.1	1.2	3.6	4.5	0.4
Total Asset Turnover 34	0.4	•	2.9	4.0	1.7	1.5	1.2	1.2	1.1	0.7	0.3
Inventory Turnover 35	5.2	•	8.3	20.4	4.7	4.2	3.8	3.7	3.7	2.9	6.5
Receivables Turnover 36	2.2	•	20.9	11.1	8.3	7.1	6.6	6.7	7.2	3.9	1.3
Total Liabilities to Net Worth 37	2.9	•	2.8	11.3	1.6	0.6	1.2	1.2	0.6	0.7	3.9
Current Assets to Working Capital 38	6.3	•	1.3	16.8	3.0	2.2	2.2	2.4	1.6	2.0	11.6
Current Liabilities to Working Capital 39	5.3	•	0.3	15.8	2.0	1.2	1.2	1.4	0.6	1.0	10.6
Working Capital to Net Sales 40	0.1	•	0.2	0.0	0.1	0.1	0.2	0.2	0.3	0.3	0.1
Inventory to Working Capital 41	0.8	•	0.4	1.8	1.3	1.0	0.9	1.0	0.7	0.8	0.8
Total Receipts to Cash Flow 42	10.2	39.4	9.4	6.5	13.3	8.1	10.8	13.7	9.6	8.2	10.1
Cost of Goods to Cash Flow 43	6.9	28.2	5.0	3.1	8.5	5.5	7.3	9.5	6.8	5.2	7.2
Cash Flow to Total Debt 44	0.1	•	0.4	0.7	0.2	0.5	0.2	0.2	0.3	0.2	0.0

Selected Financial Factors (in Percentages)

Debt Ratio 45	74.7	•	73.7	91.9	61.6	36.6	55.4	54.6	38.1	42.4	79.5
Return on Total Assets 46	1.0	•	2.6	1.3	3.1	10.2	4.2	2.4	4.9	3.9	0.4
Return on Equity Before Income Taxes 47	•	•	•	0.6	2.4	13.9	4.9	0.7	5.6	5.3	•
Return on Equity After Income Taxes 48	•	•	•	•	2.3	13.6	3.0	•	4.0	3.7	•
Profit Margin (Before Income Tax) 49	•	•	•	0.0	0.5	5.7	1.8	0.3	3.2	4.1	•
Profit Margin (After Income Tax) 50	•	•	•	•	0.5	5.6	1.1	•	2.3	2.9	•

Table II

Corporations with Net Income

CLAY, REFRACTORY AND OTHER NONMETALLIC MINERAL PRODUCT

MONEY AMOUNTS AND SIZE OF ASSETS IN THOUSANDS OF DOLLARS

Item Description for Accounting Period 7/02 Through 6/03	Total	Zero Assets	Under 500	500 to 1,000	1,000 to 5,000	5,000 to 10,000	10,000 to 25,000	25,000 to 50,000	50,000 to 100,000	100,000 to 250,000	250,000 to 500,000	500,000 to 2,500,000	2,500,000 and over
Number of Enterprises 1	726	0	189	167	223	52	49	14	0	0	•	3	•
Revenues ($ in Thousands)													
Net Sales 2	7013123	0	257303	454349	838309	707594	1118930	631801	0	0	•	934378	•
Interest 3	62954	0	55	413	600	47	1176	880	0	0	•	49820	•
Rents 4	3715	0	0	0	0	92	339	172	0	0	•	793	•
Royalties 5	4777	0	0	0	0	0	495	48	0	0	•	3018	•
Other Portfolio Income 6	12623	0	466	0	163	261	2982	806	0	0	•	0	•
Other Receipts 7	142947	0	25	1148	1133	4646	9536	2091	0	0	•	117255	•
Total Receipts 8	7240139	0	257849	455910	840205	712640	1133458	635798	0	0	•	1105264	•
Average Total Receipts 9	9973	•	1364	2730	3768	13705	23132	45414	•	•	•	368421	•
Operating Costs/Operating Income (%)													
Cost of Operations 10	64.0	•	57.1	45.5	65.6	67.2	65.4	62.8	•	•	•	66.2	•
Salaries and Wages 11	7.2	•	14.8	3.8	5.9	6.7	7.0	6.9	•	•	•	6.8	•
Taxes Paid 12	2.3	•	2.9	3.3	2.6	1.6	2.5	1.9	•	•	•	2.5	•
Interest Paid 13	1.9	•	1.3	0.1	0.9	0.8	1.0	1.3	•	•	•	7.7	•
Depreciation 14	5.0	•	6.8	0.9	1.9	3.4	4.1	5.1	•	•	•	7.8	•
Amortization and Depletion 15	0.5	•	0.0	0.0	0.1	1.0	0.3	0.3	•	•	•	1.2	•
Pensions and Other Deferred Comp. 16	0.8	•	0.5	1.3	0.6	0.5	0.5	1.0	•	•	•	1.3	•
Employee Benefits 17	1.9	•	2.7	0.4	1.4	0.8	2.2	3.1	•	•	•	3.2	•
Advertising 18	0.6	•	0.1	0.9	0.2	1.1	0.9	0.6	•	•	•	0.7	•
Other Expenses 19	9.3	•	7.6	20.4	11.2	7.4	8.7	7.7	•	•	•	9.9	•
Officers' Compensation 20	3.4	•	3.3	22.8	4.6	3.1	2.3	2.1	•	•	•	0.4	•
Operating Margin 21	3.1	•	2.8	0.6	5.0	6.7	5.2	7.2	•	•	•	7.2	•
Operating Margin Before Officers' Comp. 22	6.5	•	6.1	23.3	9.7	9.8	7.5	9.3	•	•	•	9.3	•

Selected Average Balance Sheet ($ in Thousands)

Net Receivables 23	1436	134	154	352	1572	2869	5324	•	84138
Inventories 24	1429	104	58	614	1824	3425	9586	•	69309
Net Property, Plant and Equipment 25	2576	205	44	373	2377	5290	13481	•	135284
Total Assets 26	11721	458	630	1516	7988	16890	36410	•	1424471
Notes and Loans Payable 27	1925	225	73	483	1589	3789	10663	•	144916
All Other Liabilities 28	5069	46	456	441	1017	3474	4920	•	943144
Net Worth 29	4726	187	101	591	5383	9627	20827	•	336411

Selected Financial Ratios (Times to 1)

Current Ratio 30	1.3	5.8	1.0	1.7	2.0	2.1	3.1	•	0.9
Quick Ratio 31	0.7	3.8	0.9	0.8	1.0	1.1	1.4	•	0.4
Net Sales to Working Capital 32	7.6	6.5	•	9.1	6.7	4.7	3.5	•	•
Coverage Ratio 33	4.3	3.4	7.9	6.9	10.8	7.8	7.2	•	2.4
Total Asset Turnover 34	0.8	3.0	4.3	2.5	1.7	1.4	1.2	•	0.2
Inventory Turnover 35	4.3	7.5	21.4	4.0	5.0	4.4	3.0	•	3.0
Receivables Turnover 36	5.3	9.8	17.1	8.2	7.6	8.5	5.9	•	1.6
Total Liabilities to Net Worth 37	1.5	1.5	5.3	1.6	0.5	0.8	0.7	•	3.2
Current Assets to Working Capital 38	4.0	1.2	•	2.5	2.0	1.9	1.5	•	•
Current Liabilities to Working Capital 39	3.0	0.2	•	1.5	1.0	0.9	0.5	•	•
Working Capital to Net Sales 40	0.1	0.2	•	0.1	0.2	0.2	0.3	•	•
Inventory to Working Capital 41	1.0	0.4	•	1.2	0.9	0.7	0.6	•	•
Total Receipts to Cash Flow 42	7.6	10.4	5.9	10.4	7.4	7.4	7.1	•	5.7
Cost of Goods to Cash Flow 43	4.9	5.9	2.7	6.8	5.0	4.8	4.4	•	3.8
Cash Flow to Total Debt 44	0.2	0.5	0.9	0.4	0.7	0.4	0.4	•	0.0

Selected Financial Factors (in Percentages)

Debt Ratio 45	59.7	59.3	84.0	61.0	32.6	43.0	42.8	•	76.4
Return on Total Assets 46	6.8	12.8	4.5	15.2	13.9	10.9	11.3	•	4.0
Return on Equity Before Income Taxes 47	13.0	22.2	24.7	33.2	18.7	16.7	17.0	•	9.7
Return on Equity After Income Taxes 48	11.2	18.9	22.7	33.1	18.5	14.5	12.7	•	8.4
Profit Margin (Before Income Tax) 49	6.4	3.0	0.9	5.2	7.4	7.0	7.8	•	10.5
Profit Margin (After Income Tax) 50	5.5	2.6	0.8	5.2	7.3	6.1	5.9	•	9.0

Table I
Corporations with and without Net Income

GLASS AND GLASS PRODUCT

MONEY AMOUNTS AND SIZE OF ASSETS IN THOUSANDS OF DOLLARS

Item Description for Accounting Period 7/02 Through 6/03	Total	Zero Assets	Under 500	500 to 1,000	1,000 to 5,000	5,000 to 10,000	10,000 to 25,000	25,000 to 50,000	50,000 to 100,000	100,000 to 250,000	250,000 to 500,000	500,000 to 2,500,000	2,500,000 and over
Number of Enterprises 1	2117	10	1512	231	247	49	35	8	6	6	4	9	0
Revenues ($ in Thousands)													
Net Sales 2	25090900	10725	1572268	453740	1135459	525901	808835	357890	540978	1126289	2180941	16377874	0
Interest 3	106442	18	2	0	1009	44	1242	327	111	29685	2501	71503	0
Rents 4	18073	0	0	0	22	0	822	499	0	2478	962	13291	0
Royalties 5	102395	1553	0	0	0	0	409	71	0	20167	865	79330	0
Other Portfolio Income 6	134225	0	49	0	14982	41	524	3091	1434	1322	20945	91836	0
Other Receipts 7	194639	6	927	1475	2857	674	2714	642	-185	22174	11749	151606	0
Total Receipts 8	25646674	12302	1573246	455215	1154329	526660	814546	362520	542338	1202115	2217963	16785440	0
Average Total Receipts 9	12115	1230	1041	1971	4673	10748	23273	45315	90390	200352	554491	1865049	•
Operating Costs/Operating Income (%)													
Cost of Operations 10	64.7	88.1	53.0	45.5	69.0	73.9	72.1	65.9	74.3	64.4	58.5	65.8	•
Salaries and Wages 11	7.4	•	11.3	8.4	8.8	5.3	6.6	6.9	3.3	11.5	9.4	6.7	•
Taxes Paid 12	2.4	0.0	2.8	2.7	2.5	1.6	2.2	2.0	2.3	3.4	2.5	2.3	•
Interest Paid 13	3.3	2.4	0.5	2.0	1.2	1.5	1.2	2.6	1.3	3.3	1.1	4.3	•
Depreciation 14	5.1	6.4	2.2	6.6	3.0	3.9	4.3	4.1	4.8	4.7	6.1	5.5	•
Amortization and Depletion 15	0.5	•	0.0	0.0	0.0	0.1	0.2	0.2	0.2	0.4	0.2	0.7	•
Pensions and Other Deferred Comp. 16	0.7	•	0.1	0.0	0.2	0.2	0.4	0.3	0.3	0.9	0.4	0.8	•
Employee Benefits 17	3.0	•	0.6	1.2	1.6	0.7	1.6	2.5	2.4	3.7	3.7	3.4	•
Advertising 18	0.5	0.0	1.3	0.2	0.3	0.3	0.5	0.1	0.1	2.1	0.5	0.4	•
Other Expenses 19	13.0	13.0	17.8	24.4	12.0	9.8	10.9	10.9	4.6	13.8	12.5	12.9	•
Officers' Compensation 20	1.2	1.1	6.9	7.6	4.6	1.5	1.6	1.3	0.9	0.7	0.5	0.3	•
Operating Margin 21	•	3.5	1.4	1.4	•	1.3	•	3.2	5.4	•	4.7	•	•
Operating Margin Before Officers' Comp. 22	•	10.4	8.9	1.3	2.7	0.0	4.5	6.3	5.1	•	•	•	•

Selected Average Balance Sheet ($ in Thousands)

Net Receivables 23	1338	0	76	155	605	1269	2550	6720	10742	28998	64101	203606	•
Inventories 24	1521	0	51	155	523	1146	2756	6666	10374	23801	66270	257364	•
Net Property, Plant and Equipment 25	4074	0	38	482	580	3225	5682	12478	32982	46728	161794	747793	•
Total Assets 26	14021	0	230	824	2022	6699	15202	36432	73835	155321	437228	2707759	•
Notes and Loans Payable 27	5561	0	98	469	776	3598	5508	15318	30566	27522	125686	1109068	•
All Other Liabilities 28	3198	0	67	158	560	1218	3480	8794	10748	51350	95282	609782	•
Net Worth 29	5262	0	65	197	687	1883	6214	12321	32520	76449	216261	988909	•

Selected Financial Ratios (Times to 1)

Current Ratio 30	1.3	•	2.2	1.2	1.9	1.7	1.5	1.4	1.1	2.8	1.5	1.2
Quick Ratio 31	0.6	•	1.4	0.6	1.0	1.0	0.8	0.7	0.6	1.7	0.7	0.5
Net Sales to Working Capital 32	13.1	•	12.3	38.3	7.2	8.5	9.7	10.3	29.0	3.6	10.8	18.2
Coverage Ratio 33	1.3	2.5	7.8	1.9	•	2.0	0.2	2.7	5.3	0.3	6.6	1.0
Total Asset Turnover 34	0.8	•	4.5	2.4	2.3	1.6	1.5	1.2	1.2	1.2	1.2	0.7
Inventory Turnover 35	5.0	•	10.8	5.7	6.1	6.9	6.0	4.4	6.5	5.1	4.8	4.7
Receivables Turnover 36	8.7	•	27.5	9.3	8.4	4.9	8.5	5.9	6.9	8.1	7.6	8.9
Total Liabilities to Net Worth 37	1.7	•	2.6	3.2	1.9	2.6	1.4	2.0	1.3	1.0	1.0	1.7
Current Assets to Working Capital 38	4.0	•	1.9	6.5	2.1	2.4	3.1	3.5	7.7	1.6	3.0	5.8
Current Liabilities to Working Capital 39	3.0	•	0.9	5.5	1.1	1.4	2.1	2.5	6.7	0.6	2.0	4.8
Working Capital to Net Sales 40	0.1	•	0.1	0.0	0.1	0.1	0.1	0.1	0.0	0.3	0.1	0.1
Inventory to Working Capital 41	1.7	•	0.6	3.1	0.8	0.9	1.2	1.4	3.0	0.5	1.2	2.5
Total Receipts to Cash Flow 42	10.7	6.0	6.2	6.2	14.2	11.1	13.0	7.8	12.0	14.4	6.4	12.5
Cost of Goods to Cash Flow 43	6.9	5.3	3.3	2.8	9.8	8.2	9.4	5.2	8.9	9.3	3.7	8.3
Cash Flow to Total Debt 44	0.1	•	1.0	0.5	0.2	0.2	0.2	0.2	0.2	0.2	0.4	0.1

Selected Financial Factors (in Percentages)

Debt Ratio 45	62.5	•	71.9	76.1	66.0	71.9	59.1	66.2	56.0	50.8	50.5	63.5
Return on Total Assets 46	3.5	•	18.5	8.8	•	4.7	0.4	8.6	8.6	1.2	9.4	3.0
Return on Equity Before Income Taxes 47	2.1	•	57.4	16.9	8.1	•	16.0	15.9	•	16.2	0.3	
Return on Equity After Income Taxes 48	0.5	•	57.4	15.8	6.4	•	8.0	11.8	•	14.5	•	
Profit Margin (Before Income Tax) 49	0.9	3.7	3.6	1.7	1.4	•	4.4	5.7	•	6.4	0.1	•
Profit Margin (After Income Tax) 50	0.2	3.7	3.6	1.6	1.1	•	2.2	4.2	•	5.8	•	

Table II

Corporations with Net Income

GLASS AND GLASS PRODUCT

MONEY AMOUNTS AND SIZE OF ASSETS IN THOUSANDS OF DOLLARS

Item Description for Accounting Period 7/02 Through 6/03	Total	Zero Assets	Under 500	500 to 1000	251 to 500	501 to 1,000	1,001 to 5,000	5,001 to 10,000	10,001 to 25,000	25,001 to 50,000	50,001 to 100,000	100,001 to 250,000	250,001 and over
Number of Enterprises **1**	1331	0	910	231	122	35	17	3	0	0	0	3	0
Revenues ($ in Thousands)													
Net Sales **2**	15166157	0	1096783	453740	751193	394814	493915	179103	0	0	0	9349107	0
Interest **3**	30120	0	0	0	1006	44	792	267	0	0	0	25682	0
Rents **4**	3774	0	0	0	22	0	197	472	0	0	0	2383	0
Royalties **5**	19562	0	0	0	0	0	371	0	0	0	0	16773	0
Other Portfolio Income **6**	84756	0	49	0	592	41	400	557	0	0	0	70112	0
Other Receipts **7**	54848	0	534	1475	92	635	971	175	0	0	0	44629	0
Total Receipts **8**	15359217	0	1097366	455215	752905	395534	496646	180574	0	0	0	9508686	0
Average Total Receipts **9**	11540	•	1206	1971	6171	11301	29214	60191	•	•	•	3169562	•
Operating Costs/Operating Income (%)													
Cost of Operations **10**	63.4	•	49.2	45.5	68.9	75.9	72.0	67.9	•	•	•	65.8	•
Salaries and Wages **11**	7.3	•	11.3	8.4	7.5	5.4	4.7	4.5	•	•	•	6.8	•
Taxes Paid **12**	2.4	•	2.8	2.7	2.5	1.5	2.1	1.9	•	•	•	2.4	•
Interest Paid **13**	1.8	•	0.7	2.0	0.5	0.7	0.7	0.5	•	•	•	2.4	•
Depreciation **14**	5.5	•	2.5	6.6	1.8	2.4	3.1	3.1	•	•	•	6.1	•
Amortization and Depletion **15**	0.5	•	0.0	0.0	0.0	0.0	0.1	0.1	•	•	•	0.7	•
Pensions and Other Deferred Comp. **16**	0.6	•	0.1	0.0	0.3	0.2	0.2	0.4	•	•	•	0.9	•
Employee Benefits **17**	2.5	•	0.2	1.2	1.2	1.0	1.3	2.6	•	•	•	2.7	•
Advertising **18**	0.4	•	1.2	0.2	0.2	0.4	0.5	0.1	•	•	•	0.4	•
Other Expenses **19**	11.4	•	17.1	24.4	9.4	7.2	10.1	5.5	•	•	•	10.6	•
Officers' Compensation **20**	1.4	•	7.3	7.6	6.2	1.3	1.1	0.8	•	•	•	0.3	•
Operating Margin **21**	2.8	•	7.7	1.4	1.4	4.1	4.1	12.5	•	•	•	1.1	•
Operating Margin Before Officers' Comp. **22**	4.2	•	15.0	8.9	7.7	5.4	5.2	13.3	•	•	•	1.4	•

Selected Average Balance Sheet ($ in Thousands)

Net Receivables 23	1293	105	155	730	1540	3066	9509	367662
Inventories 24	1581	49	84	524	699	2773	9142	513940
Net Property, Plant and Equipment 25	3621	48	482	397	1994	5386	13084	1213677
Total Assets 26	10002	300	824	1974	5762	15362	40373	3371740
Notes and Loans Payable 27	3236	112	469	541	2142	3863	5853	1148690
All Other Liabilities 28	2807	63	158	479	787	3553	13268	981887
Net Worth 29	3960	125	197	954	2833	7946	21252	1241163

Selected Financial Ratios (Times to 1)

Current Ratio 30	1.3	3.2	1.2	2.7	3.1	1.8	1.3	1.2
Quick Ratio 31	0.7	2.3	0.6	1.7	2.0	1.0	0.7	0.6
Net Sales to Working Capital 32	13.6	8.8	38.3	6.8	5.2	7.8	12.4	20.2
Coverage Ratio 33	3.7	12.7	1.9	4.2	7.0	7.8	27.0	2.7
Total Asset Turnover 34	1.1	4.0	2.4	3.1	2.0	1.9	1.5	0.9
Inventory Turnover 35	4.6	12.1	10.6	8.1	12.2	7.5	4.0	4.0
Receivables Turnover 36	7.8	13.7	18.8	7.4	8.9	8.7	5.3	7.4
Total Liabilities to Net Worth 37	1.5	1.4	3.2	1.1	1.0	0.9	0.9	1.7
Current Assets to Working Capital 38	3.9	1.5	6.5	1.6	1.5	2.3	4.3	6.4
Current Liabilities to Working Capital 39	2.9	0.5	5.5	0.6	0.5	1.3	3.3	5.4
Working Capital to Net Sales 40	0.1	0.1	0.0	0.1	0.2	0.1	0.0	0.0
Inventory to Working Capital 41	1.5	0.3	3.1	0.4	0.5	0.7	1.6	2.6
Total Receipts to Cash Flow 42	8.4	5.2	6.2	11.2	8.9	7.8	5.9	10.1
Cost of Goods to Cash Flow 43	5.3	2.6	2.8	7.7	6.8	5.6	4.0	6.6
Cash Flow to Total Debt 44	0.2	1.3	0.5	0.5	0.4	0.5	0.5	0.1

Selected Financial Factors (in Percentages)

Debt Ratio 45	60.4	58.3	76.1	51.7	50.8	48.3	47.4	63.2
Return on Total Assets 46	7.6	34.0	8.8	6.9	9.7	10.0	20.3	6.0
Return on Equity Before Income Taxes 47	14.0	75.1	16.9	10.8	17.0	16.9	37.2	10.2
Return on Equity After Income Taxes 48	10.8	75.1	15.8	9.8	15.3	12.3	24.8	6.8
Profit Margin (Before Income Tax) 49	4.8	7.8	1.7	1.7	4.3	4.6	13.2	4.1
Profit Margin (After Income Tax) 50	3.7	7.8	1.6	1.5	3.8	3.4	8.8	2.7

Table I

Corporations with and without Net Income

CEMENT, CONCRETE, LIME AND GYPSUM PRODUCT

MONEY AMOUNTS AND SIZE OF ASSETS IN THOUSANDS OF DOLLARS

Item Description for Accounting Period 7/02 Through 6/03	Total	Zero Assets	Under 500	500 to 1,000	1,000 to 5,000	5,000 to 10,000	10,000 to 25,000	25,000 to 50,000	50,000 to 100,000	100,000 to 250,000	250,000 to 500,000	500,000 to 2,500,000	2,500,000 and over
Number of Enterprises 1	4450	350	2044	475	1064	256	146	49	19	18	8	16	6
Revenues ($ in Thousands)													
Net Sales 2	50378556	809389	1519249	1070412	5097498	2825805	3637674	2260396	1820647	2952354	2350980	10344782	15689370
Interest 3	746654	1141	342	1709	7230	3410	4395	4496	1954	8813	50166	356036	306961
Rents 4	85294	836	0	3821	9930	1085	4108	1782	3539	6747	3716	32419	17310
Royalties 5	34649	0	0	0	0	0	795	100	63	2818	8078	10684	12111
Other Portfolio Income 6	274587	25565	18	765	23840	8772	32441	3131	25036	14661	13233	27964	99165
Other Receipts 7	716996	1504	2038	9001	67006	13336	33953	23174	16617	79909	12683	125643	332129
Total Receipts 8	52236736	838435	1521647	1085708	5205504	2852408	3713366	2293079	1867856	3065302	2438856	10897528	16457046
Average Total Receipts 9	11739	2396	744	2286	4892	11142	25434	46798	98308	170295	304857	681096	2742841
Operating Costs/Operating Income (%)													
Cost of Operations 10	65.4	58.8	48.5	53.0	63.6	66.0	69.2	68.3	70.0	64.9	61.4	68.0	66.0
Salaries and Wages 11	6.7	7.4	15.7	19.1	7.2	6.7	6.6	6.3	4.8	4.9	8.9	3.8	6.8
Taxes Paid 12	2.3	2.1	4.6	1.9	3.0	2.3	2.4	2.3	2.3	2.7	2.0	2.3	1.9
Interest Paid 13	4.1	2.3	1.6	0.7	1.4	0.8	0.9	1.4	1.6	1.2	5.5	6.5	6.4
Depreciation 14	6.4	7.5	5.3	3.6	5.1	5.3	4.7	6.0	6.0	6.1	6.8	8.5	6.4
Amortization and Depletion 15	1.0	0.8	0.0	0.0	0.1	0.3	0.2	0.4	0.8	0.8	2.0	1.5	1.6
Pensions and Other Deferred Comp. 16	0.7	0.6	*	0.8	0.8	0.4	0.5	0.7	0.7	0.8	0.6	0.7	0.7
Employee Benefits 17	2.5	2.7	0.9	3.2	1.8	1.7	1.4	2.0	2.8	5.6	1.4	2.4	3.1
Advertising 18	0.4	0.2	0.3	0.5	0.3	0.7	0.4	0.5	0.4	0.7	0.2	0.2	0.5
Other Expenses 19	10.1	13.9	24.1	14.0	14.2	9.7	9.8	8.4	6.3	7.6	10.0	9.6	8.5
Officers' Compensation 20	1.2	1.1	4.0	3.7	3.6	2.7	1.8	2.2	1.1	0.8	0.8	0.4	0.2
Operating Margin 21	*	2.5	*	*	*	3.3	2.2	1.6	3.3	3.8	0.3	*	*
Operating Margin Before Officers' Comp. 22	0.4	3.5	*	3.1	2.5	6.0	3.9	3.8	4.4	4.7	1.1	*	*

Selected Average Balance Sheet ($ in Thousands)

Line Item													
Net Receivables 23	2168	0	29	204	571	1415	3682	7086	14420	20801	45753	90043	864102
Inventories 24	895	0	15	97	227	573	1651	4078	7559	10966	31898	72672	219653
Net Property, Plant and Equipment 25	5981	0	100	225	868	2672	6047	13527	35324	58987	152568	657962	1611592
Total Assets 26	13970		174	700	2347	6804	15486	32381	71907	150484	356992	1215305	4502591
Notes and Loans Payable 27	4507	0	86	179	1042	1904	4389	10558	16708	35210	165189	351802	1523012
All Other Liabilities 28	4230	0	81	263	548	1394	2841	6783	13335	27004	53913	336088	1716496
Net Worth 29	5233	0	8	258	757	3506	8256	15040	41865	88270	137890	527415	1263082

Selected Financial Ratios (Times to 1)

Line Item													
Current Ratio 30	1.2	•	0.7	1.5	1.7	1.8	2.0	1.5	2.0	1.6	2.3	1.1	1.0
Quick Ratio 31	0.8	•	0.6	1.1	1.2	1.3	1.4	0.9	1.4	1.0	1.4	0.5	0.7
Net Sales to Working Capital 32	16.3	•	•	14.5	9.0	8.0	6.3	9.6	6.7	8.3	5.0	35.5	•
Coverage Ratio 33	1.7	3.6	•	2.2	1.8	6.0	5.8	3.2	4.7	7.2	1.8	1.3	1.5
Total Asset Turnover 34	0.8	•	4.3	3.2	2.0	1.6	1.6	1.4	1.3	1.1	0.8	0.5	0.6
Inventory Turnover 35	8.3	•	23.5	12.3	13.4	12.7	10.4	7.7	8.9	9.7	5.7	6.0	7.9
Receivables Turnover 36	5.5	•	23.5	9.2	7.6	8.2	6.7	6.3	5.7	7.6	5.6	7.7	3.5
Total Liabilities to Net Worth 37	1.7	•	21.9	1.7	2.1	0.9	0.9	1.2	0.7	0.7	1.6	1.3	2.6
Current Assets to Working Capital 38	6.1	•	•	2.9	2.4	2.3	2.0	3.2	2.0	2.6	1.8	11.8	•
Current Liabilities to Working Capital 39	5.1	•	•	1.9	1.4	1.3	1.0	2.2	1.0	1.6	0.8	10.8	•
Working Capital to Net Sales 40	0.1	•	•	0.1	0.1	0.1	0.2	0.1	0.1	0.1	0.2	0.0	•
Inventory to Working Capital 41	1.3	•	•	0.6	0.4	0.5	0.4	0.8	0.5	0.6	0.4	4.2	•
Total Receipts to Cash Flow 42	10.3	6.9	7.8	8.8	9.8	9.4	9.7	11.4	10.9	8.1	8.5	11.2	11.9
Cost of Goods to Cash Flow 43	6.8	4.1	3.8	4.6	6.3	6.2	6.7	7.8	7.6	5.2	5.2	7.6	7.8
Cash Flow to Total Debt 44	0.1	•	0.6	0.6	0.3	0.4	0.4	0.2	0.3	0.1	0.2	0.1	0.1

Selected Financial Factors (in Percentages)

Line Item													
Debt Ratio 45	62.5	•	95.6	63.1	67.8	48.5	46.7	53.6	41.8	41.3	61.4	56.6	71.9
Return on Total Assets 46	5.7	•	•	5.1	5.0	8.1	8.3	6.3	9.9	9.7	8.0	4.3	5.4
Return on Equity Before Income Taxes 47	6.2	•	•	7.5	6.9	13.2	12.9	9.3	13.5	14.2	8.8	2.1	6.1
Return on Equity After Income Taxes 48	4.1	•	•	7.2	5.8	11.6	11.5	7.4	11.3	10.3	5.9	0.4	3.8
Profit Margin (Before Income Tax) 49	2.9	6.1	•	0.9	1.1	4.2	4.3	3.0	5.9	7.6	4.1	1.7	2.9
Profit Margin (After Income Tax) 50	1.9	4.7	•	0.8	0.9	3.7	3.8	2.4	4.9	5.5	2.8	0.3	1.8

Table II
Corporations with Net Income

CEMENT, CONCRETE, LIME AND GYPSUM PRODUCT

MONEY AMOUNTS AND SIZE OF ASSETS IN THOUSANDS OF DOLLARS

Item Description for Accounting Period 7/02 Through 6/03	Total	Zero Assets	Under 500	500 to 1,000	1,000 to 5,000	5,000 to 10,000	10,000 to 25,000	25,000 to 50,000	50,000 to 100,000	100,000 to 250,000	250,000 to 500,000	500,000 to 2,500,000	2,500,000 and over
Number of Enterprises 1	2593	89	1179	339	613	172	111	40	0	14	0	9	0
Revenues ($ in Thousands)													
Net Sales 2	35989674	803591	1025120	725539	3216005	2106078	2737251	1915850	0	2235069	0	6661723	0
Interest 3	379830	1012	236	1471	4356	3116	3183	2037	0	8813	0	95863	0
Rents 4	69254	836	0	3821	5593	990	3514	1782	0	6747	0	22255	0
Royalties 5	32098	0	0	0	0	0	795	100	0	2818	0	9840	0
Other Portfolio Income 6	221024	24602	12	62	21518	1046	26568	2886	0	13909	0	12074	0
Other Receipts 7	616274	1496	1716	8777	56673	6683	29171	22070	0	66573	0	74846	0
Total Receipts 8	37308154	831537	1027084	739670	3304145	2117913	2800482	1944725	0	2333929	0	6876601	0
Average Total Receipts 9	14388	9343	871	2182	5390	12313	25230	48618	•	166709	•	764067	•
Operating Costs/Operating Income (%)													
Cost of Operations 10	64.6	58.2	54.8	59.8	59.8	63.0	68.0	67.0	•	62.6	•	68.3	•
Salaries and Wages 11	6.8	7.4	12.0	9.5	7.7	6.6	6.6	5.9	•	5.0	•	4.4	•
Taxes Paid 12	2.3	2.1	3.9	2.2	2.9	2.2	2.4	2.2	•	2.6	•	2.3	•
Interest Paid 13	3.3	2.3	1.6	0.8	0.8	0.6	0.8	0.9	•	1.3	•	3.1	•
Depreciation 14	5.9	7.5	4.9	4.6	4.6	4.6	4.5	6.0	•	5.3	•	7.4	•
Amortization and Depletion 15	1.0	0.9	•	0.0	0.0	0.3	0.2	0.3	•	0.6	•	1.5	•
Pensions and Other Deferred Comp. 16	0.6	0.6	•	1.2	0.6	0.5	0.5	0.6	•	0.7	•	0.4	•
Employee Benefits 17	2.7	2.7	1.1	1.5	1.8	1.4	1.3	1.8	•	6.4	•	2.7	•
Advertising 18	0.4	0.2	0.2	0.3	0.4	0.9	0.4	0.5	•	0.9	•	0.1	•
Other Expenses 19	8.7	12.3	14.9	13.6	15.0	9.4	9.1	7.5	•	7.6	•	6.3	•
Officers' Compensation 20	1.3	1.1	4.2	4.0	3.7	2.9	1.8	2.2	•	0.8	•	0.5	•
Operating Margin 21	2.4	4.7	2.5	2.4	2.6	7.6	4.4	5.1	•	6.2	•	3.0	•
Operating Margin Before Officers' Comp. 22	3.7	5.8	6.6	6.5	6.4	10.6	6.2	7.3	•	7.0	•	3.5	•

Selected Average Balance Sheet ($ in Thousands)

Net Receivables 23	3157	0	36	248	578	1588	3582	7191	•	19190	•	116455	•
Inventories 24	1016	0	13	69	247	671	1753	4156	•	10475	•	108728	•
Net Property, Plant and Equipment 25	6321	0	100	274	772	2567	5535	14251	•	54388	•	593700	•
Total Assets 26	16470	0	189	725	2298	6891	15170	33000	•	153644	•	1244664	•
Notes and Loans Payable 27	5427	0	52	164	598	1729	3561	7838	•	36211	•	368420	•
All Other Liabilities 28	4029	0	45	185	497	1432	2554	6358	•	27646	•	270353	•
Net Worth 29	7014	0	92	376	1203	3730	9055	18804	•	89786	•	605892	•

Selected Financial Ratios (Times to 1)

Current Ratio 30	1.6	•	1.6	1.9	1.9	1.9	2.3	2.0	•	1.5	•	1.5	•
Quick Ratio 31	1.1	•	1.4	1.5	1.4	1.3	1.7	1.3	•	0.9	•	0.9	•
Net Sales to Working Capital 32	7.1	•	31.2	10.7	8.5	7.5	5.4	6.3	•	9.3	•	9.0	•
Coverage Ratio 33	2.9	4.5	2.6	6.3	7.3	14.5	9.7	8.6	•	9.1	•	3.1	•
Total Asset Turnover 34	0.8	•	4.6	3.0	2.3	1.8	1.6	1.5	•	1.0	•	0.6	•
Inventory Turnover 35	8.8	•	37.3	18.7	12.7	11.5	9.6	7.7	•	9.5	•	4.7	•
Receivables Turnover 36	4.7	•	18.4	9.8	7.2	8.1	6.6	6.3	•	7.4	•	2.5	•
Total Liabilities to Net Worth 37	1.3	•	1.0	0.9	0.9	0.8	0.7	0.8	•	0.7	•	1.1	•
Current Assets to Working Capital 38	2.8	•	2.8	2.1	2.1	2.2	1.8	2.0	•	2.9	•	2.9	•
Current Liabilities to Working Capital 39	1.8	•	1.8	1.1	1.1	1.2	0.8	1.0	•	1.9	•	1.9	•
Working Capital to Net Sales 40	0.1	•	0.0	0.1	0.1	0.1	0.2	0.2	•	0.1	•	0.1	•
Inventory to Working Capital 41	0.5	•	0.3	0.5	0.4	0.5	0.4	0.5	•	0.6	•	0.9	•
Total Receipts to Cash Flow 42	8.6	6.6	8.4	7.2	6.9	6.8	8.1	8.3	•	6.5	•	9.8	•
Cost of Goods to Cash Flow 43	5.6	3.8	4.6	4.3	4.2	4.3	5.5	5.6	•	4.1	•	6.7	•
Cash Flow to Total Debt 44	0.2	•	1.1	0.8	0.7	0.6	0.5	0.4	•	0.4	•	0.1	•

Selected Financial Factors (in Percentages)

Debt Ratio 45	57.4	•	51.2	48.2	47.7	45.9	40.3	43.0	•	41.6	•	51.3	•
Return on Total Assets 46	7.9	•	19.6	15.4	14.2	15.6	12.2	10.9	•	12.4	•	5.6	•
Return on Equity Before Income Taxes 47	12.1	•	25.0	25.0	23.4	26.8	18.4	16.9	•	18.8	•	7.7	•
Return on Equity After Income Taxes 48	9.4	•	23.6	24.7	22.3	24.7	16.7	15.0	•	13.9	•	5.1	•
Profit Margin (Before Income Tax) 49	6.1	8.2	2.6	4.4	5.4	8.2	6.7	6.6	•	10.6	•	6.3	•
Profit Margin (After Income Tax) 50	4.8	6.8	2.5	4.3	5.1	7.5	6.1	5.9	•	7.8	•	4.2	•

Table I

Corporations with and without Net Income

IRON, STEEL MILLS AND STEEL PRODUCT

MONEY AMOUNTS AND SIZE OF ASSETS IN THOUSANDS OF DOLLARS

Item Description for Accounting Period 7/02 Through 6/03	Total	Zero Assets	Under 500	500 to 1,000	1,000 to 5,000	5,000 to 10,000	10,000 to 25,000	25,000 to 50,000	50,000 to 100,000	100,000 to 250,000	250,000 to 500,000	500,000 to 2,500,000	2,500,000 and over
Number of Enterprises **1**	3581	22	2586	322	329	59	108	45	38	37	10	19	6
Revenues ($ in Thousands)													
Net Sales **2**	67742871	2619251	1438124	472741	1615321	677464	2584653	2150465	3644247	7015478	3728000	19818096	21979030
Interest **3**	436998	19004	38	1155	1164	686	2411	2298	11487	66978	39423	117623	174733
Rents **4**	66551	2955	0	124	248	3	1982	2075	4361	6050	2994	22321	23438
Royalties **5**	320474	423	0	0	0	0	23	2512	2170	18473	0	66858	230014
Other Portfolio Income **6**	653176	236207	0	7265	12	5535	1580	6288	2298	6462	69146	184637	133744
Other Receipts **7**	890945	107102	7164	1681	11574	-1021	8671	12859	48098	50004	61973	321511	261331
Total Receipts **8**	70111015	2984942	1445326	482966	1628319	682667	2599320	2176497	3712661	7163445	3901536	20531046	22802290
Average Total Receipts **9**	19579	135679	559	1500	4949	11571	24068	48367	97702	193607	390154	1080581	3800382
Operating Costs/Operating Income (%)													
Cost of Operations **10**	78.6	86.6	51.7	70.3	77.1	78.8	77.7	78.4	81.2	83.1	84.2	82.7	73.2
Salaries and Wages **11**	3.4	3.3	13.5	4.6	4.6	3.8	5.0	4.7	4.0	3.6	2.9	3.6	2.1
Taxes Paid **12**	1.6	0.8	2.0	3.6	2.0	2.6	1.7	1.7	1.3	1.2	1.8	1.4	2.0
Interest Paid **13**	2.2	2.1	0.4	1.5	1.3	1.3	1.2	4.4	1.6	2.6	1.3	2.3	2.4
Depreciation **14**	5.1	5.5	2.9	4.5	3.0	6.5	3.8	4.6	4.0	4.1	5.5	4.9	6.1
Amortization and Depletion **15**	0.3	1.0	0.1	0.1	0.1	0.3	0.1	0.3	0.3	0.4	0.1	0.4	0.3
Pensions and Other Deferred Comp. **16**	0.5	0.3	•	0.4	0.2	0.6	0.4	0.4	0.3	0.6	0.3	0.9	0.2
Employee Benefits **17**	2.1	2.2	0.9	3.9	1.3	0.6	1.4	1.6	1.4	1.3	1.2	2.1	2.9
Advertising **18**	0.1	0.0	0.2	0.2	0.2	0.1	0.3	0.1	0.1	0.3	0.0	0.1	0.0
Other Expenses **19**	11.5	51.9	21.1	14.6	6.6	7.1	7.0	10.5	7.5	6.5	6.3	6.1	15.1
Officers' Compensation **20**	0.8	1.4	8.8	4.2	5.5	2.0	2.1	1.4	0.9	0.5	0.6	0.2	0.3
Operating Margin **21**	•	•	•	•	•	•	•	•	•	•	•	•	•
Operating Margin Before Officers' Comp. **22**	•	7.2	•	•	3.7	1.4	•	•	•	•	•	•	•

Selected Average Balance Sheet ($ in Thousands)

Net Receivables 23	2197	0	54	108	740	1227	3482	5562	11636	23491	45159	131169	415722
Inventories 24	2878	0	11	79	773	1429	3628	8672	13383	34372	75078	160880	591074
Net Property, Plant and Equipment 25	7587	0	49	291	804	2842	4849	12597	25418	59409	133440	421072	2154345
Total Assets 26	17539	0	147	707	2886	7114	15231	34958	68641	154280	356808	1032947	4350275
Notes and Loans Payable 27	5708	0	73	292	1148	2235	4687	21737	28500	54383	102960	416004	1022241
All Other Liabilities 28	9188	0	60	144	704	2025	4798	14785	18161	48473	91031	523306	2971930
Net Worth 29	2643	0	15	271	1034	2855	5746	-1564	21980	51424	162816	93637	356104

Selected Financial Ratios (Times to 1)

Current Ratio 30	1.7	•	1.2	1.9	2.1	1.4	1.5	1.5	1.8	1.7	2.6	1.7	1.5
Quick Ratio 31	0.8	•	1.0	1.2	1.1	0.8	0.8	0.7	0.8	0.8	0.8	0.9	0.6
Net Sales to Working Capital 32	7.1	•	36.0	9.2	4.7	9.4	8.4	8.5	5.6	6.5	3.2	6.4	9.0
Coverage Ratio 33	•	•	•	0.2	•	0.9	•	0.6	0.2	1.8	0.5	1.0	0.7
Total Asset Turnover 34	1.1	•	3.8	2.1	1.7	1.6	1.6	1.4	1.4	1.2	1.0	1.0	0.8
Inventory Turnover 35	5.2	•	27.1	13.1	4.9	6.3	5.1	4.3	5.8	4.6	4.2	5.4	4.5
Receivables Turnover 36	9.3	•	10.8	8.5	7.9	12.8	6.7	7.8	8.5	7.6	8.8	8.1	11.4
Total Liabilities to Net Worth 37	5.6	•	9.1	1.6	1.8	1.5	1.7	•	2.1	2.0	1.2	10.0	11.2
Current Assets to Working Capital 38	2.5	•	5.7	2.1	1.9	3.3	3.2	3.2	2.2	2.4	1.6	2.5	3.0
Current Liabilities to Working Capital 39	1.5	•	4.7	1.1	0.9	2.3	2.2	2.2	1.2	1.4	0.6	1.5	2.0
Working Capital to Net Sales 40	0.1	•	0.0	0.1	0.2	0.1	0.1	0.1	0.2	0.2	0.3	0.2	0.1
Inventory to Working Capital 41	1.1	•	1.0	0.4	0.9	1.1	1.2	1.4	1.0	1.1	0.6	1.0	1.5
Total Receipts to Cash Flow 42	42.1	•	8.8	713.0	28.4	60.4	19.5	•	22.4	35.2	19.3	42.5	24.7
Cost of Goods to Cash Flow 43	33.1	•	4.6	501.5	21.9	47.6	15.1	•	18.1	29.2	16.2	35.1	18.1
Cash Flow to Total Debt 44	0.0	•	0.5	0.0	0.1	0.0	0.1	•	0.1	0.1	0.1	0.0	0.0

Selected Financial Factors (in Percentages)

Debt Ratio 45	84.9	•	90.1	61.7	64.2	59.9	62.3	104.5	68.0	66.7	54.4	90.9	91.8
Return on Total Assets 46	•	•	•	•	0.4	•	1.7	•	1.4	0.5	2.5	1.1	1.4
Return on Equity Before Income Taxes 47	•	•	•	•	•	•	•	153.5	•	•	2.5	•	•
Return on Equity After Income Taxes 48	•	•	•	•	•	•	•	161.1	•	•	1.2	•	•
Profit Margin (Before Income Tax) 49	•	•	•	•	•	•	•	•	•	•	1.1	•	•
Profit Margin (After Income Tax) 50	•	•	•	•	•	•	•	•	•	•	0.5	•	•

Table II

Corporations with Net Income

IRON, STEEL MILLS AND STEEL PRODUCT

MONEY AMOUNTS AND SIZE OF ASSETS IN THOUSANDS OF DOLLARS

Item Description for Accounting Period 7/02 Through 6/03	Total	Zero Assets	Under 500	500 to 1,000	1,000 to 5,000	5,000 to 10,000	10,000 to 25,000	25,000 to 50,000	50,000 to 100,000	100,000 to 250,000	250,000 to 500,000	500,000 to 2,500,000	2,500,000 and over
Number of Enterprises 1	1082	0	619	58	220	26	61	26	19	21	0	11	3
Revenues ($ in Thousands)													
Net Sales 2	36440258	0	463210	65235	1349852	190235	1695053	1238529	2180664	464807	0	11693463	10603384
Interest 3	228489	0	0	77	262	548	1549	1627	3266	36904	0	87204	59127
Rents 4	13637	0	0	0	0	3	991	1263	830	1912	0	4759	1264
Royalties 5	219927	0	0	0	0	0	0	0	2160	17463	0	62130	138174
Other Portfolio Income 6	551177	0	0	9	12	5360	808	686	817	4039	0	179200	82174
Other Receipts 7	624742	0	44	1	7552	734	6070	10248	10679	45140	0	252514	168779
Total Receipts 8	38078230	0	463254	65322	1357678	196880	1704471	1252353	2198416	4750265	0	12279270	11052902
Average Total Receipts 9	35192	•	748	1126	6171	7572	27942	48167	115706	226203	•	1116297	3684301
Operating Costs/Operating Income (%)													
Cost of Operations 10	78.6	•	36.3	59.9	77.9	64.3	76.5	76.8	80.1	82.2	•	84.1	72.8
Salaries and Wages 11	2.7	•	21.4	•	5.1	4.9	4.4	4.3	3.6	3.3	•	2.7	0.6
Taxes Paid 12	1.3	•	1.8	3.3	1.7	3.1	1.6	1.6	1.1	1.0	•	1.1	1.3
Interest Paid 13	1.7	•	0.3	1.4	0.9	0.3	0.7	1.5	0.7	1.5	•	2.0	2.1
Depreciation 14	5.2	•	2.7	10.2	2.4	9.5	2.9	4.0	2.7	3.1	•	5.0	7.5
Amortization and Depletion 15	0.2	•	0.3	•	0.1	0.0	0.1	0.2	0.0	0.1	•	0.4	0.1
Pensions and Other Deferred Comp. 16	0.4	•	•	0.9	0.2	0.7	0.4	0.3	0.2	0.4	•	0.4	0.3
Employee Benefits 17	1.5	•	0.0	4.6	1.0	1.2	1.2	1.4	1.3	1.2	•	1.1	2.2
Advertising 18	0.1	•	0.3	0.6	0.1	0.1	0.3	0.1	0.1	0.0	•	0.1	0.0
Other Expenses 19	8.2	•	19.0	14.7	5.5	3.5	5.7	5.5	5.4	5.9	•	4.3	14.4
Officers' Compensation 20	0.7	•	10.6	3.5	2.5	1.7	2.4	1.6	0.9	0.5	•	0.2	0.3
Operating Margin 21	•	•	7.3	1.1	2.6	10.8	3.9	2.5	4.0	0.8	•	•	•
Operating Margin Before Officers' Comp. 22	0.2	•	18.0	4.6	5.1	12.5	6.3	4.1	4.9	1.3	•	•	•

Selected Average Balance Sheet ($ in Thousands)

Net Receivables 23	3755	•	87	130	920	856	3867	5983	12082	27123	142458	250669
Inventories 24	3892	•	29	93	871	1303	3378	9107	15560	27233	128944	600676
Net Property, Plant and Equipment 25	13958	•	71	421	803	3173	3970	11922	17913	54777	437078	2388405
Total Assets 26	30968	•	229	720	3307	7648	15507	34921	64964	150125	1024134	4246881
Notes and Loans Payable 27	9496	•	47	179	825	503	3461	13628	17365	40445	459526	957694
All Other Liabilities 28	11943	•	44	56	889	751	4121	7785	16714	46758	293874	2413618
Net Worth 29	9528	•	138	485	1592	6394	7926	13509	30885	62922	270735	875568

Selected Financial Ratios (Times to 1)

Current Ratio 30	1.8	•	1.9	4.6	2.1	5.0	1.8	1.5	2.2	1.8	1.7	1.7
Quick Ratio 31	0.8	•	1.5	3.1	1.1	3.3	1.0	0.6	0.9	0.9	0.8	0.6
Net Sales to Working Capital 32	6.4	•	11.0	5.6	5.0	2.2	6.0	8.5	4.9	6.8	6.9	7.8
Coverage Ratio 33	3.4	•	27.6	1.9	4.7	57.5	7.7	3.4	7.7	3.0	2.9	2.2
Total Asset Turnover 34	1.1	•	3.3	1.6	1.9	1.0	1.8	1.4	1.8	1.5	1.0	0.8
Inventory Turnover 35	6.8	•	9.2	7.2	5.5	3.6	6.3	4.0	5.9	6.7	6.9	4.3
Receivables Turnover 36	11.6	•	7.8	2.1	8.4	17.1	7.6	7.7	10.0	9.4	9.8	28.2
Total Liabilities to Net Worth 37	2.3	•	0.7	0.5	1.1	0.2	1.0	1.6	1.1	1.4	2.8	3.9
Current Assets to Working Capital 38	2.2	•	2.1	1.3	1.9	1.3	2.2	3.2	1.8	2.3	2.5	2.4
Current Liabilities to Working Capital 39	1.2	•	1.1	0.3	0.9	0.3	1.2	2.2	0.8	1.3	1.5	1.4
Working Capital to Net Sales 40	0.2	•	0.1	0.2	0.2	0.5	0.2	0.1	0.2	0.1	0.1	0.1
Inventory to Working Capital 41	1.0	•	0.4	0.2	0.8	0.4	0.8	1.5	0.9	1.0	1.1	1.3
Total Receipts to Cash Flow 42	11.2	•	5.1	9.1	14.6	6.0	11.8	13.0	11.9	13.3	15.0	10.5
Cost of Goods to Cash Flow 43	8.8	•	1.8	5.5	11.4	3.9	9.1	10.0	9.5	11.0	12.6	7.7
Cash Flow to Total Debt 44	0.1	•	1.6	0.5	0.2	1.0	0.3	0.2	0.3	0.2	0.1	0.1

Selected Financial Factors (in Percentages)

Debt Ratio 45	69.2	•	39.7	32.6	51.8	16.4	48.9	61.3	52.5	58.1	73.6	79.4
Return on Total Assets 46	6.3	•	25.0	4.1	7.5	13.9	9.1	6.9	9.7	6.8	6.0	3.9
Return on Equity Before Income Taxes 47	14.4	•	39.9	2.9	12.3	16.4	15.5	12.6	17.8	10.9	14.8	10.5
Return on Equity After Income Taxes 48	12.3	•	39.9	2.5	11.0	14.8	14.3	11.1	15.5	8.3	11.5	9.2
Profit Margin (Before Income Tax) 49	4.1	•	7.4	1.3	3.2	14.3	4.4	3.6	4.8	3.1	3.8	2.6
Profit Margin (After Income Tax) 50	3.5	•	7.4	1.1	2.9	12.9	4.1	3.1	4.2	2.4	2.9	2.3

Table I

Corporations with and without Net Income

NONFERROUS METAL PRODUCTION AND PROCESSING

MONEY AMOUNTS AND SIZE OF ASSETS IN THOUSANDS OF DOLLARS

Item Description for Accounting Period 7/02 Through 6/03	Total	Zero Assets	Under 500	500 to 1,000	1,000 to 5,000	5,000 to 10,000	10,000 to 25,000	25,000 to 50,000	50,000 to 100,000	100,000 to 250,000	250,000 to 500,000	500,000 to 2,500,000	2,500,000 and over
Number of Enterprises **1**	1138	0	324	0	392	117	66	47	20	15	12	14	3
Revenues ($ in Thousands)													
Net Sales **2**	50808806	0	377321	0	2270046	1541952	1918122	2827520	1591372	2574628	3686517	15611964	18327327
Interest **3**	1068680	0	13	0	785	658	2244	4566	8642	6921	17210	180317	847276
Rents **4**	46046	0	0	0	2061	2336	948	713	203	55	808	31696	7226
Royalties **5**	239720	0	0	0	0	1787	0	3940	1122	408	16908	7159	208396
Other Portfolio Income **6**	724520	0	0	0	545	491	609	1160	6294	25407	9665	32637	647714
Other Receipts **7**	959578	0	6	0	14308	5660	11748	14684	254562	48991	99854	166483	342524
Total Receipts **8**	53847350	0	377340	0	2287745	1552884	1933671	2852583	1862195	2656410	3830962	16030256	20080463
Average Total Receipts **9**	47318	•	1165	•	5836	13273	29298	60693	93110	177094	319247	1145018	6793488
Operating Costs/Operating Income (%)													
Cost of Operations **10**	83.5	•	76.4	•	79.1	78.1	80.3	80.8	76.0	87.8	79.1	83.3	86.5
Salaries and Wages **11**	3.6	•	0.9	•	4.0	3.6	3.6	3.4	7.2	2.4	4.5	3.4	3.5
Taxes Paid **12**	1.1	•	1.7	•	1.9	1.9	1.6	1.5	1.3	0.7	1.4	0.9	0.8
Interest Paid **13**	3.9	•	0.7	•	0.9	0.9	1.0	1.1	1.9	2.9	2.8	3.1	6.7
Depreciation **14**	3.9	•	1.1	•	1.8	3.4	3.1	3.4	4.5	4.5	4.5	4.9	3.2
Amortization and Depletion **15**	0.6	•	0.6	•	0.0	0.0	0.1	0.2	1.4	0.2	0.8	1.0	0.4
Pensions and Other Deferred Comp. **16**	0.3	•	•	•	0.6	0.5	0.4	0.5	0.4	0.2	0.5	0.4	0.1
Employee Benefits **17**	1.4	•	2.0	•	1.8	2.2	1.4	1.6	2.2	1.5	2.6	1.4	0.9
Advertising **18**	0.2	•	0.5	•	0.1	0.1	0.2	0.1	0.1	0.0	0.1	0.2	0.4
Other Expenses **19**	7.7	•	5.8	•	7.9	4.2	5.7	5.6	17.9	4.9	7.9	7.2	8.3
Officers' Compensation **20**	0.6	•	4.3	•	2.2	2.6	1.6	1.3	0.9	0.7	0.6	0.3	0.1
Operating Margin **21**	•	•	6.0	•	•	2.4	1.0	0.5	•	•	•	•	•
Operating Margin Before Officers' Comp. **22**	•	•	10.3	•	1.9	5.0	2.6	1.9	•	•	•	•	•

Selected Average Balance Sheet ($ in Thousands)

Net Receivables 23	20689	68	•	526	1838	3621	7557	9344	20874	39840	137319	6530524
Inventories 24	5018	28	•	478	1347	3098	7096	11982	29617	36914	126523	639866
Net Property, Plant and Equipment 25	15519	183	•	637	2583	5157	12198	26416	61473	118317	415920	2455183
Total Assets 26	94720	403	•	1991	7681	15240	35184	70497	154899	357230	1163976	26304319
Notes and Loans Payable 27	31424	157	•	927	2519	5674	11428	15951	57834	116619	301915	9055607
All Other Liabilities 28	26207	60	•	385	1561	5829	9220	21075	71992	86683	527960	6232251
Net Worth 29	37089	186	•	679	3601	3736	14536	33471	25073	153929	334102	11016460

Selected Financial Ratios (Times to 1)

Current Ratio 30	1.0	6.4	•	1.5	1.5	1.2	1.6	1.6	1.4	1.6	1.3	0.9
Quick Ratio 31	0.7	5.3	•	0.9	0.9	0.7	0.9	0.8	0.6	0.6	0.6	0.8
Net Sales to Working Capital 32	•	8.2	•	13.6	12.1	21.1	8.3	7.3	10.7	7.0	12.4	•
Coverage Ratio 33	1.0	9.9	•	1.5	4.4	2.8	2.3	2.7	0.3	0.6	•	1.3
Total Asset Turnover 34	0.5	2.9	•	2.9	1.7	1.9	1.7	1.1	1.1	0.9	1.0	0.2
Inventory Turnover 35	7.4	31.3	•	9.6	7.6	7.5	6.8	5.0	5.1	6.6	7.3	8.3
Receivables Turnover 36	2.5	20.6	•	8.8	7.3	7.7	8.8	7.1	7.0	9.5	6.8	1.1
Total Liabilities to Net Worth 37	1.6	1.2	•	1.9	1.1	3.1	1.4	1.1	5.2	1.3	2.5	1.4
Current Assets to Working Capital 38	•	1.2	•	3.0	3.0	6.1	2.7	2.8	3.5	2.6	4.3	•
Current Liabilities to Working Capital 39	•	0.2	•	2.0	2.0	5.1	1.7	1.8	2.5	1.6	3.3	•
Working Capital to Net Sales 40	•	0.1	•	0.1	0.1	0.0	0.1	0.1	0.1	0.1	0.1	•
Inventory to Working Capital 41	0.2	0.2	•	1.0	1.0	2.2	1.1	0.9	1.6	1.1	1.4	•
Total Receipts to Cash Flow 42	18.7	11.0	•	15.8	16.5	15.6	17.5	5.5	66.2	18.8	43.0	13.9
Cost of Goods to Cash Flow 43	15.6	8.4	•	12.5	12.9	12.5	14.1	4.2	58.1	14.9	35.8	12.0
Cash Flow to Total Debt 44	0.0	0.5	•	0.3	0.2	0.2	0.2	0.4	0.0	0.1	0.0	0.0

Selected Financial Factors (in Percentages)

Debt Ratio 45	60.8	53.7	•	65.9	53.1	75.5	58.7	52.5	83.8	56.9	71.3	58.1
Return on Total Assets 46	1.8	19.4	•	3.7	6.9	5.3	4.3	5.8	0.8	1.5	•	2.0
Return on Equity Before Income Taxes 47	•	37.7	•	3.5	11.3	13.8	5.8	7.8	•	•	•	1.1
Return on Equity After Income Taxes 48	•	37.7	•	1.5	11.1	12.6	3.3	4.4	•	•	•	0.5
Profit Margin (Before Income Tax) 49	6.0	6.0	•	0.4	3.1	1.8	1.4	3.3	•	•	•	1.9
Profit Margin (After Income Tax) 50	6.0	•	•	0.2	3.0	1.6	0.8	1.9	•	•	•	0.8

Table II

Corporations with Net Income

NONFERROUS METAL PRODUCTION AND PROCESSING

MONEY AMOUNTS AND SIZE OF ASSETS IN THOUSANDS OF DOLLARS

Item Description for Accounting Period 7/02 Through 6/03	Total	Zero Assets	Under 500	500 to 1,000	1,000 to 5,000	5,000 to 10,000	10,000 to 25,000	25,000 to 50,000	50,000 to 100,000	100,000 to 250,000	250,000 to 500,000	500,000 to 2,500,000	2,500,000 and over
Number of Enterprises **1**	651	0	320	•	0	54	42	28	12	7	7	7	0
Revenues ($ in Thousands)													
Net Sales **2**	35522586	0	374550	•	0	945222	1374520	1875692	1082827	1718126	2469351	24442080	0
Interest **3**	929251	0	0	•	0	153	1913	3098	1016	5811	7776	908653	0
Rents **4**	16363	0	0	•	0	2336	888	708	185	31	768	9470	0
Royalties **5**	156273	0	0	•	0	0	0	3703	0	408	16898	135264	0
Other Portfolio Income **6**	664501	0	0	•	0	52	324	663	4954	20766	8610	628696	0
Other Receipts **7**	778444	0	0	•	0	4232	4570	8650	251688	29920	57903	419846	0
Total Receipts **8**	38067418	0	374550	•	0	951995	1382215	1892514	1340670	1775062	2561306	26544009	0
Average Total Receipts **9**	58475	•	1170	•	•	17630	32910	67590	111722	253580	365901	3792001	•
Operating Costs/Operating Income (%)													
Cost of Operations **10**	83.6	•	76.5	•	•	77.9	79.3	80.5	78.2	84.7	75.5	85.9	•
Salaries and Wages **11**	3.5	•	0.8	•	•	2.2	3.4	3.2	7.3	1.7	4.6	3.4	•
Taxes Paid **12**	0.9	•	1.7	•	•	1.7	1.5	1.4	1.2	0.4	1.5	0.6	•
Interest Paid **13**	3.6	•	0.7	•	•	0.7	1.0	0.8	0.5	2.5	2.2	4.6	•
Depreciation **14**	3.2	•	0.9	•	•	3.6	2.8	2.7	4.1	3.0	3.0	3.3	•
Amortization and Depletion **15**	0.3	•	0.6	•	•	0.0	0.1	0.1	1.9	0.1	0.8	0.3	•
Pensions and Other Deferred Comp. **16**	0.3	•	•	•	•	0.6	0.4	0.5	0.3	0.1	0.6	0.2	•
Employee Benefits **17**	0.9	•	2.0	•	•	2.0	0.9	1.3	2.6	0.5	2.4	0.6	•
Advertising **18**	0.3	•	0.5	•	•	0.0	0.1	0.1	0.1	0.0	0.2	0.4	•
Other Expenses **19**	6.8	•	4.3	•	•	3.5	4.9	5.3	19.8	4.6	9.4	6.6	•
Officers' Compensation **20**	0.5	•	4.3	•	•	2.0	1.5	1.3	0.8	0.6	0.7	0.1	•
Operating Margin **21**	•	•	7.7	•	•	5.7	3.9	2.8	•	1.7	•	•	•
Operating Margin Before Officers' Comp. **22**	•	•	11.9	•	•	7.8	5.4	4.1	2.3	•	•	•	•

Selected Average Balance Sheet ($ in Thousands)

Net Receivables 23	32715	68	2290	3910	8468	9401	30322	36513	2862072
Inventories 24	5436	22	1510	3098	6581	12428	40114	38903	217425
Net Property, Plant and Equipment 25	15837	185	2884	4853	11218	27012	58775	81448	1168763
Total Assets 26	129679	403	8499	15620	36454	72167	158562	336926	11061500
Notes and Loans Payable 27	41610	159	2740	5465	9771	10423	55101	98048	3583049
All Other Liabilities 28	28228	26	1940	3612	9071	22497	73554	71743	2354537
Net Worth 29	59842	218	3818	6543	17611	39247	29907	167135	5123914

Selected Financial Ratios (Times to 1)

Current Ratio 30	1.0	6.3	1.5	1.6	1.7	1.4	1.5	1.7	1.0
Quick Ratio 31	0.9	5.2	0.9	0.9	0.9	0.7	0.8	0.6	0.9
Net Sales to Working Capital 32	31.1	8.3	12.0	9.4	7.8	9.4	10.7	7.8	•
Coverage Ratio 33	2.1	12.2	10.4	5.3	5.3	16.8	3.3	2.3	1.8
Total Asset Turnover 34	0.4	2.9	2.1	2.1	1.8	1.3	1.5	1.0	0.3
Inventory Turnover 35	8.4	40.7	9.0	8.4	8.2	5.7	5.2	6.8	13.8
Receivables Turnover 36	2.0	34.2	8.8	8.5	10.9	7.4	5.6	19.3	2.2
Total Liabilities to Net Worth 37	1.2	0.9	1.2	1.4	1.1	0.8	4.3	1.0	1.2
Current Assets to Working Capital 38	23.2	1.2	3.0	2.7	2.5	3.4	3.2	2.5	•
Current Liabilities to Working Capital 39	22.2	0.2	2.0	1.7	1.5	2.4	2.2	1.5	•
Working Capital to Net Sales 40	0.0	0.1	0.1	0.1	0.1	0.1	0.1	0.1	•
Inventory to Working Capital 41	2.8	0.2	1.0	1.0	1.0	1.2	1.3	0.9	•
Total Receipts to Cash Flow 42	11.2	9.4	11.7	12.1	13.2	4.3	11.0	9.4	12.1
Cost of Goods to Cash Flow 43	9.4	7.2	9.1	9.6	10.6	3.3	9.3	7.1	10.4
Cash Flow to Total Debt 44	0.1	0.7	0.3	0.3	0.3	0.6	0.2	0.2	0.0

Selected Financial Factors (in Percentages)

Debt Ratio 45	53.9	46.0	55.1	58.1	51.7	45.6	81.1	50.4	53.7
Return on Total Assets 46	3.2	24.3	14.7	11.4	8.2	9.5	12.9	5.3	2.6
Return on Equity Before Income Taxes 47	3.7	41.2	29.6	22.2	13.9	16.5	47.4	5.9	2.6
Return on Equity After Income Taxes 48	2.7	41.2	29.2	21.2	10.4	11.7	33.5	4.8	1.7
Profit Margin (Before Income Tax) 49	4.1	7.7	6.5	4.4	3.6	7.2	5.8	2.8	3.7
Profit Margin (After Income Tax) 50	2.9	7.7	6.4	4.2	2.7	5.1	4.1	2.3	2.5

Table I

Corporations with and without Net Income

FOUNDRIES

MONEY AMOUNTS AND SIZE OF ASSETS IN THOUSANDS OF DOLLARS

Item Description for Accounting Period 7/02 Through 6/03	Total	Zero Assets	Under 500	500 to 1,000	1,000 to 5,000	5,000 to 10,000	10,000 to 25,000	25,000 to 50,000	50,000 to 100,000	100,000 to 250,000	250,000 to 500,000	500,000 to 2,500,000	2,500,000 and over
Number of Enterprises 1	1521	0	1050	0	247	87	67	18	11	3	5	7	•
Revenues ($ in Thousands)													
Net Sales 2	15356637	0	552499	0	996057	1082392	1519673	803654	986536	1089557	2345897	5923310	•
Interest 3	119150	0	15	0	1115	1320	970	506	2391	10494	8085	94232	•
Rents 4	3786	0	2	0	714	1659	157	229	19	85	636	285	•
Royalties 5	19068	0	0	0	403	0	0	3	0	0	6343	12177	•
Other Portfolio Income 6	32147	0	20	0	7347	139	5083	372	3160	1339	1923	12764	•
Other Receipts 7	121297	0	271	0	3015	2026	11879	3625	2802	11157	26697	59391	•
Total Receipts 8	15652085	0	552807	0	1008651	1087536	1537762	808389	994908	1112632	2389581	6102159	•
Average Total Receipts 9	10291	•	526	•	4084	12500	22952	44910	90446	370877	477916	871737	•
Operating Costs/Operating Income (%)													
Cost of Operations 10	74.7	•	56.2	•	79.3	72.2	76.8	75.3	74.5	79.9	77.5	73.5	•
Salaries and Wages 11	5.2	•	16.1	•	6.3	5.9	5.0	5.9	5.5	2.4	6.4	3.7	•
Taxes Paid 12	2.3	•	3.4	•	3.8	2.9	2.8	2.1	2.4	1.2	2.6	1.9	•
Interest Paid 13	3.1	•	0.8	•	1.4	0.8	1.2	1.3	1.4	2.2	2.6	5.4	•
Depreciation 14	4.9	•	4.6	•	3.6	4.2	4.3	6.2	5.9	4.4	5.4	5.0	•
Amortization and Depletion 15	0.3	•	1.1	•	0.0	0.0	0.3	0.1	0.3	0.5	0.2	0.3	•
Pensions and Other Deferred Comp. 16	0.8	•	0.5	•	0.6	0.5	0.5	0.5	0.7	0.6	0.6	1.3	•
Employee Benefits 17	2.9	•	4.5	•	3.6	2.3	2.3	2.9	0.9	1.3	1.5	4.0	•
Advertising 18	0.1	•	0.3	•	0.1	0.2	0.1	0.1	0.2	0.0	0.2	0.1	•
Other Expenses 19	5.9	•	10.6	•	2.7	7.2	6.5	5.7	5.8	7.6	5.6	5.5	•
Officers' Compensation 20	1.4	•	10.1	•	2.9	1.7	2.5	1.6	0.8	0.2	0.4	0.7	•
Operating Margin 21	•	•	•	•	•	1.9	•	•	1.7	•	•	•	•
Operating Margin Before Officers' Comp. 22	•	•	1.8	•	•	3.6	0.2	•	2.4	0.0	•	•	•

Selected Average Balance Sheet ($ in Thousands)

Net Receivables 23	1360	•	728	34	•	1956	3378	5778	15135	23407	66083	111283
Inventories 24	1162	•	427	28	•	1203	2361	3968	7903	18365	42040	134725
Net Property, Plant and Equipment 25	2777	•	848	55	•	2357	5572	15740	25238	106737	128818	263706
Total Assets 26	8875	•	2473	202	•	7114	14814	33235	68353	184434	358066	1049816
Notes and Loans Payable 27	3224	•	1451	179	•	1388	4893	9572	23056	80211	96799	393980
All Other Liabilities 28	1768	•	515	38	•	1614	3456	7373	12105	66959	74647	186724
Net Worth 29	3884	•	508	-15	•	4112	6465	16290	33193	37263	186619	469112

Selected Financial Ratios (Times to 1)

Current Ratio 30	1.6	•	2.6	2.4	•	2.2	1.5	1.8	2.0	0.5	2.6	1.5
Quick Ratio 31	0.9	•	1.5	1.4	•	1.5	0.9	1.0	1.4	0.2	1.6	0.6
Net Sales to Working Capital 32	8.0	•	9.1	4.7	•	5.3	9.3	7.6	5.1	•	5.0	8.9
Coverage Ratio 33	1.1	•	•	•	•	3.9	0.1	0.2	2.6	1.9	0.6	1.3
Total Asset Turnover 34	1.1	•	2.6	1.6	•	1.7	1.5	1.3	1.3	2.0	1.3	0.8
Inventory Turnover 35	6.5	•	10.7	7.5	•	7.5	7.4	8.5	8.5	15.8	8.6	4.6
Receivables Turnover 36	6.9	•	16.5	5.4	•	6.0	6.6	7.7	6.0	11.4	6.0	7.2
Total Liabilities to Net Worth 37	1.3	•	•	3.9	•	0.7	1.3	1.0	1.1	3.9	0.9	1.2
Current Assets to Working Capital 38	2.6	•	1.6	1.7	•	1.8	3.1	2.3	2.0	•	1.6	3.0
Current Liabilities to Working Capital 39	1.6	•	0.6	0.7	•	0.8	2.1	1.3	1.0	•	0.6	2.0
Working Capital to Net Sales 40	0.1	•	0.1	0.2	•	0.2	0.1	0.1	0.2	•	0.2	0.1
Inventory to Working Capital 41	0.9	•	0.6	0.4	•	0.5	1.0	0.7	0.5	•	0.5	1.3
Total Receipts to Cash Flow 42	24.5	•	•	•	•	13.1	27.4	33.2	15.0	•	11.7	16.8
Cost of Goods to Cash Flow 43	18.3	•	9.4	•	•	9.4	21.0	25.0	11.2	•	9.4	12.4
Cash Flow to Total Debt 44	0.1	•	•	•	•	0.3	0.1	0.1	0.2	•	0.2	0.1

Selected Financial Factors (in Percentages)

Debt Ratio 45	56.2	•	107.2	79.5	•	42.2	56.4	51.0	51.4	79.8	47.9	55.3
Return on Total Assets 46	3.9	•	•	•	•	5.5	0.1	0.3	4.8	8.3	2.0	5.9
Return on Equity Before Income Taxes 47	0.8	•	295.6	•	•	7.1	•	•	6.2	19.6	•	3.4
Return on Equity After Income Taxes 48	•	•	295.6	•	•	4.7	•	•	4.2	14.6	•	1.5
Profit Margin (Before Income Tax) 49	0.3	•	•	•	•	2.3	•	•	2.3	2.0	•	1.9
Profit Margin (After Income Tax) 50	•	•	•	•	•	1.5	•	•	1.5	1.5	•	0.8

Table II

Corporations with Net Income

FOUNDRIES

MONEY AMOUNTS AND SIZE OF ASSETS IN THOUSANDS OF DOLLARS

Item Description for Accounting Period 7/02 Through 6/03	Total	Zero Assets	Under 500	500 to 1,000	1,000 to 5,000	5,000 to 10,000	10,000 to 25,000	25,000 to 50,000	50,000 to 100,000	100,000 to 250,000	250,000 to 500,000	500,000 to 2,500,000	2,500,000 and over
Number of Enterprises 1	421	•	224	•	0	72	25	9	6	3	0	4	•
Revenues ($ in Thousands)													
Net Sales 2	10393698	•	215801	•	0	951652	626319	458927	603600	1089557	0	4881675	•
Interest 3	86386	•	0	•	0	1097	152	36	435	10494	0	70126	•
Rents 4	2943	•	0	•	0	1659	0	0	12	85	0	284	•
Royalties 5	18898	•	0	•	0	0	0	0	0	0	0	12177	•
Other Portfolio Income 6	20971	•	0	•	0	119	1761	309	3138	1339	0	12764	•
Other Receipts 7	63062	•	0	•	0	1204	2581	2037	1365	11157	0	29014	•
Total Receipts 8	10585958	•	215801	•	0	955731	630813	461309	608550	1112632	0	5006040	•
Average Total Receipts 9	25145	•	963	•	•	13274	25233	51257	101425	370877	•	1251510	•
Operating Costs/Operating Income (%)													
Cost of Operations 10	73.6	•	66.2	•	•	69.8	72.0	74.1	74.5	79.9	•	72.1	•
Salaries and Wages 11	4.7	•	•	•	•	6.4	4.6	5.3	4.3	2.4	•	3.9	•
Taxes Paid 12	2.0	•	4.0	•	•	3.1	2.3	2.0	2.5	1.2	•	1.8	•
Interest Paid 13	2.6	•	1.6	•	•	0.7	0.8	1.1	0.9	2.2	•	4.3	•
Depreciation 14	4.7	•	4.6	•	•	4.2	4.0	5.4	3.4	4.4	•	4.9	•
Amortization and Depletion 15	0.3	•	•	•	•	0.0	0.1	0.1	0.1	0.5	•	0.4	•
Pensions and Other Deferred Comp. 16	1.0	•	•	•	•	0.5	0.5	0.2	1.1	0.6	•	1.5	•
Employee Benefits 17	2.9	•	1.2	•	•	2.6	2.2	2.8	0.7	1.3	•	4.4	•
Advertising 18	0.2	•	0.1	•	•	0.2	0.1	0.0	0.1	0.0	•	0.2	•
Other Expenses 19	4.6	•	8.7	•	•	7.3	5.3	3.8	4.2	7.6	•	4.4	•
Officers' Compensation 20	1.2	•	11.5	•	•	1.8	2.4	1.6	1.0	0.2	•	0.8	•
Operating Margin 21	2.2	•	2.1	•	•	3.5	5.6	3.4	7.4	•	•	1.3	•
Operating Margin Before Officers' Comp. 22	3.5	•	13.6	•	•	5.3	8.1	5.0	8.4	0.0	•	2.1	•

Selected Average Balance Sheet ($ in Thousands)

Net Receivables 23	3077	122		2063	3780	6774	13346	23407	145622
Inventories 24	2983	63		1316	2935	3393	7394	21946	198864
Net Property, Plant and Equipment 25	6360	61		2326	5186	16341	19794	106737	346474
Total Assets 26	19431	281		7326	15035	32216	68460	184434	1201694
Notes and Loans Payable 27	5822	224		1182	3711	10574	13602	80211	424423
All Other Liabilities 28	4672	46		1573	2759	6692	12020	66959	299966
Net Worth 29	8937	11		4572	8564	14950	42837	37263	477305

Selected Financial Ratios (Times to 1)

Current Ratio 30	1.6	4.8		2.4	2.0	1.8	2.4	0.5	1.4
Quick Ratio 31	0.8	3.5		1.6	1.2	1.2	1.7	0.2	0.6
Net Sales to Working Capital 32	8.8	6.0		4.9	5.9	9.7	4.6		10.9
Coverage Ratio 33	2.6	2.3		7.0	9.3	4.5	9.9	1.9	1.9
Total Asset Turnover 34	1.3	3.4		1.8	1.7	1.6	1.5	2.0	1.0
Inventory Turnover 35	6.1	10.1		7.0	6.1	11.1	10.1	13.2	4.4
Receivables Turnover 36	7.9	8.7		12.8	6.0	7.6	7.7		8.1
Total Liabilities to Net Worth 37	1.2	24.6		0.6	0.8	1.2	0.6	3.9	1.5
Current Assets to Working Capital 38	2.7	1.3		1.7	2.0	2.3	1.7		3.3
Current Liabilities to Working Capital 39	1.7	0.3		0.7	1.0	1.3	0.7		2.3
Working Capital to Net Sales 40	0.1	0.2		0.2	0.2	0.1	0.2		0.1
Inventory to Working Capital 41	1.1	0.3		0.5	0.7	0.7	0.4		1.7
Total Receipts to Cash Flow 42	13.6	17.3		10.8	9.8	16.0	9.5	11.7	13.3
Cost of Goods to Cash Flow 43	10.0	11.5		7.5	7.0	11.8	7.1	9.4	9.6
Cash Flow to Total Debt 44	0.2	0.2		0.4	0.4	0.2	0.4	0.2	0.1

Selected Financial Factors (in Percentages)

Debt Ratio 45	54.0	96.1		37.6	43.0	53.6	37.4	79.8	60.3
Return on Total Assets 46	8.6	13.0		8.3	11.8	7.9	12.8	8.3	8.4
Return on Equity Before Income Taxes 47	11.4	187.0		11.4	18.4	13.3	18.5	19.6	10.3
Return on Equity After Income Taxes 48	8.5	187.0		8.7	17.6	12.2	15.6	14.6	6.9
Profit Margin (Before Income Tax) 49	4.1	2.1		3.9	6.3	3.9	7.9	2.0	4.0
Profit Margin (After Income Tax) 50	3.1	2.1		3.0	6.0	3.6	6.6	1.5	2.7

Table I

Corporations with and without Net Income

FORGING AND STAMPING

MONEY AMOUNTS AND SIZE OF ASSETS IN THOUSANDS OF DOLLARS

Item Description for Accounting Period 7/02 Through 6/03	Total	Zero Assets	Under 500	500 to 1,000	1,000 to 5,000	5,000 to 10,000	10,000 to 25,000	25,000 to 50,000	50,000 to 100,000	100,000 to 250,000	250,000 to 500,000	500,000 to 2,500,000	2,500,000 and over
Number of Enterprises **1**	3518	6	1678	671	704	238	130	51	27	13	•	0	•
Revenues ($ in Thousands)													
Net Sales **2**	18313455	189046	715391	1255923	2555529	3204580	3030766	2564535	2358738	2433947	•	0	•
Interest **3**	53244	370	411	314	2358	846	1461	1792	4667	41025	•	0	•
Rents **4**	6888	0	0	0	971	128	1044	1656	2481	608	•	0	•
Royalties **5**	488	0	0	0	1	0	143	7	0	337	•	0	•
Other Portfolio Income **6**	124394	6542	0	0	3158	1658	2450	5318	4921	100347	•	0	•
Other Receipts **7**	124950	-2188	270	7504	23169	19472	14914	11132	10905	39771	•	0	•
Total Receipts **8**	18623419	193770	716072	1263741	2585186	3226684	3050778	2584440	2381712	2621035	•	0	•
Average Total Receipts **9**	5294	32295	427	1883	3672	13557	23468	50675	88212	201618	•	•	•
Operating Costs/Operating Income (%)													
Cost of Operations **10**	70.7	72.7	59.5	65.5	61.7	75.0	74.6	72.5	75.1	69.7	•	•	•
Salaries and Wages **11**	5.3	4.4	3.9	5.3	7.5	4.5	5.1	4.5	4.5	6.6	•	•	•
Taxes Paid **12**	2.3	2.6	2.3	2.8	2.8	2.4	2.3	2.2	2.0	1.8	•	•	•
Interest Paid **13**	1.8	2.5	0.9	1.5	1.1	0.9	1.2	1.3	1.9	5.4	•	•	•
Depreciation **14**	4.3	4.1	4.6	2.9	3.8	3.3	4.4	4.6	4.4	6.0	•	•	•
Amortization and Depletion **15**	0.3	0.2	0.0	0.0	0.1	0.1	0.1	0.3	0.4	1.3	•	•	•
Pensions and Other Deferred Comp. **16**	0.8	0.1	•	0.4	0.6	1.5	0.5	0.7	0.4	1.1	•	•	•
Employee Benefits **17**	2.0	3.8	0.8	1.4	2.0	1.3	2.4	1.9	2.6	2.3	•	•	•
Advertising **18**	0.3	0.1	0.2	0.4	0.7	0.4	0.1	0.1	0.2	0.1	•	•	•
Other Expenses **19**	8.5	38.2	15.0	13.2	11.9	6.3	5.9	6.2	6.3	9.2	•	•	•
Officers' Compensation **20**	2.8	0.7	6.0	7.8	5.7	2.4	2.1	1.6	1.2	0.8	•	•	•
Operating Margin **21**	0.8	•	6.9	•	2.1	1.9	1.2	3.9	1.0	•	•	•	•
Operating Margin Before Officers' Comp. **22**	3.7	•	12.9	6.6	7.8	4.4	3.3	5.6	2.2	•	•	•	•

Selected Average Balance Sheet ($ in Thousands)

Net Receivables 23	732	0	43	205	472	1922	3587	7548	13764	27148
Inventories 24	584	0	10	190	432	1270	2891	4982	11105	22427
Net Property, Plant and Equipment 25	1162	0	46	181	621	2357	5658	13326	23143	65517
Total Assets 26	3325	0	153	792	2108	6370	15116	35297	70127	173156
Notes and Loans Payable 27	1216	0	61	569	499	2035	5215	9763	29108	76771
All Other Liabilities 28	808	0	48	209	454	1570	3266	7647	23225	37455
Net Worth 29	1301	0	44	14	1156	2765	6634	17887	17794	58929

Selected Financial Ratios (Times to 1)

Current Ratio 30	1.7	·	1.8	2.4	1.9	1.8	1.8	1.8	1.4	1.3
Quick Ratio 31	1.0	·	1.5	1.5	1.1	1.0	1.1	1.2	0.8	0.7
Net Sales to Working Capital 32	7.6	·	10.1	5.4	6.8	8.3	6.1	6.4	8.5	14.4
Coverage Ratio 33	2.4	·	9.1	0.6	3.9	3.9	2.5	4.6	2.0	1.6
Total Asset Turnover 34	1.6	·	2.8	2.4	1.7	2.1	1.5	1.4	1.2	1.1
Inventory Turnover 35	6.3	·	26.6	6.4	5.2	7.9	6.0	7.3	5.9	5.8
Receivables Turnover 36	6.9	·	13.4	10.5	6.4	6.8	6.7	6.7	7.0	7.9
Total Liabilities to Net Worth 37	1.6	·	2.5	55.1	0.8	1.3	1.3	1.0	2.9	1.9
Current Assets to Working Capital 38	2.5	·	2.2	1.7	2.2	2.3	2.2	2.2	3.7	4.7
Current Liabilities to Working Capital 39	1.5	·	1.2	0.7	1.2	1.3	1.2	1.2	2.7	3.7
Working Capital to Net Sales 40	0.1	·	0.1	0.2	0.1	0.1	0.2	0.2	0.1	0.1
Inventory to Working Capital 41	0.8	·	0.3	0.6	0.8	0.9	0.8	0.6	1.1	1.8
Total Receipts to Cash Flow 42	12.7	·	6.3	17.1	8.8	15.9	16.4	11.0	16.9	10.0
Cost of Goods to Cash Flow 43	9.0	·	3.7	11.2	5.4	11.9	12.2	8.0	12.7	7.0
Cash Flow to Total Debt 44	0.2	·	0.6	0.1	0.4	0.2	0.2	0.3	0.1	0.2

Selected Financial Factors (in Percentages)

Debt Ratio 45	60.9	·	71.3	98.2	45.2	56.6	56.1	49.3	74.6	66.0
Return on Total Assets 46	6.8	·	22.0	2.0	7.5	7.5	4.8	8.5	4.8	9.2
Return on Equity Before Income Taxes 47	10.0	·	68.1	·	10.2	12.8	6.6	13.1	9.5	9.9
Return on Equity After Income Taxes 48	8.5	·	61.0	·	9.3	11.4	5.7	11.4	7.5	8.3
Profit Margin (Before Income Tax) 49	2.5	·	7.0	·	3.3	2.6	1.9	4.7	1.9	3.1
Profit Margin (After Income Tax) 50	2.1	·	6.3	·	3.0	2.3	1.6	4.0	1.5	2.6

111

Table II
Corporations with Net Income

FORGING AND STAMPING

MONEY AMOUNTS AND SIZE OF ASSETS IN THOUSANDS OF DOLLARS

Item Description for Accounting Period 7/02 Through 6/03	Total	Zero Assets	Under 500	500 to 1,000	1,000 to 5,000	5,000 to 10,000	10,000 to 25,000	25,000 to 50,000	50,000 to 100,000	100,000 to 250,000	250,000 to 500,000	500,000 to 2,500,000	2,500,000 and over
Number of Enterprises **1**	2868	0	1560	489	531	143	77	38	17	0	0	0	•
Revenues ($ in Thousands)													
Net Sales **2**	13380513	0	659625	1055963	2030659	2034946	1995159	1974766	1557319	0	0	0	•
Interest **3**	48650	0	327	262	2310	544	775	1282	3762	0	0	0	•
Rents **4**	4752	0	0	0	971	120	296	902	2172	0	0	0	•
Royalties **5**	480	0	0	0	0	0	143	0	0	0	0	0	•
Other Portfolio Income **6**	118284	0	0	0	3140	1516	1015	2537	3334	0	0	0	•
Other Receipts **7**	91569	0	73	2476	10961	13767	10395	9212	5670	0	0	0	•
Total Receipts **8**	13644248	0	660025	1058701	2048041	2050893	2007783	1988699	1572257	0	0	0	•
Average Total Receipts **9**	4757	•	423	2165	3857	14342	26075	52334	92486	•	•	•	•
Operating Costs/Operating Income (%)													
Cost of Operations **10**	68.7	•	59.6	64.8	60.7	73.1	74.0	69.7	72.6	•	•	•	•
Salaries and Wages **11**	5.3	•	3.9	4.9	7.2	3.7	4.8	4.8	4.7	•	•	•	•
Taxes Paid **12**	2.2	•	2.1	2.6	2.6	2.1	2.2	2.2	1.8	•	•	•	•
Interest Paid **13**	1.7	•	0.9	0.6	0.9	0.8	0.9	1.1	1.5	•	•	•	•
Depreciation **14**	4.0	•	4.7	2.4	3.4	3.0	3.9	4.4	4.0	•	•	•	•
Amortization and Depletion **15**	0.3	•	0.0	0.0	0.1	0.1	0.0	0.3	0.2	•	•	•	•
Pensions and Other Deferred Comp. **16**	0.8	•	•	0.5	0.6	2.3	0.5	0.7	0.3	•	•	•	•
Employee Benefits **17**	1.7	•	0.7	1.2	1.6	1.0	2.0	1.9	2.9	•	•	•	•
Advertising **18**	0.3	•	0.1	0.4	0.9	0.5	0.1	0.1	0.2	•	•	•	•
Other Expenses **19**	7.4	•	14.3	10.6	11.3	4.6	4.6	5.7	4.4	•	•	•	•
Officers' Compensation **20**	2.9	•	5.3	7.4	5.6	2.6	1.9	1.7	1.4	•	•	•	•
Operating Margin **21**	4.6	•	8.4	4.7	5.0	6.2	5.2	7.4	6.0	•	•	•	•
Operating Margin Before Officers' Comp. **22**	7.5	•	13.7	12.0	10.5	8.8	7.1	9.2	7.4	•	•	•	•

Selected Average Balance Sheet ($ in Thousands)

Net Receivables 23	633	38	233	492	2067	3658	6953	15824
Inventories 24	443	9	128	425	1376	3030	4841	11298
Net Property, Plant and Equipment 25	938	46	189	513	2355	5409	13195	23111
Total Assets 26	2820	147	842	2016	6537	15006	35308	74829
Notes and Loans Payable 27	896	44	308	422	2219	3971	8138	19887
All Other Liabilities 28	592	50	190	439	1331	2771	6465	17463
Net Worth 29	1332	52	343	1155	2987	8264	20706	37479

Selected Financial Ratios (Times to 1)

Current Ratio 30	2.0	1.6	2.7	2.2	2.1	2.1	2.4	2.2
Quick Ratio 31	1.3	1.3	1.9	1.3	1.3	1.3	1.6	1.4
Net Sales to Working Capital 32	6.4	12.6	5.4	5.7	7.2	5.6	5.0	4.2
Coverage Ratio 33	4.7	10.0	9.2	7.2	9.4	7.6	8.6	5.7
Total Asset Turnover 34	1.7	2.9	2.6	1.9	2.2	1.7	1.5	1.2
Inventory Turnover 35	7.2	27.9	10.9	5.5	7.6	6.3	7.5	5.9
Receivables Turnover 36	7.7	17.3	14.3	8.1	5.7	7.0	7.5	11.6
Total Liabilities to Net Worth 37	1.1	1.8	1.5	0.7	1.2	0.8	0.7	1.0
Current Assets to Working Capital 38	2.0	2.6	1.6	1.8	1.9	1.9	1.7	1.9
Current Liabilities to Working Capital 39	1.0	1.6	0.6	0.8	0.9	0.9	0.7	0.9
Working Capital to Net Sales 40	0.2	0.1	0.2	0.2	0.1	0.2	0.2	0.2
Inventory to Working Capital 41	0.6	0.4	0.4	0.7	0.6	0.6	0.4	0.5
Total Receipts to Cash Flow 42	8.7	5.7	9.1	7.6	9.8	11.2	8.3	9.7
Cost of Goods to Cash Flow 43	6.0	3.4	5.9	4.6	7.2	8.3	5.8	7.1
Cash Flow to Total Debt 44	0.4	0.8	0.5	0.6	0.4	0.3	0.4	0.3

Selected Financial Factors (in Percentages)

Debt Ratio 45	52.8	64.4	59.2	42.7	54.3	44.9	41.4	49.9
Return on Total Assets 46	13.6	27.0	14.2	12.8	17.0	11.5	13.4	10.2
Return on Equity Before Income Taxes 47	22.8	68.1	30.9	19.3	33.3	18.2	20.1	16.8
Return on Equity After Income Taxes 48	20.9	61.7	30.7	18.1	31.0	17.0	18.1	15.3
Profit Margin (Before Income Tax) 49	6.5	8.4	4.9	5.8	7.0	5.8	8.0	6.9
Profit Margin (After Income Tax) 50	6.0	7.6	4.9	5.5	6.5	5.4	7.2	6.2

112

Table I

Corporations with and without Net Income

CUTLERY, HARDWARE, SPRING AND WIRE MACHINE SHOPS, NUT, BOLT

MONEY AMOUNTS AND SIZE OF ASSETS IN THOUSANDS OF DOLLARS

Item Description for Accounting Period 7/02 Through 6/03	Total	Zero Assets	Under 500	500 to 1,000	1,000 to 5,000	5,000 to 10,000	10,000 to 25,000	25,000 to 50,000	50,000 to 100,000	100,000 to 250,000	250,000 to 500,000	500,000 to 2,500,000	2,500,000 and over
Number of Enterprises **1**	19441	1519	12404	2149	2692	299	242	62	27	28	10	8	0
Revenues ($ in Thousands)													
Net Sales **2**	47467263	276007	4020539	3062526	9428339	3212444	5122114	2897361	2359206	4480967	2980060	9627699	0
Interest **3**	738531	768	4249	1464	10970	3189	4235	5818	3299	8133	17885	678521	0
Rents **4**	30399	8	0	1	6157	614	2524	709	83	3232	15605	1468	0
Royalties **5**	257520	0	0	0	0	0	19	164	367	1416	6879	248675	0
Other Portfolio Income **6**	360542	6570	9060	10691	16182	3928	9195	17608	5506	19688	145846	116265	0
Other Receipts **7**	759289	59752	31747	12106	21597	7995	14669	19045	8476	134683	153527	295693	0
Total Receipts **8**	49613544	343105	4065595	3086788	9483245	3228170	5152756	2940705	2376937	4648119	3319802	10968321	0
Average Total Receipts **9**	2552	226	328	1436	3523	10797	21292	47431	88035	166004	331980	1371040	•
Operating Costs/Operating Income (%)													
Cost of Operations **10**	63.1	59.7	50.1	56.7	63.9	64.6	68.3	70.6	69.9	69.2	66.6	58.8	•
Salaries and Wages **11**	8.1	10.5	9.0	7.0	6.0	6.8	6.9	6.6	6.2	8.3	6.6	12.2	•
Taxes Paid **12**	2.5	1.7	3.6	4.0	3.1	3.1	2.5	2.0	1.8	1.7	2.5	1.7	•
Interest Paid **13**	3.4	3.1	1.6	1.7	2.0	0.8	1.4	2.1	2.0	2.3	4.6	9.0	•
Depreciation **14**	4.5	9.8	4.1	7.6	5.4	4.4	4.8	5.1	3.8	4.2	4.4	2.9	•
Amortization and Depletion **15**	0.7	0.5	0.1	0.0	0.2	0.0	0.4	0.5	0.4	1.0	1.9	1.7	•
Pensions and Other Deferred Comp. **16**	0.9	0.1	0.5	0.6	0.4	0.6	0.7	0.5	0.5	0.5	1.6	1.8	•
Employee Benefits **17**	2.3	0.2	1.9	1.9	2.1	2.4	2.2	1.8	3.3	2.3	3.1	2.7	•
Advertising **18**	0.8	0.2	0.4	0.2	0.4	0.5	0.7	0.9	1.0	0.6	1.3	1.7	•
Other Expenses **19**	13.7	40.7	19.9	11.8	10.5	9.4	8.4	8.3	8.6	10.3	13.8	22.8	•
Officers' Compensation **20**	3.7	1.6	9.7	9.2	6.3	4.4	2.8	1.4	1.3	1.0	1.7	0.2	•
Operating Margin **21**	•	•	•	•	•	2.9	1.0	0.2	1.3	1.0	•	•	•
Operating Margin Before Officers' Comp. **22**	•	•	8.9	8.5	6.1	7.3	3.8	1.6	2.5	•	•	•	•

Selected Average Balance Sheet ($ in Thousands)

Net Receivables 23	390	0	25	176	434	1284	2988	5887	13619	21065	35052	367467	·
Inventories 24	333	0	19	84	483	1415	3529	7945	14956	24614	51104	172539	·
Net Property, Plant and Equipment 25	503	0	39	296	711	2099	4877	12563	17644	39008	96561	203020	·
Total Assets 26	2265	0	116	715	2211	6655	14934	33415	67428	143750	352903	2255690	·
Notes and Loans Payable 27	678	0	72	406	983	1509	4838	13162	24102	52117	161199	325099	·
All Other Liabilities 28	638	0	14	156	365	1116	2679	7288	14922	33949	98576	893379	·
Net Worth 29	949	0	30	152	864	4030	7417	12965	28405	57684	93128	1037212	·

Selected Financial Ratios (Times to 1)

Current Ratio 30	2.0	·	2.5	1.6	2.1	2.7	2.0	1.7	1.7	1.9	1.5	2.2	·
Quick Ratio 31	1.2	·	1.9	1.1	1.2	1.5	1.0	0.8	0.9	0.9	0.7	1.5	·
Net Sales to Working Capital 32	5.1	·	7.7	9.0	5.5	4.5	5.2	6.4	5.8	5.9	6.3	3.3	·
Coverage Ratio 33	1.3	·	1.2	1.1	1.2	5.2	2.1	1.8	2.0	2.0	1.7	0.9	·
Total Asset Turnover 34	1.1	·	2.8	2.0	1.6	1.6	1.4	1.4	1.3	1.1	0.8	0.5	·
Inventory Turnover 35	4.6	·	8.6	9.6	4.6	4.9	4.1	4.2	4.1	4.5	3.9	4.1	·
Receivables Turnover 36	6.3	·	12.4	8.2	7.6	8.4	6.9	7.8	7.0	7.1	9.6	3.4	·
Total Liabilities to Net Worth 37	1.4	·	2.8	3.7	1.6	0.7	1.0	1.6	1.4	1.5	2.8	1.2	·
Current Assets to Working Capital 38	2.0	·	1.7	2.5	1.9	1.6	2.0	2.4	2.4	2.1	3.2	1.8	·
Current Liabilities to Working Capital 39	1.0	·	0.7	1.5	0.9	0.6	1.0	1.4	1.4	1.1	2.2	0.8	·
Working Capital to Net Sales 40	0.2	·	0.1	0.1	0.2	0.2	0.2	0.2	0.2	0.2	0.2	0.3	·
Inventory to Working Capital 41	0.7	·	0.4	0.7	0.7	0.6	0.9	1.1	1.0	0.9	1.2	0.4	·
Total Receipts to Cash Flow 42	8.9	4.5	8.0	14.0	14.7	9.4	12.6	12.4	11.3	9.1	8.6	5.1	·
Cost of Goods to Cash Flow 43	5.6	2.7	4.0	7.9	9.4	6.1	8.6	8.8	7.9	6.3	5.7	3.0	·
Cash Flow to Total Debt 44	0.2	·	0.5	0.2	0.2	0.4	0.2	0.2	0.2	0.2	0.1	0.2	·

Selected Financial Factors (in Percentages)

Debt Ratio 45	58.1	·	74.0	78.7	60.9	39.4	50.3	61.2	57.9	59.9	73.6	54.0	·
Return on Total Assets 46	4.7	·	5.2	3.6	3.7	6.7	4.2	5.3	5.2	5.3	6.6	4.2	·
Return on Equity Before Income Taxes 47	2.3	·	3.3	0.9	1.5	8.9	4.5	6.2	6.3	6.8	10.2	·	·
Return on Equity After Income Taxes 48	0.9	·	2.3	0.4	0.7	8.4	3.3	4.5	3.9	3.9	6.6	·	·
Profit Margin (Before Income Tax) 49	0.9	·	0.3	0.1	0.1	3.3	1.6	1.7	2.0	2.4	3.2	·	·
Profit Margin (After Income Tax) 50	0.3	·	0.2	0.0	0.0	3.2	1.2	1.2	1.3	1.4	2.0	·	·

Table II

Corporations with Net Income

CUTLERY, HARDWARE, SPRING AND WIRE MACHINE SHOPS, NUT, BOLT

MONEY AMOUNTS AND SIZE OF ASSETS IN THOUSANDS OF DOLLARS

Item Description for Accounting Period 7/02 Through 6/03	Total	Zero Assets	Under 500	500 to 1,000	1,000 to 5,000	5,000 to 10,000	10,000 to 25,000	25,000 to 50,000	50,000 to 100,000	100,000 to 250,000	250,000 to 500,000	500,000 to 2,500,000	2,500,000 and over
Number of Enterprises **1**	10843	743	7072	1101	1480	229	142	35	16	17	4	4	0
Revenues ($ in Thousands)													
Net Sales **2**	26729333	105230	2774476	1506507	5402689	2490440	3225804	1706669	1345942	2614869	945930	4610778	0
Interest **3**	102968	0	1900	1062	7435	2213	2679	4237	2396	4131	17212	59701	0
Rents **4**	20500	0	0	1	1099	120	2010	435	47	778	15469	541	0
Royalties **5**	115391	0	0	0	0	0	12	0	367	1399	6875	106738	0
Other Portfolio Income **6**	284296	6570	8464	460	7065	3274	5343	3377	5293	19568	145820	79058	0
Other Receipts **7**	639464	47652	28492	8358	11573	7190	9308	3566	5633	127623	142526	247549	0
Total Receipts **8**	27891952	159452	2813332	1516388	5429861	2503237	3245156	1718284	1359678	2768368	1273832	5104365	0
Average Total Receipts **9**	2572	215	398	1377	3669	10931	22853	49094	84980	162845	318458	1276091	•
Operating Costs/Operating Income (%)													
Cost of Operations **10**	60.5	60.7	51.6	47.8	60.7	63.8	65.8	67.9	63.7	65.1	62.3	57.6	•
Salaries and Wages **11**	8.1	15.7	7.0	8.3	6.8	5.7	6.5	6.4	6.2	10.1	10.3	12.2	•
Taxes Paid **12**	2.4	2.5	3.1	3.7	2.8	2.8	2.3	2.0	1.9	1.8	3.7	1.6	•
Interest Paid **13**	1.7	3.2	1.1	1.1	1.3	0.7	0.9	1.2	1.7	1.5	4.7	3.2	•
Depreciation **14**	4.0	2.6	2.8	8.5	4.2	4.0	4.1	4.9	3.8	4.7	2.6	2.3	•
Amortization and Depletion **15**	0.6	0.2	0.1	0.0	0.2	0.0	0.1	0.3	0.5	0.8	3.3	1.5	•
Pensions and Other Deferred Comp. **16**	0.8	•	0.4	0.8	0.4	0.6	0.7	0.5	0.6	0.6	0.6	1.9	•
Employee Benefits **17**	2.0	0.1	1.0	2.1	2.1	1.6	1.8	1.7	2.8	2.1	5.7	2.2	•
Advertising **18**	1.0	0.1	0.5	0.2	0.3	0.6	0.7	0.7	1.4	0.8	0.9	2.7	•
Other Expenses **19**	12.0	27.8	18.0	11.9	9.0	9.2	8.1	6.3	9.9	9.4	16.3	19.4	•
Officers' Compensation **20**	4.0	3.7	8.9	8.8	6.6	4.7	3.0	1.5	1.4	1.0	3.9	0.2	•
Operating Margin **21**	2.9	•	5.6	6.8	5.5	6.2	5.9	6.5	6.1	2.1	•	•	•
Operating Margin Before Officers' Comp. **22**	6.9	•	14.5	15.6	12.1	11.0	8.9	8.0	7.5	3.1	•	•	•

Selected Average Balance Sheet ($ in Thousands)

Net Receivables **23**	452	0	25	164	420	1316	3241	6024	15323	19593	26806	564855	•
Inventories **24**	354	0	22	96	523	1240	3769	7610	13781	23773	46527	228851	•
Net Property, Plant and Equipment **25**	428	0	32	267	585	1899	4395	11776	15450	38379	70991	150750	•
Total Assets **26**	2074	114	708	2256	6408	14869	31830	70665	148501	346910		1958090	•
Notes and Loans Payable **27**	597	0	60	310	734	1068	3548	9522	19695	41482	66355	562118	•
All Other Liabilities **28**	405	0	11	107	288	1076	2733	6587	11073	25901	119235	451771	•
Net Worth **29**	1073	0	43	292	1234	4264	8589	15721	39897	81117	161319	944200	•

Selected Financial Ratios (Times to 1)

Current Ratio **30**	2.5	•	2.9	2.3	2.9	3.1	2.5	2.4	2.7	2.1	2.3	2.2	•
Quick Ratio **31**	1.6	•	2.2	1.6	1.8	1.8	1.4	1.2	1.4	1.1	1.1	1.7	•
Net Sales to Working Capital **32**	4.1	•	7.7	5.7	4.3	4.3	4.3	4.7	3.5	5.2	2.6	2.7	•
Coverage Ratio **33**	5.5	11.9	7.3	7.9	5.7	10.8	7.8	7.0	5.2	6.3	5.4	3.1	•
Total Asset Turnover **34**	1.2	•	3.4	1.9	1.6	1.7	1.5	1.5	1.2	1.0	0.7	0.6	•
Inventory Turnover **35**	4.2	•	9.3	6.8	4.2	5.6	4.0	4.3	3.9	4.2	3.2	2.9	•
Receivables Turnover **36**	5.2	•	13.9	6.7	7.4	8.5	6.5	8.0	6.6	7.7	8.0	2.0	•
Total Liabilities to Net Worth **37**	0.9	•	1.7	1.4	0.8	0.5	0.7	1.0	0.8	0.8	1.2	1.1	•
Current Assets to Working Capital **38**	1.7	•	1.5	1.8	1.5	1.5	1.7	1.7	1.6	1.9	1.8	1.8	•
Current Liabilities to Working Capital **39**	0.7	•	0.5	0.8	0.5	0.5	0.7	0.7	0.6	0.9	0.8	0.8	•
Working Capital to Net Sales **40**	0.2	•	0.1	0.2	0.2	0.2	0.2	0.2	0.3	0.2	0.4	0.4	•
Inventory to Working Capital **41**	0.5	•	0.3	0.5	0.5	0.6	0.7	0.7	0.7	0.8	0.5	0.4	•
Total Receipts to Cash Flow **42**	6.2	1.8	5.6	6.9	8.5	7.2	7.9	8.3	6.6	6.2	4.1	4.2	•
Cost of Goods to Cash Flow **43**	3.8	1.1	2.9	3.3	5.1	4.6	5.2	5.6	4.2	4.0	2.6	2.4	•
Cash Flow to Total Debt **44**	0.4	•	1.0	0.5	0.4	0.7	0.5	0.4	0.4	0.4	0.3	0.3	•

Selected Financial Factors (in Percentages)

Debt Ratio **45**	48.3	•	62.7	58.8	45.3	33.5	42.2	50.6	43.5	45.4	53.5	51.8	•
Return on Total Assets **46**	10.7	•	28.1	16.4	11.7	12.5	11.3	12.9	10.5	10.1	17.1	5.8	•
Return on Equity Before Income Taxes **47**	17.0	•	65.0	34.9	17.7	17.1	17.1	22.4	15.0	15.6	29.9	8.1	•
Return on Equity After Income Taxes **48**	14.7	•	63.7	34.3	16.8	16.5	15.4	19.9	12.1	12.2	24.6	5.4	•
Profit Margin (Before Income Tax) **49**	7.4	35.0	7.0	7.4	6.0	6.7	6.5	7.2	7.1	8.2	20.4	6.6	•
Profit Margin (After Income Tax) **50**	6.4	35.0	6.9	7.3	5.7	6.5	5.8	6.4	5.7	6.4	16.8	4.4	•

Table I

Corporations with and without Net Income

ARCHITECTURAL AND STRUCTURAL METALS

Money Amounts and Size of Assets in Thousands of Dollars

Item Description for Accounting Period 7/02 Through 6/03	Total	Zero Assets	Under 500	500 to 1,000	1,000 to 5,000	5,000 to 10,000	10,000 to 25,000	25,000 to 50,000	50,000 to 100,000	100,000 to 250,000	250,000 to 500,000	500,000 to 2,500,000	2,500,000 and over
Number of Enterprises **1**	5827	10	2634	1212	1388	340	151	39	17	26	6	4	•
Revenues ($ in Thousands)													
Net Sales **2**	34320958	220758	1773116	2273158	5445497	4406309	4322682	1886469	1760443	5786648	2579465	3866413	•
Interest **3**	187874	292	2742	2019	3427	4611	4241	4041	2969	30337	3101	130093	•
Rents **4**	15579	278	0	685	43	984	1132	1081	874	4208	2385	3910	•
Royalties **5**	60901	0	0	0	0	0	0	54	230	9181	2511	48925	•
Other Portfolio Income **6**	169316	51464	2206	512	1958	29530	4858	3980	39091	5409	3322	26985	•
Other Receipts **7**	345245	-4131	528	3892	36758	23625	23936	6991	54393	69286	6204	123764	•
Total Receipts **8**	35099873	268661	1778592	2280266	5487683	4465059	4356849	1902616	1858000	5905069	2596988	4200090	•
Average Total Receipts **9**	6024	26866	675	1881	3954	13133	28853	48785	109294	227118	432831	1050022	•
Operating Costs/Operating Income (%)													
Cost of Operations **10**	69.8	59.2	68.1	71.2	69.9	72.4	72.9	70.8	74.5	71.4	64.1	62.9	•
Salaries and Wages **11**	8.0	8.1	5.4	7.6	7.8	6.7	6.6	7.0	8.7	9.0	10.8	9.5	•
Taxes Paid **12**	2.3	3.1	2.4	3.2	2.7	2.2	2.1	2.0	1.8	2.1	2.1	1.8	•
Interest Paid **13**	1.9	1.1	0.8	0.5	1.1	0.8	0.9	1.4	0.9	2.0	4.9	4.9	•
Depreciation **14**	3.1	4.3	2.4	1.7	2.2	2.5	2.6	3.3	4.0	3.4	5.8	4.2	•
Amortization and Depletion **15**	0.3	0.2	0.0	0.0	0.0	0.0	0.1	0.2	0.3	0.4	1.1	0.5	•
Pensions and Other Deferred Comp. **16**	0.6	1.6	0.1	0.4	0.6	0.7	0.5	0.5	0.6	0.7	0.7	0.7	•
Employee Benefits **17**	2.1	0.8	1.6	2.9	1.7	2.2	2.0	1.4	1.7	1.9	3.2	2.5	•
Advertising **18**	0.8	0.8	0.3	0.3	0.7	0.6	0.4	0.5	0.9	0.9	1.0	1.7	•
Other Expenses **19**	9.1	16.0	12.0	8.1	9.3	8.3	7.4	7.3	9.5	7.1	9.5	14.0	•
Officers' Compensation **20**	2.6	2.1	5.8	5.9	4.6	3.7	2.4	1.5	1.3	0.9	0.5	0.5	•
Operating Margin **21**	•	2.7	1.0	•	•	•	1.9	4.0	•	0.2	•	•	•
Operating Margin Before Officers' Comp. **22**	2.1	4.8	6.8	4.2	4.0	3.6	4.3	5.5	•	1.1	•	•	•

Selected Average Balance Sheet ($ in Thousands)

Net Receivables 23	892	0	66	252	525	1833	4920	7324	15263	39105	59422	176353
Inventories 24	569	0	21	97	413	1314	2628	5965	12593	20315	41302	126726
Net Property, Plant and Equipment 25	1026	0	57	109	568	1580	3881	9582	19402	48753	126123	263999
Total Assets 26	3711	0	217	751	2098	6421	15421	33088	73969	158476	386135	933317
Notes and Loans Payable 27	1241	0	80	133	639	2083	4583	11342	29112	50642	221974	247280
All Other Liabilities 28	1039	0	61	196	409	2058	4423	8296	17894	54046	89946	287530
Net Worth 29	1430	0	77	422	1050	2281	6415	13450	26963	53788	74216	398506

Selected Financial Ratios (Times to 1)

Current Ratio 30	1.7	•	2.1	2.7	2.4	1.7	1.6	2.3	1.4	1.3	1.1	1.6
Quick Ratio 31	1.0	•	1.7	2.1	1.5	1.1	1.0	1.3	0.8	0.8	0.6	1.0
Net Sales to Working Capital 32	7.4	•	8.7	4.9	5.2	7.3	7.6	4.4	8.3	11.6	40.7	7.1
Coverage Ratio 33	2.0	22.2	2.7	•	1.2	2.6	3.8	4.3	2.5	2.1	0.4	2.2
Total Asset Turnover 34	1.6	•	3.1	2.5	1.9	2.0	1.9	1.5	1.4	1.4	1.1	1.0
Inventory Turnover 35	7.2	•	22.3	13.8	6.6	7.1	7.9	5.7	6.1	7.8	6.7	4.8
Receivables Turnover 36	6.3	•	12.3	7.0	6.2	6.7	5.9	6.3	5.8	6.0	6.5	4.9
Total Liabilities to Net Worth 37	1.6	•	1.8	0.8	1.0	1.8	1.4	1.5	1.7	1.9	4.2	1.3
Current Assets to Working Capital 38	2.5	•	1.9	1.6	1.7	2.4	2.7	1.8	3.5	4.0	11.9	2.6
Current Liabilities to Working Capital 39	1.5	•	0.9	0.6	0.7	1.4	1.7	0.8	2.5	3.0	10.9	1.6
Working Capital to Net Sales 40	0.1	•	0.1	0.2	0.2	0.1	0.1	0.2	0.1	0.1	0.0	0.1
Inventory to Working Capital 41	0.7	•	0.3	0.3	0.5	0.8	0.7	0.6	0.9	1.1	3.7	0.8
Total Receipts to Cash Flow 42	12.3	2.9	10.2	31.4	13.8	14.3	12.6	9.9	15.7	13.7	29.7	6.4
Cost of Goods to Cash Flow 43	8.6	1.7	7.0	22.4	9.6	10.3	9.2	7.0	11.7	9.8	19.1	4.0
Cash Flow to Total Debt 44	0.2	•	0.5	0.2	0.3	0.2	0.3	0.2	0.1	0.2	0.0	0.3

Selected Financial Factors (in Percentages)

Debt Ratio 45	61.5	•	64.6	43.8	50.0	64.5	58.4	59.4	63.5	66.1	80.8	57.3
Return on Total Assets 46	5.8	•	6.5	•	2.4	4.0	6.7	9.0	3.1	6.0	2.0	11.2
Return on Equity Before Income Taxes 47	7.4	•	11.7	•	0.8	6.9	11.9	17.1	5.1	9.3	•	14.3
Return on Equity After Income Taxes 48	5.0	•	11.2	•	0.1	5.1	9.4	14.5	4.1	6.2	•	9.3
Profit Margin (Before Income Tax) 49	1.8	24.3	1.3	•	0.2	1.2	2.7	4.8	1.3	2.3	•	5.9
Profit Margin (After Income Tax) 50	1.2	22.6	1.3	•	0.0	0.9	2.1	4.0	1.1	1.5	•	3.8

Table II

Corporations with Net Income

ARCHITECTURAL AND STRUCTURAL METALS

MONEY AMOUNTS AND SIZE OF ASSETS IN THOUSANDS OF DOLLARS

Item Description for Accounting Period 7/02 Through 6/03	Total	Zero Assets	Under 500	500 to 1,000	1,000 to 5,000	5,000 to 10,000	10,000 to 25,000	25,000 to 50,000	50,000 to 100,000	100,000 to 250,000	250,000 to 500,000	500,000 to 2,500,000	2,500,000 and over
Number of Enterprises **1**	3033	0	0	710	842	254	111	24	10	17	0	4	•
Revenues ($ in Thousands)													
Net Sales **2**	23318695	0	0	1414986	3493530	3464624	3304826	1338336	1121942	4349184	0	3866413	•
Interest **3**	160818	0	0	1596	1992	3027	3830	2804	2675	13911	0	130093	•
Rents **4**	7957	0	0	284	0	874	1086	379	325	822	0	3910	•
Royalties **5**	57695	0	0	0	0	0	0	0	230	8541	0	48925	•
Other Portfolio Income **6**	134252	0	0	295	784	10340	2276	1787	36410	3782	0	26985	•
Other Receipts **7**	256148	0	0	968	32832	16489	18681	1853	15808	45350	0	123764	•
Total Receipts **8**	23935565	0	0	1418129	3529138	3495354	3330699	1345159	1177390	4421590	0	4200090	•
Average Total Receipts **9**	7892	•	•	1997	4191	13761	30006	56048	117739	260094	•	1050022	•
Operating Costs/Operating Income (%)													
Cost of Operations **10**	67.8	•	•	68.4	67.0	71.4	71.7	69.2	70.5	67.1	•	62.9	•
Salaries and Wages **11**	7.8	•	•	7.1	8.0	6.2	6.5	5.7	9.5	9.2	•	9.5	•
Taxes Paid **12**	2.2	•	•	3.2	2.5	2.1	2.1	2.0	2.0	2.4	•	1.8	•
Interest Paid **13**	1.6	•	•	0.1	0.7	0.6	0.6	1.0	0.6	2.2	•	4.9	•
Depreciation **14**	2.8	•	•	1.4	1.9	2.7	2.2	3.2	2.6	3.3	•	4.2	•
Amortization and Depletion **15**	0.3	•	•	0.0	0.0	0.0	0.1	0.2	0.5	0.7	•	0.5	•
Pensions and Other Deferred Comp. **16**	0.7	•	•	0.6	0.6	0.8	0.5	0.6	0.7	0.8	•	0.7	•
Employee Benefits **17**	1.9	•	•	2.6	1.4	1.8	2.0	1.6	2.1	1.9	•	2.5	•
Advertising **18**	0.8	•	•	0.2	0.8	0.5	0.4	0.5	1.2	1.1	•	1.7	•
Other Expenses **19**	8.7	•	•	7.9	8.9	6.3	6.9	6.9	9.8	7.4	•	14.0	•
Officers' Compensation **20**	2.5	•	•	6.0	4.4	3.8	2.4	1.6	1.3	0.6	•	0.5	•
Operating Margin **21**	2.9	•	•	2.5	3.7	3.8	4.7	7.7	•	3.4	•	•	•
Operating Margin Before Officers' Comp. **22**	5.4	•	•	8.5	8.2	7.6	7.1	9.3	0.5	4.1	•	•	•

Selected Average Balance Sheet ($ in Thousands)

Net Receivables 23	1150	274	567	1975	5081	8232	14180	37120	176353
Inventories 24	770	83	420	1434	2515	6080	15004	26038	115451
Net Property, Plant and Equipment 25	1210	99	519	1574	3468	9475	17264	51810	263999
Total Assets 26	4756	779	2071	6541	15261	33318	74672	191651	933317
Notes and Loans Payable 27	1255	8	409	1940	3384	9867	32118	58624	247280
All Other Liabilities 28	1262	159	414	1702	4250	7433	18226	52390	287530
Net Worth 29	2239	613	1248	2899	7627	16017	24328	80638	398506

Selected Financial Ratios (Times to 1)

Current Ratio 30	2.0	4.1	2.7	2.1	1.9	2.4	1.3	1.7	1.6
Quick Ratio 31	1.3	3.6	1.8	1.4	1.3	1.4	0.7	0.9	1.0
Net Sales to Working Capital 32	6.0	3.9	4.8	6.0	5.9	4.6	9.3	7.8	7.1
Coverage Ratio 33	4.4	35.4	7.7	8.4	9.8	9.5	7.6	3.3	2.2
Total Asset Turnover 34	1.6	2.6	2.0	2.1	2.0	1.7	1.5	1.3	1.0
Inventory Turnover 35	6.8	16.5	6.6	6.8	8.5	6.3	5.3	6.6	5.3
Receivables Turnover 36	6.0	6.0	6.1	6.6	6.0	5.9	5.2	6.2	11.0
Total Liabilities to Net Worth 37	1.1	0.3	0.7	1.3	1.0	1.1	2.1	1.4	1.3
Current Assets to Working Capital 38	2.0	1.3	1.6	1.9	2.1	1.7	4.0	2.5	2.6
Current Liabilities to Working Capital 39	1.0	0.3	0.6	0.9	1.1	0.7	3.0	1.5	1.6
Working Capital to Net Sales 40	0.2	0.3	0.2	0.2	0.2	0.2	0.1	0.1	0.1
Inventory to Working Capital 41	0.6	0.1	0.4	0.6	0.5	0.5	1.1	0.8	0.8
Total Receipts to Cash Flow 42	8.8	13.6	8.8	11.5	9.7	7.6	13.1	10.2	6.4
Cost of Goods to Cash Flow 43	6.0	9.3	5.9	8.2	6.9	5.2	9.2	6.8	4.0
Cash Flow to Total Debt 44	0.3	0.9	0.6	0.3	0.4	0.4	0.2	0.2	0.3

Selected Financial Factors (in Percentages)

Debt Ratio 45	52.9	21.4	39.7	55.7	50.0	51.9	67.4	57.9	57.3
Return on Total Assets 46	11.6	7.2	11.0	11.1	11.9	15.4	7.2	9.7	11.2
Return on Equity Before Income Taxes 47	19.1	8.9	15.8	22.0	21.4	28.6	19.3	16.2	14.3
Return on Equity After Income Taxes 48	16.1	8.4	15.0	20.1	18.5	25.1	17.4	12.6	9.3
Profit Margin (Before Income Tax) 49	5.6	2.8	4.8	4.7	5.5	8.2	4.2	5.1	5.9
Profit Margin (After Income Tax) 50	4.7	2.6	4.5	4.3	4.7	7.2	3.8	4.0	3.8

Table I

Corporations with and without Net Income

BOILER, TANK, AND SHIPPING CONTAINER

MONEY AMOUNTS AND SIZE OF ASSETS IN THOUSANDS OF DOLLARS

Item Description for Accounting Period 7/02 Through 6/03	Total	Zero Assets	Under 500	500 to 1,000	1,000 to 5,000	5,000 to 10,000	10,000 to 25,000	25,000 to 50,000	50,000 to 100,000	100,000 to 250,000	250,000 to 500,000	500,000 to 2,500,000	2,500,000 and over
Number of Enterprises 1	584	0	214	0	173	30	36	12	5	6	4	0	3
Revenues ($ in Thousands)													
Net Sales 2	15215371	0	133347	0	650543	407317	976954	567344	370848	818817	3134891	0	7805874
Interest 3	95641	0	43	0	893	44	968	2056	1567	8268	7193	0	74555
Rents 4	27433	0	1	0	1220	85	894	46	88	1934	290	0	21573
Royalties 5	64654	0	0	0	0	0	244	0	274	41	6209	0	57887
Other Portfolio Income 6	288721	0	6848	0	11447	395	1158	1550	242	81	3556	0	263294
Other Receipts 7	269221	0	2596	0	5098	541	2684	5607	1394	11156	9017	0	221844
Total Receipts 8	15961041	0	142835	0	669201	408382	982902	576603	374413	840297	3161156	0	8445027
Average Total Receipts 9	27331	•	667	•	3868	13613	27303	48050	74883	140050	790289	•	2815009
Operating Costs/Operating Income (%)													
Cost of Operations 10	78.6	•	59.2	•	67.9	63.5	74.4	75.4	65.7	74.9	80.0	•	81.6
Salaries and Wages 11	4.6	•	4.0	•	13.3	10.9	5.6	5.2	12.1	3.9	3.3	•	3.6
Taxes Paid 12	1.2	•	0.5	•	2.0	2.2	2.2	1.9	1.7	1.6	1.3	•	0.8
Interest Paid 13	2.5	•	1.0	•	1.2	1.7	0.9	1.4	1.5	5.7	3.2	•	2.2
Depreciation 14	3.3	•	1.2	•	2.5	2.8	2.3	3.1	4.8	4.1	3.7	•	3.2
Amortization and Depletion 15	0.4	•	0.1	•	0.0	0.7	0.1	0.2	0.2	1.0	0.3	•	0.4
Pensions and Other Deferred Comp. 16	0.6	•	1.9	•	0.7	0.2	0.6	0.3	0.5	0.2	1.0	•	0.4
Employee Benefits 17	2.3	•	0.1	•	1.9	1.7	1.7	1.8	1.6	2.0	1.1	•	3.0
Advertising 18	0.1	•	0.7	•	0.1	0.6	0.7	0.3	0.6	0.4	0.1	•	0.0
Other Expenses 19	7.0	•	35.4	•	9.8	10.0	6.7	7.5	8.4	7.4	3.4	•	7.6
Officers' Compensation 20	1.0	•	•	•	2.8	3.2	1.9	2.0	1.4	1.8	0.3	•	0.6
Operating Margin 21	•	•	•	•	•	2.5	2.8	1.0	1.6	•	2.4	•	•
Operating Margin Before Officers' Comp. 22	0.6	•	•	•	0.6	5.7	4.7	3.0	3.0	•	2.7	•	•

Selected Average Balance Sheet ($ in Thousands)

Net Receivables 23	4749	•	0	•	520	1783	5191	8340	14814	13855	70500	•	627886
Inventories 24	2388	•	0	•	517	1934	3174	5624	7240	29638	47206	•	170009
Net Property, Plant and Equipment 25	5014	•	13	•	480	2124	3783	11046	21405	27112	187633	•	493316
Total Assets 26	31020	•	166	•	1964	7799	15589	35884	60622	151852	839574	•	3961227
Notes and Loans Payable 27	9423	•	213	•	853	4866	4198	9525	16074	74523	536104	•	735196
All Other Liabilities 28	13477	•	12	•	321	1272	3669	8741	16545	52685	259729	•	2029394
Net Worth 29	8121	•	-60	•	790	1662	7721	17618	28004	24644	43740	•	1196638

Selected Financial Ratios (Times to 1)

Current Ratio 30	1.4	•	3.3	•	2.3	1.2	2.0	2.1	1.7	1.1	2.9	•	1.0
Quick Ratio 31	0.7	•	3.3	•	1.3	0.6	1.3	1.1	1.0	0.3	0.8	•	0.7
Net Sales to Working Capital 32	9.0	•	12.4	•	4.8	14.0	5.2	4.3	6.3	23.9	2.5	•	•
Coverage Ratio 33	2.4	•	4.1	•	1.5	2.6	4.7	2.7	2.7	0.9	2.0	•	3.2
Total Asset Turnover 34	0.8	•	3.8	•	1.9	1.7	1.7	1.3	1.2	0.9	0.9	•	0.7
Inventory Turnover 35	8.6	•	15787.4	•	4.9	4.5	6.4	6.3	6.7	3.5	13.3	•	12.5
Receivables Turnover 36	5.5	•	36.6	•	6.5	6.6	5.5	5.4	5.2	7.2	13.0	•	8.3
Total Liabilities to Net Worth 37	2.8	•	•	•	1.5	3.7	1.0	1.0	1.2	5.2	18.2	•	2.3
Current Assets to Working Capital 38	3.8	•	1.4	•	1.7	5.3	2.0	1.9	2.3	9.6	1.5	•	•
Current Liabilities to Working Capital 39	2.8	•	0.4	•	0.7	4.3	1.0	0.9	1.3	8.6	0.5	•	•
Working Capital to Net Sales 40	0.1	•	0.1	•	0.2	0.1	0.2	0.2	0.2	0.0	0.4	•	•
Inventory to Working Capital 41	0.8	•	0.0	•	0.6	2.5	0.5	0.5	0.7	5.7	0.2	•	•
Total Receipts to Cash Flow 42	15.3	•	3.9	•	11.4	9.4	12.0	11.5	10.5	19.9	19.1	•	15.1
Cost of Goods to Cash Flow 43	12.0	•	2.3	•	7.7	5.9	8.9	8.6	6.9	14.9	15.2	•	12.3
Cash Flow to Total Debt 44	0.1	•	0.7	•	0.3	0.2	0.3	0.2	0.2	0.1	0.1	•	0.1

Selected Financial Factors (in Percentages)

Debt Ratio 45	73.8	•	136.1	•	59.8	78.7	50.5	50.9	53.8	83.8	94.8	•	69.8
Return on Total Assets 46	4.9	•	15.4	•	3.5	7.8	7.5	5.0	4.9	4.6	6.0	•	4.7
Return on Equity Before Income Taxes 47	10.8	•	•	•	2.8	22.2	12.0	6.4	6.7	•	57.4	•	10.5
Return on Equity After Income Taxes 48	6.8	•	•	•	1.8	20.9	10.6	5.1	3.9	•	43.6	•	6.3
Profit Margin (Before Income Tax) 49	3.4	•	3.1	•	0.6	2.7	3.4	2.4	2.5	3.2	3.2	•	4.8
Profit Margin (After Income Tax) 50	2.1	•	3.1	•	0.4	2.6	3.0	1.9	1.5	2.4	2.9	•	2.9

Table II

Corporations with Net Income

BOILER, TANK, AND SHIPPING CONTAINER

MONEY AMOUNTS AND SIZE OF ASSETS IN THOUSANDS OF DOLLARS

Item Description for Accounting Period 7/02 Through 6/03	Total	Zero Assets	Under 500	500 to 1,000	1,000 to 5,000	5,000 to 10,000	10,000 to 25,000	25,000 to 50,000	50,000 to 100,000	100,000 to 250,000	250,000 to 500,000	500,000 to 2,500,000	2,500,000 and over
Number of Enterprises **1**	338	•	0	0	64	14	26	9	0	0	0	3	0
Revenues ($ in Thousands)													
Net Sales **2**	11333422	•	0	0	316219	169536	714034	477599	0	0	0	7582229	0
Interest **3**	85510	•	0	0	778	44	644	2056	0	0	0	69522	0
Rents **4**	14409	•	0	0	1220	85	693	46	0	0	0	10146	0
Royalties **5**	62872	•	0	0	0	0	238	0	0	0	0	56347	0
Other Portfolio Income **6**	287980	•	0	0	11429	73	962	1533	0	0	0	263321	0
Other Receipts **7**	209059	•	0	0	4564	472	583	2117	0	0	0	195566	0
Total Receipts **8**	11993252	•	0	0	334210	170210	717154	483351	0	0	0	8177131	0
Average Total Receipts **9**	35483	•	•	•	5222	12158	27583	53706	•	•	•	2725710	•
Operating Costs/Operating Income (%)													
Cost of Operations **10**	80.4	•	•	•	70.7	63.7	74.6	74.5	•	•	•	82.8	•
Salaries and Wages **11**	4.0	•	•	•	11.3	6.1	4.9	4.9	•	•	•	3.3	•
Taxes Paid **12**	1.1	•	•	•	1.6	1.8	2.1	1.8	•	•	•	0.8	•
Interest Paid **13**	2.5	•	•	•	0.5	2.7	0.8	1.3	•	•	•	3.0	•
Depreciation **14**	3.1	•	•	•	1.9	2.0	2.3	2.9	•	•	•	3.5	•
Amortization and Depletion **15**	0.3	•	•	•	0.0	0.7	0.0	0.2	•	•	•	0.3	•
Pensions and Other Deferred Comp. **16**	0.5	•	•	•	1.4	0.2	0.7	0.3	•	•	•	0.5	•
Employee Benefits **17**	1.9	•	•	•	3.0	0.6	1.3	1.4	•	•	•	2.2	•
Advertising **18**	0.1	•	•	•	0.0	0.6	0.8	0.3	•	•	•	0.0	•
Other Expenses **19**	5.3	•	•	•	9.3	8.5	5.6	7.5	•	•	•	4.6	•
Officers' Compensation **20**	0.8	•	•	•	1.6	2.6	2.0	2.4	•	•	•	0.4	•
Operating Margin **21**	0.1	•	•	•	•	10.6	5.0	2.3	•	•	•	2.3	•
Operating Margin Before Officers' Comp. **22**	0.9	•	•	•	0.2	13.2	6.9	4.7	•	•	•	2.7	•

Selected Average Balance Sheet ($ in Thousands)

Net Receivables 23	7133	527	1393	5169	7730	632503
Inventories 24	2450	923	1016	3385	4880	211549
Net Property, Plant and Equipment 25	6041	357	2283	3590	10504	512429
Total Assets 26	36586	2288	6070	15681	37105	3360508
Notes and Loans Payable 27	11794	250	4570	3916	8890	1127200
All Other Liabilities 28	18976	389	976	3672	8375	1862400
Net Worth 29	5816	1648	524	8093	19841	370908

Selected Financial Ratios (Times to 1)

Current Ratio 30	1.4	3.5	0.8	1.9	2.2	1.3
Quick Ratio 31	0.8	2.3	0.4	1.3	1.1	0.7
Net Sales to Working Capital 32	7.7	4.1	•	5.4	4.3	7.3
Coverage Ratio 33	3.4	10.6	5.1	7.6	3.6	3.1
Total Asset Turnover 34	0.9	2.2	2.0	1.8	1.4	0.8
Inventory Turnover 35	11.0	3.8	7.6	6.0	8.1	9.9
Receivables Turnover 36	5.1	5.7	6.9	5.6	7.9	8.0
Total Liabilities to Net Worth 37	5.3	0.4	10.6	0.9	0.9	8.1
Current Assets to Working Capital 38	3.8	1.4	•	2.1	1.8	4.0
Current Liabilities to Working Capital 39	2.8	0.4	•	1.1	0.8	3.0
Working Capital to Net Sales 40	0.1	0.2	•	0.2	0.2	0.1
Inventory to Working Capital 41	0.7	0.4	•	0.6	0.5	0.6
Total Receipts to Cash Flow 42	13.4	8.7	5.4	10.2	10.4	15.8
Cost of Goods to Cash Flow 43	10.8	6.2	3.4	7.6	7.7	13.1
Cash Flow to Total Debt 44	0.1	0.9	0.4	0.4	0.3	0.1

Selected Financial Factors (in Percentages)

Debt Ratio 45	84.1	27.9	91.4	48.4	46.5	89.0
Return on Total Assets 46	7.7	10.3	27.3	10.9	6.5	7.1
Return on Equity Before Income Taxes 47	34.3	13.0	254.2	18.3	8.8	43.4
Return on Equity After Income Taxes 48	24.6	11.7	245.2	16.5	7.2	29.4
Profit Margin (Before Income Tax) 49	5.9	4.3	11.0	5.4	3.3	6.4
Profit Margin (After Income Tax) 50	4.3	3.9	10.6	4.9	2.7	4.3

Table I

Corporations with and without Net Income

COATING, ENGRAVING, HEAT TREATING, AND ALLIED ACTIVITIES

MONEY AMOUNTS AND SIZE OF ASSETS IN THOUSANDS OF DOLLARS

Item Description for Accounting Period 7/02 Through 6/03	Total	Zero Assets	Under 500	500 to 1,000	1,000 to 5,000	5,000 to 10,000	10,000 to 25,000	25,000 to 50,000	50,000 to 100,000	100,000 to 250,000	250,000 to 500,000	500,000 to 2,500,000	2,500,000 and over
Number of Enterprises **1**	3745	0	2923	0	445	73	55	18	7	5	0	•	•
Revenues ($ in Thousands)													
Net Sales **2**	8749804	0	2273658	0	1985903	530676	1229813	622390	694802	1045616	0	•	•
Interest **3**	21666	0	946	0	1711	1243	1817	456	2209	10015	0	•	•
Rents **4**	12156	0	0	0	6541	3105	926	186	105	1293	0	•	•
Royalties **5**	1040	0	0	0	0	234	363	414	0	28	0	•	•
Other Portfolio Income **6**	85859	0	15	0	10950	4877	67271	1651	889	201	0	•	•
Other Receipts **7**	133669	0	40867	0	34489	4776	5384	8348	1467	20669	0	•	•
Total Receipts **8**	9004194	0	2315486	0	2039594	544911	1305574	633445	699472	1077822	0	•	•
Average Total Receipts **9**	2404	•	792	•	4583	7465	23738	35191	99925	215564	•	•	•
Operating Costs/Operating Income (%)													
Cost of Operations **10**	52.9	•	37.8	•	49.8	59.4	69.0	61.7	71.8	51.5	•	•	•
Salaries and Wages **11**	10.8	•	19.0	•	8.9	6.1	6.0	7.4	6.0	10.9	•	•	•
Taxes Paid **12**	3.5	•	4.4	•	4.0	3.5	2.9	2.6	2.1	2.6	•	•	•
Interest Paid **13**	1.8	•	0.2	•	1.4	1.8	2.1	1.7	1.4	5.7	•	•	•
Depreciation **14**	5.1	•	1.8	•	5.6	8.8	6.4	6.8	5.8	6.8	•	•	•
Amortization and Depletion **15**	0.4	•	0.0	•	0.0	0.1	0.1	1.0	0.4	2.2	•	•	•
Pensions and Other Deferred Comp. **16**	0.6	•	0.1	•	0.6	1.6	0.4	0.8	0.9	0.9	•	•	•
Employee Benefits **17**	2.6	•	1.3	•	2.2	4.2	3.1	2.4	2.2	3.6	•	•	•
Advertising **18**	0.2	•	0.1	•	0.3	0.3	0.3	0.2	0.1	0.5	•	•	•
Other Expenses **19**	19.3	•	26.4	•	23.5	16.5	9.0	13.5	5.9	21.0	•	•	•
Officers' Compensation **20**	5.1	•	9.9	•	4.9	4.8	2.3	2.6	1.2	1.3	•	•	•
Operating Margin **21**	•	•	•	•	•	•	•	•	2.1	•	•	•	•
Operating Margin Before Officers' Comp. **22**	2.9	•	8.9	•	3.6	•	0.8	1.9	3.3	•	•	•	•

Selected Average Balance Sheet ($ in Thousands)

Net Receivables 23	273	42	686	943	2827	5098	13396	28536
Inventories 24	119	9	704	1705	2644	8251	21328	
Net Property, Plant and Equipment 25	633	72	1157	3684	7065	12971	35591	84637
Total Assets 26	1482	181	2508	6848	15127	32023	77768	257198
Notes and Loans Payable 27	566	71	1069	2319	6320	12358	27538	98031
All Other Liabilities 28	368	54	384	1613	3384	7738	18767	91712
Net Worth 29	548	56	1056	2916	5423	11927	31463	67455

Selected Financial Ratios (Times to 1)

Current Ratio 30	1.5	1.6	1.4	1.8	1.2	1.0	1.7	1.5
Quick Ratio 31	1.0	1.1	1.2	1.0	0.8	0.6	0.9	0.9
Net Sales to Working Capital 32	12.4	20.3	13.2	6.3	20.2	•	7.6	6.9
Coverage Ratio 33	1.4	4.5	2.0	•	3.1	1.6	2.9	0.3
Total Asset Turnover 34	1.6	4.3	1.8	1.1	1.5	1.1	1.3	0.8
Inventory Turnover 35	10.4	31.7	19.7	6.1	9.0	8.1	8.6	5.1
Receivables Turnover 36	8.2	20.4	6.0	6.8	7.3	7.6	7.4	6.5
Total Liabilities to Net Worth 37	1.7	2.2	1.4	1.3	1.8	1.7	1.5	2.8
Current Assets to Working Capital 38	3.2	2.5	3.3	2.3	5.5	•	2.5	2.9
Current Liabilities to Working Capital 39	2.2	1.5	2.3	1.3	4.5	•	1.5	1.9
Working Capital to Net Sales 40	0.1	0.0	0.1	0.2	0.0	•	0.1	0.1
Inventory to Working Capital 41	0.6	0.3	0.3	0.5	1.5	•	0.7	0.6
Total Receipts to Cash Flow 42	7.3	5.2	5.5	12.0	12.7	11.2	14.9	9.6
Cost of Goods to Cash Flow 43	3.8	2.0	2.7	7.1	8.7	6.9	10.7	4.9
Cash Flow to Total Debt 44	0.3	1.2	0.6	0.2	0.2	0.2	0.1	0.1

Selected Financial Factors (in Percentages)

Debt Ratio 45	63.0	69.0	57.9	57.4	64.1	62.8	59.5	73.8
Return on Total Assets 46	3.9	4.6	5.1	•	10.0	3.0	5.3	1.3
Return on Equity Before Income Taxes 47	3.0	11.5	6.1	•	18.9	3.0	8.7	•
Return on Equity After Income Taxes 48	1.5	11.4	5.1	•	17.8	1.5	5.9	•
Profit Margin (Before Income Tax) 49	0.7	0.8	1.4	•	4.6	1.0	2.7	•
Profit Margin (After Income Tax) 50	0.4	0.8	1.2	•	4.3	0.5	1.9	•

Table II
Corporations with Net Income

COATING, ENGRAVING, HEAT TREATING, AND ALLIED ACTIVITIES

MONEY AMOUNTS AND SIZE OF ASSETS IN THOUSANDS OF DOLLARS

Item Description for Accounting Period 7/02 Through 6/03	Total	Zero Assets	Under 500	500 to 1,000	1,000 to 5,000	5,000 to 10,000	10,000 to 25,000	25,000 to 50,000	50,000 to 100,000	100,000 to 250,000	250,000 to 500,000	500,000 to 2,500,000	2,500,000 and over
Number of Enterprises 1	1938	·	0	192	281	23	34	14	0	0	0	·	·
Revenues ($ in Thousands)													
Net Sales 2	5309215	·	0	317389	1434105	195174	807339	476039	0	0	0	·	·
Interest 3	7309	·	0	10	1323	994	785	443	0	0	0	·	·
Rents 4	2787	·	0	0	2369	0	232	186	0	0	0	·	·
Royalties 5	1030	·	0	0	0	234	363	404	0	0	0	·	·
Other Portfolio Income 6	74917	·	0	0	5977	26	66655	1643	0	0	0	·	·
Other Receipts 7	87614	·	0	1822	28818	1183	3762	6935	0	0	0	·	·
Total Receipts 8	5482872	·	0	319221	1472592	197611	879136	485650	0	0	0	·	·
Average Total Receipts 9	2829	·	·	1663	5241	8592	25857	34689	·	·	·	·	·
Operating Costs/Operating Income (%)													
Cost of Operations 10	53.6	·	·	47.7	47.6	44.7	67.4	58.7	·	·	·	·	·
Salaries and Wages 11	9.6	·	·	8.1	9.0	6.7	5.4	7.6	·	·	·	·	·
Taxes Paid 12	2.9	·	·	3.7	4.1	4.2	2.9	2.5	·	·	·	·	·
Interest Paid 13	1.1	·	·	0.2	0.9	0.8	1.6	1.6	·	·	·	·	·
Depreciation 14	4.1	·	·	3.9	4.6	7.0	6.4	5.9	·	·	·	·	·
Amortization and Depletion 15	0.2	·	·	·	0.0	0.1	0.1	0.3	·	·	·	·	·
Pensions and Other Deferred Comp. 16	0.5	·	·	·	0.4	3.8	0.5	0.9	·	·	·	·	·
Employee Benefits 17	2.1	·	·	6.0	1.8	4.3	2.9	2.5	·	·	·	·	·
Advertising 18	0.2	·	·	0.1	0.3	0.4	0.2	0.3	·	·	·	·	·
Other Expenses 19	17.6	·	·	14.8	25.2	7.9	9.1	10.5	·	·	·	·	·
Officers' Compensation 20	4.5	·	·	9.6	5.2	6.9	2.5	3.1	·	·	·	·	·
Operating Margin 21	3.7	·	·	5.8	0.8	12.9	1.0	6.1	·	·	·	·	·
Operating Margin Before Officers' Comp. 22	8.3	·	·	15.5	6.0	19.9	3.5	9.2	·	·	·	·	·

Selected Average Balance Sheet ($ in Thousands)

Net Receivables 23	305	183	758	1168	2502	5282
Inventories 24	122	32	75	754	1491	1791
Net Property, Plant and Equipment 25	549	371	1013	2683	6437	12330
Total Assets 26	1459	749	2480	6556	14138	31283
Notes and Loans Payable 27	476	37	827	1645	5006	7974
All Other Liabilities 28	277	64	402	478	2520	6708
Net Worth 29	705	649	1251	4434	6613	16602

Selected Financial Ratios (Times to 1)

Current Ratio 30	2.0	5.0	1.8	5.0	1.6	1.6
Quick Ratio 31	1.3	4.3	1.5	3.0	1.1	1.1
Net Sales to Working Capital 32	8.3	6.5	9.7	2.9	10.9	8.2
Coverage Ratio 33	7.6	34.8	4.7	17.8	7.0	6.1
Total Asset Turnover 34	1.9	2.2	2.1	1.3	1.7	1.1
Inventory Turnover 35	12.0	24.4	32.6	5.0	10.7	11.1
Receivables Turnover 36	8.8	8.6	6.1	6.9	8.4	9.2
Total Liabilities to Net Worth 37	1.1	0.2	1.0	0.5	1.1	0.9
Current Assets to Working Capital 38	2.0	1.3	2.3	1.2	2.7	2.7
Current Liabilities to Working Capital 39	1.0	0.3	1.3	0.2	1.7	1.7
Working Capital to Net Sales 40	0.1	0.2	0.1	0.3	0.1	0.1
Inventory to Working Capital 41	0.3	0.1	0.1	0.1	0.6	0.6
Total Receipts to Cash Flow 42	5.1	7.1	4.4	5.0	8.6	6.1
Cost of Goods to Cash Flow 43	2.7	3.4	2.1	2.2	5.8	3.6
Cash Flow to Total Debt 44	0.7	2.3	0.9	0.8	0.4	0.4

Selected Financial Factors (in Percentages)

Debt Ratio 45	51.7	13.4	49.5	32.4	53.2	46.9
Return on Total Assets 46	15.1	14.6	9.1	19.5	19.3	10.6
Return on Equity Before Income Taxes 47	27.1	16.4	14.2	27.2	35.3	16.7
Return on Equity After Income Taxes 48	24.9	16.0	12.8	22.7	33.8	15.2
Profit Margin (Before Income Tax) 49	7.0	6.4	3.5	14.2	9.8	8.1
Profit Margin (After Income Tax) 50	6.4	6.3	3.1	11.9	9.4	7.4

Table I

Corporations with and without Net Income

OTHER FABRICATED METAL PRODUCT

MONEY AMOUNTS AND SIZE OF ASSETS IN THOUSANDS OF DOLLARS

Item Description for Accounting Period 7/02 Through 6/03	Total	Zero Assets	Under 500	500 to 1,000	1,000 to 5,000	5,000 to 10,000	10,000 to 25,000	25,000 to 50,000	50,000 to 100,000	100,000 to 250,000	250,000 to 500,000	500,000 to 2,500,000	2,500,000 and over
Number of Enterprises **1**	19741	1751	10330	2376	4032	593	372	142	63	38	21	16	7
Revenues ($ in Thousands)													
Net Sales **2**	127493701	488829	4628436	4302152	17038849	8598867	9076943	6887424	5021659	6088753	7328547	15099384	42933859
Interest **3**	2135439	462	3438	1850	13919	6378	8628	9629	11696	18229	22494	308073	1730644
Rents **4**	258907	859	1283	1272	12348	620	4725	5382	4380	1468	2503	12021	212046
Royalties **5**	1783540	0	0	0	1039	155	2471	1633	1300	49605	45773		1642023
Other Portfolio Income **6**	696940	17226	16692	11832	51909	5437	31768	22799	12183	41385	42123	40283	403304
Other Receipts **7**	1134469	8187	3310	33999	21315	46166	45751	55993	32215	48031	98592	68580	672327
Total Receipts **8**	133502996	515563	4653159	4351105	17139379	8657623	9170286	6982860	5083433	6247471	7533800	15574114	47594203
Average Total Receipts **9**	6763	294	450	1831	4251	14600	24651	49175	80689	164407	358752	973382	6799172
Operating Costs/Operating Income (%)													
Cost of Operations **10**	65.9	90.5	47.3	59.7	65.8	72.3	69.5	69.5	68.4	66.4	68.2	67.6	64.3
Salaries and Wages **11**	6.8	12.9	15.2	8.7	7.0	6.0	6.8	7.1	8.5	7.8	6.9	6.2	5.6
Taxes Paid **12**	2.2	2.6	3.7	3.7	2.7	2.1	2.4	1.9	2.0	1.9	2.3	2.3	1.6
Interest Paid **13**	3.1	2.8	1.1	1.2	1.3	1.0	1.1	1.5	2.2	2.1	1.8	5.1	5.2
Depreciation **14**	3.6	2.5	3.9	3.8	3.7	2.8	3.6	3.7	3.9	4.0	4.2	4.1	3.4
Amortization and Depletion **15**	0.7	1.0	0.0	0.1	0.1	0.1	0.2	0.2	0.5	0.5	0.3	0.6	1.7
Pensions and Other Deferred Comp. **16**	0.9	0.8	0.2	0.8	0.7	0.5	0.5	0.6	0.7	0.8	0.8	2.2	0.8
Employee Benefits **17**	2.6	1.0	1.8	2.8	1.7	1.8	2.1	1.8	2.3	2.5	3.0	3.6	3.0
Advertising **18**	1.3	0.2	0.4	0.6	0.4	0.5	0.5	0.7	0.8	1.1	1.1	1.4	2.3
Other Expenses **19**	11.4	25.1	18.0	12.2	10.6	7.8	7.9	8.4	9.3	9.8	9.8	8.3	14.7
Officers' Compensation **20**	2.1	1.5	8.4	7.3	5.3	3.1	2.7	2.0	1.1	1.1	0.6	0.7	0.3
Operating Margin **21**	•	•	•	•	0.7	2.1	2.8	2.5	0.2	1.9	0.9	•	•
Operating Margin Before Officers' Comp. **22**	1.4	•	8.4	6.6	6.0	5.3	5.5	4.6	1.4	3.0	1.5	•	•

Selected Average Balance Sheet ($ in Thousands)

Net Receivables 23	1020	0	20	187	598	2076	3565	6803	11205	26674	61129	174730	1108314
Inventories 24	795	0	23	203	460	1905	3912	7252	15156	27654	67936	121319	589633
Net Property, Plant and Equipment 25	1314	0	58	225	625	1809	4481	9826	18325	41465	88618	257934	1347719
Total Assets 26	10652	0	142	758	2180	7288	15568	35210	70511	166161	351874	1264154	20675430
Notes and Loans Payable 27	3824	0	98	327	877	2256	4670	10507	26957	51620	97162	406906	7625504
All Other Liabilities 28	1553	0	30	145	466	1905	3408	7856	18616	37467	93997	386829	1978686
Net Worth 29	5275	0	14	286	837	3127	7490	16847	24938	77074	160716	470419	11071240

Selected Financial Ratios (Times to 1)

Current Ratio 30	1.6	•	1.6	2.2	1.9	2.1	1.9	2.1	1.7	2.0	2.0	1.3	1.3
Quick Ratio 31	0.9	•	1.1	1.2	1.2	1.1	1.0	1.1	0.8	0.9	1.0	0.7	0.8
Net Sales to Working Capital 32	7.3	•	15.3	6.7	6.4	5.6	5.5	4.9	5.1	3.9	4.3	10.4	11.8
Coverage Ratio 33	2.4	•	1.5	1.3	2.0	3.9	4.6	3.6	1.6	3.1	3.1	1.3	2.7
Total Asset Turnover 34	0.6	•	3.2	2.4	1.9	2.0	1.6	1.4	1.1	1.0	1.0	0.7	0.3
Inventory Turnover 35	5.4	•	9.2	5.3	6.1	5.5	4.3	4.7	3.6	3.8	3.5	5.3	6.7
Receivables Turnover 36	6.2	•	18.3	10.1	7.2	7.3	6.5	7.2	5.9	6.8	5.6	5.9	5.1
Total Liabilities to Net Worth 37	1.0	•	9.3	1.6	1.6	1.3	1.1	1.1	1.8	1.2	1.2	1.7	0.9
Current Assets to Working Capital 38	2.7	•	2.6	1.8	2.1	2.0	2.1	1.9	2.4	2.0	2.1	4.3	4.1
Current Liabilities to Working Capital 39	1.7	•	1.6	0.8	1.1	1.0	1.1	0.9	1.4	1.0	1.1	3.3	3.1
Working Capital to Net Sales 40	0.1	•	0.1	0.1	0.2	0.2	0.2	0.2	0.2	0.3	0.2	0.1	0.1
Inventory to Working Capital 41	0.9	•	0.7	0.7	0.7	0.8	0.8	0.7	1.0	0.7	0.8	1.4	1.0
Total Receipts to Cash Flow 42	7.7	•	7.5	13.4	11.5	11.9	10.7	9.6	11.8	8.0	8.9	12.8	4.9
Cost of Goods to Cash Flow 43	5.1	•	3.6	8.0	7.6	8.6	7.5	6.6	8.1	5.3	6.1	8.7	3.2
Cash Flow to Total Debt 44	0.2	•	0.5	0.3	0.3	0.3	0.3	0.3	0.1	0.2	0.2	0.1	0.1

Selected Financial Factors (in Percentages)

Debt Ratio 45	50.5	•	90.3	62.3	61.6	57.1	51.9	52.2	64.6	53.6	54.3	62.8	46.5
Return on Total Assets 46	4.6	•	5.1	3.8	4.9	7.5	7.6	7.4	4.1	6.5	5.6	4.8	4.2
Return on Equity Before Income Taxes 47	5.4	•	17.3	2.5	6.5	13.0	12.4	11.2	4.5	9.6	8.4	2.6	4.9
Return on Equity After Income Taxes 48	3.6	•	15.7	1.2	5.7	11.7	10.8	9.4	2.7	7.7	5.1	0.7	3.2
Profit Margin (Before Income Tax) 49	4.4	•	0.5	0.4	1.3	2.8	3.8	3.9	1.4	4.6	3.9	1.3	8.9
Profit Margin (After Income Tax) 50	3.0	•	0.5	0.2	1.1	2.5	3.3	3.3	0.8	3.7	0.3	0.3	5.8

Table II

Corporations with Net Income

OTHER FABRICATED METAL PRODUCT

MONEY AMOUNTS AND SIZE OF ASSETS IN THOUSANDS OF DOLLARS

Item Description for Accounting Period 7/02 Through 6/03		Total	Zero Assets	Under 500	500 to 1,000	1,000 to 5,000	5,000 to 10,000	10,000 to 25,000	25,000 to 50,000	50,000 to 100,000	100,000 to 250,000	250,000 to 500,000	500,000 to 2,500,000	2,500,000 and over
Number of Enterprises	1	11405	492	6029	1444	2573	407	261	108	34	26	14	9	7
Revenues ($ in Thousands)														
Net Sales	2	102717777	97329	3045051	2816426	11994823	6754093	6714383	5368164	3442172	4393861	5838167	9319449	42933859
Interest	3	1996068	79	1085	1505	7849	3471	5647	5448	8967	13591	12641	205141	1730644
Rents	4	235491	0	1283	0	9359	169	2349	4399	452	955	1801	2677	212046
Royalties	5	1752391	0	0	0	140	154	2471	1283	953	41705	39541	24121	1642023
Other Portfolio Income	6	618781	12304	716	4491	44092	3015	25881	19861	2082	30218	40829	31990	403304
Other Receipts	7	1013121	331	1717	27875	24433	34113	32583	41292	11091	37364	72540	57455	672327
Total Receipts	8	108333629	110043	3049852	2850297	12080696	6795015	6783314	5440447	3465717	4517694	6005519	9640833	47594203
Average Total Receipts	9	9499	224	506	1974	4695	16695	25990	50375	101933	173757	428966	1071204	6799172
Operating Costs/Operating Income (%)														
Cost of Operations	10	64.7	46.2	43.2	57.9	63.8	72.7	67.5	67.5	66.3	64.2	66.5	66.1	64.3
Salaries and Wages	11	6.6	15.8	17.0	7.6	6.3	5.6	6.7	7.2	8.3	8.1	7.2	6.0	5.6
Taxes Paid	12	2.1	4.1	3.1	3.8	2.6	2.0	2.4	1.9	1.9	2.0	2.4	2.3	1.6
Interest Paid	13	3.0	0.5	0.8	0.8	0.8	0.6	0.8	1.2	1.3	1.2	1.2	4.1	5.2
Depreciation	14	3.4	3.7	2.5	3.9	3.3	2.2	3.3	3.5	3.9	3.6	4.1	3.5	3.4
Amortization and Depletion	15	0.8	0.0	0.0	0.0	0.1	0.0	0.1	0.2	0.4	0.2	0.3	0.6	1.7
Pensions and Other Deferred Comp.	16	0.8	4.0	0.2	1.0	0.8	0.6	0.6	0.6	0.7	0.9	0.8	1.7	0.8
Employee Benefits	17	2.6	2.7	1.2	3.1	1.6	1.4	2.0	1.7	2.3	2.4	3.2	3.7	3.0
Advertising	18	1.5	0.0	0.4	0.7	0.4	0.4	0.5	0.8	0.9	1.3	1.3	1.8	2.3
Other Expenses	19	11.4	20.4	18.6	10.8	9.6	6.4	7.4	7.6	7.1	9.9	9.1	8.4	14.7
Officers' Compensation	20	1.9	4.1	7.3	7.9	5.5	3.2	2.9	2.1	1.2	1.2	0.5	0.9	0.3
Operating Margin	21	1.3	•	5.9	2.5	5.1	4.9	5.8	5.6	5.5	5.0	3.3	0.9	•
Operating Margin Before Officers' Comp.	22	3.2	2.7	13.1	10.4	10.6	8.1	8.7	7.7	6.8	6.2	3.9	1.8	•

Selected Average Balance Sheet ($ in Thousands)

Net Receivables 23	1414	0	11	162	644	2220	3758	6703	13688	27871	58741	198067	1108314
Inventories 24	1002	0	19	216	488	1746	3930	7104	17166	25690	65480	115403	528567
Net Property, Plant and Equipment 25	1715	0	39	231	581	1695	4112	9372	21431	41043	90607	247109	1347719
Total Assets 26	16270	0	111	776	2199	7342	15489	35274	72725	165305	351980	1204626	20675430
Notes and Loans Payable 27	5671	0	60	302	641	1875	4083	9275	18290	29142	79853	391721	7625504
All Other Liabilities 28	2063	0	18	141	425	1818	3337	6945	17469	40931	89052	333695	1978686
Net Worth 29	8536	0	34	333	1134	3649	8068	19055	36966	95232	183075	479210	11071240

Selected Financial Ratios (Times to 1)

Current Ratio 30	1.7	•	2.1	2.5	2.3	2.1	2.1	2.3	2.2	2.5	2.4	1.4	1.3
Quick Ratio 31	1.0	•	1.4	1.3	1.5	1.3	1.2	1.4	1.1	1.2	1.2	0.8	0.8
Net Sales to Working Capital 32	7.0	•	15.6	6.4	5.5	6.0	4.9	4.5	4.7	3.3	3.8	9.4	11.8
Coverage Ratio 33	3.4	23.6	8.4	5.4	8.1	9.7	9.2	6.7	5.8	7.8	6.2	2.1	2.7
Total Asset Turnover 34	0.6	•	4.5	2.5	2.1	2.3	1.7	1.4	1.4	1.0	1.2	0.9	0.3
Inventory Turnover 35	5.8	•	11.3	5.2	6.1	6.9	4.4	4.7	3.9	4.2	4.2	5.9	7.5
Receivables Turnover 36	6.3	•	28.4	11.9	7.1	8.2	6.6	7.6	5.9	7.4	7.3	5.7	11.1
Total Liabilities to Net Worth 37	0.9	•	2.3	1.3	0.9	1.0	0.9	0.9	1.0	0.7	0.9	1.5	0.9
Current Assets to Working Capital 38	2.5	•	1.9	1.7	1.8	1.9	1.9	1.7	1.9	1.7	1.7	3.6	4.1
Current Liabilities to Working Capital 39	1.5	•	0.9	0.7	0.8	0.9	0.9	0.7	0.9	0.7	0.7	2.6	3.1
Working Capital to Net Sales 40	0.1	•	0.1	0.2	0.2	0.2	0.2	0.2	0.2	0.3	0.3	0.1	0.1
Inventory to Working Capital 41	0.8	•	0.5	0.7	0.5	0.7	0.7	0.6	0.7	0.5	0.7	1.1	1.0
Total Receipts to Cash Flow 42	6.3	5.3	4.8	10.8	8.1	9.9	8.3	7.8	8.9	6.3	7.5	9.0	4.9
Cost of Goods to Cash Flow 43	4.1	2.5	2.1	6.2	5.2	7.2	5.6	5.3	5.9	4.0	5.0	5.9	3.2
Cash Flow to Total Debt 44	0.2	•	1.4	0.4	0.5	0.5	0.4	0.4	0.3	0.4	0.3	0.2	0.1

Selected Financial Factors (in Percentages)

Debt Ratio 45	47.5	•	69.7	57.1	48.5	50.3	47.9	46.0	49.2	42.4	48.0	60.2	46.5
Return on Total Assets 46	5.6	•	31.2	11.4	14.0	13.8	12.7	11.4	10.4	9.4	9.0	7.4	4.2
Return on Equity Before Income Taxes 47	7.6	•	90.6	21.6	23.8	25.0	21.8	18.0	17.0	14.2	14.5	9.9	4.9
Return on Equity After Income Taxes 48	5.7	•	89.5	19.7	22.9	23.3	19.6	16.0	14.7	12.0	10.1	6.5	3.2
Profit Margin (Before Income Tax) 49	7.2	11.7	6.0	3.7	5.8	5.5	6.8	6.9	6.2	8.0	6.4	4.6	8.9
Profit Margin (After Income Tax) 50	5.4	10.6	6.0	3.4	5.6	5.1	6.2	6.1	5.4	6.7	4.4	3.0	5.8

Table I
Corporations with and without Net Income

AGRICULTURE, CONSTRUCTION, AND MINING MACHINERY

MONEY AMOUNTS AND SIZE OF ASSETS IN THOUSANDS OF DOLLARS

Item Description for Accounting Period 7/02 Through 6/03	Total	Zero Assets	Under 500	500 to 1,000	1,000 to 5,000	5,000 to 10,000	10,000 to 25,000	25,000 to 50,000	50,000 to 100,000	100,000 to 250,000	250,000 to 500,000	500,000 to 2,500,000	2,500,000 and over
Number of Enterprises **1**	2964	0	0	1010	631	115	94	26	22	22	9	11	8
Revenues ($ in Thousands)													
Net Sales **2**	68889110	0	0	2106412	2412620	1125237	2086266	1001661	1806188	3332187	3021883	10583938	40514929
Interest **3**	2864654	0	0	14	4983	1745	2171	2278	2953	22744	33091	88941	2680254
Rents **4**	993853	0	0	175	565	46	3955	951	466	1203	358	10351	975410
Royalties **5**	416098	0	0	0	0	0	38	650	7477	15545	24715	92383	255343
Other Portfolio Income **6**	953442	0	0	170	24158	1547	6161	1468	22490	22657	7398	38919	810991
Other Receipts **7**	1983340	0	0	19291	14099	77173	13517	19119	38345	39898	14584	127198	1612911
Total Receipts **8**	75900497	0	0	2126062	2456425	1205748	2112108	1026127	1877919	3434234	3102029	10941730	46649838
Average Total Receipts **9**	25607	•	•	2105	3893	10485	22469	39466	85360	156102	344670	994703	5856230
Operating Costs/Operating Income (%)													
Cost of Operations **10**	75.1	•	•	69.3	66.5	71.2	70.1	73.9	65.2	71.3	77.9	76.5	77.0
Salaries and Wages **11**	6.5	•	•	7.1	8.3	5.6	9.1	7.4	9.6	9.4	7.3	7.4	5.4
Taxes Paid **12**	1.0	•	•	1.0	2.7	2.3	1.9	2.0	1.9	1.2	1.7	1.0	0.6
Interest Paid **13**	4.6	•	•	0.5	1.2	1.0	1.6	2.2	1.6	2.0	3.2	3.0	6.1
Depreciation **14**	3.9	•	•	2.8	1.8	1.9	2.8	3.2	2.8	3.2	2.8	2.0	4.8
Amortization and Depletion **15**	0.9	•	•	0.0	0.1	0.3	0.2	0.3	0.4	0.8	0.4	0.5	1.2
Pensions and Other Deferred Comp. **16**	2.0	•	•	0.0	0.5	0.4	0.5	0.6	0.6	0.9	0.5	0.8	3.0
Employee Benefits **17**	1.5	•	•	0.4	2.2	0.6	2.1	1.6	2.2	1.8	1.1	1.3	1.5
Advertising **18**	0.5	•	•	0.8	0.9	1.4	1.1	0.8	1.1	0.9	0.9	0.8	0.2
Other Expenses **19**	14.8	•	•	8.4	10.7	12.8	9.6	14.5	10.8	8.9	7.1	13.7	17.3
Officers' Compensation **20**	0.8	•	•	5.8	4.4	5.4	2.0	1.7	1.1	0.6	0.9	0.2	0.2
Operating Margin **21**	•	•	•	3.9	0.5	•	•	•	2.7	•	•	•	•
Operating Margin Before Officers' Comp. **22**	•	•	•	9.7	4.9	2.6	1.0	•	3.8	•	•	•	•

Selected Average Balance Sheet ($ in Thousands)

Item													
Net Receivables 23	10512	•	•	138	414	1571	3240	7240	13329	31595	68558	209248	3271655
Inventories 24	3689	•	•	196	1079	2261	5378	8111	19226	36018	84984	177760	642768
Net Property, Plant and Equipment 25	4659	•	•	159	273	868	3394	8677	12601	39109	66029	123701	1210989
Total Assets 26	41406	•	•	736	2460	7119	15165	34352	72430	151611	363054	1182006	12003571
Notes and Loans Payable 27	18756	•	•	212	835	1388	6447	9059	18895	37405	103537	374354	5922477
All Other Liabilities 28	11243	•	•	157	446	1794	4277	9999	21883	38688	126588	321779	3249735
Net Worth 29	11407	•	•	367	1179	3936	4442	15295	31552	75519	132929	485872	2831360

Selected Financial Ratios (Times to 1)

Item													
Current Ratio 30	1.5	•	•	2.4	2.8	2.2	1.5	1.8	1.6	1.8	2.1	1.5	
Quick Ratio 31	1.0	•	•	1.1	1.1	1.1	0.7	1.0	0.7	0.9	1.0	1.0	
Net Sales to Working Capital 32	3.8	•	•	7.1	3.2	3.3	6.1	4.2	5.3	4.2	3.7	6.8	3.2
Coverage Ratio 33	1.1	•	•	10.5	3.0	5.6	1.2	•	5.2	2.1	0.8	•	1.1
Total Asset Turnover 34	0.6	•	•	2.8	1.6	1.4	1.5	1.1	1.1	1.0	0.9	0.8	0.4
Inventory Turnover 35	4.7	•	•	7.4	2.4	3.1	2.9	3.5	2.8	3.0	3.1	4.1	6.1
Receivables Turnover 36	2.0	•	•	20.2	9.0	5.9	6.8	5.1	5.5	5.3	4.6	4.4	1.4
Total Liabilities to Net Worth 37	2.6	•	•	1.0	1.1	0.8	2.4	1.2	1.3	1.0	1.7	1.4	3.2
Current Assets to Working Capital 38	2.9	•	•	1.7	1.5	1.8	2.9	2.2	2.6	2.2	1.9	3.2	3.1
Current Liabilities to Working Capital 39	1.9	•	•	0.7	0.5	0.8	1.9	1.2	1.6	1.2	0.9	2.2	2.1
Working Capital to Net Sales 40	0.3	•	•	0.1	0.3	0.3	0.2	0.2	0.2	0.2	0.3	0.1	0.3
Inventory to Working Capital 41	0.6	•	•	0.9	0.9	0.7	1.5	0.9	1.2	1.0	0.9	1.2	0.4
Total Receipts to Cash Flow 42	8.3	•	•	8.4	10.6	6.8	12.1	13.4	6.5	10.6	21.7	12.0	7.1
Cost of Goods to Cash Flow 43	6.2	•	•	5.8	7.0	4.8	8.5	9.9	4.3	7.5	16.9	9.2	5.5
Cash Flow to Total Debt 44	0.1	•	•	0.7	0.3	0.5	0.2	0.2	0.3	0.2	0.1	0.1	0.1

Selected Financial Factors (in Percentages)

Item													
Debt Ratio 45	72.5	•	•	50.1	52.1	44.7	70.7	55.5	56.4	50.2	63.4	58.9	76.4
Return on Total Assets 46	2.8	•	•	15.0	5.4	7.4	2.7	•	9.3	4.2	2.3	•	2.9
Return on Equity Before Income Taxes 47	1.0	•	•	27.2	7.5	11.0	1.4	•	17.2	4.5	•	•	1.5
Return on Equity After Income Taxes 48	•	•	•	27.2	6.5	9.7	•	•	15.2	2.5	•	•	•
Profit Margin (Before Income Tax) 49	0.5	•	•	4.8	2.3	4.4	0.3	•	6.6	2.2	•	•	0.9
Profit Margin (After Income Tax) 50	•	•	•	4.8	2.0	3.9	•	•	5.9	1.2	•	•	•

Table II
Corporations with Net Income

AGRICULTURE, CONSTRUCTION, AND MINING MACHINERY

MONEY AMOUNTS AND SIZE OF ASSETS IN THOUSANDS OF DOLLARS

Item Description for Accounting Period 7/02 Through 6/03	Total	Zero Assets	Under 500	500 to 1,000	1,000 to 5,000	5,000 to 10,000	10,000 to 25,000	25,000 to 50,000	50,000 to 100,000	100,000 to 250,000	250,000 to 500,000	500,000 to 2,500,000	2,500,000 and over
Number of Enterprises **1**	2036	12	561	0	384	97	58	17	19	16	3	4	0
Revenues ($ in Thousands)													
Net Sales **2**	32834300	13514	131575	0	1553400	900390	1406190	717927	1703762	2479588	780593	5527713	0
Interest **3**	1048612	164	0	0	3891	1733	1317	2005	2832	11782	3232	38709	0
Rents **4**	368596	0	350	0	467	46	3590	37	447	454	223	550	0
Royalties **5**	143004	0	0	0	0	0	21	630	6826	15535	2295	47852	0
Other Portfolio Income **6**	615900	1896	10906	0	17360	1547	1762	1140	22438	22428	4373	19932	0
Other Receipts **7**	660596	8546	3168	0	11548	77146	10565	12979	38061	32955	6798	68936	0
Total Receipts **8**	35671008	24120	145999	0	1586666	980862	1423445	734718	1774366	2562742	797514	5703692	0
Average Total Receipts **9**	17520	2010	260	*	4132	10112	24542	43219	93388	160171	265838	1425923	*
Operating Costs/Operating Income (%)													
Cost of Operations **10**	71.6	67.3	28.9	*	64.3	72.5	68.1	63.1	65.5	71.4	60.5	78.7	*
Salaries and Wages **11**	6.2	38.1	15.1	*	7.3	6.0	8.8	7.8	9.7	9.8	12.2	5.7	*
Taxes Paid **12**	1.0	5.2	4.4	*	2.6	2.5	1.8	2.1	2.0	1.2	2.4	1.0	*
Interest Paid **13**	3.4	3.8	2.6	*	1.2	1.0	1.4	2.3	1.5	1.9	4.0	2.0	*
Depreciation **14**	4.0	14.4	3.8	*	2.1	2.1	2.4	2.9	2.8	3.0	4.0	1.9	*
Amortization and Depletion **15**	0.6	*	*	*	0.2	0.3	0.1	0.4	0.4	0.2	1.1	0.2	*
Pensions and Other Deferred Comp. **16**	1.0	2.6	*	*	0.7	0.4	0.6	0.7	0.6	1.1	0.7	0.5	*
Employee Benefits **17**	1.4	0.4	*	*	1.4	0.6	1.9	1.5	2.2	2.0	1.8	0.8	*
Advertising **18**	0.6	0.2	0.4	*	1.3	1.5	1.0	0.9	0.9	0.9	0.9	1.0	*
Other Expenses **19**	12.9	19.8	20.8	*	11.6	10.3	7.8	9.9	10.1	7.0	10.0	9.9	*
Officers' Compensation **20**	1.1	3.4	5.3	*	4.0	4.8	2.3	1.7	1.2	0.7	1.2	0.1	*
Operating Margin **21**	*	*	18.7	*	3.5	*	3.7	6.8	3.1	0.9	1.3	*	*
Operating Margin Before Officers' Comp. **22**	*	*	24.0	*	7.5	2.7	6.1	8.4	4.3	1.5	2.5	*	*

Selected Average Balance Sheet ($ in Thousands)

	•	•	•	•	•	•	•	•	•	•	•
Net Receivables 23	7316	6	•	421	1362	3458	7821	14063	29283	47470	219842
Inventories 24	2837	0	•	1026	2147	4825	7766	17012	37718	62513	230870
Net Property, Plant and Equipment 25	3056	0	88	319	933	3235	8537	13337	33274	69704	134044
Total Assets 26	20271	0	109	2520	6937	15119	34313	70743	148425	410140	1212520
Notes and Loans Payable 27	9563	0	91	800	1429	4297	7365	20551	36769	162683	376890
All Other Liabilities 28	4297	0	8	473	1496	4114	6977	21226	33397	107047	259889
Net Worth 29	6411	0	10	1248	4013	6708	19971	28965	78259	140409	575742

Selected Financial Ratios (Times to 1)

	•	•	•	•	•	•	•	•	•	•	•
Current Ratio 30	3.1	2.6	•	2.8	2.3	1.9	2.5	1.6	2.2	2.1	1.6
Quick Ratio 31	2.1	2.5	•	1.1	1.0	0.9	1.4	0.7	1.1	0.8	0.8
Net Sales to Working Capital 32	2.0	17.7	•	3.3	3.2	4.6	3.4	5.8	3.6	4.2	7.6
Coverage Ratio 33	3.3	12.3	•	5.7	8.1	4.5	5.2	5.9	3.4	2.2	2.0
Total Asset Turnover 34	0.8	2.1	7.2	1.6	1.3	1.6	1.2	1.3	1.0	0.6	1.1
Inventory Turnover 35	4.1	185.6	•	2.5	3.1	3.4	3.4	3.5	2.9	2.5	4.7
Receivables Turnover 36	1.7	49.2	•	10.0	5.7	7.7	5.3	6.1	10.6	11.0	4.8
Total Liabilities to Net Worth 37	2.2	10.2	•	1.0	0.7	1.3	0.7	1.4	0.9	1.9	1.1
Current Assets to Working Capital 38	1.5	1.6	•	1.6	1.8	2.1	1.7	2.8	1.8	1.9	2.6
Current Liabilities to Working Capital 39	0.5	0.6	•	0.6	0.8	1.1	0.7	1.8	0.8	0.9	1.6
Working Capital to Net Sales 40	0.5	0.1	•	0.3	0.3	0.2	0.3	0.2	0.3	0.2	0.1
Inventory to Working Capital 41	0.3	0.0	•	0.9	0.7	1.0	0.6	1.2	0.9	1.0	1.0
Total Receipts to Cash Flow 42	6.2	2.1	2.8	7.3	7.0	8.7	5.6	6.6	10.2	9.8	9.7
Cost of Goods to Cash Flow 43	4.4	0.6	1.9	4.7	5.1	5.9	3.5	4.3	7.3	5.9	7.7
Cash Flow to Total Debt 44	0.2	1.1	•	0.4	0.5	0.3	0.5	0.3	0.2	0.1	0.2

Selected Financial Factors (in Percentages)

	•	•	•	•	•	•	•	•	•	•	•
Debt Ratio 45	68.4	91.1	•	50.5	42.2	55.6	41.8	59.1	47.3	65.8	52.5
Return on Total Assets 46	8.9	69.5	•	10.9	10.5	10.2	14.8	11.0	6.6	5.5	4.5
Return on Equity Before Income Taxes 47	19.6	713.8	•	18.2	15.9	17.9	20.6	22.3	8.9	8.7	4.6
Return on Equity After Income Taxes 48	14.1	713.8	•	16.7	14.4	15.5	18.0	19.8	6.3	8.0	3.0
Profit Margin (Before Income Tax) 49	7.8	23.2	29.7	5.6	6.9	5.0	9.7	7.2	4.5	4.7	1.9
Profit Margin (After Income Tax) 50	5.6	21.7	29.7	5.2	6.2	4.3	8.5	6.4	3.2	4.3	1.2

Table I

Corporations with and without Net Income

INDUSTRIAL MACHINERY

MONEY AMOUNTS AND SIZE OF ASSETS IN THOUSANDS OF DOLLARS

Item Description for Accounting Period 7/02 Through 6/03	Total	Zero Assets	Under 500	500 to 1,000	1,000 to 5,000	5,000 to 10,000	10,000 to 25,000	25,000 to 50,000	50,000 to 100,000	100,000 to 250,000	250,000 to 500,000	500,000 to 2,500,000	2,500,000 and over
Number of Enterprises **1**	5117	1111	2587	315	608	201	149	62	35	27	8	13	0
Revenues ($ in Thousands)													
Net Sales **2**	29431353	228603	600162	566165	3348622	1935457	2827806	2349960	2504775	3675188	3102311	8292304	0
Interest **3**	196739	368	836	280	1799	1495	9057	7093	14258	44512	21560	95481	0
Rents **4**	23562	0	0	0	3925	1362	1707	3209	2025	8797	457	2079	0
Royalties **5**	100380	46	0	0	78	0	3346	1169	11415	17032	14272	53023	0
Other Portfolio Income **6**	423845	9605	1388	800	4377	1138	6499	6976	12884	74682	9047	296451	0
Other Receipts **7**	357180	4819	28561	1892	37671	11007	25089	34977	33394	69581	6457	103730	0
Total Receipts **8**	30533059	243441	630947	569137	3396472	1950459	2873504	2403384	2578751	3889792	3154104	8843068	0
Average Total Receipts **9**	5967	219	244	1807	5586	9704	19285	38764	73679	144066	394263	680236	•
Operating Costs/Operating Income (%)													
Cost of Operations **10**	65.8	66.3	43.9	60.3	65.2	66.1	66.1	66.5	67.3	71.9	67.7	63.6	•
Salaries and Wages **11**	11.5	8.7	13.5	5.5	10.0	11.1	10.5	10.5	11.8	16.7	10.1	11.5	•
Taxes Paid **12**	2.4	2.7	4.3	3.6	3.1	2.6	2.5	2.5	1.9	2.2	1.9	2.4	•
Interest Paid **13**	2.5	0.6	1.3	1.5	0.9	1.2	1.5	1.8	1.9	2.5	2.0	4.7	•
Depreciation **14**	3.2	1.0	5.1	5.0	1.8	2.2	4.2	2.7	3.6	3.1	2.1	4.1	•
Amortization and Depletion **15**	0.9	0.1	0.1	0.3	0.0	0.3	0.4	0.8	0.7	0.8	1.0	1.7	•
Pensions and Other Deferred Comp. **16**	0.9	1.1	0.0	0.0	0.9	0.4	0.8	0.6	0.8	0.7	1.2	1.4	•
Employee Benefits **17**	2.8	4.9	4.1	4.1	1.9	1.9	2.1	2.4	2.4	4.1	3.3	2.8	•
Advertising **18**	0.7	0.3	0.9	0.2	0.9	0.5	0.7	0.7	0.6	0.6	0.4	0.7	•
Other Expenses **19**	12.2	15.7	26.1	13.2	12.4	9.0	10.7	10.3	9.3	13.0	9.1	14.4	•
Officers' Compensation **20**	2.3	0.2	12.7	4.9	4.8	7.4	2.8	1.8	1.5	1.3	0.6	0.6	•
Operating Margin **21**	•	•	•	1.5	•	•	•	•	•	•	0.5	•	•
Operating Margin Before Officers' Comp. **22**	•	•	0.7	6.4	2.8	4.7	0.6	1.2	•	•	•	1.1	•

Selected Average Balance Sheet ($ in Thousands)

Net Receivables 23	1235	0	41	181	821	1742	3395	7892	14174	33295	76566	177314
Inventories 24	974	0	32	73	783	2270	4028	7018	14070	24947	41977	108406
Net Property, Plant and Equipment 25	993	0	37	321	492	1357	3439	6983	14137	24905	48188	139486
Total Assets 26	6408	0	131	789	2478	7034	15620	35620	69884	167742	358332	1146572
Notes and Loans Payable 27	2138	0	106	415	604	2745	4676	11052	22999	39991	61377	450827
All Other Liabilities 28	1964	0	23	153	922	1921	4630	9133	19734	58136	112785	351883
Net Worth 29	2306	0	2	221	952	2368	6315	15435	27151	69615	184170	343863

Selected Financial Ratios (Times to 1)

Current Ratio 30	1.7	•	3.2	1.8	1.7	1.5	1.6	1.8	1.6	1.8	1.7	1.9
Quick Ratio 31	1.0	•	1.8	1.3	1.0	0.9	0.8	1.0	0.8	1.0	1.2	1.2
Net Sales to Working Capital 32	4.8	•	3.8	8.8	7.3	6.3	5.2	4.4	5.2	3.3	6.0	4.2
Coverage Ratio 33	0.5	10.0	•	2.3	0.4	•	0.6	2.0	1.6	•	2.3	1.0
Total Asset Turnover 34	0.9	•	1.8	2.3	2.2	1.4	1.2	1.1	1.0	0.8	1.1	0.6
Inventory Turnover 35	3.9	•	3.2	14.8	4.6	2.8	3.1	3.6	3.4	3.9	6.3	3.7
Receivables Turnover 36	4.5	•	6.4	12.8	6.7	4.1	5.0	5.3	4.7	4.2	4.4	3.5
Total Liabilities to Net Worth 37	1.8	•	68.8	2.6	1.6	2.0	1.5	1.3	1.6	1.4	0.9	2.3
Current Assets to Working Capital 38	2.4	•	1.5	2.2	2.4	3.0	2.7	2.3	2.8	2.3	2.5	2.2
Current Liabilities to Working Capital 39	1.4	•	0.5	1.2	1.4	2.0	1.7	1.3	1.8	1.3	1.5	1.2
Working Capital to Net Sales 40	0.2	•	0.3	0.1	0.1	0.2	0.2	0.2	0.2	0.3	0.2	0.2
Inventory to Working Capital 41	0.7	•	0.5	0.6	0.8	1.1	1.1	0.8	1.0	0.6	0.5	0.6
Total Receipts to Cash Flow 42	12.9	8.8	10.2	7.9	12.4	19.9	12.2	10.1	12.3	•	10.6	9.6
Cost of Goods to Cash Flow 43	8.5	5.9	4.5	4.8	8.1	13.2	8.1	6.7	8.3	•	7.1	6.1
Cash Flow to Total Debt 44	0.1	•	0.2	0.4	0.3	0.1	0.2	0.2	0.1	•	0.2	0.1

Selected Financial Factors (in Percentages)

Debt Ratio 45	64.0	•	98.6	71.9	61.6	66.3	59.6	56.7	61.1	58.5	48.6	70.0
Return on Total Assets 46	1.2	•	•	8.2	0.9	•	1.0	3.7	3.1	3.1	5.1	2.5
Return on Equity Before Income Taxes 47	•	•	•	16.6	•	•	•	4.1	3.1	•	5.7	•
Return on Equity After Income Taxes 48	•	•	8.9	•	•	•	1.9	1.4	•	2.6	•	
Profit Margin (Before Income Tax) 49	•	5.0	•	2.0	•	•	•	1.7	1.2	•	2.7	•
Profit Margin (After Income Tax) 50	•	4.8	1.1	•	•	0.8	0.5	•	1.2	•		

125

Table II

Corporations with Net Income

INDUSTRIAL MACHINERY

MONEY AMOUNTS AND SIZE OF ASSETS IN THOUSANDS OF DOLLARS

Item Description for Accounting Period 7/02 Through 6/03		Total	Zero Assets	Under 500	500 to 1,000	1,000 to 5,000	5,000 to 10,000	10,000 to 25,000	25,000 to 50,000	50,000 to 100,000	100,000 to 250,000	250,000 to 500,000	500,000 to 2,500,000	2,500,000 and over
Number of Enterprises	1	2288	447	1077	164	372	75	81	33	19	10	4	7	0
Revenues ($ in Thousands)														
Net Sales	2	16740970	146517	366964	281079	1999487	732454	1713139	1554428	1481833	1494836	1820396	5149836	0
Interest	3	81757	364	1	225	1176	270	2989	3817	11631	2764	11112	47408	0
Rents	4	14209	0	0	0	2886	254	680	1264	1091	7507	36	490	0
Royalties	5	30430	46	0	0	78	0	1534	563	11398	3511	7716	5583	0
Other Portfolio Income	6	197849	9605	1067	0	3637	256	4715	4581	10622	20538	8776	134054	0
Other Receipts	7	212839	4820	13575	78	27650	2223	18772	26144	24403	61698	3131	30346	0
Total Receipts	8	17278054	161352	381607	281382	2034914	735457	1741829	1590797	1540978	1590854	1851167	5367717	0
Average Total Receipts	9	7552	361	354	1716	5470	9806	21504	48206	81104	159085	462792	766817	•
Operating Costs/Operating Income (%)														
Cost of Operations	10	62.5	66.9	41.1	54.6	58.6	51.6	63.4	65.2	64.2	70.5	65.9	62.1	•
Salaries and Wages	11	10.8	7.7	11.5	4.4	11.2	11.5	10.0	10.2	12.6	10.4	10.6	11.2	•
Taxes Paid	12	2.3	1.0	4.8	4.1	2.8	2.4	2.3	2.4	1.5	2.2	1.3	2.3	•
Interest Paid	13	1.6	0.8	1.7	1.4	0.4	0.7	1.0	1.1	1.9	1.3	0.8	2.9	•
Depreciation	14	3.0	1.0	3.7	4.9	1.7	2.0	2.9	2.6	3.8	2.7	1.9	4.0	•
Amortization and Depletion	15	0.7	0.1	•	0.2	0.0	0.1	0.3	0.3	0.6	0.6	0.6	1.6	•
Pensions and Other Deferred Comp.	16	1.0	1.7	0.1	•	0.7	0.4	0.9	0.7	0.6	0.7	1.1	1.7	•
Employee Benefits	17	2.3	2.1	6.2	5.2	1.9	1.6	2.1	2.2	2.4	2.0	2.7	2.1	•
Advertising	18	0.7	0.1	1.3	0.2	1.3	0.4	0.8	0.5	0.6	0.4	0.5	0.7	•
Other Expenses	19	10.3	12.9	17.4	9.1	12.1	7.7	9.9	8.6	7.6	9.6	6.7	12.2	•
Officers' Compensation	20	2.7	0.3	13.6	5.6	5.9	13.3	2.8	1.7	1.6	1.6	0.7	0.5	•
Operating Margin	21	2.1	5.3	•	10.3	3.3	8.3	3.7	4.6	2.5	•	7.2	•	•
Operating Margin Before Officers' Comp.	22	4.8	5.6	12.1	15.9	9.2	21.6	6.6	6.2	4.1	•	7.9	•	•

Selected Average Balance Sheet ($ in Thousands)

Net Receivables **23**	1376	0	42	154	867	1309	3810	9291	14323	32104	122380	136928	•
Inventories **24**	1065	0	40	46	682	2781	3931	6370	11282	24729	34676	113678	•
Net Property, Plant and Equipment **25**	1253	0	34	305	418	1674	3176	7203	12607	30018	53504	178803	•
Total Assets **26**	8005	0	150	829	2621	7190	15723	36391	70263	166138	366338	1366656	•
Notes and Loans Payable **27**	2110	0	54	287	484	1884	3782	10890	19705	44072	39908	394428	•
All Other Liabilities **28**	1867	0	17	100	771	1529	4435	9157	19060	44813	150883	251357	•
Net Worth **29**	4028	0	79	442	1366	3777	7506	16344	31498	77253	175546	720871	•

Selected Financial Ratios (Times to 1)

Current Ratio **30**	1.8	•	4.1	2.9	2.1	1.6	1.8	1.9	1.7	2.1	1.9	1.5	•
Quick Ratio **31**	1.1	•	2.2	2.3	1.3	1.2	0.9	1.2	1.0	1.3	1.4	0.9	•
Net Sales to Working Capital **32**	5.2	•	4.0	5.2	5.2	6.0	4.7	4.5	4.9	3.4	4.1	7.4	•
Coverage Ratio **33**	4.7	19.4	2.5	8.4	13.7	13.8	6.7	7.1	4.4	4.9	13.0	2.6	•
Total Asset Turnover **34**	0.9	•	2.3	2.1	2.1	1.4	1.3	1.3	1.1	0.9	1.2	0.5	•
Inventory Turnover **35**	4.3	•	3.5	20.2	4.6	1.8	3.4	4.8	4.4	4.3	8.7	4.0	•
Receivables Turnover **36**	5.2	•	7.8	19.9	7.3	3.0	5.2	6.4	4.7	4.6	5.2	4.8	•
Total Liabilities to Net Worth **37**	1.0	•	0.9	0.9	0.9	0.9	1.1	1.2	1.2	1.2	1.1	0.9	•
Current Assets to Working Capital **38**	2.3	•	1.3	1.5	1.9	2.6	2.3	2.1	2.4	1.9	2.2	3.1	•
Current Liabilities to Working Capital **39**	1.3	•	0.3	0.5	0.9	1.6	1.3	1.1	1.4	0.9	1.2	2.1	•
Working Capital to Net Sales **40**	0.2	•	0.3	0.2	0.2	0.2	0.2	0.2	0.2	0.3	0.2	0.1	•
Inventory to Working Capital **41**	0.7	•	0.5	0.3	0.7	0.6	0.9	0.6	0.7	0.5	0.3	1.0	•
Total Receipts to Cash Flow **42**	7.4	5.0	7.6	5.4	7.2	6.9	7.5	7.3	8.5	8.1	7.0	7.3	•
Cost of Goods to Cash Flow **43**	4.6	3.4	3.1	2.9	4.2	3.6	4.7	4.7	5.5	5.7	4.6	4.6	•
Cash Flow to Total Debt **44**	0.3	•	0.6	0.8	0.6	0.4	0.3	0.3	0.2	0.2	0.3	0.2	•

Selected Financial Factors (in Percentages)

Debt Ratio **45**	49.7	•	47.3	46.7	47.9	47.5	52.3	55.1	55.2	53.5	52.1	47.3	•
Return on Total Assets **46**	7.0	•	9.5	24.4	11.3	12.7	8.5	10.4	9.3	5.5	13.2	4.1	•
Return on Equity Before Income Taxes **47**	11.0	•	10.8	40.3	20.1	22.4	15.2	19.9	16.0	9.5	25.5	4.8	•
Return on Equity After Income Taxes **48**	8.9	•	10.8	33.0	18.4	21.7	13.6	15.9	13.4	7.1	19.0	3.4	•
Profit Margin (Before Income Tax) **49**	6.1	15.5	2.5	10.4	5.1	8.7	5.4	6.9	6.5	4.9	9.8	4.7	•
Profit Margin (After Income Tax) **50**	4.9	15.2	2.5	8.5	4.7	8.4	4.8	5.5	5.4	3.6	7.3	3.3	•

Table I

Corporations with and without Net Income

COMMERCIAL AND SERVICE INDUSTRY MACHINERY

MONEY AMOUNTS AND SIZE OF ASSETS IN THOUSANDS OF DOLLARS

Item Description for Accounting Period 7/02 Through 6/03	Total	Zero Assets	Under 500	500 to 1,000	1,000 to 5,000	5,000 to 10,000	10,000 to 25,000	25,000 to 50,000	50,000 to 100,000	100,000 to 250,000	250,000 to 500,000	500,000 to 2,500,000	2,500,000 and over
Number of Enterprises **1**	2185	28	1260	209	455	110	60	25	12	9	4	8	5
Revenues ($ in Thousands)													
Net Sales **2**	44017279	8157	767215	538296	1560410	1009216	1625802	856412	1115145	1353585	1007431	6106589	28069022
Interest **3**	1323279	89	293	0	1928	831	4744	2232	3036	2677	19225	151882	1136342
Rents **4**	641793	63	3989	0	3319	1669	2784	1215	220	3077	31051	82807	511598
Royalties **5**	854288	0	0	0	0	0	12106	343	7331	4347	15254	18673	796236
Other Portfolio Income **6**	761193	514	266	0	11252	1137	7574	2811	4137	3483	81826	109393	538800
Other Receipts **7**	2469921	-2095	2827	14	81208	12741	143578	8949	5665	16091	8089	259005	1933849
Total Receipts **8**	50067753	6728	774590	538310	1658117	1025594	1796588	871962	1135534	1383260	1162876	6728349	32985847
Average Total Receipts **9**	22914	240	615	2576	3644	9324	29943	34878	94628	153696	290719	841044	6597169
Operating Costs/Operating Income (%)													
Cost of Operations **10**	53.4	39.4	30.0	78.3	53.5	68.2	64.7	64.7	56.4	60.7	61.4	59.6	49.9
Salaries and Wages **11**	16.8	54.0	35.1	0.5	16.9	8.8	14.7	12.5	10.8	12.1	5.5	16.1	18.2
Taxes Paid **12**	2.3	2.9	4.5	3.1	3.0	1.7	4.7	2.4	2.3	1.8	1.1	2.0	2.3
Interest Paid **13**	5.3	5.1	0.4	0.2	1.1	0.9	1.2	1.9	1.7	2.9	2.3	4.8	6.8
Depreciation **14**	7.6	6.2	2.2	0.8	2.0	2.7	5.8	3.6	4.0	3.9	4.4	5.1	9.5
Amortization and Depletion **15**	0.7	0.1	0.1	0.0	0.1	0.2	0.4	0.8	0.8	0.8	0.6	0.6	0.8
Pensions and Other Deferred Comp. **16**	1.4	0.1	0.5	•	0.7	0.5	0.5	0.7	0.9	0.5	1.1	0.3	1.9
Employee Benefits **17**	4.9	8.2	1.7	2.2	2.9	1.2	1.7	1.6	3.6	2.0	2.7	2.6	6.4
Advertising **18**	1.7	0.2	2.0	0.2	0.8	0.6	2.1	0.7	1.8	1.4	2.3	0.7	1.9
Other Expenses **19**	18.7	92.4	18.2	13.7	14.0	10.7	60.5	11.1	11.6	17.8	15.2	15.2	18.3
Officers' Compensation **20**	0.9	1.6	5.9	2.3	5.5	3.1	2.0	1.6	2.0	1.0	1.3	0.7	0.4
Operating Margin **21**	•	•	•	•	•	1.3	•	•	4.2	•	2.3	•	•
Operating Margin Before Officers' Comp. **22**	•	•	5.4	1.1	5.0	4.4	•	0.0	6.2	•	3.5	•	•

Selected Average Balance Sheet ($ in Thousands)

	1	2	3	4	5	6	7	8	9	10	11	12	13
Net Receivables 23	5904	0	19	397	537	1220	2943	5846	16693	22005	129668	156259	1984987
Inventories 24	1689	0	36	244	574	2026	4650	7238	12789	35810	40631	76976	295412
Net Property, Plant and Equipment 25	5586	0	53	39	451	1630	3685	7145	16365	25442	32320	134464	1943264
Total Assets 26	37870	122	784	2206	6864	15919	37075	65876	142499	351076	1040982		13396579
Notes and Loans Payable 27	14086	0	159	307	1084	1016	4761	10466	13583	53734	38484	256161	5302494
All Other Liabilities 28	13145	0	5	282	525	2023	19112	8761	18983	48644	151519	369362	4520720
Net Worth 29	10638	-42	196	596	3825	-7953	17848	33310	40121	161072	415459		3573365

Selected Financial Ratios (Times to 1)

	1	2	3	4	5	6	7	8	9	10	11	12	13
Current Ratio 30	1.0	•	3.1	2.6	2.1	1.8	0.5	1.6	2.2	1.4	1.5	1.9	0.9
Quick Ratio 31	0.7	•	2.1	1.5	1.1	0.8	0.3	0.8	1.3	0.7	1.1	1.2	0.6
Net Sales to Working Capital 32	•	•	13.5	5.6	4.5	4.8	•	4.7	4.4	7.6	3.6	4.6	•
Coverage Ratio 33	1.2	•	2.1	•	6.3	4.3	•	1.3	4.7	0.1	8.7	1.6	1.4
Total Asset Turnover 34	0.5	•	5.0	3.3	1.6	1.3	1.7	0.9	1.4	1.1	0.7	0.7	0.4
Inventory Turnover 35	6.4	•	5.1	8.3	3.2	3.1	3.8	3.1	4.1	2.5	3.8	5.9	9.5
Receivables Turnover 36	3.4	•	27.6	7.4	6.5	8.4	7.5	6.0	5.3	3.1	3.9	4.7	2.8
Total Liabilities to Net Worth 37	2.6	•	•	3.0	2.7	0.8	•	1.1	1.0	2.6	1.2	1.5	2.7
Current Assets to Working Capital 38	•	•	1.5	1.6	1.9	2.3	2.6	1.8	3.3	2.9	2.1	•	•
Current Liabilities to Working Capital 39	•	•	0.5	0.6	1.3	0.9	1.6	0.8	2.3	1.9	1.1	•	•
Working Capital to Net Sales 40	•	•	0.1	0.2	0.2	0.2	0.2	0.2	0.1	0.1	0.3	0.2	•
Inventory to Working Capital 41	•	•	0.5	0.7	0.7	1.2	1.1	0.6	1.2	0.6	0.6	0.5	•
Total Receipts to Cash Flow 42	7.8	•	7.0	19.2	6.4	8.2	10.4	6.3	8.2	3.3	7.1		6.7
Cost of Goods to Cash Flow 43	4.2	•	2.1	15.0	3.4	5.6	6.7	3.5	5.0	2.0	4.2		3.4
Cash Flow to Total Debt 44	0.1	•	0.5	0.2	0.3	0.4	0.2	0.5	0.2	0.4	0.2		0.1

Selected Financial Factors (in Percentages)

	1	2	3	4	5	6	7	8	9	10	11	12	13
Debt Ratio 45	71.9	•	134.5	75.0	73.0	44.3	150.0	51.9	49.4	71.8	54.1	60.1	73.3
Return on Total Assets 46	3.4	•	4.2	•	10.7	5.0	•	2.2	11.1	0.2	14.7	5.6	3.9
Return on Equity Before Income Taxes 47	1.9	•	•	•	33.3	6.9	160.1	1.0	17.2	•	28.3	5.1	3.9
Return on Equity After Income Taxes 48	•	•	•	•	30.9	6.5	161.8	14.2	•	•	23.1	3.2	2.2
Profit Margin (Before Income Tax) 49	1.0	0.4	5.8	2.9	5.8	2.9	0.5	6.2	14.2	18.1	2.8	2.5	
Profit Margin (After Income Tax) 50	•	0.3	•	5.4	2.7	•	5.1	6.2	14.8	18.1	1.7	1.4	

127

Table II

Corporations with Net Income

COMMERCIAL AND SERVICE INDUSTRY MACHINERY

MONEY AMOUNTS AND SIZE OF ASSETS IN THOUSANDS OF DOLLARS

Item Description for Accounting Period 7/02 Through 6/03	Total	Zero Assets	Under 500	500 to 1,000	1,000 to 5,000	5,000 to 10,000	10,000 to 25,000	25,000 to 50,000	50,000 to 100,000	100,000 to 250,000	250,000 to 500,000	500,000 to 2,500,000	2,500,000 and over
Number of Enterprises 1	1349	0	832	•	324	100	34	0	0	4	0	0	0
Revenues ($ in Thousands)													
Net Sales 2	36864685	0	742527	•	1357711	867699	836375	0	0	599023	0	0	0
Interest 3	1169026	0	293	•	1305	209	1003	0	0	173	0	0	0
Rents 4	594684	0	3989	•	3319	1585	147	0	0	2354	0	0	0
Royalties 5	811103	0	0	•	0	0	516	0	0	4202	0	0	0
Other Portfolio Income 6	713177	0	266	•	1507	1012	440	0	0	2705	0	0	0
Other Receipts 7	1170254	0	2318	•	74852	12164	2293	0	0	10131	0	0	0
Total Receipts 8	41322929	0	749393	•	1438694	882669	840774	0	0	618588	0	0	0
Average Total Receipts 9	30632	•	901	•	4440	8827	24729	•	•	154647	•	•	•
Operating Costs/Operating Income (%)													
Cost of Operations 10	55.7	•	26.4	•	53.8	69.6	63.5	•	•	54.1	•	•	•
Salaries and Wages 11	15.2	•	36.2	•	14.4	5.6	9.1	•	•	13.0	•	•	•
Taxes Paid 12	2.1	•	4.6	•	2.6	1.5	2.5	•	•	1.5	•	•	•
Interest Paid 13	4.6	•	0.4	•	0.5	0.4	0.8	•	•	1.4	•	•	•
Depreciation 14	5.4	•	2.1	•	1.5	2.7	2.3	•	•	3.6	•	•	•
Amortization and Depletion 15	0.6	•	•	•	0.1	0.0	0.1	•	•	0.8	•	•	•
Pensions and Other Deferred Comp. 16	0.9	•	0.5	•	0.7	0.5	0.9	•	•	1.1	•	•	•
Employee Benefits 17	5.2	•	1.7	•	2.1	0.9	1.9	•	•	2.8	•	•	•
Advertising 18	1.7	•	1.9	•	0.7	0.4	0.7	•	•	1.3	•	•	•
Other Expenses 19	16.2	•	16.2	•	12.3	9.7	9.3	•	•	19.9	•	•	•
Officers' Compensation 20	0.9	•	6.1	•	5.6	3.2	2.7	•	•	1.0	•	•	•
Operating Margin 21	•	•	3.9	•	5.7	5.4	6.3	•	•	•	•	•	•
Operating Margin Before Officers' Comp. 22	•	•	10.0	•	11.3	8.6	9.0	•	•	0.5	•	•	•

Selected Average Balance Sheet ($ in Thousands)

Net Receivables 23	7831	22	668	1152	3701	22853
Inventories 24	1990	34	542	2038	5581	25162
Net Property, Plant and Equipment 25	6374	80	206	1677	2791	23917
Total Assets 26	48481	176	2165	6731	15860	145690
Notes and Loans Payable 27	13863	112	363	771	2896	54642
All Other Liabilities 28	17900	7	596	1805	4653	56844
Net Worth 29	16718	56	1206	4154	8311	34204

Selected Financial Ratios (Times to 1)

Current Ratio 30	1.1	3.2	2.1	1.8	2.2	1.2
Quick Ratio 31	0.7	2.1	1.1	0.8	1.1	0.6
Net Sales to Working Capital 32	17.5	13.8	5.1	4.5	4.1	19.8
Coverage Ratio 33	2.0	12.6	26.8	16.7	9.7	3.0
Total Asset Turnover 34	0.6	5.1	1.9	1.3	1.6	1.0
Inventory Turnover 35	7.6	6.9	4.2	3.0	2.8	3.2
Receivables Turnover 36	3.4	42.9	6.5	8.3	5.2	3.8
Total Liabilities to Net Worth 37	1.9	2.1	0.8	0.6	0.9	3.3
Current Assets to Working Capital 38	10.2	1.5	1.9	2.2	1.8	7.3
Current Liabilities to Working Capital 39	9.2	0.5	0.9	1.2	0.8	6.3
Working Capital to Net Sales 40	0.1	0.1	0.2	0.2	0.2	0.1
Inventory to Working Capital 41	1.4	0.5	0.7	1.2	0.8	2.8
Total Receipts to Cash Flow 42	6.1	5.6	4.8	6.4	6.8	5.0
Cost of Goods to Cash Flow 43	3.4	1.5	2.6	4.5	4.3	2.7
Cash Flow to Total Debt 44	0.1	1.3	0.9	0.5	0.5	0.3

Selected Financial Factors (in Percentages)

Debt Ratio 45	65.5	68.0	44.3	38.3	47.6	76.5
Return on Total Assets 46	5.2	26.6	23.5	9.7	11.8	4.2
Return on Equity Before Income Taxes 47	7.7	76.5	40.6	14.7	20.2	11.8
Return on Equity After Income Taxes 48	5.7	74.5	39.0	14.3	17.4	10.5
Profit Margin (Before Income Tax) 49	4.7	4.8	11.7	7.1	6.8	2.7
Profit Margin (After Income Tax) 50	3.5	4.7	11.2	6.9	5.9	2.4

VENTILATION, HEATING, A.C. & COMMERCIAL REFRIGERATION EQUIP.

Table I
Corporations with and without Net Income

MONEY AMOUNTS AND SIZE OF ASSETS IN THOUSANDS OF DOLLARS

Item Description for Accounting Period 7/02 Through 6/03	Total	Zero Assets	Under 500	500 to 1,000	1,000 to 5,000	5,000 to 10,000	10,000 to 25,000	25,000 to 50,000	50,000 to 100,000	100,000 to 250,000	250,000 to 500,000	500,000 to 2,500,000	2,500,000 and over
Number of Enterprises **1**	869	235	134	187	135	48	66	33	10	12	0	8	0
Revenues ($ in Thousands)													
Net Sales **2**	24292259	8645	119601	320124	356386	593944	1857935	1818963	1021341	2819477	0	15575843	0
Interest **3**	43928	452	0	213	416	339	2577	1569	2640	1968	0	33754	0
Rents **4**	9563	0	0	638	0	117	791	1066	1139	1520	0	4292	0
Royalties **5**	264753	74	0	0	0	0	386	1204	627	2385	0	260078	0
Other Portfolio Income **6**	131400	6	108	635	0	0	6259	1614	2085	31321	0	89369	0
Other Receipts **7**	235827	5	0	6706	100	6691	18022	8025	5288	9718	0	181275	0
Total Receipts **8**	24977730	9182	119709	328316	356902	601091	1885970	1832441	1033120	2866389	0	15944611	0
Average Total Receipts **9**	28743	39	893	1756	2644	12523	28575	55529	103312	238866	•	1993076	•
Operating Costs/Operating Income (%)													
Cost of Operations **10**	72.2	55.5	83.3	64.5	66.0	57.2	70.2	66.5	63.8	72.6	•	74.4	•
Salaries and Wages **11**	7.1	3.4	12.5	8.3	6.1	8.8	8.2	8.0	8.3	7.2	•	6.7	•
Taxes Paid **12**	1.2	3.9	0.3	2.4	2.7	3.4	2.2	1.8	1.4	1.3	•	0.8	•
Interest Paid **13**	2.1	2.2	0.3	0.1	2.8	0.7	0.9	1.0	0.6	1.8	•	2.6	•
Depreciation **14**	2.2	2.8	1.3	2.2	1.8	4.9	2.5	2.8	3.1	2.0	•	2.0	•
Amortization and Depletion **15**	0.4	0.9	0.3	•	0.2	0.0	0.1	0.3	0.3	0.5	•	0.4	•
Pensions and Other Deferred Comp. **16**	0.7	0.0	•	1.4	0.0	0.9	0.7	0.6	0.7	0.6	•	0.8	•
Employee Benefits **17**	2.1	8.1	0.2	1.8	1.1	11.7	1.8	1.9	2.6	1.9	•	1.9	•
Advertising **18**	1.1	1.8	2.6	0.6	1.4	0.3	0.7	0.8	1.0	1.0	•	1.3	•
Other Expenses **19**	9.8	55.3	15.0	6.1	11.2	10.6	9.9	9.0	9.4	8.6	•	10.0	•
Officers' Compensation **20**	1.1	5.4	•	15.4	5.2	2.5	2.1	2.2	1.4	0.8	•	0.5	•
Operating Margin **21**	•	•	•	•	1.4	•	0.5	5.2	7.3	1.7	•	•	•
Operating Margin Before Officers' Comp. **22**	1.1	•	•	12.6	6.6	1.5	2.7	7.3	8.8	2.5	•	•	•

Selected Average Balance Sheet ($ in Thousands)

	1	2	3	4	5	6	7	8	9	10	11
Net Receivables 23	4315	0	23	143	243	2642	4260	7894	18715	26173	314711
Inventories 24	2833	0	0	122	504	781	3644	6957	16272	31878	164567
Net Property, Plant and Equipment 25	3931	0	0	189	148	2708	4246	9112	16656	28511	267644
Total Assets 26	27295	82	635	1720	7410	16492	35634	70210	169341		2250379
Notes and Loans Payable 27	6560	0	0	64	901	1695	4601	8051	8150	47517	533137
All Other Liabilities 28	13909	85	160	318	1769	4082	7404	19884	45066		1333012
Net Worth 29	6826	-3	411	500	3946	7809	20180	42176	76758		384231

Selected Financial Ratios (Times to 1)

	1	2	3	4	5	6	7	8	9	10	11
Current Ratio 30	1.0	•	1.0	1.8	2.2	1.6	2.0	2.5	2.1	1.7	0.8
Quick Ratio 31	0.5	•	0.3	1.1	1.0	1.2	1.1	1.4	1.2	0.8	0.4
Net Sales to Working Capital 32	5042.0	•	•	11.5	5.5	8.2	5.3	4.6	4.9	8.8	•
Coverage Ratio 33	2.6	•	•	•	1.6	1.2	3.2	7.4	14.9	3.1	2.3
Total Asset Turnover 34	1.0	•	10.9	2.7	1.5	1.7	1.7	1.5	1.5	1.4	0.9
Inventory Turnover 35	7.1	•	•	9.0	3.5	9.1	5.4	5.3	4.0	5.4	8.7
Receivables Turnover 36	6.1	•	76.3	12.7	7.3	6.3	6.6	6.9	4.2	9.0	5.7
Total Liabilities to Net Worth 37	3.0	•	•	0.5	2.4	0.9	1.1	0.8	0.7	1.2	4.9
Current Assets to Working Capital 38	1760.4	•	•	2.3	1.9	2.8	2.0	1.7	1.9	2.5	•
Current Liabilities to Working Capital 39	1759.4	•	•	1.3	0.9	1.8	1.0	0.7	0.9	1.5	•
Working Capital to Net Sales 40	0.0	•	•	0.1	0.2	0.1	0.2	0.2	0.2	0.1	•
Inventory to Working Capital 41	515.6	•	•	0.7	0.9	0.5	0.7	0.6	0.7	1.1	•
Total Receipts to Cash Flow 42	9.2	5.8	31.3	9.6	14.1	10.0	7.6	5.9	10.0		9.3
Cost of Goods to Cash Flow 43	6.7	3.2	20.2	6.3	8.1	7.0	5.0	3.8	7.2		6.9
Cash Flow to Total Debt 44	0.1	•	0.2	0.2	0.3	0.3	0.5	0.6	0.3		0.1

Selected Financial Factors (in Percentages)

	1	2	3	4	5	6	7	8	9	10	11
Debt Ratio 45	75.0	•	103.1	35.3	70.9	46.7	52.6	43.4	39.9	54.7	82.9
Return on Total Assets 46	5.6	•	•	6.6	1.4	5.1	10.9	13.4	7.7		5.0
Return on Equity Before Income Taxes 47	13.9	•	5468.7	8.2	0.5	7.3	16.6	20.7	11.5		16.2
Return on Equity After Income Taxes 48	9.5	•	5468.7	•	•	5.0	13.8	14.0	8.3		10.9
Profit Margin (Before Income Tax) 49	3.4	•	•	1.5	0.1	2.0	6.1	8.6	3.8		3.2
Profit Margin (After Income Tax) 50	2.3	•	•	•	•	1.4	5.0	5.8	2.7		2.2

VENTILATION, HEATING, A.C. & COMMERCIAL REFRIGERATION EQUIP.

Table II

Corporations with Net Income

MONEY AMOUNTS AND SIZE OF ASSETS IN THOUSANDS OF DOLLARS

Item Description for Accounting Period 7/02 Through 6/03	Total	Zero Assets	Under 500	500 to 1,000	1,000 to 5,000	5,000 to 10,000	10,000 to 25,000	25,000 to 50,000	50,000 to 100,000	100,000 to 250,000	250,000 to 500,000	500,000 to 2,500,000	2,500,000 and over
Number of Enterprises **1**	320	•	27	0	49	29	42	27	0	8	0	0	0
Revenues ($ in Thousands)													
Net Sales **2**	20398481	•	110621	0	167581	418159	1305739	1570058	0	1491927	0	0	0
Interest **3**	36174	•	0	0	105	298	1314	1460	0	649	0	0	0
Rents **4**	6618	•	0	0	0	0	777	1042	0	1475	0	0	0
Royalties **5**	172485	•	0	0	0	0	33	1204	0	738	0	0	0
Other Portfolio Income **6**	125334	•	108	0	0	0	3986	1325	0	27955	0	0	0
Other Receipts **7**	210603	•	-1	0	36	4918	6494	4847	0	8144	0	0	0
Total Receipts **8**	20949695	•	110728	0	167722	423375	1318343	1579936	0	1530888	0	0	0
Average Total Receipts **9**	65468	•	4101	•	3423	14599	31389	58516	•	191361	•	•	•
Operating Costs/Operating Income (%)													
Cost of Operations **10**	71.5	•	85.7	•	59.6	54.5	69.2	65.4	•	68.2	•	•	•
Salaries and Wages **11**	6.8	•	3.0	•	5.0	5.5	8.0	7.8	•	6.5	•	•	•
Taxes Paid **12**	1.1	•	0.3	•	3.0	3.8	2.0	1.8	•	1.4	•	•	•
Interest Paid **13**	1.9	•	•	•	3.3	0.3	0.7	0.7	•	1.2	•	•	•
Depreciation **14**	2.1	•	0.2	•	2.8	2.8	2.1	2.8	•	1.9	•	•	•
Amortization and Depletion **15**	0.3	•	•	•	0.2	•	0.1	0.2	•	0.2	•	•	•
Pensions and Other Deferred Comp. **16**	0.8	•	•	•	0.1	1.1	0.7	0.7	•	0.6	•	•	•
Employee Benefits **17**	2.2	•	0.3	•	0.6	14.2	1.4	1.9	•	2.0	•	•	•
Advertising **18**	1.3	•	0.4	•	1.1	0.4	0.6	0.9	•	1.7	•	•	•
Other Expenses **19**	9.4	•	5.2	•	7.9	4.9	8.5	8.6	•	10.6	•	•	•
Officers' Compensation **20**	1.0	•	•	•	5.0	2.7	1.8	2.3	•	0.8	•	•	•
Operating Margin **21**	1.6	•	5.0	•	11.5	9.8	4.9	6.9	•	4.9	•	•	•
Operating Margin Before Officers' Comp. **22**	2.6	•	5.0	•	16.4	12.5	6.7	9.2	•	5.7	•	•	•

Selected Average Balance Sheet ($ in Thousands)

Net Receivables 23	10180	·	116	398	3543	4407	8332	·	24894
Inventories 24	5252	·	0	284	696	3466	7003	·	28749
Net Property, Plant and Equipment 25	8691	·	0	240	1948	4084	9182	·	24253
Total Assets 26	63135	·	406	2297	7807	16538	35167	·	164880
Notes and Loans Payable 27	13740	·	0	1223	1221	4231	7277	·	26630
All Other Liabilities 28	33384	·	421	365	1786	3411	7154	·	38390
Net Worth 29	16011	·	-14	708	4800	8896	20736	·	99860

Selected Financial Ratios (Times to 1)

Current Ratio 30	0.9	·	0.9	2.3	2.7	2.6	2.5	·	1.9
Quick Ratio 31	0.5	·	0.3	1.3	2.1	1.6	1.5	·	0.9
Net Sales to Working Capital 32	·	·	6.1	4.1	4.7	4.7	·	·	6.4
Coverage Ratio 33	3.5	·	4.5	33.6	9.1	11.7	·	·	7.9
Total Asset Turnover 34	1.0	10.1	1.5	1.8	1.9	1.7	·	·	1.1
Inventory Turnover 35	8.7	·	7.2	11.3	6.2	5.4	·	·	4.4
Receivables Turnover 36	6.3	·	13.8	5.9	7.3	6.9	·	·	15.0
Total Liabilities to Net Worth 37	2.9	·	2.2	0.6	0.9	0.7	·	·	0.7
Current Assets to Working Capital 38	·	·	1.8	1.6	1.6	1.7	·	·	2.1
Current Liabilities to Working Capital 39	·	·	0.8	0.6	0.6	0.7	·	·	1.1
Working Capital to Net Sales 40	·	·	0.2	0.2	0.2	0.2	·	·	0.2
Inventory to Working Capital 41	·	·	0.7	0.2	0.5	0.6	·	·	1.0
Total Receipts to Cash Flow 42	8.3	11.1	5.9	7.1	8.0	6.9	·	·	6.6
Cost of Goods to Cash Flow 43	6.0	9.5	3.5	3.9	5.5	4.5	·	·	4.5
Cash Flow to Total Debt 44	0.2	0.9	0.4	0.7	0.5	0.6	·	·	0.4

Selected Financial Factors (in Percentages)

Debt Ratio 45	74.6	103.6	69.2	38.5	46.2	41.0	·	·	39.4
Return on Total Assets 46	6.9	51.4	22.2	20.9	12.4	13.9	·	·	10.7
Return on Equity Before Income Taxes 47	19.5	·	55.8	33.1	20.5	21.5	·	·	15.4
Return on Equity After Income Taxes 48	14.5	·	39.3	31.8	17.3	18.2	·	·	11.7
Profit Margin (Before Income Tax) 49	4.9	5.1	11.6	11.0	5.9	7.7	·	·	8.3
Profit Margin (After Income Tax) 50	3.6	5.1	8.1	10.6	4.9	6.5	·	·	6.3

Table I

Corporations with and without Net Income

METALWORKING MACHINERY

MONEY AMOUNTS AND SIZE OF ASSETS IN THOUSANDS OF DOLLARS

Item Description for Accounting Period 7/02 Through 6/03		Total	Zero Assets	Under 500	500 to 1,000	1,000 to 5,000	5,000 to 10,000	10,000 to 25,000	25,000 to 50,000	50,000 to 100,000	100,000 to 250,000	250,000 to 500,000	500,000 to 2,500,000	2,500,000 and over
Number of Enterprises	1	6307	11	4147	700	1066	197	107	46	18	12	0	3	0
Revenues ($ in Thousands)														
Net Sales	2	20070255	39805	1610262	819076	3964726	1724433	1991452	1544814	1260279	1579869	0	5535540	0
Interest	3	231659	36	2543	2227	2904	2323	2062	7034	4207	13790	0	194533	0
Rents	4	19398	0	0	1487	1405	8198	1345	640	671	3862	0	1789	0
Royalties	5	154522	0	0	0	0	0	513	279	24	3261	0	150445	0
Other Portfolio Income	6	76496	1839	450	2248	3012	1906	19336	6168	8932	26574	0	6032	0
Other Receipts	7	189063	78	2939	2467	9845	7744	20040	15142	3882	53000	0	73925	0
Total Receipts	8	20741393	41758	1616194	827505	3981892	1744604	2034748	1574077	1277995	1680356	0	5962264	0
Average Total Receipts	9	3289	3796	390	1182	3735	8856	19016	34219	71000	140030	·	1987421	·
Operating Costs/Operating Income (%)														
Cost of Operations	10	65.0	64.3	45.7	57.7	65.0	67.2	69.2	70.1	69.1	70.2	·	65.7	·
Salaries and Wages	11	7.9	14.1	5.4	6.1	4.8	5.7	7.6	7.9	10.8	13.4	·	9.6	·
Taxes Paid	12	2.9	4.6	3.4	5.0	3.4	3.8	3.1	3.5	2.5	2.2	·	1.9	·
Interest Paid	13	3.7	6.7	1.9	2.4	1.0	1.3	1.8	2.2	2.3	5.2	·	8.2	·
Depreciation	14	4.7	2.4	5.1	7.0	5.0	5.8	5.4	5.2	4.9	4.0	·	3.4	·
Amortization and Depletion	15	0.4	1.7	0.1	0.3	0.0	0.1	0.2	0.6	0.5	0.5	·	0.8	·
Pensions and Other Deferred Comp.	16	0.5	0.3	0.3	0.8	0.4	0.7	0.4	0.6	1.0	0.7	·	0.2	·
Employee Benefits	17	2.8	1.1	2.0	4.1	2.1	4.6	2.6	3.1	2.7	2.6	·	2.9	·
Advertising	18	0.5	1.2	0.1	0.6	0.3	0.2	0.4	0.4	0.6	1.0	·	0.8	·
Other Expenses	19	12.3	20.9	28.4	9.9	10.5	8.7	8.1	7.6	6.1	8.6	·	15.7	·
Officers' Compensation	20	3.3	1.9	8.5	8.2	5.9	4.1	2.8	2.1	1.6	1.1	·	0.6	·
Operating Margin	21	·	·	·	·	1.5	·	·	·	·	·	·	·	·
Operating Margin Before Officers' Comp.	22	·	·	7.7	6.0	7.4	1.8	1.2	·	·	·	·	·	·

Selected Average Balance Sheet ($ in Thousands)

Net Receivables 23	765	0	51	178	528	1403	3564	7958	14209	53356	668418
Inventories 24	474	0	14	106	362	1541	3126	7194	12658	40642	262291
Net Property, Plant and Equipment 25	710	0	48	301	819	2379	5086	9475	18627	30995	345006
Total Assets 26	3630	0	161	793	2213	6408	15191	33209	66502	180292	3845290
Notes and Loans Payable 27	1681	0	109	473	634	2133	6024	10673	16088	117742	1961124
All Other Liabilities 28	930	0	31	140	369	1996	3010	9564	15258	55572	1050966
Net Worth 29	1019	0	22	180	1210	2278	6157	12971	35156	6978	833199

Selected Financial Ratios (Times to 1)

Current Ratio 30	1.4	•	1.9	1.8	1.8	1.3	1.6	1.6	2.0	0.8	1.4
Quick Ratio 31	0.9	•	1.5	1.4	1.2	0.7	0.9	0.8	1.1	0.5	0.9
Net Sales to Working Capital 32	7.0	•	8.4	5.8	6.8	9.5	6.1	4.4	4.2	•	5.3
Coverage Ratio 33	0.8	•	0.7	0.5	2.8	0.2	1.3	0.3	0.8	0.4	0.8
Total Asset Turnover 34	0.9	•	2.4	1.5	1.7	1.4	1.2	1.0	1.1	0.7	0.5
Inventory Turnover 35	4.4	•	12.4	6.4	6.7	3.8	4.1	3.3	3.8	2.3	4.6
Receivables Turnover 36	4.4	•	9.2	5.0	6.6	6.5	4.9	4.9	5.1	2.5	3.1
Total Liabilities to Net Worth 37	2.6	•	6.5	3.4	0.8	1.8	1.5	1.6	0.9	24.8	3.6
Current Assets to Working Capital 38	3.6	•	2.1	2.2	2.2	4.0	2.7	2.6	2.0	•	3.7
Current Liabilities to Working Capital 39	2.6	•	1.1	1.2	1.2	3.0	1.7	1.6	1.0	•	2.7
Working Capital to Net Sales 40	0.1	•	0.1	0.2	0.1	0.1	0.2	0.2	0.2	•	0.2
Inventory to Working Capital 41	1.0	•	0.4	0.5	0.7	1.8	0.9	1.0	0.7	•	0.7
Total Receipts to Cash Flow 42	11.6	19.7	4.6	18.6	11.1	26.5	20.0	23.6	24.8	53.6	8.4
Cost of Goods to Cash Flow 43	7.6	12.7	2.1	10.7	7.2	17.8	13.8	16.6	17.2	37.6	5.5
Cash Flow to Total Debt 44	0.1	•	0.6	0.1	0.3	0.1	0.1	0.1	0.1	0.0	0.1

Selected Financial Factors (in Percentages)

Debt Ratio 45	71.9	•	86.6	77.4	45.3	64.4	59.5	60.9	47.1	96.1	78.3
Return on Total Assets 46	2.6	•	3.2	1.8	4.9	0.3	2.8	0.7	1.9	1.6	3.0
Return on Equity Before Income Taxes 47	•	•	•	•	5.8	•	1.5	•	•	•	•
Return on Equity After Income Taxes 48	•	•	•	•	5.5	•	0.4	•	•	•	•
Profit Margin (Before Income Tax) 49	•	•	•	•	1.9	•	0.5	•	•	•	•
Profit Margin (After Income Tax) 50	•	•	•	•	1.8	•	0.1	•	•	•	•

Table II
Corporations with Net Income

METALWORKING MACHINERY

MONEY AMOUNTS AND SIZE OF ASSETS IN THOUSANDS OF DOLLARS

Item Description for Accounting Period 7/02 Through 6/03	Total	Zero Assets	Under 500	500 to 1,000	1,000 to 5,000	5,000 to 10,000	10,000 to 25,000	25,000 to 50,000	50,000 to 100,000	100,000 to 250,000	250,000 to 500,000	500,000 to 2,500,000	2,500,000 and over
Number of Enterprises **1**	3280	0	2049	0	563	110	55	22	9	3	·	·	·
Revenues ($ in Thousands)													
Net Sales **2**	7636296	0	628061	0	2560374	967062	1158697	810343	738830	210019	·	·	·
Interest **3**	14513	0	65	0	496	1016	1336	2907	986	6307	·	·	·
Rents **4**	5984	0	0	0	178	2142	365	56	348	2896	·	·	·
Royalties **5**	87	0	0	0	0	0	0	63	24	0	·	·	·
Other Portfolio Income **6**	56759	0	448	0	1544	1202	15549	3081	7684	23266	·	·	·
Other Receipts **7**	57949	0	550	0	4531	1270	9564	8067	1273	32005	·	·	·
Total Receipts **8**	7771588	0	629124	0	2567123	972692	1185511	824517	749145	274493	·	·	·
Average Total Receipts **9**	2369	·	307	·	4560	8843	21555	37478	83238	91498	·	·	·
Operating Costs/Operating Income (%)													
Cost of Operations **10**	63.7	·	43.9	·	66.2	64.1	67.4	69.0	63.7	75.5	·	·	·
Salaries and Wages **11**	5.1	·	3.6	·	3.1	3.4	6.4	6.4	10.7	11.3	·	·	·
Taxes Paid **12**	3.1	·	4.0	·	3.0	3.3	2.7	3.0	2.3	3.1	·	·	·
Interest Paid **13**	1.4	·	1.4	·	0.6	1.1	1.3	1.6	1.2	5.9	·	·	·
Depreciation **14**	5.1	·	5.7	·	4.2	7.0	4.5	4.9	4.3	5.0	·	·	·
Amortization and Depletion **15**	0.2	·	0.0	·	0.0	0.1	0.1	0.7	0.3	1.4	·	·	·
Pensions and Other Deferred Comp. **16**	0.6	·	0.5	·	0.4	0.7	0.5	0.7	1.2	0.5	·	·	·
Employee Benefits **17**	2.3	·	2.6	·	1.8	3.2	2.1	2.7	2.3	2.4	·	·	·
Advertising **18**	0.3	·	0.1	·	0.2	0.2	0.3	0.3	0.4	0.3	·	·	·
Other Expenses **19**	8.6	·	18.8	·	9.1	6.6	7.3	4.3	8.7	3.8	·	·	·
Officers' Compensation **20**	4.9	·	11.2	·	5.3	5.0	2.9	1.9	1.8	2.8	·	·	·
Operating Margin **21**	4.7	·	8.2	·	6.1	5.4	4.3	4.4	3.2	·	·	·	·
Operating Margin Before Officers' Comp. **22**	9.6	·	19.4	·	11.4	10.3	7.3	6.3	5.0	·	·	·	·

Selected Average Balance Sheet ($ in Thousands)

Net Receivables 23	496	41	•	673	1582	3602	8880	18286	116964
Inventories 24	351	9	•	317	1124	3037	7584	10511	121106
Net Property, Plant and Equipment 25	485	37	•	746	2125	4454	9094	18788	24101
Total Assets 26	1626	120	•	2248	6067	15031	34954	70919	178398
Notes and Loans Payable 27	512	102	•	511	1631	4937	9781	18108	36137
All Other Liabilities 28	356	11	•	440	1552	2977	7237	15912	72855
Net Worth 29	758	7	•	1297	2884	7117	17937	36899	69406

Selected Financial Ratios (Times to 1)

Current Ratio 30	1.8	2.5	•	1.9	1.9	1.8	2.1	2.0	1.3
Quick Ratio 31	1.2	2.1	•	1.4	1.1	1.0	1.2	1.2	1.1
Net Sales to Working Capital 32	5.1	6.3	•	6.8	5.2	5.4	3.1	4.0	2.2
Coverage Ratio 33	5.8	6.8	•	10.8	6.5	6.0	4.7	5.1	4.2
Total Asset Turnover 34	1.4	2.6	•	2.0	1.4	1.4	1.1	1.2	0.4
Inventory Turnover 35	4.2	15.3	•	9.5	5.0	4.7	3.4	5.0	0.4
Receivables Turnover 36	3.8	8.5	•	6.8	6.4	5.7	5.2	5.0	0.3
Total Liabilities to Net Worth 37	1.1	15.7	•	0.7	1.1	1.1	0.9	0.9	1.6
Current Assets to Working Capital 38	2.2	1.7	•	2.1	2.2	2.3	1.9	2.0	4.6
Current Liabilities to Working Capital 39	1.2	0.7	•	1.1	1.2	1.3	0.9	1.0	3.6
Working Capital to Net Sales 40	0.2	0.2	•	0.1	0.2	0.2	0.3	0.3	0.4
Inventory to Working Capital 41	0.6	0.2	•	0.5	0.7	0.8	0.6	0.6	0.5
Total Receipts to Cash Flow 42	8.5	4.8	•	8.1	9.9	10.1	11.2	8.5	10.7
Cost of Goods to Cash Flow 43	5.4	2.1	•	5.4	6.3	6.8	7.7	5.4	8.1
Cash Flow to Total Debt 44	0.3	0.6	•	0.6	0.3	0.3	0.2	0.3	0.1

Selected Financial Factors (in Percentages)

Debt Ratio 45	53.4	94.0	•	42.3	52.5	52.7	48.7	48.0	61.1
Return on Total Assets 46	11.3	25.1	•	14.2	10.2	11.2	8.2	7.1	9.7
Return on Equity Before Income Taxes 47	20.1	356.7	•	22.3	18.2	19.7	12.6	11.0	18.9
Return on Equity After Income Taxes 48	18.6	352.6	•	21.8	16.1	17.9	10.6	9.6	17.1
Profit Margin (Before Income Tax) 49	6.5	8.4	•	6.4	6.0	6.7	6.1	5.0	18.8
Profit Margin (After Income Tax) 50	6.1	8.3	•	6.2	5.3	6.0	5.1	4.3	16.9

Table I
Corporations with and without Net Income

ENGINE, TURBINE AND POWER TRANSMISSION EQUIPMENT

MONEY AMOUNTS AND SIZE OF ASSETS IN THOUSANDS OF DOLLARS

Item Description for Accounting Period 7/02 Through 6/03	Total	Zero Assets	Under 500	500 to 1,000	1,000 to 5,000	5,000 to 10,000	10,000 to 25,000	25,000 to 50,000	50,000 to 100,000	100,000 to 250,000	250,000 to 500,000	500,000 to 2,500,000	2,500,000 and over
Number of Enterprises **1**	394	0	0	0	252	49	29	8	5	12	0	6	4
Revenues ($ in Thousands)													
Net Sales **2**	39385112	0	0	0	814341	597984	703871	356844	371620	2841338	0	3219441	30470541
Interest **3**	742033	0	0	0	271	714	557	977	9751	20409	0	27660	681678
Rents **4**	292837	0	0	0	0	741	347	119	894	1116	0	27839	261781
Royalties **5**	239887	0	0	0	0	0	0	197	3994	14182	0	5960	215556
Other Portfolio Income **6**	211021	0	0	0	129	1350	456	934	229	8743	0	34611	164569
Other Receipts **7**	608732	0	0	0	4934	4568	6702	1394	9079	55026	0	85269	441640
Total Receipts **8**	41479622	0	0	0	819675	605357	711933	360465	395567	2940814	0	3400780	32235765
Average Total Receipts **9**	105278	•	•	•	3253	12354	24549	45058	79113	245068	•	566797	8058941
Operating Costs/Operating Income (%)													
Cost of Operations **10**	65.3	•	•	•	71.1	68.2	72.3	66.0	76.6	72.7	•	73.1	63.3
Salaries and Wages **11**	14.0	•	•	•	7.3	4.2	5.7	8.1	8.4	6.9	•	11.0	15.7
Taxes Paid **12**	2.4	•	•	•	2.6	2.8	1.8	1.6	1.6	2.0	•	1.4	2.6
Interest Paid **13**	2.6	•	•	•	1.7	2.6	1.3	3.3	4.0	1.7	•	2.9	2.7
Depreciation **14**	3.4	•	•	•	1.7	3.8	3.7	3.3	3.2	3.7	•	4.2	3.3
Amortization and Depletion **15**	0.5	•	•	•	0.6	0.2	0.1	0.2	1.5	1.7	•	1.1	0.3
Pensions and Other Deferred Comp. **16**	1.5	•	•	•	0.7	0.3	0.8	0.5	2.0	0.7	•	1.4	1.6
Employee Benefits **17**	2.4	•	•	•	1.7	2.7	2.2	1.9	2.2	2.6	•	1.2	2.5
Advertising **18**	0.7	•	•	•	0.8	0.3	0.4	0.2	0.7	0.6	•	0.9	0.7
Other Expenses **19**	10.3	•	•	•	13.7	8.4	7.4	11.0	13.0	7.7	•	6.4	10.9
Officers' Compensation **20**	0.7	•	•	•	4.7	3.7	1.9	3.6	1.0	0.8	•	0.7	0.5
Operating Margin **21**	•	•	•	•	•	2.9	2.6	0.4	•	•	•	•	•
Operating Margin Before Officers' Comp. **22**	•	•	•	•	•	6.6	4.5	3.9	•	•	•	•	•

Selected Average Balance Sheet ($ in Thousands)

Net Receivables 23	18529	347	1651	3319	8226	14370	36077	300241	1165935
Inventories 24	12266	449	1061	3916	8481	14023	30576	91592	868812
Net Property, Plant and Equipment 25	15426	293	2489	5731	7743	17368	45516	150714	1028092
Total Assets 26	94141	1980	7569	16391	33086	72906	228554	988824	6611946
Notes and Loans Payable 27	24605	881	4161	5343	13266	38596	52313	392852	1457403
All Other Liabilities 28	54770	637	1705	4422	12454	30521	75739	406393	4401820
Net Worth 29	14766	461	1703	6626	7367	3790	100502	187579	752723

Selected Financial Ratios (Times to 1)

Current Ratio 30	1.3	1.6	1.4	1.6	1.5	1.2	1.7	1.8	1.1
Quick Ratio 31	0.7	0.7	0.7	0.8	0.8	0.6	1.0	1.3	0.6
Net Sales to Working Capital 32	10.7	7.7	11.2	6.5	6.5	14.2	4.9	2.1	24.3
Coverage Ratio 33	1.6		2.6	4.0	1.4		2.6	1.6	1.7
Total Asset Turnover 34	1.1	1.6	1.6	1.5	1.3	1.0	1.0	0.5	1.2
Inventory Turnover 35	5.3	5.1	7.8	4.5	3.5	4.1	5.6	4.3	5.5
Receivables Turnover 36	5.8	11.5	10.2	7.6	5.1	10.3	8.4	1.8	7.1
Total Liabilities to Net Worth 37	5.4	3.3	3.4	1.5	3.5	18.2	1.3	4.3	7.8
Current Assets to Working Capital 38	4.6	2.7	3.7	2.6	2.9	7.3	2.5	2.2	8.7
Current Liabilities to Working Capital 39	3.6	1.7	2.7	1.6	1.9	6.3	1.5	1.2	7.7
Working Capital to Net Sales 40	0.1	0.1	0.1	0.2	0.2	0.1	0.2	0.5	0.0
Inventory to Working Capital 41	1.3	1.2	1.4	1.1	0.9	2.7	0.7	0.4	2.7
Total Receipts to Cash Flow 42	10.8	17.4	9.3	10.7	9.6	30.9	11.7	16.0	10.2
Cost of Goods to Cash Flow 43	7.0	12.4	6.4	7.8	6.3	23.7	8.5	11.7	6.4
Cash Flow to Total Debt 44	0.1	0.1	0.2	0.2	0.2	0.0	0.2	0.0	0.1

Selected Financial Factors (in Percentages)

Debt Ratio 45	84.3	76.7	77.5	59.6	77.7	94.8	56.0	81.0	88.6
Return on Total Assets 46	4.5		10.8	7.4	6.3		4.6	2.6	5.1
Return on Equity Before Income Taxes 47	10.9		29.6	13.8	8.2		6.4	5.4	17.8
Return on Equity After Income Taxes 48	7.2		21.1	12.0	2.4		3.2	2.0	13.8
Profit Margin (Before Income Tax) 49	1.6		4.1	3.8	1.4		2.7	1.9	1.8
Profit Margin (After Income Tax) 50	1.1		2.9	3.3	0.4		1.4	0.7	1.4

Table II
Corporations with Net Income

ENGINE, TURBINE AND POWER TRANSMISSION EQUIPMENT

MONEY AMOUNTS AND SIZE OF ASSETS IN THOUSANDS OF DOLLARS

Item Description for Accounting Period 7/02 Through 6/03	Total	Zero Assets	Under 500	500 to 1,000	1,000 to 5,000	5,000 to 10,000	10,000 to 25,000	25,000 to 50,000	50,000 to 100,000	100,000 to 250,000	250,000 to 500,000	500,000 to 2,500,000	2,500,000 and over
Number of Enterprises **1**	92	•	•	0	16	37	18	0	0	7	0	0	0

Revenues ($ in Thousands)

	Total	Zero Assets	Under 500	500 to 1,000	1,000 to 5,000	5,000 to 10,000	10,000 to 25,000	25,000 to 50,000	50,000 to 100,000	100,000 to 250,000	250,000 to 500,000	500,000 to 2,500,000	2,500,000 and over
Net Sales **2**	32138625	•	•	0	60376	487766	487627	0	0	1568441	0	0	0
Interest **3**	687862	•	•	0	80	560	315	0	0	8702	0	0	0
Rents **4**	261939	•	•	0	0	731	334	0	0	1043	0	0	0
Royalties **5**	109995	•	•	0	0	0	0	0	0	14094	0	0	0
Other Portfolio Income **6**	178842	•	•	0	129	86	351	0	0	7214	0	0	0
Other Receipts **7**	407855	•	•	0	94	3442	6079	0	0	9861	0	0	0
Total Receipts **8**	33784918	•	•	0	60679	492585	494706	0	0	1609355	0	0	0
Average Total Receipts **9**	367227	•	•	•	3792	13313	27484	•	•	229908	•	•	•

Operating Costs/Operating Income (%)

	Total	Zero Assets	Under 500	500 to 1,000	1,000 to 5,000	5,000 to 10,000	10,000 to 25,000	25,000 to 50,000	50,000 to 100,000	100,000 to 250,000	250,000 to 500,000	500,000 to 2,500,000	2,500,000 and over
Cost of Operations **10**	63.3	•	•	•	42.0	63.4	69.2	•	•	70.7	•	•	•
Salaries and Wages **11**	15.4	•	•	•	4.7	4.6	5.7	•	•	7.8	•	•	•
Taxes Paid **12**	2.5	•	•	•	3.8	3.1	1.8	•	•	2.1	•	•	•
Interest Paid **13**	2.6	•	•	•	1.3	2.8	1.0	•	•	1.2	•	•	•
Depreciation **14**	3.4	•	•	•	8.0	3.9	3.4	•	•	3.7	•	•	•
Amortization and Depletion **15**	0.4	•	•	•	0.0	0.2	0.1	•	•	0.4	•	•	•
Pensions and Other Deferred Comp. **16**	1.5	•	•	•	5.6	0.4	1.1	•	•	0.7	•	•	•
Employee Benefits **17**	1.7	•	•	•	3.7	3.0	2.2	•	•	1.9	•	•	•
Advertising **18**	0.8	•	•	•	1.8	0.3	0.4	•	•	1.0	•	•	•
Other Expenses **19**	9.3	•	•	•	6.7	9.0	7.0	•	•	8.1	•	•	•
Officers' Compensation **20**	0.6	•	•	•	4.1	4.4	1.9	•	•	0.8	•	•	•
Operating Margin **21**	•	•	•	•	18.4	4.9	6.2	•	•	1.5	•	•	•
Operating Margin Before Officers' Comp. **22**	•	•	•	•	22.5	9.3	8.1	•	•	2.3	•	•	•

Selected Average Balance Sheet ($ in Thousands)

Net Receivables 23	55608	•	526	1853	3611	37596
Inventories 24	25959	•	2478	773	3778	40135
Net Property, Plant and Equipment 25	47926	•	1318	2704	5802	46611
Total Assets 26	305924	•	3275	8094	16861	186624
Notes and Loans Payable 27	62208	•	916	4635	4974	40179
All Other Liabilities 28	191521	•	483	1484	4525	54939
Net Worth 29	52195	•	1876	1975	7361	91506

Selected Financial Ratios (Times to 1)

Current Ratio 30	1.3	•	4.7	1.5	1.8	2.4
Quick Ratio 31	0.7	•	2.9	0.8	1.0	1.3
Net Sales to Working Capital 32	11.6	•	2.4	9.6	5.8	3.9
Coverage Ratio 33	2.4	•	15.5	3.1	8.8	4.7
Total Asset Turnover 34	1.1	•	1.2	1.6	1.6	1.2
Inventory Turnover 35	8.5	•	0.6	10.8	5.0	3.9
Receivables Turnover 36	9.1	•	3.0	12.9	7.7	11.9
Total Liabilities to Net Worth 37	4.9	•	0.7	3.1	1.3	1.0
Current Assets to Working Capital 38	4.5	•	1.3	3.1	2.2	1.7
Current Liabilities to Working Capital 39	3.5	•	0.3	2.1	1.2	0.7
Working Capital to Net Sales 40	0.1	•	0.4	0.1	0.2	0.3
Inventory to Working Capital 41	1.4	•	0.2	1.0	0.9	0.7
Total Receipts to Cash Flow 42	9.8	•	4.5	7.7	7.6	9.2
Cost of Goods to Cash Flow 43	6.2	•	1.9	4.9	5.3	6.5
Cash Flow to Total Debt 44	0.1	•	0.6	0.3	0.4	0.3

Selected Financial Factors (in Percentages)

Debt Ratio 45	82.9	•	42.7	75.6	56.3	51.0
Return on Total Assets 46	7.2	•	23.1	14.1	13.9	6.7
Return on Equity Before Income Taxes 47	24.3	•	37.7	39.3	28.2	10.7
Return on Equity After Income Taxes 48	19.8	•	24.9	29.6	25.6	8.1
Profit Margin (Before Income Tax) 49	3.6	•	18.7	5.9	7.7	4.4
Profit Margin (After Income Tax) 50	3.0	•	12.4	4.4	7.0	3.3

Table I

Corporations with and without Net Income

OTHER GENERAL PURPOSE MACHINERY

MONEY AMOUNTS AND SIZE OF ASSETS IN THOUSANDS OF DOLLARS

Item Description for Accounting Period 7/02 Through 6/03	Total	Zero Assets	Under 500	500 to 1,000	1,000 to 5,000	5,000 to 10,000	10,000 to 25,000	25,000 to 50,000	50,000 to 100,000	100,000 to 250,000	250,000 to 500,000	500,000 to 2,500,000	2,500,000 and over
Number of Enterprises **1**	6291	379	4168	490	859	138	127	42	23	31	10	17	8
Revenues ($ in Thousands)													
Net Sales **2**	56120296	223561	1640382	653716	3709223	1464977	2572966	2073387	1624519	4923305	2993872	9844252	24396136
Interest **3**	628001	534	1187	1037	2682	6605	4856	2586	10142	34877	15490	68425	479582
Rents **4**	29105	430	0	0	3006	25	3963	633	152	9770	5488	1561	4077
Royalties **5**	486163	0	0	0	0	10	2295	66	0	30261	6890	154263	292378
Other Portfolio Income **6**	625047	3698	34	0	1706	2958	6931	9898	5131	44451	12639	117132	420467
Other Receipts **7**	506166	8101	5705	6433	16606	7791	25998	15876	25332	39622	22989	106182	225532
Total Receipts **8**	58394778	236324	1647308	661186	3733223	1482366	2617009	2102446	1665276	5082286	3057368	10291815	25818172
Average Total Receipts **9**	9282	624	395	1349	4346	10742	20606	50058	72403	163945	305737	605401	3227272
Operating Costs/Operating Income (%)													
Cost of Operations **10**	64.2	73.9	37.9	63.6	69.6	64.3	66.5	69.5	74.2	65.2	69.3	67.8	61.3
Salaries and Wages **11**	10.0	9.2	17.9	11.9	8.2	9.4	10.5	8.0	9.8	9.2	7.5	9.6	10.5
Taxes Paid **12**	2.0	2.0	3.8	2.1	2.3	2.2	2.7	2.0	1.5	1.8	2.3	2.0	1.8
Interest Paid **13**	3.9	1.9	1.9	1.1	1.1	1.4	1.1	1.6	1.7	3.1	1.9	2.9	6.2
Depreciation **14**	3.2	2.5	3.8	1.2	2.3	2.0	3.3	2.9	2.5	3.7	3.2	3.8	3.0
Amortization and Depletion **15**	0.9	1.5	0.1	0.1	0.1	0.2	0.2	0.4	0.5	1.0	0.9	1.7	1.0
Pensions and Other Deferred Comp. **16**	1.3	0.2	0.2	0.3	0.6	1.0	0.7	0.7	0.4	0.5	0.6	0.8	2.2
Employee Benefits **17**	2.7	0.6	3.3	2.5	1.3	2.0	2.4	1.5	2.2	2.6	1.9	3.6	2.9
Advertising **18**	0.8	1.7	1.1	0.9	0.5	0.7	0.8	0.7	0.6	0.9	0.9	0.4	1.0
Other Expenses **19**	13.4	18.6	20.7	12.6	10.1	12.1	9.5	9.2	9.6	10.5	9.8	11.1	16.5
Officers' Compensation **20**	1.5	3.3	7.7	5.9	5.0	3.6	2.7	1.8	1.2	1.9	0.7	0.8	0.3
Operating Margin **21**	•	•	1.6	•	•	1.0	•	1.7	•	•	1.0	•	•
Operating Margin Before Officers' Comp. **22**	•	•	9.3	3.9	3.9	4.6	2.1	3.5	•	1.5	1.7	•	•

Selected Average Balance Sheet ($ in Thousands)

Net Receivables 23	1838	0	34	172	501	1951	3489	8123	15110	26297	64040	140324	708428
Inventories 24	1213	0	31	236	677	2094	3729	8659	17827	21235	51627	78336	345056
Net Property, Plant and Equipment 25	1475	0	39	36	493	1085	3556	8247	10595	31895	58424	100670	525534
Total Assets 26	17028		138	682	2230	7160	14991	36491	69344	153170	329364	816270	9545116
Notes and Loans Payable 27	4910	0	92	449	1015	2006	4761	12489	23266	53138	108760	235679	2591544
All Other Liabilities 28	4162	0	20	184	664	2153	3449	9510	18577	47054	124450	273546	2065363
Net Worth 29	7956	0	25	49	551	3001	6782	14492	27502	52978	96155	307044	4888210

Selected Financial Ratios (Times to 1)

Current Ratio 30	1.3	•	3.1	2.7	1.7	2.0	1.9	1.8	1.4	1.4	1.2	1.6	1.0
Quick Ratio 31	0.7	•	1.9	1.3	0.8	1.1	1.0	0.9	0.7	0.8	0.6	0.9	0.6
Net Sales to Working Capital 32	10.5	•	6.5	3.8	6.7	3.9	4.6	5.5	6.8	8.7	13.7	5.1	278.2
Coverage Ratio 33	1.2	•	2.1	0.2	0.5	2.6	2.0	3.2	•	2.2	2.6	1.5	0.9
Total Asset Turnover 34	0.5	•	2.8	2.0	1.9	1.5	1.4	1.4	1.0	1.0	0.9	0.7	0.3
Inventory Turnover 35	4.7	•	4.8	3.6	4.4	3.3	3.6	4.0	2.9	4.9	4.0	5.0	5.4
Receivables Turnover 36	4.5	•	13.0	6.8	7.9	6.5	6.0	5.8	3.8	5.6	4.1	3.8	4.0
Total Liabilities to Net Worth 37	1.1	•	4.4	12.9	3.0	1.4	1.2	1.5	1.5	1.9	2.4	1.7	1.0
Current Assets to Working Capital 38	4.8	•	1.5	1.6	2.4	2.0	2.1	2.3	3.7	3.6	7.2	2.8	124.0
Current Liabilities to Working Capital 39	3.8	•	0.5	0.6	1.4	1.0	1.1	1.3	2.7	2.6	6.2	1.8	123.0
Working Capital to Net Sales 40	0.1	•	0.2	0.3	0.1	0.3	0.2	0.2	0.1	0.1	0.1	0.2	0.0
Inventory to Working Capital 41	1.4	•	0.5	0.8	1.2	0.7	0.8	0.9	1.4	1.1	2.4	0.6	31.2
Total Receipts to Cash Flow 42	9.1	33.3	6.4	12.1	13.8	8.5	11.7	9.3	17.2	8.4	8.7	10.7	8.1
Cost of Goods to Cash Flow 43	5.8	24.6	2.4	7.7	9.6	5.4	7.8	6.5	12.8	5.5	6.0	7.2	5.0
Cash Flow to Total Debt 44	0.1	•	0.5	0.2	0.2	0.3	0.2	0.2	0.1	0.1	0.1	0.1	0.1

Selected Financial Factors (in Percentages)

Debt Ratio 45	53.3	•	81.6	92.8	75.3	58.1	54.8	60.3	60.3	65.4	70.8	62.4	48.8
Return on Total Assets 46	2.4	•	11.3	0.4	1.2	5.4	3.1	6.9	•	7.0	4.5	3.0	1.8
Return on Equity Before Income Taxes 47	0.7	•	31.6	•	•	8.0	3.4	12.0	•	11.0	9.5	2.5	•
Return on Equity After Income Taxes 48	•	•	31.1	•	•	6.4	1.5	9.9	•	6.1	4.9	•	•
Profit Margin (Before Income Tax) 49	0.7	•	2.0	•	•	2.3	1.1	3.5	•	3.7	3.1	1.3	•
Profit Margin (After Income Tax) 50	•	•	2.0	•	•	1.8	0.5	2.9	•	2.0	1.6	•	•

Table II

Corporations with Net Income

OTHER GENERAL PURPOSE MACHINERY

MONEY AMOUNTS AND SIZE OF ASSETS IN THOUSANDS OF DOLLARS

Item Description for Accounting Period 7/02 Through 6/03		Total	Zero Assets	Under 500	500 to 1,000	1,000 to 5,000	5,000 to 10,000	10,000 to 25,000	25,000 to 50,000	50,000 to 100,000	100,000 to 250,000	250,000 to 500,000	500,000 to 2,500,000	2,500,000 and over
Number of Enterprises	1	3747	3	2695	320	457	104	80	34	10	24	6	9	5
Revenues ($ in Thousands)														
Net Sales	2	34449120	146855	1193170	373774	2625357	1057832	1859096	1636528	686915	3937482	1895470	6365039	12671601
Interest	3	315859	327	137	16	1205	2539	2122	2287	2280	25583	11222	51678	216463
Rents	4	17159	430	0	0	2346	0	3363	132	66	4837	4509	353	1125
Royalties	5	399455	0	0	0	0	0	1213	56	0	27349	3571	152223	215044
Other Portfolio Income	6	498592	3698	34	0	311	2906	3502	8983	1220	40997	9618	106377	320945
Other Receipts	7	281089	5348	4242	2050	6517	4227	14111	14984	20363	28902	19263	48415	112667
Total Receipts	8	35961274	156658	1197583	375840	2635736	1067504	1883407	1662970	710844	4065150	1943653	6724085	13537845
Average Total Receipts	9	9597	52219	444	1174	5767	10264	23543	48911	71084	169381	323942	747121	2707569
Operating Costs/Operating Income (%)														
Cost of Operations	10	65.2	77.6	31.4	63.7	71.1	63.6	65.0	68.5	73.2	64.1	65.7	70.4	64.1
Salaries and Wages	11	9.1	6.6	21.9	9.1	7.7	8.5	9.4	7.5	5.3	8.7	6.1	8.2	9.7
Taxes Paid	12	1.9	1.5	3.6	1.2	1.8	2.2	2.5	2.1	1.5	1.7	3.1	2.0	1.4
Interest Paid	13	2.6	0.4	1.0	1.4	0.8	0.8	1.1	1.6	1.3	2.6	1.3	2.9	3.7
Depreciation	14	3.0	2.5	4.3	0.4	1.2	2.2	2.9	2.9	3.4	3.6	3.3	3.0	3.0
Amortization and Depletion	15	0.5	0.3	0.0	0.0	0.0	0.1	0.3	0.4	0.5	0.8	0.7	1.1	0.3
Pensions and Other Deferred Comp.	16	0.7	0.0	0.3	0.0	0.7	0.9	0.7	0.9	0.4	0.6	0.7	0.8	0.7
Employee Benefits	17	2.1	0.5	2.9	0.7	0.8	1.8	2.3	1.5	1.7	2.6	2.4	2.4	2.2
Advertising	18	0.8	1.5	0.8	0.4	0.5	0.5	0.8	0.7	0.5	1.0	1.0	0.5	0.9
Other Expenses	19	12.2	9.9	19.0	9.7	7.5	8.3	8.4	8.6	8.6	10.1	9.8	9.2	16.7
Officers' Compensation	20	1.5	0.6	5.9	5.1	4.7	2.4	2.6	2.0	1.4	1.9	0.7	0.8	0.4
Operating Margin	21	0.4	•	9.0	8.2	3.2	8.8	4.0	3.2	2.2	2.3	5.1	•	•
Operating Margin Before Officers' Comp.	22	1.9	•	14.9	13.3	7.9	11.2	6.6	5.1	3.6	4.2	5.8	•	•

Selected Average Balance Sheet ($ in Thousands)

Net Receivables 23	1982		36	142	562	1928	3748	7589	14923	24914	66248	171161	716754
Inventories 24	1178	0	12	220	689	1524	3559	6485	16146	20508	46153	88179	297213
Net Property, Plant and Equipment 25	1558	0	50	21	414	978	3553	8359	11726	32431	70753	141743	448235
Total Assets 26	18004	0	129	623	2158	6679	14933	37269	65930	158011	339528	973116	9504901
Notes and Loans Payable 27	4359	0	85	293	574	1156	4101	12978	18184	47119	80158	239989	2180637
All Other Liabilities 28	3328	0	17	185	865	1366	3568	9253	17036	48626	113035	309686	1285018
Net Worth 29	10317	0	26	144	719	4157	7265	15038	30710	62265	146336	423441	6039246

Selected Financial Ratios (Times to 1)

Current Ratio 30	1.6	•	3.0	2.7	1.6	3.1	2.2	1.9	1.4	1.8	1.4	2.4	1.2
Quick Ratio 31	0.9	•	2.2	1.5	0.8	1.9	1.2	1.0	0.7	1.0	0.7	1.5	0.7
Net Sales to Working Capital 32	5.7	•	9.6	3.7	8.9	3.0	4.4	5.0	6.7	5.4	6.6	3.1	10.1
Coverage Ratio 33	3.2	16.3	10.7	7.4	5.3	13.7	5.8	4.3	5.5	3.5	6.9	3.1	2.2
Total Asset Turnover 34	0.5	•	3.4	1.9	2.7	1.5	1.6	1.3	1.0	1.0	0.9	0.7	0.3
Inventory Turnover 35	5.1	•	11.3	3.4	5.9	4.2	4.2	5.1	3.1	5.1	4.5	5.6	5.5
Receivables Turnover 36	4.9	•	16.8	5.9	8.3	6.7	6.7	7.0	4.2	13.2	3.6	3.9	7.1
Total Liabilities to Net Worth 37	0.7	•	3.9	3.3	2.0	0.6	1.1	1.5	1.1	1.5	1.3	1.3	0.6
Current Assets to Working Capital 38	2.8	•	1.5	1.6	2.5	1.5	1.8	2.1	3.4	2.2	3.6	1.7	5.6
Current Liabilities to Working Capital 39	1.8	•	0.5	0.6	1.5	0.5	0.8	1.1	2.4	1.2	2.6	0.7	4.6
Working Capital to Net Sales 40	0.2	•	0.1	0.3	0.1	0.3	0.2	0.2	0.1	0.2	0.2	0.3	0.1
Inventory to Working Capital 41	0.7	•	0.4	0.7	1.1	0.5	0.7	0.7	1.5	0.7	0.9	0.4	1.2
Total Receipts to Cash Flow 42	6.9	8.6	4.7	5.9	10.7	6.4	8.3	8.5	8.0	7.0	6.2	8.4	6.0
Cost of Goods to Cash Flow 43	4.5	6.7	1.5	3.8	7.6	4.1	5.4	5.8	5.8	4.5	4.1	5.9	3.8
Cash Flow to Total Debt 44	0.2	•	0.9	0.4	0.4	0.6	0.4	0.3	0.2	0.2	0.3	0.2	0.1

Selected Financial Factors (in Percentages)

Debt Ratio 45	42.7	•	79.7	76.9	66.7	37.8	51.4	59.7	53.4	60.6	56.9	56.5	36.5
Return on Total Assets 46	4.2	•	35.6	19.0	11.7	16.0	10.1	9.0	7.3	9.5	8.2	6.5	2.2
Return on Equity Before Income Taxes 47	5.0	•	158.6	71.1	28.5	23.8	17.1	17.1	12.8	17.2	16.3	10.1	1.9
Return on Equity After Income Taxes 48	3.7	•	157.9	71.1	26.3	22.2	14.4	14.5	9.0	11.7	11.3	6.6	1.3
Profit Margin (Before Income Tax) 49	5.6	5.4	9.4	8.8	3.6	9.7	5.3	5.3	5.7	6.5	7.6	6.1	4.5
Profit Margin (After Income Tax) 50	4.2	4.3	9.3	8.8	3.3	9.1	4.5	4.5	4.0	4.4	5.2	4.0	3.1

Table I

Corporations with and without Net Income

COMPUTER AND PERIPHERAL EQUIPMENT

MONEY AMOUNTS AND SIZE OF ASSETS IN THOUSANDS OF DOLLARS

Item Description for Accounting Period 7/02 Through 6/03	Total	Zero Assets	Under 500	500 to 1,000	1,000 to 5,000	5,000 to 10,000	10,000 to 25,000	25,000 to 50,000	50,000 to 100,000	100,000 to 250,000	250,000 to 500,000	500,000 to 2,500,000	2,500,000 and over
Number of Enterprises **1**	1934	163	627	382	391	112	113	47	30	23	16	21	9
Revenues ($ in Thousands)													
Net Sales **2**	180341835	2171259	803072	621250	1632063	1283919	2444637	1180398	2833917	3542831	4361714	16717024	142743751
Interest **3**	6133563	1491	121	642	5428	2498	13558	20355	8568	28464	41235	162105	5849097
Rents **4**	1374272	0	0	0	102	1026	1516	292	213	153	2333	62601	1306035
Royalties **5**	17200644	0	0	0	0	640	711	10620	14327	13113	33976	252024	16875233
Other Portfolio Income **6**	3501984	1073	0	67	5039	313	5155	4780	7673	53612	12740	329423	3082108
Other Receipts **7**	10360279	7756	172	-4980	71622	5351	20915	7912	21484	48369	38597	1197996	8945087
Total Receipts **8**	218912577	2181579	803365	616979	1714254	1293747	2486492	1224357	2892182	3686542	4490595	18721173	178801311
Average Total Receipts **9**	113192	13384	1281	1615	4384	11551	22004	26050	96406	160284	280662	891484	19866812
Operating Costs/Operating Income (%)													
Cost of Operations **10**	65.3	91.9	53.2	57.3	59.3	68.9	70.2	63.5	74.5	67.3	60.7	74.1	63.8
Salaries and Wages **11**	16.2	3.5	22.0	13.3	22.0	16.1	19.4	29.3	12.1	11.0	15.9	15.6	16.5
Taxes Paid **12**	1.4	0.3	4.9	2.3	2.9	2.2	2.0	3.6	1.0	1.5	1.7	1.6	1.3
Interest Paid **13**	2.5	0.4	1.4	1.0	1.1	1.3	1.5	2.1	1.4	1.7	1.9	1.1	2.8
Depreciation **14**	6.7	0.7	2.8	1.5	2.0	2.5	3.3	6.2	2.0	3.3	3.0	3.8	7.6
Amortization and Depletion **15**	0.4	1.7	0.2	0.5	1.0	0.6	0.9	1.8	1.0	0.7	0.7	1.1	0.2
Pensions and Other Deferred Comp. **16**	2.5	0.0	0.2	0.4	0.5	0.1	0.2	0.6	0.3	0.1	0.1	0.5	3.0
Employee Benefits **17**	2.3	0.2	7.5	0.4	1.4	1.9	2.1	2.6	1.2	1.5	1.5	1.9	2.4
Advertising **18**	2.2	0.0	0.1	0.2	0.7	0.4	1.1	1.6	0.8	0.9	2.6	1.5	2.5
Other Expenses **19**	21.1	4.8	21.1	18.1	20.4	13.2	19.6	29.0	9.3	13.2	17.6	13.2	22.8
Officers' Compensation **20**	0.4	0.3	1.9	10.8	6.4	4.2	2.9	3.5	1.1	0.9	0.8	0.7	0.2
Operating Margin **21**	•	•	•	•	•	•	•	•	•	•	•	•	•
Operating Margin Before Officers' Comp. **22**	•	•	•	5.0	•	•	•	•	•	•	•	•	•

Selected Average Balance Sheet ($ in Thousands)

Item													
Net Receivables 23	32191	0	25	181	519	1668	3601	6630	20671	38300	66891	138713	6175512
Inventories 24	7080	0	33	135	564	1999	2549	4738	9602	20503	34908	65424	1108053
Net Property, Plant and Equipment 25	20808	0	52	48	341	1140	2568	4376	7655	14795	31168	108211	4010369
Total Assets 26	150358	0	102	616	2315	6509	16652	35671	67045	168250	327823	1015326	28094642
Notes and Loans Payable 27	36995	0	270	267	2576	1721	5376	6917	17805	27712	57664	153316	7092261
All Other Liabilities 28	42262	0	196	130	1117	2297	5859	9924	27533	60061	101583	323038	7680307
Net Worth 29	71101	0	-364	218	-1379	2491	5417	18830	21708	80477	168575	538972	13322075

Selected Financial Ratios (Times to 1)

Item													
Current Ratio 30	1.6	•	0.2	1.7	1.1	1.7	1.7	2.1	1.8	1.5	2.1	1.8	1.5
Quick Ratio 31	1.1	•	0.2	0.9	0.7	1.2	1.2	1.4	1.2	1.1	1.3	1.3	1.0
Net Sales to Working Capital 32	4.0	•	•	7.0	22.1	5.7	4.4	2.0	4.6	4.1	2.5	3.6	3.9
Coverage Ratio 33	1.9	•	•	•	•	•	•	•	2.3	•	•	•	2.6
Total Asset Turnover 34	0.6	•	12.5	2.6	1.8	1.8	1.3	0.7	1.4	0.9	0.8	0.8	0.6
Inventory Turnover 35	8.6	•	20.6	6.9	4.4	4.0	6.0	3.4	7.3	5.1	4.7	9.0	9.1
Receivables Turnover 36	2.9	•	39.9	9.3	7.8	5.2	5.6	3.2	5.1	4.4	3.9	5.1	2.6
Total Liabilities to Net Worth 37	1.1	•	•	1.8	•	1.6	2.1	0.9	2.1	1.1	0.9	0.9	1.1
Current Assets to Working Capital 38	2.8	•	•	2.4	7.9	2.4	2.3	1.9	2.3	2.9	1.9	2.2	2.9
Current Liabilities to Working Capital 39	1.8	•	•	1.4	6.9	1.4	1.3	0.9	1.3	1.9	0.9	1.2	1.9
Working Capital to Net Sales 40	0.3	•	•	0.1	0.0	0.2	0.2	0.5	0.2	0.2	0.4	0.3	0.3
Inventory to Working Capital 41	0.3	•	•	0.7	2.5	0.6	0.5	0.3	0.4	0.6	0.3	0.2	0.2
Total Receipts to Cash Flow 42	5.6	•	18.3	24.9	•	•	•	•	23.2	8.6	8.5	15.9	4.7
Cost of Goods to Cash Flow 43	3.6	•	10.5	14.8	•	•	•	•	17.3	5.8	5.1	11.8	3.0
Cash Flow to Total Debt 44	0.2	•	0.2	0.0	•	•	•	•	0.1	0.2	0.2	0.1	0.2

Selected Financial Factors (in Percentages)

Item													
Debt Ratio 45	52.7	•	455.4	64.5	159.6	61.7	67.5	47.2	67.6	52.2	48.6	46.9	52.6
Return on Total Assets 46	3.0	•	•	•	•	•	•	•	3.5	•	•	•	4.1
Return on Equity Before Income Taxes 47	3.1	•	53.1	38.3	•	•	•	•	4.1	•	•	•	5.3
Return on Equity After Income Taxes 48	•	•	53.1	39.9	•	•	•	•	1.9	•	•	•	1.9
Profit Margin (Before Income Tax) 49	2.3	•	•	•	•	•	•	•	2.2	•	•	•	4.5
Profit Margin (After Income Tax) 50	•	•	•	•	•	•	•	•	1.0	•	•	•	1.6

Table II

Corporations with Net Income

COMPUTER AND PERIPHERAL EQUIPMENT

MONEY AMOUNTS AND SIZE OF ASSETS IN THOUSANDS OF DOLLARS

Item Description for Accounting Period 7/02 Through 6/03		Total	Zero Assets	Under 500	500 to 1,000	1,000 to 5,000	5,000 to 10,000	10,000 to 25,000	25,000 to 50,000	50,000 to 100,000	100,000 to 250,000	250,000 to 500,000	500,000 to 2,500,000	2,500,000 and over
Number of Enterprises	1	697	12	•	338	189	53	43	12	14	14	6	10	5
Revenues ($ in Thousands)														
Net Sales	2	123342730	1561183	•	581654	657730	721134	1344916	547616	1531588	2549129	1670393	10853520	101323865
Interest	3	4903963	952		0	1117	166	1990	3430	3067	11934	11378	81450	4788480
Rents	4	567991	0	•	•	0	756	1021	84	0	71	2025	6221	557813
Royalties	5	14877911	0	•	0	0	35	0	14327	516	8379	29830	102242	14723098
Other Portfolio Income	6	3185140	31	•	0	1331	271	3018	214	516	51806	4600	96183	3027169
Other Receipts	7	4463769	4561	•	2332	56174	1610	11778	982	7567	41926	22514	691176	3623151
Total Receipts	8	151341504	1566727	•	583986	716352	723937	1362758	552326	1557065	2663245	1740740	11830792	128043576
Average Total Receipts	9	217133	130561	•	1728	3790	13659	31692	46027	111219	190232	290123	1183079	25608715
Operating Costs/Operating Income (%)														
Cost of Operations	10	59.9	93.4	•	55.6	66.4	61.4	65.1	63.9	73.5	63.2	51.7	72.9	57.7
Salaries and Wages	11	13.7	0.8	•	9.7	7.8	11.0	10.3	9.9	9.8	10.7	17.3	13.1	14.1
Taxes Paid	12	1.6	0.1	•	2.0	2.7	1.5	1.4	1.5	0.9	1.6	1.7	1.3	1.7
Interest Paid	13	2.6	0.1	•	1.0	0.7	1.3	0.5	1.0	1.1	1.5	0.7	0.6	3.0
Depreciation	14	7.5	0.2	•	1.3	0.7	1.1	2.2	2.6	1.5	3.0	2.4	2.8	8.7
Amortization and Depletion	15	0.2	0.0	•	•	0.6	0.7	0.3	0.7	0.5	0.4	0.3	0.6	0.2
Pensions and Other Deferred Comp.	16	3.5	•	•	0.4	0.3	0.1	0.1	0.6	0.4	0.1	0.1	0.6	4.1
Employee Benefits	17	2.1	0.1	•	0.0	0.5	1.1	1.0	0.7	1.0	1.5	1.0	1.6	2.3
Advertising	18	2.1	0.0	•	0.2	0.7	0.2	0.8	0.4	0.5	0.5	1.6	1.0	2.3
Other Expenses	19	21.2	1.7	•	15.0	12.0	10.9	10.4	11.8	5.9	12.2	18.3	9.0	23.7
Officers' Compensation	20	0.4	0.1	•	10.7	4.1	3.3	1.9	2.1	1.0	0.9	1.1	0.5	0.2
Operating Margin	21	•	3.5	•	4.2	3.5	7.5	5.9	4.8	3.9	4.3	3.8	•	•
Operating Margin Before Officers' Comp.	22	•	3.6	•	14.8	7.6	10.7	7.9	6.9	4.9	5.2	4.8	•	•

Selected Average Balance Sheet ($ in Thousands)

Net Receivables 23	50350	0	•	197	432	1548	4560	10517	22047	37122	82589	185521	6272431
Inventories 24	9950	0	•	84	773	1983	3262	5781	9766	21730	29820	56979	1050736
Net Property, Plant and Equipment 25	44297	0	•	46	267	1056	2715	4509	7456	14379	42587	115811	5772581
Total Assets 26	240838	0	•	614	2297	6329	16721	37120	70250	176141	328261	1079933	29900878
Notes and Loans Payable 27	65686	0	•	164	451	1803	3571	2673	8608	26624	24299	153591	8637257
All Other Liabilities 28	69058	0	•	96	511	1346	5917	10987	32450	70507	93579	366697	8375366
Net Worth 29	106094	0	•	353	1335	3180	7234	23460	29192	79010	210382	559645	12888256

Selected Financial Ratios (Times to 1)

Current Ratio 30	1.8	•	•	2.9	1.7	2.5	1.9	2.0	1.8	1.8	2.3	2.0	1.8
Quick Ratio 31	1.2	•	•	1.4	1.2	1.7	1.2	1.5	1.3	1.2	1.2	1.3	1.2
Net Sales to Working Capital 32	3.4	•	•	4.7	7.6	5.1	5.7	3.4	5.5	3.5	2.5	3.7	3.3
Coverage Ratio 33	4.8	53.3	•	5.6	19.7	7.0	15.8	6.9	6.1	6.8	12.6	9.7	4.6
Total Asset Turnover 34	0.7	•	•	2.8	1.5	2.1	1.9	1.2	1.6	1.0	0.8	1.0	0.7
Inventory Turnover 35	10.7	•	•	11.4	3.0	4.2	6.2	5.0	8.2	5.3	4.8	13.9	11.1
Receivables Turnover 36	3.3	•	•	13.9	5.5	5.1	6.6	3.5	6.1	5.9	3.5	7.8	2.9
Total Liabilities to Net Worth 37	1.3	•	•	0.7	0.7	1.0	1.3	0.6	1.4	1.2	0.6	0.9	1.3
Current Assets to Working Capital 38	2.2	•	•	1.5	2.4	1.6	2.1	2.0	2.3	2.3	1.8	2.0	2.2
Current Liabilities to Working Capital 39	1.2	•	•	0.5	1.4	0.6	1.1	1.0	1.3	1.3	0.8	1.0	1.2
Working Capital to Net Sales 40	0.3	•	•	0.2	0.1	0.2	0.2	0.3	0.2	0.3	0.4	0.3	0.3
Inventory to Working Capital 41	0.2	•	•	0.4	0.7	0.5	0.6	0.3	0.5	0.6	0.3	0.3	0.2
Total Receipts to Cash Flow 42	3.9	18.8	•	6.8	4.5	5.7	6.5	6.2	9.8	5.8	4.1	8.5	3.5
Cost of Goods to Cash Flow 43	2.3	17.5	•	3.8	3.0	3.5	4.2	4.0	7.2	3.7	2.1	6.2	2.0
Cash Flow to Total Debt 44	0.3	•	•	1.0	0.8	0.8	0.5	0.5	0.3	0.3	0.6	0.2	0.3

Selected Financial Factors (in Percentages)

Debt Ratio 45	55.9	•	•	42.4	41.9	49.8	56.7	36.8	58.4	55.1	35.9	48.2	56.9
Return on Total Assets 46	9.3	•	•	15.6	19.9	19.6	14.5	8.2	10.4	10.9	7.6	6.0	9.4
Return on Equity Before Income Taxes 47	16.7	•	•	22.2	32.5	33.5	31.3	11.0	20.8	20.7	11.0	10.4	17.0
Return on Equity After Income Taxes 48	10.9	•	•	22.2	29.0	28.5	25.8	9.4	16.2	17.0	7.9	8.5	10.8
Profit Margin (Before Income Tax) 49	10.0	3.8	•	4.6	12.5	7.8	7.2	5.7	5.6	9.0	8.3	5.4	10.8
Profit Margin (After Income Tax) 50	6.5	2.5	•	4.6	11.1	6.7	6.0	4.8	4.3	7.4	6.0	4.4	6.8

Table I

Corporations with and without Net Income

COMMUNICATIONS EQUIPMENT

MONEY AMOUNTS AND SIZE OF ASSETS IN THOUSANDS OF DOLLARS

Item Description for Accounting Period 7/02 Through 6/03	Total	Zero Assets	Under 500	500 to 1,000	1,000 to 5,000	5,000 to 10,000	10,000 to 25,000	25,000 to 50,000	50,000 to 100,000	100,000 to 250,000	250,000 to 500,000	500,000 to 2,500,000	2,500,000 and over
Number of Enterprises **1**	2109	124	999	210	445	67	112	40	40	26	11	22	13
Revenues ($ in Thousands)													
Net Sales **2**	87991695	113109	132236	300055	1251009	528279	1319676	941006	2141379	5266782	2496529	13390458	60111176
Interest **3**	1574496	11436	197	84	5360	2903	15624	14560	32067	51721	32898	177154	1230492
Rents **4**	80043	0	0	5	432	20	417	1502	1701	585	4445	3781	67154
Royalties **5**	2903144	445	0	0	0	41	2534	573	27963	5866	198	95858	2769666
Other Portfolio Income **6**	4354507	6423	1632	1840	62020	8873	5670	547	18493	5496	1282	231090	4011139
Other Receipts **7**	2312055	2017	64464	27498	20793	16067	29335	43904	14848	49942	96030	719600	1227559
Total Receipts **8**	99215940	133430	198529	329482	1339614	556183	1373256	1002092	2236451	5380392	2631382	14617941	69417186
Average Total Receipts **9**	47044	1076	199	1569	3010	8301	12261	25052	55911	206938	239217	664452	5339784
Operating Costs/Operating Income (%)													
Cost of Operations **10**	71.9	102.1	82.0	68.6	42.8	61.5	61.8	61.7	63.5	75.0	67.0	65.0	74.7
Salaries and Wages **11**	15.6	52.6	14.1	25.8	33.6	29.7	37.5	36.0	25.4	12.5	15.2	10.5	15.2
Taxes Paid **12**	1.7	6.6	3.8	2.9	3.2	3.7	4.7	3.5	2.4	1.7	1.0	1.4	1.5
Interest Paid **13**	3.5	8.1	1.0	1.5	2.8	1.5	3.9	2.7	1.8	1.0	2.8	3.7	3.9
Depreciation **14**	6.1	20.2	2.3	1.3	4.3	5.8	8.4	7.2	5.6	3.5	9.9	4.0	6.6
Amortization and Depletion **15**	1.0	11.0	0.0	0.2	1.3	1.5	2.9	6.6	1.2	1.0	1.7	0.8	0.9
Pensions and Other Deferred Comp. **16**	0.7	0.3	•	1.1	0.7	0.2	0.4	0.3	0.8	0.3	0.3	1.2	0.6
Employee Benefits **17**	2.2	12.2	0.2	2.1	2.5	3.2	4.0	3.9	3.9	1.4	6.0	2.0	2.1
Advertising **18**	1.1	0.4	6.7	0.7	0.7	1.0	1.1	1.5	0.9	0.4	0.5	1.7	1.0
Other Expenses **19**	25.4	97.3	37.3	19.1	29.6	28.5	44.0	34.7	30.5	15.8	17.4	21.0	26.6
Officers' Compensation **20**	0.8	4.5	15.1	3.6	7.4	6.1	5.2	3.8	2.1	0.6	0.9	0.5	0.4
Operating Margin **21**	•	•	•	•	•	•	•	•	•	•	•	•	•
Operating Margin Before Officers' Comp. **22**	•	•	•	•	•	•	•	•	•	•	•	•	•

Selected Average Balance Sheet ($ in Thousands)

Net Receivables 23	10969	0	16	211	447	920	2174	4789	10871	34948	64194	122536	1356322
Inventories 24	4704	0	28	147	518	872	2239	4531	7016	22261	22681	89342	466580
Net Property, Plant and Equipment 25	8004	0	6	59	430	851	2613	4058	9529	18435	42386	114044	947918
Total Assets 26	83418	0	104	730	2402	6997	16448	33596	67527	165210	351599	1194838	10292195
Notes and Loans Payable 27	16992	0	32	297	3528	836	5549	7416	13790	12727	56026	226251	2055593
All Other Liabilities 28	33298	0	19	153	1529	3030	5211	10158	25113	48220	75459	321965	4471514
Net Worth 29	33128	0	52	280	-2655	3131	5689	16022	28624	104262	220113	646622	3765088

Selected Financial Ratios (Times to 1)

Current Ratio 30	1.6	•	1.9	1.8	1.6	1.4	1.8	2.1	1.8	2.4	2.9	1.6	1.5
Quick Ratio 31	0.9	•	1.3	1.4	1.0	1.0	1.3	1.5	1.3	1.5	2.3	0.9	0.8
Net Sales to Working Capital 32	3.6	•	2.9	5.7	4.3	6.5	2.4	1.8	2.7	3.3	2.0	4.0	3.8
Coverage Ratio 33	•	•	•	•	•	•	•	•	•	•	•	0.4	•
Total Asset Turnover 34	0.5	•	1.3	2.0	1.2	1.1	0.7	0.7	0.8	1.2	0.6	0.5	0.4
Inventory Turnover 35	6.4	•	3.8	6.7	2.3	5.6	3.3	3.2	4.8	6.8	6.7	4.4	7.4
Receivables Turnover 36	3.0	•	13.5	6.5	6.4	9.5	5.5	4.8	5.0	5.3	3.6	4.4	2.6
Total Liabilities to Net Worth 37	1.5	•	1.0	1.6	•	1.2	1.9	1.1	1.4	0.6	0.6	0.8	1.7
Current Assets to Working Capital 38	2.8	•	2.1	2.2	2.8	3.6	2.2	1.9	2.3	1.7	1.5	2.8	3.0
Current Liabilities to Working Capital 39	1.8	•	1.1	1.2	1.8	2.6	1.2	0.9	1.3	0.7	0.5	1.8	2.0
Working Capital to Net Sales 40	0.3	•	0.4	0.2	0.2	0.2	0.4	0.6	0.4	0.3	0.5	0.2	0.3
Inventory to Working Capital 41	0.3	•	0.7	0.4	0.8	0.6	0.4	0.3	0.3	0.3	0.1	0.5	0.3
Total Receipts to Cash Flow 42	34.7	•	8.5	•	•	•	•	•	48.8	•	•	7.1	30.0
Cost of Goods to Cash Flow 43	24.9	•	7.0	•	•	•	•	•	36.7	•	•	4.6	22.4
Cash Flow to Total Debt 44	0.0	•	0.3	•	•	•	•	•	0.1	•	•	0.2	0.0

Selected Financial Factors (in Percentages)

Debt Ratio 45	60.3	•	49.4	61.6	210.6	55.2	65.4	52.3	57.6	36.9	37.4	45.9	63.4
Return on Total Assets 46	•	•	•	•	•	•	•	•	•	•	•	0.7	•
Return on Equity Before Income Taxes 47	•	•	•	•	23.1	•	•	•	•	•	•	•	•
Return on Equity After Income Taxes 48	•	•	•	•	24.3	•	•	•	•	•	•	•	•
Profit Margin (Before Income Tax) 49	•	•	•	•	•	•	•	•	•	•	•	•	•
Profit Margin (After Income Tax) 50	•	•	•	•	•	•	•	•	•	•	•	•	•

Table II
Corporations with Net Income

COMMUNICATIONS EQUIPMENT

MONEY AMOUNTS AND SIZE OF ASSETS IN THOUSANDS OF DOLLARS

Item Description for Accounting Period 7/02 Through 6/03	Total	Zero Assets	Under 500	500 to 1,000	1,000 to 5,000	5,000 to 10,000	10,000 to 25,000	25,000 to 50,000	50,000 to 100,000	100,000 to 250,000	250,000 to 500,000	500,000 to 2,500,000	2,500,000 and over
Number of Enterprises **1**	463	•	49	129	174	35	30	8	11	11	0	13	3
Revenues ($ in Thousands)													
Net Sales **2**	43505490	•	79246	186990	451372	362814	648791	320296	1134597	3618831	0	10437094	26265458
Interest **3**	523653	•	0	1	694	250	1848	1554	2757	8911	0	107365	400273
Rents **4**	14342	•	0	0	0	0	207	574	659	3240	0	3781	5881
Royalties **5**	1831644	•	0	0	0	41	21	0	26142	227	0	87434	1717779
Other Portfolio Income **6**	3091360	•	0	0	54043	889	3902	463	4503	3722	0	177935	2845900
Other Receipts **7**	982263	•	63422	-2956	16031	3825	16198	587	-2381	12217	0	92554	782771
Total Receipts **8**	49948752	•	142668	184035	522140	367819	670967	323474	1166277	3647148	0	10906163	32018062
Average Total Receipts **9**	107881	•	2912	1427	3001	10509	22366	40434	106025	331559	•	838936	10672687
Operating Costs/Operating Income (%)													
Cost of Operations **10**	66.9	•	74.8	68.0	29.1	61.8	54.7	46.7	57.4	81.3	•	61.0	68.9
Salaries and Wages **11**	11.5	•	8.1	12.5	20.4	13.2	13.1	18.3	17.8	4.7	•	9.5	12.7
Taxes Paid **12**	1.7	•	4.1	3.2	2.4	1.9	2.4	2.0	1.5	1.1	•	1.4	1.9
Interest Paid **13**	2.8	•	0.0	0.6	3.3	0.1	0.8	1.1	0.6	0.8	•	1.9	3.7
Depreciation **14**	5.4	•	0.3	0.4	2.4	1.0	2.6	3.5	2.8	1.6	•	3.4	7.2
Amortization and Depletion **15**	0.5	•	0.0	•	1.9	1.0	0.4	1.5	0.3	0.3	•	0.7	0.5
Pensions and Other Deferred Comp. **16**	0.9	•	•	1.7	1.2	0.2	0.6	0.5	0.7	0.4	•	1.5	0.8
Employee Benefits **17**	1.9	•	•	2.6	1.2	0.9	2.2	2.4	3.1	0.7	•	2.1	1.9
Advertising **18**	1.7	•	10.7	1.0	0.1	0.2	0.7	0.5	0.8	0.3	•	2.1	1.8
Other Expenses **19**	8.4	•	16.7	2.3	15.6	8.9	10.7	12.3	11.4	7.1	•	13.9	6.1
Officers' Compensation **20**	0.9	•	20.7	5.5	7.8	3.8	3.4	2.9	1.9	0.3	•	0.5	0.7
Operating Margin **21**	•	•	•	2.1	14.5	6.9	8.4	8.2	1.8	1.5	•	1.9	•
Operating Margin Before Officers' Comp. **22**	•	•	•	7.6	22.4	10.7	11.9	11.0	3.7	1.8	•	2.4	•

Selected Average Balance Sheet ($ in Thousands)

Net Receivables 23	16127	•	40	105	445	941	3619	5652	11872	56882	•	180753	1360455
Inventories 24	7672	•	116	197	498	687	3467	4689	11565	30888	•	114474	438846
Net Property, Plant and Equipment 25	13049	•	105	11	594	203	1862	6238	11524	16385	•	117125	1329785
Total Assets 26	113744	•	345	599	2327	6510	15434	32056	65700	177114	•	1196977	10995192
Notes and Loans Payable 27	28847	•	0	132	665	269	1590	1962	13391	22060	•	155074	3550748
All Other Liabilities 28	50677	•	209	85	241	1827	3633	9172	14749	60310	•	293279	6171918
Net Worth 29	34420	•	135	382	1421	4414	10212	20923	37560	94744	•	748624	1272525

Selected Financial Ratios (Times to 1)

Current Ratio 30	1.7	•	1.1	3.3	4.0	2.1	2.6	2.2	2.1	1.9	•	2.3	1.4
Quick Ratio 31	1.0	•	0.5	2.4	2.2	1.2	1.7	1.5	1.4	1.2	•	1.4	0.9
Net Sales to Working Capital 32	4.6	•	84.9	3.5	2.5	5.3	3.3	3.5	4.6	6.5	•	2.6	6.5
Coverage Ratio 33	5.6	•	35465.0	1.8	10.3	61.9	15.6	9.3	14.1	3.9	•	4.6	5.6
Total Asset Turnover 34	0.8	•	4.7	2.4	1.1	1.6	1.4	1.2	1.6	1.9	•	0.7	0.8
Inventory Turnover 35	8.2	•	10.4	5.0	1.5	9.3	3.4	4.0	5.1	8.7	•	4.3	13.7
Receivables Turnover 36	6.7	•	81.7	6.8	6.9	17.9	6.3	5.9	8.6	6.2	•	4.2	8.7
Total Liabilities to Net Worth 37	2.3	•	1.5	0.6	0.6	0.5	0.5	0.5	0.7	0.9	•	0.6	7.6
Current Assets to Working Capital 38	2.5	•	12.0	1.4	1.3	1.9	1.6	1.9	1.9	2.1	•	1.8	3.4
Current Liabilities to Working Capital 39	1.5	•	11.0	0.4	0.3	0.9	0.6	0.9	0.9	1.1	•	0.8	2.4
Working Capital to Net Sales 40	0.2	•	0.0	0.3	0.4	0.2	0.3	0.3	0.2	0.2	•	0.4	0.2
Inventory to Working Capital 41	0.4	•	6.1	0.4	0.5	0.6	0.5	0.4	0.4	0.6	•	0.3	0.5
Total Receipts to Cash Flow 42	5.4	•	1.6	188.5	3.4	6.6	5.1	5.4	7.1	12.4	•	5.5	5.0
Cost of Goods to Cash Flow 43	3.6	•	1.2	128.2	1.0	4.1	2.8	2.5	4.1	10.1	•	3.4	3.4
Cash Flow to Total Debt 44	0.2	•	4.7	0.0	0.8	0.7	0.8	0.7	0.5	0.3	•	0.3	0.2

Selected Financial Factors (in Percentages)

Debt Ratio 45	69.7	•	60.8	36.2	38.9	32.2	33.8	34.7	42.8	46.5	•	37.5	88.4
Return on Total Assets 46	13.1	•	209.9	2.8	37.3	13.0	17.7	12.6	13.4	5.7	•	5.8	16.6
Return on Equity Before Income Taxes 47	35.7	•	534.9	2.0	55.1	18.8	25.1	17.3	21.8	8.0	•	7.3	117.7
Return on Equity After Income Taxes 48	23.8	•	534.9	1.7	49.0	16.9	20.9	12.3	16.4	6.5	•	4.9	76.2
Profit Margin (Before Income Tax) 49	13.1	•	44.8	0.5	30.2	8.0	11.8	9.0	8.0	2.3	•	6.8	17.1
Profit Margin (After Income Tax) 50	8.7	•	44.8	0.4	26.8	7.2	9.9	6.4	6.0	1.9	•	4.6	11.1

140

AUDIO AND VIDEO EQUIP., REPRODUCING MAGNETIC & OPTICAL MEDIA

Table I

Corporations with and without Net Income

MONEY AMOUNTS AND SIZE OF ASSETS IN THOUSANDS OF DOLLARS

Item Description for Accounting Period 7/02 Through 6/03	Total	Zero Assets	Under 500	500 to 1,000	1,000 to 5,000	5,000 to 10,000	10,000 to 25,000	25,000 to 50,000	50,000 to 100,000	100,000 to 250,000	250,000 to 500,000	500,000 to 2,500,000	2,500,000 and over
Number of Enterprises **1**	1294	7	518	257	301	71	54	36	17	18	6	10	0
Revenues ($ in Thousands)													
Net Sales **2**	22171685	75759	301849	794018	952901	710044	896844	1313598	1143019	2439615	1402059	12141978	0
Interest **3**	301608	483	129	518	971	3298	4386	8079	6635	23138	9124	244848	0
Rents **4**	10120	0	0	744	19	551	40	835	5349	351	735	1497	0
Royalties **5**	375342	0	0	0	30	0	579	1089	0	15970	1615	356059	0
Other Portfolio Income **6**	201775	15404	214	25	3004	7195	763	916	23928	62359	7587	80380	0
Other Receipts **7**	331489	20663	106	15716	8639	6528	16567	12916	8670	55852	79872	105957	0
Total Receipts **8**	23392019	112309	302298	811021	965564	727616	919179	1337433	1187601	2597285	1500992	12930719	0
Average Total Receipts **9**	18077	16044	584	3156	3208	10248	17022	37151	69859	144294	250165	1293072	•
Operating Costs/Operating Income (%)													
Cost of Operations **10**	60.7	84.9	41.0	65.7	56.3	60.3	57.2	57.9	67.8	61.7	70.1	59.7	•
Salaries and Wages **11**	13.6	17.6	12.2	9.5	15.7	19.4	21.2	18.3	13.9	14.4	19.4	11.5	•
Taxes Paid **12**	1.7	1.4	2.2	3.3	3.7	3.3	2.6	2.2	1.7	2.0	1.9	1.1	•
Interest Paid **13**	2.3	0.8	2.7	2.4	0.5	1.8	2.9	1.6	3.4	2.1	1.5	2.6	•
Depreciation **14**	4.1	4.4	5.0	1.2	2.0	3.9	6.7	5.0	4.2	7.2	6.6	3.3	•
Amortization and Depletion **15**	0.9	0.4	0.3	0.2	0.7	0.9	2.5	0.9	1.2	0.7	2.6	0.7	•
Pensions and Other Deferred Comp. **16**	0.6	•	0.0	0.6	0.2	0.1	0.3	0.3	0.1	0.6	0.3	0.9	•
Employee Benefits **17**	1.8	1.4	0.3	1.1	0.7	2.6	2.8	1.8	1.9	1.8	3.3	1.7	•
Advertising **18**	1.7	1.9	1.0	0.4	1.1	0.8	1.6	1.7	1.6	1.5	0.4	2.1	•
Other Expenses **19**	19.7	29.1	33.2	9.6	20.1	19.8	24.0	20.3	17.5	15.1	5.9	22.3	•
Officers' Compensation **20**	1.6	0.7	6.8	7.2	6.3	3.0	3.4	2.2	1.6	2.4	0.7	0.3	•
Operating Margin **21**	•	•	•	•	•	•	•	•	•	•	•	•	•
Operating Margin Before Officers' Comp. **22**	•	•	2.1	6.0	•	•	•	•	•	•	•	•	•

Selected Average Balance Sheet ($ in Thousands)

Net Receivables 23	3432	0	59	462	491	1319	2868	8827	17314	23019	52646	255324
Inventories 24	1901	0	49	84	420	1359	2215	4726	15152	24868	24323	104892
Net Property, Plant and Equipment 25	2548	0	56	54	353	1430	3474	6821	13494	24793	76531	147792
Total Assets 26	19160	0	186	803	2432	6672	16038	35813	68139	151911	309628	1537872
Notes and Loans Payable 27	4679	0	225	545	669	1209	4855	7986	16285	40579	53446	363279
All Other Liabilities 28	7282	0	50	317	796	1139	5631	11154	24153	43510	154252	616980
Net Worth 29	7200	0	-89	-58	967	4324	5552	16672	27701	67822	101930	557614

Selected Financial Ratios (Times to 1)

Current Ratio 30	1.4	•	1.4	0.8	1.8	2.6	1.5	1.8	1.6	1.7	1.5	1.2
Quick Ratio 31	0.8	•	0.8	0.7	1.3	1.7	1.1	1.1	1.0	1.1	1.0	0.6
Net Sales to Working Capital 32	6.8	•	15.6	•	4.0	3.3	4.9	3.4	4.3	4.4	6.0	9.9
Coverage Ratio 33	•	8.2	•	1.4	•	•	•	•	•	•	•	1.2
Total Asset Turnover 34	0.9	•	3.1	•	1.3	1.5	1.0	1.0	1.0	0.9	0.8	0.8
Inventory Turnover 35	5.5	•	4.9	24.2	3.8	4.4	4.3	4.5	3.0	3.4	6.7	6.9
Receivables Turnover 36	5.2	•	12.8	12.4	7.3	6.7	5.1	4.3	3.8	4.7	5.1	5.0
Total Liabilities to Net Worth 37	1.7	•	•	•	1.5	0.5	1.9	1.1	1.5	1.2	2.0	1.8
Current Assets to Working Capital 38	3.7	•	3.3	•	2.2	1.6	2.9	2.2	2.7	2.4	3.0	5.6
Current Liabilities to Working Capital 39	2.7	•	2.3	•	1.2	0.6	1.9	1.2	1.7	1.4	2.0	4.6
Working Capital to Net Sales 40	0.1	•	0.1	•	0.3	0.3	0.2	0.3	0.2	0.2	0.2	0.1
Inventory to Working Capital 41	0.8	•	1.2	•	0.6	0.5	0.6	0.5	0.8	0.6	0.7	1.0
Total Receipts to Cash Flow 42	7.5	8.7	5.1	12.3	11.9	40.8	•	14.1	113.9	13.1	•	4.8
Cost of Goods to Cash Flow 43	4.5	7.4	2.1	8.1	6.7	24.6	•	8.2	77.3	8.1	•	2.9
Cash Flow to Total Debt 44	0.2	•	0.4	0.3	0.2	0.1	0.6	0.1	0.0	0.1	•	0.3

Selected Financial Factors (in Percentages)

Debt Ratio 45	62.4	•	147.5	107.3	60.2	35.2	65.4	53.4	59.3	55.4	67.1	63.7
Return on Total Assets 46	•	•	•	12.9	•	•	•	•	•	•	•	2.3
Return on Equity Before Income Taxes 47	•	•	29.5	•	•	•	•	•	•	•	•	0.8
Return on Equity After Income Taxes 48	•	•	33.6	•	•	•	•	•	•	•	•	•
Profit Margin (Before Income Tax) 49	•	5.5	1.0	•	•	•	•	•	•	•	•	0.4
Profit Margin (After Income Tax) 50	•	5.5	0.8	•	•	•	•	•	•	•	•	•

Table II

Corporations with Net Income

AUDIO AND VIDEO EQUIP., REPRODUCING MAGNETIC & OPTICAL MEDIA

MONEY AMOUNTS AND SIZE OF ASSETS IN THOUSANDS OF DOLLARS

Item Description for Accounting Period 7/02 Through 6/03	Total	Zero Assets	Under 500	500 to 1,000	1,000 to 5,000	5,000 to 10,000	10,000 to 25,000	25,000 to 50,000	50,000 to 100,000	100,000 to 250,000	250,000 to 500,000	500,000 to 2,500,000	2,500,000 and over
Number of Enterprises **1**	730	0	214	0	187	45	21	16	5	9	0	0	3
Revenues ($ in Thousands)													
Net Sales **2**	10520704	0	54012	0	723086	583586	556525	818751	291073	1799892	0	0	4929887
Interest **3**	25924	0	10	0	86	1792	1344	2521	701	10815	0	0	8216
Rents **4**	1827	0	0	0	0	551	0	0	179	354	0	0	0
Royalties **5**	14261	0	0	0	0	0	0	1037	0	194	0	0	13030
Other Portfolio Income **6**	77282	0	0	0	76	6920	697	348	12613	27632	0	0	13568
Other Receipts **7**	164430	0	0	0	5430	621	12187	5719	4348	51949	0	0	48984
Total Receipts **8**	10804428	0	54022	0	728678	593470	570753	828376	308914	1890836	0	0	5013685
Average Total Receipts **9**	14801	•	252	•	3897	13188	27179	51774	61783	210093	•	•	1671228
Operating Costs/Operating Income (%)													
Cost of Operations **10**	56.5	•	39.6	•	51.5	61.5	56.4	56.2	59.7	64.0	•	•	52.5
Salaries and Wages **11**	8.6	•	•	•	13.1	12.0	11.0	12.4	11.8	11.1	•	•	5.6
Taxes Paid **12**	1.4	•	1.8	•	3.6	2.8	2.0	1.3	2.0	1.4	•	•	0.5
Interest Paid **13**	0.6	•	3.1	•	0.3	0.5	1.2	0.9	2.5	1.6	•	•	0.1
Depreciation **14**	3.2	•	1.2	•	1.4	1.0	3.2	2.2	3.5	7.9	•	•	2.4
Amortization and Depletion **15**	0.2	•	0.3	•	0.3	0.2	1.0	0.2	0.5	0.6	•	•	0.0
Pensions and Other Deferred Comp. **16**	0.6	•	•	•	0.3	0.1	0.3	0.4	0.1	0.3	•	•	1.0
Employee Benefits **17**	1.5	•	•	•	0.5	2.4	1.3	1.1	2.3	1.0	•	•	1.8
Advertising **18**	2.2	•	5.4	•	1.2	0.6	1.4	1.9	1.7	0.7	•	•	3.6
Other Expenses **19**	18.3	•	26.8	•	14.6	11.7	12.0	14.7	10.6	11.2	•	•	25.3
Officers' Compensation **20**	1.6	•	•	•	5.7	2.0	2.3	2.1	1.8	0.6	•	•	0.3
Operating Margin **21**	5.3	•	21.7	•	7.6	5.2	7.8	6.7	3.7	•	•	•	6.8
Operating Margin Before Officers' Comp. **22**	6.9	•	21.7	•	13.3	7.2	10.2	8.8	5.5	0.2	•	•	7.1

Selected Average Balance Sheet ($ in Thousands)

Net Receivables 23	2402	38	·	432	1630	3763	10092	22342	33146	·	275038
Inventories 24	1594	63	·	302	1624	3127	6471	16126	30226	·	148415
Net Property, Plant and Equipment 25	1448	0	·	131	1113	3074	3611	17184	41400	·	130449
Total Assets 26	9141	122	·	1675	6718	17582	35149	59411	182881	·	990146
Notes and Loans Payable 27	1501	39	·	667	395	4073	8620	21771	47801	·	38047
All Other Liabilities 28	2827	19	·	441	1608	4698	12721	15099	73763	·	269605
Net Worth 29	4813	64	·	567	4715	8812	13807	22541	61317	·	682494

Selected Financial Ratios (Times to 1)

Current Ratio 30	2.0	6.1	·	2.1	3.4	1.8	1.8	1.8	2.1	·	1.9
Quick Ratio 31	1.1	2.5	·	1.1	2.0	1.2	1.1	1.2	1.2	·	1.0
Net Sales to Working Capital 32	5.5	2.6	·	5.9	3.4	5.8	4.3	3.8	5.0	·	6.8
Coverage Ratio 33	13.5	8.1	·	31.8	14.6	9.8	9.9	5.0	3.9	·	64.6
Total Asset Turnover 34	1.6	2.1	·	2.3	1.9	1.5	1.5	1.0	1.1	·	1.7
Inventory Turnover 35	5.1	1.6	·	6.6	4.9	4.8	4.4	2.2	4.2	·	5.8
Receivables Turnover 36	5.7	13.4	·	12.7	9.9	5.7	5.7	2.5	6.4	·	11.9
Total Liabilities to Net Worth 37	0.9	0.9	·	2.0	0.4	1.0	1.5	1.6	2.0	·	0.5
Current Assets to Working Capital 38	2.0	1.2	·	1.9	1.4	2.2	2.2	2.3	1.9	·	2.1
Current Liabilities to Working Capital 39	1.0	0.2	·	0.9	0.4	1.2	1.2	1.3	0.9	·	1.1
Working Capital to Net Sales 40	0.2	0.4	·	0.2	0.3	0.2	0.2	0.3	0.2	·	0.1
Inventory to Working Capital 41	0.6	0.6	·	0.8	0.5	0.5	0.6	0.7	0.6	·	0.6
Total Receipts to Cash Flow 42	4.2	2.1	·	5.2	6.1	5.0	4.8	6.7	7.9	·	3.1
Cost of Goods to Cash Flow 43	2.3	0.8	·	2.7	3.7	2.8	2.7	4.0	5.1	·	1.6
Cash Flow to Total Debt 44	0.8	2.1	·	0.7	1.1	0.6	0.5	0.2	0.2	·	1.7

Selected Financial Factors (in Percentages)

Debt Ratio 45	47.4	47.5	·	66.1	29.8	49.9	60.7	62.1	66.5	·	31.1
Return on Total Assets 46	13.6	51.4	·	20.0	14.3	17.3	12.8	12.0	6.8	·	14.3
Return on Equity Before Income Taxes 47	23.9	85.7	·	57.1	19.0	30.9	29.4	25.3	15.0	·	20.4
Return on Equity After Income Taxes 48	18.4	72.1	·	55.8	16.1	26.2	24.2	24.0	11.7	·	13.3
Profit Margin (Before Income Tax) 49	8.0	21.7	·	8.4	6.9	10.3	7.9	9.8	4.6	·	8.5
Profit Margin (After Income Tax) 50	6.1	18.3	·	8.2	5.9	8.7	6.5	9.3	3.6	·	5.5

Table I

Corporations with and without Net Income

SEMICONDUCTOR AND OTHER ELECTRONIC COMPONENT

MONEY AMOUNTS AND SIZE OF ASSETS IN THOUSANDS OF DOLLARS

Item Description for Accounting Period 7/02 Through 6/03	Total	Zero Assets	Under 500	500 to 1,000	1,000 to 5,000	5,000 to 10,000	10,000 to 25,000	25,000 to 50,000	50,000 to 100,000	100,000 to 250,000	250,000 to 500,000	500,000 to 2,500,000	2,500,000 and over
Number of Enterprises **1**	6222	497	3218	539	1079	401	207	59	53	56	39	54	19
Revenues ($ in Thousands)													
Net Sales **2**	14284883	573047	2214690	515571	4670213	5131687	3304096	1633953	3686512	7619922	8719727	32883867	73331598
Interest **3**	2613603	773	1029	991	7189	9820	15762	15538	23524	76462	130431	734871	1597215
Rents **4**	101355	4	8396	0	681	1516	2935	5097	1226	5519	13273	29869	32838
Royalties **5**	2233556	0	0	0	151	1565	23175	1555	611	171598	55514	394757	1584630
Other Portfolio Income **6**	2306185	19427	1923	0	37419	48187	13195	33505	44372	68327	82900	427928	1529003
Other Receipts **7**	1618996	2662	6397	388	56416	41405	41731	21959	17402	188704	234883	536174	470874
Total Receipts **8**	153158578	595913	2232435	516950	4772069	5234180	3400894	1711607	3773647	8130532	9236728	35007466	78546158
Average Total Receipts **9**	24616	1199	694	959	4423	13053	16429	29010	71201	145188	236839	648286	4134008
Operating Costs/Operating Income (%)													
Cost of Operations **10**	72.5	66.6	52.6	54.6	57.6	67.5	67.5	69.4	71.0	69.9	79.7	74.6	73.3
Salaries and Wages **11**	12.0	14.4	11.7	3.7	16.4	12.5	16.4	18.6	13.8	13.3	13.1	13.6	10.2
Taxes Paid **12**	1.5	1.9	2.9	3.9	3.4	2.7	3.0	2.5	2.0	1.7	1.4	1.6	1.0
Interest Paid **13**	3.1	1.7	0.9	0.7	0.9	1.2	1.8	3.4	1.3	1.8	2.3	3.1	3.8
Depreciation **14**	7.1	6.4	1.2	4.7	4.4	3.4	5.9	7.3	6.1	6.3	6.4	8.6	7.4
Amortization and Depletion **15**	1.1	2.6	0.3	0.9	0.5	0.4	1.0	1.2	1.0	0.7	1.2	1.3	1.2
Pensions and Other Deferred Comp. **16**	0.5	0.2	0.2	1.5	0.6	0.3	0.6	0.3	0.4	0.2	0.3	0.4	0.7
Employee Benefits **17**	2.1	2.2	1.1	0.7	2.3	1.9	2.2	1.9	2.1	1.8	1.6	1.9	2.3
Advertising **18**	0.7	0.2	0.6	0.1	0.6	0.5	0.8	0.7	0.5	0.9	0.5	0.4	0.8
Other Expenses **19**	14.8	19.6	22.1	186.1	15.4	14.5	16.6	18.0	13.8	13.4	14.5	12.7	14.4
Officers' Compensation **20**	1.1	5.8	9.6	10.7	4.9	3.6	3.5	2.7	1.6	1.3	0.7	0.9	0.3
Operating Margin **21**	•	•	•	•	•	•	•	•	•	•	•	•	•
Operating Margin Before Officers' Comp. **22**	•	•	6.4	•	•	•	•	•	•	•	•	•	•

Selected Average Balance Sheet ($ in Thousands)

Net Receivables 23	5222	0	61	68	619	1757	2404	4656	13890	27564	54987	156165	908376
Inventories 24	3518	0	28	45	546	1873	2686	6422	9443	22295	32460	79634	641423
Net Property, Plant and Equipment 25	6250	0	20	127	569	1584	3619	7646	13923	30933	63537	189351	1112094
Total Assets 26	41989	0	171	677	2428	7441	15286	34168	71472	174767	354515	1211810	8248222
Notes and Loans Payable 27	9469	0	65	1977	836	2922	3711	8825	15186	30528	64822	275961	1806959
All Other Liabilities 28	10121	0	75	476	639	2170	3618	8130	19656	43399	83629	336959	1829300
Net Worth 29	22400	0	32	-1776	953	2349	7957	17214	36630	100840	206064	598890	4611963

Selected Financial Ratios (Times to 1)

Current Ratio 30	2.0	•	1.4	2.4	2.0	1.6	2.2	2.4	1.9	2.6	2.3	2.3	1.8
Quick Ratio 31	1.2	•	1.0	1.0	1.2	0.9	1.4	1.4	1.2	1.5	1.4	1.6	1.0
Net Sales to Working Capital 32	2.7	•	18.1	3.4	5.5	6.2	3.0	2.4	3.4	2.2	2.0	1.9	3.1
Coverage Ratio 33	•	•	•	•	•	•	•	•	•	•	•	•	•
Total Asset Turnover 34	0.6	•	4.0	1.4	1.8	1.7	1.0	0.8	1.0	0.8	0.6	0.5	0.5
Inventory Turnover 35	4.8	•	12.9	11.6	4.6	4.6	4.0	3.0	5.2	4.3	5.5	5.7	4.4
Receivables Turnover 36	4.2	•	11.9	14.5	7.1	7.9	6.3	4.7	4.8	5.1	4.3	3.3	4.1
Total Liabilities to Net Worth 37	0.9	•	4.4	•	1.5	2.2	0.9	1.0	1.0	0.7	0.7	1.0	0.8
Current Assets to Working Capital 38	2.0	•	3.6	1.7	2.0	2.6	1.8	1.7	2.1	1.6	1.7	1.8	2.3
Current Liabilities to Working Capital 39	1.0	•	2.6	0.7	1.0	1.6	0.8	0.7	1.1	0.6	0.7	0.8	1.3
Working Capital to Net Sales 40	0.4	•	0.1	0.3	0.2	0.2	0.3	0.4	0.3	0.4	0.5	0.5	0.3
Inventory to Working Capital 41	0.4	•	0.9	0.2	0.7	1.0	0.5	0.4	0.5	0.3	0.3	0.2	0.5
Total Receipts to Cash Flow 42	•	•	7.1	•	20.7	26.9	•	•	•	18.8	•	•	56.6
Cost of Goods to Cash Flow 43	•	•	3.7	•	11.9	18.1	•	•	•	13.2	•	•	41.5
Cash Flow to Total Debt 44	•	•	0.7	•	0.1	0.1	•	•	•	0.1	•	•	0.0

Selected Financial Factors (in Percentages)

Debt Ratio 45	46.7	•	81.4	362.3	60.7	68.4	47.9	49.6	48.7	42.3	41.9	50.6	44.1
Return on Total Assets 46	•	•	•	•	•	•	•	•	•	•	•	•	•
Return on Equity Before Income Taxes 47	•	•	•	90.1	•	•	•	•	•	•	•	•	•
Return on Equity After Income Taxes 48	•	•	•	90.2	•	•	•	•	•	•	•	•	•
Profit Margin (Before Income Tax) 49	•	•	•	•	•	•	•	•	•	•	•	•	•
Profit Margin (After Income Tax) 50	•	•	•	•	•	•	•	•	•	•	•	•	•

143

Table II
Corporations with Net Income

SEMICONDUCTOR AND OTHER ELECTRONIC COMPONENT

MONEY AMOUNTS AND SIZE OF ASSETS IN THOUSANDS OF DOLLARS

Item Description for Accounting Period 7/02 Through 6/03	Total	Zero Assets	Under 500	500 to 1,000	1,000 to 5,000	5,000 to 10,000	10,000 to 25,000	25,000 to 50,000	50,000 to 100,000	100,000 to 250,000	250,000 to 500,000	500,000 to 2,500,000	2,500,000 and over
Number of Enterprises 1	3242	43	2153	222	493	169	82	17	18	22	7	11	4
Revenues ($ in Thousands)													
Net Sales 2	31307534	101181	1978641	286992	3086702	2342122	1890560	610761	1864999	4118369	1591590	7177576	6258041
Interest 3	358530	113	454	702	3098	2225	2699	1748	4856	25709	41023	54766	221135
Rents 4	50885	0	8396	0	124	1501	1225	3919	0	3279	478	2518	29444
Royalties 5	1004354	0	0	0	13	0	22040	0	84	101401	1534	29226	850057
Other Portfolio Income 6	370201	134	1923	0	34270	7695	6862	28025	22457	34759	14448	89732	129897
Other Receipts 7	369600	1122	5985	0	30796	10008	12351	3453	6923	53619	59321	196328	-10304
Total Receipts 8	33461104	102550	1995399	287694	3155003	2363551	1935737	647906	1899319	4337136	1708394	7550146	7478270
Average Total Receipts 9	10321	2385	927	1296	6400	13986	23607	38112	105518	197143	244056	686377	1869568
Operating Costs/Operating Income (%)													
Cost of Operations 10	61.0	49.6	51.4	40.6	54.0	59.5	61.2	65.9	69.2	68.3	83.6	63.6	52.7
Salaries and Wages 11	12.8	6.5	10.7	0.6	13.4	10.7	10.1	9.9	8.5	8.2	8.3	12.1	21.8
Taxes Paid 12	1.9	2.8	2.2	4.8	3.1	2.3	2.5	1.8	1.5	1.1	0.9	1.4	2.3
Interest Paid 13	1.2	0.2	0.6	0.1	0.5	0.6	0.9	3.6	0.8	0.8	0.9	1.1	2.4
Depreciation 14	4.3	1.9	0.4	1.8	3.0	2.8	2.9	3.0	2.4	4.0	2.2	6.5	6.2
Amortization and Depletion 15	0.5	0.2	0.0	*	0.2	0.2	0.2	1.5	0.4	0.2	0.0	0.6	0.9
Pensions and Other Deferred Comp. 16	0.4	0.4	0.3	2.1	0.6	0.2	0.7	0.2	0.5	0.2	0.4	0.2	0.4
Employee Benefits 17	2.3	0.5	1.1	0.5	1.9	1.9	1.5	0.9	1.0	1.6	1.1	1.9	5.0
Advertising 18	0.6	1.0	0.6	0.0	0.5	0.6	0.8	1.0	0.1	1.1	0.3	0.5	0.4
Other Expenses 19	10.1	9.8	18.3	13.3	10.9	12.3	9.0	4.7	10.2	9.8	2.3	7.7	11.7
Officers' Compensation 20	2.5	2.3	8.8	16.9	3.7	3.0	3.0	1.9	1.2	1.2	0.5	1.4	2.1
Operating Margin 21	2.6	24.7	5.5	19.2	8.0	5.9	7.1	5.5	4.2	3.4	*	3.0	*
Operating Margin Before Officers' Comp. 22	5.1	27.0	14.4	36.1	11.7	8.9	10.2	7.4	5.4	4.6	*	4.5	*

Selected Average Balance Sheet ($ in Thousands)

Net Receivables 23	1949	79	0	53	735	2049	3551	5229	19424	34506	32600	140949	539988
Inventories 24	1416	23	0	56	660	2230	3850	6723	12223	28697	28963	51970	381870
Net Property, Plant and Equipment 25	2085	10	0	140	647	1369	3290	4350	9415	30380	46885	249222	476509
Total Assets 26	11903	195	0	586	2935	7216	15148	34013	74709	174725	323540	1032728	3684998
Notes and Loans Payable 27	1601	34	0	20	591	1421	3374	11654	12602	20287	21991	100100	544604
All Other Liabilities 28	2661	90	0	78	543	1753	3372	8943	23008	43672	78909	278099	608756
Net Worth 29	7642	71	0	488	1801	4043	8403	13415	39099	110766	222639	654529	2531638

Selected Financial Ratios (Times to 1)

Current Ratio 30	2.6	1.7	•	3.6	2.8	2.3	2.5	2.1	2.1	2.5	2.1	2.6	3.2
Quick Ratio 31	1.7	1.4	•	2.9	1.7	1.2	1.4	1.4	1.4	1.4	1.4	1.8	2.1
Net Sales to Working Capital 32	2.4	13.5	•	5.2	5.1	4.6	3.7	3.2	3.9	2.9	2.6	1.8	1.4
Coverage Ratio 33	9.3	11.8	124.0	132.5	20.3	11.7	11.5	4.2	9.0	12.4	8.3	8.9	7.3
Total Asset Turnover 34	0.8	4.7	•	2.2	2.1	1.9	1.5	1.1	1.4	1.1	0.7	0.6	0.4
Inventory Turnover 35	4.2	20.4	•	9.4	5.1	3.7	3.7	3.5	5.9	4.5	6.6	8.0	2.2
Receivables Turnover 36	4.5	12.0	•	13.5	8.4	7.0	6.1	6.2	5.6	5.9	5.0	9.3	2.4
Total Liabilities to Net Worth 37	0.6	1.8	•	0.2	0.6	0.8	0.8	1.5	0.9	0.6	0.5	0.6	0.5
Current Assets to Working Capital 38	1.6	2.4	•	1.4	1.5	1.8	1.6	1.9	1.9	1.7	1.9	1.6	1.5
Current Liabilities to Working Capital 39	0.6	1.4	•	0.4	0.5	0.8	0.6	0.9	0.9	0.7	0.9	0.6	0.5
Working Capital to Net Sales 40	0.4	0.1	•	0.2	0.2	0.2	0.3	0.3	0.3	0.3	0.4	0.6	0.7
Inventory to Working Capital 41	0.2	0.4	•	0.2	0.5	0.7	0.6	0.5	0.4	0.4	0.3	0.1	0.1
Total Receipts to Cash Flow 42	6.0	5.0	2.9	3.9	6.1	6.3	6.1	10.5	7.2	6.0	12.8	7.0	4.4
Cost of Goods to Cash Flow 43	3.6	2.6	1.4	1.6	3.3	3.8	3.8	6.9	5.0	4.1	10.7	4.4	2.3
Cash Flow to Total Debt 44	0.4	1.5	•	3.3	0.9	0.7	0.6	0.2	0.4	0.5	0.2	0.2	0.3

Selected Financial Factors (in Percentages)

Debt Ratio 45	35.8	63.8	•	16.8	38.6	44.0	44.5	60.6	47.7	36.6	31.2	36.6	31.3
Return on Total Assets 46	9.1	32.7	•	43.2	22.9	14.3	15.8	15.8	9.4	11.2	5.4	6.2	7.6
Return on Equity Before Income Taxes 47	12.7	82.7	•	51.5	35.5	23.3	26.1	30.4	16.0	16.3	6.9	8.7	9.5
Return on Equity After Income Taxes 48	10.5	81.9	•	50.3	31.4	21.2	23.4	26.4	13.7	13.3	5.8	6.0	8.2
Profit Margin (Before Income Tax) 49	10.0	6.4	25.9	19.4	10.2	6.8	9.5	11.4	6.0	9.7	6.8	8.7	15.4
Profit Margin (After Income Tax) 50	8.3	6.3	18.6	19.0	9.0	6.2	8.5	9.8	5.2	7.9	5.7	6.0	13.2

Table I

Corporations with and without Net Income

NAVIGATIONAL, MEASURING, ELECTROMEDICAL, AND CONTROL

MONEY AMOUNTS AND SIZE OF ASSETS IN THOUSANDS OF DOLLARS

Item Description for Accounting Period 7/02 Through 6/03	Total	Zero Assets	Under 500	500 to 1,000	1,000 to 5,000	5,000 to 10,000	10,000 to 25,000	25,000 to 50,000	50,000 to 100,000	100,000 to 250,000	250,000 to 500,000	500,000 to 2,500,000	2,500,000 and over
Number of Enterprises 1	2814	110	1404	392	558	137	80	37	32	26	16	12	9
Revenues ($ in Thousands)													
Net Sales 2	46492987	217638	505889	344200	2348089	1313202	1395449	1507922	2149860	2968135	4932642	6598269	22211693
Interest 3	865311	296	727	192	3631	1779	3595	4043	12121	35404	43516	93647	666361
Rents 4	94564	50	2413	0	1120	3920	1439	1086	10930	2197	2498	11000	57911
Royalties 5	604747	76	0	0	39	0	449	1337	1845	12268	49484	23760	515489
Other Portfolio Income 6	976360	2	12711	0	7892	1525	4550	5143	16445	12349	83127	191715	640903
Other Receipts 7	931809	3935	533	236	22718	13937	22340	14841	26943	19012	114899	239557	452852
Total Receipts 8	49965778	221997	522273	344628	2383489	1334363	1427822	1534372	2218144	3049365	5226166	7157948	24545209
Average Total Receipts 9	17756	2018	372	879	4271	9740	17848	41470	69317	117283	326635	596496	2727245
Operating Costs/Operating Income (%)													
Cost of Operations 10	61.0	51.2	50.8	64.6	53.5	57.7	55.6	59.0	57.3	58.5	59.6	55.8	65.4
Salaries and Wages 11	16.6	25.8	2.9	9.1	14.7	14.8	16.1	15.7	15.1	19.0	16.9	21.4	15.7
Taxes Paid 12	2.4	1.7	3.0	2.3	3.1	2.8	2.4	2.2	2.1	2.7	2.6	1.1	2.7
Interest Paid 13	3.3	2.9	1.2	2.0	1.3	1.6	0.8	1.3	1.5	1.0	3.3	2.9	4.5
Depreciation 14	3.9	2.6	2.2	2.1	2.6	3.1	2.6	3.1	2.8	3.9	2.8	4.4	4.6
Amortization and Depletion 15	1.5	1.1	0.5	0.1	0.4	0.4	0.5	0.6	0.7	1.4	2.0	2.4	1.5
Pensions and Other Deferred Comp. 16	1.3	0.3	1.7	0.6	0.2	0.6	0.5	0.7	0.9	1.4	0.5	0.8	1.9
Employee Benefits 17	2.9	3.9	2.0	1.0	1.8	2.2	2.1	2.5	2.1	2.7	3.5	3.7	2.8
Advertising 18	1.0	1.1	0.8	1.0	0.9	1.7	1.6	1.6	2.7	1.9	0.7	0.6	0.7
Other Expenses 19	16.4	23.1	28.9	8.7	18.7	14.1	15.6	17.2	17.1	15.1	14.8	21.1	15.1
Officers' Compensation 20	1.4	4.2	16.9	8.5	5.1	4.3	2.6	2.1	2.1	1.9	1.0	0.8	0.3
Operating Margin 21	•	•	•	0.2	•	•	•	•	•	•	•	•	•
Operating Margin Before Officers' Comp. 22	•	•	6.0	8.7	2.8	1.1	2.2	•	•	•	•	•	•

Selected Average Balance Sheet ($ in Thousands)

Net Receivables 23	3303	0	56	114	761	1836	3281	6946	14556	28086	72566	120493	463655
Inventories 24	2663	0	35	178	609	2366	3322	6599	12038	21065	40389	97021	384080
Net Property, Plant and Equipment 25	3028	0	10	87	504	1501	2404	6333	8307	25059	41977	142959	472693
Total Assets 26	23620	0	158	666	2356	7663	14413	35183	69770	165883	372994	997873	4075189
Notes and Loans Payable 27	6878	0	48	287	813	2365	2549	6658	10260	15767	137820	196160	1405455
All Other Liabilities 28	6271	0	47	87	908	1731	3429	9614	21777	30884	98421	230497	1147902
Net Worth 29	10472	0	63	292	635	3567	8435	18911	37734	119232	136754	571216	1521832

Selected Financial Ratios (Times to 1)

Current Ratio 30	1.5	•	2.2	2.4	1.7	2.2	2.5	2.0	2.0	3.0	1.7	1.9	1.2
Quick Ratio 31	1.0	•	1.6	1.1	1.1	1.2	1.5	1.1	1.3	2.0	1.1	1.3	0.7
Net Sales to Working Capital 32	5.1	•	6.0	4.6	6.3	3.5	2.9	4.3	3.2	1.7	4.4	2.9	14.2
Coverage Ratio 33	0.1	•	•	1.1	0.4	•	3.5	•	0.5	•	0.5	•	0.3
Total Asset Turnover 34	0.7	•	2.3	1.3	1.8	1.3	1.2	1.2	1.0	0.7	0.8	0.6	0.6
Inventory Turnover 35	3.8	•	5.3	3.2	3.7	2.3	2.9	3.6	3.2	3.2	4.5	3.2	4.2
Receivables Turnover 36	3.8	•	5.2	6.7	5.0	4.4	4.9	5.6	4.9	4.8	4.3	3.2	3.4
Total Liabilities to Net Worth 37	1.3	•	1.5	1.3	2.7	1.1	0.7	0.9	0.8	0.4	1.7	0.7	1.7
Current Assets to Working Capital 38	2.9	•	1.9	1.7	2.5	1.8	1.7	2.0	2.0	1.5	2.4	2.1	7.3
Current Liabilities to Working Capital 39	1.9	•	0.9	0.7	1.5	0.8	0.7	1.0	1.0	0.5	1.4	1.1	6.3
Working Capital to Net Sales 40	0.2	•	0.2	0.2	0.2	0.3	0.3	0.2	0.3	0.6	0.2	0.4	0.1
Inventory to Working Capital 41	0.7	•	0.5	0.9	0.8	0.7	0.5	0.6	0.6	0.3	0.4	0.5	1.9
Total Receipts to Cash Flow 42	11.9	143.0	7.3	13.1	6.9	10.4	6.6	9.7	7.9	18.6	11.2	8.1	17.4
Cost of Goods to Cash Flow 43	7.3	73.3	3.7	8.5	3.7	6.0	3.6	5.7	4.6	10.9	6.6	4.5	11.3
Cash Flow to Total Debt 44	0.1	•	0.5	0.2	0.4	0.2	0.4	0.3	0.3	0.1	0.1	0.2	0.1

Selected Financial Factors (in Percentages)

Debt Ratio 45	55.7	•	60.0	56.2	73.0	53.5	41.5	46.3	45.9	28.1	63.3	42.8	62.7
Return on Total Assets 46	0.1	•	•	2.9	0.9	•	3.3	•	0.8	•	1.4	•	0.8
Return on Equity Before Income Taxes 47	•	•	•	0.8	•	4.0	•	•	•	•	•	•	•
Return on Equity After Income Taxes 48	•	•	•	•	•	1.9	•	•	•	•	•	•	•
Profit Margin (Before Income Tax) 49	•	•	•	0.3	•	1.9	•	•	•	•	•	•	•
Profit Margin (After Income Tax) 50	•	•	•	•	•	0.9	•	•	•	•	•	•	•

Table II
Corporations with Net Income

NAVIGATIONAL, MEASURING, ELECTROMEDICAL, AND CONTROL

MONEY AMOUNTS AND SIZE OF ASSETS IN THOUSANDS OF DOLLARS

Item Description for Accounting Period 7/02 Through 6/03	Total	Zero Assets	Under 500	500 to 1,000	1,000 to 5,000	5,000 to 10,000	10,000 to 25,000	25,000 to 50,000	50,000 to 100,000	100,000 to 250,000	250,000 to 500,000	500,000 to 2,500,000	2,500,000 and over
Number of Enterprises 1	1135	0	441	0	347	71	52	19	17	14	9	6	6
Revenues ($ in Thousands)													
Net Sales 2	27921134	0	368383	0	1540214	846166	994936	934808	1268636	1878037	3529406	3384421	12890944
Interest 3	287559	0	54	0	2366	709	1881	1335	6346	6723	21309	18933	227716
Rents 4	63242	0	2413	0	0	945	848	696	10655	608	1267	7392	38417
Royalties 5	295282	0	0	0	0	0	0	89	29	1	39165	7153	248846
Other Portfolio Income 6	741270	0	9531	0	7878	1449	4495	1465	8216	6181	23430	172066	506560
Other Receipts 7	514851	0	112	0	18045	1686	18197	12239	11125	9197	26024	70035	345412
Total Receipts 8	29823338	0	380493	0	1568503	850955	1020357	950632	1305007	1900747	3640601	3660000	14257895
Average Total Receipts 9	26276	•	863	•	4520	11985	19622	50033	76765	135768	404511	610000	2376316
Operating Costs/Operating Income (%)													
Cost of Operations 10	59.2	•	61.7	•	54.2	53.7	52.4	57.7	56.1	55.6	62.4	58.2	61.1
Salaries and Wages 11	13.7	•	2.8	•	11.7	13.6	14.8	12.7	12.6	14.2	13.5	14.3	14.2
Taxes Paid 12	2.0	•	3.1	•	3.0	2.5	2.3	2.1	2.1	2.3	2.5	1.1	1.9
Interest Paid 13	2.5	•	1.5	•	1.2	1.0	0.6	1.1	0.7	0.8	1.9	2.0	3.7
Depreciation 14	3.8	•	1.9	•	2.4	2.2	2.1	2.3	2.5	3.5	2.4	3.1	5.0
Amortization and Depletion 15	1.1	•	0.6	•	0.2	0.1	0.2	0.6	0.3	1.0	0.9	1.8	1.3
Pensions and Other Deferred Comp. 16	1.1	•	•	•	0.2	0.6	0.6	0.8	1.1	1.7	0.6	1.4	1.3
Employee Benefits 17	2.8	•	2.7	•	1.7	2.3	2.2	2.1	1.6	2.8	3.4	2.3	3.2
Advertising 18	0.9	•	1.1	•	0.7	1.6	1.9	1.8	4.0	0.9	0.6	0.5	0.6
Other Expenses 19	13.3	•	11.7	•	14.1	10.6	11.7	13.6	15.2	12.0	10.6	15.1	13.6
Officers' Compensation 20	1.3	•	11.3	•	4.1	4.1	2.6	2.0	1.6	1.8	0.9	0.9	0.4
Operating Margin 21	•	•	1.6	•	6.4	7.7	8.6	3.3	2.3	3.4	0.3	•	•
Operating Margin Before Officers' Comp. 22	•	•	13.0	•	10.5	11.8	11.2	5.3	3.9	5.2	1.2	•	0.0

Selected Average Balance Sheet ($ in Thousands)

Net Receivables 23	3937	100	•	854	1602	3455	8249	13923	30400	86828	97017	271365
Inventories 24	3779	97	•	689	2619	3640	8122	11443	19749	49145	82200	341529
Net Property, Plant and Equipment 25	4023	23	•	604	1962	2314	5946	9449	22471	47181	97350	412627
Total Assets 26	31376	293	•	2393	7831	14474	34992	66505	153091	359692	754636	3596898
Notes and Loans Payable 27	8977	149	•	755	1517	2324	7744	5928	16713	96174	158996	1221193
All Other Liabilities 28	7171	86	•	679	1552	2911	10775	16122	33704	105215	198320	749596
Net Worth 29	15228	58	•	959	4762	9239	16473	44455	102674	158303	397320	1626109

Selected Financial Ratios (Times to 1)

Current Ratio 30	1.2	2.3	•	2.1	2.7	2.8	1.8	2.3	2.1	1.4	1.1	0.9
Quick Ratio 31	0.7	1.4	•	1.5	1.5	1.5	1.1	1.5	1.3	1.0	0.6	0.5
Net Sales to Working Capital 32	13.7	6.8	•	4.9	3.6	3.0	5.9	3.0	3.3	9.3	15.3	•
Coverage Ratio 33	3.7	4.3	•	8.0	9.6	19.9	5.4	10.1	7.0	3.0	6.1	2.7
Total Asset Turnover 34	0.8	2.8	•	1.9	1.5	1.3	1.4	1.1	0.9	1.1	0.7	0.6
Inventory Turnover 35	3.9	5.3	•	3.5	2.4	2.8	3.5	3.7	3.8	5.0	4.0	3.8
Receivables Turnover 36	4.0	8.8	•	4.4	5.9	5.1	5.4	5.8	5.4	4.4	3.6	3.4
Total Liabilities to Net Worth 37	1.1	4.0	•	1.5	0.6	0.6	1.1	0.5	0.5	1.3	0.9	1.2
Current Assets to Working Capital 38	6.4	1.8	•	1.9	1.6	1.6	2.3	1.8	1.9	3.6	7.9	•
Current Liabilities to Working Capital 39	5.4	0.8	•	0.9	0.6	0.6	1.3	0.8	0.9	2.6	6.9	•
Working Capital to Net Sales 40	0.1	0.1	•	0.2	0.3	0.3	0.2	0.3	0.3	0.1	0.1	•
Inventory to Working Capital 41	1.8	0.6	•	0.5	0.6	0.6	0.7	0.5	0.5	0.7	1.9	•
Total Receipts to Cash Flow 42	6.8	12.6	•	5.0	5.7	4.7	6.0	5.7	7.3	9.1	4.7	8.0
Cost of Goods to Cash Flow 43	4.0	7.8	•	2.7	3.0	2.5	3.5	3.2	4.1	5.7	2.7	4.9
Cash Flow to Total Debt 44	0.2	0.3	•	0.6	0.7	0.8	0.4	0.6	0.4	0.2	0.3	0.1

Selected Financial Factors (in Percentages)

Debt Ratio 45	51.5	80.2	•	59.9	39.2	36.2	52.9	33.2	32.9	56.0	47.3	54.8
Return on Total Assets 46	7.1	18.3	•	17.4	14.1	15.5	8.5	7.7	4.9	6.3	9.3	5.8
Return on Equity Before Income Taxes 47	10.6	70.8	•	38.1	20.8	23.0	14.7	10.4	6.2	9.5	14.8	8.0
Return on Equity After Income Taxes 48	8.0	62.2	•	35.6	17.4	20.1	11.5	7.9	4.7	7.2	10.4	5.8
Profit Margin (Before Income Tax) 49	6.6	4.9	•	8.2	8.3	11.1	4.9	6.2	4.8	3.8	10.4	6.1
Profit Margin (After Income Tax) 50	5.0	4.3	•	7.7	6.9	9.7	3.9	4.7	3.6	2.9	7.3	4.4

ELECTRICAL LIGHTING EQUIPMENT AND HOUSEHOLD APPLIANCE

Table I
Corporations with and without Net Income

MONEY AMOUNTS AND SIZE OF ASSETS IN THOUSANDS OF DOLLARS

Item Description for Accounting Period 7/02 Through 6/03	Total	Zero Assets	Under 500	500 to 1,000	1,000 to 5,000	5,000 to 10,000	10,000 to 25,000	25,000 to 50,000	50,000 to 100,000	100,000 to 250,000	250,000 to 500,000	500,000 to 2,500,000	2,500,000 and over
Number of Enterprises **1**	1555	0	1075	0	292	73	42	20	9	20	0	7	4
Revenues ($ in Thousands)													
Net Sales **2**	133991882	0	205374	0	1406853	1348269	1230740	1187353	1067435	4794796	0	11377166	111271763
Interest **3**	19441950	0	0	0	90	408	1106	358	1074	10180	0	49035	19379303
Rents **4**	33850	0	0	0	0	212	601	106	364	1160	0	20112	9265
Royalties **5**	1870796					4	15	661	46	7999		34496	1827573
Other Portfolio Income **6**	5172355	0	0	0	1398	141	937	1441	245	7455	0	48738	5109020
Other Receipts **7**	13614409	0	5768	0	1133	23856	4283	9315	16129	28819	0	116819	13351956
Total Receipts **8**	174125242	0	211142	0	1409474	1372890	1237682	1199234	1085293	4850409	0	11646366	150948880
Average Total Receipts **9**	111978		196	•	4827	18807	29469	59962	120588	242520		1663767	37737220
Operating Costs/Operating Income (%)													
Cost of Operations **10**	61.5	•	52.1	•	65.7	70.7	67.4	66.8	62.8	63.5	•	74.3	59.9
Salaries and Wages **11**	11.2	•	4.7	•	8.4	10.9	7.9	6.8	9.5	6.5	•	6.4	12.1
Taxes Paid **12**	0.9	•	2.6	•	1.9	3.4	1.9	1.7	1.8	1.5	•	1.5	0.7
Interest Paid **13**	17.4	•	1.2	•	0.9	1.0	0.8	1.2	1.5	1.1	•	2.0	20.6
Depreciation **14**	11.2	•	0.8	•	2.1	1.5	2.1	1.9	2.3	2.6	•	2.7	13.0
Amortization and Depletion **15**	1.3	•	0.0	•	0.9	0.1	0.1	0.5	0.4	0.4	•	0.8	1.4
Pensions and Other Deferred Comp. **16**	0.6	•	•	•	0.1	0.1	0.5	0.4	0.5	0.4	•	0.7	0.7
Employee Benefits **17**	1.3	•	0.0	•	2.0	1.0	2.0	1.0	2.2	1.6	•	1.1	1.3
Advertising **18**	0.9	•	2.7	•	0.7	2.5	1.1	4.3	2.6	5.1	•	1.1	0.7
Other Expenses **19**	21.0	•	29.9	•	14.5	10.6	11.2	13.3	12.7	10.6	•	12.0	22.7
Officers' Compensation **20**	0.4	•	12.7	•	3.6	1.5	2.5	1.5	1.1	1.0	•	0.2	0.2
Operating Margin **21**	•	•	•	•	•	•	•	0.6	2.7	5.9	•	•	•
Operating Margin Before Officers' Comp. **22**	•	•	5.9	•	2.7	•	5.0	2.1	3.7	6.9	•	•	•

Selected Average Balance Sheet ($ in Thousands)

Item										
Net Receivables 23	89015	•	527	1923	3640	10495	17926	35489	•	229013	33817722
Inventories 24	5709	•	637	2695	4461	8566	19283	32417	•	170434	1526100
Net Property, Plant and Equipment 25	35593	•	377	1304	3431	5503	15694	35796	•	251399	13061556
Total Assets 26	476612	•	2159	7278	15646	33780	71433	178864	•	1350326	181220043
Notes and Loans Payable 27	212994	•	686	2643	6063	8894	22055	36241	•	338484	81738886
All Other Liabilities 28	105514	•	789	3648	3913	11026	17974	48985	•	484327	39658348
Net Worth 29	158103	•	684	987	5670	13860	31404	93637	•	527515	59822808

Selected Financial Ratios (Times to 1)

Item											
Current Ratio 30	0.7	•	1.4	1.3	1.2	1.9	1.9	1.8	2.3	•	1.5	0.6
Quick Ratio 31	0.6	•	0.7	0.7	0.6	1.0	1.0	0.9	1.1	•	0.8	0.5
Net Sales to Working Capital 32	•	•	12.0	19.9	18.9	5.8	5.6	5.4	4.3	•	10.3	•
Coverage Ratio 33	1.2	•	0.2	•	•	4.6	2.5	3.9	7.4	•	0.8	1.2
Total Asset Turnover 34	0.2	•	2.2	2.8	2.5	1.9	1.8	1.7	1.3	•	1.2	0.2
Inventory Turnover 35	9.3	•	5.0	6.4	4.8	4.4	4.6	3.9	4.7	•	7.1	10.9
Receivables Turnover 36	0.9	•	10.2	9.5	9.1	7.7	5.7	6.6	6.5	•	9.9	0.8
Total Liabilities to Net Worth 37	2.0	•	2.2	•	6.4	1.8	1.4	1.3	0.9	•	1.6	2.0
Current Assets to Working Capital 38	•	•	3.7	4.8	5.7	2.1	2.2	2.2	1.8	•	3.0	•
Current Liabilities to Working Capital 39	•	•	2.7	3.8	4.7	1.1	1.2	1.2	0.8	•	2.0	•
Working Capital to Net Sales 40	•	•	0.1	0.1	0.1	0.2	0.2	0.2	0.2	•	0.1	•
Inventory to Working Capital 41	•	•	1.8	2.2	2.7	0.9	0.8	0.9	0.6	•	1.2	•
Total Receipts to Cash Flow 42	5.1	•	9.4	5.5	12.8	8.1	7.5	6.6	6.0	•	9.8	4.7
Cost of Goods to Cash Flow 43	3.1	•	6.2	2.8	9.1	5.5	5.0	4.1	3.8	•	7.3	2.8
Cash Flow to Total Debt 44	0.1	•	0.3	0.3	0.2	0.4	0.4	0.5	0.5	•	0.2	0.0

Selected Financial Factors (in Percentages)

Item											
Debt Ratio 45	66.8	•	204.0	68.3	86.4	63.8	59.0	56.0	47.6	•	60.9	67.0
Return on Total Assets 46	3.8	•	0.4	•	•	7.1	5.5	9.7	10.9	•	1.9	3.8
Return on Equity Before Income Taxes 47	2.1	•	10.8	•	•	15.4	8.1	16.4	18.0	•	•	2.0
Return on Equity After Income Taxes 48	1.4	•	10.8	•	•	12.6	5.4	14.7	15.2	•	•	1.4
Profit Margin (Before Income Tax) 49	3.8	•	•	•	•	3.0	1.9	4.3	7.0	•	•	4.4
Profit Margin (After Income Tax) 50	2.6	•	•	•	•	2.4	1.3	3.9	6.0	•	•	3.0

Table II

Corporations with Net Income

ELECTRICAL LIGHTING EQUIPMENT AND HOUSEHOLD APPLIANCE

MONEY AMOUNTS AND SIZE OF ASSETS IN THOUSANDS OF DOLLARS

Item Description for Accounting Period 7/02 Through 6/03		Total	Zero Assets	Under 500	500 to 1,000	1,000 to 5,000	5,000 to 10,000	10,000 to 25,000	25,000 to 50,000	50,000 to 100,000	100,000 to 250,000	250,000 to 500,000	500,000 to 2,500,000	2,500,000 and over
Number of Enterprises	1	794	•	506	0	181	25	33	14	0	20	0	0	0
Revenues ($ in Thousands)														
Net Sales	2	126062060	•	85456	0	1088286	493193	1114986	831249	0	4794796	0	0	0
Interest	3	18983257	•	0	0	0	249	460	273	0	10180	0	0	0
Rents	4	21317	•	0	0	0	0	601	6	0	1160	0	0	0
Royalties	5	1674226	•	0	0	0	4	15	0	0	7999	0	0	0
Other Portfolio Income	6	5141115	•	0	0	0	138	458	1208	0	7455	0	0	0
Other Receipts	7	13449657	•	3	0	1071	3750	3616	1688	0	28819	0	0	0
Total Receipts	8	165331632	•	85459	0	1089357	497334	1120136	834424	0	4850409	0	0	0
Average Total Receipts	9	208226	•	169	•	6019	19893	33944	59602	•	242520	•	•	•
Operating Costs/Operating Income (%)														
Cost of Operations	10	61.2	•	51.7	•	66.4	63.9	66.9	66.3	•	63.5	•	•	•
Salaries and Wages	11	11.3	•	4.6	•	7.8	7.1	6.8	7.2	•	6.5	•	•	•
Taxes Paid	12	0.8	•	2.8	•	1.7	2.4	1.7	1.5	•	1.5	•	•	•
Interest Paid	13	17.9	•	2.2	•	0.6	0.3	0.8	0.9	•	1.1	•	•	•
Depreciation	14	11.8	•	1.4	•	1.6	2.0	1.9	2.1	•	2.6	•	•	•
Amortization and Depletion	15	1.2	•	•	•	0.1	•	0.1	0.2	•	0.4	•	•	•
Pensions and Other Deferred Comp.	16	0.6	•	•	•	0.2	0.2	0.5	0.4	•	0.4	•	•	•
Employee Benefits	17	1.3	•	0.0	•	2.0	1.2	1.9	1.1	•	1.6	•	•	•
Advertising	18	0.9	•	0.4	•	0.7	0.6	1.1	1.8	•	5.1	•	•	•
Other Expenses	19	21.0	•	15.6	•	11.9	17.5	10.0	11.7	•	10.6	•	•	•
Officers' Compensation	20	0.3	•	8.5	•	3.6	3.0	2.4	1.6	•	1.0	•	•	•
Operating Margin	21	•	•	12.8	•	3.5	1.8	6.0	5.4	•	5.9	•	•	•
Operating Margin Before Officers' Comp.	22	•	•	21.3	•	7.0	4.8	8.3	7.0	•	6.9	•	•	•

Selected Average Balance Sheet ($ in Thousands)

Net Receivables 23	172519	18	624	2867	4018	9575	35489
Inventories 24	10090	21	669	4462	4545	7397	34877
Net Property, Plant and Equipment 25	68297	41	331	1671	3754	5537	35796
Total Assets 26	920331	76	2016	7232	15680	32849	178864
Notes and Loans Payable 27	413860	68	475	1501	3958	5897	36241
All Other Liabilities 28	199389	-8	530	2213	3839	8086	48985
Net Worth 29	307082	15	1011	3518	7882	18866	93637

Selected Financial Ratios (Times to 1)

Current Ratio 30	0.7	3.3	2.1	1.8	2.0	2.5	2.3
Quick Ratio 31	0.6	1.5	1.0	1.3	1.0	1.4	1.1
Net Sales to Working Capital 32		6.1	6.9	8.1	6.2	4.6	4.3
Coverage Ratio 33	1.3	6.7	6.6	11.3	9.3	8.3	7.4
Total Asset Turnover 34	0.2	2.2	3.0	2.7	2.2	1.8	1.3
Inventory Turnover 35	9.6	4.1	6.0	2.8	5.0	5.3	4.4
Receivables Turnover 36	0.9	15.5	12.0	4.5	8.1	6.3	13.5
Total Liabilities to Net Worth 37	2.0	4.0	1.0	1.1	1.0	0.7	0.9
Current Assets to Working Capital 38		1.4	1.9	2.2	2.0	1.7	1.8
Current Liabilities to Working Capital 39		0.4	0.9	1.2	1.0	0.7	0.8
Working Capital to Net Sales 40		0.2	0.1	0.1	0.2	0.2	0.2
Inventory to Working Capital 41		0.8	0.9	0.7	0.9	0.7	0.6
Total Receipts to Cash Flow 42	5.0	4.3	7.6	5.5	6.8	6.3	6.0
Cost of Goods to Cash Flow 43	3.0	2.2	5.1	3.5	4.6	4.2	3.8
Cash Flow to Total Debt 44	0.1	0.6	0.8	1.0	0.6	0.7	0.5

Selected Financial Factors (in Percentages)

Debt Ratio 45	66.6	80.0	49.8	51.4	49.7	42.6	47.6
Return on Total Assets 46	3.9	33.4	12.6	7.9	15.5	12.8	10.9
Return on Equity Before Income Taxes 47	2.3	142.2	21.2	14.9	27.5	19.6	18.0
Return on Equity After Income Taxes 48	1.6	142.2	20.7	11.7	24.9	16.8	15.2
Profit Margin (Before Income Tax) 49	4.5	12.8	3.6	2.7	6.4	6.2	7.0
Profit Margin (After Income Tax) 50	3.2	12.8	3.5	2.1	5.8	5.3	6.0

Table I
Corporations with and without Net Income

ELECTRICAL EQUIPMENT

MONEY AMOUNTS AND SIZE OF ASSETS IN THOUSANDS OF DOLLARS

Item Description for Accounting Period 7/02 Through 6/03	Total	Zero Assets	Under 500	500 to 1,000	1,000 to 5,000	5,000 to 10,000	10,000 to 25,000	25,000 to 50,000	50,000 to 100,000	100,000 to 250,000	250,000 to 500,000	500,000 to 2,500,000	2,500,000 and over
Number of Enterprises 1	1464	0	453	0	297	79	57	30	9	13	6	5	3
Revenues ($ in Thousands)													
Net Sales 2	31008458	0	360333	0	1164129	946676	1359319	1884752	592037	2177019	1453997	4692026	15940562
Interest 3	356218	0	25	0	626	845	1508	4558	8925	4731	5913	19162	309820
Rents 4	82114	0	0	0	751	0	1018	2745	896	406	0	68	76229
Royalties 5	274438	0	0	0	0	19	59	804	415	121775	3155	12520	135692
Other Portfolio Income 6	545940	0	6693	0	4968	319	1032	5449	2110	7227	22937	49795	445407
Other Receipts 7	371402	0	3344	0	20716	2139	6970	3277	715	16726	55132	18182	244140
Total Receipts 8	32638570	0	370395	0	1191190	949998	1369906	1901585	605098	2327884	1541134	4791753	17151850
Average Total Receipts 9	22294	•	818	•	4011	12025	24033	63386	67233	179068	256856	958351	5717283
Operating Costs/Operating Income (%)													
Cost of Operations 10	68.6	•	37.7	•	66.5	72.3	69.6	78.4	61.4	67.6	61.3	74.8	67.2
Salaries and Wages 11	6.8	•	8.7	•	10.9	4.9	9.6	5.4	9.9	10.8	11.1	5.1	5.7
Taxes Paid 12	1.9	•	4.1	•	3.4	2.0	2.3	1.3	1.8	2.1	2.7	0.7	2.0
Interest Paid 13	3.0	•	0.3	•	1.6	0.7	1.1	0.6	3.0	1.6	1.7	0.9	4.8
Depreciation 14	3.1	•	1.7	•	2.4	1.7	2.9	2.5	5.6	2.8	5.4	2.5	3.3
Amortization and Depletion 15	1.3	•	0.1	•	0.0	0.3	0.3	0.3	2.0	0.6	0.9	1.0	1.8
Pensions and Other Deferred Comp. 16	1.1	•	0.0	•	0.9	0.3	0.5	0.3	0.5	0.9	1.9	0.2	1.6
Employee Benefits 17	2.7	•	0.8	•	3.2	2.0	2.1	1.8	4.0	1.6	2.7	0.8	3.6
Advertising 18	0.6	•	0.4	•	0.7	0.1	0.8	0.3	1.1	0.9	0.5	1.0	0.4
Other Expenses 19	12.2	•	29.9	•	15.2	9.4	10.4	7.0	13.9	10.4	14.6	10.6	12.6
Officers' Compensation 20	1.1	•	15.5	•	4.4	3.1	2.0	1.0	1.9	1.4	0.9	0.4	0.5
Operating Margin 21	•	•	0.8	•	•	3.2	•	1.2	•	•	•	2.0	•
Operating Margin Before Officers' Comp. 22	•	•	16.2	•	•	6.3	0.4	2.1	•	0.8	•	•	2.5

Selected Average Balance Sheet ($ in Thousands)

Net Receivables 23	8291	•	794	1759	3905	9112	9594	26418	73650	258818	2994900
Inventories 24	2422	•	690	1227	3500	7860	10967	24752	44913	274934	428621
Net Property, Plant and Equipment 25	3738	•	425	766	2902	7813	15611	34796	84719	124179	1043905
Total Assets 26	43728	•	2403	6031	15276	34569	68014	151173	369540	1526634	16041835
Notes and Loans Payable 27	6543	•	1081	1600	4276	7010	15363	39400	63264	276584	2039688
All Other Liabilities 28	8914	•	749	3166	3838	10288	16107	38801	76458	351175	3046461
Net Worth 29	28271	•	572	1266	7162	17271	36544	72972	229819	898876	10955686

Selected Financial Ratios (Times to 1)

Current Ratio 30	1.3	•	1.9	1.2	2.1	1.8	1.7	1.7	2.7	1.4	1.1
Quick Ratio 31	0.9	•	1.0	0.8	1.2	1.0	0.8	0.9	1.8	1.0	0.9
Net Sales to Working Capital 32	8.1	•	4.5	17.0	4.5	6.2	6.2	5.9	2.2	5.8	20.3
Coverage Ratio 33	2.3	13.9	•	5.7	0.2	4.3	0.2	4.9	2.9	6.9	2.2
Total Asset Turnover 34	0.5	•	1.6	2.0	1.6	1.8	1.0	1.1	0.7	0.6	0.3
Inventory Turnover 35	6.0	•	3.8	7.1	4.7	6.3	3.7	4.6	3.3	2.6	8.3
Receivables Turnover 36	2.8	•	5.2	7.5	6.2	7.0	4.5	5.9	4.5	1.0	3.5
Total Liabilities to Net Worth 37	0.5	•	3.2	3.8	1.1	1.0	0.9	1.1	0.6	0.7	0.5
Current Assets to Working Capital 38	4.7	•	2.2	5.5	1.9	2.2	2.4	2.4	1.6	3.2	13.9
Current Liabilities to Working Capital 39	3.7	•	1.2	4.5	0.9	1.2	1.4	1.4	0.6	2.2	12.9
Working Capital to Net Sales 40	0.1	•	0.2	0.1	0.2	0.2	0.2	0.2	0.5	0.2	0.0
Inventory to Working Capital 41	0.9	•	0.9	1.7	0.6	0.8	0.7	0.8	0.4	0.8	1.6
Total Receipts to Cash Flow 42	8.1	•	21.4	8.3	13.4	12.5	11.6	6.8	6.7	7.7	7.6
Cost of Goods to Cash Flow 43	5.5	•	14.2	6.0	9.3	9.8	7.1	4.6	4.1	5.7	5.1
Cash Flow to Total Debt 44	0.2	•	0.1	0.3	0.2	0.3	0.2	0.3	0.3	0.2	0.1

Selected Financial Factors (in Percentages)

Debt Ratio 45	35.3	•	76.2	79.0	53.1	50.0	46.3	51.7	37.8	41.1	31.7
Return on Total Assets 46	3.4	7.6	•	8.5	0.4	4.9	0.5	8.8	3.3	3.6	3.4
Return on Equity Before Income Taxes 47	3.0	10.2	•	•	33.4	7.5	•	14.6	3.4	5.3	2.7
Return on Equity After Income Taxes 48	1.6	10.2	•	29.1	•	5.1	•	7.8	1.2	3.7	1.6
Profit Margin (Before Income Tax) 49	4.0	3.6	•	3.5	2.1	2.1	6.4	3.3	5.1	3.6	5.5
Profit Margin (After Income Tax) 50	2.2	3.6	•	3.1	1.4	1.4	3.4	1.1	3.6	3.3	3.3

Table II

Corporations with Net Income

ELECTRICAL EQUIPMENT

MONEY AMOUNTS AND SIZE OF ASSETS IN THOUSANDS OF DOLLARS

Item Description for Accounting Period 7/02 Through 6/03	Total	Zero Assets	Under 500	500 to 1,000	1,000 to 5,000	5,000 to 10,000	10,000 to 25,000	25,000 to 50,000	50,000 to 100,000	100,000 to 250,000	250,000 to 500,000	500,000 to 2,500,000	2,500,000 and over
Number of Enterprises **1**	651	•	348	73	93	62	31	20	0	9	0	0	0
Revenues ($ in Thousands)													
Net Sales **2**	27594327	•	358128	128325	564433	910580	852186	1280867	0	1813355	0	0	0
Interest **3**	342824	•	24	0	179	649	558	4063	0	3419	0	0	0
Rents **4**	77840	•	0	0	256	0	0	445	0	406	0	0	0
Royalties **5**	270447	•	0	0	0	0	0	804	0	120095	0	0	0
Other Portfolio Income **6**	535317	•	6166	0	236	224	570	3269	0	5783	0	0	0
Other Receipts **7**	336814	•	3112	0	18303	547	2559	1315	0	16049	0	0	0
Total Receipts **8**	29157569	•	367430	128325	583407	912000	855873	1290763	0	1959107	0	0	0
Average Total Receipts **9**	44789	•	1056	1758	6273	14710	27609	64538	•	217679	•	•	•
Operating Costs/Operating Income (%)													
Cost of Operations **10**	68.5	•	37.5	67.6	63.3	71.9	69.2	77.6	•	65.6	•	•	•
Salaries and Wages **11**	6.4	•	8.7	8.0	10.9	4.4	8.2	5.2	•	10.9	•	•	•
Taxes Paid **12**	1.9	•	4.1	1.2	2.2	1.9	2.3	1.4	•	2.1	•	•	•
Interest Paid **13**	2.8	•	0.2	0.6	1.6	0.7	1.1	0.5	•	0.6	•	•	•
Depreciation **14**	3.0	•	1.7	0.1	1.0	1.6	2.1	2.1	•	2.4	•	•	•
Amortization and Depletion **15**	1.3	•	0.1	•	0.0	0.0	0.2	0.3	•	0.6	•	•	•
Pensions and Other Deferred Comp. **16**	1.1	•	0.0	•	0.4	0.3	0.5	0.3	•	0.6	•	•	•
Employee Benefits **17**	2.7	•	0.8	0.1	3.3	2.0	1.6	1.6	•	1.0	•	•	•
Advertising **18**	0.6	•	0.3	0.2	1.0	0.1	0.6	0.3	•	1.4	•	•	•
Other Expenses **19**	11.4	•	29.4	17.2	11.6	8.4	7.7	5.8	•	0.9	•	•	•
Officers' Compensation **20**	1.0	•	15.5	0.8	1.9	3.1	1.8	1.0	•	10.0	•	•	•
Operating Margin **21**	•	•	1.5	4.2	2.7	5.6	4.7	3.9	•	1.5	•	•	•
Operating Margin Before Officers' Comp. **22**	0.3	•	17.1	5.0	4.6	8.7	6.5	4.9	•	3.1	•	•	•

Selected Average Balance Sheet ($ in Thousands)

Net Receivables 23	17780	•	162	216	1933	2098	4515	9701	•	29411
Inventories 24	4529	•	89	493	1365	1460	3662	8293	•	23482
Net Property, Plant and Equipment 25	7412	•	52	4	267	870	2511	8282	•	37986
Total Assets 26	83934	•	456	943	3535	5969	16449	35301	•	169818
Notes and Loans Payable 27	13109	•	114	381	1317	1971	4877	6082	•	27413
All Other Liabilities 28	16728	•	51	218	924	2135	3935	11405	•	47273
Net Worth 29	54097	•	291	344	1293	1863	7636	17814	•	95132

Selected Financial Ratios (Times to 1)

Current Ratio 30	1.3	•	7.8	1.2	2.7	1.2	2.1	1.8	•	1.7
Quick Ratio 31	1.0	•	5.3	0.4	1.9	0.8	1.2	0.9	•	0.9
Net Sales to Working Capital 32	8.1	•	3.0	15.5	3.0	22.1	4.6	6.2	•	6.2
Coverage Ratio 33	3.1	•	17.6	7.7	4.8	8.9	5.6	10.1	•	19.7
Total Asset Turnover 34	0.5	•	2.3	1.9	1.7	2.5	1.7	1.8	•	1.2
Inventory Turnover 35	6.4	•	4.4	2.4	2.8	7.2	5.2	6.0	•	5.6
Receivables Turnover 36	2.7	•	10.7	6.2	3.2	7.6	6.1	6.6	•	8.0
Total Liabilities to Net Worth 37	0.6	•	0.6	1.7	1.7	2.2	1.2	1.0	•	0.8
Current Assets to Working Capital 38	4.9	•	1.1	6.3	1.6	6.9	1.9	2.2	•	2.5
Current Liabilities to Working Capital 39	3.9	•	0.1	5.3	0.6	5.9	0.9	1.2	•	1.5
Working Capital to Net Sales 40	0.1	•	0.3	0.1	0.3	0.0	0.2	0.2	•	0.2
Inventory to Working Capital 41	0.9	•	0.4	4.3	0.5	2.1	0.7	0.7	•	0.8
Total Receipts to Cash Flow 42	7.3	•	4.3	5.2	6.5	7.5	9.0	10.2	•	5.2
Cost of Goods to Cash Flow 43	5.0	•	1.6	3.5	4.1	5.4	6.2	7.9	•	3.4
Cash Flow to Total Debt 44	0.2	•	1.5	0.6	0.4	0.5	0.3	0.4	•	0.5

Selected Financial Factors (in Percentages)

Debt Ratio 45	35.5	•	36.2	63.5	63.4	68.8	53.6	49.5	•	44.0
Return on Total Assets 46	4.5	•	9.9	9.0	13.0	16.0	10.4	9.5	•	14.0
Return on Equity Before Income Taxes 47	4.8	•	14.6	21.5	28.2	45.6	18.5	17.0	•	23.7
Return on Equity After Income Taxes 48	3.2	•	14.6	17.6	22.4	41.8	16.3	13.6	•	16.3
Profit Margin (Before Income Tax) 49	6.1	•	4.1	4.2	6.0	5.8	5.1	4.7	•	11.2
Profit Margin (After Income Tax) 50	4.1	•	4.1	3.4	4.8	5.3	4.5	3.8	•	7.7

Table I

Corporations with and without Net Income

OTHER ELECTRICAL EQUIPMENT AND COMPONENT

MONEY AMOUNTS AND SIZE OF ASSETS IN THOUSANDS OF DOLLARS

Item Description for Accounting Period 7/02 Through 6/03	Total	Zero Assets	Under 500	500 to 1,000	1,000 to 5,000	5,000 to 10,000	10,000 to 25,000	25,000 to 50,000	50,000 to 100,000	100,000 to 250,000	250,000 to 500,000	500,000 to 2,500,000	2,500,000 and over
Number of Enterprises 1	5782	859	2310	721	1113	315	233	89	63	44	16	14	3
Revenues ($ in Thousands)													
Net Sales 2	46660584	235443	1453820	1147777	5331814	3603533	5445720	4154573	4896784	5225633	3874082	7159898	4131506
Interest 3	346950	2668	84	2452	4771	2368	9247	12582	18221	67093	41471	81059	104932
Rents 4	32236	45	0	871	823	746	2225	1609	7469	2381	298	1222	14546
Royalties 5	100336	410	0	166	0	163	261	360	32200	16922	13244	10088	26523
Other Portfolio Income 6	211453	414	891	1	1779	30375	13482	20206	23993	50399	18217	9757	41941
Other Receipts 7	616596	16831	24404	27635	26626	57415	42993	29169	28984	74374	28539	141240	118385
Total Receipts 8	47968155	255811	1479199	1178902	5365813	3694600	5513928	4218499	5007651	5436802	3975851	7403264	4437833
Average Total Receipts 9	8296	298	640	1635	4821	11729	23665	47399	79487	123564	248491	528805	1479278
Operating Costs/Operating Income (%)													
Cost of Operations 10	65.7	66.0	63.5	54.0	63.6	70.5	67.9	73.0	66.9	68.7	56.6	68.3	57.3
Salaries and Wages 11	10.6	16.9	10.8	14.5	11.0	9.6	10.5	10.8	10.7	12.1	9.7	8.7	12.1
Taxes Paid 12	2.2	1.2	3.8	2.9	2.6	2.3	2.2	1.8	2.2	2.0	2.2	1.9	1.9
Interest Paid 13	2.5	27.4	0.6	2.9	1.1	1.3	1.0	1.9	1.9	2.9	2.0	4.7	4.2
Depreciation 14	4.0	43.1	1.0	2.5	2.8	2.4	3.0	3.6	4.3	5.0	5.3	4.5	4.2
Amortization and Depletion 15	0.8	•	0.1	0.3	0.2	0.2	0.3	0.5	0.7	1.0	1.0	2.3	0.2
Pensions and Other Deferred Comp. 16	0.6	0.1	0.0	0.1	0.7	0.3	0.5	0.3	0.6	0.3	0.9	0.6	1.9
Employee Benefits 17	2.7	2.3	1.7	0.8	1.2	1.5	2.0	1.9	2.0	3.0	5.1	4.3	3.7
Advertising 18	1.0	0.2	0.3	2.1	0.6	0.8	0.7	0.6	0.9	1.1	1.1	0.9	2.4
Other Expenses 19	14.3	45.7	19.0	19.2	10.4	10.3	11.6	10.3	12.5	16.3	17.6	18.7	14.0
Officers' Compensation 20	2.2	1.9	6.1	5.9	4.7	3.4	2.6	1.6	1.8	0.9	1.1	1.1	0.6
Operating Margin 21	•	•	•	•	1.1	•	•	•	•	•	•	•	•
Operating Margin Before Officers' Comp. 22	•	•	0.7	0.7	5.8	0.7	0.3	•	•	•	•	•	•

Selected Average Balance Sheet ($ in Thousands)

Item													
Net Receivables 23	1327	0	42	152	714	1673	3652	7942	14256	22918	65078	83613	156194
Inventories 24	1277	0	34	164	775	2139	3598	8549	13464	21339	42712	73307	185264
Net Property, Plant and Equipment 25	1516	0	19	155	682	1161	3276	7317	15593	32318	67978	128480	259608
Total Assets 26	9188	182	686	2780	6836	15622	33684	69357	151696	363376	999862		3155892
Notes and Loans Payable 27	2617	0	95	832	891	2151	4025	10111	21972	43115	85322	379472	282142
All Other Liabilities 28	2755	0	91	2361	673	2113	3706	10042	18838	33136	73528	280230	1033921
Net Worth 29	3815	0	-4	-2507	1215	2571	7891	13531	28547	75445	204526	340160	1839829

Selected Financial Ratios (Times to 1)

Item													
Current Ratio 30	1.7	•	1.5	2.0	2.0	1.5	2.0	1.9	2.1	2.0	2.3	1.0	2.1
Quick Ratio 31	0.9	•	1.0	1.1	1.1	0.7	1.1	1.0	1.1	1.2	1.2	0.6	0.6
Net Sales to Working Capital 32	5.0	•	16.4	25.5	5.3	7.3	4.6	4.5	3.8	3.1	2.5	•	4.1
Coverage Ratio 33	•	•	•	0.1	2.5	0.9	•	•	•	•	1.1	•	2.4
Total Asset Turnover 34	0.9	•	3.5	2.3	1.7	1.7	1.5	1.4	1.1	0.8	0.7	0.5	0.4
Inventory Turnover 35	4.2	•	11.8	5.3	3.9	3.8	4.4	4.0	3.9	3.8	3.2	4.8	4.3
Receivables Turnover 36	5.9	•	17.9	11.4	6.8	6.7	6.4	5.4	5.7	5.6	3.8	5.2	7.7
Total Liabilities to Net Worth 37	1.4	•	•	•	1.3	1.7	1.0	1.5	1.4	1.0	0.8	1.9	0.7
Current Assets to Working Capital 38	2.4	•	3.1	7.2	2.0	3.1	2.0	2.1	1.9	2.0	1.8	•	1.9
Current Liabilities to Working Capital 39	1.4	•	2.1	6.2	1.0	2.1	1.0	1.1	0.9	1.0	0.8	•	0.9
Working Capital to Net Sales 40	0.2	•	0.1	0.0	0.2	0.1	0.2	0.2	0.3	0.3	0.4	•	0.2
Inventory to Working Capital 41	0.7	•	0.9	3.1	0.8	1.4	0.7	0.7	0.6	0.5	0.4	•	0.4
Total Receipts to Cash Flow 42	13.6	•	20.7	9.6	10.7	12.7	12.0	33.0	12.7	28.1	6.3	29.1	6.7
Cost of Goods to Cash Flow 43	8.9	•	13.1	5.2	6.8	8.9	8.1	24.1	8.5	19.3	3.6	19.9	3.9
Cash Flow to Total Debt 44	0.1	•	0.2	0.1	0.3	0.2	0.3	0.1	0.1	0.1	0.2	0.0	0.2

Selected Financial Factors (in Percentages)

Item													
Debt Ratio 45	58.5	•	102.4	465.3	56.3	62.4	49.5	59.8	58.8	50.3	43.7	66.0	41.7
Return on Total Assets 46	•	•	•	0.9	4.9	1.9	•	•	•	•	1.4	•	4.4
Return on Equity Before Income Taxes 47	•	•	746.0	1.6	6.8	•	•	•	•	•	0.2	•	4.3
Return on Equity After Income Taxes 48	•	•	748.0	1.6	5.2	•	•	•	•	•	•	•	3.0
Profit Margin (Before Income Tax) 49	•	•	•	1.7	•	•	•	•	•	•	0.1	•	5.8
Profit Margin (After Income Tax) 50	•	•	1.3	•	•	•	•	•	•	•	•	•	4.0

Table II

Corporations with Net Income

OTHER ELECTRICAL EQUIPMENT AND COMPONENT

MONEY AMOUNTS AND SIZE OF ASSETS IN THOUSANDS OF DOLLARS

Item Description for Accounting Period 7/02 Through 6/03	Total	Zero Assets	Under 500	500 to 1000	251 to 500	501 to 1,000	1,001 to 5,000	5,001 to 10,000	10,001 to 25,000	25,001 to 50,000	50,001 to 100,000	100,001 to 250,000	250,001 and over
Number of Enterprises **1**	2973	0	1481	462	590	192	135	40	36	18	0	6	3
Revenues ($ in Thousands)													
Net Sales **2**	28078550	0	946509	869084	3332867	2546194	3558234	1957866	2955424	2514637	0	2846289	4131506
Interest **3**	174587	0	40	2053	2764	371	3806	3370	8213	21051	0	14029	104932
Rents **4**	25934	0	0	871	799	67	1529	1245	4993	667	0	1076	14546
Royalties **5**	82561	0	0	166	0	156	261	360	30617	10513	0	731	26523
Other Portfolio Income **6**	155682	0	0	1	1474	28070	10403	17055	18005	24481	0	3891	41941
Other Receipts **7**	385497	0	5	27535	8470	22090	19168	6851	19151	56701	0	98914	118385
Total Receipts **8**	28902811	0	946554	899710	3346374	2596948	3593401	1986747	3036403	2628050	0	2964930	4437833
Average Total Receipts **9**	9722	•	639	1947	5672	13526	26618	49669	84345	146003	•	494155	1479278
Operating Costs/Operating Income (%)													
Cost of Operations **10**	61.8	•	60.5	51.8	58.4	70.9	65.0	66.9	63.4	66.1	•	60.5	57.3
Salaries and Wages **11**	9.8	•	10.6	11.5	10.7	7.6	8.8	9.4	10.5	9.8	•	8.6	12.1
Taxes Paid **12**	2.1	•	3.3	2.9	2.5	1.8	2.1	1.8	2.1	1.6	•	2.2	1.9
Interest Paid **13**	1.9	•	0.2	0.9	0.6	0.9	0.6	1.2	1.2	1.3	•	5.5	4.2
Depreciation **14**	3.0	•	0.5	2.2	2.4	1.8	2.2	2.7	3.4	3.9	•	2.7	4.2
Amortization and Depletion **15**	0.4	•	0.1	0.1	0.1	0.1	0.1	0.2	0.4	0.8	•	1.1	0.2
Pensions and Other Deferred Comp. **16**	0.7	•	0.0	0.0	0.6	0.3	0.5	0.4	0.6	0.2	•	1.0	1.9
Employee Benefits **17**	2.2	•	0.8	0.6	1.4	0.7	2.0	1.7	2.0	2.3	•	2.5	3.7
Advertising **18**	1.1	•	0.1	2.0	0.5	0.6	0.7	0.8	1.1	0.9	•	0.9	2.4
Other Expenses **19**	11.2	•	13.5	17.0	9.1	8.5	8.8	6.9	9.6	10.9	•	13.9	14.0
Officers' Compensation **20**	2.3	•	4.9	7.1	5.1	3.2	2.4	1.6	1.8	1.0	•	1.6	0.6
Operating Margin **21**	3.5	•	5.2	4.0	8.5	3.5	6.7	6.3	3.9	1.3	•	•	•
Operating Margin Before Officers' Comp. **22**	5.8	•	10.2	11.1	13.6	6.7	9.2	7.9	5.7	2.3	•	1.1	•

Selected Average Balance Sheet ($ in Thousands)

Net Receivables 23	1474	50	177	684	2130	3938	9429	15113	22508	82404	156194
Inventories 24	1333	34	193	869	1855	3740	10759	12103	21614	76760	147314
Net Property, Plant and Equipment 25	1313	20	188	492	1013	2896	6530	12441	26294	69353	259608
Total Assets 26	9666	187	740	2649	6903	15451	34353	66745	158186	669396	3155892
Notes and Loans Payable 27	1823	50	252	543	1778	2931	7984	12894	29850	242120	282142
All Other Liabilities 28	3354	65	3470	676	2357	3554	8097	15505	35003	284902	1033921
Net Worth 29	4489	73	-2982	1430	2768	8966	18272	38345	93333	142375	1839829

Selected Financial Ratios (Times to 1)

Current Ratio 30	2.2	1.7	1.4	2.1	1.5	2.4	2.4	2.6	2.0	2.0	2.1
Quick Ratio 31	1.2	1.2	0.8	1.2	0.9	1.4	1.4	1.4	1.3	1.2	0.6
Net Sales to Working Capital 32	4.0	13.1	11.1	5.8	7.3	4.1	3.5	3.4	3.4	4.2	4.1
Coverage Ratio 33	4.4	23.4	9.8	15.6	7.0	13.3	7.4	6.7	5.8	1.7	2.4
Total Asset Turnover 34	1.0	3.4	2.5	2.1	1.9	1.7	1.4	1.2	0.9	0.7	0.4
Inventory Turnover 35	4.4	11.3	5.1	3.8	5.1	4.6	3.0	4.3	4.3	3.7	5.4
Receivables Turnover 36	6.5	15.8	11.4	6.9	7.4	6.7	4.7	6.1	12.4	11.5	17.6
Total Liabilities to Net Worth 37	1.2	1.6	0.9	0.9	1.5	0.7	0.9	0.7	0.7	3.7	0.7
Current Assets to Working Capital 38	1.8	2.4	3.3	1.9	2.9	1.7	1.7	1.6	2.0	2.0	1.9
Current Liabilities to Working Capital 39	0.8	1.4	2.3	0.9	1.9	0.7	0.7	0.6	1.0	1.0	0.9
Working Capital to Net Sales 40	0.2	0.1	0.1	0.2	0.1	0.2	0.3	0.3	0.3	0.2	0.2
Inventory to Working Capital 41	0.6	0.7	1.4	0.7	1.1	0.6	0.6	0.5	0.5	0.7	0.4
Total Receipts to Cash Flow 42	6.6	7.5	5.3	6.7	8.1	6.7	7.7	7.1	6.7	6.5	6.7
Cost of Goods to Cash Flow 43	4.1	4.5	2.7	3.9	5.8	4.3	5.2	4.5	4.4	3.9	3.9
Cash Flow to Total Debt 44	0.3	0.7	0.1	0.7	0.4	0.6	0.4	0.4	0.3	0.1	0.2

Selected Financial Factors (in Percentages)

Debt Ratio 45	53.6	61.2	502.9	46.0	59.9	42.0	46.8	42.5	41.0	78.7	41.7
Return on Total Assets 46	8.3	18.6	21.3	20.3	12.2	14.2	12.9	9.7	6.5	6.5	4.4
Return on Equity Before Income Taxes 47	13.8	46.0		35.2	26.2	22.6	20.9	14.4	9.1	12.4	4.3
Return on Equity After Income Taxes 48	11.3	45.8		32.6	22.9	19.9	17.1	11.1	6.9	9.3	3.0
Profit Margin (Before Income Tax) 49	6.6	5.2	7.5	8.9	5.5	7.7	7.8	6.7	6.1	3.7	5.8
Profit Margin (After Income Tax) 50	5.4	5.2	7.4	8.2	4.8	6.8	6.4	5.2	4.6	2.8	4.0

Table I

Corporations with and without Net Income

MOTOR VEHICLES AND PARTS

MONEY AMOUNTS AND SIZE OF ASSETS IN THOUSANDS OF DOLLARS

Item Description for Accounting Period 7/02 Through 6/03		Total	Zero Assets	Under 500	500 to 1,000	1,000 to 5,000	5,000 to 10,000	10,000 to 25,000	25,000 to 50,000	50,000 to 100,000	100,000 to 250,000	250,000 to 500,000	500,000 to 2,500,000	2,500,000 and over
Number of Enterprises	1	3786	377	1426	396	783	199	219	113	98	88	27	42	17
Revenues ($ in Thousands)														
Net Sales	2	560677790	4296078	1529581	724890	5320897	2780482	6114804	6374286	11035469	21646459	13225540	50821286	436807016
Interest	3	38480867	19695	210	55	3288	1603	6882	7820	28849	45084	73293	298419	37995672
Rents	4	21099994	1344	4	0	160	0	2314	4892	1895	8212	46597	12700	21021876
Royalties	5	7841245	1281	0	0	721	0	1082	2003	1809	36908	42618	239337	7515487
Other Portfolio Income	6	11377144	339742	9515	137	6285	15426	9286	6153	7367	94228	30908	320993	10537103
Other Receipts	7	18177868	13831	31556	51401	14148	26419	45954	71027	103924	234187	120623	447571	17017226
Total Receipts	8	657654908	4671971	1570866	776483	5345499	2823930	6180322	6466181	11179313	22065078	13540579	52140306	530894380
Average Total Receipts	9	173707	12392	1102	1961	6827	14191	28221	57223	114075	250740	501503	1241436	31229081
Operating Costs/Operating Income (%)														
Cost of Operations	10	78.1	83.7	82.5	79.4	74.5	79.5	75.8	78.0	79.9	79.9	79.9	77.4	77.9
Salaries and Wages	11	4.0	1.3	3.7	5.5	6.9	5.4	5.5	4.7	3.9	4.6	4.1	5.3	3.7
Taxes Paid	12	1.1	0.4	2.0	3.4	2.0	1.6	2.0	1.6	1.6	1.5	1.5	1.4	1.0
Interest Paid	13	6.1	1.5	0.3	1.6	1.0	0.9	1.3	1.2	1.3	1.2	2.2	2.9	7.3
Depreciation	14	9.3	3.7	1.0	1.9	1.8	2.9	3.2	4.2	4.2	4.1	4.5	3.7	10.9
Amortization and Depletion	15	0.3	0.2	0.8	0.0	0.1	0.1	0.2	0.3	0.3	0.4	0.4	0.2	0.4
Pensions and Other Deferred Comp.	16	2.4	1.8	0.0	0.7	0.3	0.1	0.5	0.3	0.3	0.4	0.6	0.9	3.0
Employee Benefits	17	1.6	0.6	0.3	1.5	1.4	1.1	1.7	2.1	1.8	1.7	1.6	2.4	1.5
Advertising	18	1.6	0.1	0.7	0.3	0.3	1.1	0.5	0.5	0.3	0.2	0.3	0.3	2.0
Other Expenses	19	12.5	5.5	6.8	8.7	9.7	7.7	8.4	7.1	5.4	5.4	5.1	7.4	14.2
Officers' Compensation	20	0.2	0.1	2.7	3.2	2.8	2.0	1.7	0.7	0.6	0.4	0.4	0.3	0.1
Operating Margin	21	•	1.2	•	•	•	•	•	•	0.4	0.2	•	•	•
Operating Margin Before Officers' Comp.	22	•	1.4	1.9	•	2.0	•	1.0	•	1.0	0.6	•	•	•

Selected Average Balance Sheet ($ in Thousands)

Net Receivables 23	94661	0	27	216	490	1482	3615	6956	14936	35151	55979	155550	20200226
Inventories 24	8791	0	84	310	835	1594	3749	8225	10866	24208	50307	98482	1272159
Net Property, Plant and Equipment 25	49527	0	23	232	579	2396	4984	12547	25216	50423	109726	247011	9629381
Total Assets 26	321961	0	171	735	2525	6990	16044	35948	70353	152216	357353	1049238	66674040
Notes and Loans Payable 27	124826	0	64	416	1239	4151	6175	13253	24277	43426	130066	404619	25940257
All Other Liabilities 28	131434	0	63	121	838	2894	5298	10160	23032	53081	82429	387067	27560089
Net Worth 29	65700	0	44	198	448	-55	4570	12535	23044	55709	144858	257552	13173694

Selected Financial Ratios (Times to 1)

Current Ratio 30	1.2	•	1.7	2.9	1.4	1.1	1.3	1.4	1.2	1.3	1.6	1.2	1.2
Quick Ratio 31	0.9	•	0.7	1.5	0.6	0.5	0.7	0.8	0.7	0.7	0.9	0.7	0.9
Net Sales to Working Capital 32	5.3	•	19.1	5.6	12.8	39.7	11.8	10.3	18.4	14.3	8.4	17.7	4.5
Coverage Ratio 33	1.1	7.6	6.6	1.5	•	1.3	1.5	2.3	2.8	1.9	1.2	1.1	1.1
Total Asset Turnover 34	0.5	•	6.3	2.5	2.7	2.0	1.7	1.6	1.6	1.6	1.4	1.2	0.4
Inventory Turnover 35	13.2	•	10.5	4.7	6.1	7.0	5.6	5.4	8.3	8.1	7.8	9.5	15.7
Receivables Turnover 36	1.5	•	34.3	11.3	13.2	10.7	8.2	7.7	8.5	7.1	8.8	7.5	1.2
Total Liabilities to Net Worth 37	3.9	•	2.9	2.7	4.6	•	2.5	1.9	2.1	1.7	1.5	3.1	4.1
Current Assets to Working Capital 38	5.1	•	2.5	1.5	3.4	12.1	4.0	3.4	5.7	4.4	2.7	5.3	5.2
Current Liabilities to Working Capital 39	4.1	•	1.5	0.5	2.4	11.1	3.0	2.4	4.7	3.4	1.7	4.3	4.2
Working Capital to Net Sales 40	0.2	•	0.1	0.2	0.1	0.0	0.1	0.1	0.1	0.1	0.1	0.1	0.2
Inventory to Working Capital 41	0.3	•	1.5	0.7	1.7	5.6	1.7	1.3	2.0	1.4	0.9	1.4	0.2
Total Receipts to Cash Flow 42	9.0	7.2	14.8	11.6	15.9	19.8	15.2	16.1	17.8	16.4	16.9	16.8	8.0
Cost of Goods to Cash Flow 43	7.0	6.0	12.2	9.2	11.8	15.7	11.5	12.6	14.2	13.1	13.5	13.0	6.2
Cash Flow to Total Debt 44	0.1	•	0.6	0.3	0.2	0.1	0.2	0.1	0.1	0.2	0.1	0.1	0.1

Selected Financial Factors (in Percentages)

Debt Ratio 45	79.6	•	74.5	73.0	82.2	100.8	71.5	65.1	67.2	63.4	59.5	75.5	80.2
Return on Total Assets 46	3.1	•	13.6	5.7	1.8	•	2.8	3.0	4.8	5.6	5.6	4.0	3.0
Return on Equity Before Income Taxes 47	1.3	•	45.2	6.6	•	258.9	2.0	3.0	8.3	9.8	6.4	2.6	0.7
Return on Equity After Income Taxes 48	•	•	39.7	6.3	•	294.5	•	•	5.3	6.8	2.2	•	•
Profit Margin (Before Income Tax) 49	0.6	10.0	1.8	0.7	•	•	0.3	1.7	1.7	2.2	1.9	0.5	0.4
Profit Margin (After Income Tax) 50	•	9.9	1.6	0.7	•	•	•	•	1.5	0.6	•	•	•

153

Table II

Corporations with Net Income

MOTOR VEHICLES AND PARTS

MONEY AMOUNTS AND SIZE OF ASSETS IN THOUSANDS OF DOLLARS

Item Description for Accounting Period 7/02 Through 6/03	Total	Zero Assets	Under 500	500 to 1,000	1,000 to 5,000	5,000 to 10,000	10,000 to 25,000	25,000 to 50,000	50,000 to 100,000	100,000 to 250,000	250,000 to 500,000	500,000 to 2,500,000	2,500,000 and over
Number of Enterprises **1**	2352	6	1189	205	492	87	133	68	67	56	17	22	10
Revenues ($ in Thousands)													
Net Sales **2**	352330075	4030959	1250719	403114	4005426	1577789	4396488	4360920	7969691	15202692	9571127	29777515	269783633
Interest **3**	17300347	19462	38	0	1482	1043	4595	4803	12327	33671	26189	205904	16990833
Rents **4**	7426518	1344	0	0	160	0	1648	3936	1506	2701	4824	3326	7407073
Royalties **5**	2153478	1281	0	0	283	0	316	1873	1441	17482	42293	211087	1877423
Other Portfolio Income **6**	7606116	339735	771	0	3388	15285	5465	1130	3846	89777	6173	258596	6881946
Other Receipts **7**	10568199	13226	31103	48878	10741	19119	21469	27237	85366	198908	72157	192925	9847076
Total Receipts **8**	397384733	4406007	1282631	451992	4021480	1613236	4429981	4399899	8074177	15545231	9722763	30649353	312787984
Average Total Receipts **9**	168956	734334	1079	2205	8174	18543	33308	64704	120510	277593	571927	1393152	31278798
Operating Costs/Operating Income (%)													
Cost of Operations **10**	77.9	83.9	84.3	78.2	72.6	75.7	74.4	76.9	77.8	79.1	79.9	76.2	78.0
Salaries and Wages **11**	3.9	1.2	2.7	6.7	7.6	4.8	5.1	4.3	4.4	4.0	4.0	4.6	3.7
Taxes Paid **12**	1.2	0.3	2.0	3.6	1.8	1.3	1.9	1.5	1.7	1.5	1.4	1.5	1.1
Interest Paid **13**	3.9	1.5	0.1	1.4	0.8	0.8	0.9	0.9	1.0	0.8	0.6	2.0	4.7
Depreciation **14**	6.4	3.8	0.4	1.7	1.5	3.5	2.6	3.9	3.7	3.9	3.8	4.0	7.2
Amortization and Depletion **15**	0.4	0.1	0.1	0.0	0.0	0.0	0.1	0.1	0.2	0.3	0.1	•	0.5
Pensions and Other Deferred Comp. **16**	3.5	1.9	•	0.9	0.2	0.1	0.3	0.3	0.4	0.4	0.3	0.8	4.5
Employee Benefits **17**	1.4	0.5	0.0	1.6	1.3	0.5	1.5	1.8	1.9	1.5	1.8	2.4	1.2
Advertising **18**	1.5	0.1	0.6	0.0	0.4	1.6	0.5	0.5	0.3	0.2	0.3	0.4	1.9
Other Expenses **19**	9.8	4.8	3.7	9.3	7.8	6.7	6.8	5.6	4.9	5.2	3.4	7.1	11.1
Officers' Compensation **20**	0.2	0.1	1.6	5.3	2.5	2.9	1.6	0.7	0.6	0.5	0.4	0.2	0.1
Operating Margin **21**	•	1.8	4.4	•	3.5	2.1	4.5	3.6	3.2	2.7	4.1	1.2	•
Operating Margin Before Officers' Comp. **22**	•	1.9	6.0	•	6.0	5.0	6.1	4.3	3.7	3.1	4.5	1.4	•

Selected Average Balance Sheet ($ in Thousands)

Net Receivables 23	89919	0	29	320	551	1524	4258	7843	14808	35697	67053	174808	20190990
Inventories 24	6826	0	69	209	799	1489	3857	7725	11351	22047	54212	106008	1104791
Net Property, Plant and Equipment 25	34179	0	12	249	495	2752	4194	12368	23870	49595	109996	273346	6618182
Total Assets 26	231898	0	145	811	2595	6876	16322	36255	70698	152138	341230	1026784	49692864
Notes and Loans Payable 27	101009	0	33	442	1030	2695	4821	9245	22057	36304	59360	333519	22357572
All Other Liabilities 28	102002	0	58	120	768	2080	4724	10024	20184	50822	84678	340536	22481610
Net Worth 29	28887	0	54	249	797	2101	6778	16986	28457	65012	197192	352730	4853682

Selected Financial Ratios (Times to 1)

Current Ratio 30	1.4	•	1.9	2.8	1.9	1.3	1.7	1.6	1.3	1.4	1.8	1.3	1.4
Quick Ratio 31	1.2	•	0.8	1.9	0.8	0.7	0.9	0.8	0.7	0.8	1.0	0.8	1.2
Net Sales to Working Capital 32	4.5	•	16.9	5.4	9.1	19.1	7.1	8.8	13.1	12.3	6.9	15.0	3.8
Coverage Ratio 33	1.9	8.2	135.2	3.4	6.2	6.4	7.1	6.1	5.5	7.0	10.8	3.3	1.7
Total Asset Turnover 34	0.6	•	7.3	2.4	3.1	2.6	2.0	1.8	1.7	1.8	1.6	1.3	0.5
Inventory Turnover 35	17.1	•	12.9	7.4	7.4	9.2	6.4	6.4	8.1	9.7	8.3	9.7	19.0
Receivables Turnover 36	1.8	•	33.2	11.0	16.5	11.3	9.3	8.4	9.0	8.1	9.2	15.5	2.7
Total Liabilities to Net Worth 37	7.0	•	1.7	2.3	2.3	2.3	1.4	1.1	1.5	1.3	0.7	1.9	9.2
Current Assets to Working Capital 38	3.6	•	2.1	1.5	2.2	4.2	2.3	2.8	4.0	3.6	2.3	4.4	3.6
Current Liabilities to Working Capital 39	2.6	•	1.1	0.5	1.2	3.2	1.3	1.8	3.0	2.6	1.3	3.4	2.6
Working Capital to Net Sales 40	0.2	•	0.1	0.2	0.1	0.1	0.1	0.1	0.1	0.1	0.1	0.1	0.3
Inventory to Working Capital 41	0.2	•	1.2	0.5	1.1	1.7	1.0	1.1	1.5	1.1	0.8	1.2	0.2
Total Receipts to Cash Flow 42	8.9	6.9	9.6	8.2	10.6	10.0	10.0	11.2	12.1	11.2	12.3	10.5	8.5
Cost of Goods to Cash Flow 43	7.0	5.8	8.1	6.4	7.7	7.5	7.5	8.6	9.4	8.9	9.9	8.0	6.6
Cash Flow to Total Debt 44	0.1	•	1.2	0.4	0.4	0.4	0.3	0.3	0.2	0.3	0.3	0.2	0.1

Selected Financial Factors (in Percentages)

Debt Ratio 45	87.5	•	62.8	69.3	69.3	69.4	58.5	53.1	59.7	57.3	42.2	65.6	90.2
Return on Total Assets 46	4.8	•	51.0	11.6	14.6	13.6	12.3	9.5	9.2	10.5	10.3	8.6	4.2
Return on Equity Before Income Taxes 47	18.4	•	136.1	26.7	39.9	37.6	25.5	16.9	18.7	21.1	16.1	17.5	17.1
Return on Equity After Income Taxes 48	13.2	•	130.7	26.1	38.1	35.5	21.4	13.0	15.0	17.0	11.2	13.8	11.4
Profit Margin (Before Income Tax) 49	3.6	11.1	7.0	3.4	3.9	4.4	5.2	4.5	4.5	5.1	5.6	4.6	3.1
Profit Margin (After Income Tax) 50	2.5	11.0	6.7	3.3	3.7	4.1	4.4	3.5	3.6	4.1	3.9	3.6	2.0

Table I

Corporations with and without Net Income

AEROSPACE PRODUCT AND PARTS

MONEY AMOUNTS AND SIZE OF ASSETS IN THOUSANDS OF DOLLARS

Item Description for Accounting Period 7/02 Through 6/03	Total	Zero Assets	Under 500	500 to 1,000	1,000 to 5,000	5,000 to 10,000	10,000 to 25,000	25,000 to 50,000	50,000 to 100,000	100,000 to 250,000	250,000 to 500,000	500,000 to 2,500,000	2,500,000 and over
Number of Enterprises 1	1451	20	0	0	225	98	64	35	21	14	11	11	9
Revenues ($ in Thousands)													
Net Sales 2	171685849	103538	0	0	826562	1071471	1105577	1343270	1566098	1833775	3677629	7776621	152014647
Interest 3	2454712	34	0	0	513	208	1067	3372	15919	3405	8694	131916	2289204
Rents 4	1920065	31	0	0	0	29	538	1865	1025	9642	5720	53452	1847763
Royalties 5	1500842	0	0	0	0	0	1	24	3218	2	4422	32623	1460553
Other Portfolio Income 6	1037749	62	0	0	10064	749	2701	866	17541	8048	10440	91805	888207
Other Receipts 7	4407923	151	0	0	8560	11177	13157	2373	28855	13425	12258	31481	4286398
Total Receipts 8	183007140	103816	0	0	845699	1083634	1123041	1351770	1632656	1868297	3719163	8117898	162786772
Average Total Receipts 9	126125	5191	*	*	3759	11057	17548	38622	77746	133450	338106	737991	18087419
Operating Costs/Operating Income (%)													
Cost of Operations 10	67.8	72.7	*	*	60.5	72.8	67.7	69.9	67.2	72.3	65.4	69.2	67.7
Salaries and Wages 11	11.9	11.3	*	*	11.9	4.5	6.1	8.8	7.5	8.7	6.3	7.4	12.5
Taxes Paid 12	1.8	1.1	*	*	3.1	2.9	2.7	2.5	2.0	2.4	2.0	2.1	1.8
Interest Paid 13	2.9	0.6	*	*	1.2	2.2	6.2	2.1	3.4	3.2	5.1	5.4	2.7
Depreciation 14	3.8	2.9	*	*	7.2	3.5	4.2	3.3	5.2	3.7	3.6	4.2	3.8
Amortization and Depletion 15	0.5	0.1	*	*	0.1	0.1	0.4	0.9	2.3	1.0	1.5	1.1	0.4
Pensions and Other Deferred Comp. 16	1.3	0.2	*	*	0.3	0.1	0.6	0.4	1.0	0.5	1.0	1.0	1.3
Employee Benefits 17	2.3	0.0	*	*	2.4	1.1	2.7	2.1	2.1	3.6	2.9	2.5	2.3
Advertising 18	0.3	0.2	*	*	0.5	0.2	0.4	0.6	0.2	0.2	0.2	0.3	0.3
Other Expenses 19	10.8	38.5	*	*	12.1	8.7	10.9	12.0	10.4	7.1	7.9	9.5	10.9
Officers' Compensation 20	0.4	0.1	*	*	2.8	2.0	3.3	2.2	1.1	1.9	1.3	0.5	0.2
Operating Margin 21	*	*	*	*	*	1.9	*	*	*	*	2.5	*	*
Operating Margin Before Officers' Comp. 22	*	*	*	*	0.7	3.9	*	*	*	*	3.8	*	*

Selected Average Balance Sheet ($ in Thousands)

Net Receivables 23	24801	0	•	397	1496	2625	4854	14771	21380	51883	197399	3560191
Inventories 24	16384	0	•	648	3346	5310	10683	17581	48371	56899	156098	2118762
Net Property, Plant and Equipment 25	23345	0	•	983	1517	3571	5651	16410	35778	61145	186780	3274038
Total Assets 26	168737	0	•	2371	7807	15201	34059	70019	147770	368646	1180782	24510440
Notes and Loans Payable 27	52810	0	•	721	3972	9199	9978	20936	62155	221154	329661	7516915
All Other Liabilities 28	71172	0	•	577	2539	3769	8021	23808	36034	95580	496266	10533680
Net Worth 29	44755	0	•	1073	1295	2233	16060	25275	49582	51911	354854	6459846

Selected Financial Ratios (Times to 1)

Current Ratio 30	1.3	•	•	2.7	1.4	1.8	2.1	2.1	1.9	2.0	1.6	1.2
Quick Ratio 31	0.7	•	•	1.7	0.6	0.7	0.8	1.0	0.8	1.0	0.9	0.6
Net Sales to Working Capital 32	9.3	•	•	4.3	8.0	3.9	3.5	2.7	3.2	4.9	4.5	11.0
Coverage Ratio 33	2.1	•	•	1.2	2.4	0.4	•	1.5	0.1	1.7	1.3	2.3
Total Asset Turnover 34	0.7	•	•	1.5	1.4	1.1	1.1	1.1	0.9	0.9	0.6	0.7
Inventory Turnover 35	4.9	•	•	3.4	2.4	2.2	2.5	2.8	2.0	3.8	3.1	5.4
Receivables Turnover 36	4.9	•	•	7.5	6.3	8.4	4.9	4.9	5.7	6.1	4.8	4.9
Total Liabilities to Net Worth 37	2.8	•	•	1.2	5.0	1.1	1.8	2.0	2.0	6.1	2.3	2.8
Current Assets to Working Capital 38	4.8	•	•	1.6	3.4	1.9	1.9	1.9	2.2	2.0	2.6	5.6
Current Liabilities to Working Capital 39	3.8	•	•	0.6	2.4	1.2	0.9	0.9	1.2	1.0	1.6	4.6
Working Capital to Net Sales 40	0.1	•	•	0.2	0.1	0.3	0.3	0.4	0.3	0.2	0.2	0.1
Inventory to Working Capital 41	1.2	•	•	0.6	2.0	1.2	1.0	0.5	1.1	0.8	1.0	1.3
Total Receipts to Cash Flow 42	8.5	20.5	•	12.3	10.1	30.0	19.9	10.0	49.8	10.1	12.1	8.1
Cost of Goods to Cash Flow 43	5.7	14.9	•	7.4	7.3	20.3	13.9	6.7	36.0	6.6	8.4	5.5
Cash Flow to Total Debt 44	0.1	•	•	0.2	0.2	0.0	0.1	0.2	0.0	0.1	0.1	0.1

Selected Financial Factors (in Percentages)

Debt Ratio 45	73.5	•	•	54.7	83.4	85.3	52.8	63.9	66.4	85.9	69.9	73.6
Return on Total Assets 46	4.2	•	•	2.2	7.3	2.9	•	5.6	0.2	8.0	4.1	4.2
Return on Equity Before Income Taxes 47	8.1	•	•	0.9	25.4	•	•	5.3	•	23.6	2.9	8.9
Return on Equity After Income Taxes 48	4.6	•	•	•	24.3	•	•	1.8	•	16.5	1.5	5.2
Profit Margin (Before Income Tax) 49	3.1	•	•	0.3	3.0	•	•	1.8	•	3.7	1.5	3.4
Profit Margin (After Income Tax) 50	1.7	•	•	•	2.9	•	•	0.6	•	2.6	0.7	2.0

Table II

Corporations with Net Income

AEROSPACE PRODUCT AND PARTS

MONEY AMOUNTS AND SIZE OF ASSETS IN THOUSANDS OF DOLLARS

Item Description for Accounting Period 7/02 Through 6/03	Total	Zero Assets	Under 500	500 to 1,000	1,000 to 5,000	5,000 to 10,000	10,000 to 25,000	25,000 to 50,000	50,000 to 100,000	100,000 to 250,000	250,000 to 500,000	500,000 to 2,500,000	2,500,000 and over
Number of Enterprises **1**	692	0	0	128	123	53	40	19	13	7	0	0	6
Revenues ($ in Thousands)													
Net Sales **2**	140857743	0	0	135173	584432	879818	704780	718020	1103317	1001871	0	5833778	12874486
Interest **3**	1928734	0	0	0	461	37	548	1068	2495	1913	0	112839	1800513
Rents **4**	1412147	0	0	0	0	0	205	234	1025	5447	0	10369	1389167
Royalties **5**	744586	0	0	0	0	0	1	24	6	0	0	27362	713043
Other Portfolio Income **6**	666353	0	0	7258	68	153	1774	774	4822	7563	0	82674	551571
Other Receipts **7**	3855393	0	0	0	-774	8409	11117	4866	12414	7517	0	18157	3785678
Total Receipts **8**	149465956	0	0	142431	584187	888417	718425	724986	1124079	1024311	0	6085179	135114458
Average Total Receipts **9**	215991	•	•	1113	4749	16763	17961	38157	86468	146330	•	760647	22519076
Operating Costs/Operating Income (%)													
Cost of Operations **10**	64.8	•	•	58.0	60.6	72.8	65.1	65.0	66.0	72.6	•	69.6	64.5
Salaries and Wages **11**	13.2	•	•	6.2	8.8	3.6	5.3	5.5	8.0	5.0	•	6.3	14.0
Taxes Paid **12**	1.9	•	•	1.5	1.6	2.6	2.7	2.3	1.7	2.1	•	1.9	1.9
Interest Paid **13**	2.6	•	•	0.9	0.6	1.3	1.4	1.0	1.2	1.0	•	4.2	2.5
Depreciation **14**	4.0	•	•	1.0	3.5	2.6	4.0	2.4	3.3	2.4	•	3.8	4.1
Amortization and Depletion **15**	0.4	•	•	•	0.0	0.0	0.1	0.3	0.1	0.4	•	0.7	0.3
Pensions and Other Deferred Comp. **16**	1.1	•	•	1.8	0.2	0.1	0.5	0.6	1.2	0.3	•	0.8	1.1
Employee Benefits **17**	2.4	•	•	1.8	1.2	0.5	1.7	1.4	2.0	2.4	•	2.7	2.4
Advertising **18**	0.2	•	•	1.6	0.7	0.1	0.4	0.3	0.2	0.1	•	0.3	0.2
Other Expenses **19**	10.3	•	•	13.6	6.4	5.0	7.8	9.5	9.4	7.8	•	10.3	10.5
Officers' Compensation **20**	0.4	•	•	11.0	2.9	2.0	3.8	2.8	0.8	2.6	•	0.6	0.3
Operating Margin **21**	•	•	•	2.7	13.4	9.3	7.2	8.9	6.2	3.2	•	•	•
Operating Margin Before Officers' Comp. **22**	•	•	•	13.7	16.3	11.3	11.0	11.7	7.0	5.7	•	•	•

Selected Average Balance Sheet ($ in Thousands)

Net Receivables 23	38328	53	522	2290	3071	5204	17830	24561	236632	3891309
Inventories 24	25854	594	815	3352	5001	12623	14598	57684	149679	2290322
Net Property, Plant and Equipment 25	38745	12	764	1766	3375	3913	14120	23014	190940	4004123
Total Assets 26	261840	658	2512	7919	14484	31604	71489	155962	1237690	27302715
Notes and Loans Payable 27	76303	198	493	3242	3734	4776	15810	46070	236656	7961212
All Other Liabilities 28	117618	45	705	1826	2319	6631	23279	31685	599194	12458287
Net Worth 29	67920	416	1315	2852	8431	20197	32400	78207	401840	6883216

Selected Financial Ratios (Times to 1)

Current Ratio 30	1.2	6.9	2.7	2.1	3.0	3.2	1.9	1.9	1.5	1.2
Quick Ratio 31	0.6	0.7	1.7	1.0	1.4	1.4	1.2	1.0	0.8	0.6
Net Sales to Working Capital 32	10.6	1.9	4.3	5.4	2.7	2.5	4.0	3.0	5.2	12.6
Coverage Ratio 33	3.0	10.1	23.2	9.2	7.6	10.6	7.6	5.5	1.8	3.0
Total Asset Turnover 34	0.8	1.6	1.9	2.1	1.2	1.2	1.2	0.9	0.6	0.8
Inventory Turnover 35	5.1	1.0	3.5	3.6	2.3	1.9	3.8	1.8	3.4	6.0
Receivables Turnover 36	5.2	8.0	7.6	6.3	5.5	6.5	9.5	5.7	4.4	10.9
Total Liabilities to Net Worth 37	2.9	0.6	0.9	1.8	0.7	0.6	1.2	1.0	2.1	3.0
Current Assets to Working Capital 38	5.2	1.2	1.6	1.9	1.5	1.5	2.1	2.2	3.2	6.1
Current Liabilities to Working Capital 39	4.2	0.2	0.6	0.9	0.5	0.5	1.1	1.2	2.2	5.1
Working Capital to Net Sales 40	0.1	0.5	0.2	0.2	0.4	0.4	0.3	0.3	0.2	0.1
Inventory to Working Capital 41	1.3	1.0	0.6	1.0	0.7	0.7	0.7	1.0	1.2	1.4
Total Receipts to Cash Flow 42	7.5	7.3	5.6	7.2	7.0	6.0	6.6	8.8	9.1	7.4
Cost of Goods to Cash Flow 43	4.9	4.2	3.4	5.3	4.6	3.9	4.3	6.4	6.3	4.8
Cash Flow to Total Debt 44	0.1	0.6	0.7	0.5	0.4	0.6	0.3	0.2	0.1	0.1

Selected Financial Factors (in Percentages)

Debt Ratio 45	74.1	36.8	47.7	64.0	41.8	36.1	54.7	49.9	67.5	74.8
Return on Total Assets 46	6.0	14.4	26.4	24.3	12.8	12.9	10.8	5.2	4.5	5.8
Return on Equity Before Income Taxes 47	15.2	20.5	48.2	60.0	19.0	18.4	20.7	8.6	6.2	15.4
Return on Equity After Income Taxes 48	10.3	14.7	45.3	59.1	17.0	16.7	16.3	7.7	4.5	10.1
Profit Margin (Before Income Tax) 49	5.1	8.1	13.3	10.3	9.1	9.8	7.9	4.7	3.4	5.0
Profit Margin (After Income Tax) 50	3.4	5.8	12.5	10.2	8.1	8.9	6.2	4.2	2.5	3.3

Table I

Corporations with and without Net Income

SHIP AND BOAT BUILDING

MONEY AMOUNTS AND SIZE OF ASSETS IN THOUSANDS OF DOLLARS

Item Description for Accounting Period 7/02 Through 6/03	Total	Zero Assets	Under 500	500 to 1,000	1,000 to 5,000	5,000 to 10,000	10,000 to 25,000	25,000 to 50,000	50,000 to 100,000	100,000 to 250,000	250,000 to 500,000	500,000 to 2,500,000	2,500,000 and over
Number of Enterprises **1**	2747	341	1803	•	448	62	57	16	9	5	6	0	0
Revenues ($ in Thousands)													
Net Sales **2**	23354114	33577	413245	•	1785881	943535	1910240	1077633	930137	900279	15359587	0	0
Interest **3**	25917	264	562	•	2676	614	1664	503	1307	3921	14405	0	0
Rents **4**	41765	0	0	•	4532	3239	175	30	12	52	33726	0	0
Royalties **5**	4693	0	0	•	0	0	264	0	65	0	4364	0	0
Other Portfolio Income **6**	65509	2347	724	•	241	25	1689	342	242	309	59587	0	0
Other Receipts **7**	289985	2954	225	•	10793	10278	12733	9630	9940	2433	231003	0	0
Total Receipts **8**	23781983	39142	414756	•	1804123	957691	1926765	1088138	941703	906994	15702672	0	0
Average Total Receipts **9**	8657	115	230	•	4027	15447	33803	68009	104634	181399	2617112	•	•
Operating Costs/Operating Income (%)													
Cost of Operations **10**	75.2	77.8	51.2	•	68.3	81.0	78.2	72.2	76.7	76.6	75.9	•	•
Salaries and Wages **11**	3.8	4.3	12.4	•	6.5	1.1	4.2	4.5	4.3	4.6	3.2	•	•
Taxes Paid **12**	2.0	0.5	3.0	•	2.2	1.5	2.0	2.1	1.8	2.7	2.0	•	•
Interest Paid **13**	0.8	1.2	0.8	•	1.0	0.7	0.9	1.0	0.6	1.2	0.8	•	•
Depreciation **14**	2.1	2.0	3.0	•	2.6	2.2	2.2	2.5	2.3	4.4	1.9	•	•
Amortization and Depletion **15**	1.0	0.0	0.4	•	0.1	0.0	0.1	0.3	•	0.1	1.4	•	•
Pensions and Other Deferred Comp. **16**	0.6	0.0	0.2	•	0.2	0.1	0.2	0.4	0.3	1.4	0.7	•	•
Employee Benefits **17**	1.5	1.0	1.7	•	1.3	0.6	1.4	1.9	2.0	1.7	1.5	•	•
Advertising **18**	0.5	0.3	1.0	•	0.8	0.7	1.0	1.7	1.3	0.1	0.3	•	•
Other Expenses **19**	8.3	24.3	18.7	•	13.7	9.5	6.6	7.1	9.8	6.0	7.6	•	•
Officers' Compensation **20**	1.4	2.3	9.1	•	5.2	2.0	1.8	1.5	0.6	1.1	0.7	•	•
Operating Margin **21**	2.9	•	•	•	•	0.5	1.4	4.8	0.3	0.1	4.1	•	•
Operating Margin Before Officers' Comp. **22**	4.2	•	7.6	•	3.4	2.6	3.2	6.3	0.9	1.2	4.8	•	•

Selected Average Balance Sheet ($ in Thousands)

Net Receivables 23	819	0	12	•	167	1220	2482	5286	6536	19225	282474
Inventories 24	1486	0	22	•	797	591	3852	7432	14667	7004	552275
Net Property, Plant and Equipment 25	1328	0	22	•	703	1780	4978	12724	20328	67775	362409
Total Assets 26	9466	0	112	•	2086	7424	16477	33582	61089	150736	3604555
Notes and Loans Payable 27	1416	0	54	•	1039	2410	6694	7208	14750	31397	398498
All Other Liabilities 28	3606	0	20	•	620	4660	6625	8650	11879	48065	1406675
Net Worth 29	4444	0	37	•	427	355	3159	17724	34460	71273	1799382

Selected Financial Ratios (Times to 1)

Current Ratio 30	1.3	•	2.1	•	1.5	1.4	1.3	1.9	2.0	1.2	1.3
Quick Ratio 31	0.3	•	1.3	•	0.4	0.6	0.6	0.9	0.7	0.7	0.3
Net Sales to Working Capital 32	8.6	•	6.8	•	9.5	11.1	13.2	8.1	6.9	17.1	8.0
Coverage Ratio 33	6.7	3.3	•	•	0.2	4.0	3.4	6.8	3.5	1.8	9.1
Total Asset Turnover 34	0.9	•	2.0	•	1.9	2.0	2.0	2.0	1.7	1.2	0.7
Inventory Turnover 35	4.3	•	5.4	•	3.4	20.9	6.8	6.5	5.4	19.7	3.5
Receivables Turnover 36	4.6	•	15.7	•	23.3	13.1	13.3	12.7	15.7	6.4	18.1
Total Liabilities to Net Worth 37	1.1	•	2.0	•	3.9	19.9	4.2	0.9	0.8	1.1	1.0
Current Assets to Working Capital 38	4.1	•	1.9	•	2.8	3.7	3.9	2.1	2.0	5.7	4.5
Current Liabilities to Working Capital 39	3.1	•	0.9	•	1.8	2.7	2.9	1.1	1.0	4.7	3.5
Working Capital to Net Sales 40	0.1	•	0.1	•	0.1	0.1	0.1	0.1	0.1	0.1	0.1
Inventory to Working Capital 41	1.6	•	0.8	•	1.6	0.4	1.6	0.9	1.1	0.3	1.7
Total Receipts to Cash Flow 42	8.7	4.3	9.8	•	10.0	10.6	13.9	8.6	9.2	24.1	7.8
Cost of Goods to Cash Flow 43	6.5	3.3	5.0	•	6.8	8.6	10.8	6.2	7.1	18.5	5.9
Cash Flow to Total Debt 44	0.2	•	0.3	•	0.2	0.2	0.2	0.5	0.4	0.1	0.2

Selected Financial Factors (in Percentages)

Debt Ratio 45	53.1	66.7	•	79.5	95.2	80.8	47.2	43.6	52.7	50.1
Return on Total Assets 46	5.0	•	•	0.5	5.5	6.4	13.5	3.6	2.5	5.1
Return on Equity Before Income Taxes 47	9.1	•	•	•	87.0	23.6	21.8	4.6	2.2	9.1
Return on Equity After Income Taxes 48	6.1	•	•	•	74.3	18.4	19.3	1.4	1.1	6.0
Profit Margin (Before Income Tax) 49	4.7	2.9	•	•	2.0	2.2	5.7	1.5	0.9	6.4
Profit Margin (After Income Tax) 50	3.2	2.9	•	•	1.7	1.7	5.1	0.5	0.4	4.2

157

Table II

Corporations with Net Income

SHIP AND BOAT BUILDING

MONEY AMOUNTS AND SIZE OF ASSETS IN THOUSANDS OF DOLLARS

Item Description for Accounting Period 7/02 Through 6/03	Total	Zero Assets	Under 500	500 to 1,000	1,000 to 5,000	5,000 to 10,000	10,000 to 25,000	25,000 to 50,000	50,000 to 100,000	100,000 to 250,000	250,000 to 500,000	500,000 to 2,500,000	2,500,000 and over
Number of Enterprises **1**	1228	10	905	•	212	41	35	13	4	0	0	0	0
Revenues ($ in Thousands)													
Net Sales **2**	20239472	32444	346107	•	1470847	655208	1428154	989701	531835	0	0	0	0
Interest **3**	18488	9	25	•	1290	393	1167	425	904	0	0	0	0
Rents **4**	37709	0	0	•	3997	144	109	18	12	0	0	0	0
Royalties **5**	4219	0	0	•	0	0	250	0	0	0	0	0	0
Other Portfolio Income **6**	53910	2347	0	•	166	2	820	85	239	0	0	0	0
Other Receipts **7**	265627	2954	0	•	10068	10212	11947	6971	7093	0	0	0	0
Total Receipts **8**	20619425	37754	346132	•	1486368	665959	1442447	997200	540083	0	0	0	0
Average Total Receipts **9**	16791	3775	382	•	7011	16243	41213	76708	135021	•	•	•	•
Operating Costs/Operating Income (%)													
Cost of Operations **10**	75.4	77.0	39.5	•	69.2	79.3	76.3	71.7	77.0	•	•	•	•
Salaries and Wages **11**	3.3	4.5	13.3	•	6.3	1.0	3.7	4.4	3.8	•	•	•	•
Taxes Paid **12**	2.0	0.5	2.7	•	1.8	1.2	2.0	2.2	1.4	•	•	•	•
Interest Paid **13**	0.7	1.3	0.6	•	0.6	0.5	0.6	0.7	0.3	•	•	•	•
Depreciation **14**	1.9	2.0	2.7	•	1.6	1.8	1.8	2.3	1.2	•	•	•	•
Amortization and Depletion **15**	1.1	0.0	0.0	•	0.0	0.0	0.0	0.2	0.1	•	•	•	•
Pensions and Other Deferred Comp. **16**	0.6	0.0	0.3	•	0.2	0.0	0.2	0.3	0.4	•	•	•	•
Employee Benefits **17**	1.4	1.0	2.1	•	1.0	0.4	1.1	1.9	1.5	•	•	•	•
Advertising **18**	0.4	0.3	0.5	•	1.0	0.9	1.0	1.6	1.6	•	•	•	•
Other Expenses **19**	7.0	14.8	17.0	•	12.0	11.0	6.2	6.8	8.0	•	•	•	•
Officers' Compensation **20**	1.3	2.3	7.6	•	5.5	1.6	1.6	1.5	0.7	•	•	•	•
Operating Margin **21**	5.0	•	13.6	•	0.7	2.2	5.4	6.3	4.1	•	•	•	•
Operating Margin Before Officers' Comp. **22**	6.2	•	21.2	•	6.2	3.9	7.0	7.8	4.8	•	•	•	•

Selected Average Balance Sheet ($ in Thousands)

Net Receivables 23	1598	0	19	•	181	644	2813	5337	4456
Inventories 24	2934	0	24	•	847	540	3020	7244	19650
Net Property, Plant and Equipment 25	2344	0	27	•	566	1706	4536	12621	15420
Total Assets 26	19185	0	135	•	2144	7984	15124	33434	58392
Notes and Loans Payable 27	2159	0	37	•	695	2627	3581	5645	7557
All Other Liabilities 28	7392	0	14	•	779	6317	5567	8737	13950
Net Worth 29	9635	0	83	•	670	-960	5977	19052	36885

Selected Financial Ratios (Times to 1)

Current Ratio 30	1.4	•	3.2	•	1.6	1.4	1.6	1.9	2.4
Quick Ratio 31	0.3	•	2.4	•	0.4	0.5	0.9	1.0	0.8
Net Sales to Working Capital 32	7.2	•	6.6	•	12.8	10.3	11.6	8.3	6.8
Coverage Ratio 33	11.2	10.7	23.0	•	3.7	8.4	11.9	11.1	23.1
Total Asset Turnover 34	0.9	•	2.8	•	3.2	2.0	2.7	2.3	2.3
Inventory Turnover 35	4.2	•	6.4	•	5.7	23.5	10.3	7.5	5.2
Receivables Turnover 36	4.2	•	14.4	•	29.4	21.2	15.2	15.1	59.7
Total Liabilities to Net Worth 37	1.0	•	0.6	•	2.2	•	1.5	0.8	0.6
Current Assets to Working Capital 38	3.5	•	1.5	•	2.8	3.6	2.7	2.1	1.7
Current Liabilities to Working Capital 39	2.5	•	0.5	•	1.8	2.6	1.7	1.1	0.7
Working Capital to Net Sales 40	0.1	•	0.2	•	0.1	0.1	0.1	0.1	0.1
Inventory to Working Capital 41	1.3	•	0.3	•	1.8	0.5	1.0	0.9	1.0
Total Receipts to Cash Flow 42	8.0	4.3	4.3	•	9.0	7.7	8.8	7.9	7.5
Cost of Goods to Cash Flow 43	6.1	3.3	1.7	•	6.2	6.1	6.8	5.6	5.8
Cash Flow to Total Debt 44	0.2	•	1.7	•	0.5	0.2	0.5	0.7	0.8

Selected Financial Factors (in Percentages)

Debt Ratio 45	49.8	•	38.2	•	68.8	112.0	60.5	43.0	36.8
Return on Total Assets 46	6.5	•	40.4	•	7.6	8.8	18.8	17.7	13.3
Return on Equity Before Income Taxes 47	11.7	•	62.6	•	17.7	•	43.6	28.3	20.1
Return on Equity After Income Taxes 48	8.7	•	62.5	•	15.2	•	39.2	25.5	13.5
Profit Margin (Before Income Tax) 49	6.9	12.5	13.6	•	1.7	3.9	6.4	7.1	5.6
Profit Margin (After Income Tax) 50	5.1	12.5	13.6	•	1.5	3.4	5.7	6.4	3.8

Table I

Corporations with and without Net Income

OTHER TRANSPORTATION EQUIPMENT AND RAILROAD ROLLING STOCK

MONEY AMOUNTS AND SIZE OF ASSETS IN THOUSANDS OF DOLLARS

Item Description for Accounting Period 7/02 Through 6/03	Total	Zero Assets	Under 500	500 to 1,000	1,000 to 5,000	5,000 to 10,000	10,000 to 25,000	25,000 to 50,000	50,000 to 100,000	100,000 to 250,000	250,000 to 500,000	500,000 to 2,500,000	2,500,000 and over
Number of Enterprises **1**	897	267	0	0	332	65	35	19	13	9	4	6	0
Revenues ($ in Thousands)													
Net Sales **2**	19639776	86787	0	0	1230658	942233	1090351	1085341	1145526	2438437	2059665	9483810	0
Interest **3**	427601	146	0	0	1088	484	537	1397	1267	11388	7384	403911	0
Rents **4**	13345	0	0	0	0	3331	166	7053	0	0	623	2173	0
Royalties **5**	58834	1	0	0	0	3069	2868	104	0	96	818	51878	0
Other Portfolio Income **6**	133595	2090	0	0	82	224	1245	4695	508	8627	18642	95730	0
Other Receipts **7**	202741	-25305	0	0	6946	1643	3252	5104	8981	23356	29746	141974	0
Total Receipts **8**	20475892	63719	0	0	1238774	950984	1098419	1103694	1156282	2481904	2116878	10179476	0
Average Total Receipts **9**	22827	239	•	•	3731	14631	31383	58089	88945	275767	529220	1696579	•
Operating Costs/Operating Income (%)													
Cost of Operations **10**	71.7	78.6	•	•	75.3	77.6	75.8	74.7	79.4	80.4	77.3	65.4	•
Salaries and Wages **11**	5.8	11.2	•	•	5.4	8.4	5.6	6.9	5.0	3.6	5.9	6.1	•
Taxes Paid **12**	1.5	1.2	•	•	2.5	2.3	1.7	2.4	1.4	1.2	1.3	1.3	•
Interest Paid **13**	2.1	7.3	•	•	0.9	1.2	0.9	1.3	1.4	1.8	2.9	2.5	•
Depreciation **14**	5.7	7.5	•	•	1.9	2.0	2.0	3.1	2.5	3.0	5.4	8.4	•
Amortization and Depletion **15**	0.7	6.9	•	•	0.2	0.3	0.2	0.6	0.5	0.5	0.9	0.6	•
Pensions and Other Deferred Comp. **16**	0.5	0.9	•	•	0.2	0.0	0.3	0.4	0.3	0.6	0.3	0.8	•
Employee Benefits **17**	2.7	6.6	•	•	1.8	1.9	1.5	1.6	0.9	1.5	1.9	3.9	•
Advertising **18**	0.9	5.1	•	•	0.6	1.0	0.6	0.5	0.6	1.0	0.2	1.2	•
Other Expenses **19**	10.2	177.4	•	•	10.5	11.2	6.9	7.0	6.3	7.6	9.8	10.2	•
Officers' Compensation **20**	0.8	3.1	•	•	4.6	1.3	1.7	1.9	0.3	0.4	0.1	0.1	•
Operating Margin **21**	•	•	•	•	•	•	2.8	•	1.3	•	•	•	•
Operating Margin Before Officers' Comp. **22**	•	•	•	•	0.7	•	4.5	1.4	1.6	•	•	•	•

Selected Average Balance Sheet ($ in Thousands)

Net Receivables 23	3365	0	•	•	430	1685	3582	7803	15355	21859	61239	305719	•
Inventories 24	2589	0	•	•	489	3069	5484	6030	18767	37750	68786	130600	•
Net Property, Plant and Equipment 25	6107	0	•	•	247	957	3444	7896	12492	30088	148556	671118	•
Total Assets 26	21972	0	•	•	1880	6157	16020	35728	72392	162061	422493	2207470	•
Notes and Loans Payable 27	5241	0	•	•	667	5407	3871	11774	19337	52413	157073	399714	•
All Other Liabilities 28	8203	0	•	•	4356	2339	4978	8897	30823	56212	151159	649334	•
Net Worth 29	8528	0	•	•	-3142	-1590	7170	15056	22231	53435	114261	1158423	•

Selected Financial Ratios (Times to 1)

Current Ratio 30	1.4	•	•	1.7	2.0	1.8	1.5	1.2	1.3	1.6	1.4
Quick Ratio 31	0.7	•	•	0.9	0.8	0.8	0.8	0.5	0.6	0.8	0.7
Net Sales to Working Capital 32	8.5	•	•	6.6	5.9	6.3	8.9	9.7	14.5	8.2	8.8
Coverage Ratio 33	1.8	•	•	•	•	4.9	2.0	2.6	1.1	•	3.7
Total Asset Turnover 34	1.0	•	•	2.0	2.4	1.9	1.6	1.2	1.7	1.2	0.7
Inventory Turnover 35	6.1	•	•	5.7	3.7	4.3	7.1	3.7	5.8	5.8	7.9
Receivables Turnover 36	6.1	•	•	7.5	7.9	8.1	9.9	6.7	8.0	8.2	4.8
Total Liabilities to Net Worth 37	1.6	•	•	•	•	1.2	1.4	2.3	2.0	2.7	0.9
Current Assets to Working Capital 38	3.3	•	•	2.4	2.0	2.2	3.0	5.2	4.4	2.7	3.7
Current Liabilities to Working Capital 39	2.3	•	•	1.4	1.0	1.2	2.0	4.2	3.4	1.7	2.7
Working Capital to Net Sales 40	0.1	•	•	0.2	0.2	0.2	0.1	0.1	0.1	0.1	0.1
Inventory to Working Capital 41	1.0	•	•	0.9	1.1	1.0	1.2	2.3	1.5	1.1	0.8
Total Receipts to Cash Flow 42	10.7	•	•	58.1	53.4	11.1	16.5	13.9	15.9	24.8	6.3
Cost of Goods to Cash Flow 43	7.6	•	•	43.8	41.5	8.4	12.3	11.0	12.8	19.2	4.1
Cash Flow to Total Debt 44	0.2	•	•	0.0	0.0	0.3	0.2	0.1	0.2	0.1	0.2

Selected Financial Factors (in Percentages)

Debt Ratio 45	61.2	•	•	267.1	125.8	55.2	57.9	69.3	67.0	73.0	47.5
Return on Total Assets 46	3.7	•	•	•	•	8.6	4.0	4.4	3.3	•	6.7
Return on Equity Before Income Taxes 47	4.1	•	•	3.9	58.1	15.2	4.6	8.8	1.0	•	9.3
Return on Equity After Income Taxes 48	•	•	•	3.9	58.2	13.7	3.1	5.4	•	•	5.0
Profit Margin (Before Income Tax) 49	1.6	•	•	•	•	3.5	1.2	2.2	0.2	•	6.8
Profit Margin (After Income Tax) 50	•	•	•	•	•	3.1	0.8	1.4	•	•	3.7

Table II
Corporations with Net Income

OTHER TRANSPORTATION EQUIPMENT AND RAILROAD ROLLING STOCK

MONEY AMOUNTS AND SIZE OF ASSETS IN THOUSANDS OF DOLLARS

Item Description for Accounting Period 7/02 Through 6/03	Total	Zero Assets	Under 500	500 to 1,000	1,000 to 5,000	5,000 to 10,000	10,000 to 25,000	25,000 to 50,000	50,000 to 100,000	100,000 to 250,000	250,000 to 500,000	500,000 to 2,500,000	2,500,000 and over
Number of Enterprises 1	268	0	0	67	118	29	25	10	8	0	4	0	0
Revenues ($ in Thousands)													
Net Sales 2	11067211	0	0	74175	401736	401731	876096	580091	776860	0	6499928	0	0
Interest 3	311194	0	0	0	21	134	314	90	1095	0	301576	0	0
Rents 4	5872	0	0	0	0	3331	166	48	0	0	2328	0	0
Royalties 5	44159	0	0	0	0	0	2868	86	0	0	41184	0	0
Other Portfolio Income 6	37041	0	0	1755	82	13	632	2117	197	0	26804	0	0
Other Receipts 7	134837	0	0	6474	3719	357	2424	3227	6088	0	90532	0	0
Total Receipts 8	11600314	0	0	82404	405558	405566	882500	585659	784240	0	6961352	0	0
Average Total Receipts 9	43285	•	•	1230	3437	13985	35300	58566	98030	•	1740338	•	•
Operating Costs/Operating Income (%)													
Cost of Operations 10	67.1	•	•	63.5	64.4	79.5	74.1	72.3	78.5	•	61.4	•	•
Salaries and Wages 11	5.8	•	•	2.7	4.2	5.4	5.3	8.5	4.4	•	6.3	•	•
Taxes Paid 12	1.5	•	•	5.6	3.0	1.9	1.5	2.3	1.6	•	1.3	•	•
Interest Paid 13	1.5	•	•	1.0	1.4	0.8	0.8	0.6	0.6	•	1.8	•	•
Depreciation 14	3.5	•	•	4.4	2.4	1.1	1.7	2.2	2.7	•	4.7	•	•
Amortization and Depletion 15	0.5	•	•	0.1	0.0	0.0	0.1	0.3	0.1	•	0.7	•	•
Pensions and Other Deferred Comp. 16	0.5	•	•	0.2	0.0	0.0	0.3	0.3	0.3	•	0.6	•	•
Employee Benefits 17	3.3	•	•	0.0	1.4	0.9	1.5	1.1	1.2	•	4.7	•	•
Advertising 18	1.4	•	•	0.9	0.8	1.2	0.7	0.7	0.5	•	1.6	•	•
Other Expenses 19	9.1	•	•	14.5	12.7	7.3	6.5	5.4	5.3	•	10.2	•	•
Officers' Compensation 20	0.7	•	•	11.7	6.9	0.6	1.9	1.5	0.5	•	0.0	•	•
Operating Margin 21	5.2	•	•	•	2.8	1.3	5.6	5.0	4.3	•	6.6	•	•
Operating Margin Before Officers' Comp. 22	5.9	•	•	7.2	9.7	1.9	7.5	6.5	4.7	•	6.6	•	•

Selected Average Balance Sheet ($ in Thousands)

Net Receivables 23	7934	248	509	1903	3560	7121	15119	402288
Inventories 24	4395	124	762	2459	4712	6599	13837	109896
Net Property, Plant and Equipment 25	6860	113	242	735	3415	6986	16026	361430
Total Assets 26	27800	547	1564	5920	16177	32033	68139	1281210
Notes and Loans Payable 27	4115	175	472	5736	3878	8747	15558	94956
All Other Liabilities 28	10315	65	380	2448	3973	7400	17849	515776
Net Worth 29	13370	307	711	-2263	8326	15886	34732	670478

Selected Financial Ratios (Times to 1)

Current Ratio 30	1.7	1.8	2.2	2.5	2.1	1.9	1.8	1.6
Quick Ratio 31	0.9	1.3	1.2	1.0	1.1	1.0	0.8	0.9
Net Sales to Working Capital 32	5.6	5.9	5.0	4.6	6.0	6.6	5.0	5.4
Coverage Ratio 33	7.9	7.9	3.6	4.0	8.6	10.3	10.2	8.7
Total Asset Turnover 34	1.5	2.0	2.2	2.3	2.2	1.8	1.4	1.3
Inventory Turnover 35	6.3	5.7	2.9	4.5	5.5	6.4	5.5	9.1
Receivables Turnover 36	5.2		4.0	10.1	9.5	10.4	6.8	8.1
Total Liabilities to Net Worth 37	1.1	0.8	1.2		0.9	1.0	1.0	0.9
Current Assets to Working Capital 38	2.4	2.2	1.8	1.7	1.9	2.2	2.3	2.6
Current Liabilities to Working Capital 39	1.4	1.2	0.8	0.7	0.9	1.2	1.3	1.6
Working Capital to Net Sales 40	0.2	0.2	0.2	0.2	0.2	0.2	0.2	0.2
Inventory to Working Capital 41	0.5	0.7	0.8	0.9	0.8	0.9	0.7	0.4
Total Receipts to Cash Flow 42	5.6	5.7	9.8	13.3	8.8	10.0	10.8	4.4
Cost of Goods to Cash Flow 43	3.8	3.6	6.3	10.6	6.5	7.2	8.5	2.7
Cash Flow to Total Debt 44	0.5	0.8	0.4	0.1	0.5	0.4	0.3	0.6

Selected Financial Factors (in Percentages)

Debt Ratio 45	51.9	43.9	54.5	138.2	48.5	50.4	49.0	47.7
Return on Total Assets 46	17.2	15.4	11.2	7.0	15.5	11.9	8.2	19.7
Return on Equity Before Income Taxes 47	31.3	23.9	17.8		26.6	21.7	14.5	33.3
Return on Equity After Income Taxes 48	21.8	22.5	17.6		24.7	19.0	11.0	22.0
Profit Margin (Before Income Tax) 49	10.1	6.6	3.7	2.2	6.3	5.9	5.2	13.8
Profit Margin (After Income Tax) 50	7.1	6.2	3.7	2.2	5.9	5.2	3.9	9.1

Table I

Corporations with and without Net Income

FURNITURE AND RELATED PRODUCT MANUFACTURING

MONEY AMOUNTS AND SIZE OF ASSETS IN THOUSANDS OF DOLLARS

Item Description for Accounting Period 7/02 Through 6/03

		Total	Zero Assets	Under 500	500 to 1,000	1,000 to 5,000	5,000 to 10,000	10,000 to 25,000	25,000 to 50,000	50,000 to 100,000	100,000 to 250,000	250,000 to 500,000	500,000 to 2,500,000	2,500,000 and over
Number of Enterprises	1	11801	813	7870	1239	1338	250	175	49	28	17	11	11	0
Revenues ($ in Thousands)														
Net Sales	2	57668629	339301	3529865	2526092	7534924	4334551	5614479	3134323	3897612	3489544	5847273	17420663	0
Interest	3	140232	1821	586	1509	3077	1247	2709	3195	1650	28418	31739	64281	0
Rents	4	67700	0	1659	1867	164	427	1698	2380	567	3016	6520	49403	0
Royalties	5	58374	0	0	0	0	0	338	239	233	5630	11456	40477	0
Other Portfolio Income	6	432758	214969	2814	174	3686	2676	6614	6251	4464	21896	22445	146770	0
Other Receipts	7	645955	73	3485	4891	37763	13188	37053	23192	15760	14713	136918	358921	0
Total Receipts	8	59013648	556164	3538409	2534533	7579614	4352089	5662891	3169580	3920286	3563217	6056351	18080515	0
Average Total Receipts	9	5001	684	450	2046	5665	17408	32359	64685	140010	209601	550577	1643683	•
Operating Costs/Operating Income (%)														
Cost of Operations	10	67.6	60.2	57.3	70.4	66.7	66.0	70.2	72.0	71.9	68.3	67.0	67.6	•
Salaries and Wages	11	7.7	8.0	8.4	6.8	7.7	9.4	6.9	6.8	6.3	5.2	6.3	8.9	•
Taxes Paid	12	2.4	3.4	3.3	2.7	2.9	2.0	2.1	2.3	2.1	2.0	2.2	2.3	•
Interest Paid	13	1.3	1.6	1.0	0.8	0.8	0.9	1.0	1.1	1.2	1.1	2.4	1.4	•
Depreciation	14	2.6	2.5	2.4	1.3	1.9	1.9	2.2	2.4	2.4	2.4	2.1	3.7	•
Amortization and Depletion	15	0.4	7.9	0.1	0.0	0.1	0.1	0.2	0.2	0.2	0.5	0.5	0.6	•
Pensions and Other Deferred Comp.	16	0.5	0.3	0.1	0.2	0.3	0.4	0.3	0.6	0.5	0.5	0.4	0.9	•
Employee Benefits	17	2.0	3.3	1.2	1.4	1.3	0.9	1.8	2.4	2.1	2.4	1.7	2.8	•
Advertising	18	1.6	3.4	0.4	0.7	0.8	1.1	1.3	1.3	1.3	2.3	3.7	1.9	•
Other Expenses	19	11.7	138.9	19.4	13.4	12.7	9.4	9.7	7.9	7.0	12.4	11.6	9.7	•
Officers' Compensation	20	2.1	6.0	6.7	4.2	3.7	4.0	2.1	1.5	1.1	1.0	0.8	0.6	•
Operating Margin	21	0.2	•	•	•	1.1	3.8	2.2	1.5	4.0	1.8	1.3	•	•
Operating Margin Before Officers' Comp.	22	2.3	•	6.5	2.4	4.8	7.9	4.3	3.0	5.1	2.9	2.1	0.2	•

Selected Average Balance Sheet ($ in Thousands)

Net Receivables 23	531	0	30	165	589	2013	3741	7581	16394	25860	64356	173512	•
Inventories 24	503	0	25	226	577	1727	3936	8124	16099	33509	47524	148107	•
Net Property, Plant and Equipment 25	701	0	32	129	482	1428	4367	9908	21956	37259	92177	304226	•
Total Assets 26	3009	0	117	733	2222	6792	15365	34606	72958	148947	369497	1453077	•
Notes and Loans Payable 27	881	0	49	323	874	2233	4866	10036	22834	55765	131412	319090	•
All Other Liabilities 28	828	0	42	221	687	1753	3555	9534	15595	34167	86948	431768	•
Net Worth 29	1299	0	26	189	661	2806	6944	15036	34529	59015	151137	702218	•

Selected Financial Ratios (Times to 1)

Current Ratio 30	1.7	•	1.4	1.6	1.8	2.1	1.8	1.9	2.3	2.8	1.7	1.5	•
Quick Ratio 31	0.9	•	0.9	0.9	1.0	1.1	0.9	0.9	1.1	1.4	0.9	0.7	•
Net Sales to Working Capital 32	8.2	•	20.6	9.6	8.2	6.8	7.5	6.7	5.8	4.5	9.3	9.7	•
Coverage Ratio 33	3.1	•	1.0	•	3.1	5.7	4.0	3.3	4.9	4.6	3.1	3.5	•
Total Asset Turnover 34	1.6	•	3.8	2.8	2.5	2.6	2.1	1.8	1.9	1.4	1.4	1.1	•
Inventory Turnover 35	6.6	•	10.3	6.3	6.5	6.6	5.7	5.7	6.2	4.2	7.5	7.2	•
Receivables Turnover 36	9.0	•	18.8	8.5	9.8	10.3	8.7	8.5	9.3	7.3	8.7	8.0	•
Total Liabilities to Net Worth 37	1.3	•	3.5	2.9	2.4	1.4	1.2	1.3	1.1	1.5	1.4	1.1	•
Current Assets to Working Capital 38	2.4	•	3.4	2.6	2.3	1.9	2.3	2.1	1.8	1.6	2.5	3.1	•
Current Liabilities to Working Capital 39	1.4	•	2.4	1.6	1.3	0.9	1.3	1.1	0.8	0.6	1.5	2.1	•
Working Capital to Net Sales 40	0.1	•	0.0	0.1	0.1	0.1	0.1	0.1	0.2	0.2	0.1	0.1	•
Inventory to Working Capital 41	0.9	•	1.3	1.0	0.9	0.8	0.9	0.9	0.8	0.7	0.9	0.9	•
Total Receipts to Cash Flow 42	8.9	5.1	7.3	16.6	9.4	9.2	9.3	11.6	9.6	6.9	6.9	9.2	•
Cost of Goods to Cash Flow 43	6.0	3.1	4.2	11.7	6.3	6.1	6.5	8.3	6.9	4.7	4.6	6.2	•
Cash Flow to Total Debt 44	0.3	•	0.7	0.2	0.4	0.5	0.4	0.3	0.4	0.3	0.4	0.2	•

Selected Financial Factors (in Percentages)

Debt Ratio 45	56.8	•	77.8	74.2	70.2	58.7	54.8	56.5	52.7	60.4	59.1	51.7	•
Return on Total Assets 46	6.3	3.8	•	•	6.3	13.1	8.6	6.8	10.9	7.1	10.5	5.5	•
Return on Equity Before Income Taxes 47	9.9	0.5	•	•	14.3	26.1	14.2	11.0	18.4	14.1	17.4	8.1	•
Return on Equity After Income Taxes 48	7.0	•	•	•	11.7	24.8	11.8	8.8	16.6	10.6	14.1	4.9	•
Profit Margin (Before Income Tax) 49	2.6	0.0	•	•	1.7	4.2	3.1	2.6	4.6	4.0	4.9	3.6	•
Profit Margin (After Income Tax) 50	1.9	•	•	•	1.4	4.0	2.6	2.1	4.1	3.0	4.0	2.2	•

Table II

Corporations with Net Income

FURNITURE AND RELATED PRODUCT MANUFACTURING

MONEY AMOUNTS AND SIZE OF ASSETS IN THOUSANDS OF DOLLARS

Item Description for Accounting Period 7/02 Through 6/03	Total	Zero Assets	Under 500	500 to 1,000	1,000 to 5,000	5,000 to 10,000	10,000 to 25,000	25,000 to 50,000	50,000 to 100,000	100,000 to 250,000	250,000 to 500,000	500,000 to 2,500,000	2,500,000 and over
Number of Enterprises **1**	7969	669	5430	550	929	169	139	35	22	12	7	7	0
Revenues ($ in Thousands)													
Net Sales **2**	42792584	272093	2186667	942709	5818551	2958430	4803579	2400575	3096992	2978160	4548053	12786776	0
Interest **3**	90778	255	203	905	2904	1161	2102	2654	1129	28160	21848	29456	0
Rents **4**	18208	0	1290	0	164	341	529	2374	541	2467	6520	3983	0
Royalties **5**	48253	0	0	0	0	0	318	239	87	5630	11456	30523	0
Other Portfolio Income **6**	188629	57479	0	0	3014	1930	4547	5558	3055	18397	17811	76839	0
Other Receipts **7**	569942	53	2426	1451	18878	10212	29957	19706	11845	13505	130495	331411	0
Total Receipts **8**	43708394	329880	2190586	945065	5843511	2972074	4841032	2431106	3113649	3046319	4736183	13258988	0
Average Total Receipts **9**	5485	493	403	1718	6290	17586	34828	69460	141530	253860	676598	1894141	•
Operating Costs/Operating Income (%)													
Cost of Operations **10**	66.7	57.5	55.8	68.5	65.5	64.4	69.4	71.5	70.8	67.6	66.3	66.7	•
Salaries and Wages **11**	6.9	7.4	7.9	6.0	7.5	9.0	6.8	6.5	5.9	5.3	6.6	6.8	•
Taxes Paid **12**	2.3	3.4	3.0	2.2	2.9	2.2	2.1	1.9	2.0	2.0	2.5	2.1	•
Interest Paid **13**	1.0	0.3	0.5	0.4	0.7	0.5	0.9	0.9	0.7	0.8	1.2	1.4	•
Depreciation **14**	2.3	2.4	2.5	0.9	1.9	1.6	2.0	2.1	2.2	2.3	1.8	3.0	•
Amortization and Depletion **15**	0.3	0.2	0.0	0.1	0.1	0.1	0.1	0.1	0.0	0.4	0.1	0.8	•
Pensions and Other Deferred Comp. **16**	0.5	0.2	0.1	0.4	0.3	0.6	0.3	0.7	0.3	0.5	0.4	0.7	•
Employee Benefits **17**	1.8	3.8	0.7	0.3	1.0	1.0	1.5	2.4	2.0	2.5	1.8	2.4	•
Advertising **18**	1.8	1.4	0.2	0.4	0.9	1.0	1.3	1.4	1.2	2.6	3.7	2.4	•
Other Expenses **19**	11.1	14.9	18.3	12.8	11.6	9.1	9.6	7.5	6.6	11.5	12.0	11.7	•
Officers' Compensation **20**	2.0	7.1	6.8	5.1	3.9	3.1	2.0	1.5	1.2	1.0	0.9	0.5	•
Operating Margin **21**	3.5	1.5	4.1	3.0	3.6	7.5	4.1	3.5	6.9	3.5	2.7	1.6	•
Operating Margin Before Officers' Comp. **22**	5.4	8.6	10.9	8.1	7.6	10.6	6.1	5.0	8.1	4.5	3.6	2.2	•

Selected Average Balance Sheet ($ in Thousands)

Net Receivables 23	575	0	26	152	633	2015	4002	8203	16332	26218	74311	198452	·
Inventories 24	529	0	13	275	514	1585	3733	7851	15228	33007	50284	195782	·
Net Property, Plant and Equipment 25	702	0	24	67	489	1362	4316	9434	21771	38937	104806	303912	·
Total Assets 26	2926	0	90	729	2276	6678	15610	35557	71136	145581	352245	1428159	·
Notes and Loans Payable 27	796	0	33	249	680	1332	4609	8686	16220	42811	74038	406025	·
All Other Liabilities 28	702	0	17	247	663	1589	3533	9393	11990	36761	80995	340938	·
Net Worth 29	1428	0	40	234	933	3757	7468	17478	42927	66010	197212	681197	·

Selected Financial Ratios (Times to 1)

Current Ratio 30	2.0	·	1.9	1.5	2.2	2.7	1.9	2.1	2.6	3.0	1.9	1.8	·
Quick Ratio 31	1.1	·	1.4	0.9	1.2	1.5	1.0	1.1	1.4	1.5	1.0	0.9	·
Net Sales to Working Capital 32	7.1	·	14.8	9.2	7.1	5.8	7.3	6.1	5.6	4.8	8.1	7.8	·
Coverage Ratio 33	6.8	85.0	8.8	9.6	6.8	16.9	6.3	6.4	11.4	8.8	6.6	4.9	·
Total Asset Turnover 34	1.8	·	4.5	2.3	2.8	2.6	2.2	1.9	2.0	1.7	1.8	1.3	·
Inventory Turnover 35	6.8	·	17.5	4.3	8.0	7.1	6.4	6.2	6.5	5.1	8.6	6.2	·
Receivables Turnover 36	8.9	·	20.6	5.2	10.4	9.6	9.3	8.8	9.3	8.7	9.6	7.5	·
Total Liabilities to Net Worth 37	1.0	·	1.3	2.1	1.4	0.8	1.1	1.0	0.7	1.2	0.8	1.1	·
Current Assets to Working Capital 38	2.0	·	2.1	2.9	1.9	1.6	2.1	1.9	1.6	1.5	2.1	2.3	·
Current Liabilities to Working Capital 39	1.0	·	1.1	1.9	0.9	0.6	1.1	0.9	0.6	0.5	1.1	1.3	·
Working Capital to Net Sales 40	0.1	·	0.1	0.1	0.1	0.2	0.1	0.2	0.2	0.2	0.1	0.1	·
Inventory to Working Capital 41	0.7	·	0.5	1.1	0.6	0.6	0.9	0.8	0.7	0.6	0.8	0.8	·
Total Receipts to Cash Flow 42	7.0	3.0	6.1	9.2	8.3	6.7	8.0	9.6	7.7	6.4	5.9	6.7	·
Cost of Goods to Cash Flow 43	4.7	1.7	3.4	6.3	5.5	4.3	5.5	6.8	5.4	4.3	3.9	4.5	·
Cash Flow to Total Debt 44	0.5	·	1.3	0.4	0.6	0.9	0.5	0.4	0.6	0.5	0.7	0.4	·

Selected Financial Factors (in Percentages)

Debt Ratio 45	51.2	·	55.8	68.0	59.0	43.7	52.2	50.8	39.7	54.7	44.0	52.3	·
Return on Total Assets 46	12.3	·	21.6	8.5	13.0	22.2	12.7	10.9	16.1	11.3	15.0	9.0	·
Return on Equity Before Income Taxes 47	21.4	·	43.4	23.7	27.1	37.2	22.4	18.6	24.3	22.1	22.7	15.1	·
Return on Equity After Income Taxes 48	17.6	·	41.4	23.0	24.5	35.8	19.5	16.1	22.5	17.7	18.7	9.8	·
Profit Margin (Before Income Tax) 49	5.7	22.7	4.3	3.2	4.0	8.0	4.8	4.8	7.4	5.9	6.9	5.6	·
Profit Margin (After Income Tax) 50	4.7	22.2	4.1	3.1	3.6	7.7	4.2	4.1	4.8	4.7	5.7	3.7	·

Table I

Corporations with and without Net Income

MEDICAL EQUIPMENT AND SUPPLIES

MONEY AMOUNTS AND SIZE OF ASSETS IN THOUSANDS OF DOLLARS

Item Description for Accounting Period 7/02 Through 6/03		Total	Zero Assets	Under 500	500 to 1,000	1,000 to 5,000	5,000 to 10,000	10,000 to 25,000	25,000 to 50,000	50,000 to 100,000	100,000 to 250,000	250,000 to 500,000	500,000 to 2,500,000	2,500,000 and over
Number of Enterprises	1	8756	421	6225	714	822	147	193	77	57	37	24	27	12
Revenues ($ in Thousands)														
Net Sales	2	74148379	557412	1988013	1732919	3054777	1619550	3682517	2950718	3683044	4666070	5217260	17720103	27275997
Interest	3	997656	904	2402	801	4565	4797	17164	18196	19976	28294	61999	102936	735622
Rents	4	61418	0	18	4	2459	39	1935	684	3461	8975	10687	11753	21402
Royalties	5	1551921	0	0	0	334	33861	8817	242	6687	13645	27647	82630	1378057
Other Portfolio Income	6	550693	6250	2400	427	1986	9684	27319	25146	13055	41709	24569	159714	238432
Other Receipts	7	2008626	32540	10573	1496	31630	10486	30694	18754	68823	33707	94872	596528	1078525
Total Receipts	8	79318693	597106	2003406	1735647	3095751	1678417	3768446	3013740	3795046	4792400	5437034	18673664	30728035
Average Total Receipts	9	9059	1418	322	2431	3766	11418	19526	39139	66580	129524	226543	691617	2560670
Operating Costs/Operating Income (%)														
Cost of Operations	10	48.8	65.3	33.6	32.9	53.8	49.9	50.1	50.6	41.2	50.7	45.5	47.4	51.9
Salaries and Wages	11	16.0	3.0	18.1	30.4	13.0	22.6	18.2	16.6	18.6	14.6	14.2	12.5	17.3
Taxes Paid	12	2.3	0.6	3.8	8.8	3.4	3.6	2.6	2.2	2.1	2.0	2.2	2.2	1.6
Interest Paid	13	3.1	7.0	1.0	0.8	1.2	1.1	1.2	2.0	1.4	3.0	2.1	2.5	4.8
Depreciation	14	3.7	4.6	2.5	2.6	2.8	2.4	3.3	4.0	3.8	3.9	4.5	3.3	4.0
Amortization and Depletion	15	1.5	1.8	0.0	0.0	0.4	0.8	0.8	1.2	1.1	2.1	1.6	1.3	2.2
Pensions and Other Deferred Comp.	16	0.8	0.1	0.5	0.0	1.0	0.3	0.4	0.6	0.4	0.4	1.0	0.7	1.1
Employee Benefits	17	2.2	0.2	1.9	0.8	1.5	2.1	2.1	2.3	2.5	2.4	2.6	2.2	2.2
Advertising	18	1.2	3.9	0.8	0.5	1.9	1.5	1.6	1.9	3.7	1.4	1.3	1.1	0.7
Other Expenses	19	21.0	26.7	21.4	14.1	22.2	21.8	21.1	19.3	21.6	19.1	18.6	19.7	22.7
Officers' Compensation	20	1.9	2.2	16.8	5.3	6.1	5.5	3.7	2.6	2.0	1.9	1.2	1.1	0.3
Operating Margin	21	•	•	•	3.7	•	•	•	•	1.4	•	4.7	5.7	•
Operating Margin Before Officers' Comp.	22	•	•	16.3	9.0	•	•	•	•	3.4	0.3	5.9	6.9	•

Selected Average Balance Sheet ($ in Thousands)

Net Receivables 23	2350	0	15	87	452	1665	3079	5709	15053	26508	49732	133965	1010226
Inventories 24	1132	0	12	124	422	1551	2863	5307	10035	18760	33390	94112	300178
Net Property, Plant and Equipment 25	1486	0	22	267	416	1160	2537	6292	12663	24502	51917	112013	441006
Total Assets 26	13833	0	71	642	1878	6814	15960	34435	72556	160484	360393	901103	5741230
Notes and Loans Payable 27	3415	0	57	323	646	1762	4003	8107	11572	35368	62454	223601	1468858
All Other Liabilities 28	3976	0	34	209	484	1708	4110	8984	13698	35077	70684	223084	1877348
Net Worth 29	6442	0	-19	111	749	3343	7847	17344	47286	90038	227255	454417	2395024

Selected Financial Ratios (Times to 1)

Current Ratio 30	1.5	•	0.9	1.5	1.7	2.3	2.3	2.1	2.7	2.6	2.1	2.2	1.1
Quick Ratio 31	1.0	•	0.6	1.0	1.1	1.4	1.5	1.3	1.7	1.5	1.2	1.2	0.8
Net Sales to Working Capital 32	5.0	•	•	22.0	6.8	4.1	3.3	3.8	2.6	2.8	2.9	3.7	11.3
Coverage Ratio 33	2.7	•	1.3	5.8	•	•	•	0.5	4.5	1.7	5.4	5.5	2.2
Total Asset Turnover 34	0.6	•	4.5	3.8	2.0	1.6	1.2	1.1	0.9	0.8	0.6	0.7	0.4
Inventory Turnover 35	3.7	•	8.9	6.5	4.7	3.5	3.3	3.7	2.7	3.4	3.0	3.3	3.9
Receivables Turnover 36	3.4	•	25.1	13.0	8.0	5.4	6.2	5.8	4.2	4.5	3.8	5.1	2.1
Total Liabilities to Net Worth 37	1.1	•	•	4.8	1.5	1.0	1.0	1.0	0.5	0.8	0.6	1.0	1.4
Current Assets to Working Capital 38	3.0	•	•	3.0	2.4	1.8	1.8	1.9	1.6	1.6	1.9	1.8	8.8
Current Liabilities to Working Capital 39	2.0	•	•	2.0	1.4	0.8	0.8	0.9	0.6	0.6	0.9	0.8	7.8
Working Capital to Net Sales 40	0.2	•	0.0	0.0	0.1	0.2	0.3	0.3	0.4	0.4	0.3	0.3	0.1
Inventory to Working Capital 41	0.7	•	•	1.0	0.7	0.6	0.5	0.5	0.4	0.4	0.5	0.5	1.5
Total Receipts to Cash Flow 42	4.4	9.7	6.5	6.2	8.8	9.8	6.8	6.6	4.3	5.7	4.0	3.5	4.0
Cost of Goods to Cash Flow 43	2.1	6.3	2.2	2.0	4.7	4.9	3.4	3.3	1.8	2.9	1.8	1.7	2.1
Cash Flow to Total Debt 44	0.3	•	0.5	0.7	0.4	0.3	0.3	0.3	0.6	0.3	0.4	0.4	0.2

Selected Financial Factors (in Percentages)

Debt Ratio 45	53.4	•	126.8	82.7	60.1	50.9	50.8	49.6	34.8	43.9	36.9	49.6	58.3
Return on Total Assets 46	5.2	•	5.6	17.5	•	•	•	1.0	5.7	4.1	6.9	10.2	4.2
Return on Equity Before Income Taxes 47	7.1	•	•	83.9	•	•	•	•	6.8	3.1	8.9	16.6	5.5
Return on Equity After Income Taxes 48	3.9	•	•	65.2	•	•	•	•	3.4	•	6.3	11.3	3.1
Profit Margin (Before Income Tax) 49	5.4	•	0.3	3.8	•	•	•	•	5.0	2.2	9.3	11.5	5.8
Profit Margin (After Income Tax) 50	3.0	•	0.0	3.0	•	•	•	•	2.5	•	6.6	7.8	3.3

Table II

Corporations with Net Income

MEDICAL EQUIPMENT AND SUPPLIES

MONEY AMOUNTS AND SIZE OF ASSETS IN THOUSANDS OF DOLLARS

Item Description for Accounting Period 7/02 Through 6/03	Total	Zero Assets	Under 500	500 to 1,000	1,000 to 5,000	5,000 to 10,000	10,000 to 25,000	25,000 to 50,000	50,000 to 100,000	100,000 to 250,000	250,000 to 500,000	500,000 to 2,500,000	2,500,000 and over
Number of Enterprises **1**	5702	412	3884	0	466	102	108	41	38	17	19	0	0
Revenues ($ in Thousands)													
Net Sales **2**	63838872	491027	1366730	0	2165380	1476640	2723270	2064536	2971509	2365455	4649972	0	0
Interest **3**	652505	609	2195	0	1220	1402	7446	8811	9236	15823	55608	0	0
Rents **4**	50155	0	18	0	2090	0	1889	399	1095	1282	10227	0	0
Royalties **5**	1422149	0	0	0	334	33510	7246	68	6638	7661	19109	0	0
Other Portfolio Income **6**	516203	44	2400	0	1914	7286	21122	15134	12930	39905	24569	0	0
Other Receipts **7**	1742670	34897	-2712	0	21671	5610	20230	14725	9695	6972	68137	0	0
Total Receipts **8**	68222554	526577	1368631	0	2192609	1524448	2781203	2103673	3011103	2437098	4827622	0	0
Average Total Receipts **9**	11965	1278	352	•	4705	14946	25752	51309	79240	143359	254085	•	•
Operating Costs/Operating Income (%)													
Cost of Operations **10**	48.1	67.2	34.3	•	51.8	48.7	49.4	49.6	41.6	46.6	45.1	•	•
Salaries and Wages **11**	15.4	0.7	16.0	•	9.7	17.4	13.7	13.8	14.8	11.9	14.1	•	•
Taxes Paid **12**	2.2	0.3	3.7	•	3.1	3.1	2.2	2.1	2.0	1.7	2.6	•	•
Interest Paid **13**	2.2	7.0	0.2	•	0.8	0.8	1.0	1.0	1.3	1.1	1.5	•	•
Depreciation **14**	3.5	4.8	2.2	•	2.0	1.7	2.4	3.2	2.9	3.1	4.1	•	•
Amortization and Depletion **15**	1.5	1.9	•	•	0.1	0.3	0.4	0.8	1.1	1.0	1.5	•	•
Pensions and Other Deferred Comp. **16**	0.8	0.1	0.7	•	0.4	0.3	0.5	0.6	0.4	0.4	1.1	•	•
Employee Benefits **17**	2.1	0.1	0.7	•	1.1	1.7	1.6	1.8	2.0	2.2	2.6	•	•
Advertising **18**	1.1	4.2	0.6	•	1.5	1.4	1.5	1.7	3.6	1.6	1.2	•	•
Other Expenses **19**	18.1	12.6	18.6	•	15.9	14.3	14.7	13.7	18.0	18.0	18.0	•	•
Officers' Compensation **20**	1.5	0.4	12.9	•	5.3	4.7	3.1	2.2	1.7	1.3	1.1	•	•
Operating Margin **21**	3.4	0.7	10.1	•	8.4	5.6	9.4	9.4	10.6	11.1	7.2	•	•
Operating Margin Before Officers' Comp. **22**	4.9	1.0	23.0	•	13.7	10.3	12.5	11.6	12.3	12.4	8.3	•	•

Selected Average Balance Sheet ($ in Thousands)

Net Receivables 23	3054	0	15	•	608	1874	3725	6942	16592	30350	51983
Inventories 24	1411	0	9	•	572	1569	3045	6661	9812	15665	36602
Net Property, Plant and Equipment 25	1863	0	19	•	342	1163	2751	6656	12101	24327	48200
Total Assets 26	17107	0	75	•	1854	6769	15736	34946	73799	159485	349882
Notes and Loans Payable 27	3862	0	17	•	453	1719	4250	6652	13765	25164	33729
All Other Liabilities 28	4871	0	15	•	371	1481	3986	8351	15005	25485	63970
Net Worth 29	8374	0	43	•	1030	3570	7500	19943	45028	108837	252184

Selected Financial Ratios (Times to 1)

Current Ratio 30	1.6	•	2.1	•	2.5	2.5	2.1	2.7	2.5	3.1	2.4
Quick Ratio 31	1.0	•	1.5	•	1.6	1.4	1.2	1.6	1.5	1.9	1.4
Net Sales to Working Capital 32	5.0	•	16.2	•	5.6	5.2	4.6	3.9	3.3	2.6	2.8
Coverage Ratio 33	6.1	2.1	48.4	•	13.7	12.6	14.5	12.9	10.7	15.4	8.7
Total Asset Turnover 34	0.7	•	4.7	•	2.5	2.1	1.6	1.4	1.1	0.9	0.7
Inventory Turnover 35	3.8	•	13.5	•	4.2	4.5	4.1	3.8	3.3	4.1	3.0
Receivables Turnover 36	3.6	•	30.2	•	6.9	7.1	7.1	6.0	5.1	4.8	3.8
Total Liabilities to Net Worth 37	1.0	•	0.8	•	0.8	0.9	1.1	0.8	0.6	0.5	0.4
Current Assets to Working Capital 38	2.8	•	1.9	•	1.7	1.7	1.9	1.6	1.7	1.5	1.7
Current Liabilities to Working Capital 39	1.8	•	0.9	•	0.7	0.7	0.9	0.6	0.7	0.5	0.7
Working Capital to Net Sales 40	0.2	•	0.1	•	0.2	0.2	0.2	0.3	0.3	0.4	0.4
Inventory to Working Capital 41	0.6	•	0.4	•	0.5	0.7	0.6	0.4	0.5	0.3	0.4
Total Receipts to Cash Flow 42	3.8	5.0	4.4	•	4.7	4.9	4.3	4.4	3.6	3.3	3.8
Cost of Goods to Cash Flow 43	1.8	3.3	1.5	•	2.4	2.4	2.1	2.2	1.5	1.5	1.7
Cash Flow to Total Debt 44	0.3	•	2.4	•	1.2	0.9	0.7	0.8	0.8	0.8	0.7

Selected Financial Factors (in Percentages)

Debt Ratio 45	51.0	•	43.6	•	44.4	47.3	52.3	42.9	39.0	31.8	27.9
Return on Total Assets 46	8.9	•	48.8	•	26.2	20.4	22.1	17.6	14.8	15.2	9.0
Return on Equity Before Income Taxes 47	15.2	•	84.7	•	43.7	35.6	43.2	28.5	22.0	20.8	11.1
Return on Equity After Income Taxes 48	11.4	•	81.6	•	42.9	30.9	36.4	24.9	16.5	15.0	8.2
Profit Margin (Before Income Tax) 49	11.4	7.9	10.2	•	9.7	8.8	12.8	11.3	12.6	16.3	11.4
Profit Margin (After Income Tax) 50	8.5	6.0	9.9	•	9.5	7.6	10.8	9.9	9.5	11.7	8.4

Table I

Corporations with and without Net Income

OTHER MISCELLANEOUS MANUFACTURING

MONEY AMOUNTS AND SIZE OF ASSETS IN THOUSANDS OF DOLLARS

Item Description for Accounting Period 7/02 Through 6/03	Total	Zero Assets	Under 500	500 to 1,000	1,000 to 5,000	5,000 to 10,000	10,000 to 25,000	25,000 to 50,000	50,000 to 100,000	100,000 to 250,000	250,000 to 500,000	500,000 to 2,500,000	2,500,000 and over
Number of Enterprises 1	25887	1968	18526	1463	2640	497	435	177	76	63	25	12	4
Revenues ($ in Thousands)													
Net Sales 2	93907889	746324	7625269	2833330	12989146	5875169	10991233	8730840	6846622	8932492	9900611	8876922	9559932
Interest 3	855461	1027	1325	1032	7472	7082	13498	14854	22991	43135	73227	165488	504329
Rents 4	51647	409	1123	2348	1524	219	4106	3560	4890	4635	19630	7035	2169
Royalties 5	444059	597	196	0	39	458	4077	8251	10082	13108	27050	43591	336610
Other Portfolio Income 6	431341	5193	27356	2976	28440	17872	17605	12415	35359	83096	65429	111605	23989
Other Receipts 7	1454967	52103	40396	14866	62581	64653	77018	60647	105202	120196	43078	62970	751262
Total Receipts 8	97145364	805653	7695665	2854552	13089202	5965453	11107537	8830567	7025146	9196662	10129025	9267611	11178291
Average Total Receipts 9	3753	409	415	1951	4958	12003	25535	49890	92436	145979	405161	772301	2794573
Operating Costs/Operating Income (%)													
Cost of Operations 10	63.1	74.6	58.2	53.1	61.9	59.2	66.8	67.4	64.2	65.4	62.5	64.0	61.5
Salaries and Wages 11	9.2	5.9	10.2	15.7	8.6	9.8	9.2	8.4	8.5	8.7	8.5	8.5	9.9
Taxes Paid 12	2.0	1.7	3.1	4.2	2.4	2.1	2.1	1.8	1.6	1.6	1.4	1.7	1.9
Interest Paid 13	2.7	0.9	1.4	0.7	1.1	1.2	1.5	1.8	2.0	3.5	4.0	2.5	8.7
Depreciation 14	2.8	2.4	1.6	1.9	2.2	3.1	2.8	3.1	3.5	3.8	3.2	3.4	2.4
Amortization and Depletion 15	0.3	0.2	0.2	0.1	0.2	0.2	0.3	0.5	0.8	1.1	1.5	0.6	•
Pensions and Other Deferred Comp. 16	0.6	0.3	0.4	0.3	0.5	0.8	0.4	0.6	0.5	0.5	0.4	0.9	0.8
Employee Benefits 17	1.6	1.4	1.5	0.9	1.5	1.5	1.4	1.8	1.4	1.6	1.9	2.1	2.0
Advertising 18	1.8	0.2	1.7	1.1	1.2	2.1	1.5	1.5	1.6	1.5	2.4	2.3	3.0
Other Expenses 19	13.9	19.6	18.0	14.8	13.8	14.0	10.9	10.2	13.5	10.9	11.3	10.6	25.1
Officers' Compensation 20	2.7	1.6	6.9	7.0	5.7	3.8	2.5	1.9	1.7	0.9	0.7	0.8	0.3
Operating Margin 21	•	•	•	0.3	1.0	2.2	0.7	1.0	0.7	0.4	2.2	2.7	•
Operating Margin Before Officers' Comp. 22	2.0	•	3.8	7.2	6.6	6.0	3.1	2.9	2.4	1.3	2.9	3.5	•

Selected Average Balance Sheet ($ in Thousands)

Net Receivables 23	599	0	34	181	568	1726	3921	8040	15530	25703	66372	196235	573866
Inventories 24	538	0	30	204	730	1935	3948	8085	14034	23373	55864	125726	394891
Net Property, Plant and Equipment 25	555	0	26	142	468	1510	3416	8194	13752	31318	58628	153461	606301
Total Assets 26	3085	0	126	705	2274	7206	15714	34779	70324	150433	366941	900338	4781012
Notes and Loans Payable 27	1074	0	76	252	870	2218	5380	12725	24143	68366	158845	234430	1277073
All Other Liabilities 28	814	0	54	176	568	1987	4156	8445	16611	31457	98042	264068	1292905
Net Worth 29	1197	0	-4	276	836	3001	6179	13609	29571	50610	110054	401840	2211034

Selected Financial Ratios (Times to 1)

Current Ratio 30	1.7	•	1.5	2.3	2.0	1.8	1.7	1.8	1.8	1.8	1.5	1.8	1.3
Quick Ratio 31	0.9	•	0.9	1.3	1.0	1.0	0.9	1.0	1.0	1.0	0.8	1.2	0.6
Net Sales to Working Capital 32	6.0	•	15.2	6.6	6.1	5.6	6.0	5.3	5.1	4.8	6.3	4.2	7.7
Coverage Ratio 33	2.1	0.1	•	2.6	2.6	4.0	2.2	2.2	2.7	2.0	2.2	4.2	1.5
Total Asset Turnover 34	1.2	•	3.3	2.7	2.2	1.6	1.6	1.4	1.3	0.9	1.1	0.8	0.5
Inventory Turnover 35	4.3	•	8.0	5.0	4.2	3.6	4.3	4.1	4.1	4.0	4.4	3.8	3.7
Receivables Turnover 36	5.9	•	12.7	9.1	8.5	6.5	6.5	6.2	5.4	5.0	6.2	3.4	4.4
Total Liabilities to Net Worth 37	1.6	•	•	1.6	1.7	1.4	1.5	1.6	1.4	2.0	2.3	1.2	1.2
Current Assets to Working Capital 38	2.5	•	3.2	1.8	2.0	2.2	2.4	2.2	2.2	2.2	2.9	2.2	4.6
Current Liabilities to Working Capital 39	1.5	•	2.2	0.8	1.0	1.2	1.4	1.2	1.2	1.2	1.9	1.2	3.6
Working Capital to Net Sales 40	0.2	0.1	•	0.2	0.2	0.2	0.2	0.2	0.2	0.2	0.2	0.2	0.1
Inventory to Working Capital 41	0.9	•	1.1	0.7	0.9	1.0	1.0	0.9	0.7	0.7	0.9	0.7	1.4
Total Receipts to Cash Flow 42	7.3	7.7	9.9	8.2	8.6	6.8	9.6	9.4	6.9	8.5	7.1	6.4	4.1
Cost of Goods to Cash Flow 43	4.6	5.7	5.8	4.3	5.3	4.0	6.4	6.3	4.4	5.6	4.4	4.1	2.5
Cash Flow to Total Debt 44	0.3	•	0.3	0.6	0.4	0.4	0.3	0.2	0.3	0.2	0.2	0.2	0.2

Selected Financial Factors (in Percentages)

Debt Ratio 45	61.2	•	103.0	60.8	63.3	58.4	60.7	60.9	58.0	66.4	70.0	55.4	53.8
Return on Total Assets 46	6.7	•	•	4.7	6.0	8.0	5.1	5.6	7.0	6.5	9.6	8.5	6.6
Return on Equity Before Income Taxes 47	9.1	•	242.4	7.3	10.1	14.3	7.0	7.7	10.5	9.6	17.5	14.6	5.0
Return on Equity After Income Taxes 48	6.3	•	264.9	7.1	8.3	13.0	5.1	5.7	7.0	7.0	10.6	11.0	3.1
Profit Margin (Before Income Tax) 49	3.0	•	•	1.0	1.7	3.6	1.7	2.1	3.4	3.4	4.9	7.9	4.6
Profit Margin (After Income Tax) 50	2.1	•	•	1.0	1.4	3.3	1.2	1.6	2.3	2.5	2.9	6.0	2.9

Table II

Corporations with Net Income

OTHER MISCELLANEOUS MANUFACTURING

MONEY AMOUNTS AND SIZE OF ASSETS IN THOUSANDS OF DOLLARS

Item Description for Accounting Period 7/02 Through 6/03	Total	Zero Assets	Under 500	500 to 1,000	1,000 to 5,000	5,000 to 10,000	10,000 to 25,000	25,000 to 50,000	50,000 to 100,000	100,000 to 250,000	250,000 to 500,000	500,000 to 2,500,000	2,500,000 and over
Number of Enterprises 1	10877	694	6392	0	2051	343	286	110	42	44	17	0	0
Revenues ($ in Thousands)													
Net Sales 2	69922597	373367	3568255	0	10591948	4363592	7913389	5782277	4598906	6931838	6985426	0	0
Interest 3	727451	250	347	0	5837	3663	6889	6985	6231	15244	31724	0	0
Rents 4	36978	155	748	0	1061	181	2244	1810	828	2823	15605	0	0
Royalties 5	419546	597	196	0	0	458	3322	4847	8864	10427	10639	0	0
Other Portfolio Income 6	373307	5174	24756	0	26942	15585	6095	8988	23225	70534	54968	0	0
Other Receipts 7	1195397	41358	25643	0	48045	51375	43692	35300	44022	54052	24357	0	0
Total Receipts 8	72675276	420901	3619945	0	10673833	4434854	7975631	5840207	4682076	7084918	7122719	0	0
Average Total Receipts 9	6682	606	566	•	5204	12930	27887	53093	111478	161021	418983	•	•
Operating Costs/Operating Income (%)													
Cost of Operations 10	61.0	71.4	49.5	•	60.9	57.7	65.2	64.9	61.0	64.1	57.7	•	•
Salaries and Wages 11	8.9	4.6	11.8	•	7.8	8.7	8.5	8.5	7.6	8.0	8.9	•	•
Taxes Paid 12	2.0	1.8	3.3	•	2.3	1.8	2.0	1.9	1.5	1.6	1.4	•	•
Interest Paid 13	2.5	0.7	1.3	•	1.0	0.9	1.0	1.1	1.1	2.4	3.0	•	•
Depreciation 14	2.6	1.8	1.6	•	2.2	2.4	2.3	2.7	2.7	3.8	3.1	•	•
Amortization and Depletion 15	0.1	•	0.1	•	0.1	0.1	0.2	0.3	0.5	0.7	1.3	•	•
Pensions and Other Deferred Comp. 16	0.6	0.3	0.6	•	0.6	0.9	0.4	0.6	0.4	0.5	0.4	•	•
Employee Benefits 17	1.6	1.8	1.7	•	1.2	1.4	1.2	1.6	1.2	1.7	1.7	•	•
Advertising 18	1.9	0.2	1.7	•	1.0	1.7	1.6	1.7	1.7	1.5	2.5	•	•
Other Expenses 19	13.1	16.2	16.3	•	12.8	12.7	9.2	8.8	13.2	9.6	12.6	•	•
Officers' Compensation 20	2.6	1.1	7.5	•	5.6	4.0	2.6	2.1	1.6	0.8	0.7	•	•
Operating Margin 21	3.2	0.1	4.7	•	4.6	7.7	5.8	5.9	7.4	5.2	6.8	•	•
Operating Margin Before Officers' Comp. 22	5.8	1.2	12.2	•	10.1	11.7	8.4	8.0	9.0	6.0	7.6	•	•

Selected Average Balance Sheet ($ in Thousands)

Net Receivables 23	1082	0	39	•	569	1758	4032	7856	17692	27095	76351
Inventories 24	912	0	38	•	729	1889	3902	8073	15692	22233	54697
Net Property, Plant and Equipment 25	968	0	30	•	495	1459	3251	7684	12423	33813	57780
Total Assets 26	5192	0	148	•	2305	7202	15487	34136	72132	149293	364900
Notes and Loans Payable 27	1628	0	66	•	819	1592	4512	10072	19318	61072	118482
All Other Liabilities 28	1437	0	52	•	502	1694	3768	7336	17697	32540	103358
Net Worth 29	2126	0	30	•	984	3916	7208	16727	35117	55680	143061

Selected Financial Ratios (Times to 1)

Current Ratio 30	1.8	•	2.0	•	2.3	2.3	2.0	2.1	1.9	1.9	1.9
Quick Ratio 31	1.0	•	1.2	•	1.2	1.4	1.0	1.2	1.1	1.0	1.0
Net Sales to Working Capital 32	5.4	•	10.7	•	5.7	4.8	5.3	4.9	5.0	4.9	4.7
Coverage Ratio 33	3.9	20.2	5.9	•	6.3	11.8	7.5	7.3	9.2	4.1	4.1
Total Asset Turnover 34	1.2	•	3.8	•	2.2	1.8	1.8	1.5	1.5	1.1	1.1
Inventory Turnover 35	4.3	•	7.3	•	4.3	3.9	4.6	4.2	4.3	4.5	4.3
Receivables Turnover 36	6.2	•	12.1	•	9.2	6.9	7.1	6.5	6.3	5.9	7.3
Total Liabilities to Net Worth 37	1.4	•	3.9	•	1.3	0.8	1.1	1.0	1.1	1.7	1.6
Current Assets to Working Capital 38	2.2	•	2.0	•	1.8	1.8	2.0	1.9	2.1	2.1	2.1
Current Liabilities to Working Capital 39	1.2	•	1.0	•	0.8	0.8	1.0	0.9	1.1	1.1	1.1
Working Capital to Net Sales 40	0.2	•	0.1	•	0.2	0.2	0.2	0.2	0.2	0.2	0.2
Inventory to Working Capital 41	0.8	•	0.7	•	0.8	0.6	0.8	0.8	0.7	0.7	0.7
Total Receipts to Cash Flow 42	5.7	4.0	6.1	•	7.0	5.1	7.2	7.1	4.9	6.8	5.1
Cost of Goods to Cash Flow 43	3.5	2.8	3.0	•	4.2	3.0	4.7	4.6	3.0	4.4	2.9
Cash Flow to Total Debt 44	0.4	•	0.8	•	0.6	0.8	0.5	0.4	0.6	0.2	0.4

Selected Financial Factors (in Percentages)

Debt Ratio 45	59.0	•	79.6	•	57.3	45.6	53.5	51.0	51.3	62.7	60.8
Return on Total Assets 46	12.2	•	28.0	•	14.2	17.9	13.5	12.3	15.9	10.6	13.8
Return on Equity Before Income Taxes 47	22.3	•	114.2	•	28.0	30.1	25.1	21.6	29.2	21.4	26.6
Return on Equity After Income Taxes 48	18.5	•	106.1	•	25.9	28.6	22.5	19.0	23.9	18.0	18.8
Profit Margin (Before Income Tax) 49	7.4	13.0	6.1	•	5.3	9.3	6.5	6.9	9.4	7.6	9.3
Profit Margin (After Income Tax) 50	6.1	11.6	5.7	•	4.9	8.8	5.9	6.0	7.7	6.4	6.5

166

Table I

Corporations with and without Net Income

MOTOR VEHICLE AND MOTOR VEHICLE PARTS AND SUPPLIES

MONEY AMOUNTS AND SIZE OF ASSETS IN THOUSANDS OF DOLLARS

Item Description for Accounting Period 7/02 Through 6/03		Total	Zero Assets	Under 500	500 to 1,000	1,000 to 5,000	5,000 to 10,000	10,000 to 25,000	25,000 to 50,000	50,000 to 100,000	100,000 to 250,000	250,000 to 500,000	500,000 to 2,500,000	2,500,000 and over
Number of Enterprises	1	15088	1238	8237	2478	2331	356	248	95	44	23	15	14	8
Revenues ($ in Thousands)														
Net Sales	2	228080173	1729939	10844843	5244551	12503453	7016302	8530811	7985309	5973407	10045662	9880221	31869060	116456616
Interest	3	2291555	129239	3097	593	23022	5611	6110	11021	7346	16350	84299	245034	1759834
Rents	4	1399201	107683	5896	626	5158	1476	5476	5766	3034	2620	4328	109151	1147990
Royalties	5	230716	0	1816	0	0	392	144	123	287	1380	2127	68585	155863
Other Portfolio Income	6	1980067	45143	1256	11403	9632	1044	14416	14179	8752	9055	38514	214734	1611940
Other Receipts	7	2410728	4662	13720	7701	126233	47976	60771	62304	23872	38984	109524	332560	1582415
Total Receipts	8	236392440	2016666	10870628	5264874	12667498	7072801	8617728	8078702	6016698	10114051	10118471	32772666	122714658
Average Total Receipts	9	15668	1629	1320	2125	5434	19867	34749	85039	136743	439741	679031	2340905	15339332
Operating Costs/Operating Income (%)														
Cost of Operations	10	82.0	71.0	87.0	75.2	76.9	76.3	74.9	79.1	76.9	83.3	81.9	84.4	83.1
Salaries and Wages	11	4.0	3.2	2.6	6.8	7.4	9.6	8.9	7.4	7.6	5.2	5.8	3.0	2.5
Taxes Paid	12	0.8	1.8	0.9	1.7	1.3	1.1	1.3	1.1	1.5	0.9	1.2	0.7	0.5
Interest Paid	13	1.2	7.0	0.2	0.7	0.5	0.7	0.7	0.8	0.7	0.7	1.3	0.5	1.6
Depreciation	14	4.7	13.1	0.3	0.9	0.7	0.9	1.3	1.4	1.7	0.9	1.9	2.3	7.6
Amortization and Depletion	15	0.1	0.0	0.1	0.0	0.0	0.0	0.1	0.1	0.1	0.3	0.2	0.1	0.1
Pensions and Other Deferred Comp.	16	0.2	0.3	0.1	0.2	0.2	0.2	0.2	0.2	0.2	0.1	0.1	0.1	0.2
Employee Benefits	17	0.4	1.0	0.3	0.7	0.7	0.5	0.8	0.8	0.9	0.7	0.8	0.5	0.3
Advertising	18	2.6	3.3	0.4	0.7	0.7	0.4	0.5	0.6	0.6	0.6	1.0	3.9	3.6
Other Expenses	19	5.5	17.0	6.5	8.4	8.7	6.2	8.1	6.9	7.3	5.4	8.6	6.0	3.9
Officers' Compensation	20	0.7	0.7	3.1	4.0	3.3	2.8	1.7	1.2	0.7	0.4	0.5	0.2	0.1
Operating Margin	21	•	•	•	0.6	•	•	1.4	0.5	1.8	1.6	•	•	•
Operating Margin Before Officers' Comp.	22	•	•	1.7	4.6	3.0	4.1	3.1	1.7	2.5	2.0	•	•	•

Selected Average Balance Sheet ($ in Thousands)

Net Receivables 23	2340	0	42	127	484	1887	4028	9032	11751	32144	78622	275442	3087766
Inventories 24	1571	0	67	370	748	3488	6424	12386	25487	59007	87283	288886	1080293
Net Property, Plant and Equipment 25	2077	0	14	62	209	660	2017	5556	11410	20834	57300	177100	3125095
Total Assets 26	8873	0	167	669	1841	7065	15298	34258	64916	160707	330563	1058151	11332587
Notes and Loans Payable 27	3472	0	49	256	475	2204	5087	13588	20572	42306	123322	215359	5019013
All Other Liabilities 28	3249	0	79	170	595	2333	4933	10262	19243	57271	83251	488120	4161330
Net Worth 29	2152	0	39	243	771	2528	5277	10408	25101	61130	123990	354672	2152244

Selected Financial Ratios (Times to 1)

Current Ratio 30	1.2	•	1.7	2.3	2.0	1.7	1.6	1.4	1.6	1.4	1.2	1.1	
Quick Ratio 31	0.6	•	0.8	0.8	0.9	0.6	0.7	0.6	0.6	0.6	0.7	0.6	
Net Sales to Working Capital 32	14.1	24.0	6.4	7.3	7.9	11.2	8.1	13.5	10.9	16.1	19.1		
Coverage Ratio 33	2.4	0.7	2.4	2.9	4.3	3.2	4.5	4.5	3.8	2.2	1.3		
Total Asset Turnover 34	1.7	7.9	3.2	2.9	2.8	2.2	2.5	2.1	2.7	2.0	2.2	1.3	
Inventory Turnover 35	7.9	17.2	4.3	5.5	4.3	5.4	4.1	6.2	6.2	6.6	11.2		
Receivables Turnover 36	•	•	•	•	•	•	•	•	•	•	•	•	
Total Liabilities to Net Worth 37	3.1	3.3	1.8	1.4	1.8	2.3	1.6	1.6	1.7	2.0	4.3		
Current Assets to Working Capital 38	5.0	2.5	1.8	2.0	2.5	3.3	2.7	3.2	3.3	5.1	8.1		
Current Liabilities to Working Capital 39	4.0	1.5	0.8	1.0	1.5	2.3	1.7	2.2	2.3	4.1	7.1		
Working Capital to Net Sales 40	0.1	0.0	0.2	0.1	0.1	0.1	0.1	0.1	0.1	0.1	0.1		
Inventory to Working Capital 41	1.5	1.2	1.1	1.0	1.4	1.7	1.5	1.8	1.4	2.0	1.4		
Total Receipts to Cash Flow 42	16.6	7.0	26.9	14.8	13.8	15.5	15.7	13.0	16.0	15.5	18.5		
Cost of Goods to Cash Flow 43	13.6	5.0	23.4	11.1	10.6	11.3	12.3	8.8	10.0	13.1	13.1	15.4	
Cash Flow to Total Debt 44	0.1	•	0.4	0.3	0.4	0.3	0.2	0.3	0.3	0.2	0.1		

Selected Financial Factors (in Percentages)

Debt Ratio 45	75.7	76.5	63.7	58.1	64.2	65.5	69.6	61.3	62.0	62.5	66.5	81.0	
Return on Total Assets 46	4.7	•	5.6	4.4	8.0	7.2	5.9	6.8	8.0	2.1	3.8	4.6	
Return on Equity Before Income Taxes 47	11.0	•	8.9	6.9	17.1	16.0	13.3	13.6	16.4	8.3	13.4		
Return on Equity After Income Taxes 48	7.0	•	7.5	5.7	15.5	13.7	10.5	9.6	12.7	4.8	8.1		
Profit Margin (Before Income Tax) 49	1.6	•	1.0	1.0	2.2	2.5	1.7	2.5	2.3	1.3	2.0		
Profit Margin (After Income Tax) 50	1.0	•	0.9	0.8	2.0	2.1	1.3	1.8	1.8	0.7	1.2		

167

Table II
Corporations with Net Income

MOTOR VEHICLE AND MOTOR VEHICLE PARTS AND SUPPLIES

MONEY AMOUNTS AND SIZE OF ASSETS IN THOUSANDS OF DOLLARS

Item Description for Accounting Period 7/02 Through 6/03	Total	Zero Assets	Under 500	500 to 1,000	1,000 to 5,000	5,000 to 10,000	10,000 to 25,000	25,000 to 50,000	50,000 to 100,000	100,000 to 250,000	250,000 to 500,000	500,000 to 2,500,000	2,500,000 and over
Number of Enterprises 1	8601	3	4201	1829	1891	326	198	76	35	17	0	11	0
Revenues ($ in Thousands)													
Net Sales 2	172891223	22340	4369557	4104146	10531791	6371364	7341258	6630745	5219558	8806603	0	23104988	0
Interest 3	1333306	67	1641	414	16094	5545	4754	4574	6877	10681	0	83239	0
Rents 4	1149734	0	5888	26	4977	1089	4512	1674	1557	2376	0	4584	0
Royalties 5	227416	0	1816	0	0	392	102	123	247	1340	0	1656	0
Other Portfolio Income 6	981186	77	746	167	3959	815	11185	6592	7912	7551	0	78317	0
Other Receipts 7	1233798	446	7012	4471	123655	30676	36702	60275	20074	35194	0	305418	0
Total Receipts 8	177816663	22930	4386660	4109224	10680476	6409881	7398513	6703983	5256225	8863745	0	23578202	0
Average Total Receipts 9	20674	7643	1044	2247	5648	19662	37366	88210	150178	521397	•	2143473	•
Operating Costs/Operating Income (%)													
Cost of Operations 10	81.8	62.1	81.7	74.9	76.9	75.4	74.8	78.5	76.9	84.5	•	81.6	•
Salaries and Wages 11	4.4	15.1	4.2	6.7	7.1	9.7	8.7	7.2	7.2	4.6	•	3.5	•
Taxes Paid 12	0.8	3.1	1.0	1.7	1.2	1.1	1.3	1.1	1.4	0.8	•	0.7	•
Interest Paid 13	0.8	0.4	0.3	0.6	0.4	0.6	0.6	0.5	0.6	0.4	•	0.4	•
Depreciation 14	2.3	1.0	0.3	0.9	0.6	0.9	1.2	1.1	1.3	0.7	•	1.7	•
Amortization and Depletion 15	0.1	•	0.1	0.1	0.0	0.1	0.1	0.0	0.1	0.2	•	0.1	•
Pensions and Other Deferred Comp. 16	0.2	0.6	0.0	0.2	0.2	0.2	0.3	0.2	0.2	0.1	•	0.1	•
Employee Benefits 17	0.4	0.7	0.4	0.7	0.5	0.6	0.7	0.7	0.8	0.6	•	0.6	•
Advertising 18	2.5	0.4	0.8	0.5	0.6	0.3	0.4	0.7	0.6	0.5	•	4.2	•
Other Expenses 19	5.3	11.9	5.7	7.5	8.2	6.3	7.7	6.0	6.8	4.1	•	6.5	•
Officers' Compensation 20	0.8	2.5	3.7	3.9	3.2	3.0	1.6	1.3	0.7	0.4	•	0.3	•
Operating Margin 21	0.7	2.3	1.9	2.4	0.9	1.8	2.6	2.6	3.4	3.1	•	0.3	•
Operating Margin Before Officers' Comp. 22	1.4	4.7	5.6	6.3	4.2	4.8	4.2	3.8	4.1	3.5	•	0.6	•

Selected Average Balance Sheet ($ in Thousands)

Net Receivables 23	2632	0	45	132	495	1950	4137	9631	12537	32896	293432
Inventories 24	2081	0	66	363	738	3341	6608	13124	24990	61640	304666
Net Property, Plant and Equipment 25	1809	0	12	58	189	639	2070	4934	9457	18146	183018
Total Assets 26	10043	0	185	666	1842	7012	15388	33968	64734	163149	1018956
Notes and Loans Payable 27	2803	0	36	191	389	1903	4612	11359	18948	32742	211160
All Other Liabilities 28	4005	0	74	168	561	2459	4877	10365	21122	51048	421822
Net Worth 29	3234	0	75	306	892	2650	5899	12244	24664	79359	385974

Selected Financial Ratios (Times to 1)

Current Ratio 30	1.2	•	1.8	2.5	2.2	1.8	1.6	1.5	1.6	1.9	1.3
Quick Ratio 31	0.6	•	1.0	0.9	1.0	0.7	0.7	0.7	0.6	0.7	0.6
Net Sales to Working Capital 32	17.1	•	15.9	6.5	7.1	7.5	7.9	9.3	8.4	9.9	11.8
Coverage Ratio 33	5.4	14.0	9.8	5.2	6.3	4.9	6.4	7.9	7.6	10.9	6.6
Total Asset Turnover 34	2.0	•	5.6	3.4	3.0	2.8	2.4	2.6	2.3	3.2	2.1
Inventory Turnover 35	7.9	•	12.9	4.6	5.8	4.4	4.2	5.2	4.6	7.1	5.6
Receivables Turnover 36	•	•	•	•	•	•	•	•	•	•	•
Total Liabilities to Net Worth 37	2.1	•	1.5	1.2	1.1	1.6	1.6	1.8	1.6	1.1	1.6
Current Assets to Working Capital 38	5.3	•	2.2	1.7	1.9	2.3	2.6	2.8	2.7	2.1	4.0
Current Liabilities to Working Capital 39	4.3	•	1.2	0.7	0.9	1.3	1.6	1.8	1.7	1.1	3.0
Working Capital to Net Sales 40	0.1	•	0.1	0.2	0.1	0.1	0.1	0.1	0.1	0.1	0.1
Inventory to Working Capital 41	1.8	•	1.0	1.1	0.9	1.3	1.4	1.4	1.4	1.2	1.7
Total Receipts to Cash Flow 42	12.8	6.4	16.1	12.6	11.7	14.0	10.9	12.3	11.4	14.5	12.5
Cost of Goods to Cash Flow 43	10.4	4.0	13.2	9.4	9.0	10.6	8.2	9.7	8.7	12.3	10.2
Cash Flow to Total Debt 44	0.2	•	0.6	0.5	0.5	0.3	0.4	0.3	0.3	0.4	0.3

Selected Financial Factors (in Percentages)

Debt Ratio 45	67.8	•	59.5	54.0	51.6	62.2	61.7	64.0	61.9	51.4	62.1
Return on Total Assets 46	8.7	•	14.2	10.7	8.4	8.7	9.7	10.8	10.7	13.1	5.7
Return on Equity Before Income Taxes 47	22.0	•	31.5	18.7	14.6	18.2	21.3	26.2	24.4	24.5	12.7
Return on Equity After Income Taxes 48	17.3	•	29.8	17.2	13.3	16.6	18.8	23.2	19.3	20.7	8.6
Profit Margin (Before Income Tax) 49	3.5	4.9	2.3	2.6	2.3	2.5	3.4	3.7	4.0	3.8	2.3
Profit Margin (After Income Tax) 50	2.8	4.9	2.1	2.4	2.1	2.2	3.0	3.3	3.2	3.2	1.6

LUMBER AND OTHER CONSTRUCTION MATERIALS

Table I

Corporations with and without Net Income

MONEY AMOUNTS AND SIZE OF ASSETS IN THOUSANDS OF DOLLARS

Item Description for Accounting Period 7/02 Through 6/03	Total	Zero Assets	Under 500	500 to 1,000	1,000 to 5,000	5,000 to 10,000	10,000 to 25,000	25,000 to 50,000	50,000 to 100,000	100,000 to 250,000	250,000 to 500,000	500,000 to 2,500,000	2,500,000 and over
Number of Enterprises 1	16306	2142	7709	1828	3539	609	327	101	31	12	5	4	•

Revenues ($ in Thousands)

	Total	Zero Assets	Under 500	500 to 1,000	1,000 to 5,000	5,000 to 10,000	10,000 to 25,000	25,000 to 50,000	50,000 to 100,000	100,000 to 250,000	250,000 to 500,000	500,000 to 2,500,000	2,500,000 and over
Net Sales 2	91264588	809107	3728931	3964644	28483119	12259067	14078222	10074393	5550016	4431404	2649531	5236155	•
Interest 3	191202	692	4213	4325	26284	7082	9072	6565	10067	11492	1967	109442	•
Rents 4	107700	5	0	3516	3728	3753	9664	1334	1402	2310	365	81624	•
Royalties 5	1343	0	0	0	0	9	84	0	0	0	1248	2	•
Other Portfolio Income 6	279257	26358	6312	125	47737	3825	16220	8111	2383	2755	2170	163262	•
Other Receipts 7	755164	10947	4113	17661	229903	53423	73838	52451	18268	36951	6578	251030	•
Total Receipts 8	92599254	847109	3743569	3990271	28790771	12327159	14187100	10142854	5582136	4484912	2661859	5841515	•
Average Total Receipts 9	5679	395	486	2183	8135	20242	43386	100424	180069	373743	532372	1460379	•

Operating Costs/Operating Income (%)

	Total	Zero Assets	Under 500	500 to 1,000	1,000 to 5,000	5,000 to 10,000	10,000 to 25,000	25,000 to 50,000	50,000 to 100,000	100,000 to 250,000	250,000 to 500,000	500,000 to 2,500,000	2,500,000 and over
Cost of Operations 10	80.0	82.7	65.8	73.7	80.8	78.8	79.2	82.7	78.6	84.7	78.6	87.3	•
Salaries and Wages 11	6.7	5.5	6.7	7.3	6.4	6.8	7.9	6.4	7.6	5.5	6.6	4.4	•
Taxes Paid 12	1.2	1.0	2.5	1.6	1.1	1.2	1.2	1.0	1.2	0.8	1.5	1.1	•
Interest Paid 13	0.8	1.4	0.3	0.4	0.5	0.7	0.6	0.6	0.8	0.7	2.1	4.3	•
Depreciation 14	1.3	0.9	0.8	1.5	1.2	1.0	1.1	0.9	1.6	1.3	2.8	2.6	•
Amortization and Depletion 15	0.1	0.6	0.0	0.0	0.0	0.1	0.0	0.1	0.1	0.3	1.0	0.8	•
Pensions and Other Deferred Comp. 16	0.4	0.1	2.6	0.3	0.3	0.3	0.3	0.2	0.2	0.3	0.5	0.1	•
Employee Benefits 17	0.6	0.3	0.8	0.5	0.5	0.7	0.7	0.6	0.8	0.3	1.0	1.0	•
Advertising 18	0.3	0.1	0.9	1.0	0.3	0.4	0.3	0.3	0.3	0.2	0.1	0.2	•
Other Expenses 19	6.2	7.9	12.7	8.8	6.1	6.0	5.7	5.1	6.4	5.3	5.3	5.3	•
Officers' Compensation 20	2.0	0.4	6.8	5.4	2.2	2.3	1.4	1.0	0.7	0.5	0.2	1.0	•
Operating Margin 21	0.4	•	•	•	0.6	1.6	1.5	1.2	1.5	•	0.4	•	•
Operating Margin Before Officers' Comp. 22	2.4	•	6.7	4.9	2.8	4.0	3.0	2.2	2.2	0.3	0.6	•	•

Selected Average Balance Sheet ($ in Thousands)

Net Receivables 23	594	0	22	225	823	2139	4971	11048	22399	40029	75710	148140	•
Inventories 24	556	0	24	230	847	2293	4839	10565	20381	29133	47114	50238	•
Net Property, Plant and Equipment 25	392	0	14	122	327	1010	2412	5269	15468	24707	115853	400925	•
Total Assets 26	2052	0	124	738	2503	6983	15091	34433	69429	147281	323365	1025937	•
Notes and Loans Payable 27	770	0	52	188	733	2417	4758	11343	28533	37826	172534	711379	•
All Other Liabilities 28	489	0	36	281	608	1413	3744	7742	14457	45815	75959	195382	•
Net Worth 29	793	0	35	269	1162	3152	6589	15348	26439	63640	74873	119176	•

Selected Financial Ratios (Times to 1)

Current Ratio 30	1.8	•	2.2	1.6	2.2	2.0	1.8	1.9	1.9	1.4	1.3	1.0	•
Quick Ratio 31	1.0	•	1.6	0.9	1.2	1.0	0.9	1.0	1.0	0.8	0.8	0.7	•
Net Sales to Working Capital 32	8.9	•	9.6	10.6	7.4	7.5	8.7	8.2	8.1	15.7	17.2	414.4	•
Coverage Ratio 33	3.2	4.0	2.0	1.4	4.3	4.2	4.9	4.2	3.5	2.4	1.4	1.8	•
Total Asset Turnover 34	2.7	•	3.9	2.9	3.2	2.9	2.9	2.9	2.6	2.5	1.6	1.3	•
Inventory Turnover 35	8.1	•	13.4	6.9	7.7	6.9	7.0	7.8	6.9	10.7	8.8	22.7	•
Receivables Turnover 36	•	•	•	•	•	•	•	•	•	•	•	•	•
Total Liabilities to Net Worth 37	1.6	•	2.5	1.7	1.2	1.2	1.3	1.2	1.6	1.3	3.3	7.6	•
Current Assets to Working Capital 38	2.2	•	1.9	2.7	1.9	2.0	2.3	2.1	2.2	3.4	4.5	82.9	•
Current Liabilities to Working Capital 39	1.2	•	0.9	1.7	0.9	1.0	1.3	1.1	1.2	2.4	3.5	81.9	•
Working Capital to Net Sales 40	0.1	•	0.1	0.1	0.1	0.1	0.1	0.1	0.1	0.1	0.1	0.0	•
Inventory to Working Capital 41	0.9	•	0.5	1.1	0.8	1.0	1.0	0.9	1.2	1.5	1.5	15.9	•
Total Receipts to Cash Flow 42	16.1	15.4	10.3	16.7	16.7	15.3	16.1	18.5	15.2	19.8	21.0	14.2	•
Cost of Goods to Cash Flow 43	12.9	12.7	6.8	12.3	13.5	12.1	12.8	15.3	12.0	16.8	16.5	12.4	•
Cash Flow to Total Debt 44	0.3	•	0.5	0.3	0.4	0.3	0.3	0.3	0.3	0.2	0.1	0.1	•

Selected Financial Factors (in Percentages)

Debt Ratio 45	61.3	•	71.5	63.6	53.6	54.9	56.3	55.4	61.9	56.8	76.8	88.4	•
Return on Total Assets 46	7.3	•	2.6	1.7	7.0	8.3	8.3	7.2	7.7	4.4	4.7	9.9	•
Return on Equity Before Income Taxes 47	13.0	•	4.6	1.3	11.5	14.0	15.0	12.3	14.4	5.9	5.8	38.0	•
Return on Equity After Income Taxes 48	11.3	•	2.1	0.7	10.6	13.2	13.5	11.1	12.5	3.4	4.6	27.0	•
Profit Margin (Before Income Tax) 49	1.8	4.1	0.3	0.2	1.7	2.2	2.3	1.9	2.1	1.0	0.8	3.5	•
Profit Margin (After Income Tax) 50	1.6	2.8	0.2	0.1	1.5	2.1	2.1	1.7	1.9	0.6	0.7	2.5	•

169

Table II
Corporations with Net Income

LUMBER AND OTHER CONSTRUCTION MATERIALS

MONEY AMOUNTS AND SIZE OF ASSETS IN THOUSANDS OF DOLLARS

Item Description for Accounting Period 7/02 Through 6/03	Total	Zero Assets	Under 500	500 to 1,000	1,000 to 5,000	5,000 to 10,000	10,000 to 25,000	25,000 to 50,000	50,000 to 100,000	100,000 to 250,000	250,000 to 500,000	500,000 to 2,500,000	2,500,000 and over
Number of Enterprises **1**	9763	916	3987	1329	2672	466	274	79	25	0	0	0	•
Revenues ($ in Thousands)													
Net Sales **2**	74850533	687347	2343567	3292861	23737819	10060572	12272249	8113810	4696134	0	0	0	•
Interest **3**	168490	689	1632	3835	18164	5350	7456	2536	9230	0	0	0	•
Rents **4**	96985	5	0	3514	2440	484	6024	900	590	0	0	0	•
Royalties **5**	1250	0	0	0	0	0	1	0	0	0	0	0	•
Other Portfolio Income **6**	236071	26358	2673	117	24375	2947	5321	5486	1823	0	0	0	•
Other Receipts **7**	495993	10024	3296	14328	164192	49379	66474	46341	18567	0	0	0	•
Total Receipts **8**	75849322	724423	2351168	3314655	23946990	10118732	12357525	8169073	4726344	0	0	0	•
Average Total Receipts **9**	7769	791	590	2494	8962	21714	45100	103406	189054			•	
Operating Costs/Operating Income (%)													
Cost of Operations **10**	79.5	83.7	64.9	74.1	80.1	79.2	78.9	82.2	77.9	•	•	•	•
Salaries and Wages **11**	6.5	4.2	5.6	6.5	6.4	6.0	7.9	6.4	8.2	•	•	•	•
Taxes Paid **12**	1.2	1.0	2.6	1.4	1.1	1.1	1.2	1.0	1.2	•	•	•	•
Interest Paid **13**	0.8	0.5	0.2	0.3	0.4	0.6	0.5	0.5	0.8	•	•	•	•
Depreciation **14**	1.2	0.8	0.8	1.1	1.1	0.9	1.0	0.9	1.4	•	•	•	•
Amortization and Depletion **15**	0.1	0.7	0.0	0.0	0.0	0.2	0.0	0.1	0.1	•	•	•	•
Pensions and Other Deferred Comp. **16**	0.3	0.1	1.2	0.3	0.3	0.3	0.3	0.2	0.3	•	•	•	•
Employee Benefits **17**	0.6	0.4	0.8	0.4	0.5	0.6	0.6	0.5	0.8	•	•	•	•
Advertising **18**	0.4	0.0	1.1	1.1	0.3	0.4	0.3	0.3	0.3	•	•	•	•
Other Expenses **19**	5.8	6.8	11.4	6.8	5.7	5.6	5.4	4.8	6.4	•	•	•	•
Officers' Compensation **20**	2.0	0.4	6.6	5.3	2.2	2.3	1.4	1.1	0.6	•	•	•	•
Operating Margin **21**	1.7	1.6	4.6	2.6	1.8	2.7	2.3	2.1	2.0	•	•	•	•
Operating Margin Before Officers' Comp. **22**	3.6	2.0	11.3	7.9	4.0	5.0	3.7	3.2	2.6	•	•	•	•

Selected Average Balance Sheet ($ in Thousands)

Net Receivables 23	818	0	31	252	866	2214	5202	11279	23504
Inventories 24	742	0	31	186	924	2278	5009	11122	20996
Net Property, Plant and Equipment 25	485	0	10	142	340	939	2388	5224	14779
Total Assets 26	2675		144	760	2625	7021	15163	34616	69119
Notes and Loans Payable 27	991	0	28	143	709	2438	4594	10688	28515
All Other Liabilities 28	622	0	41	205	615	1430	3666	8301	12888
Net Worth 29	1061	0	75	412	1300	3152	6903	15627	27717

Selected Financial Ratios (Times to 1)

Current Ratio 30	1.9	•	2.7	2.2	2.2	2.0	1.9	2.0	2.0
Quick Ratio 31	1.1	•	1.9	1.4	1.2	1.0	1.0	1.1	1.0
Net Sales to Working Capital 32	8.6	•	8.4	8.1	7.5	8.0	8.3	7.7	7.8
Coverage Ratio 33	4.8	15.2	24.2	12.1	7.2	6.1	6.7	6.5	4.4
Total Asset Turnover 34	2.9	•	4.1	3.3	3.4	3.1	3.0	3.0	2.7
Inventory Turnover 35	8.2	•	12.3	9.9	7.7	7.5	7.1	7.6	7.0
Receivables Turnover 36	•	•	•	•	•	•	•	•	•
Total Liabilities to Net Worth 37	1.5	•	0.9	0.8	1.0	1.2	1.2	1.2	1.5
Current Assets to Working Capital 38	2.1	•	1.6	1.8	1.8	2.0	2.2	2.0	2.1
Current Liabilities to Working Capital 39	1.1	•	0.6	0.8	0.8	1.0	1.2	1.0	1.1
Working Capital to Net Sales 40	0.1	•	0.1	0.1	0.1	0.1	0.1	0.1	0.1
Inventory to Working Capital 41	0.8	•	0.4	0.6	0.8	0.8	0.9	0.8	0.9
Total Receipts to Cash Flow 42	14.3	12.0	7.5	13.1	15.0	13.4	14.8	16.5	14.3
Cost of Goods to Cash Flow 43	11.3	10.0	4.9	9.7	12.0	10.6	11.7	13.5	11.1
Cash Flow to Total Debt 44	0.3	•	1.1	0.5	0.4	0.4	0.4	0.3	0.3

Selected Financial Factors (in Percentages)

Debt Ratio 45	60.3	•	47.8	45.8	50.5	55.1	54.5	54.9	59.9
Return on Total Assets 46	10.8	•	21.1	11.4	10.5	12.1	10.4	9.8	9.3
Return on Equity Before Income Taxes 47	21.6	•	38.7	19.4	18.1	22.6	19.4	18.5	18.0
Return on Equity After Income Taxes 48	19.5	•	36.5	18.8	17.0	21.5	17.6	17.0	15.9
Profit Margin (Before Income Tax) 49	3.0	7.0	4.9	3.2	2.7	3.3	3.0	2.8	2.7
Profit Margin (After Income Tax) 50	2.7	5.5	4.7	3.1	2.5	3.1	2.7	2.6	2.3

Table I
Corporations with and without Net Income

PROFESSIONAL AND COMMERCIAL EQUIPMENT AND SUPPLIES

MONEY AMOUNTS AND SIZE OF ASSETS IN THOUSANDS OF DOLLARS

Item Description for Accounting Period 7/02 Through 6/03	Total	Zero Assets	Under 500	500 to 1,000	1,000 to 5,000	5,000 to 10,000	10,000 to 25,000	25,000 to 50,000	50,000 to 100,000	100,000 to 250,000	250,000 to 500,000	500,000 to 2,500,000	2,500,000 and over
Number of Enterprises 1	29353	3004	20175	2507	2665	559	251	82	46	29	16	13	5
Revenues ($ in Thousands)													
Net Sales 2	153948533	2596833	9339566	7172356	23535696	11688115	10874022	5428901	7348598	9288901	10399201	27632222	28646122
Interest 3	429617	1456	2264	3705	8110	5562	9129	12461	12193	16060	50338	150450	157890
Rents 4	250269	304	3725	3721	9231	1629	3307	2037	4016	3735	35864	268	182432
Royalties 5	148055	0	0	0	90	328	1937	3427	5238	22714	12316	100837	1168
Other Portfolio Income 6	322939	23095	69357	1990	7147	13887	31718	16048	4585	30700	56776	60261	7373
Other Receipts 7	1273747	11647	93985	57387	133480	82314	61797	66824	50854	100410	155445	290329	169277
Total Receipts 8	156373160	2633335	9508897	7239159	23693754	11789835	10981910	5529698	7425484	9462520	10709940	28234367	29164262
Average Total Receipts 9	5327	877	471	2888	8891	21091	43753	67435	161424	326294	669371	2171874	5832852
Operating Costs/Operating Income (%)													
Cost of Operations 10	76.6	89.9	57.6	74.9	78.9	77.2	78.2	72.5	79.1	79.6	76.6	83.1	72.2
Salaries and Wages 11	8.2	4.3	11.0	7.1	8.3	8.7	8.3	10.6	7.7	6.5	9.0	7.6	8.3
Taxes Paid 12	1.0	0.4	2.0	1.2	1.1	1.1	1.0	1.3	0.8	1.0	0.9	0.7	0.9
Interest Paid 13	0.9	0.2	0.5	0.4	0.4	0.6	0.6	0.8	0.7	0.8	1.0	1.1	1.6
Depreciation 14	2.3	0.2	1.2	0.7	0.8	1.0	0.9	1.5	1.4	1.1	2.7	0.9	7.4
Amortization and Depletion 15	0.2	0.0	0.1	0.0	0.0	0.2	0.2	0.3	0.2	0.4	0.5	0.4	0.4
Pensions and Other Deferred Comp. 16	0.3	0.0	0.2	0.1	0.3	0.2	0.2	0.3	0.2	0.1	0.2	0.3	0.4
Employee Benefits 17	0.7	0.2	0.7	0.7	0.5	0.8	0.6	0.9	0.9	0.9	1.1	0.7	0.8
Advertising 18	0.8	0.4	1.1	0.4	0.5	0.6	0.8	0.7	0.8	1.3	0.8	0.7	0.9
Other Expenses 19	8.0	5.8	17.0	10.1	6.8	7.9	8.1	9.3	7.0	8.1	10.1	4.1	8.7
Officers' Compensation 20	1.4	0.8	7.6	3.7	2.2	1.7	1.3	1.2	0.7	0.5	0.4	0.3	0.1
Operating Margin 21	•	•	1.0	0.7	0.2	•	•	0.6	0.6	•	•	0.2	•
Operating Margin Before Officers' Comp. 22	1.0	•	8.6	4.3	2.4	1.5	1.1	1.8	1.2	0.3	•	0.6	•

Selected Average Balance Sheet ($ in Thousands)

Net Receivables **23**	710	0	27	267	770	2390	5442	10616	24378	47397	105384	379359	977051
Inventories **24**	409	0	23	186	521	2081	4549	9367	16901	36678	60129	143570	391567
Net Property, Plant and Equipment **25**	184	0	17	77	290	615	1471	4490	7182	12449	35928	47268	226595
Total Assets **26**	2371	0	96	727	2135	6732	15822	35699	71560	155832	346825	1164184	4199867
Notes and Loans Payable **27**	672	0	57	244	661	2190	4183	8839	18407	47702	86026	162194	1493677
All Other Liabilities **28**	951	0	47	308	979	2894	7504	13970	28563	50928	128885	530282	1439698
Net Worth **29**	748	0	-8	175	494	1648	4135	12890	24590	57201	131914	471707	1266493

Selected Financial Ratios (Times to 1)

Current Ratio **30**	1.4	•	1.0	1.6	1.4	1.5	1.3	1.5	1.4	1.5	1.3	1.7	1.2
Quick Ratio **31**	0.8	•	0.7	1.0	0.9	0.8	0.7	0.8	0.9	0.8	0.8	1.2	0.7
Net Sales to Working Capital **32**	13.8	•	167.9	13.6	19.6	12.5	14.6	7.7	10.0	8.9	13.4	8.5	23.7
Coverage Ratio **33**	2.4	•	6.6	5.5	3.1	2.0	2.3	4.1	3.2	3.3	0.8	3.3	1.2
Total Asset Turnover **34**	2.2	•	4.8	3.9	4.1	3.1	2.7	1.9	2.2	2.1	1.9	1.8	1.4
Inventory Turnover **35**	9.8	•	11.6	11.5	13.4	7.8	7.5	5.1	7.5	6.9	8.3	12.3	10.6
Receivables Turnover **36**	•	•	•	•	•	•	•	•	•	•	•	•	•
Total Liabilities to Net Worth **37**	2.2	•	•	3.2	3.3	3.1	2.8	1.8	1.9	1.7	1.6	1.5	2.3
Current Assets to Working Capital **38**	3.7	•	25.8	2.8	3.6	3.2	4.1	3.0	3.3	3.0	4.6	2.5	7.6
Current Liabilities to Working Capital **39**	2.7	•	24.8	1.8	2.6	2.2	3.1	2.0	2.3	2.0	3.6	1.5	6.6
Working Capital to Net Sales **40**	0.1	•	0.0	0.1	0.1	0.1	0.1	0.1	0.1	0.1	0.1	0.1	0.0
Inventory to Working Capital **41**	1.1	•	8.3	0.9	1.2	1.2	1.5	1.1	1.1	1.0	1.2	0.6	1.6
Total Receipts to Cash Flow **42**	13.6	32.9	6.5	10.0	16.6	14.2	13.3	9.9	13.4	12.1	14.9	19.0	13.9
Cost of Goods to Cash Flow **43**	10.4	29.5	3.8	7.5	13.1	11.0	10.4	7.2	10.6	9.6	11.4	15.8	10.0
Cash Flow to Total Debt **44**	0.2	•	0.7	0.5	0.3	0.3	0.3	0.3	0.3	0.3	0.2	0.2	0.1

Selected Financial Factors (in Percentages)

Debt Ratio **45**	68.4	•	108.6	76.0	76.9	75.5	73.9	63.9	65.6	63.3	62.0	59.5	69.8
Return on Total Assets **46**	4.6	16.0	•	7.6	5.3	3.8	3.9	6.0	5.3	5.3	1.5	6.4	2.5
Return on Equity Before Income Taxes **47**	8.5	•	•	25.9	15.5	7.7	8.5	12.5	10.5	10.0	•	11.0	1.2
Return on Equity After Income Taxes **48**	5.6	•	•	24.7	12.7	5.1	5.7	8.5	7.5	6.7	•	7.3	•
Profit Margin (Before Income Tax) **49**	1.2	•	2.8	1.6	0.9	0.6	0.8	2.4	1.6	1.8	•	2.4	0.3
Profit Margin (After Income Tax) **50**	0.8	•	2.7	1.5	0.7	0.4	0.5	1.7	1.2	1.2	•	1.6	•

Table II

Corporations with Net Income

PROFESSIONAL AND COMMERCIAL EQUIPMENT AND SUPPLIES

MONEY AMOUNTS AND SIZE OF ASSETS IN THOUSANDS OF DOLLARS

Item Description for Accounting Period 7/02 Through 6/03	Total	Zero Assets	Under 500	500 to 1,000	1,000 to 5,000	5,000 to 10,000	10,000 to 25,000	25,000 to 50,000	50,000 to 100,000	100,000 to 250,000	250,000 to 500,000	500,000 to 2,500,000	2,500,000 and over
Number of Enterprises **1**	16745	1217	11275	1600	1986	360	177	57	27	21	12	0	0
Revenues ($ in Thousands)													
Net Sales **2**	118381149	2384167	6752437	4917568	18899249	8351215	8296006	3853375	5408348	6084451	7443482	0	0
Interest **3**	315203	1015	1846	1325	6872	3327	6261	8590	7259	8198	34181	0	0
Rents **4**	202280	304	133	194	8555	1351	1363	933	2571	3188	2124	0	0
Royalties **5**	127933	0	0	0	0	144	1937	858	342	22714	1248	0	0
Other Portfolio Income **6**	269208	22747	69276	551	7146	4888	30742	14718	1295	30653	22711	0	0
Other Receipts **7**	1007359	12465	82282	36122	116307	51551	46679	44666	41906	97396	121360	0	0
Total Receipts **8**	120303132	2420698	6905974	4955760	18838129	8412476	8382988	3923140	5461721	6246600	7625106	0	0
Average Total Receipts **9**	7184	1989	613	3097	9485	23368	47362	68827	202286	297457	635426	•	•
Operating Costs/Operating Income (%)													
Cost of Operations **10**	78.2	90.0	55.1	74.7	78.2	76.6	77.5	69.7	80.4	74.4	79.0	•	•
Salaries and Wages **11**	7.1	3.9	9.7	5.1	8.1	8.4	8.0	10.7	6.5	7.7	6.9	•	•
Taxes Paid **12**	0.9	0.2	1.7	1.2	1.1	1.0	1.0	1.4	0.8	1.2	1.0	•	•
Interest Paid **13**	0.7	0.0	0.4	0.3	0.3	0.5	0.5	0.7	0.6	0.9	0.7	•	•
Depreciation **14**	1.3	0.2	1.1	0.6	0.6	1.0	0.8	1.5	0.8	1.3	2.9	•	•
Amortization and Depletion **15**	0.2	0.0	0.0	0.0	0.0	0.0	0.2	0.2	0.2	0.4	0.4	•	•
Pensions and Other Deferred Comp. **16**	0.2	0.0	0.3	0.2	0.3	0.2	0.2	0.4	0.1	0.2	0.3	•	•
Employee Benefits **17**	0.6	0.1	0.6	0.6	0.5	0.8	0.5	1.0	0.6	1.2	0.8	•	•
Advertising **18**	0.8	0.3	1.4	0.4	0.4	0.7	0.7	0.8	0.3	1.4	0.9	•	•
Other Expenses **19**	7.2	3.9	16.9	8.8	6.3	7.2	7.3	9.0	6.1	9.3	6.5	•	•
Officers' Compensation **20**	1.4	0.6	7.2	4.1	2.3	1.5	1.3	1.3	0.7	0.6	0.5	•	•
Operating Margin **21**	1.5	0.8	5.8	3.9	1.9	2.0	1.9	3.5	2.7	1.4	0.3	•	•
Operating Margin Before Officers' Comp. **22**	2.8	1.4	13.0	8.0	4.2	3.5	3.2	4.7	3.4	2.0	0.8	•	•

Selected Average Balance Sheet ($ in Thousands)

Net Receivables 23	983	0	31	233	818	2494	5513	10438	23329	49143	111771
Inventories 24	530	0	29	178	527	2040	4758	9545	17702	33287	55681
Net Property, Plant and Equipment 25	214	0	13	67	272	592	1448	4752	6364	13648	30971
Total Assets 26	2898	0	109	727	2158	6675	16057	35780	68842	158305	334601
Notes and Loans Payable 27	658	0	45	165	465	2085	4269	8624	13296	48699	86274
All Other Liabilities 28	1128	0	39	237	956	2751	6469	13796	26249	40657	115533
Net Worth 29	1112	0	25	325	737	1839	5319	13360	29296	68949	132793

Selected Financial Ratios (Times to 1)

Current Ratio 30	1.6	•	1.7	1.9	1.5	1.5	1.5	1.5	1.6	1.8	1.4
Quick Ratio 31	1.0	•	1.1	1.2	1.0	0.9	0.9	0.8	0.9	1.0	0.9
Net Sales to Working Capital 32	10.1	•	16.7	11.4	15.9	12.9	10.6	7.9	10.0	6.4	10.0
Coverage Ratio 33	5.8	47.6	23.9	15.5	8.5	6.2	6.7	8.2	7.0	6.0	5.3
Total Asset Turnover 34	2.4	•	5.5	4.2	4.4	3.5	2.9	1.9	2.9	1.8	1.9
Inventory Turnover 35	10.4	•	11.5	12.9	14.0	8.7	7.6	4.9	9.1	6.5	8.8
Receivables Turnover 36	•	•	•	•	•	•	•	•	•	•	•
Total Liabilities to Net Worth 37	1.6	•	3.3	1.2	1.9	2.6	2.0	1.7	1.3	1.3	1.5
Current Assets to Working Capital 38	2.8	•	2.5	2.1	2.9	3.0	2.9	3.0	2.6	2.2	3.6
Current Liabilities to Working Capital 39	1.8	•	1.5	1.1	1.9	2.0	1.9	2.0	1.6	1.2	2.6
Working Capital to Net Sales 40	0.1	•	0.1	0.1	0.1	0.1	0.1	0.1	0.1	0.2	0.1
Inventory to Working Capital 41	0.8	•	0.8	0.7	0.9	1.1	1.1	1.1	0.9	0.7	0.9
Total Receipts to Cash Flow 42	11.5	21.1	5.0	8.2	13.3	11.6	11.3	7.9	11.2	8.5	13.1
Cost of Goods to Cash Flow 43	9.0	19.0	2.8	6.2	10.4	8.9	8.7	5.5	9.0	6.3	10.4
Cash Flow to Total Debt 44	0.3	1.4	0.9	0.5	0.4	0.4	0.4	0.4	0.5	0.4	0.2

Selected Financial Factors (in Percentages)

Debt Ratio 45	61.6	•	76.9	55.3	65.8	72.5	66.9	62.7	57.4	56.4	60.3
Return on Total Assets 46	9.3	•	45.9	21.2	13.0	11.4	10.2	11.3	12.7	9.4	6.5
Return on Equity Before Income Taxes 47	19.9	•	190.4	44.5	33.5	34.6	26.1	26.7	25.5	17.9	13.2
Return on Equity After Income Taxes 48	16.5	•	185.9	43.5	31.0	30.9	23.0	21.1	21.2	14.0	9.5
Profit Margin (Before Income Tax) 49	3.1	2.3	8.0	4.7	2.6	2.7	3.0	5.3	3.7	4.3	2.8
Profit Margin (After Income Tax) 50	2.6	2.1	7.8	4.6	2.4	2.5	2.6	4.2	3.1	3.3	2.0

Table I

Corporations with and without Net Income

METAL AND MINERAL (EXCEPT PETROLEUM)

MONEY AMOUNTS AND SIZE OF ASSETS IN THOUSANDS OF DOLLARS

Item Description for Accounting Period 7/02 Through 6/03	Total	Zero Assets	Under 500	500 to 1,000	1,000 to 5,000	5,000 to 10,000	10,000 to 25,000	25,000 to 50,000	50,000 to 100,000	100,000 to 250,000	250,000 to 500,000	500,000 to 2,500,000	2,500,000 and over
Number of Enterprises 1	5434	96	2967	551	1245	222	196	62	49	19	14	12	0
Revenues ($ in Thousands)													
Net Sales 2	78903783	474006	1181937	1103430	8423842	4021067	7493856	4742476	7983502	4494444	13309009	25676215	0
Interest 3	405907	708	1244	130	2457	3866	5979	7687	16636	47711	80003	239486	0
Rents 4	67423	0	1459	0	286	158	1621	1141	3263	14691	4738	40067	0
Royalties 5	5184	0	0	0	0	0	509	0	0	4003	0	672	0
Other Portfolio Income 6	268362	2649	261	1082	4466	5977	4082	9246	5425	68659	27832	138686	0
Other Receipts 7	429101	2901	9583	5202	37896	6848	31189	40306	35054	113558	56939	89620	0
Total Receipts 8	80079760	480264	1194484	1109844	8468947	4037916	7537236	4800856	8043880	4743066	13478521	26184746	0
Average Total Receipts 9	14737	5003	403	2014	6802	18189	38455	77433	164161	249635	962752	2182062	•
Operating Costs/Operating Income (%)													
Cost of Operations 10	87.1	88.6	58.5	73.3	80.0	82.1	83.8	87.5	89.7	87.0	90.9	90.3	•
Salaries and Wages 11	3.9	6.2	6.6	3.5	4.9	5.8	4.7	3.6	3.0	3.4	3.2	3.5	•
Taxes Paid 12	0.8	0.6	2.3	1.6	1.2	1.1	0.9	0.8	0.9	1.3	0.6	0.5	•
Interest Paid 13	1.1	1.0	1.2	0.6	0.7	0.7	1.0	0.9	0.8	1.8	1.0	1.5	•
Depreciation 14	1.1	0.7	2.2	0.7	1.2	0.7	0.9	0.9	0.7	1.4	1.0	1.2	•
Amortization and Depletion 15	0.1	•	0.1	•	0.0	0.0	0.3	0.0	0.1	0.3	0.2	0.2	•
Pensions and Other Deferred Comp. 16	0.2	0.0	0.5	0.1	0.5	0.2	0.2	0.2	0.1	0.5	0.3	0.2	•
Employee Benefits 17	0.7	1.4	1.6	0.3	0.8	0.7	0.6	0.6	0.4	0.8	0.7	0.8	•
Advertising 18	0.1	0.2	0.5	0.2	0.1	0.1	0.1	0.1	0.1	0.0	0.1	0.0	•
Other Expenses 19	4.8	9.2	17.6	7.8	6.3	5.1	6.0	3.8	3.7	5.9	3.8	3.9	•
Officers' Compensation 20	1.0	1.3	9.0	5.9	2.8	1.6	1.3	1.3	0.6	0.6	0.2	0.2	•
Operating Margin 21	•	•	•	6.0	1.3	1.9	0.1	0.2	•	•	•	•	•
Operating Margin Before Officers' Comp. 22	0.1	•	8.9	11.9	4.1	3.5	1.4	1.5	0.6	•	•	•	•

Selected Average Balance Sheet ($ in Thousands)

Net Receivables 23	2360	0	35	172	764	2292	4728	10243	22224	33019	63036	583933	•
Inventories 24	1830	0	35	150	782	1842	6227	12902	26516	33598	108802	241047	•
Net Property, Plant and Equipment 25	1067	0	33	64	298	898	2106	4673	8712	25359	55837	224923	•
Total Assets 26	7948	0	156	650	2554	6965	15600	35170	69261	157366	345387	1765575	•
Notes and Loans Payable 27	3234	0	75	144	742	2206	6529	11920	26847	48378	123032	823617	•
All Other Liabilities 28	2395	0	51	137	746	2133	5323	9939	20268	48464	70800	568294	•
Net Worth 29	2320	0	30	369	1066	2626	3748	13312	22146	60523	151555	373663	•

Selected Financial Ratios (Times to 1)

Current Ratio 30	1.5	•	1.3	2.4	1.9	1.7	1.6	1.7	1.5	1.4	1.6	1.3	•
Quick Ratio 31	0.8	•	0.8	1.5	1.1	1.1	0.7	0.8	0.7	0.7	0.7	0.8	•
Net Sales to Working Capital 32	8.8	•	17.1	6.9	7.6	7.4	8.2	7.1	8.6	8.6	10.3	9.5	•
Coverage Ratio 33	1.5	•	1.8	11.7	3.6	4.2	1.7	2.6	1.9	2.4	0.5	0.8	•
Total Asset Turnover 34	1.8	•	2.6	3.1	2.6	2.6	2.5	2.2	2.4	1.5	2.8	1.2	•
Inventory Turnover 35	6.9	•	6.6	9.8	6.9	8.1	5.1	5.2	5.5	6.1	7.9	8.0	•
Receivables Turnover 36	•	•	•	•	•	•	•	•	•	•	•	•	•
Total Liabilities to Net Worth 37	2.4	•	4.1	0.8	1.4	1.7	3.2	1.6	2.1	1.6	1.3	3.7	•
Current Assets to Working Capital 38	3.2	•	4.2	1.7	2.2	2.4	2.7	2.5	2.9	3.3	2.5	4.5	•
Current Liabilities to Working Capital 39	2.2	•	3.2	0.7	1.2	1.4	1.7	1.5	1.9	2.3	1.5	3.5	•
Working Capital to Net Sales 40	0.1	•	0.1	0.1	0.1	0.1	0.1	0.1	0.1	0.1	0.1	0.1	•
Inventory to Working Capital 41	1.1	•	1.5	0.5	0.9	0.8	1.3	1.2	1.4	1.2	1.2	1.1	•
Total Receipts to Cash Flow 42	25.0	•	7.0	8.0	15.7	16.9	19.7	22.6	27.8	16.6	45.6	40.1	•
Cost of Goods to Cash Flow 43	21.7	•	4.1	5.9	12.6	13.9	16.5	19.7	24.9	14.4	41.4	36.2	•
Cash Flow to Total Debt 44	0.1	•	0.5	0.9	0.3	0.2	0.2	0.2	0.1	0.1	0.1	0.0	•

Selected Financial Factors (in Percentages)

Debt Ratio 45	70.8	•	80.6	43.2	58.3	62.3	76.0	62.2	68.0	61.5	56.1	78.8	•
Return on Total Assets 46	3.1	•	5.7	21.9	6.8	7.9	4.1	5.1	3.7	6.3	1.3	1.4	•
Return on Equity Before Income Taxes 47	3.4	•	12.8	35.3	11.8	16.0	7.0	8.3	5.3	9.5	•	•	•
Return on Equity After Income Taxes 48	2.2	•	11.1	35.1	11.5	14.7	4.7	6.6	2.9	6.8	•	•	•
Profit Margin (Before Income Tax) 49	0.5	•	1.0	6.5	1.9	2.3	0.7	1.4	0.7	2.4	•	•	•
Profit Margin (After Income Tax) 50	0.4	•	0.8	6.5	1.8	2.1	0.5	1.1	0.4	1.7	•	•	•

173

Table II
Corporations with Net Income

METAL AND MINERAL (EXCEPT PETROLEUM)

MONEY AMOUNTS AND SIZE OF ASSETS IN THOUSANDS OF DOLLARS

Item Description for Accounting Period 7/02 Through 6/03	Total	Zero Assets	Under 500	500 to 1,000	1,000 to 5,000	5,000 to 10,000	10,000 to 25,000	25,000 to 50,000	50,000 to 100,000	100,000 to 250,000	250,000 to 500,000	500,000 to 2,500,000	2,500,000 and over
Number of Enterprises **1**	3749	4	1955	428	920	190	141	47	37	14	8	5	•
Revenues ($ in Thousands)													
Net Sales **2**	49836664	275044	997218	718972	6769993	3692220	5731913	3445534	6839584	3020153	8985540	9360492	•
Interest **3**	172720	8	1182	64	1648	3230	2285	5890	14029	45566	21054	77763	•
Rents **4**	43081	0	1459	0	217	143	817	1125	2975	9707	460	26178	•
Royalties **5**	3873	0	0	0	0	0	479	0	0	3395	0	0	•
Other Portfolio Income **6**	142434	2630	261	1070	1759	5595	2851	4885	5422	60690	13705	43569	•
Other Receipts **7**	356462	3885	7539	1384	34198	6394	22435	36910	22873	103712	40081	77050	•
Total Receipts **8**	50555234	281567	1007659	721490	6807815	3707582	5760780	3494344	6884883	3243223	9060840	9585052	•
Average Total Receipts **9**	13485	70392	515	1686	7400	19514	40857	74348	186078	231659	1132605	1917010	•
Operating Costs/Operating Income (%)													
Cost of Operations **10**	86.8	96.8	58.3	73.7	79.9	84.4	84.0	86.1	89.8	87.5	94.5	88.5	•
Salaries and Wages **11**	3.5	1.6	4.2	1.8	4.8	4.9	4.1	3.9	2.8	3.1	1.4	4.4	•
Taxes Paid **12**	0.8	0.2	2.2	1.1	1.0	1.0	0.9	0.9	0.8	1.2	0.3	0.6	•
Interest Paid **13**	0.8	0.1	0.8	0.7	0.5	0.6	0.6	0.8	0.7	1.9	0.3	1.2	•
Depreciation **14**	0.9	0.3	1.9	0.6	0.9	0.5	0.8	0.9	0.5	1.2	0.7	1.2	•
Amortization and Depletion **15**	0.1	•	0.1	•	0.0	0.0	0.1	0.0	0.0	0.2	0.1	0.2	•
Pensions and Other Deferred Comp. **16**	0.2	0.1	0.6	0.1	0.5	0.2	0.2	0.2	0.1	0.5	0.2	0.1	•
Employee Benefits **17**	0.6	0.9	1.8	0.3	0.7	0.6	0.4	0.4	0.3	0.6	0.5	0.7	•
Advertising **18**	0.1	0.0	0.2	0.2	0.1	0.1	0.1	0.1	0.0	0.0	0.0	0.1	•
Other Expenses **19**	4.0	0.7	16.0	6.8	5.3	3.7	5.2	3.6	2.8	5.2	1.6	3.9	•
Officers' Compensation **20**	1.2	0.2	9.7	3.5	2.8	1.4	1.3	1.5	0.6	0.6	0.1	0.5	•
Operating Margin **21**	1.1	•	4.3	11.0	3.3	2.5	2.2	1.5	1.5	•	0.2	•	•
Operating Margin Before Officers' Comp. **22**	2.3	•	14.1	14.6	6.2	3.9	3.5	3.1	2.1	•	0.3	•	•

Selected Average Balance Sheet ($ in Thousands)

Net Receivables 23	1544	0	39	134	799	2141	4931	9759	23705	24324	61458	330111
Inventories 24	1638	0	28	139	784	1807	6338	13686	30713	30710	87747	231509
Net Property, Plant and Equipment 25	727	0	36	55	263	776	1837	4661	5801	21971	53879	162096
Total Assets 26	5798	0	172	617	2595	6797	15511	35602	70353	153741	344605	1216864
Notes and Loans Payable 27	2002	0	55	111	610	1920	4923	12015	26284	45767	109280	535722
All Other Liabilities 28	1468	0	61	90	712	2030	4830	8688	22089	44863	62365	254447
Net Worth 29	2328	0	56	415	1273	2847	5759	14899	21981	63112	172960	426695

Selected Financial Ratios (Times to 1)

Current Ratio 30	1.6	•	1.2	3.4	2.0	1.9	1.7	1.8	1.6	1.3	1.6	1.4
Quick Ratio 31	0.8	•	0.8	2.3	1.1	1.2	0.8	0.8	0.7	0.6	0.8	0.6
Net Sales to Working Capital 32	8.7	•	36.4	5.1	7.7	7.3	7.6	6.1	8.5	11.0	13.2	8.3
Coverage Ratio 33	4.3	12.2	8.1	16.7	8.4	5.6	5.4	4.5	4.0	3.7	4.9	1.9
Total Asset Turnover 34	2.3	•	3.0	2.7	2.8	2.9	2.6	2.1	2.6	1.4	3.3	1.5
Inventory Turnover 35	7.0	•	10.7	8.9	7.5	9.1	5.4	4.6	5.4	6.1	12.1	7.2
Receivables Turnover 36	•	•	•	•	•	•	•	•	•	•	•	•
Total Liabilities to Net Worth 37	1.5	•	2.1	0.5	1.0	1.4	1.7	1.4	2.2	1.4	1.0	1.9
Current Assets to Working Capital 38	2.7	•	7.5	1.4	2.0	2.2	2.4	2.3	2.8	4.1	2.7	3.7
Current Liabilities to Working Capital 39	1.7	•	6.5	0.4	1.0	1.2	1.4	1.3	1.8	3.1	1.7	2.7
Working Capital to Net Sales 40	0.1	•	0.0	0.2	0.1	0.1	0.1	0.2	0.1	0.1	0.1	0.1
Inventory to Working Capital 41	1.1	2.0	2.0	0.4	0.8	0.7	1.2	1.1	1.4	1.6	1.0	1.0
Total Receipts to Cash Flow 42	18.6	53.4	5.7	6.0	13.1	18.1	15.7	17.6	23.8	12.8	44.4	25.6
Cost of Goods to Cash Flow 43	16.2	51.7	3.3	4.4	10.4	15.2	13.2	15.1	21.3	11.2	42.0	22.7
Cash Flow to Total Debt 44	0.2	•	0.8	1.4	0.4	0.3	0.3	0.2	0.2	0.2	0.1	0.1

Selected Financial Factors (in Percentages)

Debt Ratio 45	59.9	•	67.2	32.7	50.9	58.1	62.9	58.2	68.8	58.9	49.8	64.9
Return on Total Assets 46	7.6	•	18.2	32.6	12.6	10.2	8.6	7.8	7.5	10.0	4.6	3.4
Return on Equity Before Income Taxes 47	14.5	•	48.6	45.5	22.6	20.0	18.8	14.4	17.9	17.8	7.3	4.7
Return on Equity After Income Taxes 48	12.9	•	47.2	45.3	22.1	18.6	16.7	12.4	14.6	14.3	6.4	3.3
Profit Margin (Before Income Tax) 49	2.5	1.5	5.4	11.3	3.9	2.9	2.7	2.9	2.1	5.2	1.1	1.1
Profit Margin (After Income Tax) 50	2.3	1.5	5.2	11.2	3.8	2.7	2.4	2.5	1.7	4.2	1.0	0.8

Table I

Corporations with and without Net Income

ELECTRICAL GOODS

MONEY AMOUNTS AND SIZE OF ASSETS IN THOUSANDS OF DOLLARS

Item Description for Accounting Period 7/02 Through 6/03	Total	Zero Assets	Under 500	500 to 1,000	1,000 to 5,000	5,000 to 10,000	10,000 to 25,000	25,000 to 50,000	50,000 to 100,000	100,000 to 250,000	250,000 to 500,000	500,000 to 2,500,000	2,500,000 and over
Number of Enterprises **1**	20871	395	13965	1989	3285	546	379	143	80	38	22	22	6
Revenues ($ in Thousands)													
Net Sales **2**	206136367	10558716	4436093	4871994	21050220	8977048	14221676	12448041	11833010	14246542	14856765	42502396	46613866
Interest **3**	626822	50472	2210	4533	12615	3741	11514	10917	23251	44654	32396	223047	207473
Rents **4**	193514	23137	618	4971	2099	2467	4282	4337	25863	366	4513	20935	99927
Royalties **5**	528825	11561	0	0	324	67	1757	920	8722	289	15808	33745	455631
Other Portfolio Income **6**	751152	28971	19441	1718	10780	12944	8468	5313	20911	8937	50467	23192	560010
Other Receipts **7**	2849212	405775	151922	60425	84055	66738	100825	137569	142523	221532	185413	630069	662366
Total Receipts **8**	211085892	11078632	4610284	4943641	21160093	9063005	14348522	12607097	12054280	14522320	15145362	43433384	48119273
Average Total Receipts **9**	10114	28047	330	2485	6441	16599	37859	88162	150678	382166	688426	1974245	8019879
Operating Costs/Operating Income (%)													
Cost of Operations **10**	79.6	72.7	57.7	76.4	76.8	74.7	79.9	82.3	82.2	85.1	88.4	83.5	76.1
Salaries and Wages **11**	6.8	6.4	10.2	7.2	7.6	10.1	8.1	7.5	6.9	4.5	5.1	6.0	6.8
Taxes Paid **12**	0.9	1.1	2.3	1.2	1.2	1.4	1.0	0.9	0.9	0.6	0.7	0.6	0.7
Interest Paid **13**	0.9	0.7	0.4	1.3	0.4	0.8	0.5	0.6	0.5	0.7	0.7	1.2	1.2
Depreciation **14**	1.1	1.5	0.9	0.9	0.6	0.9	1.0	1.0	1.0	0.8	0.6	1.4	1.2
Amortization and Depletion **15**	1.8	9.7	0.1	0.0	0.0	0.1	0.1	0.2	0.1	0.1	0.5	0.3	5.3
Pensions and Other Deferred Comp. **16**	0.3	0.1	0.8	0.3	0.3	0.2	0.2	0.2	0.3	0.2	0.1	0.4	0.4
Employee Benefits **17**	0.6	0.8	1.2	0.4	0.6	0.9	0.6	0.8	0.6	0.5	0.4	0.7	0.6
Advertising **18**	1.2	5.6	1.1	0.9	0.5	0.4	0.5	0.6	0.8	1.1	0.5	1.3	1.4
Other Expenses **19**	8.0	9.4	21.3	9.4	8.3	8.1	6.8	7.2	7.4	7.1	3.8	6.6	9.8
Officers' Compensation **20**	1.0	0.1	8.8	4.8	2.9	2.0	1.3	0.9	0.6	0.3	0.3	0.2	0.1
Operating Margin **21**	•	•	•	•	0.6	0.3	•	•	•	•	•	•	•
Operating Margin Before Officers' Comp. **22**	•	•	3.9	2.0	3.6	2.4	1.2	•	•	•	•	•	•

Selected Average Balance Sheet ($ in Thousands)

Net Receivables 23	1343	0	26	181	699	2477	5187	12218	21779	52180	83919	289986	1331598
Inventories 24	1043	0	23	221	639	2077	4916	10263	19688	48004	58338	221518	813188
Net Property, Plant and Equipment 25	435	0	19	67	229	677	1370	3687	6388	11972	18819	108811	456415
Total Assets 26	4960		108	742	2070	6771	15105	35006	68947	161087	342540	1022677	6273896
Notes and Loans Payable 27	1258	0	50	378	534	2197	3797	9662	14090	38075	70509	213336	1703987
All Other Liabilities 28	1975	0	33	293	781	2367	6168	14201	29534	77738	107536	408702	2546629
Net Worth 29	1727	0	25	70	755	2207	5140	11143	25324	45274	164494	400638	2023280

Selected Financial Ratios (Times to 1)

Current Ratio 30	1.4	•	1.9	1.8	1.7	1.6	1.5	1.6	1.5	1.5	1.8	1.5	1.0
Quick Ratio 31	0.8	•	1.3	1.1	1.0	0.9	0.8	0.9	0.8	0.8	1.1	0.8	0.6
Net Sales to Working Capital 32	11.7	•	8.7	8.4	9.1	7.7	8.9	8.1	8.4	9.5	7.2	9.2	117.6
Coverage Ratio 33	1.4	•	•	0.0	3.6	2.7	2.4	•	1.9	2.2	2.6	1.2	1.7
Total Asset Turnover 34	2.0	•	2.9	3.3	3.1	2.4	2.5	2.5	2.1	2.3	2.0	1.9	1.2
Inventory Turnover 35	7.5	•	7.9	8.5	7.7	5.9	6.1	7.0	6.2	6.6	10.2	7.3	7.2
Receivables Turnover 36	•	•	•	•	•	•	•	•	•	•	•	•	•
Total Liabilities to Net Worth 37	1.9	•	3.3	9.5	1.7	2.1	1.9	2.1	1.7	2.6	1.1	1.6	2.1
Current Assets to Working Capital 38	3.6	•	2.1	2.2	2.4	2.6	2.9	2.6	3.1	3.1	2.3	3.0	42.0
Current Liabilities to Working Capital 39	2.6	•	1.1	1.2	1.4	1.6	1.9	1.6	2.1	2.1	1.3	2.0	41.0
Working Capital to Net Sales 40	0.1	•	0.1	0.1	0.1	0.1	0.1	0.1	0.1	0.1	0.1	0.1	0.0
Inventory to Working Capital 41	1.2	•	0.6	0.8	0.9	1.0	1.2	1.0	1.1	1.2	0.6	1.1	12.4
Total Receipts to Cash Flow 42	15.3	20.2	6.5	15.5	12.7	13.2	16.7	21.2	15.6	15.2	26.9	18.4	12.8
Cost of Goods to Cash Flow 43	12.2	14.7	3.8	11.8	9.8	9.9	13.4	17.4	12.8	12.9	23.8	15.3	9.7
Cash Flow to Total Debt 44	0.2	0.6	0.2	0.2	0.4	0.3	0.2	0.2	0.2	0.2	0.1	0.2	0.1

Selected Financial Factors (in Percentages)

Debt Ratio 45	65.2	•	76.6	90.5	63.5	67.4	66.0	68.2	63.3	71.9	52.0	60.8	67.8
Return on Total Assets 46	2.4	•	•	0.0	4.8	5.0	3.2	•	2.2	3.6	3.4	2.5	2.4
Return on Equity Before Income Taxes 47	1.9	•	•	•	9.5	9.6	5.4	•	2.9	6.8	4.4	0.9	3.0
Return on Equity After Income Taxes 48	0.2	•	•	•	6.8	7.9	3.7	•	0.5	3.2	2.6	•	1.8
Profit Margin (Before Income Tax) 49	0.3	•	•	•	1.1	1.3	0.7	•	0.5	0.8	1.1	0.2	0.8
Profit Margin (After Income Tax) 50	0.0	•	•	•	0.8	1.1	0.5	•	0.1	0.4	0.6	•	0.5

Table II

Corporations with Net Income

ELECTRICAL GOODS

MONEY AMOUNTS AND SIZE OF ASSETS IN THOUSANDS OF DOLLARS

Item Description for Accounting Period 7/02 Through 6/03	Total	Zero Assets	Under 500	500 to 1,000	1,000 to 5,000	5,000 to 10,000	10,000 to 25,000	25,000 to 50,000	50,000 to 100,000	100,000 to 250,000	250,000 to 500,000	500,000 to 2,500,000	2,500,000 and over
Number of Enterprises **1**	10312	105	5852	1164	2404	334	257	90	52	27	12	14	0
Revenues ($ in Thousands)													
Net Sales **2**	129938706	845010	2315191	3864825	16220567	6154789	10541988	8430877	7836281	11465954	10564258	51158965	0
Interest **3**	207642	138	1347	1546	8316	2386	5853	5947	10386	14881	17402	139440	0
Rents **4**	134545	0	0	0	1200	2042	1749	1085	24219	245	3939	100065	0
Royalties **5**	480400	337	0	0	0	16	0	241	8717	31	7901	463156	0
Other Portfolio Income **6**	698179	28971	19433	1183	5229	6447	6471	1689	6089	8670	48534	565463	0
Other Receipts **7**	1452919	7142	141495	5283	64790	43667	74310	79986	117162	114140	157236	647711	0
Total Receipts **8**	132372391	881598	2477466	3872837	16300102	6209347	10630371	8519825	8002854	11603921	10799270	53074800	0
Average Total Receipts **9**	12837	8396	423	3327	6780	18591	41363	94665	153901	429775	899939	3791057	·
Operating Costs/Operating Income (%)													
Cost of Operations **10**	78.3	89.8	52.3	79.8	76.2	74.3	78.9	82.1	80.2	84.9	90.0	75.3	·
Salaries and Wages **11**	6.4	3.7	8.1	4.5	6.9	9.2	7.6	6.5	7.0	4.0	3.9	6.7	·
Taxes Paid **12**	0.9	0.4	2.1	0.9	1.2	1.1	1.0	0.8	1.0	0.6	0.7	0.8	·
Interest Paid **13**	0.4	0.1	0.2	0.1	0.3	0.5	0.4	0.4	0.5	0.4	0.2	0.5	·
Depreciation **14**	1.0	0.2	0.8	0.8	0.5	0.7	0.7	0.7	0.8	0.7	0.5	1.5	·
Amortization and Depletion **15**	1.9	1.5	0.2	0.0	0.0	0.0	0.1	0.1	0.1	0.1	0.1	4.8	·
Pensions and Other Deferred Comp. **16**	0.4	0.0	1.4	0.2	0.4	0.2	0.3	0.2	0.3	0.2	0.1	0.5	·
Employee Benefits **17**	0.6	0.4	0.9	0.4	0.5	0.5	0.6	0.6	0.6	0.5	0.3	0.6	·
Advertising **18**	1.0	0.5	0.7	1.0	0.5	0.5	0.5	0.6	0.8	1.2	0.4	1.4	·
Other Expenses **19**	7.4	2.6	18.6	7.6	7.6	7.8	5.9	5.5	7.1	5.8	2.9	8.8	·
Officers' Compensation **20**	1.1	0.2	11.0	3.4	3.1	2.0	1.4	1.0	0.6	0.3	0.2	0.1	·
Operating Margin **21**	0.8	0.5	3.7	1.4	3.0	3.2	2.7	1.6	1.0	1.5	0.8	·	·
Operating Margin Before Officers' Comp. **22**	1.9	0.7	14.7	4.7	6.1	5.1	4.1	2.5	1.6	1.7	1.0	·	·

Selected Average Balance Sheet ($ in Thousands)

	•	•	•	•	•	•	•	•	•	•	•	•
Net Receivables 23	1775	0	28	204	704	2802	5459	13154	20288	59348	98326	632048	•
Inventories 24	1388	0	15	196	638	2198	5160	10980	20538	51404	63596	442835	•
Net Property, Plant and Equipment 25	596	0	6	92	207	546	1366	3178	7250	11883	23268	264978	•
Total Assets 26	6022	0	105	696	2028	6858	15068	34302	68693	166218	332010	2464327	•
Notes and Loans Payable 27	1268	0	25	130	401	2014	3307	7952	12746	35505	26706	545211	•
All Other Liabilities 28	2654	0	26	238	791	2113	5470	12976	24384	81329	116797	1206170	•
Net Worth 29	2100	0	54	329	836	2731	6291	13373	31564	49384	188507	712946	•

Selected Financial Ratios (Times to 1)

	•	•	•	•	•	•	•	•	•	•	•	•
Current Ratio 30	1.3	•	3.0	2.3	1.9	1.8	1.8	1.8	1.7	1.5	1.9	1.0	•
Quick Ratio 31	0.8	•	2.4	1.4	1.1	1.1	1.0	1.0	0.9	0.8	1.2	0.6	•
Net Sales to Working Capital 32	13.2	•	6.8	10.0	8.2	7.0	7.3	7.4	6.8	10.3	7.4	•	•
Coverage Ratio 33	8.6	43.8	49.7	13.7	12.8	9.5	8.8	7.6	7.6	7.3	16.7	6.4	•
Total Asset Turnover 34	2.1	•	3.8	4.8	3.3	2.7	2.7	2.7	2.2	2.6	2.7	1.5	•
Inventory Turnover 35	7.1	•	13.5	13.5	8.1	6.2	6.3	7.0	5.9	7.0	12.5	6.2	•
Receivables Turnover 36	•	•	•	•	•	•	•	•	•	•	•	•	•
Total Liabilities to Net Worth 37	1.9	•	0.9	1.1	1.4	1.5	1.4	1.6	1.2	2.4	0.8	2.5	•
Current Assets to Working Capital 38	4.2	•	1.5	1.8	2.1	2.2	2.2	2.3	2.5	3.2	2.1	•	•
Current Liabilities to Working Capital 39	3.2	•	0.5	0.8	1.1	1.2	1.2	1.3	1.5	2.2	1.1	•	•
Working Capital to Net Sales 40	0.1	•	0.1	0.1	0.1	0.1	0.1	0.1	0.1	0.1	0.1	•	•
Inventory to Working Capital 41	1.5	•	0.3	0.6	0.8	0.8	0.9	0.9	0.9	1.2	0.5	•	•
Total Receipts to Cash Flow 42	11.6	27.4	4.1	12.4	10.5	9.9	12.4	14.2	11.5	13.1	19.8	11.2	•
Cost of Goods to Cash Flow 43	9.1	24.6	2.1	9.9	8.0	7.3	9.8	11.6	9.2	11.1	17.8	8.5	•
Cash Flow to Total Debt 44	0.3	•	1.9	0.7	0.5	0.5	0.4	0.3	0.4	0.3	0.3	0.2	•

Selected Financial Factors (in Percentages)

	•	•	•	•	•	•	•	•	•	•	•	•
Debt Ratio 45	65.1	•	48.7	52.8	58.8	60.2	58.3	61.0	54.1	70.3	43.2	71.1	•
Return on Total Assets 46	7.4	•	41.2	8.0	12.4	12.2	10.7	8.4	7.8	7.9	9.3	4.9	•
Return on Equity Before Income Taxes 47	18.8	•	78.6	15.8	27.7	27.3	22.8	18.8	14.7	22.9	15.4	14.2	•
Return on Equity After Income Taxes 48	15.8	•	74.6	13.6	24.5	25.0	20.7	16.3	11.8	18.2	12.5	11.4	•
Profit Margin (Before Income Tax) 49	3.1	4.8	10.7	1.6	3.4	4.0	3.5	2.7	3.1	2.7	3.3	2.8	•
Profit Margin (After Income Tax) 50	2.6	3.2	10.2	1.3	3.0	3.7	3.2	2.3	2.5	2.1	2.7	2.2	•

Table I

Corporations with and without Net Income

HARDWARE, PLUMBING, HEATING EQUIPMENT, AND SUPPLIES

MONEY AMOUNTS AND SIZE OF ASSETS IN THOUSANDS OF DOLLARS

Item Description for Accounting Period 7/02 Through 6/03	Total	Zero Assets	Under 500	500 to 1,000	1,000 to 5,000	5,000 to 10,000	10,000 to 25,000	25,000 to 50,000	50,000 to 100,000	100,000 to 250,000	250,000 to 500,000	500,000 to 2,500,000	2,500,000 and over
Number of Enterprises **1**	14774	1033	8177	2052	2632	485	267	69	35	13	4	8	0
Revenues ($ in Thousands)													
Net Sales **2**	78249405	415877	3774493	4010668	14812387	8256606	9152255	6078729	5695407	4198532	2338318	19516132	0
Interest **3**	100778	1634	418	2650	18473	4765	8079	6621	4746	4053	11684	37657	0
Rents **4**	20854	262	479	1109	3208	637	2241	1728	3450	457	939	6344	0
Royalties **5**	63118	0	0	0	0	1	86	131	110	4473	0	58318	0
Other Portfolio Income **6**	149514	8029	22622	1929	9053	11790	9700	24249	2270	2056	1687	56130	0
Other Receipts **7**	1123694	7941	9273	115771	179935	48357	70390	7947	65186	146529	5563	466801	0
Total Receipts **8**	79707363	433743	3807285	4132127	15023056	8322156	9242751	6119405	5771169	4356100	2358191	20141382	0
Average Total Receipts **9**	5395	420	466	2014	5708	17159	34617	88687	164891	335085	589548	2517673	•
Operating Costs/Operating Income (%)													
Cost of Operations **10**	74.6	73.4	56.9	68.6	71.4	73.8	74.9	78.3	78.4	71.8	72.5	80.7	•
Salaries and Wages **11**	9.7	10.4	11.7	10.6	10.6	10.1	9.8	9.0	7.9	11.3	10.1	8.6	•
Taxes Paid **12**	1.4	1.8	2.4	2.4	1.6	1.3	1.3	1.4	1.1	1.3	1.3	1.2	•
Interest Paid **13**	1.1	0.4	0.5	0.9	0.6	0.7	0.7	0.8	1.1	1.2	1.8	1.9	•
Depreciation **14**	1.0	0.9	0.9	1.2	1.1	0.7	0.9	0.8	1.1	1.5	1.5	0.9	•
Amortization and Depletion **15**	0.2	0.4	0.0	0.2	0.0	0.0	0.1	0.1	0.2	0.3	0.4	0.3	•
Pensions and Other Deferred Comp. **16**	0.4	0.6	0.4	0.7	0.4	0.3	0.4	0.4	0.2	0.4	0.4	0.2	•
Employee Benefits **17**	0.8	0.3	0.4	1.5	0.8	0.8	0.8	0.8	0.8	1.3	1.6	0.7	•
Advertising **18**	0.5	0.7	0.3	0.5	0.6	0.5	0.6	0.4	0.7	0.8	0.9	0.2	•
Other Expenses **19**	8.1	10.6	15.4	9.5	8.9	7.7	7.1	6.3	6.4	10.3	8.5	6.8	•
Officers' Compensation **20**	2.4	2.9	9.4	7.0	4.3	2.8	2.0	0.9	0.8	0.5	0.2	0.1	•
Operating Margin **21**	•	•	1.7	•	•	1.2	1.6	0.8	1.2	•	0.8	•	•
Operating Margin Before Officers' Comp. **22**	2.3	0.6	11.0	3.9	4.1	4.1	3.5	1.8	2.0	•	1.0	•	•

Selected Average Balance Sheet ($ in Thousands)

Net Receivables 23	672	0	34	178	651	2258	4854	11282	22536	36679	104279	339379
Inventories 24	755	0	41	228	880	2823	5734	12058	22843	48808	87766	315793
Net Property, Plant and Equipment 25	263	0	11	104	214	583	1500	3872	9965	26952	45761	148454
Total Assets 26	2223	0	123	678	2299	6603	14705	35421	66654	159598	351090	1126395
Notes and Loans Payable 27	787	0	54	229	602	1823	4296	11964	22245	46608	163995	529677
All Other Liabilities 28	659	0	38	246	654	1983	3933	9944	19450	48130	89890	353452
Net Worth 29	777	0	31	203	1043	2796	6477	13513	24959	64859	97205	243266

Selected Financial Ratios (Times to 1)

Current Ratio 30	1.9	•	2.2	1.6	2.0	2.0	1.9	1.9	1.8	1.6	1.5	2.0
Quick Ratio 31	1.0	•	1.3	0.9	1.0	0.9	0.9	0.9	0.9	0.7	0.9	1.0
Net Sales to Working Capital 32	6.7	•	8.3	10.1	6.0	6.1	6.0	6.8	7.2	8.5	7.3	6.6
Coverage Ratio 33	2.6	5.6	6.6	1.0	3.1	4.0	4.7	2.8	3.2	3.5	1.9	1.8
Total Asset Turnover 34	2.4	•	3.7	2.9	2.4	2.6	2.3	2.5	2.4	2.0	1.7	2.2
Inventory Turnover 35	5.2	•	6.4	5.9	4.6	4.4	4.5	5.7	5.6	4.8	4.8	6.2
Receivables Turnover 36	•	•	•	•	•	•	•	•	•	•	•	•
Total Liabilities to Net Worth 37	1.9	•	3.0	2.3	1.2	1.4	1.3	1.6	1.7	1.5	2.6	3.6
Current Assets to Working Capital 38	2.1	•	1.9	2.6	2.0	2.0	2.1	2.1	2.2	2.6	2.9	2.0
Current Liabilities to Working Capital 39	1.1	•	0.9	1.6	1.0	1.0	1.1	1.1	1.2	1.6	1.9	1.0
Working Capital to Net Sales 40	0.1	•	0.1	0.1	0.2	0.2	0.2	0.1	0.1	0.1	0.1	0.2
Inventory to Working Capital 41	1.0	•	0.7	1.2	0.9	1.0	1.0	0.9	1.0	1.3	1.1	0.9
Total Receipts to Cash Flow 42	13.0	10.8	6.8	15.0	12.6	12.5	13.1	18.1	13.9	9.2	12.6	15.7
Cost of Goods to Cash Flow 43	9.7	7.9	3.8	10.3	9.0	9.2	9.8	14.2	10.9	6.6	9.1	12.7
Cash Flow to Total Debt 44	0.3	•	0.7	0.3	0.4	0.4	0.3	0.2	0.3	0.4	0.2	0.2

Selected Financial Factors (in Percentages)

Debt Ratio 45	65.0	•	74.7	70.1	54.6	57.6	56.0	61.8	62.6	59.4	72.3	78.4
Return on Total Assets 46	6.8	•	11.2	2.6	4.5	6.9	7.5	5.8	8.9	8.5	5.8	7.4
Return on Equity Before Income Taxes 47	12.0	•	37.5	•	6.7	12.2	13.5	9.8	16.4	14.9	9.8	15.3
Return on Equity After Income Taxes 48	9.4	•	36.5	•	5.3	11.3	11.3	7.3	12.6	12.0	8.6	9.5
Profit Margin (Before Income Tax) 49	1.8	2.0	2.5	•	1.2	2.0	2.5	1.5	2.5	3.0	1.6	1.5
Profit Margin (After Income Tax) 50	1.4	0.1	2.5	•	1.0	1.8	2.1	1.1	1.9	2.4	1.4	0.9

177

Table II
Corporations with Net Income

HARDWARE, PLUMBING, HEATING EQUIPMENT, AND SUPPLIES

MONEY AMOUNTS AND SIZE OF ASSETS IN THOUSANDS OF DOLLARS

Item Description for Accounting Period 7/02 Through 6/03	Total	Zero Assets	Under 500	500 to 1,000	1,000 to 5,000	5,000 to 10,000	10,000 to 25,000	25,000 to 50,000	50,000 to 100,000	100,000 to 250,000	250,000 to 500,000	500,000 to 2,500,000	2,500,000 and over
Number of Enterprises **1**	8929	344	5172	790	1974	319	227	58	25	0	0	5	0
Revenues ($ in Thousands)													
Net Sales **2**	58135134	327980	2574930	1439100	12446783	5157964	8016930	5319796	3813198	0	0	13905277	0
Interest **3**	83892	1630	376	698	15504	4220	7125	4438	3438	0	0	30961	0
Rents **4**	14525	262	479	874	2324	329	1752	1022	2840	0	0	3979	0
Royalties **5**	58743	0	0	0	0	1	0	63	110	0	0	54096	0
Other Portfolio Income **6**	64023	8028	21409	1777	6412	11774	9256	1716	1132	0	0	695	0
Other Receipts **7**	630524	8759	6832	10820	182812	29766	59239	53259	49642	0	0	79903	0
Total Receipts **8**	58986841	346659	2604026	1453269	12653835	5204054	8094302	5380294	3870360	0	0	14074911	0
Average Total Receipts **9**	6606	1008	503	1840	6410	16314	35658	92764	154814	·	·	2814982	·
Operating Costs/Operating Income (%)													
Cost of Operations **10**	73.6	70.6	52.8	67.5	71.3	70.8	74.7	78.5	74.9	·	·	78.1	·
Salaries and Wages **11**	9.7	10.9	13.2	10.0	10.0	11.6	9.6	8.6	8.5	·	·	9.3	·
Taxes Paid **12**	1.4	2.0	2.4	2.1	1.5	1.4	1.3	1.4	1.4	·	·	1.3	·
Interest Paid **13**	1.0	0.5	0.3	0.7	0.5	0.6	0.6	0.6	0.9	·	·	1.9	·
Depreciation **14**	0.9	0.6	0.9	1.4	1.1	0.8	0.8	0.7	1.1	·	·	0.7	·
Amortization and Depletion **15**	0.1	0.2	0.0	0.1	0.0	0.0	0.1	0.0	0.2	·	·	0.3	·
Pensions and Other Deferred Comp. **16**	0.3	0.7	0.5	0.0	0.5	0.4	0.3	0.4	0.3	·	·	0.2	·
Employee Benefits **17**	0.7	0.1	0.3	1.3	0.7	0.9	0.8	0.8	0.8	·	·	0.5	·
Advertising **18**	0.5	0.6	0.2	0.4	0.6	0.7	0.6	0.4	0.9	·	·	0.1	·
Other Expenses **19**	7.6	8.5	15.3	8.7	8.3	7.1	7.0	5.8	7.1	·	·	6.3	·
Officers' Compensation **20**	2.2	3.6	8.8	4.5	4.3	2.7	1.9	0.9	0.9	·	·	0.1	·
Operating Margin **21**	1.9	1.7	5.3	3.4	1.2	2.8	2.3	1.8	3.0	·	·	1.1	·
Operating Margin Before Officers' Comp. **22**	4.0	5.3	14.1	7.9	5.5	5.5	4.2	2.8	3.9	·	·	1.2	·

Selected Average Balance Sheet ($ in Thousands)

Net Receivables 23	847	0	31	207	725	2094	4881	11996	22684	•	410849
Inventories 24	895	0	33	141	896	2682	5690	12846	21639	•	350870
Net Property, Plant and Equipment 25	307	0	11	126	228	619	1447	3938	9595	•	140814
Total Assets 26	2712	0	116	653	2328	6390	14641	35340	65214	•	1332078
Notes and Loans Payable 27	930	0	35	174	574	1664	4143	9681	22021	•	648593
All Other Liabilities 28	767	0	30	289	675	2031	3761	10389	15747	•	371234
Net Worth 29	1014	0	52	191	1079	2695	6737	15270	27446	•	312251

Selected Financial Ratios (Times to 1)

Current Ratio 30	2.0	•	2.5	1.4	2.0	1.9	2.0	2.0	2.0	•	2.4
Quick Ratio 31	1.0	•	1.7	0.9	1.0	0.9	1.0	1.0	1.0	•	1.3
Net Sales to Working Capital 32	6.3	•	8.2	14.2	6.3	6.4	5.9	6.6	6.2	•	5.5
Coverage Ratio 33	4.4	17.0	19.8	7.3	6.5	6.7	6.3	5.7	5.9	•	2.2
Total Asset Turnover 34	2.4	•	4.3	2.8	2.7	2.5	2.4	2.6	2.3	•	2.1
Inventory Turnover 35	5.4	•	8.0	8.7	5.0	4.3	4.6	5.6	5.3	•	6.2
Receivables Turnover 36	•	•	•	•	•	•	•	•	•	•	•
Total Liabilities to Net Worth 37	1.7	•	1.3	2.4	1.2	1.4	1.2	1.3	1.4	•	3.3
Current Assets to Working Capital 38	2.0	•	1.7	3.4	2.0	2.2	2.0	2.0	2.0	•	1.7
Current Liabilities to Working Capital 39	1.0	•	0.7	2.4	1.0	1.2	1.0	1.0	1.0	•	0.7
Working Capital to Net Sales 40	0.2	•	0.1	0.1	0.2	0.2	0.2	0.2	0.2	•	0.2
Inventory to Working Capital 41	0.9	•	0.5	1.1	0.9	1.1	1.0	0.9	0.9	•	0.7
Total Receipts to Cash Flow 42	11.1	8.4	5.2	9.7	11.0	11.1	12.2	14.6	11.1	•	14.3
Cost of Goods to Cash Flow 43	8.2	5.9	2.8	6.5	7.9	7.9	9.1	11.5	7.8	•	11.1
Cash Flow to Total Debt 44	0.3	•	1.5	0.4	0.5	0.4	0.4	0.3	0.4	•	0.2

Selected Financial Factors (in Percentages)

Debt Ratio 45	62.6	•	55.6	70.8	53.6	57.8	54.0	56.8	57.9	•	76.6
Return on Total Assets 46	10.4	•	29.2	14.0	9.2	10.9	9.2	9.3	12.5	•	8.8
Return on Equity Before Income Taxes 47	21.4	•	62.4	41.5	16.8	22.0	16.9	17.8	24.7	•	20.8
Return on Equity After Income Taxes 48	18.1	•	61.5	39.3	15.0	20.5	14.5	15.2	19.9	•	13.6
Profit Margin (Before Income Tax) 49	3.3	7.4	6.5	4.3	2.9	3.7	3.2	3.0	4.5	•	2.3
Profit Margin (After Income Tax) 50	2.8	5.0	6.4	4.1	2.6	3.4	2.8	2.5	3.6	•	1.5

Table I

Corporations with and without Net Income

MACHINERY, EQUIPMENT, AND SUPPLIES

MONEY AMOUNTS AND SIZE OF ASSETS IN THOUSANDS OF DOLLARS

Item Description for Accounting Period 7/02 Through 6/03	Total	Zero Assets	Under 500	500 to 1,000	1,000 to 5,000	5,000 to 10,000	10,000 to 25,000	25,000 to 50,000	50,000 to 100,000	100,000 to 250,000	250,000 to 500,000	500,000 to 2,500,000	2,500,000 and over
Number of Enterprises **1**	51578	3725	32788	4676	8137	1202	687	182	80	63	19	16	0
Revenues ($ in Thousands)													
Net Sales **2**	164742117	3139519	15268887	8649171	41438957	18622752	19133770	10399097	7679165	13035211	6476973	20899615	0
Interest **3**	489737	4056	3644	11659	32386	16035	30535	17759	24568	40832	29431	278833	0
Rents **4**	314732	63	2333	3653	22968	27033	17192	12117	6090	42834	17864	162585	0
Royalties **5**	21368	0	0	2539	9	0	5867	802	4770	333	300	6749	0
Other Portfolio Income **6**	1179075	68462	120559	5265	75366	54392	141930	71362	65860	93086	98038	384756	0
Other Receipts **7**	1707149	27965	59656	74583	533041	246074	218619	111503	80262	167797	80316	107330	0
Total Receipts **8**	168454178	3240065	15455079	8746870	42102727	18966286	19547913	10611640	7860715	13380093	6702922	21839868	0
Average Total Receipts **9**	3266	870	471	1871	5174	15779	28454	58306	98259	212382	352785	1364992	·
Operating Costs/Operating Income (%)													
Cost of Operations **10**	73.6	84.4	69.3	68.8	73.4	77.3	75.7	76.5	75.0	76.4	76.1	67.6	·
Salaries and Wages **11**	8.8	3.1	8.0	9.1	9.5	8.3	8.8	8.9	9.1	7.7	8.1	10.3	·
Taxes Paid **12**	1.4	0.9	1.5	1.8	1.5	1.1	1.3	1.3	1.3	1.1	1.1	1.4	·
Interest Paid **13**	1.2	0.5	0.9	0.9	0.7	1.0	1.0	1.1	1.2	1.6	2.4	2.5	·
Depreciation **14**	2.5	0.7	1.1	1.4	1.2	1.5	2.5	2.2	3.5	4.8	6.3	4.7	·
Amortization and Depletion **15**	0.1	0.2	0.1	0.0	0.1	0.1	0.1	0.2	0.2	0.2	0.2	0.3	·
Pensions and Other Deferred Comp. **16**	0.3	0.7	0.3	0.1	0.4	0.2	0.3	0.3	0.3	0.2	0.2	0.6	·
Employee Benefits **17**	1.0	0.3	0.6	0.7	0.8	0.7	1.0	0.9	1.1	1.6	1.5	1.3	·
Advertising **18**	0.5	0.3	0.4	0.9	0.5	0.5	0.5	0.6	0.4	0.4	0.3	0.4	·
Other Expenses **19**	9.8	8.9	13.7	12.7	9.0	7.2	7.9	8.5	8.9	8.7	7.8	13.9	·
Officers' Compensation **20**	2.3	4.3	5.4	4.3	3.1	2.3	1.6	1.3	1.0	0.6	0.6	0.5	·
Operating Margin **21**	·	·	·	·	·	·	·	·	·	·	·	·	·
Operating Margin Before Officers' Comp. **22**	0.8	·	4.2	3.4	3.0	2.1	0.8	·	·	·	·	·	·

Selected Average Balance Sheet ($ in Thousands)

Net Receivables 23	444	0	32	189	576	1849	3744	8616	16311	34808	76641	310156	•
Inventories 24	602	0	35	243	944	3241	6014	13113	20001	53144	97077	240585	•
Net Property, Plant and Equipment 25	268	0	19	77	261	820	2319	5162	12365	30366	76627	176960	•
Total Assets 26	1757	0	119	704	2213	7050	15073	34281	68411	147033	309342	1234151	•
Notes and Loans Payable 27	648	0	87	263	745	2734	5410	12926	24072	47517	151703	381681	•
All Other Liabilities 28	502	0	36	215	637	2314	4651	10613	18242	47910	83263	282962	•
Net Worth 29	608	0	-4	227	831	2002	5012	10741	26097	51606	74376	569509	•

Selected Financial Ratios (Times to 1)

Current Ratio 30	1.7	•	1.6	1.8	1.9	1.5	1.5	1.5	1.6	1.5	1.5	1.8	•
Quick Ratio 31	0.8	•	0.9	0.9	0.9	0.6	0.6	0.6	0.8	0.6	0.7	1.0	•
Net Sales to Working Capital 32	6.3	•	13.3	7.1	5.8	8.4	6.9	6.5	5.6	6.0	5.5	4.0	•
Coverage Ratio 33	1.7	•	1.1	1.3	3.1	2.6	2.3	1.3	1.4	0.5	0.5	1.5	•
Total Asset Turnover 34	1.8	•	3.9	2.6	2.3	2.2	1.8	1.7	1.4	1.4	1.1	1.1	•
Inventory Turnover 35	3.9	•	9.2	5.2	4.0	3.7	3.5	3.3	3.6	3.0	2.7	3.7	•
Receivables Turnover 36	•	•	•	•	•	•	•	•	•	•	•	•	•
Total Liabilities to Net Worth 37	1.9	•	•	2.1	1.7	2.5	2.0	2.2	1.6	1.8	3.2	1.2	•
Current Assets to Working Capital 38	2.5	•	2.6	2.2	2.1	3.1	2.8	2.9	2.6	3.0	3.0	2.2	•
Current Liabilities to Working Capital 39	1.5	•	1.6	1.2	1.1	2.1	1.8	1.9	1.6	2.0	2.0	1.2	•
Working Capital to Net Sales 40	0.2	•	0.1	0.1	0.2	0.1	0.1	0.2	0.2	0.2	0.2	0.2	•
Inventory to Working Capital 41	1.2	•	1.0	0.9	1.1	1.8	1.5	1.5	1.2	1.6	1.6	0.7	•
Total Receipts to Cash Flow 42	12.6	18.4	9.7	10.1	11.7	13.6	13.6	14.4	14.0	16.8	22.8	11.6	•
Cost of Goods to Cash Flow 43	9.3	15.6	6.7	7.0	8.6	10.5	10.3	11.0	10.5	12.8	17.4	7.9	•
Cash Flow to Total Debt 44	0.2	•	0.4	0.4	0.3	0.2	0.2	0.2	0.2	0.1	0.1	0.2	•

Selected Financial Factors (in Percentages)

Debt Ratio 45	65.4	•	103.4	67.8	62.4	71.6	66.8	68.7	61.9	64.9	76.0	53.9	•
Return on Total Assets 46	3.8	•	4.1	3.1	5.3	5.9	4.5	2.4	2.3	1.2	1.4	4.0	•
Return on Equity Before Income Taxes 47	4.4	•	•	2.3	9.5	12.8	7.7	1.6	1.7	•	•	2.9	•
Return on Equity After Income Taxes 48	1.9	•	•	1.3	8.3	10.1	6.1	•	0.2	•	•	•	•
Profit Margin (Before Income Tax) 49	0.8	•	0.1	0.3	1.6	1.6	1.4	0.3	0.5	•	•	1.3	•
Profit Margin (After Income Tax) 50	0.4	•	0.0	0.2	1.4	1.3	1.1	•	0.1	•	•	•	•

Table II

Corporations with Net Income

MACHINERY, EQUIPMENT, AND SUPPLIES

MONEY AMOUNTS AND SIZE OF ASSETS IN THOUSANDS OF DOLLARS

Item Description for Accounting Period 7/02 Through 6/03	Total	Zero Assets	Under 500	500 to 1,000	1,000 to 5,000	5,000 to 10,000	10,000 to 25,000	25,000 to 50,000	50,000 to 100,000	100,000 to 250,000	250,000 to 500,000	500,000 to 2,500,000	2,500,000 and over
Number of Enterprises **1**	26909	1284	15987	2673	5504	829	432	109	47	26	10	8	0
Revenues ($ in Thousands)													
Net Sales **2**	111269740	2745552	8452225	5649256	31003969	13510680	12675973	6696029	4437999	6072139	4081636	15944282	0
Interest **3**	237180	3629	1335	6785	24266	8981	16731	11096	16876	15284	5173	127025	0
Rents **4**	229859	36	2038	302	15575	13802	8875	7118	2982	18431	3266	157433	0
Royalties **5**	14417	0	0	7	9	0	2144	728	4770	121	240	6399	0
Other Portfolio Income **6**	553459	61250	50864	5207	45206	31760	81707	43493	37487	28314	30082	138089	0
Other Receipts **7**	1124343	13933	18034	46715	415894	150398	154392	78820	55729	61887	68713	59824	0
Total Receipts **8**	113428998	2824400	8524496	5708272	31504919	13715621	12939822	6837284	4555843	6196176	4189110	16433052	0
Average Total Receipts **9**	4215	2200	533	2136	5724	16545	29953	62727	96933	238314	418911	2054132	•
Operating Costs/Operating Income (%)													
Cost of Operations **10**	73.8	85.8	66.7	65.8	73.3	76.7	75.2	76.3	72.4	78.5	79.0	71.5	•
Salaries and Wages **11**	8.2	2.0	6.1	9.4	8.9	8.0	8.3	8.2	9.3	6.1	7.1	9.6	•
Taxes Paid **12**	1.3	0.5	1.3	1.8	1.4	1.1	1.3	1.3	1.4	0.9	0.8	1.4	•
Interest Paid **13**	0.8	0.2	0.6	0.6	0.6	0.9	0.8	0.8	1.1	1.2	1.3	1.0	•
Depreciation **14**	1.6	0.5	1.2	1.1	1.1	1.3	1.9	1.6	3.2	3.3	3.2	2.1	•
Amortization and Depletion **15**	0.1	0.0	0.0	0.0	0.0	0.1	0.1	0.1	0.2	0.1	0.1	0.3	•
Pensions and Other Deferred Comp. **16**	0.4	0.8	0.1	0.1	0.5	0.3	0.3	0.4	0.4	0.2	0.2	0.7	•
Employee Benefits **17**	0.8	0.3	0.5	0.5	0.7	0.7	0.8	0.8	1.0	1.4	1.6	1.1	•
Advertising **18**	0.4	0.1	0.3	0.9	0.4	0.5	0.4	0.5	0.4	0.2	0.3	0.4	•
Other Expenses **19**	7.8	5.4	12.6	12.1	8.0	6.2	7.1	7.2	8.6	6.8	6.2	6.8	•
Officers' Compensation **20**	2.3	3.6	5.4	4.2	3.0	2.4	1.7	1.3	1.2	0.6	0.5	0.4	•
Operating Margin **21**	2.4	0.8	5.0	3.4	2.2	1.8	1.9	1.6	0.9	0.6	•	4.6	•
Operating Margin Before Officers' Comp. **22**	4.7	4.4	10.4	7.7	5.2	4.2	3.6	2.9	2.1	1.2	0.2	5.0	•

Selected Average Balance Sheet ($ in Thousands)

												•
Net Receivables 23	512	0	31	186	622	1899	3865	8871	16193	34152	76526	341640
Inventories 24	719	0	41	208	945	3432	5875	12807	18209	62322	106439	327698
Net Property, Plant and Equipment 25	259	0	15	76	242	669	1959	4439	11664	23761	64569	187246
Total Assets 26	1981	0	125	679	2225	7034	14818	33892	68746	149025	291651	1411803
Notes and Loans Payable 27	594	0	69	150	607	2428	4592	10517	19626	46033	106247	351589
All Other Liabilities 28	538	0	31	181	634	2327	4701	9964	18150	46528	91341	249463
Net Worth 29	849	0	26	348	985	2280	5526	13411	30970	56464	94062	810751

Selected Financial Ratios (Times to 1)

												•
Current Ratio 30	1.9	•	2.0	2.3	2.1	1.5	1.7	1.8	1.9	1.6	1.7	2.3
Quick Ratio 31	0.9	•	1.1	1.3	1.0	0.6	0.7	0.8	1.0	0.6	0.7	1.2
Net Sales to Working Capital 32	5.9	•	10.4	6.8	5.7	7.7	6.4	5.5	4.5	5.7	5.3	4.1
Coverage Ratio 33	6.5	16.8	10.9	8.7	7.4	4.7	5.8	5.5	4.3	3.2	2.8	9.0
Total Asset Turnover 34	2.1	•	4.2	3.1	2.5	2.3	2.0	1.8	1.4	1.6	1.4	1.4
Inventory Turnover 35	4.2	•	8.7	6.7	4.4	3.6	3.8	3.7	3.8	2.9	3.0	4.4
Receivables Turnover 36	•	•	•	•	•	•	•	•	•	•	•	•
Total Liabilities to Net Worth 37	1.3	•	3.9	1.0	1.3	2.1	1.7	1.5	1.2	1.6	2.1	0.7
Current Assets to Working Capital 38	2.1	•	2.0	1.8	1.9	2.8	2.5	2.3	2.1	2.7	2.5	1.7
Current Liabilities to Working Capital 39	1.1	•	1.0	0.8	0.9	1.8	1.5	1.3	1.1	1.7	1.5	0.7
Working Capital to Net Sales 40	0.2	•	0.1	0.1	0.2	0.1	0.2	0.2	0.2	0.2	0.2	0.2
Inventory to Working Capital 41	1.0	•	0.8	0.7	1.0	1.6	1.3	1.1	0.9	1.5	1.4	0.7
Total Receipts to Cash Flow 42	9.7	14.3	6.8	7.2	10.0	12.2	10.7	10.6	10.0	13.2	14.5	7.7
Cost of Goods to Cash Flow 43	7.1	12.3	4.5	4.7	7.3	9.3	8.0	8.1	7.3	10.4	11.5	5.5
Cash Flow to Total Debt 44	0.4	•	0.8	0.9	0.5	0.3	0.3	0.3	0.2	0.2	0.1	0.4

Selected Financial Factors (in Percentages)

												•
Debt Ratio 45	57.1	•	79.5	48.8	55.8	67.6	62.7	60.4	55.0	62.1	67.7	42.6
Return on Total Assets 46	10.8	•	27.5	15.8	11.1	9.8	9.5	8.1	6.3	6.1	4.9	12.4
Return on Equity Before Income Taxes 47	21.3	•	122.0	27.2	21.6	23.8	21.1	16.9	10.8	11.1	9.8	19.1
Return on Equity After Income Taxes 48	17.9	•	119.6	26.1	20.1	20.4	18.8	13.9	8.6	9.5	7.3	12.5
Profit Margin (Before Income Tax) 49	4.4	3.7	5.9	4.5	3.8	3.3	4.0	3.7	3.5	2.7	2.2	7.8
Profit Margin (After Income Tax) 50	3.7	3.4	5.8	4.3	3.5	2.9	3.5	3.0	2.8	2.3	1.7	5.1

Table I
Corporations with and without Net Income

FURNITURE, SPORTS, TOYS, JEWELRY, OTHER DURABLE GOODS

MONEY AMOUNTS AND SIZE OF ASSETS IN THOUSANDS OF DOLLARS

Item Description for Accounting Period 7/02 Through 6/03	Total	Zero Assets	Under 500	500 to 1,000	1,000 to 5,000	5,000 to 10,000	10,000 to 25,000	25,000 to 50,000	50,000 to 100,000	100,000 to 250,000	250,000 to 500,000	500,000 to 2,500,000	2,500,000 and over
Number of Enterprises **1**	66030	7323	42655	6406	7208	1290	747	208	99	50	29	14	0
Revenues ($ in Thousands)													
Net Sales **2**	195301825	1273018	19020151	11485698	39377729	20873337	24833987	15884805	12991434	11289167	13711929	24560571	0
Interest **3**	392706	588	12792	14120	18985	11867	27270	30084	15980	47549	66751	146718	0
Rents **4**	107652	914	1252	1907	18280	5378	5047	7687	6848	4028	18324	37988	0
Royalties **5**	365911	3283	18	1558	29961	2923	2583	5658	23749	70949	13818	211411	0
Other Portfolio Income **6**	315716	238	21048	37705	50090	8220	30190	19426	23237	19730	68286	37544	0
Other Receipts **7**	1684641	49144	217146	54753	188250	127446	166594	147837	73422	99098	226366	334587	0
Total Receipts **8**	198168451	1327185	19272407	11595741	39683295	21029171	25065671	16095497	13134670	11530521	14105474	25328819	0
Average Total Receipts **9**	3001	181	452	1810	5505	16302	33555	77382	132673	230610	486396	1809201	•
Operating Costs/Operating Income (%)													
Cost of Operations **10**	75.0	60.0	60.7	69.0	73.4	79.2	76.2	77.7	77.9	72.9	80.1	82.2	•
Salaries and Wages **11**	6.8	13.1	7.8	7.8	7.4	6.0	7.0	6.4	6.4	7.3	5.4	5.4	•
Taxes Paid **12**	1.2	1.9	1.6	1.5	1.3	1.1	1.2	1.1	1.1	1.2	1.0	0.7	•
Interest Paid **13**	0.9	1.8	0.6	0.7	0.7	0.6	0.9	0.8	0.9	1.2	1.3	1.4	•
Depreciation **14**	0.9	1.4	0.9	1.0	0.9	0.7	0.9	0.9	1.0	1.5	1.4	0.8	•
Amortization and Depletion **15**	0.2	0.3	0.1	0.0	0.1	0.0	0.1	0.1	0.4	0.4	0.5	0.5	•
Pensions and Other Deferred Comp. **16**	0.3	0.3	0.7	0.3	0.3	0.2	0.2	0.2	0.1	0.2	0.1	0.4	•
Employee Benefits **17**	0.5	0.8	0.4	0.6	0.5	0.4	0.5	0.5	0.7	0.9	0.8	0.5	•
Advertising **18**	1.4	2.2	0.7	0.9	1.0	0.7	1.0	1.4	1.4	2.4	2.1	2.6	•
Other Expenses **19**	9.9	23.0	19.2	13.5	9.6	7.5	8.5	8.3	7.9	10.1	7.3	7.5	•
Officers' Compensation **20**	2.4	4.2	7.0	5.0	3.4	2.3	1.8	1.2	1.0	0.8	0.5	0.3	•
Operating Margin **21**	0.6	•	0.4	•	1.4	1.3	1.7	1.5	1.3	1.2	•	•	•
Operating Margin Before Officers' Comp. **22**	3.0	•	7.4	4.8	4.9	3.6	3.5	2.7	2.2	2.0	•	•	•

Selected Average Balance Sheet ($ in Thousands)

Net Receivables 23	375	0	22	170	594	2198	5113	11040	20083	38396	70826	252514	•
Inventories 24	410	0	36	289	813	2538	5517	11434	19422	34044	64111	184263	•
Net Property, Plant and Equipment 25	148	0	16	69	260	592	1378	3523	7932	15273	35495	120182	•
Total Assets 26	1443	0	111	716	2138	6797	15342	34969	69267	151456	348781	1324079	•
Notes and Loans Payable 27	461	0	58	265	622	1916	4771	10980	22711	45821	113766	401543	•
All Other Liabilities 28	519	0	51	275	848	2740	5912	13048	21182	50047	102234	427605	•
Net Worth 29	463	0	2	176	668	2141	4659	10941	25373	55588	132781	494930	•

Selected Financial Ratios (Times to 1)

Current Ratio 30	1.5	•	1.3	2.0	1.7	1.5	1.5	1.5	1.6	1.6	1.4	1.2	•
Quick Ratio 31	0.8	•	0.7	1.0	0.8	0.8	0.8	0.8	0.9	0.9	0.7	0.6	•
Net Sales to Working Capital 32	8.9	•	20.9	6.0	7.7	8.3	7.8	8.1	6.9	5.9	9.9	20.5	•
Coverage Ratio 33	3.3	•	4.0	2.0	4.3	4.3	4.0	4.5	3.5	3.9	2.8	1.7	•
Total Asset Turnover 34	2.0	•	4.0	2.5	2.6	2.4	2.2	2.2	1.9	1.5	1.4	1.3	•
Inventory Turnover 35	5.4	•	7.6	4.3	4.9	5.1	4.6	5.2	5.3	4.8	5.9	7.8	•
Receivables Turnover 36	•	•	•	•	•	•	•	•	•	•	•	•	•
Total Liabilities to Net Worth 37	2.1	•	72.7	3.1	2.2	2.3	2.2	2.2	1.7	1.7	1.6	1.7	•
Current Assets to Working Capital 38	3.0	•	3.9	2.0	2.4	3.0	3.0	2.9	2.6	2.6	3.7	7.3	•
Current Liabilities to Working Capital 39	2.0	•	2.9	1.0	1.4	2.0	2.0	1.9	1.6	1.6	2.7	6.3	•
Working Capital to Net Sales 40	0.1	•	0.0	0.2	0.1	0.1	0.1	0.1	0.1	0.2	0.1	0.0	•
Inventory to Working Capital 41	1.2	•	1.7	1.0	1.1	1.3	1.3	1.2	1.0	0.9	1.3	2.2	•
Total Receipts to Cash Flow 42	10.5	6.7	6.2	9.3	11.0	12.9	10.8	10.4	11.7	9.0	12.2	14.8	•
Cost of Goods to Cash Flow 43	7.8	4.0	3.7	6.4	8.1	10.2	8.2	8.1	9.1	6.6	9.7	12.1	•
Cash Flow to Total Debt 44	0.3	•	0.7	0.4	0.3	0.3	0.3	0.3	0.3	0.3	0.2	0.1	•

Selected Financial Factors (in Percentages)

Debt Ratio 45	67.9	•	98.6	75.4	68.8	68.5	69.6	68.7	63.4	63.3	61.9	62.6	•
Return on Total Assets 46	6.0	•	9.5	3.4	7.4	6.3	7.7	8.0	6.2	6.7	5.0	3.1	•
Return on Equity Before Income Taxes 47	13.1	•	524.0	7.0	18.1	15.3	19.0	19.8	12.2	13.6	8.4	3.5	•
Return on Equity After Income Taxes 48	10.9	•	497.0	4.7	17.0	13.3	16.4	16.3	9.7	10.0	6.0	2.0	•
Profit Margin (Before Income Tax) 49	2.1	•	1.8	0.7	2.2	2.0	2.7	2.8	2.4	3.3	2.4	1.0	•
Profit Margin (After Income Tax) 50	1.7	•	1.7	0.5	2.1	1.8	2.3	2.3	1.9	2.5	1.7	0.6	•

Table II

Corporations with Net Income

FURNITURE, SPORTS, TOYS, JEWELRY, OTHER DURABLE GOODS

MONEY AMOUNTS AND SIZE OF ASSETS IN THOUSANDS OF DOLLARS

Item Description for Accounting Period 7/02 Through 6/03	Total	Zero Assets	Under 500	500 to 1,000	1,000 to 5,000	5,000 to 10,000	10,000 to 25,000	25,000 to 50,000	50,000 to 100,000	100,000 to 250,000	250,000 to 500,000	500,000 to 2,500,000	2,500,000 and over
Number of Enterprises 1	34772	1632	21763	4077	5374	1035	579	172	70	38	23	9	0
Revenues ($ in Thousands)													
Net Sales 2	147192777	445125	12894217	7703500	31804093	18493472	20238289	13966044	7683376	9237126	12549369	12178166	0
Interest 3	221634	406	4809	11824	14000	9210	14200	13092	9299	28029	55234	61530	0
Rents 4	73018	914	1252	959	15011	5200	2482	4332	5492	3908	18321	15148	0
Royalties 5	252676	0	0	1558	29277	2858	1560	5398	16751	25328	7313	162635	0
Other Portfolio Income 6	216606	166	3424	36138	31564	5231	15208	11615	12619	19494	55754	25395	0
Other Receipts 7	1342536	41565	91459	45197	148737	114335	115355	138191	65402	82625	222938	276727	0
Total Receipts 8	149299247	488176	12995161	7799176	32042682	18630306	20387094	14138672	7792939	9396510	12908929	12719601	0
Average Total Receipts 9	4294	299	597	1913	5963	18000	35211	82202	111328	247277	561258	1413289	•
Operating Costs/Operating Income (%)													
Cost of Operations 10	73.8	40.8	59.6	66.1	73.5	79.6	75.5	78.1	71.8	72.9	80.9	73.9	•
Salaries and Wages 11	6.7	10.9	8.0	7.6	6.8	5.6	6.9	5.9	7.2	6.7	5.1	7.9	•
Taxes Paid 12	1.2	1.2	1.4	1.5	1.2	1.0	1.2	1.0	1.3	1.1	0.9	1.0	•
Interest Paid 13	0.8	0.3	0.6	0.6	0.6	0.5	0.7	0.7	0.9	0.9	1.0	1.8	•
Depreciation 14	0.9	0.8	0.8	0.9	0.7	0.7	0.8	0.8	1.2	1.5	1.4	1.2	•
Amortization and Depletion 15	0.2	0.1	0.1	0.0	0.0	0.0	0.1	0.1	0.2	0.4	0.3	0.9	•
Pensions and Other Deferred Comp. 16	0.3	0.6	0.6	0.3	0.3	0.2	0.2	0.2	0.2	0.2	0.1	0.5	•
Employee Benefits 17	0.5	0.0	0.4	0.6	0.4	0.3	0.5	0.5	0.7	0.8	0.8	0.7	•
Advertising 18	1.5	2.3	0.7	0.9	0.9	0.6	1.0	1.2	1.8	2.2	2.0	5.2	•
Other Expenses 19	9.0	31.0	16.6	13.1	9.0	7.0	7.6	7.2	9.0	9.3	6.9	7.7	•
Officers' Compensation 20	2.3	2.7	5.6	5.3	3.5	1.8	1.8	1.3	1.4	0.7	0.5	0.3	•
Operating Margin 21	2.8	9.3	5.6	3.2	3.1	2.6	3.8	3.1	4.1	3.3	0.1	•	•
Operating Margin Before Officers' Comp. 22	5.1	12.0	11.2	8.5	6.6	4.4	5.6	4.3	5.5	4.1	0.6	•	•

Selected Average Balance Sheet ($ in Thousands)

Net Receivables 23	513	0	27	169	603	2297	5304	11402	19003	40348	73248	151407
Inventories 24	592	0	40	284	834	2686	5600	11937	21235	36159	66167	178497
Net Property, Plant and Equipment 25	192	0	15	65	241	583	1261	3339	8131	16296	41827	81919
Total Assets 26	1990	0	124	737	2173	6782	15334	35391	69967	156552	351418	1211634
Notes and Loans Payable 27	532	0	59	157	528	1749	4350	9938	17804	46473	104218	254525
All Other Liabilities 28	683	0	37	274	827	2730	5508	12971	18235	52796	92149	414350
Net Worth 29	775	0	28	307	818	2302	5476	12482	33929	57284	155051	542759

Selected Financial Ratios (Times to 1)

Current Ratio 30	1.6	•	2.0	2.1	1.9	1.6	1.6	1.6	1.9	1.7	1.5	1.2
Quick Ratio 31	0.8	•	1.1	1.1	0.9	0.8	0.8	0.8	1.0	0.9	0.7	0.4
Net Sales to Working Capital 32	7.7	•	12.4	5.6	6.9	8.4	6.9	7.9	4.6	5.7	8.8	21.1
Coverage Ratio 33	6.6	58.9	12.5	8.9	7.9	7.4	7.7	7.1	6.9	6.7	4.2	2.9
Total Asset Turnover 34	2.1	•	4.8	2.6	2.7	2.6	2.3	2.3	1.6	1.6	1.6	1.1
Inventory Turnover 35	5.3	•	8.8	4.4	5.2	5.3	4.7	5.3	3.7	4.9	6.7	5.6
Receivables Turnover 36	•	•	•	•	•	•	•	•	•	•	•	•
Total Liabilities to Net Worth 37	1.6	•	3.5	1.4	1.7	1.9	1.8	1.8	1.1	1.7	1.3	1.2
Current Assets to Working Capital 38	2.6	•	2.0	1.9	2.1	2.7	2.6	2.8	2.1	2.5	3.0	7.4
Current Liabilities to Working Capital 39	1.6	•	1.0	0.9	1.1	1.7	1.6	1.8	1.1	1.5	2.0	6.4
Working Capital to Net Sales 40	0.1	•	0.1	0.2	0.1	0.1	0.1	0.1	0.2	0.2	0.1	0.0
Inventory to Working Capital 41	1.1	•	0.8	0.8	1.0	1.3	1.1	1.2	0.9	0.9	1.1	2.8
Total Receipts to Cash Flow 42	9.0	2.1	5.3	7.0	9.8	11.6	9.6	9.9	7.9	8.3	11.8	10.8
Cost of Goods to Cash Flow 43	6.6	0.8	3.1	4.6	7.2	9.2	7.3	7.7	5.7	6.0	9.5	8.0
Cash Flow to Total Debt 44	0.4	•	1.2	0.6	0.4	0.3	0.4	0.4	0.4	0.3	0.2	0.2

Selected Financial Factors (in Percentages)

Debt Ratio 45	61.0	•	77.5	58.4	62.4	66.1	64.3	64.7	51.5	63.4	55.9	55.2
Return on Total Assets 46	10.7	•	33.4	12.7	11.9	10.2	11.9	11.5	10.1	9.3	6.2	5.9
Return on Equity Before Income Taxes 47	23.4	•	136.8	27.1	27.7	25.9	29.1	28.1	17.9	21.6	10.8	8.7
Return on Equity After Income Taxes 48	20.9	•	133.9	25.0	26.4	23.6	26.2	24.4	15.3	17.1	8.2	6.6
Profit Margin (Before Income Tax) 49	4.3	19.7	6.4	4.4	3.8	3.3	4.6	4.3	5.5	5.1	3.1	3.5
Profit Margin (After Income Tax) 50	3.8	19.0	6.3	4.1	3.7	3.0	4.1	3.7	4.7	4.0	2.3	2.6

Table I

Corporations with and without Net Income

PAPER AND PAPER PRODUCT

MONEY AMOUNTS AND SIZE OF ASSETS IN THOUSANDS OF DOLLARS

Item Description for Accounting Period 7/02 Through 6/03	Total	Zero Assets	Under 500	500 to 1,000	1,000 to 5,000	5,000 to 10,000	10,000 to 25,000	25,000 to 50,000	50,000 to 100,000	100,000 to 250,000	250,000 to 500,000	500,000 to 2,500,000	2,500,000 and over
Number of Enterprises **1**	9794	457	7128	781	1090	160	104	41	16	12	0	6	0
Revenues ($ in Thousands)													
Net Sales **2**	47889915	543255	3033547	1437923	8076943	3843878	5310377	4924398	4088606	5949011	0	10681977	0
Interest **3**	37256	765	364	1710	1488	2044	2407	2207	2311	3687	0	20272	0
Rents **4**	8163	6	0	0	2912	309	1001	806	663	8	0	2456	0
Royalties **5**	35481	21920	0	0	0	0	5198	27	0	2321	0	6016	0
Other Portfolio Income **6**	29772	891	107	655	5253	8663	931	1033	473	6655	0	5111	0
Other Receipts **7**	257247	29497	7205	11302	96103	12422	24452	17791	23828	24632	0	10017	0
Total Receipts **8**	48257834	596334	3041223	1451590	8182699	3867316	5344366	4946262	4115881	5986314	0	10725849	0
Average Total Receipts **9**	4927	1305	427	1859	7507	24171	51388	120641	257243	498860	•	1787642	•
Operating Costs/Operating Income (%)													
Cost of Operations **10**	78.9	66.3	68.4	70.0	78.9	79.7	83.5	77.0	88.8	85.7	•	74.6	•
Salaries and Wages **11**	6.7	20.9	5.9	6.8	6.0	7.2	6.4	6.7	3.7	5.4	•	8.5	•
Taxes Paid **12**	0.9	1.6	1.6	1.8	0.9	1.0	0.8	0.8	0.5	0.6	•	1.1	•
Interest Paid **13**	0.9	1.4	0.5	0.4	0.4	0.4	0.5	0.4	0.6	1.3	•	2.0	•
Depreciation **14**	1.1	3.2	1.1	0.8	0.7	0.5	0.8	0.5	0.6	0.7	•	2.2	•
Amortization and Depletion **15**	0.3	0.5	0.0	0.0	0.1	0.0	0.0	0.1	0.1	0.3	•	0.9	•
Pensions and Other Deferred Comp. **16**	0.3	0.2	0.3	0.2	0.4	0.1	0.3	0.2	0.2	0.2	•	0.5	•
Employee Benefits **17**	0.6	3.8	0.2	0.5	0.6	0.3	0.5	0.5	0.1	0.5	•	1.0	•
Advertising **18**	0.2	1.0	0.5	0.2	0.2	0.1	0.3	0.2	0.0	0.1	•	0.3	•
Other Expenses **19**	8.2	19.3	14.8	12.9	7.8	7.1	5.1	12.1	4.4	4.3	•	9.1	•
Officers' Compensation **20**	1.8	0.9	8.5	5.1	3.8	1.5	1.4	0.8	0.6	0.5	•	0.1	•
Operating Margin **21**	0.1	•	•	1.2	0.3	2.0	0.4	0.7	0.4	0.4	•	•	•
Operating Margin Before Officers' Comp. **22**	1.9	•	6.7	6.4	4.1	3.5	1.8	1.5	0.9	0.9	•	•	•

Selected Average Balance Sheet ($ in Thousands)

Net Receivables 23	629	0	36	216	702	2637	6742	16102	35217	71000	295445	•
Inventories 24	369	0	14	222	466	2128	3697	9716	11927	30899	191481	•
Net Property, Plant and Equipment 25	280	0	12	33	190	550	2012	2932	9863	19222	268952	•
Total Assets 26	2155	0	94	705	1786	6910	15374	35539	70322	179806	1749812	•
Notes and Loans Payable 27	780	0	68	88	629	1836	4838	10553	23651	85461	628062	•
All Other Liabilities 28	1142	0	42	117	698	2342	6215	14476	29708	57897	1208992	•
Net Worth 29	233	0	-16	500	459	2732	4321	10510	16964	36448	-87242	•

Selected Financial Ratios (Times to 1)

Current Ratio 30	1.1	•	1.4	4.9	1.7	1.7	1.4	1.6	1.7	1.6	0.6	•
Quick Ratio 31	0.6	•	1.1	2.8	1.0	1.0	0.9	1.0	1.2	1.1	0.3	•
Net Sales to Working Capital 32	67.6	•	20.1	4.0	12.9	9.6	14.4	11.1	11.6	11.9	•	•
Coverage Ratio 33	1.9	•	•	6.9	4.9	7.7	3.1	3.5	2.7	1.8	1.1	•
Total Asset Turnover 34	2.3	•	4.5	2.6	4.1	3.5	3.3	3.4	3.6	2.8	1.0	•
Inventory Turnover 35	10.5	•	20.9	5.8	12.6	9.0	11.5	9.5	19.0	13.7	6.9	•
Receivables Turnover 36	•	•	•	•	•	•	•	•	•	•	•	•
Total Liabilities to Net Worth 37	8.3	•	•	0.4	2.9	1.5	2.6	2.4	3.1	3.9	0.6	•
Current Assets to Working Capital 38	17.0	•	3.4	1.3	2.4	2.3	3.4	2.8	2.5	2.7	•	•
Current Liabilities to Working Capital 39	16.0	•	2.4	0.3	1.4	1.3	2.4	1.8	1.5	1.7	•	•
Working Capital to Net Sales 40	0.0	•	0.0	0.2	0.1	0.1	0.1	0.1	0.1	0.1	0.1	•
Inventory to Working Capital 41	5.1	•	0.7	0.5	0.8	0.8	1.0	0.9	0.5	0.7	0.7	•
Total Receipts to Cash Flow 42	14.0	14.0	10.0	8.3	14.0	13.0	20.1	8.7	23.3	23.3	13.7	•
Cost of Goods to Cash Flow 43	11.0	9.3	6.9	5.8	11.0	10.4	16.8	6.7	20.7	20.0	10.2	•
Cash Flow to Total Debt 44	0.2	•	0.4	1.1	0.4	0.4	0.2	0.6	0.2	0.1	0.1	•

Selected Financial Factors (in Percentages)

Debt Ratio 45	89.2	•	117.1	29.0	74.3	60.5	71.9	70.4	75.9	79.7	105.0	•
Return on Total Assets 46	4.0	•	•	6.6	8.2	10.3	5.3	5.2	5.9	6.6	2.2	•
Return on Equity Before Income Taxes 47	17.6	•	40.3	8.0	25.5	22.7	12.7	12.4	15.4	14.5	•	•
Return on Equity After Income Taxes 48	12.2	•	42.5	6.2	23.4	19.7	10.2	11.3	11.9	12.5	5.8	•
Profit Margin (Before Income Tax) 49	0.8	•	•	2.2	1.6	2.6	1.1	1.1	1.0	1.1	0.2	•
Profit Margin (After Income Tax) 50	0.6	•	•	1.7	1.5	2.2	0.9	1.0	0.8	0.9	•	•

Table II

Corporations with Net Income

PAPER AND PAPER PRODUCT

MONEY AMOUNTS AND SIZE OF ASSETS IN THOUSANDS OF DOLLARS

Item Description for Accounting Period 7/02 Through 6/03	Total	Zero Assets	Under 500	500 to 1,000	1,000 to 5,000	5,000 to 10,000	10,000 to 25,000	25,000 to 50,000	50,000 to 100,000	100,000 to 250,000	250,000 to 500,000	500,000 to 2,500,000	2,500,000 and over
Number of Enterprises **1**	4756	0	2958	0	925	149	82	35	12	7	4	0	•
Revenues ($ in Thousands)													
Net Sales **2**	35468359	0	2119323	0	7167929	3758862	4409375	4253535	3295179	3546766	5823938	0	•
Interest **3**	24895	0	0	0	909	1971	1859	1679	2145	2477	12673	0	•
Rents **4**	3387	0	0	0	0	48	829	806	663	0	1041	0	•
Royalties **5**	11327	0	0	0	0	0	5198	0	0	0	6130	0	•
Other Portfolio Income **6**	22568	0	107	0	3136	8663	766	673	473	2742	5480	0	•
Other Receipts **7**	203046	0	268	0	94877	11378	22110	7795	15804	22185	12007	0	•
Total Receipts **8**	35733582	0	2119698	0	7266851	3780922	4440137	4264488	3314264	3574170	5861269	0	•
Average Total Receipts **9**	7513	•	717	•	7856	25375	54148	121843	276189	510596	1465317	•	•
Operating Costs/Operating Income (%)													
Cost of Operations **10**	80.0	•	70.4	•	79.4	80.0	83.0	75.4	88.2	88.1	77.8	•	•
Salaries and Wages **11**	5.6	•	4.4	•	5.7	7.2	6.4	6.6	3.9	4.6	5.1	•	•
Taxes Paid **12**	0.9	•	1.4	•	0.9	1.0	0.8	0.7	0.5	0.5	1.1	•	•
Interest Paid **13**	0.6	•	0.5	•	0.3	0.3	0.4	0.4	0.4	0.8	1.8	•	•
Depreciation **14**	0.8	•	0.6	•	0.6	0.4	0.8	0.5	0.4	0.3	2.2	•	•
Amortization and Depletion **15**	0.2	•	0.0	•	0.1	0.0	0.0	0.0	0.1	0.3	0.7	•	•
Pensions and Other Deferred Comp. **16**	0.3	•	0.1	•	0.4	0.1	0.3	0.1	0.1	0.2	0.6	•	•
Employee Benefits **17**	0.5	•	0.1	•	0.6	0.2	0.4	0.5	0.1	0.4	0.8	•	•
Advertising **18**	0.2	•	0.6	•	0.2	0.1	0.4	0.2	0.0	0.1	0.1	•	•
Other Expenses **19**	7.5	•	13.3	•	7.4	6.9	4.2	12.6	4.9	3.9	7.0	•	•
Officers' Compensation **20**	1.9	•	7.0	•	3.5	1.6	1.5	0.9	0.5	0.4	0.1	•	•
Operating Margin **21**	1.6	•	1.6	•	0.9	2.2	1.8	2.0	0.8	0.5	2.7	•	•
Operating Margin Before Officers' Comp. **22**	3.5	•	8.5	•	4.5	3.8	3.3	2.8	1.4	0.9	2.9	•	•

Selected Average Balance Sheet ($ in Thousands)

•	•	•	•	•	•	•	•	•	•	•
Net Receivables 23 832	•	51	•	693	2786	6484	15589	37737	70475	149918
Inventories 24 499	•	8	•	506	2255	3859	9814	13656	26432	103452
Net Property, Plant and Equipment 25 296	•	9	•	168	418	2062	2683	6436	11156	180990
Total Assets 26 2371	•	107	•	1818	7000	15272	35389	71789	129920	889958
Notes and Loans Payable 27 691	•	56	•	625	1768	4352	9139	21292	51690	241897
All Other Liabilities 28 1063	•	68	•	699	2357	5414	14503	29140	55246	527798
Net Worth 29 617	•	-17	•	493	2874	5506	11748	21356	22983	120263

Selected Financial Ratios (Times to 1)

•	•	•	•	•	•	•	•	•	•	•
Current Ratio 30 1.4	•	1.0	•	1.8	1.8	1.6	1.7	1.8	1.5	0.8
Quick Ratio 31 0.9	•	0.9	•	1.1	1.0	1.0	1.0	1.3	1.1	0.4
Net Sales to Working Capital 32 15.8	•	•	•	12.0	9.2	12.3	10.2	10.0	13.9	•
Coverage Ratio 33 4.6	•	4.3	•	7.7	10.1	6.9	7.0	4.2	2.6	2.9
Total Asset Turnover 34 3.1	•	6.7	•	4.3	3.6	3.5	3.4	3.8	3.9	1.6
Inventory Turnover 35 12.0	•	63.0	•	12.2	8.9	11.6	9.3	17.7	16.9	10.9
Receivables Turnover 36 •	•	•	•	•	•	•	•	•	•	•
Total Liabilities to Net Worth 37 2.8	•	•	•	2.7	1.4	1.8	2.0	2.4	4.7	6.4
Current Assets to Working Capital 38 3.4	•	•	•	2.2	2.3	2.8	2.5	2.2	2.8	•
Current Liabilities to Working Capital 39 2.4	•	•	•	1.2	1.3	1.8	1.5	1.2	1.8	•
Working Capital to Net Sales 40 0.1	•	•	•	0.1	0.1	0.1	0.1	0.1	0.1	•
Inventory to Working Capital 41 1.1	•	•	•	0.8	0.8	0.9	0.8	0.5	0.7	•
Total Receipts to Cash Flow 42 12.4	•	8.2	•	12.9	12.8	17.9	7.6	20.0	23.4	11.9
Cost of Goods to Cash Flow 43 9.9	•	5.8	•	10.3	10.3	14.8	5.7	17.6	20.6	9.3
Cash Flow to Total Debt 44 0.3	•	0.7	•	0.5	0.5	0.3	0.7	0.3	0.2	0.2

Selected Financial Factors (in Percentages)

•	•	•	•	•	•	•	•	•	•	•
Debt Ratio 45 74.0	•	115.9	•	72.9	58.9	63.9	66.8	70.3	82.3	86.5
Return on Total Assets 46 9.4	•	13.9	•	11.3	11.1	10.1	8.9	7.1	8.1	8.5
Return on Equity Before Income Taxes 47 28.4	•	•	•	36.1	24.4	24.0	23.1	18.2	28.0	40.8
Return on Equity After Income Taxes 48 24.2	•	•	•	33.8	21.4	21.5	21.9	14.5	25.5	28.5
Profit Margin (Before Income Tax) 49 2.3	•	1.6	•	2.3	2.8	2.5	2.2	1.4	1.3	3.4
Profit Margin (After Income Tax) 50 2.0	•	1.5	•	2.2	2.4	2.2	2.1	1.1	1.2	2.4

Table I

Corporations with and without Net Income

DRUGS AND DRUGGISTS' SUNDRIES

MONEY AMOUNTS AND SIZE OF ASSETS IN THOUSANDS OF DOLLARS

Item Description for Accounting Period 7/02 Through 6/03	Total	Zero Assets	Under 500	500 to 1,000	1,000 to 5,000	5,000 to 10,000	10,000 to 25,000	25,000 to 50,000	50,000 to 100,000	100,000 to 250,000	250,000 to 500,000	500,000 to 2,500,000	2,500,000 and over
Number of Enterprises **1**	3795	55	2093	628	665	139	87	36	27	22	14	18	11
Revenues ($ in Thousands)													
Net Sales **2**	228854779	73962	2333737	735128	4693031	2337619	3649945	2693015	5371728	7627139	10947648	19277283	169214543
Interest **3**	704006	8131	438	3164	4164	1432	3735	5078	9205	12934	24458	167600	463666
Rents **4**	362365	0	0	54	812	0	1258	870	678	605	2903	6620	348564
Royalties **5**	1127328	0	747	0	604	1380	207	16813	4562	22352	211861	317676	551127
Other Portfolio Income **6**	1073780	406	2	6881	4980	12	617	319	20609	12384	4851	71380	951341
Other Receipts **7**	3465149	4088	25465	1008	7101	50895	39858	61757	125475	89103	107313	523285	2429801
Total Receipts **8**	235687407	86587	2360389	746235	4710692	2391338	3695620	2777852	5532257	7764517	11299034	20363844	173959042
Average Total Receipts **9**	62105	1574	1128	1188	7084	17204	42478	77163	204898	352933	807074	1131325	15814458
Operating Costs/Operating Income (%)													
Cost of Operations **10**	83.4	53.3	80.0	56.7	76.7	58.9	74.6	72.3	86.7	76.7	81.6	40.6	89.7
Salaries and Wages **11**	4.5	8.3	2.7	11.1	5.9	12.1	7.0	8.1	3.7	9.2	4.5	11.4	3.3
Taxes Paid **12**	0.4	1.3	0.5	1.4	1.0	1.5	1.0	0.8	0.4	0.9	0.4	1.3	0.3
Interest Paid **13**	0.6	11.5	0.4	1.0	0.7	1.1	0.7	0.9	0.4	0.8	0.6	1.9	0.5
Depreciation **14**	0.6	1.3	0.2	1.0	0.3	1.7	0.7	1.0	0.5	0.6	0.7	1.9	0.5
Amortization and Depletion **15**	0.4	3.2	0.0	0.0	0.1	0.1	0.2	0.5	0.2	0.6	0.7	0.9	0.3
Pensions and Other Deferred Comp. **16**	0.1	0.2	0.3	0.2	0.2	0.3	0.2	0.3	0.1	0.2	0.2	0.3	0.1
Employee Benefits **17**	0.5	0.9	0.3	0.6	0.8	0.5	0.5	0.6	0.3	0.5	0.6	1.1	0.4
Advertising **18**	1.1	14.0	1.6	0.5	1.6	3.2	2.0	3.4	1.7	0.5	1.2	2.6	0.8
Other Expenses **19**	7.1	108.9	11.2	24.5	8.2	18.0	11.2	11.9	7.9	8.2	8.7	28.9	3.9
Officers' Compensation **20**	0.3	0.7	2.6	6.1	2.7	2.2	2.0	0.8	0.5	0.6	0.4	0.7	0.1
Operating Margin **21**	0.8	•	0.3	•	1.9	0.3	•	•	•	1.1	0.5	8.4	0.1
Operating Margin Before Officers' Comp. **22**	1.1	•	2.9	2.8	4.6	2.5	1.9	0.1	•	1.6	0.9	9.1	0.1

Selected Average Balance Sheet ($ in Thousands)

Net Receivables 23	7116	0	49	268	670	2054	4832	8799	24479	34945	73746	146790	1833078
Inventories 24	6861	0	27	67	615	2640	4377	8415	18528	34839	81537	110881	1825136
Net Property, Plant and Equipment 25	2228	0	5	79	97	840	1348	3893	5138	12377	29772	178212	356279
Total Assets 26	31457	0	143	686	2316	6974	15532	34747	70030	156644	372209	1065567	7619183
Notes and Loans Payable 27	5968	0	186	241	1096	3087	4569	11959	13551	47236	53410	296803	1147877
All Other Liabilities 28	14128	0	152	447	954	2701	7460	12815	34520	54284	156859	308453	3729480
Net Worth 29	11361	0	-194	-1	266	1186	3502	9973	21959	55125	161940	460310	2741825

Selected Financial Ratios (Times to 1)

Current Ratio 30	1.3	•	0.7	1.1	1.9	1.3	1.3	1.3	1.3	1.4	1.4	1.4	1.3
Quick Ratio 31	0.7	•	0.4	0.8	1.0	0.6	0.7	0.7	0.7	0.7	0.6	0.8	0.7
Net Sales to Working Capital 32	12.6	•	•	36.9	7.0	12.6	16.4	13.5	16.8	14.5	12.8	6.3	13.8
Coverage Ratio 33	7.0	•	4.6	•	4.3	3.3	2.7	3.6	2.6	4.6	7.5	8.6	7.3
Total Asset Turnover 34	1.9	•	7.8	1.7	3.0	2.4	2.7	2.2	2.8	2.2	2.1	1.0	2.0
Inventory Turnover 35	7.3	•	33.5	9.9	8.8	3.8	7.2	6.4	9.3	7.6	7.8	3.9	7.6
Receivables Turnover 36	•	•	•	•	•	•	•	•	•	•	•	•	•
Total Liabilities to Net Worth 37	1.8	•	•	•	7.7	4.9	3.4	2.5	2.2	1.8	1.3	1.3	1.8
Current Assets to Working Capital 38	3.9	•	•	14.6	2.1	4.3	4.7	4.2	4.7	3.7	3.8	3.3	4.0
Current Liabilities to Working Capital 39	2.9	•	•	13.6	1.1	3.3	3.7	3.2	3.7	2.7	2.8	2.3	3.0
Working Capital to Net Sales 40	0.1	•	0.0	0.1	0.1	0.1	0.1	0.1	0.1	0.1	0.1	0.2	0.1
Inventory to Working Capital 41	1.4	•	•	2.1	0.6	2.0	1.7	1.5	1.6	1.5	1.3	0.6	1.6
Total Receipts to Cash Flow 42	10.0	•	8.9	5.3	11.4	5.5	9.1	7.6	14.0	9.7	8.7	2.4	15.9
Cost of Goods to Cash Flow 43	8.3	•	7.2	3.0	8.8	3.3	6.8	5.5	12.2	7.4	7.1	1.0	14.2
Cash Flow to Total Debt 44	0.3	•	0.4	0.3	0.3	0.5	0.4	0.4	0.3	0.4	0.4	0.7	0.2

Selected Financial Factors (in Percentages)

Debt Ratio 45	63.9	•	236.3	100.2	88.5	83.0	77.5	71.3	68.6	64.8	56.5	56.8	64.0
Return on Total Assets 46	8.6	•	14.7	•	9.1	9.0	4.9	7.3	3.0	8.3	8.9	16.2	7.2
Return on Equity Before Income Taxes 47	20.4	•	•	2024.0	60.4	37.0	13.7	18.5	5.9	18.4	17.7	33.0	17.1
Return on Equity After Income Taxes 48	13.8	•	•	2267.6	49.8	28.6	10.5	11.8	1.2	14.9	11.7	20.0	12.2
Profit Margin (Before Income Tax) 49	3.8	•	1.5	•	2.3	2.6	1.1	2.5	0.7	2.9	3.7	14.2	3.1
Profit Margin (After Income Tax) 50	2.6	•	1.4	•	1.9	2.0	0.9	1.6	0.1	2.4	2.4	8.6	2.2

Table II

Corporations with Net Income

DRUGS AND DRUGGISTS' SUNDRIES

MONEY AMOUNTS AND SIZE OF ASSETS IN THOUSANDS OF DOLLARS

Item Description for Accounting Period 7/02 Through 6/03	Total	Zero Assets	Under 500	500 to 1,000	1,000 to 5,000	5,000 to 10,000	10,000 to 25,000	25,000 to 50,000	50,000 to 100,000	100,000 to 250,000	250,000 to 500,000	500,000 to 2,500,000	2,500,000 and over
Number of Enterprises **1**	2070	0	1121	273	427	88	60	27	19	18	11	13	0
Revenues ($ in Thousands)													
Net Sales **2**	217334108	0	2071300	314299	2558159	1667128	2964427	2065426	3854460	6836255	10496247	15255639	0
Interest **3**	606675	0	390	2958	1871	1413	1617	4467	5148	10106	18260	96771	0
Rents **4**	358280	0	0	54	808	0	95	819	528	605	423	6383	0
Royalties **5**	1110767	0	747	0	0	731	0	15800	4562	22352	211654	303795	0
Other Portfolio Income **6**	1050609	0	2	4649	2283	11	347	319	20603	12384	4837	53833	0
Other Receipts **7**	3258375	0	22484	371	7503	12186	20810	52018	104378	43426	108262	457136	0
Total Receipts **8**	223718814	0	2094923	322331	2570624	1681469	2987296	2138849	3989679	6925128	10839683	16173557	0
Average Total Receipts **9**	108077	·	1869	1181	6020	19108	49788	79217	209983	384729	985426	1244120	·
Operating Costs/Operating Income (%)													
Cost of Operations **10**	84.5	·	81.9	25.7	70.0	60.2	77.3	70.3	87.6	78.3	83.7	38.8	·
Salaries and Wages **11**	4.2	·	2.7	16.8	7.1	13.1	6.3	8.4	3.9	8.6	4.1	9.2	·
Taxes Paid **12**	0.4	·	0.4	1.8	1.3	1.6	0.9	0.9	0.4	0.9	0.4	1.2	·
Interest Paid **13**	0.6	·	0.2	0.2	0.7	0.9	0.5	0.7	0.3	0.8	0.3	1.7	·
Depreciation **14**	0.6	·	0.2	0.8	0.4	1.2	0.6	0.9	0.4	0.6	0.6	1.4	·
Amortization and Depletion **15**	0.4	·	·	0.0	0.0	0.0	0.2	0.2	0.2	0.4	0.5	0.9	·
Pensions and Other Deferred Comp. **16**	0.1	·	0.3	0.7	0.2	0.4	0.2	0.3	0.1	0.2	0.2	0.3	·
Employee Benefits **17**	0.5	·	0.3	0.5	0.3	0.3	0.4	0.7	0.3	0.4	0.5	0.8	·
Advertising **18**	1.0	·	0.8	0.8	1.3	1.9	1.1	3.0	1.5	0.3	0.9	2.9	·
Other Expenses **19**	6.2	·	7.4	42.1	8.1	13.3	8.0	12.1	4.9	6.6	7.5	27.3	·
Officers' Compensation **20**	0.3	·	2.5	8.0	2.8	1.8	1.8	0.9	0.6	0.5	0.4	0.6	·
Operating Margin **21**	1.5	·	3.4	2.8	7.9	5.2	2.7	1.6	·	2.6	1.0	14.8	·
Operating Margin Before Officers' Comp. **22**	1.7	·	5.9	10.8	10.6	7.0	4.5	2.5	0.4	3.1	1.3	15.5	·

Selected Average Balance Sheet ($ in Thousands)

Net Receivables 23	12351	64	128	727	2396	5178	9059	25097	36671	81245	168370
Inventories 24	11978	20	45	674	3101	4920	8474	18191	36611	96911	117499
Net Property, Plant and Equipment 25	3186	5	100	82	654	1425	3824	4055	13451	33526	128858
Total Assets 26	53051	153	737	2176	7505	15449	35345	68137	158126	375672	1068219
Notes and Loans Payable 27	9616	255	105	521	2319	4762	8454	11253	48634	35596	349399
All Other Liabilities 28	24374	188	459	785	2674	5365	13303	29586	57673	150899	352457
Net Worth 29	19061	-290	173	870	2512	5322	13588	27298	51818	189177	366363

Selected Financial Ratios (Times to 1)

Current Ratio 30	1.3	0.6	1.0	2.4	1.4	1.6	1.4	1.4	1.3	1.5	1.2
Quick Ratio 31	0.7	0.4	0.5	1.4	0.7	0.9	0.8	0.8	0.7	0.8	0.7
Net Sales to Working Capital 32	13.3			5.1	10.9	10.9	10.3	13.7	16.2	11.4	10.5
Coverage Ratio 33	8.9	22.9	32.8	13.4	7.5	8.1	8.7	12.6	6.2	14.0	13.6
Total Asset Turnover 34	2.0	12.1	1.6	2.8	2.5	3.2	2.2	3.0	2.4	2.5	1.1
Inventory Turnover 35	7.4	76.5	6.6	6.2	3.7	7.8	6.3	9.8	8.1	8.2	3.9
Receivables Turnover 36											
Total Liabilities to Net Worth 37	1.8		3.3	1.5	2.0	1.9	1.6	1.5	2.1	1.0	1.9
Current Assets to Working Capital 38	4.0			1.7	3.7	2.7	3.2	3.6	3.9	2.8	5.3
Current Liabilities to Working Capital 39	3.0			0.7	2.7	1.7	2.2	2.6	2.9	1.8	4.3
Working Capital to Net Sales 40	0.1		0.2	0.1	0.1	0.1	0.1	0.1	0.1	0.1	0.1
Inventory to Working Capital 41	1.5			0.6	1.8	1.1	1.1	1.2	1.6	1.2	1.0
Total Receipts to Cash Flow 42	10.1	9.3	2.4	6.8	5.8	9.6	6.2	12.8	10.2	9.1	2.1
Cost of Goods to Cash Flow 43	8.5	7.6	0.6	4.7	3.5	7.4	4.3	11.2	8.0	7.6	0.8
Cash Flow to Total Debt 44	0.3	0.4	0.9	0.7	0.7	0.5	0.6	0.4	0.1	0.6	0.8

Selected Financial Factors (in Percentages)

Debt Ratio 45	64.1	289.3	76.5	60.0	66.5	65.5	61.6	59.9	67.2	49.6	65.7
Return on Total Assets 46	10.1	56.9	8.7	24.8	17.5	12.8	12.7	12.3	11.2	11.6	24.9
Return on Equity Before Income Taxes 47	25.0		35.7	57.4	45.4	32.6	29.2	28.3	28.8	21.4	67.4
Return on Equity After Income Taxes 48	17.8		32.0	52.4	39.2	29.5	22.7	22.9	24.2	14.9	44.6
Profit Margin (Before Income Tax) 49	4.5	4.5	5.4	8.3	6.0	3.5	5.2	3.8	3.9	4.2	21.0
Profit Margin (After Income Tax) 50	3.2	4.5	4.8	7.6	5.2	3.2	4.0	3.1	3.3	2.9	13.9

Table I

Corporations with and without Net Income

APPAREL, PIECE GOODS, AND NOTIONS

MONEY AMOUNTS AND SIZE OF ASSETS IN THOUSANDS OF DOLLARS

Item Description for Accounting Period 7/02 Through 6/03		Total	Zero Assets	Under 500	500 to 1,000	1,000 to 5,000	5,000 to 10,000	10,000 to 25,000	25,000 to 50,000	50,000 to 100,000	100,000 to 250,000	250,000 to 500,000	500,000 to 2,500,000	2,500,000 and over
Number of Enterprises	1	24510	3004	17055	1221	2425	369	270	79	45	24	9	8	0
Revenues ($ in Thousands)														
Net Sales	2	82108885	1197826	10753233	1903602	14085366	6543693	10650170	6054459	5782694	5737408	5786781	13613653	0
Interest	3	184077	1510	3075	4290	4170	3396	5088	4001	6371	8805	30675	112696	0
Rents	4	39797	9	3804	981	4649	1623	1777	2111	8368	4273	5044	7156	0
Royalties	5	722891	202	1121	0	0	1890	7478	3276	14567	30145	47508	616705	0
Other Portfolio Income	6	379051	1332	4305	5	3563	3515	6819	1683	4653	21323	253	331601	0
Other Receipts	7	844744	37317	155901	2041	149141	84191	137749	41119	62181	19610	-125929	281425	0
Total Receipts	8	84279445	1238196	10921439	1910919	14246889	6638308	10809081	6106649	5878834	5821564	5744332	14963236	0
Average Total Receipts	9	3439	412	640	1565	5875	17990	40034	77299	130641	242565	638259	1870404	·
Operating Costs/Operating Income (%)														
Cost of Operations	10	69.3	72.8	67.2	77.1	71.1	73.1	74.3	71.8	69.9	63.5	78.6	59.0	·
Salaries and Wages	11	8.3	5.6	6.4	4.8	9.2	8.4	7.5	7.3	8.5	9.2	6.7	10.8	·
Taxes Paid	12	2.2	3.1	1.3	1.3	2.7	2.5	2.4	2.3	2.3	2.2	1.2	2.3	·
Interest Paid	13	1.2	0.9	0.3	0.9	0.9	0.9	0.9	1.0	1.2	1.6	1.6	2.4	·
Depreciation	14	1.1	0.9	0.8	0.4	0.4	0.6	0.5	0.6	1.3	1.6	1.2	2.9	·
Amortization and Depletion	15	0.2	0.1	0.2	0.3	0.1	0.0	0.1	0.2	0.2	0.6	0.4	0.4	·
Pensions and Other Deferred Comp.	16	0.2	0.5	0.4	·	0.2	0.2	0.2	0.2	0.2	0.2	0.1	0.2	·
Employee Benefits	17	0.4	0.3	0.3	0.3	0.3	0.4	0.5	0.4	0.7	0.9	0.4	0.3	·
Advertising	18	1.8	0.8	1.6	1.1	0.6	1.3	0.8	1.3	1.9	2.6	2.0	4.3	·
Other Expenses	19	12.2	24.7	16.1	14.3	10.8	9.1	8.7	9.0	10.6	11.5	8.7	17.2	·
Officers' Compensation	20	2.5	1.0	6.5	2.5	3.2	2.1	2.4	2.3	1.0	1.6	0.7	1.0	·
Operating Margin	21	0.6	·	·	·	0.5	1.4	1.7	3.5	2.1	4.5	·	·	·
Operating Margin Before Officers' Comp.	22	3.1	·	5.5	·	3.8	3.5	4.1	5.8	3.1	6.1	·	0.2	·

Selected Average Balance Sheet ($ in Thousands)

Item													
Net Receivables 23	405	0	25	231	697	1836	4709	10513	17547	38188	72301	299664	•
Inventories 24	415	0	40	190	602	2927	5474	11571	22095	37561	66148	227542	•
Net Property, Plant and Equipment 25	195	0	14	26	123	473	939	2434	8519	18452	42778	298249	•
Total Assets 26	1734	0	126	705	2005	7085	15272	33961	72094	142172	334976	1942441	•
Notes and Loans Payable 27	473	0	53	362	647	1460	4978	11247	23978	41042	168808	291615	•
All Other Liabilities 28	562	0	53	230	978	2935	5139	11356	15890	37038	81002	565023	•
Net Worth 29	699	0	21	113	380	2690	5155	11358	32227	64091	85165	1085803	•

Selected Financial Ratios (Times to 1)

Item													
Current Ratio 30	1.7	•	1.5	1.5	1.7	1.6	1.6	1.9	2.3	1.5	2.0		•
Quick Ratio 31	0.9	•	0.8	1.0	0.7	0.8	0.7	0.9	1.3	0.7	1.1		•
Net Sales to Working Capital 32	7.0	•	19.2	7.8	9.7	6.8	7.8	7.5	5.0	4.0	9.0	4.4	•
Coverage Ratio 33	4.0	•	2.9	•	3.0	4.0	4.6	5.2	4.3	4.7	•	5.7	•
Total Asset Turnover 34	1.9	•	5.0	2.2	2.9	2.5	2.6	2.3	1.8	1.7	1.9	0.9	•
Inventory Turnover 35	5.6	•	10.6	6.3	6.9	4.4	5.4	4.8	4.1	4.0	7.6	4.4	•
Receivables Turnover 36	•	•	•	•	•	•	•	•	•	•	•	•	•
Total Liabilities to Net Worth 37	1.5	•	5.0	5.2	4.3	1.6	2.0	2.0	1.2	1.2	2.9	0.8	•
Current Assets to Working Capital 38	2.4	•	3.1	2.9	3.0	2.4	2.6	2.7	2.1	1.8	3.0	2.0	•
Current Liabilities to Working Capital 39	1.4	•	2.1	1.9	2.0	1.4	1.6	1.7	1.1	0.8	2.0	1.0	•
Working Capital to Net Sales 40	0.1	•	0.1	0.1	0.1	0.1	0.1	0.1	0.2	0.2	0.1	0.2	•
Inventory to Working Capital 41	0.9	•	1.2	1.0	1.0	1.1	1.1	1.1	0.9	0.6	0.9	0.6	•
Total Receipts to Cash Flow 42	7.9	7.0	8.4	11.4	9.8	9.8	9.8	8.7	8.5	6.9	25.7	4.3	•
Cost of Goods to Cash Flow 43	5.5	5.1	5.6	8.8	7.0	7.2	7.3	6.2	6.0	4.4	20.2	2.6	•
Cash Flow to Total Debt 44	0.4	•	0.7	0.2	0.4	0.4	0.4	0.4	0.4	0.4	0.1	0.5	•

Selected Financial Factors (in Percentages)

Item													
Debt Ratio 45	59.7	•	83.5	84.0	81.0	62.0	66.2	66.6	55.3	54.9	74.6	44.1	•
Return on Total Assets 46	9.2	•	4.4	•	7.4	9.5	10.4	12.3	8.9	12.7	•	12.1	•
Return on Equity Before Income Taxes 47	17.1	•	17.5	•	25.7	18.9	24.3	29.6	15.2	22.1	•	17.9	•
Return on Equity After Income Taxes 48	12.2	•	15.9	22.3	22.3	17.5	22.7	27.4	11.0	16.3	•	11.6	•
Profit Margin (Before Income Tax) 49	3.6	•	0.6	1.7	1.7	2.9	3.2	4.4	3.8	5.9	•	11.4	•
Profit Margin (After Income Tax) 50	2.5	•	0.5	1.5	1.5	2.7	3.0	4.1	2.7	4.4	•	7.4	•

187

Table II

Corporations with Net Income

APPAREL, PIECE GOODS, AND NOTIONS

MONEY AMOUNTS AND SIZE OF ASSETS IN THOUSANDS OF DOLLARS

Item Description for Accounting Period 7/02 Through 6/03	Total	Zero Assets	Under 500	500 to 1,000	1,000 to 5,000	5,000 to 10,000	10,000 to 25,000	25,000 to 50,000	50,000 to 100,000	100,000 to 250,000	250,000 to 500,000	500,000 to 2,500,000	2,500,000 and over
Number of Enterprises **1**	12283	1387	7919	0	1583	282	216	62	31	18	5	0	0
Revenues ($ in Thousands)													
Net Sales **2**	61349351	375809	6957960	0	10766955	5630368	9051309	4994691	4185048	4590428	2327192	0	0
Interest **3**	87752	1244	792	0	2110	1682	3610	2818	5012	6668	7342	0	0
Rents **4**	25512	0	3804	0	1241	1623	1010	308	8147	1162	3924	0	0
Royalties **5**	567599	0	0	0	0	1890	2010	1704	13911	26487	46173	0	0
Other Portfolio Income **6**	370132	6	3344	0	264	3434	4411	1388	4149	21323	253	0	0
Other Receipts **7**	727865	58013	141275	0	58607	25690	97784	35782	64587	13661	12366	0	0
Total Receipts **8**	63128211	435072	7107175	0	10829177	5664687	9160134	5036691	4280854	4659729	2397250	0	0
Average Total Receipts **9**	5139	314	897	•	6841	20088	42408	81237	138092	258874	479450		•
Operating Costs/Operating Income (%)													
Cost of Operations **10**	67.0	52.6	66.0	•	69.4	73.6	73.7	71.5	67.4	61.3	61.5	•	•
Salaries and Wages **11**	8.4	9.7	5.0	•	9.1	7.0	7.2	6.7	8.6	9.5	10.4	•	•
Taxes Paid **12**	2.3	1.7	1.2	•	3.0	2.5	2.5	2.5	2.5	2.4	2.1	•	•
Interest Paid **13**	0.9	0.9	0.2	•	0.6	0.8	0.8	0.9	1.1	1.4	1.7	•	•
Depreciation **14**	1.1	1.5	0.8	•	0.3	0.4	0.4	0.5	1.2	1.2	2.0	•	•
Amortization and Depletion **15**	0.1	0.0	0.0	•	0.1	0.0	0.0	0.2	0.2	0.5	0.7	•	•
Pensions and Other Deferred Comp. **16**	0.3	1.5	0.7	•	0.2	0.2	0.2	0.2	0.3	0.3	0.2	•	•
Employee Benefits **17**	0.4	0.4	0.3	•	0.3	0.4	0.4	0.4	0.8	0.8	0.6	•	•
Advertising **18**	2.0	0.3	2.4	•	0.3	1.3	0.6	1.2	2.2	2.3	4.2	•	•
Other Expenses **19**	11.1	17.8	14.0	•	9.2	7.7	7.8	8.2	10.2	11.3	12.5	•	•
Officers' Compensation **20**	2.7	2.7	7.8	•	3.5	2.0	2.6	2.5	1.1	1.8	1.6	•	•
Operating Margin **21**	3.7	11.0	1.7	•	4.0	4.2	3.7	5.4	4.4	7.2	2.6	•	•
Operating Margin Before Officers' Comp. **22**	6.4	13.6	9.5	•	7.6	6.1	6.3	7.9	5.5	9.0	4.2	•	•

Selected Average Balance Sheet ($ in Thousands)

Net Receivables 23	573	0	41	•	740	1327	4822	10511	19397	41836	73110	•
Inventories 24	636	0	58	•	580	3306	5781	11270	22323	37892	82866	•
Net Property, Plant and Equipment 25	283	0	21	•	121	487	860	1914	8891	13668	46795	•
Total Assets 26	2569	0	184	•	2064	7054	15421	33525	73522	146034	350630	•
Notes and Loans Payable 27	567	0	40	•	550	1028	4574	10033	25023	42016	108819	•
All Other Liabilities 28	688	0	66	•	852	3116	4805	11099	15871	32999	74083	•
Net Worth 29	1314	0	78	•	662	2910	6042	12394	32628	71019	167729	•

Selected Financial Ratios (Times to 1)

Current Ratio 30	2.1	•	2.0	•	1.9	1.7	1.8	1.6	2.0	2.9	2.7	•
Quick Ratio 31	1.0	•	1.2	•	1.1	0.6	0.8	0.8	1.0	1.7	1.3	•
Net Sales to Working Capital 32	5.7	•	11.7	•	7.9	8.1	7.1	7.4	4.7	3.5	3.1	•
Coverage Ratio 33	9.0	30.5	19.4	•	9.2	7.1	7.4	8.3	7.1	7.0	4.4	•
Total Asset Turnover 34	1.9	•	4.8	•	3.3	2.8	2.7	2.4	1.8	1.7	1.3	•
Inventory Turnover 35	5.3	•	10.1	•	8.1	4.4	5.3	5.1	4.1	4.1	3.5	•
Receivables Turnover 36	•	•	•	•	•	•	•	•	•	•	•	•
Total Liabilities to Net Worth 37	1.0	•	1.4	•	2.1	1.4	1.6	1.7	1.3	1.1	1.1	•
Current Assets to Working Capital 38	1.9	•	2.0	•	2.1	2.4	2.3	2.6	2.0	1.5	1.6	•
Current Liabilities to Working Capital 39	0.9	•	1.0	•	1.1	1.4	1.3	1.6	1.0	0.5	0.6	•
Working Capital to Net Sales 40	0.2	•	0.1	•	0.1	0.1	0.1	0.1	0.2	0.3	0.3	•
Inventory to Working Capital 41	0.7	•	0.8	•	0.7	1.3	1.0	1.0	0.8	0.5	0.5	•
Total Receipts to Cash Flow 42	6.5	2.4	7.1	•	8.4	9.0	8.8	7.7	7.0	5.8	6.7	•
Cost of Goods to Cash Flow 43	4.4	1.3	4.7	•	5.8	6.6	6.5	5.5	4.7	3.5	4.1	•
Cash Flow to Total Debt 44	0.6	•	1.2	•	0.6	0.5	0.5	0.5	0.5	0.6	0.4	•

Selected Financial Factors (in Percentages)

Debt Ratio 45	48.9	•	57.8	•	67.9	58.7	60.8	63.0	55.6	51.4	52.2	•
Return on Total Assets 46	15.4	•	19.5	•	17.0	15.6	15.4	17.1	14.5	17.6	9.9	•
Return on Equity Before Income Taxes 47	26.8	•	43.8	•	47.1	32.6	34.0	40.8	28.0	31.0	16.1	•
Return on Equity After Income Taxes 48	21.5	•	42.9	•	44.1	30.9	32.3	38.1	21.8	24.1	10.6	•
Profit Margin (Before Income Tax) 49	7.1	26.7	3.9	•	4.6	4.7	4.9	6.3	6.8	8.6	5.8	•
Profit Margin (After Income Tax) 50	5.7	24.5	3.8	•	4.3	4.5	4.7	5.9	5.3	6.7	3.8	•

GROCERY AND RELATED PRODUCT

Table I
Corporations with and without Net Income

MONEY AMOUNTS AND SIZE OF ASSETS IN THOUSANDS OF DOLLARS

Item Description for Accounting Period 7/02 Through 6/03	Total	Zero Assets	Under 500	500 to 1,000	1,000 to 5,000	5,000 to 10,000	10,000 to 25,000	25,000 to 50,000	50,000 to 100,000	100,000 to 250,000	250,000 to 500,000	500,000 to 2,500,000	2,500,000 and over
Number of Enterprises **1**	34003	1440	23294	3154	4625	755	451	145	68	36	14	17	3
Revenues ($ in Thousands)													
Net Sales **2**	336368112	2767457	18934659	13810642	52799433	23275938	28530707	20334994	18827453	22604374	19005755	52211491	63265211
Interest **3**	593269	4278	7039	2688	21425	9871	10716	26136	5153	23502	36625	195900	249936
Rents **4**	370891	17462	2822	6511	18559	8009	10724	6318	3480	28792	22609	109132	136471
Royalties **5**	738164	0	0	0	17085	371	2188	1263	221	1540	197	15302	699998
Other Portfolio Income **6**	221097	15660	14753	3833	21456	12910	14885	10791	3572	8923	15538	42720	56056
Other Receipts **7**	3960132	109579	172924	16861	235949	166877	160578	217053	140362	237921	172202	1240427	1089398
Total Receipts **8**	342251665	2914436	19132197	13840535	53113907	23473976	28729798	20596555	18980241	22905052	19252926	53814972	65497070
Average Total Receipts **9**	10065	2024	821	4388	11484	31091	63702	142045	279121	636251	1375209	3165587	21832357
Operating Costs/Operating Income (%)													
Cost of Operations **10**	85.1	83.6	76.6	82.7	83.8	86.4	85.2	85.0	89.1	87.0	82.3	86.2	86.7
Salaries and Wages **11**	5.2	7.3	5.5	4.6	4.4	4.3	5.1	5.7	3.7	4.5	7.1	5.2	6.0
Taxes Paid **12**	0.8	1.0	1.2	1.2	0.8	0.8	0.8	0.8	0.6	1.2	0.8	0.7	0.8
Interest Paid **13**	0.6	0.5	0.4	0.2	0.3	0.3	0.4	0.5	0.4	0.5	0.8	0.8	1.2
Depreciation **14**	0.9	0.9	1.0	0.9	0.7	0.6	0.8	0.8	0.7	0.7	1.5	0.8	1.1
Amortization and Depletion **15**	0.1	0.1	0.1	0.2	0.0	0.0	0.0	0.1	0.1	0.1	0.2	0.2	0.2
Pensions and Other Deferred Comp. **16**	0.2	0.2	0.1	0.2	0.2	0.1	0.2	0.2	0.1	0.2	0.2	0.3	0.4
Employee Benefits **17**	0.6	1.1	0.5	0.6	0.4	0.4	0.5	0.5	0.3	0.5	0.3	0.7	0.7
Advertising **18**	0.4	0.4	0.3	0.2	0.2	0.3	0.4	0.5	0.7	0.6	0.4	0.7	0.1
Other Expenses **19**	6.1	9.2	9.2	6.0	6.4	5.0	4.6	5.4	3.7	4.9	6.0	7.2	6.2
Officers' Compensation **20**	1.0	0.5	4.1	2.5	2.2	1.2	1.0	0.6	0.6	0.4	0.3	0.2	0.1
Operating Margin **21**	*	*	1.0	0.7	0.5	0.6	1.0	*	0.1	*	*	*	*
Operating Margin Before Officers' Comp. **22**	0.0	*	5.1	3.1	2.7	1.7	2.0	0.5	0.7	*	*	*	*

Selected Average Balance Sheet ($ in Thousands)

Net Receivables 23	586	0	26	217	819	2655	4972	10187	21564	37375	76486	157461	849369
Inventories 24	513	0	27	141	481	1664	3887	8700	18232	41635	65947	176725	1076730
Net Property, Plant and Equipment 25	487	0	34	130	342	879	2789	6089	11951	30897	123552	167993	1489765
Total Assets 26	2313		142	710	2244	6933	15120	34454	69384	151128	371428	980783	4548701
Notes and Loans Payable 27	759	0	74	170	604	1689	4687	11099	20837	55070	114039	315710	1803039
All Other Liabilities 28	878	0	40	191	911	2725	5127	11576	28513	54357	141714	368684	1972343
Net Worth 29	675		28	348	728	2518	5306	11778	20034	41702	115674	296389	773319

Selected Financial Ratios (Times to 1)

Current Ratio 30	1.4	•	1.7	2.3	1.5	1.6	1.5	1.4	1.6	1.3	0.9		
Quick Ratio 31	0.7	•	1.1	1.5	1.0	1.0	0.9	0.8	0.8	0.7	0.4		
Net Sales to Working Capital 32	25.5	•	22.5	15.6	21.1	15.1	17.4	14.8	21.3	18.7	34.4	22.6	
Coverage Ratio 33	2.3	2.4	6.2	5.6	4.6	5.3	5.0	3.7	3.7	2.7	1.9	0.9	
Total Asset Turnover 34	4.3	•	5.7	6.2	5.1	4.4	4.2	4.1	4.0	4.2	3.7	3.1	4.6
Inventory Turnover 35	16.4	•	23.3	25.8	19.9	16.0	13.9	13.7	13.5	13.1	16.9	15.0	17.0
Receivables Turnover 36	•	•	•	•	•	•	•	•	•	•	•	•	•
Total Liabilities to Net Worth 37	2.4	•	4.1	1.0	2.1	1.8	1.8	1.9	2.5	2.6	2.2	2.3	4.9
Current Assets to Working Capital 38	3.7	•	2.4	1.8	3.1	2.7	3.0	2.6	3.7	2.8	4.3	3.6	
Current Liabilities to Working Capital 39	2.7	•	1.4	0.8	2.1	1.7	2.0	1.6	2.7	1.8	3.3	2.6	
Working Capital to Net Sales 40	0.0	•	0.0	0.1	0.0	0.1	0.1	0.1	0.0	0.1	0.0	0.0	
Inventory to Working Capital 41	1.3	•	0.7	0.5	0.9	0.8	1.1	0.9	1.4	1.2	1.7	1.3	
Total Receipts to Cash Flow 42	18.3	13.0	11.6	19.0	17.3	19.7	19.5	18.2	26.1	22.0	18.8	17.2	20.0
Cost of Goods to Cash Flow 43	15.6	10.9	8.8	15.7	14.5	17.0	16.6	15.5	23.2	19.1	15.4	14.8	17.4
Cash Flow to Total Debt 44	0.3	•	0.6	0.6	0.4	0.4	0.3	0.3	0.2	0.3	0.3	0.3	0.3

Selected Financial Factors (in Percentages)

Debt Ratio 45	70.8	•	80.3	50.9	67.5	63.7	64.9	65.8	71.1	72.4	68.9	69.8	83.0
Return on Total Assets 46	5.9	•	13.8	6.5	7.0	7.9	8.8	6.9	5.3	5.2	5.7	2.6	4.9
Return on Equity Before Income Taxes 47	11.4	•	58.9	10.9	16.9	17.6	20.1	14.6	13.3	11.8	8.8	0.5	
Return on Equity After Income Taxes 48	9.4	•	57.3	10.3	15.2	15.2	18.3	11.8	11.5	9.2	6.5	•	
Profit Margin (Before Income Tax) 49	0.8	0.6	2.0	0.9	1.1	1.4	1.7	1.2	1.0	0.8	0.7	0.1	
Profit Margin (After Income Tax) 50	0.6	0.3	2.0	0.8	1.0	1.2	1.5	1.0	0.8	0.6	•		

189

Table II

Corporations with Net Income

GROCERY AND RELATED PRODUCT

MONEY AMOUNTS AND SIZE OF ASSETS IN THOUSANDS OF DOLLARS

Item Description for Accounting Period 7/02 Through 6/03	Total	Zero Assets	Under 500	500 to 1,000	1,000 to 5,000	5,000 to 10,000	10,000 to 25,000	25,000 to 50,000	50,000 to 100,000	100,000 to 250,000	250,000 to 500,000	500,000 to 2,500,000	2,500,000 and over
Number of Enterprises **1**	20940	699	13100	2523	3443	0	367	117	54	28	0	11	0
Revenues ($ in Thousands)													
Net Sales **2**	228187435	674858	12819468	11374455	41850224	0	24567459	17278550	14818492	18926407	0	49601393	0
Interest **3**	186078	1694	3884	2127	13572	0	8689	14354	3618	16247	0	101211	0
Rents **4**	175827	511	1755	5217	17091	0	8832	5428	3363	14601	0	97862	0
Royalties **5**	45980	0	0	0	17085	0	2186	1263	221	841	0	24380	0
Other Portfolio Income **6**	107046	13858	13804	3240	11501	0	14015	4329	1698	6577	0	11118	0
Other Receipts **7**	2884144	23341	109739	7045	208235	0	141005	155263	112996	203858	0	1614333	0
Total Receipts **8**	231586510	714262	12948650	11392084	42117708	0	24742186	17459187	14940388	19168531	0	51450297	0
Average Total Receipts **9**	11060	1022	988	4515	12233	•	67417	149224	276674	684590	•	4677300	•
Operating Costs/Operating Income (%)													
Cost of Operations **10**	85.1	83.6	76.6	83.3	83.3	•	85.0	85.4	88.5	87.5	•	88.1	•
Salaries and Wages **11**	4.9	5.2	4.7	4.3	4.3	•	5.0	5.3	3.7	4.7	•	5.2	•
Taxes Paid **12**	0.8	0.9	1.1	1.1	0.8	•	0.8	0.8	0.6	0.6	•	0.7	•
Interest Paid **13**	0.4	0.3	0.3	0.2	0.3	•	0.4	0.4	0.3	0.5	•	0.8	•
Depreciation **14**	0.8	0.6	0.9	0.7	0.7	•	0.7	0.7	0.7	0.6	•	1.0	•
Amortization and Depletion **15**	0.1	0.1	0.2	0.2	0.0	•	0.0	0.1	0.1	0.1	•	0.2	•
Pensions and Other Deferred Comp. **16**	0.2	0.1	0.2	0.1	0.2	•	0.2	0.2	0.1	0.1	•	0.3	•
Employee Benefits **17**	0.5	0.6	0.5	0.6	0.3	•	0.5	0.5	0.3	0.5	•	0.9	•
Advertising **18**	0.4	0.0	0.2	0.2	0.2	•	0.4	0.5	0.8	0.6	•	0.5	•
Other Expenses **19**	5.3	5.0	7.5	5.5	6.2	•	4.4	4.7	3.7	4.6	•	4.9	•
Officers' Compensation **20**	1.2	1.0	4.1	2.4	2.4	•	1.0	0.6	0.6	0.4	•	0.1	•
Operating Margin **21**	0.2	2.6	3.9	1.3	1.2	•	1.5	0.7	0.7	•	•	•	•
Operating Margin Before Officers' Comp. **22**	1.4	3.5	8.0	3.7	3.6	•	2.5	1.4	1.3	0.1	•	•	•

Selected Average Balance Sheet ($ in Thousands)

Net Receivables 23	617	0	27	231	867	•	5180	10369	20790	39045	•	110312
Inventories 24	570	0	20	140	471	•	3884	8996	20129	45303	•	275851
Net Property, Plant and Equipment 25	520	0	37	111	334	•	2611	6046	10939	29750	•	356174
Total Assets 26	2505	0	151	715	2227	•	15255	34393	68481	155587	•	1344601
Notes and Loans Payable 27	757	0	58	171	534	•	4358	10920	19530	56350	•	450645
All Other Liabilities 28	885	0	36	192	854	•	5263	11067	27486	57550	•	461366
Net Worth 29	863	0	58	351	839	•	5634	12407	21464	41686	•	432590

Selected Financial Ratios (Times to 1)

Current Ratio 30	1.4	•	2.3	2.4	1.6	•	1.5	1.7	1.4	1.7	•	0.9
Quick Ratio 31	0.8	•	1.6	1.5	1.1	•	0.9	0.9	0.7	0.8	•	0.3
Net Sales to Working Capital 32	24.6	•	19.2	15.2	19.2	•	16.9	14.5	18.5	16.9	•	•
Coverage Ratio 33	4.9	25.1	17.5	8.8	8.2	•	6.6	5.3	5.8	3.3	•	2.2
Total Asset Turnover 34	4.4	•	6.5	6.3	5.5	•	4.4	4.3	4.0	4.3	•	3.4
Inventory Turnover 35	16.3	•	36.9	26.9	21.5	•	14.7	14.0	12.1	13.1	•	14.4
Receivables Turnover 36	•	•	•	•	•	•	•	•	•	•	•	•
Total Liabilities to Net Worth 37	1.9	•	1.6	1.0	1.7	•	1.7	1.8	2.2	2.7	•	2.1
Current Assets to Working Capital 38	3.4	•	1.8	1.7	2.6	•	2.8	2.5	3.4	2.5	•	•
Current Liabilities to Working Capital 39	2.4	•	0.8	0.7	1.6	•	1.8	1.5	2.4	1.5	•	•
Working Capital to Net Sales 40	0.0	•	0.1	0.1	0.1	•	0.1	0.1	0.1	0.1	•	•
Inventory to Working Capital 41	1.3	•	0.4	0.5	0.7	•	1.0	0.9	1.4	1.1	•	•
Total Receipts to Cash Flow 42	17.7	8.5	9.6	18.6	15.7	•	18.4	18.2	22.3	21.5	•	21.9
Cost of Goods to Cash Flow 43	15.1	7.1	7.4	15.5	13.1	•	15.7	15.5	19.7	18.8	•	19.2
Cash Flow to Total Debt 44	0.4	•	1.1	0.7	0.6	•	0.4	0.4	0.3	0.3	•	0.2

Selected Financial Factors (in Percentages)

Debt Ratio 45	65.6	•	61.8	50.9	62.3	•	63.1	63.9	68.7	73.2	•	67.8
Return on Total Assets 46	9.5	•	33.5	10.0	11.5	•	11.3	9.5	7.6	6.5	•	5.6
Return on Equity Before Income Taxes 47	21.8	•	82.8	18.1	26.8	•	26.1	21.3	20.0	17.0	•	9.5
Return on Equity After Income Taxes 48	19.3	•	81.4	17.3	24.7	•	24.0	18.0	18.0	13.7	•	6.7
Profit Margin (Before Income Tax) 49	1.7	8.4	4.9	1.4	1.8	•	2.2	1.8	1.6	1.0	•	0.9
Profit Margin (After Income Tax) 50	1.5	7.0	4.8	1.3	1.7	•	2.0	1.5	1.4	0.8	•	0.6

190

Table I

Corporations with and without Net Income

FARM PRODUCT RAW MATERIAL

MONEY AMOUNTS AND SIZE OF ASSETS IN THOUSANDS OF DOLLARS

Item Description for Accounting Period 7/02 Through 6/03	Total	Zero Assets	Under 500	500 to 1,000	1,000 to 5,000	5,000 to 10,000	10,000 to 25,000	25,000 to 50,000	50,000 to 100,000	100,000 to 250,000	250,000 to 500,000	500,000 to 2,500,000	2,500,000 and over
Number of Enterprises 1	6563	1308	2608	1033	1262	182	98	29	22	11	4	3	3
Revenues ($ in Thousands)													
Net Sales 2	88595516	738170	1436504	2902055	10057538	4548692	5039463	2481073	3841288	7833819	3003642	2326005	44387267
Interest 3	707265	4439	3763	2571	8458	4849	4461	5805	14753	11606	22052	3763	620746
Rents 4	104293	0	456	2696	6343	912	2552	989	4605	1731	1222	277	82511
Royalties 5	50443	38	0	84	0	126	4275	2891	180	7938	8458	2	26451
Other Portfolio Income 6	612001	10	16756	1942	15839	825	3886	5945	5494	2854	10368	132	547950
Other Receipts 7	1064835	600	7773	106775	158523	49950	67530	28270	31384	31774	24623	18380	539253
Total Receipts 8	91134353	743257	1465252	3016123	10246701	4605354	5122167	2524973	3897704	7889722	3070365	2348559	46204178
Average Total Receipts 9	13886	568	562	2920	8119	25304	52267	87068	177168	717247	767591	782853	15401393
Operating Costs/Operating Income (%)													
Cost of Operations 10	91.2	98.0	74.4	85.5	88.6	86.8	90.6	87.5	89.5	95.1	91.6	88.8	92.8
Salaries and Wages 11	2.5	0.3	0.9	3.3	3.6	3.8	3.2	3.6	1.9	1.6	3.3	4.1	2.0
Taxes Paid 12	0.6	0.2	0.5	0.8	0.7	0.6	1.0	0.7	0.5	0.2	0.5	0.4	0.7
Interest Paid 13	1.3	0.1	1.7	0.4	0.6	0.6	0.6	0.8	0.9	0.3	0.8	1.9	1.9
Depreciation 14	1.4	0.3	2.4	1.8	1.3	0.9	0.9	1.3	1.1	0.5	0.9	1.3	1.8
Amortization and Depletion 15	0.1	*	0.1	0.3	0.0	0.0	0.4	0.0	0.0	0.1	0.0	0.1	0.1
Pensions and Other Deferred Comp. 16	0.4	0.0	0.4	0.0	0.1	0.4	0.1	0.1	0.1	0.1	0.2	0.0	0.7
Employee Benefits 17	0.2	0.2	0.2	0.2	0.3	0.2	0.3	0.3	0.3	0.3	0.6	1.0	0.1
Advertising 18	0.1	0.4	0.8	0.2	0.2	0.2	0.2	0.1	0.1	0.1	0.1	0.0	0.1
Other Expenses 19	3.8	2.1	15.0	7.9	4.8	4.9	4.0	4.8	4.6	1.8	3.6	2.6	3.1
Officers' Compensation 20	0.7	0.4	3.5	1.8	1.3	1.3	0.7	0.6	0.5	0.3	0.1	0.4	0.4
Operating Margin 21	*	*	0.2	*	*	0.3	*	*	0.4	*	*	*	*
Operating Margin Before Officers' Comp. 22	*	*	3.7	*	*	1.6	*	0.6	0.9	0.0	*	*	*

Selected Average Balance Sheet ($ in Thousands)

Net Receivables 23	2656	0	20	111	650	2454	5054	10212	17797	41111	131500	97899	4515476
Inventories 24	1261	0	3	79	448	2325	3454	8181	21745	50657	69970	251514	1516393
Net Property, Plant and Equipment 25	1071	0	38	241	655	1065	3145	6553	15087	26139	58308	70409	1366592
Total Assets 26	9381	0	109	739	2478	6710	15062	35796	73181	162470	353055	657008	15624802
Notes and Loans Payable 27	2589	0	87	288	916	2039	4876	10950	21267	56159	168314	407159	3721205
All Other Liabilities 28	3884	0	20	78	994	2649	5445	12147	23216	54274	128033	126127	6913603
Net Worth 29	2907	0	3	373	567	2023	4742	12698	28698	52037	56708	123722	4989994

Selected Financial Ratios (Times to 1)

Current Ratio 30	1.2	2.1	•	2.6	1.2	1.3	1.2	1.2	1.4	1.4	1.2	2.0	1.1
Quick Ratio 31	0.7	2.0	•	1.9	0.8	0.8	0.7	0.7	0.6	0.6	0.7	0.4	0.6
Net Sales to Working Capital 32	19.8	16.2	•	14.5	33.2	17.9	18.7	19.3	12.7	22.9	18.6	2.9	27.3
Coverage Ratio 33	1.6	2.3	•	5.0	1.7	3.7	0.6	3.2	3.1	2.5	1.6	1.2	1.4
Total Asset Turnover 34	1.4	5.0	•	3.8	3.2	3.7	3.4	2.4	2.4	4.4	2.1	1.2	0.9
Inventory Turnover 35	9.8	119.2	•	30.5	15.8	9.3	13.5	9.1	7.2	13.4	9.8	2.7	9.1
Receivables Turnover 36	•	•	•	•	•	•	•	•	•	•	•	•	•
Total Liabilities to Net Worth 37	2.2	37.6	•	1.0	3.4	2.3	2.2	1.8	1.6	2.1	5.2	4.3	2.1
Current Assets to Working Capital 38	7.4	1.9	•	1.6	6.6	3.8	3.9	5.2	3.5	3.5	5.9	2.0	14.1
Current Liabilities to Working Capital 39	6.4	0.9	•	0.6	5.6	2.8	2.9	4.2	2.5	2.5	4.9	1.0	13.1
Working Capital to Net Sales 40	0.1	0.1	•	0.1	0.0	0.1	0.1	0.1	0.1	0.0	0.1	0.3	0.0
Inventory to Working Capital 41	1.9	0.1	•	0.4	1.9	1.7	1.3	1.9	1.6	1.6	1.7	1.0	2.8
Total Receipts to Cash Flow 42	33.3	8.7	479.6	12.8	25.6	20.4	36.0	18.5	18.1	51.9	31.8	63.9	50.1
Cost of Goods to Cash Flow 43	30.3	6.4	469.9	11.0	22.6	17.7	32.6	16.2	16.2	49.3	29.1	56.7	46.5
Cash Flow to Total Debt 44	0.1	0.6	•	0.6	0.2	0.3	0.1	0.2	0.2	0.1	0.1	0.0	0.0

Selected Financial Factors (in Percentages)

Debt Ratio 45	69.0	97.4	•	49.5	77.1	69.9	68.5	64.5	60.8	68.0	83.9	81.2	68.1
Return on Total Assets 46	3.0	19.5	•	7.4	3.2	7.8	1.1	6.1	6.7	3.4	2.6	2.6	2.6
Return on Equity Before Income Taxes 47	3.7	427.4	•	11.7	5.6	18.9	•	11.8	11.6	6.3	5.9	1.9	2.5
Return on Equity After Income Taxes 48	2.5	331.9	•	10.5	4.9	16.2	•	8.7	8.4	4.4	4.7	1.3	1.5
Profit Margin (Before Income Tax) 49	0.8	2.2	•	1.6	0.4	1.5	•	1.8	1.9	0.5	0.4	0.3	0.8
Profit Margin (After Income Tax) 50	0.5	1.7	•	1.4	0.3	1.3	•	1.3	1.4	0.3	0.4	0.2	0.5

Table II

Corporations with Net Income

FARM PRODUCT RAW MATERIAL

MONEY AMOUNTS AND SIZE OF ASSETS IN THOUSANDS OF DOLLARS

Item Description for Accounting Period 7/02 Through 6/03	Total	Zero Assets	Under 500	500 to 1,000	1,000 to 5,000	5,000 to 10,000	10,000 to 25,000	25,000 to 50,000	50,000 to 100,000	100,000 to 250,000	250,000 to 500,000	500,000 to 2,500,000	2,500,000 and over
Number of Enterprises **1**	3503	101	1684	597	836	159	74	24	18	7	0	3	0
Revenues ($ in Thousands)													
Net Sales **2**	63627392	689520	1310923	1934027	8013582	4104993	4248585	2206814	2790543	5328202	0	33000204	0
Interest **3**	550614	4437	3723	1967	6433	4555	3227	5002	7878	22039	0	491353	0
Rents **4**	94165	0	456	157	3767	912	1966	930	4589	2583	0	78804	0
Royalties **5**	42106	0	0	0	0	1	4142	2891	163	8458	0	26451	0
Other Portfolio Income **6**	541412	10	16756	1879	7806	766	1269	4126	5489	9422	0	493888	0
Other Receipts **7**	747210	599	4050	45103	102639	46255	53803	27802	26534	35598	0	404827	0
Total Receipts **8**	65602899	694566	1335908	1983133	8134227	4157482	4312992	2247565	2835196	5406302	0	34495527	0
Average Total Receipts **9**	18728	6877	793	3322	9730	26148	58284	93649	157511	772329	•	11498509	•
Operating Costs/Operating Income (%)													
Cost of Operations **10**	90.5	96.3	73.5	86.2	88.4	86.8	90.1	87.7	87.6	92.9	•	92.3	•
Salaries and Wages **11**	2.5	0.2	0.6	2.6	3.4	3.6	3.1	3.6	2.2	2.4	•	2.1	•
Taxes Paid **12**	0.7	0.1	0.5	0.7	0.7	0.6	1.0	0.7	0.6	0.4	•	0.8	•
Interest Paid **13**	1.3	0.1	1.8	0.1	0.4	0.5	0.4	0.7	1.0	0.5	•	2.0	•
Depreciation **14**	1.6	0.3	2.5	1.1	1.0	0.9	0.8	1.3	1.5	0.7	•	2.1	•
Amortization and Depletion **15**	0.1	•	0.1	0.4	0.0	0.0	0.0	0.0	0.0	0.0	•	0.1	•
Pensions and Other Deferred Comp. **16**	0.5	0.0	0.4	0.0	0.1	0.4	0.1	0.1	0.1	0.2	•	0.8	•
Employee Benefits **17**	0.1	0.2	0.1	0.1	0.3	0.2	0.2	0.3	0.3	0.4	•	0.0	•
Advertising **18**	0.2	0.4	0.8	0.2	0.2	0.2	0.2	0.1	0.1	0.1	•	0.1	•
Other Expenses **19**	3.6	1.9	13.3	6.3	4.2	4.7	3.4	4.3	4.8	2.4	•	2.8	•
Officers' Compensation **20**	0.8	0.4	3.8	1.4	1.3	1.4	0.7	0.6	0.5	0.3	•	0.5	•
Operating Margin **21**	•	0.1	2.6	0.9	•	0.7	•	0.5	1.3	•	•	•	•
Operating Margin Before Officers' Comp. **22**	•	0.4	6.4	2.3	1.2	2.1	0.6	1.0	1.8	0.1	•	•	•

Selected Average Balance Sheet ($ in Thousands)

Net Receivables 23	4307	0	30	138	774	2449	5438	11015	15085	87475	•	4122372
Inventories 24	1376	0	5	20	408	2177	3478	7997	21739	51968	•	969542
Net Property, Plant and Equipment 25	1536	0	56	151	602	1003	2973	6850	18408	31896	•	1198084
Total Assets 26	13922	0	162	748	2680	6515	15226	37487	72867	220397	•	13297358
Notes and Loans Payable 27	3469	0	66	249	789	1781	4191	10584	20593	95921	•	3113651
All Other Liabilities 28	5420	0	27	56	1138	2613	5740	13157	21556	54331	•	5343805
Net Worth 29	5034	0	69	444	752	2121	5295	13746	30718	70146	•	4839901

Selected Financial Ratios (Times to 1)

Current Ratio 30	1.2	•	2.2	4.0	1.2	1.4	1.4	1.2	1.5	1.4	•	1.1
Quick Ratio 31	0.7	•	2.1	3.6	0.9	0.8	0.9	0.7	0.6	0.9	•	0.7
Net Sales to Working Capital 32	17.6	•	14.7	14.3	27.8	17.5	17.2	19.2	11.2	16.6	•	17.0
Coverage Ratio 33	2.2	11.2	3.5	37.8	4.3	5.2	4.7	4.2	4.0	3.4	•	1.6
Total Asset Turnover 34	1.3	•	4.8	4.3	3.6	4.0	3.8	2.5	2.1	3.5	•	0.8
Inventory Turnover 35	11.9	•	107.5	136.5	20.8	10.3	14.9	10.1	6.2	13.6	•	10.5
Receivables Turnover 36	•	•	•	•	•	•	•	•	•	•	•	•
Total Liabilities to Net Worth 37	1.8	•	1.3	0.7	2.6	2.1	1.9	1.7	1.4	2.1	•	1.7
Current Assets to Working Capital 38	7.0	•	1.8	1.3	5.2	3.5	3.3	5.0	3.2	3.5	•	10.0
Current Liabilities to Working Capital 39	6.0	•	0.8	0.3	4.2	2.5	2.3	4.0	2.2	2.5	•	9.0
Working Capital to Net Sales 40	0.1	•	0.1	0.1	0.0	0.1	0.1	0.1	0.1	0.1	•	0.1
Inventory to Working Capital 41	1.3	•	0.1	0.1	1.2	1.5	1.0	1.7	1.6	1.1	•	1.5
Total Receipts to Cash Flow 42	28.7	46.1	8.3	11.8	22.0	19.6	24.6	17.7	14.4	30.8	•	51.2
Cost of Goods to Cash Flow 43	25.9	44.4	6.1	10.2	19.5	17.0	22.2	15.5	12.6	28.6	•	47.2
Cash Flow to Total Debt 44	0.1	•	1.0	0.9	0.2	0.3	0.2	0.2	0.3	0.2	•	0.0

Selected Financial Factors (in Percentages)

Debt Ratio 45	63.8	•	57.4	40.7	71.9	67.4	65.2	63.3	57.8	68.2	•	63.6
Return on Total Assets 46	3.8	•	30.3	15.4	6.6	9.7	7.0	7.4	8.2	6.2	•	2.7
Return on Equity Before Income Taxes 47	5.8	•	50.6	25.2	18.0	24.0	15.8	15.3	14.6	13.9	•	3.0
Return on Equity After Income Taxes 48	4.5	•	44.6	23.4	17.2	21.0	13.5	11.9	10.9	11.1	•	2.0
Profit Margin (Before Income Tax) 49	1.6	0.8	4.5	3.5	1.4	2.0	1.5	2.3	2.9	1.3	•	1.3
Profit Margin (After Income Tax) 50	1.2	0.7	4.0	3.2	1.4	1.7	1.2	1.8	2.2	1.0	•	0.9

Table I

Corporations with and without Net Income

CHEMICAL AND ALLIED PRODUCTS

MONEY AMOUNTS AND SIZE OF ASSETS IN THOUSANDS OF DOLLARS

Item Description for Accounting Period 7/02 Through 6/03	Total	Zero Assets	Under 500	500 to 1,000	1,000 to 5,000	5,000 to 10,000	10,000 to 25,000	25,000 to 50,000	50,000 to 100,000	100,000 to 250,000	250,000 to 500,000	500,000 to 2,500,000	2,500,000 and over
Number of Enterprises **1**	10476	1497	6549	486	1400	290	152	50	24	11	7	9	0
Revenues ($ in Thousands)													
Net Sales **2**	52426603	669376	3136095	1506888	8249862	5829964	5391165	3798837	3004559	2386277	3796140	14657440	0
Interest **3**	104600	709	770	291	9104	6169	4048	2874	5933	13661	21675	39365	0
Rents **4**	35761	0	0	0	1933	381	1321	259	1378	5823	859	23806	0
Royalties **5**	104878	123	0	0	0	0	191	444	64	0	45307	58749	0
Other Portfolio Income **6**	127516	2170	1565	113	5825	8858	1903	2882	3809	5386	2006	92998	0
Other Receipts **7**	796534	21844	19602	226	45272	41803	91302	20343	123315	13539	94511	324781	0
Total Receipts **8**	53595892	694222	3158032	1507518	8311996	5887175	5489930	3825639	3139058	2424686	3960498	15197139	0
Average Total Receipts **9**	5116	464	482	3102	5937	20301	36118	76513	130794	220426	565785	1688571	•
Operating Costs/Operating Income (%)													
Cost of Operations **10**	74.3	76.3	73.7	66.7	72.1	81.7	77.7	81.4	83.5	80.3	84.1	64.9	•
Salaries and Wages **11**	6.9	3.2	4.9	10.9	10.2	4.5	7.3	5.0	5.3	5.6	3.7	7.8	•
Taxes Paid **12**	1.1	1.1	1.2	1.3	1.3	0.8	1.0	0.9	1.0	1.1	0.6	1.2	•
Interest Paid **13**	1.2	1.0	0.5	0.3	0.6	0.4	0.9	0.5	0.8	1.7	1.3	2.2	•
Depreciation **14**	1.9	0.6	0.7	1.1	1.2	0.8	1.4	1.1	1.7	2.3	1.1	3.7	•
Amortization and Depletion **15**	0.3	0.1	0.0	0.1	0.0	0.0	0.1	0.1	0.1	0.4	0.3	0.7	•
Pensions and Other Deferred Comp. **16**	0.5	0.0	0.3	0.3	0.6	0.3	0.3	0.3	0.3	0.3	0.1	0.8	•
Employee Benefits **17**	1.0	0.4	0.9	1.3	0.6	0.4	0.7	0.5	0.6	1.0	0.7	1.8	•
Advertising **18**	0.9	0.4	0.1	0.4	0.4	0.1	0.3	0.2	0.1	0.5	0.3	2.6	•
Other Expenses **19**	10.2	14.8	10.5	12.7	9.6	6.7	8.5	5.5	9.0	8.4	7.0	14.7	•
Officers' Compensation **20**	2.0	4.2	8.0	5.5	2.8	2.2	1.8	1.4	1.1	0.9	0.5	0.7	•
Operating Margin **21**	•	•	•	•	0.5	1.9	0.1	3.0	•	•	•	•	•
Operating Margin Before Officers' Comp. **22**	1.8	2.0	7.2	5.1	3.4	4.2	1.9	4.4	•	•	0.8	0.8	•

Selected Average Balance Sheet ($ in Thousands)

Net Receivables 23	646	0	24	360	721	2456	5225	11686	23350	37330	109815	177222	•
Inventories 24	483	0	18	164	443	2146	4102	8621	16037	29945	32341	180599	•
Net Property, Plant and Equipment 25	613	0	13	99	320	673	2389	4503	14189	33193	48875	445035	•
Total Assets 26	2934	0	99	832	2172	7078	15039	35411	70722	151925	363834	1625064	•
Notes and Loans Payable 27	920	0	59	240	653	1761	4777	9832	21384	50886	119494	508523	•
All Other Liabilities 28	1071	0	36	396	914	3343	5813	11953	24306	50087	88387	588896	•
Net Worth 29	944	0	3	196	604	1974	4448	13627	25032	50952	155954	527645	•

Selected Financial Ratios (Times to 1)

Current Ratio 30	1.3	•	1.1	1.5	1.5	1.4	1.5	1.5	1.5	1.2	1.5	1.1	•
Quick Ratio 31	0.8	•	0.7	1.1	1.0	0.8	0.9	0.9	0.9	0.6	1.0	0.6	•
Net Sales to Working Capital 32	14.2	•	109.0	13.3	10.5	11.7	9.4	9.0	8.4	19.6	10.8	34.5	•
Coverage Ratio 33	2.8	2.4	0.9	•	3.0	7.4	3.2	7.9	2.4	0.6	4.6	2.3	•
Total Asset Turnover 34	1.7	•	4.9	3.7	2.7	2.8	2.4	2.1	1.8	1.4	1.5	1.0	•
Inventory Turnover 35	7.7	•	19.2	12.6	9.6	7.7	6.7	7.2	6.5	5.8	14.1	5.9	•
Receivables Turnover 36	•	•	•	•	•	•	•	•	•	•	•	•	•
Total Liabilities to Net Worth 37	2.1	•	31.5	3.2	2.6	2.6	2.4	1.6	1.8	2.0	1.3	2.1	•
Current Assets to Working Capital 38	4.0	•	15.5	3.0	2.9	3.4	3.0	2.9	3.1	7.0	3.2	9.7	•
Current Liabilities to Working Capital 39	3.0	•	14.5	2.0	1.9	2.4	2.0	1.9	2.1	6.0	2.2	8.7	•
Working Capital to Net Sales 40	0.1	0.0	0.0	0.1	0.1	0.1	0.1	0.1	0.1	0.1	0.1	0.0	•
Inventory to Working Capital 41	1.4	•	4.2	0.7	0.8	1.2	1.1	1.0	1.1	2.7	0.6	3.8	•
Total Receipts to Cash Flow 42	9.9	7.0	12.9	9.4	11.1	12.5	11.5	12.6	11.3	16.9	9.7	7.2	•
Cost of Goods to Cash Flow 43	7.3	5.3	9.5	6.2	8.0	10.2	9.0	10.3	9.4	13.6	8.1	4.7	•
Cash Flow to Total Debt 44	0.3	0.4	0.5	0.3	0.3	0.3	0.3	0.3	0.2	0.1	0.3	0.2	•

Selected Financial Factors (in Percentages)

Debt Ratio 45	67.8	96.9	76.5	72.2	72.1	70.4	61.5	64.6	66.5	57.1	67.5		•
Return on Total Assets 46	5.7	2.2			9.5	5.2	6.6	9.1	3.4	1.5	8.9	5.1	•
Return on Equity Before Income Taxes 47	11.4				29.5	12.5	15.4	20.7	5.6	16.3	8.7		•
Return on Equity After Income Taxes 48	8.0				26.2	10.0	12.9	17.5	3.2	12.2	4.7		•
Profit Margin (Before Income Tax) 49	2.2	1.5			2.9	1.3	1.9	3.7	1.1	4.7	2.8		•
Profit Margin (After Income Tax) 50	1.5	1.3		1.0	2.6	1.0	1.6	3.1	0.6	3.5	1.5		•

Table II
Corporations with Net Income

CHEMICAL AND ALLIED PRODUCTS

MONEY AMOUNTS AND SIZE OF ASSETS IN THOUSANDS OF DOLLARS

Item Description for Accounting Period 7/02 Through 6/03	Total	Zero Assets	Under 500	500 to 1,000	1,000 to 5,000	5,000 to 10,000	10,000 to 25,000	25,000 to 50,000	50,000 to 100,000	100,000 to 250,000	250,000 to 500,000	500,000 to 2,500,000	2,500,000 and over
Number of Enterprises **1**	6259	819	3740	0	975	265	119	42	17	6	0	4	0
Revenues ($ in Thousands)													
Net Sales **2**	38677950	532124	2207943	0	6564316	5326635	4514735	3413718	2176232	1476005	0	8100300	0
Interest **3**	65710	219	404	0	8031	5515	2964	1725	5407	11088	0	19420	0
Rents **4**	25987	0	0	0	1424	265	784	74	1268	5415	0	16051	0
Royalties **5**	68682	0	0	0	0	0	53	444	64	0	0	23579	0
Other Portfolio Income **6**	76668	2170	1565	0	4828	8771	740	2876	3469	5038	0	45194	0
Other Receipts **7**	559020	27388	301	0	36245	34243	74660	24895	9845	15788	0	259455	0
Total Receipts **8**	39474017	561901	2210213	0	6614844	5375429	4593936	3443732	2196285	1513334	0	8463999	0
Average Total Receipts **9**	6307	686	591	·	6784	20285	38605	81994	129193	252222	·	2116000	·
Operating Costs/Operating Income (%)													
Cost of Operations **10**	74.8	76.1	75.5	·	72.4	81.9	77.2	82.0	82.3	83.8	·	59.2	·
Salaries and Wages **11**	6.0	2.3	2.4	·	8.9	4.3	7.3	4.7	5.5	3.9	·	7.6	·
Taxes Paid **12**	1.0	1.1	0.7	·	1.2	0.8	1.0	0.9	1.1	1.2	·	1.3	·
Interest Paid **13**	0.7	0.7	0.2	·	0.5	0.4	0.5	0.4	0.5	1.7	·	1.1	·
Depreciation **14**	1.4	0.5	0.5	·	1.3	0.8	1.2	1.0	1.3	2.1	·	2.5	·
Amortization and Depletion **15**	0.2	·	0.0	·	0.0	0.0	0.1	0.0	0.1	0.2	·	0.8	·
Pensions and Other Deferred Comp. **16**	0.5	0.0	0.5	·	0.4	0.3	0.3	0.3	0.3	0.1	·	1.1	·
Employee Benefits **17**	0.8	0.2	0.6	·	0.7	0.4	0.6	0.5	0.6	1.0	·	1.4	·
Advertising **18**	1.2	0.4	0.1	·	0.4	0.1	0.3	0.2	0.1	0.1	·	4.6	·
Other Expenses **19**	9.2	13.3	7.7	·	8.5	6.2	7.7	4.9	5.2	5.3	·	17.4	·
Officers' Compensation **20**	2.0	5.3	6.4	·	2.9	2.2	1.9	1.4	1.3	1.1	·	0.8	·
Operating Margin **21**	2.3	0.1	5.3	·	2.7	2.6	1.9	3.7	1.6	·	·	1.9	·
Operating Margin Before Officers' Comp. **22**	4.3	5.4	11.7	·	5.6	4.8	3.8	5.1	2.9	0.7	·	2.7	·

Selected Average Balance Sheet ($ in Thousands)

Net Receivables 23	818	0	12	•	769	2484	5494	11802	21340	38150	•	279211
Inventories 24	559	0	9	•	445	2090	4119	9440	18910	31798	•	210007
Net Property, Plant and Equipment 25	477	0	10	•	376	691	2175	4101	10990	29466	•	327210
Total Assets 26	3017	0	80	•	2370	7046	14839	34956	70030	149476	•	1681375
Notes and Loans Payable 27	706	0	10	•	574	1610	3307	7791	18839	47120	•	313240
All Other Liabilities 28	1215	0	12	•	832	3170	5731	12535	24775	66096	•	803245
Net Worth 29	1096	0	58	•	964	2266	5800	14631	26416	36260	•	564889

Selected Financial Ratios (Times to 1)

Current Ratio 30	1.4	•	3.3	•	1.9	1.5	1.6	1.5	1.5	1.2	•	0.9
Quick Ratio 31	0.8	•	2.5	•	1.2	0.9	0.9	0.9	0.8	0.6	•	0.5
Net Sales to Working Capital 32	13.9	•	15.8	•	8.1	10.6	9.1	9.8	8.1	19.9	•	•
Coverage Ratio 33	7.4	9.4	23.1	•	8.0	10.3	8.0	11.7	5.9	2.4	•	7.1
Total Asset Turnover 34	2.0	•	7.3	•	2.8	2.9	2.6	2.3	1.8	1.6	•	1.2
Inventory Turnover 35	8.3	•	48.9	•	11.0	7.9	7.1	7.1	5.6	6.5	•	5.7
Receivables Turnover 36	•	•	•	•	•	•	•	•	•	•	•	•
Total Liabilities to Net Worth 37	1.8	•	0.4	•	1.5	2.1	1.6	1.4	1.7	3.1	•	2.0
Current Assets to Working Capital 38	3.8	•	1.4	•	2.1	3.1	2.7	3.0	3.0	6.3	•	•
Current Liabilities to Working Capital 39	2.8	•	0.4	•	1.1	2.1	1.7	2.0	2.0	5.3	•	•
Working Capital to Net Sales 40	0.1	•	0.1	•	0.1	0.1	0.1	0.1	0.1	0.1	•	•
Inventory to Working Capital 41	1.3	•	0.2	•	0.5	1.1	1.0	1.1	1.2	2.6	•	•
Total Receipts to Cash Flow 42	8.5	5.9	9.0	•	9.7	12.3	10.3	12.0	15.4	16.4	•	4.8
Cost of Goods to Cash Flow 43	6.4	4.5	6.8	•	7.0	10.1	7.9	9.8	12.7	13.7	•	2.8
Cash Flow to Total Debt 44	0.4	•	2.9	•	0.5	0.3	0.4	0.3	0.2	0.1	•	0.4

Selected Financial Factors (in Percentages)

Debt Ratio 45	63.7	•	28.0	•	59.3	67.8	60.9	58.1	62.3	75.7	•	66.4
Return on Total Assets 46	10.5	•	41.6	•	11.4	10.9	10.7	11.7	5.7	6.9	•	9.4
Return on Equity Before Income Taxes 47	25.1	•	55.4	•	24.4	30.7	23.9	25.6	12.6	16.7	•	24.1
Return on Equity After Income Taxes 48	20.1	•	53.8	•	22.1	27.6	21.5	22.0	9.3	12.8	•	15.7
Profit Margin (Before Income Tax) 49	4.4	5.7	5.4	•	3.5	3.5	3.6	4.6	2.6	2.5	•	6.7
Profit Margin (After Income Tax) 50	3.6	5.5	5.3	•	3.2	3.3	3.3	4.0	1.9	1.9	•	4.4

Table I

Corporations with and without Net Income

PETROLEUM AND PETROLEUM PRODUCTS

MONEY AMOUNTS AND SIZE OF ASSETS IN THOUSANDS OF DOLLARS

Item Description for Accounting Period 7/02 Through 6/03	Total	Zero Assets	Under 500	500 to 1,000	1,000 to 5,000	5,000 to 10,000	10,000 to 25,000	25,000 to 50,000	50,000 to 100,000	100,000 to 250,000	250,000 to 500,000	500,000 to 2,500,000	2,500,000 and over
Number of Enterprises **1**	9722	131	5292	688	2780	364	299	96	29	20	10	7	5
Revenues ($ in Thousands)													
Net Sales **2**	215286605	26722785	3512252	2816271	31681589	11553352	23170480	14814490	10231501	15735784	17248034	19498000	38302068
Interest **3**	1777479	8885	3350	1182	17638	7399	16021	7967	8228	4415	8608	50453	1643334
Rents **4**	292561	340	4764	1195	31060	27744	43023	18305	7670	6455	55463	417	96125
Royalties **5**	130202	0	0	0	208	576	542	0	174	5	0	246	128451
Other Portfolio Income **6**	2088281	24421	12043	1028	67836	27466	48743	15774	5570	9026	251	5487	1870635
Other Receipts **7**	2007114	24321	9915	1375	262562	84173	132683	81998	69640	40406	47243	119451	1133345
Total Receipts **8**	221582242	26780752	3542324	2821051	32060893	11700710	23411492	14938534	10322783	15796091	17359599	19674054	43173958
Average Total Receipts **9**	22792	204433	669	4100	11533	32145	78299	155610	355958	789805	1735960	2810579	8634792
Operating Costs/Operating Income (%)													
Cost of Operations **10**	90.4	98.8	84.0	86.7	88.5	86.0	90.8	91.2	93.7	95.2	95.6	97.7	78.7
Salaries and Wages **11**	2.4	0.6	3.3	3.9	3.6	3.3	3.0	3.0	2.4	1.4	1.1	0.8	3.3
Taxes Paid **12**	1.1	0.2	1.3	0.7	1.3	5.0	0.7	0.9	0.4	0.2	0.2	0.1	2.0
Interest Paid **13**	1.9	0.2	0.7	0.3	0.3	0.5	0.4	0.4	0.4	0.4	0.4	0.6	8.9
Depreciation **14**	1.6	0.1	0.9	0.8	1.1	1.1	1.2	1.2	0.9	0.6	0.4	0.5	5.2
Amortization and Depletion **15**	0.6	0.0	0.1	0.0	0.0	0.0	0.0	0.1	0.0	0.1	0.0	0.1	3.1
Pensions and Other Deferred Comp. **16**	0.1	0.0	0.2	0.1	0.1	0.1	0.1	0.1	0.1	0.0	0.0	0.0	0.1
Employee Benefits **17**	0.2	0.0	0.2	0.3	0.2	0.2	0.2	0.2	0.2	0.2	0.1	0.1	0.5
Advertising **18**	0.1	0.0	0.2	0.1	0.1	0.1	0.1	0.1	0.1	0.0	0.0	0.0	0.0
Other Expenses **19**	4.2	0.7	6.8	4.6	4.4	3.7	3.6	3.0	2.5	1.7	3.3	0.8	10.8
Officers' Compensation **20**	0.5	0.0	2.4	2.4	1.1	0.6	0.5	0.5	0.2	0.3	0.1	0.1	0.3
Operating Margin **21**	•	•	•	0.0	•	•	•	•	•	•	•	•	•
Operating Margin Before Officers' Comp. **22**	•	•	2.3	2.5	0.3	0.1	•	0.0	•	0.1	•	•	•

Selected Average Balance Sheet ($ in Thousands)

Net Receivables 23	2854	0	35	286	729	2009	4199	9988	24621	51676	135607	295185	3444107
Inventories 24	576	0	19	164	246	672	1576	4098	9105	24108	79028	120099	243419
Net Property, Plant and Equipment 25	5233	0	38	136	619	2401	5277	12436	16897	40708	61754	97568	8522717
Total Assets 26	15389	0	153	684	2142	7102	15206	33754	66645	155774	345130	933175	23393823
Notes and Loans Payable 27	4238	0	68	198	616	2759	4992	12552	17036	44134	121200	218540	6234616
All Other Liabilities 28	4532	0	37	194	637	2082	5394	11374	34945	72529	219659	393408	6216608
Net Worth 29	6619	0	49	291	889	2262	4819	9828	14663	39111	4272	321227	10942599

Selected Financial Ratios (Times to 1)

Current Ratio 30	1.3	•	2.7	2.3	1.6	1.6	1.2	1.2	1.2	1.1	1.1	1.3	1.3
Quick Ratio 31	1.0	•	2.0	1.5	1.2	1.1	0.8	0.9	0.8	0.6	0.6	0.8	1.0
Net Sales to Working Capital 32	23.0	•	11.4	13.7	23.4	20.5	74.0	50.7	45.5	59.3	57.0	24.2	8.1
Coverage Ratio 33	1.2	•	2.0	1.8	2.3	2.5	2.0	1.8	1.2	1.7	•	1.4	1.1
Total Asset Turnover 34	1.4	•	4.3	6.0	5.3	4.5	5.1	4.6	5.3	5.1	5.0	3.0	0.3
Inventory Turnover 35	34.7	•	30.0	21.6	41.0	40.6	44.7	34.3	36.3	31.1	20.9	22.6	24.8
Receivables Turnover 36	•	•	•	•	•	•	•	•	•	•	•	•	•
Total Liabilities to Net Worth 37	1.3	•	2.1	1.3	1.4	2.1	2.2	2.4	3.5	3.0	79.8	1.9	1.1
Current Assets to Working Capital 38	4.6	•	1.6	1.8	2.7	2.6	7.3	5.7	5.7	7.1	8.8	4.3	5.0
Current Liabilities to Working Capital 39	3.6	•	0.6	0.8	1.7	1.6	6.3	4.7	4.7	6.1	7.8	3.3	4.0
Working Capital to Net Sales 40	0.0	•	0.1	0.1	0.0	0.0	0.0	0.0	0.0	0.0	0.0	0.0	0.1
Inventory to Working Capital 41	0.6	•	0.3	0.6	0.5	0.4	1.5	1.3	1.2	1.8	2.6	1.0	0.3
Total Receipts to Cash Flow 42	31.5	504.3	17.5	27.8	29.6	29.7	36.4	42.7	61.9	65.2	51.3	127.1	12.2
Cost of Goods to Cash Flow 43	28.5	498.3	14.7	24.1	26.2	25.5	33.0	38.9	58.0	62.1	49.0	124.1	9.6
Cash Flow to Total Debt 44	0.1	•	0.4	0.4	0.3	0.2	0.2	0.2	0.1	0.1	0.1	0.0	0.1

Selected Financial Factors (in Percentages)

Debt Ratio 45	57.0	•	68.1	57.4	58.5	68.2	68.3	70.9	78.0	74.9	98.8	65.6	53.2
Return on Total Assets 46	3.1	•	6.5	2.8	3.7	5.5	4.3	3.5	2.3	3.2	•	2.5	3.2
Return on Equity Before Income Taxes 47	1.0	•	10.3	3.0	5.1	10.4	6.8	5.3	1.7	5.0	•	2.0	0.6
Return on Equity After Income Taxes 48	0.5	•	7.0	2.1	4.1	9.2	4.9	3.7	•	2.7	•	0.2	0.4
Profit Margin (Before Income Tax) 49	0.3	•	0.8	0.2	0.4	0.7	0.4	0.3	0.1	0.3	•	0.2	0.9
Profit Margin (After Income Tax) 50	0.2	•	0.5	0.2	0.3	0.7	0.3	0.2	•	0.1	•	0.0	0.6

Table II
Corporations with Net Income

PETROLEUM AND PETROLEUM PRODUCTS

MONEY AMOUNTS AND SIZE OF ASSETS IN THOUSANDS OF DOLLARS

Item Description for Accounting Period 7/02 Through 6/03	Total	Zero Assets	Under 500	500 to 1,000	1,000 to 5,000	5,000 to 10,000	10,000 to 25,000	25,000 to 50,000	50,000 to 100,000	100,000 to 250,000	250,000 to 500,000	500,000 to 2,500,000	2,500,000 and over
Number of Enterprises 1	4064	120	1646	383	1377	258	181	55	19	14	3	0	0
Revenues ($ in Thousands)													
Net Sales 2	134784633	2914594	1665561	1989796	18015532	8083976	15793050	9915088	7663111	12898226	6233153	0	0
Interest 3	1653573	2282	2718	477	13050	5796	12095	5990	5325	3089	2226	0	0
Rents 4	162381	299	0	24	18296	15830	32826	10066	3381	6455	5439	0	0
Royalties 5	63231	0	0	0	154	576	533	0	0	5	0	0	0
Other Portfolio Income 6	1844586	24421	12043	0	51750	25547	29796	8844	3325	8398	250	0	0
Other Receipts 7	1622148	23352	2328	381	159947	56288	91431	60848	54203	31086	8265	0	0
Total Receipts 8	140130552	2964948	1682650	1990678	18258729	8188013	15959731	10000836	7729345	12947259	6249333	0	0
Average Total Receipts 9	34481	24708	1022	5198	13260	31736	88175	181833	406808	924804	2083111	•	•
Operating Costs/Operating Income (%)													
Cost of Operations 10	89.2	97.7	76.5	88.1	88.7	84.5	91.4	92.0	95.4	95.6	97.8	•	•
Salaries and Wages 11	2.2	0.9	3.1	3.0	3.1	3.0	2.6	2.5	1.5	1.2	0.7	•	•
Taxes Paid 12	1.3	0.2	1.0	0.6	1.3	6.5	0.6	1.1	0.2	0.2	0.1	•	•
Interest Paid 13	2.5	0.4	0.7	0.1	0.3	0.4	0.3	0.3	0.1	0.2	0.3	•	•
Depreciation 14	1.9	0.5	1.0	0.7	1.1	1.0	1.0	1.0	0.6	0.5	0.2	•	•
Amortization and Depletion 15	0.8	0.2	0.2	0.0	0.1	0.0	0.0	0.0	0.0	0.1	0.0	•	•
Pensions and Other Deferred Comp. 16	0.1	0.0	0.4	0.1	0.1	0.1	0.1	0.1	0.1	0.0	0.0	•	•
Employee Benefits 17	0.2	0.1	0.5	0.1	0.2	0.2	0.2	0.2	0.2	0.2	0.0	•	•
Advertising 18	0.0	0.0	0.4	0.0	0.1	0.1	0.1	0.0	0.1	0.0	0.0	•	•
Other Expenses 19	4.1	0.7	9.3	3.5	3.7	3.4	3.1	2.6	1.5	1.4	0.8	•	•
Officers' Compensation 20	0.5	0.2	4.3	2.9	1.2	0.6	0.5	0.3	0.2	0.2	0.1	•	•
Operating Margin 21	•	•	2.8	1.0	0.2	0.1	0.1	•	0.0	0.3	0.0	•	•
Operating Margin Before Officers' Comp. 22	•	•	7.1	3.8	1.4	0.6	0.6	0.3	0.2	0.6	0.1	•	•

Selected Average Balance Sheet ($ in Thousands)

Net Receivables 23	4472	0	43	296	867	2071	4730	11686	30552	54984	120942
Inventories 24	963	0	12	183	263	694	1676	4035	9270	27619	141683
Net Property, Plant and Equipment 25	10666	0	16	151	654	2285	4696	11512	11594	41007	44400
Total Assets 26	26933	0	173	725	2399	7262	15162	34644	66420	161083	357052
Notes and Loans Payable 27	7619	0	87	144	544	2622	4303	9949	11700	43325	155386
All Other Liabilities 28	7211	0	51	255	737	2086	5551	12630	36479	75575	153359
Net Worth 29	12104	0	35	326	1117	2554	5307	12065	18241	42183	48307

Selected Financial Ratios (Times to 1)

Current Ratio 30	1.4	•	1.8	2.2	1.8	1.7	1.3	1.3	1.3	1.2	1.6
Quick Ratio 31	1.0	•	1.4	1.4	1.4	1.2	1.0	0.9	1.0	0.8	0.7
Net Sales to Working Capital 32	15.7	18.7	16.9	19.1	18.1		49.1	42.9	35.0	52.9	18.6
Coverage Ratio 33	1.5	3.6	6.8	9.3	6.4	4.1	4.5	3.9	7.3	4.4	2.1
Total Asset Turnover 34	1.2	•	5.9	7.2	5.5	4.3	5.8	5.2	6.1	5.7	5.8
Inventory Turnover 35	30.7	•	65.3	25.0	44.1	38.1	47.6	41.1	41.5	31.9	14.3
Receivables Turnover 36	•	•	•	•	•	•	•	•	•	•	•
Total Liabilities to Net Worth 37	1.2	•	4.0	1.2	1.1	1.8	1.9	1.9	2.6	2.8	6.4
Current Assets to Working Capital 38	3.4	•	2.3	1.8	2.3	2.4	4.7	4.6	4.3	5.9	2.7
Current Liabilities to Working Capital 39	2.4	•	1.3	0.8	1.3	1.4	3.7	3.6	3.3	4.9	1.7
Working Capital to Net Sales 40	0.1	•	0.1	0.1	0.1	0.1	0.0	0.0	0.0	0.0	0.1
Inventory to Working Capital 41	0.5	•	0.2	0.6	0.4	0.4	0.9	1.0	0.8	1.6	1.3
Total Receipts to Cash Flow 42	24.1	87.9	9.8	26.3	24.7	26.3	31.3	37.5	51.4	56.3	156.4
Cost of Goods to Cash Flow 43	21.5	85.8	7.5	23.2	21.9	22.2	28.6	34.5	49.0	53.8	153.1
Cash Flow to Total Debt 44	0.1	•	0.7	0.5	0.4	0.3	0.3	0.2	0.2	0.1	0.0

Selected Financial Factors (in Percentages)

Debt Ratio 45	55.1	•	80.0	55.0	53.4	64.8	65.0	65.2	72.5	73.8	86.5
Return on Total Assets 46	4.8	•	26.2	8.0	10.1	7.7	8.7	5.9	6.4	5.4	3.1
Return on Equity Before Income Taxes 47	3.8	•	111.9	15.9	18.4	16.7	19.3	12.7	20.2	15.8	12.3
Return on Equity After Income Taxes 48	3.2	•	96.7	14.5	16.8	15.2	16.4	10.4	17.1	12.7	6.6
Profit Margin (Before Income Tax) 49	1.4	1.0	3.8	1.0	1.6	1.4	1.2	0.8	0.9	0.7	0.3
Profit Margin (After Income Tax) 50	1.2	1.0	3.3	0.9	1.4	1.2	1.0	0.7	0.8	0.6	0.2

Table I

Corporations with and without Net Income

BEER, WINE, AND DISTILLED ALCOHOLIC BEVERAGE

MONEY AMOUNTS AND SIZE OF ASSETS IN THOUSANDS OF DOLLARS

Item Description for Accounting Period 7/02 Through 6/03	Total	Zero Assets	Under 500	500 to 1,000	1,000 to 5,000	5,000 to 10,000	10,000 to 25,000	25,000 to 50,000	50,000 to 100,000	100,000 to 250,000	250,000 to 500,000	500,000 to 2,500,000	2,500,000 and over
Number of Enterprises **1**	3563	264	1395	182	982	382	218	73	37	20	5	6	0
Revenues ($ in Thousands)													
Net Sales **2**	67387611	426978	523513	186930	11515598	10127187	11137993	6621779	6298289	5908570	4865194	9775581	0
Interest **3**	26216	192	3981	0	2515	2265	1330	1690	1121	5404	1674	6044	0
Rents **4**	77138	0	0	0	6198	2785	340	751	988	3222	11796	51058	0
Royalties **5**	224797	0	0	0	0	0	0	0	0	4574	28225	191998	0
Other Portfolio Income **6**	212198	0	19394	0	5407	4099	9886	2924	6659	25810	14999	123019	0
Other Receipts **7**	746414	7376	11950	114	50788	95174	113308	155146	81284	68983	18998	143292	0
Total Receipts **8**	68674374	434546	558838	187044	11580506	10231510	11262857	6782290	6388341	6016563	4940886	10290992	0
Average Total Receipts **9**	19274	1646	401	1028	11793	26784	51664	92908	172658	300828	988177	1715165	•
Operating Costs/Operating Income (%)													
Cost of Operations **10**	75.2	56.5	66.6	71.2	75.8	76.0	74.5	76.6	74.2	73.0	77.3	75.8	•
Salaries and Wages **11**	8.2	5.0	8.2	12.5	9.0	8.4	8.3	8.4	8.6	7.6	6.2	8.2	•
Taxes Paid **12**	3.1	1.3	2.0	2.1	1.5	3.4	3.3	3.0	2.4	3.6	4.6	3.9	•
Interest Paid **13**	0.8	3.8	0.8	0.0	0.5	0.6	0.6	0.6	0.7	0.6	1.2	1.8	•
Depreciation **14**	0.9	3.6	0.4	1.8	0.8	1.2	1.0	1.0	1.1	0.6	0.8	0.7	•
Amortization and Depletion **15**	0.4	5.3	0.0	•	0.2	0.2	0.4	0.5	0.2	0.3	0.6	0.6	•
Pensions and Other Deferred Comp. **16**	0.4	•	3.1	•	0.4	0.4	0.4	0.3	0.3	0.2	0.4	0.2	•
Employee Benefits **17**	0.7	2.0	1.1	0.0	0.6	0.7	0.8	0.8	0.7	0.8	0.6	0.7	•
Advertising **18**	1.4	18.5	0.3	1.2	0.8	0.6	1.0	1.4	1.9	2.0	1.1	2.0	•
Other Expenses **19**	6.0	3.5	12.4	13.8	6.7	5.4	5.7	5.2	5.3	6.9	4.8	6.8	•
Officers' Compensation **20**	1.2	0.1	11.4	0.0	2.0	1.2	1.4	0.9	1.2	0.7	0.5	0.5	•
Operating Margin **21**	1.7	0.3	•	•	1.7	2.1	2.6	1.4	3.4	3.7	1.9	•	•
Operating Margin Before Officers' Comp. **22**	2.9	0.4	5.2	•	3.7	3.3	4.0	2.3	4.6	4.4	2.4	•	•

Selected Average Balance Sheet ($ in Thousands)

Net Receivables 23	1255	0	15	195	445	1109	2683	5865	11439	32600	50524	202168	•
Inventories 24	1604	0	28	126	732	1947	2993	5869	15828	32345	63548	259770	•
Net Property, Plant and Equipment 25	974	0	5	49	517	1309	2746	5346	12326	9721	44479	97301	•
Total Assets 26	7236	0	139	546	2673	7130	15914	32664	68786	140044	345215	1202362	•
Notes and Loans Payable 27	2242	0	74	108	944	2458	5384	9703	22822	40948	110475	316681	•
All Other Liabilities 28	2537	0	25	359	707	1452	3406	8185	16779	45946	96275	721306	•
Net Worth 29	2457	0	40	79	1022	3220	7124	14776	29185	53150	138464	164374	•

Selected Financial Ratios (Times to 1)

Current Ratio 30	1.6	•	4.2	1.0	1.6	2.3	1.6	1.8	1.7	1.7	1.3	1.2	•
Quick Ratio 31	0.8	•	3.1	0.7	0.8	1.2	0.9	1.0	0.8	0.9	0.6	0.5	•
Net Sales to Working Capital 32	13.8	•	4.5	56.9	19.0	10.8	17.1	12.5	11.0	9.2	26.2	15.5	•
Coverage Ratio 33	5.5	1.5	1.7	•	5.2	6.5	7.3	7.2	7.8	9.6	3.9	3.7	•
Total Asset Turnover 34	2.6	•	2.7	1.9	4.4	3.7	3.2	2.8	2.5	2.1	2.8	1.4	•
Inventory Turnover 35	8.9	•	9.0	5.8	12.1	10.3	12.7	11.8	8.0	6.7	11.8	4.8	•
Receivables Turnover 36	•	•	•	•	•	•	•	•	•	•	•	•	•
Total Liabilities to Net Worth 37	1.9	•	2.5	5.9	1.6	1.2	1.2	1.2	1.4	1.6	1.5	6.3	•
Current Assets to Working Capital 38	2.7	•	1.3	22.8	2.6	1.8	2.7	2.3	2.5	2.4	4.0	5.1	•
Current Liabilities to Working Capital 39	1.7	•	0.3	21.8	1.6	0.8	1.7	1.3	1.5	1.4	3.0	4.1	•
Working Capital to Net Sales 40	0.1	•	0.2	0.0	0.1	0.1	0.1	0.1	0.1	0.1	0.0	0.1	•
Inventory to Working Capital 41	1.2	•	0.3	7.0	1.2	0.8	1.0	0.8	1.0	1.0	1.7	2.5	•
Total Receipts to Cash Flow 42	12.3	19.7	13.6	12.3	13.6	14.3	12.9	13.0	11.1	8.7	13.9	11.3	•
Cost of Goods to Cash Flow 43	9.3	11.1	9.1	8.8	10.3	10.9	9.6	10.0	8.2	6.4	10.7	8.6	•
Cash Flow to Total Debt 44	0.3	•	0.3	0.2	0.5	0.5	0.5	0.4	0.4	0.4	0.3	0.1	•

Selected Financial Factors (in Percentages)

Debt Ratio 45	66.0	•	71.6	85.5	61.8	54.8	55.2	54.8	57.6	62.0	59.9	86.3	•
Return on Total Assets 46	11.9	•	3.5	•	12.2	13.7	13.8	12.2	13.7	13.0	13.1	8.7	•
Return on Equity Before Income Taxes 47	28.6	•	5.0	•	25.8	25.6	26.7	23.3	28.2	30.8	24.4	46.4	•
Return on Equity After Income Taxes 48	25.5	•	3.2	•	24.6	24.4	25.9	21.5	27.1	27.0	18.3	34.7	•
Profit Margin (Before Income Tax) 49	3.7	2.1	0.5	•	2.2	3.1	3.7	3.8	4.8	5.5	3.5	4.7	•
Profit Margin (After Income Tax) 50	3.3	1.5	0.3	0.2	2.1	3.0	3.6	3.5	4.7	4.8	2.6	3.5	•

Table II
Corporations with Net Income

BEER, WINE, AND DISTILLED ALCOHOLIC BEVERAGE

MONEY AMOUNTS AND SIZE OF ASSETS IN THOUSANDS OF DOLLARS

Item Description for Accounting Period 7/02 Through 6/03	Total	Zero Assets	Under 500	500 to 1,000	1,000 to 5,000	5,000 to 10,000	10,000 to 25,000	25,000 to 50,000	50,000 to 100,000	100,000 to 250,000	250,000 to 500,000	500,000 to 2,500,000	2,500,000 and over
Number of Enterprises 1	2088	0	672	0	692	342	196	64	33	16	0	6	0
Revenues ($ in Thousands)													
Net Sales 2	61662135	0	273537	0	9908353	9650185	10121765	6073534	5923382	5087687	0	9775581	0
Interest 3	22561	0	3147	0	1603	2231	1128	1223	1087	4643	0	6044	0
Rents 4	64504	0	0	0	6198	2775	306	749	988	1927	0	51058	0
Royalties 5	223102	0	0	0	0	0	0	0	0	4419	0	191998	0
Other Portfolio Income 6	196453	0	19394	0	5363	3550	8910	2580	6238	24055	0	123019	0
Other Receipts 7	713460	0	8514	0	30631	93324	109740	147161	81318	73351	0	143292	0
Total Receipts 8	62882215	0	304592	0	9952148	9752065	10241849	6225247	6013013	5196082	0	10290992	0
Average Total Receipts 9	30116	•	453	•	14382	28515	52254	97269	182213	324755	•	1715165	•
Operating Costs/Operating Income (%)													
Cost of Operations 10	75.1	•	44.2	•	75.9	76.1	74.3	76.6	74.0	73.3	•	75.8	•
Salaries and Wages 11	8.2	•	9.5	•	8.8	8.1	8.2	8.2	8.5	7.6	•	8.2	•
Taxes Paid 12	3.1	•	2.6	•	1.3	3.5	3.3	3.1	2.5	3.6	•	3.9	•
Interest Paid 13	0.7	•	1.4	•	0.4	0.5	0.5	0.6	0.7	0.6	•	1.8	•
Depreciation 14	0.9	•	0.6	•	0.8	1.1	0.9	0.9	1.0	0.6	•	0.7	•
Amortization and Depletion 15	0.3	•	0.1	•	0.1	0.2	0.4	0.5	0.2	0.2	•	0.6	•
Pensions and Other Deferred Comp. 16	0.4	•	5.9	•	0.4	0.4	0.4	0.3	0.3	0.2	•	0.2	•
Employee Benefits 17	0.7	•	0.8	•	0.6	0.7	0.8	0.7	0.6	0.6	•	0.7	•
Advertising 18	1.4	•	0.5	•	0.7	0.5	1.0	1.4	2.0	2.1	•	2.0	•
Other Expenses 19	5.7	•	20.9	•	6.0	5.1	5.6	5.0	5.1	5.9	•	6.8	•
Officers' Compensation 20	1.2	•	19.7	•	1.8	1.2	1.4	0.9	1.3	0.6	•	0.5	•
Operating Margin 21	2.3	•	•	•	2.9	2.7	3.1	1.8	3.9	4.5	•	•	•
Operating Margin Before Officers' Comp. 22	3.5	•	13.4	•	4.7	3.9	4.5	2.7	5.1	5.1	•	•	•

Selected Average Balance Sheet ($ in Thousands)

Net Receivables 23	1905	31	429	1073	2764	5871	12101	32354	202168
Inventories 24	2471	10	789	1841	3016	6187	16875	34422	259770
Net Property, Plant and Equipment 25	1510	10	666	1212	2692	5239	12764	10927	97301
Total Assets 26	11010	193	2980	7089	15928	32759	69759	138711	1202362
Notes and Loans Payable 27	3224	85	931	2219	4989	9357	24341	41549	316681
All Other Liabilities 28	3851	47	732	1430	3410	8554	16908	39986	721306
Net Worth 29	3936	60	1317	3441	7530	14847	28510	57175	164374

Selected Financial Ratios (Times to 1)

Current Ratio 30	1.6	2.8	1.7	2.6	1.6	1.7	1.7	1.8	1.2
Quick Ratio 31	0.8	2.5	0.8	1.4	0.9	0.9	0.8	0.9	0.5
Net Sales to Working Capital 32	13.7	4.7	20.8	10.6	16.2	13.7	11.2	8.8	15.5
Coverage Ratio 33	6.9	4.6	8.9	8.6	8.8	8.3	8.6	11.7	3.7
Total Asset Turnover 34	2.7	2.1	4.8	4.0	3.2	2.9	2.6	2.3	1.4
Inventory Turnover 35	9.0	18.8	13.8	11.7	12.7	11.7	7.9	6.8	4.8
Receivables Turnover 36	•	•	•	•	•	•	•	•	•
Total Liabilities to Net Worth 37	1.8	2.2	1.3	1.1	1.1	1.2	1.4	1.4	6.3
Current Assets to Working Capital 38	2.7	1.6	2.4	1.6	2.6	2.4	2.5	2.2	5.1
Current Liabilities to Working Capital 39	1.7	0.6	1.4	0.6	1.6	1.4	1.5	1.2	4.1
Working Capital to Net Sales 40	0.1	0.2	0.0	0.1	0.1	0.1	0.1	0.1	0.1
Inventory to Working Capital 41	1.2	0.1	1.1	0.7	0.9	0.9	1.0	0.9	2.5
Total Receipts to Cash Flow 42	11.7	6.2	12.8	13.6	12.1	12.4	10.7	8.6	11.3
Cost of Goods to Cash Flow 43	8.8	2.7	9.7	10.4	9.0	9.5	7.9	6.3	8.6
Cash Flow to Total Debt 44	0.4	0.5	0.7	0.6	0.5	0.4	0.4	0.5	0.1

Selected Financial Factors (in Percentages)

Debt Ratio 45	64.3	68.8	55.8	51.5	52.7	54.7	59.1	58.8	86.3
Return on Total Assets 46	13.7	13.6	17.9	16.8	15.5	14.0	15.7	16.6	8.7
Return on Equity Before Income Taxes 47	32.7	34.0	35.9	30.5	29.1	27.2	33.9	36.8	46.4
Return on Equity After Income Taxes 48	29.4	31.6	34.7	29.2	28.3	25.2	32.7	32.4	34.7
Profit Margin (Before Income Tax) 49	4.4	5.0	3.3	3.7	4.2	4.2	5.4	6.6	4.7
Profit Margin (After Income Tax) 50	3.9	4.7	3.2	3.6	4.1	3.9	5.2	5.8	3.5

Table I

Corporations with and without Net Income

MISCELLANEOUS NONDURABLE GOODS

MONEY AMOUNTS AND SIZE OF ASSETS IN THOUSANDS OF DOLLARS

Item Description for Accounting Period 7/02 Through 6/03	Total	Zero Assets	Under 500	500 to 1,000	1,000 to 5,000	5,000 to 10,000	10,000 to 25,000	25,000 to 50,000	50,000 to 100,000	100,000 to 250,000	250,000 to 500,000	500,000 to 2,500,000	2,500,000 and over
Number of Enterprises **1**	36689	5048	23156	4010	3393	534	333	106	49	34	12	13	0
Revenues ($ in Thousands)													
Net Sales **2**	124651812	1001670	10475584	9797602	23487011	14197938	14384614	10337697	7960779	8321097	9130911	15556908	0
Interest **3**	325232	436	8012	8006	26004	13126	12436	8482	9166	84057	55416	100090	0
Rents **4**	54971	0	2089	1089	4851	4583	5958	698	5581	8623	2209	19292	0
Royalties **5**	56019	102	0	9	1267	1698	9295	466	2184	9600	3697	27701	0
Other Portfolio Income **6**	255859	38	11208	3790	72379	14237	14786	8128	10254	9062	8672	103304	0
Other Receipts **7**	1231868	9211	124810	36916	196099	58462	108290	83099	114471	166203	76569	257737	0
Total Receipts **8**	126575761	1011457	10621703	9847412	23787611	14290044	14535379	10438570	8102435	8598642	9277474	16065032	0
Average Total Receipts **9**	3450	200	459	2456	7011	26760	43650	98477	165356	252901	773123	1235772	.
Operating Costs/Operating Income (%)													
Cost of Operations **10**	76.7	70.4	70.1	72.4	78.5	82.3	80.1	83.0	74.1	73.7	86.2	66.7	.
Salaries and Wages **11**	6.5	4.6	6.4	7.9	5.7	4.8	6.4	5.4	7.8	8.1	5.0	8.9	.
Taxes Paid **12**	1.4	11.1	1.3	1.6	1.5	1.4	1.8	1.1	1.3	1.0	0.7	1.4	.
Interest Paid **13**	1.0	1.8	0.4	0.6	0.6	0.4	0.6	0.5	1.1	2.7	0.8	2.3	.
Depreciation **14**	1.2	0.7	0.8	1.1	0.8	0.5	0.8	0.8	1.3	1.5	0.6	3.9	.
Amortization and Depletion **15**	0.2	0.4	0.2	0.0	0.0	0.0	0.1	0.2	0.4	0.5	0.2	0.8	.
Pensions and Other Deferred Comp. **16**	0.3	0.0	0.3	0.4	0.2	0.2	0.2	0.2	0.2	0.3	0.1	0.5	.
Employee Benefits **17**	0.6	0.5	0.4	0.4	0.4	0.4	0.5	0.4	0.7	0.9	0.6	1.0	.
Advertising **18**	0.7	0.5	0.4	0.6	0.4	0.4	0.7	0.6	3.2	0.5	0.2	1.0	.
Other Expenses **19**	9.4	12.9	14.0	11.2	9.3	6.3	6.7	6.0	9.0	11.7	4.4	14.5	.
Officers' Compensation **20**	1.9	2.1	5.3	3.0	2.5	2.2	1.3	1.0	0.9	0.7	0.5	0.6	.
Operating Margin **21**	0.0	.	0.5	0.7	.	1.1	0.8	0.6	.	.	.	.	.
Operating Margin Before Officers' Comp. **22**	1.9	.	5.8	3.8	2.4	3.3	2.1	1.6	0.8	1.3	0.8	.	.

Selected Average Balance Sheet ($ in Thousands)

Net Receivables 23	391	0	23	206	758	2344	4627	10275	17771	36031	120175	231427	•
Inventories 24	334	0	19	159	676	2244	4534	9538	17910	31437	73047	179951	•
Net Property, Plant and Equipment 25	245	0	17	152	262	630	2004	4094	13107	23323	32866	294066	•
Total Assets 26	1600	0	95	750	2208	6995	15125	33663	71206	170115	391932	1515094	•
Notes and Loans Payable 27	530	0	114	269	673	2213	4598	10455	23373	62524	97639	399716	•
All Other Liabilities 28	562	0	45	240	817	2921	5441	13242	27867	59261	169598	434415	•
Net Worth 29	509	0	-63	241	718	1861	5086	9967	19966	48331	124695	680963	•

Selected Financial Ratios (Times to 1)

Current Ratio 30	1.3	•	0.6	1.6	1.5	1.5	1.5	1.5	1.4	1.5	1.3	1.2	•
Quick Ratio 31	0.8	•	0.4	1.0	0.9	0.8	0.8	0.8	0.8	0.8	0.8	0.7	•
Net Sales to Working Capital 32	14.0	•	•	13.0	10.2	14.0	11.3	11.2	11.5	6.8	15.4	14.3	•
Coverage Ratio 33	2.7	•	5.2	3.1	2.8	4.9	4.0	4.0	2.6	1.7	4.2	2.1	•
Total Asset Turnover 34	2.1	•	4.8	3.3	3.1	3.8	2.9	2.9	2.3	1.4	1.9	0.8	•
Inventory Turnover 35	7.8	•	16.6	11.1	8.0	9.8	7.6	8.5	6.7	5.7	9.0	4.4	•
Receivables Turnover 36	•	•	•	•	•	•	•	•	•	•	•	•	•
Total Liabilities to Net Worth 37	2.1	•	•	2.1	2.1	2.8	2.0	2.4	2.6	2.5	2.1	1.2	•
Current Assets to Working Capital 38	4.0	•	•	2.7	2.6	3.0	3.0	3.0	3.3	2.9	4.9	6.7	•
Current Liabilities to Working Capital 39	3.0	•	•	1.7	1.6	2.0	2.0	2.0	2.3	1.9	3.9	5.7	•
Working Capital to Net Sales 40	0.1	•	•	0.1	0.1	0.1	0.1	0.1	0.1	0.1	0.1	0.1	•
Inventory to Working Capital 41	1.4	•	•	0.8	1.0	1.2	1.2	1.1	1.3	0.9	1.5	2.1	•
Total Receipts to Cash Flow 42	11.0	15.6	7.6	9.8	11.7	15.1	13.9	15.6	11.2	8.5	18.1	7.7	•
Cost of Goods to Cash Flow 43	8.5	11.0	5.3	7.1	9.1	12.4	11.1	13.0	8.3	6.2	15.6	5.1	•
Cash Flow to Total Debt 44	0.3	•	0.4	0.5	0.4	0.3	0.3	0.3	0.3	0.2	0.2	0.2	•

Selected Financial Factors (in Percentages)

Debt Ratio 45	68.2	•	166.2	67.9	67.5	73.4	66.4	70.4	72.0	71.6	68.2	55.1	•
Return on Total Assets 46	5.7	•	11.1	6.1	5.7	8.3	6.9	6.2	6.4	6.4	6.2	3.8	•
Return on Equity Before Income Taxes 47	11.4	•	•	12.8	11.3	24.8	15.4	15.7	14.1	9.0	14.8	4.4	•
Return on Equity After Income Taxes 48	8.4	•	•	11.6	9.5	22.4	12.7	12.5	10.2	6.6	9.7	1.9	•
Profit Margin (Before Income Tax) 49	1.7	•	1.9	1.3	1.2	1.7	1.8	1.6	1.7	1.8	2.4	2.5	•
Profit Margin (After Income Tax) 50	1.3	•	1.7	1.1	1.0	1.6	1.5	1.3	1.2	1.3	1.6	1.1	•

Table II

Corporations with Net Income

MISCELLANEOUS NONDURABLE GOODS

MONEY AMOUNTS AND SIZE OF ASSETS IN THOUSANDS OF DOLLARS

Item Description for Accounting Period 7/02 Through 6/03	Total	Zero Assets	Under 500	500 to 1,000	1,000 to 5,000	5,000 to 10,000	10,000 to 25,000	25,000 to 50,000	50,000 to 100,000	100,000 to 250,000	250,000 to 500,000	500,000 to 2,500,000	2,500,000 and over
Number of Enterprises **1**	19013	1371	11813	2634	2335	0	253	75	31	21	0	9	0
Revenues ($ in Thousands)													
Net Sales **2**	97699902	825539	7358924	7523370	1816287	0	12014690	7541603	5090453	4879899	0	11253539	0
Interest **3**	166793	144	5628	6081	14879	0	7955	5523	2717	23979	0	36335	0
Rents **4**	22317	0	799	0	3582	0	4391	513	1176	5079	0	98	0
Royalties **5**	34175	102	0	9	1267	0	457	251	996	1432	0	27229	0
Other Portfolio Income **6**	199837	38	10030	3566	70249	0	14007	2555	2339	5412	0	70904	0
Other Receipts **7**	896398	8272	66500	36357	76749	0	91592	57337	92430	146407	0	205729	0
Total Receipts **8**	99019422	834095	7441881	7569383	18993013	0	12133092	7607782	5190111	5062208	0	11593834	0
Average Total Receipts **9**	5208	608	630	2874	8130	•	47957	101437	167423	241058	•	1288204	•
Operating Costs/Operating Income (%)													
Cost of Operations **10**	76.4	66.5	68.1	72.2	78.8	•	80.6	82.9	70.5	66.1	•	64.0	•
Salaries and Wages **11**	6.1	4.1	4.7	7.9	5.1	•	5.8	5.2	7.6	9.6	•	9.4	•
Taxes Paid **12**	1.4	12.5	1.2	1.4	1.6	•	1.9	0.8	1.6	1.1	•	1.4	•
Interest Paid **13**	0.7	2.0	0.3	0.4	0.5	•	0.5	0.5	1.2	2.1	•	1.1	•
Depreciation **14**	1.0	0.7	0.6	1.0	0.7	•	0.7	0.8	1.3	1.3	•	3.5	•
Amortization and Depletion **15**	0.2	0.2	0.1	0.0	0.0	•	0.1	0.1	0.4	0.7	•	0.7	•
Pensions and Other Deferred Comp. **16**	0.3	0.0	0.4	0.4	0.2	•	0.2	0.3	0.3	0.4	•	0.5	•
Employee Benefits **17**	0.5	0.4	0.3	0.3	0.4	•	0.4	0.4	0.8	0.8	•	1.0	•
Advertising **18**	0.7	0.2	0.3	0.3	0.4	•	0.5	0.5	4.5	0.6	•	1.2	•
Other Expenses **19**	8.2	8.1	12.8	10.4	7.4	•	6.2	4.9	7.9	13.4	•	13.5	•
Officers' Compensation **20**	1.9	2.3	6.1	2.6	2.6	•	1.3	1.1	1.0	0.8	•	0.5	•
Operating Margin **21**	2.5	2.8	5.0	3.0	2.3	•	2.0	2.7	3.0	3.1	•	3.0	•
Operating Margin Before Officers' Comp. **22**	4.5	5.1	11.1	5.7	4.9	•	3.3	3.8	3.9	3.9	•	3.5	•

Selected Average Balance Sheet ($ in Thousands)

Net Receivables 23	542	0	25	239	825	4806	10816	17105	32164	185191
Inventories 24	492	0	21	179	662	4713	9802	20355	26947	226980
Net Property, Plant and Equipment 25	282	0	19	119	223	1715	4193	11516	22204	232540
Total Assets 26	2105	0	111	757	2233	14997	33501	70266	159932	1331084
Notes and Loans Payable 27	515	0	44	216	559	3867	9810	22189	55854	199808
All Other Liabilities 28	676	0	26	234	717	5380	10862	25079	42162	347473
Net Worth 29	914	0	42	307	958	5750	12829	22998	61916	783803

Selected Financial Ratios (Times to 1)

Current Ratio 30	1.7	•	2.3	1.7	1.9	1.6	1.7	1.7	1.9	2.0
Quick Ratio 31	1.0	•	1.6	1.2	1.1	0.9	0.9	0.9	1.1	0.9
Net Sales to Working Capital 32	8.9	•	14.6	11.4	9.2	10.4	9.6	8.2	5.1	4.3
Coverage Ratio 33	7.0	2.9	18.5	10.4	7.6	7.3	8.3	5.2	4.1	7.6
Total Asset Turnover 34	2.4	•	5.6	3.8	3.6	3.2	3.0	2.3	1.5	0.9
Inventory Turnover 35	8.0	•	20.0	11.5	9.6	8.1	8.5	5.7	5.7	3.5
Receivables Turnover 36	•	•	•	•	•	•	•	•	•	•
Total Liabilities to Net Worth 37	1.3	•	1.6	1.5	1.3	1.6	1.6	2.1	1.6	0.7
Current Assets to Working Capital 38	2.4	•	1.8	2.4	2.1	2.6	2.5	2.5	2.1	2.0
Current Liabilities to Working Capital 39	1.4	•	0.8	1.4	1.1	1.6	1.5	1.5	1.1	1.0
Working Capital to Net Sales 40	0.1	•	0.1	0.1	0.1	0.1	0.1	0.1	0.2	0.2
Inventory to Working Capital 41	0.9	•	0.5	0.7	0.8	1.0	0.9	1.0	0.6	0.8
Total Receipts to Cash Flow 42	9.7	10.3	6.0	8.5	11.2	12.5	13.5	8.8	5.5	6.0
Cost of Goods to Cash Flow 43	7.4	6.8	4.1	6.1	8.8	10.1	11.2	6.2	3.6	3.8
Cash Flow to Total Debt 44	0.4	•	1.5	0.7	0.6	0.4	0.4	0.4	0.4	0.4

Selected Financial Factors (in Percentages)

Debt Ratio 45	56.6	•	62.1	59.4	57.1	61.7	61.7	67.3	61.3	41.1
Return on Total Assets 46	11.5	•	36.0	15.3	13.2	10.9	12.2	14.1	12.9	7.9
Return on Equity Before Income Taxes 47	22.7	•	89.9	34.1	26.8	24.5	27.9	34.9	25.3	11.7
Return on Equity After Income Taxes 48	19.5	•	86.2	32.6	24.9	21.3	24.3	29.6	22.3	8.5
Profit Margin (Before Income Tax) 49	4.0	3.9	6.1	3.7	3.2	3.0	3.6	4.9	6.7	7.3
Profit Margin (After Income Tax) 50	3.5	3.3	5.8	3.5	3.0	2.6	3.1	4.1	5.9	5.3

Table I

Corporations with and without Net Income

WHOLESALE ELECTRONIC MARKETS AND AGENTS AND BROKERS

MONEY AMOUNTS AND SIZE OF ASSETS IN THOUSANDS OF DOLLARS

Item Description for Accounting Period 7/02 Through 6/03	Total	Zero Assets	Under 500	500 to 1,000	1,000 to 5,000	5,000 to 10,000	10,000 to 25,000	25,000 to 50,000	50,000 to 100,000	100,000 to 250,000	250,000 to 500,000	500,000 to 2,500,000	2,500,000 and over
Number of Enterprises **1**	1358	403	936	0	19	0	0	0	0	0	0	0	0
Revenues ($ in Thousands)													
Net Sales **2**	140693	15698	109227	0	15769	0	0	0	0	0	0	0	0
Interest **3**	1012	0	1012	0	0	0	0	0	0	0	0	0	0
Rents **4**	0	0	0	0	0	0	0	0	0	0	0	0	0
Royalties **5**	0	0	0	0	0	0	0	0	0	0	0	0	0
Other Portfolio Income **6**	4	0	4	0	0	0	0	0	0	0	0	0	0
Other Receipts **7**	0	0	0	0	0	0	0	0	0	0	0	0	0
Total Receipts **8**	141709	15698	110243	0	15769	0	0	0	0	0	0	0	0
Average Total Receipts **9**	104	39	118	•	830	•	•	•	•	•	•	•	•
Operating Costs/Operating Income (%)													
Cost of Operations **10**	0.0	•	•	•	0.3	•	•	•	•	•	•	•	•
Salaries and Wages **11**	24.8	27.7	27.4	•	3.9	•	•	•	•	•	•	•	•
Taxes Paid **12**	5.2	5.7	5.5	•	2.1	•	•	•	•	•	•	•	•
Interest Paid **13**	0.9	•	1.2	•	•	•	•	•	•	•	•	•	•
Depreciation **14**	3.0	1.6	3.3	•	1.9	•	•	•	•	•	•	•	•
Amortization and Depletion **15**	•	•	•	•	•	•	•	•	•	•	•	•	•
Pensions and Other Deferred Comp. **16**	0.0	•	0.0	•	•	•	•	•	•	•	•	•	•
Employee Benefits **17**	4.2	•	5.4	•	•	•	•	•	•	•	•	•	•
Advertising **18**	0.6	•	0.7	•	•	•	•	•	•	•	•	•	•
Other Expenses **19**	34.6	34.5	26.9	•	87.7	•	•	•	•	•	•	•	•
Officers' Compensation **20**	35.2	36.9	39.0	•	7.2	•	•	•	•	•	•	•	•
Operating Margin **21**	•	•	•	•	•	•	•	•	•	•	•	•	•
Operating Margin Before Officers' Comp. **22**	26.9	30.4	29.6	•	4.1	•	•	•	•	•	•	•	•

Selected Average Balance Sheet ($ in Thousands)

Item				
Net Receivables 23	46	0	0	3277
Inventories 24	0	0	0	0
Net Property, Plant and Equipment 25	33	0	48	21
Total Assets 26	119	0	105	3332
Notes and Loans Payable 27	28	0	41	1
All Other Liabilities 28	50	0	4	3377
Net Worth 29	41	0	60	-46

Selected Financial Ratios (Times to 1)

Item			
Current Ratio 30	1.6	8.4	1.0
Quick Ratio 31	1.6	8.0	1.0
Net Sales to Working Capital 32	3.1	2.4	
Coverage Ratio 33			
Total Asset Turnover 34	0.9	1.1	0.2
Inventory Turnover 35			
Receivables Turnover 36			
Total Liabilities to Net Worth 37	1.9	0.7	
Current Assets to Working Capital 38	2.6	1.1	
Current Liabilities to Working Capital 39	1.6	0.1	
Working Capital to Net Sales 40	0.3	0.4	
Inventory to Working Capital 41			
Total Receipts to Cash Flow 42	4.3	3.6	7.1	1.2
Cost of Goods to Cash Flow 43	0.0	0.0	
Cash Flow to Total Debt 44	0.3	0.4	0.2

Selected Financial Factors (in Percentages)

Item			
Debt Ratio 45	65.7	42.7	101.4
Return on Total Assets 46			
Return on Equity Before Income Taxes 47	56.3		
Return on Equity After Income Taxes 48	56.3		
Profit Margin (Before Income Tax) 49			
Profit Margin (After Income Tax) 50			

Table II
Corporations with Net Income

WHOLESALE ELECTRONIC MARKETS AND AGENTS AND BROKERS

MONEY AMOUNTS AND SIZE OF ASSETS IN THOUSANDS OF DOLLARS

Item Description for Accounting Period 7/02 Through 6/03	Total	Zero Assets	Under 500	500 to 1000	251 to 500	501 to 1,000	1,001 to 5,000	5,001 to 10,000	10,001 to 25,000	25,001 to 50,000	50,001 to 100,000	100,001 to 250,000	250,001 and over
Number of Enterprises **1**	252	0	252	0	0	0	0	0	0	0	0	0	0
Revenues ($ in Thousands)													
Net Sales **2**	12593	0	12593	0	0	0	0	0	0	0	0	0	0
Interest **3**	0	0	0	0	0	0	0	0	0	0	0	0	0
Rents **4**	0	0	0	0	0	0	0	0	0	0	0	0	0
Royalties **5**	0	0	0	0	0	0	0	0	0	0	0	0	0
Other Portfolio Income **6**	0	0	0	0	0	0	0	0	0	0	0	0	0
Other Receipts **7**	0	0	0	0	0	0	0	0	0	0	0	0	0
Total Receipts **8**	12593	0	12593	0	0	0	0	0	0	0	0	0	0
Average Total Receipts **9**	50	•	50	•	•	•	•	•	•	•	•	•	•
Operating Costs/Operating Income (%)													
Cost of Operations **10**	•	•	•	•	•	•	•	•	•	•	•	•	•
Salaries and Wages **11**	•	•	•	•	•	•	•	•	•	•	•	•	•
Taxes Paid **12**	6.3	•	6.3	•	•	•	•	•	•	•	•	•	•
Interest Paid **13**	•	•	•	•	•	•	•	•	•	•	•	•	•
Depreciation **14**	•	•	•	•	•	•	•	•	•	•	•	•	•
Amortization and Depletion **15**	•	•	•	•	•	•	•	•	•	•	•	•	•
Pensions and Other Deferred Comp. **16**	•	•	•	•	•	•	•	•	•	•	•	•	•
Employee Benefits **17**	•	•	•	•	•	•	•	•	•	•	•	•	•
Advertising **18**	•	•	•	•	•	•	•	•	•	•	•	•	•
Other Expenses **19**	18.6	•	18.6	•	•	•	•	•	•	•	•	•	•
Officers' Compensation **20**	74.8	•	74.8	•	•	•	•	•	•	•	•	•	•
Operating Margin **21**	0.3	•	0.3	•	•	•	•	•	•	•	•	•	•
Operating Margin Before Officers' Comp. **22**	75.1	•	75.1	•	•	•	•	•	•	•	•	•	•

Selected Average Balance Sheet ($ in Thousands)

Net Receivables 23	0
Inventories 24	0
Net Property, Plant and Equipment 25	0
Total Assets 26	2
Notes and Loans Payable 27	0
All Other Liabilities 28	0
Net Worth 29	2

Selected Financial Ratios (Times to 1)

Current Ratio 30	
Quick Ratio 31	
Net Sales to Working Capital 32	40.9
Coverage Ratio 33	
Total Asset Turnover 34	32.8
Inventory Turnover 35	
Receivables Turnover 36	
Total Liabilities to Net Worth 37	
Current Assets to Working Capital 38	1.0
Current Liabilities to Working Capital 39	
Working Capital to Net Sales 40	0.0
Inventory to Working Capital 41	
Total Receipts to Cash Flow 42	6.3
Cost of Goods to Cash Flow 43	
Cash Flow to Total Debt 44	

Selected Financial Factors (in Percentages)

Debt Ratio 45	
Return on Total Assets 46	9.6
Return on Equity Before Income Taxes 47	9.6
Return on Equity After Income Taxes 48	8.1
Profit Margin (Before Income Tax) 49	0.3
Profit Margin (After Income Tax) 50	0.2

Table I

Corporations with and without Net Income

NEW AND USED CAR DEALERS

MONEY AMOUNTS AND SIZE OF ASSETS IN THOUSANDS OF DOLLARS

Item Description for Accounting Period 7/02 Through 6/03	Total	Zero Assets	Under 500	500 to 1,000	1,000 to 5,000	5,000 to 10,000	10,000 to 25,000	25,000 to 50,000	50,000 to 100,000	100,000 to 250,000	250,000 to 500,000	500,000 to 2,500,000	2,500,000 and over
Number of Enterprises 1	43939	2249	20646	3138	9433	4634	3099	575	119	29	9	9	0
Revenues ($ in Thousands)													
Net Sales 2	624685599	3637750	19950622	9174803	107143271	136823577	190483907	71390466	25759596	11379954	5886216	43055437	0
Interest 3	1872745	98794	22838	29725	198948	174129	186977	79573	33651	45260	121240	881612	0
Rents 4	232090	5	8203	3251	20138	22099	42354	42237	20240	30607	5329	37626	0
Royalties 5	139137	0	0	0	0	5533	764	75	0	5104	0	127661	0
Other Portfolio Income 6	556692	6016	15910	16057	55720	51620	79201	51629	35701	31399	14830	198612	0
Other Receipts 7	10350058	104708	83539	58777	1712304	2343944	3396815	1378934	523610	244002	195391	308029	0
Total Receipts 8	637836321	3847273	20081112	9282613	109130381	139420902	194190018	72942914	26372798	11736326	6223006	44608977	0
Average Total Receipts 9	14516	1711	973	2958	11569	30087	62662	126857	221620	404701	691445	4956553	•
Operating Costs/Operating Income (%)													
Cost of Operations 10	88.3	92.3	86.5	89.8	88.3	88.7	88.7	88.7	87.5	88.1	82.3	85.5	•
Salaries and Wages 11	4.9	4.3	2.4	2.6	4.5	4.8	5.0	5.0	5.4	5.4	6.3	6.2	•
Taxes Paid 12	0.8	0.8	1.2	0.7	0.8	0.8	0.7	0.7	0.8	0.8	1.3	1.2	•
Interest Paid 13	0.6	0.9	0.6	0.7	0.5	0.3	0.3	0.4	0.5	0.6	1.2	2.4	•
Depreciation 14	0.5	0.8	0.2	0.2	0.3	0.3	0.4	0.7	0.8	1.5	1.4	1.1	•
Amortization and Depletion 15	0.1	0.1	0.0	0.0	0.0	0.0	0.0	0.0	0.1	0.0	0.3	0.4	•
Pensions and Other Deferred Comp. 16	0.1	0.0	0.1	0.0	0.0	0.1	0.1	0.1	0.1	0.1	0.1	0.0	•
Employee Benefits 17	0.4	0.5	0.1	0.2	0.5	0.4	0.4	0.4	0.4	0.5	0.6	0.4	•
Advertising 18	1.1	0.9	0.8	0.7	1.1	1.2	1.1	1.1	1.2	1.1	0.8	1.1	•
Other Expenses 19	3.7	5.9	7.2	4.6	4.0	3.5	3.3	3.2	3.8	3.3	9.3	3.9	•
Officers' Compensation 20	0.8	0.4	1.9	1.4	1.1	0.9	0.8	0.7	0.6	0.6	0.4	0.1	•
Operating Margin 21	•	•	•	•	•	•	•	•	•	•	•	•	•
Operating Margin Before Officers' Comp. 22	•	0.9	0.9	0.6	•	•	•	•	•	•	•	•	•

Selected Average Balance Sheet ($ in Thousands)

	•	•	•	•	•	•	•	•	•	•	•
Net Receivables 23	499	0	17	181	344	752	1767	4458	8942	24217	57423	440117
Inventories 24	1931	0	97	297	1914	4482	7862	14950	27664	43589	75859	542290
Net Property, Plant and Equipment 25	397	0	16	28	175	527	1451	4537	10554	21476	63444	377863
Total Assets 26	3835	0	158	691	2809	7130	14745	33435	65807	139285	321916	2653000
Notes and Loans Payable 27	2501	0	106	440	1890	5264	10632	23130	42871	96987	170936	931270
All Other Liabilities 28	580	0	30	96	332	737	1466	3690	8934	12400	61456	1042330
Net Worth 29	755	0	22	155	586	1129	2647	6615	14002	29899	89524	679400

Selected Financial Ratios (Times to 1)

	•	•	•	•	•	•	•	•	•	•	•
Current Ratio 30	1.2	•	2.2	2.6	1.4	1.2	1.2	1.2	1.2	1.3	1.2	0.8
Quick Ratio 31	0.3	•	0.6	1.1	0.3	0.3	0.4	0.4	0.4	0.5	0.5	0.4
Net Sales to Working Capital 32	26.4	•	13.4	7.3	16.1	26.7	28.1	26.1	28.1	18.3	24.4	•
Coverage Ratio 33	2.7	•	0.5	1.4	2.3	3.5	4.3	4.2	3.7	3.1	2.3	1.6
Total Asset Turnover 34	3.7	•	6.1	4.2	4.0	4.1	4.2	3.7	3.3	2.8	2.0	1.8
Inventory Turnover 35	6.5	•	8.6	8.8	5.2	5.8	6.9	7.4	6.8	7.9	7.1	7.5
Receivables Turnover 36	29.0	•	55.2	17.2	30.8	38.4	36.4	31.2	24.3	17.9	17.7	10.6
Total Liabilities to Net Worth 37	4.1	•	6.0	3.5	3.8	5.3	4.6	4.1	3.7	3.7	2.6	2.9
Current Assets to Working Capital 38	5.6	•	1.8	1.6	3.6	5.6	5.7	5.6	6.3	4.5	7.3	•
Current Liabilities to Working Capital 39	4.6	•	0.8	0.6	2.6	4.6	4.7	4.6	5.3	3.5	6.3	•
Working Capital to Net Sales 40	0.0	•	0.1	0.1	0.1	0.0	0.0	0.0	0.0	0.1	0.0	•
Inventory to Working Capital 41	3.9	•	1.2	0.9	2.6	4.2	4.1	3.7	4.0	2.6	3.1	•
Total Receipts to Cash Flow 42	27.9	30.3	20.8	28.1	27.9	30.9	29.8	28.4	24.4	27.7	10.5	24.5
Cost of Goods to Cash Flow 43	24.7	28.0	18.0	25.3	24.6	27.5	26.5	25.2	21.4	24.4	8.6	21.0
Cash Flow to Total Debt 44	0.2	•	0.3	0.2	0.2	0.2	0.2	0.2	0.2	0.1	0.3	0.1

Selected Financial Factors (in Percentages)

	•	•	•	•	•	•	•	•	•	•	•
Debt Ratio 45	80.3	•	85.8	77.6	79.1	84.2	82.0	80.2	78.7	78.5	72.2	74.4
Return on Total Assets 46	5.5	•	1.7	4.3	4.8	4.8	5.8	6.1	6.1	4.9	5.7	6.8
Return on Equity Before Income Taxes 47	17.6	•	•	5.7	12.7	21.5	24.8	23.4	20.9	15.5	11.6	9.7
Return on Equity After Income Taxes 48	15.5	•	•	5.0	11.7	20.1	23.5	21.7	18.3	11.8	8.4	5.4
Profit Margin (Before Income Tax) 49	0.9	•	•	0.3	0.7	0.8	1.1	1.2	1.4	1.2	1.6	1.4
Profit Margin (After Income Tax) 50	0.8	•	•	0.3	0.6	0.8	1.0	1.2	0.9	1.2	1.2	0.8

Table II

Corporations with Net Income

NEW AND USED CAR DEALERS

MONEY AMOUNTS AND SIZE OF ASSETS IN THOUSANDS OF DOLLARS

Item Description for Accounting Period 7/02 Through 6/03	Total	Zero Assets	Under 500	500 to 1,000	1,000 to 5,000	5,000 to 10,000	10,000 to 25,000	25,000 to 50,000	50,000 to 100,000	100,000 to 250,000	250,000 to 500,000	500,000 to 2,500,000	2,500,000 and over
Number of Enterprises **1**	26525	43	11410	2192	6352	0	2448	453	106	26	0	0	0
Revenues ($ in Thousands)													
Net Sales **2**	506711775	2296059	13123785	6823420	78945903	0	156948208	59446181	23618458	10598731	0	0	0
Interest **3**	1696955	98704	814	21201	132707	0	154167	64737	29559	43176	0	0	0
Rents **4**	166133	5	8161	0	16996	0	27975	33977	7147	14184	0	0	0
Royalties **5**	137360	0	0	0	0	0	644	75	0	5104	0	0	0
Other Portfolio Income **6**	450082	5724	8430	211	39106	0	57964	42365	28249	10789	0	0	0
Other Receipts **7**	8402894	105192	45925	31391	1215361	0	2805879	1144329	478186	227710	0	0	0
Total Receipts **8**	517565199	2505684	13187115	6876223	80350073	0	159994837	60731664	24161599	10899694	0	0	0
Average Total Receipts **9**	19512	58272	1156	3137	12650	•	65357	134065	227940	419219	•	•	•
Operating Costs/Operating Income (%)													
Cost of Operations **10**	88.1	89.0	84.8	89.2	87.9	•	88.6	88.6	87.6	88.3	•	•	•
Salaries and Wages **11**	4.9	6.1	2.1	2.2	4.4	•	5.0	5.0	5.4	5.3	•	•	•
Taxes Paid **12**	0.8	0.8	1.2	0.7	0.8	•	0.7	0.7	0.8	0.8	•	•	•
Interest Paid **13**	0.5	1.1	0.4	0.6	0.4	•	0.3	0.4	0.5	0.5	•	•	•
Depreciation **14**	0.4	0.4	0.2	0.2	0.3	•	0.4	0.6	0.6	0.8	•	•	•
Amortization and Depletion **15**	0.1	0.1	0.0	0.0	0.0	•	0.0	0.0	0.0	0.0	•	•	•
Pensions and Other Deferred Comp. **16**	0.1	0.0	0.0	0.0	0.0	•	0.1	0.1	0.1	0.1	•	•	•
Employee Benefits **17**	0.4	0.7	0.1	0.1	0.4	•	0.4	0.4	0.4	0.5	•	•	•
Advertising **18**	1.1	1.2	0.7	0.6	1.1	•	1.0	1.0	1.1	1.1	•	•	•
Other Expenses **19**	3.6	7.2	6.2	3.8	3.9	•	3.1	3.1	3.6	3.3	•	•	•
Officers' Compensation **20**	0.8	0.3	1.9	1.6	1.1	•	0.8	0.7	0.6	0.6	•	•	•
Operating Margin **21**	•	•	2.5	1.1	•	•	•	•	•	•	•	•	•
Operating Margin Before Officers' Comp. **22**	0.2	•	4.4	2.7	0.7	•	0.3	0.1	•	•	•	•	•

Selected Average Balance Sheet ($ in Thousands)

Net Receivables 23	677	0	16	210	353	•	1799	4438	8812	24564
Inventories 24	2545	0	98	334	2025	•	8158	15768	28012	44904
Net Property, Plant and Equipment 25	508	0	18	19	171	•	1400	4365	10286	20701
Total Assets 26	5071	0	170	720	2865	•	14818	33739	65803	139103
Notes and Loans Payable 27	3125	0	91	421	1814	•	10374	22793	42700	94590
All Other Liabilities 28	817	0	35	98	354	•	1467	3443	8771	13234
Net Worth 29	1128	0	45	200	698	•	2977	7502	14331	31279

Selected Financial Ratios (Times to 1)

Current Ratio 30	1.2	•	2.9	2.6	1.5	•	1.2	1.3	1.2	1.3
Quick Ratio 31	0.4	•	0.8	1.1	0.3	•	0.3	0.4	0.4	0.5
Net Sales to Working Capital 32	24.8	•	11.8	7.5	15.3	•	26.1	23.5	27.3	16.7
Coverage Ratio 33	4.0	3.0	8.3	4.4	4.6	•	6.0	5.5	4.5	3.7
Total Asset Turnover 34	3.8	•	6.7	4.3	4.3	•	4.3	3.9	3.4	2.9
Inventory Turnover 35	6.6	•	9.9	8.3	5.4	•	7.0	7.4	7.0	8.0
Receivables Turnover 36	29.1	•	141.4	17.5	33.1	•	36.3	32.3	26.1	18.2
Total Liabilities to Net Worth 37	3.5	•	2.8	2.6	3.1	•	4.0	3.5	3.6	3.4
Current Assets to Working Capital 38	5.1	•	1.5	1.6	3.2	•	5.1	4.9	6.0	4.1
Current Liabilities to Working Capital 39	4.1	•	0.5	0.6	2.2	•	4.1	3.9	5.0	3.1
Working Capital to Net Sales 40	0.0	•	0.1	0.1	0.1	•	0.0	0.0	0.0	0.1
Inventory to Working Capital 41	3.5	•	1.0	0.9	2.4	•	3.7	3.2	3.9	2.4
Total Receipts to Cash Flow 42	24.5	12.6	13.4	21.6	23.3	•	27.2	25.9	23.6	25.8
Cost of Goods to Cash Flow 43	21.6	11.2	11.3	19.3	20.5	•	24.1	23.0	20.6	22.8
Cash Flow to Total Debt 44	0.2	•	0.7	0.3	0.2	•	0.2	0.2	0.2	0.1

Selected Financial Factors (in Percentages)

Debt Ratio 45	77.8	•	73.6	72.2	75.7	•	79.9	77.8	78.2	77.5
Return on Total Assets 46	7.8	•	22.5	10.6	8.0	•	7.7	7.8	7.0	6.0
Return on Equity Before Income Taxes 47	26.1	•	75.1	29.6	25.7	•	32.0	28.7	25.1	19.4
Return on Equity After Income Taxes 48	23.8	•	73.7	28.8	24.4	•	30.5	26.8	22.2	15.5
Profit Margin (Before Income Tax) 49	1.5	2.1	2.9	1.9	1.4	•	1.5	1.6	1.6	1.5
Profit Margin (After Income Tax) 50	1.4	1.6	1.8	1.8	1.4	•	1.4	1.5	1.4	1.2

Table I

Corporations with and without Net Income

OTHER MOTOR VEHICLE AND PARTS DEALERS

MONEY AMOUNTS AND SIZE OF ASSETS IN THOUSANDS OF DOLLARS

Item Description for Accounting Period 7/02 Through 6/03	Total	Zero Assets	Under 500	500 to 1,000	1,000 to 5,000	5,000 to 10,000	10,000 to 25,000	25,000 to 50,000	50,000 to 100,000	100,000 to 250,000	250,000 to 500,000	500,000 to 2,500,000	2,500,000 and over
Number of Enterprises **1**	45373	2713	29952	5445	5984	781	355	74	40	19	4	5	0
Revenues ($ in Thousands)													
Net Sales **2**	113767148	741045	14454011	8974643	31151388	13116511	12805558	6521041	5903935	4526165	2705505	12867345	0
Interest **3**	128697	153	7779	6489	26608	13054	17366	12316	7715	21404	10528	5284	0
Rents **4**	95856	0	6607	4595	18183	14592	8223	6686	27890	2721	2551	3809	0
Royalties **5**	219084	0	0	0	0	290	272	3	2	8633	0	209884	0
Other Portfolio Income **6**	304210	18873	58242	22090	27858	13448	31062	10098	38666	82678	165	1027	0
Other Receipts **7**	2598840	17232	32006	86228	382169	190739	138192	68086	92776	29424	33613	1528380	0
Total Receipts **8**	117713835	777303	14558645	9094045	31606206	13348634	13000673	6618230	6070984	4671025	2752362	14615729	0
Average Total Receipts **9**	2581	287	486	1670	5282	17092	36622	89436	151775	245843	688090	2923146	·
Operating Costs/Operating Income (%)													
Cost of Operations **10**	72.6	57.9	65.3	68.8	77.0	79.6	81.0	81.5	76.5	71.3	57.1	55.5	·
Salaries and Wages **11**	9.8	16.5	10.2	11.1	7.6	7.6	7.1	7.4	8.9	9.3	18.6	18.3	·
Taxes Paid **12**	1.9	1.9	2.8	2.0	1.5	1.3	1.1	1.2	1.4	1.6	2.1	4.1	·
Interest Paid **13**	1.1	1.8	1.0	1.1	1.1	1.0	1.0	1.1	1.2	1.4	1.2	1.6	·
Depreciation **14**	1.6	1.6	1.4	1.3	1.0	1.6	1.4	1.3	3.4	4.0	1.5	2.3	·
Amortization and Depletion **15**	0.1	1.8	0.1	0.0	0.1	0.0	0.0	0.1	0.2	0.4	1.0	0.1	·
Pensions and Other Deferred Comp. **16**	0.2	0.0	0.1	0.1	0.1	0.2	0.2	0.2	0.2	0.7	0.3	0.2	·
Employee Benefits **17**	0.8	0.5	0.4	0.5	0.5	0.9	0.6	0.7	0.9	1.0	1.0	1.7	·
Advertising **18**	1.1	3.0	1.5	1.2	1.3	0.8	0.9	0.7	0.9	0.8	1.9	1.1	·
Other Expenses **19**	10.1	26.8	13.5	11.1	7.4	5.8	6.1	5.8	7.9	8.5	15.7	22.3	·
Officers' Compensation **20**	1.8	0.7	5.0	2.9	2.0	1.6	1.1	0.6	0.7	0.5	0.3	0.2	·
Operating Margin **21**	·	·	·	·	0.4	·	·	·	·	0.6	·	·	·
Operating Margin Before Officers' Comp. **22**	0.6	·	3.8	2.8	2.3	1.3	0.5	·	·	1.0	·	·	·

Selected Average Balance Sheet ($ in Thousands)

Item													
Net Receivables 23	102	0	14	71	177	685	1864	5348	9155	21094	64291	35058	•
Inventories 24	555	0	64	413	1343	3644	7914	16178	30126	45659	69337	753891	•
Net Property, Plant and Equipment 25	204	0	23	112	278	1115	2338	5696	15476	44931	44002	502875	•
Total Assets 26	1079	0	128	709	2094	6888	14941	33953	68544	156808	317202	1709654	•
Notes and Loans Payable 27	507	0	80	296	966	3311	8568	19025	39477	60134	142173	572091	•
All Other Liabilities 28	286	0	30	166	594	1586	4121	8323	15272	29778	62351	576728	•
Net Worth 29	286	0	18	247	534	1991	2252	6605	13795	66895	112677	560835	•

Selected Financial Ratios (Times to 1)

Item												
Current Ratio 30	1.5	•	2.5	1.6	1.4	1.3	1.3	1.3	1.2	1.3	2.0	1.1
Quick Ratio 31	0.3	•	0.8	0.3	0.3	0.3	0.4	0.4	0.4	0.5	0.9	0.1
Net Sales to Working Capital 32	10.0	•	8.5	8.0	10.4	12.1	17.5	17.5	16.7	13.1	8.4	53.8
Coverage Ratio 33	2.5	•	0.5	2.7	2.5	2.0	1.7	1.6	4.1	1.8	4.9	
Total Asset Turnover 34	2.3	•	3.8	2.3	2.5	2.4	2.4	2.6	2.2	1.5	2.1	1.5
Inventory Turnover 35	3.3	•	4.9	2.7	3.0	3.7	3.7	4.4	3.7	3.7	5.6	1.9
Receivables Turnover 36	22.4	•	28.2	18.4	27.7	26.3	18.7	15.9	15.4	8.9	10.8	59.0
Total Liabilities to Net Worth 37	2.8	•	6.3	1.9	2.9	2.5	5.6	4.1	4.0	1.3	1.8	2.0
Current Assets to Working Capital 38	3.0	•	1.7	1.7	3.3	3.3	3.9	4.9	5.1	4.4	2.0	17.5
Current Liabilities to Working Capital 39	2.0	•	0.7	0.7	1.7	2.3	2.9	3.9	4.1	3.4	1.0	16.5
Working Capital to Net Sales 40	0.1	•	0.1	0.2	0.1	0.1	0.1	0.1	0.1	0.1	0.1	0.0
Inventory to Working Capital 41	2.2	•	1.1	1.2	2.1	2.4	2.8	3.4	3.4	2.4	0.9	14.2
Total Receipts to Cash Flow 42	11.3	8.8	12.1	10.5	14.4	18.5	19.7	21.0	16.2	10.0	9.0	4.3
Cost of Goods to Cash Flow 43	8.2	5.1	7.9	7.2	11.1	14.7	16.0	17.1	12.4	7.1	5.1	2.4
Cash Flow to Total Debt 44	0.3	•	0.4	0.3	0.2	0.2	0.1	0.2	0.2	0.3	0.4	0.5

Selected Financial Factors (in Percentages)

Item												
Debt Ratio 45	73.5	•	86.2	65.1	74.5	71.1	84.9	80.5	79.9	57.3	64.5	67.2
Return on Total Assets 46	6.7	•	1.9	5.3	7.2	5.8	4.7	4.9	4.4	9.0	4.5	11.8
Return on Equity Before Income Taxes 47	15.3	•	•	7.8	18.1	12.0	15.4	10.4	8.4	16.0	5.7	28.5
Return on Equity After Income Taxes 48	11.7	•	•	7.3	16.8	10.0	12.4	8.2	6.6	10.1	3.4	19.4
Profit Margin (Before Income Tax) 49	1.7	•	•	1.2	1.9	1.4	1.0	0.8	0.8	4.5	1.0	6.2
Profit Margin (After Income Tax) 50	1.3	•	•	1.1	1.7	1.2	0.8	0.6	0.6	2.8	0.6	4.2

Table II
Corporations with Net Income

OTHER MOTOR VEHICLE AND PARTS DEALERS

MONEY AMOUNTS AND SIZE OF ASSETS IN THOUSANDS OF DOLLARS

Item Description for Accounting Period 7/02 Through 6/03	Total	Zero Assets	Under 500	500 to 1,000	1,000 to 5,000	5,000 to 10,000	10,000 to 25,000	25,000 to 50,000	50,000 to 100,000	100,000 to 250,000	250,000 to 500,000	500,000 to 2,500,000	2,500,000 and over
Number of Enterprises **1**	24921	1104	14680	3650	4499	0	247	51	25	13	0	0	0
Revenues ($ in Thousands)													
Net Sales **2**	89844658	459037	8188464	6748555	25573304	0	9599874	4811385	4378908	3640094	0	0	0
Interest **3**	103037	0	5782	5210	20223	0	13257	8253	3544	20882	0	0	0
Rents **4**	69788	0	4634	4595	11775	0	5259	5891	26110	2069	0	0	0
Royalties **5**	218788	0	0	0	0	0	270	0	0	8633	0	0	0
Other Portfolio Income **6**	227205	10558	47208	21777	22291	0	22263	6656	14938	72052	0	0	0
Other Receipts **7**	2342596	9685	19354	70432	288190	0	106871	52975	59460	24368	0	0	0
Total Receipts **8**	92806072	479280	8265442	6850569	25915783	0	9747794	4885160	4482960	3768098	0	0	0
Average Total Receipts **9**	3724	434	563	1877	5760	*	39465	95787	179318	289854	*	*	*
Operating Costs/Operating Income (%)													
Cost of Operations **10**	71.8	47.0	63.2	68.4	76.1	*	80.6	81.5	78.4	70.6	*	*	*
Salaries and Wages **11**	10.0	20.2	9.4	10.6	7.7	*	7.1	7.4	8.2	9.8	*	*	*
Taxes Paid **12**	1.9	2.3	2.4	2.2	1.5	*	1.1	1.2	1.2	1.7	*	*	*
Interest Paid **13**	1.0	0.1	0.8	0.9	0.9	*	0.9	0.9	0.9	1.2	*	*	*
Depreciation **14**	1.3	0.8	1.4	1.3	0.9	*	1.1	1.1	1.6	2.4	*	*	*
Amortization and Depletion **15**	0.1	0.0	0.0	0.0	0.1	*	0.0	0.1	0.1	0.5	*	*	*
Pensions and Other Deferred Comp. **16**	0.2	0.0	0.1	0.1	0.2	*	0.2	0.2	0.2	0.7	*	*	*
Employee Benefits **17**	0.8	0.3	0.3	0.5	0.5	*	0.6	0.7	0.7	1.1	*	*	*
Advertising **18**	1.1	3.4	1.5	1.0	1.2	*	0.9	0.7	1.0	0.8	*	*	*
Other Expenses **19**	9.9	20.5	12.0	10.6	7.3	*	5.7	5.1	6.9	8.6	*	*	*
Officers' Compensation **20**	1.7	0.5	5.4	2.9	2.0	*	1.2	0.6	0.7	0.5	*	*	*
Operating Margin **21**	0.1	4.9	3.2	1.5	1.5	*	0.6	0.4	0.1	2.1	*	*	*
Operating Margin Before Officers' Comp. **22**	1.8	5.3	8.6	4.4	3.5	*	1.8	1.0	0.8	2.6	*	*	*

Selected Average Balance Sheet ($ in Thousands)

Net Receivables 23	136	0	17	64	191	•	1734	5331	9614	23745
Inventories 24	757	0	62	396	1340	•	8182	16063	31580	55975
Net Property, Plant and Equipment 25	274	0	25	133	277	•	2165	5071	12209	34043
Total Assets 26	1507	0	146	712	2122	•	14955	34724	70457	156303
Notes and Loans Payable 27	632	0	62	278	879	•	8024	17738	37972	48741
All Other Liabilities 28	398	0	25	144	612	•	3220	8946	17825	28431
Net Worth 29	477	0	58	289	631	•	3711	8040	14660	79132

Selected Financial Ratios (Times to 1)

Current Ratio 30	1.5	•	3.0	2.5	1.7	•	1.4	1.3	1.2	1.6
Quick Ratio 31	0.3	•	1.2	0.7	0.3	•	0.3	0.4	0.3	0.6
Net Sales to Working Capital 32	9.9	•	8.0	5.6	7.7	•	11.6	15.7	17.7	8.2
Coverage Ratio 33	4.4	84.1	6.2	4.3	4.3	•	3.4	3.1	3.7	6.2
Total Asset Turnover 34	2.4	•	3.8	2.6	2.7	•	2.6	2.7	2.5	1.8
Inventory Turnover 35	3.4	•	5.7	3.2	3.2	•	3.8	4.8	4.3	3.5
Receivables Turnover 36	25.0	•	66.8	20.0	28.9	•	20.7	18.3	19.2	8.3
Total Liabilities to Net Worth 37	2.2	•	1.5	1.5	2.4	•	3.0	3.3	3.8	1.0
Current Assets to Working Capital 38	2.9	•	1.5	1.7	2.4	•	3.6	4.2	5.2	2.5
Current Liabilities to Working Capital 39	1.9	•	0.5	0.7	1.4	•	2.6	3.2	4.2	1.5
Working Capital to Net Sales 40	0.1	•	0.1	0.2	0.1	•	0.1	0.1	0.1	0.1
Inventory to Working Capital 41	2.2	•	0.9	1.2	1.9	•	2.7	2.9	3.6	1.4
Total Receipts to Cash Flow 42	9.6	4.3	8.6	9.1	12.7	•	16.8	18.2	13.9	8.6
Cost of Goods to Cash Flow 43	6.9	2.0	5.4	6.2	9.7	•	13.6	14.9	10.9	6.0
Cash Flow to Total Debt 44	0.4	•	0.7	0.5	0.3	•	0.2	0.2	0.2	0.4

Selected Financial Factors (in Percentages)

Debt Ratio 45	68.3	•	60.1	59.4	70.2	•	75.2	76.8	79.2	49.4
Return on Total Assets 46	10.6	•	18.8	10.3	10.1	•	7.9	7.8	8.3	13.9
Return on Equity Before Income Taxes 47	25.8	•	39.5	19.5	25.9	•	22.4	22.6	29.0	23.0
Return on Equity After Income Taxes 48	21.8	•	38.2	18.8	24.5	•	19.8	19.9	26.3	15.7
Profit Margin (Before Income Tax) 49	3.4	9.3	4.1	3.0	2.9	•	2.1	1.9	2.4	6.5
Profit Margin (After Income Tax) 50	2.9	9.3	4.0	2.9	2.7	•	1.9	1.7	2.2	4.4

Table I

Corporations with and without Net Income

FURNITURE AND HOME FURNISHINGS STORES

MONEY AMOUNTS AND SIZE OF ASSETS IN THOUSANDS OF DOLLARS

Item Description for Accounting Period 7/02 Through 6/03	Total	Zero Assets	Under 500	500 to 1,000	1,000 to 5,000	5,000 to 10,000	10,000 to 25,000	25,000 to 50,000	50,000 to 100,000	100,000 to 250,000	250,000 to 500,000	500,000 to 2,500,000	2,500,000 and over
Number of Enterprises **1**	42078	3104	31162	3939	3328	303	149	41	21	16	5	9	0
Revenues ($ in Thousands)													
Net Sales **2**	79512483	1018872	17225266	7445650	17473558	4210980	5564486	3664449	3540225	5303559	2289783	11775655	0
Interest **3**	287386	205	7681	26154	65680	10107	11628	3079	25463	47109	2594	87686	0
Rents **4**	39304	36	6186	1022	1842	5919	3977	464	627	4537	2065	12627	0
Royalties **5**	81962	0	0	0	0	0	7	169	149	3029	293	78314	0
Other Portfolio Income **6**	92047	1144	11546	6748	4657	1205	2348	4617	1023	6118	45849	6793	0
Other Receipts **7**	750255	7243	55756	49012	104026	50186	89081	63834	44666	130837	2474	153143	0
Total Receipts **8**	80763437	1027500	17306435	7528586	17649763	4278397	5671527	3736612	3612153	5495189	2343058	12114218	0
Average Total Receipts **9**	1919	331	555	1911	5303	14120	38064	91137	172007	343449	468612	1346024	•
Operating Costs/Operating Income (%)													
Cost of Operations **10**	59.9	71.6	63.4	60.6	62.5	63.7	62.1	58.3	59.3	54.0	56.9	51.0	•
Salaries and Wages **11**	11.8	6.5	8.2	10.9	12.1	12.7	13.3	14.3	14.2	13.0	11.7	14.5	•
Taxes Paid **12**	2.3	2.8	2.5	2.9	2.1	2.0	1.9	2.1	2.0	2.4	2.5	2.5	•
Interest Paid **13**	0.8	0.6	0.8	0.8	0.6	0.6	0.6	0.6	0.8	1.1	1.2	1.0	•
Depreciation **14**	1.5	0.9	1.0	0.9	1.1	1.0	1.4	1.5	1.4	1.9	2.7	3.1	•
Amortization and Depletion **15**	0.2	0.2	0.1	0.0	0.1	0.0	0.1	0.2	0.8	0.3	0.1	0.4	•
Pensions and Other Deferred Comp. **16**	0.2	0.0	0.1	0.3	0.2	0.4	0.2	0.2	0.1	0.3	0.4	0.3	•
Employee Benefits **17**	0.8	0.4	0.5	0.8	0.5	0.6	0.9	1.1	0.5	1.0	1.6	1.5	•
Advertising **18**	3.9	4.6	2.2	4.0	3.7	4.1	4.5	4.3	4.9	6.7	6.5	4.0	•
Other Expenses **19**	15.0	22.1	15.9	13.3	13.4	12.9	14.7	14.4	14.7	20.3	13.8	15.5	•
Officers' Compensation **20**	2.9	0.8	5.7	4.3	3.3	2.4	1.6	1.4	0.9	0.5	0.7	0.8	•
Operating Margin **21**	0.7	•	•	1.0	0.5	•	•	1.7	0.3	•	1.9	5.4	•
Operating Margin Before Officers' Comp. **22**	3.6	•	5.3	5.4	3.8	2.0	0.3	3.1	1.2	•	2.7	6.3	•

Selected Average Balance Sheet ($ in Thousands)

	1	2	3	4	5	6	7	8	9	10	11	12	13
Net Receivables 23	112	0	18	134	417	1052	3119	5972	12097	18749	64630	34434	•
Inventories 24	288	0	53	281	881	2426	5339	12275	22975	44526	79703	311245	•
Net Property, Plant and Equipment 25	184	0	28	126	374	1132	2880	7844	16193	44501	77348	288973	•
Total Assets 26	885	0	140	724	2089	6481	14959	34200	71697	162748	332125	1301390	•
Notes and Loans Payable 27	237	0	67	229	597	1458	4530	9211	23663	46541	85789	200619	•
All Other Liabilities 28	360	0	49	156	772	2571	7511	13110	20085	54488	100725	687477	•
Net Worth 29	289	0	24	340	720	2452	2919	11879	27949	61719	145612	413294	•

Selected Financial Ratios (Times to 1)

	1	2	3	4	5	6	7	8	9	10	11	12	13
Current Ratio 30	1.7	•	1.9	3.0	1.7	1.7	1.2	1.4	1.6	1.7	1.7	1.7	•
Quick Ratio 31	0.6	•	0.7	1.3	0.6	0.6	0.5	0.5	0.7	0.6	0.7	0.4	•
Net Sales to Working Capital 32	8.1	•	12.5	5.1	8.1	7.2	19.6	12.2	10.0	8.6	5.9	5.0	•
Coverage Ratio 33	3.9	•	1.1	3.5	3.4	3.0	2.1	7.3	4.1	2.8	6.0	9.3	•
Total Asset Turnover 34	2.1	•	3.9	2.6	2.5	2.1	2.5	2.6	2.4	2.0	1.4	1.0	•
Inventory Turnover 35	3.9	•	6.6	4.1	3.7	3.6	4.3	4.2	4.4	4.0	3.3	2.1	•
Receivables Turnover 36	17.7	•	33.2	13.5	13.3	15.3	12.1	17.4	14.5	15.3	8.5	38.8	•
Total Liabilities to Net Worth 37	2.1	•	4.9	1.1	1.9	1.6	4.1	1.9	1.6	1.6	1.3	2.1	•
Current Assets to Working Capital 38	2.4	•	2.2	1.5	2.4	2.4	5.8	3.3	2.6	2.4	2.4	2.5	•
Current Liabilities to Working Capital 39	1.4	•	1.2	0.5	1.4	1.4	4.8	2.3	1.6	1.4	1.4	1.5	•
Working Capital to Net Sales 40	0.1	•	0.1	0.2	0.1	0.1	0.1	0.1	0.1	0.1	0.2	0.2	•
Inventory to Working Capital 41	1.3	•	1.2	0.8	1.4	1.3	2.8	1.9	1.4	1.2	1.3	1.3	•
Total Receipts to Cash Flow 42	8.9	21.8	10.9	9.0	10.3	12.1	9.8	8.0	8.9	6.5	6.6	6.2	•
Cost of Goods to Cash Flow 43	5.3	15.6	6.9	5.4	6.5	7.7	6.1	4.6	5.3	3.5	3.8	3.2	•
Cash Flow to Total Debt 44	0.4	•	0.4	0.5	0.4	0.3	0.3	0.5	0.4	0.5	0.4	0.2	•

Selected Financial Factors (in Percentages)

	1	2	3	4	5	6	7	8	9	10	11	12	13
Debt Ratio 45	67.3	•	83.0	53.1	65.5	62.2	80.5	65.3	61.0	62.1	56.2	68.2	•
Return on Total Assets 46	6.7	•	3.6	7.8	5.4	3.8	3.3	11.2	7.3	6.3	9.7	9.3	•
Return on Equity Before Income Taxes 47	15.3	•	1.8	11.9	11.0	6.7	8.8	27.9	14.1	10.5	18.4	26.2	•
Return on Equity After Income Taxes 48	11.3	•	0.2	11.1	9.4	5.5	6.2	26.3	12.9	7.6	12.8	17.6	•
Profit Margin (Before Income Tax) 49	2.3	•	0.1	2.1	1.5	1.2	0.7	3.7	2.3	2.0	5.8	8.3	•
Profit Margin (After Income Tax) 50	1.7	•	0.0	2.0	1.3	1.0	0.5	3.5	2.1	1.4	4.1	5.5	•

Table II

Corporations with Net Income

FURNITURE AND HOME FURNISHINGS STORES

MONEY AMOUNTS AND SIZE OF ASSETS IN THOUSANDS OF DOLLARS

Item Description for Accounting Period 7/02 Through 6/03	Total	Zero Assets	Under 500	500 to 1,000	1,000 to 5,000	5,000 to 10,000	10,000 to 25,000	25,000 to 50,000	50,000 to 100,000	100,000 to 250,000	250,000 to 500,000	500,000 to 2,500,000	2,500,000 and over
Number of Enterprises **1**	20141	552	14090	2607	2516	195	111	32	15	0	5	0	0
Revenues ($ in Thousands)													
Net Sales **2**	59652070	308908	9696549	5393098	14238779	2949771	4373065	3119185	2748997	0	2289783	0	0
Interest **3**	244397	0	3542	23369	52275	3740	7600	878	25227	0	2594	0	0
Rents **4**	35088	0	6186	183	1143	4738	3476	121	478	0	2065	0	0
Royalties **5**	81763	0	0	0	0	0	0	169	149	0	293	0	0
Other Portfolio Income **6**	88123	0	11545	6370	4604	761	1004	4522	1022	0	45849	0	0
Other Receipts **7**	592593	898	40081	46147	80367	36748	88929	59521	40739	0	2474	0	0
Total Receipts **8**	60694034	309806	9757903	5469167	14377168	2995758	4474074	3184396	2816612	0	2343058	0	0
Average Total Receipts **9**	3013	561	693	2098	5714	15363	40307	99512	187774	•	468612	•	•
Operating Costs/Operating Income (%)													
Cost of Operations **10**	59.0	53.3	62.7	61.5	61.8	65.8	62.8	57.8	60.6	•	56.9	•	•
Salaries and Wages **11**	11.7	2.4	6.6	10.6	11.7	11.6	12.9	14.0	14.4	•	11.7	•	•
Taxes Paid **12**	2.3	0.3	2.6	2.9	2.1	2.0	1.8	2.0	1.8	•	2.5	•	•
Interest Paid **13**	0.7	0.2	0.6	0.7	0.6	0.4	0.5	0.5	0.6	•	1.2	•	•
Depreciation **14**	1.5	0.7	0.9	0.9	0.8	1.1	1.0	1.5	1.3	•	2.7	•	•
Amortization and Depletion **15**	0.2	•	0.1	0.0	0.1	0.0	0.0	0.1	0.8	•	0.1	•	•
Pensions and Other Deferred Comp. **16**	0.2	•	0.1	0.1	0.2	0.4	0.2	0.2	0.2	•	0.4	•	•
Employee Benefits **17**	0.8	•	0.3	0.8	0.5	0.5	0.9	1.1	0.4	•	1.6	•	•
Advertising **18**	3.7	9.0	2.2	3.4	3.5	3.4	4.4	4.4	4.1	•	6.5	•	•
Other Expenses **19**	13.9	27.4	14.4	12.2	13.0	10.4	11.8	14.1	12.9	•	13.8	•	•
Officers' Compensation **20**	2.7	•	5.7	4.1	3.5	2.2	1.5	1.4	0.9	•	0.7	•	•
Operating Margin **21**	3.3	6.7	3.9	2.8	2.3	2.1	2.1	3.0	2.1	•	1.9	•	•
Operating Margin Before Officers' Comp. **22**	6.0	6.7	9.6	6.9	5.7	4.3	3.6	4.4	2.9	•	2.7	•	•

Selected Average Balance Sheet ($ in Thousands)

Net Receivables 23	175	0	20	124	431	1102	3302	4659	15124	•	64630
Inventories 24	451	0	55	260	860	2551	5440	12182	29958	•	79703
Net Property, Plant and Equipment 25	305	0	33	136	359	1160	2590	7988	19249	•	77348
Total Assets 26	1349	0	159	735	2072	6292	14960	34153	76721	•	332125
Notes and Loans Payable 27	309	0	48	184	545	1300	3135	7147	23978	•	85789
All Other Liabilities 28	454	0	53	157	742	1962	5606	12644	23913	•	100725
Net Worth 29	586	0	58	394	786	3029	6219	14363	28831	•	145612

Selected Financial Ratios (Times to 1)

Current Ratio 30	1.8	•	1.9	3.0	1.8	1.8	1.7	1.6	1.7	•	1.7
Quick Ratio 31	0.7	•	0.9	1.4	0.7	0.7	0.8	0.6	0.6	•	0.7
Net Sales to Working Capital 32	7.5	•	13.1	5.7	8.1	7.4	8.5	10.3	8.4	•	5.9
Coverage Ratio 33	8.6	31.5	8.8	6.8	6.6	9.3	9.2	12.2	8.0	•	6.0
Total Asset Turnover 34	2.2	•	4.3	2.8	2.7	2.4	2.6	2.9	2.4	•	1.4
Inventory Turnover 35	3.9	•	7.8	4.9	4.1	3.9	4.5	4.6	3.7	•	3.3
Receivables Turnover 36	17.2	•	35.0	15.1	13.5	16.2	11.5	23.2	24.2	•	8.5
Total Liabilities to Net Worth 37	1.3	•	1.8	0.9	1.6	1.1	1.4	1.4	1.7	•	1.3
Current Assets to Working Capital 38	2.3	•	2.1	1.5	2.2	2.3	2.4	2.6	2.4	•	2.4
Current Liabilities to Working Capital 39	1.3	•	1.1	0.5	1.2	1.3	1.4	1.6	1.4	•	1.4
Working Capital to Net Sales 40	0.1	•	0.1	0.2	0.1	0.1	0.1	0.1	0.1	•	0.2
Inventory to Working Capital 41	1.2	•	1.0	0.8	1.2	1.3	1.2	1.5	1.4	•	1.3
Total Receipts to Cash Flow 42	7.4	3.8	7.7	8.0	8.8	10.4	8.6	7.4	7.6	•	6.6
Cost of Goods to Cash Flow 43	4.4	2.0	4.8	4.9	5.4	6.9	5.4	4.3	4.6	•	3.8
Cash Flow to Total Debt 44	0.5	•	0.9	0.8	0.5	0.4	0.5	0.7	0.5	•	0.4

Selected Financial Factors (in Percentages)

Debt Ratio 45	56.6	•	63.8	46.4	62.1	51.9	58.4	57.9	62.4	•	56.2
Return on Total Assets 46	12.7	•	22.0	13.9	10.5	9.8	13.0	15.8	12.4	•	9.7
Return on Equity Before Income Taxes 47	25.8	•	53.8	22.1	23.4	18.2	27.8	34.4	28.9	•	18.4
Return on Equity After Income Taxes 48	21.6	•	52.3	21.1	21.4	16.6	26.1	32.7	27.2	•	12.8
Profit Margin (Before Income Tax) 49	5.1	7.0	4.5	4.2	3.2	3.6	4.4	5.1	4.5	•	5.8
Profit Margin (After Income Tax) 50	4.3	7.0	4.4	4.0	3.3	3.3	4.1	4.8	4.3	•	4.1

Table I

Corporations with and without Net Income

ELECTRONICS AND APPLIANCE STORES

MONEY AMOUNTS AND SIZE OF ASSETS IN THOUSANDS OF DOLLARS

Item Description for Accounting Period 7/02 Through 6/03	Total	Zero Assets	Under 500	500 to 1,000	1,000 to 5,000	5,000 to 10,000	10,000 to 25,000	25,000 to 50,000	50,000 to 100,000	100,000 to 250,000	250,000 to 500,000	500,000 to 2,500,000	2,500,000 and over
Number of Enterprises 1	28932	2252	21705	2047	2424	278	134	28	23	20	9	12	0
Revenues ($ in Thousands)													
Net Sales 2	88715266	631648	13508791	3703515	15114836	4661231	5347850	1936164	3461383	5998587	5852199	28499062	0
Interest 3	837416	689	4461	5266	9626	9497	10974	6314	6697	32992	12611	738289	0
Rents 4	53137	0	1653	2271	1947	81	1849	0	1390	145	3228	40574	0
Royalties 5	151241	0	0	0	368	18	4805	5023	241	1940	9609	129236	0
Other Portfolio Income 6	179146	399	4905	45161	10788	1648	10720	701	1867	2536	8538	91879	0
Other Receipts 7	2752525	14546	110357	127891	119331	45230	93636	15203	63880	214517	122580	1825360	0
Total Receipts 8	92688731	647282	13630167	3884104	15256896	4717705	5469834	1963405	3535458	6250717	6008765	31324400	0
Average Total Receipts 9	3204	287	628	1897	6294	16970	40820	70122	153716	312536	667641	2610367	·
Operating Costs/Operating Income (%)													
Cost of Operations 10	69.9	73.3	64.3	62.5	71.4	63.0	71.4	67.4	73.9	70.4	72.0	72.5	·
Salaries and Wages 11	12.4	11.4	11.9	14.3	10.7	16.2	13.0	15.9	11.0	14.4	11.7	12.3	·
Taxes Paid 12	2.0	1.8	2.1	2.7	1.4	2.0	1.5	1.6	1.5	1.6	1.3	2.5	·
Interest Paid 13	0.8	0.1	0.5	0.6	0.5	0.6	0.6	0.4	0.4	1.4	0.2	1.2	·
Depreciation 14	1.6	1.2	0.8	1.5	1.1	1.8	1.4	1.1	2.2	2.8	1.9	1.8	·
Amortization and Depletion 15	0.2	0.8	0.0	0.1	0.1	0.2	0.3	0.5	0.2	0.7	0.3	0.2	·
Pensions and Other Deferred Comp. 16	0.2	0.0	0.1	0.4	0.2	0.5	0.2	0.3	0.1	0.1	0.1	0.2	·
Employee Benefits 17	0.7	0.4	0.7	1.5	0.6	1.1	0.8	0.9	1.2	0.9	0.4	0.6	·
Advertising 18	2.0	1.0	1.9	1.5	2.3	1.3	1.1	0.9	1.3	2.4	1.7	2.4	·
Other Expenses 19	11.3	14.4	13.0	14.2	9.2	10.7	8.5	11.0	8.9	12.7	10.2	11.9	·
Officers' Compensation 20	2.2	0.4	5.6	5.9	2.9	3.6	2.3	2.1	1.0	0.6	0.9	0.3	·
Operating Margin 21	·	·	·	·	·	·	·	·	·	·	·	·	·
Operating Margin Before Officers' Comp. 22	·	·	4.6	0.8	2.5	2.5	1.2	·	0.2	·	0.2	·	·

Selected Average Balance Sheet ($ in Thousands)

Net Receivables 23	250	0	20	132	477	1958	4730	9836	18908	25256	59689	201796	•
Inventories 24	280	0	39	176	480	841	2431	4416	12315	25179	93658	284664	•
Net Property, Plant and Equipment 25	196	0	17	149	303	702	1833	1866	12042	25057	64535	199989	•
Total Assets 26	1364	0	125	698	1869	7082	15236	33223	70198	154725	371898	1483528	•
Notes and Loans Payable 27	313	0	72	175	474	2702	3134	5703	36488	43332	25936	226111	•
All Other Liabilities 28	560	0	68	205	852	3143	7592	19529	24300	60551	128819	573668	•
Net Worth 29	491	0	-15	319	543	1237	4511	7991	9410	50842	217142	683749	•

Selected Financial Ratios (Times to 1)

Current Ratio 30	1.4	•	1.2	1.8	1.6	1.3	1.4	1.1	1.6	1.3	1.8	1.3
Quick Ratio 31	0.8	•	0.6	1.1	0.9	0.9	1.0	0.8	1.0	0.8	0.9	0.7
Net Sales to Working Capital 32	12.1	•	46.1	9.0	11.9	19.6	11.8	26.4	8.1	14.5	6.5	10.1
Coverage Ratio 33	2.8	•	0.7	0.7	2.1	1.1	3.0	•	1.7	•	9.5	4.6
Total Asset Turnover 34	2.2	•	5.0	2.6	3.3	2.4	2.6	2.1	2.1	1.9	1.7	1.6
Inventory Turnover 35	7.6	•	10.2	6.4	9.3	12.6	11.7	10.6	9.0	8.4	5.0	6.1
Receivables Turnover 36	12.1	•	31.2	10.1	13.9	10.7	8.0	6.4	7.7	12.5	7.0	12.4
Total Liabilities to Net Worth 37	1.8	•	•	1.2	2.4	4.7	2.4	3.2	6.5	2.0	0.7	1.2
Current Assets to Working Capital 38	3.5	•	6.6	2.2	2.7	5.0	3.2	9.6	2.6	4.4	2.3	4.0
Current Liabilities to Working Capital 39	2.5	•	5.6	1.2	1.7	4.0	2.2	8.6	1.6	3.4	1.3	3.0
Working Capital to Net Sales 40	0.1	•	0.0	0.1	0.1	0.1	0.1	0.0	0.1	0.1	0.2	0.1
Inventory to Working Capital 41	1.1	•	3.2	0.8	0.9	0.9	0.8	1.3	0.6	1.3	1.0	1.2
Total Receipts to Cash Flow 42	11.2	12.9	10.5	10.2	13.6	12.0	13.3	13.2	14.7	18.1	12.8	9.0
Cost of Goods to Cash Flow 43	7.8	9.5	6.8	6.4	9.7	7.6	9.5	8.9	10.8	12.7	9.2	6.5
Cash Flow to Total Debt 44	0.3	•	0.4	0.5	0.3	0.2	0.3	0.2	0.2	0.2	0.3	0.3

Selected Financial Factors (in Percentages)

Debt Ratio 45	64.0	•	112.2	54.4	70.9	82.5	70.4	75.9	86.6	67.1	41.6	53.9
Return on Total Assets 46	4.9	•	1.5	1.0	3.4	1.7	4.7	1.3	1.3	•	3.8	9.0
Return on Equity Before Income Taxes 47	8.8	•	6.5	•	6.2	1.2	10.6	4.0	4.0	•	5.8	15.4
Return on Equity After Income Taxes 48	4.1	•	9.7	•	4.5	•	7.4	0.0	0.0	•	4.0	9.0
Profit Margin (Before Income Tax) 49	1.4	•	•	•	0.5	0.1	1.2	0.3	0.3	•	2.0	4.4
Profit Margin (After Income Tax) 50	0.6	•	•	•	0.4	•	0.8	0.0	0.0	•	1.3	2.6

Table II

Corporations with Net Income

ELECTRONICS AND APPLIANCE STORES

MONEY AMOUNTS AND SIZE OF ASSETS IN THOUSANDS OF DOLLARS

Item Description for Accounting Period 7/02 Through 6/03	Total	Zero Assets	Under 500	500 to 1,000	1,000 to 5,000	5,000 to 10,000	10,000 to 25,000	25,000 to 50,000	50,000 to 100,000	100,000 to 250,000	250,000 to 500,000	500,000 to 2,500,000	2,500,000 and over
Number of Enterprises **1**	14323	435	10811	1140	1637	164	93	12	0	7	0	7	0
Revenues ($ in Thousands)													
Net Sales **2**	68629063	575575	9491366	2002600	10956188	3123003	4312286	1001132	0	2449502	0	26679062	0
Interest **3**	739240	368	3104	4411	4829	1948	3630	3415	0	16559	0	691185	0
Rents **4**	35940	0	326	2271	1116	27	1334	0	0	113	0	27494	0
Royalties **5**	21389	0	0	0	0	0	4693	0	0	1940	0	5148	0
Other Portfolio Income **6**	89534	399	1444	44755	9973	734	2146	155	0	1765	0	20837	0
Other Receipts **7**	2427426	13177	95332	100873	53569	17244	43414	14122	0	128913	0	1802511	0
Total Receipts **8**	71942592	590519	9591572	2154910	11025675	3142956	4367503	1018824	0	2598792	0	29226237	0
Average Total Receipts **9**	5023	1358	887	1890	6735	19164	46962	84902	•	371256	•	4175177	•
Operating Costs/Operating Income (%)													
Cost of Operations **10**	71.3	74.5	66.2	59.7	72.2	67.2	72.4	58.1	•	75.8	•	73.0	•
Salaries and Wages **11**	10.8	9.7	9.7	13.9	9.9	11.9	10.9	17.7	•	10.6	•	11.4	•
Taxes Paid **12**	1.9	1.7	1.8	2.5	1.2	1.8	1.4	2.1	•	1.3	•	2.5	•
Interest Paid **13**	0.7	0.0	0.4	0.7	0.4	0.4	0.4	0.4	•	0.9	•	1.1	•
Depreciation **14**	1.3	1.0	0.7	1.3	0.8	1.2	1.2	0.9	•	3.3	•	1.6	•
Amortization and Depletion **15**	0.1	0.9	0.0	0.1	0.0	0.2	0.1	0.2	•	0.1	•	0.1	•
Pensions and Other Deferred Comp. **16**	0.2	•	0.1	0.6	0.3	0.6	0.2	0.4	•	0.1	•	0.2	•
Employee Benefits **17**	0.5	0.3	0.4	1.9	0.5	1.1	0.5	0.7	•	0.3	•	0.5	•
Advertising **18**	1.9	0.9	1.1	1.7	2.4	0.6	1.1	1.3	•	2.1	•	2.5	•
Other Expenses **19**	9.5	5.7	11.6	13.7	6.9	7.6	6.7	11.9	•	6.2	•	10.8	•
Officers' Compensation **20**	1.8	0.2	4.9	7.1	2.7	2.9	2.2	1.6	•	0.5	•	0.2	•
Operating Margin **21**	•	5.0	3.0	•	2.7	4.4	2.8	4.8	•	•	•	•	•
Operating Margin Before Officers' Comp. **22**	1.6	5.2	8.0	3.9	5.4	7.3	5.0	6.4	•	•	•	•	•

Selected Average Balance Sheet ($ in Thousands)

Net Receivables **23**	299	0	26	148	498	1507	4969	10987	26005	198900
Inventories **24**	457	0	45	223	485	1058	2695	6818	38969	477075
Net Property, Plant and Equipment **25**	287	0	20	78	255	611	1816	2185	37820	301141
Total Assets **26**	1764	0	158	677	1816	6700	14890	32790	143281	1808456
Notes and Loans Payable **27**	288	0	61	150	424	1041	2283	5584	41607	206983
All Other Liabilities **28**	645	0	89	189	795	2368	6821	16428	50815	554190
Net Worth **29**	831	0	8	339	598	3291	5786	10778	50859	1047284

Selected Financial Ratios (Times to 1)

Current Ratio **30**	1.7	•	1.2	2.4	1.9	1.7	1.6	1.3	1.3	1.7
Quick Ratio **31**	0.9	•	0.7	1.3	1.1	1.1	1.1	0.9	0.7	0.9
Net Sales to Working Capital **32**	9.5	•	39.1	6.2	9.8	11.0	10.3	12.7	14.9	7.0
Coverage Ratio **33**	8.0	230.6	12.3	6.9	9.7	12.8	11.9	18.1	6.2	6.3
Total Asset Turnover **34**	2.7	•	5.6	2.6	3.7	2.8	3.1	2.5	2.4	2.1
Inventory Turnover **35**	7.5	•	12.8	4.7	10.0	12.1	12.5	7.1	6.8	5.8
Receivables Turnover **36**	15.5	•	33.9	7.4	16.0	12.9	9.2	7.0	10.0	20.0
Total Liabilities to Net Worth **37**	1.1	•	19.9	1.0	2.0	1.0	1.6	2.0	1.8	0.7
Current Assets to Working Capital **38**	2.5	•	5.2	1.7	2.1	2.4	2.6	4.0	3.9	2.4
Current Liabilities to Working Capital **39**	1.5	•	4.2	0.7	1.1	1.4	1.6	3.0	2.9	1.4
Working Capital to Net Sales **40**	0.1	•	0.0	0.2	0.1	0.1	0.1	0.1	0.1	0.1
Inventory to Working Capital **41**	0.9	•	2.3	0.7	0.7	0.5	0.7	1.0	1.3	0.9
Total Receipts to Cash Flow **42**	9.2	10.9	7.9	7.6	11.9	9.3	11.0	6.6	10.4	8.2
Cost of Goods to Cash Flow **43**	6.6	8.1	5.2	4.5	8.6	6.3	8.0	3.8	7.9	6.0
Cash Flow to Total Debt **44**	0.6	•	0.7	0.7	0.5	0.6	0.5	0.6	0.4	0.6

Selected Financial Factors (in Percentages)

Debt Ratio **45**	52.9	•	95.2	49.9	67.1	50.9	61.1	67.1	64.5	42.1
Return on Total Assets **46**	14.3	•	24.7	13.2	13.7	15.4	14.0	17.7	14.2	14.0
Return on Equity Before Income Taxes **47**	26.5	•	475.5	22.6	37.3	28.9	32.9	50.7	33.6	20.4
Return on Equity After Income Taxes **48**	20.9	•	462.6	20.6	35.1	27.9	29.4	43.7	29.9	13.2
Profit Margin (Before Income Tax) **49**	4.6	7.4	4.1	4.4	3.3	5.0	4.1	6.6	4.9	5.6
Profit Margin (After Income Tax) **50**	3.6	4.8	4.0	3.1	4.8	3.7	5.6	•	4.3	3.6

Table I

Corporations with and without Net Income

HOMES CENTERS; PAINT AND WALLPAPER STORES

MONEY AMOUNTS AND SIZE OF ASSETS IN THOUSANDS OF DOLLARS

Item Description for Accounting Period 7/02 Through 6/03	Total	Zero Assets	Under 500	500 to 1,000	1,000 to 5,000	5,000 to 10,000	10,000 to 25,000	25,000 to 50,000	50,000 to 100,000	100,000 to 250,000	250,000 to 500,000	500,000 to 2,500,000	2,500,000 and over
Number of Enterprises **1**	4550	402	3325	271	456	43	30	8	11	.	.	0	3
Revenues ($ in Thousands)													
Net Sales **2**	97753629	238479	1774615	443923	2530607	989035	998389	761888	2427839	.	.	0	87588853
Interest **3**	416881	0	614	69	3584	2219	2129	1	31442	.	.	0	376825
Rents **4**	16746	0	0	394	3305	0	713	0	4373	.	.	0	7961
Royalties **5**	2224772	0	0	0	0	0	1203	0	0	.	.	0	2223569
Other Portfolio Income **6**	154759	6495	171	3252	4010	950	8311	207	59519	.	.	0	71845
Other Receipts **7**	1133334	-19	9155	6840	11190	31535	5072	7023	47159	.	.	0	1015377
Total Receipts **8**	101700121	244955	1784555	454478	2552696	1023739	1015817	769119	2570332	.	.	0	91284430
Average Total Receipts **9**	22352	609	537	1677	5598	23808	33861	96140	233667	.	.	.	30428143
Operating Costs/Operating Income (%)													
Cost of Operations **10**	68.8	60.2	62.7	67.5	67.7	75.2	71.1	71.4	70.3	.	.	.	68.8
Salaries and Wages **11**	12.1	16.4	10.6	11.5	11.5	10.9	12.0	13.3	13.5	.	.	.	12.1
Taxes Paid **12**	1.9	1.4	4.4	1.5	2.3	1.1	1.7	1.6	1.4	.	.	.	1.9
Interest Paid **13**	0.8	0.9	0.4	1.7	0.6	0.6	0.8	0.6	2.3	.	.	.	0.7
Depreciation **14**	2.7	1.4	0.7	1.3	1.1	2.0	1.4	1.8	2.4	.	.	.	2.8
Amortization and Depletion **15**	0.0	.	0.0	0.0	0.0	0.0	0.0	0.0	0.3	.	.	.	0.0
Pensions and Other Deferred Comp. **16**	0.1	.	0.1	0.3	0.3	0.2	0.2	0.2	0.2	.	.	.	0.1
Employee Benefits **17**	0.3	.	0.5	0.5	1.2	0.7	0.9	1.0	2.8	.	.	.	0.2
Advertising **18**	1.2	4.0	1.0	0.9	1.1	1.1	1.4	0.8	0.5	.	.	.	1.2
Other Expenses **19**	8.7	16.7	13.4	12.1	8.3	7.5	8.5	7.6	12.7	.	.	.	8.5
Officers' Compensation **20**	0.3	7.6	4.2	4.3	3.3	1.4	1.1	1.0	0.6	.	.	.	0.1
Operating Margin **21**	3.1	.	2.0	.	2.7	.	1.0	0.8	.	.	.	.	3.5
Operating Margin Before Officers' Comp. **22**	3.4	.	6.3	2.6	6.0	0.7	2.1	1.7	.	.	.	.	3.6

Selected Average Balance Sheet ($ in Thousands)

Net Receivables 23	603	0	24	115	508	1492	2600	7747	16116	·	673650
Inventories 24	2897	0	61	358	723	3876	5405	15161	18207	·	3949852
Net Property, Plant and Equipment 25	5659	0	31	220	270	1620	3017	9595	39248	·	8264733
Total Assets 26	19479	0	135	723	2014	7291	14667	35969	152885	·	28115088
Notes and Loans Payable 27	2383	0	67	374	611	1711	4349	11768	33945	·	3190096
All Other Liabilities 28	3330	0	47	240	440	2239	3038	7520	49590	·	4645033
Net Worth 29	13766	0	21	109	963	3341	7280	16681	69350	·	20279959

Selected Financial Ratios (Times to 1)

Current Ratio 30	1.6	·	2.0	1.5	2.6	1.8	1.9	3.0	2.0	·	1.5
Quick Ratio 31	0.5	·	0.7	0.4	1.3	0.8	0.7	1.1	1.2	·	0.5
Net Sales to Working Capital 32	11.6	·	10.4	9.7	5.6	10.3	7.4	5.8	5.7	·	12.6
Coverage Ratio 33	10.4	·	6.8	1.4	7.2	5.5	4.5	3.9	0.5	·	11.7
Total Asset Turnover 34	1.1	·	4.0	2.3	2.8	3.2	2.3	2.6	1.4	·	1.0
Inventory Turnover 35	5.1	·	5.5	3.1	5.2	4.5	4.4	4.5	8.5	·	5.1
Receivables Turnover 36	37.7	·	19.9	11.0	9.5	13.8	12.1	12.4	17.2	·	48.7
Total Liabilities to Net Worth 37	0.4	·	5.5	5.6	1.1	1.2	1.0	1.2	1.2	·	0.4
Current Assets to Working Capital 38	2.7	·	2.0	2.8	1.6	2.2	2.2	1.5	2.0	·	2.8
Current Liabilities to Working Capital 39	1.7	·	1.0	1.8	0.6	1.2	1.2	0.5	1.0	·	1.8
Working Capital to Net Sales 40	0.1	·	0.1	0.1	0.2	0.1	0.1	0.2	0.2	·	0.1
Inventory to Working Capital 41	1.7	·	1.3	2.1	0.8	1.2	1.3	0.9	0.6	·	1.9
Total Receipts to Cash Flow 42	7.3	24.4	8.8	12.3	10.4	13.0	12.7	14.9	11.0	·	7.0
Cost of Goods to Cash Flow 43	5.0	14.7	5.5	8.3	7.1	9.8	9.1	10.6	7.7	·	4.8
Cash Flow to Total Debt 44	0.5	·	0.5	0.2	0.5	0.4	0.4	0.3	0.2	·	0.5

Selected Financial Factors (in Percentages)

Debt Ratio 45	29.3	·	84.6	84.9	52.2	54.2	50.4	53.6	54.6	·	27.9
Return on Total Assets 46	8.6	·	12.1	5.5	11.4	10.6	7.9	6.1	1.7	·	8.7
Return on Equity Before Income Taxes 47	11.0	·	66.9	11.1	20.6	18.9	12.4	9.8	·	·	11.1
Return on Equity After Income Taxes 48	7.5	·	64.3	10.2	19.6	13.8	10.8	9.6	·	·	7.5
Profit Margin (Before Income Tax) 49	7.1	·	2.6	0.7	3.6	2.7	2.7	1.7	·	·	7.7
Profit Margin (After Income Tax) 50	4.8	·	2.5	0.7	3.4	2.0	2.4	1.7	·	·	5.2

Table II
Corporations with Net Income

HOMES CENTERS; PAINT AND WALLPAPER STORES

MONEY AMOUNTS AND SIZE OF ASSETS IN THOUSANDS OF DOLLARS

Item Description for Accounting Period 7/02 Through 6/03	Total	Zero Assets	Under 500	500 to 1,000	1,000 to 5,000	5,000 to 10,000	10,000 to 25,000	25,000 to 50,000	50,000 to 100,000	100,000 to 250,000	250,000 to 500,000	500,000 to 2,500,000	2,500,000 and over
Number of Enterprises **1**	2648	8	1879	0	428	43	25	0	8	•	•	0	3
Revenues ($ in Thousands)													
Net Sales **2**	96018130	115116	1446361	0	2194236	989035	885374	0	1727149	•	•	0	87588853
Interest **3**	384626	0	44	0	3572	2219	458	0	1439	•	•	0	376825
Rents **4**	11875	0	0	0	2585	0	710	0	225	•	•	0	7961
Royalties **5**	2223569	0	0	0	0	0	0	0	0	•	•	0	2223569
Other Portfolio Income **6**	145409	0	171	0	4010	950	8213	0	56761	•	•	0	71845
Other Receipts **7**	1108778	0	9066	0	9230	31535	3844	0	28099	•	•	0	1015377
Total Receipts **8**	99892387	115116	1455642	0	2213633	1023739	898599	0	1813673	•	•	0	91284430
Average Total Receipts **9**	37724	14390	775	•	5172	23808	35944	•	226709	•	•	•	30428143
Operating Costs/Operating Income (%)													
Cost of Operations **10**	68.8	61.4	64.6	•	66.3	75.2	71.8	•	72.9	•	•	•	68.8
Salaries and Wages **11**	12.0	19.1	9.4	•	11.8	10.9	11.7	•	11.9	•	•	•	12.1
Taxes Paid **12**	1.9	0.3	4.7	•	2.0	1.1	1.6	•	0.7	•	•	•	1.9
Interest Paid **13**	0.7	0.5	0.4	•	0.6	0.6	0.6	•	1.6	•	•	•	0.7
Depreciation **14**	2.7	2.9	0.4	•	1.1	2.0	1.3	•	2.5	•	•	•	2.8
Amortization and Depletion **15**	0.0	•	0.0	•	0.1	0.0	0.0	•	0.4	•	•	•	0.0
Pensions and Other Deferred Comp. **16**	0.1	•	0.1	•	0.3	0.2	0.2	•	0.2	•	•	•	0.1
Employee Benefits **17**	0.3	•	0.6	•	1.2	0.7	0.9	•	2.4	•	•	•	0.2
Advertising **18**	1.2	5.2	0.8	•	1.1	1.1	1.3	•	0.3	•	•	•	1.2
Other Expenses **19**	8.6	8.1	12.1	•	8.8	7.5	7.5	•	7.9	•	•	•	8.5
Officers' Compensation **20**	0.3	3.9	3.9	•	3.5	1.4	1.0	•	0.6	•	•	•	0.1
Operating Margin **21**	3.3	2.5	2.9	•	3.4	•	2.0	•	•	•	•	•	3.5
Operating Margin Before Officers' Comp. **22**	3.6	2.5	6.8	•	6.8	0.7	3.0	•	•	•	•	•	3.6

Selected Average Balance Sheet ($ in Thousands)

Net Receivables 23	993	0	35	•	490	1492	2837	•	14556	•	673650
Inventories 24	4889	0	86	•	631	3303	5638	•	23533	•	3949852
Net Property, Plant and Equipment 25	9617	0	9	•	260	1620	3064	•	33444	•	8264733
Total Assets 26	33047	0	143	•	1916	7291	14725	•	119672	•	28115088
Notes and Loans Payable 27	3967	0	41	•	568	1711	4148	•	33506	•	3190096
All Other Liabilities 28	5570	0	78	•	450	2239	2707	•	24811	•	4645033
Net Worth 29	23509	0	25	•	899	3341	7869	•	61355	•	20279959

Selected Financial Ratios (Times to 1)

Current Ratio 30	1.6	•	1.6	•	2.7	1.8	1.9	•	2.5	•	1.5
Quick Ratio 31	0.5	•	0.7	•	1.4	0.8	0.7	•	1.0	•	0.5
Net Sales to Working Capital 32	11.9	•	14.6	•	5.3	10.3	7.3	•	7.6	•	12.6
Coverage Ratio 33	11.1	5.9	9.8	•	8.4	5.5	7.1	•	3.4	•	11.7
Total Asset Turnover 34	1.1	•	5.4	•	2.7	3.2	2.4	•	1.8	•	1.0
Inventory Turnover 35	5.1	•	5.8	•	5.4	5.2	4.5	•	6.7	•	5.1
Receivables Turnover 36	39.1	•	18.4	•	10.9	14.7	12.5	•	29.7	•	48.7
Total Liabilities to Net Worth 37	0.4	•	4.7	•	1.1	1.2	0.9	•	1.0	•	0.4
Current Assets to Working Capital 38	2.7	•	2.5	•	1.6	2.2	2.1	•	1.7	•	2.8
Current Liabilities to Working Capital 39	1.7	•	1.5	•	0.6	1.2	1.1	•	0.7	•	1.8
Working Capital to Net Sales 40	0.1	•	0.1	•	0.2	0.1	0.1	•	0.1	•	0.1
Inventory to Working Capital 41	1.7	•	1.5	•	0.7	1.2	1.2	•	0.8	•	1.9
Total Receipts to Cash Flow 42	7.2	12.7	8.7	•	9.5	13.0	12.6	•	10.3	•	7.0
Cost of Goods to Cash Flow 43	5.0	7.8	5.6	•	6.3	9.8	9.0	•	7.5	•	4.8
Cash Flow to Total Debt 44	0.5	•	0.7	•	0.5	0.4	0.4	•	0.4	•	0.5

Selected Financial Factors (in Percentages)

Debt Ratio 45	28.9	•	82.5	•	53.1	54.2	46.6	•	48.7	•	27.9
Return on Total Assets 46	8.8	•	21.3	•	13.0	10.6	9.8	•	9.6	•	8.7
Return on Equity Before Income Taxes 47	11.3	•	108.9	•	24.4	18.9	15.8	•	13.3	•	11.1
Return on Equity After Income Taxes 48	7.8	•	105.2	•	23.3	13.8	14.0	•	11.1	•	7.5
Profit Margin (Before Income Tax) 49	7.3	2.5	3.5	•	4.3	2.7	3.5	•	3.8	•	7.7
Profit Margin (After Income Tax) 50	5.0	1.6	3.4	•	4.1	2.0	3.1	•	3.1	•	5.2

Table I

Corporations with and without Net Income

HARDWARE STORES

MONEY AMOUNTS AND SIZE OF ASSETS IN THOUSANDS OF DOLLARS

Item Description for Accounting Period 7/02 Through 6/03	Total	Zero Assets	Under 500	500 to 1,000	1,000 to 5,000	5,000 to 10,000	10,000 to 25,000	25,000 to 50,000	50,000 to 100,000	100,000 to 250,000	250,000 to 500,000	500,000 to 2,500,000	2,500,000 and over
Number of Enterprises **1**	10614	1293	5623	2112	1414	115	47	7	3	0	•	•	•

Revenues ($ in Thousands)

	Total	Zero Assets	Under 500	500 to 1,000	1,000 to 5,000	5,000 to 10,000	10,000 to 25,000	25,000 to 50,000	50,000 to 100,000	100,000 to 250,000	250,000 to 500,000	500,000 to 2,500,000	2,500,000 and over
Net Sales **2**	16496203	63291	3479329	2961895	5088998	1764719	1715858	642952	779160	0	•	•	•
Interest **3**	21314	0	4236	4612	7974	983	2637	872	0	0	•	•	•
Rents **4**	8122	44	8	1990	2720	0	2163	1198	0	0	•	•	•
Royalties **5**	36	0	0	35	1	0	0	0	0	0	•	•	•
Other Portfolio Income **6**	30035	0	12542	1834	12117	557	2870	36	80	0	•	•	•
Other Receipts **7**	188087	716	19829	44958	47649	32426	18782	1197	22529	0	•	•	•
Total Receipts **8**	16743797	64051	3515944	3015324	5159459	1798685	1742310	646255	801769	0	•	•	•
Average Total Receipts **9**	1578	50	625	1428	3649	15641	37070	92322	267256	•	•	•	•

Operating Costs/Operating Income (%)

	Total	Zero Assets	Under 500	500 to 1,000	1,000 to 5,000	5,000 to 10,000	10,000 to 25,000	25,000 to 50,000	50,000 to 100,000	100,000 to 250,000	250,000 to 500,000	500,000 to 2,500,000	2,500,000 and over
Cost of Operations **10**	65.0	71.9	61.8	62.5	65.7	61.9	70.0	62.4	82.2	•	•	•	•
Salaries and Wages **11**	13.2	5.0	12.8	11.7	14.0	17.1	12.8	13.2	7.1	•	•	•	•
Taxes Paid **12**	2.3	2.7	2.7	2.5	2.3	2.0	1.9	2.0	1.1	•	•	•	•
Interest Paid **13**	0.9	0.9	1.1	0.9	1.0	0.5	0.6	0.4	0.6	•	•	•	•
Depreciation **14**	1.4	0.5	1.9	1.4	1.4	1.4	1.1	1.5	0.9	•	•	•	•
Amortization and Depletion **15**	0.0	0.0	0.0	0.0	0.1	0.0	0.0	0.0	0.0	•	•	•	•
Pensions and Other Deferred Comp. **16**	0.3	0.0	0.1	0.4	0.2	0.3	0.5	0.5	0.2	•	•	•	•
Employee Benefits **17**	1.1	0.1	1.3	1.0	1.1	1.1	1.2	1.6	0.9	•	•	•	•
Advertising **18**	1.6	1.4	1.5	1.7	1.4	1.4	1.6	3.9	0.6	•	•	•	•
Other Expenses **19**	10.5	25.8	14.5	10.3	9.5	10.0	7.6	10.6	6.4	•	•	•	•
Officers' Compensation **20**	3.4	3.8	5.4	5.3	2.7	2.4	1.0	0.7	0.8	•	•	•	•
Operating Margin **21**	0.3	•	•	2.4	0.5	2.0	1.6	3.2	•	•	•	•	•
Operating Margin Before Officers' Comp. **22**	3.7	•	2.3	7.7	3.2	4.4	2.6	3.9	•	•	•	•	•

Selected Average Balance Sheet ($ in Thousands)

Net Receivables 23	83	0	23	88	213	1188	2250	2387	2676
Inventories 24	293	0	138	268	688	2217	5861	17324	45659
Net Property, Plant and Equipment 25	140	0	42	114	359	1838	4059	7526	15454
Total Assets 26	687	0	249	696	1695	7170	14992	33935	85659
Notes and Loans Payable 27	240	0	134	245	559	1160	3941	4793	45293
All Other Liabilities 28	143	0	51	101	347	1875	3426	9820	25101
Net Worth 29	304	0	64	350	788	4135	7625	19322	15265

Selected Financial Ratios (Times to 1)

Current Ratio 30	2.8	•	2.3	5.5	3.1	2.0	1.8	2.1	2.4
Quick Ratio 31	1.0	•	0.5	2.2	1.2	0.8	0.6	0.4	0.9
Net Sales to Working Capital 32	5.1	•	6.3	3.3	4.6	6.8	8.5	7.6	7.3
Coverage Ratio 33	3.1	•	•	5.6	2.8	9.5	6.3	9.4	4.0
Total Asset Turnover 34	2.3	•	2.5	2.0	2.1	2.1	2.4	2.7	3.0
Inventory Turnover 35	3.5	•	2.8	3.3	3.4	4.3	4.4	3.3	4.7
Receivables Turnover 36	18.4	•	23.6	18.9	15.2	14.9	17.7	21.9	67.6
Total Liabilities to Net Worth 37	1.3	•	2.9	1.0	1.1	0.7	1.0	0.8	4.6
Current Assets to Working Capital 38	1.6	•	1.8	1.2	1.5	2.0	2.2	1.9	1.7
Current Liabilities to Working Capital 39	0.6	•	0.8	0.2	0.5	1.0	1.2	0.9	0.7
Working Capital to Net Sales 40	0.2	•	0.2	0.3	0.2	0.1	0.1	0.1	0.1
Inventory to Working Capital 41	1.0	•	1.3	0.7	0.9	1.0	1.4	1.5	1.0
Total Receipts to Cash Flow 42	12.0	22.7	17.2	8.9	12.6	9.8	12.3	9.9	15.8
Cost of Goods to Cash Flow 43	7.8	16.3	10.6	5.6	8.3	6.1	8.6	6.2	13.0
Cash Flow to Total Debt 44	0.3	•	0.2	0.5	0.3	0.5	0.4	0.6	0.2

Selected Financial Factors (in Percentages)

Debt Ratio 45	55.7	74.3	•	49.8	53.5	42.3	49.1	43.1	82.2
Return on Total Assets 46	6.1	•	•	10.2	6.2	9.3	9.0	11.3	7.6
Return on Equity Before Income Taxes 47	9.3	•	•	16.7	8.6	14.4	14.8	17.8	31.9
Return on Equity After Income Taxes 48	8.3	•	•	16.5	7.5	13.8	13.4	14.5	31.9
Profit Margin (Before Income Tax) 49	1.8	•	•	4.2	1.9	3.9	3.1	3.7	1.9
Profit Margin (After Income Tax) 50	1.6	•	•	4.1	1.6	3.7	2.8	3.0	1.9

Table II

Corporations with Net Income

HARDWARE STORES

MONEY AMOUNTS AND SIZE OF ASSETS IN THOUSANDS OF DOLLARS

Item Description for Accounting Period 7/02 Through 6/03	Total	Zero Assets	Under 500	500 to 1,000	1,000 to 5,000	5,000 to 10,000	10,000 to 25,000	25,000 to 50,000	50,000 to 100,000	100,000 to 250,000	250,000 to 500,000	500,000 to 2,500,000	2,500,000 and over
Number of Enterprises **1**	5361	373	2247	0	1021	100	39	0	•	0	•	•	•
Revenues ($ in Thousands)													
Net Sales **2**	11138764	36151	1327337	0	3773444	1569842	1516336	0	•	0	•	•	•
Interest **3**	11782	0	2649	0	4408	983	2035	0	•	0	•	•	•
Rents **4**	4917	44	0	0	2268	0	1373	0	•	0	•	•	•
Royalties **5**	36	0	0	0	1	0	0	0	•	0	•	•	•
Other Portfolio Income **6**	26313	0	10228	0	10995	539	2826	0	•	0	•	•	•
Other Receipts **7**	131567	31	11013	0	35001	28134	17240	0	•	0	•	•	•
Total Receipts **8**	11313379	36226	1351227	0	3826117	1599498	1539810	0	•	0	•	•	•
Average Total Receipts **9**	2110	97	601	•	3747	15995	39482	•	•	•	•	•	•
Operating Costs/Operating Income (%)													
Cost of Operations **10**	63.0	50.1	57.2	•	65.0	61.3	70.2	•	•	•	•	•	•
Salaries and Wages **11**	13.4	1.7	11.8	•	13.6	17.2	12.6	•	•	•	•	•	•
Taxes Paid **12**	2.3	3.6	2.5	•	2.5	1.9	1.8	•	•	•	•	•	•
Interest Paid **13**	0.8	1.6	1.2	•	0.9	0.5	0.5	•	•	•	•	•	•
Depreciation **14**	1.5	0.6	2.8	•	1.4	1.4	1.1	•	•	•	•	•	•
Amortization and Depletion **15**	0.0	0.0	0.0	•	0.1	0.0	0.0	•	•	•	•	•	•
Pensions and Other Deferred Comp. **16**	0.3	0.0	0.0	•	0.3	0.3	0.5	•	•	•	•	•	•
Employee Benefits **17**	1.0	•	1.1	•	0.8	1.1	1.2	•	•	•	•	•	•
Advertising **18**	1.6	2.0	1.3	•	1.4	1.1	1.5	•	•	•	•	•	•
Other Expenses **19**	10.1	27.5	14.5	•	9.2	9.8	7.2	•	•	•	•	•	•
Officers' Compensation **20**	3.1	0.2	4.5	•	2.9	2.5	1.0	•	•	•	•	•	•
Operating Margin **21**	3.0	12.7	3.3	•	2.0	2.8	2.2	•	•	•	•	•	•
Operating Margin Before Officers' Comp. **22**	6.1	12.9	7.7	•	4.9	5.2	3.2	•	•	•	•	•	•

Selected Average Balance Sheet ($ in Thousands)

Net Receivables 23	108	0	29	197	1296	2200
Inventories 24	403	0	174	682	2007	6261
Net Property, Plant and Equipment 25	211	0	71	371	2030	3995
Total Assets 26	961	0	280	1743	7427	15141
Notes and Loans Payable 27	266	0	139	480	1210	3354
All Other Liabilities 28	172	0	32	308	1970	3250
Net Worth 29	523	0	109	955	4247	8537

Selected Financial Ratios (Times to 1)

Current Ratio 30	3.0		2.7	3.4	1.9	2.1
Quick Ratio 31	1.1		0.8	1.3	0.9	0.7
Net Sales to Working Capital 32	4.8		5.4	4.5	7.4	7.7
Coverage Ratio 33	6.9	9.2	5.2	4.7	10.9	8.1
Total Asset Turnover 34	2.2		2.1	2.1	2.1	2.6
Inventory Turnover 35	3.2		1.9	3.5	4.8	4.4
Receivables Turnover 36	17.1		16.0	15.2	24.2	17.9
Total Liabilities to Net Worth 37	0.8		1.6	0.8	0.7	0.8
Current Assets to Working Capital 38	1.5		1.6	1.4	2.1	1.9
Current Liabilities to Working Capital 39	0.5		0.6	0.4	1.1	0.9
Working Capital to Net Sales 40	0.2		0.2	0.2	0.1	0.1
Inventory to Working Capital 41	0.9		1.1	0.8	0.9	1.2
Total Receipts to Cash Flow 42	9.1	3.0	8.0	10.4	9.2	11.7
Cost of Goods to Cash Flow 43	5.7	1.5	4.5	6.7	5.6	8.2
Cash Flow to Total Debt 44	0.5		0.4	0.5	0.5	0.5

Selected Financial Factors (in Percentages)

Debt Ratio 45	45.6		61.1	45.2	42.8	43.6
Return on Total Assets 46	11.6		13.2	9.0	10.7	11.0
Return on Equity Before Income Taxes 47	18.2		27.4	13.0	17.1	17.1
Return on Equity After Income Taxes 48	17.0		25.4	11.7	16.4	15.5
Profit Margin (Before Income Tax) 49	4.6	12.9	5.1	3.3	4.6	3.8
Profit Margin (After Income Tax) 50	4.3	12.9	4.7	3.0	4.4	3.4

Table I

Corporations with and without Net Income

OTHER BUILDING MATERIAL DEALERS

MONEY AMOUNTS AND SIZE OF ASSETS IN THOUSANDS OF DOLLARS

Item Description for Accounting Period 7/02 Through 6/03		Total	Zero Assets	Under 500	500 to 1,000	1,000 to 5,000	5,000 to 10,000	10,000 to 25,000	25,000 to 50,000	50,000 to 100,000	100,000 to 250,000	250,000 to 500,000	500,000 to 2,500,000	2,500,000 and over
Number of Enterprises	1	16613	1345	9272	2389	2994	397	146	42	14	8	3	3	•
Revenues ($ in Thousands)														
Net Sales	2	55252191	104329	5879728	5544941	15659293	7512619	5399359	3482611	2439315	3227550	1353557	4648890	•
Interest	3	113319	97	570	3588	26658	2568	7711	5924	2830	10093	8673	44607	•
Rents	4	43694	64	0	669	5508	531	5254	5958	1590	18939	4973	208	•
Royalties	5	1586	2	0	0	0	0	24	1557	0	2	0	0	•
Other Portfolio Income	6	133192	3270	5313	1624	15139	7370	8459	4624	1938	51242	31840	2373	•
Other Receipts	7	338364	841	35456	42208	91071	56666	43029	38884	16685	8383	281	4858	•
Total Receipts	8	55582346	108603	5921067	5593030	15797669	7579754	5463836	3539558	2462358	3316209	1399324	4700936	•
Average Total Receipts	9	3364	81	639	2341	5276	19093	37424	84275	175883	414526	466441	1566979	•
Operating Costs/Operating Income (%)														
Cost of Operations	10	73.4	84.0	65.3	72.3	72.9	76.7	73.3	76.9	77.6	74.1	76.1	75.0	•
Salaries and Wages	11	9.5	12.1	7.9	9.4	9.3	9.4	10.5	10.0	8.8	10.9	8.4	10.4	•
Taxes Paid	12	1.7	2.3	2.1	2.2	1.8	1.4	1.7	1.5	1.2	1.5	1.1	1.2	•
Interest Paid	13	0.8	0.7	0.5	0.5	0.6	0.8	0.5	0.8	0.6	1.5	0.6	1.6	•
Depreciation	14	1.4	1.0	1.9	1.4	1.2	1.4	1.7	1.2	1.1	1.3	2.2	1.6	•
Amortization and Depletion	15	0.1	•	0.1	0.0	0.0	0.0	0.0	0.1	0.0	0.3	0.3	0.4	•
Pensions and Other Deferred Comp.	16	0.3	0.1	0.2	0.4	0.4	0.2	0.4	0.3	0.4	0.3	0.0	0.1	•
Employee Benefits	17	0.8	0.5	0.3	0.8	0.7	0.9	0.9	1.1	0.7	1.3	0.4	1.5	•
Advertising	18	0.6	1.7	1.4	0.5	0.5	0.5	0.5	0.4	0.5	0.4	0.8	0.3	•
Other Expenses	19	7.9	47.9	13.6	7.9	7.7	6.4	6.6	6.3	6.2	8.6	8.0	6.5	•
Officers' Compensation	20	2.4	2.9	5.9	3.8	3.1	1.4	1.9	0.8	0.8	0.6	0.3	0.3	•
Operating Margin	21	1.1	0.9	0.9	1.0	1.7	0.9	1.8	0.7	2.1	•	1.7	1.1	•
Operating Margin Before Officers' Comp.	22	3.5	•	6.8	4.8	4.8	2.4	3.7	1.5	2.8	•	2.1	1.4	•

Selected Average Balance Sheet ($ in Thousands)

Net Receivables 23	356	0	36	236	544	2134	4824	10730	21678	50120	43449	183843	•
Inventories 24	359	0	48	264	676	1905	3911	7499	15653	35063	74247	165142	•
Net Property, Plant and Equipment 25	243	0	45	83	326	1358	3485	7692	14121	31844	73631	135222	•
Total Assets 26	1310	0	161	703	2078	6719	15228	32773	65487	157186	391921	913135	•
Notes and Loans Payable 27	387	0	64	193	576	2911	4014	10558	15725	65420	43035	196876	•
All Other Liabilities 28	312	0	43	215	426	1478	3313	8092	14925	36755	82961	279268	•
Net Worth 29	610	0	54	294	1077	2330	7901	14123	34837	55011	265926	436991	•

Selected Financial Ratios (Times to 1)

Current Ratio 30	2.1	•	1.7	2.3	2.7	1.6	2.1	1.9	2.4	2.8	2.2	1.6	•
Quick Ratio 31	1.1	•	0.9	1.2	1.4	0.8	1.2	1.1	1.5	1.6	0.9	0.8	•
Net Sales to Working Capital 32	7.2	•	15.3	7.1	5.2	10.9	6.7	7.9	6.7	6.4	4.5	10.8	•
Coverage Ratio 33	3.9	•	4.1	4.7	5.0	3.2	6.5	3.9	6.3	2.3	8.9	2.3	•
Total Asset Turnover 34	2.5	•	3.9	3.3	2.5	2.8	2.4	2.5	2.7	2.6	1.2	1.7	•
Inventory Turnover 35	6.8	•	8.6	6.3	5.6	7.6	6.9	8.5	8.6	8.5	4.6	7.0	•
Receivables Turnover 36	9.5	•	22.9	10.1	8.6	9.9	7.7	8.5	7.9	8.4	8.4	9.7	•
Total Liabilities to Net Worth 37	1.1	•	2.0	1.4	0.9	1.9	0.9	1.3	0.9	1.9	0.5	1.1	•
Current Assets to Working Capital 38	1.9	•	2.5	1.8	1.6	2.8	1.9	2.1	1.7	1.6	1.8	2.8	•
Current Liabilities to Working Capital 39	0.9	•	1.5	0.8	0.6	1.8	0.9	1.1	0.7	0.6	0.8	1.8	•
Working Capital to Net Sales 40	0.1	•	0.1	0.1	0.2	0.1	0.2	0.1	0.1	0.2	0.2	0.1	•
Inventory to Working Capital 41	0.8	•	1.0	0.8	0.7	1.2	0.7	0.8	0.6	0.6	0.6	1.2	•
Total Receipts to Cash Flow 42	12.9	•	8.8	13.6	12.4	16.7	12.9	15.1	13.3	14.7	10.3	14.7	•
Cost of Goods to Cash Flow 43	9.5	•	5.7	9.9	9.1	12.8	9.5	11.6	10.3	10.9	7.8	11.0	•
Cash Flow to Total Debt 44	0.4	•	0.7	0.4	0.4	0.3	0.4	0.3	0.4	0.3	0.3	0.2	•

Selected Financial Factors (in Percentages)

Debt Ratio 45	53.4	•	66.6	58.1	48.2	65.3	48.1	56.9	46.8	65.0	32.1	52.1	•
Return on Total Assets 46	7.6	•	8.3	7.9	8.0	7.5	8.7	7.8	9.5	8.8	6.6	6.5	•
Return on Equity Before Income Taxes 47	12.2	•	18.9	14.9	12.4	14.9	14.1	13.5	15.0	14.2	8.6	7.8	•
Return on Equity After Income Taxes 48	11.0	•	18.0	14.1	11.6	14.2	13.1	10.9	12.9	11.8	7.7	6.2	•
Profit Margin (Before Income Tax) 49	2.2	•	1.6	1.9	2.5	1.8	3.0	2.3	3.0	1.9	5.1	2.2	•
Profit Margin (After Income Tax) 50	2.0	•	1.5	1.8	2.4	1.7	2.8	1.9	2.6	1.6	4.6	1.7	•

Table II
Corporations with Net Income

OTHER BUILDING MATERIAL DEALERS

MONEY AMOUNTS AND SIZE OF ASSETS IN THOUSANDS OF DOLLARS

Item Description for Accounting Period 7/02 Through 6/03	Total	Zero Assets	Under 500	500 to 1,000	1,000 to 5,000	5,000 to 10,000	10,000 to 25,000	25,000 to 50,000	50,000 to 100,000	100,000 to 250,000	250,000 to 500,000	500,000 to 2,500,000	2,500,000 and over
Number of Enterprises **1**	9634	0	5105	1594	2413	341	123	0	11	0	3	3	•
Revenues ($ in Thousands)													
Net Sales **2**	45105071	0	3584787	3837771	12867293	6747478	4731478	0	2015663	0	1353557	4648890	•
Interest **3**	104129	0	341	2598	22457	2194	6754	0	2066	0	8673	44607	•
Rents **4**	36571	0	0	647	4153	529	4696	0	925	0	4973	208	•
Royalties **5**	28	0	0	0	0	0	24	0	0	0	0	0	•
Other Portfolio Income **6**	114024	0	2037	1234	8753	7291	6830	0	1327	0	31840	2373	•
Other Receipts **7**	286063	0	32761	39668	73555	52822	40603	0	12832	0	281	4858	•
Total Receipts **8**	45645886	0	3619926	3881918	12976211	6810314	4790385	0	2032813	0	1399324	4700936	•
Average Total Receipts **9**	4738	•	709	2435	5378	19972	38946	•	184801	•	466441	1566979	•
Operating Costs/Operating Income (%)													
Cost of Operations **10**	73.2	•	62.7	73.2	72.8	76.7	72.8	•	76.4	•	76.1	75.0	•
Salaries and Wages **11**	9.4	•	8.7	7.6	8.6	9.3	10.7	•	9.0	•	8.4	10.4	•
Taxes Paid **12**	1.6	•	1.9	1.8	1.8	1.3	1.8	•	1.2	•	1.1	1.2	•
Interest Paid **13**	0.7	•	0.5	0.4	0.6	0.8	0.5	•	0.6	•	0.6	1.6	•
Depreciation **14**	1.4	•	2.2	1.3	1.2	1.3	1.6	•	1.2	•	2.2	1.6	•
Amortization and Depletion **15**	0.1	•	0.0	0.0	0.0	0.0	0.0	•	0.1	•	0.3	0.4	•
Pensions and Other Deferred Comp. **16**	0.3	•	0.1	0.3	0.4	0.2	0.4	•	0.5	•	0.0	0.1	•
Employee Benefits **17**	0.8	•	0.3	0.7	0.6	0.8	0.9	•	0.6	•	0.4	1.5	•
Advertising **18**	0.6	•	1.3	0.4	0.5	0.5	0.6	•	0.5	•	0.8	0.3	•
Other Expenses **19**	7.4	•	12.3	7.8	7.4	6.3	6.3	•	6.0	•	8.0	6.5	•
Officers' Compensation **20**	2.4	•	5.8	4.3	3.4	1.3	1.8	•	0.8	•	0.3	0.3	•
Operating Margin **21**	2.1	•	4.2	2.2	2.7	1.3	2.6	•	3.1	•	1.7	1.1	•
Operating Margin Before Officers' Comp. **22**	4.5	•	10.0	6.4	6.1	2.6	4.4	•	3.9	•	2.1	1.4	•

Selected Average Balance Sheet ($ in Thousands)

Net Receivables 23	497	40	250	542	2160	4957	18806	43449	183343
Inventories 24	511	55	283	689	1942	4021	16838	62293	166142
Net Property, Plant and Equipment 25	338	54	71	302	1412	3167	15989	73631	135222
Total Assets 26	1862	189	711	2060	6691	15239	64833	391921	913135
Notes and Loans Payable 27	505	75	180	495	3009	3639	13832	43035	196876
All Other Liabilities 28	432	43	225	385	1510	3231	15709	82961	279268
Net Worth 29	926	70	307	1180	2172	8369	35291	265926	436991

Selected Financial Ratios (Times to 1)

Current Ratio 30	2.2	2.1	2.1	3.2	1.5	2.3	2.3	2.2	1.6
Quick Ratio 31	1.2	1.2	1.3	1.7	0.8	1.3	1.3	0.9	0.8
Net Sales to Working Capital 32	6.9	11.2	7.5	4.9	12.6	6.3	7.6	4.5	10.8
Coverage Ratio 33	5.7	11.3	10.4	7.4	3.7	8.9	7.9	8.9	2.3
Total Asset Turnover 34	2.5	3.7	3.4	2.6	3.0	2.5	2.8	1.2	1.7
Inventory Turnover 35	6.7	8.0	6.2	5.6	7.8	7.0	8.3	5.5	7.0
Receivables Turnover 36	9.3	24.1	9.1	8.3	10.6	7.7	8.8	20.8	9.7
Total Liabilities to Net Worth 37	1.0	1.7	1.3	0.7	2.1	0.8	0.8	0.5	1.1
Current Assets to Working Capital 38	1.8	1.9	1.9	1.5	3.0	1.8	1.8	1.8	2.8
Current Liabilities to Working Capital 39	0.8	0.9	0.9	0.5	2.0	0.8	0.8	0.8	1.8
Working Capital to Net Sales 40	0.1	0.1	0.1	0.2	0.1	0.2	0.1	0.2	0.1
Inventory to Working Capital 41	0.7	0.8	0.7	0.6	1.4	0.6	0.6	0.6	1.2
Total Receipts to Cash Flow 42	11.9	7.2	11.8	11.3	16.2	11.9	11.7	10.3	14.7
Cost of Goods to Cash Flow 43	8.7	4.5	8.6	8.2	12.4	8.6	8.9	7.8	11.0
Cash Flow to Total Debt 44	0.4	0.8	0.5	0.5	0.3	0.5	0.5	0.3	0.2

Selected Financial Factors (in Percentages)

Debt Ratio 45	50.3	63.0	56.9	42.7	67.5	45.1	45.6	32.1	52.1
Return on Total Assets 46	10.2	21.2	12.4	10.6	8.9	10.9	12.8	6.6	6.5
Return on Equity Before Income Taxes 47	16.9	52.2	25.9	16.0	20.2	17.6	20.5	8.6	7.8
Return on Equity After Income Taxes 48	15.5	50.8	24.8	15.1	19.2	16.4	17.9	7.7	6.2
Profit Margin (Before Income Tax) 49	3.3	5.2	3.3	3.5	2.2	3.8	3.9	5.1	2.2
Profit Margin (After Income Tax) 50	3.1	5.1	3.2	3.3	2.1	3.6	3.4	4.6	1.7

Table I
Corporations with and without Net Income

LAWN AND GARDEN EQUIPMENT AND SUPPLIES STORES

MONEY AMOUNTS AND SIZE OF ASSETS IN THOUSANDS OF DOLLARS

Item Description for Accounting Period 7/02 Through 6/03	Total	Zero Assets	Under 500	500 to 1,000	1,000 to 5,000	5,000 to 10,000	10,000 to 25,000	25,000 to 50,000	50,000 to 100,000	100,000 to 250,000	250,000 to 500,000	500,000 to 2,500,000	2,500,000 and over
Number of Enterprises **1**	11482	450	8792	1235	880	91	26	4	4	0	0	0	•
Revenues ($ in Thousands)													
Net Sales **2**	13761481	37220	4137283	2642359	3967835	1472682	812395	318299	373408	•	•	•	•
Interest **3**	10838	50	761	805	5703	843	794	99	1782	•	•	•	•
Rents **4**	5591	0	128	0	4536	20	289	58	560	0	0	0	•
Royalties **5**	0	0	0	0	0	0	0	0	0	0	0	0	•
Other Portfolio Income **6**	8682	0	2151	1023	1308	33	3150	99	917	0	0	0	•
Other Receipts **7**	147813	21	9877	15343	25866	16075	5168	203	75264	0	0	0	•
Total Receipts **8**	13934405	37291	4150200	2659530	4005248	1489653	821796	318758	451931	•	•	•	•
Average Total Receipts **9**	1214	83	472	2153	4551	16370	31608	79690	112983	•	•	•	•
Operating Costs/Operating Income (%)													
Cost of Operations **10**	71.8	83.4	65.8	67.4	76.2	85.3	72.3	61.0	76.2	•	•	•	•
Salaries and Wages **11**	9.6	5.7	11.2	10.7	8.7	3.5	9.5	15.3	12.7	•	•	•	•
Taxes Paid **12**	2.0	0.8	3.1	2.5	1.3	0.8	1.3	1.2	2.6	•	•	•	•
Interest Paid **13**	0.9	0.9	0.6	0.8	1.1	0.6	1.2	0.9	2.2	•	•	•	•
Depreciation **14**	1.4	3.6	1.2	1.7	1.3	0.8	1.6	1.2	3.5	•	•	•	•
Amortization and Depletion **15**	0.0	0.0	0.0	0.0	0.0	0.0	0.0	0.7	0.0	•	•	•	•
Pensions and Other Deferred Comp. **16**	0.2	0.1	•	0.3	0.4	0.1	0.2	0.1	0.0	•	•	•	•
Employee Benefits **17**	0.5	0.8	0.2	0.5	0.6	0.4	0.8	2.0	0.3	•	•	•	•
Advertising **18**	1.2	0.5	1.2	1.2	1.1	0.7	1.3	2.3	2.2	•	•	•	•
Other Expenses **19**	10.6	8.1	13.8	10.0	7.0	6.8	10.7	12.4	29.9	•	•	•	•
Officers' Compensation **20**	3.0	1.4	4.8	3.3	2.5	0.7	1.0	1.2	0.9	•	•	•	•
Operating Margin **21**	•	•	•	1.5	•	0.2	•	1.8	•	•	•	•	•
Operating Margin Before Officers' Comp. **22**	1.9	•	2.9	4.8	2.3	0.9	1.0	3.0	•	•	•	•	•

Selected Average Balance Sheet ($ in Thousands)

Net Receivables 23	63	0	31	60	220	375	3250	4737	11302
Inventories 24	244	0	64	308	1125	5739	7364	10503	28070
Net Property, Plant and Equipment 25	102	0	32	241	409	653	2821	7718	18400
Total Assets 26	531	0	152	802	2303	7971	14876	33986	124392
Notes and Loans Payable 27	215	0	81	243	872	2444	5691	7624	72812
All Other Liabilities 28	185	0	59	161	681	3159	5817	11338	79690
Net Worth 29	132	0	12	399	751	2368	3367	15023	-28110

Selected Financial Ratios (Times to 1)

Current Ratio 30	1.5	•	1.6	2.2	1.7	1.5	1.3	1.4	0.5
Quick Ratio 31	0.4	•	0.6	0.8	0.4	0.2	0.4	0.5	0.2
Net Sales to Working Capital 32	9.5	•	10.7	7.3	6.4	7.2	13.0	15.5	•
Coverage Ratio 33	1.2	•	•	3.6	1.7	3.1	1.9	3.1	•
Total Asset Turnover 34	2.3	•	3.1	2.7	2.0	2.0	2.1	2.3	0.8
Inventory Turnover 35	3.5	•	4.8	4.7	3.1	2.4	3.1	4.6	2.5
Receivables Turnover 36	20.0	•	16.0	34.3	23.1	33.3	10.3	11.4	12.3
Total Liabilities to Net Worth 37	3.0	•	11.5	1.0	2.1	2.4	3.4	1.3	•
Current Assets to Working Capital 38	3.0	•	2.6	1.8	2.4	3.2	4.7	3.3	•
Current Liabilities to Working Capital 39	2.0	•	1.6	0.8	1.4	2.2	3.7	2.3	•
Working Capital to Net Sales 40	0.1	•	0.1	0.1	0.2	0.1	0.1	0.1	•
Inventory to Working Capital 41	2.0	•	1.5	1.1	1.8	2.7	2.8	2.1	•
Total Receipts to Cash Flow 42	13.5	102.0	12.2	12.0	16.2	13.6	10.4	10.8	•
Cost of Goods to Cash Flow 43	9.7	85.1	8.1	8.1	12.3	11.6	7.5	6.6	•
Cash Flow to Total Debt 44	0.2	•	0.3	0.4	0.2	0.2	0.3	0.4	•

Selected Financial Factors (in Percentages)

Debt Ratio 45	75.2	•	92.0	50.3	67.4	70.3	77.4	55.8	122.6
Return on Total Assets 46	2.3	•	•	8.0	3.7	4.1	4.9	6.6	•
Return on Equity Before Income Taxes 47	1.3	•	•	11.6	4.8	9.5	10.1	10.1	31.8
Return on Equity After Income Taxes 48	0.5	•	•	11.1	3.8	9.4	8.5	10.1	32.0
Profit Margin (Before Income Tax) 49	0.1	•	•	2.2	0.8	1.4	1.1	1.9	•
Profit Margin (After Income Tax) 50	0.1	•	•	2.1	0.6	1.4	0.9	1.9	•

Table II
Corporations with Net Income

LAWN AND GARDEN EQUIPMENT AND SUPPLIES STORES

MONEY AMOUNTS AND SIZE OF ASSETS IN THOUSANDS OF DOLLARS

Item Description for Accounting Period 7/02 Through 6/03	Total	Zero Assets	Under 500	500 to 1,000	1,000 to 5,000	5,000 to 10,000	10,000 to 25,000	25,000 to 50,000	50,000 to 100,000	100,000 to 250,000	250,000 to 500,000	500,000 to 2,500,000	2,500,000 and over
Number of Enterprises **1**	5574	18	3985	881	594	72	20	4	0	•	•	•	•
Revenues ($ in Thousands)													
Net Sales **2**	10298150	35053	2796465	2054931	3137578	1217523	712106	344493	•	•	•	•	•
Interest **3**	7060	50	204	199	5572	621	347	66	0	•	•	•	•
Rents **4**	2524	0	0	0	2215	20	289	0	0	•	•	•	•
Royalties **5**	0	0	0	0	0	0	0	0	0				
Other Portfolio Income **6**	3377	0	368	773	1252	16	872	96	0	•	•	•	•
Other Receipts **7**	65547	20	6624	13203	24615	13980	4997	2111	0	•	•	•	•
Total Receipts **8**	10376658	35123	2803661	2069106	3171232	1232160	718611	346766	0	•	•	•	•
Average Total Receipts **9**	1862	1951	704	2349	5339	17113	35931	86692	•	•	•	•	•
Operating Costs/Operating Income (%)													
Cost of Operations **10**	72.6	85.2	66.6	67.7	76.7	84.5	72.7	69.9	•	•	•	•	•
Salaries and Wages **11**	8.0	4.2	8.0	10.2	7.7	3.4	9.5	10.8	•	•	•	•	•
Taxes Paid **12**	1.8	0.5	3.0	2.3	1.1	0.8	1.2	0.7	•	•	•	•	•
Interest Paid **13**	0.6	0.7	0.4	0.4	0.7	0.6	1.1	1.1	•	•	•	•	•
Depreciation **14**	1.1	0.5	0.7	1.7	1.1	0.8	1.1	1.8	•	•	•	•	•
Amortization and Depletion **15**	0.0	0.0	0.7	0.0	0.0	0.0	0.0	0.1	•	•	•	•	•
Pensions and Other Deferred Comp. **16**	0.2	0.2	•	0.2	0.4	0.1	0.3	0.0	•	•	•	•	•
Employee Benefits **17**	0.5	0.8	0.3	0.5	0.6	0.4	0.8	1.9	•	•	•	•	•
Advertising **18**	1.1	0.4	1.4	1.1	1.1	0.7	1.4	1.2	•	•	•	•	•
Other Expenses **19**	9.0	6.1	12.0	9.5	6.3	7.4	10.1	9.7	•	•	•	•	•
Officers' Compensation **20**	3.1	0.4	5.5	3.1	2.6	0.7	1.0	1.0	•	•	•	•	•
Operating Margin **21**	1.9	1.1	2.2	3.2	1.5	0.6	0.8	1.8	•	•	•	•	•
Operating Margin Before Officers' Comp. **22**	5.0	1.5	7.7	6.4	4.1	1.3	1.8	2.8	•	•	•	•	•

Selected Average Balance Sheet ($ in Thousands)

Net Receivables 23	89	0	28	69	286	441	3437	12658
Inventories 24	347	0	80	273	1151	5827	7272	23750
Net Property, Plant and Equipment 25	121	0	33	240	347	767	2107	7650
Total Assets 26	682	0	181	761	2250	8035	15037	49490
Notes and Loans Payable 27	198	0	61	118	749	2204	5363	10818
All Other Liabilities 28	242	0	87	175	656	3240	5993	26853
Net Worth 29	243	0	33	468	845	2591	3680	11818

Selected Financial Ratios (Times to 1)

Current Ratio 30	1.6	•	1.5	2.1	1.8	1.5	1.3	1.2
Quick Ratio 31	0.4	•	0.5	0.8	0.4	0.2	0.4	0.4
Net Sales to Working Capital 32	9.1	•	15.0	8.8	6.5	7.5	14.4	13.6
Coverage Ratio 33	5.4	2.9	7.2	10.4	4.6	3.9	2.6	3.3
Total Asset Turnover 34	2.7	•	3.9	3.1	2.3	2.1	2.4	1.7
Inventory Turnover 35	3.9	•	5.8	5.8	3.5	2.5	3.6	2.5
Receivables Turnover 36	22.1	•	26.6	36.9	20.8	76.6	10.8	13.6
Total Liabilities to Net Worth 37	1.8	•	4.5	0.6	1.7	2.1	3.1	3.2
Current Assets to Working Capital 38	2.6	•	2.9	1.9	2.3	3.1	4.8	6.1
Current Liabilities to Working Capital 39	1.6	•	1.9	0.9	1.3	2.1	3.8	5.1
Working Capital to Net Sales 40	0.1	•	0.1	0.1	0.2	0.1	0.1	0.1
Inventory to Working Capital 41	1.8	•	1.9	1.1	1.6	2.6	3.0	3.7
Total Receipts to Cash Flow 42	10.9	17.6	8.9	10.5	13.4	12.1	10.4	12.1
Cost of Goods to Cash Flow 43	7.9	15.0	5.9	7.1	10.3	10.2	7.5	8.4
Cash Flow to Total Debt 44	0.4	•	0.5	0.8	0.3	0.3	0.3	0.2

Selected Financial Factors (in Percentages)

Debt Ratio 45	64.5	•	81.9	38.5	62.4	67.8	75.5	76.1
Return on Total Assets 46	8.9	•	11.2	13.4	7.9	5.1	6.5	6.1
Return on Equity Before Income Taxes 47	20.3	•	53.1	19.6	16.3	11.7	16.3	17.7
Return on Equity After Income Taxes 48	19.5	•	52.4	19.1	15.0	11.7	14.4	17.2
Profit Margin (Before Income Tax) 49	2.7	1.3	2.5	3.9	2.6	1.8	1.7	2.4
Profit Margin (After Income Tax) 50	2.6	0.9	2.4	3.8	2.4	1.8	1.5	2.4

Table I

Corporations with and without Net Income

FOOD AND BEVERAGE STORES

MONEY AMOUNTS AND SIZE OF ASSETS IN THOUSANDS OF DOLLARS

Item Description for Accounting Period 7/02 Through 6/03	Total	Zero Assets	Under 500	500 to 1,000	1,000 to 5,000	5,000 to 10,000	10,000 to 25,000	25,000 to 50,000	50,000 to 100,000	100,000 to 250,000	250,000 to 500,000	500,000 to 2,500,000	2,500,000 and over
Number of Enterprises **1**	71407	4872	56672	5369	3713	367	216	73	55	28	7	25	9
Revenues ($ in Thousands)													
Net Sales **2**	437866769	647600	36243467	15879379	30524063	11288255	14075347	9898254	14330528	14294779	6714157	67243300	216729639
Interest **3**	487750	895	3754	5183	16074	4865	8236	5385	11044	12963	2014	123144	294193
Rents **4**	1075837	0	8778	5010	28199	10666	19691	16559	12267	16796	13943	190220	753709
Royalties **5**	1434406	0	31	0	27	0	5	0	1343	26205	0	133641	1273154
Other Portfolio Income **6**	297408	628	30168	19761	30191	14469	22357	44359	4708	7350	16178	43449	63793
Other Receipts **7**	6395883	2767	446566	132354	287934	276692	169026	137047	157131	179524	91661	660649	3854530
Total Receipts **8**	447758053	651890	36732764	16041687	30886488	11592947	14294662	10101604	14517021	14537617	6837953	68394403	222969018
Average Total Receipts **9**	6268	134	648	2988	8318	31588	66179	138378	263946	519201	976850	2735776	24774335
Operating Costs/Operating Income (%)													
Cost of Operations **10**	73.4	69.3	73.0	76.0	76.0	78.5	75.3	73.6	72.9	72.4	69.2	71.5	73.2
Salaries and Wages **11**	10.4	7.3	7.7	8.8	9.0	8.9	10.6	10.6	10.9	12.2	13.8	11.5	10.6
Taxes Paid **12**	1.6	2.4	2.0	1.4	1.5	1.4	1.5	1.5	2.0	1.7	1.8	1.9	1.5
Interest Paid **13**	1.0	0.6	0.5	0.7	0.4	0.6	0.5	0.5	0.6	0.8	0.5	1.0	1.3
Depreciation **14**	2.2	1.6	1.2	1.2	1.3	1.3	1.5	1.6	1.8	2.0	1.9	2.5	2.6
Amortization and Depletion **15**	0.1	0.3	0.2	0.1	0.1	0.1	0.1	0.9	0.1	0.1	0.1	0.2	0.1
Pensions and Other Deferred Comp. **16**	0.3	0.0	0.0	0.1	0.1	0.2	0.2	0.3	0.4	0.4	0.6	0.4	0.5
Employee Benefits **17**	1.3	0.2	0.3	0.3	0.7	0.8	1.0	1.1	1.1	1.6	1.9	1.9	1.5
Advertising **18**	0.8	0.3	0.7	0.7	1.0	1.1	1.0	1.1	1.1	0.9	1.0	0.9	0.6
Other Expenses **19**	9.1	19.6	12.6	9.2	9.0	9.0	8.6	9.1	9.3	8.2	8.9	8.1	8.9
Officers' Compensation **20**	0.6	3.1	3.0	1.8	1.3	0.6	0.6	0.7	0.4	0.3	0.2	0.2	0.1
Operating Margin **21**	•	•	•	•	•	•	•	•	•	•	0.0	•	•
Operating Margin Before Officers' Comp. **22**	•	1.8	1.5	0.9	•	•	•	•	•	•	0.2	•	0.1

Selected Average Balance Sheet ($ in Thousands)

Net Receivables 23	135	0	4	41	143	352	951	2156	4867	6834	13076	51185	701238
Inventories 24	386	0	36	143	418	1685	3168	6676	11850	27573	61874	155010	1738958
Net Property, Plant and Equipment 25	963	0	36	234	693	2793	6125	14027	31204	74149	128178	506370	4684135
Total Assets 26	2270	0	117	661	1867	7077	15492	34988	69861	158172	353638	1034268	11101801
Notes and Loans Payable 27	792	0	84	358	786	3035	6312	11218	27581	47290	73415	353095	3495504
All Other Liabilities 28	864	0	22	140	487	1876	5046	9697	23849	45745	111998	314114	4909950
Net Worth 29	614	0	11	163	594	2167	4134	14073	18431	65136	168225	367060	2696347

Selected Financial Ratios (Times to 1)

Current Ratio 30	1.0	•	2.2	1.9	1.6	1.3	1.2	1.3	1.0	1.2	1.2	1.3	0.8
Quick Ratio 31	0.3	•	0.7	0.8	0.7	0.5	0.5	0.5	0.4	0.4	0.5	0.4	0.2
Net Sales to Working Capital 32	•	•	20.1	19.9	24.7	45.7	64.5	44.4	271.3	72.4	55.8	40.9	•
Coverage Ratio 33	2.5	•	1.3	2.1	2.8	1.4	2.6	3.1	2.1	2.4	4.7	2.6	2.5
Total Asset Turnover 34	2.7	•	5.5	4.5	4.4	4.3	4.2	3.9	3.7	3.2	2.7	2.6	2.2
Inventory Turnover 35	11.7	•	12.9	15.7	14.9	14.3	15.5	14.9	16.0	13.4	10.7	12.4	10.1
Receivables Turnover 36	49.4	•	152.2	77.1	56.9	85.4	66.5	65.3	59.9	68.1	70.1	55.4	38.6
Total Liabilities to Net Worth 37	2.7	•	9.8	3.1	2.1	2.3	2.7	1.5	2.8	1.4	1.1	1.8	3.1
Current Assets to Working Capital 38	•	•	1.9	2.1	2.8	4.4	7.0	4.7	26.2	7.0	6.3	4.8	•
Current Liabilities to Working Capital 39	•	•	0.9	1.1	1.8	3.4	6.0	3.7	25.2	6.0	5.3	3.8	•
Working Capital to Net Sales 40	•	•	0.0	0.1	0.0	0.0	0.0	0.0	0.0	0.0	0.0	0.0	•
Inventory to Working Capital 41	•	•	1.2	1.1	1.2	2.4	3.2	2.0	12.7	3.9	2.8	2.6	•
Total Receipts to Cash Flow 42	13.5	15.5	12.3	15.0	14.4	16.3	16.3	14.3	15.5	17.0	13.6	14.7	12.6
Cost of Goods to Cash Flow 43	9.9	10.7	9.0	11.4	11.0	12.8	12.3	10.6	11.3	12.3	9.4	10.5	9.2
Cash Flow to Total Debt 44	0.3	•	0.5	0.4	0.4	0.4	0.4	0.5	0.3	0.3	0.4	0.3	0.2

Selected Financial Factors (in Percentages)

Debt Ratio 45	72.9	•	90.7	75.4	68.2	69.4	73.3	59.8	73.6	58.8	52.4	64.5	75.7
Return on Total Assets 46	6.6	•	3.6	6.1	5.5	3.6	5.2	6.0	4.9	5.8	6.4	6.8	7.1
Return on Equity Before Income Taxes 47	14.6	•	9.5	12.7	11.2	3.7	11.9	10.1	9.6	8.2	10.7	11.9	17.7
Return on Equity After Income Taxes 48	9.9	•	7.0	11.5	9.3	1.3	8.8	8.6	6.9	5.5	9.7	7.9	11.6
Profit Margin (Before Income Tax) 49	1.5	•	0.2	0.7	0.8	0.3	0.8	1.0	0.7	1.1	1.9	1.6	2.0
Profit Margin (After Income Tax) 50	1.0	•	0.1	0.6	0.7	0.1	0.6	0.9	0.5	0.7	1.1	1.1	1.3

Table II

Corporations with Net Income

FOOD AND BEVERAGE STORES

MONEY AMOUNTS AND SIZE OF ASSETS IN THOUSANDS OF DOLLARS

Item Description for Accounting Period 7/02 Through 6/03	Total	Zero Assets	Under 500	500 to 1,000	1,000 to 5,000	5,000 to 10,000	10,000 to 25,000	25,000 to 50,000	50,000 to 100,000	100,000 to 250,000	250,000 to 500,000	500,000 to 2,500,000	2,500,000 and over
Number of Enterprises **1**	36410	0	29211	3090	2350	0	154	0	40	21	0	21	0
Revenues ($ in Thousands)													
Net Sales **2**	377922656	0	24025579	9839096	22969355	0	11028052	0	10916386	11953985	0	52813945	0
Interest **3**	455914	0	1946	4880	11607	0	5909	0	8135	11157	0	120234	0
Rents **4**	990604	0	5	921	21927	0	12572	0	10970	15994	0	138838	0
Royalties **5**	1408128	0	0	0	0	0	5	0	1331	0	0	133639	0
Other Portfolio Income **6**	240240	0	14873	19656	26840	0	20791	0	4185	5286	0	40556	0
Other Receipts **7**	5621258	0	332962	102732	178768	0	123472	0	128359	119157	0	577463	0
Total Receipts **8**	386638800	0	24375365	9967285	23208497	0	11190801	0	11069366	12105579	0	53824675	0
Average Total Receipts **9**	10592	•	834	3226	9876	•	72668	•	276734	576456	•	2563080	•
Operating Costs/Operating Income (%)													
Cost of Operations **10**	73.4	•	74.3	76.0	75.6	•	75.2	•	73.5	74.0	•	71.5	•
Salaries and Wages **11**	10.4	•	7.2	8.5	8.5	•	10.5	•	11.1	11.8	•	11.3	•
Taxes Paid **12**	1.6	•	1.8	1.3	1.4	•	1.5	•	1.7	1.6	•	2.1	•
Interest Paid **13**	1.0	•	0.4	0.3	0.5	•	0.4	•	0.4	0.3	•	1.0	•
Depreciation **14**	2.1	•	0.8	1.0	0.8	•	1.3	•	1.6	1.8	•	2.5	•
Amortization and Depletion **15**	0.1	•	0.1	0.1	0.1	•	0.1	•	0.1	0.0	•	0.2	•
Pensions and Other Deferred Comp. **16**	0.4	•	0.0	0.2	0.1	•	0.1	•	0.4	0.4	•	0.4	•
Employee Benefits **17**	1.3	•	0.2	0.3	0.6	•	0.9	•	1.2	1.3	•	1.8	•
Advertising **18**	0.7	•	0.6	0.6	1.0	•	1.0	•	1.1	0.7	•	0.8	•
Other Expenses **19**	8.6	•	11.0	8.2	8.2	•	7.9	•	8.3	6.7	•	7.4	•
Officers' Compensation **20**	0.5	•	2.8	2.2	1.2	•	0.6	•	0.4	0.4	•	0.2	•
Operating Margin **21**	•	•	0.8	1.6	1.5	•	0.5	•	0.1	1.0	•	0.7	•
Operating Margin Before Officers' Comp. **22**	0.4	•	3.6	3.8	2.7	•	1.2	•	0.5	1.3	•	0.9	•

Selected Average Balance Sheet ($ in Thousands)

Net Receivables 23	228	•	5	29	144	916	•	4286	7421	43388
Inventories 24	667	•	48	152	440	3272	•	12945	26781	147608
Net Property, Plant and Equipment 25	1636	•	35	181	600	6033	•	30061	81855	495210
Total Assets 26	3926	•	131	632	1882	15446	•	69734	159115	1017096
Notes and Loans Payable 27	1216	•	64	254	487	4491	•	19102	30671	346277
All Other Liabilities 28	1524	•	24	109	520	4326	•	20597	44200	287597
Net Worth 29	1186	•	43	269	875	6630	•	30035	84245	383223

Selected Financial Ratios (Times to 1)

Current Ratio 30	1.0	•	2.3	2.4	1.8	1.4	•	1.3	1.3	1.3
Quick Ratio 31	0.3	•	0.8	1.2	0.8	0.6	•	0.6	0.4	0.4
Net Sales to Working Capital 32	•	•	19.3	16.7	21.4	38.0	•	48.7	46.3	39.8
Coverage Ratio 33	3.2	•	6.8	6.5	9.4	6.3	•	4.6	7.4	3.6
Total Asset Turnover 34	2.6	•	6.3	5.0	5.2	4.6	•	3.9	3.6	2.5
Inventory Turnover 35	11.4	•	12.8	15.8	16.9	16.5	•	15.5	15.7	12.2
Receivables Turnover 36	48.3	•	171.7	111.8	59.4	76.4	•	65.0	81.2	115.9
Total Liabilities to Net Worth 37	2.3	•	2.0	1.4	1.2	1.3	•	1.3	0.9	1.7
Current Assets to Working Capital 38	•	•	1.8	1.7	2.2	3.8	•	4.5	4.4	4.7
Current Liabilities to Working Capital 39	•	•	0.8	0.7	1.2	2.8	•	3.5	3.4	3.7
Working Capital to Net Sales 40	•	•	0.1	0.1	0.0	0.0	•	0.0	0.0	0.0
Inventory to Working Capital 41	•	•	1.1	0.8	1.0	1.8	•	2.2	2.3	2.3
Total Receipts to Cash Flow 42	12.7	•	10.7	11.9	12.2	14.3	•	15.1	16.2	13.4
Cost of Goods to Cash Flow 43	9.3	•	7.9	9.0	9.3	10.8	•	11.1	12.0	9.6
Cash Flow to Total Debt 44	0.3	•	0.9	0.7	0.8	0.6	•	0.5	0.5	0.3

Selected Financial Factors (in Percentages)

Debt Ratio 45	69.8	•	66.7	57.4	53.5	57.1	•	56.9	47.1	62.3
Return on Total Assets 46	8.4	•	16.7	17.2	15.0	11.1	•	7.8	9.2	9.1
Return on Equity Before Income Taxes 47	19.2	•	42.8	34.2	28.9	21.8	•	14.3	14.9	17.4
Return on Equity After Income Taxes 48	14.5	•	41.6	33.0	26.9	19.5	•	12.0	12.2	12.9
Profit Margin (Before Income Tax) 49	2.2	•	2.3	2.9	2.6	2.0	•	1.6	2.2	2.7
Profit Margin (After Income Tax) 50	1.7	•	2.2	2.8	2.4	1.8	•	1.3	1.8	2.0

Table I
Corporations with and without Net Income

BEER, WINE, AND LIQUOR STORES

MONEY AMOUNTS AND SIZE OF ASSETS IN THOUSANDS OF DOLLARS

Item Description for Accounting Period 7/02 Through 6/03	Total	Zero Assets	Under 500	500 to 1,000	1,000 to 5,000	5,000 to 10,000	10,000 to 25,000	25,000 to 50,000	50,000 to 100,000	100,000 to 250,000	250,000 to 500,000	500,000 to 2,500,000	2,500,000 and over
Number of Enterprises **1**	14600	400	12123	1360	667	26	19	5	•	0	•	•	•
Revenues ($ in Thousands)													
Net Sales **2**	19291399	1404	9765127	3760057	3568520	791224	594934	810134	•	0	•	•	•
Interest **3**	6518	0	859	2708	1954	348	371	278	•	0	•	•	•
Rents **4**	5043	0	0	0	3879	0	668	497	•	0	•	•	•
Royalties **5**	0	0	0	0	0	0	0	0		0			
Other Portfolio Income **6**	13576	0	5550	185	4684	1415	58	1681	•	0	•	•	•
Other Receipts **7**	274849	5	133234	22998	91764	7216	16816	2815	•	0	•	•	•
Total Receipts **8**	19591385	1409	9904770	3785948	3670801	800203	612847	815405	•	0	•	•	•
Average Total Receipts **9**	1342	4	817	2784	5503	30777	32255	163081					
Operating Costs/Operating Income (%)													
Cost of Operations **10**	79.3	76.4	79.2	80.5	79.9	76.5	77.0	76.8	•	•	•	•	•
Salaries and Wages **11**	5.6	9.8	4.7	4.6	6.8	10.2	7.9	7.8	•	•	•	•	•
Taxes Paid **12**	2.0	26.8	2.4	2.2	1.1	2.0	1.4	1.2	•	•	•	•	•
Interest Paid **13**	0.6	0.5	0.7	0.4	0.7	0.6	0.8	0.3	•	•	•	•	•
Depreciation **14**	0.8	0.2	0.8	0.4	0.9	0.7	1.0	1.4	•	•	•	•	•
Amortization and Depletion **15**	0.2	•	0.2	0.2	0.2	0.4	0.2	0.1	•	•	•	•	•
Pensions and Other Deferred Comp. **16**	0.1	•	0.1	0.1	0.2	0.0	0.1	0.1	•	•	•	•	•
Employee Benefits **17**	0.3	0.8	0.3	0.1	0.4	0.7	0.5	1.2	•	•	•	•	•
Advertising **18**	0.6	0.8	0.3	0.7	0.8	0.4	2.0	1.0	•	•	•	•	•
Other Expenses **19**	8.2	847.2	8.6	6.8	7.9	9.1	7.7	8.9	•	•	•	•	•
Officers' Compensation **20**	2.6	1.4	3.4	1.8	1.8	2.2	2.1	0.5	•	•	•	•	•
Operating Margin **21**	•	•	•	2.2	•	•	•	0.7	•	•	•	•	•
Operating Margin Before Officers' Comp. **22**	2.3	•	2.6	4.0	1.2	•	1.5	1.2	•	•	•	•	•

Selected Average Balance Sheet ($ in Thousands)

Net Receivables 23	8	•	0	2	7	83	140	362	2476
Inventories 24	164	•	0	93	362	687	4298	6070	19129
Net Property, Plant and Equipment 25	69	•	0	45	56	340	744	2823	15846
Total Assets 26	374	•	0	203	743	1856	7282	14818	55678
Notes and Loans Payable 27	204	•	0	131	480	791	2372	4385	12777
All Other Liabilities 28	86	•	0	36	195	485	2776	4596	14973
Net Worth 29	84	•	0	37	68	580	2135	5837	27928

Selected Financial Ratios (Times to 1)

Current Ratio 30	2.2	•	2.9	2.7	1.7	1.2	1.7	1.8
Quick Ratio 31	0.6	•	0.7	0.8	0.5	0.2	0.3	0.3
Net Sales to Working Capital 32	10.1	•	10.2	7.6	11.5	43.1	8.7	12.9
Coverage Ratio 33	3.2	•	2.1	8.7	4.1	•	4.0	5.3
Total Asset Turnover 34	3.5	•	4.0	3.7	2.9	4.2	2.1	2.9
Inventory Turnover 35	6.4	•	6.9	6.1	6.2	5.4	4.0	6.5
Receivables Turnover 36	140.2	•	310.0	699.2	70.6	31.5	51.2	60.1
Total Liabilities to Net Worth 37	3.4	•	4.5	10.0	2.2	2.4	1.5	1.0
Current Assets to Working Capital 38	1.8	•	1.5	1.6	2.5	6.2	2.5	2.2
Current Liabilities to Working Capital 39	0.8	•	0.5	0.6	1.5	5.2	1.5	1.2
Working Capital to Net Sales 40	0.1	•	0.1	0.1	0.1	0.0	0.1	0.1
Inventory to Working Capital 41	1.3	•	1.2	1.1	1.6	4.6	1.7	1.7
Total Receipts to Cash Flow 42	15.6	•	16.3	14.5	13.5	36.6	14.1	16.7
Cost of Goods to Cash Flow 43	12.4	•	12.9	11.7	10.8	28.0	10.9	12.9
Cash Flow to Total Debt 44	0.3	•	0.3	0.3	0.3	0.2	0.2	0.3

Selected Financial Factors (in Percentages)

Debt Ratio 45	77.5	•	81.9	90.9	68.7	70.7	60.6	49.8
Return on Total Assets 46	6.8	•	5.4	12.0	8.5	•	6.8	4.7
Return on Equity Before Income Taxes 47	20.8	•	15.4	116.6	20.5	•	12.9	7.6
Return on Equity After Income Taxes 48	19.1	•	14.6	113.3	19.0	•	9.1	5.6
Profit Margin (Before Income Tax) 49	1.3	•	0.7	2.9	2.2	•	2.4	1.3
Profit Margin (After Income Tax) 50	1.2	•	0.7	2.8	2.1	•	1.7	1.0

Table II
Corporations with Net Income

BEER, WINE, AND LIQUOR STORES

MONEY AMOUNTS AND SIZE OF ASSETS IN THOUSANDS OF DOLLARS

Item Description for Accounting Period 7/02 Through 6/03	Total	Zero Assets	Under 500	500 to 1,000	1,000 to 5,000	5,000 to 10,000	10,000 to 25,000	25,000 to 50,000	50,000 to 100,000	100,000 to 250,000	250,000 to 500,000	500,000 to 2,500,000	2,500,000 and over
Number of Enterprises **1**	8469	0	6825	1144	473	0	12	0	0	0	•	•	•
Revenues ($ in Thousands)													
Net Sales **2**	14262830	0	6859910	3052819	3051189	0	359478	0	0	0	•	•	•
Interest **3**	5985	0	555	2654	1849	0	330	0	0	0	•	•	•
Rents **4**	4400	0	0	0	3879	0	25	0	0	0	•	•	•
Royalties **5**	0	0	0	0	0	0	0	0	0	0	•	•	•
Other Portfolio Income **6**	8078	0	5515	185	644	0	38	0	0	0	•	•	•
Other Receipts **7**	204667	0	79327	17135	90511	0	12347	0	0	0	•	•	•
Total Receipts **8**	14485960	0	6945307	3072793	3148072	0	372218	0	0	0	•	•	•
Average Total Receipts **9**	1710	•	1018	2686	6656	•	31018	•	•	•	•	•	•
Operating Costs/Operating Income (%)													
Cost of Operations **10**	79.2	•	78.6	80.5	80.5	•	77.2	•	•	•	•	•	•
Salaries and Wages **11**	5.4	•	4.8	4.5	6.4	•	7.2	•	•	•	•	•	•
Taxes Paid **12**	1.8	•	2.5	1.2	1.1	•	1.4	•	•	•	•	•	•
Interest Paid **13**	0.4	•	0.4	0.5	0.5	•	0.6	•	•	•	•	•	•
Depreciation **14**	0.5	•	0.4	0.5	0.6	•	0.8	•	•	•	•	•	•
Amortization and Depletion **15**	0.2	•	0.2	0.2	0.1	•	0.2	•	•	•	•	•	•
Pensions and Other Deferred Comp. **16**	0.1	•	0.1	0.1	0.3	•	0.0	•	•	•	•	•	•
Employee Benefits **17**	0.3	•	0.3	0.1	0.2	•	0.5	•	•	•	•	•	•
Advertising **18**	0.6	•	0.3	0.9	0.7	•	1.3	•	•	•	•	•	•
Other Expenses **19**	7.5	•	7.6	6.6	7.7	•	6.6	•	•	•	•	•	•
Officers' Compensation **20**	2.7	•	3.6	2.2	1.8	•	2.5	•	•	•	•	•	•
Operating Margin **21**	1.3	•	1.2	2.9	0.0	•	1.6	•	•	•	•	•	•
Operating Margin Before Officers' Comp. **22**	4.1	•	4.8	5.1	1.8	•	4.2	•	•	•	•	•	•

Selected Average Balance Sheet ($ in Thousands)

Net Receivables 23	10	2	0	102	268
Inventories 24	210	112	360	813	6560
Net Property, Plant and Equipment 25	66	41	60	240	2177
Total Assets 26	460	245	760	1882	14798
Notes and Loans Payable 27	221	121	513	702	4617
All Other Liabilities 28	114	47	180	612	4622
Net Worth 29	126	76	66	568	5559

Selected Financial Ratios (Times to 1)

Current Ratio 30	2.3	3.1	2.9	1.6	1.6
Quick Ratio 31	0.6	0.8	0.8	0.6	0.3
Net Sales to Working Capital 32	9.4	9.5	7.2	12.0	8.9
Coverage Ratio 33	7.9	7.7	8.9	7.3	9.0
Total Asset Turnover 34	3.7	4.1	3.5	3.4	2.0
Inventory Turnover 35	6.4	7.1	6.0	6.4	3.5
Receivables Turnover 36	132.7	321.1	5088.0	67.0	72.5
Total Liabilities to Net Worth 37	2.7	2.2	10.4	2.3	1.7
Current Assets to Working Capital 38	1.8	1.5	1.5	2.5	2.7
Current Liabilities to Working Capital 39	0.8	0.5	0.5	1.5	1.7
Working Capital to Net Sales 40	0.1	0.1	0.1	0.1	0.1
Inventory to Working Capital 41	1.2	1.1	1.1	1.6	1.8
Total Receipts to Cash Flow 42	13.5	14.0	13.6	12.2	11.1
Cost of Goods to Cash Flow 43	10.7	11.0	11.0	9.8	8.6
Cash Flow to Total Debt 44	0.4	0.4	0.3	0.4	0.3

Selected Financial Factors (in Percentages)

Debt Ratio 45	72.6	68.9	91.3	69.8	62.4
Return on Total Assets 46	12.0	11.6	14.2	12.6	11.8
Return on Equity Before Income Taxes 47	38.5	32.4	144.4	36.2	27.9
Return on Equity After Income Taxes 48	36.5	31.6	140.5	34.0	21.5
Profit Margin (Before Income Tax) 49	2.9	2.5	3.6	3.2	5.2
Profit Margin (After Income Tax) 50	2.7	2.4	3.5	3.0	4.0

Table I

Corporations with and without Net Income

HEALTH AND PERSONAL CARE STORES

MONEY AMOUNTS AND SIZE OF ASSETS IN THOUSANDS OF DOLLARS

Item Description for Accounting Period 7/02 Through 6/03	Total	Zero Assets	Under 500	500 to 1,000	1,000 to 5,000	5,000 to 10,000	10,000 to 25,000	25,000 to 50,000	50,000 to 100,000	100,000 to 250,000	250,000 to 500,000	500,000 to 2,500,000	2,500,000 and over
Number of Enterprises **1**	35909	2682	27432	3730	1799	139	52	29	15	15	5	6	4
Revenues ($ in Thousands)													
Net Sales **2**	194997743	605198	22956633	13117916	11566133	3248258	2346126	2844967	2736166	5587104	1078210	24253923	104657110
Interest **3**	911126	3567	3891	6325	6057	2212	1685	1665	2643	9021	10774	63940	799345
Rents **4**	111970	210	753	1125	3411	1422	6077	1240	780	3141	0	23607	70204
Royalties **5**	202426	819	0	0	0	0	7780	9991	0	0	33575	43762	106499
Other Portfolio Income **6**	123332	35905	7400	17359	8656	1519	7483	824	562	7598	2900	16507	16615
Other Receipts **7**	1738843	23698	110590	40601	54889	20679	23530	18385	11933	64453	15247	570106	784735
Total Receipts **8**	198085440	669397	23079267	13183326	11639146	3274090	2392681	2877072	2752084	5671317	1140706	24971845	106434508
Average Total Receipts **9**	5516	250	841	3534	6470	23555	46013	99209	183472	378088	228141	4161974	26608627
Operating Costs/Operating Income (%)													
Cost of Operations **10**	76.3	71.7	68.9	74.4	70.0	76.7	60.3	67.1	61.7	69.8	51.2	77.5	80.3
Salaries and Wages **11**	8.8	5.0	8.1	7.2	11.4	7.7	12.1	14.0	16.3	11.6	8.2	9.0	8.3
Taxes Paid **12**	1.1	0.9	1.6	1.3	1.4	1.2	1.5	1.5	1.8	1.7	1.7	1.1	0.8
Interest Paid **13**	1.0	1.1	0.4	0.2	0.4	0.5	0.5	0.9	2.0	1.5	2.8	1.2	1.2
Depreciation **14**	1.0	1.1	0.7	0.5	1.0	1.1	1.2	1.2	1.9	1.4	2.7	1.0	1.1
Amortization and Depletion **15**	0.2	3.4	0.1	0.0	0.1	0.2	0.3	0.5	0.4	0.3	1.0	0.6	0.2
Pensions and Other Deferred Comp. **16**	0.2	0.0	0.2	0.6	0.3	0.2	0.2	0.1	0.2	0.1	0.2	0.2	0.2
Employee Benefits **17**	0.5	0.5	0.3	0.2	0.5	0.7	0.6	0.7	1.5	1.1	0.9	0.9	0.5
Advertising **18**	0.9	2.5	1.1	0.5	1.0	1.2	5.4	1.9	1.9	1.3	1.9	0.9	0.7
Other Expenses **19**	8.1	22.3	11.2	8.3	8.7	7.7	12.4	10.4	16.2	9.6	37.6	8.2	6.5
Officers' Compensation **20**	1.4	2.7	5.7	5.1	3.5	1.8	1.8	1.0	0.7	0.5	1.5	0.2	0.0
Operating Margin **21**	0.5	•	1.7	1.7	1.8	1.1	3.8	0.7	•	1.0	•	•	0.4
Operating Margin Before Officers' Comp. **22**	1.8	•	7.4	6.7	5.2	2.9	5.6	1.7	•	1.6	•	•	0.4

Selected Average Balance Sheet ($ in Thousands)

Net Receivables 23	210	0	21	86	362	2126	3918	8786	11502	24325	19694	145225	932938
Inventories 24	461	0	62	220	494	1462	4388	9575	20884	40378	42885	183279	2550127
Net Property, Plant and Equipment 25	364	0	24	89	221	1413	2678	5437	18531	29494	37375	249816	2195224
Total Assets 26	1792	0	153	673	1680	7144	15385	35846	72835	145979	303683	1564062	9394342
Notes and Loans Payable 27	541	0	70	175	414	2064	3942	9825	26882	67891	93658	384621	2779152
All Other Liabilities 28	542	0	41	203	542	3038	5821	15287	33069	45353	96511	640121	2479956
Net Worth 29	709	0	42	295	724	2042	5622	10734	12885	32735	113514	539320	4135234

Selected Financial Ratios (Times to 1)

Current Ratio 30	1.6	•	2.6	2.3	2.0	1.5	1.5	1.2	0.9	1.9	1.3	1.0	1.6
Quick Ratio 31	0.6	•	1.2	1.2	1.0	1.0	0.8	0.6	0.3	0.8	0.4	0.4	0.5
Net Sales to Working Capital 32	16.6	•	11.8	12.3	10.2	14.5	14.0	25.2	•	9.6	9.7	184.5	16.5
Coverage Ratio 33	3.1	0.3	6.3	9.8	7.3	4.9	13.8	3.0	•	2.7	•	2.9	2.7
Total Asset Turnover 34	3.0	•	5.5	5.2	3.8	3.3	2.9	2.7	2.5	2.6	0.7	2.6	2.8
Inventory Turnover 35	9.0	•	9.3	11.9	9.1	12.3	6.2	6.9	5.4	6.4	2.6	17.1	8.2
Receivables Turnover 36	25.8	•	41.2	33.1	19.6	13.0	11.3	11.8	13.7	21.6	6.2	30.4	27.0
Total Liabilities to Net Worth 37	1.5	•	2.7	1.3	1.3	2.5	1.7	2.3	4.7	3.5	1.7	1.9	1.3
Current Assets to Working Capital 38	2.7	•	1.6	1.8	2.0	3.0	3.2	5.7	•	2.1	5.0	25.5	2.6
Current Liabilities to Working Capital 39	1.7	•	0.6	0.8	1.0	2.0	2.2	4.7	•	1.1	4.0	24.5	1.6
Working Capital to Net Sales 40	0.1	•	0.1	0.1	0.1	0.1	0.1	0.0	•	0.1	0.1	0.0	0.1
Inventory to Working Capital 41	1.4	•	0.8	0.8	0.8	1.0	1.3	2.5	•	1.2	1.9	9.8	1.6
Total Receipts to Cash Flow 42	14.0	7.4	10.4	12.9	11.1	12.7	6.8	10.8	16.6	12.5	4.6	12.8	17.5
Cost of Goods to Cash Flow 43	10.7	5.3	7.2	9.6	7.8	9.8	4.1	7.3	10.3	8.7	2.4	9.9	14.0
Cash Flow to Total Debt 44	0.4	•	0.7	0.7	0.6	0.4	0.7	0.4	0.2	0.3	0.2	0.3	0.3

Selected Financial Factors (in Percentages)

Debt Ratio 45	60.4	•	72.9	56.2	56.9	71.4	63.5	70.1	82.3	77.6	62.6	65.5	56.0
Return on Total Assets 46	9.3	•	14.7	12.6	10.5	7.8	18.3	7.6	•	10.3	•	8.9	9.1
Return on Equity Before Income Taxes 47	15.8	•	45.6	25.8	21.1	21.8	46.4	16.9	•	29.0	•	17.1	13.1
Return on Equity After Income Taxes 48	11.5	•	43.6	24.0	19.3	17.8	42.0	13.1	•	23.5	•	11.0	8.5
Profit Margin (Before Income Tax) 49	2.1	•	2.3	2.2	2.4	1.9	5.8	1.8	•	2.6	•	2.3	2.1
Profit Margin (After Income Tax) 50	1.5	•	2.2	2.0	2.2	1.6	5.2	1.4	•	2.1	•	1.5	1.3

Table II

Corporations with Net Income

HEALTH AND PERSONAL CARE STORES

MONEY AMOUNTS AND SIZE OF ASSETS IN THOUSANDS OF DOLLARS

Item Description for Accounting Period 7/02 Through 6/03		Total	Zero Assets	Under 500	500 to 1,000	1,000 to 5,000	5,000 to 10,000	10,000 to 25,000	25,000 to 50,000	50,000 to 100,000	100,000 to 250,000	250,000 to 500,000	500,000 to 2,500,000	2,500,000 and over
Number of Enterprises	1	24046	0	18373	2706	1413	0	38	20	8	15	0	0	0
Revenues ($ in Thousands)														
Net Sales	2	16281294	0	18514529	9892904	8689212	0	1986266	2063739	1749195	5329308	0	0	0
Interest	3	589306	0	2546	5335	3530	0	552	781	453	14408	0	0	0
Rents	4	57743	0	753	964	2619	0	5711	47	694	2305	0	0	0
Royalties	5	143895	0	0	0	0	0	62	3739	0	31861	0	0	0
Other Portfolio Income	6	114057	0	3117	17351	8067	0	6491	158	307	8440	0	0	0
Other Receipts	7	1105296	0	48877	38705	31984	0	13464	15975	7769	63118	0	0	0
Total Receipts	8	164891591	0	18569822	9955259	8735412	0	2012546	2084439	1758418	5449440	0	0	0
Average Total Receipts	9	6857	•	1011	3679	6182	•	52962	104222	219802	363296	•	•	•
Operating Costs/Operating Income (%)														
Cost of Operations	10	78.1	•	70.0	74.1	74.1	•	60.3	66.5	71.4	68.7	•	•	•
Salaries and Wages	11	7.9	•	7.2	6.9	9.4	•	10.3	12.5	13.1	11.6	•	•	•
Taxes Paid	12	0.9	•	1.6	1.1	1.3	•	1.4	1.4	1.4	1.8	•	•	•
Interest Paid	13	0.7	•	0.3	0.2	0.3	•	0.4	0.8	0.7	1.5	•	•	•
Depreciation	14	0.9	•	0.6	0.5	0.8	•	1.1	1.2	1.4	1.5	•	•	•
Amortization and Depletion	15	0.2	•	0.1	0.0	0.0	•	0.2	0.3	0.1	0.4	•	•	•
Pensions and Other Deferred Comp.	16	0.2	•	0.3	0.5	0.3	•	0.2	0.1	0.2	0.1	•	•	•
Employee Benefits	17	0.4	•	0.3	0.2	0.5	•	0.6	0.5	1.3	1.2	•	•	•
Advertising	18	0.7	•	0.9	0.4	0.5	•	6.1	2.0	0.8	1.3	•	•	•
Other Expenses	19	6.9	•	9.4	8.5	5.7	•	11.2	10.9	6.8	10.1	•	•	•
Officers' Compensation	20	1.2	•	5.0	4.5	3.3	•	1.7	1.1	0.8	0.6	•	•	•
Operating Margin	21	1.8	•	4.3	2.9	3.9	•	6.5	2.7	1.9	1.2	•	•	•
Operating Margin Before Officers' Comp.	22	3.0	•	9.3	7.4	7.1	•	8.2	3.8	2.7	1.8	•	•	•

Selected Average Balance Sheet ($ in Thousands)

Net Receivables 23	251	23	89	324	4231	8824	11852	20062
Inventories 24	538	73	234	474	4230	9402	27880	35536
Net Property, Plant and Equipment 25	424	23	103	171	2517	4869	20662	31512
Total Assets 26	2180	169	705	1534	15675	34565	71751	172198
Notes and Loans Payable 27	522	64	136	337	3364	8750	18685	62038
All Other Liabilities 28	600	42	188	413	6176	15136	22702	41789
Net Worth 29	1059	63	380	784	6135	10679	30363	68371

Selected Financial Ratios (Times to 1)

Current Ratio 30	1.6	2.8	2.6	2.3	1.5	1.5	1.8	2.1
Quick Ratio 31	0.7	1.4	1.4	1.2	0.8	0.7	0.7	0.7
Net Sales to Working Capital 32	16.8	11.9	11.5	9.4	14.5	14.4	11.1	8.1
Coverage Ratio 33	5.5	14.3	16.9	16.4	22.5	5.7	4.4	3.3
Total Asset Turnover 34	3.1	6.0	5.2	4.0	3.3	3.0	3.0	2.1
Inventory Turnover 35	9.8	9.6	11.6	9.6	7.5	7.3	5.6	6.9
Receivables Turnover 36	27.1	43.7	29.1	20.4	13.6	13.9	13.6	24.9
Total Liabilities to Net Worth 37	1.1	1.7	0.9	1.0	1.6	2.2	1.4	1.5
Current Assets to Working Capital 38	2.5	1.6	1.6	1.8	3.0	3.2	2.2	1.9
Current Liabilities to Working Capital 39	1.5	0.6	0.6	0.8	2.0	2.2	1.2	0.9
Working Capital to Net Sales 40	0.1	0.1	0.1	0.1	0.1	0.1	0.1	0.1
Inventory to Working Capital 41	1.3	0.8	0.7	0.6	1.2	1.4	1.1	1.0
Total Receipts to Cash Flow 42	13.4	9.2	10.4	11.9	6.2	8.7	16.3	10.8
Cost of Goods to Cash Flow 43	10.5	6.4	7.7	8.8	3.8	5.8	11.6	7.4
Cash Flow to Total Debt 44	0.4	1.0	1.1	0.7	0.9	0.5	0.3	0.3

Selected Financial Factors (in Percentages)

Debt Ratio 45	51.4	62.5	46.0	48.9	60.9	69.1	57.7	60.3
Return on Total Assets 46	11.7	29.5	19.5	18.7	27.3	13.4	9.7	10.0
Return on Equity Before Income Taxes 47	19.6	73.2	34.0	34.3	66.6	35.7	17.6	17.7
Return on Equity After Income Taxes 48	15.3	71.3	32.0	32.2	61.1	30.2	15.0	15.0
Profit Margin (Before Income Tax) 49	3.1	4.6	3.5	4.4	7.8	3.7	2.4	3.4
Profit Margin (After Income Tax) 50	2.4	4.5	3.3	4.1	7.2	3.1	2.1	2.9

Table I

Corporations with and without Net Income

GASOLINE STATIONS

MONEY AMOUNTS AND SIZE OF ASSETS IN THOUSANDS OF DOLLARS

Item Description for Accounting Period 7/02 Through 6/03	Total	Zero Assets	Under 500	500 to 1,000	1,000 to 5,000	5,000 to 10,000	10,000 to 25,000	25,000 to 50,000	50,000 to 100,000	100,000 to 250,000	250,000 to 500,000	500,000 to 2,500,000	2,500,000 and over
Number of Enterprises **1**	36982	3397	25343	4174	3467	327	172	53	23	14	7	6	0
Revenues ($ in Thousands)													
Net Sales **2**	141339411	1921839	41474178	9607464	25054424	8367447	10481198	7167146	4536665	7493654	10212347	15023049	
Interest **3**	57837	209	2419	4513	9900	2397	6636	2796	1112	6166	4954	16735	0
Rents **4**	107122	2656	7913	13800	12233	10315	9898	8046	7157	7132	13948	14024	0
Royalties **5**	17273	3493	0	0	0	0	142	413	521	923	0	11781	0
Other Portfolio Income **6**	230559	266	35489	2727	113812	5453	18992	9206	4682	2750	13266	23915	0
Other Receipts **7**	1579763	247618	427710	85170	201719	112659	118959	32703	67438	82056	93576	110156	0
Total Receipts **8**	143331965	2176081	41947709	9713674	25392088	8498271	10635825	7220310	4617575	7592681	10338091	15199660	0
Average Total Receipts **9**	3876	641	1655	2327	7324	25989	61836	136232	200764	542334	1476870	2533277	·
Operating Costs/Operating Income (%)													
Cost of Operations **10**	85.2	85.7	85.6	82.9	85.5	81.6	86.6	84.6	86.1	85.2	84.4	86.2	·
Salaries and Wages **11**	5.0	4.8	3.7	5.3	4.9	9.0	4.8	5.0	5.2	5.9	6.1	5.2	·
Taxes Paid **12**	1.5	1.8	1.9	1.9	1.1	2.5	1.2	2.6	0.9	0.9	1.1	0.8	·
Interest Paid **13**	0.7	0.6	0.3	0.9	1.0	1.0	0.8	0.6	1.2	0.7	0.6	0.9	·
Depreciation **14**	1.6	1.1	0.7	2.3	1.7	1.9	1.6	1.8	2.1	2.3	2.1	2.7	·
Amortization and Depletion **15**	0.2	9.6	0.1	0.1	0.1	0.1	0.1	0.0	0.1	0.1	0.1	0.2	·
Pensions and Other Deferred Comp. **16**	0.1	0.0	0.0	0.0	0.0	0.0	0.0	0.0	0.1	0.1	0.1	0.1	·
Employee Benefits **17**	0.2	0.3	0.1	0.1	0.1	0.6	0.2	0.3	0.3	0.5	0.4	0.3	·
Advertising **18**	0.2	0.1	0.2	0.1	0.2	0.1	0.2	0.2	0.2	0.2	0.3	0.2	·
Other Expenses **19**	6.2	8.5	7.5	6.6	6.3	5.4	5.8	4.8	5.4	4.8	6.0	4.8	·
Officers' Compensation **20**	0.7	1.8	1.2	0.9	0.7	0.4	0.4	0.4	0.4	0.2	0.2	0.1	·
Operating Margin **21**	·	·	·	·	·	·	·	·	·	·	·	·	·
Operating Margin Before Officers' Comp. **22**	·	·	·	·	·	·	·	0.0	·	·	·	·	·

Selected Average Balance Sheet ($ in Thousands)

Net Receivables 23	71	0	14	25	120	596	1387	2261	6674	13510	70499	62805	•
Inventories 24	96	0	45	60	146	494	1331	3108	5080	15582	41258	79049	•
Net Property, Plant and Equipment 25	452	0	56	409	1115	3880	8460	19788	33632	83588	188147	448845	•
Total Assets 26	853	0	188	679	1888	6263	15068	33631	66408	158666	365233	778663	•
Notes and Loans Payable 27	437	0	107	420	1247	3763	7608	14374	28638	61792	115500	294285	•
All Other Liabilities 28	205	0	40	82	285	1600	3562	8197	18856	48571	162050	237559	•
Net Worth 29	210	0	41	178	356	901	3898	11060	18914	48302	87683	246820	•

Selected Financial Ratios (Times to 1)

Current Ratio 30	1.3	•	2.4	1.9	1.6	0.8	1.1	0.8	1.3	1.0	1.0	1.0	•
Quick Ratio 31	0.7	•	1.0	1.2	0.9	0.5	0.6	0.5	0.6	0.6	0.6	0.5	•
Net Sales to Working Capital 32	59.4	•	30.8	25.1	35.3	•	117.7	44.3	•	•	•	627.5	•
Coverage Ratio 33	0.7	•	0.5	0.9	0.7	•	0.8	1.0	1.2	0.6	0.6	0.6	•
Total Asset Turnover 34	4.5	•	8.7	3.4	3.8	4.1	4.0	4.0	3.0	3.4	4.0	3.2	•
Inventory Turnover 35	33.9	•	31.1	32.1	42.4	42.2	39.6	36.8	33.4	29.3	29.8	27.3	•
Receivables Turnover 36	58.6	•	114.4	92.3	72.1	50.3	47.5	56.9	30.0	42.6	23.9	45.6	•
Total Liabilities to Net Worth 37	3.1	•	3.6	2.8	4.3	6.0	2.9	2.0	2.5	2.3	3.2	2.2	•
Current Assets to Working Capital 38	4.3	•	1.7	2.1	2.6	•	8.8	4.7	•	•	•	56.9	•
Current Liabilities to Working Capital 39	3.3	•	0.7	1.1	1.6	•	7.8	3.7	•	•	•	55.9	•
Working Capital to Net Sales 40	0.0	•	0.0	0.0	0.0	•	0.0	0.0	•	•	•	0.0	•
Inventory to Working Capital 41	1.6	•	0.9	0.6	0.8	•	2.8	1.2	•	•	•	21.6	•
Total Receipts to Cash Flow 42	28.2	30.3	26.5	24.1	27.1	36.2	27.3	26.6	28.1	28.0	29.9	37.4	•
Cost of Goods to Cash Flow 43	24.0	25.9	22.7	20.0	23.2	29.5	23.6	22.5	24.2	23.9	25.2	32.2	•
Cash Flow to Total Debt 44	0.2	•	0.4	0.2	0.2	0.1	0.2	0.2	0.1	0.2	0.2	0.1	•

Selected Financial Factors (in Percentages)

Debt Ratio 45	75.4	•	78.2	73.8	81.1	85.6	74.1	67.1	71.5	69.6	76.0	68.3	•
Return on Total Assets 46	2.1	•	1.3	2.8	2.5	•	2.7	4.1	3.3	2.9	1.4	1.7	•
Return on Equity Before Income Taxes 47	•	•	•	•	•	•	•	4.9	•	1.9	•	•	•
Return on Equity After Income Taxes 48	•	•	•	•	•	•	•	4.5	•	0.1	•	•	•
Profit Margin (Before Income Tax) 49	•	•	•	•	•	•	•	0.4	•	0.2	•	0.2	•
Profit Margin (After Income Tax) 50	•	•	•	•	•	•	•	0.4	•	0.0	•	•	•

225

Table II
Corporations with Net Income

GASOLINE STATIONS

MONEY AMOUNTS AND SIZE OF ASSETS IN THOUSANDS OF DOLLARS

Item Description for Accounting Period 7/02 Through 6/03	Total	Zero Assets	Under 500	500 to 1,000	1,000 to 5,000	5,000 to 10,000	10,000 to 25,000	25,000 to 50,000	50,000 to 100,000	100,000 to 250,000	250,000 to 500,000	500,000 to 2,500,000	2,500,000 and over
Number of Enterprises **1**	18879	1202	13750	2161	1494	131	83	33	12	6	4	3	0
Revenues ($ in Thousands)													
Net Sales **2**	77755178	643102	23589018	6093650	14804457	2455255	5452180	4528692	2386672	3703983	6595150	7503019	0
Interest **3**	44775	0	1184	4473	6446	1709	4206	1473	336	4892	3709	16347	0
Rents **4**	59359	0	5438	3266	7704	4818	6890	2504	3747	4341	6627	14024	0
Royalties **5**	11921	0	0	0	0	0	141	0	0	0	0	11781	0
Other Portfolio Income **6**	163499	0	20420	2496	84655	1437	12067	8122	1963	644	9490	22204	0
Other Receipts **7**	882400	42015	308253	47262	129598	17964	73557	19400	34803	65929	75397	68222	0
Total Receipts **8**	78917132	685117	23924313	6151147	15032860	2481183	5549041	4560191	2427521	3779789	6690373	7635597	0
Average Total Receipts **9**	4180	570	1740	2846	10062	18940	66856	138188	202293	629965	1672593	2545199	•
Operating Costs/Operating Income (%)													
Cost of Operations **10**	84.9	84.7	85.3	83.4	85.3	83.5	86.7	85.6	85.2	82.8	83.9	84.6	•
Salaries and Wages **11**	4.6	3.0	3.2	4.1	5.1	4.0	4.8	4.5	5.0	7.0	6.3	5.6	•
Taxes Paid **12**	1.5	3.2	1.9	2.0	1.0	2.9	1.1	1.6	1.0	0.9	1.0	0.9	•
Interest Paid **13**	0.6	•	0.3	0.6	0.6	1.2	0.5	0.6	1.1	0.5	0.6	1.1	•
Depreciation **14**	1.3	0.1	0.6	1.2	1.2	1.7	1.5	1.6	2.0	1.9	2.2	2.6	•
Amortization and Depletion **15**	0.1	•	0.1	0.1	0.1	0.1	0.1	0.0	0.0	0.0	0.0	0.2	•
Pensions and Other Deferred Comp. **16**	0.1	•	0.0	0.0	0.2	0.1	0.0	0.0	0.1	0.0	0.1	0.1	•
Employee Benefits **17**	0.2	•	0.1	0.1	0.1	0.2	0.2	0.3	0.3	0.6	0.4	0.5	•
Advertising **18**	0.2	•	0.2	0.1	0.2	0.2	0.1	0.2	0.2	0.3	0.4	0.4	•
Other Expenses **19**	6.0	6.6	7.1	6.1	6.0	5.5	5.4	4.7	5.0	5.0	5.4	5.2	•
Officers' Compensation **20**	0.7	0.1	1.1	0.9	0.6	0.8	0.4	0.4	0.4	0.2	0.2	0.2	•
Operating Margin **21**	•	2.2	0.1	1.4	•	•	•	0.4	•	0.1	•	•	•
Operating Margin Before Officers' Comp. **22**	0.5	2.4	1.2	2.3	0.2	0.6	•	0.8	0.3	0.4	0.2	0.4	•

Selected Average Balance Sheet ($ in Thousands)

Net Receivables 23	68	0	16	22	111	418	1635	2161	5114	12193	58833	70364	•
Inventories 24	107	0	51	62	180	553	1507	3451	6056	17148	37247	65100	•
Net Property, Plant and Equipment 25	410	0	52	367	1061	3330	8301	18475	34571	94424	176858	408641	•
Total Assets 26	824	0	194	664	1991	5899	15268	32886	65687	163880	366066	703419	•
Notes and Loans Payable 27	367	0	85	339	1069	3617	5710	13700	25036	49212	124860	310255	•
All Other Liabilities 28	183	0	30	60	321	913	3959	7033	19497	47340	136430	229264	•
Net Worth 29	274	0	80	265	601	1368	5598	12153	21154	67327	104776	163900	•

Selected Financial Ratios (Times to 1)

Current Ratio 30	1.6	•	3.6	3.3	1.9	1.4	1.2	1.1	1.6	1.2	1.2	0.9	•
Quick Ratio 31	0.9	•	1.6	2.2	1.0	0.8	0.7	0.6	0.6	0.6	0.8	0.4	•
Net Sales to Working Capital 32	36.0	•	22.3	20.6	32.3	40.5	79.3	278.8	23.0	70.2	77.5	•	•
Coverage Ratio 33	3.4	•	6.7	4.6	2.8	1.7	2.6	2.9	2.4	5.1	2.3	1.6	•
Total Asset Turnover 34	5.0	•	8.8	4.2	5.0	3.2	4.3	4.2	3.0	3.8	4.5	3.6	•
Inventory Turnover 35	32.6	•	28.6	37.7	47.0	28.3	37.8	34.0	28.0	29.8	37.2	32.5	•
Receivables Turnover 36	58.1	•	115.3	119.6	93.2	31.3	44.3	56.2	36.1	40.1	56.0	71.1	•
Total Liabilities to Net Worth 37	2.0	•	1.4	1.5	2.3	3.3	1.7	1.7	2.1	1.4	2.5	3.3	•
Current Assets to Working Capital 38	2.6	•	1.4	1.4	2.2	3.7	6.3	20.5	2.6	5.9	5.5	•	•
Current Liabilities to Working Capital 39	1.6	•	0.4	0.4	1.2	2.7	5.3	19.5	1.6	4.9	4.5	•	•
Working Capital to Net Sales 40	0.0	•	0.0	0.0	0.0	0.0	0.0	0.0	0.0	0.0	0.0	•	•
Inventory to Working Capital 41	0.9	•	0.7	0.4	0.6	1.4	1.9	6.3	0.7	2.7	1.8	•	•
Total Receipts to Cash Flow 42	20.1	8.1	18.9	16.1	21.5	21.0	22.3	23.2	19.0	17.2	24.0	25.4	•
Cost of Goods to Cash Flow 43	17.1	6.9	16.1	13.4	18.3	17.5	19.4	19.9	16.2	14.3	20.1	21.5	•
Cash Flow to Total Debt 44	0.4	•	0.8	0.4	0.3	0.2	0.3	0.3	0.2	0.4	0.3	0.2	•

Selected Financial Factors (in Percentages)

Debt Ratio 45	66.7	•	59.1	60.1	69.8	76.8	63.3	63.0	67.8	58.9	71.4	76.7	•
Return on Total Assets 46	9.6	•	15.6	12.7	8.7	6.7	6.1	7.1	7.9	10.2	5.9	6.1	•
Return on Equity Before Income Taxes 47	20.3	•	32.3	24.9	18.4	12.4	10.2	12.7	14.5	20.0	11.8	9.6	•
Return on Equity After Income Taxes 48	19.2	•	31.9	24.5	17.3	11.6	9.2	12.1	12.9	17.0	10.3	7.2	•
Profit Margin (Before Income Tax) 49	1.4	8.8	1.5	2.3	1.1	0.9	0.9	1.1	1.5	2.2	0.8	0.6	•
Profit Margin (After Income Tax) 50	1.3	8.8	1.5	2.3	1.1	0.8	0.8	1.1	1.4	1.9	0.7	0.5	•

Table I

Corporations with and without Net Income

CLOTHING AND CLOTHING ACCESSORIES STORES

MONEY AMOUNTS AND SIZE OF ASSETS IN THOUSANDS OF DOLLARS

Item Description for Accounting Period 7/02 Through 6/03	Total	Zero Assets	Under 500	500 to 1,000	1,000 to 5,000	5,000 to 10,000	10,000 to 25,000	25,000 to 50,000	50,000 to 100,000	100,000 to 250,000	250,000 to 500,000	500,000 to 2,500,000	2,500,000 and over
Number of Enterprises **1**	52089	3738	41022	4262	2480	284	141	53	31	32	21	20	5
Revenues ($ in Thousands)													
Net Sales **2**	144073291	845397	15658659	6019861	7642847	4008496	4703886	3862450	3983185	10118956	14904969	32517958	39806629
Interest **3**	693206	814	6920	2091	10327	6193	11669	4816	7127	11874	135138	249895	246343
Rents **4**	108961	345	94	3276	4603	4200	2728	2700	747	11126	30375	26910	21858
Royalties **5**	675225	0	33	9	0	6507	320	134	16996	9344	123715	193688	324479
Other Portfolio Income **6**	249865	6375	30471	5687	8156	3665	1219	4390	46326	5610	15958	85817	36188
Other Receipts **7**	2348804	72961	40743	25273	48435	75939	56083	60328	80268	119053	232363	371376	1165980
Total Receipts **8**	148149352	925892	15736920	6056197	7714368	4105000	4775905	3934818	4134649	10275963	15442518	33445644	41601477
Average Total Receipts **9**	2844	248	384	1421	3111	14454	33872	74242	133376	321124	735358	1672282	8320295
Operating Costs/Operating Income (%)													
Cost of Operations **10**	56.0	51.4	55.9	58.5	57.9	60.3	56.6	57.2	55.9	55.8	60.7	53.0	55.5
Salaries and Wages **11**	14.3	13.3	10.1	11.9	13.5	15.6	13.7	14.4	15.8	14.9	12.7	14.8	16.2
Taxes Paid **12**	2.2	2.7	2.3	2.1	2.1	2.1	2.3	2.3	2.9	2.3	2.2	2.2	2.3
Interest Paid **13**	1.0	0.3	0.9	0.7	0.8	0.9	0.8	1.2	1.5	0.9	1.0	0.8	1.2
Depreciation **14**	2.7	3.3	0.9	0.6	1.2	1.2	1.6	1.8	2.1	2.9	2.9	3.4	3.7
Amortization and Depletion **15**	0.3	0.0	0.2	0.1	0.1	0.1	0.6	0.2	0.2	0.2	0.1	0.2	0.6
Pensions and Other Deferred Comp. **16**	0.3	0.6	0.2	0.3	0.5	0.1	0.2	0.1	0.2	0.1	0.1	0.2	0.4
Employee Benefits **17**	1.0	1.1	0.5	0.6	0.7	0.5	0.6	1.2	1.2	1.0	0.7	1.3	1.4
Advertising **18**	2.3	1.0	2.2	2.9	2.6	2.2	3.5	2.3	2.9	2.1	2.2	2.5	2.1
Other Expenses **19**	17.7	25.7	19.4	16.2	17.1	15.9	18.1	19.3	21.2	18.8	17.9	18.6	15.8
Officers' Compensation **20**	1.9	7.6	6.2	5.8	5.0	1.7	2.3	1.5	1.2	0.7	1.0	0.8	0.6
Operating Margin **21**	0.3	•	1.3	0.5	•	•	•	•	•	•	1.3	2.3	0.3
Operating Margin Before Officers' Comp. **22**	2.2	0.5	7.5	6.3	3.5	1.1	2.2	0.2	•	1.1	3.1	•	0.8

Selected Average Balance Sheet ($ in Thousands)

Net Receivables 23	106	0	8	40	93	831	1815	3140	6094	6877	35983	53909	374546
Inventories 24	517	0	75	399	1018	3270	7191	15834	28081	52576	111380	335687	1041825
Net Property, Plant and Equipment 25	383	0	11	77	270	1078	2759	7815	15040	48311	109811	259183	1579476
Total Assets 26	1594	0	141	701	1819	6918	16215	34975	72229	163330	349828	1038703	5608772
Notes and Loans Payable 27	394	0	52	246	461	3364	4552	12183	29004	35393	53785	147946	1568022
All Other Liabilities 28	525	0	47	178	582	3141	5991	11893	28548	64952	113004	265306	2045207
Net Worth 29	674	0	42	276	775	413	5672	10899	14677	62985	183039	625451	1995542

Selected Financial Ratios (Times to 1)

Current Ratio 30	1.9	•	2.1	2.8	2.0	1.4	1.6	1.7	1.5	1.2	1.8	1.9	2.1
Quick Ratio 31	0.6	•	0.7	0.8	0.5	0.4	0.4	0.4	0.4	0.3	0.6	0.4	1.1
Net Sales to Working Capital 32	6.3	•	6.4	3.7	4.4	9.4	7.6	7.7	8.8	23.7	7.6	6.8	5.0
Coverage Ratio 33	4.4	7.6	3.1	2.6	0.2	3.1	2.9	1.4	0.3	3.2	2.8	7.3	5.5
Total Asset Turnover 34	1.7	•	2.7	2.0	1.7	2.0	2.1	2.1	1.8	1.9	2.0	1.6	1.4
Inventory Turnover 35	3.0	•	2.8	2.1	1.8	2.6	2.6	2.6	2.6	3.4	3.9	2.6	4.2
Receivables Turnover 36	19.8	•	47.2	40.2	30.3	23.8	19.3	24.5	24.8	37.8	20.4	30.4	10.6
Total Liabilities to Net Worth 37	1.4	•	2.4	1.5	1.3	15.7	1.9	2.2	3.9	1.6	0.9	0.7	1.8
Current Assets to Working Capital 38	2.1	•	1.9	1.5	2.0	3.6	2.7	2.5	3.1	6.6	2.2	2.2	1.9
Current Liabilities to Working Capital 39	1.1	•	0.9	0.5	1.0	2.6	1.7	1.5	2.1	5.6	1.2	1.2	0.9
Working Capital to Net Sales 40	0.2	•	0.2	0.3	0.2	0.1	0.1	0.1	0.1	0.0	0.1	0.1	0.2
Inventory to Working Capital 41	1.2	•	1.3	1.1	1.4	2.5	1.7	1.6	1.9	4.0	1.2	1.4	0.8
Total Receipts to Cash Flow 42	8.3	6.8	7.8	9.6	11.2	10.8	8.6	9.0	10.4	9.1	9.8	7.3	7.8
Cost of Goods to Cash Flow 43	4.6	3.5	4.4	5.6	6.5	6.5	4.9	5.2	5.8	5.1	6.0	3.9	4.3
Cash Flow to Total Debt 44	0.4	•	0.5	0.3	0.3	0.2	0.4	0.3	0.2	0.3	0.4	0.5	0.3

Selected Financial Factors (in Percentages)

Debt Ratio 45	57.7	•	70.2	60.6	57.4	94.0	65.0	68.8	79.7	61.4	47.7	39.8	64.4
Return on Total Assets 46	7.5	•	7.3	3.6	0.2	5.5	4.6	3.6	0.8	5.6	5.9	9.4	9.6
Return on Equity Before Income Taxes 47	13.7	•	16.5	5.7	•	62.5	8.7	3.5	•	10.0	7.2	13.4	22.0
Return on Equity After Income Taxes 48	8.7	•	14.4	4.2	•	60.1	6.6	0.0	•	4.2	3.3	8.8	14.3
Profit Margin (Before Income Tax) 49	3.3	2.3	1.8	1.1	•	1.8	1.5	0.5	•	2.0	1.9	5.2	5.5
Profit Margin (After Income Tax) 50	2.1	0.6	1.6	0.8	•	1.8	1.1	0.0	•	0.8	3.4	3.4	3.6

Table II

Corporations with Net Income

CLOTHING AND CLOTHING ACCESSORIES STORES

MONEY AMOUNTS AND SIZE OF ASSETS IN THOUSANDS OF DOLLARS

Item Description for Accounting Period 7/02 Through 6/03	Total	Zero Assets	Under 500	500 to 1,000	1,000 to 5,000	5,000 to 10,000	10,000 to 25,000	25,000 to 50,000	50,000 to 100,000	100,000 to 250,000	250,000 to 500,000	500,000 to 2,500,000	2,500,000 and over
Number of Enterprises **1**	28824	1607	22650	2898	1259	0	93	34	16	20	13	0	5
Revenues ($ in Thousands)													
Net Sales **2**	117382375	600148	10786538	4359430	4797568	0	3256032	2769624	2634416	6599938	8238199	0	39806629
Interest **3**	562177	733	3532	1734	6858	0	9709	2383	904	9341	45618	0	246343
Rents **4**	94828	345	94	715	2835	0	2535	358	747	11126	27276	0	21858
Royalties **5**	657134	0	0	0	0	0	0	0	8445	9329	120068	0	324479
Other Portfolio Income **6**	145985	6268	29722	3216	6584	0	611	1333	2951	5606	12846	0	36188
Other Receipts **7**	2105700	46690	23835	19983	32657	0	46886	41329	72141	82489	144141	0	1165980
Total Receipts **8**	120948199	654184	10843721	4385078	4846502	0	3315773	2815027	2719604	6717829	8558148	0	41601477
Average Total Receipts **9**	4196	407	479	1513	3849	•	35653	82795	169975	335891	660627	•	8320295
Operating Costs/Operating Income (%)													
Cost of Operations **10**	54.7	41.2	54.7	57.7	56.0	•	56.2	57.7	55.5	53.9	53.3	•	55.5
Salaries and Wages **11**	14.4	14.8	9.6	11.6	12.5	•	12.8	13.3	15.3	14.8	14.8	•	16.2
Taxes Paid **12**	2.2	2.7	2.2	2.0	2.0	•	2.0	2.1	3.0	2.3	2.5	•	2.3
Interest Paid **13**	0.8	0.2	0.8	0.7	0.5	•	0.6	0.8	0.8	0.5	0.2	•	1.2
Depreciation **14**	2.8	3.6	0.6	0.6	1.0	•	1.4	1.3	1.9	3.0	3.7	•	3.7
Amortization and Depletion **15**	0.3	0.0	0.1	0.0	0.0	•	0.7	0.2	•	0.1	0.1	•	0.6
Pensions and Other Deferred Comp. **16**	0.3	0.9	0.2	0.2	0.7	•	0.3	0.1	0.2	0.0	0.1	•	0.4
Employee Benefits **17**	1.1	1.5	0.5	0.6	0.6	•	0.6	0.9	1.0	0.9	0.7	•	1.4
Advertising **18**	2.3	0.2	1.9	3.0	2.8	•	3.4	2.1	3.3	1.6	1.9	•	2.1
Other Expenses **19**	17.2	19.0	18.8	14.2	16.0	•	15.3	17.6	18.3	17.3	20.2	•	15.8
Officers' Compensation **20**	1.7	10.0	5.5	5.1	5.2	•	2.7	1.4	0.9	0.8	1.3	•	0.6
Operating Margin **21**	2.2	5.8	5.1	4.3	2.6	•	4.2	2.6	•	4.8	1.2	•	0.3
Operating Margin Before Officers' Comp. **22**	3.8	15.8	10.6	9.4	7.8	•	6.9	4.0	0.7	5.6	2.5	•	0.8

Selected Average Balance Sheet ($ in Thousands)

Net Receivables 23	156	0	10	46	88	2057	3636	5814	4994	32822	•	374546
Inventories 24	700	0	85	380	1373	7601	15928	29697	51261	132575	•	1210163
Net Property, Plant and Equipment 25	580	0	11	66	222	2464	6722	16471	47960	112730	•	1579476
Total Assets 26	2360		166	702	2031	16128	35643	71350	165445	360746	•	5608772
Notes and Loans Payable 27	504	0	36	195	468	3068	8023	20107	27904	25483	•	1568022
All Other Liabilities 28	774	0	62	176	527	5949	11967	24804	52157	100593	•	2045207
Net Worth 29	1082	0	69	332	1036	7112	15654	26439	85384	234670	•	1995542

Selected Financial Ratios (Times to 1)

Current Ratio 30	2.1	•	2.1	3.1	2.6	1.8	1.9	1.6	1.6	2.4	•	2.1
Quick Ratio 31	0.8	•	0.8	1.0	0.6	0.6	0.5	0.4	0.5	0.8	•	1.1
Net Sales to Working Capital 32	5.7	•	6.5	3.6	3.8	6.6	6.9	9.8	9.5	5.3	•	5.0
Coverage Ratio 33	7.5	75.9	8.1	8.0	7.4	11.1	6.4	5.1	14.5	24.0	•	5.5
Total Asset Turnover 34	1.7	•	2.9	2.1	1.9	2.2	2.3	2.3	2.0	1.8	•	1.4
Inventory Turnover 35	3.2	•	3.1	2.3	1.6	2.6	2.9	3.1	3.5	2.5	•	3.7
Receivables Turnover 36	26.1	•	53.1	39.6	28.0	17.3	25.5	56.6	78.9	19.5	•	42.5
Total Liabilities to Net Worth 37	1.2	•	1.4	1.1	1.0	1.3	1.3	1.7	0.9	0.5	•	1.8
Current Assets to Working Capital 38	1.9	•	1.9	1.5	1.6	2.3	2.1	2.7	2.7	1.7	•	1.9
Current Liabilities to Working Capital 39	0.9	•	0.9	0.5	0.6	1.3	1.1	1.7	1.7	0.7	•	0.9
Working Capital to Net Sales 40	0.2	•	0.2	0.3	0.3	0.2	0.1	0.1	0.1	0.2	•	0.2
Inventory to Working Capital 41	1.1	•	1.1	0.9	1.2	1.4	1.4	1.8	1.5	0.9	•	0.8
Total Receipts to Cash Flow 42	7.2	4.2	6.2	7.1	7.8	6.6	6.9	7.6	6.7	7.1	•	7.8
Cost of Goods to Cash Flow 43	3.9	1.7	3.4	4.1	4.4	3.7	4.0	4.2	3.6	3.8	•	4.3
Cash Flow to Total Debt 44	0.4	•	0.8	0.6	0.5	0.6	0.6	0.5	0.6	0.7	•	0.3

Selected Financial Factors (in Percentages)

Debt Ratio 45	54.1	•	58.6	52.8	49.0	55.9	56.1	62.9	48.4	34.9	•	64.4
Return on Total Assets 46	10.9	•	18.4	11.9	7.7	14.4	11.3	9.0	13.9	9.7	•	9.6
Return on Equity Before Income Taxes 47	20.5	•	39.0	22.0	13.0	29.8	21.7	19.5	25.1	14.3	•	22.0
Return on Equity After Income Taxes 48	14.9	•	36.7	20.0	11.6	27.3	17.9	16.7	18.2	9.4	•	14.3
Profit Margin (Before Income Tax) 49	5.5	14.5	5.6	4.8	3.5	6.0	4.2	3.1	6.5	5.3	•	5.5
Profit Margin (After Income Tax) 50	4.0	12.2	5.3	4.4	3.2	5.5	3.4	2.7	4.7	3.5	•	3.6

Table I

Corporations with and without Net Income

SPORTING GOODS, HOBBY, BOOK, AND MUSIC STORES

MONEY AMOUNTS AND SIZE OF ASSETS IN THOUSANDS OF DOLLARS

Item Description for Accounting Period 7/02 Through 6/03	Total	Zero Assets	Under 500	500 to 1,000	1,000 to 5,000	5,000 to 10,000	10,000 to 25,000	25,000 to 50,000	50,000 to 100,000	100,000 to 250,000	250,000 to 500,000	500,000 to 2,500,000	2,500,000 and over
Number of Enterprises **1**	34676	3590	26321	2511	1945	170	69	22	17	9	9	13	0
Revenues ($ in Thousands)													
Net Sales **2**	73351521	527218	8722640	4370273	10112760	2361744	2133388	1392100	2757282	2953765	6331373	31688978	0
Interest **3**	126881	34	1650	1381	11977	1236	2609	1256	2930	2992	10564	90252	0
Rents **4**	39729	0	1490	2604	5002	450	1036	1781	664	391	1890	24422	0
Royalties **5**	482214	0	0	0	0	8	96	8998	181	9450	70204	393278	0
Other Portfolio Income **6**	121710	43578	3542	889	5839	5594	1092	31598	297	1846	1238	26200	0
Other Receipts **7**	1114362	1849	55969	29282	160977	35448	25150	15814	8946	15559	149243	616120	0
Total Receipts **8**	75236417	572679	8785291	4404429	10296555	2404480	2163371	1451547	2770300	2984003	6564512	32839250	0
Average Total Receipts **9**	2170	160	334	1754	5294	14144	31353	65979	162959	331556	729390	2526096	•
Operating Costs/Operating Income (%)													
Cost of Operations **10**	62.6	63.6	60.9	61.4	62.7	64.5	63.5	61.0	61.9	62.0	66.1	62.4	•
Salaries and Wages **11**	12.2	11.6	8.5	11.9	13.5	12.2	13.1	13.7	13.4	13.5	11.5	12.6	•
Taxes Paid **12**	2.1	2.6	1.8	2.9	1.9	1.8	1.9	1.9	2.1	2.3	1.9	2.2	•
Interest Paid **13**	1.0	0.9	0.9	1.0	0.8	1.1	1.0	0.8	0.7	1.2	1.4	1.1	•
Depreciation **14**	2.2	2.0	1.1	1.0	1.2	1.4	2.7	2.1	2.0	2.6	2.3	3.1	•
Amortization and Depletion **15**	0.2	0.3	0.3	0.0	0.1	0.1	0.3	0.9	0.1	1.2	0.2	0.1	•
Pensions and Other Deferred Comp. **16**	0.2	0.0	0.2	0.1	0.3	0.1	0.1	0.2	0.1	0.6	0.1	0.2	•
Employee Benefits **17**	0.6	0.7	0.6	0.3	0.6	0.7	0.6	0.7	0.6	1.0	0.6	0.6	•
Advertising **18**	2.1	1.2	1.9	2.7	2.3	2.8	4.0	4.4	3.0	2.4	3.0	1.5	•
Other Expenses **19**	16.3	29.4	18.9	14.9	13.6	16.1	17.4	17.3	13.3	15.1	13.3	17.4	•
Officers' Compensation **20**	1.7	4.3	5.0	3.5	2.8	1.5	2.1	1.2	0.9	1.0	0.4	0.5	•
Operating Margin **21**	•	•	•	0.3	0.2	•	•	•	1.8	•	•	•	•
Operating Margin Before Officers' Comp. **22**	0.4	•	4.9	3.8	3.0	•	•	•	2.8	•	•	•	•

Selected Average Balance Sheet ($ in Thousands)

	•	•	•	•	•	•	•	•	•	•	•	•
Net Receivables 23	70	0	4	52	226	672	1946	3902	5433	16015	40895	61069
Inventories 24	492	0	57	359	1102	3589	5796	18016	31848	100461	174093	621781
Net Property, Plant and Equipment 25	275	0	12	161	251	1004	2357	5770	15895	32990	82048	504582
Total Assets 26	1162	0	106	691	2156	7368	15091	34727	75898	167755	334635	1746050
Notes and Loans Payable 27	336	0	57	264	741	2733	4345	12355	18879	35347	64736	444912
All Other Liabilities 28	443	0	36	199	687	3983	7618	13323	29207	80904	146801	657506
Net Worth 29	383	0	14	227	728	652	3128	9049	27812	51503	123098	643631

Selected Financial Ratios (Times to 1)

	•	•	•	•	•	•	•	•	•	•	•	•
Current Ratio 30	1.6	•	2.1	2.2	1.9	1.3	1.1	1.8	1.5	1.5	1.4	1.5
Quick Ratio 31	0.3	•	0.5	0.6	0.5	0.3	0.4	0.5	0.3	0.3	0.3	0.3
Net Sales to Working Capital 32	7.9	•	7.2	6.2	6.4	9.9	28.5	5.9	9.5	7.8	10.4	8.0
Coverage Ratio 33	2.3	•	1.7	2.1	3.5	0.5	•	1.1	4.4	•	3.1	2.8
Total Asset Turnover 34	1.8	•	3.1	2.5	2.4	1.9	2.0	1.8	2.1	2.0	2.1	1.4
Inventory Turnover 35	2.7	•	3.5	3.0	3.0	2.5	3.4	2.1	3.2	2.0	2.7	2.4
Receivables Turnover 36	34.5	•	91.2	31.9	25.1	22.2	17.2	11.9	27.7	26.4	23.1	48.1
Total Liabilities to Net Worth 37	2.0	•	6.8	2.0	2.0	10.3	3.8	2.8	1.7	2.3	1.7	1.7
Current Assets to Working Capital 38	2.7	•	1.9	1.8	2.1	4.0	9.5	2.3	3.0	2.9	3.4	2.9
Current Liabilities to Working Capital 39	1.7	•	0.9	0.8	1.1	3.0	8.5	1.3	2.0	1.9	2.4	1.9
Working Capital to Net Sales 40	0.1	•	0.1	0.2	0.2	0.1	0.0	0.2	0.1	0.1	0.1	0.1
Inventory to Working Capital 41	1.9	•	1.4	1.3	1.4	2.6	5.6	1.4	2.2	2.1	2.6	2.1
Total Receipts to Cash Flow 42	9.8	12.4	8.1	10.4	10.3	11.9	14.8	10.7	11.3	19.3	9.4	9.2
Cost of Goods to Cash Flow 43	6.1	7.9	5.0	6.4	6.5	7.7	9.4	6.6	7.0	12.0	6.2	5.7
Cash Flow to Total Debt 44	0.3	•	0.4	0.4	0.4	0.2	0.2	0.2	0.3	0.1	0.4	0.2

Selected Financial Factors (in Percentages)

	•	•	•	•	•	•	•	•	•	•	•	•
Debt Ratio 45	67.0	•	87.2	67.1	66.2	91.2	79.3	73.9	63.4	69.3	63.2	63.1
Return on Total Assets 46	4.3	•	4.7	5.2	6.7	1.1	•	1.7	6.4	•	9.0	4.4
Return on Equity Before Income Taxes 47	7.3	•	14.8	8.2	14.1	•	•	0.5	13.4	•	16.6	7.7
Return on Equity After Income Taxes 48	4.6	•	13.5	7.2	12.6	•	•	•	10.6	•	11.0	5.1
Profit Margin (Before Income Tax) 49	1.3	•	0.6	1.1	2.0	•	•	0.1	2.3	•	2.9	2.0
Profit Margin (After Income Tax) 50	0.8	•	0.6	0.9	1.8	•	•	•	1.8	•	1.9	1.4

Table II

Corporations with Net Income

SPORTING GOODS, HOBBY, BOOK, AND MUSIC STORES

MONEY AMOUNTS AND SIZE OF ASSETS IN THOUSANDS OF DOLLARS

Item Description for Accounting Period 7/02 Through 6/03	Total	Zero Assets	Under 500	500 to 1,000	1,000 to 5,000	5,000 to 10,000	10,000 to 25,000	25,000 to 50,000	50,000 to 100,000	100,000 to 250,000	250,000 to 500,000	500,000 to 2,500,000	2,500,000 and over
Number of Enterprises 1	16685	1284	12190	1472	1548	96	47	12	13	5	0	0	0
Revenues ($ in Thousands)													
Net Sales 2	57448502	314390	4456074	2212569	8241195	1479034	1393304	935248	2274460	1493433	0	0	0
Interest 3	114183	2	700	763	11687	297	1585	914	2392	625	0	0	0
Rents 4	33495	0	0	1818	3470	422	529	1249	442	391	0	0	0
Royalties 5	435045	0	0	0	0	0	96	36	181	0	0	0	0
Other Portfolio Income 6	87002	43578	0	388	5838	5256	829	2907	271	800	0	0	0
Other Receipts 7	952655	996	28312	16514	117063	24790	14170	13818	5568	11289	0	0	0
Total Receipts 8	59070882	358966	4485086	2232052	8379253	1509799	1410513	954172	2283314	1506538	0	0	0
Average Total Receipts 9	3540	280	368	1516	5413	15727	30011	79514	175640	301308	.	.	.
Operating Costs/Operating Income (%)													
Cost of Operations 10	62.4	51.7	58.7	61.3	61.9	66.7	59.8	59.2	60.9	62.0	.	.	.
Salaries and Wages 11	12.1	13.3	7.5	10.8	13.1	10.5	12.6	13.4	13.7	12.7	.	.	.
Taxes Paid 12	2.1	2.8	1.7	3.6	1.9	1.5	1.8	1.9	2.0	2.2	.	.	.
Interest Paid 13	1.0	0.1	0.6	0.9	0.8	0.9	0.9	0.5	0.7	0.7	.	.	.
Depreciation 14	2.4	1.6	0.9	1.2	1.3	1.3	1.1	2.0	2.0	1.7	.	.	.
Amortization and Depletion 15	0.1	0.1	0.4	.	0.1	0.0	0.3	0.1	0.1	0.5	.	.	.
Pensions and Other Deferred Comp. 16	0.2	.	0.3	0.2	0.3	0.2	0.2	0.3	0.1	1.0	.	.	.
Employee Benefits 17	0.6	0.6	0.5	0.3	0.5	0.6	0.6	0.7	0.6	1.3	.	.	.
Advertising 18	2.0	1.4	1.7	2.3	2.0	2.6	4.6	5.6	3.0	2.5	.	.	.
Other Expenses 19	15.0	22.8	16.5	11.2	13.0	11.1	13.2	12.4	12.8	12.7	.	.	.
Officers' Compensation 20	1.4	7.0	4.8	3.9	3.2	1.8	2.0	1.4	1.0	1.6	.	.	.
Operating Margin 21	0.6	.	6.4	4.3	1.9	2.8	2.9	2.7	3.0	1.3	.	.	.
Operating Margin Before Officers' Comp. 22	2.0	5.7	11.2	8.2	5.1	4.7	4.9	4.1	4.0	2.8	.	.	.

Selected Average Balance Sheet ($ in Thousands)

Net Receivables 23	98	0	4	69	227	384	1736	4070	5822	23641
Inventories 24	778	0	68	370	1064	3858	6310	20322	41892	78141
Net Property, Plant and Equipment 25	502	0	10	153	228	1089	2397	6191	17177	22837
Total Assets 26	1984	0	114	702	2167	7506	14790	36752	78733	163573
Notes and Loans Payable 27	507	0	56	228	597	1214	3977	5625	18708	35142
All Other Liabilities 28	701	0	31	189	638	3243	4816	13268	25352	66585
Net Worth 29	776	0	27	286	932	3049	5997	17859	34673	61847

Selected Financial Ratios (Times to 1)

Current Ratio 30	1.7	•	2.7	2.3	2.0	1.3	1.7	2.0	1.9	2.1
Quick Ratio 31	0.4	•	0.7	0.7	0.5	0.3	0.5	0.7	0.4	0.6
Net Sales to Working Capital 32	7.1	•	5.9	5.0	6.3	13.1	7.2	5.5	6.8	4.5
Coverage Ratio 33	4.5	104.3	13.5	7.0	5.7	6.4	5.4	11.1	6.1	4.1
Total Asset Turnover 34	1.7	•	3.2	2.1	2.5	2.1	2.0	2.1	2.2	1.8
Inventory Turnover 35	2.8	•	3.2	2.5	3.1	2.7	2.8	2.3	2.5	2.4
Receivables Turnover 36	37.6	•	93.6	22.1	27.6	25.0	17.2	10.2	60.1	25.3
Total Liabilities to Net Worth 37	1.6	•	3.3	1.5	1.3	1.5	1.5	1.1	1.3	1.6
Current Assets to Working Capital 38	2.4	•	1.6	1.8	2.0	4.5	2.5	2.0	2.2	1.9
Current Liabilities to Working Capital 39	1.4	•	0.6	0.8	1.0	3.5	1.5	1.0	1.2	0.9
Working Capital to Net Sales 40	0.1	•	0.2	0.2	0.2	0.1	0.1	0.2	0.1	0.2
Inventory to Working Capital 41	1.7	•	1.2	1.2	1.4	3.5	1.6	1.1	1.6	1.2
Total Receipts to Cash Flow 42	8.8	3.8	5.7	8.4	9.3	10.2	7.9	8.1	10.0	13.2
Cost of Goods to Cash Flow 43	5.5	2.0	3.3	5.2	5.7	6.8	4.7	4.8	6.1	8.2
Cash Flow to Total Debt 44	0.3	•	0.7	0.4	0.4	0.5	0.3	0.4	0.5	0.2

Selected Financial Factors (in Percentages)

Debt Ratio 45	60.9	•	76.6	59.3	57.0	59.4	59.5	51.4	56.0	62.2
Return on Total Assets 46	7.6	•	24.4	12.9	10.6	11.9	10.0	11.0	9.0	5.2
Return on Equity Before Income Taxes 47	15.2	•	96.7	27.2	20.4	24.8	20.2	20.6	17.0	10.4
Return on Equity After Income Taxes 48	12.5	•	95.3	25.9	18.9	23.2	17.1	16.0	14.1	7.8
Profit Margin (Before Income Tax) 49	3.4	12.9	7.0	5.2	3.6	4.9	4.1	4.7	3.4	2.1
Profit Margin (After Income Tax) 50	2.8	12.9	6.9	4.9	3.3	4.6	3.5	3.7	2.8	1.6

Table I

Corporations with and without Net Income

GENERAL MERCHANDISE STORES

MONEY AMOUNTS AND SIZE OF ASSETS IN THOUSANDS OF DOLLARS

Item Description for Accounting Period 7/02 Through 6/03	Total	Zero Assets	Under 500	500 to 1,000	1,000 to 5,000	5,000 to 10,000	10,000 to 25,000	25,000 to 50,000	50,000 to 100,000	100,000 to 250,000	250,000 to 500,000	500,000 to 2,500,000	2,500,000 and over
Number of Enterprises **1**	11077	835	8664	735	689	33	46	22	9	13	9	8	14
Revenues ($ in Thousands)													
Net Sales **2**	512821902	11341022	3147591	881477	4428840	1725806	1536158	1559542	3262737	4250292	4929437	27457084	448301917
Interest **3**	3256914	61109	4008	1858	2316	6489	1129	4776	13634	6300	49770	173976	2931550
Rents **4**	755396	0	7526	510	5515	301	2259	150	9531	13239	3809	24671	687885
Royalties **5**	1350465	0	0	0	107	0	5442	0	0	0	2118	324153	1018644
Other Portfolio Income **6**	304640	0	0	34	1605	398	3214	236	11587	518	1319	6656	279073
Other Receipts **7**	10039787	46090	42534	18300	24096	8298	15915	30819	36988	152588	79547	560855	9023756
Total Receipts **8**	528529104	11448221	3201659	902179	4462479	1741292	1564117	1595523	3334477	4422937	5066000	28547395	462242825
Average Total Receipts **9**	47714	13710	370	1227	6477	52766	34003	72524	370497	340226	562889	3568424	33017345
Operating Costs/Operating Income (%)													
Cost of Operations **10**	71.9	66.0	61.0	70.9	66.0	85.3	68.7	64.4	73.1	67.0	65.9	70.2	72.4
Salaries and Wages **11**	11.0	10.0	9.5	8.2	13.3	7.3	12.7	16.9	13.8	12.6	11.7	10.8	11.0
Taxes Paid **12**	1.7	2.2	3.3	1.6	2.4	1.0	1.7	2.2	2.1	2.1	1.6	2.6	1.6
Interest Paid **13**	1.2	1.1	0.5	1.0	0.5	0.2	0.6	0.9	1.2	1.4	1.2	0.9	1.3
Depreciation **14**	2.2	3.0	1.1	0.7	0.7	0.3	1.4	2.1	2.0	2.7	3.0	2.1	2.2
Amortization and Depletion **15**	0.1	0.0	0.2	0.2	0.0	0.0	0.2	0.1	1.8	0.2	0.3	0.1	0.1
Pensions and Other Deferred Comp. **16**	0.6	1.9	0.1	0.0	0.5	0.1	0.2	0.2	0.2	0.3	0.2	0.3	0.6
Employee Benefits **17**	0.8	1.3	0.2	0.3	0.6	0.7	0.9	1.7	0.9	1.0	1.5	1.4	0.8
Advertising **18**	1.4	0.1	0.8	0.9	1.3	0.4	1.5	2.2	3.4	1.8	2.0	1.1	1.5
Other Expenses **19**	9.6	10.6	21.9	12.2	12.2	6.2	11.2	16.3	16.0	21.2	12.1	11.9	9.1
Officers' Compensation **20**	0.1	0.0	4.4	2.3	2.1	0.9	1.1	1.2	0.4	1.1	0.8	0.2	0.1
Operating Margin **21**	•	3.9	•	1.6	0.4	•	•	•	•	•	•	•	•
Operating Margin Before Officers' Comp. **22**	•	3.9	1.4	3.9	2.6	•	1.0	•	•	•	0.4	•	•

Selected Average Balance Sheet ($ in Thousands)

Net Receivables 23	6265	0	0	35	113	1390	1422	2354	10552	12461	31709	140069	4819342
Inventories 24	5614	0	63	189	1083	1888	6304	12675	20875	78687	97064	531520	3841601
Net Property, Plant and Equipment 25	7031	0	29	135	262	1080	2932	7730	16663	32447	81547	486190	5129416
Total Assets 26	27798	0	134	724	2046	9162	14712	37494	70854	157905	340115	1412070	20426258
Notes and Loans Payable 27	8776	0	77	271	444	1110	4466	21073	8299	36549	58163	276225	6574940
All Other Liabilities 28	9740	0	25	88	641	5968	3574	16777	131406	98841	99873	454056	7102673
Net Worth 29	9282	0	31	365	961	2085	6672	-355	-68851	22515	182079	681789	6748645

Selected Financial Ratios (Times to 1)

Current Ratio 30	1.3	•	3.1	3.2	2.4	1.2	2.2	1.1	0.4	2.5	1.5	1.9	1.2
Quick Ratio 31	0.7	•	0.9	1.0	0.6	0.7	0.7	0.4	0.2	0.8	0.4	0.5	0.7
Net Sales to Working Capital 32	16.9	•	5.9	3.6	7.1	40.9	5.7	30.3	•	4.8	9.4	9.6	17.9
Coverage Ratio 33	3.0	5.6	•	4.8	3.4	•	3.6	•	•	•	2.9	3.6	3.1
Total Asset Turnover 34	1.7	•	2.7	1.7	3.1	5.7	2.3	1.9	5.1	2.1	1.6	2.4	1.6
Inventory Turnover 35	5.9	•	3.5	4.5	3.9	23.6	3.6	3.6	12.7	2.8	3.7	4.5	6.0
Receivables Turnover 36	7.6	•	135.0	55.0	58.6	28.2	24.4	28.1	36.8	13.5	20.2	18.6	6.8
Total Liabilities to Net Worth 37	2.0	•	3.3	1.0	1.1	3.4	1.2	•	•	6.0	0.9	1.1	2.0
Current Assets to Working Capital 38	4.9	•	1.5	1.4	1.7	5.8	1.8	9.9	•	1.6	2.9	2.1	5.4
Current Liabilities to Working Capital 39	3.9	•	0.5	0.4	0.7	4.8	0.8	8.9	•	0.6	1.9	1.1	4.4
Working Capital to Net Sales 40	0.1	•	0.2	0.3	0.1	0.0	0.2	0.0	0.0	0.2	0.1	0.1	0.1
Inventory to Working Capital 41	2.1	•	1.0	0.7	1.3	2.0	1.1	5.3	•	1.0	1.9	1.4	2.2
Total Receipts to Cash Flow 42	11.3	9.6	11.6	8.8	11.9	43.8	12.1	49.6	•	16.1	10.2	9.1	11.3
Cost of Goods to Cash Flow 43	8.1	6.3	7.1	6.3	7.9	37.3	8.3	31.9	•	10.8	6.8	6.4	8.2
Cash Flow to Total Debt 44	0.2	•	0.3	0.4	0.5	0.2	0.3	0.0	•	0.1	0.3	0.5	0.2

Selected Financial Factors (in Percentages)

Debt Ratio 45	66.6	•	76.7	49.6	53.0	77.2	54.7	100.9	197.2	85.7	46.5	51.7	67.0
Return on Total Assets 46	6.1	•	•	8.2	5.3	•	5.3	•	•	•	5.8	8.0	6.1
Return on Equity Before Income Taxes 47	12.1	•	•	13.0	8.0	•	8.4	1166.0	65.4	•	7.2	11.9	12.6
Return on Equity After Income Taxes 48	6.7	•	•	12.9	6.7	•	7.2	1226.4	66.2	•	5.3	7.7	7.1
Profit Margin (Before Income Tax) 49	2.4	4.9	•	3.9	1.2	•	1.7	•	•	•	2.4	2.4	2.7
Profit Margin (After Income Tax) 50	1.4	4.9	•	3.9	1.0	•	1.4	•	•	•	1.8	1.5	1.5

Table II

Corporations with Net Income

GENERAL MERCHANDISE STORES

MONEY AMOUNTS AND SIZE OF ASSETS IN THOUSANDS OF DOLLARS

Item Description for Accounting Period 7/02 Through 6/03	Total	Zero Assets	Under 500	500 to 1,000	1,000 to 5,000	5,000 to 10,000	10,000 to 25,000	25,000 to 50,000	50,000 to 100,000	100,000 to 250,000	250,000 to 500,000	500,000 to 2,500,000	2,500,000 and over
Number of Enterprises **1**	5486	579	3747	535	537	0	34	10	0	10	6	8	10
Revenues ($ in Thousands)													
Net Sales **2**	423706804	11286622	1881081	574526	3452977	0	1295585	1016260	0	3555267	3113545	27457084	368746178
Interest **3**	2921538	61109	306	513	1737	0	571	358	0	2622	32055	173976	2635430
Rents **4**	546883	0	0	510	1224	0	1382	5	0	11009	223	24671	499062
Royalties **5**	1319094	0	0	0	107	0	5442	0	0	0	1800	324153	987591
Other Portfolio Income **6**	240066	0	0	33	621	0	2466	228	0	518	1013	6656	228390
Other Receipts **7**	6083835	46477	27043	18002	7286	0	9104	10938	0	90957	43383	560855	5257783
Total Receipts **8**	434818220	11394208	1908430	593584	3463952	0	1314550	1027789	0	3660373	3192019	28547395	378354434
Average Total Receipts **9**	79260	19679	509	1110	6451	•	38663	102779	•	366037	532003	3568424	37835443
Operating Costs/Operating Income (%)													
Cost of Operations **10**	72.4	66.0	58.2	66.1	65.5	•	68.5	67.5	•	61.5	68.2	70.2	73.2
Salaries and Wages **11**	10.4	10.0	8.0	9.9	12.5	•	11.9	14.1	•	12.6	9.5	10.8	10.3
Taxes Paid **12**	1.6	2.2	3.8	1.7	2.1	•	1.6	1.6	•	2.1	1.3	2.6	1.5
Interest Paid **13**	1.2	1.1	0.3	0.7	0.4	•	0.5	0.7	•	0.7	0.6	0.9	1.2
Depreciation **14**	2.1	2.9	1.1	0.3	0.6	•	1.3	1.8	•	2.2	2.9	2.1	2.1
Amortization and Depletion **15**	0.1	•	0.0	0.4	0.0	•	0.2	0.1	•	0.1	0.1	0.1	0.1
Pensions and Other Deferred Comp. **16**	0.5	1.9	0.2	0.1	0.6	•	0.2	0.2	•	0.2	0.1	0.3	0.5
Employee Benefits **17**	0.8	1.3	0.0	0.3	0.4	•	0.9	0.5	•	0.6	1.5	1.4	0.8
Advertising **18**	1.0	0.0	0.4	1.3	1.2	•	1.4	1.2	•	1.8	1.1	1.1	1.0
Other Expenses **19**	8.4	10.4	20.9	13.0	11.0	•	10.3	9.9	•	16.0	11.8	11.9	7.9
Officers' Compensation **20**	0.1	0.0	3.8	2.2	2.2	•	1.2	0.4	•	1.1	1.1	0.2	0.0
Operating Margin **21**	1.3	4.3	3.2	4.0	3.4	•	2.1	2.1	•	1.0	1.9	1.4	•
Operating Margin Before Officers' Comp. **22**	1.4	4.3	7.1	6.2	5.7	•	3.3	2.5	•	2.1	3.0	1.5	•

Net Receivables 23	11810	0	0	42	120	1256	1083	•	15248	41997	140069	6304246
Inventories 24	9126	0	75	186	991	6489	15675	•	93393	104329	418028	4152778
Net Property, Plant and Equipment 25	11454	0	47	105	242	2985	9644	•	32869	71336	486190	5749574
Total Assets 26	46550	0	169	724	1852	15177	36377	•	173495	322994	1412070	23700959
Notes and Loans Payable 27	14374	0	65	236	329	4160	8547	•	37375	47188	276225	7515700
All Other Liabilities 28	15889	0	25	98	584	3736	11493	•	57711	81539	454056	8163342
Net Worth 29	16287	0	78	389	939	7281	16337	•	78409	194268	681789	8021918

Selected Financial Ratios (Times to 1)

Current Ratio 30	1.2	3.8	2.7	2.4	2.2	1.8	•	2.6	1.7	1.9	1.2
Quick Ratio 31	0.7	1.6	1.0	0.7	0.6	0.5	•	0.6	0.5	0.5	0.7
Net Sales to Working Capital 32	19.4	6.7	3.4	7.6	6.3	9.6	•	4.8	7.3	9.6	22.6
Coverage Ratio 33	4.4	17.3	11.8	9.5	7.8	5.5	5.9	6.8	8.0	3.6	4.3
Total Asset Turnover 34	1.7	3.0	1.5	3.5	2.5	2.8	•	2.0	1.6	2.4	1.6
Inventory Turnover 35	6.1	3.9	3.8	4.3	4.0	4.4	•	2.3	3.4	5.8	6.5
Receivables Turnover 36	6.6	103.8	41.5	56.6	34.0	60.8	•	13.8	24.7	19.2	11.7
Total Liabilities to Net Worth 37	1.9	1.2	0.9	1.0	1.1	1.2	•	1.2	0.7	1.1	2.0
Current Assets to Working Capital 38	5.6	1.4	1.6	1.7	1.8	2.2	•	1.6	2.5	2.1	6.8
Current Liabilities to Working Capital 39	4.6	0.4	0.6	0.7	0.8	1.2	•	0.6	1.5	1.1	5.8
Working Capital to Net Sales 40	0.1	0.1	0.3	0.1	0.2	0.1	•	0.2	0.1	0.1	0.0
Inventory to Working Capital 41	2.2	0.8	0.7	1.2	1.2	1.4	•	1.1	1.5	1.4	2.5
Total Receipts to Cash Flow 42	10.2	6.6	6.4	10.0	10.0	12.9	9.4	6.9	8.2	9.1	10.5
Cost of Goods to Cash Flow 43	7.4	3.8	4.3	6.6	6.9	8.7	6.2	4.2	5.6	6.4	7.7
Cash Flow to Total Debt 44	0.2	0.8	0.5	0.7	0.5	0.4	•	0.5	0.5	0.5	0.2

Selected Financial Factors (in Percentages)

Debt Ratio 45	65.0	53.6	46.2	49.3	52.0	55.1	•	54.8	39.9	51.7	66.2
Return on Total Assets 46	8.6	14.9	11.9	14.6	10.3	11.0	•	9.6	8.3	8.0	8.2
Return on Equity Before Income Taxes 47	18.8	30.2	20.2	25.7	18.6	20.1	•	18.1	12.1	11.9	18.6
Return on Equity After Income Taxes 48	12.7	29.4	20.1	24.0	17.1	17.2	13.9	13.9	9.4	7.7	12.1
Profit Margin (Before Income Tax) 49	4.0	4.7	7.3	3.8	3.6	3.2	5.2	4.0	4.5	2.4	4.0
Profit Margin (After Income Tax) 50	2.7	4.6	7.3	3.5	3.3	2.8	5.2	3.1	3.5	1.5	2.6

Table I

Corporations with and without Net Income

MISCELLANEOUS STORE RETAILERS

MONEY AMOUNTS AND SIZE OF ASSETS IN THOUSANDS OF DOLLARS

Item Description for Accounting Period 7/02 Through 6/03	Total	Zero Assets	Under 500	500 to 1,000	1,000 to 5,000	5,000 to 10,000	10,000 to 25,000	25,000 to 50,000	50,000 to 100,000	100,000 to 250,000	250,000 to 500,000	500,000 to 2,500,000	2,500,000 and over
Number of Enterprises **1**	98391	8318	79171	5318	4869	398	198	56	23	22	3	15	0
Revenues ($ in Thousands)													
Net Sales **2**	127401589	1308808	31821684	9203224	21663536	4926428	5907175	4279293	2913896	5876498	1240161	38260886	0
Interest **3**	424345	55532	16843	10188	33725	5812	12109	10191	9348	55422	8097	207078	0
Rents **4**	119389	0	17237	7908	16032	909	2944	4946	4073	4132	6469	54739	0
Royalties **5**	68415	1846	62	0	2069	0	1253	151	775	27908	6256	28096	0
Other Portfolio Income **6**	372303	69813	23333	15855	28101	10252	11195	20648	17462	10216	80117	85309	0
Other Receipts **7**	2479744	187989	218603	68125	199728	124139	86261	85824	51324	138039	27983	1291730	0
Total Receipts **8**	130865785	1623988	32097762	9305300	21943191	5067540	6020937	4401053	2996878	6112215	1369083	39927838	0
Average Total Receipts **9**	1330	195	405	1750	4507	12733	30409	78590	130299	277828	456361	2661856	·
Operating Costs/Operating Income (%)													
Cost of Operations **10**	62.1	64.2	56.9	61.6	68.2	63.4	65.1	66.6	64.5	59.4	47.8	62.5	·
Salaries and Wages **11**	12.1	11.7	11.3	11.2	11.0	12.4	12.6	11.6	12.3	13.3	15.9	13.4	·
Taxes Paid **12**	2.1	3.0	2.5	2.2	2.0	1.6	1.8	1.7	1.9	2.1	1.9	1.9	·
Interest Paid **13**	1.2	3.9	0.8	1.0	0.8	1.0	1.1	1.7	1.0	2.8	2.5	1.5	·
Depreciation **14**	2.2	2.0	1.3	1.4	1.2	2.4	1.8	2.4	2.2	2.8	4.1	3.5	·
Amortization and Depletion **15**	0.2	0.9	0.2	0.2	0.0	0.1	0.2	0.6	0.1	0.3	2.1	0.3	·
Pensions and Other Deferred Comp. **16**	0.2	0.1	0.2	0.3	0.3	0.3	0.2	0.2	0.1	0.1	1.0	0.1	·
Employee Benefits **17**	0.8	0.7	0.5	0.5	0.8	0.9	0.9	0.9	1.2	1.0	2.6	1.0	·
Advertising **18**	2.3	1.6	1.5	2.7	0.9	1.4	1.6	1.4	2.4	2.3	1.8	4.0	·
Other Expenses **19**	15.2	57.2	18.6	14.8	11.4	13.0	12.9	14.9	14.6	16.4	26.6	13.3	·
Officers' Compensation **20**	2.8	4.7	5.8	4.6	3.6	2.8	1.7	1.1	1.4	0.9	2.1	0.2	·
Operating Margin **21**	·	0.4	·	·	·	0.9	·	·	·	·	·	·	·
Operating Margin Before Officers' Comp. **22**	1.6	6.3	4.0	3.5	3.6	3.6	1.6	·	·	·	·	·	·

Selected Average Balance Sheet ($ in Thousands)

	•	•	•	•	•	•	•	•	•	•	•	•
Net Receivables 23	95	0	14	85	311	1057	2588	4979	13807	13720	19831	289826
Inventories 24	185	0	43	275	788	2920	5444	12383	21533	44374	140540	308523
Net Property, Plant and Equipment 25	122	0	21	131	332	1205	3092	7058	11467	32050	72756	357330
Total Assets 26	616	0	111	675	1800	6805	15153	35853	68079	162846	349718	1703342
Notes and Loans Payable 27	214	0	59	323	680	2232	5213	18905	17061	53447	153957	426530
All Other Liabilities 28	189	0	27	135	469	1649	4928	10883	27392	54471	56750	615898
Net Worth 29	213	0	25	218	651	2924	5012	6065	23626	54928	139011	660914

Selected Financial Ratios (Times to 1)

	•	•	•	•	•	•	•	•	•	•	•	•
Current Ratio 30	1.6	•	2.2	2.1	1.8	2.0	1.4	1.7	1.5	1.6	1.9	1.4
Quick Ratio 31	0.7	•	0.9	0.7	0.8	0.7	0.6	0.6	0.6	0.5	0.5	0.7
Net Sales to Working Capital 32	9.0	•	9.6	7.1	7.5	5.1	9.4	7.6	7.7	8.0	5.8	12.0
Coverage Ratio 33	2.3	•	2.6	1.5	2.5	4.8	2.6	0.8	1.9	2.0	2.7	2.9
Total Asset Turnover 34	2.1	•	3.6	2.6	2.5	1.8	2.0	2.1	1.9	1.6	1.2	1.5
Inventory Turnover 35	4.4	•	5.3	3.9	3.9	2.7	3.6	4.1	3.8	3.6	1.4	5.2
Receivables Turnover 36	14.8	•	25.3	21.1	13.7	10.7	12.8	16.5	11.7	20.9	12.8	10.9
Total Liabilities to Net Worth 37	1.9	•	3.4	2.1	1.8	1.3	2.0	4.9	1.9	2.0	1.5	1.6
Current Assets to Working Capital 38	2.6	•	1.8	1.9	2.2	2.0	3.2	2.5	3.0	2.7	2.1	3.9
Current Liabilities to Working Capital 39	1.6	•	0.8	0.9	1.2	1.0	2.2	1.5	2.0	1.7	1.1	2.9
Working Capital to Net Sales 40	0.1	•	0.1	0.1	0.1	0.2	0.1	0.1	0.1	0.1	0.2	0.1
Inventory to Working Capital 41	1.3	•	1.0	1.2	1.2	1.2	1.7	1.4	1.4	1.5	1.4	1.5
Total Receipts to Cash Flow 42	9.3	•	8.2	10.0	11.5	8.6	10.1	10.7	9.9	8.2	5.9	9.7
Cost of Goods to Cash Flow 43	5.8	3.8	4.7	6.1	7.8	5.5	6.6	7.1	6.4	4.8	2.8	6.0
Cash Flow to Total Debt 44	0.3	•	0.6	0.4	0.3	0.4	0.3	0.2	0.3	0.3	0.3	0.3

Selected Financial Factors (in Percentages)

	•	•	•	•	•	•	•	•	•	•	•	•
Debt Ratio 45	65.5	•	77.2	67.7	63.8	57.0	66.9	83.1	65.3	66.3	60.3	61.2
Return on Total Assets 46	5.8	•	7.6	4.1	4.8	8.6	5.8	3.0	3.7	9.1	8.0	6.4
Return on Equity Before Income Taxes 47	9.5	•	20.5	4.5	8.0	15.8	10.9	•	5.1	13.5	12.6	10.9
Return on Equity After Income Taxes 48	6.3	•	19.5	3.6	6.3	13.8	9.0	•	3.3	8.4	8.1	6.6
Profit Margin (Before Income Tax) 49	1.6	•	1.3	0.6	1.2	3.7	1.8	•	1.0	2.8	4.2	2.8
Profit Margin (After Income Tax) 50	1.0	•	1.2	0.5	0.9	3.3	1.5	•	0.6	1.7	2.7	1.7

Table II

Corporations with Net Income

MISCELLANEOUS STORE RETAILERS

MONEY AMOUNTS AND SIZE OF ASSETS IN THOUSANDS OF DOLLARS

Item Description for Accounting Period 7/02 Through 6/03	Total	Zero Assets	Under 500	500 to 1,000	1,000 to 5,000	5,000 to 10,000	10,000 to 25,000	25,000 to 50,000	50,000 to 100,000	100,000 to 250,000	250,000 to 500,000	500,000 to 2,500,000	2,500,000 and over
Number of Enterprises 1	49214	2661	39368	3596	3121	260	132	33	15	14	3	11	0
Revenues ($ in Thousands)													
Net Sales 2	92535293	99235	20434387	6609727	14620842	4202457	4356956	2074900	2013271	4475424	1240161	32407934	0
Interest 3	166119	1239	7615	7597	26644	5452	4101	4446	5354	53712	8097	41862	0
Rents 4	77827	0	1791	3473	12312	907	1562	1601	594	3205	6469	45914	0
Royalties 5	46071	0	0	0	2067	0	0	151	775	18078	6256	18744	0
Other Portfolio Income 6	278921	17965	12308	15683	24855	9055	7862	9651	7739	8440	80117	85246	0
Other Receipts 7	1457193	12234	136492	22942	126487	117894	64461	45767	13316	61743	27983	827871	0
Total Receipts 8	94561424	130673	20592593	6659422	14813207	4335765	4434942	2136516	2041049	4620602	1369083	33427571	0
Average Total Receipts 9	1921	49	523	1852	4746	16676	33598	64743	136070	330043	456361	3038870	•
Operating Costs/Operating Income (%)													
Cost of Operations 10	61.3	35.5	57.2	60.9	66.2	64.6	64.7	59.5	61.8	58.3	47.8	61.9	•
Salaries and Wages 11	12.0	0.4	10.3	10.8	11.1	12.0	11.9	12.1	12.0	12.3	15.9	13.5	•
Taxes Paid 12	1.9	3.7	2.1	2.1	1.9	1.4	1.8	1.9	1.9	1.9	1.9	1.9	•
Interest Paid 13	1.1	1.6	0.6	0.7	0.7	0.8	0.9	1.1	0.7	2.5	2.5	1.4	•
Depreciation 14	2.2	1.3	0.9	1.2	1.1	1.7	1.7	2.7	1.6	2.9	4.1	3.8	•
Amortization and Depletion 15	0.2	•	0.1	0.1	0.0	0.0	0.1	0.2	0.1	0.3	2.1	0.3	•
Pensions and Other Deferred Comp. 16	0.2	•	0.2	0.3	0.3	0.3	0.3	0.2	0.1	0.1	1.0	0.1	•
Employee Benefits 17	0.8	0.0	0.4	0.5	0.8	0.9	0.8	1.1	1.0	0.9	2.6	1.0	•
Advertising 18	2.1	0.7	1.3	3.0	0.9	1.3	1.4	1.8	2.9	2.5	1.8	3.1	•
Other Expenses 19	13.5	40.7	16.7	13.8	11.0	11.6	11.4	15.4	13.2	14.1	26.6	12.4	•
Officers' Compensation 20	2.6	0.3	5.4	4.7	3.8	2.8	1.9	1.6	1.5	1.1	2.1	0.2	•
Operating Margin 21	2.2	16.0	4.7	1.9	2.2	2.6	3.1	2.5	3.1	3.0	•	0.6	•
Operating Margin Before Officers' Comp. 22	4.7	16.3	10.2	6.6	6.0	5.4	5.0	4.1	4.6	4.1	•	0.8	•

Selected Average Balance Sheet ($ in Thousands)

Net Receivables **23**	141	0	19	81	357	1299	2836	4618	12955	13745	19831	317656	•
Inventories **24**	240	0	46	291	744	3412	5336	11349	21421	39509	97328	318441	•
Net Property, Plant and Equipment **25**	173	0	19	111	304	1054	3140	6111	9667	41679	72756	416229	•
Total Assets **26**	879		124	672	1829	6951	15382	34472	63899	163870	349718	1908575	•
Notes and Loans Payable **27**	268	0	39	269	609	2245	4980	9823	13281	47846	153957	536307	•
All Other Liabilities **28**	255	0	31	115	466	1843	4659	9132	26133	54631	56750	612746	•
Net Worth **29**	356	0	54	288	755	2863	5744	15517	24485	61392	139011	759522	•

Selected Financial Ratios (Times to 1)

Current Ratio **30**	1.7	•	2.4	2.0	1.8	1.5	2.0	1.7	1.6	1.9	1.4		•
Quick Ratio **31**	0.8	•	1.1	0.8	0.9	0.7	0.7	0.6	0.6	0.5	0.7		•
Net Sales to Working Capital **32**	8.9	•	10.0	6.5	6.9	6.6	8.9	5.6	7.0	9.3	5.8	11.7	•
Coverage Ratio **33**	5.2	30.7	9.9	4.9	6.0	8.2	6.7	6.2	7.4	3.5	2.7	3.7	•
Total Asset Turnover **34**	2.1	•	4.2	2.7	2.6	2.3	2.1	1.8	2.1	2.0	1.2	1.5	•
Inventory Turnover **35**	4.8	•	6.5	3.8	4.2	3.1	4.0	3.3	3.9	4.7	2.0	5.7	•
Receivables Turnover **36**	14.6	•	24.0	21.8	12.6	10.5	12.9	12.8	20.7	33.4	41.7	11.8	•
Total Liabilities to Net Worth **37**	1.5	•	1.3	1.3	1.4	1.7	1.7	1.2	1.6	1.7	1.5	1.5	•
Current Assets to Working Capital **38**	2.4	•	1.7	1.7	2.0	2.8	2.0	2.0	2.5	2.6	2.1	3.6	•
Current Liabilities to Working Capital **39**	1.4	•	0.7	0.7	1.0	1.8	1.0	1.0	1.5	1.6	1.1	2.6	•
Working Capital to Net Sales **40**	0.1	•	0.1	0.2	0.1	0.1	0.2	0.2	0.1	0.1	0.2	0.1	•
Inventory to Working Capital **41**	1.1	•	0.8	1.1	1.0	1.4	1.4	1.1	1.1	1.4	1.4	1.3	•
Total Receipts to Cash Flow **42**	7.9	1.8	6.4	8.7	9.0	8.3	8.0	5.8	7.8	6.8	5.9	9.2	•
Cost of Goods to Cash Flow **43**	4.8	0.6	3.7	5.3	5.9	5.4	5.2	3.4	4.8	4.0	2.8	5.7	•
Cash Flow to Total Debt **44**	0.5	1.2	1.2	0.6	0.5	0.4	0.5	0.6	0.4	0.5	0.3	0.3	•

Selected Financial Factors (in Percentages)

Debt Ratio **45**	59.5	56.5	57.1	58.7	62.7	55.0	61.7	62.5	60.3	60.2			•
Return on Total Assets **46**	11.8	25.7	9.2	10.7	12.4	12.0	10.9	17.4	8.0	8.2			•
Return on Equity Before Income Taxes **47**	23.5	53.2	17.1	21.5	28.2	22.3	24.6	33.2	12.6	15.1			•
Return on Equity After Income Taxes **48**	19.8	52.4	16.1	19.2	25.8	20.0	21.9	26.0	8.1	10.0			•
Profit Margin (Before Income Tax) **49**	4.4	47.7	5.5	2.7	3.5	4.9	5.5	4.5	6.4	4.2	3.9		•
Profit Margin (After Income Tax) **50**	3.7	45.7	5.4	2.5	3.1	5.2	4.0	4.5	5.0	2.7	2.6		•

Table I

Corporations with and without Net Income

NONSTORE RETAILERS

MONEY AMOUNTS AND SIZE OF ASSETS IN THOUSANDS OF DOLLARS

Item Description for Accounting Period 7/02 Through 6/03	Total	Zero Assets	Under 500	500 to 1,000	1,000 to 5,000	5,000 to 10,000	10,000 to 25,000	25,000 to 50,000	50,000 to 100,000	100,000 to 250,000	250,000 to 500,000	500,000 to 2,500,000	2,500,000 and over
Number of Enterprises **1**	42556	6008	30568	2708	2667	295	145	72	31	33	9	19	0
Revenues ($ in Thousands)													
Net Sales **2**	96267052	1292613	10870703	6831806	14686773	5582232	6557240	5460675	3773527	10269537	6236646	24705300	0
Interest **3**	466446	2248	3262	6601	12122	6501	6308	10953	13581	29392	107810	267668	0
Rents **4**	90088	17	2741	6705	8209	1084	3416	3917	4694	13677	1636	43992	0
Royalties **5**	196714	0	0	0	14599	0	6382	2255	20227	4687	9875	138690	0
Other Portfolio Income **6**	216925	43182	182	7641	47533	5559	4811	30805	3280	23820	12459	37654	0
Other Receipts **7**	1975881	109314	35746	39009	134621	91459	89155	101239	58893	130349	104951	1081143	0
Total Receipts **8**	99213106	1447374	10912634	6891762	14903857	5686835	6667312	5609844	3874202	10471462	6473377	26274447	0
Average Total Receipts **9**	2331	241	357	2545	5588	19277	45981	77914	124974	317317	719264	1382866	•
Operating Costs/Operating Income (%)													
Cost of Operations **10**	63.2	40.6	54.4	71.1	63.1	68.3	64.3	62.8	59.5	59.6	71.4	64.7	•
Salaries and Wages **11**	10.4	22.3	9.8	8.1	11.0	11.9	10.2	9.2	12.8	8.4	7.2	11.4	•
Taxes Paid **12**	1.7	2.2	2.7	3.3	1.9	1.4	1.4	1.4	1.8	1.2	1.1	1.3	•
Interest Paid **13**	1.2	0.8	0.7	1.0	1.0	0.6	0.7	1.0	1.6	1.0	1.5	1.9	•
Depreciation **14**	2.1	2.8	2.4	2.4	2.4	1.9	2.1	2.5	2.5	1.8	1.5	1.9	•
Amortization and Depletion **15**	0.6	0.2	0.2	0.1	0.2	0.6	0.5	0.4	1.2	0.7	0.5	0.9	•
Pensions and Other Deferred Comp. **16**	0.3	0.3	0.3	0.2	0.4	0.7	0.2	0.2	0.3	0.2	0.2	0.3	•
Employee Benefits **17**	0.8	0.5	0.5	0.7	0.7	0.6	0.7	1.2	1.2	0.6	0.7	1.2	•
Advertising **18**	3.4	1.5	1.1	0.5	1.9	3.8	4.8	6.1	4.1	6.3	2.1	4.3	•
Other Expenses **19**	16.8	20.1	8.9	8.9	14.8	10.9	14.1	16.9	16.6	17.0	16.9	19.7	•
Officers' Compensation **20**	2.5	5.1	7.4	4.9	3.7	1.7	1.4	1.2	1.1	0.9	0.5	0.8	•
Operating Margin **21**	•	0.2	•	•	•	•	•	•	•	2.2	•	•	•
Operating Margin Before Officers' Comp. **22**	7.6	•	7.6	3.8	2.5	•	1.0	•	•	•	3.2	•	•

Selected Average Balance Sheet ($ in Thousands)

Item												
Net Receivables 23	167	0	15	147	391	901	3468	6626	14117	27560	83198	99583
Inventories 24	165	0	15	141	332	1123	2970	6964	10345	26185	75844	112550
Net Property, Plant and Equipment 25	195	0	24	194	564	1509	3680	6178	10476	22710	34127	143629
Total Assets 26	1143	0	75	700	2045	6455	15496	35097	66577	162302	334372	1152041
Notes and Loans Payable 27	376	0	41	516	896	1942	4943	10361	27204	29783	89449	331423
All Other Liabilities 28	375	0	31	211	704	2235	6367	14292	20245	45542	102842	363597
Net Worth 29	392	0	4	-27	445	2278	4185	10444	19129	86976	142082	457021

Selected Financial Ratios (Times to 1)

Item												
Current Ratio 30	1.4	•	1.4	1.4	1.5	1.3	1.4	1.5	1.7	1.8	2.0	1.3
Quick Ratio 31	0.8	•	0.9	0.9	0.8	0.9	0.8	0.8	0.8	1.1	1.3	0.6
Net Sales to Working Capital 32	12.9	•	29.0	18.7	19.4	16.6	17.6	9.9	7.3	6.7	7.3	13.7
Coverage Ratio 33	1.1	6.5	1.9	0.8	1.3	0.1	2.9	0.9	0.9	5.2	1.2	•
Total Asset Turnover 34	2.0	•	4.8	3.6	2.7	2.9	2.9	2.2	1.8	1.9	2.1	1.1
Inventory Turnover 35	8.7	•	12.6	12.7	10.4	11.5	9.8	6.8	7.0	7.1	6.5	7.5
Receivables Turnover 36	12.7	•	26.7	17.5	14.2	21.0	13.9	11.4	8.3	11.3	7.7	10.4
Total Liabilities to Net Worth 37	1.9	•	20.0	•	3.6	1.8	2.7	2.4	2.5	0.9	1.4	1.5
Current Assets to Working Capital 38	3.4	•	3.8	3.0	4.2	3.3	3.8	2.9	2.5	2.2	2.0	4.9
Current Liabilities to Working Capital 39	2.4	•	2.8	2.0	3.2	2.3	2.8	1.9	1.5	1.2	1.0	3.9
Working Capital to Net Sales 40	0.1	•	0.0	0.1	0.1	0.1	0.1	0.1	0.1	0.1	0.1	0.1
Inventory to Working Capital 41	0.9	•	1.2	1.0	1.1	1.1	1.1	0.8	0.8	0.6	0.5	1.3
Total Receipts to Cash Flow 42	7.0	3.3	6.1	14.7	7.8	12.9	7.4	7.0	6.8	5.3	6.2	6.6
Cost of Goods to Cash Flow 43	4.4	1.3	3.3	10.4	4.9	8.8	4.8	4.4	4.0	3.2	4.5	4.3
Cash Flow to Total Debt 44	0.4	•	0.8	0.2	0.4	0.4	0.5	0.4	0.4	0.8	0.6	0.3

Selected Financial Factors (in Percentages)

Item												
Debt Ratio 45	65.7	•	95.2	103.8	78.2	64.7	73.0	70.2	71.3	46.4	57.5	60.3
Return on Total Assets 46	2.8	•	6.4	2.8	3.6	0.2	5.8	2.0	2.8	10.0	3.7	•
Return on Equity Before Income Taxes 47	0.9	•	62.3	•	22.9	3.4	•	14.0	•	•	15.0	1.5
Return on Equity After Income Taxes 48	•	•	55.1	•	28.6	0.3	•	11.7	•	•	11.8	•
Profit Margin (Before Income Tax) 49	0.2	4.3	0.6	0.6	0.3	0.3	1.3	•	•	4.2	0.3	•
Profit Margin (After Income Tax) 50	•	4.0	0.6	0.0	0.0	•	1.1	•	•	3.3	•	•

Table II

Corporations with Net Income

NONSTORE RETAILERS

MONEY AMOUNTS AND SIZE OF ASSETS IN THOUSANDS OF DOLLARS

Item Description for Accounting Period 7/02 Through 6/03	Total	Zero Assets	Under 500	500 to 1,000	1,000 to 5,000	5,000 to 10,000	10,000 to 25,000	25,000 to 50,000	50,000 to 100,000	100,000 to 250,000	250,000 to 500,000	500,000 to 2,500,000	2,500,000 and over
Number of Enterprises **1**	20941	1708	15394	1777	1705	176	90	41	18	18	5	9	0
Revenues ($ in Thousands)													
Net Sales **2**	60341154	1029014	7193693	4907983	11236507	3629016	4651737	3366542	2615267	7400537	3697807	10613051	0
Interest **3**	316179	765	2489	3748	5941	2940	2905	6159	11658	13255	105145	161172	0
Rents **4**	67585	17	2741	416	6116	685	2822	1119	3913	11174	1636	36947	0
Royalties **5**	119932	0	0	0	0	0	1	2154	17253	4687	3301	92536	0
Other Portfolio Income **6**	167539	40269	182	5801	44929	2154	2262	17008	2769	23572	152	28442	0
Other Receipts **7**	882613	25611	17886	32097	99211	81212	74208	55145	55258	68390	41095	332501	0
Total Receipts **8**	61895002	1095676	7216991	4950045	11392704	3716007	4733935	3448127	2706118	7521615	3849136	11264649	0
Average Total Receipts **9**	2956	641	469	2786	6682	21114	52599	84101	150340	417868	769827	1251628	•
Operating Costs/Operating Income (%)													
Cost of Operations **10**	62.2	35.6	55.7	71.7	63.3	68.9	64.1	62.2	62.8	60.3	71.8	58.0	•
Salaries and Wages **11**	9.3	24.1	7.7	8.4	9.9	10.4	9.8	7.7	12.2	6.6	6.6	10.5	•
Taxes Paid **12**	1.7	1.7	2.8	2.5	1.8	1.2	1.4	1.3	1.9	0.9	0.9	1.5	•
Interest Paid **13**	0.7	0.7	0.3	0.6	0.5	0.3	0.5	0.8	0.9	0.5	0.7	1.3	•
Depreciation **14**	1.7	2.5	1.0	2.3	1.8	1.2	1.8	1.9	1.9	1.3	0.7	2.2	•
Amortization and Depletion **15**	0.3	0.1	0.0	0.0	0.1	0.0	0.4	0.3	0.6	0.4	0.3	0.7	•
Pensions and Other Deferred Comp. **16**	0.4	0.3	0.4	0.2	0.4	1.0	0.2	0.3	0.4	0.1	0.2	0.6	•
Employee Benefits **17**	0.7	0.3	0.4	0.6	0.6	0.7	0.6	1.1	1.2	0.4	0.3	1.4	•
Advertising **18**	3.1	1.3	0.9	0.5	1.5	4.1	5.0	6.7	2.6	7.5	3.2	2.2	•
Other Expenses **19**	13.8	16.0	16.9	8.6	13.7	8.7	12.1	14.4	14.2	13.2	16.2	15.8	•
Officers' Compensation **20**	2.7	6.1	7.7	3.3	3.8	1.5	1.3	0.9	1.1	0.7	0.5	1.6	•
Operating Margin **21**	3.6	11.3	6.1	1.4	2.5	1.9	2.7	2.5	0.3	8.1	•	4.0	•
Operating Margin Before Officers' Comp. **22**	6.3	17.4	13.8	4.7	6.3	3.4	4.0	3.4	1.4	8.8	•	5.7	•

Selected Average Balance Sheet ($ in Thousands)

Net Receivables 23	212	0	18	130	423	1047	3774	7869	15288	33286	96762	110127
Inventories 24	211	0	19	147	365	1178	3192	7386	13745	34361	86627	127588
Net Property, Plant and Equipment 25	213	0	17	191	447	1006	3500	5383	9934	23748	29554	181624
Total Assets 26	1171	0	83	684	2053	6033	15724	34103	69755	168771	321197	971581
Notes and Loans Payable 27	230	0	25	174	607	958	4325	8128	22301	31392	21652	124206
All Other Liabilities 28	365	0	24	193	705	1856	5440	11828	19920	46412	87087	309496
Net Worth 29	576	0	34	317	740	3220	5960	14148	27534	90966	212458	537879

Selected Financial Ratios (Times to 1)

Current Ratio 30	1.7	•	2.0	1.7	1.6	1.9	1.4	1.5	1.8	1.8	2.2	1.5
Quick Ratio 31	0.9	•	1.4	1.1	1.0	1.1	0.8	0.9	0.8	0.9	1.4	0.7
Net Sales to Working Capital 32	10.4	•	14.9	16.2	12.7	10.2	17.1	10.7	6.6	7.8	6.5	8.2
Coverage Ratio 33	10.3	26.0	23.7	4.9	8.3	13.4	9.7	7.5	5.4	20.4	4.7	8.9
Total Asset Turnover 34	2.5	•	5.6	4.0	3.2	3.4	3.3	2.4	2.1	2.4	2.3	1.2
Inventory Turnover 35	8.5	•	13.9	13.5	11.4	12.1	10.4	6.9	6.6	7.2	6.1	5.4
Receivables Turnover 36	13.4	•	27.2	19.4	14.6	19.2	14.1	11.1	10.2	13.0	6.2	10.9
Total Liabilities to Net Worth 37	1.0	•	1.4	1.2	1.8	0.9	1.6	1.4	1.5	0.9	0.5	0.8
Current Assets to Working Capital 38	2.4	•	2.0	2.3	2.6	2.1	3.4	2.8	2.2	2.2	1.8	2.8
Current Liabilities to Working Capital 39	1.4	•	1.0	1.3	1.6	1.1	2.4	1.8	1.2	1.2	0.8	1.8
Working Capital to Net Sales 40	0.1	•	0.1	0.1	0.1	0.1	0.1	0.1	0.2	0.1	0.2	0.1
Inventory to Working Capital 41	0.8	•	0.6	0.9	0.7	0.8	1.1	0.7	0.8	0.7	0.4	1.0
Total Receipts to Cash Flow 42	5.6	3.3	5.0	11.2	6.4	8.7	6.7	5.7	6.1	4.8	5.5	4.1
Cost of Goods to Cash Flow 43	3.5	1.2	2.8	8.0	4.0	6.0	4.3	3.6	3.8	2.9	4.0	2.4
Cash Flow to Total Debt 44	0.9	•	1.9	0.7	0.8	0.8	0.8	0.7	0.6	1.1	1.2	0.7

Selected Financial Factors (in Percentages)

Debt Ratio 45	50.8	•	59.0	53.7	63.9	46.6	62.1	58.5	60.5	46.1	33.9	44.6
Return on Total Assets 46	17.0	•	38.0	11.4	14.2	15.9	16.5	13.8	9.6	24.9	8.1	14.3
Return on Equity Before Income Taxes 47	31.2	•	88.7	19.7	34.7	27.6	39.1	28.8	19.8	43.9	9.6	22.9
Return on Equity After Income Taxes 48	26.3	•	87.2	18.9	31.8	26.1	36.6	26.6	17.0	38.2	6.8	15.5
Profit Margin (Before Income Tax) 49	6.2	18.0	6.5	2.3	3.9	4.3	4.5	5.0	3.7	9.7	2.8	10.4
Profit Margin (After Income Tax) 50	5.3	17.7	6.4	2.2	3.6	4.1	4.2	4.6	3.2	8.5	2.0	7.1

Table I

Corporations with and without Net Income

AIR TRANSPORTATION

MONEY AMOUNTS AND SIZE OF ASSETS IN THOUSANDS OF DOLLARS

Item Description for Accounting Period 7/02 Through 6/03	Total	Zero Assets	Under 500	500 to 1,000	1,000 to 5,000	5,000 to 10,000	10,000 to 25,000	25,000 to 50,000	50,000 to 100,000	100,000 to 250,000	250,000 to 500,000	500,000 to 2,500,000	2,500,000 and over
Number of Enterprises **1**	9705	698	7089	538	984	162	142	44	9	12	9	10	8
Revenues ($ in Thousands)													
Net Sales **2**	106264108	500311	1905581	276912	2821950	536897	2001816	1340950	628640	2641646	4297523	10112805	79199077
Interest **3**	866269	757	1738	0	6882	1157	2829	5265	2704	4514	24260	82439	733724
Rents **4**	228895	5	0	0	35	38	503	334	0	1838	9551	117000	99592
Royalties **5**	383265	0	0	0	0	0	9	0	0	0	0	16813	366443
Other Portfolio Income **6**	1888178	53322	3328	3509	12508	26063	13868	8270	483	9035	69802	57395	1630595
Other Receipts **7**	3003443	5085	28425	1834	-12357	-15501	77925	23194	4566	122481	101506	149634	2516650
Total Receipts **8**	112634158	559480	1939072	282255	2829018	548654	2096950	1378013	636393	2779514	4502642	10536086	84546081
Average Total Receipts **9**	11606	802	274	525	2875	3387	14767	31318	70710	231626	500294	1053609	10568260
Operating Costs/Operating Income (%)													
Cost of Operations **10**	15.5	51.3	11.6	63.6	41.6	35.5	51.4	59.5	11.4	30.6	25.4	13.0	11.8
Salaries and Wages **11**	30.0	4.7	6.0	13.7	10.2	9.7	11.9	9.6	18.9	17.7	20.6	21.7	34.5
Taxes Paid **12**	2.6	1.4	1.4	1.3	1.7	5.7	1.8	1.9	1.7	2.7	2.4	3.8	2.5
Interest Paid **13**	3.7	0.5	2.1	6.3	1.3	8.2	2.4	2.3	2.8	1.5	2.3	3.1	4.1
Depreciation **14**	12.9	7.2	8.4	12.8	9.5	31.6	11.8	9.8	6.3	4.4	9.2	8.5	14.3
Amortization and Depletion **15**	•	0.3	0.0	0.0	0.1	0.2	0.2	0.3	1.1	0.4	1.5	1.5	•
Pensions and Other Deferred Comp. **16**	1.6	0.0	0.3	•	0.1	0.2	0.2	0.3	0.0	0.7	0.5	0.4	2.0
Employee Benefits **17**	3.1	0.3	1.4	0.0	0.9	0.7	1.2	1.1	1.5	2.3	1.5	3.3	3.5
Advertising **18**	1.0	0.3	0.4	0.1	0.4	0.3	0.4	0.7	0.1	0.9	0.7	0.8	1.1
Other Expenses **19**	50.3	56.5	69.1	24.6	39.4	48.6	34.5	35.8	68.1	42.7	41.5	53.0	51.1
Officers' Compensation **20**	0.5	1.3	2.5	4.2	3.6	0.9	1.2	1.3	0.7	0.8	0.5	0.5	0.2
Operating Margin **21**	•	•	•	•	•	•	•	•	•	•	•	•	•
Operating Margin Before Officers' Comp. **22**	•	•	•	•	•	•	•	•	•	•	•	•	•

Selected Average Balance Sheet ($ in Thousands)

Net Receivables 23	659	0	15	216	211	780	1844	2710	10219	23744	19289	86760	504344
Inventories 24	271	0	0	3	103	94	670	741	632	10762	14890	17589	242410
Net Property, Plant and Equipment 25	9308	0	41	258	1280	3822	9770	15309	29935	58661	189976	461288	9833624
Total Assets 26	14941	0	84	792	2145	6500	15663	34015	60979	159015	358175	1052577	15111070
Notes and Loans Payable 27	6688	0	185	825	1657	5040	8818	14205	35850	47641	154865	449715	6504770
All Other Liabilities 28	7937	0	24	83	500	418	6813	12161	16105	67475	136461	354978	8628110
Net Worth 29	316	0	-125	-116	-12	1042	31	7650	9023	43900	66848	247884	-21809

Selected Financial Ratios (Times to 1)

Current Ratio 30	0.8	•	1.2	5.5	0.9	2.3	0.9	0.9	0.7	1.1	1.0	1.6	0.7
Quick Ratio 31	0.5	•	1.1	3.1	0.6	1.8	0.6	0.6	0.6	0.7	0.7	1.1	0.5
Net Sales to Working Capital 32	•	•	52.5	1.2	•	2.9	•	•	•	35.0	118.1	6.9	•
Coverage Ratio 33	•	•	0.3	•	•	•	•	•	•	1.4	0.4	•	•
Total Asset Turnover 34	0.7	•	3.2	0.6	1.3	0.5	0.9	0.9	1.1	1.4	1.3	1.0	0.7
Inventory Turnover 35	6.3	•	145.6	121.6	11.6	12.5	10.8	24.4	12.6	6.3	8.1	7.5	4.8
Receivables Turnover 36	14.7	•	25.1	2.1	16.0	5.5	7.9	10.3	10.5	7.7	23.0	10.5	16.4
Total Liabilities to Net Worth 37	46.3	•	•	•	•	5.2	507.2	3.4	5.8	2.6	4.4	3.2	•
Current Assets to Working Capital 38	•	•	7.1	1.2	•	1.8	•	•	•	12.3	29.6	2.8	•
Current Liabilities to Working Capital 39	•	•	6.1	0.2	•	0.8	•	•	•	11.3	28.6	1.8	•
Working Capital to Net Sales 40	•	•	0.0	0.8	•	0.3	•	•	•	0.0	0.0	0.1	•
Inventory to Working Capital 41	•	•	•	•	•	0.1	•	•	•	1.3	3.6	0.1	•
Total Receipts to Cash Flow 42	5.8	2.6	•	5.6	2.0	14.2	•	•	3.9	5.5	5.0	3.6	6.4
Cost of Goods to Cash Flow 43	0.9	1.3	0.2	2.3	•	7.3	•	•	0.4	1.7	1.3	0.5	0.8
Cash Flow to Total Debt 44	0.1	0.6	•	0.2	0.1	•	0.1	•	0.3	0.4	0.3	0.3	0.1

Selected Financial Factors (in Percentages)

Debt Ratio 45	97.9	•	247.4	114.6	100.6	84.0	99.8	77.5	85.2	72.4	81.3	76.4	100.1
Return on Total Assets 46	•	•	1.8	•	•	•	•	•	•	2.8	1.4	•	•
Return on Equity Before Income Taxes 47	•	•	3.2	109.6	1991.2	•	•	•	•	2.7	•	•	7806.7
Return on Equity After Income Taxes 48	•	•	3.2	112.8	2024.6	•	•	•	•	1.2	•	•	7806.7
Profit Margin (Before Income Tax) 49	•	•	•	•	•	•	•	•	•	0.5	•	•	•
Profit Margin (After Income Tax) 50	•	•	•	•	•	•	•	•	•	0.2	•	•	•

Table II

Corporations with Net Income

AIR TRANSPORTATION

MONEY AMOUNTS AND SIZE OF ASSETS IN THOUSANDS OF DOLLARS

Item Description for Accounting Period 7/02 Through 6/03	Total	Zero Assets	Under 500	500 to 1,000	1,000 to 5,000	5,000 to 10,000	10,000 to 25,000	25,000 to 50,000	50,000 to 100,000	100,000 to 250,000	250,000 to 500,000	500,000 to 2,500,000	2,500,000 and over
Number of Enterprises **1**	3483	247	2821	69	242	33	43	11	3	6	4	4	•
Revenues ($ in Thousands)													
Net Sales **2**	11597687	130726	1703228	244086	1685978	197798	911747	608152	206262	1664505	1894997	2350206	•
Interest **3**	46772	165	474	0	1880	713	1591	1585	679	1044	18037	20605	•
Rents **4**	48367	0	0	0	35	38	142	40	0	1708	9530	36874	•
Royalties **5**	0	0	0	0	0	0	0	0	0	0	0	0	•
Other Portfolio Income **6**	144768	53313	0	3509	9945	24882	5250	696	483	6761	30671	9255	•
Other Receipts **7**	165927	1853	27890	1834	11574	-15352	26810	10475	3682	31881	54030	11251	•
Total Receipts **8**	12003521	186057	1731592	249429	1709412	208079	945540	620948	211106	1705899	2007265	2428191	•
Average Total Receipts **9**	3446	753	614	3615	7064	6305	21989	56450	70369	284316	501816	607048	•
Operating Costs/Operating Income (%)													
Cost of Operations **10**	22.1	0.9	9.4	72.2	52.4	22.9	47.2	68.4	•	20.4	4.6	1.0	•
Salaries and Wages **11**	15.7	12.3	4.6	8.6	10.9	11.2	12.7	8.7	16.3	17.7	26.2	21.3	•
Taxes Paid **12**	2.0	2.9	1.1	0.1	0.9	3.5	1.7	1.7	1.5	2.4	2.6	3.0	•
Interest Paid **13**	1.4	1.3	0.9	0.2	0.4	5.2	1.0	0.9	1.7	1.2	2.0	2.1	•
Depreciation **14**	5.0	1.1	4.5	0.7	1.4	18.5	4.0	2.7	4.4	3.4	7.0	7.9	•
Amortization and Depletion **15**	1.0	1.1	0.0	•	0.1	0.0	0.1	0.0	1.8	0.3	2.7	2.2	•
Pensions and Other Deferred Comp. **16**	0.4	0.0	0.4	•	0.2	0.1	0.2	0.4	0.0	0.8	0.6	0.5	•
Employee Benefits **17**	1.1	0.7	0.8	0.0	0.7	0.8	1.2	2.0	0.9	1.5	1.6	1.0	•
Advertising **18**	0.2	1.1	0.3	0.1	0.3	0.1	0.3	0.2	0.0	0.1	0.1	0.1	•
Other Expenses **19**	46.4	73.1	63.9	9.9	28.4	24.8	29.6	12.7	64.6	48.5	53.9	56.7	•
Officers' Compensation **20**	1.2	0.9	2.6	4.7	1.4	0.4	1.6	1.0	0.9	0.7	0.5	0.7	•
Operating Margin **21**	3.5	4.5	11.4	3.4	2.9	12.4	0.4	1.3	7.8	3.0	•	3.5	•
Operating Margin Before Officers' Comp. **22**	4.8	5.5	14.0	8.1	4.3	12.8	2.0	2.3	8.7	3.8	•	4.2	•

Selected Average Balance Sheet ($ in Thousands)

	•	•	•	•	•	•	•	•	•	•	•	•
Net Receivables 23	286	0	33	590	756	2722	3234	5267	2787	30238	18710	31420
Inventories 24	112	0	1	20	216	168	787	1206	0	15834	20276	26185
Net Property, Plant and Equipment 25	885	0	60	49	407	2814	7062	10296	33712	45852	165950	314777
Total Assets 26	2209	0	143	774	2472	6428	15588	34818	59383	158439	339428	722238
Notes and Loans Payable 27	740	0	86	191	838	5510	4725	9721	9584	33486	160732	188968
All Other Liabilities 28	685	0	52	510	1008	367	3599	15199	8758	71838	95771	196494
Net Worth 29	784	0	5	73	625	551	7264	9898	41040	53116	82926	336776

Selected Financial Ratios (Times to 1)

	•	•	•	•	•	•	•	•	•	•	•	•
Current Ratio 30	1.5	•	1.1	1.4	1.3	7.2	1.7	1.2	2.4	1.2	1.2	2.0
Quick Ratio 31	1.0	•	1.1	1.3	1.1	6.0	1.2	0.9	1.9	0.8	0.7	1.1
Net Sales to Working Capital 32	9.9	•	66.7	16.5	19.6	1.6	7.2	20.2	5.4	19.4	27.2	4.1
Coverage Ratio 33	6.2	38.2	15.3	27.0	12.3	4.4	5.3	4.8	6.9	5.5	3.1	4.5
Total Asset Turnover 34	1.5	•	4.2	4.6	2.8	0.9	1.4	1.6	1.2	1.8	1.4	0.8
Inventory Turnover 35	6.6	•	105.9	128.6	16.9	8.2	12.7	31.4	•	3.6	1.1	0.2
Receivables Turnover 36	11.8	•	26.6	3.7	11.5	3.4	7.0	10.2	49.3	8.8	16.4	16.2
Total Liabilities to Net Worth 37	1.8	•	26.7	9.6	3.0	10.7	1.1	2.5	0.4	2.0	3.1	1.1
Current Assets to Working Capital 38	3.0	•	8.8	3.4	4.2	1.2	2.4	7.0	1.7	5.8	7.3	2.0
Current Liabilities to Working Capital 39	2.0	•	7.8	2.4	3.2	0.2	1.4	6.0	0.7	4.8	6.3	1.0
Working Capital to Net Sales 40	0.1	•	0.0	0.1	0.1	0.6	0.1	0.0	0.2	0.1	0.0	0.2
Inventory to Working Capital 41	0.3	•	•	•	0.2	0.1	0.3	0.6	•	0.9	0.9	0.2
Total Receipts to Cash Flow 42	2.8	1.0	1.6	7.0	3.3	3.4	4.4	11.3	2.0	4.1	3.3	2.4
Cost of Goods to Cash Flow 43	0.6	0.0	0.2	5.1	1.7	0.8	2.1	7.7	•	0.8	0.1	0.0
Cash Flow to Total Debt 44	0.8	•	2.7	0.7	1.1	0.3	0.6	0.2	1.9	0.6	0.6	0.6

Selected Financial Factors (in Percentages)

	•	•	•	•	•	•	•	•	•	•	•	•
Debt Ratio 45	64.5	•	96.4	90.6	74.7	91.4	53.4	71.6	30.9	66.5	75.6	53.4
Return on Total Assets 46	12.9	•	59.1	26.6	13.2	21.2	6.9	6.9	13.7	11.5	8.8	7.8
Return on Equity Before Income Taxes 47	30.3	•	1528.4	270.8	47.9	191.4	12.1	19.2	17.0	28.1	24.3	13.0
Return on Equity After Income Taxes 48	27.1	•	1527.8	231.1	45.5	179.4	10.7	16.8	12.0	25.7	22.0	9.2
Profit Margin (Before Income Tax) 49	7.1	46.9	13.1	5.6	4.3	17.6	4.1	3.4	10.1	5.4	4.3	7.4
Profit Margin (After Income Tax) 50	6.4	44.8	13.0	4.8	4.1	16.5	3.7	3.0	7.2	4.9	3.9	5.3

Table I

Corporations with and without Net Income

RAIL TRANSPORTATION

MONEY AMOUNTS AND SIZE OF ASSETS IN THOUSANDS OF DOLLARS

Item Description for Accounting Period 7/02 Through 6/03	Total	Zero Assets	Under 500	500 to 1,000	1,000 to 5,000	5,000 to 10,000	10,000 to 25,000	25,000 to 50,000	50,000 to 100,000	100,000 to 250,000	250,000 to 500,000	500,000 to 2,500,000	2,500,000 and over
Number of Enterprises **1**	354	8	175	•	66	45	19	11	11	4	4	4	8
Revenues ($ in Thousands)													
Net Sales **2**	44368189	8041	61720	•	328480	23909	221108	145273	417370	164018	534378	1356060	41107833
Interest **3**	1532451	0	835	•	3134	1808	370	1657	2596	1786	6973	13598	1499693
Rents **4**	582145	0	0	•	3142	472	1563	1896	7450	3079	7125	12108	545310
Royalties **5**	17901	0	0	•	70	0	0	0	189	0	0	0	17642
Other Portfolio Income **6**	1100955	0	0	•	758	912	2157	398	4957	3206	3405	78539	1006620
Other Receipts **7**	2358652	0	58	•	4472	3844	10621	11106	9807	3511	26633	110339	2178265
Total Receipts **8**	49960293	8041	62613	•	340056	30945	235819	160330	442369	175600	578514	1570644	46355363
Average Total Receipts **9**	141131	1005	358	•	5152	688	12412	14575	40215	43900	144628	392661	5794420
Operating Costs/Operating Income (%)													
Cost of Operations **10**	26.3	235.0	•	•	1.5	50.4	32.8	7.1	30.1	32.2	29.9	12.8	26.8
Salaries and Wages **11**	21.4	•	•	•	30.6	3.7	12.9	21.9	16.4	9.5	13.0	24.2	21.5
Taxes Paid **12**	7.7	•	0.1	•	8.0	7.7	5.5	5.8	5.6	7.2	3.8	8.4	7.7
Interest Paid **13**	9.0	9.0	•	•	1.5	0.7	2.7	3.3	2.4	6.5	5.9	6.7	9.3
Depreciation **14**	12.7	•	0.0	•	5.8	13.1	11.4	14.8	9.2	15.8	13.0	16.1	12.7
Amortization and Depletion **15**	0.2	•	•	•	•	•	0.3	0.2	0.1	0.2	0.9	0.6	0.2
Pensions and Other Deferred Comp. **16**	0.9	•	•	•	1.3	4.8	0.3	1.8	1.5	0.2	1.0	0.1	0.9
Employee Benefits **17**	4.2	•	•	•	5.5	0.6	1.8	5.0	5.1	7.8	5.1	2.5	4.2
Advertising **18**	0.1	•	•	•	0.7	•	0.4	0.2	0.1	0.0	0.0	0.1	0.1
Other Expenses **19**	29.1	70.6	•	•	45.4	12.6	29.0	21.9	31.9	21.8	30.0	64.6	27.8
Officers' Compensation **20**	0.3	•	•	•	0.7	•	3.5	2.5	1.5	2.2	1.6	0.6	0.2
Operating Margin **21**	•	•	29.3	•	•	6.4	•	15.6	•	•	•	•	•
Operating Margin Before Officers' Comp. **22**	•	•	29.3	•	•	6.4	•	18.0	•	•	•	•	•

Selected Average Balance Sheet ($ in Thousands)

Net Receivables 23	14835	0	63	•	331	135	2327	3045	7388	15600	30291	57454	580063
Inventories 24	2619	0	97	•	33	21	259	1612	2074	790	4407	5382	102392
Net Property, Plant and Equipment 25	299300	0	65	•	1328	1814	10753	19824	52650	78706	217624	723027	12586594
Total Assets 26	490279	0	329	•	2964	7865	16654	35097	74165	138314	330517	990604	20699462
Notes and Loans Payable 27	114330	0	0	•	1077	370	5047	7237	15910	38464	137874	267069	4782628
All Other Liabilities 28	170937	0	0	•	964	1356	4306	8722	22848	47723	95854	307110	7269418
Net Worth 29	205012	0	329	•	923	6140	7301	19139	35408	52128	96790	416424	8647417

Selected Financial Ratios (Times to 1)

Current Ratio 30	0.6	•	2851.6	•	0.8	2.4	1.3	1.0	0.6	1.0	0.8	1.1	0.6
Quick Ratio 31	0.4	•	1629.6	•	0.6	2.3	1.0	0.7	0.4	0.8	0.6	0.6	0.4
Net Sales to Working Capital 32	•	•	1.4	•	•	0.4	10.7	•	•	•	•	22.3	•
Coverage Ratio 33	1.1	•	•	•	2.7	52.3	3.2	8.8	1.9	1.6	1.7	•	1.1
Total Asset Turnover 34	0.3	•	1.1	•	1.7	0.1	0.7	0.4	0.5	0.3	0.4	0.3	0.2
Inventory Turnover 35	12.6	•	•	•	2.2	12.8	14.7	0.6	5.5	16.7	9.1	8.1	13.5
Receivables Turnover 36	8.6	•	4.0	•	8.8	3.6	5.9	4.0	5.1	3.6	3.6	5.0	9.1
Total Liabilities to Net Worth 37	1.4	•	0.0	•	2.2	0.3	1.3	0.8	1.1	1.7	2.4	1.4	1.4
Current Assets to Working Capital 38	•	•	1.0	•	•	1.7	4.4	•	•	•	•	10.9	•
Current Liabilities to Working Capital 39	•	•	0.0	•	•	0.7	3.4	•	•	•	•	9.9	•
Working Capital to Net Sales 40	•	•	0.7	•	•	2.8	0.1	•	•	•	•	0.0	•
Inventory to Working Capital 41	•	•	0.1	•	•	0.0	0.2	•	•	•	•	0.3	•
Total Receipts to Cash Flow 42	6.7	•	1.0	•	3.2	2.1	3.9	2.3	3.9	14.4	4.5	•	6.7
Cost of Goods to Cash Flow 43	1.8	•	•	•	0.0	1.1	1.3	0.2	1.2	4.6	1.3	•	1.8
Cash Flow to Total Debt 44	0.1	•	3899.2	•	0.8	0.1	0.3	0.4	0.3	0.0	0.1	•	0.1

Selected Financial Factors (in Percentages)

Debt Ratio 45	58.2	•	0.0	•	68.9	21.9	56.2	45.5	52.3	62.3	70.7	58.0	58.2
Return on Total Assets 46	2.5	•	33.0	•	6.6	2.5	6.2	11.0	2.3	3.0	4.0	•	2.6
Return on Equity Before Income Taxes 47	0.5	•	33.0	•	13.3	3.1	9.7	17.9	2.4	2.9	5.4	•	0.7
Return on Equity After Income Taxes 48	0.0	•	33.0	•	9.8	2.3	8.4	13.6	0.7	0.3	3.7	•	0.3
Profit Margin (Before Income Tax) 49	0.8	•	30.7	•	2.5	35.6	6.1	25.9	2.2	3.7	3.9	•	1.2
Profit Margin (After Income Tax) 50	0.0	•	30.7	•	1.8	26.5	5.2	19.7	0.6	0.4	2.7	•	0.5

Table II

Corporations with Net Income

RAIL TRANSPORTATION

MONEY AMOUNTS AND SIZE OF ASSETS IN THOUSANDS OF DOLLARS

Item Description for Accounting Period 7/02 Through 6/03	Total	Zero Assets	Under 500	500 to 1,000	1,000 to 5,000	5,000 to 10,000	10,000 to 25,000	25,000 to 50,000	50,000 to 100,000	100,000 to 250,000	250,000 to 500,000	500,000 to 2,500,000	2,500,000 and over
Number of Enterprises **1**	289	•	0	•	66	12	11	0	8	0	4	0	5
Revenues ($ in Thousands)													
Net Sales **2**	39654837	•	0	•	328480	23595	144314	0	226229	0	1116472	0	37615313
Interest **3**	1428734	•	0	•	3134	552	250	0	1814	0	16482	0	1404455
Rents **4**	474748	•	0	•	3142	472	1282	0	5373	0	5482	0	457728
Royalties **5**	17745	•	0	•	70	0	0	0	189	0	0	0	17486
Other Portfolio Income **6**	961378	•	0	•	758	912	1960	0	3864	0	16027	0	937460
Other Receipts **7**	1270943	•	0	•	4472	3843	10615	0	6428	0	55053	0	1185581
Total Receipts **8**	43808385	•	0	•	340056	29374	158421	0	243897	0	1209516	0	41618023
Average Total Receipts **9**	151586	•	•	•	5152	2448	14402	•	30487	•	302379	•	8323605
Operating Costs/Operating Income (%)													
Cost of Operations **10**	26.9	•	•	•	1.5	51.1	39.2	•	13.3	•	22.3	•	27.4
Salaries and Wages **11**	19.3	•	•	•	30.6	0.7	8.9	•	15.8	•	19.0	•	19.3
Taxes Paid **12**	7.2	•	•	•	8.0	7.8	6.1	•	7.3	•	6.7	•	7.3
Interest Paid **13**	8.7	•	•	•	1.5	0.4	1.3	•	2.8	•	3.5	•	9.0
Depreciation **14**	12.2	•	•	•	5.8	9.3	7.7	•	12.7	•	13.5	•	12.3
Amortization and Depletion **15**	0.2	•	•	•	•	•	0.1	•	0.2	•	0.1	•	0.2
Pensions and Other Deferred Comp. **16**	1.0	•	•	•	1.3	•	0.3	•	0.6	•	0.0	•	1.0
Employee Benefits **17**	3.6	•	•	•	5.5	0.1	1.8	•	3.4	•	4.2	•	3.6
Advertising **18**	0.0	•	•	•	0.7	•	0.4	•	0.1	•	0.0	•	0.0
Other Expenses **19**	26.7	•	•	•	45.4	11.5	24.7	•	31.7	•	30.0	•	26.4
Officers' Compensation **20**	0.3	•	•	•	0.7	•	3.9	•	2.7	•	0.3	•	0.2
Operating Margin **21**	•	•	•	•	•	19.1	5.5	•	9.4	•	0.4	•	•
Operating Margin Before Officers' Comp. **22**	•	•	•	•	•	19.1	9.4	•	12.1	•	0.6	•	•

Selected Average Balance Sheet ($ in Thousands)

Net Receivables 23	15660	331	505	3254	3293	53364	837231
Inventories 24	2080	25	62	383	1649	6254	109656
Net Property, Plant and Equipment 25	299118	1328	1802	9769	56616	488167	16723562
Total Assets 26	513738	2964	8313	16858	80904	641438	28880678
Notes and Loans Payable 27	111905	1077	0	2992	21407	145545	6283543
All Other Liabilities 28	186013	964	1305	5657	16641	258216	10477772
Net Worth 29	215821	923	7008	8209	42856	237678	12119364

Selected Financial Ratios (Times to 1)

Current Ratio 30	0.6	0.8	2.7	1.1	0.6	0.7	0.6
Quick Ratio 31	0.4	0.6	2.5	1.0	0.3	0.6	0.4
Net Sales to Working Capital 32	•	•	1.4	19.3	•	•	•
Coverage Ratio 33	1.5	2.7	98.6	12.5	7.2	3.5	1.4
Total Asset Turnover 34	0.3	1.7	0.2	0.8	0.3	0.4	0.3
Inventory Turnover 35	17.7	2.9	16.3	13.4	2.3	9.9	18.8
Receivables Turnover 36	10.7	14.7	3.6	4.6	7.3	10.5	11.5
Total Liabilities to Net Worth 37	1.4	2.2	0.2	1.1	0.9	1.7	1.4
Current Assets to Working Capital 38	•	•	1.6	8.6	•	•	•
Current Liabilities to Working Capital 39	•	•	0.6	7.6	•	•	•
Working Capital to Net Sales 40	•	•	0.7	0.1	•	•	•
Inventory to Working Capital 41	•	•	0.0	0.5	•	•	•
Total Receipts to Cash Flow 42	5.8	3.2	1.8	3.3	2.7	4.8	6.0
Cost of Goods to Cash Flow 43	1.5	0.0	0.9	1.3	0.4	1.1	1.6
Cash Flow to Total Debt 44	0.1	0.8	0.8	0.5	0.3	0.1	0.1

Selected Financial Factors (in Percentages)

Debt Ratio 45	58.0	68.9	51.3	47.0	62.9	•	58.0
Return on Total Assets 46	3.5	6.6	10.4	13.0	7.0	5.3	3.4
Return on Equity Before Income Taxes 47	2.8	13.3	12.2	24.5	11.3	10.2	2.5
Return on Equity After Income Taxes 48	2.3	9.8	9.6	22.3	7.8	9.5	2.0
Profit Margin (Before Income Tax) 49	4.4	2.5	43.4	15.3	17.2	8.7	4.0
Profit Margin (After Income Tax) 50	3.6	1.8	34.2	14.0	11.9	8.1	3.2

Table I
Corporations with and without Net Income

WATER TRANSPORTATION

MONEY AMOUNTS AND SIZE OF ASSETS IN THOUSANDS OF DOLLARS

Item Description for Accounting Period 7/02 Through 6/03	Total	Zero Assets	Under 500	500 to 1,000	1,000 to 5,000	5,000 to 10,000	10,000 to 25,000	25,000 to 50,000	50,000 to 100,000	100,000 to 250,000	250,000 to 500,000	500,000 to 2,500,000	2,500,000 and over
Number of Enterprises 1	2143	96	1013	348	425	122	59	24	23	16	6	11	•
Revenues ($ in Thousands)													
Net Sales 2	18659765	61990	2298015	1240073	478979	981334	1166260	881546	1037862	1470092	656180	8387432	•
Interest 3	171152	6519	2403	1601	1637	1729	3144	630	24319	3227	14905	111039	•
Rents 4	141175	0	10158	0	0	457	3126	1090	12461	1678	435	111770	•
Royalties 5	2	0	0	0	0	0	0	0	2	0	0	0	•
Other Portfolio Income 6	357044	42349	39493	34	43548	1209	3732	3832	43407	5027	640	173774	•
Other Receipts 7	1575643	-791	58134	181	13362	8048	32074	6239	29223	169004	-26806	1286977	•
Total Receipts 8	20904781	110067	2408203	1241889	537526	992777	1208336	893337	1147274	1649028	645354	10070992	•
Average Total Receipts 9	9755	1147	2377	3569	1265	8138	20480	37222	49881	103064	107559	915545	•
Operating Costs/Operating Income (%)													
Cost of Operations 10	54.8	75.6	90.0	57.4	42.8	64.8	45.3	46.2	41.0	51.4	42.8	49.7	•
Salaries and Wages 11	9.8	9.2	3.9	13.8	5.3	7.7	11.5	12.1	12.2	7.1	10.0	11.1	•
Taxes Paid 12	1.9	3.2	0.6	2.0	4.0	1.5	3.1	1.9	2.4	1.5	3.4	1.8	•
Interest Paid 13	3.3	45.8	0.1	0.7	5.9	1.2	2.6	2.3	6.1	3.6	12.3	3.4	•
Depreciation 14	7.2	7.9	0.7	1.6	9.3	3.8	6.6	6.2	14.3	11.2	26.2	7.3	•
Amortization and Depletion 15	0.3	0.4	0.0	0.0	0.2	0.0	0.2	0.1	0.2	0.4	0.9	0.5	•
Pensions and Other Deferred Comp. 16	0.7	•	0.1	0.5	0.3	0.1	0.3	0.4	0.6	0.4	0.1	1.1	•
Employee Benefits 17	2.0	0.1	0.2	0.2	1.7	0.8	2.3	4.5	1.8	1.5	1.6	2.8	•
Advertising 18	0.3	0.0	0.0	0.7	2.8	0.1	0.7	0.1	0.3	0.1	0.6	0.1	•
Other Expenses 19	29.0	61.2	7.4	16.4	25.6	16.6	28.2	25.8	29.8	30.9	16.5	39.3	•
Officers' Compensation 20	1.5	1.0	2.6	2.6	6.7	1.8	2.0	1.0	1.4	1.4	0.2	0.8	•
Operating Margin 21	•	•	•	4.1	•	1.6	•	•	•	•	•	•	•
Operating Margin Before Officers' Comp. 22	•	•	•	6.7	2.0	3.4	•	0.5	•	•	•	•	•

Selected Average Balance Sheet ($ in Thousands)

Net Receivables 23	1191	0	32	104	399	1636	2678	4891	8946	18693	13294	114121
Inventories 24	97	0	0	0	55	36	274	317	290	1933	744	10364
Net Property, Plant and Equipment 25	5409	39	274	1458	2572	7687	19719	45164	87771	163178	•	561249
Total Assets 26	10964	208	603	2568	7166	15560	34109	75660	154953	338770	•	1192872
Notes and Loans Payable 27	4258	121	298	1350	2591	6359	17757	37930	57776	166613	•	400997
All Other Liabilities 28	2616	64	229	495	2111	4417	6842	15374	36881	52941	•	300633
Net Worth 29	4090	23	77	723	2464	4784	9511	22356	60296	119216	•	491242

Selected Financial Ratios (Times to 1)

Current Ratio 30	1.2	•	1.3	0.7	1.6	1.5	1.2	1.1	1.0	1.1	1.7	1.2
Quick Ratio 31	0.9	•	1.0	0.7	1.1	1.4	0.9	0.8	0.7	0.8	1.1	0.9
Net Sales to Working Capital 32	22.6	•	72.7	•	3.8	7.1	18.8	42.5	•	52.4	3.6	29.7
Coverage Ratio 33	1.5	0.4	•	7.3	2.3	3.4	1.3	1.3	1.1	1.8	•	1.8
Total Asset Turnover 34	0.8	•	10.9	5.9	0.4	1.1	1.3	1.1	0.6	0.6	0.3	0.6
Inventory Turnover 35	49.2	•	•	•	8.7	145.3	32.7	53.5	63.7	24.4	62.9	36.5
Receivables Turnover 36	7.3	•	46.1	30.4	3.6	5.7	8.2	8.3	5.6	4.1	9.1	6.4
Total Liabilities to Net Worth 37	1.7	8.2	6.8	•	2.6	1.9	2.3	2.6	2.4	1.6	1.8	1.4
Current Assets to Working Capital 38	6.2	4.7	•	•	2.7	3.0	5.9	12.4	•	18.4	2.4	7.6
Current Liabilities to Working Capital 39	5.2	3.7	•	•	1.7	2.0	4.9	11.4	•	17.4	1.4	6.6
Working Capital to Net Sales 40	0.0	0.0	•	0.3	0.3	0.1	0.0	0.0	•	0.0	0.3	0.0
Inventory to Working Capital 41	0.3	•	•	•	0.2	0.0	0.2	0.3	•	1.2	0.0	0.4
Total Receipts to Cash Flow 42	4.5	21.9	6.4	5.4	6.7	5.1	5.9	5.9	4.3	5.9	•	3.0
Cost of Goods to Cash Flow 43	2.4	19.7	3.7	2.3	4.3	2.3	2.7	3.0	1.8	3.0	•	1.5
Cash Flow to Total Debt 44	0.3	0.6	1.0	0.1	0.3	0.4	0.3	0.2	0.2	0.2	•	0.4

Selected Financial Factors (in Percentages)

Debt Ratio 45	62.7	89.1	87.2	71.9	65.6	69.3	72.1	70.5	61.1	64.8	•	58.8
Return on Total Assets 46	3.8	•	29.0	5.9	4.5	4.2	3.3	4.0	•	3.7	•	3.9
Return on Equity Before Income Taxes 47	3.1	195.9	•	11.7	9.2	3.1	3.0	1.0	•	4.1	•	4.3
Return on Equity After Income Taxes 48	1.3	193.0	•	8.0	6.8	0.4	0.8	•	•	2.2	•	2.5
Profit Margin (Before Income Tax) 49	1.5	4.2	•	7.5	2.8	0.7	0.8	0.5	•	2.7	•	2.8
Profit Margin (After Income Tax) 50	0.6	4.2	•	5.2	2.1	0.1	0.2	•	•	1.5	•	1.6

Table II
Corporations with Net Income

WATER TRANSPORTATION

MONEY AMOUNTS AND SIZE OF ASSETS IN THOUSANDS OF DOLLARS

Item Description for Accounting Period 7/02 Through 6/03	Total	Zero Assets	Under 500	500 to 1,000	1,000 to 5,000	5,000 to 10,000	10,000 to 25,000	25,000 to 50,000	50,000 to 100,000	100,000 to 250,000	250,000 to 500,000	500,000 to 2,500,000	2,500,000 and over
Number of Enterprises **1**	1218	54	0	205	213	88	29	0	11	12	0	0	8
Revenues ($ in Thousands)													
Net Sales **2**	13039169	58829	0	991273	309001	962525	571012	0	583305	1126749	0	0	5740510
Interest **3**	60055	677	0	1601	1610	1729	1669	0	10790	7307	0	0	31820
Rents **4**	120231	0	0	0	0	457	1716	0	4510	2114	0	0	111434
Royalties **5**	0	0	0	0	0	0	0	0	0	0	0	0	0
Other Portfolio Income **6**	309181	42349	0	34	41262	1209	930	0	39825	4806	0	0	136755
Other Receipts **7**	1544851	0	0	181	11590	8036	24023	0	26869	165520	0	0	1248466
Total Receipts **8**	15073487	101855	0	993089	363463	973956	599350	0	665299	1306496	0	0	7266985
Average Total Receipts **9**	12376	1886	•	4844	1706	11068	20667	•	60482	108875	•	•	908623
Operating Costs/Operating Income (%)													
Cost of Operations **10**	54.1	79.6	•	71.9	47.2	66.1	25.5	•	39.3	49.9	•	•	41.3
Salaries and Wages **11**	9.8	9.0	•	5.9	5.3	7.5	13.6	•	14.7	7.6	•	•	12.8
Taxes Paid **12**	1.8	2.7	•	1.4	2.7	1.5	4.5	•	2.7	3.0	•	•	1.7
Interest Paid **13**	1.8	3.6	•	0.3	2.5	1.2	1.4	•	3.9	3.5	•	•	2.3
Depreciation **14**	5.7	1.6	•	0.5	5.1	2.6	6.3	•	12.9	10.1	•	•	7.9
Amortization and Depletion **15**	0.3	•	•	•	0.0	0.0	0.1	•	0.1	0.4	•	•	0.5
Pensions and Other Deferred Comp. **16**	0.6	•	•	0.5	0.4	0.1	0.6	•	0.6	0.5	•	•	1.1
Employee Benefits **17**	2.1	•	•	0.2	1.6	0.8	2.9	•	1.6	1.9	•	•	2.9
Advertising **18**	0.2	•	•	0.9	0.2	0.1	0.7	•	0.5	0.4	•	•	0.1
Other Expenses **19**	31.7	6.4	•	10.0	17.0	14.7	36.5	•	27.3	30.3	•	•	50.3
Officers' Compensation **20**	1.6	1.0	•	2.4	8.5	1.8	2.7	•	1.3	1.3	•	•	0.9
Operating Margin **21**	•	•	•	5.9	9.4	3.6	5.1	•	•	•	•	•	•
Operating Margin Before Officers' Comp. **22**	•	•	•	8.3	17.9	5.4	7.8	•	•	•	•	•	•

Selected Average Balance Sheet ($ in Thousands)

Net Receivables 23	1352	0	•	176	426	2268	1423	•	12158	20587	•	103666
Inventories 24	127	0	•	0	54	0	114	•	263	2384	•	12533
Net Property, Plant and Equipment 25	6266	0	•	78	1002	1702	7855	•	37227	99532	•	650268
Total Assets 26	13409	0	•	640	2369	7727	16304	•	78106	193452	•	1357552
Notes and Loans Payable 27	3896	0	•	177	692	1813	4631	•	31397	46183	•	398194
All Other Liabilities 28	3388	0	•	210	536	2926	2880	•	20164	53812	•	326963
Net Worth 29	6126	0	•	253	1141	2988	8793	•	26545	93458	•	632395

Selected Financial Ratios (Times to 1)

Current Ratio 30	1.3	•	•	1.2	1.6	1.5	1.8	•	1.0	1.3	•	1.2
Quick Ratio 31	1.0	•	•	1.2	1.0	1.3	1.3	•	0.7	1.0	•	0.9
Net Sales to Working Capital 32	16.5	•	•	66.8	3.9	7.4	7.1	•	•	7.3	•	19.6
Coverage Ratio 33	4.4	20.5	•	21.9	11.8	5.1	7.9	•	3.4	3.0	•	3.3
Total Asset Turnover 34	0.8	•	•	7.6	0.6	1.4	1.2	•	0.7	0.5	•	0.5
Inventory Turnover 35	45.6	•	•	•	12.7	•	43.9	•	79.2	19.6	•	23.6
Receivables Turnover 36	7.9	•	•	24.3	3.4	5.7	8.4	•	4.6	5.2	•	7.3
Total Liabilities to Net Worth 37	1.2	•	•	1.5	1.1	1.6	0.9	•	1.9	1.1	•	1.1
Current Assets to Working Capital 38	4.6	•	•	5.0	2.7	3.1	2.3	•	•	4.2	•	5.5
Current Liabilities to Working Capital 39	3.6	•	•	4.0	1.7	2.1	1.3	•	•	3.2	•	4.5
Working Capital to Net Sales 40	0.1	•	•	0.0	0.3	0.1	0.1	•	0.1	0.1	•	0.1
Inventory to Working Capital 41	0.2	•	•	•	•	•	0.0	•	0.2	0.2	•	0.4
Total Receipts to Cash Flow 42	3.3	•	•	7.3	2.7	6.5	2.8	•	3.3	5.1	•	2.1
Cost of Goods to Cash Flow 43	1.8	1.3	•	5.3	1.3	4.3	0.7	•	1.3	2.5	•	0.9
Cash Flow to Total Debt 44	0.4	1.1	•	1.7	0.4	0.4	0.9	•	0.3	0.2	•	0.5

Selected Financial Factors (in Percentages)

Debt Ratio 45	54.3	•	•	60.5	51.8	61.3	46.1	•	66.0	51.7	•	53.4
Return on Total Assets 46	6.3	•	•	48.5	18.1	8.4	13.9	•	9.0	5.1	•	4.1
Return on Equity Before Income Taxes 47	10.6	•	•	117.2	34.4	17.5	22.5	•	18.7	7.1	•	6.1
Return on Equity After Income Taxes 48	8.6	•	•	115.7	29.7	14.7	19.6	•	15.9	5.2	•	4.3
Profit Margin (Before Income Tax) 49	6.1	69.4	•	6.1	27.0	4.8	10.1	•	9.3	7.1	•	5.4
Profit Margin (After Income Tax) 50	4.9	69.2	•	6.0	23.4	4.0	8.7	•	8.0	5.1	•	3.8

Table I

Corporations with and without Net Income

TRUCK TRANSPORTATION

MONEY AMOUNTS AND SIZE OF ASSETS IN THOUSANDS OF DOLLARS

Item Description for Accounting Period 7/02 Through 6/03	Total	Zero Assets	Under 500	500 to 1,000	1,000 to 5,000	5,000 to 10,000	10,000 to 25,000	25,000 to 50,000	50,000 to 100,000	100,000 to 250,000	250,000 to 500,000	500,000 to 2,500,000	2,500,000 and over
Number of Enterprises 1	90938	11421	67245	6252	4952	495	354	92	61	34	13	19	0
Revenues ($ in Thousands)													
Net Sales 2	167135948	1774413	32616577	15054296	29968018	8356359	13260460	6016913	6977413	8518271	7261112	37332117	0
Interest 3	290208	4339	11483	4500	24351	9089	12301	10625	7704	20045	21770	163999	0
Rents 4	644539	230	5015	2585	32269	12281	18542	23594	14949	26196	6049	502828	0
Royalties 5	104415	2142	0	128	6	0	2	6	7	1	51889	50234	0
Other Portfolio Income 6	1163167	73257	168140	92672	229558	40360	66246	62700	60245	54796	42059	273129	0
Other Receipts 7	2177039	38334	111877	37650	150772	40751	104079	97236	43304	239006	963620	350418	0
Total Receipts 8	171515316	1892715	32913092	15191831	30404974	8458840	13461630	6211074	7103622	8858315	8346499	38672725	0
Average Total Receipts 9	1886	166	489	2430	6140	17089	38027	67512	116453	260539	642038	2035407	•
Operating Costs/Operating Income (%)													
Cost of Operations 10	30.3	17.4	25.4	25.7	36.0	33.4	39.5	31.5	30.2	34.9	31.4	27.2	•
Salaries and Wages 11	19.6	12.6	19.7	15.6	15.7	17.8	16.6	21.3	21.7	18.9	29.4	23.4	•
Taxes Paid 12	4.0	3.8	3.9	3.6	3.3	3.8	4.1	4.5	4.5	5.1	4.5	4.5	•
Interest Paid 13	1.3	2.1	1.1	1.1	1.4	1.0	1.2	1.6	1.6	1.4	1.9	1.2	•
Depreciation 14	5.6	8.1	4.8	6.5	5.4	4.6	5.1	5.9	7.6	7.9	8.0	5.1	•
Amortization and Depletion 15	0.1	0.1	0.0	0.0	0.0	0.1	0.1	0.2	0.1	0.3	0.1	0.3	•
Pensions and Other Deferred Comp. 16	0.6	0.2	0.1	0.1	0.4	0.5	0.4	0.5	0.2	0.5	1.2	1.6	•
Employee Benefits 17	2.6	0.7	1.2	1.2	1.6	1.8	2.2	2.1	2.8	3.4	5.2	5.1	•
Advertising 18	0.2	0.1	0.2	0.2	0.2	0.2	0.2	0.3	0.2	0.3	0.1	0.2	•
Other Expenses 19	35.6	52.4	39.0	43.2	35.4	36.0	30.1	33.4	31.6	28.7	29.0	34.7	•
Officers' Compensation 20	2.0	5.9	4.6	3.0	2.2	1.9	1.3	0.9	0.7	0.7	0.4	0.3	•
Operating Margin 21	•	•	•	•	•	•	•	•	•	•	•	•	•
Operating Margin Before Officers' Comp. 22	0.0	2.5	4.4	2.7	0.6	0.8	0.6	•	•	•	•	•	•

Selected Average Balance Sheet ($ in Thousands)

	1	2	3	4	5	6	7	8	9	10	11	12
Net Receivables 23	169	0	14	140	531	2024	4005	8595	12781	30519	77269	258702
Inventories 24	7	0	1	5	19	57	170	629	653	1483	1891	7541
Net Property, Plant and Equipment 25	360	0	50	378	905	2825	7233	17104	40985	94140	201499	456895
Total Assets 26	778	91	694	1961	6852	15173	34240	69536	163397	372693	1266594	
Notes and Loans Payable 27	341	78	388	1074	3044	6963	14882	28661	55070	137233	383638	
All Other Liabilities 28	217	18	113	490	1877	3702	8605	18156	38967	97372	454413	
Net Worth 29	221	-5	193	397	1932	4507	10753	22719	69360	138088	428543	

Selected Financial Ratios (Times to 1)

	1	2	3	4	5	6	7	8	9	10	11	12
Current Ratio 30	1.1	•	1.1	1.3	1.1	1.1	1.2	1.1	1.0	1.3	1.7	1.1
Quick Ratio 31	0.9	•	0.9	1.2	1.0	0.9	0.9	0.9	0.7	1.0	1.3	0.8
Net Sales to Working Capital 32	51.2	•	123.7	37.0	78.9	63.4	40.9	50.8	•	24.9	11.1	54.4
Coverage Ratio 33	1.5	2.6	1.7	1.5	0.9	1.1	1.6	1.7	1.5	2.3	3.0	1.1
Total Asset Turnover 34	2.4	•	5.3	3.5	3.1	2.5	2.5	1.9	1.6	1.5	1.5	1.6
Inventory Turnover 35	84.4	119.4	119.5	114.0	98.4	87.2	32.8	52.8	59.0	92.9	70.9	
Receivables Turnover 36	11.4	39.1	20.3	12.2	8.8	9.4	8.3	9.6	7.2	8.4	7.9	
Total Liabilities to Net Worth 37	2.5	•	2.6	3.9	2.5	2.4	2.2	2.1	1.4	1.7	2.0	
Current Assets to Working Capital 38	7.9	8.5	3.9	11.3	13.0	7.0	10.1	•	4.9	2.5	11.7	
Current Liabilities to Working Capital 39	6.9	7.5	2.9	10.3	12.0	6.0	9.1	•	3.9	1.5	10.7	
Working Capital to Net Sales 40	0.0	0.0	0.0	0.0	0.0	0.0	0.0	•	0.0	0.1	0.0	
Inventory to Working Capital 41	0.2	0.4	0.1	0.3	0.2	0.2	0.6	•	0.1	0.0	0.2	
Total Receipts to Cash Flow 42	3.8	3.5	3.0	4.0	5.2	4.7	4.4	4.6	5.4	3.8	3.5	
Cost of Goods to Cash Flow 43	1.2	0.9	0.8	1.4	1.7	1.8	1.4	1.4	1.9	1.2	1.0	
Cash Flow to Total Debt 44	0.9	1.4	1.6	1.0	0.7	0.8	0.6	0.5	0.5	0.6	0.7	

Selected Financial Factors (in Percentages)

	1	2	3	4	5	6	7	8	9	10	11	12
Debt Ratio 45	71.6	•	105.0	72.2	79.7	71.8	70.3	68.6	67.3	57.6	62.9	66.2
Return on Total Assets 46	4.4	•	9.7	5.9	3.8	2.8	4.7	5.1	3.8	4.9	8.2	2.0
Return on Equity Before Income Taxes 47	5.0	•	•	7.0	•	1.0	6.1	6.7	3.8	6.5	14.7	0.4
Return on Equity After Income Taxes 48	3.0	•	5.8	•	•	•	4.6	4.6	2.7	5.1	10.9	•
Profit Margin (Before Income Tax) 49	0.6	3.2	0.7	0.6	•	0.1	0.7	1.1	0.8	1.8	3.6	0.1
Profit Margin (After Income Tax) 50	0.4	2.7	0.7	0.5	•	•	0.5	0.8	0.5	1.4	2.7	•

Table II

Corporations with Net Income

TRUCK TRANSPORTATION

MONEY AMOUNTS AND SIZE OF ASSETS IN THOUSANDS OF DOLLARS

Item Description for Accounting Period 7/02 Through 6/03	Total	Zero Assets	Under 500	500 to 1,000	1,000 to 5,000	5,000 to 10,000	10,000 to 25,000	25,000 to 50,000	50,000 to 100,000	100,000 to 250,000	250,000 to 500,000	500,000 to 2,500,000	2,500,000 and over
Number of Enterprises **1**	49570	5065	37338	3571	2931	329	211	0	32	20	0	12	0
Revenues ($ in Thousands)													
Net Sales **2**	104944635	974921	18812532	8736371	17740574	6144267	8442919	0	3903053	5973976	0	24457265	0
Interest **3**	167459	4292	4780	3692	17514	7188	7849	0	6259	5733	0	84720	0
Rents **4**	472428	225	2539	2518	24613	7134	11098	0	5777	1084	0	391599	0
Royalties **5**	95787	2142	0	128	6	0	0	0	7	1	0	46908	0
Other Portfolio Income **6**	780934	64895	119116	61104	116310	23340	37558	0	42307	37717	0	206417	0
Other Receipts **7**	877736	37392	62857	23506	107187	19130	62910	0	33205	189690	0	269085	0
Total Receipts **8**	107338979	1083867	19001824	8827319	18006204	6201059	8562334	0	3990608	6208201	0	25455994	0
Average Total Receipts **9**	2165	214	509	2472	6143	18848	40580	•	124706	310410	•	2121333	•
Operating Costs/Operating Income (%)													
Cost of Operations **10**	29.3	3.3	20.8	26.3	37.3	27.2	39.7	•	36.1	36.4	•	25.0	•
Salaries and Wages **11**	18.7	13.2	21.1	14.3	14.6	18.0	15.4	•	18.0	16.6	•	21.4	•
Taxes Paid **12**	4.0	4.2	4.1	3.1	3.1	3.3	4.0	•	4.1	5.4	•	4.7	•
Interest Paid **13**	1.0	2.4	0.9	0.8	0.9	0.8	0.9	•	1.4	1.0	•	1.0	•
Depreciation **14**	5.2	5.3	4.3	5.2	4.0	3.9	4.1	•	7.1	7.4	•	5.9	•
Amortization and Depletion **15**	0.1	0.1	0.0	0.1	0.0	0.0	0.1	•	0.1	0.2	•	0.1	•
Pensions and Other Deferred Comp. **16**	0.5	0.4	0.1	0.2	0.3	0.5	0.3	•	0.2	0.5	•	1.2	•
Employee Benefits **17**	2.5	1.2	1.5	0.9	1.5	1.8	1.9	•	2.3	3.0	•	5.0	•
Advertising **18**	0.2	0.1	0.2	0.2	0.2	0.2	0.2	•	0.2	0.3	•	0.2	•
Other Expenses **19**	35.6	58.1	39.3	44.4	34.2	40.1	30.1	•	29.3	28.8	•	37.4	•
Officers' Compensation **20**	1.8	5.8	4.0	2.4	2.4	2.1	1.4	•	0.8	0.7	•	0.4	•
Operating Margin **21**	1.0	5.9	3.7	2.3	1.3	2.0	1.8	•	0.5	•	•	•	•
Operating Margin Before Officers' Comp. **22**	2.9	11.6	7.7	4.7	3.7	4.1	3.2	•	1.3	0.6	•	•	•

Selected Average Balance Sheet ($ in Thousands)

	•	•	•	•	•	•	•	•	•	•
Net Receivables 23	201	0	16	168	581	2389	4260	13516	37947	253184
Inventories 24	7	0	1	4	12	20	183	655	1363	9255
Net Property, Plant and Equipment 25	400	0	47	313	757	2491	6293	43126	106358	517508
Total Assets 26	880	0	92	699	1930	6897	14776	71005	178183	1286788
Notes and Loans Payable 27	325	0	68	245	817	2526	5573	27571	44003	416166
All Other Liabilities 28	242	0	16	127	454	1860	3526	17499	43787	451021
Net Worth 29	313	0	8	327	658	2510	5678	25935	90393	419601

Selected Financial Ratios (Times to 1)

	•	•	•	•	•	•	•	•	•	•
Current Ratio 30	1.3	·	1.2	1.6	1.4	1.2	1.4	1.1	1.5	1.1
Quick Ratio 31	1.0	·	1.0	1.4	1.2	1.1	1.1	0.8	1.2	0.8
Net Sales to Working Capital 32	30.1	·	77.8	21.8	22.5	25.2	21.5	117.0	16.1	69.6
Coverage Ratio 33	4.5	8.0	6.0	5.5	4.1	4.8	4.5	3.0	4.9	2.8
Total Asset Turnover 34	2.4	·	5.5	3.5	3.1	2.7	2.7	1.7	1.7	1.6
Inventory Turnover 35	93.8	·	180.8	143.2	189.7	250.9	86.9	67.2	79.7	55.1
Receivables Turnover 36	11.6	·	39.8	17.4	11.5	9.5	9.1	10.3	7.8	9.0
Total Liabilities to Net Worth 37	1.8	·	10.6	1.1	1.9	1.7	1.6	1.7	1.0	2.1
Current Assets to Working Capital 38	4.8	·	5.5	2.7	3.6	5.2	3.7	20.5	3.2	13.7
Current Liabilities to Working Capital 39	3.8	·	4.5	1.7	2.6	4.2	2.7	19.5	2.2	12.7
Working Capital to Net Sales 40	0.0	·	0.0	0.0	0.0	0.0	0.0	0.0	0.1	0.0
Inventory to Working Capital 41	0.1	·	0.1	0.0	0.1	0.0	0.1	0.6	0.1	0.4
Total Receipts to Cash Flow 42	3.5	1.7	3.2	2.6	4.1	4.0	4.2	4.8	5.1	3.1
Cost of Goods to Cash Flow 43	1.0	0.1	0.7	0.7	1.5	1.1	1.7	1.7	1.9	0.8
Cash Flow to Total Debt 44	1.1	·	1.9	2.5	1.2	1.1	1.1	0.6	0.7	0.7

Selected Financial Factors (in Percentages)

	•	•	•	•	•	•	•	•	•	•
Debt Ratio 45	64.5	·	91.4	53.2	65.9	63.6	61.6	63.5	49.3	67.4
Return on Total Assets 46	10.3	·	30.7	14.5	11.6	9.9	11.2	7.1	8.0	4.3
Return on Equity Before Income Taxes 47	22.4	·	296.4	25.3	25.7	21.6	22.7	13.1	12.5	8.6
Return on Equity After Income Taxes 48	19.9	·	289.2	24.1	24.0	17.5	20.6	11.3	10.8	6.2
Profit Margin (Before Income Tax) 49	3.3	17.0	4.7	3.4	2.8	2.9	3.2	2.8	3.8	1.8
Profit Margin (After Income Tax) 50	2.9	16.0	4.5	3.2	2.6	2.3	2.9	2.4	3.3	1.3

Table I

Corporations with and without Net Income

TRANSIT AND GROUND PASSENGER TRANSPORTATION

MONEY AMOUNTS AND SIZE OF ASSETS IN THOUSANDS OF DOLLARS

Item Description for Accounting Period 7/02 Through 6/03	Total	Zero Assets	Under 500	500 to 1,000	1,000 to 5,000	5,000 to 10,000	10,000 to 25,000	25,000 to 50,000	50,000 to 100,000	100,000 to 250,000	250,000 to 500,000	500,000 to 2,500,000	2,500,000 and over
Number of Enterprises **1**	27680	3296	22106	671	1320	205	52	16	6	0	3	4	0
Revenues ($ in Thousands)													
Net Sales **2**	23230426	92039	3989182	747339	5675927	2428190	1192425	796503	544676	0	1139839	6624307	0
Interest **3**	430008	257	2085	816	5083	2325	1902	2734	1531	0	19441	393835	0
Rents **4**	52053	0	3487	0	26522	2101	3271	1359	1356	0	8624	5333	0
Royalties **5**	0	0	0	0	0	0	0	0	0	0	0	0	0
Other Portfolio Income **6**	61807	4154	4662	67	13790	8585	5195	3841	2502	0	13212	5797	0
Other Receipts **7**	296659	17	20070	3170	55844	8977	6170	55057	7957	0	5206	134191	0
Total Receipts **8**	24070953	96467	4019486	751392	5777166	2450178	1208963	859494	558022	0	1186322	7163463	0
Average Total Receipts **9**	870	29	182	1120	4377	11952	23249	53718	93004	•	395441	1790866	•
Operating Costs/Operating Income (%)													
Cost of Operations **10**	28.3	13.3	17.2	2.6	47.8	31.5	48.3	31.7	29.4	•	39.3	14.1	•
Salaries and Wages **11**	22.8	0.8	19.9	24.2	14.9	22.7	14.2	29.0	23.6	•	18.5	33.1	•
Taxes Paid **12**	4.3	3.7	4.2	3.8	3.2	3.9	4.1	4.7	4.2	•	5.9	5.3	•
Interest Paid **13**	4.1	6.8	2.4	2.1	1.2	2.1	1.6	2.2	1.9	•	6.6	8.8	•
Depreciation **14**	6.4	4.6	5.3	6.2	4.9	7.9	8.7	8.2	6.7	•	7.4	6.9	•
Amortization and Depletion **15**	0.7	1.6	0.4	0.5	0.2	0.3	0.1	0.5	0.3	•	1.2	1.5	•
Pensions and Other Deferred Comp. **16**	0.5	•	1.0	•	0.3	0.6	1.1	0.6	0.4	•	0.7	0.3	•
Employee Benefits **17**	2.1	0.1	0.9	0.9	1.3	2.5	2.7	7.1	3.2	•	5.4	2.0	•
Advertising **18**	0.6	0.2	1.3	0.9	0.6	0.6	0.4	0.4	0.3	•	0.3	0.5	•
Other Expenses **19**	31.8	68.6	40.6	55.4	24.1	23.9	16.9	19.9	31.1	•	26.4	38.0	•
Officers' Compensation **20**	2.2	0.7	6.9	3.2	2.1	2.2	1.8	1.5	1.7	•	0.2	0.1	•
Operating Margin **21**	•	•	•	0.1	•	1.7	0.2	•	•	•	•	•	•
Operating Margin Before Officers' Comp. **22**	•	0.3	6.8	3.3	1.4	3.9	2.0	•	•	•	•	•	•

Selected Average Balance Sheet ($ in Thousands)

Net Receivables 23	69	0	6	39	338	905	2194	5695	13290	55047	165468
Inventories 24	7	0	0	5	21	76	313	733	1122	7053	22477
Net Property, Plant and Equipment 25	236	0	28	371	810	3641	7642	15012	28117	125754	668695
Total Assets 26	603	0	107	733	1968	7051	15140	38012	86082	321801	1725367
Notes and Loans Payable 27	388	0	82	388	939	4245	6636	15492	26628	218030	1285015
All Other Liabilities 28	111	0	11	93	479	1190	2706	9781	28078	80130	297410
Net Worth 29	104	0	14	252	550	1616	5798	12740	31376	23640	142942

Selected Financial Ratios (Times to 1)

Current Ratio 30	1.3	•	1.8	1.7	1.2	1.0	1.3	0.9	1.2	0.9	1.6
Quick Ratio 31	0.9	•	1.4	1.4	0.7	0.7	0.8	0.7	0.7	0.7	1.0
Net Sales to Working Capital 32	20.2	•	17.9	15.9	35.8	130.8	20.1	•	16.2	•	10.0
Coverage Ratio 33	0.9	1.6	1.3	1.3	1.8	2.2	1.9	2.0	0.8	•	0.7
Total Asset Turnover 34	1.4	•	1.7	1.5	2.2	1.7	1.5	1.3	1.1	1.2	1.0
Inventory Turnover 35	33.9	•	455.0	5.3	98.1	49.2	35.4	21.5	23.7	21.2	10.4
Receivables Turnover 36	9.7	•	36.8	21.6	12.1	14.2	10.2	7.2	9.5	13.8	5.5
Total Liabilities to Net Worth 37	4.8	•	6.4	1.9	2.6	3.4	1.6	2.0	1.7	12.6	11.1
Current Assets to Working Capital 38	4.4	•	2.3	2.5	7.3	24.6	4.8	•	6.4	•	2.8
Current Liabilities to Working Capital 39	3.4	•	1.3	1.5	6.3	23.6	3.8	•	5.4	•	1.8
Working Capital to Net Sales 40	0.0	•	0.1	0.1	0.0	0.0	0.0	0.0	0.1	•	0.1
Inventory to Working Capital 41	0.1	•	0.0	0.1	0.2	1.1	0.2	•	0.2	•	0.1
Total Receipts to Cash Flow 42	4.1	1.9	3.0	2.4	5.5	4.9	6.9	6.5	4.9	25.5	3.4
Cost of Goods to Cash Flow 43	1.2	0.3	0.5	0.1	2.6	1.5	3.3	2.1	1.4	10.0	0.5
Cash Flow to Total Debt 44	0.4	•	0.6	1.0	0.6	0.4	0.4	0.3	0.3	0.0	0.3

Selected Financial Factors (in Percentages)

Debt Ratio 45	82.7	•	86.5	65.6	72.1	77.1	61.7	66.5	63.6	92.7	91.7
Return on Total Assets 46	5.4	•	5.3	4.1	5.0	8.0	4.8	5.7	1.6	•	6.2
Return on Equity Before Income Taxes 47	•	•	8.5	2.9	8.1	19.4	6.1	8.3	•	•	•
Return on Equity After Income Taxes 48	•	•	6.3	1.9	7.8	18.0	4.1	7.2	•	•	•
Profit Margin (Before Income Tax) 49	•	4.4	0.7	0.7	1.0	2.6	1.5	2.1	•	•	•
Profit Margin (After Income Tax) 50	•	4.3	0.5	0.4	1.0	2.5	1.0	1.8	0.3	•	•

Table II

Corporations with Net Income

TRANSIT AND GROUND PASSENGER TRANSPORTATION

MONEY AMOUNTS AND SIZE OF ASSETS IN THOUSANDS OF DOLLARS

Item Description for Accounting Period 7/02 Through 6/03	Total	Zero Assets	Under 500	500 to 1,000	1,000 to 5,000	5,000 to 10,000	10,000 to 25,000	25,000 to 50,000	50,000 to 100,000	100,000 to 250,000	250,000 to 500,000	500,000 to 2,500,000	2,500,000 and over
Number of Enterprises **1**	14650	1636	11678	363	782	148	32	11	0	0	0	0	0
Revenues ($ in Thousands)													
Net Sales **2**	10184204	53478	2366915	496504	4139934	1689229	809238	628905	0	0	0	0	0
Interest **3**	9650	0	721	816	2594	1489	1548	2482	0	0	0	0	0
Rents **4**	31553	0	3487	0	21868	1555	3237	1406	0	0	0	0	0
Royalties **5**	0	0	0	0	0	0	0	0	0	0	0	0	0
Other Portfolio Income **6**	24430	0	4434	67	7363	7853	1581	3133	0	0	0	0	0
Other Receipts **7**	77690	0	10004	3171	41949	4667	5032	12866	0	0	0	0	0
Total Receipts **8**	10327527	53478	2385561	500558	4213708	1704793	820636	648792	0	0	0	0	0
Average Total Receipts **9**	705	33	204	1379	5388	11519	25645	58981	•	•	•	•	•
Operating Costs/Operating Income (%)													
Cost of Operations **10**	39.3	19.6	22.7	4.0	52.6	36.9	46.6	41.2	•	•	•	•	•
Salaries and Wages **11**	16.5	0.1	18.1	24.7	14.2	18.7	13.9	17.9	•	•	•	•	•
Taxes Paid **12**	3.5	1.8	3.9	3.8	2.8	3.6	4.2	5.5	•	•	•	•	•
Interest Paid **13**	1.4	1.6	1.5	1.0	1.0	2.1	1.3	1.8	•	•	•	•	•
Depreciation **14**	4.9	3.2	4.2	5.7	3.0	8.2	7.7	6.8	•	•	•	•	•
Amortization and Depletion **15**	0.2	0.0	0.1	0.3	0.2	0.4	0.1	0.3	•	•	•	•	•
Pensions and Other Deferred Comp. **16**	0.7	•	1.8	•	0.3	0.4	1.0	0.2	•	•	•	•	•
Employee Benefits **17**	1.0	0.1	0.3	1.1	0.5	1.6	2.2	2.7	•	•	•	•	•
Advertising **18**	0.5	0.2	0.6	1.1	0.3	0.4	0.4	0.4	•	•	•	•	•
Other Expenses **19**	25.0	46.7	34.1	51.8	20.2	21.1	17.2	19.6	•	•	•	•	•
Officers' Compensation **20**	3.2	•	6.3	4.8	2.2	2.5	2.1	1.2	•	•	•	•	•
Operating Margin **21**	3.9	26.8	6.4	1.8	2.6	4.2	3.4	2.4	•	•	•	•	•
Operating Margin Before Officers' Comp. **22**	7.1	26.8	12.6	6.6	4.8	6.7	5.5	3.6	•	•	•	•	•

Selected Average Balance Sheet ($ in Thousands)

Net Receivables 23	52	0	9	71	445	904	2452	6737
Inventories 24	3	0	0	18	49	86		761
Net Property, Plant and Equipment 25	122	0	21	284	629	3748	6640	15724
Total Assets 26	333	0	90	710	1973	7160	15425	43070
Notes and Loans Payable 27	158	0	53	207	880	4182	5356	13431
All Other Liabilities 28	69	0	10	111	593	1207	2694	10301
Net Worth 29	106	0	26	393	500	1771	7375	19338

Selected Financial Ratios (Times to 1)

Current Ratio 30	1.4	•	2.2	2.4	1.3	1.1	1.7	1.1
Quick Ratio 31	1.0	•	2.0	2.0	0.8	0.8	1.2	0.9
Net Sales to Working Capital 32	17.2	•	12.0	7.6	20.3	81.6	9.3	39.4
Coverage Ratio 33	4.9	18.1	5.6	3.7	5.4	3.5	4.7	4.1
Total Asset Turnover 34	2.1	•	2.3	1.9	2.7	1.6	1.6	1.3
Inventory Turnover 35	86.4	•	357.9	5.8	151.9	86.6	136.2	30.9
Receivables Turnover 36	13.8	•	27.9	27.0	12.0	17.1	20.6	8.4
Total Liabilities to Net Worth 37	2.2	•	2.5	0.8	2.9	3.0	1.1	1.2
Current Assets to Working Capital 38	3.5	•	1.8	1.7	4.3	16.5	2.4	10.4
Current Liabilities to Working Capital 39	2.5	•	0.8	0.7	3.3	15.5	1.4	9.4
Working Capital to Net Sales 40	0.1	•	0.1	0.1	0.0	0.0	0.1	0.0
Inventory to Working Capital 41	0.1	•	0.0	0.1	0.0	0.5	0.0	0.8
Total Receipts to Cash Flow 42	4.3	1.5	3.1	2.2	5.5	4.9	5.4	5.8
Cost of Goods to Cash Flow 43	1.7	0.3	0.7	0.1	2.9	1.8	2.5	2.4
Cash Flow to Total Debt 44	0.7	•	1.0	2.0	0.7	0.4	0.6	0.4

Selected Financial Factors (in Percentages)

Debt Ratio 45	68.3	•	71.1	44.7	74.7	75.3	52.2	55.1
Return on Total Assets 46	13.9	•	19.7	6.9	14.5	11.5	9.8	9.8
Return on Equity Before Income Taxes 47	34.8	•	55.9	9.1	46.6	33.2	16.3	16.5
Return on Equity After Income Taxes 48	33.2	•	53.6	8.0	46.1	31.5	13.8	14.5
Profit Margin (Before Income Tax) 49	5.3	26.8	7.1	2.6	4.4	5.1	4.7	5.6
Profit Margin (After Income Tax) 50	5.0	26.6	6.9	2.3	4.3	4.9	4.0	4.9

Table I

Corporations with and without Net Income

PIPELINE TRANSPORTATION

MONEY AMOUNTS AND SIZE OF ASSETS IN THOUSANDS OF DOLLARS

Item Description for Accounting Period 7/02 Through 6/03	Total	Zero Assets	Under 500	500 to 1,000	1,000 to 5,000	5,000 to 10,000	10,000 to 25,000	25,000 to 50,000	50,000 to 100,000	100,000 to 250,000	250,000 to 500,000	500,000 to 2,500,000	2,500,000 and over
Number of Enterprises 1	342	0	0	137	118	0	14	9	6	8	3	4	0
Revenues ($ in Thousands)													
Net Sales 2	3394210	0	0	233581	144405	0	238739	440876	328422	222998	387022	1292122	0
Interest 3	45289	0	0	0	1176	0	1385	667	972	5959	1559	32103	0
Rents 4	5775	0	0	0	0	0	67	187	1	5106	0	3	0
Royalties 5	0	0	0	0	0	0	0	0	0	0	0	0	0
Other Portfolio Income 6	23427	0	0	0	0	0	2634	464	23	11620	0	6324	0
Other Receipts 7	118328	0	0	5228	6658	0	8724	870	7868	80219	1243	5120	0
Total Receipts 8	3587029	0	0	238809	152239	0	251549	443064	337286	325902	389824	1335672	0
Average Total Receipts 9	10488	•	•	1743	1290	•	17968	49229	56214	40738	129941	333918	•
Operating Costs/Operating Income (%)													
Cost of Operations 10	22.2	•	•	39.2	50.8	•	51.2	43.6	17.7	2.4	•	14.6	•
Salaries and Wages 11	7.6	•	•	15.6	13.3	•	3.0	2.4	24.5	2.8	2.8	5.8	•
Taxes Paid 12	3.9	•	•	2.1	2.5	•	3.6	4.2	4.4	2.0	4.6	4.2	•
Interest Paid 13	8.5	•	•	1.4	3.0	•	2.3	1.3	2.0	15.5	4.1	16.0	•
Depreciation 14	12.9	•	•	1.2	14.0	•	4.3	4.3	5.7	13.0	13.8	20.9	•
Amortization and Depletion 15	0.5	•	•	0.7	0.3	•	0.1	0.0	0.4	3.2	0.0	0.2	•
Pensions and Other Deferred Comp. 16	0.6	•	•	0.1	0.2	•	0.0	0.2	0.9	0.5	1.1	0.7	•
Employee Benefits 17	1.1	•	•	•	1.4	•	0.4	0.7	3.6	2.1	0.6	0.9	•
Advertising 18	0.1	•	•	0.6	0.5	•	0.0	0.0	0.0	0.0	•	0.1	•
Other Expenses 19	30.8	•	•	13.7	18.2	•	14.2	26.0	33.5	86.7	40.3	26.9	•
Officers' Compensation 20	0.7	•	•	4.9	3.0	•	0.5	0.4	0.1	•	0.2	0.2	•
Operating Margin 21	11.3	•	•	20.5	•	•	20.4	16.9	7.2	•	32.5	9.5	•
Operating Margin Before Officers' Comp. 22	11.9	•	•	25.4	•	•	20.8	17.3	7.3	•	32.7	9.8	•

Selected Average Balance Sheet ($ in Thousands)

Net Receivables 23	79386	14975	3342	8518	4168	4250	153	550	1863
Inventories 24	2443	4366	901	285	1260	215	164	1	186
Net Property, Plant and Equipment 25	1161823	255280	62919	37907	21736	7173	58	1201	19492
Total Assets 26	1669066	322109	148946	62662	34073	14715	644	3510	30759
Notes and Loans Payable 27	773180	229162	64055	22021	11527	4564	216	1110	14049
All Other Liabilities 28	539391	64265	67711	24110	8189	3974	67	1239	9836
Net Worth 29	356496	28682	17180	16531	14357	6178	361	1161	6874

Selected Financial Ratios (Times to 1)

Current Ratio 30	0.8	0.3	0.8	0.9	0.7	1.7	6.4	1.9	0.8
Quick Ratio 31	0.5	0.2	0.6	0.7	0.6	1.5	4.0	1.3	0.5
Net Sales to Working Capital 32	•	•	•	•	•	6.6	4.7	2.6	•
Coverage Ratio 33	1.8	9.1	2.2	5.9	14.2	12.1	17.0	0.4	3.0
Total Asset Turnover 34	0.2	0.4	0.2	0.9	1.4	1.2	2.6	0.3	0.3
Inventory Turnover 35	19.3	•	0.7	33.9	16.9	40.7	4.1	1019.4	11.8
Receivables Turnover 36	4.2	17.2	3.9	6.4	7.2	5.4	12.6	2.6	5.2
Total Liabilities to Net Worth 37	3.7	10.2	7.7	2.8	1.4	1.4	0.8	2.0	3.5
Current Assets to Working Capital 38	•	•	•	•	•	2.5	1.2	2.1	•
Current Liabilities to Working Capital 39	•	•	•	•	•	1.5	0.2	1.1	•
Working Capital to Net Sales 40	•	•	•	•	•	0.2	0.2	0.4	•
Inventory to Working Capital 41	•	•	•	•	•	0.1	0.4	0.0	•
Total Receipts to Cash Flow 42	2.8	1.4	1.0	2.9	2.5	2.7	3.0	7.7	2.3
Cost of Goods to Cash Flow 43	0.4	•	0.0	0.5	1.1	1.4	1.2	3.9	0.5
Cash Flow to Total Debt 44	0.1	0.3	0.2	0.4	1.0	0.7	2.0	0.1	0.2

Selected Financial Factors (in Percentages)

Debt Ratio 45	78.6	91.1	88.5	73.6	57.9	58.0	44.0	66.9	77.7
Return on Total Assets 46	5.6	15.0	6.2	10.4	26.9	32.5	64.0	0.4	8.2
Return on Equity Before Income Taxes 47	11.7	149.5	29.0	32.6	59.4	71.0	107.5	•	24.5
Return on Equity After Income Taxes 48	6.2	97.2	17.3	20.5	38.0	47.4	107.5	•	15.7
Profit Margin (Before Income Tax) 49	12.9	33.2	17.9	9.9	17.4	25.7	22.7	•	16.9
Profit Margin (After Income Tax) 50	6.8	21.6	10.6	6.2	11.1	17.2	22.7	•	10.9

Table II
Corporations with Net Income

PIPELINE TRANSPORTATION

MONEY AMOUNTS AND SIZE OF ASSETS IN THOUSANDS OF DOLLARS

Item Description for Accounting Period 7/02 Through 6/03		Total	Zero Assets	Under 500	500 to 1,000	1,000 to 5,000	5,000 to 10,000	10,000 to 25,000	25,000 to 50,000	50,000 to 100,000	100,000 to 250,000	250,000 to 500,000	500,000 to 2,500,000	2,500,000 and over
Number of Enterprises	1	265	0	·	137	74	21	11	0	0	0	0	0	0
Revenues ($ in Thousands)														
Net Sales	2	2886114	0	·	233581	31763	77238	228284	0	0	0	0	0	0
Interest	3	15622	0	·	0	1141	412	1385	0	0	0	0	0	0
Rents	4	5760	0	·	0	0	412	67	0	0	0	0	0	0
Royalties	5	0	0	·	0	0	0	0	0	0	0	0	0	0
Other Portfolio Income	6	3481	0	·	0	0	31	2377	0	0	0	0	0	0
Other Receipts	7	109509	0	·	5228	6792	839	7310	0	0	0	0	0	0
Total Receipts	8	3020486	0	·	238809	39696	78932	239423	0	0	0	0	0	0
Average Total Receipts	9	11398	·	·	1743	536	3759	21766	·	·	·	·	·	·
Operating Costs/Operating Income (%)														
Cost of Operations	10	19.7	·	·	39.2	56.7	27.8	53.6	·	·	·	·	·	·
Salaries and Wages	11	6.3	·	·	15.6	·	·	2.5	·	·	·	·	·	·
Taxes Paid	12	4.1	·	·	2.1	0.6	5.8	3.3	·	·	·	·	·	·
Interest Paid	13	7.4	·	·	1.4	4.7	·	1.2	·	·	·	·	·	·
Depreciation	14	13.0	·	·	1.2	20.0	9.9	4.2	·	·	·	·	·	·
Amortization and Depletion	15	0.2	·	·	0.7	0.0	0.0	0.1	·	·	·	·	·	·
Pensions and Other Deferred Comp.	16	0.5	·	·	0.1	·	0.0	0.1	·	·	·	·	·	·
Employee Benefits	17	0.8	·	·	·	·	·	·	·	·	·	·	·	·
Advertising	18	0.1	·	·	0.6	·	·	0.4	·	·	·	·	·	·
Other Expenses	19	26.9	·	·	13.7	5.8	34.2	11.9	·	·	·	·	·	·
Officers' Compensation	20	0.6	·	·	4.9	·	·	0.2	·	·	·	·	·	·
Operating Margin	21	20.3	·	·	20.5	12.2	22.3	22.6	·	·	·	·	·	·
Operating Margin Before Officers' Comp.	22	20.9	·	·	25.4	12.2	22.3	22.8	·	·	·	·	·	·

Selected Average Balance Sheet ($ in Thousands)

Net Receivables 23	1259	153	638	595	2524
Inventories 24	172	164	0	71	349
Net Property, Plant and Equipment 25	21486	58	585	3049	8898
Total Assets 26	29764	644	2914	7812	14175
Notes and Loans Payable 27	13708	216	1556	82	2906
All Other Liabilities 28	8927	67	-323	1573	4731
Net Worth 29	7129	361	1680	6156	6539

Selected Financial Ratios (Times to 1)

Current Ratio 30	0.9	6.4	4.0	1.2	1.2
Quick Ratio 31	0.5	4.0	2.4	1.0	1.1
Net Sales to Working Capital 32	•	4.7	0.5	12.4	22.1
Coverage Ratio 33	4.4	17.0	8.9	•	23.4
Total Asset Turnover 34	0.4	2.6	0.1	0.5	1.5
Inventory Turnover 35	12.5	4.1	•	14.4	31.8
Receivables Turnover 36	8.8	12.6	1.3	2.1	16.4
Total Liabilities to Net Worth 37	3.2	0.8	0.7	0.3	1.2
Current Assets to Working Capital 38	•	1.2	1.3	6.5	5.2
Current Liabilities to Working Capital 39	•	0.2	0.3	5.5	4.2
Working Capital to Net Sales 40	•	0.2	2.0	0.1	0.0
Inventory to Working Capital 41	•	0.4	•	0.3	0.4
Total Receipts to Cash Flow 42	2.0	3.0	3.2	1.7	2.6
Cost of Goods to Cash Flow 43	0.4	1.2	1.8	0.5	1.4
Cash Flow to Total Debt 44	0.2	2.0	0.1	1.3	1.0

Selected Financial Factors (in Percentages)

Debt Ratio 45	76.0	44.0	42.3	21.2	53.9
Return on Total Assets 46	11.8	64.0	6.2	11.5	42.1
Return on Equity Before Income Taxes 47	38.1	107.5	9.5	14.6	87.3
Return on Equity After Income Taxes 48	27.2	107.5	9.5	10.0	59.0
Profit Margin (Before Income Tax) 49	24.9	22.7	37.2	24.5	27.5
Profit Margin (After Income Tax) 50	17.8	22.7	37.1	16.7	18.6

Table I

Corporations with and without Net Income

OTHER TRANSPORTATION AND SUPPORT ACTIVITIES

MONEY AMOUNTS AND SIZE OF ASSETS IN THOUSANDS OF DOLLARS

Item Description for Accounting Period 7/02 Through 6/03	Total	Zero Assets	Under 500	500 to 1,000	1,000 to 5,000	5,000 to 10,000	10,000 to 25,000	25,000 to 50,000	50,000 to 100,000	100,000 to 250,000	250,000 to 500,000	500,000 to 2,500,000	2,500,000 and over
Number of Enterprises **1**	39609	5331	29839	2058	1910	186	163	50	20	31	7	10	3
Revenues ($ in Thousands)													
Net Sales **2**	130860532	680846	15135721	6272164	10140918	4373676	5617945	3544068	2262171	5999210	2506324	11394119	62933371
Interest **3**	542599	470	5047	3499	9977	3030	7714	13968	4310	26671	13537	152516	301859
Rents **4**	159921	0	270	6396	4859	1244	5883	792	9239	39338	5408	29170	57321
Royalties **5**	805485	0	0	0	0	6	0	381	0	31968	0	37010	736121
Other Portfolio Income **6**	345456	414	25675	23322	11682	22680	14246	32647	9334	12566	10218	136744	45931
Other Receipts **7**	880066	-3074	15877	34299	107180	21239	114705	88708	40930	73320	59680	123502	203696
Total Receipts **8**	133594059	678656	15182590	6339680	10274616	4421875	5760493	3680564	2325984	6183073	2595167	11873061	64278299
Average Total Receipts **9**	3373	127	509	3081	5379	23774	35340	73611	116299	199454	370738	1187306	21426100
Operating Costs/Operating Income (%)													
Cost of Operations **10**	37.8	20.4	47.4	60.8	63.8	71.5	53.1	65.6	58.1	48.9	69.0	34.3	21.5
Salaries and Wages **11**	19.5	7.7	12.1	8.6	12.8	10.2	15.2	10.9	11.5	19.8	17.1	23.4	24.6
Taxes Paid **12**	3.3	3.4	2.7	1.2	4.4	1.5	3.8	3.8	4.8	2.8	3.0	3.0	3.6
Interest Paid **13**	1.0	4.0	0.7	0.3	0.8	0.5	0.8	1.5	1.3	2.0	1.8	1.7	0.9
Depreciation **14**	3.8	6.0	2.7	2.4	1.7	0.9	2.4	2.0	2.9	3.0	1.6	3.4	5.2
Amortization and Depletion **15**	0.3	2.0	0.0	0.1	0.2	0.2	0.2	0.4	0.3	0.7	0.9	0.5	0.3
Pensions and Other Deferred Comp. **16**	2.1	0.5	0.3	0.2	0.2	0.1	0.6	0.1	0.2	0.6	0.3	1.0	3.9
Employee Benefits **17**	3.1	0.9	0.4	0.7	1.1	0.9	2.1	1.6	1.7	2.7	1.7	3.1	4.7
Advertising **18**	0.5	1.0	0.3	0.2	0.2	0.2	0.4	0.2	0.3	0.4	0.1	0.2	0.8
Other Expenses **19**	26.1	27.5	21.1	13.5	10.1	10.0	21.8	16.3	19.4	21.4	11.5	32.1	30.1
Officers' Compensation **20**	1.5	0.8	5.5	4.2	3.2	2.8	1.6	1.0	0.9	0.8	0.6	0.4	0.2
Operating Margin **21**	1.2	•	0.4	0.2	•	1.2	•	•	•	•	•	•	•
Operating Margin Before Officers' Comp. **22**	2.6	•	5.9	4.4	1.3	4.0	•	•	•	•	•	4.1	4.3

Selected Average Balance Sheet ($ in Thousands)

Net Receivables 23	374	20	255	617	2668	4919	10813	18717	34790	50875	228886	2186429
Inventories 24	31	1	8	64	148	502	1368	3726	3748	2005	37307	194097
Net Property, Plant and Equipment 25	730	38	180	617	1647	4611	10214	23158	39546	33219	245069	6762339
Total Assets 26	1995	96	686	2159	6925	15542	34266	69167	151123	350329	1017694	15468359
Notes and Loans Payable 27	526	72	243	1014	2155	4534	11724	20103	53402	139783	236851	3048338
All Other Liabilities 28	716	27	248	719	2318	6956	14243	22257	54936	100433	382407	5575190
Net Worth 29	753	-3	195	425	2451	4052	8299	26807	42785	110113	398436	6844830

Selected Financial Ratios (Times to 1)

Current Ratio 30	1.1	1.5	1.3	1.4	1.4	1.1	1.2	1.4	1.2	0.8	1.4	1.0
Quick Ratio 31	0.9	1.2	1.2	1.0	1.2	0.9	0.9	1.1	0.9	0.5	1.0	0.8
Net Sales to Working Capital 32	40.6	32.7	30.7	15.8	20.4	67.6	26.1	10.3	18.5	•	10.8	712.6
Coverage Ratio 33	4.3	2.0	5.1	0.3	6.1	1.7	1.4	2.0	1.1	•	1.8	7.7
Total Asset Turnover 34	1.7	5.3	4.4	2.5	3.4	2.2	2.1	1.6	1.3	1.0	1.1	1.4
Inventory Turnover 35	40.4	178.9	226.9	53.1	113.3	36.5	34.0	17.6	25.3	123.1	10.5	23.2
Receivables Turnover 36	8.9	25.6	14.4	9.4	10.5	6.9	7.6	4.6	5.1	6.3	2.0	19.2
Total Liabilities to Net Worth 37	1.7	•	2.5	4.1	1.8	2.8	3.1	1.6	2.5	2.2	1.6	1.3
Current Assets to Working Capital 38	8.3	3.2	3.9	3.6	3.7	16.9	6.7	3.3	5.9	•	3.5	133.2
Current Liabilities to Working Capital 39	7.3	2.2	2.9	2.6	2.7	15.9	5.7	2.3	4.9	•	2.5	132.2
Working Capital to Net Sales 40	0.0	0.0	0.0	0.1	0.0	0.0	0.0	0.1	0.1	•	0.1	0.0
Inventory to Working Capital 41	0.4	0.1	0.0	0.2	0.1	1.0	0.4	0.3	0.3	•	0.1	6.6
Total Receipts to Cash Flow 42	4.4	4.3	6.4	11.0	12.1	6.0	8.9	7.2	6.8	17.1	3.8	3.5
Cost of Goods to Cash Flow 43	1.7	2.0	3.9	7.0	8.7	3.2	5.8	4.2	3.3	11.8	1.3	0.8
Cash Flow to Total Debt 44	0.6	1.2	1.0	0.3	0.4	0.5	0.3	0.4	0.3	0.1	0.5	0.7

Selected Financial Factors (in Percentages)

Debt Ratio 45	62.3	102.7	71.6	80.3	64.6	73.9	75.8	61.2	71.7	68.6	60.8	55.7
Return on Total Assets 46	7.2	7.5	7.0	0.7	9.4	3.0	4.1	4.2	2.8	•	3.5	9.8
Return on Equity Before Income Taxes 47	14.6	•	19.7	•	22.1	4.6	4.4	5.4	0.5	•	4.1	19.3
Return on Equity After Income Taxes 48	9.1	•	18.6	•	19.1	0.3	0.1	3.2	•	•	1.2	12.6
Profit Margin (Before Income Tax) 49	3.3	0.7	1.3	•	2.3	0.5	0.5	1.3	0.1	•	1.4	6.3
Profit Margin (After Income Tax) 50	2.1	0.6	1.2	•	2.0	0.0	0.0	0.8	•	•	0.4	4.1

Table II

Corporations with Net Income

OTHER TRANSPORTATION AND SUPPORT ACTIVITIES

MONEY AMOUNTS AND SIZE OF ASSETS IN THOUSANDS OF DOLLARS

Item Description for Accounting Period 7/02 Through 6/03	Total	Zero Assets	Under 500	500 to 1,000	1,000 to 5,000	5,000 to 10,000	10,000 to 25,000	25,000 to 50,000	50,000 to 100,000	100,000 to 250,000	250,000 to 500,000	500,000 to 2,500,000	2,500,000 and over
Number of Enterprises 1	17375	934	13387	1715	1021	152	99	31	13	14	0	6	3
Revenues ($ in Thousands)													
Net Sales 2	107607161	319487	8847641	5630633	6756852	3584134	3746615	2651457	1677605	3484667	0	7974699	62933371
Interest 3	429781	0	2407	2775	3880	2741	3108	12142	2975	7574	0	90319	301859
Rents 4	127077	0	0	5977	4804	1244	4806	792	5610	25003	0	21520	57321
Royalties 5	764236	0	0	0	0	0	0	2	0	1010	0	27103	736121
Other Portfolio Income 6	292574	0	21980	20745	8159	22595	12567	32621	7974	20865	0	99138	45931
Other Receipts 7	677101	1050	2284	33147	71030	15299	79199	79284	27221	53897	0	110994	203696
Total Receipts 8	109897930	320537	8874312	5693277	6844725	3626013	3846295	2776298	1721385	3593016	0	8323773	64278299
Average Total Receipts 9	6325	343	663	3320	6704	23855	38851	89558	132414	256644	•	1387296	21426100
Operating Costs/Operating Income (%)													
Cost of Operations 10	35.0	6.3	53.6	65.9	61.1	75.9	56.2	62.2	58.1	53.3	•	27.4	21.5
Salaries and Wages 11	19.9	6.7	9.1	7.7	12.6	9.7	13.5	11.4	10.3	14.1	•	25.4	24.6
Taxes Paid 12	3.3	4.3	2.0	1.0	5.3	1.5	4.0	4.6	2.6	2.8	•	3.2	3.6
Interest Paid 13	0.9	2.6	0.3	0.3	0.6	0.4	0.7	1.2	0.5	1.4	•	2.1	0.9
Depreciation 14	3.9	2.4	1.7	1.8	1.1	0.7	1.9	1.7	2.7	2.4	•	3.6	5.2
Amortization and Depletion 15	0.2	0.9	0.0	0.1	0.1	0.2	0.1	0.2	0.1	0.3	•	0.4	0.3
Pensions and Other Deferred Comp. 16	2.5	0.8	0.2	0.2	0.3	0.2	0.6	0.1	0.2	0.8	•	1.2	3.9
Employee Benefits 17	3.4	0.3	0.4	0.8	1.1	1.0	2.2	1.9	1.8	2.2	•	3.2	4.7
Advertising 18	0.6	0.0	0.2	0.1	0.1	0.2	0.3	0.2	0.2	0.2	•	0.2	0.8
Other Expenses 19	26.1	23.7	16.6	16.6	12.2	6.2	17.1	17.2	20.7	21.2	•	33.6	30.1
Officers' Compensation 20	1.1	0.6	4.5	4.3	3.3	1.7	1.7	1.1	1.0	0.8	•	0.8	0.2
Operating Margin 21	3.1	4.0	4.4	1.3	2.1	2.4	1.7	•	1.7	0.6	•	4.1	•
Operating Margin Before Officers' Comp. 22	4.2	4.6	8.9	5.6	5.4	4.2	3.4	•	2.7	1.5	•	4.3	•

Selected Average Balance Sheet ($ in Thousands)

Net Receivables 23	690	0	26	276	674	2478	5577	12655	20792	50758	•	270828	2186429
Inventories 24	44	0	1	9	25	145	496	1309	3046	4208	•	34963	194097
Net Property, Plant and Equipment 25	1445	0	33	155	441	1782	4275	8549	19190	39870	•	316182	6762339
Total Assets 26	3742	0	101	700	2176	7106	15150	35175	70418	193218	•	1090491	15468359
Notes and Loans Payable 27	783	0	33	175	599	1901	3880	10733	12701	57653	•	188978	3048338
All Other Liabilities 28	1388	0	32	263	901	2249	6054	13772	24648	69372	•	487281	5575190
Net Worth 29	1570	0	35	262	675	2957	5215	10670	33069	66193	•	414233	6844830

Selected Financial Ratios (Times to 1)

Current Ratio 30	1.2	•	2.1	1.4	1.5	1.4	1.3	1.1	1.5	1.2	•	1.9	1.0
Quick Ratio 31	1.0	•	1.8	1.3	1.1	1.2	1.1	0.9	1.2	0.9	•	1.3	0.8
Net Sales to Working Capital 32	32.4	•	20.1	28.7	13.7	19.3	18.2	33.6	9.3	21.3	•	6.2	712.6
Coverage Ratio 33	6.9	2.7	16.7	10.0	6.8	11.1	7.6	3.5	9.4	3.7	•	3.0	7.7
Total Asset Turnover 34	1.7	•	6.6	4.7	3.0	3.3	2.5	2.4	1.8	1.3	•	1.2	1.4
Inventory Turnover 35	48.9	•	399.0	228.4	161.8	123.6	42.9	40.6	24.6	31.5	•	10.4	23.2
Receivables Turnover 36	9.4	•	28.2	16.5	10.5	11.1	7.2	8.5	7.6	4.6	•	1.7	19.2
Total Liabilities to Net Worth 37	1.4	•	1.9	1.7	2.2	1.4	1.9	2.3	1.1	1.9	•	1.6	1.3
Current Assets to Working Capital 38	6.5	•	1.9	3.7	3.0	3.4	4.2	7.7	2.9	7.4	•	2.2	133.2
Current Liabilities to Working Capital 39	5.5	•	0.9	2.7	2.0	2.4	3.2	6.7	1.9	6.4	•	1.2	132.2
Working Capital to Net Sales 40	0.0	•	0.0	0.0	0.1	0.1	0.1	0.0	0.1	0.0	•	0.2	0.0
Inventory to Working Capital 41	0.2	•	0.0	0.0	0.0	0.1	0.3	0.4	0.2	0.2	•	0.0	6.6
Total Receipts to Cash Flow 42	4.0	1.4	3.9	8.1	8.1	13.2	6.0	7.0	5.8	5.4	•	3.3	3.5
Cost of Goods to Cash Flow 43	1.4	0.1	2.1	5.4	4.9	10.0	3.4	4.3	3.4	2.9	•	0.9	0.8
Cash Flow to Total Debt 44	0.7	•	2.6	0.9	0.5	0.4	0.6	0.5	0.6	0.4	•	0.6	0.7

Selected Financial Factors (in Percentages)

Debt Ratio 45	58.0	•	65.0	62.6	69.0	58.4	65.6	69.7	53.0	65.7	•	62.0	55.7
Return on Total Assets 46	10.2	•	32.7	12.5	11.9	13.1	12.7	10.0	8.7	6.6	•	7.6	9.8
Return on Equity Before Income Taxes 47	20.7	•	87.6	30.2	32.8	28.7	32.1	23.7	16.6	14.2	•	13.4	19.3
Return on Equity After Income Taxes 48	14.7	•	84.3	29.2	29.4	25.6	26.6	18.3	13.9	10.4	•	8.7	12.6
Profit Margin (Before Income Tax) 49	5.3	4.3	4.7	2.4	3.4	3.6	4.4	3.0	4.3	3.8	•	4.2	6.3
Profit Margin (After Income Tax) 50	3.7	4.0	4.5	2.3	3.0	3.2	3.7	2.3	3.6	2.8	•	2.7	4.1

WAREHOUSING AND STORAGE

Table I
Corporations with and without Net Income

MONEY AMOUNTS AND SIZE OF ASSETS IN THOUSANDS OF DOLLARS

Item Description for Accounting Period 7/02 Through 6/03	Total	Zero Assets	Under 500	500 to 1,000	1,000 to 5,000	5,000 to 10,000	10,000 to 25,000	25,000 to 50,000	50,000 to 100,000	100,000 to 250,000	250,000 to 500,000	500,000 to 2,500,000	2,500,000 and over
Number of Enterprises 1	6975	0	3793	1109	1045	0	102	24	18	11	7	0	0
Revenues ($ in Thousands)													
Net Sales 2	16903820	0	1837838	1605179	3385815	0	1468263	918328	1865977	742819	2471154	0	0
Interest 3	104982	0	1020	3677	3454	0	2731	768	5151	11743	73035	0	0
Rents 4	36462	0	3634	3170	4969	0	6110	1301	7386	3451	2482	0	0
Royalties 5	1124	0	0	0	0	0	85	0	0	809	229	0	0
Other Portfolio Income 6	54497	0	128	343	4617	0	9468	1136	889	11059	19406	0	0
Other Receipts 7	245685	0	3320	5955	70181	0	33678	21595	36591	2109	32894	0	0
Total Receipts 8	17346570	0	1845940	1618324	3469036	0	1520335	943128	1915994	771990	2599200	0	0
Average Total Receipts 9	2487	•	487	1459	3320	•	14905	39297	106444	70181	371314	•	•
Operating Costs/Operating Income (%)													
Cost of Operations 10	36.0	•	46.2	35.3	48.9	•	37.7	19.8	30.1	11.5	9.9	•	•
Salaries and Wages 11	18.6	•	7.0	15.1	13.2	•	15.1	20.9	31.7	30.6	31.7	•	•
Taxes Paid 12	3.7	•	4.4	3.7	2.2	•	3.9	3.1	3.0	4.8	5.2	•	•
Interest Paid 13	2.8	•	0.5	1.3	1.2	•	2.3	2.2	1.3	4.7	10.5	•	•
Depreciation 14	4.7	•	2.1	2.6	3.5	•	4.8	4.8	3.2	11.1	10.2	•	•
Amortization and Depletion 15	0.6	•	0.0	0.4	0.1	•	0.2	0.2	0.2	0.5	3.3	•	•
Pensions and Other Deferred Comp. 16	0.4	•	0.2	0.5	0.2	•	0.7	0.4	0.4	1.2	0.3	•	•
Employee Benefits 17	2.5	•	1.8	1.3	1.2	•	2.0	4.1	7.2	2.3	2.8	•	•
Advertising 18	0.3	•	0.4	0.8	0.1	•	0.2	0.1	0.1	0.1	0.6	•	•
Other Expenses 19	29.4	•	33.2	36.2	25.4	•	29.5	42.5	20.4	38.2	34.6	•	•
Officers' Compensation 20	2.1	•	6.3	2.4	1.5	•	3.5	1.7	0.6	1.2	0.2	•	•
Operating Margin 21	•	•	•	0.4	2.4	•	0.3	0.1	1.8	•	•	•	•
Operating Margin Before Officers' Comp. 22	1.1	•	4.2	2.8	4.0	•	3.7	1.8	2.4	•	•	•	•

Selected Average Balance Sheet ($ in Thousands)

Net Receivables 23	318	·	21	144	253	·	2402	7102	14049	16810	100419
Inventories 24	47	·	3	7	48	·	607	291	1442	1599	2832
Net Property, Plant and Equipment 25	931	·	58	245	978	·	6592	18572	33920	70447	267860
Total Assets 26	2466	·	116	700	2040	·	15051	36781	73229	162463	990169
Notes and Loans Payable 27	1103	·	69	336	772	·	5595	15041	22328	49618	531950
All Other Liabilities 28	624	·	30	157	503	·	2837	6387	15118	43401	296152
Net Worth 29	739	·	17	207	764	·	6619	15353	35783	69444	162067

Selected Financial Ratios (Times to 1)

Current Ratio 30	1.4	·	0.8	1.8	2.3	·	1.5	1.3	1.7	1.4	1.2
Quick Ratio 31	1.1	·	0.7	1.5	1.9	·	1.1	1.0	1.2	1.0	1.1
Net Sales to Working Capital 32	11.9	·	·	10.1	8.6	·	7.6	14.2	10.2	7.1	9.0
Coverage Ratio 33	1.6	·	·	2.0	5.2	·	2.6	2.3	4.5	0.5	0.6
Total Asset Turnover 34	1.0	·	4.2	2.1	1.6	·	1.0	1.0	1.4	0.4	0.4
Inventory Turnover 35	18.5	·	81.4	68.9	32.8	·	8.9	26.0	21.6	4.8	12.4
Receivables Turnover 36	7.4	·	25.9	9.7	13.7	·	6.0	6.4	8.3	3.4	3.1
Total Liabilities to Net Worth 37	2.3	·	5.7	2.4	1.7	·	1.3	1.4	1.0	1.3	5.1
Current Assets to Working Capital 38	3.5	·	·	2.3	1.8	·	2.9	4.3	2.5	3.7	5.2
Current Liabilities to Working Capital 39	2.5	·	·	1.3	0.8	·	1.9	3.3	1.5	2.7	4.2
Working Capital to Net Sales 40	0.1	·	·	0.1	0.1	·	0.1	0.1	0.1	0.1	0.1
Inventory to Working Capital 41	0.2	·	·	0.1	0.1	·	0.3	0.2	0.2	0.1	0.1
Total Receipts to Cash Flow 42	5.3	·	6.9	5.4	4.5	·	4.9	3.0	6.4	4.0	5.4
Cost of Goods to Cash Flow 43	1.9	·	3.2	1.9	2.2	·	1.8	0.6	1.9	0.5	0.5
Cash Flow to Total Debt 44	0.3	·	0.7	0.5	0.6	·	0.3	0.6	0.4	0.2	0.1

Selected Financial Factors (in Percentages)

Debt Ratio 45	70.1	·	85.1	70.4	62.5	·	56.0	58.3	51.1	57.3	83.6
Return on Total Assets 46	4.3	·	·	5.1	9.5	·	5.8	5.3	8.1	1.0	2.2
Return on Equity Before Income Taxes 47	5.2	·	·	8.5	20.5	·	8.2	7.1	12.9	·	·
Return on Equity After Income Taxes 48	3.9	·	·	7.8	19.1	·	6.8	5.8	9.5	·	·
Profit Margin (Before Income Tax) 49	1.6	·	·	1.2	4.8	·	3.8	2.8	4.5	·	·
Profit Margin (After Income Tax) 50	1.2	·	·	1.1	4.5	·	3.1	2.3	3.3	·	·

Table II
Corporations with Net Income

WAREHOUSING AND STORAGE

MONEY AMOUNTS AND SIZE OF ASSETS IN THOUSANDS OF DOLLARS

Item Description for Accounting Period 7/02 Through 6/03	Total	Zero Assets	Under 100	100 to 250	251 to 500	501 to 1,000	1,001 to 5,000	5,001 to 10,000	10,001 to 25,000	25,001 to 50,000	50,001 to 100,000	100,001 to 250,000	250,001 and over
Number of Enterprises **1**	4375	658	2042	740	707	122	63	16	0	0	0	0	0
Revenues ($ in Thousands)													
Net Sales **2**	12851285	5138	1473715	1029275	2841863	2072240	1059073	754208	0	0	0	0	0
Interest **3**	43868	484	101	3582	1952	2784	2368	611	0	0	0	0	0
Rents **4**	19169	0	0	118	618	2572	3532	1301	0	0	0	0	0
Royalties **5**	76	0	0	0	0	0	76	0	0	0	0	0	0
Other Portfolio Income **6**	49117	2782	128	251	1393	4272	8505	999	0	0	0	0	0
Other Receipts **7**	164852	21	3	5547	34518	30068	32680	12101	0	0	0	0	0
Total Receipts **8**	13128367	8425	1473947	1038773	2880344	2111936	1106234	769220	0	0	0	0	0
Average Total Receipts **9**	3001	13	722	1404	4074	17311	17559	48076	•	•	•	•	•
Operating Costs/Operating Income (%)													
Cost of Operations **10**	39.6	•	44.2	46.1	49.8	58.7	42.0	21.5	•	•	•	•	•
Salaries and Wages **11**	16.2	•	4.1	12.5	11.6	9.2	13.1	18.8	•	•	•	•	•
Taxes Paid **12**	3.2	0.7	2.0	3.1	1.9	3.7	3.7	2.8	•	•	•	•	•
Interest Paid **13**	2.2	12.6	0.5	1.4	0.7	0.8	1.8	2.1	•	•	•	•	•
Depreciation **14**	4.1	6.5	1.4	2.6	2.6	2.2	4.1	4.7	•	•	•	•	•
Amortization and Depletion **15**	0.5	2.1	•	0.6	0.2	0.0	0.1	0.1	•	•	•	•	•
Pensions and Other Deferred Comp. **16**	0.3	•	•	0.7	0.1	0.2	0.1	0.3	•	•	•	•	•
Employee Benefits **17**	2.5	•	1.1	1.6	1.3	1.1	1.4	3.8	•	•	•	•	•
Advertising **18**	0.2	•	0.3	0.9	0.1	0.0	0.2	0.1	•	•	•	•	•
Other Expenses **19**	25.7	44.3	35.3	23.2	23.8	19.9	25.9	41.9	•	•	•	•	•
Officers' Compensation **20**	2.0	•	6.9	2.4	1.2	1.6	3.4	1.4	•	•	•	•	•
Operating Margin **21**	3.5	33.8	4.1	4.9	6.6	2.7	3.6	2.4	•	•	•	•	•
Operating Margin Before Officers' Comp. **22**	5.5	33.8	11.0	7.2	7.8	4.3	7.0	3.8	•	•	•	•	•

Selected Average Balance Sheet ($ in Thousands)

Net Receivables 23	353	0	24	124	290	983	2481	7656
Inventories 24	44	0	5	11	37	476	753	259
Net Property, Plant and Equipment 25	1043	0	65	291	956	2369	6452	22412
Total Assets 26	2572	0	134	707	1992	7138	15072	40353
Notes and Loans Payable 27	956	0	82	372	523	3445	5412	16280
All Other Liabilities 28	704	0	15	151	690	1716	2919	6526
Net Worth 29	912	0	37	184	779	1976	6742	17547

Selected Financial Ratios (Times to 1)

Current Ratio 30	1.6	•	1.4	2.0	2.3	1.2	1.7	1.2
Quick Ratio 31	1.3	•	1.2	1.7	1.9	0.7	1.2	0.9
Net Sales to Working Capital 32	8.8	•	40.9	8.3	9.1	32.9	6.7	20.7
Coverage Ratio 33	3.6	8.8	9.1	5.0	11.7	7.1	5.4	3.1
Total Asset Turnover 34	1.1	•	5.4	2.0	2.0	2.4	1.1	1.2
Inventory Turnover 35	26.6	•	62.5	58.9	54.0	20.9	9.4	39.1
Receivables Turnover 36	9.9	•	31.8	8.0	14.6	15.3	6.8	8.0
Total Liabilities to Net Worth 37	1.8	•	2.6	2.8	1.6	2.6	1.2	1.3
Current Assets to Working Capital 38	2.6	•	3.5	2.0	1.8	7.4	2.5	5.5
Current Liabilities to Working Capital 39	1.6	•	2.5	1.0	0.8	6.4	1.5	4.5
Working Capital to Net Sales 40	0.1	•	0.0	0.1	0.1	0.0	0.1	0.0
Inventory to Working Capital 41	0.2	•	0.1	0.1	0.1	1.6	0.3	0.2
Total Receipts to Cash Flow 42	4.9	1.3	4.8	4.7	4.0	9.2	4.4	2.8
Cost of Goods to Cash Flow 43	1.9	•	2.1	2.2	2.0	5.4	1.8	0.6
Cash Flow to Total Debt 44	0.4	•	1.5	0.6	0.8	0.4	0.5	0.7

Selected Financial Factors (in Percentages)

Debt Ratio 45	64.5	•	72.2	74.0	60.9	72.3	55.3	56.5
Return on Total Assets 46	9.0	•	24.8	14.2	17.5	12.8	11.0	7.5
Return on Equity Before Income Taxes 47	18.2	•	79.4	43.6	40.9	39.8	20.1	11.7
Return on Equity After Income Taxes 48	16.4	•	75.2	42.5	38.8	37.1	18.0	10.0
Profit Margin (Before Income Tax) 49	5.6	97.7	4.1	5.8	7.9	4.6	8.1	4.4
Profit Margin (After Income Tax) 50	5.1	86.3	3.9	5.6	7.5	4.3	7.2	3.7

Table I

Corporations with and without Net Income

NEWSPAPER PUBLISHERS

MONEY AMOUNTS AND SIZE OF ASSETS IN THOUSANDS OF DOLLARS

Item Description for Accounting Period 7/02 Through 6/03		Total	Zero Assets	Under 500	500 to 1,000	1,000 to 5,000	5,000 to 10,000	10,000 to 25,000	25,000 to 50,000	50,000 to 100,000	100,000 to 250,000	250,000 to 500,000	500,000 to 2,500,000	2,500,000 and over
Number of Enterprises	1	7121	1124	4869	626	251	55	82	39	26	13	8	19	9
Revenues ($ in Thousands)														
Net Sales	2	47963721	120436	1941548	774382	1342839	577237	1538678	1294680	1425857	1691228	1734046	10245729	25277062
Interest	3	517884	31	558	1105	1980	252	4407	3253	4013	11170	8996	185201	296919
Rents	4	139608	0	116	0	0	1078	1880	2476	3243	6001	10618	20146	94051
Royalties	5	700671	0	0	0	0	0	38	1377	54	0	1693	80727	616782
Other Portfolio Income	6	314976	0	349	264	9274	412	26440	7087	6807	60057	21054	75528	107700
Other Receipts	7	1766563	2188	7165	940	13830	14944	30839	77236	27900	30533	8668	460681	1091639
Total Receipts	8	51403423	122655	1949736	776691	1367923	593923	1602282	1386109	1467874	1798989	1785075	11068012	27484153
Average Total Receipts	9	7219	109	400	1241	5450	10799	19540	35541	56457	138384	223134	582527	3053795
Operating Costs/Operating Income (%)														
Cost of Operations	10	25.2	88.1	32.3	43.8	35.0	39.3	25.4	31.0	36.8	22.2	31.9	16.4	25.2
Salaries and Wages	11	23.9	1.6	19.7	16.8	16.2	23.3	25.4	26.1	16.8	28.4	20.9	26.9	23.9
Taxes Paid	12	3.4	0.4	3.2	3.9	3.0	3.4	3.8	3.8	3.2	3.6	4.0	3.9	3.2
Interest Paid	13	4.1	0.3	1.5	1.0	1.3	0.4	1.6	2.8	3.3	2.3	3.8	6.6	4.1
Depreciation	14	5.1	0.1	1.2	1.9	3.8	3.0	4.3	4.6	5.6	7.5	8.0	6.0	5.0
Amortization and Depletion	15	2.9	0.1	0.0	1.5	0.3	0.4	1.1	1.9	1.9	2.8	4.3	6.3	2.2
Pensions and Other Deferred Comp.	16	2.2	0.1	0.1	0.6	0.2	0.9	1.0	1.5	0.7	1.1	0.8	2.7	2.8
Employee Benefits	17	2.9	0.1	1.0	2.7	1.0	2.1	3.0	2.9	2.8	2.6	2.4	3.6	3.0
Advertising	18	1.8	0.2	0.7	0.6	2.5	0.4	4.2	1.5	0.7	2.0	1.7	2.0	1.7
Other Expenses	19	25.1	17.5	30.5	18.0	31.7	14.9	24.5	24.8	21.2	26.1	16.9	24.8	25.6
Officers' Compensation	20	1.9	0.2	8.0	3.1	2.7	5.4	3.4	1.9	2.0	1.4	1.2	1.3	1.5
Operating Margin	21	1.5	•	1.9	6.3	2.3	6.5	2.5	•	5.0	•	4.1	•	1.9
Operating Margin Before Officers' Comp.	22	3.4	•	9.8	9.4	5.0	11.9	5.9	•	7.0	1.4	5.3	0.8	3.4

Selected Average Balance Sheet ($ in Thousands)

Net Receivables 23	971	0	23	126	439	911	2517	4117	8913	16855	25890	86695	432273
Inventories 24	90	0	2	12	28	220	264	529	729	2003	4209	8556	35314
Net Property, Plant and Equipment 25	2256	0	26	151	777	1547	4246	9937	19940	53552	104899	207784	981221
Total Assets 26	12019	0	101	760	2176	6370	16351	36128	70356	166503	353126	1160677	5789488
Notes and Loans Payable 27	3868	0	38	326	953	1180	4833	13315	26789	42298	110389	495065	1600326
All Other Liabilities 28	2571	0	49	106	638	1276	4001	7169	15822	34123	64175	72318	1602796
Net Worth 29	5580	0	14	328	586	3914	7517	15644	27745	90082	178562	593294	2586366

Selected Financial Ratios (Times to 1)

Current Ratio 30	1.0	•	1.5	2.2	1.3	1.9	1.5	1.5	1.0	2.6	1.4	1.4	0.7
Quick Ratio 31	0.7	•	1.4	2.1	1.1	1.4	1.2	1.1	0.8	2.1	1.1	1.0	0.5
Net Sales to Working Capital 32	•	•	24.1	8.3	31.3	9.5	8.9	10.4	141.9	4.4	14.7	11.0	•
Coverage Ratio 33	3.1	•	2.5	7.6	4.2	25.3	5.2	2.5	3.4	3.8	2.8	2.2	3.7
Total Asset Turnover 34	0.6	•	4.0	1.6	2.5	1.6	1.1	0.9	0.8	0.8	0.6	0.5	0.5
Inventory Turnover 35	18.9	•	62.1	44.8	66.5	18.8	18.1	19.5	27.7	14.4	16.4	10.4	20.0
Receivables Turnover 36	7.5	•	17.1	11.7	12.4	10.9	7.5	8.0	5.9	8.5	6.4	7.0	7.3
Total Liabilities to Net Worth 37	1.2	•	6.3	1.3	2.7	0.6	1.2	1.3	1.5	0.8	1.0	1.0	1.2
Current Assets to Working Capital 38	•	•	2.8	1.8	4.8	2.2	2.8	3.1	49.7	1.6	3.6	3.7	•
Current Liabilities to Working Capital 39	•	•	1.8	0.8	3.8	1.2	1.8	2.1	48.7	0.6	2.6	2.7	•
Working Capital to Net Sales 40	•	•	0.0	0.0	0.0	0.1	0.1	0.1	0.0	0.2	0.1	0.1	•
Inventory to Working Capital 41	•	•	0.1	0.1	0.1	0.2	0.1	0.2	2.1	0.1	0.2	0.2	•
Total Receipts to Cash Flow 42	3.3	13.7	3.5	5.1	3.1	4.6	3.8	3.8	3.8	3.9	4.7	3.4	3.0
Cost of Goods to Cash Flow 43	0.8	12.1	1.1	2.2	1.1	1.8	1.0	1.2	1.4	0.9	1.5	0.6	0.8
Cash Flow to Total Debt 44	0.3	•	1.3	0.6	1.1	0.9	0.6	0.4	0.3	0.4	0.3	0.3	0.3

Selected Financial Factors (in Percentages)

Debt Ratio 45	53.6	•	86.3	56.9	73.1	38.6	54.0	56.7	60.6	45.9	49.4	48.9	55.3
Return on Total Assets 46	7.2	•	15.1	12.3	13.3	16.1	9.3	6.5	8.8	6.7	6.7	6.6	7.2
Return on Equity Before Income Taxes 47	10.6	•	65.8	24.8	37.7	25.1	16.4	8.9	15.8	9.1	8.6	7.0	11.7
Return on Equity After Income Taxes 48	7.1	•	63.9	24.7	32.9	24.1	14.5	6.4	12.8	6.3	6.3	4.0	7.8
Profit Margin (Before Income Tax) 49	8.8	•	2.3	6.6	4.1	9.4	6.6	4.2	8.0	6.3	7.0	7.7	10.8
Profit Margin (After Income Tax) 50	5.9	•	2.2	6.5	3.6	9.0	5.8	3.0	6.5	4.3	4.3	4.4	7.2

Table II

Corporations with Net Income

NEWSPAPER PUBLISHERS

MONEY AMOUNTS AND SIZE OF ASSETS IN THOUSANDS OF DOLLARS

Item Description for Accounting Period 7/02 Through 6/03	Total	Zero Assets	Under 500	500 to 1,000	1,000 to 5,000	5,000 to 10,000	10,000 to 25,000	25,000 to 50,000	50,000 to 100,000	100,000 to 250,000	250,000 to 500,000	500,000 to 2,500,000	2,500,000 and over
Number of Enterprises **1**	4176	848	2589	351	188	55	63	27	19	10	5	0	0
Revenues ($ in Thousands)													
Net Sales **2**	38727044	109749	1205677	580964	641471	577237	1280090	947425	1192522	1273391	1188107	0	0
Interest **3**	376799	31	549	6	1814	252	2644	2441	2752	9570	8521	0	0
Rents **4**	94572	0	116	0	0	1078	1512	2339	2843	6001	9273	0	0
Royalties **5**	685819	0	0	0	0	0	21	1377	54	0	1693	0	0
Other Portfolio Income **6**	255112	0	349	0	9132	412	26007	6034	5896	59895	13343	0	0
Other Receipts **7**	1617766	2157	658	-14	13593	14944	27891	74692	26534	25638	7924	0	0
Total Receipts **8**	41757112	111937	1207349	580956	666010	593923	1338165	1034308	1230601	1374495	1228861	0	0
Average Total Receipts **9**	9999	132	466	1655	3543	10799	21241	38308	64768	137450	245772	•	•
Operating Costs/Operating Income (%)													
Cost of Operations **10**	25.7	84.7	28.4	48.7	26.1	39.3	25.9	28.0	37.2	23.4	34.3	•	•
Salaries and Wages **11**	23.4	•	21.1	9.8	19.7	23.3	24.6	27.7	15.6	25.6	16.1	•	•
Taxes Paid **12**	3.4	0.1	3.4	3.8	3.5	3.4	3.7	4.1	3.0	3.9	4.3	•	•
Interest Paid **13**	4.0	0.3	1.9	1.3	2.6	0.4	1.2	1.9	2.1	2.4	3.1	•	•
Depreciation **14**	5.1	0.1	1.0	2.3	5.4	3.0	3.9	4.5	5.0	8.1	5.4	•	•
Amortization and Depletion **15**	2.7	•	0.0	2.0	0.3	0.4	0.8	1.0	1.6	2.6	3.9	•	•
Pensions and Other Deferred Comp. **16**	2.5	0.1	0.0	0.5	0.2	0.9	1.1	1.9	0.8	1.2	0.8	•	•
Employee Benefits **17**	2.8	•	0.7	2.6	1.8	2.1	2.9	3.0	2.9	2.5	2.0	•	•
Advertising **18**	1.9	0.2	0.6	0.6	2.2	0.4	4.8	1.6	0.8	1.7	1.9	•	•
Other Expenses **19**	22.2	13.2	24.5	14.9	25.4	14.9	22.2	24.3	21.0	23.4	17.4	•	•
Officers' Compensation **20**	1.9	•	9.8	3.5	4.8	5.4	3.4	2.3	2.2	1.5	1.6	•	•
Operating Margin **21**	4.2	1.4	8.6	10.2	8.1	6.5	5.5	•	8.0	3.8	9.3	•	•
Operating Margin Before Officers' Comp. **22**	6.2	1.4	18.3	13.7	12.9	11.9	8.9	2.0	10.1	5.3	10.8	•	•

Selected Average Balance Sheet ($ in Thousands)

Net Receivables 23	1345	0	26	155	399	911	2487	3958	10080	18004	26309
Inventories 24	121	0	3	22	33	206	276	485	808	1867	3113
Net Property, Plant and Equipment 25	3174	0	39	236	852	1547	4192	11124	20194	58519	88672
Total Assets 26	17432	0	106	794	2145	6370	16691	35977	70591	166775	359440
Notes and Loans Payable 27	5520	0	27	328	1072	1180	3910	9997	22338	43295	99780
All Other Liabilities 28	3421	0	55	104	347	1276	4275	7157	17662	29378	62589
Net Worth 29	8490	0	25	361	726	3914	8507	18824	30591	94102	197070

Selected Financial Ratios (Times to 1)

Current Ratio 30	0.9	•	3.1	2.4	2.0	1.9	1.7	1.9	1.2	2.6	1.4
Quick Ratio 31	0.7	•	3.0	2.2	1.7	1.4	1.4	1.5	1.0	2.1	1.1
Net Sales to Working Capital 32	•	•	11.5	9.1	10.1	9.5	7.7	6.4	21.2	4.3	15.5
Coverage Ratio 33	4.0	12.7	5.6	8.9	5.5	25.3	9.6	5.7	6.2	5.9	5.1
Total Asset Turnover 34	0.5	•	4.4	2.1	1.6	1.6	1.2	1.0	0.9	0.8	0.7
Inventory Turnover 35	19.8	•	49.9	36.2	26.8	20.0	19.1	20.3	28.8	16.0	26.2
Receivables Turnover 36	7.4	•	15.4	21.4	7.8	12.1	8.9	9.5	7.9	8.5	18.1
Total Liabilities to Net Worth 37	1.1	•	3.3	1.2	2.0	0.6	1.0	0.9	1.3	0.8	0.8
Current Assets to Working Capital 38	•	•	1.5	1.7	2.0	2.2	2.4	2.1	7.6	1.6	3.4
Current Liabilities to Working Capital 39	•	•	0.5	0.7	1.0	1.2	1.4	1.1	6.6	0.6	2.4
Working Capital to Net Sales 40	•	•	0.1	0.1	0.1	0.1	0.1	0.2	0.0	0.2	0.1
Inventory to Working Capital 41	•	•	0.0	0.1	0.1	0.2	0.1	0.1	0.3	0.1	0.2
Total Receipts to Cash Flow 42	3.2	6.0	3.6	4.8	2.9	4.6	3.6	3.3	3.4	3.6	3.6
Cost of Goods to Cash Flow 43	0.8	5.1	1.0	2.4	0.8	1.8	0.9	0.9	1.3	0.8	1.2
Cash Flow to Total Debt 44	0.3	•	1.6	0.8	0.8	0.9	0.7	0.6	0.5	0.5	0.4

Selected Financial Factors (in Percentages)

Debt Ratio 45	51.3	•	76.8	54.5	66.1	38.6	49.0	47.7	56.7	43.6	45.2
Return on Total Assets 46	8.6	•	46.4	24.0	23.1	16.1	13.6	10.4	11.8	10.8	10.5
Return on Equity Before Income Taxes 47	13.2	•	164.3	46.8	55.9	25.1	23.9	16.3	22.9	15.8	15.3
Return on Equity After Income Taxes 48	9.4	•	162.3	46.7	50.8	24.1	21.7	13.3	19.3	12.3	10.6
Profit Margin (Before Income Tax) 49	12.1	3.4	8.7	10.2	11.9	9.4	8.8	8.8	11.2	11.7	12.7
Profit Margin (After Income Tax) 50	8.6	3.2	8.6	10.2	10.8	9.0	9.1	7.1	9.4	9.1	8.8

Table I

Corporations with and without Net Income

PERIODICAL PUBLISHERS

MONEY AMOUNTS AND SIZE OF ASSETS IN THOUSANDS OF DOLLARS

Item Description for Accounting Period 7/02 Through 6/03	Total	Zero Assets	Under 500	500 to 1,000	1,000 to 5,000	5,000 to 10,000	10,000 to 25,000	25,000 to 50,000	50,000 to 100,000	100,000 to 250,000	250,000 to 500,000	500,000 to 2,500,000	2,500,000 and over
Number of Enterprises **1**	8453	2066	5025	391	715	119	67	30	11	10	10	9	0
Revenues ($ in Thousands)													
Net Sales **2**	21349155	187965	2502419	359401	4253268	1216702	1705251	1240591	803591	1178348	2198341	5703279	0
Interest **3**	223645	812	914	3132	3537	3938	5505	4177	5773	4572	32174	159111	0
Rents **4**	36196	0	1312	0	656	5669	673	612	2783	3533	11627	9331	0
Royalties **5**	280627	302	46	0	5	1	5	398	2822	1406	118234	157407	0
Other Portfolio Income **6**	434427	2060	887	2	707	14499	1875	4198	4700	304598	45571	55333	0
Other Receipts **7**	489827	2727	942	5338	108735	61940	13578	8994	25689	80207	35944	145729	0
Total Receipts **8**	22813877	193866	2506520	367873	4366908	1302749	1726887	1258970	845358	1572664	2441891	6230190	0
Average Total Receipts **9**	2699	94	499	941	6108	10947	25774	41966	76851	157266	244189	692243	•
Operating Costs/Operating Income (%)													
Cost of Operations **10**	40.0	49.4	36.2	11.8	52.1	40.5	43.5	34.6	49.9	41.1	40.5	32.4	•
Salaries and Wages **11**	18.1	14.5	21.3	25.1	16.5	17.3	16.6	19.1	12.8	21.9	19.9	17.1	•
Taxes Paid **12**	2.2	2.0	2.7	3.3	2.1	2.3	2.4	2.2	1.5	2.8	2.5	1.8	•
Interest Paid **13**	4.1	0.9	0.5	1.3	0.6	2.1	1.4	1.8	4.5	2.9	5.3	10.0	•
Depreciation **14**	2.3	3.4	0.9	1.2	1.2	2.8	1.8	2.5	1.5	2.6	4.9	2.9	•
Amortization and Depletion **15**	2.5	0.1	0.0	2.5	0.9	1.1	1.0	1.6	1.8	2.8	3.9	5.2	•
Pensions and Other Deferred Comp. **16**	0.6	0.1	0.2	•	0.5	1.2	0.4	0.4	0.5	1.4	1.0	0.6	•
Employee Benefits **17**	1.7	0.3	0.8	1.9	1.9	1.4	1.7	2.2	1.2	1.9	2.1	2.0	•
Advertising **18**	1.9	1.7	1.1	0.3	1.4	0.6	1.6	1.6	1.5	2.5	6.4	1.4	•
Other Expenses **19**	26.8	28.9	26.8	42.6	17.6	23.0	22.6	28.4	21.6	29.2	22.8	35.9	•
Officers' Compensation **20**	4.5	1.4	8.6	10.8	4.1	19.2	3.0	2.4	1.5	9.0	2.3	0.7	•
Operating Margin **21**	•	•	0.8	•	1.0	•	4.1	3.3	1.6	•	•	•	•
Operating Margin Before Officers' Comp. **22**	•	•	9.5	10.1	5.1	7.7	7.0	5.7	3.1	•	•	•	•

Selected Average Balance Sheet ($ in Thousands)

Net Receivables 23	338	0	21	320	718	990	2740	6995	11450	19602	30317	108439
Inventories 24	69	0	7	3	81	399	800	1147	4052	3651	4981	12041
Net Property, Plant and Equipment 25	205	0	11	45	255	1240	2447	4771	6131	21749	20284	59123
Total Assets 26	3922	103	791	2387	7208	15902	35557	72151	159922	362204	2401870	
Notes and Loans Payable 27	1344	56	174	684	3022	4635	13061	22380	40956	103914	863147	
All Other Liabilities 28	895	57	228	1400	3139	7767	18880	33591	53676	99609	313926	
Net Worth 29	1683	-10	389	303	1046	3500	3615	16179	65290	158681	1224797	

Selected Financial Ratios (Times to 1)

Current Ratio 30	1.0	1.0	1.6	1.1	1.1	1.1	1.0	1.6	1.6	1.7	0.7	
Quick Ratio 31	0.7	0.7	1.5	0.8	0.9	0.7	0.7	1.0	1.1	1.2	1.3	0.4
Net Sales to Working Capital 32	•	140.6	5.6	42.6	30.0	27.8	51.3	5.4	5.5	5.6	•	
Coverage Ratio 33	1.6	1.5	2.9	2.2	7.0	•	4.9	3.5	1.2	2.4	6.3	1.0
Total Asset Turnover 34	0.6	•	4.8	1.2	2.5	1.4	1.6	1.2	1.0	0.7	0.6	0.3
Inventory Turnover 35	14.6	27.1	39.1	38.1	10.4	13.8	12.5	9.0	13.3	17.9	17.1	
Receivables Turnover 36	6.7	30.5	4.0	9.0	8.2	9.0	6.4	5.6	6.1	7.0	8.1	
Total Liabilities to Net Worth 37	1.3	•	1.0	•	5.9	3.5	8.8	3.5	1.4	1.3	1.0	
Current Assets to Working Capital 38	•	23.5	2.6	10.4	8.9	8.8	22.8	2.6	2.8	2.5	•	
Current Liabilities to Working Capital 39	•	22.5	1.6	9.4	7.9	7.8	21.8	1.6	1.8	1.5	•	
Working Capital to Net Sales 40	0.0	0.0	0.2	0.0	0.0	0.0	0.0	0.2	0.2	0.2	0.2	
Inventory to Working Capital 41	•	2.2	0.0	0.6	1.0	0.9	1.7	0.2	0.2	0.1	•	
Total Receipts to Cash Flow 42	4.2	4.3	2.5	5.4	7.1	4.0	3.3	3.9	6.8	6.0	3.2	
Cost of Goods to Cash Flow 43	1.7	1.6	0.3	2.8	2.9	1.7	1.1	1.9	2.8	2.4	1.0	
Cash Flow to Total Debt 44	0.3	1.0	0.9	0.5	0.2	0.5	0.4	0.3	0.2	0.2	0.2	

Selected Financial Factors (in Percentages)

Debt Ratio 45	57.1	109.9	50.8	87.3	85.5	78.0	89.8	77.6	59.2	56.2	49.0	
Return on Total Assets 46	4.2	7.5	3.4	10.8	•	10.9	7.5	11.2	13.3	3.3	2.6	
Return on Equity Before Income Taxes 47	3.6	•	3.9	72.6	•	39.6	52.7	29.6	27.4	0.1	•	
Return on Equity After Income Taxes 48	2.0	•	3.6	65.8	•	36.2	45.3	22.5	16.0	•	•	
Profit Margin (Before Income Tax) 49	2.4	0.4	1.6	3.7	•	5.4	4.6	6.5	15.2	0.1	•	
Profit Margin (After Income Tax) 50	1.3	0.4	1.5	3.4	•	5.0	4.0	5.0	8.8	•	•	

Table II

Corporations with Net Income

PERIODICAL PUBLISHERS

MONEY AMOUNTS AND SIZE OF ASSETS IN THOUSANDS OF DOLLARS

Item Description for Accounting Period 7/02 Through 6/03	Total	Zero Assets	Under 500	500 to 1,000	1,000 to 5,000	5,000 to 10,000	10,000 to 25,000	25,000 to 50,000	50,000 to 100,000	100,000 to 250,000	250,000 to 500,000	500,000 to 2,500,000	2,500,000 and over
Number of Enterprises 1	4926	1272	2811	204	477	74	43	19	8	7	7	4	0
Revenues ($ in Thousands)													
Net Sales 2	13855487	167717	1223677	144298	2636424	796140	1310145	1041740	707172	843151	1392572	3592452	0
Interest 3	179083	405	181	2981	3093	2769	1795	2460	5541	3678	7899	148280	0
Rents 4	26935	0	0	0	656	5654	641	431	2783	3000	4491	9279	0
Royalties 5	235349	0	0	0	0	0	0	388	2562	1406	100283	130711	0
Other Portfolio Income 6	376269	2060	842	0	576	12846	1040	1994	2369	303057	23747	27736	0
Other Receipts 7	370186	2631	302	14	80723	55045	10004	5877	23945	74042	28848	88755	0
Total Receipts 8	15043309	172813	1225002	147293	2721472	872454	1323625	1052890	744372	1228334	1557840	3997213	0
Average Total Receipts 9	3054	136	436	722	5705	11790	30782	55415	93046	175476	222549	999303	•
Operating Costs/Operating Income (%)													
Cost of Operations 10	38.5	45.8	30.0	2.9	41.0	33.3	43.1	37.3	53.8	37.1	41.3	36.7	•
Salaries and Wages 11	16.6	14.4	11.7	12.7	20.9	13.8	16.1	17.2	12.1	21.9	19.7	14.5	•
Taxes Paid 12	2.3	2.0	2.5	1.9	2.7	2.1	2.4	2.3	1.4	2.8	2.3	2.0	•
Interest Paid 13	2.7	0.0	0.5	3.3	0.5	0.6	0.6	1.4	4.8	1.6	2.7	6.5	•
Depreciation 14	2.3	3.1	1.6	0.2	1.5	2.2	1.5	2.4	1.5	3.0	4.9	2.3	•
Amortization and Depletion 15	1.5	•	0.0	5.9	0.3	0.6	0.5	1.2	1.8	0.9	1.9	3.5	•
Pensions and Other Deferred Comp. 16	0.8	0.1	0.4	•	0.5	1.8	0.5	0.4	0.4	1.7	1.2	0.9	•
Employee Benefits 17	1.8	0.3	0.8	0.0	2.4	1.0	1.6	2.2	1.3	2.0	2.7	1.7	•
Advertising 18	2.0	1.4	0.3	0.3	2.1	0.6	1.6	1.3	1.6	2.4	6.9	1.3	•
Other Expenses 19	25.8	26.6	28.7	55.9	19.5	18.9	19.4	25.6	16.9	30.0	17.4	36.3	•
Officers' Compensation 20	5.1	0.6	11.7	7.1	3.5	28.2	3.2	2.6	1.3	11.1	2.4	0.7	•
Operating Margin 21	0.6	5.6	11.8	9.9	5.0	•	9.5	6.1	3.0	•	•	•	•
Operating Margin Before Officers' Comp. 22	5.7	6.3	23.5	17.0	8.6	25.1	12.7	8.7	4.3	•	•	•	•

Selected Average Balance Sheet ($ in Thousands)

	•	•	•	•	•	•	•	•	•	•	•	•
Net Receivables 23	405	0	17	335	729	839	2574	9503	13430	19638	27309	184895
Inventories 24	87	0	11	0	103	433	877	1449	4865	4760	5723	35013
Net Property, Plant and Equipment 25	238	0	12	8	262	1202	2373	5920	7763	20813	21041	88575
Total Assets 26	5182	0	106	926	2252	7235	15828	35387	74962	147435	360340	4481244
Notes and Loans Payable 27	1132	0	16	332	529	1179	3658	11246	24381	15325	62090	1003892
All Other Liabilities 28	1185	0	50	36	1080	3560	7604	24660	40370	49218	104456	678794
Net Worth 29	2866	0	40	557	643	2495	4565	-519	10211	82893	193794	2798556

Selected Financial Ratios (Times to 1)

	•	•	•	•	•	•	•	•	•	•	•	•
Current Ratio 30	1.3	•	1.8	3.3	1.5	1.6	1.2	1.0	1.7	2.3	1.9	1.0
Quick Ratio 31	1.0	•	1.3	3.3	1.2	1.4	0.8	0.7	1.0	1.9	1.6	0.6
Net Sales to Working Capital 32	11.2	187.4	10.8	2.7	11.0	8.1	17.9	70.4	5.8	3.2	4.5	•
Coverage Ratio 33	4.6	•	23.1	4.7	17.7	11.1	18.5	6.1	2.7	19.8	4.3	1.9
Total Asset Turnover 34	0.5	•	4.1	0.8	2.5	1.5	1.9	1.5	1.2	0.8	0.6	0.2
Inventory Turnover 35	12.4	•	11.6	•	22.1	8.3	15.0	14.1	9.8	9.4	14.3	9.4
Receivables Turnover 36	6.6	•	29.4	4.2	8.5	11.7	11.5	7.5	6.8	6.0	7.5	9.7
Total Liabilities to Net Worth 37	0.8	•	1.6	0.7	2.5	1.9	2.5	•	6.3	0.8	0.9	0.6
Current Assets to Working Capital 38	4.0	•	2.2	1.4	2.9	2.6	5.2	25.0	2.5	1.8	2.1	•
Current Liabilities to Working Capital 39	3.0	•	1.2	0.4	1.9	1.6	4.2	24.0	1.5	0.8	1.1	•
Working Capital to Net Sales 40	0.1	•	0.1	0.4	0.1	0.1	0.1	0.0	0.2	0.3	0.2	•
Inventory to Working Capital 41	0.4	•	0.3	•	0.2	0.3	0.5	2.4	0.2	0.1	0.1	•
Total Receipts to Cash Flow 42	3.4	3.3	2.7	1.5	4.1	4.5	3.6	3.3	4.5	4.4	4.7	2.6
Cost of Goods to Cash Flow 43	1.3	1.5	0.8	0.0	1.7	1.5	1.6	1.2	2.4	1.6	1.9	1.0
Cash Flow to Total Debt 44	0.4	•	2.4	1.2	0.8	0.5	0.7	0.5	0.3	0.4	0.3	0.2

Selected Financial Factors (in Percentages)

	•	•	•	•	•	•	•	•	•	•	•	•
Debt Ratio 45	44.7	•	62.2	39.8	71.4	65.5	71.2	101.5	86.4	43.8	46.2	37.5
Return on Total Assets 46	6.6	•	51.2	11.7	21.4	10.0	21.8	13.2	15.5	26.5	6.4	2.5
Return on Equity Before Income Taxes 47	9.4	•	129.8	15.2	70.9	26.5	71.4	•	71.7	44.8	9.1	2.0
Return on Equity After Income Taxes 48	7.7	•	129.7	14.9	66.1	21.4	67.3	•	56.4	31.9	6.7	1.4
Profit Margin (Before Income Tax) 49	9.5	8.7	11.9	12.0	8.2	6.1	10.7	7.1	8.3	30.8	8.9	6.1
Profit Margin (After Income Tax) 50	7.9	8.7	11.9	11.7	7.7	5.0	10.1	6.4	6.5	21.9	6.6	4.2

Table I

Corporations with and without Net Income

BOOK PUBLISHERS

MONEY AMOUNTS AND SIZE OF ASSETS IN THOUSANDS OF DOLLARS

Item Description for Accounting Period 7/02 Through 6/03	Total	Zero Assets	Under 500	500 to 1,000	1,000 to 5,000	5,000 to 10,000	10,000 to 25,000	25,000 to 50,000	50,000 to 100,000	100,000 to 250,000	250,000 to 500,000	500,000 to 2,500,000	2,500,000 and over
Number of Enterprises 1	6021	950	4534	92	306	37	54	18	5	13	3	4	5
Revenues ($ in Thousands)													
Net Sales 2	23139491	26678	150302	107494	682274	505303	1065448	694039	404595	1511536	552981	2520937	14917904
Interest 3	719482	31	1192	1900	111	25	996	1577	393	6614	5638	13494	687513
Rents 4	69550	0	0	0	0	1664	918	449	0	271	0	4000	62248
Royalties 5	304633	0	0	0	27129	0	1628	17925	200	17703	4579	50353	185117
Other Portfolio Income 6	214402	0	144	4241	2252	25	2089	568	448	19673	107	19392	165461
Other Receipts 7	718422	2218	60159	4003	14915	722	13303	17401	8255	66658	29425	59796	441564
Total Receipts 8	25165980	28927	211797	117638	726681	507739	1084382	731959	413891	1622455	592730	2667972	16459807
Average Total Receipts 9	4180	30	47	1279	2375	13723	20081	40664	82778	124804	197577	666993	3291961
Operating Costs/Operating Income (%)													
Cost of Operations 10	28.2	32.4	38.0	42.5	46.4	16.9	45.9	47.1	48.6	34.7	43.3	41.4	21.3
Salaries and Wages 11	21.8	31.2	12.2	3.5	9.8	34.0	16.2	17.0	16.9	18.4	16.7	17.4	24.2
Taxes Paid 12	2.5	3.9	3.1	2.9	1.3	3.7	2.1	2.1	2.0	1.5	2.0	2.8	2.7
Interest Paid 13	6.6	0.9	0.1	3.1	1.8	0.6	1.1	1.2	0.6	4.8	8.1	3.1	8.7
Depreciation 14	4.7	0.4	4.3	1.3	1.2	3.9	2.1	2.1	1.8	1.3	1.7	4.0	5.8
Amortization and Depletion 15	2.9	0.1	•	0.0	1.7	0.0	1.6	1.7	0.2	4.6	6.4	2.3	3.1
Pensions and Other Deferred Comp. 16	0.9	0.3	0.0	•	1.2	1.1	0.6	0.6	0.8	0.7	0.7	0.8	1.1
Employee Benefits 17	2.2	0.9	1.0	1.7	0.8	3.9	1.3	1.5	1.2	2.0	2.5	2.6	2.3
Advertising 18	3.0	5.1	2.2	2.1	1.2	2.8	3.2	3.6	3.7	2.8	4.8	1.8	3.2
Other Expenses 19	29.4	51.8	38.2	29.9	25.9	24.3	20.4	19.5	15.3	31.5	25.2	27.3	31.5
Officers' Compensation 20	1.8	2.6	•	22.7	8.2	5.3	4.0	2.8	3.4	1.5	1.1	1.0	1.1
Operating Margin 21	•	•	0.8	•	0.5	3.6	1.5	0.7	5.5	•	•	•	•
Operating Margin Before Officers' Comp. 22	•	•	0.8	12.9	8.7	8.9	5.5	3.6	9.0	•	•	•	•

Selected Average Balance Sheet ($ in Thousands)

Net Receivables 23	842	0	1	47	255	1686	3812	7516	17374	21793	41338	166843	683933
Inventories 24	529	0	11	163	532	2156	3973	7488	21665	10951	29244	155951	312884
Net Property, Plant and Equipment 25	507	0	16	132	225	1663	1498	3218	6661	6569	10738	162722	378720
Total Assets 26	8828	0	36	721	2030	6605	15518	33378	77395	156069	323935	1392533	8332974
Notes and Loans Payable 27	3713	0	24	435	710	4041	3618	7198	7900	131567	171144	460226	3482093
All Other Liabilities 28	2574	0	8	172	500	3075	6082	10569	30231	56563	79992	192219	2552843
Net Worth 29	2541	0	3	114	821	-510	5818	15611	39264	-32062	72799	740088	2298038

Selected Financial Ratios (Times to 1)

Current Ratio 30	1.3	•	1.1	0.3	2.0	0.8	1.4	1.8	1.7	0.8	1.4	1.7	1.3
Quick Ratio 31	0.3	•	0.5	0.1	0.8	0.4	0.7	0.8	1.0	0.4	0.6	0.8	0.2
Net Sales to Working Capital 32	3.7	•	26.5	•	3.7	•	6.1	4.0	3.4	•	6.8	3.4	2.9
Coverage Ratio 33	1.8	•	385.6	0.9	4.8	8.2	3.9	6.0	15.1	1.8	0.4	1.5	1.7
Total Asset Turnover 34	0.4	•	0.9	1.6	1.1	2.1	1.3	1.2	1.0	0.7	0.6	0.5	0.4
Inventory Turnover 35	2.0	•	1.2	3.0	1.9	1.1	2.3	2.4	1.8	3.7	2.7	1.7	2.0
Receivables Turnover 36	4.9	•	29.3	14.1	8.5	5.3	5.1	4.8	3.4	6.0	4.3	3.5	5.1
Total Liabilities to Net Worth 37	2.5	•	9.8	5.3	1.5	•	1.7	1.1	1.0	•	3.4	0.9	2.6
Current Assets to Working Capital 38	4.0	•	14.8	•	2.0	•	3.2	2.3	2.3	•	3.8	2.3	4.0
Current Liabilities to Working Capital 39	3.0	•	13.8	•	1.0	•	2.2	1.3	1.3	•	2.8	1.3	3.0
Working Capital to Net Sales 40	0.3	•	0.0	•	0.3	•	0.2	0.3	0.3	•	0.1	0.3	0.3
Inventory to Working Capital 41	0.5	•	6.3	•	0.8	•	1.2	0.8	0.6	•	1.0	0.8	0.3
Total Receipts to Cash Flow 42	3.3	4.9	1.4	4.2	3.4	4.1	4.8	4.5	4.8	3.3	5.8	4.3	3.0
Cost of Goods to Cash Flow 43	0.9	1.6	0.5	1.8	1.6	0.7	2.2	2.1	2.3	1.1	2.5	1.8	0.7
Cash Flow to Total Debt 44	0.2	•	0.7	0.5	0.5	0.5	0.4	0.5	0.4	0.2	0.1	0.2	0.2

Selected Financial Factors (in Percentages)

Debt Ratio 45	71.2	•	90.7	84.2	59.6	107.7	62.5	53.2	49.3	120.5	77.5	46.9	72.4
Return on Total Assets 46	5.1	•	38.7	4.4	9.7	9.7	5.6	8.6	9.0	6.2	1.6	2.1	5.2
Return on Equity Before Income Taxes 47	7.6	•	416.1	•	19.1	•	11.1	15.2	16.6	•	•	1.3	7.5
Return on Equity After Income Taxes 48	4.8	•	415.5	•	14.9	•	7.7	13.0	13.0	•	•	0.8	4.4
Profit Margin (Before Income Tax) 49	5.0	•	41.7	•	7.0	4.1	3.3	6.2	8.0	3.6	•	1.5	5.8
Profit Margin (After Income Tax) 50	3.2	•	41.7	•	5.5	4.1	2.3	5.3	6.3	2.3	•	1.0	3.4

Table II

Corporations with Net Income

BOOK PUBLISHERS

MONEY AMOUNTS AND SIZE OF ASSETS IN THOUSANDS OF DOLLARS

Item Description for Accounting Period 7/02 Through 6/03	Total	Zero Assets	Under 500	500 to 1,000	1,000 to 5,000	5,000 to 10,000	10,000 to 25,000	25,000 to 50,000	50,000 to 100,000	100,000 to 250,000	250,000 to 500,000	500,000 to 2,500,000	2,500,000 and over
Number of Enterprises **1**	1585	•	1213	68	196	37	36	14	5	10	0	0	0
Revenues ($ in Thousands)													
Net Sales **2**	14454543	•	128062	51270	465324	505303	734223	545342	404595	1302780	0	0	0
Interest **3**	63258	•	360	1891	60	25	675	1466	393	9816	0	0	0
Rents **4**	42148	•	0	0	0	1664	618	449	0	231	0	0	0
Royalties **5**	234951	•	0	0	27129	0	546	17033	200	14266	0	0	0
Other Portfolio Income **6**	212375	•	144	4241	2252	25	627	567	448	19692	0	0	0
Other Receipts **7**	629569	•	48419	1006	1247	722	7827	14339	8255	90045	0	0	0
Total Receipts **8**	15636844	•	176985	58408	496012	507739	744516	579196	413891	1436830	0	0	0
Average Total Receipts **9**	9866	•	146	859	2531	13723	20681	41371	82778	143683	•	•	•
Operating Costs/Operating Income (%)													
Cost of Operations **10**	21.1	•	36.4	19.9	35.2	16.9	49.7	41.8	48.6	42.6	•	•	•
Salaries and Wages **11**	22.7	•	14.3	0.9	9.4	34.0	13.8	18.2	16.9	16.5	•	•	•
Taxes Paid **12**	2.7	•	2.3	3.1	1.3	3.7	1.8	2.3	2.0	1.7	•	•	•
Interest Paid **13**	3.0	•	•	3.3	1.2	0.6	0.8	1.3	0.6	3.5	•	•	•
Depreciation **14**	4.3	•	3.0	0.1	1.5	3.9	1.5	2.4	1.8	0.9	•	•	•
Amortization and Depletion **15**	2.7	•	•	0.0	0.1	0.0	0.4	1.5	0.2	1.0	•	•	•
Pensions and Other Deferred Comp. **16**	1.3	•	•	•	1.7	1.1	0.6	0.7	0.8	0.8	•	•	•
Employee Benefits **17**	2.3	•	1.2	3.6	0.3	3.9	1.0	1.6	1.2	1.8	•	•	•
Advertising **18**	3.6	•	2.3	1.9	0.7	2.8	2.6	2.3	3.7	4.4	•	•	•
Other Expenses **19**	31.7	•	15.9	24.9	26.8	24.3	17.5	21.3	15.3	28.2	•	•	•
Officers' Compensation **20**	2.1	•	•	47.6	10.7	5.3	3.9	3.0	3.4	0.8	•	•	•
Operating Margin **21**	2.5	•	24.6	•	11.2	3.6	6.5	3.6	5.5	•	•	•	•
Operating Margin Before Officers' Comp. **22**	4.7	•	24.6	42.3	21.9	8.9	10.4	6.7	9.0	•	•	•	•

Selected Average Balance Sheet ($ in Thousands)

Net Receivables 23	1841	3	14	276	1686	4186	7283	17374	26439
Inventories 24	1264	30	182	378	1689	4209	7706	15399	10414
Net Property, Plant and Equipment 25	993	55	0	323	1663	1532	3629	6661	8209
Total Assets 26	14887	99	644	2029	6605	14838	33509	77395	170532
Notes and Loans Payable 27	4662	36	392	550	4041	3060	6498	7900	74276
All Other Liabilities 28	5045	3	50	302	3075	5539	10310	30231	52122
Net Worth 29	5179	61	201	1177	-510	6239	16701	39264	44135

Selected Financial Ratios (Times to 1)

Current Ratio 30	1.2	1.1	0.2	3.1	0.8	1.9	1.9	1.7	1.3
Quick Ratio 31	0.6	0.4	0.1	1.6	0.4	0.9	0.9	1.0	0.6
Net Sales to Working Capital 32	10.7	24.5	•	2.9	•	3.9	3.7	3.4	9.0
Coverage Ratio 33	4.7	•	3.6	15.8	8.2	11.1	8.6	15.1	3.3
Total Asset Turnover 34	0.6	1.1	1.2	1.2	2.1	1.4	1.2	1.0	0.8
Inventory Turnover 35	1.5	1.3	0.8	2.2	1.4	2.4	2.1	2.6	5.3
Receivables Turnover 36	5.3	27.1	8.7	8.8	6.5	5.1	5.0	9.3	7.1
Total Liabilities to Net Worth 37	1.9	0.6	2.2	0.7	•	1.4	1.0	1.0	2.9
Current Assets to Working Capital 38	5.2	9.5	•	1.5	•	2.1	2.1	2.3	4.9
Current Liabilities to Working Capital 39	4.2	8.5	•	0.5	•	1.1	1.1	1.3	3.9
Working Capital to Net Sales 40	0.1	0.0	•	0.3	•	0.3	0.3	0.3	0.1
Inventory to Working Capital 41	1.5	5.7	•	0.5	•	0.8	0.8	0.6	1.1
Total Receipts to Cash Flow 42	2.6	1.3	4.0	2.4	4.1	4.4	3.6	4.8	3.0
Cost of Goods to Cash Flow 43	0.6	0.5	0.8	0.9	0.7	2.2	1.5	2.3	1.3
Cash Flow to Total Debt 44	0.4	2.0	0.4	1.1	0.5	0.5	0.6	0.4	0.3

Selected Financial Factors (in Percentages)

Debt Ratio 45	65.2	39.1	68.7	42.0	107.7	58.0	50.2	49.3	74.1
Return on Total Assets 46	8.5	66.7	13.9	22.2	9.7	11.8	12.9	9.0	8.8
Return on Equity Before Income Taxes 47	19.4	109.5	31.9	35.8	•	25.6	22.9	16.6	23.5
Return on Equity After Income Taxes 48	14.2	109.3	25.1	31.2	•	20.9	20.2	13.0	18.8
Profit Margin (Before Income Tax) 49	11.0	62.8	8.5	17.8	4.1	7.8	9.8	8.0	8.0
Profit Margin (After Income Tax) 50	8.1	62.8	6.7	15.5	4.1	6.4	8.7	6.3	6.4

Table I

Corporations with and without Net Income

DATABASE, DIRECTORY, AND OTHER PUBLISHERS

MONEY AMOUNTS AND SIZE OF ASSETS IN THOUSANDS OF DOLLARS

Item Description for Accounting Period 7/02 Through 6/03	Total	Zero Assets	Under 500	500 to 1,000	1,000 to 5,000	5,000 to 10,000	10,000 to 25,000	25,000 to 50,000	50,000 to 100,000	100,000 to 250,000	250,000 to 500,000	500,000 to 2,500,000	2,500,000 and over
Number of Enterprises 1	6349	1366	3826	774	268	39	37	12	7	5	6	4	5
Revenues ($ in Thousands)													
Net Sales 2	25200243	62496	183018	1262037	884513	515738	989066	506765	356220	659855	944003	2195193	16641339
Interest 3	1203846	115	238	1864	1491	236	1183	1766	506	2290	9415	13386	1171356
Rents 4	61055	0	0	0	0	0	31	859	0	0	0	0	60165
Royalties 5	723104	4	0	0	116	0	51	127	17	10188	16955	0	695647
Other Portfolio Income 6	168033	2202	6251	0	7489	154	813	20	16184	633	69770	3241	61276
Other Receipts 7	475628	12	0	13672	3212	6611	11760	3677	8380	31645	90146	151534	154978
Total Receipts 8	27831909	64829	189507	1277573	896821	522739	1002904	513214	381307	704611	1130289	2363354	18784761
Average Total Receipts 9	4384	47	50	1651	3346	13404	27106	42768	54472	140922	188382	590838	3756952
Operating Costs/Operating Income (%)													
Cost of Operations 10	28.3	5.4	37.6	20.5	31.9	20.5	39.9	26.2	31.9	18.8	27.2	19.6	29.8
Salaries and Wages 11	23.2	7.9	6.7	29.4	23.4	21.1	23.6	24.8	28.7	24.1	22.5	39.3	20.8
Taxes Paid 12	3.3	3.0	2.6	2.5	3.5	2.6	2.5	2.5	2.8	2.1	3.3	3.6	3.4
Interest Paid 13	10.1	0.2	10.5	0.0	0.7	0.7	0.5	1.2	3.1	2.0	15.8	4.4	13.5
Depreciation 14	4.3	3.5	12.6	1.3	4.4	4.2	2.3	2.3	3.0	2.2	2.7	3.0	5.0
Amortization and Depletion 15	4.2	0.2	1.6	0.0	0.2	1.0	0.5	2.3	3.1	5.1	2.8	4.0	5.2
Pensions and Other Deferred Comp. 16	1.3	•	•	1.3	0.4	0.8	0.6	0.2	0.3	0.2	0.4	0.1	1.8
Employee Benefits 17	2.1	5.9	0.0	2.0	0.7	0.8	1.6	2.0	4.9	1.8	2.0	3.5	2.1
Advertising 18	2.2	1.3	0.3	2.1	3.0	4.4	2.1	4.1	3.1	3.5	3.9	3.0	1.8
Other Expenses 19	28.6	65.6	44.2	34.6	26.7	36.4	19.9	29.3	26.3	46.0	25.6	24.6	28.3
Officers' Compensation 20	1.9	12.2	10.0	8.0	8.7	6.3	3.6	2.5	2.4	1.3	1.3	0.3	0.9
Operating Margin 21	•	•	•	•	•	1.1	3.0	2.7	•	•	•	•	•
Operating Margin Before Officers' Comp. 22	•	7.1	•	6.2	5.1	7.4	6.6	5.2	•	•	•	•	•

Selected Average Balance Sheet ($ in Thousands)

Net Receivables 23	921	0	2	149	532	415	3870	9562	13368	66373	50586	380493	611383
Inventories 24	269	0	8	81	247	1340	2797	2330	6924	4482	2886		284902
Net Property, Plant and Equipment 25	563	0	27	46	379	1930	2226	3306	10858	5326	17724	42524	551521
Total Assets 26	7530	0	66	628	1625	7296	15140	36766	71695	187279	349313	1000604	7561869
Notes and Loans Payable 27	4070	0	55	178	453	3973	2199	9940	23550	28028	510115	312979	4079563
All Other Liabilities 28	2112	0	32	267	482	2171	7684	19205	24388	74047	81500	320724	2008068
Net Worth 29	1347	0	-21	184	690	1152	5257	7620	23758	85205	-242301	366900	1474238

Selected Financial Ratios (Times to 1)

Current Ratio 30	1.1	•	11.6	1.5	1.7	0.6	1.2	1.7	1.0	1.2	1.9	1.4	1.0
Quick Ratio 31	0.7	•	3.3	1.0	1.5	0.5	0.8	1.3	0.7	1.0	1.1	1.3	0.6
Net Sales to Working Capital 32	22.8	•	1.8	8.8	7.9	•	19.9	4.3	76.3	10.2	2.7	4.7	•
Coverage Ratio 33	1.1	•	•	•	•	4.3	9.2	4.4	0.2	0.9	1.9	1.5	1.1
Total Asset Turnover 34	0.5	•	0.7	2.6	2.0	1.8	1.8	1.1	0.7	0.7	0.5	0.5	0.4
Inventory Turnover 35	4.2	•	2.4	4.1	35.7	11.0	8.0	4.0	7.0	3.6	9.6	37.4	3.5
Receivables Turnover 36	4.7	•	15.7	13.2	6.0	11.0	7.5	3.5	4.0	1.9	2.4	2.1	5.7
Total Liabilities to Net Worth 37	4.6	•	•	2.4	1.4	5.3	1.9	3.8	2.0	1.2	•	1.7	4.1
Current Assets to Working Capital 38	9.8	•	1.1	2.9	2.4	•	6.9	2.4	34.1	6.5	2.2	3.7	•
Current Liabilities to Working Capital 39	8.8	•	0.1	1.9	1.4	•	5.9	1.4	33.1	5.5	1.2	2.7	•
Working Capital to Net Sales 40	0.0	•	0.6	0.1	0.1	•	0.1	0.2	0.0	0.1	0.4	0.2	•
Inventory to Working Capital 41	1.6	•	0.2	0.4	0.1	•	1.0	0.3	3.5	0.4	0.1	0.0	•
Total Receipts to Cash Flow 42	4.9	2.2	13.9	4.7	6.0	2.9	4.7	3.4	7.0	2.4	3.0	4.4	5.6
Cost of Goods to Cash Flow 43	1.4	0.1	5.2	1.0	1.9	0.6	1.9	0.9	2.2	0.5	0.8	0.9	1.7
Cash Flow to Total Debt 44	0.1	•	0.0	0.8	0.6	0.7	0.6	0.4	0.2	0.5	0.1	0.2	0.1

Selected Financial Factors (in Percentages)

Debt Ratio 45	82.1	•	132.1	70.8	57.6	84.2	65.3	79.3	66.9	54.5	169.4	63.3	80.5
Return on Total Assets 46	6.0	•	•	•	•	5.7	8.6	5.9	0.3	1.2	13.2	3.6	6.3
Return on Equity Before Income Taxes 47	3.6	•	50.3	•	•	27.9	22.1	21.9	•	•	•	3.2	1.9
Return on Equity After Income Taxes 48	1.2	•	50.9	•	•	27.9	21.2	19.0	•	•	•	1.4	0.3
Profit Margin (Before Income Tax) 49	1.2	•	•	•	•	2.4	4.3	3.9	•	•	13.6	2.1	0.8
Profit Margin (After Income Tax) 50	0.4	•	•	•	•	2.4	4.2	3.4	•	•	9.6	0.9	0.2

Table II

Corporations with Net Income

DATABASE, DIRECTORY, AND OTHER PUBLISHERS

MONEY AMOUNTS AND SIZE OF ASSETS IN THOUSANDS OF DOLLARS

Item Description for Accounting Period 7/02 Through 6/03	Total	Zero Assets	Under 500	500 to 1,000	1,000 to 5,000	5,000 to 10,000	10,000 to 25,000	25,000 to 50,000	50,000 to 100,000	100,000 to 250,000	250,000 to 500,000	500,000 to 2,500,000	2,500,000 and over
Number of Enterprises **1**	2898	281	1814	0	169	35	26	7	7	0	6	0	0
Revenues ($ in Thousands)													
Net Sales **2**	15792150	55574	74653	0	618845	481398	728989	256401	561671	0	944003	0	0
Interest **3**	665305	26	238	0	1302	0	1021	1298	2729	0	9415	0	0
Rents **4**	52517	0	0	0	0	0	11	0	0	0	0	0	0
Royalties **5**	518724	0	0	0	0	0	4	127	17	0	16955	0	0
Other Portfolio Income **6**	149657	2202	6251	0	7352	154	251	20	3811	0	69770	0	0
Other Receipts **7**	183823	10	0	0	1423	3798	11140	890	20292	0	90146	0	0
Total Receipts **8**	17362176	57812	81142	0	628922	485350	741416	258736	588520	0	1130289	0	0
Average Total Receipts **9**	5991	206	45	•	3721	13867	28516	36962	84074	•	188382	•	•
Operating Costs/Operating Income (%)													
Cost of Operations **10**	25.3	1.2	63.5	•	32.5	17.7	39.7	26.5	30.9	•	27.2	•	•
Salaries and Wages **11**	22.1	6.1	•	•	21.2	18.7	22.6	24.4	20.2	•	22.5	•	•
Taxes Paid **12**	3.4	2.0	1.0	•	3.2	2.4	2.2	2.6	2.4	•	3.3	•	•
Interest Paid **13**	9.4	•	0.7	•	0.7	0.4	0.4	1.2	1.5	•	15.8	•	•
Depreciation **14**	4.7	•	1.2	•	3.4	4.1	1.6	3.5	2.1	•	2.7	•	•
Amortization and Depletion **15**	3.4	•	0.0	•	0.1	1.0	0.6	1.3	0.9	•	2.8	•	•
Pensions and Other Deferred Comp. **16**	1.5	•	•	•	0.6	0.9	0.7	0.2	0.4	•	0.4	•	•
Employee Benefits **17**	1.8	6.2	•	•	0.7	0.6	1.7	1.8	2.7	•	2.0	•	•
Advertising **18**	2.2	0.0	0.5	•	4.0	4.3	2.5	4.1	3.8	•	3.9	•	•
Other Expenses **19**	29.3	60.0	23.2	•	21.9	35.3	18.0	21.6	29.7	•	25.6	•	•
Officers' Compensation **20**	2.0	13.7	•	•	6.0	6.2	3.9	2.1	1.7	•	1.3	•	•
Operating Margin **21**	•	10.9	9.9	•	5.6	8.6	6.2	10.8	3.7	•	•	•	•
Operating Margin Before Officers' Comp. **22**	•	24.5	9.9	•	11.7	14.8	10.1	12.9	5.4	•	•	•	•

Selected Average Balance Sheet ($ in Thousands)

Net Receivables 23	871	0	4	655	350	4065	8975	46461	50586
Inventories 24	430	0	13	24	227	1140	4540	2541	4969
Net Property, Plant and Equipment 25	856	0	0	366	2064	1897	2989	10427	17724
Total Assets 26	8701	0	65	1546	7285	15839	37805	96533	349313
Notes and Loans Payable 27	3775	0	17	395	3615	1695	6806	18082	510115
All Other Liabilities 28	2662	0	17	438	1388	7399	13260	31191	81500
Net Worth 29	2264	0	31	713	2282	6745	17740	47260	-242301

Selected Financial Ratios (Times to 1)

Current Ratio 30	1.3	15.8	•	2.0	0.9	1.4	1.9	2.1	1.9
Quick Ratio 31	0.8	4.8	•	1.9	0.8	1.0	1.3	1.8	1.1
Net Sales to Working Capital 32	10.6	0.8	•	6.4	•	10.4	3.1	2.5	2.7
Coverage Ratio 33	1.6	27.0	•	11.1	27.0	21.2	10.5	6.8	1.9
Total Asset Turnover 34	0.6	0.6	•	2.4	1.9	1.8	1.0	0.8	0.5
Inventory Turnover 35	3.2	2.1	•	50.5	10.7	9.8	2.1	9.8	8.6
Receivables Turnover 36	5.5	9.4	•	5.7	28.5	8.3	3.3	3.5	6.2
Total Liabilities to Net Worth 37	2.8	1.1	•	1.2	2.2	1.3	1.1	1.0	•
Current Assets to Working Capital 38	4.0	1.1	•	2.0	•	3.6	2.1	1.9	2.2
Current Liabilities to Working Capital 39	3.0	0.1	•	1.0	•	2.6	1.1	0.9	1.2
Working Capital to Net Sales 40	0.1	1.2	•	0.2	•	0.1	0.3	0.4	0.4
Inventory to Working Capital 41	0.8	0.2	•	0.0	•	0.4	0.4	0.1	0.1
Total Receipts to Cash Flow 42	4.0	3.0	1.9	4.3	2.4	4.4	3.3	3.0	3.0
Cost of Goods to Cash Flow 43	1.0	1.9	0.0	1.4	0.4	1.7	0.9	0.9	0.8
Cash Flow to Total Debt 44	0.2	0.4	•	1.0	1.1	0.7	0.5	0.5	0.1

Selected Financial Factors (in Percentages)

Debt Ratio 45	74.0	51.8	•	53.9	68.7	57.4	53.1	51.0	169.4
Return on Total Assets 46	9.1	12.2	•	18.9	18.5	14.6	12.6	8.3	13.2
Return on Equity Before Income Taxes 47	12.5	24.3	•	37.3	56.8	32.6	24.2	14.5	•
Return on Equity After Income Taxes 48	9.5	23.5	•	33.1	56.8	31.6	22.1	10.8	•
Profit Margin (Before Income Tax) 49	5.2	14.9	18.6	7.3	9.4	7.8	11.7	8.5	13.6
Profit Margin (After Income Tax) 50	3.9	14.9	18.0	6.4	9.4	7.6	10.7	6.3	9.6

Table I

Corporations with and without Net Income

SOFTWARE PUBLISHERS

MONEY AMOUNTS AND SIZE OF ASSETS IN THOUSANDS OF DOLLARS

Item Description for Accounting Period 7/02 Through 6/03	Total	Zero Assets	Under 500	500 to 1,000	1,000 to 5,000	5,000 to 10,000	10,000 to 25,000	25,000 to 50,000	50,000 to 100,000	100,000 to 250,000	250,000 to 500,000	500,000 to 2,500,000	2,500,000 and over
Number of Enterprises 1	9485	1957	5336	599	858	275	217	73	52	44	35	29	9
Revenues ($ in Thousands)													
Net Sales 2	76250838	544629	2155710	742812	2459074	1681220	2262462	1826440	3208796	3473525	6524051	15147871	36224249
Interest 3	1329377	4141	4698	2379	23861	14114	31290	23880	31476	63665	134398	304897	690577
Rents 4	53151	231	37	24	101	175	454	244	792	2983	16066	31146	898
Royalties 5	2746449	13	0	0	9336	24542	11369	23629	35763	102065	210375	965797	1363560
Other Portfolio Income 6	1541643	217945	44857	5578	59023	19509	29457	5025	4023	117046	38470	103453	897253
Other Receipts 7	10529242	39753	144951	6060	65093	40719	97381	70190	34314	209717	80514	527895	9212659
Total Receipts 8	92450700	806712	2350253	756853	2616488	1780279	2432413	1949408	3315164	3969001	7003874	17081059	48389196
Average Total Receipts 9	9747	412	440	1264	3050	6474	11209	26704	63753	90205	200111	589002	5376577
Operating Costs/Operating Income (%)													
Cost of Operations 10	19.1	38.3	21.1	7.2	28.2	20.6	17.6	25.0	24.6	17.5	18.3	30.9	12.9
Salaries and Wages 11	40.5	34.1	34.9	66.5	52.6	52.8	60.3	46.2	38.3	42.6	38.3	33.8	40.8
Taxes Paid 12	3.3	5.6	5.2	7.1	4.8	5.4	5.5	4.0	4.0	3.7	3.3	2.2	3.0
Interest Paid 13	1.3	1.9	2.1	2.4	2.6	1.7	2.0	1.4	0.8	1.1	1.0	1.7	1.1
Depreciation 14	4.0	7.7	3.7	4.2	4.1	5.2	6.0	4.3	4.2	4.2	4.3	4.2	3.5
Amortization and Depletion 15	1.8	1.9	0.5	2.4	2.1	1.7	2.9	3.1	1.4	1.9	2.7	2.7	1.2
Pensions and Other Deferred Comp. 16	0.3	0.2	0.5	0.4	0.5	0.3	0.5	0.5	0.3	0.7	0.5	0.5	0.1
Employee Benefits 17	3.3	2.6	3.2	3.2	3.6	3.6	4.4	4.3	3.1	3.3	4.1	3.7	2.9
Advertising 18	5.2	3.8	0.7	5.0	2.1	2.4	2.7	2.5	2.2	1.9	2.5	4.4	7.5
Other Expenses 19	31.8	70.8	39.2	48.2	43.2	40.4	46.4	39.1	32.1	38.0	37.3	25.3	29.2
Officers' Compensation 20	2.6	3.0	12.8	10.0	7.8	7.0	7.8	3.3	2.4	2.3	1.8	1.4	1.7
Operating Margin 21	•	•	•	•	•	•	•	•	•	•	•	•	•
Operating Margin Before Officers' Comp. 22	•	•	•	•	•	•	•	•	•	•	•	•	•

Selected Average Balance Sheet ($ in Thousands)

Net Receivables 23	1772	0	24	145	359	1305	2394	7193	15336	25200	55038	114470	858217
Inventories 24	155	0	11	25	48	162	153	356	395	737	1858	10697	91317
Net Property, Plant and Equipment 25	962	0	35	94	202	570	1267	2717	5088	7518	24683	76750	487350
Total Assets 26	17157	0	134	703	2273	7151	15002	35033	68250	153028	356708	951413	11278289
Notes and Loans Payable 27	1418	0	252	682	1172	957	2538	3503	6262	11079	29521	95470	556211
All Other Liabilities 28	5459	0	68	285	1167	3346	7384	13679	32816	42161	102477	257985	3565737
Net Worth 29	10280	0	-186	-264	-65	2848	5081	17850	29172	99788	224709	597958	7156342

Selected Financial Ratios (Times to 1)

Current Ratio 30	1.2	•	0.7	0.8	1.1	1.7	1.8	1.7	1.6	2.3	2.3	2.0	0.8
Quick Ratio 31	0.8	•	0.5	0.8	1.0	1.4	1.5	1.4	1.3	1.8	1.8	1.4	0.4
Net Sales to Working Capital 32	8.5	•	•	•	19.7	2.8	2.2	2.6	3.8	1.5	1.7	2.4	•
Coverage Ratio 33	8.1	•	•	•	•	•	•	•	•	•	•	3.3	30.0
Total Asset Turnover 34	0.5	•	3.0	1.8	1.3	0.9	0.7	0.7	0.9	0.5	0.5	0.5	0.4
Inventory Turnover 35	9.9	•	7.9	3.5	16.8	7.7	12.1	17.6	38.4	18.7	18.4	15.1	5.7
Receivables Turnover 36	4.1	•	19.6	7.1	7.2	5.4	4.1	3.8	4.1	2.8	3.1	4.3	4.1
Total Liabilities to Net Worth 37	0.7	•	•	•	•	1.5	2.0	1.0	1.3	0.5	0.6	0.6	0.6
Current Assets to Working Capital 38	6.3	•	•	•	9.4	2.4	2.2	2.4	2.7	1.8	1.8	2.1	•
Current Liabilities to Working Capital 39	5.3	•	•	•	8.4	1.4	1.2	1.4	1.7	0.8	0.8	1.1	•
Working Capital to Net Sales 40	0.1	•	•	•	0.1	0.4	0.4	0.4	0.3	0.7	0.6	0.4	•
Inventory to Working Capital 41	0.1	•	•	•	0.3	0.1	0.0	0.0	0.0	0.0	0.0	0.1	•
Total Receipts to Cash Flow 42	2.9	•	6.2	•	•	•	•	41.1	6.7	3.5	4.1	4.4	1.8
Cost of Goods to Cash Flow 43	0.6	•	1.3	•	•	•	•	10.3	1.7	0.6	0.7	1.4	0.2
Cash Flow to Total Debt 44	0.4	•	0.2	•	•	•	•	0.0	0.2	0.4	0.3	0.3	0.5

Selected Financial Factors (in Percentages)

Debt Ratio 45	40.1	•	238.2	137.5	102.9	60.2	66.1	49.0	57.3	34.8	37.0	37.2	36.5
Return on Total Assets 46	5.1	•	•	•	•	•	•	•	•	•	•	3.0	11.9
Return on Equity Before Income Taxes 47	7.4	•	32.4	257.1	1981.4	•	•	•	•	•	•	3.4	18.1
Return on Equity After Income Taxes 48	2.9	•	33.1	257.1	2013.1	•	•	•	•	•	•	1.8	12.1
Profit Margin (Before Income Tax) 49	9.5	•	•	•	•	•	•	•	•	•	•	3.8	32.2
Profit Margin (After Income Tax) 50	3.7	•	•	•	•	•	•	•	•	•	•	2.0	21.5

Table II

Corporations with Net Income

SOFTWARE PUBLISHERS

MONEY AMOUNTS AND SIZE OF ASSETS IN THOUSANDS OF DOLLARS

Item Description for Accounting Period 7/02 Through 6/03	Total	Zero Assets	Under 500	500 to 1,000	1,000 to 5,000	5,000 to 10,000	10,000 to 25,000	25,000 to 50,000	50,000 to 100,000	100,000 to 250,000	250,000 to 500,000	500,000 to 2,500,000	2,500,000 and over
Number of Enterprises 1	4617	543	3407	0	308	90	42	15	20	20	14	18	0
Revenues ($ in Thousands)													
Net Sales 2	58147070	319494	1570347	0	1309874	821911	792559	587760	1539502	1965956	3449472	11135377	0
Interest 3	908882	919	1042	0	3644	2225	3040	2877	11504	29080	31946	188500	0
Rents 4	32508	0	0	0	0	0	101	84	531	227	13200	17468	0
Royalties 5	1864333	13	0	0	0	21992	5928	354	33773	52142	163273	339742	0
Other Portfolio Income 6	1367062	217201	41223	0	13591	13384	12368	519	2540	110072	27530	47716	0
Other Receipts 7	10083892	35433	49527	0	8276	23328	14390	22471	8377	139352	50117	538669	0
Total Receipts 8	72403747	573060	1662139	0	1335385	882840	828386	614065	1596227	2296829	3735538	12267472	0
Average Total Receipts 9	15682	1055	488	•	4336	9809	19723	40938	79811	114841	266824	681526	•
Operating Costs/Operating Income (%)													
Cost of Operations 10	19.2	40.5	21.1	•	35.4	13.7	14.4	24.9	17.5	14.7	19.4	36.8	•
Salaries and Wages 11	35.1	15.6	25.9	•	25.9	31.6	30.8	28.6	32.8	36.6	30.7	26.6	•
Taxes Paid 12	2.9	6.4	3.3	•	2.6	4.1	3.6	3.1	3.7	3.1	2.8	2.0	•
Interest Paid 13	1.2	1.0	0.2	•	0.5	0.7	1.3	0.2	0.3	1.0	0.5	2.0	•
Depreciation 14	3.2	1.0	3.7	•	1.1	2.3	2.8	2.3	3.1	3.4	2.8	3.4	•
Amortization and Depletion 15	1.2	2.0	0.0	•	0.1	0.0	0.7	0.7	0.9	1.7	1.5	1.8	•
Pensions and Other Deferred Comp. 16	0.3	0.2	0.6	•	0.4	0.4	1.0	0.6	0.5	0.8	0.9	0.4	•
Employee Benefits 17	2.8	1.7	2.0	•	2.3	2.1	2.2	3.6	2.3	3.3	3.6	2.8	•
Advertising 18	6.1	0.4	0.8	•	1.6	1.0	2.7	0.9	1.8	2.0	3.1	5.1	•
Other Expenses 19	26.8	34.9	26.1	•	17.0	26.9	25.6	22.7	28.0	29.8	32.2	17.8	•
Officers' Compensation 20	2.0	2.2	11.3	•	4.5	4.3	4.5	1.9	2.3	2.1	1.5	1.5	•
Operating Margin 21	•	•	4.9	•	8.7	12.8	10.3	10.4	6.7	1.5	1.0	•	•
Operating Margin Before Officers' Comp. 22	1.3	16.3	•	•	13.2	17.2	14.8	12.3	9.0	3.6	2.5	1.3	•

Selected Average Balance Sheet ($ in Thousands)

Net Receivables 23	2484	0	15	391	1919	4032	9304	18285	27990	76697	106468
Inventories 24	274	0	12	45	392	174	660	191	440	2215	16151
Net Property, Plant and Equipment 25	1300	0	47	119	562	1487	3974	6008	7859	29930	61687
Total Assets 26	27118	0	143	1837	7196	15978	33554	72863	145701	330969	939015
Notes and Loans Payable 27	1777	0	95	223	431	3272	2046	3023	9745	30251	128894
All Other Liabilities 28	8572	0	26	731	4671	6011	14475	34806	47067	91787	286619
Net Worth 29	16768	0	21	883	2094	6694	17033	35034	88888	208931	523502

Selected Financial Ratios (Times to 1)

Current Ratio 30	1.0		3.4	1.9	1.6	1.7	1.4	1.7	2.5	2.1	2.1
Quick Ratio 31	0.7		2.2	1.7	1.3	1.5	1.3	1.5	1.9	1.8	1.5
Net Sales to Working Capital 32	1541.3		7.2	7.3	3.7	4.0	6.6	3.7	1.6	2.4	2.5
Coverage Ratio 33	23.0	74.0	59.2	23.3	31.3	12.1	63.4	33.2	18.7	19.8	6.9
Total Asset Turnover 34	0.5		3.2	2.3	1.3	1.2	1.2	1.1	0.7	0.7	0.7
Inventory Turnover 35	8.8		8.3	33.3	3.2	15.7	14.8	70.5	32.9	21.6	14.1
Receivables Turnover 36	4.7		30.1	10.5	6.6	4.9	4.0	5.3	3.5	3.4	7.8
Total Liabilities to Net Worth 37	0.6		5.7	1.1	2.4	1.4	1.0	1.1	0.6	0.6	0.8
Current Assets to Working Capital 38	966.0		1.4	2.2	2.6	2.4	3.3	2.4	1.7	1.9	1.9
Current Liabilities to Working Capital 39	965.0		0.4	1.2	1.6	1.4	2.3	1.4	0.7	0.9	0.9
Working Capital to Net Sales 40	0.0		0.1	0.1	0.3	0.3	0.2	0.3	0.6	0.4	0.4
Inventory to Working Capital 41	31.2		0.2	0.1	0.1	0.0	0.0	0.0	0.0	0.0	0.1
Total Receipts to Cash Flow 42	2.1	2.5	3.1	4.3	2.6	2.8	3.0	2.9	2.4	2.7	4.1
Cost of Goods to Cash Flow 43	0.4	1.0	0.7	1.5	0.4	0.4	0.7	0.5	0.3	0.5	1.5
Cash Flow to Total Debt 44	0.6		1.2	1.0	0.7	0.7	0.8	0.7	0.7	0.8	0.4

Selected Financial Factors (in Percentages)

Debt Ratio 45	38.2		85.1	51.9	70.9	58.1	49.2	51.9	39.0	36.9	44.2
Return on Total Assets 46	12.4		35.4	25.8	26.5	19.1	17.7	11.4	13.1	7.6	8.9
Return on Equity Before Income Taxes 47	19.2		233.6	51.3	88.2	41.8	34.4	22.9	20.4	11.5	13.6
Return on Equity After Income Taxes 48	13.5		222.9	44.8	76.7	39.1	27.3	18.4	16.1	9.0	10.7
Profit Margin (Before Income Tax) 49	25.6	73.3	10.8	10.6	20.2	14.8	14.9	18.4	10.4	9.7	11.5
Profit Margin (After Income Tax) 50	18.0	71.7	10.3	9.3	17.6	13.9	11.9	14.5	8.4	7.6	9.1

Table I

Corporations with and without Net Income

MOTION PICTURE AND VIDEO INDUSTRIES (EXCEPT VIDEO RENTAL)

MONEY AMOUNTS AND SIZE OF ASSETS IN THOUSANDS OF DOLLARS

Item Description for Accounting Period 7/02 Through 6/03	Total	Zero Assets	Under 500	500 to 1,000	1,000 to 5,000	5,000 to 10,000	10,000 to 25,000	25,000 to 50,000	50,000 to 100,000	100,000 to 250,000	250,000 to 500,000	500,000 to 2,500,000	2,500,000 and over
Number of Enterprises **1**	23539	2351	18685	1347	849	121	98	35	17	15	5	10	6
Revenues ($ in Thousands)													
Net Sales **2**	62577705	1149146	4638450	2292628	3406032	1102314	1369854	1517043	844377	1599370	995255	5376941	38286294
Interest **3**	5797196	1234	5198	427	3337	659	6242	1208	1722	20976	29907	87807	5638479
Rents **4**	364399	367	0	0	65	988	412	860	1200	3320	976	5106	351104
Royalties **5**	675481	0	27900	3971	9	2	213	0	161	10251	0	202370	430604
Other Portfolio Income **6**	238617	0	1303	46	4358	3407	3248	5700	2926	9451	8099	15538	184542
Other Receipts **7**	2637359	107005	146125	-259	90037	32659	94447	16053	8254	-53183	113453	95339	1987431
Total Receipts **8**	72290757	1257752	4818976	2296813	3503838	1140029	1474416	1540864	858640	1590185	1147690	5783101	46878454
Average Total Receipts **9**	3071	535	258	1705	4127	9422	15045	44025	50508	106012	229538	578310	7813076
Operating Costs/Operating Income (%)													
Cost of Operations **10**	32.3	3.1	26.4	53.1	64.9	30.6	45.6	27.9	27.5	51.6	42.5	27.1	29.2
Salaries and Wages **11**	12.0	11.9	4.8	14.2	7.4	18.4	15.7	8.1	7.4	12.6	20.5	11.5	12.8
Taxes Paid **12**	2.1	3.6	2.8	2.5	1.4	2.4	3.3	2.0	2.2	1.7	1.6	3.2	1.9
Interest Paid **13**	12.5	2.5	0.3	1.1	1.4	1.2	1.7	2.3	3.5	4.6	4.8	4.6	18.9
Depreciation **14**	6.1	5.7	1.7	4.4	3.0	8.8	7.7	4.0	10.4	4.2	6.5	6.8	6.8
Amortization and Depletion **15**	12.3	7.6	0.1	0.2	1.4	3.5	2.7	4.9	12.9	14.9	3.9	3.0	17.8
Pensions and Other Deferred Comp. **16**	0.5	0.0	1.9	1.8	0.2	0.2	0.2	0.1	0.1	0.1	0.0	0.3	0.5
Employee Benefits **17**	1.0	0.9	0.6	0.6	0.6	1.3	1.5	0.7	0.6	0.9	1.7	1.2	1.1
Advertising **18**	4.7	2.0	0.4	0.9	0.3	0.9	1.3	5.4	1.1	1.3	1.0	2.5	6.8
Other Expenses **19**	25.0	69.6	31.7	17.3	13.5	17.7	23.5	33.8	28.4	25.9	18.4	40.7	22.1
Officers' Compensation **20**	4.0	0.4	33.3	7.4	5.9	13.2	4.5	8.9	1.8	1.7	11.0	0.9	0.1
Operating Margin **21**	•	•	•	•	•	1.7	•	1.9	4.1	•	•	•	•
Operating Margin Before Officers' Comp. **22**	•	•	29.2	4.0	5.9	14.9	•	10.8	5.9	•	•	•	•

Selected Average Balance Sheet ($ in Thousands)

Net Receivables 23	540	0	3	37	412	1336	1665	5929	10309	21092	32444	80627	1710522
Inventories 24	315	0	6	65	144	137	808	2009	1370	18422	1629	56057	1009898
Net Property, Plant and Equipment 25	745	0	13	323	490	2261	3206	9258	21341	28237	67629	312151	1878886
Total Assets 26	15556	0	77	751	2189	7198	15658	35448	72939	160452	376154	1022144	57079913
Notes and Loans Payable 27	4665	0	57	570	1296	2862	5800	18205	30605	76937	52778	372933	16608622
All Other Liabilities 28	2082	0	13	208	722	1298	4060	9895	17962	52261	93838	248816	7151677
Net Worth 29	8809	0	6	-27	171	3038	5798	7347	24372	31253	229537	400394	33319615

Selected Financial Ratios (Times to 1)

Current Ratio 30	1.3	•	2.5	1.1	1.3	1.2	1.5	1.0	1.0	1.3	1.7	1.1	1.3
Quick Ratio 31	0.6	•	1.9	0.6	1.0	1.0	1.0	0.6	0.6	0.8	1.1	0.4	0.6
Net Sales to Working Capital 32	7.2	•	10.8	113.1	16.6	17.2	9.7	11.3	327.8	6.5	5.0	15.5	5.5
Coverage Ratio 33	1.3	1.9	0.3	•	2.9	5.2	2.5	1.2	2.7	•	1.6	3.2	1.2
Total Asset Turnover 34	0.2	•	3.2	2.3	1.8	1.3	1.2	0.9	0.7	0.7	0.5	0.5	0.1
Inventory Turnover 35	2.7	•	11.8	13.8	20.4	18.1	7.9	6.0	10.0	3.0	52.0	2.6	1.8
Receivables Turnover 36	5.1	•	68.8	69.6	8.0	5.5	6.7	6.5	4.8	4.6	4.9	7.5	4.0
Total Liabilities to Net Worth 37	0.8	•	11.7	•	11.8	1.4	1.7	3.8	2.0	4.1	0.6	1.6	0.7
Current Assets to Working Capital 38	4.8	•	1.7	16.9	4.0	5.7	4.8	3.2	150.3	4.0	2.5	9.5	4.8
Current Liabilities to Working Capital 39	3.8	•	0.7	15.9	3.0	4.7	3.8	2.2	149.3	3.0	1.5	8.5	3.8
Working Capital to Net Sales 40	0.1	•	0.1	0.0	0.1	0.1	0.1	0.1	0.0	0.2	0.2	0.1	0.2
Inventory to Working Capital 41	0.9	•	0.2	5.1	0.7	0.2	0.6	0.4	8.9	1.0	0.0	1.8	1.0
Total Receipts to Cash Flow 42	4.9	4.0	3.9	10.9	7.8	5.9	5.7	3.0	3.7	•	6.3	3.2	5.0
Cost of Goods to Cash Flow 43	1.6	0.1	1.0	5.8	5.1	1.8	2.6	0.8	1.0	•	2.7	0.9	1.5
Cash Flow to Total Debt 44	0.1	•	0.9	0.2	0.3	0.4	0.2	0.5	0.3	•	0.2	0.3	0.1

Selected Financial Factors (in Percentages)

Debt Ratio 45	43.4	•	92.1	103.6	92.2	57.8	63.0	79.3	66.6	80.5	39.0	60.8	41.6
Return on Total Assets 46	2.7	0.3	•	•	7.5	8.0	1.5	7.0	6.3	•	4.1	7.8	2.6
Return on Equity Before Income Taxes 47	1.1	•	•	204.1	63.2	15.3	0.1	20.4	11.7	•	2.5	13.8	0.9
Return on Equity After Income Taxes 48	0.7	•	•	204.4	61.8	15.0	•	14.7	11.1	•	0.9	8.9	0.6
Profit Margin (Before Income Tax) 49	3.6	2.2	•	•	2.7	5.1	0.0	3.5	5.8	•	2.9	10.3	4.7
Profit Margin (After Income Tax) 50	2.2	1.9	•	•	2.6	5.0	•	2.5	5.4	•	1.1	6.6	3.0

Table II
Corporations with Net Income

Motion Picture and Video Industries (except Video Rental)

Money Amounts and Size of Assets in Thousands of Dollars

Item Description for Accounting Period 7/02 Through 6/03	Total	Zero Assets	Under 500	500 to 1,000	1,000 to 5,000	5,000 to 10,000	10,000 to 25,000	25,000 to 50,000	50,000 to 100,000	100,000 to 250,000	250,000 to 500,000	500,000 to 2,500,000	2,500,000 and over
Number of Enterprises **1**	9641	1048	7790	0	0	67	38	14	9	4	0	4	0
Revenues ($ in Thousands)													
Net Sales **2**	37926979	1046082	2451569	0	0	867489	832967	1179865	571401	451042	0	2214713	0
Interest **3**	787495	889	1736	0	0	261	2748	805	438	5367	0	31904	0
Rents **4**	287698	367	0	0	0	340	389	83	1190	0	0	2343	0
Royalties **5**	529392	0	27279	0	0	0	26	0	0	0	0	202369	0
Other Portfolio Income **6**	122725	0	78	0	0	3213	3008	1387	1733	279	0	14553	0
Other Receipts **7**	1261867	103581	148266	0	0	31604	54271	12685	3386	112675	0	43840	0
Total Receipts **8**	40916156	1150919	2628928	0	0	902907	893409	1194825	578148	569363	0	2509722	0
Average Total Receipts **9**	4244	1098	337	•	•	13476	23511	85345	64239	142341	•	627430	•
Operating Costs/Operating Income (%)													
Cost of Operations **10**	25.8	2.2	30.9	•	•	24.9	45.7	23.8	19.0	62.1	•	41.3	•
Salaries and Wages **11**	13.9	12.4	4.9	•	•	19.5	12.0	5.9	6.9	9.3	•	10.9	•
Taxes Paid **12**	2.3	3.8	2.4	•	•	1.8	2.4	1.9	2.5	1.9	•	2.5	•
Interest Paid **13**	5.2	2.3	0.3	•	•	0.5	1.2	0.5	2.9	5.7	•	2.3	•
Depreciation **14**	4.1	5.8	1.5	•	•	5.1	7.2	2.8	10.1	3.7	•	4.5	•
Amortization and Depletion **15**	11.8	2.2	0.1	•	•	4.1	2.5	0.1	12.9	0.3	•	6.2	•
Pensions and Other Deferred Comp. **16**	0.5	0.1	1.1	•	•	0.2	0.3	0.0	0.1	0.1	•	0.0	•
Employee Benefits **17**	1.0	0.9	0.6	•	•	1.4	0.8	0.5	0.3	0.4	•	1.4	•
Advertising **18**	4.2	1.8	0.5	•	•	0.9	0.9	6.3	1.0	0.7	•	3.3	•
Other Expenses **19**	25.2	71.8	22.6	•	•	15.5	20.3	35.4	32.4	28.3	•	12.8	•
Officers' Compensation **20**	3.8	•	29.1	•	•	15.5	3.0	10.4	0.9	1.1	•	1.5	•
Operating Margin **21**	2.2	•	6.1	•	•	10.4	3.7	12.4	11.1	•	•	13.2	•
Operating Margin Before Officers' Comp. **22**	5.9	•	35.2	•	•	26.0	6.8	22.8	12.0	•	•	14.8	•

Selected Average Balance Sheet ($ in Thousands)

Net Receivables 23	881	0	2	•	1883	2808	5249	10833	10537	•	61542
Inventories 24	493	0	2	•	128	751	1588	292	6406	•	74515
Net Property, Plant and Equipment 25	1152	0	13	•	1458	3785	13029	33109	44249	•	207341
Total Assets 26	12399	0	90	•	6995	14803	33994	72853	148155	•	1031884
Notes and Loans Payable 27	1695	0	18	•	1227	3809	6498	28075	44119	•	149850
All Other Liabilities 28	3257	0	8	•	1090	4470	13225	13824	70686	•	321586
Net Worth 29	7447	0	65	•	4677	6525	14272	30954	33351	•	560447

Selected Financial Ratios (Times to 1)

Current Ratio 30	1.0	•	5.4	•	2.9	1.5	1.3	1.3	1.0	•	1.2
Quick Ratio 31	0.5	•	4.4	•	2.7	1.1	0.8	1.0	0.6	•	0.3
Net Sales to Working Capital 32	•	•	8.4	•	4.9	9.1	20.0	11.2	•	•	9.0
Coverage Ratio 33	3.0	4.0	51.1	•	28.6	10.0	26.6	5.2	3.2	•	12.3
Total Asset Turnover 34	0.3	•	3.5	•	1.9	1.5	2.5	0.9	0.8	•	0.5
Inventory Turnover 35	2.1	•	57.0	•	25.3	13.3	12.7	41.2	10.9	•	3.1
Receivables Turnover 36	4.2	•	90.1	•	6.6	7.0	13.7	6.0	5.9	•	13.0
Total Liabilities to Net Worth 37	0.7	•	0.4	•	0.5	1.3	1.4	1.4	3.4	•	0.8
Current Assets to Working Capital 38	•	•	1.2	•	1.5	3.0	4.2	4.1	•	•	5.9
Current Liabilities to Working Capital 39	•	•	0.2	•	0.5	2.0	3.2	3.1	•	•	4.9
Working Capital to Net Sales 40	•	•	0.1	•	0.2	0.1	0.0	0.1	•	•	0.1
Inventory to Working Capital 41	•	•	0.1	•	0.0	0.3	0.2	0.1	•	•	2.4
Total Receipts to Cash Flow 42	3.8	3.7	3.2	•	4.0	3.8	2.2	2.7	2.7	•	2.9
Cost of Goods to Cash Flow 43	1.0	0.1	1.0	•	1.0	1.7	0.5	0.5	1.6	•	1.2
Cash Flow to Total Debt 44	0.2	•	3.9	•	1.4	0.7	2.0	0.6	0.4	•	0.4

Selected Financial Factors (in Percentages)

Debt Ratio 45	39.9	•	27.9	•	33.1	55.9	58.0	57.5	77.5	•	45.7
Return on Total Assets 46	4.9	•	47.7	•	27.8	18.0	35.2	13.2	13.9	•	15.4
Return on Equity Before Income Taxes 47	5.4	•	64.9	•	40.2	36.7	80.7	25.0	42.5	•	26.0
Return on Equity After Income Taxes 48	4.2	•	63.8	•	39.7	35.2	73.4	24.0	42.1	•	17.2
Profit Margin (Before Income Tax) 49	10.3	6.9	13.4	•	14.5	10.9	13.7	12.2	12.6	•	26.3
Profit Margin (After Income Tax) 50	7.9	6.6	13.1	•	14.4	10.5	12.4	11.7	12.5	•	17.4

Table I

Corporations with and without Net Income

SOUND RECORDING INDUSTRIES

MONEY AMOUNTS AND SIZE OF ASSETS IN THOUSANDS OF DOLLARS

Item Description for Accounting Period 7/02 Through 6/03	Total	Zero Assets	Under 500	500 to 1,000	1,000 to 5,000	5,000 to 10,000	10,000 to 25,000	25,000 to 50,000	50,000 to 100,000	100,000 to 250,000	250,000 to 500,000	500,000 to 2,500,000	2,500,000 and over
Number of Enterprises **1**	9779	1973	7343	204	182	37	21	11	0	3	0	4	0
Revenues ($ in Thousands)													
Net Sales **2**	11750282	129064	1519576	49348	234858	69517	290428	361822	0	548962	0	8546707	0
Interest **3**	175230	195	162	26	7183	0	1857	1007	0	917	0	163884	0
Rents **4**	39310	0	805	611	637	0	371	2504	0	469	0	33913	0
Royalties **5**	1746408	0	282	0	16761	0	15064	25752	0	15279	0	1673270	0
Other Portfolio Income **6**	167791	2	0	12	1556	12	468	764	0		0	164980	0
Other Receipts **7**	282176	13982	57818	10593	874	2732	14354	47853	0	10026	0	123942	0
Total Receipts **8**	14161197	143243	1578643	60590	261869	72261	322542	439702	0	575653	0	10706696	0
Average Total Receipts **9**	1448	73	215	297	1439	1953	15359	39973	•	191884	•	2676674	•
Operating Costs/Operating Income (%)													
Cost of Operations **10**	49.3	17.5	13.6	37.6	35.3	43.4	61.0	48.7	•	33.4	•	57.2	•
Salaries and Wages **11**	13.4	6.9	12.0	10.3	14.0	11.7	11.7	9.0	•	10.4	•	14.2	•
Taxes Paid **12**	5.6	0.7	3.3	1.7	3.1	2.0	1.8	6.4	•	0.6	•	6.6	•
Interest Paid **13**	3.9	1.0	0.7	8.4	8.7	0.8	2.4	1.6	•	2.9	•	4.6	•
Depreciation **14**	7.2	16.5	3.9	1.1	6.1	6.8	4.1	2.0	•	2.2	•	8.4	•
Amortization and Depletion **15**	4.5	•	0.1	•	2.8	0.1	1.2	3.1	•	2.5	•	5.8	•
Pensions and Other Deferred Comp. **16**	0.3	0.0	0.2	0.2	•	0.0	0.3	0.3	•	0.0	•	0.3	•
Employee Benefits **17**	1.8	0.2	1.4	0.0	0.4	0.3	0.6	0.5	•	1.6	•	2.1	•
Advertising **18**	7.2	5.7	1.9	2.5	5.6	0.8	2.1	3.6	•	17.0	•	8.0	•
Other Expenses **19**	28.6	66.7	56.7	24.2	47.5	51.7	21.5	35.7	•	42.3	•	21.4	•
Officers' Compensation **20**	3.1	1.3	15.3	9.9	2.0	1.6	3.3	4.1	•	0.8	•	1.1	•
Operating Margin **21**	•	•	•	4.1	•	•	•	•	•	•	•	•	•
Operating Margin Before Officers' Comp. **22**	•	•	6.3	14.0	•	•	•	•	•	•	•	•	•

Selected Average Balance Sheet ($ in Thousands)

Net Receivables 23	6196	0	8	91	305	439	2155	4133	•	35310	•	15060598
Inventories 24	173	0	6	241	49	38	1922	1610	•	10877	•	375362
Net Property, Plant and Equipment 25	229	0	21	49	553	1778	2864	3265	•	23748	•	436196
Total Assets 26	17053	0	58	836	2202	6360	13976	37933	•	241891	•	41023466
Notes and Loans Payable 27	622	0	109	875	1025	5422	6462	23124	•	107209	•	1000305
All Other Liabilities 28	6244	0	23	13	549	176	4766	56342	•	122566	•	14924083
Net Worth 29	10187	0	-75	-52	627	761	2748	-41533	•	12116	•	25099078

Selected Financial Ratios (Times to 1)

Current Ratio 30	1.1	•	1.6	15.2	1.5	2.4	1.0	0.4	•	1.0	•	1.1
Quick Ratio 31	1.1	•	0.7	8.3	0.6	0.4	0.6	0.3	•	0.5	•	1.1
Net Sales to Working Capital 32	1.8	•	15.6	1.3	3.1	0.7	110.6	•	•	64.2	•	1.3
Coverage Ratio 33	•	•	•	4.2	•	•	1.4	5.2	•	•	•	0.1
Total Asset Turnover 34	0.1	•	3.6	0.3	0.6	0.3	1.0	0.9	•	0.8	•	0.1
Inventory Turnover 35	3.4	•	4.7	0.4	9.3	21.4	4.4	9.9	•	5.6	•	3.3
Receivables Turnover 36	0.2	•	40.8	1.0	2.6	3.6	5.9	10.5	•	10.4	•	0.1
Total Liabilities to Net Worth 37	0.7	•	•	•	2.5	7.4	4.1	•	•	19.0	•	0.6
Current Assets to Working Capital 38	9.8	•	2.7	1.1	2.9	1.7	57.7	•	•	39.2	•	9.5
Current Liabilities to Working Capital 39	8.8	•	1.7	0.1	1.9	0.7	56.7	•	•	38.2	•	8.5
Working Capital to Net Sales 40	0.6	•	0.1	0.8	0.3	1.3	0.0	•	•	0.0	•	0.8
Inventory to Working Capital 41	0.1	•	0.7	0.5	0.1	0.0	11.7	•	•	3.8	•	0.1
Total Receipts to Cash Flow 42	5.1	1.9	2.5	2.1	3.1	3.0	5.3	2.7	•	3.1	•	7.4
Cost of Goods to Cash Flow 43	2.5	0.3	0.3	0.8	1.1	1.3	3.2	1.3	•	1.0	•	4.2
Cash Flow to Total Debt 44	0.0	•	0.6	0.1	0.3	0.1	0.2	0.2	•	0.3	•	0.0

Selected Financial Factors (in Percentages)

Debt Ratio 45	40.3	•	228.6	106.3	71.5	88.0	80.3	209.5	•	95.0	•	38.8
Return on Total Assets 46	•	•	•	10.2	•	•	3.3	7.4	•	•	•	0.0
Return on Equity Before Income Taxes 47	•	•	14.0	•	•	•	4.7	•	•	•	•	•
Return on Equity After Income Taxes 48	•	•	14.3	•	•	•	0.9	•	•	•	•	•
Profit Margin (Before Income Tax) 49	•	•	•	26.8	•	•	0.9	6.9	•	•	•	•
Profit Margin (After Income Tax) 50	•	•	•	26.8	•	•	0.2	5.5	•	•	•	•

Table II
Corporations with Net Income

SOUND RECORDING INDUSTRIES

MONEY AMOUNTS AND SIZE OF ASSETS IN THOUSANDS OF DOLLARS

Item Description for Accounting Period 7/02 Through 6/03	Total	Zero Assets	Under 500	500 to 1,000	1,000 to 5,000	5,000 to 10,000	10,000 to 25,000	25,000 to 50,000	50,000 to 100,000	100,000 to 250,000	250,000 to 500,000	500,000 to 2,500,000	2,500,000 and over
Number of Enterprises **1**	3276	448	2491	0	0	0	10	8	0	•	•	0	•
Revenues ($ in Thousands)													
Net Sales **2**	2138707	95563	951262	0	0	0	192074	684375	0	•	•	0	•
Interest **3**	5231	195	156	0	0	0	579	3449	0	•	•	0	•
Rents **4**	7349	0	0	0	0	0	9	6729	0	•	•	0	•
Royalties **5**	56124	0	0	0	0	0	9535	33106	0	•	•	0	•
Other Portfolio Income **6**	129468	2	0	0	0	0	457	127442	0	•	•	0	•
Other Receipts **7**	78284	5	17610	0	0	0	4655	46016	0	•	•	0	•
Total Receipts **8**	2415163	95765	969028	0	0	0	207309	901117	0	•	•	0	•
Average Total Receipts **9**	737	214	389	•	•	•	20731	112640	•	•	•		•
Operating Costs/Operating Income (%)													
Cost of Operations **10**	17.2	5.1	1.2	•	•	•	63.2	24.1	•	•	•	•	•
Salaries and Wages **11**	15.3	0.0	14.5	•	•	•	9.4	21.8	•	•	•	•	•
Taxes Paid **12**	3.9	0.0	2.6	•	•	•	1.4	7.4	•	•	•	•	•
Interest Paid **13**	2.1	1.1	0.5	•	•	•	1.0	3.6	•	•	•	•	•
Depreciation **14**	7.2	22.0	5.3	•	•	•	2.4	10.2	•	•	•	•	•
Amortization and Depletion **15**	0.7	•	0.0	•	•	•	0.3	1.8	•	•	•	•	•
Pensions and Other Deferred Comp. **16**	0.5	0.0	0.2	•	•	•	0.3	1.3	•	•	•	•	•
Employee Benefits **17**	1.7	0.0	1.2	•	•	•	0.6	3.5	•	•	•	•	•
Advertising **18**	1.8	•	0.7	•	•	•	2.3	3.7	•	•	•	•	•
Other Expenses **19**	39.7	25.4	49.0	•	•	•	15.6	36.0	•	•	•	•	•
Officers' Compensation **20**	8.7	0.1	16.0	•	•	•	2.4	3.4	•	•	•	•	•
Operating Margin **21**	1.2	46.3	8.8	•	•	•	1.0	•	•	•	•	•	•
Operating Margin Before Officers' Comp. **22**	9.8	46.3	24.7	•	•	•	3.4	•	•	•	•	•	•

Selected Average Balance Sheet ($ in Thousands)

Line Item					
Net Receivables 23	49	0	0	2304	9203
Inventories 24	399	0	0	2568	2987
Net Property, Plant and Equipment 25	406	0	50	1662	143299
Total Assets 26	984	0	88	13587	305280
Notes and Loans Payable 27	426	0	31	3008	132519
All Other Liabilities 28	350	0	24	5548	122415
Net Worth 29	208	0	34	5032	50346

Selected Financial Ratios (Times to 1)

Line Item					
Current Ratio 30	0.7	·	13.9	1.6	0.4
Quick Ratio 31	0.4	·	6.5	0.9	0.3
Net Sales to Working Capital 32	·	·	11.1	6.2	·
Coverage Ratio 33	7.6	44.6	20.5	9.6	5.2
Total Asset Turnover 34	0.7	·	4.3	1.4	0.3
Inventory Turnover 35	0.3	·	3.2	4.7	6.9
Receivables Turnover 36	0.1	·	255.4	6.9	10.7
Total Liabilities to Net Worth 37	3.7	·	1.6	1.7	5.1
Current Assets to Working Capital 38	·	·	1.1	2.8	·
Current Liabilities to Working Capital 39	·	·	0.1	1.8	·
Working Capital to Net Sales 40	·	·	0.1	0.2	·
Inventory to Working Capital 41	·	·	·	0.6	·
Total Receipts to Cash Flow 42	2.2	1.6	2.0	4.5	2.5
Cost of Goods to Cash Flow 43	0.4	0.1	0.0	2.9	0.6
Cash Flow to Total Debt 44	0.4	·	3.5	0.5	0.1

Selected Financial Factors (in Percentages)

Line Item					
Debt Ratio 45	78.8	·	61.2	63.0	83.5
Return on Total Assets 46	10.8	·	48.4	14.0	5.2
Return on Equity Before Income Taxes 47	44.3	·	118.8	33.9	25.5
Return on Equity After Income Taxes 48	42.3	·	116.7	29.5	24.3
Profit Margin (Before Income Tax) 49	14.1	46.5	10.6	8.9	15.0
Profit Margin (After Income Tax) 50	13.5	44.3	10.4	7.7	14.3

Table I

Corporations with and without Net Income

BROADCASTING (EXCEPT INTERNET)

MONEY AMOUNTS AND SIZE OF ASSETS IN THOUSANDS OF DOLLARS

Item Description for Accounting Period 7/02 Through 6/03	Total	Zero Assets	Under 500	500 to 1,000	1,000 to 5,000	5,000 to 10,000	10,000 to 25,000	25,000 to 50,000	50,000 to 100,000	100,000 to 250,000	250,000 to 500,000	500,000 to 2,500,000	2,500,000 and over
Number of Enterprises **1**	6772	1249	3617	738	754	141	119	38	36	32	11	27	9
Revenues ($ in Thousands)													
Net Sales **2**	66159220	493907	884400	977055	2003723	779251	1171714	599565	1067513	2682960	1552536	7633655	46312940
Interest **3**	1785194	17509	194	7329	2896	918	5176	4547	8580	25453	32990	394484	1285117
Rents **4**	383003	143	629	0	3301	892	2504	1246	2499	4117	8741	32289	326644
Royalties **5**	2307517	0	72051	0	174	0	0	138	0	25	0	173169	2061960
Other Portfolio Income **6**	2115982	146185	390	3227	4001	9194	30603	12282	15587	44501	172232	584528	1093251
Other Receipts **7**	-694185	-2894909	15978	18039	2658	25972	68433	7783	40230	32543	12001	183224	1793863
Total Receipts **8**	72056731	-2237165	973642	1005650	2016753	816227	1278430	625561	1134409	2789599	1778500	9001349	52873775
Average Total Receipts **9**	10640	-1791	269	1363	2675	5789	10743	16462	31511	87175	161682	333383	5874864
Operating Costs/Operating Income (%)													
Cost of Operations **10**	27.2	15.4	33.6	2.4	22.1	42.9	26.6	21.3	22.6	39.5	4.7	14.5	30.0
Salaries and Wages **11**	17.2	29.3	16.5	34.9	28.0	16.7	20.3	17.4	28.1	11.4	19.4	22.0	15.4
Taxes Paid **12**	3.9	3.9	3.3	5.4	4.4	2.5	3.6	4.0	3.8	2.6	3.3	5.2	3.8
Interest Paid **13**	8.5	14.6	2.2	3.1	2.9	2.7	4.0	4.6	7.9	7.1	15.8	19.2	7.3
Depreciation **14**	11.1	10.2	2.4	3.0	4.7	5.3	7.4	9.0	8.6	11.3	14.5	8.3	12.3
Amortization and Depletion **15**	6.2	7.7	0.8	1.0	1.9	3.6	4.1	4.7	9.8	4.4	13.0	19.3	4.4
Pensions and Other Deferred Comp. **16**	0.2	3.7	•	0.0	0.2	0.1	0.6	0.3	0.6	0.2	0.3	0.3	0.2
Employee Benefits **17**	1.0	1.3	2.1	1.7	2.1	0.8	1.3	1.4	2.3	1.2	1.7	1.4	0.8
Advertising **18**	1.9	2.5	1.4	2.1	1.4	3.5	2.2	2.8	1.7	2.2	4.1	2.6	1.7
Other Expenses **19**	35.7	46.8	32.8	28.1	33.5	20.1	31.3	45.5	31.4	25.4	39.5	48.8	34.5
Officers' Compensation **20**	1.5	9.8	18.8	19.0	4.5	1.1	3.4	2.8	3.3	1.6	1.5	1.3	0.6
Operating Margin **21**	•	•	•	•	•	0.6	•	•	•	•	•	•	•
Operating Margin Before Officers' Comp. **22**	•	•	4.9	18.4	•	1.8	•	•	•	•	•	•	•

Selected Average Balance Sheet ($ in Thousands)

Net Receivables 23	5120	0	30	175	360	620	1973	3414	5717	18280	42452	66056	3407871
Inventories 24	346	0	0	0	26	35	122	507	499	3645	1272	30458	146074
Net Property, Plant and Equipment 25	4355	0	36	199	631	1734	3077	5759	12245	39294	74837	124431	2447977
Total Assets 26	40570	0	116	690	2246	7221	15329	38143	73313	168148	380740	1411629	24167246
Notes and Loans Payable 27	14484	0	89	661	2085	3574	7740	14405	39770	77599	245831	587261	7917189
All Other Liabilities 28	9424	0	397	253	928	1811	2848	8555	9454	46655	85093	241967	5697126
Net Worth 29	16662	0	-370	-224	-767	1836	4741	15183	24089	43895	49816	582401	10552930

Selected Financial Ratios (Times to 1)

Current Ratio 30	1.2	•	0.3	0.7	1.2	1.5	1.4	1.5	1.1	1.3	1.0	1.8	1.2
Quick Ratio 31	1.0	•	0.3	0.7	0.9	1.3	1.1	1.1	0.7	1.0	0.8	1.1	1.0
Net Sales to Working Capital 32	6.8	•	•	•	15.5	5.7	6.6	4.5	21.5	10.0	•	3.0	6.9
Coverage Ratio 33	0.4	•	•	1.7	•	3.0	2.1	•	•	0.6	0.8	•	1.5
Total Asset Turnover 34	0.2	•	2.1	1.9	1.2	0.8	0.6	0.4	0.4	0.5	0.4	0.2	0.2
Inventory Turnover 35	7.7	•	3457.6	•	22.5	67.8	21.5	6.6	13.4	9.1	5.2	1.3	10.6
Receivables Turnover 36	•	•	•	•	•	•	•	•	•	•	•	•	•
Total Liabilities to Net Worth 37	1.4	•	•	•	2.9	2.2	1.5	2.0	2.8	6.6	•	1.4	1.3
Current Assets to Working Capital 38	5.2	•	•	•	5.5	3.0	3.3	3.2	15.1	4.6	•	2.2	6.0
Current Liabilities to Working Capital 39	4.2	•	•	•	4.5	2.0	2.3	2.2	14.1	3.6	•	1.2	5.0
Working Capital to Net Sales 40	0.1	•	•	0.1	0.1	0.2	0.2	0.2	0.0	0.1	0.1	0.3	0.1
Inventory to Working Capital 41	0.2	•	•	•	0.2	0.1	0.1	0.1	0.4	0.4	•	0.3	0.2
Total Receipts to Cash Flow 42	4.2	4.5	4.5	3.9	4.4	4.5	3.3	3.2	8.4	5.4	4.8	7.1	3.1
Cost of Goods to Cash Flow 43	1.1	1.5	1.5	0.1	1.0	1.9	0.9	0.7	1.9	2.2	0.2	1.0	0.9
Cash Flow to Total Debt 44	0.1	0.1	0.1	0.4	0.2	0.3	0.2	0.1	0.1	0.1	0.1	0.0	0.1

Selected Financial Factors (in Percentages)

Debt Ratio 45	58.9	•	418.6	132.4	134.2	74.6	69.1	60.2	67.1	73.9	86.9	58.7	56.3
Return on Total Assets 46	0.7	•	•	10.3	•	6.2	5.3	•	•	2.1	4.7	•	2.3
Return on Equity Before Income Taxes 47	•	•	2.5	•	17.7	16.1	8.7	•	•	•	•	•	1.7
Return on Equity After Income Taxes 48	•	•	2.9	•	20.4	13.7	5.5	•	•	•	•	•	1.3
Profit Margin (Before Income Tax) 49	•	•	2.3	2.3	4.2	5.3	•	•	•	•	•	•	3.5
Profit Margin (After Income Tax) 50	•	•	2.3	2.3	2.6	4.6	•	•	•	•	•	•	2.6

Table II
Corporations with Net Income

BROADCASTING (EXCEPT INTERNET)

MONEY AMOUNTS AND SIZE OF ASSETS IN THOUSANDS OF DOLLARS

Item Description for Accounting Period 7/02 Through 6/03	Total	Zero Assets	Under 500	500 to 1,000	1,000 to 5,000	5,000 to 10,000	10,000 to 25,000	25,000 to 50,000	50,000 to 100,000	100,000 to 250,000	250,000 to 500,000	500,000 to 2,500,000	2,500,000 and over
Number of Enterprises 1	2051	134	1151	167	383	88	67	15	15	15	0	10	6
Revenues ($ in Thousands)													
Net Sales 2	51579990	103643	325079	507538	1221652	622953	856374	273568	474895	2101252	0	2941072	42151962
Interest 3	1445723	2736	0	25	2626	672	3574	1366	2839	21619	0	221438	1188827
Rents 4	339064	0	0	0	3296	803	1894	280	2082	2744	0	7214	320752
Royalties 5	2294432	0	72051	0	0	0	0	0	0	15	0	160406	2061960
Other Portfolio Income 6	1341200	135995	0	0	4001	8781	27124	11572	10947	209355	0	496728	436696
Other Receipts 7	1668976	1618	2967	21277	5113	21800	44650	21306	6564	23145	0	99169	1421371
Total Receipts 8	58669385	243992	400097	528840	1236688	655009	933616	308092	497327	2358130	0	3926027	47581568
Average Total Receipts 9	28605	1821	348	3167	3229	7443	13935	20539	33155	157209	•	392603	7930261
Operating Costs/Operating Income (%)													
Cost of Operations 10	30.1	1.1	55.6	•	11.5	48.4	24.4	16.2	10.7	45.6	•	12.7	31.5
Salaries and Wages 11	15.7	35.2	8.0	23.5	26.7	9.7	20.1	20.2	26.2	11.3	•	24.9	14.8
Taxes Paid 12	3.8	5.8	1.6	5.1	3.9	1.8	3.9	3.6	3.3	2.6	•	4.0	3.9
Interest Paid 13	6.6	6.1	0.0	2.0	1.6	1.3	2.0	3.1	2.6	5.4	•	14.2	6.6
Depreciation 14	9.5	2.0	0.6	0.4	3.4	4.0	5.7	6.1	7.2	6.0	•	4.8	10.5
Amortization and Depletion 15	4.3	0.4	•	0.0	0.5	3.5	3.0	3.2	3.7	5.3	•	10.9	4.0
Pensions and Other Deferred Comp. 16	0.2	16.7	•	0.1	0.2	0.0	0.7	0.5	0.8	0.2	•	0.4	0.1
Employee Benefits 17	0.7	0.1	1.2	1.4	2.0	0.4	1.3	1.5	1.6	1.0	•	1.7	0.6
Advertising 18	1.8	4.2	0.8	2.9	1.5	2.4	2.3	2.5	1.6	3.1	•	2.1	1.7
Other Expenses 19	32.8	32.0	30.2	25.1	28.5	17.0	27.3	33.5	27.2	16.3	•	35.9	34.1
Officers' Compensation 20	1.2	27.9	7.2	29.6	5.9	0.6	3.5	2.8	3.3	1.3	•	1.6	0.5
Operating Margin 21	•	•	•	9.9	14.3	10.7	5.7	6.9	11.9	1.8	•	•	•
Operating Margin Before Officers' Comp. 22	•	•	2.0	39.5	20.2	11.4	9.3	9.7	15.2	3.1	•	•	•

Selected Average Balance Sheet ($ in Thousands)

Net Receivables 23	14344	0	27	284	346	777	2057	2700	4766	21643	•	103782	4588057
Inventories 24	678	0	0	0	0	27	153	1236	40	6517	•	322	209619
Net Property, Plant and Equipment 25	9475	0	8	175	441	1891	3208	4955	13705	33666	•	69411	2894367
Total Assets 26	108572	0	62	802	2025	7854	15342	38755	70578	200727	•	1233206	33833179
Notes and Loans Payable 27	32286	0	3	634	727	3664	6103	13047	24640	69850	•	396355	9920372
All Other Liabilities 28	24825	0	165	443	196	2457	2506	10994	13965	65031	•	217410	7778244
Net Worth 29	51461	0	-106	-275	1101	1734	6733	14714	31972	65845	•	619441	16134562

Selected Financial Ratios (Times to 1)

Current Ratio 30	1.2	•	0.2	0.8	3.3	1.2	2.2	2.3	2.1	1.1	•	2.6	1.2
Quick Ratio 31	1.0	•	0.2	0.8	3.0	1.0	1.7	1.5	0.8	0.7	•	1.8	0.9
Net Sales to Working Capital 32	6.5	•	•	•	4.9	14.8	4.1	2.2	3.1	20.8	•	1.6	7.9
Coverage Ratio 33	2.1	18.1	513.9	7.9	10.5	12.8	8.2	7.3	7.3	3.6	•	2.4	1.7
Total Asset Turnover 34	0.2	•	4.6	3.8	1.6	0.9	0.8	0.5	0.4	0.7	•	0.2	0.2
Inventory Turnover 35	11.2	•	•	•	•	124.9	20.4	2.4	83.9	9.8	•	115.6	10.5
Receivables Turnover 36	•	•	•	•	•	•	•	•	•	•	•	•	•
Total Liabilities to Net Worth 37	1.1	•	•	•	0.8	3.5	1.3	1.6	1.2	2.0	•	1.0	1.1
Current Assets to Working Capital 38	5.3	•	•	•	1.4	6.8	1.9	1.8	1.9	9.6	•	1.6	6.8
Current Liabilities to Working Capital 39	4.3	•	•	•	0.4	5.8	0.9	0.8	0.9	8.6	•	0.6	5.8
Working Capital to Net Sales 40	0.2	•	•	•	0.2	0.1	0.2	0.5	0.3	0.0	•	0.6	0.1
Inventory to Working Capital 41	0.2	•	•	•	•	0.1	0.0	0.1	0.0	1.0	•	0.0	0.2
Total Receipts to Cash Flow 42	2.9	2.0	2.2	2.6	2.5	3.4	2.7	2.1	2.6	5.6	•	2.6	2.8
Cost of Goods to Cash Flow 43	0.9	0.0	1.2	•	0.3	1.6	0.7	0.3	0.3	2.5	•	0.3	0.9
Cash Flow to Total Debt 44	0.2	•	•	1.1	1.4	0.3	0.5	0.4	0.3	0.2	•	0.2	0.1

Selected Financial Factors (in Percentages)

Debt Ratio 45	52.6	•	272.1	134.3	45.6	77.9	56.1	62.0	54.7	67.2	•	49.8	52.3
Return on Total Assets 46	3.2	•	•	61.1	27.1	15.5	14.0	10.6	8.5	13.6	•	8.2	2.4
Return on Equity Before Income Taxes 47	3.5	•	81.8	•	45.1	64.7	28.0	24.1	16.2	29.8	•	9.5	2.1
Return on Equity After Income Taxes 48	2.9	•	•	•	41.3	60.7	23.9	19.0	13.7	24.3	•	8.9	1.7
Profit Margin (Before Income Tax) 49	7.2	104.0	17.8	14.1	15.5	15.9	14.7	19.4	16.3	14.0	•	20.0	4.8
Profit Margin (After Income Tax) 50	6.0	97.2	16.4	14.1	14.3	14.9	12.6	15.4	13.8	11.4	•	18.7	3.8

Table I

Corporations with and without Net Income

INTERNET PUBLISHING AND BROADCASTING

MONEY AMOUNTS AND SIZE OF ASSETS IN THOUSANDS OF DOLLARS

Item Description for Accounting Period 7/02 Through 6/03	Total	Zero Assets	Under 500	500 to 1,000	1,000 to 5,000	5,000 to 10,000	10,000 to 25,000	25,000 to 50,000	50,000 to 100,000	100,000 to 250,000	250,000 to 500,000	500,000 to 2,500,000	2,500,000 and over
Number of Enterprises **1**	3137	247	2614	77	134	21	24	11	7	0	3	0	0
Revenues ($ in Thousands)													
Net Sales **2**	3265892	4255	232896	24359	374478	181833	261503	288739	232807	0	1665023	0	0
Interest **3**	29224	50	397	54	2272	946	5017	3577	6839	0	10071	0	0
Rents **4**	10321	0	4152	0	40	0	285	0	847	0	4996	0	0
Royalties **5**	17436	0	0	0	0	0	1486	194	0	0	15756	0	0
Other Portfolio Income **6**	4980	0	0	0	3480	8	676	62	51	0	702	0	0
Other Receipts **7**	137417	273	6298	55	22555	1633	6379	62501	30352	0	7374	0	0
Total Receipts **8**	3465270	4578	243743	24468	402825	184420	275346	355073	270896	0	1703922	0	0
Average Total Receipts **9**	1105	19	93	318	3006	8782	11473	32279	38699	•	567974	•	•
Operating Costs/Operating Income (%)													
Cost of Operations **10**	19.8	82.3	8.5	43.8	38.8	40.1	31.2	19.0	23.3	•	12.3	•	•
Salaries and Wages **11**	36.7	223.5	48.3	123.8	32.9	36.6	50.6	42.9	34.6	•	31.3	•	•
Taxes Paid **12**	3.4	60.6	5.0	8.7	3.0	3.9	4.3	2.2	5.3	•	2.8	•	•
Interest Paid **13**	6.9	0.9	2.0	6.6	2.0	0.8	1.2	0.7	1.9	•	12.1	•	•
Depreciation **14**	6.4	14.4	3.0	14.3	5.6	7.3	8.5	11.3	18.2	•	4.0	•	•
Amortization and Depletion **15**	5.1	82.3	0.5	6.8	1.8	0.8	2.1	9.3	9.0	•	5.9	•	•
Pensions and Other Deferred Comp. **16**	0.7	•	•	•	0.1	0.0	0.2	3.6	0.1	•	0.7	•	•
Employee Benefits **17**	2.3	10.6	2.3	14.8	1.3	1.5	3.8	4.2	2.4	•	1.9	•	•
Advertising **18**	2.2	0.0	1.3	5.2	5.5	2.2	4.4	4.6	7.2	•	•	•	•
Other Expenses **19**	38.5	225.1	61.3	49.6	35.2	50.6	45.9	41.9	57.6	•	29.6	•	•
Officers' Compensation **20**	3.3	•	4.2	19.6	3.3	7.9	6.1	2.7	3.2	•	2.2	•	•
Operating Margin **21**	•	•	•	•	•	•	•	•	•	•	•	•	•
Operating Margin Before Officers' Comp. **22**	•	•	•	•	•	•	•	•	•	•	•	•	•

Selected Average Balance Sheet ($ in Thousands)

	•	•	•	•	•	•	•	•	•	•
Net Receivables 23	154	0	9	39	256	1492	1920	9576	4859	68497
Inventories 24	14	0	0	0	158	0	389	445	67	2940
Net Property, Plant and Equipment 25	127	0	5	64	211	743	1979	3755	9479	60867
Total Assets 26	2440	0	27	724	1728	6111	15258	36871	87530	1928265
Notes and Loans Payable 27	1077	0	28	2033	1156	3669	2098	1400	12213	921884
All Other Liabilities 28	555	0	25	139	396	4275	6525	17348	33060	314008
Net Worth 29	808	0	-27	-1448	176	-1832	6635	18123	42257	692373

Selected Financial Ratios (Times to 1)

	•	•	•	•	•	•	•	•	•	•
Current Ratio 30	1.2	•	0.6	4.3	1.7	0.7	2.2	1.7	1.1	0.9
Quick Ratio 31	0.8	•	0.5	1.0	1.2	0.6	1.9	1.5	0.7	0.6
Net Sales to Working Capital 32	12.6	•	•	0.7	4.8	•	2.1	2.5	9.6	•
Coverage Ratio 33	•	•	•	•	•	•	•	•	•	1.0
Total Asset Turnover 34	0.4	•	3.3	0.4	1.6	1.4	0.7	0.7	0.4	0.3
Inventory Turnover 35	14.5	•	•	6.9	12154.8	8.7	11.2	115.5	23.3	•
Receivables Turnover 36	•	•	•	•	•	•	•	•	•	•
Total Liabilities to Net Worth 37	2.0	•	•	8.8	•	1.3	1.0	1.1	1.8	•
Current Assets to Working Capital 38	7.4	•	•	1.3	2.4	•	1.9	2.5	14.3	•
Current Liabilities to Working Capital 39	6.4	•	•	0.3	1.4	•	0.9	1.5	13.3	•
Working Capital to Net Sales 40	0.1	•	•	1.4	0.2	•	0.5	0.4	0.1	•
Inventory to Working Capital 41	0.2	•	•	•	0.3	•	0.1	0.0	•	•
Total Receipts to Cash Flow 42	9.5	6.5	•	•	•	•	5.8	21.2	4.4	•
Cost of Goods to Cash Flow 43	1.9	0.6	•	•	•	•	1.1	4.9	0.5	•
Cash Flow to Total Debt 44	0.1	0.3	•	•	•	•	0.2	0.0	0.1	•

Selected Financial Factors (in Percentages)

	•	•	•	•	•	•	•	•	•	•
Debt Ratio 45	66.9	•	200.4	299.9	89.8	130.0	56.5	50.8	51.7	64.1
Return on Total Assets 46	•	•	•	•	•	•	•	•	•	3.4
Return on Equity Before Income Taxes 47	•	•	105.5	42.1	•	238.0	•	•	•	•
Return on Equity After Income Taxes 48	•	•	105.5	42.1	•	238.0	•	•	•	•
Profit Margin (Before Income Tax) 49	•	•	•	•	•	•	•	•	•	•
Profit Margin (After Income Tax) 50	•	•	•	•	•	•	•	•	•	•

Table II
Corporations with Net Income

INTERNET PUBLISHING AND BROADCASTING

MONEY AMOUNTS AND SIZE OF ASSETS IN THOUSANDS OF DOLLARS

Item Description for Accounting Period 7/02 Through 6/03	Total	Zero Assets	Under 500	500 to 1,000	1,000 to 5,000	5,000 to 10,000	10,000 to 25,000	25,000 to 50,000	50,000 to 100,000	100,000 to 250,000	250,000 to 500,000	500,000 to 2,500,000	2,500,000 and over
Number of Enterprises **1**	1419	0	1326	0	0	0	0	7	0	0	0	0	0
Revenues ($ in Thousands)													
Net Sales **2**	937560	0	52403	0	0	0	0	498146	0	0	0	0	0
Interest **3**	7904	0	1	0	0	0	0	7402	0	0	0	0	0
Rents **4**	0	0	0	0	0	0	0	0	0	0	0	0	0
Royalties **5**	0	0	0	0	0	0	0	0	0	0	0	0	0
Other Portfolio Income **6**	2755	0	0	0	0	0	0	0	0	0	0	0	0
Other Receipts **7**	28991	0	11	0	0	0	0	3018	0	0	0	0	0
Total Receipts **8**	977210	0	52415	0	0	0	0	508566	0	0	0	0	0
Average Total Receipts **9**	689	.	40	.	.	.	.	72652	.	.	.	.	.
Operating Costs/Operating Income (%)													
Cost of Operations **10**	23.9	.	27.7	.	.	.	.	9.4	.	.	.	.	.
Salaries and Wages **11**	17.0	.	.	.	.	.	.	20.2	.	.	.	.	.
Taxes Paid **12**	1.8	.	5.3	.	.	.	.	1.5	.	.	.	.	.
Interest Paid **13**	0.2	.	0.8	.	.	.	.	0.3	.	.	.	.	.
Depreciation **14**	3.3	.	0.8	.	.	.	.	4.0	.	.	.	.	.
Amortization and Depletion **15**	2.0	.	.	.	.	.	.	3.3	.	.	.	.	.
Pensions and Other Deferred Comp. **16**	0.0	.	.	.	.	.	.	0.0	.	.	.	.	.
Employee Benefits **17**	0.5	.	.	.	.	.	.	0.7	.	.	.	.	.
Advertising **18**	3.1	.	1.1	.	.	.	.	1.7	.	.	.	.	.
Other Expenses **19**	36.2	.	51.0	.	.	.	.	51.0	.	.	.	.	.
Officers' Compensation **20**	2.5	.	.	.	.	.	.	3.4	.	.	.	.	.
Operating Margin **21**	9.2	.	13.4	.	.	.	.	4.5	.	.	.	.	.
Operating Margin Before Officers' Comp. **22**	11.8	.	13.4	.	.	.	.	7.9	.	.	.	.	.

Selected Average Balance Sheet ($ in Thousands)

Net Receivables 23	69	1	9723
Inventories 24	15	0	67
Net Property, Plant and Equipment 25	33	0	3478
Total Assets 26	474	10	71513
Notes and Loans Payable 27	58	2	575
All Other Liabilities 28	122	9	20944
Net Worth 29	294	-1	49994

Selected Financial Ratios (Times to 1)

Current Ratio 30	2.5	1.3	2.4
Quick Ratio 31	2.2	1.2	2.3
Net Sales to Working Capital 32	3.3	41.3	2.5
Coverage Ratio 33	58.7	18.5	32.5
Total Asset Turnover 34	1.4	4.0	1.0
Inventory Turnover 35	10.5		100.3
Receivables Turnover 36			
Total Liabilities to Net Worth 37	0.6		0.4
Current Assets to Working Capital 38	1.7	4.0	1.7
Current Liabilities to Working Capital 39	0.7	3.0	0.7
Working Capital to Net Sales 40	0.3	0.0	0.4
Inventory to Working Capital 41	0.1		0.0
Total Receipts to Cash Flow 42	2.2	1.6	2.0
Cost of Goods to Cash Flow 43	0.5	0.4	0.2
Cash Flow to Total Debt 44	1.6	2.2	1.7

Selected Financial Factors (in Percentages)

Debt Ratio 45	38.1	113.6	30.1
Return on Total Assets 46	20.3	56.9	8.4
Return on Equity Before Income Taxes 47	32.2		11.6
Return on Equity After Income Taxes 48	31.2		11.0
Profit Margin (Before Income Tax) 49	14.3	13.4	8.1
Profit Margin (After Income Tax) 50	13.9	13.4	7.7

Table I

Corporations with and without Net Income

TELECOMMUNICATIONS

MONEY AMOUNTS AND SIZE OF ASSETS IN THOUSANDS OF DOLLARS

Item Description for Accounting Period 7/02 Through 6/03	Total	Zero Assets	Under 500	500 to 1,000	1,000 to 5,000	5,000 to 10,000	10,000 to 25,000	25,000 to 50,000	50,000 to 100,000	100,000 to 250,000	250,000 to 500,000	500,000 to 2,500,000	2,500,000 and over
Number of Enterprises 1	17998	2751	12005	586	1372	342	409	198	124	90	31	49	40
Revenues ($ in Thousands)													
Net Sales 2	375023967	6062471	2900179	1159655	6418736	2583121	5947108	4860500	5268059	9261613	5774008	21884970	302903548
Interest 3	16117234	64422	25844	1339	12045	19613	84710	45776	53337	96122	64543	488363	15161120
Rents 4	6924300	433	0	3061	3915	3366	8691	16861	22524	37548	18426	44720	6764755
Royalties 5	1921937	0	0	0	0	0	701	0	2129	109938	9157	34187	1765776
Other Portfolio Income 6	6775574	299818	1396	34	7633	22483	122620	149874	54356	47706	20474	1209602	4839581
Other Receipts 7	19013377	232543	93125	19027	151284	254692	118431	142154	220165	327966	395744	382303	16675939
Total Receipts 8	425776389	6659687	3020544	1183116	6593663	2883275	6282261	5215165	5620570	9880893	6282352	24044145	348110719
Average Total Receipts 9	23657	2421	252	2019	4806	8431	15360	26339	45327	109788	202657	490697	8702768
Operating Costs/Operating Income (%)													
Cost of Operations 10	23.7	44.8	26.8	42.9	53.9	55.4	53.2	48.6	43.6	46.3	35.7	38.4	19.0
Salaries and Wages 11	13.3	10.5	26.1	17.8	15.5	22.6	15.9	10.9	14.7	15.9	20.5	14.7	12.7
Taxes Paid 12	2.5	2.6	2.6	5.3	1.9	2.5	2.7	2.2	2.4	2.4	3.3	2.7	2.5
Interest Paid 13	10.9	13.8	1.2	1.3	1.2	1.7	6.2	4.1	4.0	6.2	8.5	11.9	11.8
Depreciation 14	21.6	22.0	4.3	2.8	3.5	7.8	24.6	12.1	16.2	13.8	29.8	24.9	22.4
Amortization and Depletion 15	1.6	6.4	0.7	0.3	1.0	1.2	0.9	1.6	1.9	3.0	3.5	3.7	1.3
Pensions and Other Deferred Comp. 16	0.6	0.0	2.5	0.1	0.1	0.3	0.3	0.2	0.3	0.2	1.0	0.3	0.7
Employee Benefits 17	3.1	1.6	0.7	1.5	0.7	1.2	1.6	1.0	1.3	1.6	2.4	1.8	3.4
Advertising 18	2.4	2.1	1.5	2.1	1.0	1.6	1.4	1.2	1.0	1.2	1.4	2.6	2.6
Other Expenses 19	44.0	22.3	35.3	26.8	28.8	28.5	47.3	32.2	38.5	52.9	41.2	41.1	45.3
Officers' Compensation 20	0.5	1.4	11.2	5.8	4.5	3.4	1.9	1.9	1.4	1.0	0.9	0.5	0.2
Operating Margin 21	•	•	•	•	•	•	•	•	•	•	•	•	•
Operating Margin Before Officers' Comp. 22	•	•	•	•	•	•	•	•	•	•	•	•	•

Selected Average Balance Sheet ($ in Thousands)

Net Receivables 23	4240	0	5	164	502	1429	1877	4265	6621	18472	49288	112362	1596248
Inventories 24	376	0	4	60	131	279	385	790	1759	2382	4622	13506	121262
Net Property, Plant and Equipment 25	20256	0	21	129	579	2295	6200	13394	28457	55061	171857	372972	8134438
Total Assets 26	81415	0	77	703	2114	7368	16055	35347	69390	151262	369954	1257794	33741629
Notes and Loans Payable 27	29006	0	86	566	1021	2511	7378	17852	24485	69174	191329	758871	11487268
All Other Liabilities 28	21298	0	37	317	1127	2302	4174	11453	12496	51648	77000	355741	8759376
Net Worth 29	31110	0	-47	-180	-34	2554	4502	6042	32409	30440	101626	143181	13494985

Selected Financial Ratios (Times to 1)

Current Ratio 30	0.9	•	1.0	1.3	0.9	1.5	1.1	1.1	1.4	1.1	1.1	0.8	0.9
Quick Ratio 31	0.5	•	0.8	0.8	0.6	1.2	0.8	0.7	1.0	0.8	0.9	0.5	0.4
Net Sales to Working Capital 32	•	•	•	16.9	•	5.6	17.7	32.3	6.7	20.2	24.5	•	0.5
Coverage Ratio 33	0.1	•	•	•	•	•	•	•	•	•	•	•	•
Total Asset Turnover 34	0.3	•	3.2	2.8	2.2	1.0	0.9	0.7	0.6	0.5	0.5	0.4	0.2
Inventory Turnover 35	13.2	•	16.6	14.2	19.2	15.0	20.1	15.1	10.5	20.0	14.4	12.7	11.9
Receivables Turnover 36	•	•	•	•	•	•	•	•	•	•	•	•	•
Total Liabilities to Net Worth 37	1.6	•	•	•	•	1.9	2.6	4.9	1.1	4.0	2.6	7.8	1.5
Current Assets to Working Capital 38	•	•	•	4.6	•	3.1	7.7	2.6	16.9	3.3	9.9	•	12.6
Current Liabilities to Working Capital 39	•	•	•	3.6	•	2.1	6.7	1.6	15.9	2.3	8.9	•	11.6
Working Capital to Net Sales 40	•	•	•	0.1	•	0.2	0.1	0.0	0.1	0.0	0.0	•	0.0
Inventory to Working Capital 41	•	•	•	0.5	•	0.2	0.5	1.0	0.3	0.5	0.6	•	0.6
Total Receipts to Cash Flow 42	4.0	•	4.7	6.0	8.0	14.3	6.8	10.7	4.0	9.9	10.7	•	3.2
Cost of Goods to Cash Flow 43	1.0	•	1.2	2.6	4.3	7.9	3.3	4.7	2.6	7.9	7.8	•	0.6
Cash Flow to Total Debt 44	0.1	•	0.4	0.4	0.3	0.1	0.1	0.4	0.1	0.4	0.1	•	0.1

Selected Financial Factors (in Percentages)

Debt Ratio 45	61.8	•	161.0	125.7	101.6	65.3	72.0	82.9	53.3	79.9	72.5	88.6	60.0
Return on Total Assets 46	0.1	•	•	•	•	•	•	•	•	•	•	•	1.2
Return on Equity Before Income Taxes 47	•	•	44.8	51.4	1289.4	•	•	•	•	•	•	•	•
Return on Equity After Income Taxes 48	•	•	44.9	52.8	1359.4	•	•	•	•	•	•	•	•
Profit Margin (Before Income Tax) 49	•	•	•	•	•	•	•	•	•	•	•	•	•
Profit Margin (After Income Tax) 50	•	•	•	•	•	•	•	•	•	•	•	•	•

Table II
Corporations with Net Income

TELECOMMUNICATIONS

MONEY AMOUNTS AND SIZE OF ASSETS IN THOUSANDS OF DOLLARS

Item Description for Accounting Period 7/02 Through 6/03	Total	Zero Assets	Under 500	500 to 1,000	1,000 to 5,000	5,000 to 10,000	10,000 to 25,000	25,000 to 50,000	50,000 to 100,000	100,000 to 250,000	250,000 to 500,000	500,000 to 2,500,000	2,500,000 and over
Number of Enterprises **1**	6177	1434	3218	384	535	181	212	104	55	33	4	9	8
Revenues ($ in Thousands)													
Net Sales **2**	111693091	621149	1494730	696491	3537191	1199869	2612780	2409374	2891727	3427613	347478	3998776	88455912
Interest **3**	3491619	16637	2548	1171	3023	9761	19864	21074	30552	30122	11103	93075	3252691
Rents **4**	3019044	38	0	1011	1678	3019	6254	12898	20398	22093	0	15328	2936328
Royalties **5**	1825265	0	0	0	0	0	152	0	0	94313	0	31241	1699559
Other Portfolio Income **6**	3423187	135435	74	34	3658	22254	35913	127820	36980	27776	2047	1065520	1965678
Other Receipts **7**	5522395	128463	70157	1143	140488	206727	170714	100093	102921	98981	18760	152694	4331249
Total Receipts **8**	128974601	901722	1567509	699850	3686038	1441630	2845677	2671259	3082578	3700898	379388	5356634	102641417
Average Total Receipts **9**	20880	629	487	1823	6890	7965	13423	25685	56047	112148	94847	595182	12830177
Operating Costs/Operating Income (%)													
Cost of Operations **10**	30.0	54.6	26.6	31.1	56.0	49.6	41.1	41.2	45.0	44.2	49.2	40.1	26.3
Salaries and Wages **11**	8.7	22.1	33.2	20.7	13.9	13.6	11.5	6.4	9.0	11.6	7.8	9.4	7.6
Taxes Paid **12**	2.9	2.4	1.7	3.1	1.5	2.7	2.4	2.1	2.3	2.3	2.2	4.1	3.0
Interest Paid **13**	7.2	4.9	0.8	0.7	0.6	1.0	2.0	2.7	2.7	3.6	5.9	11.2	8.1
Depreciation **14**	20.2	2.1	2.2	2.4	2.8	8.0	9.1	11.0	10.7	11.5	9.5	17.7	23.0
Amortization and Depletion **15**	1.0	0.6	0.4	0.0	0.1	0.2	0.5	0.8	0.5	1.1	6.6	3.3	1.0
Pensions and Other Deferred Comp. **16**	0.5	0.3	1.2	0.1	0.1	0.5	0.4	0.3	0.4	0.4	0.1	0.2	0.6
Employee Benefits **17**	3.3	1.5	0.4	0.9	0.6	0.4	0.9	0.7	1.0	1.6	0.9	1.5	3.8
Advertising **18**	2.4	0.5	1.3	2.1	1.1	2.2	2.2	0.7	0.9	1.7	0.2	1.4	2.7
Other Expenses **19**	30.6	19.9	15.1	23.8	18.0	24.2	25.2	27.3	23.2	22.3	21.2	30.9	32.4
Officers' Compensation **20**	0.6	5.7	10.4	5.5	2.8	2.4	1.9	2.0	1.3	0.7	1.5	1.0	0.1
Operating Margin **21**	•	•	6.6	9.5	2.5	•	•	2.8	4.8	3.1	•	•	•
Operating Margin Before Officers' Comp. **22**	•	•	17.0	15.0	5.3	•	•	4.8	6.7	4.4	•	•	•

Selected Average Balance Sheet ($ in Thousands)

Net Receivables 23	3951	0	4	56	723	1177	1817	3035	6762	20029	88806	81120	2618841
Inventories 24	258	0	3	43	188	250	358	428	2576	1077	116	11970	126790
Net Property, Plant and Equipment 25	17059	0	26	118	695	3044	6723	14685	30238	62381	25731	227314	11937325
Total Assets 26	47784	0	104	680	2464	7650	16103	35359	71763	148524	380445	1245809	32898436
Notes and Loans Payable 27	12673	0	72	121	726	1244	4446	11440	22106	51134	45852	693461	8240821
All Other Liabilities 28	15481	0	5	117	715	1576	2855	4597	11403	40736	127652	382645	10986050
Net Worth 29	19630	0	27	442	1023	4830	8802	19322	38255	56654	206941	169703	13671565

Selected Financial Ratios (Times to 1)

Current Ratio 30	0.9	•	6.5	4.2	1.6	2.6	2.0	1.8	2.0	1.1	1.0	1.3	0.8
Quick Ratio 31	0.7	•	5.9	2.1	1.2	2.0	1.4	1.3	1.4	1.0	1.0	0.6	0.7
Net Sales to Working Capital 32	•	•	12.4	4.4	11.8	2.9	4.4	5.0	4.7	20.3	31.0	6.0	•
Coverage Ratio 33	2.2	7.5	15.8	14.4	12.2	16.2	6.9	6.7	4.6	2.9	1.7	2.2	2.0
Total Asset Turnover 34	0.4	•	4.5	2.7	2.7	0.9	0.8	0.7	0.7	0.7	0.2	0.4	0.3
Inventory Turnover 35	21.0	•	37.8	13.0	19.7	13.2	14.1	22.3	9.2	42.6	366.9	14.9	23.0
Receivables Turnover 36	•	•	•	•	•	•	•	•	•	•	•	•	•
Total Liabilities to Net Worth 37	1.4	•	2.9	0.5	1.4	0.6	0.8	0.8	0.9	1.6	0.8	6.3	1.4
Current Assets to Working Capital 38	•	•	1.2	1.3	2.6	1.6	2.0	2.3	2.0	8.2	43.6	4.3	•
Current Liabilities to Working Capital 39	•	•	0.2	0.3	1.6	0.6	1.0	1.3	1.0	7.2	42.6	3.3	•
Working Capital to Net Sales 40	•	•	0.1	0.2	0.1	0.3	0.2	0.2	0.2	0.0	0.0	0.2	•
Inventory to Working Capital 41	•	•	0.1	0.1	0.3	0.1	0.1	0.1	0.2	0.0	0.0	0.2	•
Total Receipts to Cash Flow 42	3.0	4.2	4.2	3.6	5.0	3.0	3.2	2.9	3.5	3.9	4.3	12.4	2.8
Cost of Goods to Cash Flow 43	0.9	2.3	1.1	1.1	2.8	1.5	1.3	1.2	1.6	1.7	2.1	5.0	0.7
Cash Flow to Total Debt 44	0.2	•	1.4	2.1	0.9	0.8	0.5	0.5	0.4	0.3	0.1	0.0	0.2

Selected Financial Factors (in Percentages)

Debt Ratio 45	58.9	•	74.5	35.0	58.5	36.9	45.3	45.4	46.7	61.9	45.6	86.4	58.4
Return on Total Assets 46	6.0	•	54.7	28.6	19.5	14.0	10.4	12.0	9.2	7.4	2.3	8.8	5.4
Return on Equity Before Income Taxes 47	8.1	•	201.3	40.9	43.0	20.8	16.4	18.7	13.5	12.8	1.7	34.9	6.6
Return on Equity After Income Taxes 48	5.9	•	200.3	40.1	39.5	16.3	13.3	15.7	10.0	9.6	1.5	31.9	4.5
Profit Margin (Before Income Tax) 49	8.8	31.5	11.5	10.0	6.7	15.2	11.7	15.6	9.8	7.0	4.1	13.3	8.2
Profit Margin (After Income Tax) 50	6.4	24.9	11.4	9.8	6.1	11.9	9.5	13.1	7.3	5.2	3.6	12.2	5.6

272

Table I

Corporations with and without Net Income

INTERNET SERVICE PROVIDERS, WEB PORTALS, AND D.P. SERVICES

MONEY AMOUNTS AND SIZE OF ASSETS IN THOUSANDS OF DOLLARS

Item Description for Accounting Period 7/02 Through 6/03	Total	Zero Assets	Under 500	500 to 1,000	1,000 to 5,000	5,000 to 10,000	10,000 to 25,000	25,000 to 50,000	50,000 to 100,000	100,000 to 250,000	250,000 to 500,000	500,000 to 2,500,000	2,500,000 and over
Number of Enterprises 1	13710	1832	10630	522	452	96	86	24	24	16	13	7	8
Revenues ($ in Thousands)													
Net Sales 2	68886241	503932	3258206	896315	2230188	699070	1474614	654078	1666316	2062361	2034415	3631999	49772745
Interest 3	4004885	4558	734	274	3821	5078	9359	8014	12709	26718	71065	121594	3740960
Rents 4	714508	107	0	0	226	104	253	8547	1705	3125	16190	327	683923
Royalties 5	1951863	0	756	0	0	10798	352	0	2303	126	0	2302	1935227
Other Portfolio Income 6	1837192	39428	82642	2	14806	7871	2343	5767	54315	17115	8175	26301	1578425
Other Receipts 7	4874008	64119	12782	3254	19965	4749	62557	85858	26729	215714	135549	76594	4166144
Total Receipts 8	82268697	612144	3355120	899845	2269006	727670	1549478	762264	1766077	2325159	2265394	3859117	61877424
Average Total Receipts 9	6001	334	316	1724	5020	7580	18017	31761	73587	145322	174261	551302	7734678
Operating Costs/Operating Income (%)													
Cost of Operations 10	27.3	13.3	28.4	30.6	33.5	39.6	30.2	35.9	46.4	39.6	23.3	20.1	26.2
Salaries and Wages 11	26.7	26.1	16.6	28.4	30.2	35.1	34.4	37.4	24.3	31.5	38.4	35.9	25.4
Taxes Paid 12	2.9	2.8	2.0	2.2	3.4	4.4	3.5	3.5	2.9	3.1	3.7	3.2	2.9
Interest Paid 13	8.4	0.5	0.9	0.9	1.5	2.7	2.5	6.0	1.7	2.3	4.8	2.3	10.8
Depreciation 14	8.1	6.8	2.3	3.1	5.6	8.8	13.6	9.8	6.6	11.1	16.7	9.9	7.9
Amortization and Depletion 15	4.8	2.4	0.3	2.2	1.4	1.8	2.6	11.9	3.2	3.1	2.5	10.9	5.1
Pensions and Other Deferred Comp. 16	0.7	0.2	0.3	0.0	0.3	0.3	0.5	0.2	0.8	0.3	1.4	0.1	0.8
Employee Benefits 17	2.4	3.5	0.6	2.6	2.1	2.1	2.8	4.4	2.6	2.3	3.5	2.6	2.4
Advertising 18	4.8	1.1	1.0	0.7	1.5	1.0	2.8	2.6	3.4	0.9	1.7	7.3	5.6
Other Expenses 19	39.7	183.6	48.9	28.6	40.3	37.8	43.4	60.2	31.4	82.5	131.5	44.7	31.9
Officers' Compensation 20	1.5	4.6	7.2	4.2	6.9	5.1	4.5	2.7	2.7	1.2	2.1	0.7	0.6
Operating Margin 21	*	*	*	*	*	*	*	*	*	*	*	*	*
Operating Margin Before Officers' Comp. 22	*	0.7	*	*	*	*	*	*	*	*	*	*	*

Selected Average Balance Sheet ($ in Thousands)

Net Receivables 23	3569	0	11	91	330	1264	2583	4415	12826	15488	23126	96727	5829968
Inventories 24	114	0	0	5	74	50	199	300	702	687	1756	2676	177550
Net Property, Plant and Equipment 25	1222	0	17	213	649	1191	3581	7553	9398	29390	68749	160521	1606734
Total Assets 26	22396	0	69	679	1911	7335	14997	36650	69066	168429	350393	1368656	35465819
Notes and Loans Payable 27	3675	0	83	516	1256	1586	4591	14255	16246	79749	61512	209870	5479962
All Other Liabilities 28	10639	0	31	196	906	4285	7611	14074	27435	39730	73645	473789	17255019
Net Worth 29	8082	0	-45	-33	-252	1464	2795	8321	25385	48950	215236	684997	12730838

Selected Financial Ratios (Times to 1)

Current Ratio 30	1.0	0.7	0.6	0.9	1.3	1.3	0.8	0.7	1.3	1.1	2.7	1.2	1.0
Quick Ratio 31	0.6	0.6	0.5	0.8	1.0	1.0	0.6	0.6	1.1	0.9	1.3	0.6	0.5
Net Sales to Working Capital 32	14.5	•	•	7.7	•	•	•	•	8.5	15.1	1.5	6.7	15.8
Coverage Ratio 33	0.1	•	•	•	•	•	•	•	•	•	•	•	1.5
Total Asset Turnover 34	0.2	4.4	2.5	2.6	1.0	1.0	1.1	0.7	1.0	0.8	0.4	0.4	0.2
Inventory Turnover 35	12.1	300.7	105.0	22.3	57.6	•	26.0	32.6	46.0	74.4	20.8	39.0	9.2
Receivables Turnover 36	•	•	•	•	•	•	•	•	•	•	•	•	•
Total Liabilities to Net Worth 37	1.8	•	•	4.0	•	4.4	3.4	•	1.7	2.4	1.0	1.0	1.8
Current Assets to Working Capital 38	23.1	•	•	4.7	•	•	•	•	4.1	8.3	1.6	6.5	31.5
Current Liabilities to Working Capital 39	22.1	•	•	3.7	•	•	•	•	3.1	7.3	0.6	5.5	30.5
Working Capital to Net Sales 40	0.1	•	•	0.1	•	•	•	•	0.1	0.1	0.6	0.1	0.1
Inventory to Working Capital 41	0.3	•	•	0.1	•	•	•	•	0.1	0.1	0.0	0.0	0.4
Total Receipts to Cash Flow 42	5.7	3.1	5.8	15.8	•	•	•	•	39.1	•	•	•	3.8
Cost of Goods to Cash Flow 43	1.6	0.9	1.8	5.3	•	•	•	•	18.1	•	•	•	1.0
Cash Flow to Total Debt 44	0.1	0.9	0.4	0.1	•	•	•	•	0.0	•	•	•	0.1

Selected Financial Factors (in Percentages)

Debt Ratio 45	63.9	164.8	104.8	113.2	80.0	81.4	77.3	63.2	80.0	70.9	38.6	50.0	64.1
Return on Total Assets 46	0.2	•	•	•	•	•	•	•	•	•	•	•	2.8
Return on Equity Before Income Taxes 47	•	37.5	160.7	488.4	•	•	•	•	•	•	•	•	2.5
Return on Equity After Income Taxes 48	•	38.2	167.3	490.6	•	•	•	•	•	•	•	•	1.8
Profit Margin (Before Income Tax) 49	•	•	•	•	•	•	•	•	•	•	•	•	5.1
Profit Margin (After Income Tax) 50	•	•	•	•	•	•	•	•	•	•	•	•	3.6

Table II

Corporations with Net Income

INTERNET SERVICE PROVIDERS, WEB PORTALS, AND D.P. SERVICES

MONEY AMOUNTS AND SIZE OF ASSETS IN THOUSANDS OF DOLLARS

Item Description for Accounting Period 7/02 Through 6/03	Total	Zero Assets	Under 500	500 to 1,000	1,000 to 5,000	5,000 to 10,000	10,000 to 25,000	25,000 to 50,000	50,000 to 100,000	100,000 to 250,000	250,000 to 500,000	500,000 to 2,500,000	2,500,000 and over
Number of Enterprises **1**	6095	0	4762	275	0	26	26	4	12	0	0	0	0
Revenues ($ in Thousands)													
Net Sales **2**	53544751	0	2489513	759531	0	343561	734679	141863	1043896	0	0	0	0
Interest **3**	1060260	0	645	157	0	501	1032	441	8305	0	0	0	0
Rents **4**	357329	0	0	0	0	19	189	0	1666	0	0	0	0
Royalties **5**	1934676	0	0	0	0	0	135	0	0	0	0	0	0
Other Portfolio Income **6**	1569285	0	82642	0	0	7231	1001	118	55920	0	0	0	0
Other Receipts **7**	4167515	0	9799	2482	0	1030	6814	44521	206492	0	0	0	0
Total Receipts **8**	62633816	0	2582599	762170	0	352342	743850	186943	1316279	0	0	0	0
Average Total Receipts **9**	10276	•	542	2772	•	13552	28610	46736	109690	•	•	•	•
Operating Costs/Operating Income (%)													
Cost of Operations **10**	24.6	•	30.9	33.3	•	43.0	21.4	28.3	40.5	•	•	•	•
Salaries and Wages **11**	25.6	•	11.8	23.5	•	14.1	25.4	36.7	25.4	•	•	•	•
Taxes Paid **12**	2.7	•	1.9	1.2	•	3.3	2.4	2.4	2.9	•	•	•	•
Interest Paid **13**	4.0	•	0.5	0.6	•	1.2	0.5	2.8	0.6	•	•	•	•
Depreciation **14**	4.6	•	1.7	1.5	•	3.5	3.6	5.3	9.0	•	•	•	•
Amortization and Depletion **15**	4.8	•	0.0	0.7	•	0.0	0.3	2.6	1.9	•	•	•	•
Pensions and Other Deferred Comp. **16**	0.8	•	0.4	0.0	•	0.2	0.7	•	1.3	•	•	•	•
Employee Benefits **17**	2.2	•	0.3	2.5	•	1.2	2.6	6.0	2.0	•	•	•	•
Advertising **18**	5.2	•	1.0	0.5	•	0.4	2.0	1.2	0.3	•	•	•	•
Other Expenses **19**	30.7	•	44.1	21.8	•	26.2	33.0	39.2	21.8	•	•	•	•
Officers' Compensation **20**	1.2	•	4.8	4.2	•	1.4	3.3	1.0	3.2	•	•	•	•
Operating Margin **21**	•	•	2.3	10.0	•	5.4	4.8	•	•	•	•	•	•
Operating Margin Before Officers' Comp. **22**	•	•	7.2	14.3	•	6.8	8.1	•	•	•	•	•	•

Selected Average Balance Sheet ($ in Thousands)

Net Receivables 23	3187		21	143		2794	3895	3304	15962
Inventories 24	235		1	2		139	410	220	516
Net Property, Plant and Equipment 25	1168		16	74		1916	2473	11784	10522
Total Assets 26	34991		96	536		7637	14232	40014	91626
Notes and Loans Payable 27	4840		69	329		1771	2503	12800	8896
All Other Liabilities 28	13604		42	222		3810	6229	12141	21194
Net Worth 29	16547		-15	35		2056	5500	15073	61536

Selected Financial Ratios (Times to 1)

Current Ratio 30	1.0	0.7	0.6		1.1	1.2	0.9	2.7
Quick Ratio 31	0.6	0.6	0.5		1.0	0.9	0.7	2.3
Net Sales to Working Capital 32	33.0	12.7			42.1	18.7		3.1
Coverage Ratio 33	3.7	12.7	18.9		7.5	13.0	3.2	29.1
Total Asset Turnover 34	0.3	5.4	4.7		1.7	2.0	0.9	0.9
Inventory Turnover 35	9.2	322.6	579.6		40.7	14.8	45.5	68.2
Receivables Turnover 36								
Total Liabilities to Net Worth 37	1.1		15.9		2.7	1.6	1.7	0.5
Current Assets to Working Capital 38	24.5				13.7	6.0		1.6
Current Liabilities to Working Capital 39	23.5				12.7	5.0		0.6
Working Capital to Net Sales 40	0.0				0.0	0.1		0.3
Inventory to Working Capital 41	0.9				0.4	0.3		0.0
Total Receipts to Cash Flow 42	3.1	2.4	3.9		4.3	3.0	2.4	3.5
Cost of Goods to Cash Flow 43	0.8	0.7	1.3		1.8	0.6	0.7	1.4
Cash Flow to Total Debt 44	0.2	2.0	1.3		0.6	1.1	0.6	0.8

Selected Financial Factors (in Percentages)

Debt Ratio 45	52.7	115.5	94.1		73.1	61.4	62.3	32.8
Return on Total Assets 46	3.7	35.8	51.6		15.8	13.0	7.9	17.1
Return on Equity Before Income Taxes 47	5.7		825.2		50.9	31.2	14.4	24.7
Return on Equity After Income Taxes 48	4.8		813.5		42.6	27.5	14.4	23.3
Profit Margin (Before Income Tax) 49	10.7	6.1	10.4		7.9	6.1	6.1	17.4
Profit Margin (After Income Tax) 50	9.0	6.0	10.2		6.6	5.3	6.1	16.5

Table I

Corporations with and without Net Income

OTHER INFORMATION SERVICES, NEWS SYNDICATES, LIBRARIES

MONEY AMOUNTS AND SIZE OF ASSETS IN THOUSANDS OF DOLLARS

Item Description for Accounting Period 7/02 Through 6/03	Total	Zero Assets	Under 500	500 to 1,000	1,000 to 5,000	5,000 to 10,000	10,000 to 25,000	25,000 to 50,000	50,000 to 100,000	100,000 to 250,000	250,000 to 500,000	500,000 to 2,500,000	2,500,000 and over
Number of Enterprises **1**	7908	836	6167	368	323	92	47	26	14	11	11	12	0
Revenues ($ in Thousands)													
Net Sales **2**	17874470	544232	943140	301872	1238597	1123727	781852	837296	1367609	1117241	3131482	6487421	0
Interest **3**	194747	12243	1476	1212	3096	5979	7907	5310	7939	9995	31722	107868	0
Rents **4**	20973	39	0	173	17	587	1115	0	101	1453	6040	11449	0
Royalties **5**	86685	0	0	0	0	2482	108	1916	0	3091	7274	71813	0
Other Portfolio Income **6**	647063	315572	14825	15334	3968	20241	788	907	13448	2461	104149	155372	0
Other Receipts **7**	686320	6003	1199	5909	55479	26281	27270	23161	21783	54915	-28020	492339	0
Total Receipts **8**	19510258	878089	960640	324500	1301157	1179297	819040	868590	1410880	1189156	3252647	7326262	0
Average Total Receipts **9**	2467	1050	156	882	4028	12818	17426	33407	100777	108105	295695	610522	•
Operating Costs/Operating Income (%)													
Cost of Operations **10**	21.9	50.5	14.1	38.9	36.3	48.7	31.5	12.6	15.0	7.4	37.5	8.9	•
Salaries and Wages **11**	26.9	18.2	33.5	34.3	25.2	29.1	32.5	34.9	22.7	36.5	19.5	27.5	•
Taxes Paid **12**	2.7	2.4	3.4	5.2	3.8	3.5	3.1	3.5	2.4	3.0	1.4	2.6	•
Interest Paid **13**	3.2	4.8	3.7	1.8	1.7	1.7	2.1	1.3	1.4	1.8	0.6	5.8	•
Depreciation **14**	4.8	3.1	3.0	7.1	5.9	5.4	7.1	9.8	3.8	7.0	3.2	4.4	•
Amortization and Depletion **15**	2.9	1.8	2.5	5.4	2.6	1.8	6.1	3.6	2.8	5.2	2.2	2.7	•
Pensions and Other Deferred Comp. **16**	1.6	0.2	1.4	0.3	0.7	0.3	0.3	0.5	0.7	1.6	0.5	3.3	•
Employee Benefits **17**	2.9	1.2	2.2	3.1	2.2	2.1	2.5	2.6	1.9	3.5	1.1	4.4	•
Advertising **18**	2.2	2.9	1.4	1.8	2.7	1.9	9.6	4.6	1.2	1.9	2.3	1.1	•
Other Expenses **19**	40.5	35.8	33.1	56.9	36.6	33.8	43.0	40.5	53.0	41.3	41.4	39.6	•
Officers' Compensation **20**	4.1	3.5	28.4	9.5	5.4	5.1	3.5	3.0	1.8	3.1	1.7	1.9	•
Operating Margin **21**	•	•	•	•	•	•	•	•	•	•	•	•	•
Operating Margin Before Officers' Comp. **22**	•	1.7	•	•	•	•	•	•	•	•	•	•	•

Selected Average Balance Sheet ($ in Thousands)

Net Receivables 23	419	0	14	99	527	1640	2258	5389	10034	18592	34726	157776	•
Inventories 24	19	0	0	2	1	10	73	354	19	624	34	5205	3866	•
Net Property, Plant and Equipment 25	260	0	7	359	526	1187	2227	5587	8578	13449	26887	65872	•
Total Assets 26	2989	71	670	2393	6749	16253	34338	74535	141871	328801	1140283	•
Notes and Loans Payable 27	1046	174	672	964	2188	3061	4589	10065	6570	20627	477763	•
All Other Liabilities 28	1312	0	307	158	980	3392	5999	15537	26334	44419	109872	420243	•
Net Worth 29	632	0	-410	-160	449	1168	7194	14212	38136	90882	198302	242277	•

Selected Financial Ratios (Times to 1)

Current Ratio 30	0.9	•	0.2	0.4	1.0	1.2	1.7	1.2	1.4	2.3	1.9	0.7	•
Quick Ratio 31	0.6	•	0.2	0.3	0.8	1.0	1.5	1.0	0.9	1.6	1.1	0.5	•
Net Sales to Working Capital 32	•	•	•	•	13.9	11.5	4.3	10.1	2.5	3.9	•
Coverage Ratio 33	•	8.8	•	•	•	•	•	•	•	•	3.0	•
Total Asset Turnover 34	0.8	•	2.2	1.2	1.6	1.8	1.0	0.9	1.3	0.7	0.9	0.5	•
Inventory Turnover 35	25.9	•	12.5	281.3	138.9	81.5	14.8	216.3	23.4	219.4	20.5	12.4	•
Receivables Turnover 36	•	•	•	•	•	•	•	•	•	•	•
Total Liabilities to Net Worth 37	3.7	•	•	•	4.3	4.8	1.3	1.4	1.0	0.6	0.7	3.7	•
Current Assets to Working Capital 38	•	•	•	•	5.4	2.4	6.1	3.5	1.7	2.1	•
Current Liabilities to Working Capital 39	•	•	•	•	4.4	1.4	5.1	2.5	0.7	1.1	•
Working Capital to Net Sales 40	•	•	•	0.1	0.2	0.1	0.1	0.4	0.3	•
Inventory to Working Capital 41	•	•	•	0.1	0.1	0.0	0.0	0.0	0.1	•
Total Receipts to Cash Flow 42	3.7	10.9	•	9.5	•	•	4.7	2.2	3.4	3.9	2.2	•
Cost of Goods to Cash Flow 43	0.8	5.5	•	3.4	•	0.6	0.3	0.3	1.5	0.2	•
Cash Flow to Total Debt 44	0.3	•	•	0.2	•	0.3	1.2	0.6	0.6	0.3	•

Selected Financial Factors (in Percentages)

Debt Ratio 45	78.9	675.9	123.9	81.2	82.7	55.7	58.6	48.8	35.9	39.7	78.8	•
Return on Total Assets 46	•	•	•	•	•	•	•	•	•	8.1
Return on Equity Before Income Taxes 47	•	9.3	291.1	•	•	•	•	•	•	25.3
Return on Equity After Income Taxes 48	•	9.4	291.1	•	•	•	•	•	•	17.0
Profit Margin (Before Income Tax) 49	•	37.1	•	•	•	•	•	•	•	11.3
Profit Margin (After Income Tax) 50	•	31.6	•	•	•	•	•	•	•	7.6

Table II
Corporations with Net Income

OTHER INFORMATION SERVICES, NEWS SYNDICATES, LIBRARIES

MONEY AMOUNTS AND SIZE OF ASSETS IN THOUSANDS OF DOLLARS

Item Description for Accounting Period 7/02 Through 6/03	Total	Zero Assets	Under 500	500 to 1,000	1,000 to 5,000	5,000 to 10,000	10,000 to 25,000	25,000 to 50,000	50,000 to 100,000	100,000 to 250,000	250,000 to 500,000	500,000 to 2,500,000	2,500,000 and over
Number of Enterprises 1	2631	644	1727	4	164	42	14	11	6	4	6	9	0

Revenues ($ in Thousands)

Net Sales 2	13199055	367482	655948	34362	1107167	830356	456042	546656	706878	527916	2504940	5461308	0
Interest 3	101321	12048	1009	16	670	1369	815	1855	1455	3782	15058	63244	0
Rents 4	20007	39	0	173	0	587	236	0	30	1453	6040	11449	0
Royalties 5	76056	0	0	0	0	0	0	1916	0	2759	3158	68222	0
Other Portfolio Income 6	426632	314845	14385	10322	3937	101	310	88	230	1726	33018	47670	0
Other Receipts 7	312338	5534	343	3515	47180	22823	13807	2909	13326	41014	41718	120171	0
Total Receipts 8	14135409	699948	671685	48388	1158954	855236	471210	553424	721919	578650	2603932	5772064	0
Average Total Receipts 9	5373	1087	389	12097	7067	20363	33658	50311	120320	144662	433989	641340	•

Operating Costs/Operating Income (%)

Cost of Operations 10	22.3	54.9	1.6	44.7	38.1	62.2	38.5	5.9	3.9	6.2	46.3	6.5	•
Salaries and Wages 11	21.0	11.8	32.1	15.6	16.3	13.5	15.1	32.6	22.7	32.8	14.2	23.6	•
Taxes Paid 12	2.5	2.0	2.8	1.2	3.1	2.3	1.8	3.4	2.1	3.5	1.3	3.0	•
Interest Paid 13	2.2	5.8	0.3	0.9	1.0	0.3	0.7	0.4	1.6	1.6	0.5	4.1	•
Depreciation 14	3.3	1.9	1.9	1.2	4.0	1.6	3.1	5.8	3.3	9.0	2.6	3.3	•
Amortization and Depletion 15	1.8	1.8	0.3	0.2	0.2	0.1	0.4	0.7	3.1	1.0	1.2	3.1	•
Pensions and Other Deferred Comp. 16	2.1	0.2	2.1	0.3	0.7	0.3	0.4	0.6	1.3	3.4	0.5	3.9	•
Employee Benefits 17	2.3	1.1	0.9	0.9	1.8	1.5	1.5	2.0	1.7	2.8	1.1	3.5	•
Advertising 18	1.9	4.2	1.2	1.7	2.0	0.3	13.1	5.9	0.2	0.9	1.6	1.2	•
Other Expenses 19	30.9	26.3	12.8	24.3	25.0	13.0	17.3	27.3	53.9	28.0	26.9	37.9	•
Officers' Compensation 20	3.7	4.0	32.7	3.6	4.1	2.5	1.6	2.4	1.8	1.7	1.7	2.0	•
Operating Margin 21	5.7	•	11.3	5.4	3.7	2.4	6.6	12.9	4.4	9.1	2.3	8.0	•
Operating Margin Before Officers' Comp. 22	9.4	•	44.0	9.0	7.8	4.9	8.1	15.3	6.1	10.8	4.0	10.0	•

Selected Average Balance Sheet ($ in Thousands)

	•	•	•	•	•	•	•	•	•	•	•	•	•
Net Receivables 23	724	0	11	416	647	2615	2651	6082	10668	19861	55349	120768	•
Inventories 24	45	0	1	12	17	147	310	38	26	0	9490	5132	•
Net Property, Plant and Equipment 25	451	0	14	46	627	1056	4161	5030	8618	22002	37425	59651	•
Total Assets 26	5734		132	832	2861	6391	14814	33424	73538	141102	352236	1158243	•
Notes and Loans Payable 27	1501	0	67	788	1148	797	2618	3384	15452	1099	17211	370480	•
All Other Liabilities 28	2178		40	926	937	3592	6200	17506	24540	35737	99521	465197	•
Net Worth 29	2055		25	-882	775	2002	5997	12535	33545	104266	235505	322566	•

Selected Financial Ratios (Times to 1)

	•	•	•	•	•	•	•	•	•	•	•	•	•
Current Ratio 30	0.9	•	5.3	0.6	1.0	1.2	1.3	0.9	1.5	2.3	1.4	0.7	•
Quick Ratio 31	0.7	•	5.2	0.6	0.9	0.9	1.0	0.8	1.0	2.1	1.0	0.4	•
Net Sales to Working Capital 32	•	•	4.1	100.5	28.2	18.6	•	12.3	3.4	9.3	•	•	•
Coverage Ratio 33	6.8	14.1	55.7	49.9	9.2	14.3	33.9	5.0	12.6	15.6	4.5	•	•
Total Asset Turnover 34	0.9	•	2.9	10.3	2.4	3.1	2.2	1.5	1.6	0.9	1.2	0.5	•
Inventory Turnover 35	24.9	•	10.0	313.8	150.0	83.5	40.4	77.5	173.5	•	20.3	7.7	•
Receivables Turnover 36	•	•	•	•	•	•	•	•	•	•	•	•	•
Total Liabilities to Net Worth 37	1.8	•	4.2	•	2.7	2.2	1.5	1.7	1.2	0.4	0.5	2.6	•
Current Assets to Working Capital 38	•	•	1.2	25.0	7.2	4.5	•	3.2	1.8	3.4	•	•	•
Current Liabilities to Working Capital 39	•	•	0.2	24.0	6.2	3.5	•	2.2	0.8	2.4	•	•	•
Working Capital to Net Sales 40	•	0.2	•	0.0	0.0	0.1	•	0.1	0.3	0.1	•	•	•
Inventory to Working Capital 41	•	0.0	•	0.3	0.2	0.2	•	0.0	•	0.2	•	•	•
Total Receipts to Cash Flow 42	2.7	6.5	4.6	2.7	3.6	6.4	4.3	2.8	1.7	2.3	3.3	2.1	•
Cost of Goods to Cash Flow 43	0.6	3.6	0.1	1.2	1.4	4.0	1.7	0.2	0.1	0.1	1.5	0.1	•
Cash Flow to Total Debt 44	0.5	0.8	1.8	0.9	0.9	0.7	0.9	0.9	1.7	1.5	1.1	0.3	•

Selected Financial Factors (in Percentages)

	•	•	•	•	•	•	•	•	•	•	•	•	•
Debt Ratio 45	64.2	•	80.8	206.0	72.9	68.7	59.5	62.5	54.4	26.1	33.1	72.2	•
Return on Total Assets 46	13.5	•	40.1	487.1	22.1	17.6	23.4	21.6	13.1	18.7	8.4	9.6	•
Return on Equity Before Income Taxes 47	32.1	•	204.6	•	72.8	53.1	53.8	56.0	22.8	23.4	11.8	26.8	•
Return on Equity After Income Taxes 48	25.5	•	197.5	•	69.7	47.1	49.9	55.2	16.7	18.5	9.4	18.5	•
Profit Margin (Before Income Tax) 49	13.2	76.5	13.7	46.2	8.4	5.4	9.9	14.1	6.5	18.5	6.7	14.3	•
Profit Margin (After Income Tax) 50	10.5	68.5	13.2	46.2	8.0	4.8	9.2	13.9	4.8	14.6	5.3	9.8	•

Table I

Corporations with and without Net Income

FINANCE AND INSURANCE

MONEY AMOUNTS AND SIZE OF ASSETS IN THOUSANDS OF DOLLARS

Item Description for Accounting Period 7/02 Through 6/03		Total	Zero Assets	Under 500	500 to 1,000	1,000 to 5,000	5,000 to 10,000	10,000 to 25,000	25,000 to 50,000	50,000 to 100,000	100,000 to 250,000	250,000 to 500,000	500,000 to 2,500,000	2,500,000 and over
Number of Enterprises	1	54554	6674	34586	3361	4096	1011	1062	880	957	953	457	374	144
Revenues ($ in Thousands)														
Net Sales	2	437252823	52675876	12230650	1995566	5595488	2732112	4453967	4988604	7518522	14143734	13607707	33198639	284111957
Interest	3	248976416	33862948	79765	80369	303384	139243	456975	1145615	2743111	7317149	8044329	17097270	177706259
Rents	4	1636876	116889	1436	634	7440	3428	8228	5929	8519	31659	30126	277024	1145565
Royalties	5	592118	8264	0	0	554	0	68	12477	94	683	2989	11258	555731
Other Portfolio Income	6	15438622	1555640	759	8308	39648	38539	56303	93084	262551	462448	517287	1655994	10744058
Other Receipts	7	170608791	17132135	12148690	1906255	5244462	2550902	3932393	3731499	4504247	6331795	5012976	14153093	93960344
Total Receipts	8	437252823	52675876	12230650	1995566	5595488	2732112	4453967	4988604	7518522	14143734	13607707	33198639	284111957
Average Total Receipts	9	8015	7893	354	594	1366	2702	4194	5669	7856	14841	29776	88766	1973000
Operating Costs/Operating Income (%)														
Cost of Operations	10	2.3	0.1	7.7	3.5	6.7	9.8	8.7	5.7	2.5	3.6	0.7	1.0	2.4
Salaries and Wages	11	10.0	9.0	28.1	34.2	22.6	21.3	23.3	24.4	19.6	17.3	15.5	15.1	6.9
Taxes Paid	12	1.4	1.1	2.6	3.0	3.0	2.7	2.8	3.1	2.9	2.6	2.6	2.3	1.0
Interest Paid	13	40.1	46.1	0.9	5.9	7.2	7.9	10.7	15.5	21.2	26.6	30.7	27.9	45.8
Depreciation	14	4.2	5.9	1.5	1.2	2.7	2.2	2.0	1.9	2.7	2.6	2.4	3.4	4.4
Amortization and Depletion	15	0.8	0.4	0.1	0.3	0.8	0.3	0.3	0.9	0.6	1.0	0.9	1.1	0.8
Pensions and Other Deferred Comp.	16	0.6	0.4	0.3	0.3	0.4	0.4	0.4	0.6	0.6	0.8	0.7	1.1	0.6
Employee Benefits	17	0.9	1.0	0.7	3.3	0.8	1.0	1.1	1.5	1.8	1.7	1.7	1.7	0.7
Advertising	18	1.4	0.3	2.0	2.0	3.1	2.0	1.6	1.8	2.2	1.0	1.0	3.1	1.3
Other Expenses	19	26.7	52.0	38.9	40.0	35.6	38.5	34.0	29.4	26.3	27.2	25.8	25.4	21.0
Officers' Compensation	20	1.5	0.7	12.1	8.0	8.5	6.3	8.0	6.1	5.8	4.1	3.7	1.5	0.5
Operating Margin	21	10.2	•	4.9	•	8.5	7.6	7.1	9.1	13.9	11.5	14.4	16.4	14.6
Operating Margin Before Officers' Comp.	22	11.7	•	17.1	6.2	16.9	13.9	15.1	15.2	19.7	15.6	18.1	17.9	15.1

Selected Average Balance Sheet ($ in Thousands)

Net Receivables **23**	13961	0	13	299	1060	3148	7137	15926	29463	55207	94579	248023	3571215
Inventories **24**	·	0	·	·	·	·	·	·	·	·	·	·	·
Net Property, Plant and Equipment **25**	780	0	16	38	167	369	415	734	1308	2710	5093	12693	200192
Total Assets **26**	77575	0	92	695	2253	7179	16220	36424	71281	157435	349400	1026426	23603625
Notes and Loans Payable **27**	44907	0	42	371	1157	4181	6902	8162	10808	24530	57112	269242	15716406
All Other Liabilities **28**	27510	0	131	443	1891	2694	8014	23589	51251	116616	256932	605628	6603395
Net Worth **29**	5158	0	-81	-119	-795	304	1303	4673	9221	16290	35356	151556	1288824

Selected Financial Ratios (Times to 1)

Current Ratio **30**	0.5	·	1.9	1.3	1.2	1.0	0.9	0.8	0.7	0.6	0.6	0.6	0.5
Quick Ratio **31**	0.4	·	1.6	1.1	1.1	0.9	0.8	0.6	0.6	0.5	0.5	0.5	0.4
Net Sales to Working Capital **32**	·	·	14.4	2.5	4.2	3.2	12.6	·	·	·	·	·	·
Coverage Ratio **33**	1.2	0.6	·	6.2	0.7	2.2	2.0	1.6	1.6	1.4	1.4	1.6	1.3
Total Asset Turnover **34**	0.1	·	3.8	0.9	0.4	0.3	1.6	0.2	0.1	0.1	0.1	0.1	0.1
Inventory Turnover **35**	·	·	·	·	·	·	·	·	·	·	·	·	·
Receivables Turnover **36**	·	·	·	·	·	·	·	·	·	·	·	·	·
Total Liabilities to Net Worth **37**	14.0	·	·	·	·	22.6	11.4	6.8	6.7	8.7	8.9	5.8	17.4
Current Assets to Working Capital **38**	2.1	·	2.1	4.9	5.5	11.4	33.1	·	·	·	·	·	·
Current Liabilities to Working Capital **39**	1.1	·	1.1	3.9	4.5	10.4	32.1	·	·	·	·	·	·
Working Capital to Net Sales **40**	·	·	0.1	0.4	0.2	0.3	0.1	·	·	·	·	·	·
Inventory to Working Capital **41**	0.0	·	0.0	0.0	0.0	0.0	0.0	·	·	·	·	·	·
Total Receipts to Cash Flow **42**	3.0	3.6	3.0	2.6	2.5	2.7	2.7	2.9	2.7	2.9	2.8	2.6	3.0
Cost of Goods to Cash Flow **43**	0.1	0.0	0.1	0.2	0.2	0.2	0.2	0.2	0.1	0.1	0.0	0.0	0.1
Cash Flow to Total Debt **44**	0.0	·	0.8	0.2	0.2	0.1	0.1	·	0.0	0.0	0.0	0.0	0.0

Selected Financial Factors (in Percentages)

Debt Ratio **45**	93.4	·	188.2	117.2	135.3	95.8	92.0	87.2	87.1	89.7	89.9	85.2	94.6
Return on Total Assets **46**	5.1	·	22.6	3.5	9.5	5.8	4.6	3.7	3.7	3.5	3.8	3.8	5.0
Return on Equity Before Income Taxes **47**	15.0	·	·	·	8.9	66.7	22.2	10.4	11.0	9.5	11.4	9.2	21.5
Return on Equity After Income Taxes **48**	8.5	·	·	·	10.1	55.9	18.7	8.7	8.5	6.1	7.2	6.0	14.0
Profit Margin (Before Income Tax) **49**	9.6	4.9	·	8.4	·	7.5	6.9	8.6	12.9	10.4	13.5	15.7	14.0
Profit Margin (After Income Tax) **50**	5.5	4.8	·	7.6	·	6.3	5.8	7.2	10.0	8.6	10.2	·	9.1

277

Table II
Corporations with Net Income

FINANCE AND INSURANCE

MONEY AMOUNTS AND SIZE OF ASSETS IN THOUSANDS OF DOLLARS

Item Description for Accounting Period 7/02 Through 6/03		Total	Zero Assets	Under 500	500 to 1,000	1,000 to 5,000	5,000 to 10,000	10,000 to 25,000	25,000 to 50,000	50,000 to 100,000	100,000 to 250,000	250,000 to 500,000	500,000 to 2,500,000	2,500,000 and over
Number of Enterprises	1	31721	3308	18253	2117	3193	794	820	689	820	862	414	327	124
Revenues ($ in Thousands)														
Net Sales	2	372278231	22041698	9837017	1627547	4718137	2442048	3785886	4152038	6750286	12104249	11796659	28667183	264355483
Interest	3	218158047	13679767	30414	45609	240002	93477	356605	858159	2396545	6283203	6948243	14473294	172752730
Rents	4	1165155	75486	530	627	7320	1756	6703	2838	8018	25647	27288	216406	792535
Royalties	5	489713	8264	0	0	554	0	67	12477	92	17	2450	60	465732
Other Portfolio Income	6	11646753	196484	757	18	36518	34358	51464	81442	244400	416386	446884	1530719	8607323
Other Receipts	7	140818563	8081697	9805316	1581293	4433743	2312457	3371047	3197122	4101231	5378996	4371794	12446704	81737163
Total Receipts	8	372278231	22041698	9837017	1627547	4718137	2442048	3785886	4152038	6750286	12104249	11796659	28667183	264355483
Average Total Receipts	9	11736	6663	539	769	1478	3076	4617	6026	8232	14042	28494	87667	2131899
Operating Costs/Operating Income (%)														
Cost of Operations	10	2.5	0.2	8.8	0.7	6.4	9.6	8.5	4.7	2.5	4.1	0.8	0.2	2.4
Salaries and Wages	11	9.9	8.6	28.5	33.8	23.8	21.5	23.2	24.9	19.0	18.0	16.4	15.5	6.9
Taxes Paid	12	1.4	1.4	2.2	2.9	3.0	2.7	2.8	3.1	2.9	2.6	2.7	2.4	1.0
Interest Paid	13	40.4	39.5	0.5	2.6	5.8	6.5	9.4	14.5	20.1	25.6	29.2	27.3	47.1
Depreciation	14	1.9	1.2	1.2	1.1	2.8	1.9	1.9	1.7	2.4	2.4	2.5	3.6	1.7
Amortization and Depletion	15	0.7	0.2	0.0	0.1	0.8	0.2	0.2	0.8	0.5	0.6	0.9	0.8	0.8
Pensions and Other Deferred Comp.	16	0.6	0.5	0.3	0.3	0.5	0.5	0.4	0.6	0.6	0.6	0.8	1.0	0.6
Employee Benefits	17	0.9	0.9	0.5	3.5	0.8	1.0	1.1	1.4	1.8	1.8	1.8	1.8	0.7
Advertising	18	1.4	0.6	1.3	1.0	1.8	1.8	1.5	1.9	2.3	1.1	1.1	3.4	1.3
Other Expenses	19	22.0	33.7	34.2	37.2	29.9	32.7	28.7	24.2	24.7	20.3	19.3	21.6	20.3
Officers' Compensation	20	1.5	0.7	11.7	8.0	8.5	6.4	8.4	6.2	5.8	4.4	4.1	1.6	0.5
Operating Margin	21	16.7	12.6	10.7	8.7	15.9	15.2	14.0	15.9	17.5	18.2	20.5	20.8	16.7
Operating Margin Before Officers' Comp.	22	18.3	13.3	22.4	16.7	24.3	21.6	22.3	22.1	23.3	22.6	24.6	22.4	17.2

Selected Average Balance Sheet ($ in Thousands)

Net Receivables 23	19315	0	10	360	1168	3192	7167	15698	29125	55129	93838	224220	3268044
Inventories 24	•	•	•	•	•	•	•	•	•	•	•	•	•
Net Property, Plant and Equipment 25	770	0	21	30	162	291	346	677	1315	2656	5284	12797	102676
Total Assets 26	123306	0	95	694	2269	7121	16287	36537	71354	157694	349078	1019358	25681374
Notes and Loans Payable 27	71905	0	23	270	1113	3855	6658	8236	10012	20793	44928	217885	17307966
All Other Liabilities 28	42875	0	11	127	427	1452	7911	23341	51914	117722	263987	645450	7016723
Net Worth 29	8526	0	60	297	728	1814	1719	4960	9428	19179	40162	156024	1356684

Selected Financial Ratios (Times to 1)

Current Ratio 30	0.5	•	3.6	2.6	2.0	1.3	1.0	0.9	0.8	0.7	0.6	0.5	0.5
Quick Ratio 31	0.4	•	3.0	2.3	1.8	1.1	0.9	0.8	0.8	0.6	0.5	0.5	0.3
Net Sales to Working Capital 32	•	•	14.0	2.3	1.8	3.2	19.1	•	•	•	•	•	•
Coverage Ratio 33	1.4	1.3	23.2	4.4	3.7	3.3	2.5	2.1	1.8	1.7	1.7	1.7	1.3
Total Asset Turnover 34	0.1	•	5.7	1.1	0.7	0.4	0.3	0.2	0.1	0.1	0.1	0.1	0.1
Inventory Turnover 35	•	•	•	•	•	•	•	•	•	•	•	•	•
Receivables Turnover 36	•	•	•	•	•	•	•	•	•	•	•	•	•
Total Liabilities to Net Worth 37	13.5	•	0.6	1.3	2.1	2.9	8.5	6.4	6.6	7.2	7.7	5.5	17.9
Current Assets to Working Capital 38	•	•	1.4	1.6	2.0	5.0	45.9	•	•	•	•	•	•
Current Liabilities to Working Capital 39	•	•	0.4	0.6	1.0	4.0	44.9	•	•	•	•	•	•
Working Capital to Net Sales 40	•	•	0.1	0.4	0.6	0.3	0.1	•	•	•	•	•	•
Inventory to Working Capital 41	•	•	•	•	•	0.0	0.0	•	•	•	•	•	•
Total Receipts to Cash Flow 42	2.8	2.3	2.5	2.4	2.4	2.2	2.5	2.7	2.6	2.8	2.7	2.6	2.9
Cost of Goods to Cash Flow 43	0.1	0.0	0.2	0.0	0.2	0.2	0.2	0.1	0.1	0.1	0.0	0.0	0.1
Cash Flow to Total Debt 44	0.0	•	6.3	0.8	0.4	0.3	0.1	0.1	0.1	0.0	0.0	0.0	0.0

Selected Financial Factors (in Percentages)

Debt Ratio 45	93.1	•	36.1	57.2	67.9	74.5	89.4	86.4	86.8	87.8	88.5	84.7	94.7
Return on Total Assets 46	5.4	•	63.9	12.5	14.1	9.4	6.6	4.9	4.2	3.8	4.0	4.1	5.2
Return on Equity Before Income Taxes 47	22.1	•	95.6	22.5	32.1	25.6	37.0	18.6	14.4	12.5	13.9	11.3	25.2
Return on Equity After Income Taxes 48	15.4	•	94.3	21.8	30.1	23.3	33.5	16.6	11.7	9.3	9.8	7.7	16.9
Profit Margin (Before Income Tax) 49	16.1	12.6	10.7	8.7	15.8	15.1	13.8	15.3	16.5	17.1	19.5	20.1	16.0
Profit Margin (After Income Tax) 50	11.2	9.0	10.6	8.4	14.8	13.8	12.5	13.6	13.4	12.8	13.8	13.8	10.8

Table I

Corporations with and without Net Income

COMMERCIAL BANKING

MONEY AMOUNTS AND SIZE OF ASSETS IN THOUSANDS OF DOLLARS

Item Description for Accounting Period 7/02 Through 6/03		Total	Zero Assets	Under 500	500 to 1,000	1,000 to 5,000	5,000 to 10,000	10,000 to 25,000	25,000 to 50,000	50,000 to 100,000	100,000 to 250,000	250,000 to 500,000	500,000 to 2,500,000	2,500,000 and over
Number of Enterprises	1	2544	284	392	•	19	57	258	420	519	418	120	48	8
Revenues ($ in Thousands)														
Net Sales	2	50797883	34995506	87623	•	10781	41123	282488	1036287	2365463	4199782	2868912	2701996	2207921
Interest	3	35456963	25933455	399	•	3988	19882	179334	597042	1440764	2519948	1537743	1773178	1451229
Rents	4	347351	57007	0	•	0	36	438	1214	3556	9674	10848	39560	225017
Royalties	5	264	0	0	•	0	0	2	0	38	17	200	7	0
Other Portfolio Income	6	1334541	644088	0	•	11	639	10682	32201	89735	168363	99013	113660	176151
Other Receipts	7	13658764	8360956	87224	•	6782	20566	92032	405830	831370	1501780	1221108	775591	355524
Total Receipts	8	50797883	34995506	87623	•	10781	41123	282488	1036287	2365463	4199782	2868912	2701996	2207921
Average Total Receipts	9	19968	123224	224	•	567	721	1095	2467	4558	10047	23908	56292	275990
Operating Costs/Operating Income (%)														
Cost of Operations	10	0.0	•	•	•	•	•	•	0.1	0.1	0.1	0.6	•	•
Salaries and Wages	11	10.6	9.6	0.0	•	9.0	11.6	14.2	12.3	14.1	13.6	12.2	15.3	10.0
Taxes Paid	12	1.6	1.1	0.0	•	2.1	2.0	3.1	2.9	2.8	3.3	2.6	3.1	2.1
Interest Paid	13	47.2	55.3	4.3	•	0.5	15.2	30.3	29.0	30.3	29.1	26.4	25.1	37.6
Depreciation	14	2.4	1.5	•	•	1.8	2.6	3.8	3.3	3.5	3.1	3.3	3.5	10.7
Amortization and Depletion	15	0.5	0.5	•	•	•	0.9	0.7	0.9	0.6	0.7	0.3	0.2	0.5
Pensions and Other Deferred Comp.	16	0.5	0.4	•	•	•	•	0.8	0.7	0.6	0.7	0.6	0.8	0.7
Employee Benefits	17	1.3	1.0	•	•	•	2.0	3.3	2.6	2.4	2.1	1.9	2.4	1.5
Advertising	18	0.3	0.1	0.0	•	0.2	0.5	1.4	1.0	0.9	0.9	0.7	1.0	0.5
Other Expenses	19	36.3	41.5	85.5	•	141.6	96.8	24.8	28.5	21.9	27.9	30.1	18.8	16.8
Officers' Compensation	20	2.4	0.8	0.0	•	15.7	17.1	13.1	10.6	8.1	6.5	4.6	3.0	4.6
Operating Margin	21	•	•	10.2	•	•	•	4.5	8.1	14.7	12.1	16.6	26.9	14.9
Operating Margin Before Officers' Comp.	22	•	•	10.2	•	•	•	17.6	18.7	22.8	18.5	21.2	29.9	19.6

Selected Average Balance Sheet ($ in Thousands)

Item												
Net Receivables 23	49423	0	0	2605	4363	9871	22030	41093	87766	193125	412704	1579541
Inventories 24	•	•	•	•	•	•	•	•	•	•	•	•
Net Property, Plant and Equipment 25	1415	0	0	87	66	291	692	1329	2758	5514	10230	29294
Total Assets 26	96133	0	3	4017	8036	17943	37095	70877	151107	333503	832313	5487338
Notes and Loans Payable 27	5342	0	0	0	0	139	335	1228	4036	8932	37479	1027214
All Other Liabilities 28	81636	0	947	2617	9292	18045	32187	61384	131981	297346	700534	4027938
Net Worth 29	9156	0	-945	1400	-1256	-241	4573	8265	15091	27224	94299	432186

Selected Financial Ratios (Times to 1)

Item												
Current Ratio 30	0.9	0.1	•	1.9	1.8	1.1	1.0	1.0	1.0	0.9	1.0	0.8
Quick Ratio 31	0.9	0.1	•	1.9	1.7	1.1	1.0	0.9	0.9	0.9	0.9	0.8
Net Sales to Working Capital 32	•	•	0.8	0.3	0.2	0.7	2.5	•	•	•	•	•
Coverage Ratio 33	0.9	3.4	•	•	1.1	1.1	1.2	1.3	1.3	1.5	2.0	1.4
Total Asset Turnover 34	0.2	85.2	•	0.1	•	0.1	0.1	0.1	0.1	0.1	0.1	0.1
Inventory Turnover 35	•	•	•	•	•	•	•	•	•	•	•	•
Receivables Turnover 36	•	•	•	•	•	•	•	•	•	•	•	•
Total Liabilities to Net Worth 37	9.5	•	•	1.9	•	•	7.1	7.6	9.0	11.3	7.8	11.7
Current Assets to Working Capital 38	•	•	•	2.1	2.3	11.1	33.7	•	•	•	•	•
Current Liabilities to Working Capital 39	•	•	•	1.1	1.3	10.1	32.7	•	•	•	•	•
Working Capital to Net Sales 40	•	•	3.2	3.2	4.6	1.3	0.4	•	•	•	•	•
Inventory to Working Capital 41	•	•	•	•	0.0	•	0.0	•	•	•	•	•
Total Receipts to Cash Flow 42	4.1	1.2	5.0	•	4.2	3.9	3.0	3.0	3.3	2.5	2.4	3.5
Cost of Goods to Cash Flow 43	0.0	•	•	•	•	•	0.0	0.0	0.0	0.0	0.0	0.0
Cash Flow to Total Debt 44	0.1	0.2	•	0.2	0.0	0.0	0.0	0.0	0.0	0.0	•	0.0

Selected Financial Factors (in Percentages)

Item												
Debt Ratio 45	90.5	36116.9	•	65.1	115.6	101.3	87.7	88.3	90.0	91.8	88.7	92.1
Return on Total Assets 46	8.9	1232.9	•	•	•	2.0	2.3	2.7	2.6	2.9	3.4	2.6
Return on Equity Before Income Taxes 47	•	•	•	•	28.7	•	3.2	6.7	6.4	12.3	14.6	9.3
Return on Equity After Income Taxes 48	•	•	•	29.9	•	1.2	1.9	5.0	3.7	8.1	10.2	6.1
Profit Margin (Before Income Tax) 49	•	10.2	•	1.8	•	•	5.8	12.2	9.6	14.0	24.5	14.5
Profit Margin (After Income Tax) 50	•	10.2	•	•	•	•	3.5	5.5	9.3	14.0	17.1	9.5

Table II

Corporations with Net Income

COMMERCIAL BANKING

MONEY AMOUNTS AND SIZE OF ASSETS IN THOUSANDS OF DOLLARS

Item Description for Accounting Period 7/02 Through 6/03	Total	Zero Assets	Under 500	500 to 1,000	1,000 to 5,000	5,000 to 10,000	10,000 to 25,000	25,000 to 50,000	50,000 to 100,000	100,000 to 250,000	250,000 to 500,000	500,000 to 2,500,000	2,500,000 and over
Number of Enterprises **1**	2098	149	389	•	0	32	186	323	444	384	116	48	0
Revenues ($ in Thousands)													
Net Sales **2**	23906944	9395594	83810	•	0	19811	223633	820415	2074878	3776545	2598217	2701996	0
Interest **3**	14933889	6064262	0	•	0	10897	140288	464604	1238319	2302137	1485034	1773178	0
Rents **4**	306601	18906	0	•	0	36	357	944	3151	9539	9089	39560	0
Royalties **5**	260	0	0	•	0	0	0	0	36	17	200	7	0
Other Portfolio Income **6**	701994	33888	0	•	0	607	9040	27471	83400	159341	98425	113660	0
Other Receipts **7**	7964200	3278538	83810	•	0	8271	73948	327396	749972	1305511	1005469	775591	0
Total Receipts **8**	23906944	9395594	83810	•	0	19811	223633	820415	2074878	3776545	2598217	2701996	0
Average Total Receipts **9**	11395	63058	215	•	•	619	1202	2540	4673	9835	22398	56292	•
Operating Costs/Operating Income (%)													
Cost of Operations **10**	0.1	•	•	•	•	•	•	•	0.1	0.1	0.6	•	•
Salaries and Wages **11**	11.1	8.2	•	•	•	10.3	11.6	10.9	12.7	13.7	13.4	15.3	•
Taxes Paid **12**	2.4	1.8	•	•	•	3.3	2.9	2.7	2.8	2.9	2.8	3.1	•
Interest Paid **13**	37.7	49.9	•	•	•	19.4	30.3	29.3	30.2	29.7	28.6	25.1	•
Depreciation **14**	3.3	1.7	•	•	•	2.1	2.4	2.7	3.2	3.1	3.6	3.5	•
Amortization and Depletion **15**	0.2	0.1	•	•	•	0.1	0.2	0.4	0.4	0.4	0.3	0.2	•
Pensions and Other Deferred Comp. **16**	0.7	0.6	•	•	•	•	1.0	0.7	0.7	0.8	0.7	0.8	•
Employee Benefits **17**	1.5	0.6	•	•	•	2.6	3.2	2.5	2.3	2.2	2.1	2.4	•
Advertising **18**	0.5	0.1	•	•	•	0.9	0.9	0.8	0.9	0.9	0.7	1.0	•
Other Expenses **19**	21.8	26.9	•	•	•	25.6	18.7	18.9	19.3	18.2	17.7	18.8	•
Officers' Compensation **20**	3.8	0.7	•	•	•	16.3	12.8	10.5	8.0	6.6	5.0	3.0	•
Operating Margin **21**	16.8	9.4	28.8	•	•	19.4	16.2	20.5	19.4	21.6	24.5	26.9	•
Operating Margin Before Officers' Comp. **22**	20.6	10.0	28.8	•	•	35.7	29.0	31.0	27.4	28.1	29.5	29.9	•

Selected Average Balance Sheet ($ in Thousands)

Net Receivables **23**	55752	0	0	•	•	5080	9617	21976	40683	89221	199122	412704
Inventories **24**	•	•	•	•	•	•	•	•	•	•	•	•
Net Property, Plant and Equipment **25**	1546	0	0	•	•	44	215	590	1295	2747	5637	10230
Total Assets **26**	108654	0	1	•	•	7946	18095	37185	70824	151656	333783	832313
Notes and Loans Payable **27**	6361	0	0	•	•	0	115	343	1251	4089	9238	37479
All Other Liabilities **28**	91308	0	6	•	•	6430	19887	32169	61273	131671	289748	700534
Net Worth **29**	10985	0	-5	•	•	1515	-1907	4673	8301	15896	34797	94299

Selected Financial Ratios (Times to 1)

Current Ratio **30**	0.9	0.2	•	•	•	1.2	1.1	1.0	1.0	1.0	1.0	1.0
Quick Ratio **31**	0.9	0.2	•	•	•	1.2	1.0	1.0	0.9	0.9	0.9	0.9
Net Sales to Working Capital **32**	•	•	•	•	•	0.4	1.0	1.8	•	•	•	•
Coverage Ratio **33**	1.4	1.2	•	•	•	1.9	1.4	1.6	1.5	1.6	1.8	2.0
Total Asset Turnover **34**	0.1	179.1	•	•	•	0.1	0.1	0.1	0.1	0.1	0.1	0.1
Inventory Turnover **35**	•	•	•	•	•	•	•	•	•	•	•	•
Receivables Turnover **36**	•	•	•	•	•	•	•	•	•	•	•	•
Total Liabilities to Net Worth **37**	8.9	•	•	•	•	4.2	•	7.0	7.5	8.5	8.6	7.8
Current Assets to Working Capital **38**	•	•	•	•	•	5.4	13.8	23.6	•	•	•	•
Current Liabilities to Working Capital **39**	•	•	•	•	•	4.4	12.8	22.6	•	•	•	•
Working Capital to Net Sales **40**	•	•	•	•	•	2.3	0.6	1.0	•	•	•	•
Inventory to Working Capital **41**	•	•	•	•	•	•	•	•	•	•	•	•
Total Receipts to Cash Flow **42**	2.9	3.1	1.1	•	•	2.4	•	2.7	2.8	2.7	2.5	2.4
Cost of Goods to Cash Flow **43**	0.0	0.0	•	•	•	0.0	•	0.0	0.0	0.0	0.0	0.0
Cash Flow to Total Debt **44**	0.0	33.1	•	•	•	0.0	0.0	0.0	0.0	0.0	0.0	0.0

Selected Financial Factors (in Percentages)

Debt Ratio **45**	89.9	499.1	•	•	•	80.9	110.5	87.4	88.3	89.5	89.6	88.7
Return on Total Assets **46**	5.6	5150.0	•	•	•	2.8	2.9	3.2	3.1	3.2	3.4	3.4
Return on Equity Before Income Taxes **47**	16.0	•	•	•	•	6.9	•	9.7	9.3	11.7	13.9	14.6
Return on Equity After Income Taxes **48**	11.7	•	•	•	•	5.2	•	8.0	7.3	8.9	10.5	10.2
Profit Margin (Before Income Tax) **49**	15.4	9.3	28.8	•	•	17.0	13.4	17.8	16.6	18.9	21.6	24.5
Profit Margin (After Income Tax) **50**	11.3	6.5	28.8	•	•	12.6	10.8	14.8	13.0	14.3	16.3	17.1

Table I

Corporations with and without Net Income

SAVINGS INSTITUTIONS AND OTHER DEPOSITORY CREDIT

MONEY AMOUNTS AND SIZE OF ASSETS IN THOUSANDS OF DOLLARS

Item Description for Accounting Period 7/02 Through 6/03	Total	Zero Assets	Under 500	500 to 1,000	1,000 to 5,000	5,000 to 10,000	10,000 to 25,000	25,000 to 50,000	50,000 to 100,000	100,000 to 250,000	250,000 to 500,000	500,000 to 2,500,000	2,500,000 and over
Number of Enterprises **1**	1856	47	390	3	48	27	71	141	238	365	260	208	58
Revenues ($ in Thousands)													
Net Sales **2**	89807048	4457652	19987	8666	101657	51491	106195	345913	1275698	3827770	6134258	14686010	58791754
Interest **3**	61834962	3060881	698	7229	61971	3647	60619	281028	919879	3188043	4882584	10292984	39075398
Rents **4**	686184	6144	0	7	258	10	537	1241	2092	9106	15519	155169	496102
Royalties **5**	1232	0	0	0	0	0	0	6	30	0	6	53	1137
Other Portfolio Income **6**	443211	61856	0	480	115	0	7157	8544	31844	135254	225733	746438	3215789
Other Receipts **7**	22851459	1328771	19289	950	39313	47834	37882	55094	321853	495367	1010416	3491366	16003328
Total Receipts **8**	89807048	4457652	19987	8666	101657	51491	106195	345913	1275698	3827770	6134258	14686010	58791754
Average Total Receipts **9**	48387	94844	51	2889	2118	1907	1496	2453	5360	10487	23593	70606	1013651
Operating Costs/Operating Income (%)													
Cost of Operations **10**	0.3	•	•	•	•	2.3	0.0	0.0	0.2	0.0	0.5	0.2	0.4
Salaries and Wages **11**	13.5	11.0	•	14.8	19.6	30.7	12.6	11.5	15.8	12.4	13.1	13.8	13.6
Taxes Paid **12**	2.3	2.2	1.6	2.8	3.8	1.6	2.7	2.7	2.8	2.8	2.6	2.2	2.2
Interest Paid **13**	35.9	42.0	83.4	41.8	54.0	12.9	28.3	40.5	36.6	40.0	38.9	38.6	34.1
Depreciation **14**	3.5	1.4	•	1.8	1.7	3.0	1.8	2.4	3.3	2.7	2.5	3.3	3.9
Amortization and Depletion **15**	1.0	0.4	•	0.1	0.0	0.6	0.2	0.2	0.2	0.2	0.4	1.1	1.1
Pensions and Other Deferred Comp. **16**	1.0	0.6	•	1.7	1.2	•	1.1	1.1	1.1	1.2	1.2	0.9	0.9
Employee Benefits **17**	1.4	0.7	2.3	2.6	1.9	3.4	1.8	2.2	2.0	2.1	2.0	1.9	1.2
Advertising **18**	1.1	0.7	•	1.2	0.5	0.9	0.8	0.9	0.8	1.1	1.2	1.0	1.1
Other Expenses **19**	15.7	16.5	237.3	41.1	27.9	144.8	28.1	19.4	18.1	15.7	17.9	16.5	14.8
Officers' Compensation **20**	1.5	1.0	14.4	6.6	1.2	•	6.8	7.0	5.2	4.6	3.1	1.9	0.9
Operating Margin **21**	23.1	23.4	•	•	•	•	15.7	12.0	13.8	17.2	16.7	18.7	25.7
Operating Margin Before Officers' Comp. **22**	24.5	24.4	•	•	•	•	22.5	19.0	19.0	21.8	19.8	20.6	26.6

Selected Average Balance Sheet ($ in Thousands)

Item												
Net Receivables 23	37043	0	0	68	2302	1087	3400	6212	13506	32198	69984	668840
Inventories 24	•	•	•	•	•	•	•	•	•	•	•	•
Net Property, Plant and Equipment 25	7187	0	0	13	650	209	527	1225	2791	5491	13036	134171
Total Assets 26	626934	11	795	1917	5382	17636	37314	73265	163304	355756	1031073	13324628
Notes and Loans Payable 27	127097	0	1723	203	2896	1035	1830	4843	12128	32744	122567	3377263
All Other Liabilities 28	467194	9679	319109	124372	39352	17949	31565	59119	138684	288806	792234	9397554
Net Worth 29	32643	-9668	-320037	-122658	-36866	-1348	3919	9302	12493	34206	116272	549811

Selected Financial Ratios (Times to 1)

Item												
Current Ratio 30	0.2	0.0	2.9	0.0	0.9	0.4	0.4	0.3	0.3	0.3	0.2	0.2
Quick Ratio 31	0.2	0.0	2.9	0.0	0.9	0.4	0.3	0.3	0.3	0.3	0.2	0.2
Net Sales to Working Capital 32	•	•	9.3	•	•	•	•	•	•	•	•	•
Coverage Ratio 33	1.6	1.6	0.7	0.8	1.5	1.3	1.4	1.4	1.4	1.4	1.5	1.7
Total Asset Turnover 34	0.1	4.7	3.6	1.1	0.4	0.1	0.1	0.1	0.1	0.1	0.1	0.1
Inventory Turnover 35	•	•	•	•	•	•	•	•	•	•	•	•
Receivables Turnover 36	•	•	•	•	•	•	•	•	•	•	•	•
Total Liabilities to Net Worth 37	18.2	•	•	•	•	•	8.5	6.9	12.1	9.4	7.9	23.2
Current Assets to Working Capital 38	•	•	1.5	•	•	•	•	•	•	•	•	•
Current Liabilities to Working Capital 39	•	•	0.5	•	•	•	•	•	•	•	•	•
Working Capital to Net Sales 40	•	•	0.1	•	•	•	•	•	•	•	•	•
Inventory to Working Capital 41	•	•	•	•	•	•	•	•	•	•	•	•
Total Receipts to Cash Flow 42	2.8	2.7	•	15.5	10.0	2.7	3.5	3.4	3.3	3.3	3.2	2.7
Cost of Goods to Cash Flow 43	0.0	•	•	•	0.0	0.0	0.0	0.0	0.0	0.0	0.0	0.0
Cash Flow to Total Debt 44	0.0	•	•	•	0.0	0.0	0.0	0.0	0.0	0.0	0.0	0.0

Selected Financial Factors (in Percentages)

Item												
Debt Ratio 45	94.8	88172.2	40373.1	6499.6	784.9	107.6	89.5	87.3	92.3	90.4	88.7	95.9
Return on Total Assets 46	4.5	•	•	98.9	46.4	3.7	3.4	3.6	3.6	3.6	3.9	4.5
Return on Equity Before Income Taxes 47	33.7	•	1.3	0.1	0.2	5.2	7.1	7.5	13.7	11.1	11.0	47.0
Return on Equity After Income Taxes 48	22.5	•	1.3	0.2	0.3	5.2	4.8	4.9	9.1	7.1	7.3	31.8
Profit Margin (Before Income Tax) 49	22.7	23.3	•	•	15.2	•	11.3	13.1	16.4	16.0	18.1	25.5
Profit Margin (After Income Tax) 50	15.2	14.5	•	•	10.4	•	7.7	8.5	10.8	10.2	12.0	17.3

281

Table II

Corporations with Net Income

SAVINGS INSTITUTIONS AND OTHER DEPOSITORY CREDIT

MONEY AMOUNTS AND SIZE OF ASSETS IN THOUSANDS OF DOLLARS

Item Description for Accounting Period 7/02 Through 6/03	Total	Zero Assets	Under 500	500 to 1,000	1,000 to 5,000	5,000 to 10,000	10,000 to 25,000	25,000 to 50,000	50,000 to 100,000	100,000 to 250,000	250,000 to 500,000	500,000 to 2,500,000	2,500,000 and over
Number of Enterprises **1**	1684	24	385	0	0	0	62	117	217	345	246	197	0
Revenues ($ in Thousands)													
Net Sales **2**	86711259	4264126	24117	0	0	0	101684	293081	1160356	3635777	5771148	13859429	0
Interest **3**	60113119	2922289	4996	0	0	0	57488	237145	853099	3049621	4668196	9727512	0
Rents **4**	323986	4148	7	0	0	0	531	1189	2089	8577	14603	146708	0
Royalties **5**	1232	0	0	0	0	0	0	6	30	0	6	53	0
Other Portfolio Income **6**	4282807	42748	0	0	0	0	6966	6737	27243	123657	216862	724590	0
Other Receipts **7**	21990115	1294941	19114	0	0	0	36699	48004	277895	453922	871481	3260566	0
Total Receipts **8**	86711259	4264126	24117	0	0	0	101684	293081	1160356	3635777	5771148	13859429	0
Average Total Receipts **9**	51491	177672	63	•	•	•	1640	2505	5347	10538	23460	70352	•
Operating Costs/Operating Income (%)													
Cost of Operations **10**	0.3	•	•	•	•	•	0.0	•	0.1	0.0	0.6	0.2	•
Salaries and Wages **11**	13.3	9.3	3.0	•	•	•	12.5	10.1	16.0	12.2	13.3	13.6	•
Taxes Paid **12**	2.3	2.2	2.0	•	•	•	2.6	2.7	2.9	2.8	2.6	2.2	•
Interest Paid **13**	35.7	40.3	8.9	•	•	•	28.4	39.6	35.8	39.2	39.4	38.1	•
Depreciation **14**	3.0	1.3	0.4	•	•	•	1.7	2.1	2.2	2.6	2.5	3.3	•
Amortization and Depletion **15**	0.9	0.3	•	•	•	•	0.1	0.1	0.1	0.2	0.4	0.8	•
Pensions and Other Deferred Comp. **16**	1.0	0.5	0.1	•	•	•	1.1	1.2	1.2	1.2	1.2	0.9	•
Employee Benefits **17**	1.4	0.6	2.4	•	•	•	1.8	2.1	2.0	2.1	2.0	1.9	•
Advertising **18**	1.1	0.7	0.2	•	•	•	0.8	0.8	0.8	1.1	1.2	1.1	•
Other Expenses **19**	14.7	11.0	37.1	•	•	•	25.6	16.3	16.9	15.0	14.3	15.3	•
Officers' Compensation **20**	1.5	0.8	13.1	•	•	•	6.3	7.0	5.3	4.7	3.0	1.9	•
Operating Margin **21**	24.9	32.9	32.7	•	•	•	19.1	18.1	16.7	18.9	19.6	20.8	•
Operating Margin Before Officers' Comp. **22**	26.3	33.7	45.9	•	•	•	25.4	25.0	22.0	23.6	22.6	22.7	•

Selected Average Balance Sheet ($ in Thousands)

Net Receivables **23**	38828	0	0	•	1123	3334	5745	12929	31610	71519
Inventories **24**	•	•	•	•	•	•	•	•	•	•
Net Property, Plant and Equipment **25**	7202	0	0	•	219	473	1223	2747	5438	12745
Total Assets **26**	669889	0	11	•	17874	37542	73374	163518	356031	1021584
Notes and Loans Payable **27**	136792	0	0	•	1181	1908	3905	11718	33162	119467
All Other Liabilities **28**	490076	0	18	•	14270	31598	60381	133507	286384	786523
Net Worth **29**	43021	0	-7	•	2422	4036	9088	18294	36484	115594

Selected Financial Ratios (Times to 1)

Current Ratio **30**	0.2	•	0.5	•	0.4	0.3	0.3	0.3	0.3	0.2
Quick Ratio **31**	0.2	•	0.5	•	0.3	0.3	0.3	0.3	0.3	0.2
Net Sales to Working Capital **32**	•	•	•	•	•	•	•	•	•	•
Coverage Ratio **33**	1.7	1.8	4.7	•	1.7	1.4	1.4	1.5	1.5	1.5
Total Asset Turnover **34**	0.1	•	5.7	•	0.1	0.1	0.1	0.1	0.1	0.1
Inventory Turnover **35**	•	•	•	•	•	•	•	•	•	•
Receivables Turnover **36**	•	•	•	•	•	•	•	•	•	•
Total Liabilities to Net Worth **37**	14.6	•	•	•	6.4	8.3	7.1	7.9	8.8	7.8
Current Assets to Working Capital **38**	•	•	•	•	•	•	•	•	•	•
Current Liabilities to Working Capital **39**	•	•	•	•	•	•	•	•	•	•
Working Capital to Net Sales **40**	•	•	•	•	•	•	•	•	•	•
Inventory to Working Capital **41**	•	•	•	•	•	•	•	•	•	•
Total Receipts to Cash Flow **42**	2.8	2.4	1.6	•	2.6	3.1	3.2	3.2	3.2	3.1
Cost of Goods to Cash Flow **43**	0.0	•	•	•	0.0	•	0.0	0.0	0.0	0.0
Cash Flow to Total Debt **44**	0.0	•	2.2	•	0.0	0.0	0.0	0.0	0.0	0.0

Selected Financial Factors (in Percentages)

Debt Ratio **45**	93.6	•	160.7	•	86.4	89.2	87.6	88.8	89.8	88.7
Return on Total Assets **46**	4.6	•	238.0	•	4.3	3.8	3.8	3.7	3.8	4.0
Return on Equity Before Income Taxes **47**	29.4	•	•	•	12.6	10.8	9.4	10.4	12.2	12.2
Return on Equity After Income Taxes **48**	20.0	•	•	•	9.2	8.2	6.4	7.0	8.2	8.3
Profit Margin (Before Income Tax) **49**	24.5	32.8	32.7	•	18.7	17.5	16.0	18.0	18.9	20.1
Profit Margin (After Income Tax) **50**	16.7	23.6	31.3	•	13.6	13.2	11.0	12.2	12.8	13.7

Table I

Corporations with and without Net Income

CREDIT CARD ISSUING AND OTHER CONSUMER CREDIT

MONEY AMOUNTS AND SIZE OF ASSETS IN THOUSANDS OF DOLLARS

Item Description for Accounting Period 7/02 Through 6/03		Total	Zero Assets	Under 500	500 to 1,000	1,000 to 5,000	5,000 to 10,000	10,000 to 25,000	25,000 to 50,000	50,000 to 100,000	100,000 to 250,000	250,000 to 500,000	500,000 to 2,500,000	2,500,000 and over
Number of Enterprises	1	7048	508	3262	1142	1385	319	228	70	35	36	18	28	17
Revenues ($ in Thousands)														
Net Sales	2	102747194	10587625	425499	301921	1365314	693604	1038869	536595	787047	1769826	1292014	2886617	81062263
Interest	3	3645260	4531993	4913	5705	123482	80037	92429	90995	97883	680117	563664	1589542	28897502
Rents	4	266058	50184	0	0	296	354	736	651	75	212	23	0	213480
Royalties	5	113519	8264	0	0	554	0	0	12457	0	0	2244	0	89999
Other Portfolio Income	6	3731102	817931	662	893	27089	8769	12537	3090	12715	11591	92	19120	2816616
Other Receipts	7	62178255	5179253	419924	295323	1213893	604444	933167	429402	676374	1077906	725967	1277932	4934666
Total Receipts	8	102747194	10587625	425499	301921	1365314	693604	1038869	536595	787047	1769826	1292014	2886617	81062263
Average Total Receipts	9	14578	20842	130	264	986	2174	4556	7666	22487	49162	71779	103093	4768368
Operating Costs/Operating Income (%)														
Cost of Operations	10	5.8	0.1	0.0	2.8	2.0	3.6	7.1	3.5	1.4	4.0	•	0.1	7.0
Salaries and Wages	11	8.0	5.1	28.0	22.5	11.4	15.1	17.0	19.6	17.8	18.2	19.1	9.3	7.3
Taxes Paid	12	1.0	0.4	3.4	2.3	1.9	2.3	2.2	2.4	2.6	1.9	1.9	1.6	0.9
Interest Paid	13	21.0	25.7	6.3	11.7	9.1	12.9	12.9	18.3	9.9	18.7	22.3	27.1	20.8
Depreciation	14	11.6	23.6	1.2	2.6	6.6	2.2	3.7	0.9	3.3	3.8	1.6	4.1	11.1
Amortization and Depletion	15	0.7	0.2	0.1	0.2	0.1	0.5	0.5	1.4	0.9	1.8	5.0	1.0	0.6
Pensions and Other Deferred Comp.	16	0.8	0.5	0.0	0.2	0.3	1.0	0.4	0.6	0.5	0.2	0.2	0.2	0.9
Employee Benefits	17	0.9	1.1	3.0	1.1	0.4	1.1	1.0	1.1	1.3	1.5	0.6	0.7	0.9
Advertising	18	2.2	0.9	2.4	2.9	3.9	1.1	1.0	1.5	2.9	0.7	2.0	0.7	2.5
Other Expenses	19	44.5	42.1	55.5	40.6	45.7	41.1	37.4	35.7	30.2	41.0	33.7	50.0	45.2
Officers' Compensation	20	0.7	0.3	21.3	5.9	5.1	8.7	6.6	7.0	3.5	0.9	1.0	0.8	0.3
Operating Margin	21	2.9	•	•	7.2	13.3	10.4	10.2	8.0	25.8	7.2	12.6	4.5	2.5
Operating Margin Before Officers' Comp.	22	3.6	0.2	0.0	13.1	18.5	19.0	16.8	15.1	29.3	8.2	13.6	5.3	2.8

Selected Average Balance Sheet ($ in Thousands)

Net Receivables 23	39550	0	60	601	1703	4516	11401	24753	37492	85355	222018	618682	14354978
Inventories 24	•	•	•	•	•	•	•	•	•	•	•	•	•
Net Property, Plant and Equipment 25	2700	0	5	26	128	126	404	370	1955	3634	3624	7621	1068821
Total Assets 26	79864	0	142	745	2209	7000	15239	34486	71010	155199	354439	1081003	29744948
Notes and Loans Payable 27	40342	0	118	395	1280	4981	9919	24423	42940	103311	198290	633755	14683763
All Other Liabilities 28	27228	0	27	122	389	724	2712	5698	12349	16928	82191	288612	10546404
Net Worth 29	12294	0	-3	228	541	1295	2608	4365	15721	34959	73957	158636	4514781

Selected Financial Ratios (Times to 1)

Current Ratio 30	1.6	•	2.4	3.1	2.8	1.6	2.0	1.5	1.9	2.2	1.6	1.4	1.6
Quick Ratio 31	1.5	•	1.7	2.9	2.7	1.4	1.9	1.4	1.7	1.9	1.5	1.2	1.5
Net Sales to Working Capital 32	0.8	•	2.0	0.6	0.8	1.0	0.7	0.8	1.0	0.8	0.8	0.5	0.7
Coverage Ratio 33	1.1	1.0	•	1.6	2.5	1.8	1.8	1.4	3.6	1.4	1.6	1.2	1.1
Total Asset Turnover 34	0.2	•	0.9	0.4	0.4	0.3	0.3	0.2	0.3	0.3	0.2	0.1	0.2
Inventory Turnover 35	•	•	•	•	•	•	•	•	•	•	•	•	•
Receivables Turnover 36	•	•	•	•	•	•	•	•	•	•	•	•	•
Total Liabilities to Net Worth 37	5.5	•	•	2.3	3.1	4.4	4.8	6.9	3.5	3.4	3.8	5.8	5.6
Current Assets to Working Capital 38	2.7	•	1.7	1.5	1.6	2.7	2.0	2.8	2.1	1.9	2.7	3.8	2.7
Current Liabilities to Working Capital 39	1.7	•	0.7	0.5	0.6	1.7	1.0	1.8	1.1	0.9	1.7	2.8	1.7
Working Capital to Net Sales 40	1.2	•	0.5	1.6	1.2	1.0	1.4	1.3	1.0	1.3	1.3	1.9	1.4
Inventory to Working Capital 41	0.0	•	•	•	•	•	0.0	0.0	0.0	0.0	0.2	0.0	0.0
Total Receipts to Cash Flow 42	2.2	2.4	3.5	2.4	1.8	2.1	2.2	2.5	2.0	2.2	2.4	1.9	2.2
Cost of Goods to Cash Flow 43	0.1	0.0	0.0	0.1	0.0	0.1	0.2	0.1	0.0	0.1	•	0.0	0.2
Cash Flow to Total Debt 44	0.1	•	0.3	0.2	0.3	0.2	0.2	0.1	0.2	0.2	0.1	0.1	0.1

Selected Financial Factors (in Percentages)

Debt Ratio 45	84.6	•	102.0	69.3	75.5	81.5	82.9	87.3	77.9	77.5	79.1	85.3	84.8
Return on Total Assets 46	4.4	•	•	6.7	10.0	7.2	6.9	5.9	11.3	8.2	7.1	3.0	3.7
Return on Equity Before Income Taxes 47	3.5	•	958.1	8.3	24.3	17.4	17.9	14.1	36.9	10.1	12.2	2.9	2.7
Return on Equity After Income Taxes 48	1.3	•	962.1	8.0	22.8	13.1	15.8	12.0	30.4	7.3	9.0	0.7	0.7
Profit Margin (Before Income Tax) 49	2.9	•	•	7.2	13.3	10.4	10.2	8.0	25.8	7.2	12.6	4.5	2.5
Profit Margin (After Income Tax) 50	1.1	•	•	6.9	12.5	7.8	9.1	6.8	21.2	5.2	9.3	1.1	0.7

Table II
Corporations with Net Income

CREDIT CARD ISSUING AND OTHER CONSUMER CREDIT

MONEY AMOUNTS AND SIZE OF ASSETS IN THOUSANDS OF DOLLARS

Item Description for Accounting Period 7/02 Through 6/03	Total	Zero Assets	Under 500	500 to 1,000	1,000 to 5,000	5,000 to 10,000	10,000 to 25,000	25,000 to 50,000	50,000 to 100,000	100,000 to 250,000	250,000 to 500,000	500,000 to 2,500,000	2,500,000 and over
Number of Enterprises **1**	4091	503	1007	834	1160	263	186	51	27	25	9	17	9

Revenues ($ in Thousands)

	Total	Zero Assets	Under 500	500 to 1,000	1,000 to 5,000	5,000 to 10,000	10,000 to 25,000	25,000 to 50,000	50,000 to 100,000	100,000 to 250,000	250,000 to 500,000	500,000 to 2,500,000	2,500,000 and over
Net Sales **2**	79185908	7206252	44729	240633	1043923	612732	904168	402413	722760	1239857	1053913	1374276	64340252
Interest **3**	31526565	4474530	1439	112	92611	59141	70698	50132	80451	334354	332295	663788	25367013
Rents **4**	262924	50184	0	0	296	354	526	178	75	209	47	23	211032
Royalties **5**	23520	8264	0	0	554	0	0	12457	0	0	2244	0	0
Other Portfolio Income **6**	1172724	105348	662	0	26939	8727	10716	1642	12701	2871	92	16673	986354
Other Receipts **7**	46200175	2567926	42628	240521	923523	544510	822228	338004	629533	902423	719235	693792	37775853
Total Receipts **8**	79185908	7206252	44729	240633	1043923	612732	904168	402413	722760	1239857	1053913	1374276	64340252
Average Total Receipts **9**	19356	14327	44	289	900	2330	4861	7890	26769	49594	117101	80840	7148917

Operating Costs/Operating Income (%)

	Total	Zero Assets	Under 500	500 to 1,000	1,000 to 5,000	5,000 to 10,000	10,000 to 25,000	25,000 to 50,000	50,000 to 100,000	100,000 to 250,000	250,000 to 500,000	500,000 to 2,500,000	2,500,000 and over
Cost of Operations **10**	7.3	0.2	0.5	3.6	2.3	4.1	5.6	2.2	1.5	5.3	•		8.7
Salaries and Wages **11**	8.6	6.2	2.9	22.5	11.9	15.5	17.1	19.1	18.3	21.4	22.9	11.7	7.8
Taxes Paid **12**	1.0	0.1	1.2	2.0	2.1	2.4	2.2	2.5	2.8	2.4	2.3	1.9	0.9
Interest Paid **13**	19.9	29.9	15.8	8.5	7.7	12.4	11.4	15.0	7.6	10.7	9.8	32.5	19.4
Depreciation **14**	2.2	0.4	1.4	3.1	8.2	2.4	3.9	0.8	3.0	2.2	2.0	7.3	2.2
Amortization and Depletion **15**	0.6	0.3	•	0.0	0.1	0.4	0.2	1.6	0.8	0.6	5.4	0.9	0.5
Pensions and Other Deferred Comp. **16**	0.8	0.2	0.0	0.2	0.4	1.1	0.4	0.7	0.5	0.3	0.3	0.3	1.0
Employee Benefits **17**	1.0	1.5	0.2	0.3	0.4	1.1	1.0	1.0	1.3	1.6	0.6	1.0	1.0
Advertising **18**	2.5	1.1	0.5	1.4	1.3	1.3	1.1	1.5	3.1	0.9	2.5	0.2	2.8
Other Expenses **19**	47.3	54.9	41.2	32.7	39.8	32.4	34.8	29.2	28.9	34.3	36.0	21.9	48.3
Officers' Compensation **20**	0.7	0.4	2.1	5.6	4.6	9.2	6.7	8.1	3.8	1.3	1.2	1.2	0.3
Operating Margin **21**	8.2	4.7	34.3	20.0	21.2	17.7	15.8	18.3	28.5	19.1	17.1	21.3	7.1
Operating Margin Before Officers' Comp. **22**	8.8	5.1	36.3	25.7	25.8	26.9	22.5	26.4	32.2	20.3	18.3	22.4	7.5

Selected Average Balance Sheet ($ in Thousands)

Item													
Net Receivables **23**	46762	0	25	705	1797	4415	11560	26528	41538	98852	256772	737266	18339394
Inventories **24**	•	•	•	•	•	•	•	•	•	•	•	•	•
Net Property, Plant and Equipment **25**	865	0	33	125	144	390	397	2085	2929	7208	8647	•	321339
Total Assets **26**	96515	0	86	758	2276	6764	15282	34521	70875	159361	357700	1190168	39527916
Notes and Loans Payable **27**	46025	0	19	275	1262	4421	9341	22739	37588	76497	96614	681249	18571010
All Other Liabilities **28**	33396	0	10	95	390	762	2533	5367	13325	37233	137384	321143	14127562
Net Worth **29**	17094	0	56	388	624	1581	3407	6416	19961	45631	123702	187776	6829344

Selected Financial Ratios (Times to 1)

Item													
Current Ratio **30**	1.9	•		3.7	4.2	2.8	1.9	2.1	1.5	2.9	1.9	1.2	2.0
Quick Ratio **31**	1.8	•		3.3	4.2	2.7	1.7	1.9	1.5	2.4	1.7	1.2	1.8
Net Sales to Working Capital **32**	0.7	•		1.2	0.5	0.8	0.7	0.8	1.0	0.6	0.8	0.6	0.6
Coverage Ratio **33**	1.4	1.2		3.1	3.3	3.8	2.4	2.2	4.8	2.8	2.7	1.7	1.4
Total Asset Turnover **34**	0.2	•		0.5	0.4	0.3	0.3	0.2	0.4	0.3	0.3	0.1	0.2
Inventory Turnover **35**	•	•	•	•	•	•	•	•	•	•	•	•	•
Receivables Turnover **36**	•	•	•	•	•	•	•	•	•	•	•	•	•
Total Liabilities to Net Worth **37**	4.6	•		0.5	1.0	2.6	3.3	3.5	4.4	2.6	1.9	5.3	4.8
Current Assets to Working Capital **38**	2.1	•		1.4	1.3	1.6	2.1	1.9	2.9	1.5	2.1	5.7	2.0
Current Liabilities to Working Capital **39**	1.1	•		0.4	0.3	0.6	1.1	0.9	1.9	0.5	1.1	4.7	1.0
Working Capital to Net Sales **40**	1.5	•		0.8	1.9	1.4	1.2	1.4	1.3	1.8	1.2	1.8	1.6
Inventory to Working Capital **41**	0.0	•	•	•	•	•		0.0	0.0	0.0	0.0	0.0	0.0
Total Receipts to Cash Flow **42**	1.9	1.7		1.4	2.1	1.7	2.1	2.1	2.2	2.0	2.1	2.3	1.9
Cost of Goods to Cash Flow **43**	0.1	0.0		0.0	0.0	0.0	0.1	0.1	0.0	0.0	0.1	•	0.2
Cash Flow to Total Debt **44**	0.1	•		1.1	0.4	0.3	0.2	0.1	0.3	0.2	0.2	0.0	0.1

Selected Financial Factors (in Percentages)

Item													
Debt Ratio **45**	82.3	•	34.4	48.8	72.6	76.6	77.7	81.4	71.8	71.4	65.4	84.2	82.7
Return on Total Assets **46**	5.6	•	25.7	10.9	11.4	10.4	8.6	7.6	13.6	9.2	8.8	3.6	4.8
Return on Equity Before Income Taxes **47**	9.2	•	26.8	14.9	30.6	26.1	22.5	22.6	38.2	20.6	16.2	9.2	7.4
Return on Equity After Income Taxes **48**	6.5	•	26.1	14.7	29.0	21.9	20.6	20.6	31.6	17.6	12.3	6.1	4.9
Profit Margin (Before Income Tax) **49**	8.1	4.7	34.0	20.0	21.2	17.7	15.8	18.3	28.5	19.0	17.1	21.3	7.1
Profit Margin (After Income Tax) **50**	5.7	3.1	33.1	19.8	20.1	14.8	14.5	16.7	23.6	16.2	13.0	14.2	4.7

Table I

Corporations with and without Net Income

REAL ESTATE CREDIT INCL. MORTGAGE BANKERS AND ORIGINATORS

MONEY AMOUNTS AND SIZE OF ASSETS IN THOUSANDS OF DOLLARS

Item Description for Accounting Period 7/02 Through 6/03	Total	Zero Assets	Under 500	500 to 1,000	1,000 to 5,000	5,000 to 10,000	10,000 to 25,000	25,000 to 50,000	50,000 to 100,000	100,000 to 250,000	250,000 to 500,000	500,000 to 2,500,000	2,500,000 and over
Number of Enterprises **1**	16587	2589	11642	468	1021	264	270	139	77	59	25	26	6
Revenues ($ in Thousands)													
Net Sales **2**	34465602	335286	6231209	177702	1946301	817627	1553755	1618401	1399557	2255107	2031341	3867891	12231424
Interest **3**	6099998	77362	17425	2328	59623	7881	64470	74154	132271	485591	712931	1178874	3287089
Rents **4**	45483	1281	523	0	4565	1493	4862	2059	177	9126	967	12452	7978
Royalties **5**	1196	0	0	0	0	0	67	13	0	666	450	0	0
Other Portfolio Income **6**	2673504	1368	0	4681	8570	1370	20731	47417	114458	111441	186214	670300	1506952
Other Receipts **7**	25645421	255275	6213261	170693	1873543	806883	1463625	1494758	1152651	1648283	1130779	2006265	7429405
Total Receipts **8**	34465602	335286	6231209	177702	1946301	817627	1553755	1618401	1399557	2255107	2031341	3867891	12231424
Average Total Receipts **9**	2078	130	535	380	1906	3097	5755	11643	18176	38222	81254	148765	2038571
Operating Costs/Operating Income (%)													
Cost of Operations **10**	4.6	7.0	4.1	14.6	10.2	12.5	7.2	6.5	7.4	3.4	2.3	0.8	4.2
Salaries and Wages **11**	25.9	32.9	38.8	30.5	26.9	23.7	27.5	35.1	28.6	30.9	21.0	22.9	18.2
Taxes Paid **12**	2.6	3.3	2.6	4.1	3.5	2.9	3.1	3.6	3.4	2.9	2.5	3.7	1.6
Interest Paid **13**	12.6	3.5	0.4	14.2	5.5	3.8	7.0	7.3	11.7	14.8	24.4	19.2	18.0
Depreciation **14**	1.2	0.8	1.1	1.0	0.9	0.9	1.2	1.0	1.2	1.1	1.5	1.7	1.2
Amortization and Depletion **15**	2.5	0.3	0.1	0.7	0.5	0.0	0.4	0.4	0.4	1.9	0.3	1.5	6.0
Pensions and Other Deferred Comp. **16**	0.4	0.1	0.3	2.5	0.4	0.1	0.3	0.4	0.4	0.8	0.1	0.4	0.5
Employee Benefits **17**	1.1	1.4	0.5	0.3	0.8	0.6	0.8	0.9	1.4	1.0	0.5	2.1	1.4
Advertising **18**	1.6	1.9	2.1	5.5	4.5	2.6	2.1	2.0	1.4	1.4	0.5	2.3	0.7
Other Expenses **19**	31.4	53.2	31.1	32.2	28.6	37.6	34.9	26.8	25.3	28.4	30.5	27.1	33.9
Officers' Compensation **20**	4.8	0.8	11.9	20.2	11.8	4.6	10.3	5.3	5.7	3.7	6.8	1.4	0.2
Operating Margin **21**	11.1	7.0	•	•	6.4	10.8	5.1	10.7	13.2	9.7	9.7	17.0	14.2
Operating Margin Before Officers' Comp. **22**	15.9	18.9	•	•	18.1	15.4	15.5	16.0	18.8	13.4	16.5	18.4	14.3

Selected Average Balance Sheet ($ in Thousands)

	1	2	3	4	5	6	7	8	9	10	11	12	13
Net Receivables 23	1394	0	5	73	632	1424	3581	5630	12395	18870	52239	270000	1645580
Inventories 24	•	•	•	•	•	•	•	•	•	•	•	•	•
Net Property, Plant and Equipment 25	115	0	16	59	247	275	505	791	736	1777	2501	9334	108779
Total Assets 26	8916	0	98	665	2315	7088	15644	35778	69712	165762	365859	988869	13833676
Notes and Loans Payable 27	4104	0	22	460	1090	3785	10303	21691	47299	97283	241646	468924	5345237
All Other Liabilities 28	3893	0	11	252	469	1848	3878	9995	13476	57209	99179	439081	7102214
Net Worth 29	919	0	64	-48	756	1455	1462	4093	8937	11270	25034	80864	1386226

Selected Financial Ratios (Times to 1)

	1	2	3	4	5	6	7	8	9	10	11	12	13
Current Ratio 30	0.5	•	4.8	0.4	1.2	0.6	0.4	0.4	0.5	0.4	0.6	0.7	0.4
Quick Ratio 31	0.4	•	4.3	0.4	1.0	0.5	0.4	0.3	0.3	0.3	0.4	0.6	0.4
Net Sales to Working Capital 32	•	•	14.1	•	8.5	•	•	•	•	•	•	•	•
Coverage Ratio 33	1.9	•	19.3	2.1	2.1	3.8	1.7	2.5	2.1	1.7	1.4	1.9	1.8
Total Asset Turnover 34	0.2	•	5.5	0.6	0.8	0.4	0.4	0.3	0.3	0.2	0.2	0.2	0.1
Inventory Turnover 35	•	•	•	•	•	•	•	•	•	•	•	•	•
Receivables Turnover 36	•	•	•	•	•	•	•	•	•	•	•	•	•
Total Liabilities to Net Worth 37	8.7	•	0.5	•	2.1	3.9	9.7	7.7	6.8	13.7	13.6	11.2	9.0
Current Assets to Working Capital 38	•	•	1.3	•	5.3	•	•	•	•	•	•	•	•
Current Liabilities to Working Capital 39	•	•	0.3	•	4.3	•	•	•	•	•	•	•	•
Working Capital to Net Sales 40	•	•	0.1	•	0.1	•	•	•	•	•	•	•	•
Inventory to Working Capital 41	•	•	•	•	0.0	•	•	•	•	•	•	•	•
Total Receipts to Cash Flow 42	3.1	2.2	3.0	2.2	3.2	2.7	3.0	3.0	2.9	2.8	2.8	2.4	3.6
Cost of Goods to Cash Flow 43	0.1	0.2	0.1	0.3	0.3	0.2	0.2	0.2	0.2	0.1	0.1	0.0	0.2
Cash Flow to Total Debt 44	0.1	•	5.3	0.4	0.2	0.1	0.1	0.1	0.1	0.1	0.1	0.1	0.0

Selected Financial Factors (in Percentages)

	1	2	3	4	5	6	7	8	9	10	11	12	13
Debt Ratio 45	89.7	•	34.3	107.2	67.3	79.5	90.7	88.6	87.2	93.2	93.2	91.8	90.0
Return on Total Assets 46	5.5	•	40.7	9.7	6.3	4.4	5.9	6.4	5.6	7.6	5.4	4.7	
Return on Equity Before Income Taxes 47	25.1	•	58.8	205.6	15.8	22.8	20.0	30.3	25.9	32.6	31.5	31.2	20.9
Return on Equity After Income Taxes 48	20.4	•	57.9	216.1	14.8	22.0	17.8	28.2	22.5	22.7	19.0	19.5	17.9
Profit Margin (Before Income Tax) 49	11.1	•	7.0	•	6.3	10.7	5.1	10.7	12.7	9.6	9.7	17.0	14.2
Profit Margin (After Income Tax) 50	9.0	•	6.9	•	5.9	10.4	4.5	9.9	11.1	6.7	5.9	10.6	12.2

Table II
Corporations with Net Income

REAL ESTATE CREDIT INCL. MORTGAGE BANKERS AND ORIGINATORS

MONEY AMOUNTS AND SIZE OF ASSETS IN THOUSANDS OF DOLLARS

Item Description for Accounting Period 7/02 Through 6/03	Total	Zero Assets	Under 500	500 to 1,000	1,000 to 5,000	5,000 to 10,000	10,000 to 25,000	25,000 to 50,000	50,000 to 100,000	100,000 to 250,000	250,000 to 500,000	500,000 to 2,500,000	2,500,000 and over
Number of Enterprises **1**	10306	677	7876	278	765	233	208	113	66	50	0	19	0
Revenues ($ in Thousands)													
Net Sales **2**	30188008	292328	5064139	136596	1713044	781562	1326781	1461471	1295630	1939744	0	3444472	0
Interest **3**	4495242	71319	3994	1407	53886	5977	47926	52913	117210	264667	0	884837	0
Rents **4**	32208	3	523	0	4520	1366	3634	192	91	3782	0	9511	0
Royalties **5**	80	0	0	0	0	0	67	13	0	0	0	0	0
Other Portfolio Income **6**	2344849	101	0	0	8406	1370	20264	44395	108470	110674	0	606788	0
Other Receipts **7**	23315629	220905	5059622	135189	1646232	772849	1254890	1363958	1069859	1560621	0	1943336	0
Total Receipts **8**	30188008	292328	5064139	136596	1713044	781562	1326781	1461471	1295630	1939744	0	3444472	0
Average Total Receipts **9**	2929	432	643	491	2239	3354	6379	12933	19631	38795	•	181288	•
Operating Costs/Operating Income (%)													
Cost of Operations **10**	4.0	8.1	5.1	2.2	7.7	11.5	7.1	5.2	7.5	3.9	•	0.9	•
Salaries and Wages **11**	26.6	37.4	40.5	25.7	28.8	23.7	27.5	35.8	28.6	33.0	•	23.5	•
Taxes Paid **12**	2.6	3.6	2.3	4.4	3.3	2.9	3.1	3.7	3.4	3.1	•	3.9	•
Interest Paid **13**	10.8	2.7	0.2	4.1	5.4	3.8	6.0	6.6	10.7	9.4	•	14.0	•
Depreciation **14**	1.2	0.9	1.1	0.3	0.7	0.7	0.9	1.0	1.1	1.0	•	1.7	•
Amortization and Depletion **15**	2.8	0.4	0.0	0.0	0.3	0.0	0.3	0.3	0.1	1.8	•	1.4	•
Pensions and Other Deferred Comp. **16**	0.4	0.1	0.3	3.2	0.4	0.1	0.3	0.3	0.4	1.0	•	0.2	•
Employee Benefits **17**	1.1	1.7	0.5	0.4	0.7	0.7	0.8	0.9	1.3	1.1	•	2.1	•
Advertising **18**	1.4	1.9	1.6	1.3	2.5	2.1	1.9	1.9	1.4	1.5	•	2.3	•
Other Expenses **19**	28.9	20.1	25.6	21.7	26.0	38.3	31.1	25.6	24.6	24.1	•	23.9	•
Officers' Compensation **20**	4.9	0.7	12.1	26.1	11.9	4.6	11.1	5.6	5.5	3.8	•	1.6	•
Operating Margin **21**	15.5	22.5	10.8	10.7	12.0	11.5	9.9	13.1	15.4	16.2	•	24.6	•
Operating Margin Before Officers' Comp. **22**	20.3	23.1	22.8	36.8	24.0	16.1	21.0	18.7	20.9	20.1	•	26.2	•

Selected Average Balance Sheet ($ in Thousands)

	(1)	(2)	(3)	(4)	(5)	(6)	(7)	(8)	(9)	(10)	(11)
Net Receivables 23	1977	0	7	0	695	1610	3514	5703	13837	22069	277071
Inventories 24	•	•	•	•	•	•	•	•	•	•	•
Net Property, Plant and Equipment 25	158	0	21	8	249	292	387	792	700	1804	10520
Total Assets 26	11661	•	100	688	2466	7046	15441	36252	69772	166135	1049737
Notes and Loans Payable 27	5113	0	16	33	1172	3820	9296	22625	48283	91107	454597
All Other Liabilities 28	5219	0	11	211	416	1699	3683	9080	12382	60291	493033
Net Worth 29	1329	0	73	445	877	1527	2462	4547	9107	14738	102107

Selected Financial Ratios (Times to 1)

	(1)	(2)	(3)	(4)	(5)	(6)	(7)	(8)	(9)	(10)	(11)
Current Ratio 30	0.5	•	5.4	1.1	1.4	0.7	0.6	0.4	0.5	0.5	0.7
Quick Ratio 31	0.4	•	4.9	1.1	1.1	0.5	0.4	0.3	0.3	0.3	0.6
Net Sales to Working Capital 32	•	•	13.4	27.2	6.7	•	•	•	•	•	•
Coverage Ratio 33	2.4	9.3	72.8	3.6	3.2	4.0	2.7	3.0	2.4	2.7	2.8
Total Asset Turnover 34	0.3	•	6.4	0.7	0.9	0.5	0.4	0.4	0.3	0.2	0.2
Inventory Turnover 35	•	•	•	•	•	•	•	•	•	•	•
Receivables Turnover 36	•	•	•	•	•	•	•	•	•	•	•
Total Liabilities to Net Worth 37	7.8	•	0.4	0.5	1.8	3.6	5.3	7.0	6.7	10.3	9.3
Current Assets to Working Capital 38	•	•	1.2	12.6	3.8	•	•	•	•	•	•
Current Liabilities to Working Capital 39	•	•	0.2	11.6	2.8	•	•	•	•	•	•
Working Capital to Net Sales 40	•	•	0.1	0.0	0.1	•	•	•	•	•	•
Inventory to Working Capital 41	•	•	•	•	•	•	•	•	•	•	•
Total Receipts to Cash Flow 42	2.9	2.5	3.1	3.7	2.9	2.1	2.7	2.9	2.7	2.7	2.2
Cost of Goods to Cash Flow 43	0.1	0.2	0.2	0.1	0.2	0.2	0.2	0.1	0.2	0.1	0.0
Cash Flow to Total Debt 44	0.1	•	7.7	0.5	0.5	0.3	0.2	0.1	0.1	0.1	0.1

Selected Financial Factors (in Percentages)

	(1)	(2)	(3)	(4)	(5)	(6)	(7)	(8)	(9)	(10)	(11)
Debt Ratio 45	88.6	•	26.7	35.4	64.4	78.3	84.1	87.5	86.9	91.1	90.3
Return on Total Assets 46	6.6	•	70.2	10.5	15.8	7.2	6.5	7.0	7.3	6.0	6.7
Return on Equity Before Income Taxes 47	34.1	•	94.4	11.8	30.4	25.0	25.5	37.2	33.2	42.6	43.6
Return on Equity After Income Taxes 48	28.9	•	93.3	9.9	29.3	24.2	23.8	34.8	29.3	33.6	31.1
Profit Margin (Before Income Tax) 49	15.5	22.5	10.8	10.7	11.9	11.4	9.9	13.1	15.4	16.2	24.6
Profit Margin (After Income Tax) 50	13.1	19.8	10.6	9.0	11.5	11.0	9.2	12.2	13.6	12.8	17.5

286

Table I

Corporations with and without Net Income

INTL. TRADE, SECONDARY FINANCING, OTHER NONDEPOSITORY CREDIT

MONEY AMOUNTS AND SIZE OF ASSETS IN THOUSANDS OF DOLLARS

Item Description for Accounting Period 7/02 Through 6/03	Total	Zero Assets	Under 500	500 to 1,000	1,000 to 5,000	5,000 to 10,000	10,000 to 25,000	25,000 to 50,000	50,000 to 100,000	100,000 to 250,000	250,000 to 500,000	500,000 to 2,500,000	2,500,000 and over
Number of Enterprises **1**	7085	653	4328	957	646	135	93	47	41	55	29	51	51
Revenues ($ in Thousands)													
Net Sales **2**	128116733	1361700	341699	267774	601284	494140	484268	464582	422158	1085604	735031	3143161	118715334
Interest **3**	107793898	244725	47206	57094	26267	9955	34733	84525	112675	369039	267808	1804383	104875489
Rents **4**	160045	0	62	627	75	0	1277	462	5	3541	2460	45059	106478
Royalties **5**	70777	0	0	0	0	0	0	0	26	0	88	11198	59465
Other Portfolio Income **6**	2679670	5652	93	2254	954	25804	2009	732	11114	19580	6235	99301	2505942
Other Receipts **7**	17272343	1111323	294338	207799	573988	458381	446249	378863	298338	693444	458440	1183220	11167960
Total Receipts **8**	128116733	1361700	341699	267774	601284	494140	484268	464582	422158	1085604	735031	3143161	118715334
Average Total Receipts **9**	18083	2085	79	280	931	3660	5207	9885	10297	19738	25346	61631	2327752
Operating Costs/Operating Income (%)													
Cost of Operations **10**	0.4	•	•	•	4.3	13.0	7.6	3.6	1.9	3.0	•	7.5	0.0
Salaries and Wages **11**	1.9	0.4	14.8	31.1	18.8	21.0	20.2	22.0	15.5	13.7	13.4	5.4	1.2
Taxes Paid **12**	0.2	0.2	4.6	5.1	3.0	3.0	2.7	2.8	2.0	0.9	3.0	0.7	0.1
Interest Paid **13**	71.6	19.8	6.7	17.5	8.8	8.5	13.9	11.2	21.5	23.0	26.1	39.4	75.4
Depreciation **14**	0.6	0.0	7.2	1.6	1.8	3.0	1.5	2.1	1.8	2.3	1.3	4.0	0.4
Amortization and Depletion **15**	0.1	0.0	0.7	0.1	4.8	0.2	0.1	3.9	0.8	0.7	0.8	0.6	0.1
Pensions and Other Deferred Comp. **16**	0.2	0.2	•	0.1	0.6	0.2	0.4	1.2	0.4	0.2	0.4	0.2	0.2
Employee Benefits **17**	0.2	0.0	1.3	0.9	1.2	1.2	0.9	1.7	1.6	1.2	1.2	0.7	0.1
Advertising **18**	0.1	0.0	1.8	4.2	1.7	1.2	1.0	1.1	0.7	0.3	1.0	0.2	0.0
Other Expenses **19**	11.5	513.4	51.6	35.7	33.2	33.0	44.6	45.9	39.5	45.0	40.6	21.5	4.3
Officers' Compensation **20**	0.5	0.0	6.6	10.4	9.7	5.1	5.1	3.4	6.8	1.4	1.8	0.2	0.3
Operating Margin **21**	12.7	•	4.7	•	12.1	10.6	2.0	1.3	7.5	8.3	10.5	19.6	17.9
Operating Margin Before Officers' Comp. **22**	13.2	•	11.2	3.8	21.8	15.7	7.1	4.6	14.2	9.7	12.2	19.8	18.2

Selected Average Balance Sheet ($ in Thousands)

Item													
Net Receivables 23	35976	0	20	215	1081	4088	8076	22639	49130	107224	205562	591955	4067971
Inventories 24	•	•	•	•	•	•	•	•	•	•	•	•	•
Net Property, Plant and Equipment 25	276	0	21	17	95	639	433	1061	1113	2217	2158	7360	19623
Total Assets 26	288055	0	122	678	2232	7680	15388	35740	74292	160114	337445	1178478	38281626
Notes and Loans Payable 27	256390	0	65	365	1443	4905	10152	18803	53994	106947	210513	788577	34471604
All Other Liabilities 28	19766	0	4	124	262	1001	2939	8900	7069	14929	59775	72850	2595142
Net Worth 29	11899	0	53	190	527	1774	2297	8037	13229	38238	67157	317051	1214880

Selected Financial Ratios (Times to 1)

Item													
Current Ratio 30	0.5	•	6.2	2.3	1.4	1.6	1.5	1.8	1.5	1.3	1.4	1.4	0.5
Quick Ratio 31	0.3	•	3.8	1.2	1.3	1.4	1.2	1.6	1.3	1.2	1.2	1.1	0.3
Net Sales to Working Capital 32	•	•	1.4	1.0	1.9	1.8	1.4	0.7	0.6	0.8	0.3	0.2	•
Coverage Ratio 33	1.2	•	1.7	0.6	2.4	2.3	1.1	1.1	1.3	1.3	1.4	1.4	1.2
Total Asset Turnover 34	0.1	•	0.6	0.4	0.4	0.5	0.3	0.3	0.1	0.1	0.1	0.1	0.1
Inventory Turnover 35	•	•	•	•	•	•	•	•	•	•	•	•	•
Receivables Turnover 36	•	•	•	•	•	•	•	•	•	•	•	•	•
Total Liabilities to Net Worth 37	23.2	•	1.3	2.6	3.2	3.3	5.7	3.4	4.6	3.2	4.0	2.7	30.5
Current Assets to Working Capital 38	•	•	1.2	1.7	3.3	2.6	3.1	2.2	3.2	4.9	3.3	3.3	•
Current Liabilities to Working Capital 39	•	•	0.2	0.7	2.3	1.6	2.1	1.2	2.2	3.9	2.3	2.3	•
Working Capital to Net Sales 40	•	•	0.7	1.1	0.5	0.6	0.7	1.3	1.7	1.2	3.3	4.1	•
Inventory to Working Capital 41	•	•	•	•	•	•	0.0	•	0.0	0.0	0.0	0.0	•
Total Receipts to Cash Flow 42	4.2	1.3	2.1	5.8	2.5	2.6	2.3	2.4	2.4	1.9	2.1	2.5	4.6
Cost of Goods to Cash Flow 43	0.0	•	•	•	0.1	0.3	0.2	0.1	0.0	0.1	0.1	0.2	0.0
Cash Flow to Total Debt 44	0.0	•	0.5	0.1	0.2	0.2	0.2	0.2	0.1	0.1	0.0	0.0	0.0

Selected Financial Factors (in Percentages)

Item													
Debt Ratio 45	95.9	•	56.3	71.9	76.4	76.9	85.1	77.5	82.2	76.1	80.1	73.1	96.8
Return on Total Assets 46	5.2	•	7.3	4.5	8.7	9.1	5.4	3.4	4.0	3.7	2.7	2.9	5.6
Return on Equity Before Income Taxes 47	17.6	•	6.9	•	21.4	21.8	4.6	1.5	5.8	3.5	3.8	3.3	32.1
Return on Equity After Income Taxes 48	8.9	•	6.1	•	19.1	19.7	0.1	•	4.3	2.3	1.0	2.0	20.9
Profit Margin (Before Income Tax) 49	11.6	•	4.7	•	12.1	10.6	2.0	1.2	7.5	6.7	9.9	16.8	16.7
Profit Margin (After Income Tax) 50	5.9	•	4.2	•	10.8	9.5	0.0	•	5.5	4.5	2.7	10.3	10.9

Table II
Corporations with Net Income

INTL. TRADE, SECONDARY FINANCING, OTHER NONDEPOSITORY CREDIT

MONEY AMOUNTS AND SIZE OF ASSETS IN THOUSANDS OF DOLLARS

Item Description for Accounting Period 7/02 Through 6/03		Total	Zero Assets	Under 500	500 to 1,000	1,000 to 5,000	5,000 to 10,000	10,000 to 25,000	25,000 to 50,000	50,000 to 100,000	100,000 to 250,000	250,000 to 500,000	500,000 to 2,500,000	2,500,000 and over
Number of Enterprises	1	3551	261	1943	456	518	103	65	31	29	45	22	36	42
Revenues ($ in Thousands)														
Net Sales	2	123790821	183706	219124	158677	548113	456089	367582	345983	355852	693747	487973	2127807	117846168
Interest	3	106288136	142963	15474	41137	15114	5905	21125	37084	84056	311725	223730	1219852	104169972
Rents	4	127881	0	0	627	0	0	1277	32	0	3540	2298	13628	106478
Royalties	5	59491	0	0	0	0	0	0	0	26	0	0	0	59465
Other Portfolio Income	6	2576537	4118	91	18	0	21697	1944	589	11114	3659	73	57943	2475290
Other Receipts	7	14738776	36625	203559	116895	532999	428487	343236	308278	260656	374823	261872	836384	11034963
Total Receipts	8	123790821	183706	219124	158677	548113	456089	367582	345983	355852	693747	487973	2127807	117846168
Average Total Receipts	9	34861	704	113	348	1058	4428	5655	11161	12271	15417	22181	59106	2805861
Operating Costs/Operating Income (%)														
Cost of Operations	10	0.2	·	·	·	4.2	11.0	6.6	4.8	2.3	4.7	·	0.3	0.0
Salaries and Wages	11	1.7	3.2	20.4	27.3	18.1	21.2	19.4	20.8	16.2	15.8	6.1	7.1	1.2
Taxes Paid	12	0.2	0.5	5.5	5.0	2.8	2.8	2.7	3.1	2.1	0.9	1.0	1.0	0.1
Interest Paid	13	73.0	64.0	6.4	7.0	7.4	5.5	11.0	10.6	17.3	30.3	29.7	37.6	75.4
Depreciation	14	0.5	0.0	2.7	2.4	1.7	1.8	1.5	2.1	2.0	2.6	0.7	4.9	0.4
Amortization and Depletion	15	0.1	0.0	0.3	0.1	5.2	0.1	0.1	4.3	0.9	1.0	0.0	0.3	0.1
Pensions and Other Deferred Comp.	16	0.2	1.2	·	0.2	0.7	0.2	0.4	1.4	0.4	0.3	0.4	0.2	0.2
Employee Benefits	17	0.2	0.3	0.1	1.0	1.2	1.3	0.9	1.5	1.7	1.1	0.8	0.9	0.1
Advertising	18	0.1	0.0	2.4	2.8	1.8	1.3	0.9	1.2	0.8	0.5	0.2	0.3	0.0
Other Expenses	19	5.1	16.7	32.2	34.5	26.3	32.7	28.2	29.3	40.2	29.4	26.5	17.9	4.1
Officers' Compensation	20	0.4	·	8.0	10.5	9.6	5.4	5.3	3.5	5.9	1.9	2.3	0.3	0.3
Operating Margin	21	18.2	14.2	22.2	9.4	21.0	16.8	23.1	17.4	10.2	11.4	32.2	29.1	18.0
Operating Margin Before Officers' Comp.	22	18.7	14.2	30.2	19.9	30.6	22.2	28.4	20.9	16.1	13.4	34.5	29.4	18.3

Selected Average Balance Sheet ($ in Thousands)

Net Receivables 23	59196	0	31	289	1124	3995	9209	23863	53111	109204	201630	510379	4248052
Inventories 24	•	•	•	•	•	•	•	•	•	•	•	•	•
Net Property, Plant and Equipment 25	444	0	6	24	107	294	376	744	1493	1878	1341	7385	23739
Total Assets 26	556187	0	120	639	2155	7572	15751	35031	75864	159561	335216	1134310	45545261
Notes and Loans Payable 27	498002	0	47	454	1130	3442	9707	18584	54242	111797	193867	644824	41235188
All Other Liabilities 28	35133	0	6	32	282	1202	2483	7207	5322	9478	55901	86531	2836897
Net Worth 29	23052	0	67	153	742	2928	3562	9240	16300	38286	85447	402954	1473176

Selected Financial Ratios (Times to 1)

Current Ratio 30	0.5	•	11.2	2.3	2.0	1.5	1.6	2.1	1.6	1.3	1.5	1.8	0.4
Quick Ratio 31	0.3	•	6.8	1.3	1.8	1.2	1.3	1.8	1.5	1.2	1.2	1.4	0.3
Net Sales to Working Capital 32	•	•	1.3	1.0	1.2	2.3	1.2	0.7	0.6	0.6	0.3	0.2	1.2
Coverage Ratio 33	1.2	1.2	4.5	2.4	3.8	4.0	3.1	2.6	1.6	1.4	2.1	1.7	1.2
Total Asset Turnover 34	0.1	•	0.9	0.5	0.5	0.6	0.4	0.3	0.2	0.1	0.1	0.1	0.1
Inventory Turnover 35	•	•	•	•	•	•	•	•	•	•	•	•	•
Receivables Turnover 36	•	•	•	•	•	•	•	•	•	•	•	•	•
Total Liabilities to Net Worth 37	23.1	•	0.8	3.2	1.9	1.6	3.4	2.8	3.7	3.2	2.9	1.8	29.9
Current Assets to Working Capital 38	•	•	1.1	1.8	2.0	2.8	2.6	1.9	2.6	4.5	3.2	2.2	•
Current Liabilities to Working Capital 39	•	•	0.1	0.8	1.0	1.8	1.6	0.9	1.6	3.5	2.2	1.2	•
Working Capital to Net Sales 40	•	•	0.8	1.0	0.8	0.4	0.8	1.4	1.8	1.7	3.7	6.0	•
Inventory to Working Capital 41	•	•	•	•	•	0.0	0.0	•	0.0	0.0	•	0.0	•
Total Receipts to Cash Flow 42	4.4	3.3	2.1	2.9	2.4	2.2	2.1	2.4	2.3	2.6	1.7	2.2	4.6
Cost of Goods to Cash Flow 43	0.0	•	•	•	0.1	0.2	0.1	0.1	0.1	0.1	•	0.0	0.0
Cash Flow to Total Debt 44	0.0	•	1.0	0.2	0.3	0.4	0.2	0.2	0.1	0.0	0.1	0.0	0.0

Selected Financial Factors (in Percentages)

Debt Ratio 45	95.9	•	44.1	76.1	65.5	61.3	77.4	73.6	78.5	76.0	74.5	64.5	96.8
Return on Total Assets 46	5.6	•	26.9	8.9	14.0	13.0	12.2	8.9	4.4	4.0	4.1	3.3	5.7
Return on Equity Before Income Taxes 47	25.9	•	37.4	21.5	29.9	25.4	36.7	20.9	7.7	4.6	8.3	3.9	32.2
Return on Equity After Income Taxes 48	17.0	•	36.0	20.1	27.9	23.7	32.5	17.4	5.9	3.1	5.5	2.5	21.0
Profit Margin (Before Income Tax) 49	17.1	14.2	22.2	9.4	21.0	16.8	23.1	17.3	10.2	11.3	32.2	26.7	16.9
Profit Margin (After Income Tax) 50	11.2	9.4	21.4	8.8	19.6	15.6	20.5	14.4	7.9	7.8	21.2	17.1	11.0

Table I

Corporations with and without Net Income

ACTIVITIES RELATED TO CREDIT INTERMEDIATION

MONEY AMOUNTS AND SIZE OF ASSETS IN THOUSANDS OF DOLLARS

Item Description for Accounting Period 7/02 Through 6/03	Total	Zero Assets	Under 500	500 to 1,000	1,000 to 5,000	5,000 to 10,000	10,000 to 25,000	25,000 to 50,000	50,000 to 100,000	100,000 to 250,000	250,000 to 500,000	500,000 to 2,500,000	2,500,000 and over
Number of Enterprises **1**	19434	2594	14572	791	978	208	141	62	46	19	5	13	4
Revenues ($ in Thousands)													
Net Sales **2**	31318363	938107	5124633	1239504	1570152	634128	988394	988827	1268599	1005645	546151	5912964	11103261
Interest **3**	1192335	14533	9125	8013	28054	17840	25389	17870	39639	74411	79598	458309	419553
Rents **4**	131755	2273	850	0	2247	1536	378	303	2613	0	285	24761	96510
Royalties **5**	405131	0	0	0	0	0	0	0	0	0	0	0	405131
Other Portfolio Income **6**	588593	24742	5	0	2908	1957	3192	1100	2685	16220	0	11175	522608
Other Receipts **7**	29002549	896559	5114653	1231491	1536943	612795	959435	967554	1223662	915014	466268	5418719	9659459
Total Receipts **8**	31318363	938107	5124633	1239504	1570152	634128	988394	986827	1268599	1005645	546151	5912964	11103261
Average Total Receipts **9**	1612	362	352	1567	1605	3049	7010	15917	27578	52929	109230	454843	2775815
Operating Costs/Operating Income (%)													
Cost of Operations **10**	6.1	0.2	13.3	2.9	7.9	11.7	16.5	14.7	4.7	32.0	*	0.6	2.5
Salaries and Wages **11**	20.9	26.4	16.7	38.4	28.6	25.1	28.6	27.9	26.3	23.4	34.3	21.2	16.2
Taxes Paid **12**	3.0	3.2	2.5	2.6	3.3	2.9	2.7	2.9	2.8	1.2	3.5	2.4	3.7
Interest Paid **13**	4.4	2.2	0.4	0.6	4.2	6.3	5.2	6.3	5.8	9.3	9.7	2.9	6.6
Depreciation **14**	2.9	2.5	1.6	0.9	1.9	3.3	1.3	2.3	2.2	1.6	2.3	3.9	3.9
Amortization and Depletion **15**	1.4	1.7	0.1	0.3	0.3	0.4	0.1	0.4	1.2	2.5	2.0	1.7	2.3
Pensions and Other Deferred Comp. **16**	1.1	0.8	0.4	0.0	0.5	0.5	0.2	0.4	0.5	1.3	0.2	3.0	0.9
Employee Benefits **17**	1.8	0.6	0.6	4.7	1.0	0.9	1.1	1.0	1.4	1.1	4.4	1.8	2.3
Advertising **18**	5.9	1.2	2.0	0.8	1.5	3.1	1.8	3.4	6.7	1.2	0.7	12.3	7.1
Other Expenses **19**	40.6	54.4	44.7	42.0	36.3	28.7	27.1	27.1	36.9	21.7	36.3	39.7	43.9
Officers' Compensation **20**	3.6	2.5	12.3	6.2	7.2	6.8	6.0	2.9	3.5	2.2	3.2	0.7	0.4
Operating Margin **21**	8.2	4.2	5.4	0.6	7.3	10.4	9.3	10.8	8.0	2.4	3.4	9.7	10.3
Operating Margin Before Officers' Comp. **22**	11.9	6.8	17.7	6.8	14.5	17.2	15.3	13.7	11.5	4.6	6.6	10.4	10.7

Selected Average Balance Sheet ($ in Thousands)

Net Receivables 23	533	0	8	98	599	2420	4526	11352	24128	48061	82540	297021	362832
Inventories 24	•	•	•	•	•	•	•	•	•	•	•	•	•
Net Property, Plant and Equipment 25	141	0	18	67	197	734	583	1537	2176	2811	9544	54859	246986
Total Assets 26	3717	0	72	660	2245	7275	15710	34595	67262	162814	369348	1029841	10291433
Notes and Loans Payable 27	1619	0	37	289	934	4318	8749	18958	25982	101180	159945	249917	4829078
All Other Liabilities 28	1515	0	11	196	551	1334	4558	9402	29532	28484	190916	375516	4838189
Net Worth 29	583	0	25	175	759	1623	2403	6235	11748	33149	18487	404409	624166

Selected Financial Ratios (Times to 1)

Current Ratio 30	0.6	•	2.4	2.3	2.0	1.1	0.9	1.0	0.9	1.1	0.4	1.3	0.3
Quick Ratio 31	0.4	•	2.2	2.1	1.6	0.9	0.7	0.8	0.9	0.9	0.3	1.1	0.1
Net Sales to Working Capital 32	•	•	16.4	6.1	2.3	5.7	•	•	•	7.1	•	3.8	•
Coverage Ratio 33	2.6	2.9	13.8	2.1	2.7	2.6	2.8	2.7	2.4	1.3	1.4	4.4	2.0
Total Asset Turnover 34	0.4	•	4.9	2.4	0.7	0.4	0.4	0.5	0.4	0.3	0.3	0.4	0.3
Inventory Turnover 35	•	•	•	•	•	•	•	•	•	•	•	•	•
Receivables Turnover 36	•	•	•	•	•	•	•	•	•	•	•	•	•
Total Liabilities to Net Worth 37	5.4	•	1.9	2.8	2.0	3.5	5.5	4.5	4.7	3.9	19.0	1.5	15.5
Current Assets to Working Capital 38	•	•	1.7	1.8	2.1	8.1	•	•	•	11.3	•	4.1	•
Current Liabilities to Working Capital 39	•	•	0.7	0.8	1.1	7.1	•	•	•	10.3	•	3.1	•
Working Capital to Net Sales 40	•	•	0.1	0.2	0.4	0.2	•	•	•	0.1	•	0.3	•
Inventory to Working Capital 41	•	•	•	•	0.0	0.0	•	•	•	0.0	•	0.0	•
Total Receipts to Cash Flow 42	2.2	1.9	2.3	2.5	2.7	2.8	3.1	3.0	2.4	4.9	3.0	2.2	1.9
Cost of Goods to Cash Flow 43	0.1	0.0	0.3	0.1	0.2	0.3	0.5	0.4	0.1	1.6	•	0.0	0.0
Cash Flow to Total Debt 44	0.2	•	3.3	1.3	0.4	0.2	0.2	0.2	0.2	0.1	0.1	0.3	0.1

Selected Financial Factors (in Percentages)

Debt Ratio 45	84.3	•	65.8	73.5	66.2	77.7	84.7	82.0	82.5	79.6	95.0	60.7	93.9
Return on Total Assets 46	4.9	•	28.5	2.9	8.2	7.0	6.4	7.8	5.6	3.8	3.9	5.6	3.6
Return on Equity Before Income Taxes 47	19.2	•	77.3	5.5	15.5	19.4	27.0	27.5	18.5	3.8	20.1	11.0	29.9
Return on Equity After Income Taxes 48	15.0	•	75.7	5.1	13.9	17.4	24.7	26.5	16.0	1.3	16.3	7.7	20.8
Profit Margin (Before Income Tax) 49	6.9	4.2	5.4	0.6	7.3	10.3	9.2	10.8	7.9	2.4	3.4	9.8	6.7
Profit Margin (After Income Tax) 50	5.4	3.9	5.3	0.6	6.6	9.3	8.5	10.4	6.8	0.8	2.8	6.8	4.7

Table II
Corporations with Net Income

ACTIVITIES RELATED TO CREDIT INTERMEDIATION

MONEY AMOUNTS AND SIZE OF ASSETS IN THOUSANDS OF DOLLARS

Item Description for Accounting Period 7/02 Through 6/03	Total	Zero Assets	Under 500	500 to 1,000	1,000 to 5,000	5,000 to 10,000	10,000 to 25,000	25,000 to 50,000	50,000 to 100,000	100,000 to 250,000	250,000 to 500,000	500,000 to 2,500,000	2,500,000 and over
Number of Enterprises **1**	9991	1695	6652	549	715	0	113	53	36	12	0	10	4

Revenues ($ in Thousands)

	Total	Zero Assets	Under 500	500 to 1,000	1,000 to 5,000	5,000 to 10,000	10,000 to 25,000	25,000 to 50,000	50,000 to 100,000	100,000 to 250,000	250,000 to 500,000	500,000 to 2,500,000	2,500,000 and over
Net Sales **2**	28495290	699692	4401097	1091642	1309239	0	862038	828676	1140809	818580	0	5159203	11103261
Interest **3**	801095	4404	4511	2955	13734	0	19079	16281	23409	20700	0	204127	419553
Rents **4**	111555	2245	0	0	2247	0	378	303	2613	0	0	6976	96510
Royalties **5**	405131	0	0	0	0	0	0	0	0	0	0	0	405131
Other Portfolio Income **6**	567843	10281	5	0	1131	0	2534	606	1473	16184	0	11066	522608
Other Receipts **7**	26609666	682762	4396581	1088687	1292127	0	840047	811486	1113314	781696	0	4937034	9665459
Total Receipts **8**	28495290	699692	4401097	1091642	1309239	0	862038	828676	1140809	818580	0	5159203	11103261
Average Total Receipts **9**	2852	413	662	1988	1831	•	7629	15635	31689	68215	•	515920	2775815

Operating Costs/Operating Income (%)

	Total	Zero Assets	Under 500	500 to 1,000	1,000 to 5,000	5,000 to 10,000	10,000 to 25,000	25,000 to 50,000	50,000 to 100,000	100,000 to 250,000	250,000 to 500,000	500,000 to 2,500,000	2,500,000 and over
Cost of Operations **10**	6.0	0.2	13.9	•	9.3	•	17.8	11.5	4.1	39.3	•	0.0	2.5
Salaries and Wages **11**	20.3	23.6	16.0	38.3	29.2	•	28.7	29.2	24.1	24.9	•	19.9	16.2
Taxes Paid **12**	2.9	2.5	1.9	2.6	3.4	•	2.8	3.1	2.7	1.3	•	2.3	3.7
Interest Paid **13**	4.1	0.6	0.4	0.4	3.0	•	4.4	6.1	5.0	2.6	•	2.9	6.6
Depreciation **14**	3.0	2.5	1.3	0.6	1.9	•	1.3	2.2	2.3	1.2	•	4.1	3.9
Amortization and Depletion **15**	1.2	0.3	0.1	0.1	0.2	•	0.1	0.4	1.2	0.6	•	1.0	2.3
Pensions and Other Deferred Comp. **16**	0.9	0.0	0.4	•	0.5	•	0.2	0.4	0.5	1.5	•	2.0	0.9
Employee Benefits **17**	1.7	0.4	0.5	4.9	1.1	•	1.2	1.1	1.3	1.0	•	1.5	2.3
Advertising **18**	6.1	1.0	1.0	0.7	1.5	•	2.0	4.0	7.2	1.3	•	13.9	7.1
Other Expenses **19**	39.7	56.3	43.3	40.6	29.0	•	22.0	25.3	35.2	15.4	•	39.9	43.9
Officers' Compensation **20**	3.4	2.6	11.8	5.9	7.0	•	6.2	3.1	3.6	1.9	•	0.8	0.4
Operating Margin **21**	10.6	9.8	9.4	5.9	13.9	•	13.2	13.7	12.8	8.8	•	11.6	10.3
Operating Margin Before Officers' Comp. **22**	14.0	12.4	21.2	11.8	21.0	•	19.5	16.8	16.3	10.7	•	12.3	10.7

Selected Average Balance Sheet ($ in Thousands)

Item													
Net Receivables 23	848	0	5	79	667	•	4769	11148	27709	25890	•	324952	362832
Inventories 24	•	•	•	•	•	•	•	•	•	•	•	•	•
Net Property, Plant and Equipment 25	231	0	32	41	175	•	461	1657	2553	3229	•	57013	246986
Total Assets 26	6537	0	92	645	2072	•	15959	34485	67321	150964	•	1111408	10291433
Notes and Loans Payable 27	2784	0	28	230	838	•	9403	19779	28680	67683	•	248206	4829078
All Other Liabilities 28	2804	0	13	210	567	•	4464	8887	25851	40269	•	454917	4838189
Net Worth 29	949	0	52	205	667	•	2092	5818	12790	43012	•	408285	624166

Selected Financial Ratios (Times to 1)

Item													
Current Ratio 30	0.6	•	1.9	1.9	1.6	•	0.8	0.9	1.0	0.9	•	1.2	0.3
Quick Ratio 31	0.3	•	1.7	1.9	1.4	•	0.6	0.8	0.9	0.6	•	1.0	0.1
Net Sales to Working Capital 32	•	•	33.7	10.0	3.2	•	•	•	•	•	•	4.7	•
Coverage Ratio 33	3.3	16.2	25.6	15.3	5.7	•	4.0	3.3	3.5	4.3	•	5.0	2.0
Total Asset Turnover 34	0.4	•	7.2	3.1	0.9	•	0.5	0.5	0.5	0.5	•	0.5	0.3
Inventory Turnover 35	•	•	•	•	•	•	•	•	•	•	•	•	•
Receivables Turnover 36	•	•	•	•	•	•	•	•	•	•	•	•	•
Total Liabilities to Net Worth 37	5.9	•	0.8	2.1	2.1	•	6.6	4.9	4.3	2.5	•	1.7	15.5
Current Assets to Working Capital 38	•	•	2.1	2.1	2.6	•	•	•	•	•	•	5.1	•
Current Liabilities to Working Capital 39	•	•	1.1	1.1	1.6	•	•	•	•	•	•	4.1	•
Working Capital to Net Sales 40	•	•	0.0	0.1	0.3	•	•	•	•	•	•	0.2	•
Inventory to Working Capital 41	•	•	•	•	•	•	•	•	•	•	•	•	•
Total Receipts to Cash Flow 42	2.1	1.6	2.1	2.3	2.7	•	3.2	2.9	2.3	4.7	•	2.1	1.9
Cost of Goods to Cash Flow 43	0.1	0.0	0.3	•	0.2	•	0.6	0.3	0.1	1.8	•	0.0	0.0
Cash Flow to Total Debt 44	0.2	•	7.7	2.0	0.5	•	0.2	0.2	0.3	0.1	•	0.3	0.1

Selected Financial Factors (in Percentages)

Item													
Debt Ratio 45	85.5	•	44.2	68.2	67.8	•	86.9	83.1	81.0	71.5	•	63.3	93.9
Return on Total Assets 46	5.8	•	70.1	19.4	14.9	•	8.4	9.0	8.4	5.2	•	6.7	3.6
Return on Equity Before Income Taxes 47	27.7	•	120.6	57.0	38.2	•	48.1	36.9	31.6	14.0	•	14.6	29.9
Return on Equity After Income Taxes 48	22.7	•	119.0	56.5	35.8	•	44.8	35.6	28.7	10.9	•	10.4	20.8
Profit Margin (Before Income Tax) 49	9.2	9.8	9.4	5.9	13.9	•	13.2	13.7	12.8	8.8	•	11.6	6.7
Profit Margin (After Income Tax) 50	7.6	9.3	9.3	5.8	13.0	•	12.3	11.6	13.2	6.9	•	8.2	4.7

Table I

Corporations with and without Net Income

INVESTMENT BANKING AND SECURITIES DEALING

MONEY AMOUNTS AND SIZE OF ASSETS IN THOUSANDS OF DOLLARS

Item Description for Accounting Period 7/02 Through 6/03	Total	Zero Assets	Under 500	500 to 1,000	1,000 to 5,000	5,000 to 10,000	10,000 to 25,000	25,000 to 50,000	50,000 to 100,000	100,000 to 250,000	250,000 to 500,000	500,000 to 2,500,000	2,500,000 and over
Number of Enterprises **1**	4083	1248	2187	243	236	49	47	27	11	12	4	6	12
Revenues ($ in Thousands)													
Net Sales **2**	105357698	212028	340260	19626	275600	401020	270530	563342	221767	357258	448677	538438	101709151
Interest **3**	50776800	9343	2089	50	4562	11994	2840	11339	4996	12488	60475	81945	50574679
Rents **4**	866478	917	0	0	4526	11330	90	71	0	0	163	1454	849928
Royalties **5**	240												240
Other Portfolio Income **6**	4337574	6970	1368	0	1453	3883	7157	20719	10269	4323	923	14490	4266019
Other Receipts **7**	49374606	194798	336803	19576	265059	373813	260443	531213	206502	340447	387116	440549	46018285
Total Receipts **8**	105357698	212028	340260	19626	275600	401020	270530	563342	221767	357258	448677	538438	101709151
Average Total Receipts **9**	25804	170	156	81	1168	8184	5756	20865	20161	29772	112169	89740	8475763
Operating Costs/Operating Income (%)													
Cost of Operations **10**	0.1	•	•	•	0.2	•	•	5.5	•	•	•	•	0.1
Salaries and Wages **11**	12.9	20.8	11.7	13.0	36.6	22.8	38.7	36.5	37.4	30.2	23.3	22.1	12.4
Taxes Paid **12**	0.8	2.3	2.4	0.1	3.0	1.2	2.8	2.7	2.6	2.7	2.2	1.4	0.7
Interest Paid **13**	39.7	14.1	2.4	•	2.7	3.5	1.4	2.6	9.6	57.1	11.5	7.6	40.8
Depreciation **14**	1.7	1.5	0.6	2.8	1.4	1.8	2.7	5.1	0.3	1.9	2.3	2.7	1.7
Amortization and Depletion **15**	0.3	0.3	0.0	1.8	0.3	0.1	1.6	0.1	0.2	0.1	0.6	0.1	0.3
Pensions and Other Deferred Comp. **16**	0.7	•	1.5	•	0.5	0.9	0.8	0.7	1.2	1.1	•	0.7	0.7
Employee Benefits **17**	0.7	4.2	1.7	1.0	1.9	1.2	1.6	2.1	1.0	1.2	0.9	1.8	0.7
Advertising **18**	0.2	0.1	0.1	•	0.1	0.3	0.6	0.4	0.1	0.6	1.1	0.1	0.2
Other Expenses **19**	35.2	35.7	75.2	8.7	36.6	85.6	34.9	41.8	31.7	21.1	34.6	44.0	34.8
Officers' Compensation **20**	2.4	8.0	17.4	1.0	8.8	9.5	10.1	9.3	7.8	5.3	4.7	14.5	2.2
Operating Margin **21**	5.2	13.0	•	71.7	7.7	•	4.8	•	8.0	•	18.9	4.9	5.4
Operating Margin Before Officers' Comp. **22**	7.6	21.0	4.5	72.7	16.5	•	14.9	2.5	15.9	•	23.6	19.5	7.6

Selected Average Balance Sheet ($ in Thousands)

Net Receivables 23	118502	0	18	0	126	1288	2043	5061	25205	50126	21055	373798	40022813
Inventories 24	•	•	•	•	•	•	•	•	•	•	•	•	•
Net Property, Plant and Equipment 25	2875	0	5	6	200	275	429	3117	224	1423	8727	6186	955941
Total Assets 26	483844	0	110	589	2025	7688	15097	36437	70817	147508	301144	1528595	163306386
Notes and Loans Payable 27	74411	0	41	0	737	2749	2242	9946	18439	19157	146549	269198	25034550
All Other Liabilities 28	374473	0	10	1	138	2023	3799	12184	20870	82965	37374	842582	126823620
Net Worth 29	34959	0	59	588	1151	2916	9056	14307	31509	45385	117221	416816	11448216

Selected Financial Ratios (Times to 1)

Current Ratio 30	0.8	•	10.5	148.1	•	2.4	1.8	1.2	1.7	1.2	2.4	1.9	0.8
Quick Ratio 31	0.4	•	5.4	29.7	•	1.0	1.5	0.7	1.4	0.8	1.5	1.4	0.4
Net Sales to Working Capital 32	•	•	3.2	0.7	•	2.2	1.6	7.0	1.2	1.6	2.8	0.2	•
Coverage Ratio 33	1.2	1.9	•	•	3.8	•	3.8	•	1.7	0.6	2.6	1.7	1.2
Total Asset Turnover 34	0.1	1.4	•	0.1	•	1.1	0.4	0.6	0.3	0.2	0.4	0.1	0.1
Inventory Turnover 35	•	•	•	•	•	•	•	•	•	•	•	•	•
Receivables Turnover 36	•	•	•	•	•	•	•	•	•	•	•	•	•
Total Liabilities to Net Worth 37	12.8	•	0.9	0.0	•	1.6	0.7	1.5	1.2	2.3	1.6	2.7	13.3
Current Assets to Working Capital 38	•	•	1.1	1.0	•	1.7	2.2	5.4	2.5	5.5	1.7	2.1	•
Current Liabilities to Working Capital 39	•	•	0.1	0.0	•	0.7	1.2	4.4	1.5	4.5	0.7	1.1	•
Working Capital to Net Sales 40	•	•	0.3	1.4	•	0.5	0.6	0.1	0.8	0.6	0.4	6.3	•
Inventory to Working Capital 41	•	•	•	•	0.0	•	0.0	•	•	•	•	•	•
Total Receipts to Cash Flow 42	2.8	2.4	2.1	1.3	•	2.5	1.9	3.8	2.9	2.0	2.0	2.3	2.8
Cost of Goods to Cash Flow 43	0.0	•	0.0	•	•	0.0	•	0.2	•	•	•	0.0	0.0
Cash Flow to Total Debt 44	0.0	•	1.4	84.1	•	0.9	0.3	0.2	0.2	0.3	0.3	0.0	0.0

Selected Financial Factors (in Percentages)

Debt Ratio 45	92.8	•	46.6	0.1	43.2	62.1	40.0	60.7	55.5	69.2	61.1	72.7	93.0
Return on Total Assets 46	2.5	•	•	9.8	5.9	•	2.1	•	4.6	7.0	11.3	0.7	2.5
Return on Equity Before Income Taxes 47	4.6	•	•	9.9	7.7	•	2.5	•	4.2	•	18.1	1.1	4.9
Return on Equity After Income Taxes 48	3.1	•	•	9.9	7.7	•	1.6	•	3.9	•	17.6	0.8	3.3
Profit Margin (Before Income Tax) 49	6.3	13.0	71.7	71.7	7.6	•	4.0	•	6.5	•	18.9	5.0	6.6
Profit Margin (After Income Tax) 50	4.1	5.6	71.7	71.7	7.6	•	2.5	•	6.2	•	18.4	3.7	4.4

Table II

Corporations with Net Income

INVESTMENT BANKING AND SECURITIES DEALING

MONEY AMOUNTS AND SIZE OF ASSETS IN THOUSANDS OF DOLLARS

Item Description for Accounting Period 7/02 Through 6/03	Total	Zero Assets	Under 500	500 to 1,000	1,000 to 5,000	5,000 to 10,000	10,000 to 25,000	25,000 to 50,000	50,000 to 100,000	100,000 to 250,000	250,000 to 500,000	500,000 to 2,500,000	2,500,000 and over
Number of Enterprises 1	1349	0	652	0	111	11	22	9	0	0	0	0	0
Revenues ($ in Thousands)													
Net Sales 2	103792562	0	162479	0	249752	94074	193738	311343	0	0	0	0	0
Interest 3	50673203	0	1596	0	3673	1548	1110	1113	0	0	0	0	0
Rents 4	859507	0	0	0	44	11330	90	35	0	0	0	0	0
Royalties 5	240	0	0	0	0	0	0	0	0	0	0	0	0
Other Portfolio Income 6	4202221	0	1347	0	730	3823	6732	3100	0	0	0	0	0
Other Receipts 7	48057391	0	159536	0	245305	77373	185806	307095	0	0	0	0	0
Total Receipts 8	103792562	0	162479	0	249752	94074	193738	311343	0	0	0	0	0
Average Total Receipts 9	76940	•	249	•	2250	8552	8806	34594	•	•	•	•	•
Operating Costs/Operating Income (%)													
Cost of Operations 10	0.1	•	•	•	•	•	•	9.9	•	•	•	•	•
Salaries and Wages 11	12.7	•	6.1	•	39.7	16.2	29.7	25.8	•	•	•	•	•
Taxes Paid 12	0.8	•	0.6	•	2.8	2.5	3.0	1.9	•	•	•	•	•
Interest Paid 13	40.0	•	0.5	•	2.0	10.1	1.1	0.8	•	•	•	•	•
Depreciation 14	1.7	•	0.0	•	1.1	4.5	1.6	1.5	•	•	•	•	•
Amortization and Depletion 15	0.3	•	0.0	•	0.0	0.0	1.9	0.0	•	•	•	•	•
Pensions and Other Deferred Comp. 16	0.7	•	0.0	•	0.5	3.2	0.8	0.9	•	•	•	•	•
Employee Benefits 17	0.7	•	2.9	•	2.0	0.0	1.1	1.6	•	•	•	•	•
Advertising 18	0.2	•	•	•	0.1	0.1	0.4	0.2	•	•	•	•	•
Other Expenses 19	34.7	•	81.1	•	29.0	24.7	14.0	39.9	•	•	•	•	•
Officers' Compensation 20	2.4	•	0.8	•	8.9	31.2	9.4	10.3	•	•	•	•	•
Operating Margin 21	5.8	•	7.9	•	13.7	7.6	37.1	7.2	•	•	•	•	•
Operating Margin Before Officers' Comp. 22	8.2	•	8.7	•	22.7	38.8	46.5	17.6	•	•	•	•	•

Selected Average Balance Sheet ($ in Thousands)

Net Receivables 23	357298		263	675	1614	4274
Inventories 24						
Net Property, Plant and Equipment 25	8584	0	178	427	335	2003
Total Assets 26	1454560	117	2258	6820	14936	36360
Notes and Loans Payable 27	223769	16	743	499	1622	5786
All Other Liabilities 28	1127554	25	246	3214	4603	8930
Net Worth 29	103238	76	1270	3108	8712	21645

Selected Financial Ratios (Times to 1)

Current Ratio 30	0.8	0.3	5.9	1.0	1.6	2.8
Quick Ratio 31	0.4	0.2	4.7	0.7	1.3	1.6
Net Sales to Working Capital 32			1.6	10452.7	2.7	2.9
Coverage Ratio 33	1.2	16.7	7.8	1.8	33.9	9.3
Total Asset Turnover 34	0.1	2.1	1.0	1.3	0.6	1.0
Inventory Turnover 35						
Receivables Turnover 36						
Total Liabilities to Net Worth 37	13.1	0.5	0.8	1.2	0.7	0.7
Current Assets to Working Capital 38			1.2	4493.8	2.6	1.6
Current Liabilities to Working Capital 39			0.2	4492.8	1.6	0.6
Working Capital to Net Sales 40			0.6	0.0	0.4	0.3
Inventory to Working Capital 41					0.1	
Total Receipts to Cash Flow 42	2.7	1.3	2.6	3.5	2.2	2.3
Cost of Goods to Cash Flow 43	0.0					0.2
Cash Flow to Total Debt 44	0.0	4.8	0.9	0.7	0.7	1.0

Selected Financial Factors (in Percentages)

Debt Ratio 45	92.9	35.0	43.8	54.4	41.7	40.5
Return on Total Assets 46	2.5	17.8	15.7	22.2	22.0	6.8
Return on Equity Before Income Taxes 47	5.1	25.7	24.3	20.9	36.6	10.1
Return on Equity After Income Taxes 48	3.5	22.9	24.3	14.7	34.4	9.8
Profit Margin (Before Income Tax) 49	6.9	7.9	13.7	7.6	36.2	6.3
Profit Margin (After Income Tax) 50	4.7	7.0	13.7	5.3	34.1	6.2

Table I

Corporations with and without Net Income

SECURITIES BROKERAGE

MONEY AMOUNTS AND SIZE OF ASSETS IN THOUSANDS OF DOLLARS

Item Description for Accounting Period 7/02 Through 6/03	Total	Zero Assets	Under 500	500 to 1,000	1,000 to 5,000	5,000 to 10,000	10,000 to 25,000	25,000 to 50,000	50,000 to 100,000	100,000 to 250,000	250,000 to 500,000	500,000 to 2,500,000	2,500,000 and over
Number of Enterprises **1**	9898	1718	6813	529	512	120	80	28	25	19	12	14	28
Revenues ($ in Thousands)													
Net Sales **2**	103068268	601655	1966358	572789	1856717	1206679	1939195	553470	1427019	1022377	2513702	3506697	85901611
Interest **3**	35896852	66773	2698	3053	18172	8267	27890	6756	15956	38297	86267	272287	35350435
Rents **4**	428748	0	0	0	212	198	342	4906	221	335	46	8661	413827
Royalties **5**	139344	0	53	0	0	0	2097	0	518	0	0	0	136677
Other Portfolio Income **6**	1579289	162277	1664	1061	2275	15123	28177	22824	11557	54936	19909	57726	1201758
Other Receipts **7**	65024035	372605	1961943	568675	1836058	1183091	1880689	518984	1398767	928809	2407480	3168023	48798914
Total Receipts **8**	103068268	601655	1966358	572789	1856717	1206679	1939195	553470	1427019	1022377	2513702	3506697	85901611
Average Total Receipts **9**	10413	350	289	1083	3626	10056	24240	19767	57081	53809	209475	250478	3067915
Operating Costs/Operating Income (%)													
Cost of Operations **10**	2.3	0.2	1.5	•	10.9	13.2	10.3	4.1	0.3	•	•	•	2.1
Salaries and Wages **11**	23.9	12.3	24.7	28.2	27.6	24.1	27.8	39.4	17.5	46.2	34.4	30.6	22.9
Taxes Paid **12**	1.8	4.2	3.8	4.0	2.9	2.8	1.7	3.0	1.9	2.8	2.2	2.6	1.6
Interest Paid **13**	28.3	4.5	0.3	0.1	0.6	0.4	1.3	1.5	1.2	3.0	1.6	8.7	33.5
Depreciation **14**	1.9	3.6	0.8	1.4	1.2	1.0	1.0	2.0	1.1	1.8	1.9	1.4	1.9
Amortization and Depletion **15**	0.9	0.7	0.0	0.1	0.2	0.0	0.2	0.1	0.3	0.8	0.2	7.3	0.7
Pensions and Other Deferred Comp. **16**	0.8	0.1	1.9	0.1	0.8	0.4	0.4	0.9	0.7	1.4	0.4	0.3	0.9
Employee Benefits **17**	1.4	0.5	1.0	0.8	0.9	1.1	0.7	1.5	0.6	2.0	1.8	1.4	1.4
Advertising **18**	0.8	5.6	1.6	0.3	0.3	0.3	0.4	1.0	1.2	0.4	0.4	2.1	0.7
Other Expenses **19**	31.6	39.4	44.1	43.4	43.4	49.6	49.6	28.9	61.2	35.0	44.7	33.6	29.3
Officers' Compensation **20**	5.6	4.2	18.2	34.5	8.5	5.4	6.5	12.1	8.0	12.4	3.4	2.4	5.1
Operating Margin **21**	0.7	24.4	2.0	•	2.7	1.6	0.3	5.4	6.0	•	9.0	9.4	•
Operating Margin Before Officers' Comp. **22**	6.3	28.7	20.2	21.5	11.2	7.0	6.8	17.6	14.0	6.6	12.4	11.8	5.0

Selected Average Balance Sheet ($ in Thousands)

Net Receivables 23	21562	0	9	46	340	751	2044	7375	21240	28402	74438	188660	7431897
Inventories 24	•	•	•	•	•	•	•	•	•	•	•	•	•
Net Property, Plant and Equipment 25	663	0	3	28	113	312	677	3357	1352	4260	11819	14966	207862
Total Assets 26	139345	0	70	698	2014	6796	14791	35777	72559	144333	342345	1363373	48093025
Notes and Loans Payable 27	22817	0	30	15	253	333	1805	3119	4560	23766	47612	100481	7953322
All Other Liabilities 28	108669	0	12	214	723	1137	5229	27483	38486	75584	164312	871178	37755231
Net Worth 29	7859	0	28	469	1039	5326	7757	5174	29512	44983	130421	391713	2384472

Selected Financial Ratios (Times to 1)

Current Ratio 30	1.0	•	2.1	2.1	2.5	2.9	1.7	1.0	1.3	1.2	1.3	0.9	1.0
Quick Ratio 31	0.3	•	1.2	2.0	2.2	1.8	1.3	0.7	1.1	0.8	0.9	0.7	0.3
Net Sales to Working Capital 32	•	•	11.0	4.4	4.8	4.6	6.1	533.7	4.8	4.1	4.6	•	•
Coverage Ratio 33	1.0	6.4	8.1	•	5.4	4.9	1.1	4.2	5.9	•	6.3	2.1	1.0
Total Asset Turnover 34	0.1	•	4.1	1.6	1.8	1.5	1.6	0.6	0.8	0.4	0.6	0.2	0.1
Inventory Turnover 35	•	•	•	•	•	•	•	•	•	•	•	•	•
Receivables Turnover 36	•	•	•	•	•	•	•	•	•	•	•	•	•
Total Liabilities to Net Worth 37	16.7	•	1.5	0.5	0.9	0.3	0.9	5.9	1.5	2.2	1.6	2.5	19.2
Current Assets to Working Capital 38	•	•	1.9	1.9	1.6	1.5	2.4	588.1	4.2	6.3	4.7	•	•
Current Liabilities to Working Capital 39	•	•	0.9	0.9	0.6	0.5	1.4	587.1	3.2	5.3	3.7	•	•
Working Capital to Net Sales 40	•	•	0.1	0.2	0.2	0.2	0.2	0.0	0.2	0.2	0.2	•	•
Inventory to Working Capital 41	•	•	•	•	•	•	0.0	0.1	•	0.2	•	•	•
Total Receipts to Cash Flow 42	3.6	3.1	2.7	4.3	2.4	2.1	2.2	3.3	1.6	5.0	2.0	2.6	4.0
Cost of Goods to Cash Flow 43	0.1	0.0	0.0	•	0.3	•	0.2	0.1	0.0	•	•	0.1	0.1
Cash Flow to Total Debt 44	0.0	•	2.6	1.1	1.5	3.3	1.6	0.2	0.9	0.1	0.5	0.1	0.0

Selected Financial Factors (in Percentages)

Debt Ratio 45	94.4	•	59.6	32.9	48.4	21.6	47.6	85.5	59.3	68.8	61.9	71.3	95.0
Return on Total Assets 46	2.2	•	9.4	•	5.9	2.7	2.3	3.5	5.5	•	6.3	3.3	2.1
Return on Equity Before Income Taxes 47	0.6	•	20.4	•	9.2	2.7	0.5	18.6	11.2	•	14.0	6.0	•
Return on Equity After Income Taxes 48	•	•	20.1	•	7.3	1.7	•	17.5	8.9	•	7.9	4.1	•
Profit Margin (Before Income Tax) 49	0.5	24.4	2.0	•	2.6	1.4	0.2	4.9	5.8	•	8.7	9.4	•
Profit Margin (After Income Tax) 50	•	13.4	2.0	•	2.1	0.9	•	4.6	4.6	•	4.9	6.5	•

Table II
Corporations with Net Income

SECURITIES BROKERAGE

MONEY AMOUNTS AND SIZE OF ASSETS IN THOUSANDS OF DOLLARS

Item Description for Accounting Period 7/02 Through 6/03	Total	Zero Assets	Under 500	500 to 1,000	1,000 to 5,000	5,000 to 10,000	10,000 to 25,000	25,000 to 50,000	50,000 to 100,000	100,000 to 250,000	250,000 to 500,000	500,000 to 2,500,000	2,500,000 and over
Number of Enterprises **1**	6116	975	4405	179	353	76	52	14	13	12	9	0	0
Revenues ($ in Thousands)													
Net Sales **2**	66133476	587787	1719222	160175	1185374	1100754	1503444	330117	1172101	834401	2277132	0	0
Interest **3**	18782715	66376	581	1866	6114	5542	21573	4678	7444	18894	72799	0	0
Rents **4**	184895	0	0	0	194	0	231	1942	0	0	46	0	0
Royalties **5**	49277	0	0	0	0	0	2097	0	518	0	0	0	0
Other Portfolio Income **6**	1362024	161750	187	934	704	4131	14376	19857	5267	34347	19867	0	0
Other Receipts **7**	45754565	359661	1718454	157375	1178362	1091081	1465167	303640	1158872	781160	2184420	0	0
Total Receipts **8**	66133476	587787	1719222	160175	1185374	1100754	1503444	330117	1172101	834401	2277132	0	0
Average Total Receipts **9**	10813	603	390	895	3358	14484	28912	23580	90162	69533	253015	·	·
Operating Costs/Operating Income (%)													
Cost of Operations **10**	3.2	0.3	1.4	·	0.7	13.9	12.2	1.0	0.4	·	·	·	·
Salaries and Wages **11**	26.7	10.5	24.5	31.1	27.7	21.8	27.0	35.1	12.0	43.2	32.5	·	·
Taxes Paid **12**	1.9	4.2	2.5	4.0	2.9	2.7	1.5	3.1	1.8	2.7	1.8	·	·
Interest Paid **13**	20.8	3.8	0.2	·	0.2	0.3	1.2	0.9	0.4	1.2	1.7	·	·
Depreciation **14**	1.9	2.0	0.8	3.4	0.9	0.9	0.6	1.5	0.6	1.3	1.8	·	·
Amortization and Depletion **15**	0.9	0.5	0.0	0.1	0.0	0.0	0.0	0.0	0.1	0.2	0.2	·	·
Pensions and Other Deferred Comp. **16**	0.7	0.1	2.1	0.3	1.2	0.4	0.3	0.5	0.5	0.4	0.3	·	·
Employee Benefits **17**	1.4	0.4	0.7	1.7	1.0	0.9	0.5	1.5	0.3	2.3	1.8	·	·
Advertising **18**	1.1	5.8	1.0	0.5	0.2	0.2	0.4	0.6	1.1	0.5	0.3	·	·
Other Expenses **19**	30.2	33.5	38.0	37.8	43.8	46.3	44.8	24.8	62.0	27.1	43.6	·	·
Officers' Compensation **20**	4.6	4.2	18.0	18.3	8.8	5.4	6.5	9.8	7.7	4.9	3.4	·	·
Operating Margin **21**	6.5	34.7	10.7	2.9	12.6	7.2	4.8	21.2	13.1	16.3	12.5	·	·
Operating Margin Before Officers' Comp. **22**	11.1	38.9	28.7	21.2	21.4	12.5	11.3	30.9	20.8	21.2	15.9	·	·

Selected Average Balance Sheet ($ in Thousands)

Item											
Net Receivables 23	29372	0	11	2	244	957	1971	9252	23726	39081	88010
Inventories 24	•	•	•	•	•	•	•	•	•	•	•
Net Property, Plant and Equipment 25	818	0	2	37	89	333	645	2978	1470	4897	13946
Total Assets 26	142316	0	73	796	1754	6793	14700	36572	75776	146501	360344
Notes and Loans Payable 27	17893	0	10	0	46	254	1526	764	4053	20624	62508
All Other Liabilities 28	115309	0	10	96	711	1459	4735	28385	35072	82745	175325
Net Worth 29	9114	0	53	700	997	5079	8440	7423	36652	43132	122511

Selected Financial Ratios (Times to 1)

Item											
Current Ratio 30	1.0	•	3.3	6.3	3.8	3.1	1.8	1.8	1.4	1.1	1.2
Quick Ratio 31	0.4	•	1.7	6.0	3.4	2.1	1.3	1.2	1.3	0.8	0.8
Net Sales to Working Capital 32	•	•	10.7	1.7	3.7	5.4	7.4	1.9	6.3	6.1	5.9
Coverage Ratio 33	1.3	10.1	51.7	•	62.5	22.5	4.7	23.6	34.4	13.5	8.1
Total Asset Turnover 34	0.1	•	5.4	1.1	1.9	2.1	2.0	0.6	1.2	0.5	0.7
Inventory Turnover 35	•	•	•	•	•	•	•	•	•	•	•
Receivables Turnover 36	•	•	•	•	•	•	•	•	•	•	•
Total Liabilities to Net Worth 37	14.6	•	0.4	0.1	0.8	0.3	0.7	3.9	1.1	2.4	1.9
Current Assets to Working Capital 38	•	•	1.4	1.2	1.4	1.5	2.3	2.3	3.5	7.7	5.3
Current Liabilities to Working Capital 39	•	•	0.4	0.2	0.4	0.5	1.3	1.3	2.5	6.7	4.3
Working Capital to Net Sales 40	•	•	0.1	0.6	0.3	0.2	0.1	0.5	0.2	0.2	0.2
Inventory to Working Capital 41	•	•	•	•	•	•	•	0.0	•	0.3	•
Total Receipts to Cash Flow 42	3.2	2.7	2.4	3.3	2.0	2.0	2.1	2.4	1.4	2.7	1.9
Cost of Goods to Cash Flow 43	0.1	0.0	0.0	•	0.0	0.3	0.3	0.0	0.0	0.0	•
Cash Flow to Total Debt 44	0.0	•	8.2	2.8	2.3	4.3	2.2	0.3	1.7	0.2	0.6

Selected Financial Factors (in Percentages)

Item											
Debt Ratio 45	93.6	•	27.6	12.1	43.2	25.2	42.6	79.7	51.6	70.6	66.0
Return on Total Assets 46	2.0	•	58.6	3.2	24.3	15.9	11.6	14.1	15.8	8.0	9.7
Return on Equity Before Income Taxes 47	7.2	•	79.3	3.7	42.1	20.3	15.9	66.4	31.7	25.0	25.1
Return on Equity After Income Taxes 48	5.1	•	79.0	3.2	39.1	18.7	13.2	64.8	28.2	18.0	16.3
Profit Margin (Before Income Tax) 49	6.1	34.7	10.7	2.9	12.5	7.1	4.7	20.9	12.9	15.5	12.1
Profit Margin (After Income Tax) 50	4.3	23.5	10.7	2.5	11.6	6.6	3.9	20.4	11.4	11.1	7.9

Table I

Corporations with and without Net Income

COMMODITY CONTRACTS DEALING AND BROKERAGE

MONEY AMOUNTS AND SIZE OF ASSETS IN THOUSANDS OF DOLLARS

Item Description for Accounting Period 7/02 Through 6/03	Total	Zero Assets	Under 500	500 to 1,000	1,000 to 5,000	5,000 to 10,000	10,000 to 25,000	25,000 to 50,000	50,000 to 100,000	100,000 to 250,000	250,000 to 500,000	500,000 to 2,500,000	2,500,000 and over
Number of Enterprises 1	1925	6	1600	58	108	77	30	15	12	10	6	0	3
Revenues ($ in Thousands)													
Net Sales 2	4790246	37712	649097	22259	627112	767288	807575	114182	245831	189905	322365	0	1006921
Interest 3	261196	415	750	45	31	1185	3526	1778	5441	7469	8991	0	231566
Rents 4	8175	0	9	0	0	0	5851	289	10	0	2016	0	0
Royalties 5	15664	0	0	0	0	0	15577	0	0	0	0	0	87
Other Portfolio Income 6	29244	4	724	121	2600	1848	122	2700	3281	1138	258	0	16444
Other Receipts 7	4475967	37293	647614	22093	624481	764255	782499	109415	237099	181298	311100	0	758824
Total Receipts 8	4790246	37712	649097	22259	627112	767288	807575	114182	245831	189905	322365	0	1006921
Average Total Receipts 9	2488	6285	406	384	5807	9965	26919	7612	20486	18990	53728	*	335640
Operating Costs/Operating Income (%)													
Cost of Operations 10	26.5	3.1	78.9	*	1.4	*	87.0	8.8	5.3	10.4	0.0	•	•
Salaries and Wages 11	27.0	1.8	1.6	29.6	63.6	43.4	5.2	56.8	18.5	18.5	15.7	•	30.4
Taxes Paid 12	1.3	3.5	1.0	4.0	0.5	1.4	0.5	4.7	1.3	3.2	1.4	•	1.7
Interest Paid 13	6.9	1.6	0.0	6.4	0.0	1.5	0.4	5.7	2.2	4.1	32.0	•	19.1
Depreciation 14	0.9	0.1	0.4	3.7	0.2	0.5	0.7	5.1	1.7	0.6	0.5	•	1.6
Amortization and Depletion 15	0.6	0.0	•	6.0	0.0	1.3	0.0	0.3	0.2	0.0	0.2	•	1.3
Pensions and Other Deferred Comp. 16	0.6	•	0.3	3.2	1.8	0.1	0.2	0.6	0.4	0.5	0.3	•	1.1
Employee Benefits 17	1.5	0.2	0.1	4.7	5.6	1.2	0.4	2.1	0.6	1.0	1.2	•	1.3
Advertising 18	0.2	0.0	0.0	0.4	0.1	0.4	0.0	0.8	0.9	0.5	0.1	•	0.2
Other Expenses 19	29.1	11.5	9.3	25.3	17.6	46.0	9.2	36.7	47.8	49.8	46.5	•	38.2
Officers' Compensation 20	3.9	2.4	8.2	16.9	5.6	5.6	1.2	5.7	2.2	4.4	2.9	•	1.0
Operating Margin 21	1.4	75.6	0.1	•	3.5	•	•	•	18.8	7.0	•	•	4.2
Operating Margin Before Officers' Comp. 22	5.3	78.0	8.3	16.8	9.1	4.1	•	•	21.0	11.4	2.1	•	5.2

Selected Average Balance Sheet ($ in Thousands)

Net Receivables 23	1320	0	22	351	59	1142	3649	6155	20111	15062	216534	165919
Inventories 24	·	·	·	·	·	·	·	·	·	·	·	·
Net Property, Plant and Equipment 25	120	0	10	60	29	105	671	2233	1307	357	14166	13775
Total Assets 26	9287	0	96	591	3132	6242	15919	35267	71513	127470	466271	3644579
Notes and Loans Payable 27	2344	0	3	314	71	1962	3600	8675	23846	13526	305721	611928
All Other Liabilities 28	6556	0	16	243	1796	2469	7685	14366	37595	77462	279117	2950057
Net Worth 29	387	0	77	33	1264	1811	4633	12226	10072	36482	-118566	82595

Selected Financial Ratios (Times to 1)

Current Ratio 30	0.8	·	3.0	0.8	1.6	1.1	1.2	1.4	0.8	1.1	0.6	0.8
Quick Ratio 31	0.3	·	2.2	0.8	0.7	0.7	0.8	0.9	0.6	0.6	0.4	0.2
Net Sales to Working Capital 32	·	·	11.5	·	5.0	25.2	16.6	1.4	4.5	·	·	·
Coverage Ratio 33	1.2	47.3	2.1	1.0	133.7	·	·	·	9.6	2.7	1.0	1.2
Total Asset Turnover 34	0.3	·	4.2	0.6	1.9	1.6	1.7	0.2	0.3	0.1	·	0.1
Inventory Turnover 35	·	·	·	·	·	·	·	·	·	·	·	·
Receivables Turnover 36	·	·	·	·	·	·	·	·	·	·	·	·
Total Liabilities to Net Worth 37	23.0	·	0.3	17.0	1.5	2.4	2.4	1.9	6.1	2.5	·	43.1
Current Assets to Working Capital 38	·	·	1.5	·	2.6	8.8	7.0	3.6	20.3	·	·	·
Current Liabilities to Working Capital 39	·	·	0.5	·	1.6	7.8	6.0	2.6	19.3	·	·	·
Working Capital to Net Sales 40	·	·	0.1	·	0.2	0.0	0.1	0.7	0.2	·	·	·
Inventory to Working Capital 41	·	·	·	·	·	0.5	·	·	·	·	·	·
Total Receipts to Cash Flow 42	3.6	1.2	12.5	4.7	5.3	2.4	28.7	22.8	1.7	2.0	2.3	2.6
Cost of Goods to Cash Flow 43	1.0	0.0	9.9	0.1	0.1	24.9	2.0	2.0	0.1	0.2	0.0	0.0
Cash Flow to Total Debt 44	0.1	·	1.6	0.1	0.6	0.9	0.1	0.0	0.2	0.1	0.0	0.0

Selected Financial Factors (in Percentages)

Debt Ratio 45	95.8	·	20.4	94.4	59.6	71.0	70.9	65.3	85.9	71.4	125.4	97.7
Return on Total Assets 46	2.2	·	0.4	4.1	6.5	0.2	·	·	6.0	1.6	3.6	2.1
Return on Equity Before Income Taxes 47	9.1	·	0.3	·	16.0	·	·	·	38.3	3.6	0.4	17.0
Return on Equity After Income Taxes 48	1.5	·	·	·	16.0	·	·	·	27.9	1.4	0.9	9.5
Profit Margin (Before Income Tax) 49	1.4	75.6	0.1	·	3.5	·	·	·	18.8	7.0	·	4.2
Profit Margin (After Income Tax) 50	0.2	54.1	·	·	3.5	·	·	·	13.7	2.6	·	2.3

Table II

Corporations with Net Income

COMMODITY CONTRACTS DEALING AND BROKERAGE

MONEY AMOUNTS AND SIZE OF ASSETS IN THOUSANDS OF DOLLARS

Item Description for Accounting Period 7/02 Through 6/03	Total	Zero Assets	Under 500	500 to 1,000	1,000 to 5,000	5,000 to 10,000	10,000 to 25,000	25,000 to 50,000	50,000 to 100,000	100,000 to 250,000	250,000 to 500,000	500,000 to 2,500,000	2,500,000 and over
Number of Enterprises **1**	1351	0	1171	0	33	40	14	9	0	0	0	4	0
Revenues ($ in Thousands)													
Net Sales **2**	3317269	0	641679	0	97881	764675	264736	127687	0	0	0	815456	0
Interest **3**	211064	0	747	0	8	57	892	1136	0	0	0	188153	0
Rents **4**	6140	0	0	0	0	0	5851	289	0	0	0	0	0
Royalties **5**	15664	0	0	0	0	0	15577	0	0	0	0	87	0
Other Portfolio Income **6**	24713	0	724	0	2557	1460	40	2680	0	0	0	16411	0
Other Receipts **7**	3059688	0	640208	0	95316	763158	242376	123582	0	0	0	610805	0
Total Receipts **8**	3317269	0	641679	0	97881	764675	264736	127687	0	0	0	815456	0
Average Total Receipts **9**	2455	•	548	•	2966	19117	18910	14187	•	•	•	203864	•
Operating Costs/Operating Income (%)													
Cost of Operations **10**	21.5	•	79.2	•	8.7	•	57.0	7.9	•	•	•	•	•
Salaries and Wages **11**	21.4	•	1.1	•	8.2	42.9	12.3	29.4	•	•	•	23.3	•
Taxes Paid **12**	1.5	•	0.8	•	2.3	1.3	1.0	3.6	•	•	•	1.4	•
Interest Paid **13**	5.9	•	0.0	•	0.1	0.5	0.4	3.3	•	•	•	19.9	•
Depreciation **14**	1.1	•	0.4	•	0.6	0.4	2.0	3.8	•	•	•	1.5	•
Amortization and Depletion **15**	0.3	•	•	•	0.0	0.8	0.0	0.2	•	•	•	0.3	•
Pensions and Other Deferred Comp. **16**	0.7	•	0.0	•	11.8	0.1	0.5	0.5	•	•	•	0.7	•
Employee Benefits **17**	0.8	•	0.1	•	1.0	1.2	1.0	1.8	•	•	•	0.7	•
Advertising **18**	0.3	•	0.0	•	0.8	0.4	0.1	0.8	•	•	•	0.0	•
Other Expenses **19**	32.5	•	5.2	•	9.8	43.2	20.2	24.6	•	•	•	43.4	•
Officers' Compensation **20**	4.2	•	7.0	•	12.4	5.5	3.0	3.7	•	•	•	1.7	•
Operating Margin **21**	9.9	•	6.0	•	44.5	3.6	2.4	20.5	•	•	•	7.0	•
Operating Margin Before Officers' Comp. **22**	14.2	•	13.0	•	56.8	9.1	5.5	24.1	•	•	•	8.7	•

Selected Average Balance Sheet ($ in Thousands)

Net Receivables 23	1555	30	161	902	5263	8651	331285
Inventories 24	·	·	·	·	·	·	·
Net Property, Plant and Equipment 25	144	14	69	179	593	3418	7683
Total Assets 26	9184	120	2687	6637	17343	35398	2304583
Notes and Loans Payable 27	1947	5	216	1627	4751	5801	514786
All Other Liabilities 28	6530	18	335	3889	7371	16676	1740893
Net Worth 29	707	98	2136	1121	5222	12921	48904

Selected Financial Ratios (Times to 1)

Current Ratio 30	1.0	3.7	4.4	0.8	1.3	1.1	1.0
Quick Ratio 31	0.4	2.7	4.3	0.5	0.9	0.7	0.3
Net Sales to Working Capital 32	·	10.6	1.6	·	5.5	8.6	10.1
Coverage Ratio 33	2.7	124.7	484.1	9.1	6.8	7.2	1.4
Total Asset Turnover 34	0.3	4.6	1.1	2.9	1.1	0.4	0.1
Inventory Turnover 35	·	·	·	·	·	·	·
Receivables Turnover 36	·	·	·	·	·	·	·
Total Liabilities to Net Worth 37	12.0	0.2	0.3	4.9	2.3	1.7	46.1
Current Assets to Working Capital 38	·	1.4	1.3	·	4.0	10.8	84.8
Current Liabilities to Working Capital 39	·	0.4	0.3	·	3.0	9.8	83.8
Working Capital to Net Sales 40	0.1	0.1	0.6	·	0.2	0.1	0.1
Inventory to Working Capital 41	·	·	·	·	0.5	·	·
Total Receipts to Cash Flow 42	2.5	9.8	2.0	2.3	4.9	2.4	2.1
Cost of Goods to Cash Flow 43	0.5	7.8	0.2	·	2.8	0.2	0.2
Cash Flow to Total Debt 44	0.1	2.5	2.8	1.5	0.3	0.3	0.0

Selected Financial Factors (in Percentages)

Debt Ratio 45	92.3	18.5	20.5	83.1	69.9	63.5	97.9
Return on Total Assets 46	4.2	27.7	49.1	11.9	3.1	9.4	2.4
Return on Equity Before Income Taxes 47	34.6	33.7	61.7	62.7	8.8	22.3	29.2
Return on Equity After Income Taxes 48	28.6	33.0	61.7	61.9	7.3	19.4	19.2
Profit Margin (Before Income Tax) 49	9.9	6.0	44.4	3.7	2.4	20.3	7.0
Profit Margin (After Income Tax) 50	8.2	5.9	44.4	3.6	2.0	17.7	4.6

SECURITIES & COMMODITY EXCHANGES, OTHER FINANCIAL INVESTMENT

Table I

Corporations with and without Net Income

MONEY AMOUNTS AND SIZE OF ASSETS IN THOUSANDS OF DOLLARS

Item Description for Accounting Period 7/02 Through 6/03	Total	Zero Assets	Under 500	500 to 1,000	1,000 to 5,000	5,000 to 10,000	10,000 to 25,000	25,000 to 50,000	50,000 to 100,000	100,000 to 250,000	250,000 to 500,000	500,000 to 2,500,000	2,500,000 and over
Number of Enterprises **1**	31105	4011	22565	1267	2209	363	366	129	70	57	19	29	20
Revenues ($ in Thousands)													
Net Sales **2**	62025191	979264	4848044	799431	3973617	2097009	3087372	1782828	1271378	2934973	1479567	8839100	29932608
Interest **3**	4548339	15617	13188	5945	29993	12018	34449	41937	41560	158748	115323	282804	3796757
Rents **4**	100870	2101	1622	702	6881	540	3473	459	2309	2955	48022	7511	24295
Royalties **5**	107515	10327	15815	0	0	6	3075	4300	128	41968	188	31691	17
Other Portfolio Income **6**	1397890	82828	17277	11783	41706	12865	52146	55960	33798	36363	8625	35269	1009271
Other Receipts **7**	55870577	868391	4800142	781001	3895037	2071580	2994229	1680172	1193583	2694939	1307409	8481825	25102268
Total Receipts **8**	62025191	979264	4848044	799431	3973617	2097009	3087372	1782828	1271378	2934973	1479567	8839100	29932608
Average Total Receipts **9**	1994	244	215	631	1799	5777	8435	13820	18163	51491	77872	304797	1496630
Operating Costs/Operating Income (%)													
Cost of Operations **10**	1.3	2.9	2.0	•	3.9	3.7	5.9	0.5	8.4	3.9	0.3	•	0.0
Salaries and Wages **11**	23.0	24.6	22.8	19.4	34.4	29.8	28.0	26.2	29.3	26.3	13.5	29.7	18.2
Taxes Paid **12**	2.4	2.5	3.5	2.3	2.5	2.6	2.6	3.2	2.6	3.2	4.2	2.6	1.9
Interest Paid **13**	4.3	1.8	0.7	1.4	1.5	1.7	2.0	4.6	5.8	6.1	8.9	3.5	5.7
Depreciation **14**	2.9	7.6	1.2	3.2	2.4	4.0	2.6	3.3	3.4	3.5	7.1	4.3	2.3
Amortization and Depletion **15**	1.1	1.9	0.2	0.2	0.8	0.4	0.8	0.7	1.7	1.7	4.4	2.0	0.9
Pensions and Other Deferred Comp. **16**	1.2	1.9	3.2	2.9	1.5	0.9	1.0	1.1	2.1	1.0	1.4	2.1	0.6
Employee Benefits **17**	2.4	1.2	1.6	0.4	1.5	1.2	1.4	1.4	1.5	1.6	1.5	3.5	2.9
Advertising **18**	2.6	1.1	0.8	0.4	0.5	0.4	0.6	0.6	0.3	1.6	1.2	2.7	4.0
Other Expenses **19**	36.9	71.8	31.3	33.5	30.3	26.1	32.3	34.0	40.5	30.4	26.7	34.5	40.7
Officers' Compensation **20**	9.2	1.4	24.0	16.4	14.5	20.8	14.3	22.4	5.3	15.4	21.4	6.5	3.8
Operating Margin **21**	12.6	•	8.6	19.9	6.1	8.6	8.5	2.1	•	5.4	9.5	8.7	18.8
Operating Margin Before Officers' Comp. **22**	21.8	•	32.6	36.3	20.6	29.4	22.8	24.5	4.5	20.7	31.0	15.1	22.7

Selected Average Balance Sheet ($ in Thousands)

Net Receivables 23	1054	·	6	42	340	461	1845	4470	7465	18530	66611	82162	1260224
Inventories 24	·	·	·	·	·	·	·	·	·	·	·	·	·
Net Property, Plant and Equipment 25	269	0	10	83	227	822	1262	2387	3253	8516	33788	71228	152801
Total Assets 26	8534	0	79	718	2178	6626	15062	34734	69953	161912	384591	1126833	9571293
Notes and Loans Payable 27	1932	0	46	308	862	1695	4782	12436	17010	48563	138075	127172	2127265
All Other Liabilities 28	3063	0	16	124	456	1568	3131	6134	14695	39370	117564	425307	3669273
Net Worth 29	3538	0	17	236	860	3363	7148	16165	38248	73979	128952	574353	3774756

Selected Financial Ratios (Times to 1)

Current Ratio 30	1.1	·	1.1	2.9	2.0	1.5	1.5	1.7	1.3	1.3	0.8	1.5	1.0
Quick Ratio 31	0.8	·	0.9	1.8	1.6	1.0	1.1	1.3	1.0	0.9	0.7	0.7	0.8
Net Sales to Working Capital 32	6.6	·	128.3	3.0	3.5	7.4	4.0	2.4	3.2	3.9	·	2.4	16.7
Coverage Ratio 33	3.9	·	12.9	15.4	5.2	6.2	5.2	1.4	0.8	1.9	2.0	3.6	4.3
Total Asset Turnover 34	0.2	·	2.7	0.9	0.8	0.9	0.6	0.4	0.3	0.3	0.2	0.3	0.2
Inventory Turnover 35	·	·	·	·	·	·	·	·	·	·	·	·	·
Receivables Turnover 36	·	·	·	·	·	·	·	·	·	·	·	·	·
Total Liabilities to Net Worth 37	1.4	·	3.7	1.5	1.5	1.0	1.1	1.1	0.8	1.2	2.0	1.0	1.5
Current Assets to Working Capital 38	11.1	·	18.2	1.5	2.0	3.2	2.8	2.4	3.9	4.0	·	3.2	42.6
Current Liabilities to Working Capital 39	10.1	·	17.2	0.5	1.0	2.2	1.8	1.4	2.9	3.0	·	2.2	41.6
Working Capital to Net Sales 40	0.2	·	0.0	0.3	0.3	0.1	0.3	0.4	0.3	0.3	·	0.4	0.1
Inventory to Working Capital 41	0.0	·	·	0.0	0.0	0.0	0.0	·	0.0	0.0	·	·	0.0
Total Receipts to Cash Flow 42	2.3	2.5	3.0	2.1	3.5	3.3	2.8	3.4	3.3	3.5	3.2	2.6	1.8
Cost of Goods to Cash Flow 43	0.0	0.1	0.1	0.1	0.1	0.1	0.2	0.0	0.3	0.1	0.0	0.0	0.0
Cash Flow to Total Debt 44	0.2	·	1.2	0.7	0.4	0.5	0.4	0.2	0.2	0.2	0.1	0.2	0.1

Selected Financial Factors (in Percentages)

Debt Ratio 45	58.5	·	78.5	60.1	60.5	49.2	52.5	53.5	45.3	54.3	66.5	49.0	60.6
Return on Total Assets 46	4.0	·	25.1	18.7	6.3	8.9	5.8	2.5	1.1	3.6	3.7	3.4	3.8
Return on Equity Before Income Taxes 47	7.1	·	107.8	43.8	12.8	14.7	9.9	1.5	·	3.6	5.6	4.9	7.5
Return on Equity After Income Taxes 48	4.5	·	106.1	43.6	10.9	13.2	9.0	0.1	·	1.6	2.7	1.8	4.8
Profit Margin (Before Income Tax) 49	12.6	·	8.5	19.8	6.1	8.5	8.4	1.8	5.2	5.2	9.2	9.2	18.9
Profit Margin (After Income Tax) 50	8.0	·	8.4	19.8	5.2	7.7	7.6	0.1	2.3	4.4	9.2	3.4	12.1

SECURITIES & COMMODITY EXCHANGES, OTHER FINANCIAL INVESTMENT

Table II

Corporations with Net Income

MONEY AMOUNTS AND SIZE OF ASSETS IN THOUSANDS OF DOLLARS

Item Description for Accounting Period 7/02 Through 6/03	Total	Zero Assets	Under 500	500 to 1,000	1,000 to 5,000	5,000 to 10,000	10,000 to 25,000	25,000 to 50,000	50,000 to 100,000	100,000 to 250,000	250,000 to 500,000	500,000 to 2,500,000	2,500,000 and over
Number of Enterprises **1**	16443	1605	12537	665	1112	166	192	63	31	27	11	18	16
Revenues ($ in Thousands)													
Net Sales **2**	52516520	354219	4434034	556637	3343334	1675585	2281866	1050063	976832	2365911	1262134	6455379	27760528
Interest **3**	3292961	9744	4413	3056	16445	8436	24537	14958	20957	77212	52606	157476	2903120
Rents **4**	49442	0	1397	702	6881	21	3002	343	545	2145	3970	6505	23933
Royalties **5**	93946	0	15815	0	0	0	2	4282	1	41966	188	31691	0
Other Portfolio Income **6**	767096	42609	8203	9672	32604	10983	41460	25401	26736	10415	6398	34274	518338
Other Receipts **7**	48313075	301866	4404206	543207	3287404	1656145	2212865	1005079	928593	2234173	1198972	6225433	24315137
Total Receipts **8**	52516520	354219	4434034	556637	3343334	1675585	2281866	1050063	976832	2365911	1262134	6455379	27760528
Average Total Receipts **9**	3194	221	354	837	3007	10094	11885	16668	31511	87626	114739	358632	1735033
Operating Costs/Operating Income (%)													
Cost of Operations **10**	1.0	7.9	0.4	•	4.0	1.8	4.9	0.2	10.6	4.7	•	•	0.0
Salaries and Wages **11**	20.5	7.6	22.5	12.8	33.2	29.7	22.4	24.3	26.2	25.6	13.8	19.3	18.1
Taxes Paid **12**	2.3	1.8	3.2	1.8	2.3	2.3	2.5	3.3	2.2	3.1	4.6	2.4	1.9
Interest Paid **13**	2.5	2.9	0.3	0.8	1.1	1.1	1.2	3.1	2.0	2.0	4.0	2.1	3.3
Depreciation **14**	2.4	0.1	0.9	2.9	1.6	1.1	1.8	2.5	1.6	2.8	4.3	3.7	2.4
Amortization and Depletion **15**	0.6	0.0	0.1	0.2	0.2	0.0	0.3	0.3	1.7	1.2	2.1	1.1	0.6
Pensions and Other Deferred Comp. **16**	1.1	0.1	2.5	1.5	1.6	0.9	0.9	1.0	2.1	0.9	1.6	1.7	0.6
Employee Benefits **17**	2.3	0.0	1.5	0.6	1.4	1.1	1.4	1.3	1.2	1.7	1.7	1.5	3.0
Advertising **18**	2.9	0.5	0.7	0.6	0.4	0.3	0.5	0.9	0.2	1.6	1.0	2.9	4.3
Other Expenses **19**	34.8	29.3	25.9	27.3	26.5	18.0	27.5	29.6	23.6	23.1	21.8	35.2	41.1
Officers' Compensation **20**	8.1	2.2	23.9	14.7	10.6	19.1	14.2	10.9	2.5	11.8	24.1	5.7	3.6
Operating Margin **21**	21.6	47.6	18.0	36.8	17.2	24.6	22.4	22.4	26.1	21.3	21.0	24.4	21.0
Operating Margin Before Officers' Comp. **22**	29.7	49.8	41.9	51.5	27.7	43.8	36.5	33.3	28.6	33.1	45.1	30.0	24.6

Selected Average Balance Sheet ($ in Thousands)

Item	1	2	3	4	5	6	7	8	9	10	11	12	13
Net Receivables 23	1714	0	6	38	482	663	2092	5028	9696	18456	88622	104444	1441639
Inventories 24	•	•	•	•	•	•	•	•	•	•	•	•	•
Net Property, Plant and Equipment 25	365	0	10	98	223	433	1187	2436	2931	9758	46086	69857	186635
Total Assets 26	11641	0	72	615	2272	6806	15223	33754	68954	155545	370811	956656	9609333
Notes and Loans Payable 27	1604	0	22	200	568	1417	3496	7971	10703	31002	140012	78833	1237112
All Other Liabilities 28	4726	0	12	82	534	2166	3995	7534	14191	36338	131506	288749	4203032
Net Worth 29	5310	0	38	332	1170	3222	7732	18250	44061	88205	99293	589074	4169189

Selected Financial Ratios (Times to 1)

Item	1	2	3	4	5	6	7	8	9	10	11	12	13
Current Ratio 30	1.2	•	2.5	4.3	2.6	1.4	1.6	2.0	1.5	1.8	0.8	1.8	1.2
Quick Ratio 31	1.1	•	2.3	3.2	2.3	0.9	1.2	1.6	1.3	1.4	0.8	1.1	1.0
Net Sales to Working Capital 32	3.4	•	18.0	3.0	3.7	9.3	4.5	2.3	3.8	3.8	•	1.9	3.1
Coverage Ratio 33	9.7	17.7	62.8	48.6	16.4	24.4	20.1	8.1	13.9	11.4	6.2	12.8	7.4
Total Asset Turnover 34	0.3	•	4.9	1.4	1.3	1.5	0.8	0.5	0.5	0.6	0.3	0.4	0.2
Inventory Turnover 35	•	•	•	•	•	•	•	•	•	•	•	•	•
Receivables Turnover 36	•	•	•	•	•	•	•	•	•	•	•	•	•
Total Liabilities to Net Worth 37	1.2	0.9	0.9	0.9	1.1	1.0	0.8	0.6	0.8	0.8	2.7	0.6	1.3
Current Assets to Working Capital 38	5.4	1.7	1.3	1.6	2.5	3.6	2.0	2.0	3.0	2.3	•	2.3	7.4
Current Liabilities to Working Capital 39	4.4	0.7	0.3	0.6	2.6	1.6	1.0	2.0	1.3	1.3	0.3	1.3	6.4
Working Capital to Net Sales 40	0.3	0.1	0.1	0.3	0.3	0.1	0.2	0.4	0.3	0.3	•	0.5	0.3
Inventory to Working Capital 41	0.0	•	0.1	0.0	0.0	•	•	0.0	0.0	0.0	•	•	0.0
Total Receipts to Cash Flow 42	1.9	1.6	2.6	2.8	2.5	2.2	2.1	2.3	2.5	2.3	2.6	1.8	1.7
Cost of Goods to Cash Flow 43	0.0	0.1	•	0.1	0.0	0.1	0.0	0.0	0.2	0.1	•	•	0.0
Cash Flow to Total Debt 44	0.3	3.9	1.8	1.0	1.1	0.7	1.1	0.5	0.6	0.5	0.2	0.5	0.2

Selected Financial Factors (in Percentages)

Item	1	2	3	4	5	6	7	8	9	10	11	12	13
Debt Ratio 45	54.4	•	47.1	46.0	48.5	52.6	49.2	45.9	36.1	43.3	73.2	38.4	56.6
Return on Total Assets 46	6.6	•	89.4	51.1	24.3	38.0	18.3	12.5	12.7	13.1	7.7	9.9	4.4
Return on Equity Before Income Taxes 47	13.0	•	166.3	92.6	44.3	77.1	34.2	20.3	18.4	21.1	24.0	14.8	8.8
Return on Equity After Income Taxes 48	9.7	•	164.9	92.4	41.6	73.7	32.6	17.7	17.2	17.5	17.5	10.0	5.7
Profit Margin (Before Income Tax) 49	21.6	47.6	18.0	36.8	17.3	24.6	22.2	22.2	25.8	21.2	20.8	24.3	21.1
Profit Margin (After Income Tax) 50	16.2	42.4	17.8	36.7	16.2	23.5	21.2	19.4	24.1	17.6	15.2	16.4	13.8

Table I

Corporations with and without Net Income

LIFE INSURANCE

MONEY AMOUNTS AND SIZE OF ASSETS IN THOUSANDS OF DOLLARS

Item Description for Accounting Period 7/02 Through 6/03		Total	Zero Assets	Under 500	500 to 1,000	1,000 to 5,000	5,000 to 10,000	10,000 to 25,000	25,000 to 50,000	50,000 to 100,000	100,000 to 250,000	250,000 to 500,000	500,000 to 2,500,000	2,500,000 and over
Number of Enterprises	1	1407	39	366	115	301	91	96	69	37	52	57	85	99
Revenues ($ in Thousands)														
Net Sales	2	817988508	16628968	85638	77923	244171	187753	675115	962206	935542	3579393	6301513	26670519	761639767
Interest	3	135153496	1017319	2078	2337	29136	22178	66362	109985	98713	373971	884284	4550954	127996178
Rents	4	5439999	4976	0	9	53	479	2283	3202	6556	10909	27729	78279	5305523
Royalties	5	11407	0	0	0	0	0	0	0	3981	223	114	56	7032
Other Portfolio Income	6	11157251	5483	391	112	5428	7059	18738	17158	14837	32864	82441	2111250	8861495
Other Receipts	7	666226355	15601190	83169	75465	209554	158037	587732	831861	811455	3161426	5306945	19929980	619469539
Total Receipts	8	817988508	16628968	85638	77923	244171	187753	675115	962206	935542	3579393	6301513	26670519	761639767
Average Total Receipts	9	581371	426384	234	678	811	2063	7032	13945	25285	68834	110553	313771	7693331
Operating Costs/Operating Income (%)														
Cost of Operations	10	45.8	79.7	30.2	25.5	33.0	29.3	40.4	47.4	41.1	43.6	38.3	42.3	45.2
Salaries and Wages	11	2.2	0.0	•	•	•	•	0.1	0.6	0.9	0.3	1.3	0.2	2.4
Taxes Paid	12	0.8	0.1	0.5	0.5	1.1	1.5	1.6	1.2	1.7	1.5	1.4	1.2	0.8
Interest Paid	13	2.2	0.0	0.1	0.0	0.7	0.2	0.1	0.1	0.3	0.3	0.7	0.5	2.4
Depreciation	14	0.6	0.1	0.0	0.0	0.3	0.2	0.3	0.3	0.5	0.3	0.3	0.4	0.7
Amortization and Depletion	15	1.0	0.2	0.3	0.6	2.1	1.4	2.1	1.4	2.4	2.2	2.6	1.9	0.9
Pensions and Other Deferred Comp.	16	0.3	0.1	•	•	0.6	0.1	0.5	0.5	0.5	0.7	0.5	0.6	0.3
Employee Benefits	17	0.2	0.0	•	0.0	0.1	0.0	0.3	0.3	3.0	0.1	0.2	0.2	0.2
Advertising	18	0.2	0.0	0.0	0.0	0.1	0.0	0.2	0.6	0.1	0.2	0.6	0.7	0.2
Other Expenses	19	45.4	19.2	57.4	56.1	60.3	47.4	42.3	38.4	41.0	45.5	52.5	43.3	46.0
Officers' Compensation	20	0.1	•	•	•	0.0	•	0.3	0.1	0.0	0.1	0.1	0.1	0.1
Operating Margin	21	1.1	0.4	11.5	17.2	1.7	19.7	11.7	9.1	8.5	5.3	1.6	8.6	0.8
Operating Margin Before Officers' Comp.	22	1.2	0.4	11.5	17.2	1.8	19.7	12.0	9.2	8.5	5.3	1.7	8.7	0.9

Selected Average Balance Sheet ($ in Thousands)

Net Receivables 23	79356	0	9	23	163	285	766	1061	317	779	5694	10987	1112278
Inventories 24	•	•	•	•	•	•	•	•	•	•	•	•	•
Net Property, Plant and Equipment 25	29652	0	•	2	17	21	159	248	553	973	2767	6157	413422
Total Assets 26	2700781	197	748	2486	7078	16757	36282	67860	163216	345421	1197362	36988623	
Notes and Loans Payable 27	108945	0	0	0	0	0	22	163	133	1242	3416	3797	1542282
All Other Liabilities 28	2197917	197	452	1425	4242	10726	24224	51338	128811	271132	1011184	30089159	
Net Worth 29	393918	0	296	1061	2835	6008	11894	16389	33163	70873	182382	5357183	

Selected Financial Ratios (Times to 1)

Current Ratio 30	1.3	5.3	1.3	6.0	5.9	2.3	2.3	1.9	1.3	1.6	1.4	1.3	
Quick Ratio 31	0.9	3.9	0.9	4.7	4.7	1.8	1.7	1.5	0.9	1.3	1.0	0.9	
Net Sales to Working Capital 32	4.9	•	1.7	5.0	0.6	0.5	1.8	1.6	2.3	6.3	2.6	3.6	4.9
Coverage Ratio 33	1.5	15.8	85.5	1918.6	3.4	90.1	116.6	66.9	29.8	18.2	3.4	19.2	1.3
Total Asset Turnover 34	0.2	•	1.2	0.9	0.3	0.4	0.4	0.4	0.4	0.3	0.3	0.2	
Inventory Turnover 35	•	•	•	•	•	•	•	•	•	•	•	•	•
Receivables Turnover 36	•	•	•	•	•	•	•	•	•	•	•	•	•
Total Liabilities to Net Worth 37	5.9	1535.5	•	1.5	1.3	1.8	2.1	3.1	5.0	3.9	3.4	5.6	5.9
Current Assets to Working Capital 38	4.2	•	1.2	4.4	1.2	1.8	1.8	2.2	5.0	2.6	3.4	4.3	
Current Liabilities to Working Capital 39	3.2	•	0.2	3.4	0.2	0.8	0.8	1.2	4.0	1.6	2.4	3.3	
Working Capital to Net Sales 40	0.2	•	0.6	0.2	1.7	0.6	0.6	0.4	0.2	0.3	0.4	0.2	
Inventory to Working Capital 41	0.0	•	•	0.0	•	0.0	0.0	•	0.0	0.0	0.0	0.0	
Total Receipts to Cash Flow 42	2.2	5.1	1.5	1.4	1.7	1.6	1.9	2.2	2.0	1.9	2.0	2.2	
Cost of Goods to Cash Flow 43	1.0	4.1	0.4	0.3	0.6	0.5	1.0	0.9	0.9	0.7	0.8	1.0	
Cash Flow to Total Debt 44	0.1	•	0.8	1.1	0.3	0.3	0.3	0.2	0.3	0.2	0.2	0.1	

Selected Financial Factors (in Percentages)

Debt Ratio 45	85.4	•	99.9	60.4	57.3	59.9	64.1	67.2	75.8	79.7	79.5	84.8	85.5
Return on Total Assets 46	0.7	•	13.7	15.6	0.8	5.8	4.9	3.4	3.2	2.3	0.7	2.3	0.6
Return on Equity Before Income Taxes 47	1.5	•	20863.8	39.4	1.3	14.3	13.6	10.1	12.9	10.8	2.5	14.6	1.0
Return on Equity After Income Taxes 48	0.6	•	17570.2	36.5	•	10.9	10.6	7.2	8.9	7.5	0.6	11.3	0.2
Profit Margin (Before Income Tax) 49	1.0	0.4	11.5	17.2	1.7	19.6	11.6	8.6	8.4	5.2	1.6	8.5	0.7
Profit Margin (After Income Tax) 50	0.4	0.3	9.6	16.0	•	15.0	9.0	6.1	5.7	3.6	0.4	6.6	0.2

Table II

Corporations with Net Income

LIFE INSURANCE

MONEY AMOUNTS AND SIZE OF ASSETS IN THOUSANDS OF DOLLARS

Item Description for Accounting Period 7/02 Through 6/03	Total	Zero Assets	Under 500	500 to 1,000	1,000 to 5,000	5,000 to 10,000	10,000 to 25,000	25,000 to 50,000	50,000 to 100,000	100,000 to 250,000	250,000 to 500,000	500,000 to 2,500,000	2,500,000 and over
Number of Enterprises **1**	1060	24	240	98	243	80	79	54	30	39	44	62	67
Revenues ($ in Thousands)													
Net Sales **2**	499972245	16610798	59151	60621	166560	142171	547405	617405	831406	2670570	4560465	19971234	453734458
Interest **3**	88360183	1016595	1765	2038	20777	19363	57001	88072	83963	280623	682351	3211578	82896058
Rents **4**	2424172	4976	0	0	0	469	1479	2729	3526	9165	23557	56450	2321822
Royalties **5**	8893	0	0	0	0	0	0	0	3981	6	114	4	4788
Other Portfolio Income **6**	7841863	5477	366	70	3681	6895	17016	14239	11806	28551	76395	2016115	5561252
Other Receipts **7**	401337134	15583750	57020	58813	142102	115444	471909	512365	728130	2352225	3778048	14687087	362850538
Total Receipts **8**	499972245	16610798	59151	60621	166560	142171	547405	617405	831406	2670570	4560465	19971234	453734458
Average Total Receipts **9**	471672	692117	246	619	685	1777	6929	11433	27714	68476	103647	322117	6772156
Operating Costs/Operating Income (%)													
Cost of Operations **10**	42.1	79.7	30.5	24.3	25.2	25.2	39.8	43.6	42.2	44.7	39.3	39.8	40.9
Salaries and Wages **11**	1.9	0.0	•	•	•	•	0.1	0.9	0.9	0.1	1.4	0.3	2.1
Taxes Paid **12**	0.8	0.1	0.4	0.6	1.2	1.7	1.6	1.4	1.7	1.5	1.8	1.2	0.8
Interest Paid **13**	2.7	0.0	0.1	0.0	0.0	0.2	0.1	0.1	0.2	0.2	0.7	0.5	2.9
Depreciation **14**	0.8	0.1	•	0.0	0.3	0.2	0.3	0.4	0.4	0.3	0.4	0.3	0.9
Amortization and Depletion **15**	1.0	0.2	0.3	0.7	1.7	1.2	1.5	1.5	2.2	2.2	3.2	1.8	0.9
Pensions and Other Deferred Comp. **16**	0.3	0.1	•	•	0.8	0.1	0.5	0.6	0.3	0.6	0.5	0.6	0.3
Employee Benefits **17**	0.2	0.0	•	0.0	0.1	0.1	0.3	0.4	3.4	0.1	0.2	0.2	0.2
Advertising **18**	0.3	0.0	0.0	0.0	0.1	0.0	0.3	0.2	0.1	0.1	0.6	0.8	0.3
Other Expenses **19**	46.4	19.2	40.5	44.9	44.9	38.8	37.1	31.3	37.0	41.5	44.8	37.2	47.9
Officers' Compensation **20**	0.2	•	•	•	•	•	0.3	0.2	0.1	0.1	0.1	0.1	0.2
Operating Margin **21**	3.4	0.5	28.1	29.5	25.7	32.5	18.0	19.3	11.5	8.5	7.0	17.2	2.7
Operating Margin Before Officers' Comp. **22**	3.6	0.5	28.1	29.5	25.7	32.5	18.4	19.5	11.5	8.6	7.1	17.2	2.9

Selected Average Balance Sheet ($ in Thousands)

Item	1	2	3	4	5	6	7	8	9	10	11	12	13
Net Receivables 23	77730	0	11	23	196	298	646	1260	340	690	4578	8956	1214986
Inventories 24	•	•	•	•	•	•	•	•	•	•	•	•	•
Net Property, Plant and Equipment 25	33181	0	0	2	11	23	112	238	258	830	3020	6181	516258
Total Assets 26	2274057	214	755	2491	6904	16911	36627	160914	67386	349084	1148983		34492687
Notes and Loans Payable 27	104609	0	0	0	0	27	173	366	113	3479	4058		1648529
All Other Liabilities 28	1796188	136	462	1165	3260	10628	24060	125035	50424	269599	932080		27241175
Net Worth 29	373260	0	78	293	1326	3644	6256	12394	16850	35513	76006	212844	5602983

Selected Financial Ratios (Times to 1)

Item	1	2	3	4	5	6	7	8	9	10	11	12	13
Current Ratio 30	1.3	•	6.3	1.4	8.0	5.2	3.6	2.7	2.6	1.1	2.8	1.6	1.3
Quick Ratio 31	0.8	•	5.0	1.0	6.0	4.1	2.8	2.1	2.2	0.9	2.3	1.2	0.8
Net Sales to Working Capital 32	4.2	•	1.7	3.5	0.5	0.5	1.2	1.3	1.9	10.9	1.4	2.7	4.3
Coverage Ratio 33	2.3	16.3	417.0	2552.0	593.3	181.0	164.9	157.6	48.5	41.1	10.7	36.8	2.0
Total Asset Turnover 34	0.2	•	1.2	0.8	0.3	0.3	0.4	0.3	0.4	0.4	0.3	0.3	0.2
Inventory Turnover 35	•	•	•	•	•	•	•	•	•	•	•	•	•
Receivables Turnover 36	•	•	•	•	•	•	•	•	•	•	•	•	•
Total Liabilities to Net Worth 37	5.1	1.7	1.7	1.6	0.9	0.9	1.1	2.0	3.0	3.5	3.6	4.4	5.2
Current Assets to Working Capital 38	4.2	1.2	1.2	3.3	1.1	1.2	1.4	1.6	1.6	8.4	1.6	2.6	4.5
Current Liabilities to Working Capital 39	3.2	0.2	0.2	2.3	0.1	0.2	0.4	0.6	0.6	7.4	0.6	1.6	3.5
Working Capital to Net Sales 40	0.2	0.6	0.6	0.3	2.1	2.0	0.8	0.8	0.5	0.1	0.7	0.4	0.2
Inventory to Working Capital 41	0.0	•	0.0	0.0	•	•	•	•	•	•	0.0	0.0	0.0
Total Receipts to Cash Flow 42	2.1	5.1	1.5	1.3	1.5	1.9	2.0	2.2	2.1	2.1	2.0	1.9	2.0
Cost of Goods to Cash Flow 43	0.9	4.1	0.4	0.3	0.4	0.4	0.9	0.9	0.9	0.9	0.8	0.7	0.8
Cash Flow to Total Debt 44	0.1	1.2	1.0	0.4	0.4	0.3	0.2	0.3	0.3	0.3	0.2	0.2	0.1

Selected Financial Factors (in Percentages)

Item	1	2	3	4	5	6	7	8	9	10	11	12	13
Debt Ratio 45	83.6	•	63.4	61.2	46.8	47.2	63.0	66.2	75.0	77.9	78.2	81.5	83.8
Return on Total Assets 46	1.3	•	32.5	24.2	7.1	8.4	7.4	5.8	4.8	3.7	2.3	4.9	1.1
Return on Equity Before Income Taxes 47	4.4	•	88.5	62.3	13.2	15.8	19.8	17.2	18.7	16.2	9.4	25.6	3.4
Return on Equity After Income Taxes 48	3.2	•	80.3	58.9	11.6	12.8	16.3	13.7	13.8	12.2	7.2	21.8	2.4
Profit Margin (Before Income Tax) 49	3.5	0.5	28.1	29.5	25.6	32.4	17.9	18.6	11.4	8.4	6.9	16.9	2.9
Profit Margin (After Income Tax) 50	2.5	0.3	25.5	27.8	22.5	26.3	14.7	14.8	8.4	6.3	5.3	14.4	2.0

Table I

Corporations with and without Net Income

LIFE INSURANCE, STOCK COMPANIES (FORM 1120L)

MONEY AMOUNTS AND SIZE OF ASSETS IN THOUSANDS OF DOLLARS

Item Description for Accounting Period 7/02 Through 6/03	Total	Zero Assets	Under 500	500 to 1,000	1,000 to 5,000	5,000 to 10,000	10,000 to 25,000	25,000 to 50,000	50,000 to 100,000	100,000 to 250,000	250,000 to 500,000	500,000 to 2,500,000	2,500,000 and over
Number of Enterprises **1**	1336	39	356	115	283	91	96	62	37	43	50	73	90
Revenues ($ in Thousands)													
Net Sales **2**	731235488	16628968	85373	77923	229995	187753	675115	881304	935542	2830757	5568651	23762670	679371436
Interest **3**	117314773	1017319	1944	2337	26724	22178	66362	93682	98713	297141	754665	3815037	111118670
Rents **4**	4400575	4976	0	9	0	479	2283	3130	6556	9190	25930	62049	4285971
Royalties **5**	9432	0	0	0	0	0	0	0	3981	6	0	0	5445
Other Portfolio Income **6**	10272023	5483	391	112	5494	7059	18738	16464	14837	27148	67351	2078317	8030630
Other Receipts **7**	599238885	15601190	83038	75465	197777	158037	587732	768028	811455	2497272	4720705	17807267	555930720
Total Receipts **8**	731235488	16628968	85373	77923	229995	187753	675115	881304	935542	2830757	5568651	23762670	679371436
Average Total Receipts **9**	547332	426384	240	678	813	2063	7032	14215	25285	65832	111373	325516	7548572
Operating Costs/Operating Income (%)													
Cost of Operations **10**	46.2	79.7	30.2	25.5	34.0	29.3	40.4	46.7	41.1	43.9	36.8	42.6	45.6
Salaries and Wages **11**	2.4	0.0	•	•	•	•	0.1	0.7	0.9	0.4	1.4	0.3	2.6
Taxes Paid **12**	0.8	0.1	0.4	0.5	1.1	1.5	1.6	1.1	1.7	1.5	1.3	1.2	0.8
Interest Paid **13**	2.4	0.0	0.1	0.0	0.6	0.2	0.1	0.1	0.3	0.3	0.7	0.5	2.5
Depreciation **14**	0.7	0.1	0.0	0.0	0.3	0.2	0.3	0.2	0.5	0.3	0.3	0.3	0.7
Amortization and Depletion **15**	0.9	0.2	0.3	0.6	2.1	1.4	2.1	1.3	2.4	2.5	2.5	1.9	0.9
Pensions and Other Deferred Comp. **16**	0.3	0.1	•	•	0.6	0.1	0.5	0.5	0.5	0.5	0.4	0.5	0.3
Employee Benefits **17**	0.2	0.0	•	0.0	0.1	0.0	0.3	0.2	3.0	0.1	0.2	0.2	0.2
Advertising **18**	0.2	0.0	•	0.0	0.1	0.0	0.2	0.6	0.1	0.2	0.6	0.7	0.2
Other Expenses **19**	44.9	19.2	57.5	56.1	59.1	47.4	42.3	39.0	41.0	43.8	54.6	42.2	45.6
Officers' Compensation **20**	0.1	•	•	•	•	•	0.3	0.1	0.0	0.1	0.1	0.1	0.1
Operating Margin **21**	0.9	0.4	11.4	17.2	2.0	19.7	11.7	9.3	8.5	6.3	1.0	9.5	0.5
Operating Margin Before Officers' Comp. **22**	0.9	0.4	11.4	17.2	2.0	19.7	12.0	9.5	8.5	6.4	1.0	9.6	0.6

Selected Average Balance Sheet ($ in Thousands)													
Net Receivables 23	79829	0	9	23	172	285	766	1177	317	934	6198	12544	1168306
Inventories 24	•	•	•	•	•	•	•	•	•	•	•	•	•
Net Property, Plant and Equipment 25	30063	0	0	2	10	21	159	240	553	812	2721	5946	438935
Total Assets 26	2538770	0	192	748	2454	7078	16757	35723	67860	157054	339661	1212401	36352535
Notes and Loans Payable 27	111003	0	0	0	0	0	22	182	133	1501	3894	4376	1641146
All Other Liabilities 28	2040677	0	198	452	1371	4242	10726	23392	51338	119879	261140	1014547	29208824
Net Worth 29	387090	0	-6	296	1082	2835	6008	12149	16389	35673	74626	193478	5502564

Selected Financial Ratios (Times to 1)													
Current Ratio 30	1.2	•	5.3	1.3	6.3	5.9	2.3	2.2	1.9	1.2	1.5	1.4	1.2
Quick Ratio 31	0.8	•	3.9	0.9	5.0	4.7	1.7	1.7	1.5	0.9	1.2	1.0	0.8
Net Sales to Working Capital 32	6.5	•	1.7	5.0	0.6	0.5	1.6	1.9	2.3	7.3	2.9	4.0	6.7
Coverage Ratio 33	1.3	15.8	85.0	1918.6	4.1	90.1	116.6	63.3	29.8	19.2	2.2	20.7	1.2
Total Asset Turnover 34	0.2	•	1.2	0.9	0.3	0.3	0.4	0.4	0.4	0.4	0.3	0.3	0.2
Inventory Turnover 35	•	•	•	•	•	•	•	•	•	•	•	•	•
Receivables Turnover 36	•	•	•	•	•	•	•	•	•	•	•	•	•
Total Liabilities to Net Worth 37	5.6	•	•	1.5	1.3	1.5	1.8	1.9	3.1	3.4	3.6	5.3	5.6
Current Assets to Working Capital 38	5.6	•	1.2	4.4	1.2	1.2	1.8	1.9	2.2	6.2	2.9	3.8	5.9
Current Liabilities to Working Capital 39	4.6	•	0.2	3.4	0.2	0.2	0.8	0.9	1.2	5.2	1.9	2.8	4.9
Working Capital to Net Sales 40	0.2	•	0.6	0.2	1.7	1.9	0.6	0.5	0.4	0.1	0.3	0.3	0.1
Inventory to Working Capital 41	0.0	•	0.0	0.0	•	•	•	•	0.4	0.1	0.0	0.0	0.0
Total Receipts to Cash Flow 42	2.2	5.1	1.5	1.4	1.7	1.6	1.9	2.1	2.1	2.0	1.8	2.0	2.2
Cost of Goods to Cash Flow 43	1.0	4.1	0.4	0.3	0.6	0.5	0.8	1.0	0.9	0.9	0.7	0.8	1.0
Cash Flow to Total Debt 44	0.1	0.8	1.1	0.3	0.3	0.3	0.3	0.3	0.2	0.3	0.2	0.2	0.1

Selected Financial Factors (in Percentages)													
Debt Ratio 45	84.8	•	103.2	60.4	55.9	59.9	64.1	66.0	75.8	77.3	78.0	84.0	84.9
Return on Total Assets 46	0.7	•	14.4	15.6	0.9	5.8	4.9	3.6	3.2	2.8	0.5	2.6	0.6
Return on Equity Before Income Taxes 47	1.2	•	•	39.4	1.5	14.3	13.6	10.3	12.9	11.5	1.4	15.7	0.7
Return on Equity After Income Taxes 48	0.3	•	•	36.5	•	10.9	10.6	7.3	8.9	8.0	•	12.4	•
Profit Margin (Before Income Tax) 49	0.8	0.4	11.4	17.2	2.0	19.6	11.6	8.8	8.4	6.2	0.9	9.3	0.5
Profit Margin (After Income Tax) 50	0.2	0.3	9.6	16.0	•	15.0	9.0	6.2	5.7	4.3	•	7.4	•

Table II

Corporations with Net Income

LIFE INSURANCE, STOCK COMPANIES (FORM 1120L)

MONEY AMOUNTS AND SIZE OF ASSETS IN THOUSANDS OF DOLLARS

Item Description for Accounting Period 7/02 Through 6/03	Total	Zero Assets	Under 500	500 to 1000	251 to 500	501 to 1,000	1,001 to 5,000	5,001 to 10,000	10,001 to 25,000	25,001 to 50,000	50,001 to 100,000	100,001 to 250,000	250,001 and over
Number of Enterprises **1**	1017	24	232	98	238	80	79	47	30	35	38	54	61

Revenues ($ in Thousands)

	Total	Zero Assets	Under 500	500 to 1000	251 to 500	501 to 1,000	1,001 to 5,000	5,001 to 10,000	10,001 to 25,000	25,001 to 50,000	50,001 to 100,000	100,001 to 250,000	250,001 and over
Net Sales **2**	418930267	16610798	58893	60621	158312	142171	547405	536504	831406	2222532	3897687	18120491	375743448
Interest **3**	71673854	1016595	1636	2038	19823	19363	57001	71769	83963	259793	578313	2765764	66797795
Rents **4**	1434357	4976	0	0	0	469	1479	2657	3526	9020	21758	49856	1340615
Royalties **5**	8278	0	0	0	0	0	0	0	3981	6	0	0	4291
Other Portfolio Income **6**	6982941	5477	366	70	3543	6895	17016	13545	11806	24719	62064	2002958	4834484
Other Receipts **7**	338830837	15583750	56891	58513	134946	115444	471909	448533	728130	1928994	3235552	13301913	302766263
Total Receipts **8**	418930267	16610798	58893	60621	158312	142171	547405	536504	831406	2222532	3897687	18120491	375743448
Average Total Receipts **9**	411927	692117	254	619	665	1777	6929	11415	27714	63501	102571	335565	6159729

Operating Costs/Operating Income (%)

	Total	Zero Assets	Under 500	500 to 1000	251 to 500	501 to 1,000	1,001 to 5,000	5,001 to 10,000	10,001 to 25,000	25,001 to 50,000	50,001 to 100,000	100,001 to 250,000	250,001 and over
Cost of Operations **10**	42.2	79.7	30.5	24.3	26.0	25.2	39.8	41.9	42.2	46.4	37.9	40.0	40.7
Salaries and Wages **11**	2.2	0.0	•	•	•	•	0.1	1.0	0.9	0.1	1.6	0.3	2.4
Taxes Paid **12**	0.8	0.1	0.4	0.6	1.2	1.7	1.6	1.3	1.7	1.5	1.7	1.2	0.8
Interest Paid **13**	3.0	0.0	0.1	0.0	0.0	0.2	0.1	0.1	0.2	0.3	0.8	0.5	3.3
Depreciation **14**	0.9	0.1	•	0.0	0.3	0.2	0.3	0.3	0.4	0.3	0.4	0.3	1.0
Amortization and Depletion **15**	0.9	0.2	0.3	0.7	1.7	1.2	1.5	1.4	2.2	2.6	3.1	1.8	0.8
Pensions and Other Deferred Comp. **16**	0.3	0.1	•	•	0.8	0.1	0.5	0.6	0.3	0.6	0.5	0.6	0.3
Employee Benefits **17**	0.2	0.0	•	0.0	0.1	0.1	0.3	0.3	3.4	0.1	0.2	0.1	0.2
Advertising **18**	0.3	0.0	0.0	0.0	0.1	0.0	0.3	0.2	0.1	0.2	0.7	0.9	0.3
Other Expenses **19**	45.7	19.2	40.5	44.9	43.0	38.8	37.1	31.3	37.0	38.5	46.1	35.8	47.4
Officers' Compensation **20**	0.1	•	•	•	•	•	0.3	0.2	0.1	0.1	0.0	0.1	0.2
Operating Margin **21**	3.4	0.5	28.1	29.5	26.6	32.5	18.0	21.3	11.5	9.3	6.9	18.3	2.6
Operating Margin Before Officers' Comp. **22**	3.5	0.5	28.1	29.5	26.6	32.5	18.4	21.5	11.5	9.4	6.9	18.4	2.8

Selected Average Balance Sheet ($ in Thousands)

Item													
Net Receivables 23	76138	0	11	23	200	298	646	1443	340	765	4927	10244	1253432
Inventories 24	•	•	•	•	•	•	•	•	•	•	•	•	•
Net Property, Plant and Equipment 25	33470	206	0	2	12	23	112	226	258	818	2938	6134	549753
Total Assets 26	1997719	•	•	755	2454	6904	16911	35942	67386	158879	343976	1183414	31849816
Notes and Loans Payable 27	104132	•	•	0	0	0	27	199	113	408	4028	4653	1729000
All Other Liabilities 28	1539277	•	134	462	1108	3260	10628	22938	50424	121943	259483	950610	24523806
Net Worth 29	354309	•	71	293	1346	3644	6256	12804	16850	36528	80465	228151	5597009

Selected Financial Ratios (Times to 1)

Item													
Current Ratio 30	1.2	•	6.3	1.4	8.1	5.2	2.6	3.6	2.6	1.1	2.8	1.6	1.2
Quick Ratio 31	0.7	•	4.9	1.0	6.2	4.1	1.9	2.8	2.2	0.9	2.3	1.2	0.7
Net Sales to Working Capital 32	6.2	•	1.7	3.5	0.5	0.5	1.2	1.2	1.9	9.8	1.3	2.9	6.7
Coverage Ratio 33	2.2	16.3	415.3	2552.0	794.2	181.0	164.9	151.9	48.5	37.6	9.4	38.6	1.9
Total Asset Turnover 34	0.2	•	1.2	0.8	0.3	0.3	0.4	0.3	0.4	0.4	0.3	0.3	0.2
Inventory Turnover 35	•	•	•	•	•	•	•	•	•	•	•	•	•
Receivables Turnover 36	•	•	•	•	•	•	•	•	•	•	•	•	•
Total Liabilities to Net Worth 37	4.6	•	1.9	1.6	0.8	0.9	1.7	1.8	3.0	3.3	3.3	4.2	4.7
Current Assets to Working Capital 38	6.4	•	1.2	3.3	1.1	1.2	1.4	1.6	1.6	8.7	1.5	2.7	7.2
Current Liabilities to Working Capital 39	5.4	•	0.2	2.3	0.1	0.2	0.4	0.6	0.6	7.7	0.5	1.7	6.2
Working Capital to Net Sales 40	0.2	•	0.6	0.3	2.2	2.0	0.8	0.8	0.5	0.1	0.7	0.3	0.1
Inventory to Working Capital 41	0.0	•	•	•	•	•	•	•	•	0.0	0.0	0.0	0.0
Total Receipts to Cash Flow 42	2.1	5.1	1.5	1.3	1.5	1.9	2.0	2.0	2.2	2.1	2.0	1.9	2.0
Cost of Goods to Cash Flow 43	0.9	4.1	0.4	0.3	0.4	0.4	0.8	0.8	0.9	1.0	0.7	0.8	0.8
Cash Flow to Total Debt 44	0.1	•	1.3	1.0	0.4	0.4	0.3	0.3	0.3	0.2	0.2	0.2	0.1

Selected Financial Factors (in Percentages)

Item													
Debt Ratio 45	82.3	•	65.3	61.2	45.1	47.2	63.0	64.4	75.0	77.0	76.6	80.7	82.4
Return on Total Assets 46	1.3	•	34.8	24.2	7.2	8.4	6.6	6.6	4.8	3.8	2.3	5.3	1.2
Return on Equity Before Income Taxes 47	4.1	•	99.9	62.3	13.1	15.8	19.8	18.3	18.7	16.0	8.7	26.6	3.1
Return on Equity After Income Taxes 48	3.0	•	90.6	58.9	11.5	12.8	16.3	14.5	13.8	11.8	6.8	22.8	2.1
Profit Margin (Before Income Tax) 49	3.5	0.5	28.1	29.5	26.6	32.4	17.9	20.5	11.4	9.2	6.8	18.1	2.8
Profit Margin (After Income Tax) 50	2.6	0.3	25.5	27.8	23.3	26.3	14.7	16.3	8.4	6.8	5.3	15.5	1.9

Table I

Corporations with and without Net Income

LIFE INSURANCE, MUTUAL COMPANIES (FORM 1120L)

MONEY AMOUNTS AND SIZE OF ASSETS IN THOUSANDS OF DOLLARS

Item Description for Accounting Period 7/02 Through 6/03	Total	Zero Assets	Under 500	500 to 1,000	1,000 to 5,000	5,000 to 10,000	10,000 to 25,000	25,000 to 50,000	50,000 to 100,000	100,000 to 250,000	250,000 to 500,000	500,000 to 2,500,000	2,500,000 and over
Number of Enterprises 1	71	•	10	0	17	0	•	7	0	9	7	12	9
Revenues ($ in Thousands)													
Net Sales 2	86753020	•	265	0	14176	0	•	80902	0	748636	732861	2907849	82268331
Interest 3	17838723	•	134	0	2412	0	•	16303	0	76830	129618	735917	16877508
Rents 4	1039424	•	0	0	53	0	•	72	0	1719	1799	16230	1019552
Royalties 5	1975	•	0	0	0	0	•	0	0	217	114	56	1587
Other Portfolio Income 6	885229	•	0	0	-67	0	•	693	0	5716	15089	32934	830864
Other Receipts 7	6987669	•	131	0	11778	0	•	63834	0	664154	586241	2122712	63538820
Total Receipts 8	86753020	•	265	0	14176	0	•	80902	0	748636	732861	2907849	82268331
Average Total Receipts 9	1221874	•	26	•	834	•	•	11557	•	83182	104694	242321	9140926
Operating Costs/Operating Income (%)													
Cost of Operations 10	42.2	•	32.5	•	16.6	•	•	55.1	•	42.6	49.1	39.7	42.2
Salaries and Wages 11	0.7	•	•	•	•	•	•	•	•	•	0.5	0.0	0.7
Taxes Paid 12	0.8	•	0.8	•	2.0	•	•	1.8	•	1.3	1.9	1.5	0.7
Interest Paid 13	0.8	•	•	•	1.3	•	•	0.0	•	0.1	0.2	0.4	0.9
Depreciation 14	0.5	•	•	•	0.3	•	•	1.3	•	0.3	0.4	0.8	0.5
Amortization and Depletion 15	1.4	•	•	•	1.7	•	•	2.4	•	1.0	3.7	2.3	1.4
Pensions and Other Deferred Comp. 16	0.3	•	•	•	0.2	•	•	0.8	•	1.4	0.8	1.2	0.3
Employee Benefits 17	0.1	•	•	•	0.4	•	•	0.8	•	0.2	0.3	0.2	0.1
Advertising 18	0.3	•	•	•	0.1	•	•	0.1	•	0.0	0.1	0.4	0.3
Other Expenses 19	49.6	•	43.0	•	80.2	•	•	31.3	•	51.8	35.9	52.2	49.7
Officers' Compensation 20	0.5	•	•	•	0.6	•	•	•	•	•	0.4	•	0.5
Operating Margin 21	2.8	•	23.4	•	•	•	•	6.3	•	1.3	6.8	1.3	2.8
Operating Margin Before Officers' Comp. 22	3.3	•	23.4	•	•	•	•	6.3	•	1.3	7.2	1.3	3.3

Selected Average Balance Sheet ($ in Thousands)

Net Receivables 23	70446	0	21	34	•	37	2087	1515	551999
Inventories 24	•	•	•	•	•	•	•	•	•
Net Property, Plant and Equipment 25	21912	0	127	317	•	1744	3101	7443	158293
Total Assets 26	5749328	381	3168	41229	•	192657	386569	1105878	43349508
Notes and Loans Payable 27	70226	0	0	0	•	0	0	273	553640
All Other Liabilities 28	5156700	160	2398	31592	•	171486	342503	990728	38892502
Net Worth 29	522403	222	770	9637	•	21171	44067	114876	3903367

Selected Financial Ratios (Times to 1)

Current Ratio 30	3.3	13.3	3.0	6.4	•	1.8	2.7	2.0	3.4
Quick Ratio 31	2.4	7.0	1.8	5.4	•	1.6	2.2	1.4	2.5
Net Sales to Working Capital 32	1.5	0.7	1.1	1.4	•	4.2	1.3	2.0	1.5
Coverage Ratio 33	4.3	•	•	1200.0	•	9.7	39.0	4.3	4.2
Total Asset Turnover 34	0.2	0.1	0.3	0.3	•	0.4	0.3	0.2	0.2
Inventory Turnover 35	•	•	•	•	•	•	•	•	•
Receivables Turnover 36	•	•	•	•	•	•	•	•	•
Total Liabilities to Net Worth 37	10.0	0.7	3.1	3.3	•	8.1	7.8	8.6	10.1
Current Assets to Working Capital 38	1.4	1.1	1.5	1.2	•	2.3	1.6	2.0	1.4
Current Liabilities to Working Capital 39	0.4	0.1	0.5	0.2	•	1.3	0.6	1.0	0.4
Working Capital to Net Sales 40	0.6	1.4	0.9	0.7	•	0.2	0.8	0.5	0.7
Inventory to Working Capital 41	•	•	•	•	•	•	•	•	•
Total Receipts to Cash Flow 42	1.9	1.5	1.3	2.7	•	1.9	2.5	1.9	1.9
Cost of Goods to Cash Flow 43	0.8	0.5	0.2	1.5	•	0.8	1.2	0.8	0.8
Cash Flow to Total Debt 44	0.1	0.1	0.3	0.1	•	0.3	0.1	0.1	0.1

Selected Financial Factors (in Percentages)

Debt Ratio 45	90.9	41.8	75.7	76.6	•	89.0	88.6	89.6	91.0
Return on Total Assets 46	0.8	1.6	•	1.7	•	0.6	1.8	0.4	0.8
Return on Equity Before Income Taxes 47	6.4	2.8	•	7.1	•	5.1	15.6	2.7	6.5
Return on Equity After Income Taxes 48	4.3	2.6	•	5.9	•	3.9	10.9	0.2	4.4
Profit Margin (Before Income Tax) 49	2.8	23.4	•	5.9	•	1.3	6.6	1.3	2.8
Profit Margin (After Income Tax) 50	1.8	21.9	•	4.9	•	1.0	4.6	0.1	1.9

Table II
Corporations with Net Income

LIFE INSURANCE, MUTUAL COMPANIES (FORM 1120L)

MONEY AMOUNTS AND SIZE OF ASSETS IN THOUSANDS OF DOLLARS

Item Description for Accounting Period 7/02 Through 6/03	Total	Zero Assets	Under 500	500 to 1,000	1,000 to 5,000	5,000 to 10,000	10,000 to 25,000	25,000 to 50,000	50,000 to 100,000	100,000 to 250,000	250,000 to 500,000	500,000 to 2,500,000	2,500,000 and over
Number of Enterprises **1**	43	•	7	0	0	0	•	7	0	4	0	8	6
Revenues ($ in Thousands)													
Net Sales **2**	81041978	•	258	0	0	0	•	80902	0	448038	0	1850744	77991010
Interest **3**	16686329	•	128	0	0	0	•	16303	0	20830	0	445813	16098264
Rents **4**	989816	•	0	0	0	0	•	72	0	144	0	6594	981207
Royalties **5**	616	•	0	0	0	0	•	0	0	0	0	4	497
Other Portfolio Income **6**	858921	•	0	0	0	0	•	693	0	3834	0	13158	826766
Other Receipts **7**	6250296	•	130	0	0	0	•	63834	0	423230	0	1385175	60084276
Total Receipts **8**	81041978	•	258	0	0	0	•	80902	0	448038	0	1850744	77991010
Average Total Receipts **9**	1884697	•	37	•	•	•	•	11557	•	112010	•	231343	12998502
Operating Costs/Operating Income (%)													
Cost of Operations **10**	41.6	•	30.2	•	•	•	•	55.1	•	36.5	•	37.6	41.7
Salaries and Wages **11**	0.7	•	•	•	•	•	•	•	•	•	•	•	0.7
Taxes Paid **12**	0.7	•	0.8	•	•	•	•	1.8	•	1.3	•	1.6	0.7
Interest Paid **13**	0.9	•	•	•	•	•	•	0.0	•	0.0	•	0.4	0.9
Depreciation **14**	0.5	•	•	•	•	•	•	1.3	•	0.3	•	0.3	0.5
Amortization and Depletion **15**	1.4	•	•	•	•	•	•	2.4	•	0.4	•	2.4	1.4
Pensions and Other Deferred Comp. **16**	0.3	•	•	•	•	•	•	0.8	•	0.8	•	1.0	0.2
Employee Benefits **17**	0.1	•	•	•	•	•	•	0.8	•	0.1	•	0.2	0.1
Advertising **18**	0.3	•	•	•	•	•	•	0.1	•	0.0	•	0.1	0.3
Other Expenses **19**	49.8	•	42.6	•	•	•	•	31.3	•	56.1	•	50.8	49.9
Officers' Compensation **20**	0.5	•	•	•	•	•	•	•	•	•	•	•	0.5
Operating Margin **21**	3.2	•	26.7	•	•	•	•	6.3	•	4.4	•	5.7	3.0
Operating Margin Before Officers' Comp. **22**	3.7	•	26.7	•	•	•	•	6.3	•	4.4	•	5.7	3.6

Selected Average Balance Sheet ($ in Thousands)

Net Receivables 23	115383	0	34	33	268	824127
Inventories 24	•	•	•	•	•	•
Net Property, Plant and Equipment 25	26361	0	317	932	6496	175726
Total Assets 26	8809787	518	41229	178718	916571	61361882
Notes and Loans Payable 27	115880	0	0	0	45	830411
All Other Liabilities 28	7872441	201	31592	152088	807003	54867755
Net Worth 29	821466	317	9637	26629	109523	5663716

Selected Financial Ratios (Times to 1)

Current Ratio 30	3.3	13.3	6.4	1.3	2.7	3.3
Quick Ratio 31	2.4	7.0	5.4	0.9	2.0	2.4
Net Sales to Working Capital 32	1.6	0.7	1.4	23.4	1.9	1.6
Coverage Ratio 33	4.5	•	1200.0	1528.6	15.3	4.3
Total Asset Turnover 34	0.2	0.1	0.3	0.6	0.3	0.2
Inventory Turnover 35	•	•	•	•	•	•
Receivables Turnover 36	•	•	•	•	•	•
Total Liabilities to Net Worth 37	9.7	0.6	3.3	5.7	7.4	9.8
Current Assets to Working Capital 38	1.4	1.1	1.2	4.6	1.6	1.4
Current Liabilities to Working Capital 39	0.4	0.1	0.2	3.6	0.6	0.4
Working Capital to Net Sales 40	0.6	1.4	0.7	0.0	0.5	0.6
Inventory to Working Capital 41	•	•	•	•	•	•
Total Receipts to Cash Flow 42	1.9	1.4	2.7	1.7	1.8	1.9
Cost of Goods to Cash Flow 43	0.8	0.4	1.5	0.6	0.7	0.8
Cash Flow to Total Debt 44	0.1	0.1	0.1	0.4	0.2	0.1

Selected Financial Factors (in Percentages)

Debt Ratio 45	90.7	38.8	76.6	85.1	88.1	90.8
Return on Total Assets 46	0.9	1.9	1.7	2.8	1.5	0.8
Return on Equity Before Income Taxes 47	7.1	3.1	7.1	18.6	11.9	6.9
Return on Equity After Income Taxes 48	4.9	2.9	5.9	16.6	7.9	4.7
Profit Margin (Before Income Tax) 49	3.1	26.4	5.9	4.4	5.7	3.0
Profit Margin (After Income Tax) 50	2.1	24.8	4.9	3.9	3.7	2.0

MUTUAL PROPERTY AND CASUALTY COMPANIES (FORM 1120-PC)

Table I

Corporations with and without Net Income

MONEY AMOUNTS AND SIZE OF ASSETS IN THOUSANDS OF DOLLARS

Item Description for Accounting Period 7/02 Through 6/03	Total	Zero Assets	Under 500	500 to 1,000	1,000 to 5,000	5,000 to 10,000	10,000 to 25,000	25,000 to 50,000	50,000 to 100,000	100,000 to 250,000	250,000 to 500,000	500,000 to 2,500,000	2,500,000 and over
Number of Enterprises 1	1603	29	116	147	574	176	190	95	74	95	28	60	19
Revenues ($ in Thousands)													
Net Sales 2	171278329	-106696	48956	67136	643541	686863	1790967	1667335	2302841	9344343	6893133	34688882	113251027
Interest 3	11365445	972	667	2436	38293	33278	88992	105134	161902	515505	305001	1804650	8308615
Rents 4	376100	0	0	83	3397	1092	2167	2492	4191	18019	15631	57785	271241
Royalties 5	196	0	0	0	0	0	0	0	0	0	0	196	0
Other Portfolio Income 6	4292237	44101	90	88	8259	7364	21537	29928	62900	165503	77000	650563	3224903
Other Receipts 7	155244351	-151769	48199	64529	593592	645129	1678271	1529781	2073848	8645316	6495501	32175688	101446268
Total Receipts 8	171278329	-106696	48956	67136	643541	686863	1790967	1667335	2302841	9344343	6893133	34688882	113251027
Average Total Receipts 9	106849	-3679	422	457	1121	3903	9426	17551	31119	98362	246183	578148	5960580
Operating Costs/Operating Income (%)													
Cost of Operations 10	65.4	•	80.8	58.3	50.3	72.4	61.6	56.9	56.9	61.8	69.3	64.4	66.1
Salaries and Wages 11	9.7	•	•	5.7	11.8	8.5	11.9	14.6	17.2	16.5	14.4	14.5	7.1
Taxes Paid 12	2.0	•	0.0	9.7	4.3	1.5	2.2	2.6	2.8	2.7	2.1	2.5	1.8
Interest Paid 13	0.4	•	•	0.4	0.3	0.1	0.2	0.1	0.1	0.2	0.0	0.3	0.4
Depreciation 14	0.9	•	•	0.2	0.5	0.2	0.4	0.4	0.9	0.9	0.7	0.9	1.0
Amortization and Depletion 15	0.3	•	•	•	0.0	0.0	0.1	0.1	0.1	0.1	0.1	0.1	0.4
Pensions and Other Deferred Comp. 16	0.3	•	•	•	0.1	0.3	0.2	0.2	0.1	0.2	0.6	0.5	0.2
Employee Benefits 17	1.0	•	•	0.6	1.0	0.6	0.7	1.3	1.7	1.5	1.2	1.7	0.7
Advertising 18	0.3	•	•	0.2	0.3	0.1	0.2	0.3	0.3	0.3	0.3	0.2	0.3
Other Expenses 19	17.7	6.4	•	22.1	23.6	16.3	21.8	18.2	18.4	12.7	7.1	10.9	20.7
Officers' Compensation 20	0.2	•	•	1.4	1.7	0.5	0.7	1.1	0.8	0.6	0.5	0.3	0.1
Operating Margin 21	1.7	225.7	12.8	1.4	6.2	•	0.2	4.2	0.7	2.6	3.6	3.5	1.2
Operating Margin Before Officers' Comp. 22	2.0	225.6	12.8	2.8	7.9	•	0.9	5.4	1.4	3.2	4.1	3.8	1.3

Selected Average Balance Sheet ($ in Thousands)

Net Receivables **23**	17967	0	15	17	136	675	1345	3522	6624	19177	37084	89346	1015696
Inventories **24**	·	·	·	·	·	·	·	·	·	·	·	·	·
Net Property, Plant and Equipment **25**	4190	0	0	15	64	73	262	407	1171	3868	8767	17216	254966
Total Assets **26**	233469	198	0	666	2334	7364	16187	36075	70922	165507	340147	1023758	14372090
Notes and Loans Payable **27**	1976	0	·	396	102	265	110	220	330	1535	2046	6762	122562
All Other Liabilities **28**	154146	571	·	595	1088	6192	11879	25754	47594	107647	202241	657078	9562527
Net Worth **29**	77347	-374	·	-325	1144	908	4199	10101	22998	56325	135861	359918	4687001

Selected Financial Ratios (Times to 1)

Current Ratio **30**	0.8	·	0.3	·	1.7	0.8	1.0	0.8	0.9	1.0	0.9	0.9	0.8
Quick Ratio **31**	0.7	·	0.3	·	1.5	0.7	0.8	0.7	0.7	0.8	0.9	0.7	0.7
Net Sales to Working Capital **32**	·	·	·	·	1.8	·	·	·	·	·	·	·	·
Coverage Ratio **33**	2.6	·	·	4.4	22.0	25.7	·	11.8	90.1	9.6	·	·	0.9
Total Asset Turnover **34**	0.5	2.1	·	0.7	·	·	0.5	0.6	0.4	0.6	0.7	0.6	0.4
Inventory Turnover **35**	·	·	·	·	·	·	·	·	·	·	·	·	·
Receivables Turnover **36**	·	·	·	·	·	·	·	·	·	·	·	·	·
Total Liabilities to Net Worth **37**	2.0	·	·	1.0	2.5	2.6	2.1	2.9	7.1	1.5	1.9	1.8	2.1
Current Assets to Working Capital **38**	·	·	·	·	2.5	·	·	·	·	·	·	·	·
Current Liabilities to Working Capital **39**	·	·	·	·	1.5	·	·	·	·	·	·	·	·
Working Capital to Net Sales **40**	·	·	·	·	0.6	·	·	·	·	·	·	·	·
Inventory to Working Capital **41**	·	·	·	·	·	·	·	·	·	·	·	·	·
Total Receipts to Cash Flow **42**	5.5	0.4	·	5.2	4.4	3.5	6.6	4.8	5.8	7.2	10.3	7.7	4.9
Cost of Goods to Cash Flow **43**	3.6	·	·	4.2	2.6	1.8	4.8	2.9	3.3	4.5	7.1	5.0	3.2
Cash Flow to Total Debt **44**	0.1	·	·	0.1	0.1	0.3	0.1	0.2	0.1	0.1	0.1	0.1	0.1

Selected Financial Factors (in Percentages)

Debt Ratio **45**	66.9	·	289.2	148.8	51.0	87.7	74.1	72.0	67.6	66.0	60.1	64.8	67.4
Return on Total Assets **46**	0.5	·	27.3	1.2	2.8	·	·	1.9	·	1.3	2.2	1.7	0.2
Return on Equity Before Income Taxes **47**	0.9	·	·	·	5.5	·	·	6.4	·	3.5	5.5	4.3	·
Return on Equity After Income Taxes **48**	·	·	·	·	4.5	·	·	3.7	·	1.6	3.3	2.3	·
Profit Margin (Before Income Tax) **49**	0.6	225.7	12.8	1.4	5.6	·	·	3.7	·	1.6	3.3	2.3	·
Profit Margin (After Income Tax) **50**	0.9	226.1	12.8	0.2	4.6	2.1	·	3.7	·	2.0	3.0	2.7	1.4

Table II

Corporations with Net Income

MUTUAL PROPERTY AND CASUALTY COMPANIES (FORM 1120-PC)

MONEY AMOUNTS AND SIZE OF ASSETS IN THOUSANDS OF DOLLARS

Item Description for Accounting Period 7/02 Through 6/03	Total	Zero Assets	Under 500	500 to 1,000	1,000 to 5,000	5,000 to 10,000	10,000 to 25,000	25,000 to 50,000	50,000 to 100,000	100,000 to 250,000	250,000 to 500,000	500,000 to 2,500,000	2,500,000 and over
Number of Enterprises 1	1056	16	63	95	419	110	113	61	40	59	19	45	15
Revenues ($ in Thousands)													
Net Sales 2	92573714	5536	47012	33158	333088	403741	1062256	1144634	1116012	6237439	5387894	27355658	49447287
Interest 3	6083868	661	527	1631	27399	17364	51810	70716	79796	304033	220014	1428567	3881349
Rents 4	237943	0	0	83	3007	725	1662	1842	1947	11393	5034	52078	160171
Royalties 5	196	0	0	0	0	0	0	0	0	0	0	196	0
Other Portfolio Income 6	2539154	0	0	50	7124	5776	14232	18818	36905	100775	38535	546406	1770531
Other Receipts 7	83712553	4875	46485	31394	295558	379876	994552	1053258	997364	5821238	5124311	25328411	43635236
Total Receipts 8	92573714	5536	47012	33158	333088	403741	1062256	1144634	1116012	6237439	5387894	27355658	49447287
Average Total Receipts 9	87665	346	746	349	795	3670	9400	18764	27900	105719	283573	607904	3296486
Operating Costs/Operating Income (%)													
Cost of Operations 10	57.6	44.7	82.5	52.3	35.4	57.0	55.3	52.9	49.2	59.4	71.1	60.6	54.7
Salaries and Wages 11	14.5	•	•	8.7	13.5	8.1	10.8	14.5	17.5	17.7	12.8	15.6	13.7
Taxes Paid 12	3.0	3.1	0.0	1.0	2.4	1.4	2.0	2.5	2.8	2.4	1.9	2.7	3.5
Interest Paid 13	0.5	0.6	•	0.5	0.1	0.2	0.2	0.2	0.0	0.1	0.0	0.3	0.7
Depreciation 14	0.9	•	0.3	0.3	0.7	0.2	0.4	0.5	0.7	0.8	0.6	1.0	0.9
Amortization and Depletion 15	0.2	•	•	0.0	0.0	0.0	0.0	0.1	0.0	0.1	0.1	0.1	0.3
Pensions and Other Deferred Comp. 16	0.4	•	•	0.1	0.1	0.3	0.2	0.2	0.2	0.2	0.7	0.5	0.4
Employee Benefits 17	1.4	•	0.8	1.1	0.8	0.6	1.3	1.3	1.7	1.3	0.9	1.8	1.2
Advertising 18	0.4	•	0.3	0.4	0.1	0.1	0.2	0.3	0.3	0.2	0.2	0.3	0.5
Other Expenses 19	15.0	25.2	2.0	22.2	21.9	13.7	21.0	14.7	17.0	10.8	5.7	11.0	18.6
Officers' Compensation 20	0.3	•	•	1.4	2.1	0.3	0.7	1.5	0.7	0.7	0.6	0.3	0.2
Operating Margin 21	5.8	26.3	15.5	12.5	22.3	17.9	8.5	11.4	10.1	6.3	5.5	5.8	5.2
Operating Margin Before Officers' Comp. 22	6.1	26.3	15.5	13.9	24.4	18.2	9.2	12.8	10.8	7.0	6.0	6.1	5.4

Selected Average Balance Sheet ($ in Thousands)

Net Receivables 23	16588	0	27	11	79	691	1332	3550	5203	17777	34317	98308	713650
Inventories 24	•	•	•	•	•	•	•	•	•	•	•	•	•
Net Property, Plant and Equipment 25	2791	0	0	21	54	46	316	476	851	4070	7669	19597	103373
Total Assets 26	193817	0	154	660	2212	7040	15831	36152	70070	162301	336902	1113403	8668027
Notes and Loans Payable 27	1988	0	0	22	134	424	147	189	154	1682	1548	8841	95549
All Other Liabilities 28	124306	0	867	432	842	3650	10346	22722	46117	102225	200505	701658	5640170
Net Worth 29	67523	0	-713	206	1237	2965	5338	13241	23800	58394	134849	402904	2932309

Selected Financial Ratios (Times to 1)

Current Ratio 30	0.9	•	0.2	1.1	2.2	1.2	1.1	0.9	1.0	1.0	0.9	0.9	0.9
Quick Ratio 31	0.8	•	0.1	1.0	2.0	1.1	0.9	0.7	0.8	0.9	0.8	0.7	0.8
Net Sales to Working Capital 32	•	•	•	9.6	1.0	4.7	18.8	•	84.9	52.7	•	•	•
Coverage Ratio 33	10.7	42.7	•	25.7	166.5	94.4	37.1	54.7	438.1	48.3	438.8	15.3	6.6
Total Asset Turnover 34	0.5	•	4.8	0.5	0.4	0.5	0.6	0.5	0.4	0.7	0.8	0.5	0.4
Inventory Turnover 35	•	•	•	•	•	•	•	•	•	•	•	•	•
Receivables Turnover 36	•	•	•	•	•	•	•	•	•	•	•	•	•
Total Liabilities to Net Worth 37	1.9	•	•	2.2	0.8	1.4	2.0	1.7	1.9	1.8	1.5	1.8	2.0
Current Assets to Working Capital 38	•	•	•	11.3	1.8	6.1	20.1	•	130.0	47.5	•	•	•
Current Liabilities to Working Capital 39	•	•	•	10.3	0.8	5.1	19.1	•	129.0	46.5	•	•	•
Working Capital to Net Sales 40	•	•	•	0.1	1.0	0.2	0.1	•	0.0	0.0	•	•	•
Inventory to Working Capital 41	•	•	•	•	•	•	•	•	•	•	•	•	•
Total Receipts to Cash Flow 42	5.3	1.9	5.7	2.9	2.4	3.2	3.5	4.1	4.0	6.4	9.5	6.6	4.7
Cost of Goods to Cash Flow 43	3.1	0.9	4.7	1.5	0.8	1.8	1.9	2.1	2.0	3.8	6.8	4.0	2.6
Cash Flow to Total Debt 44	0.1	•	0.2	0.3	0.3	0.3	0.3	0.2	0.2	0.2	0.1	•	0.1

Selected Financial Factors (in Percentages)

Debt Ratio 45	65.2	•	562.8	68.8	44.1	57.9	66.3	63.4	66.0	64.0	60.0	63.8	66.2
Return on Total Assets 46	2.4	•	74.9	6.9	7.7	9.0	4.9	5.7	3.4	3.9	4.3	2.9	1.8
Return on Equity Before Income Taxes 47	6.1	•	•	21.2	13.7	21.1	14.0	15.2	9.9	10.6	10.6	7.4	4.4
Return on Equity After Income Taxes 48	4.3	•	•	17.4	12.4	18.1	11.0	12.0	6.9	7.6	7.4	5.1	3.0
Profit Margin (Before Income Tax) 49	4.7	26.3	15.5	12.5	21.4	17.1	7.9	10.7	8.5	5.8	5.1	4.9	3.9
Profit Margin (After Income Tax) 50	3.3	19.6	15.4	10.2	19.4	14.6	6.3	8.5	5.9	4.2	3.5	3.4	2.6

Table I
Corporations with and without Net Income

STOCK PROPERTY AND CASUALTY COMPANIES (FORM 1120-PC)

MONEY AMOUNTS AND SIZE OF ASSETS IN THOUSANDS OF DOLLARS

Item Description for Accounting Period 7/02 Through 6/03	Total	Zero Assets	Under 500	500 to 1,000	1,000 to 5,000	5,000 to 10,000	10,000 to 25,000	25,000 to 50,000	50,000 to 100,000	100,000 to 250,000	250,000 to 500,000	500,000 to 2,500,000	2,500,000 and over
Number of Enterprises **1**	2580	57	841	200	572	190	215	130	83	98	46	84	65
Revenues ($ in Thousands)													
Net Sales **2**	504420442	5066073	73329	27223	465157	809325	3584549	4901221	6453704	12728494	10540863	76744185	383026317
Interest **3**	29803646	115532	3441	2370	33353	37818	79129	109589	134489	411342	415463	2767401	25693719
Rents **4**	1606539	88	0	0	861	53	2149	2964	3967	12554	8508	74953	1500441
Royalties **5**	832700	0	0	0	0	0	44	1398	0	1897	16	4752	824593
Other Portfolio Income **6**	11471604	38808	556	108	4794	6022	22238	33695	44717	163643	132411	1137861	9886749
Other Receipts **7**	460705953	4911645	69332	24745	426149	765432	3480989	4753575	6270531	12139058	9984465	72759218	345120815
Total Receipts **8**	504420442	5066073	73329	27223	465157	809325	3584549	4901221	6453704	12728494	10540863	76744185	383026317
Average Total Receipts **9**	195512	88878	87	136	813	4260	16672	37702	77755	129883	229149	913621	5892713
Operating Costs/Operating Income (%)													
Cost of Operations **10**	58.7	80.4	84.5	74.6	48.0	68.1	66.3	66.4	73.4	60.0	68.6	68.3	55.7
Salaries and Wages **11**	12.9	4.4	26.6	15.6	11.1	18.9	11.5	14.3	9.4	11.4	14.5	12.9	13.1
Taxes Paid **12**	2.1	1.0	1.3	0.0	1.0	1.7	1.9	1.7	1.8	2.0	2.0	1.7	2.2
Interest Paid **13**	1.5	0.4	1.6	•	0.1	0.3	0.2	0.2	0.2	0.3	0.5	0.4	1.8
Depreciation **14**	0.9	0.5	•	•	0.2	0.3	0.5	0.5	0.4	0.7	1.0	0.8	1.0
Amortization and Depletion **15**	0.3	0.1	0.2	0.1	0.1	0.3	0.1	0.1	0.4	0.1	0.3	0.2	0.3
Pensions and Other Deferred Comp. **16**	0.5	0.2	•	•	0.1	0.0	0.1	0.1	0.1	0.2	0.3	0.5	0.5
Employee Benefits **17**	0.9	0.2	•	•	0.1	0.5	0.5	0.6	0.5	0.9	0.8	0.8	1.0
Advertising **18**	0.4	0.1	•	•	0.0	0.7	0.1	0.3	0.4	0.4	0.3	0.3	0.4
Other Expenses **19**	18.0	10.4	9.8	21.0	11.6	12.2	18.4	14.6	11.1	21.0	10.0	11.5	19.7
Officers' Compensation **20**	0.3	0.7	0.9	•	0.7	1.6	0.9	0.8	0.4	1.0	0.5	0.4	0.2
Operating Margin **21**	3.6	1.6	•	•	26.9	•	•	0.3	1.8	2.0	1.2	2.4	4.0
Operating Margin Before Officers' Comp. **22**	3.9	2.3	•	•	27.6	•	0.4	1.1	2.2	3.1	1.7	2.8	4.3

Selected Average Balance Sheet ($ in Thousands)

Net Receivables 23	31808	0	3	0	40	360	1424	3013	8464	12607	37773	98808	1066126
Inventories 24	•	•	•	•	•	•	•	•	•	•	•	•	•
Net Property, Plant and Equipment 25	7187	•	0	0	24	66	204	651	1165	3741	6064	20959	244373
Total Assets 26	523372	214	699	2368	7358	16256	35481	73554	156599	373363	•	1230091	1841944
Notes and Loans Payable 27	37470	0	1	0	56	268	684	923	3763	6224	18790	72129	1361177
All Other Liabilities 28	287173	0	403	694	2034	5351	11838	26420	48450	109261	229326	803618	9838248
Net Worth 29	198730	0	-189	6	278	1739	3734	8138	21342	41114	125246	354344	7218519

Selected Financial Ratios (Times to 1)

Current Ratio 30	0.9	•	0.6	0.7	0.8	1.0	0.9	1.0	1.0	0.9	0.9	0.8	0.9
Quick Ratio 31	0.7	•	0.5	0.6	0.6	0.8	0.7	0.8	0.8	0.7	0.8	0.7	0.8
Net Sales to Working Capital 32	•	•	•	•	•	548.8	•	•	•	•	•	•	•
Coverage Ratio 33	2.7	4.2	•	•	281.2	1.4	•	•	10.1	6.6	2.3	5.3	2.6
Total Asset Turnover 34	0.4	•	0.4	0.2	0.3	0.6	1.0	1.1	1.1	0.8	0.6	0.7	0.3
Inventory Turnover 35	•	•	•	•	•	•	•	•	•	•	•	•	•
Receivables Turnover 36	•	•	•	•	•	•	•	•	•	•	•	•	•
Total Liabilities to Net Worth 37	1.6	•	•	119.8	7.5	3.2	3.4	3.4	2.4	2.8	2.0	2.5	1.6
Current Assets to Working Capital 38	•	•	•	•	•	•	•	322.7	•	•	•	•	•
Current Liabilities to Working Capital 39	•	•	•	•	•	•	•	321.7	•	•	•	•	•
Working Capital to Net Sales 40	•	•	•	•	•	•	•	0.0	•	•	•	•	•
Inventory to Working Capital 41	•	•	•	•	•	•	•	0.1	•	•	•	•	•
Total Receipts to Cash Flow 42	5.1	8.9	10.4	•	2.6	15.5	6.0	7.3	8.2	4.7	10.6	8.1	4.6
Cost of Goods to Cash Flow 43	3.0	7.2	7.8	•	1.3	10.5	3.9	4.8	6.0	2.8	7.3	5.6	2.5
Cash Flow to Total Debt 44	0.1	•	0.0	0.0	0.1	0.0	0.2	0.2	0.2	0.2	0.1	0.1	0.1

Selected Financial Factors (in Percentages)

Debt Ratio 45	62.0	•	188.3	99.2	88.2	76.4	77.0	77.1	71.0	73.7	66.5	71.2	60.8
Return on Total Assets 46	1.5	•	•	•	9.1	•	•	0.3	1.8	1.6	0.7	1.7	1.5
Return on Equity Before Income Taxes 47	2.5	•	11.6	•	77.4	•	•	0.4	5.4	5.2	1.2	4.7	2.3
Return on Equity After Income Taxes 48	1.0	•	12.2	•	69.9	•	•	1.3	1.3	1.0	•	1.6	1.0
Profit Margin (Before Income Tax) 49	2.5	1.3	•	•	26.5	•	•	0.1	1.5	1.6	0.7	1.8	2.8
Profit Margin (After Income Tax) 50	1.1	0.5	•	•	23.9	•	•	0.4	•	0.3	•	0.6	1.3

Table II

Corporations with Net Income

STOCK PROPERTY AND CASUALTY COMPANIES (FORM 1120-PC)

MONEY AMOUNTS AND SIZE OF ASSETS IN THOUSANDS OF DOLLARS

Item Description for Accounting Period 7/02 Through 6/03	Total	Zero Assets	Under 500	500 to 1,000	1,000 to 5,000	5,000 to 10,000	10,000 to 25,000	25,000 to 50,000	50,000 to 100,000	100,000 to 250,000	250,000 to 500,000	500,000 to 2,500,000	2,500,000 and over
Number of Enterprises **1**	1810	28	546	147	464	122	148	93	54	70	31	61	45
Revenues ($ in Thousands)													
Net Sales **2**	410438521	3485994	22386	11030	315310	468074	2253225	3517375	4091575	9954392	7538701	67223324	311557134
Interest **3**	22605091	96181	2384	2059	28546	24931	55435	77511	87091	308534	263604	2099458	19559356
Rents **4**	1333561	88	0	0	386	53	1898	2674	3096	8973	7595	47586	1261211
Royalties **5**	831252	0	0	0	0	0	0	0	0	1897	10	4752	824593
Other Portfolio Income **6**	7785559	20627	278	15	3915	2769	17580	27451	28713	114069	95179	747467	6727496
Other Receipts **7**	377883058	3369098	19724	8956	282463	440321	2178312	3409739	3972675	9520919	7172313	64324061	283184478
Total Receipts **8**	410438521	3485994	22386	11030	315310	468074	2253225	3517375	4091575	9954392	7538701	67223324	311557134
Average Total Receipts **9**	226762	124500	41	75	680	3837	15224	37821	75770	142206	243184	1102022	6923492
Operating Costs/Operating Income (%)													
Cost of Operations **10**	57.5	75.9	37.5	56.0	28.0	50.4	56.3	59.7	68.5	63.3	64.6	68.7	54.4
Salaries and Wages **11**	12.2	5.3	19.7	4.0	8.9	21.6	11.5	15.7	9.8	12.3	15.7	12.4	12.1
Taxes Paid **12**	1.8	0.9	0.5	•	1.0	1.9	2.3	1.7	2.0	2.0	2.1	1.5	1.9
Interest Paid **13**	1.3	0.3	0.0	•	0.0	0.2	0.2	0.2	0.2	0.2	0.5	0.4	1.6
Depreciation **14**	1.0	0.6	•	•	0.1	0.1	0.4	0.5	0.4	0.7	1.2	0.7	1.0
Amortization and Depletion **15**	0.3	0.1	0.3	•	0.1	0.1	0.1	0.1	0.1	0.1	0.1	0.2	0.3
Pensions and Other Deferred Comp. **16**	0.5	0.3	•	•	0.1	•	0.1	0.1	0.1	0.2	0.1	0.3	0.6
Employee Benefits **17**	0.9	0.3	•	•	0.2	0.4	0.4	0.7	0.6	0.9	0.6	0.7	1.0
Advertising **18**	0.4	0.2	•	•	0.0	0.7	0.2	0.3	0.6	0.4	0.3	0.3	0.5
Other Expenses **19**	17.4	11.2	3.0	19.2	6.6	11.8	19.7	13.4	10.8	13.0	8.8	9.9	19.5
Officers' Compensation **20**	0.3	0.9	•	•	1.0	1.7	1.0	0.8	0.6	0.5	0.5	0.4	0.2
Operating Margin **21**	6.5	3.9	38.9	20.9	54.0	11.1	8.0	7.0	6.4	6.4	5.4	4.5	6.9
Operating Margin Before Officers' Comp. **22**	6.7	4.9	38.9	20.9	55.0	12.8	8.9	7.7	6.9	6.9	5.9	4.9	7.1

Selected Average Balance Sheet ($ in Thousands)

Net Receivables 23	27944	•	•	0	5	0	24	414	1509	3145	9031	13775	38881	98605	918357
Inventories 24	•	•	•	•	•	•	•	•	•	•	•	•	•	•	•
Net Property, Plant and Equipment 25	8619	•	•	0	0	0	6	84	171	589	1195	4303	7504	23519	299436
Total Assets 26	530510	•	•	0	228	689	2268	7360	16268	35864	71521	159162	373213	1223545	18913205
Notes and Loans Payable 27	36632	•	•	0	0	0	22	48	661	518	3665	6205	16955	61948	1360108
All Other Liabilities 28	277787	•	•	0	222	735	1683	4443	10355	24705	42535	104790	216392	695238	9748069
Net Worth 29	216091	•	•	0	7	-46	563	2869	5252	10642	25321	48167	139865	466360	7805028

Selected Financial Ratios (Times to 1)

Current Ratio 30	0.9	•	0.7	0.6	0.9	1.2	1.1	1.1	1.2	1.0	1.0	0.9	0.9
Quick Ratio 31	0.8	•	0.6	0.5	0.8	1.0	0.9	1.0	1.0	0.8	0.8	0.7	0.8
Net Sales to Working Capital 32	•	•	•	•	4.1	16.5	13.8	10.8	•	•	•	•	•
Coverage Ratio 33	5.3	14.1	781.4	3373.0	65.4	39.5	42.5	41.6	27.6	10.4	11.7	4.7	•
Total Asset Turnover 34	0.4	•	0.2	0.1	0.3	0.5	0.9	1.1	1.1	0.9	0.7	0.9	0.4
Inventory Turnover 35	•	•	•	•	•	•	•	•	•	•	•	•	•
Receivables Turnover 36	•	•	•	•	•	•	•	•	•	•	•	•	•
Total Liabilities to Net Worth 37	1.5	•	33.8	•	3.0	1.6	2.1	2.4	1.8	2.3	1.7	1.6	1.4
Current Assets to Working Capital 38	•	•	•	•	5.3	11.3	8.0	6.9	•	•	•	•	•
Current Liabilities to Working Capital 39	•	•	•	•	4.3	10.3	7.0	5.9	•	•	•	•	•
Working Capital to Net Sales 40	•	•	•	•	0.2	0.1	0.1	0.1	•	•	•	•	•
Inventory to Working Capital 41	•	•	•	•	•	0.0	0.0	0.0	•	•	•	•	•
Total Receipts to Cash Flow 42	4.5	6.9	2.4	1.7	2.5	4.6	3.7	5.2	6.1	5.6	7.9	7.6	4.0
Cost of Goods to Cash Flow 43	2.6	5.3	0.9	0.5	1.4	2.3	2.1	3.1	4.2	3.5	5.1	5.2	2.2
Cash Flow to Total Debt 44	0.2	0.1	0.1	0.0	0.2	0.2	0.4	0.3	0.3	0.2	0.1	0.2	0.2

Selected Financial Factors (in Percentages)

Debt Ratio 45	59.3	•	97.1	106.7	75.2	61.0	67.7	70.3	64.6	69.7	62.5	61.9	58.7
Return on Total Assets 46	3.0	•	6.9	2.3	16.0	5.7	7.5	7.2	6.6	5.6	3.5	4.0	2.7
Return on Equity Before Income Taxes 47	5.9	•	239.1	•	64.5	14.5	22.5	23.8	18.2	17.7	8.4	9.7	5.2
Return on Equity After Income Taxes 48	4.1	•	210.6	•	59.9	10.9	17.8	17.7	13.0	12.7	5.9	6.5	3.6
Profit Margin (Before Income Tax) 49	5.6	3.5	38.3	20.9	53.5	10.8	7.8	6.7	6.1	6.0	4.8	4.1	5.9
Profit Margin (After Income Tax) 50	3.9	2.4	33.8	17.9	49.7	8.1	6.1	5.0	4.3	4.8	3.4	2.7	4.0

Table I

Corporations with and without Net Income

INSURANCE AGENCIES AND BROKERAGES

MONEY AMOUNTS AND SIZE OF ASSETS IN THOUSANDS OF DOLLARS

Item Description for Accounting Period 7/02 Through 6/03		Total	Zero Assets	Under 500	500 to 1,000	1,000 to 5,000	5,000 to 10,000	10,000 to 25,000	25,000 to 50,000	50,000 to 100,000	100,000 to 250,000	250,000 to 500,000	500,000 to 2,500,000	2,500,000 and over
Number of Enterprises	1	81779	10193	62373	4780	3615	412	251	80	34	20	9	5	6
Revenues ($ in Thousands)														
Net Sales	2	87544035	1588231	18969417	5178296	10409458	3596071	4029658	3001187	2095161	1761393	967924	3229480	32717758
Interest	3	720863	3504	18677	19724	34653	18500	22326	19604	9513	24467	9547	71095	469253
Rents	4	73213	4815	18616	615	19667	11689	3178	1972	875	8	249	96	11433
Royalties	5	5140	0	0	4560	0	1	143	0	75	0	0	41	321
Other Portfolio Income	6	568842	66557	99737	28380	16856	7286	8819	6206	2940	30274	8466	56043	237263
Other Receipts	7	86175977	1513345	18832387	5125017	10338282	3558595	3995192	2973405	2081758	1706644	949662	3102205	31999488
Total Receipts	8	87544035	1588231	18969417	5178296	10409458	3596071	4029658	3001187	2095161	1761393	967924	3229480	32717758
Average Total Receipts	9	1070	156	304	1083	2880	8728	16054	37515	61622	88070	107547	645896	5452960
Operating Costs/Operating Income (%)														
Cost of Operations	10	27.0	0.7	12.2	16.9	13.3	16.6	21.0	21.7	23.6	4.4	15.4	0.7	49.5
Salaries and Wages	11	22.5	28.8	23.4	20.8	26.0	31.3	28.4	23.0	36.6	23.9	33.2	29.7	17.2
Taxes Paid	12	2.5	3.5	3.1	3.1	2.8	3.0	2.5	2.0	2.1	2.3	3.3	3.7	1.8
Interest Paid	13	1.4	0.8	0.6	1.4	0.7	1.0	0.7	0.6	0.9	1.1	3.6	2.8	2.0
Depreciation	14	1.4	1.5	1.4	1.4	1.2	1.5	1.6	1.4	1.2	1.4	2.1	2.0	1.2
Amortization and Depletion	15	0.7	0.3	0.4	1.1	0.6	0.7	0.6	0.6	0.3	1.1	1.0	2.4	0.8
Pensions and Other Deferred Comp.	16	1.2	1.2	1.7	0.9	1.6	1.1	1.2	0.7	0.8	0.8	0.5	1.3	1.0
Employee Benefits	17	1.9	2.5	1.5	2.2	1.6	1.7	1.8	6.9	1.4	1.5	2.1	2.1	1.8
Advertising	18	0.9	1.8	1.7	1.0	0.8	1.1	0.8	0.5	0.3	0.5	1.6	2.3	0.3
Other Expenses	19	23.3	36.5	26.5	26.2	27.1	24.5	26.9	32.6	22.3	52.0	23.6	31.8	15.3
Officers' Compensation	20	9.2	13.7	16.6	15.4	13.8	10.1	8.8	5.5	4.7	5.9	5.0	6.5	3.5
Operating Margin	21	8.0	8.7	10.9	9.5	10.5	7.5	5.7	4.5	6.0	5.0	8.6	14.7	5.5
Operating Margin Before Officers' Comp.	22	17.2	22.4	27.5	24.9	24.3	17.6	14.5	10.0	10.7	10.9	13.6	21.2	9.0

Selected Average Balance Sheet ($ in Thousands)

Net Receivables 23	279	0	6	121	472	2150	4500	11022	21834	34686	103253	286159	2239924
Inventories 24	•	•	•	•	•	•	•	•	•	•	•	•	•
Net Property, Plant and Equipment 25	61	•	15	74	182	665	850	2314	3174	4200	11568	73975	280382
Total Assets 26	1271	0	78	716	2027	7001	15183	35289	68982	145118	365988	1130575	10772201
Notes and Loans Payable 27	159	0	30	238	391	1355	2152	4557	9736	9994	90079	182542	812428
All Other Liabilities 28	603	0	30	250	1198	4431	10450	23396	47437	107387	176444	490776	4629450
Net Worth 29	509	0	18	228	438	1215	2582	7336	11809	27737	99465	457258	5330322

Selected Financial Ratios (Times to 1)

Current Ratio 30	1.1	•	1.0	1.4	1.2	1.1	1.0	1.2	1.1	0.9	1.0	0.9	1.0
Quick Ratio 31	0.9	•	0.9	1.1	1.0	1.0	0.9	1.0	0.9	0.7	0.7	0.8	0.9
Net Sales to Working Capital 32	38.1	•	268.8	10.9	13.3	16.1	35.3	11.1	17.0	•	2533.8	•	46.5
Coverage Ratio 33	7.3	11.3	18.1	7.7	15.3	8.7	8.6	8.1	7.9	5.4	3.3	6.2	4.6
Total Asset Turnover 34	0.8	•	3.9	1.5	1.4	1.2	1.1	1.1	0.9	0.6	0.3	0.6	0.5
Inventory Turnover 35	•	•	•	•	•	•	•	•	•	•	•	•	•
Receivables Turnover 36	•	•	•	•	•	•	•	•	•	•	•	•	•
Total Liabilities to Net Worth 37	1.5	•	3.4	2.1	3.6	4.8	4.9	3.8	4.8	2.7	2.7	1.5	1.0
Current Assets to Working Capital 38	19.0	•	31.1	3.8	6.6	9.4	24.0	7.3	13.6	•	5347.4	•	28.1
Current Liabilities to Working Capital 39	18.0	•	30.1	2.8	5.6	8.4	23.0	6.3	12.6	•	5346.4	•	27.1
Working Capital to Net Sales 40	0.0	•	0.0	0.1	0.1	0.1	0.0	0.1	0.1	0.0	0.0	•	0.0
Inventory to Working Capital 41	0.0	•	•	0.0	0.0	0.0	0.0	0.0	0.0	0.1	0.1	•	0.1
Total Receipts to Cash Flow 42	3.7	2.8	3.1	3.3	3.0	3.6	3.4	2.9	3.9	3.6	3.6	2.5	5.7
Cost of Goods to Cash Flow 43	1.0	0.0	0.4	0.6	0.4	0.6	0.7	0.6	0.9	0.5	0.5	0.0	2.8
Cash Flow to Total Debt 44	0.4	•	1.6	0.7	0.6	0.4	0.4	0.5	0.3	0.4	0.1	0.4	0.2

Selected Financial Factors (in Percentages)

Debt Ratio 45	59.9	•	77.1	68.2	78.4	82.7	83.0	79.2	82.9	80.9	72.8	59.6	50.5
Return on Total Assets 46	8.4	•	45.0	16.2	16.0	10.4	6.7	5.4	6.1	3.7	3.5	10.0	4.7
Return on Equity Before Income Taxes 47	18.2	•	185.6	44.4	69.1	53.1	35.1	22.8	31.2	15.6	8.9	20.7	7.5
Return on Equity After Income Taxes 48	15.0	•	181.4	42.2	65.7	47.1	29.1	16.6	26.1	10.6	6.1	13.6	4.9
Profit Margin (Before Income Tax) 49	8.6	8.7	10.9	9.3	10.5	7.4	5.6	4.5	6.0	4.9	8.3	14.7	7.3
Profit Margin (After Income Tax) 50	7.1	6.6	10.6	8.9	10.0	6.6	4.7	3.3	5.0	3.3	5.6	9.6	4.8

Table II

Corporations with Net Income

INSURANCE AGENCIES AND BROKERAGES

MONEY AMOUNTS AND SIZE OF ASSETS IN THOUSANDS OF DOLLARS

Item Description for Accounting Period 7/02 Through 6/03	Total	Zero Assets	Under 500	500 to 1,000	1,000 to 5,000	5,000 to 10,000	10,000 to 25,000	25,000 to 50,000	50,000 to 100,000	100,000 to 250,000	250,000 to 500,000	500,000 to 2,500,000	2,500,000 and over
Number of Enterprises **1**	59706	5871	45658	4239	3286	326	204	62	25	15	0	0	6
Revenues ($ in Thousands)													
Net Sales **2**	80155756	1333703	15103531	4827360	9707158	3111530	3522058	2320549	1798674	1529220	0	0	32717758
Interest **3**	685059	3205	15101	13564	33816	13727	13048	15673	6562	20529	0	0	469253
Rents **4**	54032	4815	7330	455	19139	5498	2307	1972	875	8	0	0	11433
Royalties **5**	5140	0	0	4560	0	1	143	0	75	0	0	0	321
Other Portfolio Income **6**	514281	57572	67880	18252	16165	7163	7837	5038	2462	30139	0	0	237263
Other Receipts **7**	78897244	1268111	15013220	4790529	9638038	3085141	3498723	2297866	1788700	1478544	0	0	31999488
Total Receipts **8**	80155756	1333703	15103531	4827360	9707158	3111530	3522058	2320549	1798674	1529220	0	0	32717758
Average Total Receipts **9**	1343	227	331	1139	2954	9545	17265	37428	71947	101948		•	5452960
Operating Costs/Operating Income (%)													
Cost of Operations **10**	28.1	0.9	11.8	16.7	13.9	16.2	21.8	15.9	26.9	2.5	•	•	49.5
Salaries and Wages **11**	22.0	30.8	22.2	20.5	25.0	32.2	27.8	25.7	36.6	22.4	•	•	17.2
Taxes Paid **12**	2.4	3.3	2.8	3.1	2.8	3.1	2.5	2.1	1.8	2.5	•	•	1.8
Interest Paid **13**	1.4	0.4	0.5	1.3	0.7	0.6	0.6	0.6	0.6	1.1	•	•	2.0
Depreciation **14**	1.3	1.0	1.3	1.3	1.0	1.3	1.6	1.3	1.1	1.5	•	•	1.2
Amortization and Depletion **15**	0.7	0.3	0.3	1.1	0.5	0.7	0.4	0.6	0.2	1.0	•	•	0.8
Pensions and Other Deferred Comp. **16**	1.2	1.3	1.4	0.9	1.6	1.1	1.1	0.9	0.8	0.9	•	•	1.0
Employee Benefits **17**	1.7	2.5	1.3	2.2	1.6	1.8	1.8	1.5	1.3	1.5	•	•	1.8
Advertising **18**	0.8	1.4	1.8	1.1	0.7	0.7	0.8	0.5	0.3	0.5	•	•	0.3
Other Expenses **19**	21.9	30.0	24.6	24.8	25.7	21.3	24.2	36.5	18.3	54.4	•	•	15.3
Officers' Compensation **20**	8.8	11.1	16.1	15.7	14.3	10.2	8.9	6.4	4.1	4.6	•	•	3.5
Operating Margin **21**	9.7	17.2	15.8	11.3	12.2	10.8	8.6	8.1	7.9	7.0	•	•	5.5
Operating Margin Before Officers' Comp. **22**	18.5	28.3	31.9	27.0	26.6	21.0	17.4	14.4	12.0	11.7	•	•	9.0

Selected Average Balance Sheet ($ in Thousands)

Net Receivables 23	364	0	•	6	131	462	2130	4446	11692	24692	41806	•	2239924
Inventories 24	•	•	•	•	•	•	•	•	•	•	•	•	•
Net Property, Plant and Equipment 25	74	0	•	15	72	174	640	872	2302	3748	5056	•	280382
Total Assets 26	1648	0	•	82	713	2050	7139	14849	35448	70218	153391	•	10772201
Notes and Loans Payable 27	186	0	•	22	241	341	1031	1843	4221	9621	12775	•	812428
All Other Liabilities 28	765	0	•	21	256	1224	4370	10338	24870	44919	108407	•	4629450
Net Worth 29	697	0	•	39	216	486	1737	2668	6358	15678	32209	•	5330322

Selected Financial Ratios (Times to 1)

Current Ratio 30	1.1	•	1.6	1.3	1.2	1.2	1.0	1.1	1.1	1.1	0.9	•	1.0
Quick Ratio 31	0.9	•	1.4	1.1	1.0	1.1	0.9	1.1	1.0	1.0	0.8	•	0.9
Net Sales to Working Capital 32	29.0	•	23.8	12.6	12.7	13.1	40.4	12.1	19.3	•			46.5
Coverage Ratio 33	8.7	41.9	•	29.8	9.7	18.0	18.6	15.5	13.4	14.6	7.1	•	4.6
Total Asset Turnover 34	0.8	•	4.1	1.6	1.4	1.2	1.3	1.2	1.0	0.7			0.5
Inventory Turnover 35	•	•	•	•	•	•	•	•	•	•	•	•	•
Receivables Turnover 36	•	•	•	•	•	•	•	•	•	•	•	•	•
Total Liabilities to Net Worth 37	1.4	•	1.1	3.2	2.3	3.1	4.6	4.6	3.5	3.8			1.0
Current Assets to Working Capital 38	14.6	•	2.8	6.3	4.2	7.2	25.8	8.3	3.5	13.1			28.1
Current Liabilities to Working Capital 39	13.6	•	1.8	3.2	5.3	24.8	7.3	12.1					27.1
Working Capital to Net Sales 40	0.0	•	0.0	0.1	0.1	0.1	0.0	0.0	0.1				0.0
Inventory to Working Capital 41	0.0	•	0.0	•	0.0	0.0	0.0	0.0					0.1
Total Receipts to Cash Flow 42	3.6	2.6	2.9	3.2	2.9	3.5	3.4	2.4	4.2	1.8			5.7
Cost of Goods to Cash Flow 43	1.0	0.0	0.3	0.5	0.4	0.6	0.7	0.4	1.1	0.0			2.8
Cash Flow to Total Debt 44	0.4	•	0.7	0.6	0.5	0.4	0.5	0.3	0.5				0.2

Selected Financial Factors (in Percentages)

Debt Ratio 45	57.7	•	51.7	69.8	76.3	75.7	82.0	82.1	77.7	79.0			50.5
Return on Total Assets 46	9.6	•	66.4	20.2	18.7	15.2	10.6	9.2	8.7	5.3			4.7
Return on Equity Before Income Taxes 47	20.1	•	133.0	59.8	74.3	59.0	55.3	47.3	36.4	21.8			7.5
Return on Equity After Income Taxes 48	17.0	•	130.5	57.2	71.0	53.7	48.8	38.2	31.3	16.1			4.9
Profit Margin (Before Income Tax) 49	10.5	17.2	15.8	11.3	12.2	10.7	8.5	8.0	7.9	6.9			7.3
Profit Margin (After Income Tax) 50	8.8	14.7	15.5	10.8	11.7	9.8	7.5	6.5	6.8	5.1			4.8

Table I

Corporations with and without Net Income

OTHER INSURANCE RELATED ACTIVITIES

MONEY AMOUNTS AND SIZE OF ASSETS IN THOUSANDS OF DOLLARS

Item Description for Accounting Period 7/02 Through 6/03	Total	Zero Assets	Under 500	500 to 1,000	1,000 to 5,000	5,000 to 10,000	10,000 to 25,000	25,000 to 50,000	50,000 to 100,000	100,000 to 250,000	250,000 to 500,000	500,000 to 2,500,000	2,500,000 and over
Number of Enterprises **1**	15150	2254	11021	880	634	152	102	40	27	22	7	7	3
Revenues ($ in Thousands)													
Net Sales **2**	41835282	493564	4540162	1801183	1976592	2317234	2180012	2459063	1763056	4985213	2084894	2502825	14731482
Interest **3**	875820	2738	7129	7572	21864	10244	22909	14387	30563	39681	49355	48732	620645
Rents **4**	90376	124	0	5036	4095	267	629	1433	4783	10006	0	1220	62782
Royalties **5**	31818	0	0	0	0	0	0	0	0	24727	7091	0	0
Other Portfolio Income **6**	151804	22621	186	28	2997	671	12590	2495	3123	11703	5721	19399	70272
Other Receipts **7**	40685464	468081	4532847	1788547	1947636	2306052	2143884	2440748	1724587	4899096	2022727	2433474	13977783
Total Receipts **8**	41835282	493564	4540162	1801183	1976592	2317234	2180012	2459063	1763056	4985213	2084894	2502825	14731482
Average Total Receipts **9**	2761	219	412	2047	3118	15245	21373	61477	65298	226601	347482	357546	4910494
Operating Costs/Operating Income (%)													
Cost of Operations **10**	34.8	6.5	4.5	6.0	1.5	8.5	17.5	42.3	18.6	26.4	38.7	19.2	65.3
Salaries and Wages **11**	16.3	16.3	34.7	23.5	21.1	19.9	20.6	15.6	15.6	12.1	26.1	23.6	7.0
Taxes Paid **12**	2.0	2.3	4.0	2.5	2.5	2.4	2.0	3.5	1.9	1.6	2.4	1.7	1.1
Interest Paid **13**	1.1	0.6	0.4	1.3	0.6	0.6	0.8	0.8	0.5	1.3	0.4	2.8	1.3
Depreciation **14**	1.2	0.6	0.8	1.6	1.5	1.5	1.2	1.1	1.4	0.9	1.6	2.3	0.9
Amortization and Depletion **15**	0.4	0.3	0.1	0.1	0.5	0.1	0.4	0.5	0.5	0.6	0.6	1.9	0.3
Pensions and Other Deferred Comp. **16**	0.9	0.1	2.5	2.1	0.6	0.2	0.4	0.2	0.7	0.5	1.1	0.7	0.6
Employee Benefits **17**	1.8	2.0	1.9	1.6	1.3	1.6	2.1	7.6	1.7	1.2	1.8	3.2	0.9
Advertising **18**	0.4	0.9	0.9	0.2	0.5	0.2	0.6	0.3	0.5	0.5	0.2	0.6	0.2
Other Expenses **19**	31.2	50.7	29.4	48.8	60.6	59.3	51.7	23.2	55.2	49.6	20.5	25.1	12.4
Officers' Compensation **20**	3.0	10.9	14.1	4.7	5.5	3.3	2.3	1.2	1.5	1.7	1.4	1.3	0.2
Operating Margin **21**	6.9	8.7	6.8	7.4	3.6	2.3	0.3	3.7	1.9	3.5	5.2	17.5	9.6
Operating Margin Before Officers' Comp. **22**	9.9	19.5	20.8	12.1	9.1	5.6	2.6	5.0	3.4	5.2	6.7	18.8	9.8

Selected Average Balance Sheet ($ in Thousands)

Net Receivables 23	786	0	6	189	643	1371	3669	9094	13507	35300	34666	162471	2611881
Inventories 24	•	•	•	•	•	•	•	•	•	•	•	•	•
Net Property, Plant and Equipment 25	127	0	12	165	216	1317	799	2045	3316	9323	16621	37728	162406
Total Assets 26	3323	83	809	2549	7688	16200	35850	67202	166766	345910	937599	•	9573762
Notes and Loans Payable 27	378	0	29	143	256	1386	2679	7096	7451	31464	25554	169014	709878
All Other Liabilities 28	1914	30	264	1979	4696	11081	18547	42550	131100	239841	434690	•	5358298
Net Worth 29	1031	25	402	314	1606	2440	10207	17202	4202	80514	333895	•	3505585

Selected Financial Ratios (Times to 1)

Current Ratio 30	1.2	1.4	•	2.5	1.3	1.0	1.2	1.1	1.3	0.9	1.2	1.3	1.2
Quick Ratio 31	1.0	1.1	•	2.2	1.1	0.9	1.0	0.9	1.0	0.8	0.4	1.2	1.1
Net Sales to Working Capital 32	11.2	25.6	•	5.7	7.1	•	10.9	27.3	6.8	•	14.0	6.8	7.2
Coverage Ratio 33	7.5	19.7	15.3	6.8	6.5	5.0	1.3	5.9	5.0	4.0	15.4	7.2	8.6
Total Asset Turnover 34	0.8	4.9	•	2.5	1.2	2.0	1.3	1.7	1.0	1.4	1.0	0.4	0.5
Inventory Turnover 35	•	•	•	•	•	•	•	•	•	•	•	•	•
Receivables Turnover 36	•	•	•	•	•	•	•	•	•	•	•	•	•
Total Liabilities to Net Worth 37	2.2	2.3	•	1.0	7.1	3.8	5.6	2.5	2.9	38.7	3.3	1.8	1.7
Current Assets to Working Capital 38	6.2	3.4	•	1.6	4.5	•	5.5	10.4	4.1	7.1	7.1	4.7	6.1
Current Liabilities to Working Capital 39	5.2	2.4	•	0.6	3.5	•	4.5	9.4	3.1	6.1	6.1	3.7	5.1
Working Capital to Net Sales 40	0.1	0.0	•	0.2	0.1	•	0.1	0.0	0.1	0.1	0.1	0.1	0.1
Inventory to Working Capital 41	0.0	•	•	•	0.0	•	0.0	•	0.0	•	•	0.0	0.0
Total Receipts to Cash Flow 42	2.8	3.3	2.0	1.9	1.7	1.7	2.1	4.1	1.8	2.0	4.5	2.6	4.8
Cost of Goods to Cash Flow 43	1.0	0.1	•	0.1	0.0	0.1	0.4	1.7	0.3	0.5	1.7	0.5	3.1
Cash Flow to Total Debt 44	0.4	•	•	2.6	0.8	1.5	0.8	0.6	0.7	0.7	0.3	0.2	0.2

Selected Financial Factors (in Percentages)

Debt Ratio 45	69.0	69.8	•	50.3	87.7	79.1	84.9	71.5	74.4	97.5	76.7	64.4	63.4
Return on Total Assets 46	6.6	35.2	•	22.1	5.1	5.6	1.4	7.7	2.3	6.9	5.4	7.6	5.6
Return on Equity Before Income Taxes 47	18.4	110.4	•	37.8	35.3	21.7	2.1	22.4	7.1	205.4	21.9	18.5	13.4
Return on Equity After Income Taxes 48	13.1	109.3	•	32.2	30.2	18.8	•	19.7	4.0	131.4	10.8	12.0	9.0
Profit Margin (Before Income Tax) 49	6.9	6.8	8.7	7.4	3.6	2.3	0.2	3.7	1.9	3.8	5.1	17.2	9.6
Profit Margin (After Income Tax) 50	4.9	6.7	7.1	6.3	3.0	2.0	•	3.3	1.0	2.4	2.5	11.2	6.4

Table II

Corporations with Net Income

OTHER INSURANCE RELATED ACTIVITIES

MONEY AMOUNTS AND SIZE OF ASSETS IN THOUSANDS OF DOLLARS

Item Description for Accounting Period 7/02 Through 6/03		Total	Zero Assets	Under 500	500 to 1,000	1,000 to 5,000	5,000 to 10,000	10,000 to 25,000	25,000 to 50,000	50,000 to 100,000	100,000 to 250,000	250,000 to 500,000	500,000 to 2,500,000	2,500,000 and over
Number of Enterprises	1	9990	1229	7354	678	0	112	60	27	18	16	0	0	0
Revenues ($ in Thousands)														
Net Sales	2	35155840	386713	3532763	1437488	0	1318213	1183860	1926044	1528225	3703546	0	0	0
Interest	3	661126	114	4700	2838	0	5876	11736	8407	15438	21909	0	0	0
Rents	4	84524	0	0	5036	0	267	628	1270	149	9075	0	0	0
Royalties	5	31818	0	0	0	0	0	0	0	0	24727	0	0	0
Other Portfolio Income	6	86101	11217	186	28	0	671	11206	2461	2926	9391	0	0	0
Other Receipts	7	34292271	375382	3527877	1429586	0	1311399	1160290	1913906	1509712	3638444	0	0	0
Total Receipts	8	35155840	386713	3532763	1437488	0	1318213	1183860	1926044	1528225	3703546	0	0	0
Average Total Receipts	9	3519	315	480	2120	·	11770	19731	71335	84901	231472	·	·	·
Operating Costs/Operating Income (%)														
Cost of Operations	10	39.8	5.6	5.6	·	·	14.9	23.9	52.7	21.5	30.6	·	·	·
Salaries and Wages	11	16.2	14.7	36.6	26.7	·	30.7	25.2	14.9	11.0	13.3	·	·	·
Taxes Paid	12	1.9	1.8	3.1	2.7	·	3.7	2.4	4.0	1.6	1.7	·	·	·
Interest Paid	13	0.7	0.7	0.2	1.6	·	0.5	0.8	0.6	0.3	0.7	·	·	·
Depreciation	14	1.1	0.3	0.7	1.4	·	2.3	1.3	1.0	1.1	1.0	·	·	·
Amortization and Depletion	15	0.4	0.3	0.1	0.1	·	0.2	0.4	0.5	0.3	0.6	·	·	·
Pensions and Other Deferred Comp.	16	0.9	0.1	2.7	2.4	·	0.3	0.6	0.2	0.7	0.2	·	·	·
Employee Benefits	17	1.4	0.0	1.4	1.6	·	2.6	2.7	1.5	1.3	1.4	·	·	·
Advertising	18	0.4	0.9	0.5	0.2	·	0.3	0.6	0.4	0.5	0.7	·	·	·
Other Expenses	19	24.1	37.5	22.4	46.8	·	31.8	29.6	16.3	54.6	42.0	·	·	·
Officers' Compensation	20	3.1	11.3	16.1	5.4	·	5.3	3.3	1.4	1.6	2.0	·	·	·
Operating Margin	21	9.9	26.8	10.6	11.0	·	7.3	9.1	6.4	5.5	5.7	·	·	·
Operating Margin Before Officers' Comp.	22	13.0	38.1	26.7	16.4	·	12.6	12.4	7.8	7.0	7.7	·	·	·

Selected Average Balance Sheet ($ in Thousands)

Net Receivables 23	1120	0	4	224	1433	3964	10162	14434	43197
Inventories 24	•	•	•	•	•	•	•	•	•
Net Property, Plant and Equipment 25	149	0	12	99	886	772	2339	2654	10636
Total Assets 26	3974	0	81	827	7694	15808	34711	66060	167615
Notes and Loans Payable 27	400	0	15	166	994	2706	8349	9152	30586
All Other Liabilities 28	2386	0	37	300	4171	10563	14247	37927	95491
Net Worth 29	1189	0	29	361	2529	2539	12115	18981	41538

Selected Financial Ratios (Times to 1)

Current Ratio 30	1.3	•	1.5	2.7	1.2	1.3	1.2	1.3	1.5
Quick Ratio 31	1.1	•	1.0	2.4	1.2	1.1	1.0	1.0	1.4
Net Sales to Working Capital 32	7.7	•	23.1	4.8	12.7	7.9	15.8	9.3	8.1
Coverage Ratio 33	14.4	39.6	43.9	7.9	16.6	12.0	11.2	16.8	9.6
Total Asset Turnover 34	0.9	•	5.9	2.6	1.5	1.2	2.1	1.3	1.4
Inventory Turnover 35	•	•	•	•	•	•	•	•	•
Receivables Turnover 36	•	•	•	•	•	•	•	•	•
Total Liabilities to Net Worth 37	2.3	•	1.8	1.3	2.0	5.2	1.9	2.5	3.0
Current Assets to Working Capital 38	4.4	•	3.1	1.6	5.1	4.4	5.1	4.9	2.9
Current Liabilities to Working Capital 39	3.4	•	2.1	0.6	4.1	3.4	4.1	3.9	1.9
Working Capital to Net Sales 40	0.1	•	0.0	0.2	0.1	0.1	0.1	0.1	0.1
Inventory to Working Capital 41	0.0	•	•	•	•	0.0	•	0.0	0.1
Total Receipts to Cash Flow 42	3.2	1.8	3.6	1.8	2.9	2.9	4.8	1.7	2.3
Cost of Goods to Cash Flow 43	1.3	0.1	0.2	•	0.4	0.7	2.5	0.4	0.7
Cash Flow to Total Debt 44	0.4	•	2.6	2.5	0.8	0.5	0.7	1.1	0.8

Selected Financial Factors (in Percentages)

Debt Ratio 45	70.1	•	63.8	56.3	67.1	83.9	65.1	71.3	75.2
Return on Total Assets 46	9.4	•	64.3	32.3	11.9	12.3	14.5	7.4	9.4
Return on Equity Before Income Taxes 47	29.3	•	173.6	64.6	34.1	70.2	37.9	24.3	34.1
Return on Equity After Income Taxes 48	22.2	•	172.1	56.4	31.6	59.1	34.4	20.1	23.8
Profit Margin (Before Income Tax) 49	9.9	26.8	10.6	11.0	7.3	9.0	6.4	5.4	6.1
Profit Margin (After Income Tax) 50	7.5	24.8	10.5	9.6	6.8	7.6	5.8	4.5	4.3

Table I
Corporations with and without Net Income

OPEN-END INVESTMENT FUNDS (FORM 1120-RIC)

MONEY AMOUNTS AND SIZE OF ASSETS IN THOUSANDS OF DOLLARS

Item Description for Accounting Period 7/02 Through 6/03	Total	Zero Assets	Under 500	500 to 1,000	1,000 to 5,000	5,000 to 10,000	10,000 to 25,000	25,000 to 50,000	50,000 to 100,000	100,000 to 250,000	250,000 to 500,000	500,000 to 2,500,000	2,500,000 and over
Number of Enterprises **1**	11067	696	93	132	610	499	1042	1098	1367	1963	1304	1718	544
Revenues ($ in Thousands)													
Net Sales **2**	191615634	1724318	871	3927	200088	77616	522296	1081381	2980143	9783942	14231319	51988137	109021596
Interest **3**	106034061	650687	674	1312	139512	16356	218270	456730	1229061	4274145	6149104	26417467	66480745
Rents **4**	0	0	0	0	0	0	0	0	0	0	0	0	0
Royalties **5**	0	0	0	0	0	0	0	0	0	0	0	0	0
Other Portfolio Income **6**	32193777	114714	2	160	14122	12984	96818	214731	800552	2791188	4191737	11995688	11961082
Other Receipts **7**	53387796	958917	195	2455	46454	48276	207208	409920	950530	2718609	3890478	13574982	30579769
Total Receipts **8**	191615634	1724318	871	3927	200088	77616	522296	1081381	2980143	9783942	14231319	51988137	109021596
Average Total Receipts **9**	17314	2477	9	30	328	156	501	985	2180	4984	10914	30261	200407
Operating Costs/Operating Income (%)													
Cost of Operations **10**	•	•	•	•	•	•	•	•	•	•	•	•	•
Salaries and Wages **11**	0.0	0.0	1.8	1.2	0.1	0.2	0.2	0.3	0.1	0.1	0.1	0.1	0.0
Taxes Paid **12**	0.2	0.3	0.2	1.6	0.2	1.0	0.7	0.7	0.6	0.4	0.3	0.2	0.1
Interest Paid **13**	0.2	0.1	•	0.2	0.0	0.0	0.2	1.0	0.6	0.7	0.3	0.2	0.1
Depreciation **14**	0.0	•	•	•	•	•	0.0	0.0	0.0	0.0	0.0	0.0	0.0
Amortization and Depletion **15**	0.0	0.0	3.0	2.0	0.2	0.3	0.2	0.1	0.0	0.0	0.0	0.0	0.0
Pensions and Other Deferred Comp. **16**	•	•	•	•	•	•	•	•	•	•	•	•	•
Employee Benefits **17**	•	•	•	•	•	•	•	•	•	•	•	•	•
Advertising **18**	0.0	•	•	•	•	•	•	•	0.0	0.0	0.0	•	•
Other Expenses **19**	26.2	17.5	27.4	57.3	45.4	67.1	48.4	43.3	34.9	30.8	27.8	27.2	24.7
Officers' Compensation **20**	0.0	0.0	•	•	•	•	0.2	0.1	0.0	0.0	0.0	0.0	0.0
Operating Margin **21**	73.3	82.2	67.5	37.6	54.1	31.3	50.1	54.5	63.8	68.0	71.5	72.2	75.0
Operating Margin Before Officers' Comp. **22**	73.3	82.2	67.5	37.6	54.1	31.3	50.3	54.6	63.8	68.0	71.5	72.3	75.0

Selected Average Balance Sheet ($ in Thousands)

Net Receivables 23	11820	0	3	15	61	96	344	578	1304	3235	7789	19994	141724
Inventories 24	•	•	•	•	•	•	•	•	•	•	•	•	•
Net Property, Plant and Equipment 25	2	0	0	0	0	0	0	3	0	0	0	9	4
Total Assets 26	649680	0	262	796	2602	7470	17135	36600	73021	163602	356261	1046228	8168322
Notes and Loans Payable 27	537	0	0	0	0	0	21	88	271	463	620	963	3833
All Other Liabilities 28	28253	0	53	40	140	191	666	1589	2928	7207	20363	58465	303121
Net Worth 29	620890	0	208	756	2462	7279	16447	34923	69822	155932	335279	986799	7861368

Selected Financial Ratios (Times to 1)

Current Ratio 30	4.5	•	1.5	4.6	1.8	3.3	3.1	4.1	4.9	5.4	4.1	4.2	4.6
Quick Ratio 31	4.1	•	1.0	3.5	1.5	2.9	2.7	3.8	4.5	5.0	3.9	3.9	4.2
Net Sales to Working Capital 32	0.2	•	0.3	0.2	3.0	0.4	0.4	0.2	0.2	0.2	0.2	0.2	0.2
Coverage Ratio 33	324.7	1431.6	•	165.1	12033.6	16120.0	173.3	36.4	71.8	65.0	157.8	208.2	831.2
Total Asset Turnover 34	0.0	•	0.0	0.0	0.1	0.0	0.0	0.0	0.0	0.0	0.0	0.0	0.0
Inventory Turnover 35	•	•	•	•	•	•	•	•	•	•	•	•	•
Receivables Turnover 36	•	•	•	•	•	•	•	•	•	•	•	•	•
Total Liabilities to Net Worth 37	0.0	•	0.3	0.1	0.0	0.0	0.0	0.0	0.0	0.0	0.1	0.1	0.0
Current Assets to Working Capital 38	1.3	•	3.0	1.3	2.2	1.4	1.5	1.3	1.3	1.2	1.3	1.3	1.3
Current Liabilities to Working Capital 39	0.3	•	2.0	0.3	1.2	0.4	0.5	0.3	0.3	0.2	0.3	0.3	0.3
Working Capital to Net Sales 40	5.7	•	2.9	4.8	0.3	2.8	2.6	4.4	5.3	6.4	6.0	6.2	5.4
Inventory to Working Capital 41	•	•	•	•	•	•	•	•	•	•	•	•	•
Total Receipts to Cash Flow 42	1.0	1.0	1.1	1.1	1.1	1.1	1.1	1.0	1.0	1.0	1.0	1.0	1.0
Cost of Goods to Cash Flow 43	•	•	•	•	•	•	•	•	•	•	•	•	•
Cash Flow to Total Debt 44	0.6	•	0.2	0.7	2.2	0.8	0.6	0.6	0.7	0.6	0.5	0.5	0.6

Selected Financial Factors (in Percentages)

Debt Ratio 45	4.4	•	20.5	5.0	5.4	2.6	4.0	4.6	4.4	4.7	5.9	5.7	3.8
Return on Total Assets 46	1.6	•	2.4	1.4	6.8	0.4	1.2	1.0	1.2	1.3	1.4	1.5	1.7
Return on Equity Before Income Taxes 47	1.7	•	3.0	1.5	7.2	0.4	1.3	1.0	1.2	1.4	1.5	1.6	1.7
Return on Equity After Income Taxes 48	1.7	•	3.0	1.5	7.2	0.4	1.3	1.0	1.2	1.4	1.5	1.6	1.7
Profit Margin (Before Income Tax) 49	60.1	78.2	67.5	37.6	54.1	20.8	41.6	37.1	39.3	42.7	45.5	51.6	68.2
Profit Margin (After Income Tax) 50	60.1	78.2	67.5	37.6	54.1	20.8	41.6	37.1	39.3	42.7	45.5	51.6	68.2

Table II
Corporations with Net Income

OPEN-END INVESTMENT FUNDS (FORM 1120-RIC)

MONEY AMOUNTS AND SIZE OF ASSETS IN THOUSANDS OF DOLLARS

Item Description for Accounting Period 7/02 Through 6/03	Total	Zero Assets	Under 500	500 to 1,000	1,000 to 5,000	5,000 to 10,000	10,000 to 25,000	25,000 to 50,000	50,000 to 100,000	100,000 to 250,000	250,000 to 500,000	500,000 to 2,500,000	2,500,000 and over
Number of Enterprises **1**	7488	391	78	78	289	274	623	681	908	1384	959	1363	460
Revenues ($ in Thousands)													
Net Sales **2**	176103152	1639444	853	3705	191768	57199	449734	869955	2469822	8407913	12185442	47240901	102586417
Interest **3**	10907033	645392	674	1274	138006	14295	209821	434990	1188934	4158279	5984795	26053282	66077290
Rents **4**	0	0	0	0	0	0	0	0	0	0	0	0	0
Royalties **5**	0	0	0	0	0	0	0	0	0	0	0	0	0
Other Portfolio Income **6**	23750291	95446	2	160	14122	10309	75853	128879	529707	1962640	2981963	9496541	8454670
Other Receipts **7**	47445828	898606	177	2271	39640	32595	164060	306086	751181	2286994	3218684	11691078	28054457
Total Receipts **8**	176103152	1639444	853	3705	191768	57199	449734	869955	2469822	8407913	12185442	47240901	102586417
Average Total Receipts **9**	23518	4193	11	48	664	209	722	1277	2720	6075	12706	34660	223014
Operating Costs/Operating Income (%)													
Cost of Operations **10**	•	•	•	•	•	•	•	•	•	•	•	•	•
Salaries and Wages **11**	0.0	0.0	•	1.3	0.1	•	0.1	0.1	0.1	0.1	0.0	0.1	0.0
Taxes Paid **12**	0.1	0.1	0.2	1.2	0.0	0.9	0.4	0.4	0.3	0.2	0.2	0.1	0.1
Interest Paid **13**	0.2	0.1	•	0.2	•	0.0	0.2	0.5	0.6	0.7	0.3	0.3	0.1
Depreciation **14**	0.0	•	•	•	•	•	0.0	0.0	0.0	0.0	0.0	0.0	0.0
Amortization and Depletion **15**	0.0	0.0	•	2.1	0.1	0.4	0.2	0.1	0.0	0.0	0.0	0.0	0.0
Pensions and Other Deferred Comp. **16**	•	•	•	•	•	•	•	•	•	•	•	•	•
Employee Benefits **17**	•	•	•	•	•	•	•	•	•	•	•	•	•
Advertising **18**	0.0	•	•	•	•	•	0.0	0.0	0.0	0.0	0.0	0.0	0.1
Other Expenses **19**	21.1	11.9	22.3	42.0	36.3	37.3	29.0	26.6	22.9	20.7	20.0	21.1	21.2
Officers' Compensation **20**	0.0	0.0	•	0.2	•	•	0.1	0.1	0.0	0.0	0.0	0.0	0.0
Operating Margin **21**	78.5	88.0	77.5	53.1	63.5	61.1	70.0	72.2	76.0	78.3	79.4	78.4	78.5
Operating Margin Before Officers' Comp. **22**	78.5	88.0	77.5	53.1	63.5	61.1	70.1	72.3	76.0	78.3	79.4	78.4	78.5

Selected Average Balance Sheet ($ in Thousands)

Net Receivables 23	15398	0	3	18	67	61	342	518	1355	3571	9056	20422	156529
Inventories 24	•	•	•	•	•	•	•	•	•	•	•	•	•
Net Property, Plant and Equipment 25	3	0	0	0	0	0	5	0	0	0	0	11	5
Total Assets 26	814277	0	288	821	2547	7463	17186	36769	73174	164040	356706	1060680	8646581
Notes and Loans Payable 27	731	0	0	0	0	0	32	64	328	533	790	1187	4353
All Other Liabilities 28	34203	0	60	30	174	118	646	1369	2712	7458	20784	60375	303646
Net Worth 29	779343	0	228	791	2373	7345	16508	35336	70135	156049	335132	999119	8338582

Selected Financial Ratios (Times to 1)

Current Ratio 30	4.5	•	1.5	4.0	2.2	5.1	3.2	4.3	5.2	5.4	4.0	4.3	4.6
Quick Ratio 31	4.2	•	0.9	3.8	2.1	4.5	2.9	3.9	4.8	5.1	3.8	4.0	4.3
Net Sales to Working Capital 32	0.2	•	0.4	0.5	3.3	0.4	0.5	0.3	0.2	0.2	0.2	0.2	0.2
Coverage Ratio 33	368.6	1693.3	219.7	•	121821.0	29484.0	350.3	119.5	101.6	90.3	192.9	225.8	859.2
Total Asset Turnover 34	0.0	•	0.0	0.1	0.3	0.0	0.0	0.0	0.0	0.0	0.0	0.0	0.0
Inventory Turnover 35	•	•	•	•	•	•	•	•	•	•	•	•	•
Receivables Turnover 36	•	•	•	•	•	•	•	•	•	•	•	•	•
Total Liabilities to Net Worth 37	0.0	•	0.3	0.0	0.1	0.0	0.0	0.0	0.1	0.1	0.1	0.1	0.0
Current Assets to Working Capital 38	1.3	•	3.1	1.3	1.8	1.2	1.5	1.3	1.2	1.2	1.3	1.3	1.3
Current Liabilities to Working Capital 39	0.3	•	2.1	0.3	0.8	0.2	0.5	0.3	0.2	0.2	0.3	0.3	0.3
Working Capital to Net Sales 40	5.1	•	2.6	1.8	0.3	2.3	1.8	3.3	4.3	5.5	5.2	5.8	4.9
Inventory to Working Capital 41	•	•	•	•	•	•	•	•	•	•	•	•	•
Total Receipts to Cash Flow 42	1.0	1.0	1.0	1.1	1.1	1.1	1.1	1.0	1.0	1.0	1.0	1.0	1.0
Cost of Goods to Cash Flow 43	•	•	•	•	•	•	•	•	•	•	•	•	•
Cash Flow to Total Debt 44	0.6	•	0.2	1.5	3.5	1.6	0.9	0.9	0.9	0.7	0.6	0.5	0.7

Selected Financial Factors (in Percentages)

Debt Ratio 45	4.3	•	20.9	•	3.6	6.8	1.6	3.9	4.2	4.9	6.0	5.8	3.6
Return on Total Assets 46	2.0	•	2.9	3.1	16.6	1.4	2.7	2.1	2.2	2.2	2.1	2.0	1.9
Return on Equity Before Income Taxes 47	2.1	•	3.7	3.2	17.8	1.5	2.8	2.2	2.3	2.2	2.2	2.1	2.0
Return on Equity After Income Taxes 48	2.1	•	3.7	3.2	17.8	1.5	2.8	2.2	2.3	2.2	2.2	2.1	2.0
Profit Margin (Before Income Tax) 49	68.9	85.0	77.5	53.1	63.5	51.5	64.7	60.5	57.5	58.7	58.8	60.9	74.7
Profit Margin (After Income Tax) 50	68.9	84.9	77.5	53.1	63.5	51.5	64.7	60.5	57.5	58.7	58.8	60.9	74.7

Table I
Corporations with and without Net Income

REAL ESTATE INVESTMENT TRUSTS (FORM 1120-REIT)

MONEY AMOUNTS AND SIZE OF ASSETS IN THOUSANDS OF DOLLARS

Item Description for Accounting Period 7/02 Through 6/03	Total	Zero Assets	Under 500	500 to 1,000	1,000 to 5,000	5,000 to 10,000	10,000 to 25,000	25,000 to 50,000	50,000 to 100,000	100,000 to 250,000	250,000 to 500,000	500,000 to 2,500,000	2,500,000 and over
Number of Enterprises 1	1089	96	39	14	45	32	85	85	122	169	119	201	83
Revenues ($ in Thousands)													
Net Sales 2	64282029	1845786	15778	72883	225276	168364	469501	1008744	1136593	3117690	3691408	20615289	31914717
Interest 3	24094544	501188	213	130	1531	6310	33173	184854	490045	861877	1203299	7797940	13013985
Rents 4	28801394	320915	4974	11808	26766	44718	209192	167599	495325	1752281	1799262	9667026	14301528
Royalties 5	0	0	0	0	0	0	0	0	0	0	0	0	0
Other Portfolio Income 6	4178833	648309	10588	60943	175815	110756	218819	606788	79911	188993	142028	921433	1013449
Other Receipts 7	7207258	375374	3	2	21164	6580	8317	49503	71312	313539	546819	2228890	3585755
Total Receipts 8	64282029	1845786	15778	72883	225276	168364	469501	1008744	1136593	3117690	3691408	20615289	31914717
Average Total Receipts 9	59028	19227	405	5206	5006	5261	5524	11868	9316	18448	31020	102564	384515
Operating Costs/Operating Income (%)													
Cost of Operations 10	*	*	*	*	*	*	*	*	*	*	*	*	*
Salaries and Wages 11	1.6	0.1	*	*	*	*	0.5	2.1	1.3	0.9	1.1	2.0	1.7
Taxes Paid 12	2.7	0.5	0.8	0.0	0.3	0.4	2.1	1.2	3.6	2.1	2.5	3.2	2.6
Interest Paid 13	9.8	2.3	0.3	0.2	0.3	5.0	6.1	5.5	27.0	9.2	8.4	11.6	9.0
Depreciation 14	6.9	2.2	6.3	3.3	0.9	0.5	4.3	2.2	6.0	5.0	6.3	8.3	6.9
Amortization and Depletion 15	0.7	0.1	0.6	0.0	0.5	0.3	0.5	0.4	1.2	0.5	0.6	0.8	0.6
Pensions and Other Deferred Comp. 16	*	*	*	*	*	*	*	*	*	*	*	*	*
Employee Benefits 17	*	*	*	*	*	*	*	*	*	*	*	*	*
Advertising 18	0.2	0.0	0.0	*	*	*	0.2	0.1	0.3	0.2	0.1	0.4	0.2
Other Expenses 19	16.6	10.8	30.6	43.1	4.3	12.0	27.5	10.1	19.0	38.3	20.3	14.4	15.8
Officers' Compensation 20	0.3	0.1	*	*	*	*	0.1	0.0	0.2	0.4	0.4	0.4	0.3
Operating Margin 21	61.1	83.9	61.3	53.3	93.6	81.8	58.7	78.4	41.3	43.4	60.2	59.0	62.8
Operating Margin Before Officers' Comp. 22	61.4	84.1	61.3	53.3	93.6	81.8	58.8	78.4	41.5	43.9	60.6	59.4	63.1

Selected Average Balance Sheet ($ in Thousands)

Item													
Net Receivables 23	28299	0	2	107	82	349	1738	1677	10689	13529	68961	158445	
Inventories 24	•	•	•	•	•	•	•	•	•	•	•	•	•
Net Property, Plant and Equipment 25	158928	0	42	116	483	1065	4462	8197	16543	32565	72316	295431	1161783
Total Assets 26	707394	0	196	717	2838	7500	16685	36542	70563	162182	348682	1135245	5539123
Notes and Loans Payable 27	114740	0	75	0	273	2851	3398	6529	14888	27542	46396	193370	881235
All Other Liabilities 28	48826	0	2	3	164	663	140	648	2397	3872	11387	63907	456976
Net Worth 29	543827	0	120	714	2401	3985	13148	29364	53278	130768	290899	877968	4200912

Selected Financial Ratios (Times to 1)

Item													
Current Ratio 30	1.9	•	32.8	12.9	4.7	0.7	2.7	1.9	4.4	4.0	2.4	1.5	
Quick Ratio 31	1.7	•	32.4	11.2	2.4	0.7	2.1	1.6	3.3	3.6	2.1	1.4	
Net Sales to Working Capital 32	1.5	•	7.9	203.6	10.0	•	3.0	2.6	1.0	1.1	1.1	1.8	
Coverage Ratio 33	7.2	37.0	225.9	269.1	274.6	17.3	15.3	2.5	5.7	8.2	6.1	8.0	
Total Asset Turnover 34	0.1	•	2.1	7.3	1.8	0.7	0.3	0.1	0.1	0.1	0.1	0.1	
Inventory Turnover 35	•	•	•	•	•	•	•	•	•	•	•	•	•
Receivables Turnover 36	•	•	•	•	•	•	•	•	•	•	•	•	•
Total Liabilities to Net Worth 37	0.3	•	0.6	0.0	0.2	0.9	0.3	0.2	0.3	0.2	0.3	0.3	
Current Assets to Working Capital 38	2.1	•	1.0	1.1	1.3	•	1.5	1.6	2.1	1.3	1.7	2.8	
Current Liabilities to Working Capital 39	1.1	•	0.0	0.1	0.3	•	0.5	0.6	1.1	0.3	0.7	1.8	
Working Capital to Net Sales 40	0.7	•	0.1	0.0	0.1	•	0.3	0.2	0.4	0.9	0.9	0.6	
Inventory to Working Capital 41	•	•	•	•	•	•	•	•	•	•	•	•	•
Total Receipts to Cash Flow 42	1.5	1.8	4.1	7.8	4.6	3.7	3.5	2.1	3.6	1.6	1.4	1.4	
Cost of Goods to Cash Flow 43	•	•	•	•	•	•	•	•	•	•	•	•	•
Cash Flow to Total Debt 44	0.2	1.3	212.9	2.5	0.4	0.4	0.5	0.3	0.4	0.3	0.2		

Selected Financial Factors (in Percentages)

Item													
Debt Ratio 45	23.1	•	39.1	0.4	15.4	46.9	21.2	19.6	24.5	19.4	16.6	24.2	
Return on Total Assets 46	5.9	126.9	388.6	165.8	60.9	21.5	27.1	9.0	6.0	6.1	6.4	5.0	
Return on Equity Before Income Taxes 47	6.6	•	207.4	195.3	108.0	24.7	31.6	7.2	6.1	6.4	6.9	5.7	
Return on Equity After Income Taxes 48	6.6	•	207.4	195.2	108.0	24.6	31.5	7.2	6.1	6.4	6.9	5.7	
Profit Margin (Before Income Tax) 49	61.1	83.9	61.3	53.3	93.6	81.8	58.7	78.1	41.3	43.4	60.2	59.0	62.8
Profit Margin (After Income Tax) 50	61.0	83.5	61.3	53.3	93.6	81.8	58.7	77.8	41.3	43.4	60.2	58.8	62.7

Table II

Corporations with Net Income

REAL ESTATE INVESTMENT TRUSTS (FORM 1120-REIT)

MONEY AMOUNTS AND SIZE OF ASSETS IN THOUSANDS OF DOLLARS

Item Description for Accounting Period 7/02 Through 6/03	Total	Zero Assets	Under 500	500 to 1,000	1,000 to 5,000	5,000 to 10,000	10,000 to 25,000	25,000 to 50,000	50,000 to 100,000	100,000 to 250,000	250,000 to 500,000	500,000 to 2,500,000	2,500,000 and over
Number of Enterprises **1**	930	68	21	0	33	22	63	65	103	153	113	194	0
Revenues ($ in Thousands)													
Net Sales **2**	62643964	1875085	15576	0	220944	163722	453093	934043	1007986	2696981	3513152	20029135	0
Interest **3**	23733880	500918	206	0	1392	6006	27612	183202	482922	827090	1201744	7527354	0
Rents **4**	27498893	319325	4780	0	19845	39873	196513	115646	382904	1380861	1633270	9317954	0
Royalties **5**	0	0	0	0	0	0	0	0	0	0	0	0	0
Other Portfolio Income **6**	4159273	648309	10588	0	175815	110756	216554	603591	79901	176187	142028	921151	0
Other Receipts **7**	7251818	406533	2	0	23892	7087	12414	31604	62259	312843	536110	2262676	0
Total Receipts **8**	62643964	1875085	15576	0	220944	163722	453093	934043	1007986	2696981	3513152	20029135	0
Average Total Receipts **9**	67359	27575	742	•	6695	7442	7192	14370	9786	17627	31090	103243	•
Operating Costs/Operating Income (%)													
Cost of Operations **10**	•	•	•	•	•	•	•	•	•	•	•	•	•
Salaries and Wages **11**	1.6	0.1	•	•	•	•	0.3	2.2	1.1	0.5	0.7	1.9	•
Taxes Paid **12**	2.6	0.4	0.3	•	0.3	0.4	1.7	0.9	3.2	1.6	2.1	3.2	•
Interest Paid **13**	9.1	2.2	0.2	•	0.3	5.1	3.5	3.6	25.1	7.3	7.5	10.3	•
Depreciation **14**	6.6	2.1	5.9	•	0.3	0.5	2.9	1.5	5.2	3.7	5.5	7.8	•
Amortization and Depletion **15**	0.6	0.1	0.6	•	0.5	0.4	0.4	0.2	1.1	0.5	0.7	0.8	•
Pensions and Other Deferred Comp. **16**	•	•	•	•	•	•	•	•	•	•	•	•	•
Employee Benefits **17**	•	•	•	•	•	•	•	•	•	•	•	•	•
Advertising **18**	0.2	0.0	•	•	•	•	0.1	0.1	0.3	0.1	0.1	0.4	•
Other Expenses **19**	15.1	6.9	27.1	•	1.0	6.1	24.0	3.9	14.6	30.5	18.6	13.0	•
Officers' Compensation **20**	0.3	0.1	•	•	•	•	0.1	0.0	0.2	0.4	0.4	0.4	•
Operating Margin **21**	63.8	88.0	65.9	•	97.6	87.5	67.0	87.6	49.1	55.3	64.4	62.2	•
Operating Margin Before Officers' Comp. **22**	64.2	88.2	65.9	•	97.6	87.5	67.0	87.6	49.3	55.7	64.8	62.6	•

Selected Average Balance Sheet ($ in Thousands)

Net Receivables 23	32996	0	0	146	119	221	2252	1816	11783	14220	71329
Inventories 24	•	•	•	•	•	•	•	•	•	•	•
Net Property, Plant and Equipment 25	177269	•	26	659	1549	4369	6669	14246	24983	64016	295793
Total Assets 26	805485	•	156	2583	7554	17042	36504	71522	161977	348842	1131009
Notes and Loans Payable 27	123753	•	19	362	4147	3491	4918	13398	21685	39448	177669
All Other Liabilities 28	56440	•	1	191	965	-342	740	2181	3916	11619	65713
Net Worth 29	625293	•	135	2030	2442	13893	30846	55942	136377	297775	887627

Selected Financial Ratios (Times to 1)

Current Ratio 30	2.0	•	17.5	5.2	0.7	3.3	4.2	2.2	4.4	4.2	2.8
Quick Ratio 31	1.7	•	16.6	2.4	0.7	2.3	3.3	1.9	3.3	3.8	2.5
Net Sales to Working Capital 32	1.4	•	33.6	10.6	•	3.7	3.5	2.2	0.9	1.0	1.0
Coverage Ratio 33	8.0	41.0	302.9	280.8	18.0	20.2	25.1	3.0	8.6	9.6	7.0
Total Asset Turnover 34	0.1	•	4.8	2.6	1.0	0.4	0.4	0.1	0.1	0.1	0.1
Inventory Turnover 35	•	•	•	•	•	•	•	•	•	•	•
Receivables Turnover 36	•	•	•	•	•	•	•	•	•	•	•
Total Liabilities to Net Worth 37	0.3	•	0.2	0.3	2.1	0.2	0.2	0.3	0.2	0.2	0.3
Current Assets to Working Capital 38	2.0	•	1.1	1.2	•	1.4	1.3	1.9	1.3	1.3	1.6
Current Liabilities to Working Capital 39	1.0	•	0.1	0.2	•	0.4	0.3	0.9	0.3	0.3	0.6
Working Capital to Net Sales 40	0.7	•	0.0	0.1	•	0.3	0.3	0.5	1.1	1.0	1.0
Inventory to Working Capital 41	•	•	•	•	•	•	•	•	•	•	•
Total Receipts to Cash Flow 42	1.5	1.8	4.0	4.6	3.9	3.1	3.9	1.9	1.5	1.3	1.5
Cost of Goods to Cash Flow 43	•	•	•	•	•	•	•	•	•	•	•
Cash Flow to Total Debt 44	0.3	•	9.1	2.7	0.4	0.7	0.7	0.3	0.5	0.5	0.3

Selected Financial Factors (in Percentages)

Debt Ratio 45	22.4	•	13.1	21.4	67.7	18.5	15.5	21.8	15.8	14.6	21.5
Return on Total Assets 46	6.1	•	315.1	253.9	91.3	29.7	35.9	10.2	6.8	6.4	6.6
Return on Equity Before Income Taxes 47	6.9	•	361.4	322.0	266.6	34.7	40.8	8.6	7.1	6.7	7.2
Return on Equity After Income Taxes 48	6.9	•	361.4	322.0	266.6	34.6	40.6	8.6	7.1	6.7	7.2
Profit Margin (Before Income Tax) 49	63.8	88.0	65.9	97.6	87.5	67.0	87.6	49.1	55.3	64.3	62.2
Profit Margin (After Income Tax) 50	63.7	87.6	65.9	97.6	87.5	66.9	87.2	49.1	55.2	64.3	62.0

Table I

Corporations with and without Net Income

OTHER FINANCIAL VEHICLES

MONEY AMOUNTS AND SIZE OF ASSETS IN THOUSANDS OF DOLLARS

Item Description for Accounting Period 7/02 Through 6/03	Total	Zero Assets	Under 500	500 to 1,000	1,000 to 5,000	5,000 to 10,000	10,000 to 25,000	25,000 to 50,000	50,000 to 100,000	100,000 to 250,000	250,000 to 500,000	500,000 to 2,500,000	2,500,000 and over
Number of Enterprises **1**	8113	1269	4104	1287	901	150	96	45	29	48	44	96	43
Revenues ($ in Thousands)													
Net Sales **2**	14113130	350717	303198	42431	517415	76246	291868	150839	144617	405504	597011	3422843	7810441
Interest **3**	11494874	176611	58435	14333	13617	17014	52171	31943	82237	324924	570070	3100758	7052759
Rents **4**	15309	63	0	99	1791	657	915	773	1054	9957	0	0	0
Royalties **5**	234	0	0	0	0	0	0	233	1	0	0	0	0
Other Portfolio Income **6**	602730	59419	20179	7303	44077	16788	10384	5528	27703	4082	33	227639	179595
Other Receipts **7**	1999983	114624	224584	20696	457930	41787	228398	112362	33622	66541	26908	94446	578087
Total Receipts **8**	14113130	350717	303198	42431	517415	76246	291868	150839	144617	405504	597011	3422843	7810441
Average Total Receipts **9**	1740	276	74	33	574	508	3040	3352	4987	8448	13568	35655	181638
Operating Costs/Operating Income (%)													
Cost of Operations **10**	0.3	*	0.2	0.3	0.9	6.2	0.2	22.1	3.1	*	*	*	0.0
Salaries and Wages **11**	1.4	5.9	1.2	17.4	18.3	5.2	14.1	10.5	4.9	0.1	0.0	0.0	0.0
Taxes Paid **12**	0.5	1.0	2.3	19.0	3.8	2.9	2.2	2.4	0.9	0.4	0.3	0.2	0.0
Interest Paid **13**	55.5	32.9	26.7	26.8	2.9	13.3	18.2	20.4	47.7	62.8	52.6	61.7	61.1
Depreciation **14**	0.4	0.8	0.2	5.3	1.9	0.6	1.8	2.2	0.4	8.0	0.1	0.0	0.0
Amortization and Depletion **15**	0.2	0.7	1.2	1.7	0.2	0.2	0.6	6.0	0.2	0.3	*	0.3	*
Pensions and Other Deferred Comp. **16**	0.3	0.2	*	0.1	7.0	0.1	0.2	1.1	0.3	*	*	*	*
Employee Benefits **17**	2.8	0.9	1.7	0.3	2.0	0.3	0.7	34.2	0.1	4.5	3.1	*	3.6
Advertising **18**	0.1	0.6	0.5	0.0	2.2	2.4	0.9	0.8	0.1	0.0	*	0.2	*
Other Expenses **19**	16.9	44.0	69.4	138.7	43.6	46.1	48.7	51.3	16.9	21.2	10.3	11.5	11.7
Officers' Compensation **20**	1.9	6.6	42.6	0.2	9.6	61.0	3.5	2.5	4.6	*	*	0.0	0.0
Operating Margin **21**	19.6	6.4	*	*	7.8	*	9.0	*	20.9	2.6	33.5	26.4	23.5
Operating Margin Before Officers' Comp. **22**	21.6	13.1	*	*	17.4	22.7	12.5	*	25.5	2.6	33.5	26.4	23.5

Selected Average Balance Sheet ($ in Thousands)

Net Receivables 23	10610	0	7	5	174	2371	1563	3406	14787	32274	50269	186197	1468851
Inventories 24	•	•	•	•	•	•	•	•	•	•	•	•	•
Net Property, Plant and Equipment 25	41	0	3	56	28	841	173	779	1617	9	0	0	0
Total Assets 26	52731	0	67	697	1902	7613	16141	34882	69911	156801	358980	1128799	673098
Notes and Loans Payable 27	35455	0	57	226	542	3554	6215	12661	28205	90265	130031	698764	4813617
All Other Liabilities 28	5171	0	45	140	320	1883	3041	9260	11542	32717	91708	140561	485371
Net Worth 29	12104	0	-35	331	1040	2176	6884	12962	30164	33820	137240	289474	1374110

Selected Financial Ratios (Times to 1)

Current Ratio 30	0.5	•	1.0	2.2	2.3	2.1	1.3	1.6	1.4	1.2	1.0	0.4	0.5
Quick Ratio 31	0.4	•	1.0	1.3	1.5	1.6	0.9	1.1	1.0	0.9	0.8	0.4	0.4
Net Sales to Working Capital 32	•	•	179.0	0.2	1.3	0.2	2.2	0.7	0.7	0.9	12.8	•	•
Coverage Ratio 33	1.4	1.1	•	•	3.5	•	1.5	•	1.5	1.0	1.6	1.4	1.4
Total Asset Turnover 34	0.0	•	1.1	0.0	0.3	0.1	0.2	0.1	0.1	0.1	0.0	0.0	0.0
Inventory Turnover 35	•	•	•	•	•	•	•	•	•	•	•	•	•
Receivables Turnover 36	•	•	•	•	•	•	•	•	•	•	•	•	•
Total Liabilities to Net Worth 37	3.4	•	•	1.1	0.8	2.5	1.3	1.7	1.3	3.6	1.6	2.9	3.9
Current Assets to Working Capital 38	•	•	94.7	1.9	1.8	1.9	4.0	2.6	3.5	6.4	98.9	2.9	3.9
Current Liabilities to Working Capital 39	•	•	93.7	0.9	0.8	0.9	3.0	1.6	2.5	5.4	97.9	•	•
Working Capital to Net Sales 40	•	•	0.0	4.1	0.7	4.4	0.5	1.5	1.5	0.1	0.1	•	•
Inventory to Working Capital 41	•	•	•	•	•	0.0	0.0	0.1	0.0	0.0	0.0	0.0	0.0
Total Receipts to Cash Flow 42	2.9	3.4	8.7	17.4	2.5	•	2.5	2.3	2.8	4.3	2.3	2.8	2.9
Cost of Goods to Cash Flow 43	0.0	0.0	0.0	0.0	0.0	0.0	0.0	0.0	0.1	•	0.0	•	0.0
Cash Flow to Total Debt 44	0.0	•	0.1	0.0	0.3	•	0.1	0.1	0.0	0.0	0.0	0.0	0.0

Selected Financial Factors (in Percentages)

Debt Ratio 45	77.0	•	153.2	52.5	45.3	71.4	57.3	62.8	56.9	78.4	61.8	74.4	79.4
Return on Total Assets 46	2.5	•	•	•	3.1	•	5.0	•	5.0	3.5	3.3	2.8	2.3
Return on Equity Before Income Taxes 47	2.9	•	96.0	•	4.0	•	3.7	•	3.6	0.7	3.3	3.2	3.3
Return on Equity After Income Taxes 48	1.7	•	97.7	•	2.1	•	3.2	•	2.9	2.1	2.1	2.2	2.1
Profit Margin (Before Income Tax) 49	20.4	3.8	•	•	7.3	•	8.4	•	21.9	2.6	33.5	26.4	24.9
Profit Margin (After Income Tax) 50	12.2	•	•	•	3.9	•	7.3	•	17.3	•	20.7	17.8	16.2

Table II

Corporations with Net Income

OTHER FINANCIAL VEHICLES

MONEY AMOUNTS AND SIZE OF ASSETS IN THOUSANDS OF DOLLARS

Item Description for Accounting Period 7/02 Through 6/03	Total	Zero Assets	Under 500	500 to 1,000	1,000 to 5,000	5,000 to 10,000	10,000 to 25,000	25,000 to 50,000	50,000 to 100,000	100,000 to 250,000	250,000 to 500,000	500,000 to 2,500,000	2,500,000 and over
Number of Enterprises **1**	2751	197	1536	0	387	65	40	15	17	17	22	62	0
Revenues ($ in Thousands)													
Net Sales **2**	8758894	240280	119673	0	439420	53532	217787	55560	112853	179359	349849	2203133	0
Interest **3**	6710893	63340	16611	0	6109	10021	20302	18321	53527	132679	331250	1928172	0
Rents **4**	2020	29	0	0	0	9	0	771	1054	0	0	0	0
Royalties **5**	1	0	0	0	0	0	0	0	1	0	0	0	0
Other Portfolio Income **6**	554042	47738	4556	0	38862	16246	7568	3105	26800	3883	0	226167	0
Other Receipts **7**	1491938	129173	98506	0	394649	27256	189859	33363	31471	42797	18599	48794	0
Total Receipts **8**	8758894	240280	119673	0	439420	53532	217787	55560	112853	179359	349849	2203133	0
Average Total Receipts **9**	3184	1220	78	*	1135	824	5445	3704	6638	10551	15902	35534	*
Operating Costs/Operating Income (%)													
Cost of Operations **10**	0.0	*	*	*	0.0	*	0.0	*	0.3	*	*	*	*
Salaries and Wages **11**	1.2	0.0	3.1	*	12.8	*	15.2	6.0	6.3	*	0.0	0.0	*
Taxes Paid **12**	0.5	1.0	4.1	*	3.5	2.2	2.3	2.0	1.2	1.0	0.0	0.3	*
Interest Paid **13**	39.6	11.0	14.8	*	0.7	11.3	8.5	19.9	34.1	43.9	30.5	47.7	*
Depreciation **14**	0.2	0.0	0.2	*	1.1	0.2	1.9	1.0	0.4	2.7	0.2	0.0	*
Amortization and Depletion **15**	0.0	0.0	0.1	*	0.0	0.0	0.7	0.1	0.0	0.0	*	0.1	*
Pensions and Other Deferred Comp. **16**	0.4	0.2	*	*	8.2	0.0	0.2	0.3	0.3	*	*	*	*
Employee Benefits **17**	3.4	*	4.0	*	1.9	*	0.8	0.2	0.1	*	*	*	*
Advertising **18**	0.1	*	1.3	*	0.8	*	1.2	0.9	0.1	*	*	*	*
Other Expenses **19**	11.1	9.7	27.9	*	26.2	14.5	23.8	12.4	12.1	14.3	5.3	6.7	*
Officers' Compensation **20**	1.3	9.5	25.2	*	9.6	*	2.9	2.6	5.9	*	*	0.0	*
Operating Margin **21**	42.1	68.5	19.4	*	35.1	71.7	42.4	54.5	39.2	38.1	64.0	45.2	*
Operating Margin Before Officers' Comp. **22**	43.4	78.0	44.6	*	44.7	71.7	45.4	57.1	45.1	38.1	64.0	45.2	*

Selected Average Balance Sheet ($ in Thousands)

Net Receivables 23	20396	•	0	7	237	4446	1729	2327	21686	32127	41916	225988
Inventories 24	•	•	•	•	•	•	•	•	•	•	•	•
Net Property, Plant and Equipment 25	91	•	0	7	42	1800	346	60	2754	0	0	•
Total Assets 26	90967	•	73	2127	7738	15946	32093	74255	157021	376868	1117028	•
Notes and Loans Payable 27	48901	•	0	0	254	4723	6263	13218	20092	74724	85992	566622
All Other Liabilities 28	10413	•	0	3	376	4191	2701	794	13883	2006	74543	150303
Net Worth 29	31653	•	0	70	1497	-1177	6982	18081	40280	80291	216334	400103

Selected Financial Ratios (Times to 1)

Current Ratio 30	0.7	•	11.3	2.4	1.2	1.2	1.4	1.8	2.1	1.0	0.5	•
Quick Ratio 31	0.6	•	11.3	1.6	1.1	0.8	1.3	1.3	1.6	0.7	0.5	•
Net Sales to Working Capital 32	•	•	2.3	2.0	1.1	6.8	2.7	0.4	0.4	10.1	•	•
Coverage Ratio 33	2.1	7.3	2.3	48.9	7.7	6.0	3.7	2.2	1.9	3.1	1.9	•
Total Asset Turnover 34	0.0	•	1.1	0.5	0.1	0.3	0.1	0.1	0.1	0.0	0.0	•
Inventory Turnover 35	•	•	•	•	•	•	•	•	•	•	•	•
Receivables Turnover 36	•	•	•	•	•	•	•	•	•	•	•	•
Total Liabilities to Net Worth 37	1.9	•	0.0	0.4	•	1.3	0.8	0.8	1.8	1.0	0.7	1.8
Current Assets to Working Capital 38	•	•	1.1	1.7	6.9	3.8	2.3	2.3	1.9	1.9	43.4	•
Current Liabilities to Working Capital 39	•	•	0.1	0.7	5.9	5.7	2.8	1.3	0.9	0.9	42.4	•
Working Capital to Net Sales 40	0.4	•	0.5	0.9	0.1	0.4	0.4	2.3	0.1	2.8	0.1	•
Inventory to Working Capital 41	•	•	•	•	0.1	0.1	0.1	•	0.0	0.0	•	•
Total Receipts to Cash Flow 42	2.0	1.9	2.6	2.0	1.6	1.6	1.6	2.0	1.6	1.9	1.4	2.0
Cost of Goods to Cash Flow 43	0.0	•	•	•	0.0	0.0	0.0	0.0	0.0	•	•	•
Cash Flow to Total Debt 44	0.0	•	9.0	0.9	0.1	0.4	0.2	0.1	0.1	1.0	0.1	0.0

Selected Financial Factors (in Percentages)

Debt Ratio 45	65.2	•	4.7	29.6	115.2	56.2	43.7	45.8	48.9	42.6	64.2	•
Return on Total Assets 46	2.9	•	36.5	19.1	9.3	17.3	8.6	6.7	5.5	4.0	3.0	•
Return on Equity Before Income Taxes 47	4.4	•	21.7	26.6	•	33.0	11.1	6.7	5.0	4.7	4.0	•
Return on Equity After Income Taxes 48	3.0	•	20.0	23.5	•	31.8	9.5	5.7	5.0	3.1	2.8	•
Profit Margin (Before Income Tax) 49	43.5	69.4	19.3	35.0	75.7	42.3	54.4	40.6	38.1	64.0	45.2	•
Profit Margin (After Income Tax) 50	30.3	53.5	17.9	31.0	58.4	40.7	46.3	34.7	25.1	42.2	31.9	•

Table I

Corporations with and without Net Income

LESSORS OF BUILDINGS

MONEY AMOUNTS AND SIZE OF ASSETS IN THOUSANDS OF DOLLARS

Item Description for Accounting Period 7/02 Through 6/03		Total	Zero Assets	Under 500	500 to 1,000	1,000 to 5,000	5,000 to 10,000	10,000 to 25,000	25,000 to 50,000	50,000 to 100,000	100,000 to 250,000	250,000 to 500,000	500,000 to 2,500,000	2,500,000 and over
Number of Enterprises	1	214935	21152	121839	33214	32776	3568	1690	428	146	89	21	8	4
Revenues ($ in Thousands)														
Net Sales	2	33205317	1856198	3758954	2529531	7564517	3200088	3400547	2198023	1389079	2711170	1099227	802444	2695540
Interest	3	795949	47235	47523	44284	107968	65975	62398	66565	47663	86572	44921	40920	133923
Rents	4	460674	5292	126489	18291	22491	97196	14076	15075	2529	8907	2314	12910	135105
Royalties	5	39226	9927	2153	7699	227	13872	4649	228	144	271	0	0	55
Other Portfolio Income	6	2308168	658203	208804	117814	284614	133521	130011	75356	61555	417594	25431	135445	59818
Other Receipts	7	29601300	1135541	3373985	2341443	7149217	2889524	3189413	2040799	1277188	2197826	1026561	613169	2366639
Total Receipts	8	33205317	1856198	3758954	2529531	7564517	3200088	3400547	2198023	1389079	2711170	1099227	802444	2695540
Average Total Receipts	9	154	88	31	76	231	897	2012	5136	9514	30463	52344	100306	673885
Operating Costs/Operating Income (%)														
Cost of Operations	10	13.9	4.9	7.2	18.8	12.5	1.0	8.3	11.9	10.8	18.0	6.5	2.4	56.1
Salaries and Wages	11	9.9	2.3	7.2	9.7	10.8	18.7	12.5	9.8	9.7	8.3	9.6	4.6	5.6
Taxes Paid	12	10.6	8.6	10.3	11.2	12.9	16.0	13.1	10.8	10.0	5.8	9.1	8.6	2.2
Interest Paid	13	13.9	15.2	9.4	10.2	13.1	16.5	16.1	14.4	17.0	12.7	17.7	34.4	10.4
Depreciation	14	9.8	9.6	6.4	8.0	10.3	10.8	13.3	13.0	12.7	9.9	10.3	17.5	2.9
Amortization and Depletion	15	0.7	1.5	0.1	0.3	0.5	0.5	0.7	0.7	1.1	1.8	1.8	1.1	0.1
Pensions and Other Deferred Comp.	16	0.3	0.0	0.6	0.5	0.3	0.4	0.3	0.4	0.3	0.2	0.3	0.1	0.0
Employee Benefits	17	1.0	0.2	0.9	0.7	1.0	2.1	1.4	1.2	1.1	0.6	1.1	0.3	0.1
Advertising	18	0.5	0.2	0.5	0.8	0.5	0.4	0.4	0.4	0.4	0.8	0.8	0.3	0.2
Other Expenses	19	31.3	31.6	45.9	29.6	30.3	33.1	31.2	33.3	28.2	38.6	34.2	25.7	6.1
Officers' Compensation	20	3.6	0.8	8.5	4.4	5.3	3.8	2.6	2.4	1.9	1.3	1.4	0.2	0.4
Operating Margin	21	4.6	25.1	3.0	5.8	2.5	•	0.1	1.9	6.8	2.0	7.1	4.7	15.8
Operating Margin Before Officers' Comp.	22	8.3	25.9	11.5	10.2	7.8	0.5	2.8	4.3	8.7	3.3	8.5	5.0	16.2

Selected Average Balance Sheet ($ in Thousands)

Item													
Net Receivables 23	31	•	4	21	46	224	396	1241	1747	8728	4520	41910	164672
Inventories 24	•	•	•	•	•	•	•	•	•	•	•	•	•
Net Property, Plant and Equipment 25	716	0	123	521	1477	4923	10489	22050	44424	85043	192160	461214	1671086
Total Assets 26	1049	0	167	702	2009	6786	15014	34592	66346	155249	327811	820860	3648118
Notes and Loans Payable 27	657	0	116	481	1370	4488	9369	19165	40936	83955	160235	452779	1465932
All Other Liabilities 28	84	0	10	45	130	497	1233	2963	6562	26274	21689	72180	406960
Net Worth 29	307	0	41	175	509	1800	4412	12465	18848	45019	145887	295901	1775226

Selected Financial Ratios (Times to 1)

Item													
Current Ratio 30	1.8	•	2.3	1.7	1.8	1.9	1.6	1.6	1.2	1.5	1.6	3.2	3.1
Quick Ratio 31	1.3	•	1.9	1.3	1.3	1.5	1.1	1.1	0.7	1.2	1.2	2.7	1.0
Net Sales to Working Capital 32	2.2	2.6	2.2	1.9	2.0	2.2	2.5	2.4	9.0	3.5	3.7	1.0	1.3
Coverage Ratio 33	1.3	•	1.3	1.6	1.2	0.8	1.0	1.1	1.5	1.1	1.4	1.1	2.5
Total Asset Turnover 34	0.1	•	0.2	0.1	0.1	0.1	0.1	0.1	0.1	0.2	0.2	0.1	0.2
Inventory Turnover 35	•	•	•	•	•	•	•	•	•	•	•	•	•
Receivables Turnover 36	•	•	•	•	•	•	•	•	•	•	•	•	•
Total Liabilities to Net Worth 37	2.4	•	3.1	3.0	2.9	2.8	2.6	1.8	2.5	2.4	1.2	1.8	1.1
Current Assets to Working Capital 38	2.2	•	1.8	2.4	2.3	2.2	2.6	2.7	7.6	3.0	2.7	1.5	1.5
Current Liabilities to Working Capital 39	1.2	•	0.8	1.4	1.3	1.2	1.6	1.7	6.6	2.0	1.7	0.5	0.5
Working Capital to Net Sales 40	0.4	•	0.5	0.5	0.5	0.4	0.4	0.4	0.1	0.3	0.3	1.0	0.8
Inventory to Working Capital 41	0.0	•	•	•	0.0	0.0	0.0	0.0	0.1	0.0	0.0	0.0	0.0
Total Receipts to Cash Flow 42	4.6	5.5	3.2	4.4	4.7	5.2	4.6	4.0	3.9	8.6	3.3	5.4	5.6
Cost of Goods to Cash Flow 43	0.6	0.3	0.2	0.8	0.6	0.1	0.4	0.5	0.4	1.5	0.2	0.1	3.1
Cash Flow to Total Debt 44	0.0	•	0.1	0.0	0.0	0.0	0.0	0.1	0.1	0.0	0.1	0.0	0.1

Selected Financial Factors (in Percentages)

Item													
Debt Ratio 45	70.7	•	75.3	75.1	74.6	73.5	70.6	64.0	71.6	71.0	55.5	64.0	51.3
Return on Total Assets 46	2.7	•	2.3	1.7	1.8	1.7	2.1	2.4	3.6	2.9	3.9	4.8	4.8
Return on Equity Before Income Taxes 47	2.3	•	2.3	2.5	1.0	•	•	0.7	4.0	1.3	2.5	1.6	6.0
Return on Equity After Income Taxes 48	0.9	•	1.5	1.9	0.2	•	•	•	1.8	1.6	1.6	1.2	4.3
Profit Margin (Before Income Tax) 49	4.5	25.1	3.1	5.6	2.2	•	1.6	1.6	7.8	1.9	7.0	4.7	15.8
Profit Margin (After Income Tax) 50	1.8	16.9	2.0	4.4	0.4	•	•	•	3.6	•	4.4	3.5	11.4

Table II

Corporations with Net Income

LESSORS OF BUILDINGS

MONEY AMOUNTS AND SIZE OF ASSETS IN THOUSANDS OF DOLLARS

Item Description for Accounting Period 7/02 Through 6/03	Total	Zero Assets	Under 500	500 to 1,000	1,000 to 5,000	5,000 to 10,000	10,000 to 25,000	25,000 to 50,000	50,000 to 100,000	100,000 to 250,000	250,000 to 500,000	500,000 to 2,500,000	2,500,000 and over
Number of Enterprises **1**	46782	4509	26103	6609	7725	959	560	181	68	50	10	0	0
Revenues ($ in Thousands)													
Net Sales **2**	20781283	1533268	2488806	1337272	4291642	1432135	1790204	1358951	804319	1873461	584651	0	0
Interest **3**	590532	35890	31239	34639	69869	47724	39764	36649	35128	64611	30822	0	0
Rents **4**	328077	5132	120340	1923	17869	5651	9168	10488	0	7565	1926	0	0
Royalties **5**	26363	9554	1	7699	171	3600	4639	228	144	271	0	0	0
Other Portfolio Income **6**	2059118	633495	173347	110074	254363	76386	112850	61801	55310	390925	23780	0	0
Other Receipts **7**	17777193	849197	2163879	1182937	3949370	1298774	1623783	1249785	713737	1410089	528123	0	0
Total Receipts **8**	20781283	1533268	2488806	1337272	4291642	1432135	1790204	1358951	804319	1873461	584651	0	0
Average Total Receipts **9**	444	340	95	202	556	1493	3197	7508	11828	37469	58465	·	·
Operating Costs/Operating Income (%)													
Cost of Operations **10**	14.7	4.4	5.5	4.8	8.3	0.9	10.6	14.0	9.5	23.3	3.8	·	·
Salaries and Wages **11**	7.4	2.0	5.4	11.8	11.2	10.4	7.6	7.3	5.5	4.9	7.8	·	·
Taxes Paid **12**	8.0	7.3	7.2	9.5	10.6	11.6	9.2	8.3	8.5	5.8	10.0	·	·
Interest Paid **13**	11.0	13.9	6.4	8.3	8.2	14.5	13.1	9.6	14.7	11.2	12.3	·	·
Depreciation **14**	7.5	7.9	4.5	7.4	7.1	9.6	9.7	10.4	10.7	6.9	10.9	·	·
Amortization and Depletion **15**	0.5	1.6	0.0	0.2	0.4	0.4	0.6	0.6	1.2	0.4	1.4	·	·
Pensions and Other Deferred Comp. **16**	0.2	0.0	·	0.0	0.4	0.3	0.3	0.4	0.2	0.1	0.1	·	·
Employee Benefits **17**	0.6	0.2	0.6	1.0	0.8	0.8	0.8	1.0	0.5	0.4	0.7	·	·
Advertising **18**	0.4	0.1	0.1	0.2	0.5	0.7	0.3	0.4	0.3	0.6	1.1	·	·
Other Expenses **19**	24.0	18.5	42.1	24.8	26.0	28.0	26.3	25.9	22.8	17.1	31.4	·	·
Officers' Compensation **20**	3.9	0.4	9.9	4.9	6.6	4.5	3.0	2.8	1.9	1.2	1.9	·	·
Operating Margin **21**	21.9	43.7	18.2	27.1	19.8	18.2	18.6	19.3	24.1	28.0	18.6	·	·
Operating Margin Before Officers' Comp. **22**	25.8	44.1	28.1	32.0	26.4	22.7	21.6	22.2	26.0	29.2	20.5	·	·

Selected Average Balance Sheet ($ in Thousands)

Net Receivables 23	70	0	5	34	63	355	589	1133	2317	9275	5887
Inventories 24	•	•	•	•	•	•	•	•	•	•	•
Net Property, Plant and Equipment 25	889	0	108	391	1205	4442	9442	19448	41258	86594	170137
Total Assets 26	1571	0	174	711	1947	6855	15069	34383	66591	158481	326881
Notes and Loans Payable 27	789	0	120	334	994	3627	8443	16038	40669	77121	148397
All Other Liabilities 28	145	0	18	50	159	362	1467	3193	6506	18940	25542
Net Worth 29	637	0	35	327	794	2865	5159	15152	19416	62420	152941

Selected Financial Ratios (Times to 1)

Current Ratio 30	2.2	•	3.0	2.2	2.2	3.1	1.9	1.9	1.7	1.5	1.8
Quick Ratio 31	1.8	•	2.6	1.9	1.8	2.6	1.4	1.2	1.1	1.3	1.6
Net Sales to Working Capital 32	2.8	•	3.8	2.0	2.5	1.8	2.4	2.6	3.1	4.4	2.8
Coverage Ratio 33	3.0	4.1	3.9	4.2	3.4	2.2	2.4	3.0	2.8	3.5	2.5
Total Asset Turnover 34	0.3	•	0.5	0.3	0.3	0.2	0.2	0.2	0.2	0.2	0.2
Inventory Turnover 35	•	•	•	•	•	•	•	•	•	•	•
Receivables Turnover 36	•	•	•	•	•	•	•	•	•	•	•
Total Liabilities to Net Worth 37	1.5	•	4.0	1.2	1.5	1.4	1.9	1.3	2.4	1.5	1.1
Current Assets to Working Capital 38	1.8	•	1.5	1.8	1.8	1.5	2.1	2.1	2.4	2.9	2.3
Current Liabilities to Working Capital 39	0.8	•	0.5	0.8	0.8	0.5	1.1	1.1	1.4	1.9	1.3
Working Capital to Net Sales 40	0.4	•	0.3	0.5	0.4	0.6	0.4	0.4	0.3	0.2	0.4
Inventory to Working Capital 41	0.0	•	•	0.0	0.0	0.0	0.0	0.1	0.0	0.0	0.0
Total Receipts to Cash Flow 42	3.2	4.3	2.4	2.6	3.0	2.9	3.0	2.9	2.7	4.0	2.7
Cost of Goods to Cash Flow 43	0.5	0.2	0.1	0.1	0.3	0.0	0.3	0.4	0.3	0.9	0.1
Cash Flow to Total Debt 44	0.1	•	0.3	0.2	0.2	0.1	0.1	0.1	0.1	0.1	0.1

Selected Financial Factors (in Percentages)

Debt Ratio 45	59.4	•	79.8	54.0	59.2	58.2	65.8	55.9	70.8	60.6	53.2
Return on Total Assets 46	9.3	•	13.6	10.0	7.9	7.1	6.7	6.3	7.2	9.2	5.5
Return on Equity Before Income Taxes 47	15.2	•	49.8	16.6	13.7	9.4	11.4	9.5	15.9	16.7	7.0
Return on Equity After Income Taxes 48	12.1	•	45.5	15.1	11.5	7.5	8.6	7.3	11.4	11.7	5.2
Profit Margin (Before Income Tax) 49	21.8	43.7	18.3	26.8	19.6	18.1	18.4	19.2	26.1	27.9	18.4
Profit Margin (After Income Tax) 50	17.4	34.1	16.7	24.5	16.4	14.3	13.9	14.8	18.8	19.5	13.7

Table I

Corporations with and without Net Income

LESSORS OF MINIWAREHOUSES, SELF-STORAGE, OTHER REAL ESTATE

MONEY AMOUNTS AND SIZE OF ASSETS IN THOUSANDS OF DOLLARS

Item Description for Accounting Period 7/02 Through 6/03	Total	Zero Assets	Under 500	500 to 1,000	1,000 to 5,000	5,000 to 10,000	10,000 to 25,000	25,000 to 50,000	50,000 to 100,000	100,000 to 250,000	250,000 to 500,000	500,000 to 2,500,000	2,500,000 and over
Number of Enterprises **1**	52805	8294	30578	7442	5321	632	360	93	47	22	8	8	•
Revenues ($ in Thousands)													
Net Sales **2**	8025845	366281	1392624	590500	1492356	504002	834664	410587	333086	534813	220270	1346664	•
Interest **3**	262914	13509	12333	16435	39007	13176	33515	14537	21723	17801	21817	59061	•
Rents **4**	38858	9839	15488	1248	3913	162	1471	2869	545	519	209	2595	•
Royalties **5**	15052	373	3019	2817	2734	0	4191	1400	518	0	0	0	•
Other Portfolio Income **6**	1042467	158764	112186	28772	152576	36399	57653	63838	45874	229661	3766	152979	•
Other Receipts **7**	6666554	183796	1249598	541228	1294126	454265	737834	327943	264426	286832	194478	1132029	•
Total Receipts **8**	8025845	366281	1392624	590500	1492356	504002	834664	410587	333086	534813	220270	1346664	•
Average Total Receipts **9**	152	44	46	79	280	797	2319	4415	7087	24310	27534	168333	•
Operating Costs/Operating Income (%)													
Cost of Operations **10**	5.4	0.1	0.3	3.9	5.5	11.1	11.5	2.2	0.2	5.4	1.1	9.8	•
Salaries and Wages **11**	8.1	3.7	4.8	5.7	6.8	13.5	15.5	10.8	12.3	4.2	12.2	7.8	•
Taxes Paid **12**	7.0	8.6	7.0	10.8	7.4	8.2	6.3	8.7	5.9	4.1	5.0	5.8	•
Interest Paid **13**	14.1	13.1	6.9	10.2	14.3	10.3	12.0	15.9	23.5	22.7	13.8	19.5	•
Depreciation **14**	8.8	7.8	5.1	11.5	8.2	9.4	8.6	10.3	12.9	5.7	12.0	11.5	•
Amortization and Depletion **15**	0.8	0.3	0.1	0.4	0.3	0.3	0.9	0.9	1.7	0.3	0.2	2.4	•
Pensions and Other Deferred Comp. **16**	0.6	0.0	1.0	0.2	1.0	1.1	0.6	0.4	0.2	0.4	0.1	0.0	•
Employee Benefits **17**	1.1	0.6	0.9	0.4	1.3	1.3	1.6	1.1	1.1	0.8	0.7	1.1	•
Advertising **18**	1.0	0.4	0.9	2.4	0.9	1.2	1.4	0.9	0.5	0.1	0.3	1.0	•
Other Expenses **19**	36.8	44.9	47.0	32.7	37.5	36.0	29.9	31.6	48.0	18.9	64.8	30.6	•
Officers' Compensation **20**	5.3	2.8	13.6	3.3	5.4	2.8	4.6	4.3	1.2	3.2	6.4	1.7	•
Operating Margin **21**	11.1	17.5	12.3	18.5	11.3	4.8	7.0	12.8	•	34.1	•	8.8	•
Operating Margin Before Officers' Comp. **22**	16.4	20.3	25.9	21.8	16.7	7.6	11.6	17.1	•	37.3	•	10.5	•

Selected Average Balance Sheet ($ in Thousands)

	•	•	•	•	•	•	•	•	•	•	•	•
Net Receivables 23	42	•	4	21	70	441	717	1752	5150	6970	15349	44215
Inventories 24	•	•	•	•	•	•	•	•	•	•	•	•
Net Property, Plant and Equipment 25	492	0	99	481	1107	3899	7632	16741	25253	63809	76877	442182
Total Assets 26	928	•	154	584	1872	6766	15272	33048	68063	156137	323033	895990
Notes and Loans Payable 27	504	0	88	371	1100	4030	8597	18525	32608	70064	129538	479226
All Other Liabilities 28	112	0	29	16	194	766	1926	4671	17139	11480	19837	127218
Net Worth 29	312	0	36	297	578	1971	4749	9852	18316	74593	173658	289546

Selected Financial Ratios (Times to 1)

	•	•	•	•	•	•	•	•	•	•	•	•
Current Ratio 30	1.7	•	1.3	3.4	2.3	1.4	1.9	1.6	1.3	0.7	0.8	2.6
Quick Ratio 31	1.0	•	0.8	2.6	1.5	1.0	1.1	1.1	0.8	0.5	0.5	0.9
Net Sales to Working Capital 32	2.3	•	6.8	1.0	1.5	2.7	1.5	1.8	2.3	2.5	•	1.6
Coverage Ratio 33	1.8	2.3	2.8	2.8	1.4	1.5	1.8	0.7	2.5	•	•	1.5
Total Asset Turnover 34	0.2	•	0.3	0.1	0.1	0.2	0.1	0.1	0.2	0.1	•	0.2
Inventory Turnover 35	•	•	•	•	•	•	•	•	•	•	•	•
Receivables Turnover 36	•	•	•	•	•	•	•	•	•	•	•	•
Total Liabilities to Net Worth 37	2.0	•	3.2	1.3	2.2	2.4	2.2	2.4	2.7	1.1	0.9	2.1
Current Assets to Working Capital 38	2.5	•	4.6	1.4	1.8	3.6	2.2	2.7	4.8	3.8	•	1.6
Current Liabilities to Working Capital 39	1.5	•	3.6	0.4	0.8	2.6	1.2	1.7	3.8	•	•	0.6
Working Capital to Net Sales 40	0.4	•	0.1	1.0	0.7	0.4	0.7	0.6	0.4	•	•	0.6
Inventory to Working Capital 41	0.0	•	0.0	0.0	0.1	0.0	0.0	0.0	0.0	•	•	0.0
Total Receipts to Cash Flow 42	3.5	5.0	2.7	2.6	3.6	2.9	4.0	4.2	6.3	9.9	2.9	3.8
Cost of Goods to Cash Flow 43	0.2	0.0	0.0	0.1	0.2	0.4	0.5	0.1	0.0	0.5	0.0	0.4
Cash Flow to Total Debt 44	0.1	•	0.1	0.1	0.0	0.0	0.1	0.0	0.1	0.0	0.0	0.1

Selected Financial Factors (in Percentages)

	•	•	•	•	•	•	•	•	•	•	•	•
Debt Ratio 45	66.4	•	76.4	56.5	69.1	70.9	68.9	70.2	73.1	52.2	46.2	67.7
Return on Total Assets 46	4.1	•	5.7	3.3	3.8	1.7	2.8	3.8	1.7	8.8	•	5.3
Return on Equity Before Income Taxes 47	5.4	•	15.4	4.9	5.4	1.8	3.2	5.7	•	11.1	•	5.1
Return on Equity After Income Taxes 48	3.7	•	13.8	4.4	3.4	0.8	1.7	3.2	•	9.6	•	2.9
Profit Margin (Before Income Tax) 49	11.0	17.5	12.3	18.4	11.1	4.4	6.5	12.7	•	34.1	•	8.8
Profit Margin (After Income Tax) 50	7.6	8.4	11.0	16.6	7.0	2.0	3.5	7.2	•	29.5	•	4.9

Table II

Corporations with Net Income

LESSORS OF MINIWAREHOUSES, SELF-STORAGE, OTHER REAL ESTATE

MONEY AMOUNTS AND SIZE OF ASSETS IN THOUSANDS OF DOLLARS

Item Description for Accounting Period 7/02 Through 6/03	Total	Zero Assets	Under 500	500 to 1,000	1,000 to 5,000	5,000 to 10,000	10,000 to 25,000	25,000 to 50,000	50,000 to 100,000	100,000 to 250,000	250,000 to 500,000	500,000 to 2,500,000	2,500,000 and over
Number of Enterprises **1**	18864	2733	10842	2621	2170	272	145	40	20	14	3	4	•
Revenues ($ in Thousands)													
Net Sales **2**	5102209	369904	933993	465770	963981	305664	504528	295227	193188	467928	40087	561938	•
Interest **3**	172956	11941	11951	12530	28298	12021	24440	5303	8040	10207	17328	30897	•
Rents **4**	32812	9696	12639	1248	3661	162	1286	2846	545	519	209	0	•
Royalties **5**	11415	373	29	2817	2734	0	4062	1400	0	0	0	0	•
Other Portfolio Income **6**	980110	157946	106592	27556	140176	27885	45313	60399	42046	219178	44	152978	•
Other Receipts **7**	3904916	189948	802782	421619	789112	265596	429427	225279	142557	238024	22506	378063	•
Total Receipts **8**	5102209	369904	933993	465770	963981	305664	504528	295227	193188	467928	40087	561938	•
Average Total Receipts **9**	270	135	86	178	444	1124	3480	7381	9659	33423	13362	140484	•
Operating Costs/Operating Income (%)													
Cost of Operations **10**	1.5	•	0.4	3.4	0.3	1.7	4.2	1.9	•	2.7	5.1	1.4	•
Salaries and Wages **11**	5.3	1.9	1.8	4.8	5.7	8.0	15.0	7.3	2.8	4.6	4.2	3.0	•
Taxes Paid **12**	7.2	6.5	6.6	7.8	8.8	8.6	6.7	7.9	6.4	3.9	2.0	8.3	•
Interest Paid **13**	11.7	11.3	6.7	7.2	11.9	11.5	9.8	14.0	13.7	20.7	8.2	15.9	•
Depreciation **14**	6.9	4.2	5.0	10.4	7.1	9.0	6.4	8.9	12.6	4.4	9.4	7.2	•
Amortization and Depletion **15**	0.4	0.2	0.0	0.5	0.4	0.3	0.6	0.9	0.4	0.3	0.3	1.1	•
Pensions and Other Deferred Comp. **16**	0.4	0.0	0.6	0.2	0.6	1.3	0.6	0.1	0.1	0.3	•	0.3	•
Employee Benefits **17**	0.6	0.6	0.4	0.3	0.6	0.6	1.7	0.9	0.5	0.8	0.1	0.3	•
Advertising **18**	0.7	0.1	0.3	2.9	0.4	0.2	0.8	0.9	0.4	0.1	•	1.2	•
Other Expenses **19**	25.6	20.7	31.9	28.5	21.2	34.0	22.3	19.9	27.7	14.5	61.0	30.9	•
Officers' Compensation **20**	4.2	1.0	8.9	2.0	6.6	3.1	3.9	2.3	0.8	3.1	1.0	0.1	•
Operating Margin **21**	35.4	53.4	37.3	31.9	36.4	21.7	28.0	35.0	34.6	44.6	8.7	30.6	•
Operating Margin Before Officers' Comp. **22**	39.6	54.4	46.2	34.0	43.0	24.8	31.9	37.3	35.4	47.7	9.7	30.7	•

Selected Average Balance Sheet ($ in Thousands)

	1	2	3	4	5	6	7	8	9	10	11	12
Net Receivables 23	52	0	8	20	88	498	919	965	3903	10747	995	28604
Inventories 24	•	•	•	•	•	•	•	•	•	•	•	•
Net Property, Plant and Equipment 25	507	0	99	409	1020	2924	6331	18716	27845	61102	29556	313860
Total Assets 26	1119		163	685	1985	6700	15064	33080	73011	162118	378196	759714
Notes and Loans Payable 27	442		79	242	990	2981	6833	21262	20760	55426	27533	192513
All Other Liabilities 28	137		35	23	264	421	2228	4747	13158	10789	32519	110020
Net Worth 29	540		49	420	731	3298	6003	7071	39093	95904	318144	457181

Selected Financial Ratios (Times to 1)

	1	2	3	4	5	6	7	8	9	10	11	12
Current Ratio 30	2.0	•	1.4	3.5	2.2	3.0	2.2	0.9	1.5	2.2	0.8	2.4
Quick Ratio 31	1.2	•	1.0	2.5	1.7	2.2	1.4	0.6	0.8	1.6	0.7	0.4
Net Sales to Working Capital 32	2.3	•	8.9	1.5	1.9	1.3	1.5	•	1.8	2.9	•	1.1
Coverage Ratio 33	4.0	5.7	6.6	5.4	4.0	2.8	3.8	3.5	3.5	3.2	2.1	2.9
Total Asset Turnover 34	0.2	•	0.5	0.3	0.2	0.2	0.2	0.2	0.1	0.2	0.0	0.2
Inventory Turnover 35	•	•	•	•	•	•	•	•	•	•	•	•
Receivables Turnover 36	•	•	•	•	•	•	•	•	•	•	•	•
Total Liabilities to Net Worth 37	1.1	•	2.3	0.6	1.7	1.0	1.5	3.7	0.9	0.7	0.2	0.7
Current Assets to Working Capital 38	2.0	•	3.5	1.4	1.8	1.5	1.8	•	3.0	1.9	•	1.7
Current Liabilities to Working Capital 39	1.0	•	2.5	0.4	0.8	0.5	0.8	•	2.0	0.9	•	0.7
Working Capital to Net Sales 40	0.4	•	0.1	0.7	0.5	0.8	0.7	•	0.6	0.3	•	0.9
Inventory to Working Capital 41	0.0	•	0.0	0.0	0.0	0.0	0.0	•	0.0	0.0	•	0.0
Total Receipts to Cash Flow 42	2.6	3.0	2.2	2.1	2.5	2.4	2.7	3.2	2.5	7.7	1.5	2.7
Cost of Goods to Cash Flow 43	0.0	•	0.0	0.1	0.0	0.0	0.1	0.1	0.2	0.1	0.1	0.0
Cash Flow to Total Debt 44	0.2	•	0.4	0.3	0.1	0.1	0.1	0.1	0.1	0.1	0.1	0.2

Selected Financial Factors (in Percentages)

	1	2	3	4	5	6	7	8	9	10	11	12
Debt Ratio 45	51.8	•	69.7	38.7	63.2	50.8	60.2	78.6	46.5	40.8	15.9	39.8
Return on Total Assets 46	11.4	•	23.2	10.1	10.8	5.5	8.7	10.9	6.4	13.5	0.6	8.6
Return on Equity Before Income Taxes 47	17.7	•	64.8	13.5	22.0	7.2	16.1	36.5	8.6	15.6	0.4	9.4
Return on Equity After Income Taxes 48	15.0	•	61.5	12.5	18.2	5.9	13.2	28.5	6.6	13.7	0.3	6.5
Profit Margin (Before Income Tax) 49	35.3	53.4	37.2	31.9	36.2	21.2	27.8	34.9	34.7	44.6	8.7	30.6
Profit Margin (After Income Tax) 50	29.9	44.4	35.3	29.6	29.9	17.2	22.8	27.3	26.8	39.3	6.7	21.3

Table I
Corporations with and without Net Income

OFFICES OF REAL ESTATE AGENTS AND BROKERS

MONEY AMOUNTS AND SIZE OF ASSETS IN THOUSANDS OF DOLLARS

Item Description for Accounting Period 7/02 Through 6/03	Total	Zero Assets	Under 500	500 to 1,000	1,000 to 5,000	5,000 to 10,000	10,000 to 25,000	25,000 to 50,000	50,000 to 100,000	100,000 to 250,000	250,000 to 500,000	500,000 to 2,500,000	2,500,000 and over
Number of Enterprises 1	85277	6952	73869	2143	2003	188	78	18	11	9	0	7	0
Revenues ($ in Thousands)													
Net Sales 2	43306223	748552	27456978	2574760	4778541	843212	1723672	958176	597850	857069	0	2767414	0
Interest 3	153733	2616	17884	10005	28078	1064	4613	3333	13759	30427	0	41953	0
Rents 4	305882	0	14355	12011	56161	6762	18868	1563	8795	18356	0	169212	0
Royalties 5	9787	0	5700	0	64	0	0	0	123	0	0	3900	0
Other Portfolio Income 6	187346	12240	9275	26833	71342	4962	5150	9836	4715	36	0	42957	0
Other Receipts 7	42649475	733696	27409764	2525911	4622896	830424	1695241	943444	570458	808250	0	2509392	0
Total Receipts 8	43306223	748552	27456978	2574760	4778541	843212	1723672	958176	597850	857069	0	2767414	0
Average Total Receipts 9	508	108	372	1201	2386	4485	22098	53232	54350	95230	.	395345	.
Operating Costs/Operating Income (%)													
Cost of Operations 10	18.4	7.7	16.8	19.5	20.8	19.8	36.9	41.7	25.5	35.9	.	5.2	.
Salaries and Wages 11	23.6	5.8	22.1	17.8	24.1	30.2	23.9	19.1	22.5	16.2	.	49.6	.
Taxes Paid 12	1.8	1.8	1.5	1.3	2.0	1.9	1.8	1.6	1.9	1.7	.	5.3	.
Interest Paid 13	1.0	1.1	0.3	1.2	1.9	4.3	1.2	1.3	1.9	4.7	.	4.9	.
Depreciation 14	1.3	0.3	1.1	1.1	1.1	1.6	1.6	2.6	1.6	3.2	.	3.0	.
Amortization and Depletion 15	0.2	3.4	0.1	0.1	0.3	0.1	0.2	0.2	0.6	0.4	.	1.0	.
Pensions and Other Deferred Comp. 16	1.2	1.8	1.6	0.3	0.7	0.3	0.2	0.3	0.3	0.7	.	0.1	.
Employee Benefits 17	0.7	0.5	0.6	0.2	0.9	0.7	0.6	0.7	0.9	0.8	.	1.6	.
Advertising 18	3.6	2.3	4.3	3.3	2.7	2.7	3.0	3.2	3.3	2.4	.	0.7	.
Other Expenses 19	32.7	51.1	32.7	42.2	36.2	25.9	25.2	16.5	27.7	35.6	.	25.1	.
Officers' Compensation 20	8.9	12.2	11.7	4.7	4.3	2.1	2.3	7.1	3.9	1.7	.	2.0	.
Operating Margin 21	6.5	11.9	7.3	8.2	5.1	10.5	3.3	5.9	9.7	.	.	1.5	.
Operating Margin Before Officers' Comp. 22	15.4	24.0	19.0	12.9	9.4	12.6	5.5	12.9	13.6	.	.	3.5	.

Selected Average Balance Sheet ($ in Thousands)

	•	•	•	•	•	•	•	•	•	•	•
Net Receivables 23	27	2	8	135	1131	2206	4081	5327	15706	•	171013
Inventories 24	0	•	0	0	•	•	•	•	•	•	•
Net Property, Plant and Equipment 25	68	22	162	364	1794	4680	7922	17380	37835	•	248958
Total Assets 26	283	66	578	1965	6791	14860	35496	66858	175903	•	1210769
Notes and Loans Payable 27	114	29	242	1201	3164	7526	12444	26049	44554	•	374111
All Other Liabilities 28	76	14	121	464	1448	3499	12196	18943	45637	•	408314
Net Worth 29	92	23	316	300	2179	3836	10856	21867	85712	•	428344

Selected Financial Ratios (Times to 1)

	•	•	•	•	•	•	•	•	•	•	•
Current Ratio 30	1.4	1.8	2.0	1.8	1.8	1.3	1.0	1.1	1.7	•	0.9
Quick Ratio 31	0.9	1.4	1.4	0.8	1.1	0.8	0.4	0.6	1.0	•	0.8
Net Sales to Working Capital 32	16.7	28.3	8.9	5.5	3.3	13.0	•	26.1	3.1	•	1.3
Coverage Ratio 33	7.2	30.0	7.7	3.7	3.5	3.8	5.6	6.1	0.3	11.4	1.3
Total Asset Turnover 34	1.8	5.6	1.8	1.2	0.7	1.5	1.5	0.8	0.5	•	0.3
Inventory Turnover 35	•	•	•	•	•	•	•	•	•	•	•
Receivables Turnover 36	•	•	•	•	•	•	•	•	•	•	•
Total Liabilities to Net Worth 37	2.1	1.9	1.1	5.5	2.1	2.9	2.3	2.1	1.1	•	1.8
Current Assets to Working Capital 38	3.5	2.3	2.0	2.2	2.3	4.1	•	13.4	2.4	•	2.4
Current Liabilities to Working Capital 39	2.5	1.3	1.0	1.2	1.3	3.1	•	12.4	1.4	•	•
Working Capital to Net Sales 40	0.1	0.0	0.1	0.2	0.3	0.1	•	0.0	0.3	•	•
Inventory to Working Capital 41	0.0	•	•	•	0.0	0.0	•	0.6	0.1	•	•
Total Receipts to Cash Flow 42	2.9	2.8	2.2	2.8	3.0	4.3	5.8	3.3	3.5	1.7	4.9
Cost of Goods to Cash Flow 43	0.5	0.5	0.4	0.6	0.6	1.6	2.4	0.8	1.3	0.1	0.3
Cash Flow to Total Debt 44	0.9	3.1	1.5	0.5	0.3	0.5	0.4	0.4	0.3	•	0.1

Selected Financial Factors (in Percentages)

	•	•	•	•	•	•	•	•	•	•	•
Debt Ratio 45	67.3	65.2	53.5	84.7	67.9	74.2	69.4	67.3	51.3	•	64.6
Return on Total Assets 46	13.5	42.3	16.7	8.5	9.8	6.6	10.6	9.4	0.8	•	2.1
Return on Equity Before Income Taxes 47	35.6	117.4	31.2	40.5	21.6	18.8	28.6	24.0	•	•	1.4
Return on Equity After Income Taxes 48	34.5	116.0	30.6	38.0	20.8	17.0	26.1	20.7	•	•	0.7
Profit Margin (Before Income Tax) 49	6.5	7.3	8.2	5.1	10.5	3.3	5.8	9.6	•	11.9	1.6
Profit Margin (After Income Tax) 50	6.3	7.2	8.1	4.8	10.1	2.9	5.3	8.3	•	11.9	0.8

Table II

Corporations with Net Income

OFFICES OF REAL ESTATE AGENTS AND BROKERS

MONEY AMOUNTS AND SIZE OF ASSETS IN THOUSANDS OF DOLLARS

Item Description for Accounting Period 7/02 Through 6/03	Total	Zero Assets	Under 500	500 to 1,000	1,000 to 5,000	5,000 to 10,000	10,000 to 25,000	25,000 to 50,000	50,000 to 100,000	100,000 to 250,000	250,000 to 500,000	500,000 to 2,500,000	2,500,000 and over
Number of Enterprises **1**	51521	4285	44286	1521	1211	140	48	13	0	3	•	0	0
Revenues ($ in Thousands)													
Net Sales **2**	29719450	676109	16106076	2405397	4342891	698941	1443592	709145	0	487563	•	0	0
Interest **3**	96010	367	8329	5120	20001	800	2944	3324	0	2674	•	0	0
Rents **4**	229979	0	9258	4294	24637	1866	11188	1563	0	0	•	0	0
Royalties **5**	151	0	0	0	28	0	0	0	0	0	•	0	0
Other Portfolio Income **6**	161600	12069	3292	23712	58481	4320	4169	7976	0	16	•	0	0
Other Receipts **7**	29231710	663673	16085197	2372271	4239744	691955	1425291	696282	0	484873	•	0	0
Total Receipts **8**	29719450	676109	16106076	2405397	4342891	698941	1443592	709145	0	487563	•	0	0
Average Total Receipts **9**	577	158	364	1581	3586	4992	30075	54550	•	162521	•	•	•
Operating Costs/Operating Income (%)													
Cost of Operations **10**	18.3	0.0	15.4	20.9	21.5	23.8	33.3	39.7	•	63.2	•	•	•
Salaries and Wages **11**	22.9	6.4	20.8	18.7	23.0	29.9	24.8	19.1	•	9.0	•	•	•
Taxes Paid **12**	1.8	1.8	1.5	1.1	1.7	1.6	1.6	1.5	•	0.8	•	•	•
Interest Paid **13**	0.9	0.1	0.2	0.7	0.8	4.8	0.9	1.1	•	2.4	•	•	•
Depreciation **14**	1.1	0.2	0.9	0.9	0.8	1.3	1.3	1.7	•	1.7	•	•	•
Amortization and Depletion **15**	0.1	0.0	0.1	0.0	0.3	0.0	0.2	0.3	•	0.2	•	•	•
Pensions and Other Deferred Comp. **16**	0.8	2.0	1.1	0.2	0.7	0.2	0.2	0.3	•	1.1	•	•	•
Employee Benefits **17**	0.7	0.6	0.6	0.2	0.9	0.7	0.6	0.6	•	0.0	•	•	•
Advertising **18**	3.5	2.3	4.5	3.5	2.5	1.5	3.1	2.9	•	2.0	•	•	•
Other Expenses **19**	31.4	53.1	31.4	41.2	35.3	17.2	26.0	18.4	•	9.5	•	•	•
Officers' Compensation **20**	6.2	13.4	8.3	3.4	3.8	2.3	1.9	5.4	•	2.2	•	•	•
Operating Margin **21**	12.4	20.1	15.3	9.2	8.7	16.6	6.0	8.9	•	7.9	•	•	•
Operating Margin Before Officers' Comp. **22**	18.5	33.5	23.6	12.7	12.4	18.9	7.9	14.3	•	10.1	•	•	•

Selected Average Balance Sheet ($ in Thousands)

Net Receivables 23	29	0	1	12	131	1257	2120	4228	6051
Inventories 24	•	•	•	•	•	•	•	•	•
Net Property, Plant and Equipment 25	66	0	14	160	280	1155	3443	5756	12668
Total Assets 26	316	0	64	682	1856	6923	15226	35750	155420
Notes and Loans Payable 27	100	0	15	233	676	2871	6774	11444	0
All Other Liabilities 28	93	0	12	123	544	1159	3836	9913	67320
Net Worth 29	124	0	37	327	636	2892	4616	14392	88100

Selected Financial Ratios (Times to 1)

Current Ratio 30	1.5	•	2.9	2.5	1.8	3.1	1.4	1.2	1.3
Quick Ratio 31	1.0	•	2.3	1.7	0.9	2.0	0.7	0.6	0.5
Net Sales to Working Capital 32	13.6	•	16.1	9.4	8.2	2.2	13.2	20.4	8.8
Coverage Ratio 33	14.2	180.1	81.8	13.5	11.3	4.5	7.6	9.3	4.3
Total Asset Turnover 34	1.8	•	5.7	2.3	1.9	0.7	2.0	1.5	1.0
Inventory Turnover 35	•	•	•	•	•	•	•	•	•
Receivables Turnover 36	•	•	•	•	•	•	•	•	•
Total Liabilities to Net Worth 37	1.6	•	0.7	1.1	1.9	1.4	2.3	1.5	0.8
Current Assets to Working Capital 38	2.9	•	1.5	1.7	2.2	1.5	3.6	6.0	4.6
Current Liabilities to Working Capital 39	1.9	•	0.5	0.7	1.2	0.5	2.6	5.0	3.6
Working Capital to Net Sales 40	0.1	•	0.1	0.1	0.1	0.5	0.1	0.0	0.1
Inventory to Working Capital 41	0.0	•	•	•	•	0.0	•	0.6	•
Total Receipts to Cash Flow 42	2.6	1.5	2.4	2.2	2.6	3.3	3.7	4.4	7.3
Cost of Goods to Cash Flow 43	0.5	0.0	0.4	0.5	0.6	0.8	1.2	1.7	4.6
Cash Flow to Total Debt 44	1.2	•	5.7	2.1	1.2	0.4	0.8	0.6	0.3

Selected Financial Factors (in Percentages)

Debt Ratio 45	60.9	•	41.8	52.1	65.7	58.2	69.7	59.7	43.3
Return on Total Assets 46	24.2	•	88.5	23.1	18.4	15.4	13.6	15.2	10.7
Return on Equity Before Income Taxes 47	57.7	•	150.3	44.7	49.0	28.7	39.1	33.8	14.5
Return on Equity After Income Taxes 48	56.3	•	148.8	43.9	47.0	27.9	36.6	31.1	14.2
Profit Margin (Before Income Tax) 49	12.4	20.1	15.3	9.2	8.7	16.6	6.0	8.9	7.9
Profit Margin (After Income Tax) 50	12.1	20.1	15.2	9.1	8.3	16.1	5.6	8.2	7.7

Table I

Corporations with and without Net Income

OTHER REAL ESTATE ACTIVITIES

MONEY AMOUNTS AND SIZE OF ASSETS IN THOUSANDS OF DOLLARS

Item Description for Accounting Period 7/02 Through 6/03	Total	Zero Assets	Under 500	500 to 1,000	1,000 to 5,000	5,000 to 10,000	10,000 to 25,000	25,000 to 50,000	50,000 to 100,000	100,000 to 250,000	250,000 to 500,000	500,000 to 2,500,000	2,500,000 and over
Number of Enterprises **1**	163184	24449	118931	7856	9492	1200	822	259	122	41	12	0	•
Revenues ($ in Thousands)													
Net Sales **2**	43815696	1460312	19188046	1980215	6741424	2783645	3585126	2507020	2205906	1297155	2066849	0	•
Interest **3**	609187	46682	78323	63788	86842	32052	93140	57626	66530	30993	53210	0	•
Rents **4**	1532203	80327	276367	75654	226613	118167	200789	197026	133038	172998	51225	0	•
Royalties **5**	44236	4345	1295	0	25055	1774	3255	716	7482	22	292	0	•
Other Portfolio Income **6**	1534902	317549	107812	144432	212915	134938	104001	152794	98765	98879	162818	0	•
Other Receipts **7**	40095168	1011409	18724249	1696341	6189999	2496714	3183941	2098858	1900091	994263	1799304	0	•
Total Receipts **8**	43815696	1460312	19188046	1980215	6741424	2783645	3585126	2507020	2205906	1297155	2066849	0	•
Average Total Receipts **9**	269	60	161	252	710	2320	4361	9680	18081	31638	172237	•	•
Operating Costs/Operating Income (%)													
Cost of Operations **10**	7.6	6.2	3.4	11.0	10.5	10.4	16.9	17.8	8.8	2.6	4.8	•	•
Salaries and Wages **11**	27.0	13.6	29.0	19.6	29.0	26.5	29.9	19.3	13.5	21.6	40.7	•	•
Taxes Paid **12**	3.6	5.6	3.7	4.4	4.1	3.9	3.4	3.3	2.6	3.4	1.3	•	•
Interest Paid **13**	3.7	6.8	1.6	3.7	4.8	3.8	7.2	7.1	5.1	6.3	4.6	•	•
Depreciation **14**	2.6	4.1	1.7	2.7	2.4	2.6	4.4	3.8	3.5	3.8	3.6	•	•
Amortization and Depletion **15**	0.5	1.1	0.1	0.1	0.6	0.3	0.5	0.7	0.6	1.0	2.8	•	•
Pensions and Other Deferred Comp. **16**	0.7	0.1	1.0	1.7	0.6	0.2	0.3	0.1	0.4	0.7	0.4	•	•
Employee Benefits **17**	1.7	0.8	1.4	1.7	2.2	1.1	1.4	1.2	3.7	0.9	3.6	•	•
Advertising **18**	0.9	0.3	0.9	0.3	0.8	0.8	1.1	1.5	1.7	1.3	0.7	•	•
Other Expenses **19**	40.8	42.2	43.2	40.4	35.8	41.5	30.0	40.4	58.8	41.5	33.2	•	•
Officers' Compensation **20**	7.4	7.3	10.9	9.6	5.8	2.9	3.3	3.9	3.2	4.8	1.1	•	•
Operating Margin **21**	3.5	11.7	3.1	5.0	3.4	5.9	1.8	0.9	•	12.0	3.1	•	•
Operating Margin Before Officers' Comp. **22**	10.8	19.0	13.9	14.6	8.9	5.1	4.8	1.3	•	16.8	4.2	•	•

Selected Average Balance Sheet ($ in Thousands)

	•	•	•	•	•	•	•	•	•	•
Net Receivables 23	41	6	45	164	477	1195	1848	6046	10786	68632
Inventories 24	•	•	•	•	•	•	•	•	•	•
Net Property, Plant and Equipment 25	159	28	231	742	2567	4896	11230	18642	23512	47037
Total Assets 26	519	92	691	2112	6875	15044	34523	68461	142936	364042
Notes and Loans Payable 27	271	72	398	1160	4039	7741	15157	27193	46316	108497
All Other Liabilities 28	110	25	154	312	1010	2943	9083	14530	43569	110777
Net Worth 29	137	-4	139	640	1826	4360	10283	26737	53051	144768

Selected Financial Ratios (Times to 1)

	•	•	•	•	•	•	•	•	•	•
Current Ratio 30	1.7	1.9	2.3	2.1	1.5	1.6	1.3	1.6	1.3	1.6
Quick Ratio 31	1.1	1.5	1.5	1.3	0.7	0.9	0.8	1.1	0.8	1.2
Net Sales to Working Capital 32	3.9	8.8	1.8	2.1	3.8	2.5	4.3	2.6	3.3	3.4
Coverage Ratio 33	1.9	2.9	2.4	1.7	2.5	1.2	1.1	0.6	2.9	1.7
Total Asset Turnover 34	0.5	1.7	0.4	0.3	0.3	0.3	0.3	0.3	0.2	0.5
Inventory Turnover 35	•	•	•	•	•	•	•	•	•	•
Receivables Turnover 36	•	•	•	•	•	•	•	•	•	•
Total Liabilities to Net Worth 37	2.8	•	4.0	2.3	2.8	2.5	2.4	1.6	1.7	1.5
Current Assets to Working Capital 38	2.5	2.1	1.8	2.0	3.2	2.7	4.1	2.6	5.0	2.5
Current Liabilities to Working Capital 39	1.5	1.1	0.8	1.0	2.2	1.7	3.1	1.6	4.0	1.5
Working Capital to Net Sales 40	0.3	0.1	0.6	0.5	0.3	0.4	0.2	0.4	0.3	0.3
Inventory to Working Capital 41	0.0	•	0.0	0.0	0.0	0.0	0.1	0.0	0.0	0.1
Total Receipts to Cash Flow 42	3.3	3.0	3.0	3.9	4.0	4.2	3.6	2.7	2.5	3.2
Cost of Goods to Cash Flow 43	0.2	0.1	0.3	0.4	0.4	0.7	0.6	0.2	0.1	0.2
Cash Flow to Total Debt 44	0.2	0.6	0.2	0.1	0.1	0.1	0.1	0.2	0.1	0.2

Selected Financial Factors (in Percentages)

	•	•	•	•	•	•	•	•	•	•
Debt Ratio 45	73.7	104.5	79.8	69.7	73.4	71.0	70.2	60.9	62.9	60.2
Return on Total Assets 46	3.7	8.1	3.2	2.7	3.6	3.2	2.6	2.2	4.0	3.6
Return on Equity Before Income Taxes 47	6.7	•	•	9.0	3.6	7.2	1.7	0.7	7.1	3.7
Return on Equity After Income Taxes 48	4.6	•	•	6.0	2.3	4.3	0.6	•	5.1	3.2
Profit Margin (Before Income Tax) 49	3.4	11.7	3.1	5.0	3.3	5.7	1.7	0.7	11.9	3.1
Profit Margin (After Income Tax) 50	2.3	6.1	2.8	3.3	2.1	3.4	0.6	•	8.5	2.7

Table II

Corporations with Net Income

OTHER REAL ESTATE ACTIVITIES

MONEY AMOUNTS AND SIZE OF ASSETS IN THOUSANDS OF DOLLARS

Item Description for Accounting Period 7/02 Through 6/03	Total	Zero Assets	Under 500	500 to 1,000	1,000 to 5,000	5,000 to 10,000	10,000 to 25,000	25,000 to 50,000	50,000 to 100,000	100,000 to 250,000	250,000 to 500,000	500,000 to 2,500,000	2,500,000 and over
Number of Enterprises **1**	68868	10795	49718	3641	3685	477	348	124	50	24	6	0	•
Revenues ($ in Thousands)													
Net Sales **2**	28738693	974709	12863973	1584802	4401131	2248891	2149629	1245746	817528	1026680	1425604	0	•
Interest **3**	359884	27769	39868	44667	54298	18519	43511	32784	34093	19589	44787	0	•
Rents **4**	997663	38189	168127	49346	152488	75948	101944	133011	114232	149392	14985	0	•
Royalties **5**	41608	4345	0	0	25050	1774	2939	52	7449	0	0	0	•
Other Portfolio Income **6**	1209607	306270	95859	137741	181446	123062	66586	120237	73528	67818	37063	0	•
Other Receipts **7**	26129931	598136	12560119	1353048	3987849	2029588	1934649	959662	588226	789881	1328769	0	•
Total Receipts **8**	28738693	974709	12863973	1584802	4401131	2248891	2149629	1245746	817528	1026680	1425604	0	•
Average Total Receipts **9**	417	90	259	435	1194	4715	6177	10046	16351	42778	237601	•	•
Operating Costs/Operating Income (%)													
Cost of Operations **10**	7.2	1.4	2.9	10.8	11.8	8.9	17.1	13.3	17.3	3.1	6.4	•	•
Salaries and Wages **11**	25.3	3.8	28.4	17.2	21.5	28.1	24.1	21.6	17.3	21.9	41.2	•	•
Taxes Paid **12**	3.4	4.9	3.4	3.2	3.6	3.8	3.2	3.7	3.7	3.5	1.0	•	•
Interest Paid **13**	2.3	5.3	0.8	1.9	2.7	1.8	4.7	6.0	5.7	5.4	2.8	•	•
Depreciation **14**	2.0	1.7	1.3	1.4	2.2	2.1	2.8	3.5	4.4	3.8	3.1	•	•
Amortization and Depletion **15**	0.3	0.3	0.0	0.1	0.2	0.1	0.3	0.5	0.6	0.6	3.4	•	•
Pensions and Other Deferred Comp. **16**	0.8	0.1	1.4	0.5	0.5	0.2	0.3	0.2	0.5	0.5	0.0	•	•
Employee Benefits **17**	1.4	0.2	1.1	1.5	2.2	0.8	1.0	0.9	1.5	0.9	5.1	•	•
Advertising **18**	0.9	0.1	1.1	0.2	0.5	0.7	1.1	0.9	1.1	1.4	0.1	•	•
Other Expenses **19**	31.7	37.4	27.4	27.7	27.5	33.2	20.3	25.1	22.0	31.9	30.5	•	•
Officers' Compensation **20**	6.6	6.3	8.9	7.6	6.6	2.8	3.8	4.0	3.8	5.4	0.3	•	•
Operating Margin **21**	18.1	54.7	13.3	27.9	20.6	17.6	21.2	20.2	22.0	21.7	6.1	•	•
Operating Margin Before Officers' Comp. **22**	24.7	60.9	22.2	35.5	27.2	20.4	25.0	24.3	25.7	27.1	6.4	•	•

Selected Average Balance Sheet ($ in Thousands)

Net Receivables 23	47	0	7	44	178	562	1674	1690	5088	10954	86188	•
Inventories 24	•	•	•	•	•	•	•	•	•	•	•	•
Net Property, Plant and Equipment 25	133	0	18	165	605	2450	3836	10127	20609	17834	43865	•
Total Assets 26	542	0	93	671	2212	6958	15330	33976	68479	143063	400729	•
Notes and Loans Payable 27	214	0	43	232	965	3146	6934	12721	24021	34342	116194	•
All Other Liabilities 28	115	0	20	133	383	923	3119	6837	13456	56388	98898	•
Net Worth 29	214	0	30	306	864	2889	5277	14418	31002	52333	185637	•

Selected Financial Ratios (Times to 1)

Current Ratio 30	1.7	•	2.8	1.8	1.8	1.6	1.3	1.7	1.0	1.5	•
Quick Ratio 31	1.2	•	2.4	2.0	1.3	1.0	0.8	1.2	0.7	1.2	•
Net Sales to Working Capital 32	4.8	•	8.2	2.1	3.4	4.7	2.6	4.3	1.9	18.5	4.6
Coverage Ratio 33	8.8	11.3	18.0	15.6	8.6	10.5	5.5	4.3	4.8	5.0	3.2
Total Asset Turnover 34	0.8	•	2.8	0.6	0.6	0.5	0.7	0.4	0.3	0.2	0.6
Inventory Turnover 35	•	•	•	•	•	•	•	•	•	•	•
Receivables Turnover 36	•	•	•	•	•	•	•	•	•	•	•
Total Liabilities to Net Worth 37	1.5	•	2.1	1.2	1.6	1.4	1.9	1.4	1.2	1.7	1.2
Current Assets to Working Capital 38	2.4	•	1.6	1.6	2.2	2.3	2.6	4.3	2.4	23.7	2.9
Current Liabilities to Working Capital 39	1.4	•	0.6	0.6	1.2	1.3	1.6	3.3	1.4	22.7	1.9
Working Capital to Net Sales 40	0.2	•	0.1	0.5	0.3	0.2	0.4	0.2	0.5	0.1	0.2
Inventory to Working Capital 41	0.0	•	•	0.0	0.0	0.0	0.0	0.1	0.0	0.0	0.1
Total Receipts to Cash Flow 42	2.8	2.0	2.7	2.3	2.8	3.6	2.8	3.2	3.2	2.4	3.1
Cost of Goods to Cash Flow 43	0.2	0.0	0.1	0.2	0.3	0.3	0.5	0.4	0.6	0.1	0.2
Cash Flow to Total Debt 44	0.5	•	1.5	0.5	0.3	0.2	0.3	0.2	0.1	0.2	0.4

Selected Financial Factors (in Percentages)

Debt Ratio 45	60.6	•	67.8	54.3	60.9	58.5	65.6	57.6	54.7	63.4	53.7
Return on Total Assets 46	15.6	•	39.3	19.3	12.5	13.0	10.4	7.7	6.5	8.1	5.3
Return on Equity Before Income Taxes 47	35.1	•	115.2	39.6	28.3	28.3	24.7	13.9	11.5	17.7	7.8
Return on Equity After Income Taxes 48	32.0	•	111.6	36.7	25.8	23.7	22.6	12.1	9.2	14.3	7.1
Profit Margin (Before Income Tax) 49	18.0	54.6	13.3	27.9	20.5	17.4	21.1	20.0	21.7	21.7	6.1
Profit Margin (After Income Tax) 50	16.4	46.2	12.9	25.8	18.7	14.6	19.3	17.3	17.5	17.5	5.5

Table I

Corporations with and without Net Income

AUTOMOTIVE EQUIPMENT RENTAL AND LEASING

MONEY AMOUNTS AND SIZE OF ASSETS IN THOUSANDS OF DOLLARS

Item Description for Accounting Period 7/02 Through 6/03	Total	Zero Assets	Under 500	500 to 1,000	1,000 to 5,000	5,000 to 10,000	10,000 to 25,000	25,000 to 50,000	50,000 to 100,000	100,000 to 250,000	250,000 to 500,000	500,000 to 2,500,000	2,500,000 and over
Number of Enterprises **1**	11157	1690	7060	873	1144	150	147	52	18	13	0	4	6
Revenues ($ in Thousands)													
Net Sales **2**	4947603	175195	952565	418050	2391608	902011	1891771	1127552	1091958	7107652	0	3393364	30035876
Interest **3**	1017570	141	4000	500	4297	2565	5094	2384	4331	42562	0	16806	934891
Rents **4**	134261	0	81	773	12	1059	594	714	9081	2018	0	574	119356
Royalties **5**	24098	230	0	0	0	11797	0	0	0	0	0	0	12070
Other Portfolio Income **6**	1006627	14110	33824	18949	125017	22882	143678	54318	56249	125741	0	49052	362812
Other Receipts **7**	4730547	160714	914660	397828	2262282	863708	1742405	1070136	1022297	6937331	0	3326932	28606747
Total Receipts **8**	4947603	175195	952565	418050	2391608	902011	1891771	1127552	1091958	7107652	0	3393364	30035876
Average Total Receipts **9**	4436	104	135	479	2091	6013	12869	21684	60664	546742	•	848341	5005979
Operating Costs/Operating Income (%)													
Cost of Operations **10**	44.0	22.8	56.4	30.2	29.3	41.3	31.3	43.2	10.5	51.8	•	28.9	47.0
Salaries and Wages **11**	10.0	6.2	3.8	10.4	11.9	11.0	9.2	7.3	13.7	5.0	•	5.1	11.8
Taxes Paid **12**	1.9	2.0	1.0	3.0	4.7	2.2	2.1	1.9	2.3	1.1	•	0.5	2.1
Interest Paid **13**	5.1	4.1	5.4	5.1	4.3	4.6	6.2	5.1	4.6	4.4	•	4.7	5.3
Depreciation **14**	15.8	36.6	18.6	17.8	20.8	18.7	35.6	33.4	22.2	17.2	•	65.4	6.9
Amortization and Depletion **15**	0.2	0.0	0.0	•	0.0	0.0	0.1	0.1	0.2	0.0	•	0.4	0.2
Pensions and Other Deferred Comp. **16**	0.3	0.0	0.1	0.1	0.0	0.0	0.2	0.2	2.2	0.1	•	0.2	0.3
Employee Benefits **17**	1.0	0.4	0.5	0.0	0.6	0.2	0.7	0.6	1.9	0.7	•	0.6	1.2
Advertising **18**	0.9	1.2	0.5	1.8	2.4	0.2	1.0	0.6	0.4	0.8	•	0.3	0.9
Other Expenses **19**	23.7	15.2	14.8	27.0	26.5	19.9	14.7	12.0	43.7	22.0	•	3.1	26.9
Officers' Compensation **20**	0.5	1.1	2.2	7.0	1.9	0.9	1.7	1.3	1.3	0.2	•	0.3	0.2
Operating Margin **21**	•	10.4	•	•	•	0.9	•	•	•	•	•	•	•
Operating Margin Before Officers' Comp. **22**	•	11.4	•	•	4.5	1.8	•	•	•	•	•	•	•

Selected Average Balance Sheet ($ in Thousands)

Net Receivables 23	316	0	11	83	310	435	1328	4496	7820	26745	115108	263840
Inventories 24	•	•	•	•	•	•	•	•	•	•	•	•
Net Property, Plant and Equipment 25	2489	0	67	254	1390	5149	10311	22114	44993	98508	912452	2717797
Total Assets 26	4153	0	129	691	2252	8129	15688	34630	73906	179697	1460478	4567890
Notes and Loans Payable 27	2531	0	188	307	1627	5316	11121	24438	49562	168728	1221884	2185599
All Other Liabilities 28	1043	0	10	22	301	838	1369	5381	12018	37263	144208	1552774
Net Worth 29	578	0	-70	361	324	1975	3198	4911	12325	-26293	94386	829517

Selected Financial Ratios (Times to 1)

Current Ratio 30	0.5	•	3.3	2.6	0.7	0.8	0.7	0.7	1.0	1.0	0.2	0.4
Quick Ratio 31	0.3	•	2.3	2.0	0.5	0.4	0.4	0.5	0.7	0.6	0.2	0.3
Net Sales to Working Capital 32	•	•	4.8	2.5	•	•	•	•	•	222.1	•	•
Coverage Ratio 33	0.4	3.5	0.4	0.5	0.5	1.2	0.6	0.4	•	0.3	•	0.5
Total Asset Turnover 34	1.1	•	1.0	0.7	0.9	0.7	0.8	0.6	0.8	3.0	0.6	1.1
Inventory Turnover 35	•	•	•	•	•	•	•	•	•	•	•	•
Receivables Turnover 36	•	•	•	•	•	•	•	•	•	•	•	•
Total Liabilities to Net Worth 37	6.2	•	•	0.9	5.9	3.1	3.9	6.1	5.0	•	14.5	4.5
Current Assets to Working Capital 38	•	•	1.4	1.6	•	•	•	•	•	31.0	•	•
Current Liabilities to Working Capital 39	•	•	0.4	0.6	•	•	•	•	•	30.0	•	•
Working Capital to Net Sales 40	•	•	0.2	0.4	•	•	•	•	•	0.0	•	•
Inventory to Working Capital 41	•	•	0.0	0.1	•	•	•	•	•	0.3	•	•
Total Receipts to Cash Flow 42	9.4	7.9	20.8	7.6	12.2	6.5	14.5	48.1	4.2	14.4	•	7.3
Cost of Goods to Cash Flow 43	4.1	1.8	11.7	2.3	3.6	2.7	4.5	20.8	0.4	7.4	•	3.4
Cash Flow to Total Debt 44	0.1	•	0.0	0.2	0.1	0.1	0.1	0.0	0.2	0.2	•	0.2

Selected Financial Factors (in Percentages)

Debt Ratio 45	86.1	•	154.3	47.7	85.6	75.7	79.6	85.8	83.3	114.6	93.5	81.8
Return on Total Assets 46	1.9	•	2.4	1.8	1.8	4.1	2.9	•	1.4	3.5	•	2.7
Return on Equity Before Income Taxes 47	•	•	6.2	2.7	•	•	•	•	•	66.6	•	•
Return on Equity After Income Taxes 48	•	•	6.3	1.4	•	•	•	•	•	66.9	•	•
Profit Margin (Before Income Tax) 49	10.4	•	•	0.9	•	•	•	•	•	•	•	•
Profit Margin (After Income Tax) 50	10.4	•	•	0.4	•	•	•	•	•	•	•	•

Table II
Corporations with Net Income

AUTOMOTIVE EQUIPMENT RENTAL AND LEASING

MONEY AMOUNTS AND SIZE OF ASSETS IN THOUSANDS OF DOLLARS

Item Description for Accounting Period 7/02 Through 6/03	Total	Zero Assets	Under 500	500 to 1,000	1,000 to 5,000	5,000 to 10,000	10,000 to 25,000	25,000 to 50,000	50,000 to 100,000	100,000 to 250,000	250,000 to 500,000	500,000 to 2,500,000	2,500,000 and over
Number of Enterprises **1**	4295	937	2341	410	436	83	63	10	7	0	•	•	0
Revenues ($ in Thousands)													
Net Sales **2**	10515561	150264	229543	162483	781923	667746	900633	445995	664617	0	0	0	0
Interest **3**	299743	141	1499	427	2435	2479	2716	258	3090	0	0	0	0
Rents **4**	108350	0	81	692	12	744	363	114	9041	0	0	0	0
Royalties **5**	230	230	0	0	0	0	0	0	0	0	0	0	0
Other Portfolio Income **6**	278846	13848	10995	3719	78422	16203	54298	5772	18888	0	0	0	0
Other Receipts **7**	9828392	136045	216968	157645	701054	648320	843256	439851	633598	0	0	0	0
Total Receipts **8**	10515561	150264	229543	162483	781923	667746	900633	445995	664617	0	0	0	0
Average Total Receipts **9**	2448	160	98	396	1793	8045	14296	44600	94945	•	•	•	•
Operating Costs/Operating Income (%)													
Cost of Operations **10**	22.2	26.2	0.2	53.6	27.6	52.5	46.3	71.3	6.2	•	•	•	•
Salaries and Wages **11**	10.1	2.5	6.2	6.1	8.5	6.3	7.6	5.5	15.9	•	•	•	•
Taxes Paid **12**	2.4	1.9	1.6	1.7	4.9	1.7	1.9	1.3	2.1	•	•	•	•
Interest Paid **13**	7.1	2.3	10.1	2.6	4.3	3.1	3.8	2.2	2.9	•	•	•	•
Depreciation **14**	11.9	34.7	33.8	7.6	22.7	10.5	22.7	7.7	10.0	•	•	•	•
Amortization and Depletion **15**	0.3	0.0	0.0	•	0.0	0.0	0.0	0.1	0.3	•	•	•	•
Pensions and Other Deferred Comp. **16**	0.4	•	•	0.1	0.0	0.0	0.2	0.3	3.5	•	•	•	•
Employee Benefits **17**	1.2	0.3	•	0.5	0.2	0.2	0.7	0.3	2.5	•	•	•	•
Advertising **18**	1.2	0.7	1.2	1.4	0.7	0.2	0.9	0.6	0.2	•	•	•	•
Other Expenses **19**	37.8	15.6	28.6	6.1	21.5	17.7	9.5	6.5	54.8	•	•	•	•
Officers' Compensation **20**	0.8	1.2	0.0	9.3	3.0	1.2	1.6	0.7	0.9	•	•	•	•
Operating Margin **21**	4.6	14.6	18.1	11.6	6.0	6.5	4.7	3.6	0.7	•	•	•	•
Operating Margin Before Officers' Comp. **22**	5.3	15.8	18.2	20.9	9.0	7.7	6.3	4.3	1.7	•	•	•	•

Selected Average Balance Sheet ($ in Thousands)

Net Receivables 23	232	0	12	17	256	478	1494	6270	13947
Inventories 24	•	•	•	•	•	•	•	•	•
Net Property, Plant and Equipment 25	1029	0	71	192	1303	4053	9315	15876	39661
Total Assets 26	2830	139	772	2051	8139	16167	35665	73558	•
Notes and Loans Payable 27	1648	0	281	125	1481	4249	9968	14678	41937
All Other Liabilities 28	746	0	9	16	161	720	1179	10839	19216
Net Worth 29	436	0	-150	632	408	3170	5020	10147	12405

Selected Financial Ratios (Times to 1)

Current Ratio 30	0.6	•	7.6	14.8	0.7	1.2	0.9	0.8	1.9
Quick Ratio 31	0.4	•	4.7	10.5	0.5	0.6	0.5	0.5	1.4
Net Sales to Working Capital 32	•	•	1.7	1.1	•	16.5	•	•	10.0
Coverage Ratio 33	1.6	7.4	2.8	5.5	2.4	3.1	2.2	2.6	1.3
Total Asset Turnover 34	0.9	•	0.7	0.5	0.9	1.0	0.9	1.3	1.3
Inventory Turnover 35	•	•	•	•	•	•	•	•	•
Receivables Turnover 36	•	•	•	•	•	•	•	•	•
Total Liabilities to Net Worth 37	5.5	•	•	0.2	4.0	1.6	2.2	2.5	4.9
Current Assets to Working Capital 38	•	•	1.2	1.1	•	6.2	•	•	2.2
Current Liabilities to Working Capital 39	•	•	0.2	0.1	•	5.2	•	•	1.2
Working Capital to Net Sales 40	•	•	0.6	0.9	0.1	0.1	•	•	0.1
Inventory to Working Capital 41	•	•	•	0.1	•	2.2	•	•	0.2
Total Receipts to Cash Flow 42	4.3	5.2	3.4	6.1	5.6	5.1	9.5	12.7	2.8
Cost of Goods to Cash Flow 43	1.0	1.4	0.0	3.3	1.6	2.7	4.4	9.0	0.2
Cash Flow to Total Debt 44	0.2	•	0.1	0.5	0.2	0.3	0.1	0.1	0.6

Selected Financial Factors (in Percentages)

Debt Ratio 45	84.6	•	207.7	18.2	80.1	61.0	68.9	71.5	83.1
Return on Total Assets 46	10.1	•	19.9	7.3	9.0	9.6	7.5	7.3	4.6
Return on Equity Before Income Taxes 47	25.7	•	•	7.3	26.3	16.6	13.3	15.8	5.7
Return on Equity After Income Taxes 48	24.9	•	•	6.9	24.1	15.0	12.8	15.5	4.9
Profit Margin (Before Income Tax) 49	4.6	14.6	18.1	11.6	6.0	6.5	4.7	3.6	0.7
Profit Margin (After Income Tax) 50	4.4	14.6	17.9	11.0	5.5	5.9	4.5	3.5	0.6

Table I

Corporations with and without Net Income

OTHER CONSUMER GOODS AND GENERAL RENTAL CENTERS

MONEY AMOUNTS AND SIZE OF ASSETS IN THOUSANDS OF DOLLARS

Item Description for Accounting Period 7/02 Through 6/03	Total	Zero Assets	Under 500	500 to 1,000	1,000 to 5,000	5,000 to 10,000	10,000 to 25,000	25,000 to 50,000	50,000 to 100,000	100,000 to 250,000	250,000 to 500,000	500,000 to 2,500,000	2,500,000 and over
Number of Enterprises **1**	12889	276	10916	1170	393	76	33	9	7	4	5	0	*
Revenues ($ in Thousands)													
Net Sales **2**	12612322	68812	2836862	1689902	1961047	1124018	534073	367608	349486	514844	3165671	0	*
Interest **3**	11762	66	634	966	766	1600	1846	181	3358	881	1463	0	*
Rents **4**	7082	0	6060	6	8	51	308	0	0	650	0	0	*
Royalties **5**	1378	0	0	0	0	1378	0	0	0	0	0	0	*
Other Portfolio Income **6**	109404	554	49123	70	4847	13512	8336	3650	24906	4406	0	0	*
Other Receipts **7**	12482696	68192	2781045	1688860	1955426	1107477	523583	363777	321222	508907	3164208	0	*
Total Receipts **8**	12612322	68812	2836862	1689902	1961047	1124018	534073	367608	349486	514844	3165671	0	*
Average Total Receipts **9**	979	249	260	1444	4990	14790	16184	40845	49927	128711	633134	*	*
Operating Costs/Operating Income (%)													
Cost of Operations **10**	22.6	32.0	24.6	24.6	32.9	12.1	38.9	42.9	4.7	18.1	14.3	*	*
Salaries and Wages **11**	19.9	22.2	20.4	19.2	17.4	25.2	16.2	14.2	18.0	24.5	20.2	*	*
Taxes Paid **12**	3.7	5.6	3.8	3.8	4.2	3.2	2.8	2.4	2.7	3.4	3.8	*	*
Interest Paid **13**	1.9	1.9	1.3	1.3	1.4	1.2	3.4	2.5	3.3	1.5	3.0	*	*
Depreciation **14**	11.8	3.5	9.7	5.9	11.1	10.3	12.0	12.7	23.4	6.8	17.2	*	*
Amortization and Depletion **15**	2.9	0.0	0.1	0.1	1.2	0.1	0.8	0.8	2.0	10.9	8.5	*	*
Pensions and Other Deferred Comp. **16**	0.1	0.0	0.1	0.2	0.1	0.2	0.2	0.1	0.3	0.2	0.1	*	*
Employee Benefits **17**	1.1	0.0	1.2	0.6	1.2	1.5	1.2	1.1	1.6	0.8	1.0	*	*
Advertising **18**	1.9	1.0	1.9	1.8	2.7	1.7	1.9	2.1	2.1	2.8	1.3	*	*
Other Expenses **19**	29.3	29.7	28.8	31.6	22.3	38.1	20.6	21.0	55.0	31.3	29.1	*	*
Officers' Compensation **20**	3.7	1.1	7.4	5.7	3.9	2.2	1.7	2.3	1.2	1.8	1.0	*	*
Operating Margin **21**	1.1	3.0	0.7	5.3	1.5	4.0	0.3	*	*	*	0.6	*	*
Operating Margin Before Officers' Comp. **22**	4.8	4.1	8.1	11.1	5.4	6.3	2.0	0.1	*	*	1.5	*	*

Selected Average Balance Sheet ($ in Thousands)

Net Receivables 23	46	0	8	32	263	1282	2205	4745	8540	5203	14932
Inventories 24	•	•	•	•	•	•	•	•	•	•	•
Net Property, Plant and Equipment 25	314	0	78	440	1143	2641	6682	12806	21345	57268	261604
Total Assets 26	651	0	132	730	2319	6384	16071	30842	71615	137852	566720
Notes and Loans Payable 27	344	0	72	630	832	3120	8198	14529	70058	42738	258150
All Other Liabilities 28	128	0	17	69	679	1390	3559	11241	12418	30536	116480
Net Worth 29	178	0	43	31	809	1874	4313	5072	-10861	64579	192091

Selected Financial Ratios (Times to 1)

Current Ratio 30	1.1	•	1.5	2.2	1.0	1.0	0.9	1.4	0.6	1.3	1.0
Quick Ratio 31	0.6	•	0.9	1.2	0.6	0.5	0.5	0.9	0.4	1.1	0.5
Net Sales to Working Capital 32	71.9	•	20.8	10.9	•	•	•	11.1	•	12.5	•
Coverage Ratio 33	1.6	2.6	1.5	5.0	2.0	4.4	1.1	0.1	•	1.2	•
Total Asset Turnover 34	1.5	•	2.0	2.0	2.0	2.3	1.0	1.3	0.7	0.9	1.1
Inventory Turnover 35	•	•	•	•	•	•	•	•	•	•	•
Receivables Turnover 36	•	•	•	•	•	•	•	•	•	•	•
Total Liabilities to Net Worth 37	2.6	2.1	2.1	22.4	1.9	2.4	2.7	5.1	•	1.1	2.0
Current Assets to Working Capital 38	14.9	3.1	1.8	•	•	•	•	3.2	•	4.0	•
Current Liabilities to Working Capital 39	13.9	2.1	2.1	0.8	•	•	•	2.2	•	3.0	•
Working Capital to Net Sales 40	0.0	0.0	0.0	0.1	•	•	•	0.1	•	0.1	•
Inventory to Working Capital 41	3.6	0.9	0.9	0.6	•	•	•	1.0	•	0.4	•
Total Receipts to Cash Flow 42	5.7	4.2	5.5	4.0	7.9	4.2	7.3	7.7	14.5	4.8	6.3
Cost of Goods to Cash Flow 43	1.3	1.4	1.3	1.0	2.6	0.5	2.8	3.3	0.7	0.9	0.9
Cash Flow to Total Debt 44	0.4	0.5	0.5	0.5	0.4	0.8	0.2	0.2	0.0	0.4	0.3

Selected Financial Factors (in Percentages)

Debt Ratio 45	72.6	•	67.3	95.7	65.1	70.6	73.2	83.6	115.2	53.2	66.1
Return on Total Assets 46	4.5	•	3.8	13.2	6.2	12.1	3.7	0.5	•	•	4.0
Return on Equity Before Income Taxes 47	5.9	•	4.1	246.2	9.0	31.9	1.0	•	66.0	•	1.9
Return on Equity After Income Taxes 48	4.8	•	2.8	237.6	7.2	31.2	1.0	•	66.0	•	1.4
Profit Margin (Before Income Tax) 49	1.1	3.0	0.7	5.3	1.5	4.0	0.3	•	•	•	0.6
Profit Margin (After Income Tax) 50	0.9	2.0	0.5	5.1	1.2	3.9	0.3	•	•	•	0.4

Table II

Corporations with Net Income

OTHER CONSUMER GOODS AND GENERAL RENTAL CENTERS

MONEY AMOUNTS AND SIZE OF ASSETS IN THOUSANDS OF DOLLARS

Item Description for Accounting Period 7/02 Through 6/03	Total	Zero Assets	Under 500	500 to 1,000	1,000 to 5,000	5,000 to 10,000	10,000 to 25,000	25,000 to 50,000	50,000 to 100,000	100,000 to 250,000	250,000 to 500,000	500,000 to 2,500,000	2,500,000 and over
Number of Enterprises 1	6283	0	5269	395	0	69	0	0	0	0	0	0	·
Revenues ($ in Thousands)													
Net Sales 2	7699664	0	2022661	907774	0	1039633	0	0	0	0	0	0	·
Interest 3	4541	0	541	568	0	1143	0	0	0	0	0	0	·
Rents 4	7021	0	6060	0	0	0	0	0	0	0	0	0	·
Royalties 5	1378	0	0	0	0	1378	0	0	0	0	0	0	·
Other Portfolio Income 6	70677	0	48175	0	0	13486	0	0	0	0	0	0	·
Other Receipts 7	7616047	0	1967885	907206	0	1023626	0	0	0	0	0	0	·
Total Receipts 8	7699664	0	2022661	907774	0	1039633	0	0	0	0	0	0	·
Average Total Receipts 9	1225	·	384	2298	·	15067	·	·	·	·	·	·	·
Operating Costs/Operating Income (%)													
Cost of Operations 10	21.7	·	28.4	29.5	·	11.2	·	·	·	·	·	·	·
Salaries and Wages 11	17.9	·	15.8	9.4	·	25.0	·	·	·	·	·	·	·
Taxes Paid 12	3.6	·	3.7	3.3	·	3.1	·	·	·	·	·	·	·
Interest Paid 13	1.5	·	1.1	1.2	·	0.9	·	·	·	·	·	·	·
Depreciation 14	8.7	·	8.3	6.1	·	10.1	·	·	·	·	·	·	·
Amortization and Depletion 15	4.2	·	0.1	·	·	0.1	·	·	·	·	·	·	·
Pensions and Other Deferred Comp. 16	0.1	·	0.1	0.2	·	0.2	·	·	·	·	·	·	·
Employee Benefits 17	0.9	·	1.0	0.8	·	1.6	·	·	·	·	·	·	·
Advertising 18	1.3	·	1.8	0.7	·	1.6	·	·	·	·	·	·	·
Other Expenses 19	29.7	·	27.1	28.6	·	37.6	·	·	·	·	·	·	·
Officers' Compensation 20	3.9	·	6.6	6.5	·	2.3	·	·	·	·	·	·	·
Operating Margin 21	6.3	·	6.0	13.7	·	6.3	·	·	·	·	·	·	·
Operating Margin Before Officers' Comp. 22	10.2	·	12.6	20.2	·	8.5	·	·	·	·	·	·	·

Selected Average Balance Sheet ($ in Thousands)

Net Receivables 23	48	6	6	1382
Inventories 24			6	
Net Property, Plant and Equipment 25	310	75	325	2649
Total Assets 26	648	144	689	6313
Notes and Loans Payable 27	259	61	326	2765
All Other Liabilities 28	139	12	36	1234
Net Worth 29	250	71	327	2314

Selected Financial Ratios (Times to 1)

Current Ratio 30	1.3	2.9	6.1	1.0
Quick Ratio 31	0.8	1.8	3.9	0.7
Net Sales to Working Capital 32	24.2	10.7	7.6	361.1
Coverage Ratio 33	5.1	6.3	12.6	7.7
Total Asset Turnover 34	1.9	2.7	3.3	2.4
Inventory Turnover 35				
Receivables Turnover 36				
Total Liabilities to Net Worth 37	1.6	1.0	1.1	1.7
Current Assets to Working Capital 38	4.6	1.5	1.2	74.0
Current Liabilities to Working Capital 39	3.6	0.5	0.2	73.0
Working Capital to Net Sales 40	0.0	0.1	0.1	0.0
Inventory to Working Capital 41	1.1	0.4	0.1	8.0
Total Receipts to Cash Flow 42	4.4	4.6	3.0	4.0
Cost of Goods to Cash Flow 43	1.0	1.3	0.9	0.4
Cash Flow to Total Debt 44	0.7	1.1	2.1	0.9

Selected Financial Factors (in Percentages)

Debt Ratio 45	61.4	50.6	52.5	63.3
Return on Total Assets 46	14.8	19.0	49.6	17.2
Return on Equity Before Income Taxes 47	31.0	32.3	96.1	40.8
Return on Equity After Income Taxes 48	29.3	30.8	93.7	40.2
Profit Margin (Before Income Tax) 49	6.3	6.0	13.7	6.3
Profit Margin (After Income Tax) 50	6.0	5.7	13.3	6.2

COMMERCIAL AND INDUSTRIAL MACHINERY AND EQUIPMENT RENTAL

Table I

Corporations with and without Net Income

MONEY AMOUNTS AND SIZE OF ASSETS IN THOUSANDS OF DOLLARS

Item Description for Accounting Period 7/02 Through 6/03	Total	Zero Assets	Under 500	500 to 1,000	1,000 to 5,000	5,000 to 10,000	10,000 to 25,000	25,000 to 50,000	50,000 to 100,000	100,000 to 250,000	250,000 to 500,000	500,000 to 2,500,000	2,500,000 and over
Number of Enterprises **1**	29150	2569	19723	2997	2855	526	251	94	52	34	20	20	8
Revenues ($ in Thousands)													
Net Sales **2**	39066704	705451	3242242	2142494	5633555	2804678	2577540	1849389	1619263	2370853	2143417	4996430	8981392
Interest **3**	1177747	19213	6540	2416	28173	14517	19865	26718	29289	79046	131831	486403	327736
Rents **4**	21288	223	0	29	8136	3534	851	3263	937	633	1819	1562	302
Royalties **5**	107161	11866	0	0	55	17378	9	233	0	4704	0	29545	43372
Other Portfolio Income **6**	1304626	51208	83322	15433	170387	61140	79653	32813	71564	66165	123227	309891	239820
Other Receipts **7**	36461882	622941	3152380	2124616	5426804	2708109	2477162	1786362	1517473	1886540	4169029	8370162	
Total Receipts **8**	39066704	705451	3242242	2142494	5633555	2804678	2577540	1849389	1619263	2370853	2143417	4996430	8981392
Average Total Receipts **9**	1340	275	164	715	1973	5332	10269	19674	31140	69731	107171	249822	1122674
Operating Costs/Operating Income (%)													
Cost of Operations **10**	23.3	8.9	17.5	20.1	35.7	34.2	36.8	38.6	30.0	29.2	10.9	17.1	12.9
Salaries and Wages **11**	12.7	14.3	15.7	16.9	15.9	10.0	9.8	8.7	9.2	9.4	10.7	11.8	13.7
Taxes Paid **12**	2.0	1.6	3.6	3.2	2.4	2.7	2.2	1.7	1.7	1.4	1.8	1.2	1.6
Interest Paid **13**	9.0	12.6	2.8	4.6	3.1	4.0	5.8	5.4	8.0	6.8	10.8	16.4	15.2
Depreciation **14**	27.3	39.4	15.8	21.7	15.8	23.5	23.1	26.0	32.4	30.0	34.9	33.0	35.1
Amortization and Depletion **15**	0.7	2.5	0.1	0.1	0.1	0.4	0.4	0.2	0.3	1.0	0.8	1.6	1.1
Pensions and Other Deferred Comp. **16**	0.5	0.1	0.2	0.5	0.3	2.0	0.5	0.3	0.2	0.1	0.2	0.1	0.6
Employee Benefits **17**	1.4	3.0	0.5	0.8	1.2	1.3	1.1	0.7	0.9	1.5	1.1	1.7	2.3
Advertising **18**	0.5	0.2	1.3	0.7	0.4	0.7	0.4	0.4	0.3	0.4	0.5	0.5	0.3
Other Expenses **19**	26.0	89.9	32.8	25.4	23.0	24.9	17.7	17.6	15.7	23.8	29.7	30.1	24.3
Officers' Compensation **20**	2.4	1.2	9.2	6.0	2.9	2.6	2.5	1.9	1.9	1.2	1.3	0.6	0.6
Operating Margin **21**	•	•	0.6	•	•	•	•	•	•	•	•	•	•
Operating Margin Before Officers' Comp. **22**	•	•	9.8	5.9	2.0	•	2.2	0.5	1.2	2.2	•	•	•

Selected Average Balance Sheet ($ in Thousands)

Net Receivables 23	514	0	•	26	72	309	804	2022	5609	7526	28611	56666	216407	636000
Inventories 24	•	•	•	•	•	•	•	•	•	•	•	•	•	•
Net Property, Plant and Equipment 25	1217	0	•	71	383	1073	4742	8103	13975	32212	65507	124859	253212	1568208
Total Assets 26	3350	0	•	151	705	2230	7154	15710	34475	68633	160678	317440	1105320	4720990
Notes and Loans Payable 27	1735	0	•	117	608	1298	4654	10345	18433	42921	77787	120103	555778	2197325
All Other Liabilities 28	798	0	•	13	145	258	862	2144	7130	15259	32059	100420	187316	1567708
Net Worth 29	817	0	•	21	-48	675	1638	3221	8913	10452	50832	96917	362226	955957

Selected Financial Ratios (Times to 1)

Current Ratio 30	1.3	•	•	1.9	1.1	1.8	1.1	1.1	1.6	1.0	1.5	1.3	1.9	1.0
Quick Ratio 31	0.9	•	•	1.4	0.9	1.2	0.8	0.7	0.9	0.6	1.0	1.1	1.2	0.7
Net Sales to Working Capital 32	5.2	•	•	5.5	27.5	5.3	24.8	18.0	4.2	•	4.3	5.1	1.2	•
Coverage Ratio 33	0.3	•	•	1.2	1.0	0.7	•	0.9	0.7	0.9	0.3	0.8	0.2	0.5
Total Asset Turnover 34	0.4	•	•	1.1	1.0	0.9	0.7	0.7	0.6	0.5	0.4	0.3	0.2	0.2
Inventory Turnover 35	•	•	•	•	•	•	•	•	•	•	•	•	•	•
Receivables Turnover 36	•	•	•	•	•	•	•	•	•	•	•	•	•	•
Total Liabilities to Net Worth 37	3.1	•	•	6.1	•	2.3	3.4	3.9	2.9	5.6	2.2	2.3	2.1	3.9
Current Assets to Working Capital 38	3.9	•	•	2.1	9.2	2.3	7.9	8.5	2.8	•	3.1	4.5	2.1	•
Current Liabilities to Working Capital 39	2.9	•	•	1.1	8.2	1.3	6.9	7.5	1.8	•	2.1	3.5	1.1	•
Working Capital to Net Sales 40	0.2	•	•	0.2	0.0	0.2	0.0	0.1	0.2	•	0.2	0.2	0.8	•
Inventory to Working Capital 41	0.3	•	•	0.2	1.3	0.4	0.8	1.6	0.4	•	0.5	0.2	0.1	•
Total Receipts to Cash Flow 42	14.2	•	•	4.3	6.7	9.0	12.7	11.4	11.7	12.5	22.9	6.5	•	34.6
Cost of Goods to Cash Flow 43	3.3	•	•	0.7	1.4	3.2	4.3	4.2	4.5	3.8	6.7	0.7	•	4.5
Cash Flow to Total Debt 44	0.0	•	•	0.3	0.1	0.1	0.1	0.1	0.1	0.0	0.0	0.1	•	0.0

Selected Financial Factors (in Percentages)

Debt Ratio 45	75.6	•	•	85.8	106.8	69.8	77.1	79.5	74.1	84.8	68.4	69.5	67.2	79.8
Return on Total Assets 46	1.2	•	•	3.7	4.5	1.9	•	3.4	2.2	3.3	0.9	2.7	0.7	1.8
Return on Equity Before Income Taxes 47	•	•	•	4.5	1.8	•	•	•	•	•	•	•	•	•
Return on Equity After Income Taxes 48	•	•	•	2.2	4.7	•	•	•	•	•	•	•	•	•
Profit Margin (Before Income Tax) 49	•	•	•	0.6	•	•	•	•	•	•	•	•	•	•
Profit Margin (After Income Tax) 50	•	•	•	0.3	•	•	•	•	•	•	•	•	•	•

Table II
Corporations with Net Income

COMMERCIAL AND INDUSTRIAL MACHINERY AND EQUIPMENT RENTAL

MONEY AMOUNTS AND SIZE OF ASSETS IN THOUSANDS OF DOLLARS

Item Description for Accounting Period 7/02 Through 6/03	Total	Zero Assets	Under 500	500 to 1,000	1,000 to 5,000	5,000 to 10,000	10,000 to 25,000	25,000 to 50,000	50,000 to 100,000	100,000 to 250,000	250,000 to 500,000	500,000 to 2,500,000	2,500,000 and over
Number of Enterprises 1	10584	0	6763	1590	1378	177	108	36	19	17	8	0	0
Revenues ($ in Thousands)													
Net Sales 2	15432079	0	1807610	1667144	3401417	1133118	1470812	758920	894636	1328344	874175	0	0
Interest 3	246000	0	4254	1573	10678	2341	10746	8434	18854	44930	39176	0	0
Rents 4	10247	0	0	29	1888	3454	696	773	16	8	1819	0	0
Royalties 5	17332	0	0	0	0	17236	9	0	0	87	0	0	0
Other Portfolio Income 6	690139	0	76476	14801	124606	34289	39865	14142	49747	46147	71053	0	0
Other Receipts 7	14468361	0	1726880	1650741	3264245	1075798	1419496	735571	826019	1237172	762127	0	0
Total Receipts 8	15432079	0	1807610	1667144	3401417	1133118	1470812	758920	894636	1328344	874175	0	0
Average Total Receipts 9	1458	·	267	1049	2468	6402	13619	21081	47086	78138	109272	·	·
Operating Costs/Operating Income (%)													
Cost of Operations 10	23.6	·	12.7	19.6	33.2	31.4	35.7	33.4	29.7	25.0	8.2	·	·
Salaries and Wages 11	11.8	·	14.3	20.2	16.4	8.2	9.0	8.7	7.3	8.7	12.4	·	·
Taxes Paid 12	2.4	·	3.8	3.3	2.5	3.5	2.3	2.0	1.6	1.7	2.1	·	·
Interest Paid 13	6.0	·	1.9	3.4	1.5	2.3	3.8	4.6	6.2	6.1	7.3	·	·
Depreciation 14	20.2	·	11.8	16.6	12.8	21.1	16.1	22.8	26.7	24.2	35.7	·	·
Amortization and Depletion 15	0.3	·	0.0	0.1	0.1	0.3	0.3	0.1	0.2	1.2	0.6	·	·
Pensions and Other Deferred Comp. 16	0.4	·	0.4	0.6	0.4	0.9	0.6	0.3	0.2	0.1	0.1	·	·
Employee Benefits 17	0.8	·	0.4	1.1	0.6	1.5	1.0	0.5	0.6	0.8	1.5	·	·
Advertising 18	0.5	·	1.3	0.7	0.4	0.6	0.4	0.5	0.4	0.7	0.7	·	·
Other Expenses 19	20.8	·	28.9	20.0	19.1	17.6	15.6	16.5	13.8	24.1	19.9	·	·
Officers' Compensation 20	3.4	·	9.0	6.5	3.2	2.3	2.5	1.6	1.3	1.6	2.0	·	·
Operating Margin 21	9.9	·	15.4	8.0	9.8	10.5	12.7	9.0	12.0	5.7	9.5	·	·
Operating Margin Before Officers' Comp. 22	13.3	·	24.5	14.5	13.0	12.8	15.2	10.6	13.3	7.3	11.5	·	·

Selected Average Balance Sheet ($ in Thousands)

Net Receivables 23	450	•	30	60	339	1105	2743	7679	9501	34236	53160
Inventories 24	•	•	•	•	•	•	•	•	•	•	•
Net Property, Plant and Equipment 25	1001	•	71	396	1072	4074	6518	14377	28624	57278	93915
Total Assets 26	2798	•	170	705	2329	7320	15628	35001	68128	162768	298725
Notes and Loans Payable 27	1233	•	90	411	1025	5587	7675	16253	45680	77971	115066
All Other Liabilities 28	568	•	13	185	237	896	2348	6214	12124	32100	65002
Net Worth 29	998	•	68	109	1068	837	5605	12534	10324	52697	118658

Selected Financial Ratios (Times to 1)

Current Ratio 30	2.2	•	2.1	1.0	2.5	2.4	1.5	2.4	1.1	1.8	2.9
Quick Ratio 31	1.6	•	1.7	0.6	1.6	1.8	0.9	1.4	0.7	1.3	2.4
Net Sales to Working Capital 32	3.2	•	6.8	681.9	4.2	4.3	7.1	2.2	26.3	3.1	1.6
Coverage Ratio 33	2.7	•	9.1	3.3	7.5	5.6	4.4	3.0	2.9	2.0	2.3
Total Asset Turnover 34	0.5	•	1.6	1.5	1.1	0.9	0.9	0.6	0.7	0.5	0.4
Inventory Turnover 35	•	•	•	•	•	•	•	•	•	•	•
Receivables Turnover 36	•	•	•	•	•	•	•	•	•	•	•
Total Liabilities to Net Worth 37	1.8	•	1.5	5.4	1.2	7.7	1.8	1.8	5.6	2.1	1.5
Current Assets to Working Capital 38	1.9	•	1.9	160.0	1.7	1.7	3.1	1.7	12.1	2.3	1.5
Current Liabilities to Working Capital 39	0.9	•	0.9	159.0	0.7	0.7	2.1	0.7	11.1	1.3	0.5
Working Capital to Net Sales 40	0.3	•	0.1	0.0	0.2	0.2	0.1	0.5	0.0	0.3	0.6
Inventory to Working Capital 41	0.2	•	0.2	37.1	0.3	0.2	0.7	0.2	2.1	0.2	0.1
Total Receipts to Cash Flow 42	5.2	•	2.8	5.7	5.2	4.8	5.1	5.6	5.4	6.5	3.9
Cost of Goods to Cash Flow 43	1.2	•	0.4	1.1	1.7	1.5	1.8	1.9	1.6	1.6	0.3
Cash Flow to Total Debt 44	0.2	•	0.9	0.3	0.4	0.2	0.3	0.2	0.2	0.1	0.2

Selected Financial Factors (in Percentages)

Debt Ratio 45	64.3	•	59.9	84.5	54.2	88.6	64.1	64.2	84.8	67.6	60.3
Return on Total Assets 46	8.4	•	27.2	17.0	12.0	11.1	14.3	8.2	12.6	5.8	6.2
Return on Equity Before Income Taxes 47	14.9	•	60.4	76.7	22.6	80.1	30.8	15.1	54.6	8.9	8.8
Return on Equity After Income Taxes 48	13.5	•	58.3	74.2	21.4	70.7	29.6	12.6	51.3	6.4	7.1
Profit Margin (Before Income Tax) 49	10.2	•	15.4	8.0	9.8	10.5	12.7	9.0	12.0	6.0	9.5
Profit Margin (After Income Tax) 50	9.2	•	14.9	7.8	9.3	9.2	12.2	7.5	11.2	4.3	7.7

Table I

Corporations with and without Net Income

LESSORS OF NONFINAN. INTANGIBLE ASSETS (EX. COPYRIGHTED WORKS)

MONEY AMOUNTS AND SIZE OF ASSETS IN THOUSANDS OF DOLLARS

Item Description for Accounting Period 7/02 Through 6/03	Total	Zero Assets	Under 500	500 to 1,000	1,000 to 5,000	5,000 to 10,000	10,000 to 25,000	25,000 to 50,000	50,000 to 100,000	100,000 to 250,000	250,000 to 500,000	500,000 to 2,500,000	2,500,000 and over
Number of Enterprises 1	1242	115	945	113	39	4	7	6	6	4	3	0	0
Revenues ($ in Thousands)													
Net Sales 2	1127323	-1299	147388	54834	93307	22147	83599	114270	168160	241889	203028	0	0
Interest 3	23960	14	57	0	2416	334	1490	3044	195	2571	13839	0	0
Rents 4	3422	0	0	230	0	103	189	0	0	0	2901	0	0
Royalties 5	384202	0	25730	1670	0	17527	17741	47554	34701	98229	141048	0	0
Other Portfolio Income 6	8262	579	0	48	1362	206	387	21	757	4901	0	0	0
Other Receipts 7	707477	-1892	121601	52886	89529	3977	63792	63651	132507	136188	45240	0	0
Total Receipts 8	1127323	-1299	147388	54834	93307	22147	83599	114270	168160	241889	203028	0	0
Average Total Receipts 9	908	-11	156	485	2392	5537	11943	19045	28027	60472	67676	•	•
Operating Costs/Operating Income (%)													
Cost of Operations 10	5.6	•	9.8	•	4.5	•	15.7	7.6	9.4	2.9	•	•	•
Salaries and Wages 11	12.6	•	3.6	0.3	35.4	11.3	18.5	11.6	7.6	19.4	6.0	•	•
Taxes Paid 12	2.5	•	1.4	0.8	3.3	4.7	1.9	3.9	0.5	4.3	2.2	•	•
Interest Paid 13	3.3	•	2.5	•	0.9	2.5	1.0	4.7	7.8	0.1	6.0	•	•
Depreciation 14	2.6	•	0.0	•	2.7	1.5	2.3	0.5	0.5	3.5	7.4	•	•
Amortization and Depletion 15	3.4	•	0.0	0.1	1.4	6.3	2.0	2.6	11.9	3.8	0.6	•	•
Pensions and Other Deferred Comp. 16	0.1	•	•	•	0.1	0.1	0.7	0.0	•	0.1	0.3	•	•
Employee Benefits 17	1.4	•	•	•	1.3	0.0	1.1	0.2	1.4	4.1	0.7	•	•
Advertising 18	1.9	•	5.0	•	1.5	8.5	2.6	1.8	3.7	0.3	0.0	•	•
Other Expenses 19	30.6	•	31.2	11.9	27.5	43.6	24.5	29.6	13.3	64.1	8.1	•	•
Officers' Compensation 20	4.9	•	6.4	23.0	5.4	1.7	6.3	•	•	0.2	7.6	•	•
Operating Margin 21	31.0	843.0	40.1	86.8	16.0	•	23.2	35.8	43.9	•	61.2	•	•
Operating Margin Before Officers' Comp. 22	35.9	843.0	46.5	86.8	21.5	21.5	29.5	37.5	43.9	68.7	•	•	•

Selected Average Balance Sheet ($ in Thousands)

	C1	C2	C3	C4	C5	C6	C7	C8	C9	C10	C11
Net Receivables 23	153	0	4	•	1399	682	3788	2088	4112	13425	3925
Inventories 24	•	•	•	•	•	•	•	•	•	•	•
Net Property, Plant and Equipment 25	288	0	0	254	412	365	2638	1253	272	9486	81934
Total Assets 26	2453	39	751	2868	7991	16370	32708	68808	179444	446450	•
Notes and Loans Payable 27	416	0	14	•	401	1251	2130	6568	20321	49478	36380
All Other Liabilities 28	471	0	19	•	462	1105	3531	6342	16846	32562	83447
Net Worth 29	1566	6	751	2005	5635	10709	19798	31641	97406	326623	•

Selected Financial Ratios (Times to 1)

	C1	C2	C3	C4	C5	C6	C7	C8	C9	C10	C11
Current Ratio 30	2.5	•	1.2	4091.2	2.9	3.3	1.9	1.3	3.8	4.3	0.6
Quick Ratio 31	1.9	•	1.0	4041.4	2.7	2.8	1.8	1.2	3.1	2.2	0.6
Net Sales to Working Capital 32	3.8	•	26.0	1.0	2.1	2.2	3.0	21.0	7.0	1.7	•
Coverage Ratio 33	10.5	•	16.9	•	•	7.2	23.5	8.7	6.6	•	11.2
Total Asset Turnover 34	0.4	•	4.0	0.6	0.8	0.7	0.7	0.6	0.4	0.3	0.2
Inventory Turnover 35	•	•	•	•	•	•	•	•	•	•	•
Receivables Turnover 36	•	•	•	•	•	•	•	•	•	•	•
Total Liabilities to Net Worth 37	0.6	•	5.2	0.0	0.4	0.4	0.5	0.7	1.2	0.8	0.4
Current Assets to Working Capital 38	1.6	•	5.1	1.0	1.5	1.4	2.1	4.2	1.4	1.3	•
Current Liabilities to Working Capital 39	0.6	•	4.1	0.0	0.5	0.4	1.1	3.2	0.4	0.3	•
Working Capital to Net Sales 40	0.3	•	0.0	1.0	0.5	0.5	0.3	0.0	0.1	0.6	•
Inventory to Working Capital 41	0.0	•	0.0	0.0	0.0	•	0.0	0.3	0.1	0.0	•
Total Receipts to Cash Flow 42	1.7	0.6	1.4	1.0	6.4	1.8	2.3	1.6	1.8	1.7	1.5
Cost of Goods to Cash Flow 43	0.1	•	0.1	•	0.3	•	0.4	0.1	0.2	0.0	•
Cash Flow to Total Debt 44	0.6	•	3.4	4164.0	0.4	1.3	0.9	1.0	0.4	0.4	0.4

Selected Financial Factors (in Percentages)

	C1	C2	C3	C4	C5	C6	C7	C8	C9	C10	C11
Debt Ratio 45	36.2	•	83.9	0.0	30.1	29.5	34.6	39.5	54.0	45.7	26.8
Return on Total Assets 46	12.6	•	169.3	56.0	•	12.4	17.7	23.6	20.9	•	10.2
Return on Equity Before Income Taxes 47	17.9	•	991.5	56.0	•	15.1	25.9	34.4	38.5	•	12.7
Return on Equity After Income Taxes 48	14.7	•	991.5	55.7	•	9.4	23.2	23.2	37.1	•	8.2
Profit Margin (Before Income Tax) 49	30.9	843.0	40.1	86.7	•	15.4	23.2	35.8	43.5	•	61.2
Profit Margin (After Income Tax) 50	25.3	849.9	40.1	86.2	•	9.5	20.8	24.1	41.9	•	39.8

Table II

Corporations with Net Income

LESSORS OF NONFINAN. INTANGIBLE ASSETS (EX. COPYRIGHTED WORKS)

MONEY AMOUNTS AND SIZE OF ASSETS IN THOUSANDS OF DOLLARS

Item Description for Accounting Period 7/02 Through 6/03	Total	Zero Assets	Under 500	500 to 1,000	1,000 to 5,000	5,000 to 10,000	10,000 to 25,000	25,000 to 50,000	50,000 to 100,000	100,000 to 250,000	250,000 to 500,000	500,000 to 2,500,000	2,500,000 and over
Number of Enterprises **1**	728	8	548	113	0	0	0	0	0	0	3	0	0
Revenues ($ in Thousands)													
Net Sales **2**	990887	744	139084	54834	0	0	0	0	0	0	203028	0	0
Interest **3**	22453	14	0	0	0	0	0	0	0	0	13839	0	0
Rents **4**	3347	0	0	230	0	0	0	0	0	0	2901	0	0
Royalties **5**	274829	0	17700	1670	0	0	0	0	0	0	141048	0	0
Other Portfolio Income **6**	3800	579	0	48	0	0	0	0	0	0	0	0	0
Other Receipts **7**	686458	151	121384	52886	0	0	0	0	0	0	45240	0	0
Total Receipts **8**	990887	744	139084	54834	0	0	0	0	0	0	203028	0	0
Average Total Receipts **9**	1361	93	254	485	•	•	•	•	•	•	67676	•	•
Operating Costs/Operating Income (%)													
Cost of Operations **10**	5.4	•	10.4	•	•	•	•	•	•	•	•	•	•
Salaries and Wages **11**	13.0	•	3.8	0.3	•	•	•	•	•	•	6.0	•	•
Taxes Paid **12**	2.7	6.0	1.5	0.8	•	•	•	•	•	•	2.2	•	•
Interest Paid **13**	2.4	•	•	•	•	•	•	•	•	•	6.0	•	•
Depreciation **14**	2.6	7.0	0.0	•	•	•	•	•	•	•	7.4	•	•
Amortization and Depletion **15**	1.6	•	0.0	0.1	•	•	•	•	•	•	0.6	•	•
Pensions and Other Deferred Comp. **16**	0.1	•	•	•	•	•	•	•	•	•	0.3	•	•
Employee Benefits **17**	1.5	•	•	•	•	•	•	•	•	•	0.7	•	•
Advertising **18**	2.1	•	5.3	•	•	•	•	•	•	•	0.0	•	•
Other Expenses **19**	21.3	13.6	19.2	11.9	•	•	•	•	•	•	8.1	•	•
Officers' Compensation **20**	5.4	•	6.8	•	•	•	•	•	•	•	7.6	•	•
Operating Margin **21**	42.0	73.4	53.0	86.8	•	•	•	•	•	•	61.2	•	•
Operating Margin Before Officers' Comp. **22**	47.3	73.4	59.8	86.8	•	•	•	•	•	•	68.7	•	•

Selected Average Balance Sheet ($ in Thousands)

Item				
Net Receivables 23	238	0	0	3925
Inventories 24			7	
Net Property, Plant and Equipment 25	455	0	0	81934
Total Assets 26	3126	0	254 / 751	446450
Notes and Loans Payable 27	306	57	9	36380
All Other Liabilities 28	636	30	0	83447
Net Worth 29	2185	18	751	326623

Selected Financial Ratios (Times to 1)

Item					
Current Ratio 30	2.5	1.1	4091.2	0.6	
Quick Ratio 31	1.9	1.1	4041.4	0.6	
Net Sales to Working Capital 32	3.9	91.3	1.0		
Coverage Ratio 33	18.3	11.2			
Total Asset Turnover 34	0.4	4.4	0.6	0.2	
Inventory Turnover 35					
Receivables Turnover 36					
Total Liabilities to Net Worth 37	0.4	2.2	0.0	0.4	
Current Assets to Working Capital 38	1.7	15.2	1.0		
Current Liabilities to Working Capital 39	0.7	14.2	0.0		
Working Capital to Net Sales 40	0.3	0.0	1.0		
Inventory to Working Capital 41	0.0	0.0			
Total Receipts to Cash Flow 42	1.6	1.4	10.9	1.0	1.5
Cost of Goods to Cash Flow 43	0.1	0.1			
Cash Flow to Total Debt 44	0.9	4.6	4164.0	0.4	

Selected Financial Factors (in Percentages)

Item					
Debt Ratio 45	30.1	68.9	0.0		26.8
Return on Total Assets 46	19.3	235.5	56.0		10.2
Return on Equity Before Income Taxes 47	26.1	757.6	56.0		12.7
Return on Equity After Income Taxes 48	22.1	757.6	55.7		8.2
Profit Margin (Before Income Tax) 49	41.9	73.4	53.0	86.7	61.2
Profit Margin (After Income Tax) 50	35.5	61.4	53.0	86.2	39.8

Table I

Corporations with and without Net Income

LEGAL SERVICES

MONEY AMOUNTS AND SIZE OF ASSETS IN THOUSANDS OF DOLLARS

Item Description for Accounting Period 7/02 Through 6/03	Total	Zero Assets	Under 500	500 to 1,000	1,000 to 5,000	5,000 to 10,000	10,000 to 25,000	25,000 to 50,000	50,000 to 100,000	100,000 to 250,000	250,000 to 500,000	500,000 to 2,500,000	2,500,000 and over
Number of Enterprises **1**	91178	10245	75610	3181	1736	285	89	24	9	0	0	·	·
Revenues ($ in Thousands)													
Net Sales **2**	71298232	1814046	39465342	8310068	9926783	5410276	3512457	2063819	795441	0	0	·	·
Interest **3**	70732	1053	30891	9184	11179	4529	3847	3441	6609	0	0	·	·
Rents **4**	92820	2416	43357	18431	17960	7495	2517	518	127	0	0	·	·
Royalties **5**	1716	0	1017	74	267	0	63	295	0	0	0	·	·
Other Portfolio Income **6**	53328	27457	6683	3151	4010	1726	957	5832	3514	0	0	·	·
Other Receipts **7**	4008835	75657	1658952	841587	284536	760869	170983	48160	168087	0	0	·	·
Total Receipts **8**	75525663	1920629	41206242	9182495	10244735	6184895	3690824	2122065	973778	0	0	·	·
Average Total Receipts **9**	828	187	545	2887	5901	21701	41470	88419	108198				
Operating Costs/Operating Income (%)													
Cost of Operations **10**	5.1	1.1	6.0	3.3	5.2	2.6	1.9	3.6	16.6	·	·	·	·
Salaries and Wages **11**	30.6	15.5	23.7	32.8	34.4	54.9	52.5	43.6	39.4	·	·	·	·
Taxes Paid **12**	3.5	2.2	3.5	4.0	3.4	3.6	3.5	3.1	3.6	·	·	·	·
Interest Paid **13**	0.5	0.9	0.4	0.4	0.5	0.4	0.5	0.6	1.2	·	·	·	·
Depreciation **14**	1.3	0.9	1.1	1.3	1.3	1.5	1.8	2.7	2.8	·	·	·	·
Amortization and Depletion **15**	0.1	0.5	0.0	0.0	0.0	0.1	0.1	0.3	0.8	·	·	·	·
Pensions and Other Deferred Comp. **16**	2.2	0.8	2.2	2.5	2.2	2.9	2.9	1.5	0.4	·	·	·	·
Employee Benefits **17**	1.8	2.7	1.7	2.2	1.5	2.0	2.5	1.8	2.1	·	·	·	·
Advertising **18**	1.8	0.9	2.0	2.4	1.7	1.1	0.7	0.5	1.3	·	·	·	·
Other Expenses **19**	27.1	53.7	29.4	25.3	20.9	18.2	23.0	27.0	31.0	·	·	·	·
Officers' Compensation **20**	24.2	15.0	26.1	28.2	24.5	21.9	11.8	12.4	4.0	·	·	·	·
Operating Margin **21**	1.8	5.8	3.7	4.4	·	·	·	2.8	·				
Operating Margin Before Officers' Comp. **22**	26.0	20.8	29.9	28.9	25.8	12.6	10.6	15.2	0.8				

Selected Average Balance Sheet ($ in Thousands)

Net Receivables **23**	13	0	4	27	238	156	1084	5346	11022
Inventories **24**	0	0	0	1	10	25	122	18	0
Net Property, Plant and Equipment **25**	33	0	18	101	256	1409	2848	6962	6068
Total Assets **26**	184		79	699	1861	7389	15295	32978	122339
Notes and Loans Payable **27**	63	0	34	219	623	2355	4142	10082	13203
All Other Liabilities **28**	85	0	35	325	883	3276	7831	12282	67052
Net Worth **29**	36	0	10	155	355	1758	3322	10614	42084

Selected Financial Ratios (Times to 1)

Current Ratio **30**	1.2	•	1.1	1.5	1.1	1.3	1.2	1.5	1.5
Quick Ratio **31**	0.8	•	0.8	0.8	0.8	0.7	0.6	1.0	1.2
Net Sales to Working Capital **32**	38.6	•	98.9	16.6	48.1	15.7	23.6	14.6	7.5
Coverage Ratio **33**	18.2	13.8	20.4	21.1	17.4	13.7	9.3	9.9	17.5
Total Asset Turnover **34**	4.3	•	6.6	3.7	3.1	2.6	2.6	2.6	0.7
Inventory Turnover **35**	93.2	•	3088.3	116.0	30.0	20.0	6.1	170.3	•
Receivables Turnover **36**	68.8	•	139.2	116.2	28.5	156.0	38.0	18.4	13.5
Total Liabilities to Net Worth **37**	4.1	•	7.1	3.5	4.2	3.2	3.6	2.1	1.9
Current Assets to Working Capital **38**	5.6	•	8.9	3.1	11.0	3.9	6.0	3.1	3.0
Current Liabilities to Working Capital **39**	4.6	•	7.9	2.1	10.0	2.9	5.0	2.1	2.0
Working Capital to Net Sales **40**	0.0	•	0.0	0.1	0.0	0.1	0.0	0.1	0.1
Inventory to Working Capital **41**	0.0	•	0.0	•	0.1	0.0	0.1	0.0	•
Total Receipts to Cash Flow **42**	3.5	1.7	3.3	3.7	4.4	5.8	4.9	4.0	2.2
Cost of Goods to Cash Flow **43**	0.2	0.0	0.2	0.1	0.2	0.2	0.1	0.1	0.4
Cash Flow to Total Debt **44**	1.5	•	2.3	1.3	0.9	0.6	0.7	1.0	0.5

Selected Financial Factors (in Percentages)

Debt Ratio **45**	80.5	•	87.7	77.8	80.9	76.2	78.3	67.8	65.6
Return on Total Assets **46**	34.9	•	56.8	31.7	24.9	13.7	11.3	16.3	14.7
Return on Equity Before Income Taxes **47**	168.9	•	437.9	136.2	123.0	53.3	46.4	45.6	40.2
Return on Equity After Income Taxes **48**	164.7	•	434.2	133.5	119.5	49.2	41.3	39.0	34.2
Profit Margin (Before Income Tax) **49**	7.8	11.7	8.1	8.1	7.6	4.9	3.9	5.6	19.1
Profit Margin (After Income Tax) **50**	7.6	11.6	8.1	7.9	7.4	4.6	3.5	4.8	16.3

Table II

Corporations with Net Income

LEGAL SERVICES

MONEY AMOUNTS AND SIZE OF ASSETS IN THOUSANDS OF DOLLARS

Item Description for Accounting Period 7/02 Through 6/03	Total	Zero Assets	Under 500	500 to 1,000	1,000 to 5,000	5,000 to 10,000	10,000 to 25,000	25,000 to 50,000	50,000 to 100,000	100,000 to 250,000	250,000 to 500,000	500,000 to 2,500,000	2,500,000 and over
Number of Enterprises **1**	59329	5254	50169	2298	1275	226	77	21	9	0	0	•	•
Revenues ($ in Thousands)													
Net Sales **2**	51655626	872172	26491292	6155374	8155814	3979266	3317843	1888423	795441	0	0	•	•
Interest **3**	43061	184	12240	4431	9378	3265	3553	3401	6609	0	0	•	•
Rents **4**	39987	0	7931	17526	4120	7248	2517	518	127	0	0	•	•
Royalties **5**	697	0	0	74	267	0	61	295	0	0	0	•	•
Other Portfolio Income **6**	45928	27457	4809	3039	2890	1620	608	1991	3514	0	0	•	•
Other Receipts **7**	2265328	74814	979237	484549	192418	178642	142513	45070	168087	0	0	•	•
Total Receipts **8**	54050627	974627	27495509	6664993	8364887	4170041	3467095	1939698	973778	•	•	•	•
Average Total Receipts **9**	911	186	548	2900	6561	18452	45027	92367	108198	•	•	•	•
Operating Costs/Operating Income (%)													
Cost of Operations **10**	4.9	0.4	5.7	4.4	4.6	3.5	2.0	1.7	16.6	•	•	•	•
Salaries and Wages **11**	30.8	13.8	22.6	32.5	35.6	49.8	53.2	44.3	39.4	•	•	•	•
Taxes Paid **12**	3.4	3.0	3.4	3.8	3.4	3.5	3.5	3.1	3.6	•	•	•	•
Interest Paid **13**	0.4	0.6	0.4	0.4	0.4	0.4	0.4	0.5	1.2	•	•	•	•
Depreciation **14**	1.3	1.2	1.1	1.3	1.4	1.7	1.8	2.6	2.8	•	•	•	•
Amortization and Depletion **15**	0.0	0.0	0.0	0.0	0.0	0.0	0.1	0.2	0.8	•	•	•	•
Pensions and Other Deferred Comp. **16**	1.9	1.6	1.7	1.8	2.0	2.7	2.9	1.6	0.4	•	•	•	•
Employee Benefits **17**	1.6	1.7	1.5	2.0	1.5	1.6	2.6	1.9	2.1	•	•	•	•
Advertising **18**	1.9	1.7	2.1	3.1	1.9	0.9	0.6	0.5	1.3	•	•	•	•
Other Expenses **19**	26.1	35.7	28.6	25.2	21.4	20.4	21.3	27.2	31.0	•	•	•	•
Officers' Compensation **20**	20.2	23.9	23.1	21.5	20.4	12.2	11.1	11.3	4.0	•	•	•	•
Operating Margin **21**	7.5	16.5	10.0	4.1	7.4	3.3	0.5	4.9	•	•	•	•	•
Operating Margin Before Officers' Comp. **22**	27.6	40.4	33.1	25.5	27.8	15.5	11.6	16.2	0.8	•	•	•	•

Selected Average Balance Sheet ($ in Thousands)

Net Receivables 23	17	0	4	31	288	196	1200	5008	11022
Inventories 24	1	0	0	0	14	47	141	28	0
Net Property, Plant and Equipment 25	39	0	19	92	298	1564	2989	7359	6068
Total Assets 26	219	0	83	699	1939	7634	15545	33305	122339
Notes and Loans Payable 27	58	0	27	157	548	1918	3836	7850	13203
All Other Liabilities 28	96	0	30	333	919	3151	8215	13224	67052
Net Worth 29	65	0	26	209	473	2565	3495	12231	42084

Selected Financial Ratios (Times to 1)

Current Ratio 30	1.4	•	1.3	1.6	1.2	1.5	1.2	1.4	1.5
Quick Ratio 31	0.9	•	1.0	1.0	0.9	0.8	0.6	0.9	1.2
Net Sales to Working Capital 32	23.9	•	42.9	13.6	23.6	9.9	25.3	18.4	7.5
Coverage Ratio 33	30.8	48.6	37.8	35.0	26.1	20.3	12.6	14.9	17.5
Total Asset Turnover 34	4.0	•	6.3	3.8	3.3	2.3	2.8	2.7	0.7
Inventory Turnover 35	71.0	1498000.0	•	•	21.7	13.2	6.1	54.8	•
Receivables Turnover 36	62.4	•	130.8	162.4	28.3	180.0	38.4	35.9	16.0
Total Liabilities to Net Worth 37	2.3	•	2.2	2.3	3.1	2.0	3.4	1.7	1.9
Current Assets to Working Capital 38	3.7	•	3.9	2.6	5.2	2.9	6.1	3.7	3.0
Current Liabilities to Working Capital 39	2.7	•	2.9	1.6	4.2	1.9	5.1	2.7	2.0
Working Capital to Net Sales 40	0.0	•	0.0	0.1	0.0	0.1	0.0	0.1	0.1
Inventory to Working Capital 41	0.0	•	0.0	•	0.0	0.0	0.1	0.0	•
Total Receipts to Cash Flow 42	3.2	1.9	2.8	3.2	3.9	4.7	5.1	3.7	2.2
Cost of Goods to Cash Flow 43	0.2	0.0	0.2	0.1	0.2	0.2	0.1	0.1	0.4
Cash Flow to Total Debt 44	1.8	•	3.3	1.7	1.1	0.7	0.7	1.2	0.5

Selected Financial Factors (in Percentages)

Debt Ratio 45	70.1	•	68.6	70.1	75.6	66.4	77.5	63.3	65.6
Return on Total Assets 46	49.7	•	89.8	48.7	34.0	19.5	15.0	22.0	14.7
Return on Equity Before Income Taxes 47	161.0	•	278.2	158.2	134.2	55.3	61.6	55.9	40.2
Return on Equity After Income Taxes 48	157.4	•	276.2	155.4	130.6	51.7	56.0	49.3	34.2
Profit Margin (Before Income Tax) 49	12.1	28.3	13.8	12.3	9.9	8.0	5.0	7.6	19.1
Profit Margin (After Income Tax) 50	11.8	28.0	13.7	12.1	9.6	7.5	4.5	6.7	16.3

Table I

Corporations with and without Net Income

ACCOUNTING, TAX PREPARATION, BOOKKEEPING, AND PAYROLL SERVICES

MONEY AMOUNTS AND SIZE OF ASSETS IN THOUSANDS OF DOLLARS

Item Description for Accounting Period 7/02 Through 6/03	Total	Zero Assets	Under 500	500 to 1,000	1,000 to 5,000	5,000 to 10,000	10,000 to 25,000	25,000 to 50,000	50,000 to 100,000	100,000 to 250,000	250,000 to 500,000	500,000 to 2,500,000	2,500,000 and over
Number of Enterprises 1	59894	9183	49629	425	500	103	29	16	4	4	0	0	0

Revenues ($ in Thousands)

Net Sales 2	24441800	636747	14577218	1136822	1980700	714162	402553	1488586	500207	3004806	0	0	0
Interest 3	274496	420	17327	7309	3324	1500	1963	4050	4053	234551	0	0	0
Rents 4	10348	0	0	9073	104	0	114	0	1058	0	0	0	0
Royalties 5	481357	0	0	0	0	0	1070	4902	0	475385	0	0	0
Other Portfolio Income 6	150847	0	17061	0	18971	116	244	10043	295	104115	0	0	0
Other Receipts 7	1945857	19305	66219	6591	20617	278483	22059	5373	1128	1526082	0	0	0
Total Receipts 8	27304705	656472	14677825	1159795	2023716	994261	428003	1512954	506741	5344939	0	0	0
Average Total Receipts 9	456	71	296	2729	4047	9653	14759	94560	126685	1336235	•	•	•

Operating Costs/Operating Income (%)

Cost of Operations 10	11.2	0.2	2.9	6.2	28.6	7.5	61.0	86.5	0.8	3.2	•	•	•
Salaries and Wages 11	31.4	12.3	28.9	44.8	24.6	44.0	21.2	3.9	65.2	53.2	•	•	•
Taxes Paid 12	4.7	3.5	4.4	4.3	5.2	9.5	1.9	4.3	2.8	5.7	•	•	•
Interest Paid 13	1.5	1.2	0.8	0.8	0.8	0.7	0.7	0.4	1.4	6.6	•	•	•
Depreciation 14	2.1	1.7	1.7	1.7	2.3	2.0	1.5	0.5	2.2	4.7	•	•	•
Amortization and Depletion 15	0.7	0.0	0.3	0.6	0.6	0.3	0.5	0.0	1.9	3.1	•	•	•
Pensions and Other Deferred Comp. 16	1.4	0.1	1.9	1.9	0.6	2.3	0.6	0.1	1.8	0.4	•	•	•
Employee Benefits 17	2.2	1.3	2.5	4.1	1.5	6.3	1.0	1.1	0.9	0.5	•	•	•
Advertising 18	1.3	1.2	0.6	0.4	1.7	0.8	0.6	0.3	0.0	5.8	•	•	•
Other Expenses 19	29.6	44.4	25.4	24.4	19.3	44.7	15.8	3.1	18.5	68.6	•	•	•
Officers' Compensation 20	16.4	23.3	22.3	11.7	12.7	19.2	2.3	0.8	0.7	1.7	•	•	•
Operating Margin 21	•	10.7	8.1	•	2.2	•	•	•	3.8	•	•	•	•
Operating Margin Before Officers' Comp. 22	13.8	34.0	30.4	10.8	14.8	•	•	•	4.5	•	•	•	•

Selected Average Balance Sheet ($ in Thousands)

Net Receivables 23	33	0	6	168	317	828	4123	5733	31022	258449
Inventories 24	6	0	0	1	23	22	12	971	82	58202
Net Property, Plant and Equipment 25	22	0	12	274	368	346	715	2376	8746	79801
Total Assets 26	233	0	54	749	1804	6318	15959	33576	71477	2034204
Notes and Loans Payable 27	123	0	32	585	743	2058	2773	7023	16093	1162742
All Other Liabilities 28	81	0	11	197	939	3546	9829	36142	34782	598788
Net Worth 29	30	0	11	-34	121	713	3357	-9589	20602	272674

Selected Financial Ratios (Times to 1)

Current Ratio 30	0.9	•	1.2	0.5	0.8	1.0	1.3	0.6	1.6	0.9
Quick Ratio 31	0.7	•	1.0	0.5	0.7	0.8	1.0	0.4	1.5	0.7
Net Sales to Working Capital 32	•	•	77.0	•	•	59.9	5.0	•	8.2	•
Coverage Ratio 33	7.0	12.3	11.5	2.3	6.3	3.2	•	2.6	4.6	4.6
Total Asset Turnover 34	1.7	•	5.4	3.6	2.2	1.1	0.9	2.8	1.7	0.4
Inventory Turnover 35	7.1	•	30.1	194.4	49.1	23.9	732.8	82.9	11.9	0.4
Receivables Turnover 36	10.1	•	52.0	16.8	8.9	7.7	3.8	18.7	1.8	5.8
Total Liabilities to Net Worth 37	6.9	•	3.9	•	7.9	3.8	3.8	•	2.5	6.5
Current Assets to Working Capital 38	•	•	6.2	•	37.8	4.1	•	2.6	•	•
Current Liabilities to Working Capital 39	•	•	5.2	•	36.8	3.1	•	1.6	•	•
Working Capital to Net Sales 40	•	•	0.0	•	0.0	0.0	0.2	0.1	0.1	•
Inventory to Working Capital 41	•	•	0.1	•	•	0.3	0.0	0.0	0.0	•
Total Receipts to Cash Flow 42	3.1	2.1	3.7	6.4	5.7	2.5	8.2	42.2	5.1	1.2
Cost of Goods to Cash Flow 43	0.4	0.0	0.1	0.4	1.6	0.2	5.0	36.5	0.0	0.0
Cash Flow to Total Debt 44	0.6	•	1.8	0.5	0.4	0.5	0.1	0.1	0.5	0.4

Selected Financial Factors (in Percentages)

Debt Ratio 45	87.3	•	79.8	104.6	93.3	88.7	79.0	128.6	71.2	86.6
Return on Total Assets 46	18.7	•	52.1	6.7	11.3	2.6	•	2.6	11.4	11.4
Return on Equity Before Income Taxes 47	125.5	•	235.2	•	141.6	15.7	•	•	30.8	66.7
Return on Equity After Income Taxes 48	108.3	•	231.5	•	120.0	14.1	•	•	21.2	42.7
Profit Margin (Before Income Tax) 49	9.1	13.8	8.8	1.1	4.3	1.6	•	0.6	5.1	24.2
Profit Margin (After Income Tax) 50	7.9	13.7	8.6	1.1	3.7	1.4	•	0.6	3.5	15.5

Table II
Corporations with Net Income

ACCOUNTING, TAX PREPARATION, BOOKKEEPING, AND PAYROLL SERVICES

MONEY AMOUNTS AND SIZE OF ASSETS IN THOUSANDS OF DOLLARS

Item Description for Accounting Period 7/02 Through 6/03	Total	Zero Assets	Under 500	500 to 1,000	1,000 to 5,000	5,000 to 10,000	10,000 to 25,000	25,000 to 50,000	50,000 to 100,000	100,000 to 250,000	250,000 to 500,000	500,000 to 2,500,000	2,500,000 and over
Number of Enterprises 1	42189	6057	35420	333	298	50	17	0	4	0	0	0	0
Revenues ($ in Thousands)													
Net Sales 2	20461735	561600	11695180	877359	1668910	650002	97372	0	500207	0	0	0	0
Interest 3	262107	344	12847	5598	3230	1488	1527	0	4053	0	0	0	0
Rents 4	9930	0	0	8758	0	0	114	0	1058	0	0	0	0
Royalties 5	476454	0	0	0	0	0	1070	0	0	0	0	0	0
Other Portfolio Income 6	141087	0	8205	0	18865	10	239	0	295	0	0	0	0
Other Receipts 7	1903735	20577	42326	5996	20206	278482	8049	0	1128	0	0	0	0
Total Receipts 8	23255048	582521	11758558	897711	1711211	929982	108371	0	506741	0	0	0	0
Average Total Receipts 9	551	96	332	2696	5742	18600	6375	•	126685	•	•	•	•
Operating Costs/Operating Income (%)													
Cost of Operations 10	11.7	0.1	3.3	0.5	33.8	8.1	3.2	•	0.8	•	•	•	•
Salaries and Wages 11	31.2	11.4	28.2	46.0	22.9	42.5	31.5	•	65.2	•	•	•	•
Taxes Paid 12	4.8	3.8	4.4	4.5	5.2	9.9	4.6	•	2.8	•	•	•	•
Interest Paid 13	1.6	0.9	0.9	0.8	0.6	0.6	2.0	•	1.4	•	•	•	•
Depreciation 14	2.0	1.8	1.7	1.6	1.7	2.0	2.4	•	2.2	•	•	•	•
Amortization and Depletion 15	0.8	0.0	0.4	0.8	0.3	0.1	0.8	•	1.9	•	•	•	•
Pensions and Other Deferred Comp. 16	1.3	0.2	1.7	1.8	0.5	2.4	0.9	•	1.8	•	•	•	•
Employee Benefits 17	2.0	1.4	2.4	3.7	1.0	6.6	1.3	•	0.9	•	•	•	•
Advertising 18	1.4	0.9	0.6	0.5	1.8	0.7	1.6	•	0.0	•	•	•	•
Other Expenses 19	29.7	38.9	25.1	26.4	12.7	45.4	34.7	•	18.5	•	•	•	•
Officers' Compensation 20	14.7	25.0	20.4	13.3	10.8	19.7	6.5	•	0.7	•	•	•	•
Operating Margin 21	•	15.7	11.1	0.2	8.6	•	10.5	•	3.8	•	•	•	•
Operating Margin Before Officers' Comp. 22	13.4	40.7	31.5	13.5	19.4	•	17.0	•	4.5	•	•	•	•

Selected Average Balance Sheet ($ in Thousands)

Net Receivables 23	39	0	5	118	372	993	3547	•	31022
Inventories 24	9	0	0	1	2	0	10	•	82
Net Property, Plant and Equipment 25	25	0	13	311	334	601	520	•	8746
Total Assets 26	284	0	59	771	1909	6876	16268	•	71477
Notes and Loans Payable 27	155	0	33	610	703	2216	2640	•	16093
All Other Liabilities 28	80	0	11	229	297	3504	9142	•	34782
Net Worth 29	49	0	15	-68	909	1155	4487	•	20602

Selected Financial Ratios (Times to 1)

Current Ratio 30	1.0	•	1.1	0.4	4.5	0.9	1.4	•	1.6
Quick Ratio 31	0.8	•	0.9	0.4	3.6	0.6	1.0	•	1.5
Net Sales to Working Capital 32	•	•	257.9	•	6.7	•	1.8	•	8.2
Coverage Ratio 33	8.5	21.9	14.5	4.1	19.2	8.8	11.7	•	4.6
Total Asset Turnover 34	1.7	•	5.6	3.4	2.9	1.9	0.4	•	1.7
Inventory Turnover 35	6.7	•	886.2	11.4	878.0	2115.0	18.1	•	11.9
Receivables Turnover 36	10.0	•	64.8	21.7	11.6	9.5	1.5	•	2.5
Total Liabilities to Net Worth 37	4.8	•	3.0	•	1.1	5.0	2.6	•	2.5
Current Assets to Working Capital 38	•	•	18.5	•	1.3	•	3.6	•	2.6
Current Liabilities to Working Capital 39	•	•	17.5	•	0.3	•	2.6	•	1.6
Working Capital to Net Sales 40	•	•	0.0	•	0.1	•	0.6	•	0.1
Inventory to Working Capital 41	•	•	0.0	•	•	•	0.0	•	0.0
Total Receipts to Cash Flow 42	2.8	1.9	3.4	5.6	5.4	2.3	2.1	•	5.1
Cost of Goods to Cash Flow 43	0.3	0.0	0.1	0.0	1.8	0.2	0.1	•	0.0
Cash Flow to Total Debt 44	0.7	•	2.2	0.6	1.0	1.0	0.2	•	0.5

Selected Financial Factors (in Percentages)

Debt Ratio 45	82.7	•	75.1	108.8	52.4	83.2	72.4	•	71.2
Return on Total Assets 46	23.8	•	70.0	11.6	34.5	10.6	8.4	•	11.4
Return on Equity Before Income Taxes 47	121.7	•	261.6	•	68.6	56.1	27.8	•	30.8
Return on Equity After Income Taxes 48	106.9	•	257.7	•	63.8	54.0	26.1	•	21.2
Profit Margin (Before Income Tax) 49	12.3	19.4	11.7	2.6	11.1	5.0	21.8	•	5.1
Profit Margin (After Income Tax) 50	10.8	19.3	11.5	2.5	10.4	4.8	20.4	•	3.5

ARCHITECTURAL, ENGINEERING, AND RELATED SERVICES

Table I

Corporations with and without Net Income

MONEY AMOUNTS AND SIZE OF ASSETS IN THOUSANDS OF DOLLARS

Item Description for Accounting Period 7/02 Through 6/03	Total	Zero Assets	Under 500	500 to 1,000	1,000 to 5,000	5,000 to 10,000	10,000 to 25,000	25,000 to 50,000	50,000 to 100,000	100,000 to 250,000	250,000 to 500,000	500,000 to 2,500,000	2,500,000 and over
Number of Enterprises 1	83030	10317	65991	2714	3134	456	227	88	36	42	8	13	4
Revenues ($ in Thousands)													
Net Sales 2	132174555	2295114	43383321	6876735	18630107	6694663	7336709	5839544	5096152	9743666	1577811	11831411	12869322
Interest 3	443603	8313	31589	2738	20921	12418	8232	12760	8316	38099	21840	192609	85769
Rents 4	200958	1048	987	0	8684	2109	2523	5831	6855	6639	8496	15368	142418
Royalties 5	101876	66	0	0	1400	0	520	431	361	13681	4512	1000	79906
Other Portfolio Income 6	289346	85863	15632	1738	19730	3609	10914	32561	22851	12359	303	43105	40681
Other Receipts 7	1536281	-25943	377913	194220	119131	40276	83135	107823	35393	53008	28018	267113	256191
Total Receipts 8	134746619	2364461	43809442	7075431	18799973	6753075	7442033	5998950	5169928	9867452	1640980	12350606	13474287
Average Total Receipts 9	1623	229	664	2607	5999	14809	32784	68170	143609	234939	205122	950047	3368572
Operating Costs/Operating Income (%)													
Cost of Operations 10	40.8	22.1	25.6	32.0	35.5	36.8	43.1	49.1	45.4	46.3	65.1	61.9	76.3
Salaries and Wages 11	20.0	22.4	21.8	24.6	23.6	24.0	21.7	17.0	20.8	18.6	6.7	10.4	15.1
Taxes Paid 12	3.1	3.0	3.3	3.5	3.9	3.4	3.5	2.8	2.9	2.6	1.6	3.1	1.3
Interest Paid 13	0.8	1.9	0.3	0.5	0.6	0.6	0.6	0.8	0.8	1.1	4.8	2.0	1.4
Depreciation 14	2.0	3.2	1.6	2.0	2.6	2.3	2.3	1.9	2.2	2.2	3.5	2.6	1.1
Amortization and Depletion 15	0.2	0.4	0.0	0.2	0.1	0.1	0.2	0.3	0.2	0.5	1.0	0.4	0.2
Pensions and Other Deferred Comp. 16	1.1	1.2	1.2	1.6	1.5	0.9	1.3	1.0	1.1	0.8	0.1	1.0	0.8
Employee Benefits 17	2.3	1.4	1.8	1.1	2.5	2.8	2.6	2.3	1.8	2.9	1.1	2.5	3.5
Advertising 18	0.3	0.4	0.4	0.3	0.4	0.5	0.3	0.3	0.3	0.3	0.2	0.2	0.1
Other Expenses 19	20.8	32.2	25.4	23.5	20.2	19.1	20.4	21.5	21.2	21.7	22.1	18.2	4.4
Officers' Compensation 20	8.2	12.0	16.0	10.9	7.4	6.3	3.9	2.8	2.4	1.6	0.9	2.1	0.4
Operating Margin 21	0.4	•	2.5	0.0	1.5	3.3	0.0	0.3	0.9	1.3	•	•	•
Operating Margin Before Officers' Comp. 22	8.6	11.9	18.5	10.9	8.9	9.5	3.9	3.0	3.3	2.9	•	•	•

Selected Average Balance Sheet ($ in Thousands)

Net Receivables 23	210	0	8	190	631	2444	6095	15498	27744	45842	82319	370624	524324
Inventories 24	21	0	1	30	59	250	558	1639	2741	4893	6607	29244	148656
Net Property, Plant and Equipment 25	102	0	29	141	460	1127	2883	4436	8322	18943	58146	60020	200873
Total Assets 26	745	0	74	700	1959	6585	15115	35633	70978	144678	345188	1045056	3608523
Notes and Loans Payable 27	196	0	40	206	568	1726	3725	7761	12922	40460	134834	188718	815389
All Other Liabilities 28	310	0	20	261	708	2046	6258	15814	30114	53190	100076	510055	1753367
Net Worth 29	239	0	13	233	683	2814	5132	12058	27942	51029	110278	346283	1039767

Selected Financial Ratios (Times to 1)

Current Ratio 30	1.3	•	1.3	1.7	1.5	1.7	1.5	1.5	1.6	1.5	2.2	1.3	0.9
Quick Ratio 31	0.9	•	1.1	1.4	1.3	1.3	1.1	1.2	1.2	1.1	1.8	1.0	0.4
Net Sales to Working Capital 32	16.6	•	81.4	14.7	14.0	8.4	10.3	7.7	8.4	8.8	2.7	8.2	•
Coverage Ratio 33	3.8	2.6	11.1	6.5	4.9	8.0	3.3	4.7	4.0	3.3	0.3	1.1	1.1
Total Asset Turnover 34	2.1	•	8.9	3.6	3.0	2.2	2.1	1.9	2.0	1.6	0.6	0.9	0.9
Inventory Turnover 35	31.0	•	202.2	27.4	35.6	21.6	25.0	19.9	23.5	21.9	19.4	19.3	16.5
Receivables Turnover 36	8.0	•	76.1	15.5	8.7	6.3	5.2	4.7	4.2	5.3	2.0	2.5	12.3
Total Liabilities to Net Worth 37	2.1	•	4.6	2.0	1.9	1.3	1.9	2.0	1.5	1.8	2.1	2.0	2.5
Current Assets to Working Capital 38	4.2	•	4.4	2.5	2.9	2.5	3.2	3.0	2.8	3.2	1.9	4.6	•
Current Liabilities to Working Capital 39	3.2	•	3.4	1.5	1.9	1.5	2.2	2.0	1.8	2.2	0.9	3.6	•
Working Capital to Net Sales 40	0.1	•	0.0	0.1	0.1	0.1	0.1	0.1	0.1	0.1	0.4	0.1	•
Inventory to Working Capital 41	0.2	•	0.1	0.2	0.1	0.1	0.2	0.2	0.1	0.2	0.1	0.1	•
Total Receipts to Cash Flow 42	5.3	3.5	4.1	4.5	5.4	5.4	5.7	4.9	5.2	5.0	7.4	6.8	48.5
Cost of Goods to Cash Flow 43	2.2	0.8	1.1	1.4	1.9	2.0	2.5	2.4	2.4	2.3	4.8	4.2	37.0
Cash Flow to Total Debt 44	0.6	•	2.6	1.2	0.9	0.7	0.6	0.6	0.6	0.5	0.1	0.2	0.0

Selected Financial Factors (in Percentages)

Debt Ratio 45	67.9	•	82.2	66.7	65.1	57.3	66.0	66.2	60.6	64.7	68.1	66.9	71.2
Return on Total Assets 46	6.9	•	33.9	12.3	9.2	10.5	4.5	7.0	6.4	6.0	0.9	1.9	1.4
Return on Equity Before Income Taxes 47	15.8	•	173.2	31.4	21.0	21.5	9.1	16.4	12.2	11.8	•	0.7	0.5
Return on Equity After Income Taxes 48	12.9	•	168.7	28.7	16.5	17.9	5.1	13.0	8.2	7.2	•	•	•
Profit Margin (Before Income Tax) 49	2.4	2.9	3.5	2.9	2.4	4.1	1.5	3.0	2.4	2.6	•	0.3	0.2
Profit Margin (After Income Tax) 50	1.9	2.3	3.4	2.6	1.9	3.4	0.8	2.4	1.6	1.6	•	•	•

Table II
Corporations with Net Income

ARCHITECTURAL, ENGINEERING, AND RELATED SERVICES

MONEY AMOUNTS AND SIZE OF ASSETS IN THOUSANDS OF DOLLARS

Item Description for Accounting Period 7/02 Through 6/03	Total	Zero Assets	Under 500	500 to 1,000	1,000 to 5,000	5,000 to 10,000	10,000 to 25,000	25,000 to 50,000	50,000 to 100,000	100,000 to 250,000	250,000 to 500,000	500,000 to 2,500,000	2,500,000 and over
Number of Enterprises **1**	48952	5267	38784	2049	2234	0	147	65	25	27	4	8	0
Revenues ($ in Thousands)													
Net Sales **2**	102436189	1457840	31955484	5823122	14700197	0	5585213	4841145	4027597	7513793	621056	9279481	0
Interest **3**	339679	3345	22750	2616	16272	0	4755	8902	4906	24239	16854	145738	0
Rents **4**	160080	9	610	0	8233	0	1667	5788	4692	4922	0	9438	0
Royalties **5**	86734	0	0	0	0	0	0	429	361	13565	4450	1000	0
Other Portfolio Income **6**	227186	78692	14337	1686	8229	0	5985	30504	10522	11467	265	34947	0
Other Receipts **7**	1260304	5233	276883	187218	81680	0	45326	98517	23657	40062	16792	229133	0
Total Receipts **8**	104510172	1545119	32270064	6014642	14814611	0	5642946	4985285	4071735	7608048	659417	9699737	0
Average Total Receipts **9**	2135	293	832	2935	6631	•	38387	76697	162869	281780	164854	1212467	•
Operating Costs/Operating Income (%)													
Cost of Operations **10**	40.7	20.4	26.8	29.7	34.7	•	43.1	51.1	38.9	45.9	33.7	58.9	•
Salaries and Wages **11**	19.4	18.6	20.6	23.6	23.5	•	20.9	16.1	22.8	17.8	12.7	10.2	•
Taxes Paid **12**	3.0	3.0	3.0	3.4	4.0	•	3.4	2.8	3.1	2.7	1.8	3.2	•
Interest Paid **13**	0.7	1.3	0.3	0.4	0.4	•	0.5	0.6	0.7	0.9	5.7	1.6	•
Depreciation **14**	1.6	1.7	1.3	1.5	2.0	•	1.8	1.7	2.4	1.9	6.3	1.2	•
Amortization and Depletion **15**	0.1	0.0	0.0	0.2	0.1	•	0.2	0.1	0.1	0.5	0.4	0.3	•
Pensions and Other Deferred Comp. **16**	1.1	1.4	1.0	1.8	1.4	•	1.4	1.1	1.3	0.9	0.3	0.8	•
Employee Benefits **17**	2.3	1.0	1.6	1.1	2.6	•	2.5	2.4	1.8	2.9	2.5	2.5	•
Advertising **18**	0.3	0.2	0.4	0.2	0.3	•	0.2	0.3	0.3	0.3	0.5	0.1	•
Other Expenses **19**	19.5	28.4	24.1	23.8	18.2	•	17.9	18.6	22.2	21.1	34.1	20.0	•
Officers' Compensation **20**	7.8	10.4	15.3	11.1	7.6	•	4.0	2.9	2.4	1.8	1.0	2.3	•
Operating Margin **21**	3.6	13.5	5.7	3.2	5.1	•	4.0	2.4	3.9	3.3	1.0	1.0	•
Operating Margin Before Officers' Comp. **22**	11.3	24.0	21.0	14.3	12.8	•	8.0	5.3	6.3	5.1	2.0	1.0	•

Selected Average Balance Sheet ($ in Thousands)

Net Receivables 23	276	0	10	181	696	6936	16202	29674	56294	73837	544253
Inventories 24	21	0	1	33	65	539	1432	1962	4229	402	10358
Net Property, Plant and Equipment 25	106	0	29	113	350	2639	4536	8130	20225	28205	53723
Total Assets 26	900	0	84	681	1945	15441	35487	72592	153734	308271	1254972
Notes and Loans Payable 27	194	0	32	151	391	3247	6495	13050	40733	116037	156594
All Other Liabilities 28	369	0	21	214	627	6297	15632	31728	57128	85592	649058
Net Worth 29	337	0	31	316	926	5896	13361	27814	55874	106642	449320

Selected Financial Ratios (Times to 1)

Current Ratio 30	1.4	•	1.7	1.8	2.0	1.6	1.6	1.6	1.6	2.5	1.6
Quick Ratio 31	1.0	•	1.5	1.5	1.7	1.3	1.3	1.2	1.2	1.9	1.3
Net Sales to Working Capital 32	13.0	•	46.1	13.8	9.8	9.2	7.4	8.3	7.7	2.4	4.6
Coverage Ratio 33	9.5	15.9	27.1	18.7	15.0	10.5	10.6	7.9	6.0	2.3	3.0
Total Asset Turnover 34	2.3	•	9.9	4.2	3.4	2.5	2.1	2.2	1.8	0.5	0.9
Inventory Turnover 35	41.4	•	233.7	25.9	35.3	30.4	26.6	31.9	30.2	130.1	66.0
Receivables Turnover 36	8.4	•	91.8	18.9	9.1	5.6	5.0	5.1	4.6	4.2	2.4
Total Liabilities to Net Worth 37	1.7	•	1.7	1.2	1.1	1.6	1.7	1.6	1.8	1.9	1.8
Current Assets to Working Capital 38	3.3	•	2.5	2.2	2.0	2.7	2.6	2.6	2.7	1.7	2.8
Current Liabilities to Working Capital 39	2.3	•	1.5	1.2	1.0	1.7	1.6	1.6	1.7	0.7	1.8
Working Capital to Net Sales 40	0.1	•	0.0	0.1	0.1	0.1	0.1	0.1	0.1	0.4	0.2
Inventory to Working Capital 41	0.2	•	0.0	0.1	0.1	0.1	0.2	0.1	0.1	0.0	0.1
Total Receipts to Cash Flow 42	4.7	2.4	3.8	3.9	5.0	5.3	5.1	4.5	4.6	2.7	5.1
Cost of Goods to Cash Flow 43	1.9	0.5	1.0	1.1	1.7	2.3	2.6	1.7	2.1	0.9	3.0
Cash Flow to Total Debt 44	0.8	•	4.1	2.0	1.3	0.8	0.7	0.8	0.6	0.3	0.3

Selected Financial Factors (in Percentages)

Debt Ratio 45	62.6	•	63.4	53.6	52.4	61.8	62.4	61.7	63.7	65.4	64.2
Return on Total Assets 46	14.6	•	68.0	28.4	21.4	13.6	12.4	12.8	9.8	6.5	4.5
Return on Equity Before Income Taxes 47	34.8	•	178.9	58.0	42.0	32.3	29.9	29.2	22.6	10.5	8.5
Return on Equity After Income Taxes 48	31.3	•	175.7	55.3	37.4	26.8	25.8	23.4	16.1	8.3	5.6
Profit Margin (Before Income Tax) 49	5.6	19.5	6.6	6.4	5.9	5.0	5.4	5.0	4.5	7.2	3.3
Profit Margin (After Income Tax) 50	5.0	18.6	6.5	6.1	5.3	4.2	4.6	4.0	3.2	5.7	2.2

Table I
Corporations with and without Net Income

SPECIALIZED DESIGN SERVICES

MONEY AMOUNTS AND SIZE OF ASSETS IN THOUSANDS OF DOLLARS

Item Description for Accounting Period 7/02 Through 6/03	Total	Zero Assets	Under 500	500 to 1,000	1,000 to 5,000	5,000 to 10,000	10,000 to 25,000	25,000 to 50,000	50,000 to 100,000	100,000 to 250,000	250,000 to 500,000	500,000 to 2,500,000	2,500,000 and over
Number of Enterprises 1	36731	4055	31280	669	619	82	18	5	0	4	0	0	•
Revenues ($ in Thousands)													
Net Sales 2	15588802	459405	8238307	1525800	2728444	864798	253120	266282	0	1252646	0	0	•
Interest 3	29765	41	3531	114	1846	289	473	1256	0	22215	0	0	•
Rents 4	2185	625	0	903	0	0	0	625	0	32	0	0	•
Royalties 5	28368	0	0	0	0	0	10739	808	0	16821	0	0	•
Other Portfolio Income 6	9379	3175	1824	1312	569	193	39	0	0	2267	0	0	•
Other Receipts 7	136519	291	63449	28552	14792	-1090	11617	1527	0	17380	0	0	•
Total Receipts 8	15795018	463537	8307111	1556681	2745651	864190	275988	270498	0	1311361	0	0	•
Average Total Receipts 9	430	114	266	2327	4436	10539	15333	54100	•	327840	•	•	•
Operating Costs/Operating Income (%)													
Cost of Operations 10	49.4	45.2	45.4	65.3	59.8	55.3	50.9	63.7	•	27.8	•	•	•
Salaries and Wages 11	13.3	7.0	8.5	9.4	14.0	16.1	27.4	14.0	•	45.1	•	•	•
Taxes Paid 12	2.4	2.1	2.3	1.4	2.2	2.3	3.2	1.2	•	4.2	•	•	•
Interest Paid 13	0.6	0.8	0.6	0.3	0.3	0.3	1.1	0.2	•	2.1	•	•	•
Depreciation 14	1.9	1.0	1.5	1.0	1.4	1.3	4.0	2.3	•	7.5	•	•	•
Amortization and Depletion 15	0.1	0.0	0.1	0.0	0.1	0.0	0.0	0.6	•	0.9	•	•	•
Pensions and Other Deferred Comp. 16	0.8	0.0	1.0	0.9	0.8	0.4	0.3	0.2	•	0.4	•	•	•
Employee Benefits 17	1.1	0.7	0.9	0.6	0.8	1.2	1.0	1.1	•	3.8	•	•	•
Advertising 18	0.8	1.2	0.8	0.7	0.9	0.6	0.4	0.2	•	0.6	•	•	•
Other Expenses 19	21.0	32.7	26.7	11.6	13.4	13.5	12.0	19.4	•	14.9	•	•	•
Officers' Compensation 20	7.5	4.1	9.8	7.2	6.0	4.5	7.5	0.9	•	1.0	•	•	•
Operating Margin 21	1.0	5.3	2.4	1.6	0.3	4.4	•	•	•	•	•	•	•
Operating Margin Before Officers' Comp. 22	8.5	9.3	12.2	8.8	6.3	8.9	•	•	•	•	•	•	•

Selected Average Balance Sheet ($ in Thousands)

Net Receivables 23	33	0	11	148	636	1415	2839	13919	•	36228
Inventories 24	15	0	4	279	190	604	968	1188	•	14243
Net Property, Plant and Equipment 25	31	0	15	123	201	1290	2259	4490	•	67681
Total Assets 26	164	0	59	706	1782	6725	14824	41259	•	394961
Notes and Loans Payable 27	51	0	34	56	339	1181	3213	4530	•	99542
All Other Liabilities 28	62	0	22	362	939	4452	4947	12118	•	69921
Net Worth 29	50	0	4	288	504	1092	6665	24611	•	225498

Selected Financial Ratios (Times to 1)

Current Ratio 30	1.6	•	1.4	1.5	1.5	0.9	1.7	1.9	•	3.4
Quick Ratio 31	1.2	•	1.1	0.8	1.0	0.6	1.1	1.3	•	3.0
Net Sales to Working Capital 32	10.0	•	26.4	12.4	9.0	•	4.2	5.1	•	1.7
Coverage Ratio 33	4.6	8.6	6.2	13.1	3.8	14.0	2.4	•		
Total Asset Turnover 34	2.6	•	4.4	3.2	2.5	1.6	0.9	1.3	•	0.8
Inventory Turnover 35	13.6	•	28.1	5.3	13.9	9.7	7.4	28.6	•	6.1
Receivables Turnover 36	12.0	•	23.5	15.4	6.3	5.9	5.7	4.4	•	7.4
Total Liabilities to Net Worth 37	2.3	•	15.4	1.4	2.5	5.2	1.2	0.7	•	0.8
Current Assets to Working Capital 38	2.6	•	3.6	3.0	2.9	•	2.4	2.1	•	1.4
Current Liabilities to Working Capital 39	1.6	•	2.6	2.0	1.9	•	1.4	1.1	•	0.4
Working Capital to Net Sales 40	0.1	•	0.0	0.1	0.1	•	0.2	0.2	•	0.6
Inventory to Working Capital 41	0.4	•	0.5	1.2	0.5	•	0.5	0.1	•	0.1
Total Receipts to Cash Flow 42	5.6	3.5	4.2	9.1	9.7	6.9	11.2	8.4	•	24.7
Cost of Goods to Cash Flow 43	2.8	1.6	1.9	6.0	5.8	3.8	5.7	5.3	•	6.9
Cash Flow to Total Debt 44	0.7	•	1.1	0.6	0.4	0.3	0.2	0.4	•	0.1

Selected Financial Factors (in Percentages)

Debt Ratio 45	69.3	•	93.9	59.1	71.7	83.8	55.0	40.4	•	42.9
Return on Total Assets 46	7.8	•	17.2	12.7	3.1	7.3	2.5	•		
Return on Equity Before Income Taxes 47	19.9	•	237.2	28.7	7.9	41.7	3.2	•		
Return on Equity After Income Taxes 48	18.1	•	230.1	28.1	5.1	39.8	0.8	•		
Profit Margin (Before Income Tax) 49	2.4	6.2	3.3	3.6	0.9	4.3	1.5	•		
Profit Margin (After Income Tax) 50	2.1	5.8	3.2	3.5	0.6	4.1	0.4	•		

Table II

Corporations with Net Income

SPECIALIZED DESIGN SERVICES

MONEY AMOUNTS AND SIZE OF ASSETS IN THOUSANDS OF DOLLARS

Item Description for Accounting Period 7/02 Through 6/03	Total	Zero Assets	Under 500	500 to 1,000	1,000 to 5,000	5,000 to 10,000	10,000 to 25,000	25,000 to 50,000	50,000 to 100,000	100,000 to 250,000	250,000 to 500,000	500,000 to 2,500,000	2,500,000 and over
Number of Enterprises **1**	22002	2797	18237	577	313	0	13	0	•	0	0	•	•
Revenues ($ in Thousands)													
Net Sales **2**	11413174	320276	5917444	1361494	1916339	0	233912	0	•	0	0	•	•
Interest **3**	3855	41	1646	101	1198	0	361	0	•	0	0	•	•
Rents **4**	1536	625	0	903	0	0	0	0	•	0	0	•	•
Royalties **5**	1686	0	0	0	0	0	0	0	•	0	0	•	•
Other Portfolio Income **6**	5420	3175	708	1312	68	0	39	0	•	0	0	•	•
Other Receipts **7**	121446	292	60152	18836	11201	0	11545	0	•	0	0	•	•
Total Receipts **8**	11547117	324409	5979950	1382646	1928806	0	245857	0	•	0	0	•	•
Average Total Receipts **9**	525	116	328	2396	6162	•	18912	•	•	•	•	•	•
Operating Costs/Operating Income (%)													
Cost of Operations **10**	49.0	42.7	45.5	68.8	59.5	•	54.3	•	•	•	•	•	•
Salaries and Wages **11**	11.6	7.6	8.1	6.8	14.0	•	19.6	•	•	•	•	•	•
Taxes Paid **12**	2.2	2.4	2.2	1.0	2.0	•	2.7	•	•	•	•	•	•
Interest Paid **13**	0.5	0.6	0.5	0.3	0.3	•	0.8	•	•	•	•	•	•
Depreciation **14**	1.3	1.2	1.1	0.7	1.1	•	1.8	•	•	•	•	•	•
Amortization and Depletion **15**	0.2	0.1	0.0	0.0	0.2	•	0.0	•	•	•	•	•	•
Pensions and Other Deferred Comp. **16**	0.9	•	1.2	1.0	0.8	•	0.3	•	•	•	•	•	•
Employee Benefits **17**	1.0	0.8	0.7	0.5	0.9	•	0.9	•	•	•	•	•	•
Advertising **18**	0.5	1.5	0.5	0.8	0.2	•	0.4	•	•	•	•	•	•
Other Expenses **19**	18.9	30.8	22.2	10.5	11.2	•	10.5	•	•	•	•	•	•
Officers' Compensation **20**	6.8	2.7	9.0	6.3	4.5	•	6.0	•	•	•	•	•	•
Operating Margin **21**	7.1	9.7	9.0	3.2	5.2	•	2.6	•	•	•	•	•	•
Operating Margin Before Officers' Comp. **22**	13.9	12.4	18.0	9.5	9.7	•	8.6	•	•	•	•	•	•

Selected Average Balance Sheet ($ in Thousands)

Net Receivables 23	36	0	13	106	734	3289
Inventories 24	17	0	4	247	171	829
Net Property, Plant and Equipment 25	30	0	15	129	267	1961
Total Assets 26	160	0	72	717	2074	14414
Notes and Loans Payable 27	34	0	23	49	487	2024
All Other Liabilities 28	64	0	25	382	1073	5400
Net Worth 29	61	0	25	286	514	6991

Selected Financial Ratios (Times to 1)

Current Ratio 30	1.5	·	1.5	1.5	1.5	1.6
Quick Ratio 31	1.0	·	1.2	0.8	1.0	1.1
Net Sales to Working Capital 32	14.4	·	20.7	12.8	10.9	5.6
Coverage Ratio 33	18.9	19.4	21.2	16.9	18.1	11.2
Total Asset Turnover 34	3.2	·	4.5	3.3	3.0	1.2
Inventory Turnover 35	15.3	·	36.0	6.6	21.3	11.8
Receivables Turnover 36	14.6	·	29.2	18.2	8.1	6.7
Total Liabilities to Net Worth 37	1.6	·	1.9	1.5	3.0	1.1
Current Assets to Working Capital 38	3.0	·	3.0	3.0	3.1	2.7
Current Liabilities to Working Capital 39	2.0	·	2.0	2.0	2.1	1.7
Working Capital to Net Sales 40	0.1	·	0.0	0.1	0.1	0.2
Inventory to Working Capital 41	0.6	·	0.2	1.3	0.5	0.4
Total Receipts to Cash Flow 42	4.5	3.5	3.8	8.8	7.2	6.8
Cost of Goods to Cash Flow 43	2.2	1.5	1.7	6.1	4.3	3.7
Cash Flow to Total Debt 44	1.2	·	1.8	0.6	0.5	0.4

Selected Financial Factors (in Percentages)

Debt Ratio 45	61.6	·	66.0	60.1	75.2	51.5
Return on Total Assets 46	28.3	·	47.0	16.7	18.2	11.1
Return on Equity Before Income Taxes 47	70.0	·	131.6	39.3	69.3	20.9
Return on Equity After Income Taxes 48	67.5	·	129.8	38.6	63.8	17.7
Profit Margin (Before Income Tax) 49	8.3	11.0	10.0	4.8	5.8	8.1
Profit Margin (After Income Tax) 50	8.0	10.4	9.9	4.7	5.4	6.9

Table I

Corporations with and without Net Income

COMPUTER SYSTEMS DESIGN AND RELATED SERVICES

MONEY AMOUNTS AND SIZE OF ASSETS IN THOUSANDS OF DOLLARS

Item Description for Accounting Period 7/02 Through 6/03	Total	Zero Assets	Under 500	500 to 1,000	1,000 to 5,000	5,000 to 10,000	10,000 to 25,000	25,000 to 50,000	50,000 to 100,000	100,000 to 250,000	250,000 to 500,000	500,000 to 2,500,000	2,500,000 and over
Number of Enterprises **1**	112004	22770	81869	2915	3081	628	401	151	80	60	21	21	6
Revenues ($ in Thousands)													
Net Sales **2**	119156751	4172050	21718682	6657425	15686599	6190760	7944675	6233322	5363691	6659624	4730229	14254216	19545477
Interest **3**	1275414	9372	8932	8314	31960	34383	46837	36269	53771	102001	40639	190566	712370
Rents **4**	145928	2536	3986	86	1110	1920	2372	1631	2926	10415	22319	37573	59054
Royalties **5**	1795490	4555	3485	753	3844	9555	19496	29739	3443	51165	111680	880621	677153
Other Portfolio Income **6**	766446	81810	28372	35700	40648	37916	51959	55441	64195	32779	25134	266348	46142
Other Receipts **7**	2248487	62185	84454	41562	259978	103345	162867	56113	97394	386424	96011	771669	126489
Total Receipts **8**	125388516	4332508	21847911	6743840	16024139	6377879	8228206	6412515	5585420	7242408	5026012	16400993	21166685
Average Total Receipts **9**	1120	190	267	2313	5201	10156	20519	42467	69818	120707	239334	781000	3527781
Operating Costs/Operating Income (%)													
Cost of Operations **10**	32.4	23.0	20.1	40.4	40.5	43.4	45.0	42.0	41.5	31.1	40.6	40.8	16.9
Salaries and Wages **11**	29.1	37.4	23.6	25.4	30.6	32.7	31.0	29.7	30.1	40.0	31.1	27.4	28.4
Taxes Paid **12**	4.1	3.8	3.6	3.3	4.3	4.0	3.4	3.7	3.6	3.6	2.9	3.5	6.0
Interest Paid **13**	1.7	1.3	0.7	1.1	0.9	1.4	1.3	1.2	1.5	2.6	1.7	1.4	4.1
Depreciation **14**	3.2	2.2	1.5	2.1	2.1	3.1	3.9	3.6	3.7	5.6	2.9	4.3	4.4
Amortization and Depletion **15**	1.8	1.2	0.1	0.6	0.8	3.5	1.4	1.6	1.8	3.3	2.8	2.1	3.6
Pensions and Other Deferred Comp. **16**	0.8	1.1	1.2	0.5	0.9	0.5	0.5	0.3	0.5	0.4	0.3	0.9	0.8
Employee Benefits **17**	2.5	1.3	1.6	1.9	2.1	2.9	2.8	2.8	3.3	2.6	2.8	3.7	2.9
Advertising **18**	0.9	0.4	0.8	0.5	0.8	1.3	1.0	0.9	0.8	0.7	0.9	2.1	0.3
Other Expenses **19**	30.3	36.4	31.5	24.8	27.2	22.7	27.6	23.9	25.0	32.7	26.5	30.6	38.9
Officers' Compensation **20**	5.7	8.4	15.9	8.7	7.0	5.2	3.6	2.4	2.3	2.1	1.2	0.7	0.8
Operating Margin **21**	•	•	•	•	•	•	•	•	•	•	•	•	•
Operating Margin Before Officers' Comp. **22**	•	•	15.3	•	•	•	•	•	•	•	•	•	•

Selected Average Balance Sheet ($ in Thousands)

Item													
Net Receivables 23	263	0	199	635	1645	3993	8687	12617	25672	73520	167008		2454681
Inventories 24	13	0	30	54	124	321	553	960	2281	1488	9722		47628
Net Property, Plant and Equipment 25	84	0	96	257	703	1769	3555	7068	14850	17096	69864		409887
Total Assets 26	980	52	685	2086	6842	15520	35547	70299	155554	328848	881811		6800303
Notes and Loans Payable 27	272	36	472	920	1620	5025	5157	12419	45316	41899	129812		2023246
All Other Liabilities 28	338	22	325	950	2772	6329	13738	21179	43890	143777	274987		2123521
Net Worth 29	370	-6	-112	217	2451	4166	16652	36701	66348	143172	477012		2653536

Selected Financial Ratios (Times to 1)

Item													
Current Ratio 30	1.4	1.2	0.9	1.3	1.7	1.7	1.5	1.8	1.4	1.5	2.1		1.2
Quick Ratio 31	1.2	1.0	0.8	1.1	1.5	1.4	1.2	1.5	1.1	1.1	1.7		1.1
Net Sales to Working Capital 32	6.9	58.5	•	16.5	5.2	4.6	5.8	3.9	5.1	4.4	2.6		6.5
Coverage Ratio 33	•	1.0	•	•	•	•	•	•	•	•	•		1.6
Total Asset Turnover 34	1.1	5.1	3.3	2.4	1.4	1.3	1.2	1.0	0.7	0.7	0.8		0.5
Inventory Turnover 35	26.7	26.4	30.8	37.9	34.7	27.8	31.3	29.0	15.1	61.4	28.5		11.6
Receivables Turnover 36	4.2	36.1	11.9	8.4	6.2	5.1	4.6	4.6	3.6	2.6	3.5		1.6
Total Liabilities to Net Worth 37	1.6	•	•	8.6	1.8	2.7	1.1	0.9	1.3	1.3	0.8		1.6
Current Assets to Working Capital 38	3.3	7.1	•	4.4	2.4	2.5	3.0	2.2	3.5	3.1	1.9		6.0
Current Liabilities to Working Capital 39	2.3	6.1	•	3.4	1.4	1.5	2.0	1.2	2.5	2.1	0.9		5.0
Working Capital to Net Sales 40	0.1	0.0	•	0.1	0.2	0.2	0.2	0.3	0.2	0.2	0.4		0.2
Inventory to Working Capital 41	0.1	0.5	•	0.2	0.1	0.1	0.1	0.1	0.1	0.0	0.0		0.1
Total Receipts to Cash Flow 42	5.7	3.9	8.5	14.8	•	27.3	10.3	12.1	11.6	7.4	4.7		2.7
Cost of Goods to Cash Flow 43	1.9	0.8	3.4	6.0	•	12.3	4.3	5.0	3.6	3.0	1.9		0.5
Cash Flow to Total Debt 44	0.3	1.2	0.3	0.2	0.1	0.1	0.2	0.2	0.1	0.2	0.4		0.3

Selected Financial Factors (in Percentages)

Item													
Debt Ratio 45	62.2	•	112.0	116.4	89.6	64.2	73.2	53.2	47.8	57.3	56.5	45.9	61.0
Return on Total Assets 46	•	3.3	•	•	•	•	•	•	•	•	•	•	3.1
Return on Equity Before Income Taxes 47	•	1.1	161.4	•	•	•	•	•	•	•	•	•	3.0
Return on Equity After Income Taxes 48	•	6.2	162.2	•	•	•	•	•	•	•	•	•	1.2
Profit Margin (Before Income Tax) 49	•	•	•	•	•	•	•	•	•	•	•	•	2.4
Profit Margin (After Income Tax) 50	•	•	•	•	•	•	•	•	•	•	•	•	1.0

Table II
Corporations with Net Income

COMPUTER SYSTEMS DESIGN AND RELATED SERVICES

MONEY AMOUNTS AND SIZE OF ASSETS IN THOUSANDS OF DOLLARS

Item Description for Accounting Period 7/02 Through 6/03	Total	Zero Assets	Under 500	500 to 1,000	1,000 to 5,000	5,000 to 10,000	10,000 to 25,000	25,000 to 50,000	50,000 to 100,000	100,000 to 250,000	250,000 to 500,000	500,000 to 2,500,000	2,500,000 and over
Number of Enterprises **1**	58928	8974	46485	1320	1636	0	134	54	28	20	7	10	0
Revenues ($ in Thousands)													
Net Sales **2**	70947485	2542632	14347199	5143093	11307626	0	4445518	3285435	2603643	2253429	1655781	8386520	0
Interest **3**	359897	2694	3760	1405	6376	0	7021	9917	7797	38883	16363	66472	0
Rents **4**	84166	270	3946	0	345	0	131	606	1510	3020	21758	14296	0
Royalties **5**	1537701	4554	0	0	815	0	12282	10942	2007	46316	68684	710765	0
Other Portfolio Income **6**	570246	77902	2008	22894	28453	0	39368	47041	14233	3629	15263	254818	0
Other Receipts **7**	1085410	13405	83013	23183	137490	0	38006	11660	70512	18093	-87	669857	0
Total Receipts **8**	74584905	2641457	14439926	5190575	11481105	0	4542326	3365601	2699702	2363370	1777762	10102728	0
Average Total Receipts **9**	1266	294	311	3932	7018	•	33898	62326	96418	118168	253966	1010273	•
Operating Costs/Operating Income (%)													
Cost of Operations **10**	34.0	13.9	20.0	40.8	43.0	•	47.3	43.9	40.7	16.4	53.8	45.1	•
Salaries and Wages **11**	22.7	40.3	16.8	20.2	23.1	•	20.1	22.5	24.5	40.1	16.0	24.0	•
Taxes Paid **12**	4.0	3.3	2.8	2.6	3.5	•	2.7	3.1	3.7	3.2	3.2	3.7	•
Interest Paid **13**	0.8	0.3	0.3	0.6	0.3	•	0.6	0.5	0.8	1.3	1.7	1.2	•
Depreciation **14**	2.1	1.3	1.1	0.9	1.0	•	1.9	1.8	2.6	3.4	2.5	4.0	•
Amortization and Depletion **15**	0.9	0.1	0.0	0.1	0.1	•	0.3	0.6	0.5	1.9	1.6	1.4	•
Pensions and Other Deferred Comp. **16**	0.9	1.2	1.3	0.5	0.9	•	0.7	0.3	0.4	0.4	0.3	1.1	•
Employee Benefits **17**	2.1	0.6	1.2	1.3	1.4	•	2.0	2.3	3.3	3.0	2.3	4.3	•
Advertising **18**	0.5	0.2	0.7	0.3	0.8	•	0.4	0.8	0.4	0.4	0.4	0.2	•
Other Expenses **19**	22.4	24.2	28.2	21.0	14.7	•	15.7	14.7	15.5	25.3	19.0	23.7	•
Officers' Compensation **20**	5.8	8.2	15.5	6.4	6.0	•	2.8	2.0	2.0	2.7	0.9	0.4	•
Operating Margin **21**	3.8	6.4	12.0	5.3	5.2	•	5.5	7.6	5.5	1.9	•	•	•
Operating Margin Before Officers' Comp. **22**	9.6	14.6	27.5	11.7	11.1	•	8.3	9.6	7.5	4.5	•	•	•

Selected Average Balance Sheet ($ in Thousands)

	C1	C2	C3	C4	C5	C6	C7	C8	C9	C10	C11	C12	C13
Net Receivables 23	270	0	8	260	799	•	5702	12129	17471	20210	118064	218661	•
Inventories 24	12	0	2	38	58	•	450	510	1221	467	1768	7842	•
Net Property, Plant and Equipment 25	67	0	11	103	187	•	1538	2460	8009	8627	16569	79760	•
Total Assets 26	832	0	55	670	1987	•	15673	35169	72234	147683	320602	896108	•
Notes and Loans Payable 27	217	0	17	356	412	•	2831	3429	13329	8341	35244	159640	•
All Other Liabilities 28	243	0	13	336	671	•	6732	16350	21592	45450	139333	233812	•
Net Worth 29	371	0	25	-21	904	•	6110	15391	37313	93892	146025	502655	•

Selected Financial Ratios (Times to 1)

	C1	C2	C3	C4	C5	C6	C7	C8	C9	C10	C11	C12	C13
Current Ratio 30	1.5	•	2.1	0.9	2.2	•	1.6	1.5	2.0	1.9	1.3	2.3	•
Quick Ratio 31	1.3	•	1.8	0.8	2.0	•	1.4	1.2	1.7	1.5	1.2	2.0	•
Net Sales to Working Capital 32	7.9	•	16.0	•	8.1	•	7.8	7.8	4.3	3.0	7.1	2.9	•
Coverage Ratio 33	12.0	31.0	38.3	12.0	26.7	•	14.9	21.3	12.2	6.3	4.4	10.4	•
Total Asset Turnover 34	1.4	•	5.6	5.8	3.5	•	2.1	1.7	1.3	0.8	0.7	0.9	•
Inventory Turnover 35	32.9	•	29.7	41.9	51.6	•	34.8	52.4	31.0	39.6	72.0	48.2	•
Receivables Turnover 36	4.6	•	38.1	15.8	9.7	•	6.0	5.8	4.7	4.1	1.8	7.7	•
Total Liabilities to Net Worth 37	1.2	•	1.2	•	1.2	•	1.6	1.3	0.9	0.6	1.2	0.8	•
Current Assets to Working Capital 38	3.2	•	1.9	•	1.8	•	2.7	3.1	2.0	2.1	4.6	1.8	•
Current Liabilities to Working Capital 39	2.2	•	0.9	•	0.8	•	1.7	2.1	1.0	1.1	3.6	0.8	•
Working Capital to Net Sales 40	0.1	•	0.1	•	0.1	•	0.1	0.1	0.2	0.3	0.1	0.3	•
Inventory to Working Capital 41	0.1	•	0.1	•	0.1	•	0.1	0.1	0.1	0.0	0.0	0.0	•
Total Receipts to Cash Flow 42	3.7	3.3	2.7	4.3	5.4	•	5.0	4.5	4.8	3.7	4.8	3.5	•
Cost of Goods to Cash Flow 43	1.2	0.5	1.8	1.8	2.3	•	2.4	2.0	1.9	0.6	2.6	1.6	•
Cash Flow to Total Debt 44	0.7	•	3.7	1.3	1.2	•	0.7	0.7	0.6	0.6	0.3	0.6	•

Selected Financial Factors (in Percentages)

	C1	C2	C3	C4	C5	C6	C7	C8	C9	C10	C11	C12	C13
Debt Ratio 45	55.4	•	54.7	103.2	54.5	•	61.0	56.2	48.3	36.4	54.5	43.9	•
Return on Total Assets 46	14.7	•	72.5	39.4	24.2	•	17.4	18.2	13.3	6.2	5.5	12.2	•
Return on Equity Before Income Taxes 47	30.2	•	155.7	•	51.2	•	41.5	39.5	23.6	8.2	9.3	19.6	•
Return on Equity After Income Taxes 48	26.6	•	153.5	•	47.8	•	35.7	35.3	21.2	6.5	6.6	16.0	•
Profit Margin (Before Income Tax) 49	9.3	10.3	12.7	6.2	6.7	•	7.7	10.0	9.5	6.8	5.7	11.8	•
Profit Margin (After Income Tax) 50	8.2	9.2	12.5	6.2	6.3	•	6.6	8.9	8.5	5.4	4.1	9.6	•

Table I
Corporations with and without Net Income

MANAGEMENT, SCIENTIFIC, AND TECHNICAL CONSULTING SERVICES

MONEY AMOUNTS AND SIZE OF ASSETS IN THOUSANDS OF DOLLARS

Item Description for Accounting Period 7/02 Through 6/03	Total	Zero Assets	Under 500	500 to 1,000	1,000 to 5,000	5,000 to 10,000	10,000 to 25,000	25,000 to 50,000	50,000 to 100,000	100,000 to 250,000	250,000 to 500,000	500,000 to 2,500,000	2,500,000 and over
Number of Enterprises 1	205268	34866	160039	4856	4336	482	411	123	62	50	18	21	3
Revenues ($ in Thousands)													
Net Sales 2	131368171	2335029	50736617	10045856	14740386	5544020	8717871	5373345	3412999	6734965	4552308	17613989	1560786
Interest 3	762221	7961	34561	27449	40635	12150	33973	28196	46502	70495	116811	237855	105632
Rents 4	94732	119	2368	1009	3660	2045	5765	5646	11598	12670	226	47591	2034
Royalties 5	611468	0	398	2989	13023	849	16181	127229	2	6982	14663	429151	0
Other Portfolio Income 6	537359	50774	84873	22316	43822	20250	71786	25481	25156	33001	60606	98709	587
Other Receipts 7	3543979	-37288	998379	8733	622415	208166	245977	216380	213273	297298	172351	584957	13340
Total Receipts 8	136917930	2356595	51857196	10108352	15463941	5787480	9091553	5776277	3709530	7155441	4916965	19012252	1682379
Average Total Receipts 9	667	68	324	2082	3566	12007	22121	46962	59831	143108	273165	905345	560793
Operating Costs/Operating Income (%)													
Cost of Operations 10	28.6	6.3	34.3	9.2	37.7	21.7	36.7	35.4	19.7	41.0	28.6	14.4	1.3
Salaries and Wages 11	25.2	21.4	16.7	31.4	22.5	32.7	28.0	27.6	36.0	21.6	30.4	41.9	34.5
Taxes Paid 12	3.0	3.3	2.7	2.8	3.2	3.5	2.9	2.8	3.5	2.8	3.0	3.3	3.8
Interest Paid 13	1.1	1.0	0.5	0.8	0.9	1.4	1.3	1.3	1.6	2.0	3.0	1.5	10.5
Depreciation 14	1.8	2.4	1.1	1.1	1.8	2.2	2.3	2.2	2.8	2.0	2.4	3.0	3.4
Amortization and Depletion 15	0.9	0.3	0.2	0.3	0.2	0.2	0.6	0.5	0.8	9.7	2.3	0.7	1.5
Pensions and Other Deferred Comp. 16	1.6	2.1	1.6	1.2	1.2	0.7	1.2	1.3	1.6	0.6	0.9	3.2	3.8
Employee Benefits 17	1.9	1.5	1.3	2.2	2.0	3.2	2.4	2.9	3.0	1.4	1.6	2.4	2.2
Advertising 18	0.7	2.1	0.6	0.2	0.9	0.6	0.5	0.5	0.5	0.8	0.6	0.9	0.4
Other Expenses 19	27.7	40.4	22.3	36.8	23.4	31.6	26.2	27.6	37.6	38.7	27.2	30.5	57.3
Officers' Compensation 20	8.7	16.5	13.9	9.7	8.1	5.4	3.9	3.1	3.8	6.9	2.6	1.6	1.2
Operating Margin 21	*	2.7	4.6	4.3	*	*	*	*			*	*	*
Operating Margin Before Officers' Comp. 22	7.4	19.2	18.6	13.9	6.1	2.2	*	*				*	*

Selected Average Balance Sheet ($ in Thousands)

Net Receivables 23	98	0	7	64	483	1636	3704	9136	13214	35203	109506	223676	1260378
Inventories 24	5	0	1	21	35	47	203	941	1345	2995	3568	8951	2106
Net Property, Plant and Equipment 25	47	0	12	122	255	989	1962	4928	9027	15839	20002	112773	56732
Total Assets 26	438	0	55	702	2006	6693	15323	36167	69489	158918	372230	986609	5118373
Notes and Loans Payable 27	149	0	40	505	706	3448	4885	12161	14477	50097	146594	203529	1076724
All Other Liabilities 28	146	0	17	174	635	2159	5138	11889	26193	45220	111361	435164	1346950
Net Worth 29	143	0	-1	23	665	1086	5300	12117	28819	63601	114275	347915	2694700

Selected Financial Ratios (Times to 1)

Current Ratio 30	1.4	•	1.3	1.9	1.6	1.3	1.5	1.2	1.4	1.4	2.1	1.1	1.4
Quick Ratio 31	1.1	•	1.2	1.4	1.2	1.0	1.1	1.0	1.1	1.1	1.7	0.8	1.3
Net Sales to Working Capital 32	11.6	•	42.1	13.0	8.1	13.6	8.3	12.7	6.4	6.5	2.4	19.7	1.2
Coverage Ratio 33	3.7	4.6	15.2	6.8	4.1	1.8	•	3.0	•	•	2.7	4.6	•
Total Asset Turnover 34	1.5	•	5.8	2.9	1.7	1.7	1.4	1.2	0.8	0.8	0.7	0.9	0.1
Inventory Turnover 35	34.8	•	144.5	9.2	36.9	53.3	38.3	16.4	8.1	18.5	20.3	13.5	3.3
Receivables Turnover 36	6.8	•	45.7	24.5	7.3	7.5	5.7	4.9	4.0	4.3	2.6	2.8	0.8
Total Liabilities to Net Worth 37	2.1	•	•	29.6	2.0	5.2	1.9	2.0	1.4	1.5	2.3	1.8	0.9
Current Assets to Working Capital 38	3.7	•	4.1	2.1	2.7	4.7	3.2	5.1	3.7	3.5	1.9	10.9	3.5
Current Liabilities to Working Capital 39	2.7	•	3.1	1.1	1.7	3.7	2.2	4.1	2.7	2.5	0.9	9.9	2.5
Working Capital to Net Sales 40	0.1	•	0.0	0.1	0.1	0.1	0.1	0.1	0.2	0.2	0.4	0.1	0.8
Inventory to Working Capital 41	0.1	•	0.1	0.1	0.1	0.1	0.1	0.2	0.1	0.2	0.0	0.2	0.0
Total Receipts to Cash Flow 42	3.8	2.6	3.9	2.5	4.9	3.6	5.0	4.1	3.4	8.9	3.8	3.4	2.5
Cost of Goods to Cash Flow 43	1.1	0.2	1.4	0.2	1.8	0.8	1.8	1.5	0.7	3.7	1.1	0.5	0.0
Cash Flow to Total Debt 44	0.6	•	1.4	1.2	0.5	0.6	0.4	0.4	0.4	0.2	0.3	0.4	0.1

Selected Financial Factors (in Percentages)

Debt Ratio 45	67.3	•	102.3	96.7	66.8	83.8	65.4	66.5	58.5	60.0	69.3	64.7	47.4
Return on Total Assets 46	6.1	•	42.3	16.6	6.4	4.5	•	4.7	•	•	5.6	5.7	•
Return on Equity Before Income Taxes 47	13.7	•	•	434.5	14.7	12.4	•	9.4	•	•	11.4	12.8	•
Return on Equity After Income Taxes 48	10.7	•	425.5	•	12.7	5.6	•	5.0	•	•	6.8	7.9	•
Profit Margin (Before Income Tax) 49	3.1	3.6	6.9	4.8	2.9	1.2	2.6	2.6	•	•	5.2	5.3	•
Profit Margin (After Income Tax) 50	2.4	2.8	6.8	4.7	2.5	0.5	1.4	1.4	•	•	3.1	3.3	•

Table II
Corporations with Net Income

MANAGEMENT, SCIENTIFIC, AND TECHNICAL CONSULTING SERVICES

MONEY AMOUNTS AND SIZE OF ASSETS IN THOUSANDS OF DOLLARS

Item Description for Accounting Period 7/02 Through 6/03	Total	Zero Assets	Under 500	500 to 1,000	1,000 to 5,000	5,000 to 10,000	10,000 to 25,000	25,000 to 50,000	50,000 to 100,000	100,000 to 250,000	250,000 to 500,000	500,000 to 2,500,000	2,500,000 and over
Number of Enterprises 1	117468	14784	96033	3614	2406	0	211	66	32	21	11	0	0
Revenues ($ in Thousands)													
Net Sales 2	87581757	1383643	31278593	4467255	11277300	0	5494320	3477404	2076263	3579600	3396223	0	0
Interest 3	475565	7373	20310	13114	30490	0	12048	14425	14761	40183	29737	0	0
Rents 4	71580	119	135	1009	2448	0	4129	4810	8036	5731	0	0	0
Royalties 5	526129	0	11	2989	12740	0	5418	124297	2	206	14663	0	0
Other Portfolio Income 6	371843	50774	47043	4868	14656	0	58971	4170	13316	20111	56901	0	0
Other Receipts 7	2387260	43174	746918	39201	296929	0	183395	52126	130388	259414	41972	0	0
Total Receipts 8	91414134	1485083	32093010	4528436	11634563	0	5758281	3677232	2242766	3905245	3539496	0	0
Average Total Receipts 9	778	100	334	1253	4836	•	27290	55716	70086	185964	321772	•	•
Operating Costs/Operating Income (%)													
Cost of Operations 10	22.7	6.0	19.0	18.2	36.1	•	38.9	30.9	22.1	35.9	27.0	•	•
Salaries and Wages 11	24.9	10.1	18.4	23.8	19.0	•	24.1	25.6	32.5	18.8	27.6	•	•
Taxes Paid 12	3.0	2.1	3.0	2.4	2.9	•	2.9	2.9	3.7	2.2	2.9	•	•
Interest Paid 13	0.9	0.6	0.5	0.8	0.5	•	0.8	0.8	1.4	1.4	1.2	•	•
Depreciation 14	1.7	2.0	1.1	1.1	1.4	•	1.5	1.6	2.7	1.7	2.0	•	•
Amortization and Depletion 15	0.3	0.2	0.1	0.2	0.1	•	0.3	0.3	0.7	0.6	1.7	•	•
Pensions and Other Deferred Comp. 16	1.8	1.6	1.7	1.5	1.5	•	0.9	1.5	1.3	0.6	1.2	•	•
Employee Benefits 17	1.7	1.1	1.0	0.8	1.8	•	2.3	3.1	2.5	0.9	1.0	•	•
Advertising 18	0.7	2.7	0.7	0.4	0.6	•	0.4	0.4	0.2	1.3	0.5	•	•
Other Expenses 19	25.6	37.2	25.1	22.1	20.2	•	20.0	25.0	27.8	31.3	26.5	•	•
Officers' Compensation 20	9.0	9.5	16.6	10.4	8.4	•	4.1	3.2	3.3	6.4	2.5	•	•
Operating Margin 21	7.6	26.9	12.7	18.2	7.6	•	4.0	4.7	1.7	•	5.8	•	•
Operating Margin Before Officers' Comp. 22	16.6	36.4	29.2	28.7	16.0	•	8.1	7.9	5.1	5.4	8.3	•	•

Selected Average Balance Sheet ($ in Thousands)

Net Receivables 23	125	0	8	67	531	•	4191	10397	16522	23490	117842	•
Inventories 24	6	0	1	19	47	•	194	776	1431	5664	4544	•
Net Property, Plant and Equipment 25	50	0	11	119	-238	•	1788	4209	9114	19115	17587	•
Total Assets 26	468	0	60	688	2005	•	15037	36234	67069	162109	361120	•
Notes and Loans Payable 27	132	0	29	254	543	•	3377	9952	13018	27761	106637	•
All Other Liabilities 28	166	0	17	143	585	•	4818	12086	21277	40462	81212	•
Net Worth 29	169	0	14	292	877	•	6842	14196	32773	93886	173271	•

Selected Financial Ratios (Times to 1)

Current Ratio 30	1.4	•	1.6	2.5	1.8	•	1.6	1.3	1.6	1.6	1.6	•
Quick Ratio 31	1.2	•	1.4	1.9	1.5	•	1.3	1.1	1.3	1.2	1.4	•
Net Sales to Working Capital 32	10.6	•	23.5	6.1	7.9	•	7.9	12.3	5.4	7.9	5.0	•
Coverage Ratio 33	14.0	60.2	29.2	24.6	21.7	•	12.3	13.4	8.1	6.7	9.2	•
Total Asset Turnover 34	1.6	•	5.4	1.8	2.3	•	1.7	1.5	1.0	1.1	0.9	•
Inventory Turnover 35	28.1	•	98.0	11.9	36.0	•	52.1	21.0	10.0	10.8	18.3	•
Receivables Turnover 36	6.1	•	38.7	16.0	8.4	•	6.3	5.4	4.1	5.9	2.6	•
Total Liabilities to Net Worth 37	1.8	•	3.2	1.4	1.3	•	1.2	1.6	1.0	0.7	1.1	•
Current Assets to Working Capital 38	3.4	•	2.7	1.7	2.2	•	2.6	4.2	2.8	2.8	2.7	•
Current Liabilities to Working Capital 39	2.4	•	1.7	0.7	1.2	•	1.6	3.2	1.8	1.8	1.7	•
Working Capital to Net Sales 40	0.1	•	0.0	0.2	0.1	•	0.1	0.1	0.2	0.1	0.2	•
Inventory to Working Capital 41	0.1	•	0.1	0.0	0.1	•	0.1	0.2	0.1	0.3	0.0	•
Total Receipts to Cash Flow 42	3.0	1.6	2.7	2.6	4.0	•	3.9	3.2	3.1	2.8	3.3	•
Cost of Goods to Cash Flow 43	0.7	0.1	0.5	0.5	1.4	•	1.5	1.0	0.7	1.0	0.9	•
Cash Flow to Total Debt 44	0.8	•	2.6	1.2	1.0	•	0.8	0.8	0.6	0.9	0.5	•

Selected Financial Factors (in Percentages)

Debt Ratio 45	63.8	•	76.4	57.6	56.3	•	54.5	60.8	51.1	42.1	52.0	•
Return on Total Assets 46	20.7	•	85.4	36.7	26.3	•	16.6	16.5	10.7	10.0	9.6	•
Return on Equity Before Income Taxes 47	53.1	•	350.1	83.1	57.5	•	33.5	38.9	19.1	14.7	17.8	•
Return on Equity After Income Taxes 48	48.8	•	346.4	82.2	54.8	•	30.1	32.1	15.5	12.2	12.8	•
Profit Margin (Before Income Tax) 49	12.1	34.3	15.3	19.6	10.7	•	8.8	10.5	9.7	8.1	10.0	•
Profit Margin (After Income Tax) 50	11.1	33.1	15.1	19.4	10.3	•	7.9	8.6	7.8	6.7	7.2	•

SCIENTIFIC RESEARCH AND DEVELOPMENT SERVICES

Table I
Corporations with and without Net Income

MONEY AMOUNTS AND SIZE OF ASSETS IN THOUSANDS OF DOLLARS

Item Description for Accounting Period 7/02 Through 6/03	Total	Zero Assets	Under 500	500 to 1,000	1,000 to 5,000	5,000 to 10,000	10,000 to 25,000	25,000 to 50,000	50,000 to 100,000	100,000 to 250,000	250,000 to 500,000	500,000 to 2,500,000	2,500,000 and over
Number of Enterprises **1**	8242	1006	4832	570	1125	215	243	113	59	40	23	15	0
Revenues ($ in Thousands)													
Net Sales **2**	25665333	1573745	1956426	775640	2594631	1221573	1737340	1531037	1178076	2164359	1640062	9292445	0
Interest **3**	849391	23118	949	3209	11900	17149	43610	54144	69838	100455	156857	368160	0
Rents **4**	34754	5802	0	3392	497	2261	1094	1360	144	838	15445	3919	0
Royalties **5**	1389497	365038	0	45274	868	918	26565	20397	82403	6887	340361	500786	0
Other Portfolio Income **6**	799791	96036	1	2723	16984	13080	26660	28498	24930	5756	28896	556227	0
Other Receipts **7**	1489941	61701	72763	78088	152445	49589	148502	120486	65829	187896	179373	373273	0
Total Receipts **8**	30228707	2125440	2030139	908326	2777325	1304570	1983771	1755922	1421220	2466191	2360994	11094810	0
Average Total Receipts **9**	3668	2113	420	1594	2469	6068	8164	15539	24088	61655	102652	739654	•
Operating Costs/Operating Income (%)													
Cost of Operations **10**	32.8	75.0	9.1	51.5	18.6	18.1	35.1	44.9	39.8	15.9	32.9	35.5	•
Salaries and Wages **11**	34.4	22.9	31.4	22.7	47.7	39.4	46.3	40.5	45.1	39.0	39.0	27.2	•
Taxes Paid **12**	4.6	0.8	4.0	4.1	5.0	4.1	6.3	6.4	5.8	4.9	4.8	4.4	•
Interest Paid **13**	3.0	2.4	0.9	1.4	1.5	2.3	2.4	2.6	3.9	3.0	7.5	3.4	•
Depreciation **14**	5.3	7.0	2.4	3.1	4.9	6.0	8.2	8.5	11.3	8.8	6.8	3.0	•
Amortization and Depletion **15**	2.3	3.9	0.1	0.5	1.2	2.4	4.7	1.9	6.3	3.2	3.5	1.7	•
Pensions and Other Deferred Comp. **16**	1.9	7.5	2.1	1.9	1.7	0.7	1.3	2.3	1.4	1.5	0.8	1.6	•
Employee Benefits **17**	3.2	0.3	1.1	1.7	4.3	3.8	5.1	5.7	4.9	4.7	3.8	2.5	•
Advertising **18**	1.0	0.6	2.6	0.2	1.6	0.6	1.1	1.0	1.7	0.9	1.4	0.5	•
Other Expenses **19**	52.1	27.1	54.3	39.1	49.3	75.1	67.8	69.8	69.7	64.1	100.8	35.4	•
Officers' Compensation **20**	5.4	2.4	9.1	21.6	9.2	8.2	8.9	7.1	7.2	3.9	4.6	1.6	•
Operating Margin **21**	•	•	•	•	•	•	•	•	•	•	•	•	•
Operating Margin Before Officers' Comp. **22**	•	•	•	•	•	•	•	•	•	•	•	•	•

Selected Average Balance Sheet ($ in Thousands)

Item													
Net Receivables 23	661	0	22	146	424	780	1679	2782	3708	11516	27202	172373	•
Inventories 24	97	0	1	28	111	161	331	444	882	3541	7513	8226	•
Net Property, Plant and Equipment 25	764	0	19	217	347	1205	2272	4800	10280	27280	39820	115044	•
Total Assets 26	6296	0	114	716	2148	7143	15448	34805	69406	156574	367473	1365376	•
Notes and Loans Payable 27	1368	0	62	414	654	1147	2203	5488	8874	19495	85201	356287	•
All Other Liabilities 28	1565	0	60	375	824	2051	3087	6570	11563	28262	83477	386916	•
Net Worth 29	3362	0	-7	-73	671	3946	10158	22747	48968	108816	198794	622173	•

Selected Financial Ratios (Times to 1)

Item													
Current Ratio 30	2.7	•	1.1	1.6	1.8	1.9	3.3	3.4	3.3	2.9	3.0	2.7	•
Quick Ratio 31	1.7	•	0.9	1.4	1.5	1.6	2.7	2.6	2.2	1.8	1.8	1.4	•
Net Sales to Working Capital 32	1.4	•	89.7	9.9	4.0	2.9	1.0	0.9	0.8	1.0	0.6	1.4	•
Coverage Ratio 33	•	•	•	•	•	•	•	•	•	•	1.8	•	•
Total Asset Turnover 34	0.5	•	3.5	1.9	1.1	0.8	0.5	0.4	0.3	0.3	0.2	0.5	•
Inventory Turnover 35	10.5	•	29.5	24.8	3.9	6.4	7.6	13.7	9.0	2.4	3.1	26.7	•
Receivables Turnover 36	4.6	•	25.6	6.2	6.0	5.0	4.6	5.4	4.9	3.7	2.7	3.6	•
Total Liabilities to Net Worth 37	0.9	•	•	•	2.2	0.8	0.5	0.5	0.4	0.4	0.8	1.2	•
Current Assets to Working Capital 38	1.6	•	16.0	2.8	2.2	2.1	1.4	1.4	1.4	1.5	1.5	1.6	•
Current Liabilities to Working Capital 39	0.6	•	15.0	1.8	1.2	1.1	0.4	0.4	0.4	0.5	0.5	0.6	•
Working Capital to Net Sales 40	0.7	•	0.0	0.1	0.3	0.3	1.0	1.2	1.3	1.0	1.7	0.7	•
Inventory to Working Capital 41	0.0	•	0.2	0.1	0.2	0.1	0.0	0.0	0.0	0.1	0.1	0.0	•
Total Receipts to Cash Flow 42	7.2	•	18.7	2.9	95.3	81.1	7.6	•	•	5.0	3.6	3.6	•
Cost of Goods to Cash Flow 43	2.3	•	14.0	0.3	49.1	15.1	1.4	•	•	0.8	1.2	1.3	•
Cash Flow to Total Debt 44	0.1	•	1.1	0.0	0.0	0.2	•	•	•	0.1	0.1	0.2	•

Selected Financial Factors (in Percentages)

Item													
Debt Ratio 45	46.6	•	106.5	110.2	68.8	44.8	34.2	34.6	29.4	30.5	45.9	54.4	•
Return on Total Assets 46	•	•	•	•	•	•	•	•	•	•	•	2.8	•
Return on Equity Before Income Taxes 47	•	•	725.5	574.0	•	•	•	•	•	•	•	2.6	•
Return on Equity After Income Taxes 48	•	•	728.1	603.8	•	•	•	•	•	•	•	2.6	•
Profit Margin (Before Income Tax) 49	•	•	•	•	•	•	•	•	•	•	•	2.6	•
Profit Margin (After Income Tax) 50	•	•	•	•	•	•	•	•	•	•	•	2.6	•

SCIENTIFIC RESEARCH AND DEVELOPMENT SERVICES

Table II
Corporations with Net Income

MONEY AMOUNTS AND SIZE OF ASSETS IN THOUSANDS OF DOLLARS

Item Description for Accounting Period 7/02 Through 6/03	Total	Zero Assets	Under 500	500 to 1,000	1,000 to 5,000	5,000 to 10,000	10,000 to 25,000	25,000 to 50,000	50,000 to 100,000	100,000 to 250,000	250,000 to 500,000	500,000 to 2,500,000	2,500,000 and over
Number of Enterprises 1	3499	89	2520	258	492	42	48	22	6	13	0	9	0
Revenues ($ in Thousands)													
Net Sales 2	17837528	84715	1590555	446283	1927884	800521	1127221	1075469	373365	1387973	0	9023541	0
Interest 3	221554	53	0	1777	2266	337	3512	3593	2520	13370	0	194126	0
Rents 4	8726	6	0	3392	0	1939	762	658	0	335	0	1634	0
Royalties 5	843608	0	0	45227	34	0	4518	3777	16735	324040	0	449278	0
Other Portfolio Income 6	617547	8	1	230	15186	11078	13702	19846	9640	2769	0	545088	0
Other Receipts 7	613895	68151	38862	2854	87383	27798	88063	26780	6504	9728	0	257772	0
Total Receipts 8	20142858	152933	1629418	499763	2032753	841673	1237778	1130123	408764	1738215	0	10471439	0
Average Total Receipts 9	5757	1718	647	1937	4132	20040	25787	51369	68127	133709	•	1163493	•
Operating Costs/Operating Income (%)													
Cost of Operations 10	28.5	13.5	3.1	28.0	18.9	1.6	33.0	50.8	46.1	10.2	•	36.4	•
Salaries and Wages 11	25.3	36.3	28.3	16.6	35.2	26.7	23.8	13.1	19.4	27.9	•	24.4	•
Taxes Paid 12	3.8	3.7	3.7	2.3	4.1	2.6	3.5	3.2	2.1	3.6	•	4.2	•
Interest Paid 13	1.7	1.8	0.4	0.4	0.4	0.2	0.6	0.7	2.2	1.6	•	2.7	•
Depreciation 14	2.8	6.7	1.9	1.9	2.4	2.2	3.4	2.3	4.7	5.6	•	2.6	•
Amortization and Depletion 15	1.0	0.1	0.0	0.4	0.1	0.4	0.4	0.3	1.0	2.0	•	1.5	•
Pensions and Other Deferred Comp. 16	1.7	0.1	2.1	1.9	2.0	0.7	1.5	2.7	0.4	2.1	•	1.6	•
Employee Benefits 17	2.3	2.7	0.9	1.1	3.1	2.1	3.3	3.0	2.5	3.5	•	2.1	•
Advertising 18	0.7	0.2	3.1	0.3	1.0	0.0	0.5	0.4	0.5	0.4	•	0.4	•
Other Expenses 19	30.1	59.5	37.3	17.3	24.8	55.6	24.0	15.0	20.0	53.2	•	27.5	•
Officers' Compensation 20	3.1	0.3	4.8	27.1	5.8	2.0	3.5	2.4	2.5	1.6	•	1.4	•
Operating Margin 21	•	•	14.3	2.8	2.2	5.7	2.6	6.1	•	•	•	•	•
Operating Margin Before Officers' Comp. 22	2.0	•	19.1	29.9	8.0	7.7	6.1	8.4	1.0	•	•	•	•

Selected Average Balance Sheet ($ in Thousands)

Net Receivables 23	1238	0	19	128	763	2101	5265	10340	13809	51473	283629
Inventories 24	88	0	0	17	148	66	407	303	1348	4482	10993
Net Property, Plant and Equipment 25	681	0	20	245	251	1253	3185	5194	12781	37278	140565
Total Assets 26	6180		95	694	1898	6237	15205	34754	70044	195997	1727224
Notes and Loans Payable 27	1266	0	31	80	198	507	1756	6471	13661	17642	408500
All Other Liabilities 28	2071	0	14	108	498	3050	4703	8446	17769	65483	604742
Net Worth 29	2842	0	51	505	1202	2680	8746	19838	38614	112871	713981

Selected Financial Ratios (Times to 1)

Current Ratio 30	2.1	•	3.1	3.2	3.5	1.5	2.1	2.7	1.7	1.6	2.2
Quick Ratio 31	1.4	•	2.1	3.0	2.9	1.4	1.7	2.4	1.4	1.3	1.3
Net Sales to Working Capital 32	2.8	•	19.8	6.8	3.4	14.4	4.5	3.3	5.2	2.6	2.1
Coverage Ratio 33	7.9	32.4	38.5	41.9	19.6	45.7	20.5	17.0	4.7	9.4	5.3
Total Asset Turnover 34	0.8	•	6.6	2.5	2.1	3.1	1.5	1.4	0.9	0.5	0.6
Inventory Turnover 35	16.6	•	•	28.3	5.0	4.7	19.0	82.1	21.3	2.4	33.2
Receivables Turnover 36	4.8	•	55.7	6.6	5.7	5.4	5.1	5.5	3.7	2.5	4.8
Total Liabilities to Net Worth 37	1.2	•	0.9	0.4	0.6	1.3	0.7	0.8	0.8	0.7	1.4
Current Assets to Working Capital 38	1.9	•	1.5	1.5	1.4	3.2	2.0	1.6	2.4	2.6	1.9
Current Liabilities to Working Capital 39	0.9	•	0.5	0.5	0.4	2.2	1.0	0.6	1.4	1.6	0.9
Working Capital to Net Sales 40	0.4	•	0.1	0.1	0.3	0.1	0.2	0.3	0.2	0.4	0.5
Inventory to Working Capital 41	0.0	•	•	0.1	0.2	0.0	0.1	0.0	0.2	0.0	0.0
Total Receipts to Cash Flow 42	2.9	1.3	2.1	3.3	4.0	1.6	3.3	4.8	4.3	1.7	3.4
Cost of Goods to Cash Flow 43	0.8	0.2	0.1	0.9	0.8	0.0	1.1	2.5	2.0	0.2	1.3
Cash Flow to Total Debt 44	0.5	•	6.9	2.8	1.4	3.4	1.1	0.7	0.5	0.8	0.3

Selected Financial Factors (in Percentages)

Debt Ratio 45	54.0	•	46.6	27.1	36.7	57.0	42.5	42.9	44.9	42.4	58.7
Return on Total Assets 46	11.2	•	114.1	37.7	16.6	33.8	20.2	16.7	9.0	8.2	8.1
Return on Equity Before Income Taxes 47	21.2	•	208.2	50.5	24.9	77.0	33.4	27.5	12.9	12.8	15.9
Return on Equity After Income Taxes 48	17.4	•	207.5	41.0	23.4	71.3	29.1	22.7	11.4	8.7	11.9
Profit Margin (Before Income Tax) 49	11.8	55.5	16.8	14.8	7.6	10.8	12.4	11.1	8.0	13.5	11.3
Profit Margin (After Income Tax) 50	9.7	55.3	16.7	12.0	7.2	10.0	10.8	9.2	7.0	9.2	8.5

Table I

Corporations with and without Net Income

ADVERTISING AND RELATED SERVICES

MONEY AMOUNTS AND SIZE OF ASSETS IN THOUSANDS OF DOLLARS

Item Description for Accounting Period 7/02 Through 6/03	Total	Zero Assets	Under 500	500 to 1,000	1,000 to 5,000	5,000 to 10,000	10,000 to 25,000	25,000 to 50,000	50,000 to 100,000	100,000 to 250,000	250,000 to 500,000	500,000 to 2,500,000	2,500,000 and over
Number of Enterprises **1**	44508	5167	34419	2783	1674	192	152	58	21	22	7	6	7
Revenues ($ in Thousands)													
Net Sales **2**	63533541	1833117	10248784	6949435	12659143	2735935	4641435	3045586	1728431	2568511	1987536	3512901	11622728
Interest **3**	778264	24219	2771	6965	10477	3901	8257	9561	6118	13908	56370	115197	520519
Rents **4**	69329	6162	9325	4614	1915	430	610	521	0	366	23	1360	44001
Royalties **5**	126644	1144	0	0	0	0	32944	375	9807	1014	13445	12881	55035
Other Portfolio Income **6**	629713	20393	137343	12375	10663	229	3172	3964	15626	47322	3279	5111	370236
Other Receipts **7**	1565646	206679	172453	145949	81363	416489	84912	41592	45144	31826	3289	34488	301465
Total Receipts **8**	66703137	2091714	10570676	7119338	12763561	3156984	4771330	3101599	1805126	2662947	2063942	3681938	12913984
Average Total Receipts **9**	1499	405	307	2558	7625	16443	31390	53476	85958	121043	294849	613656	1844855
Operating Costs/Operating Income (%)													
Cost of Operations **10**	40.1	18.6	37.9	58.9	57.5	67.0	54.3	38.6	55.9	41.0	37.5	35.8	2.7
Salaries and Wages **11**	20.7	32.0	9.3	16.9	11.6	12.7	16.3	14.8	21.0	19.1	26.9	30.2	42.7
Taxes Paid **12**	2.4	4.5	2.3	2.1	1.6	1.4	1.7	1.9	1.7	1.9	2.4	2.7	4.2
Interest Paid **13**	3.3	2.5	0.6	0.5	0.6	0.4	0.7	1.3	1.7	2.0	4.8	3.3	13.0
Depreciation **14**	2.1	3.5	1.8	1.1	1.1	1.2	1.7	2.4	1.9	2.0	5.1	3.0	3.5
Amortization and Depletion **15**	1.0	1.5	0.2	0.2	0.1	0.2	0.3	0.7	1.9	1.8	1.4	1.9	2.9
Pensions and Other Deferred Comp. **16**	0.7	0.8	1.0	0.4	0.5	0.4	0.5	0.4	0.3	0.4	0.2	0.6	1.2
Employee Benefits **17**	1.2	2.0	0.8	0.9	0.7	0.7	1.1	1.2	1.2	0.9	4.2	1.7	1.5
Advertising **18**	5.4	7.4	6.2	1.0	1.0	11.1	4.8	17.9	2.8	0.5	0.7	3.4	0.2
Other Expenses **19**	22.1	32.8	27.6	13.7	10.7	11.3	17.3	21.7	21.6	31.8	18.3	23.5	35.4
Officers' Compensation **20**	4.9	3.0	10.7	6.1	4.6	4.3	3.1	2.1	1.5	2.2	0.7	1.7	4.2
Operating Margin **21**	*		1.4		0.6								
Operating Margin Before Officers' Comp. **22**	1.0		12.1	4.3	5.1		1.3						

Selected Average Balance Sheet ($ in Thousands)

Net Receivables 23	509	0	11	218	717	3322	5794	11369	17612	33561	70124	362380	2072988
Inventories 24	18	0	2	17	57	167	415	749	1121	1799	3793	7265	47613
Net Property, Plant and Equipment 25	141	0	19	141	337	792	2276	5069	4011	7479	47277	80293	401611
Total Assets 26	2195		67	678	2213	7334	14844	34748	66876	157910	314219	1487796	9731387
Notes and Loans Payable 27	411	0	33	229	582	984	2994	10989	18969	31719	87995	122222	1690091
All Other Liabilities 28	994	0	24	253	1325	5114	9658	16156	40666	65354	106387	758214	4217121
Net Worth 29	790	0	10	197	305	1236	2192	7602	7241	60838	119837	607360	3824174

Selected Financial Ratios (Times to 1)

Current Ratio 30	0.8	•	1.1	1.5	1.1	1.5	1.0	1.2	0.9	1.1	1.2	1.0	0.7
Quick Ratio 31	0.7	•	0.9	1.3	0.9	1.4	0.9	0.9	0.8	0.9	1.0	0.8	0.5
Net Sales to Working Capital 32	•	81.3	17.3	101.9	6.8	80.3	16.2	•	15.5	15.2	•	•	
Coverage Ratio 33	1.4	3.7	8.3	2.1	3.2	2.1	2.4	0.1	1.5	1.1	1.3	0.2	1.1
Total Asset Turnover 34	0.7	•	4.4	3.7	3.4	1.9	2.1	1.5	0.7	0.9	0.4	0.2	
Inventory Turnover 35	31.2	•	57.5	85.7	75.8	57.3	40.0	27.1	41.1	26.6	28.1	28.9	1.0
Receivables Turnover 36	3.4	•	23.8	11.1	10.4	4.9	5.6	4.6	4.4	3.5	4.3	1.4	1.1
Total Liabilities to Net Worth 37	1.8	•	5.5	2.4	6.3	4.9	5.8	3.6	8.2	1.6	1.6	1.4	1.5
Current Assets to Working Capital 38	•	•	10.5	3.0	20.6	2.9	7.4	8.8	6.5	•	•	
Current Liabilities to Working Capital 39	•	•	9.5	2.0	19.6	1.9	6.4	7.8	5.5	•	•	
Working Capital to Net Sales 40	•	•	0.0	0.1	0.0	0.1	0.1	0.1	0.1	0.1	•	
Inventory to Working Capital 41	•	•	0.5	0.1	0.8	0.1	1.3	0.2	0.1	0.3	•	•	
Total Receipts to Cash Flow 42	5.7	3.2	3.9	9.1	11.4	7.6	6.5	6.3	12.7	3.6	6.1	7.2	4.0
Cost of Goods to Cash Flow 43	2.3	0.6	1.5	5.4	6.6	5.1	3.5	2.5	7.1	1.5	2.3	2.6	0.1
Cash Flow to Total Debt 44	0.2	1.3	0.6	0.3	0.3	0.3	0.4	0.3	0.1	0.3	0.2	0.1	0.1

Selected Financial Factors (in Percentages)

Debt Ratio 45	64.0	•	84.6	70.9	86.2	83.2	85.2	78.1	89.2	61.5	61.9	59.2	60.7
Return on Total Assets 46	3.0	•	22.7	4.0	6.9	9.8	3.5	0.2	1.6	5.7	0.2	2.3	
Return on Equity Before Income Taxes 47	2.4	•	129.9	7.3	34.2	54.2	14.1	•	0.3	3.7	0.3		
Return on Equity After Income Taxes 48	1.2	•	127.7	2.3	30.6	50.8	10.1	•	•	•		
Profit Margin (Before Income Tax) 49	1.3	6.6	4.5	0.6	1.4	4.7	1.0	•	0.2	1.5	0.7		
Profit Margin (After Income Tax) 50	0.7	4.6	4.4	0.2	1.2	4.4	0.7	•	•	•		

Table II

Corporations with Net Income

ADVERTISING AND RELATED SERVICES

MONEY AMOUNTS AND SIZE OF ASSETS IN THOUSANDS OF DOLLARS

Item Description for Accounting Period 7/02 Through 6/03	Total	Zero Assets	Under 500	500 to 1,000	1,000 to 5,000	5,000 to 10,000	10,000 to 25,000	25,000 to 50,000	50,000 to 100,000	100,000 to 250,000	250,000 to 500,000	500,000 to 2,500,000	2,500,000 and over
Number of Enterprises **1**	22075	1861	17337	1646	958	114	104	30	11	8	3	0	4
Revenues ($ in Thousands)													
Net Sales **2**	37223201	1309430	6399425	4586732	8114592	2443469	3482544	1779655	1200023	1380383	1581797	0	4945151
Interest **3**	474979	18798	652	6837	6619	1619	2401	4302	1902	6954	20002	0	404893
Rents **4**	58661	6162	9325	4614	1320	430	489	276	0	0	7	0	36037
Royalties **5**	57056	0	0	0	0	0	32944	375	0	1014	22057	0	666
Other Portfolio Income **6**	486560	12130	132832	10491	1630	173	1596	3202	1578	44393	4144	0	274390
Other Receipts **7**	677998	19398	34397	121132	100394	27136	50388	27229	33356	18847	-7448	0	253170
Total Receipts **8**	38978455	1365918	6576631	4729806	8224555	2472827	3570362	1815039	1236859	1451591	1620559	0	5914307
Average Total Receipts **9**	1766	734	379	2874	8585	21691	34330	60501	112442	181449	540186	•	1478577
Operating Costs/Operating Income (%)													
Cost of Operations **10**	42.4	14.6	30.5	63.9	56.2	72.5	54.1	45.7	58.4	22.3	29.9	•	4.3
Salaries and Wages **11**	16.8	34.3	8.9	9.3	10.5	7.9	15.5	14.7	18.4	20.8	29.1	•	40.1
Taxes Paid **12**	2.1	4.0	2.1	1.6	1.6	1.0	1.7	2.0	1.4	2.1	2.7	•	4.1
Interest Paid **13**	2.2	1.1	0.5	0.2	0.6	0.3	0.4	0.7	0.6	1.1	2.5	•	12.4
Depreciation **14**	1.5	2.9	1.5	1.0	1.0	0.9	1.2	1.9	1.6	1.6	4.8	•	1.6
Amortization and Depletion **15**	0.4	0.6	0.2	0.0	0.0	0.2	0.2	0.3	0.4	0.3	0.4	•	2.1
Pensions and Other Deferred Comp. **16**	0.7	0.8	0.9	0.6	0.5	0.4	0.5	0.4	0.5	0.5	0.6	•	1.3
Employee Benefits **17**	0.9	1.8	0.7	0.8	0.7	0.5	1.1	1.4	0.9	1.0	3.7	•	0.5
Advertising **18**	3.3	0.2	2.5	1.4	8.7	0.6	4.4	3.4	3.0	0.6	0.3	•	0.3
Other Expenses **19**	20.7	25.5	31.2	11.0	11.1	6.2	14.6	22.7	14.0	43.0	17.8	•	37.3
Officers' Compensation **20**	5.1	3.6	10.1	7.5	4.2	3.6	3.1	2.3	1.6	2.1	1.4	•	4.3
Operating Margin **21**	3.9	10.6	10.9	2.9	5.0	5.9	3.3	4.5	•	4.6	6.8	•	•
Operating Margin Before Officers' Comp. **22**	9.0	14.2	21.0	10.4	9.2	9.5	6.4	6.8	0.7	6.7	8.1	•	•

Selected Average Balance Sheet ($ in Thousands)

Net Receivables 23	745	0	9	185	706	2820	6309	13345	19972	52850	402762	• 3018085
Inventories 24	17	0	1	23	47	159	428	948	212	3125	2316	• 27463
Net Property, Plant and Equipment 25	121	0	19	163	264	798	1908	5426	5224	10863	122696	• 217278
Total Assets 26	2099	0	75	677	2377	6448	15001	35453	65799	163819	919434	8369416
Notes and Loans Payable 27	397	0	33	78	405	1168	2186	5542	7113	26342	139914	• 1611515
All Other Liabilities 28	1204	0	15	170	1365	3228	9574	18501	51945	97158	623409	• 4901151
Net Worth 29	497	0	28	429	607	2052	3240	11410	6741	40319	156111	• 1856749

Selected Financial Ratios (Times to 1)

Current Ratio 30	0.9	•	1.6	2.4	1.2	1.4	1.2	1.3	0.9	1.2	1.0	0.8
Quick Ratio 31	0.7	•	1.3	2.1	1.0	1.3	1.0	1.1	0.7	0.8	0.9	0.6
Net Sales to Working Capital 32	•	•	22.9	10.7	34.9	13.4	18.9	10.3	•	11.8	•	•
Coverage Ratio 33	5.2	15.9	26.4	34.5	12.4	26.7	14.5	9.9	4.8	9.7	4.9	2.1
Total Asset Turnover 34	0.8	•	4.9	4.1	3.6	3.3	2.2	1.7	1.7	1.1	0.6	0.1
Inventory Turnover 35	43.0	•	83.0	78.7	100.5	97.7	42.3	28.6	300.8	12.3	68.2	1.9
Receivables Turnover 36	2.8	•	36.1	12.2	11.7	8.5	5.8	4.3	10.9	3.8	2.6	0.8
Total Liabilities to Net Worth 37	3.2	•	1.7	0.6	2.9	2.1	3.6	2.1	8.8	3.1	4.9	3.5
Current Assets to Working Capital 38	•	•	2.7	1.7	7.2	3.2	6.5	4.4	•	7.7	•	•
Current Liabilities to Working Capital 39	•	•	1.7	0.7	6.2	2.2	5.5	3.4	6.7	•	•	•
Working Capital to Net Sales 40	•	•	0.0	0.0	0.0	0.1	0.1	0.1	•	0.1	•	•
Inventory to Working Capital 41	•	•	0.1	0.1	0.2	0.1	0.3	0.2	0.0	0.0	•	•
Total Receipts to Cash Flow 42	4.1	3.1	2.6	7.3	7.0	8.5	5.6	4.3	7.5	2.0	4.5	2.5
Cost of Goods to Cash Flow 43	1.7	0.5	0.8	4.6	4.0	6.2	3.0	1.9	4.4	0.4	1.3	0.1
Cash Flow to Total Debt 44	0.3	•	3.0	1.5	0.7	0.6	0.5	0.6	0.2	0.7	0.2	0.1

Selected Financial Factors (in Percentages)

Debt Ratio 45	76.3	•	63.0	36.6	74.5	68.2	78.4	67.8	89.8	75.4	83.0	77.8
Return on Total Assets 46	9.0	•	69.5	25.3	24.5	24.5	13.8	12.1	4.5	11.5	7.0	3.9
Return on Equity Before Income Taxes 47	30.6	•	180.8	38.7	88.2	74.1	59.6	33.7	35.1	42.0	33.1	9.2
Return on Equity After Income Taxes 48	26.9	•	179.2	35.7	85.0	70.6	55.6	31.2	31.9	33.1	21.6	6.3
Profit Margin (Before Income Tax) 49	9.0	16.3	13.6	6.0	6.3	7.1	5.8	6.5	2.2	9.8	9.8	13.9
Profit Margin (After Income Tax) 50	7.9	13.4	13.5	5.5	6.1	6.8	5.4	6.0	2.0	7.7	6.4	9.5

Table I
Corporations with and without Net Income

OTHER PROFESSIONAL, SCIENTIFIC, AND TECHNICAL SERVICES

MONEY AMOUNTS AND SIZE OF ASSETS IN THOUSANDS OF DOLLARS

Item Description for Accounting Period 7/02 Through 6/03	Total	Zero Assets	Under 500	500 to 1,000	1,000 to 5,000	5,000 to 10,000	10,000 to 25,000	25,000 to 50,000	50,000 to 100,000	100,000 to 250,000	250,000 to 500,000	500,000 to 2,500,000	2,500,000 and over
Number of Enterprises **1**	95151	11307	77465	3111	2584	331	202	71	38	31	6	4	0
Revenues ($ in Thousands)													
Net Sales **2**	68765717	1649449	27412564	3994694	12791174	3686314	5725734	3028639	2867094	4567789	1249460	1792806	0
Interest **3**	184835	7135	36536	7260	16519	12008	14651	12865	15151	46300	15695	714	0
Rents **4**	25169	531	2463	218	7095	391	3677	4371	2262	3198	572	391	0
Royalties **5**	156077	0	3740	62	0	995	31624	70765	13852	33610	1430	0	0
Other Portfolio Income **6**	297742	10231	59794	6325	24113	17477	16713	48111	20548	92371	203	1858	0
Other Receipts **7**	1839919	25522	287234	206653	563317	51938	190681	109449	47577	193299	115662	48586	0
Total Receipts **8**	71269459	1692868	27802331	4215212	13402218	3769123	5983080	3274200	2966484	4936567	1383022	1844355	0
Average Total Receipts **9**	749	150	359	1355	5187	11387	29619	46115	78065	159244	230504	461089	•
Operating Costs/Operating Income (%)													
Cost of Operations **10**	31.1	16.5	17.6	44.4	48.7	30.2	47.0	22.5	36.2	45.3	32.2	13.9	•
Salaries and Wages **11**	21.2	21.8	22.2	16.6	16.1	23.8	18.8	22.2	32.0	21.3	25.3	33.9	•
Taxes Paid **12**	3.5	2.7	3.5	4.8	3.8	2.6	2.5	2.8	4.1	3.1	2.3	5.0	•
Interest Paid **13**	1.1	0.8	0.7	0.7	0.8	0.4	1.2	1.6	2.3	3.4	2.8	2.3	•
Depreciation **14**	2.2	1.5	1.5	2.0	2.3	2.3	2.3	3.7	4.4	3.2	2.6	2.9	•
Amortization and Depletion **15**	0.6	0.3	0.2	0.4	0.3	0.5	0.5	1.3	1.8	1.9	2.0	1.7	•
Pensions and Other Deferred Comp. **16**	1.1	0.8	1.6	1.3	0.6	0.5	0.4	0.4	0.7	0.8	0.3	3.4	•
Employee Benefits **17**	1.9	1.6	1.6	1.1	1.6	4.1	1.7	2.2	2.2	2.4	1.7	2.8	•
Advertising **18**	1.0	0.5	1.0	0.4	1.2	0.5	0.8	0.9	1.0	1.5	0.2	1.4	•
Other Expenses **19**	29.2	42.2	32.6	20.0	21.5	33.3	28.2	48.1	24.3	20.7	42.4	24.8	•
Officers' Compensation **20**	8.1	10.2	13.0	11.6	6.1	5.9	2.7	2.4	1.8	1.6	1.9	1.3	•
Operating Margin **21**	•	0.9	4.4	•	•	•	•	•	•	•	•	6.6	•
Operating Margin Before Officers' Comp. **22**	7.2	11.2	17.4	8.4	3.1	1.8	•	•	•	•	•	8.0	•

Selected Average Balance Sheet ($ in Thousands)

Net Receivables 23	67	0	5	125	557	1650	4086	10319	15512	28422	38967	80704	•
Inventories 24	14	0	3	20	50	171	413	709	2545	2794	32911	92781	•
Net Property, Plant and Equipment 25	64	0	19	126	577	1056	2187	5867	14549	17574	18201	72415	•
Total Assets 26	387	0	80	678	2191	7155	15696	35533	71000	169124	334134	1209020	•
Notes and Loans Payable 27	146	0	44	287	865	1369	4642	12200	25105	53107	48045	548787	•
All Other Liabilities 28	122	0	22	168	768	2975	6857	13638	25751	48281	185220	117338	•
Net Worth 29	119	0	14	223	559	2811	4198	9695	20144	67736	100870	542895	•

Selected Financial Ratios (Times to 1)

Current Ratio 30	1.4	•	1.7	1.5	1.3	1.3	1.3	1.3	1.1	1.7	1.2	1.3
Quick Ratio 31	1.1	•	1.2	1.2	1.1	1.1	1.0	1.1	0.7	1.3	0.5	1.2
Net Sales to Working Capital 32	15.2	22.9	11.4	17.7	12.0	13.7	9.5	41.1	5.3	8.0	5.3	12.5
Coverage Ratio 33	3.5	5.4	9.7	4.3	3.3	•	0.9	•	1.9	1.9	•	5.3
Total Asset Turnover 34	1.9	•	4.4	1.9	1.6	1.8	1.8	1.2	1.1	0.9	0.6	0.4
Inventory Turnover 35	15.6	•	21.0	28.2	19.7	32.2	13.5	48.0	10.7	23.9	2.0	0.7
Receivables Turnover 36	10.1	58.1	9.1	9.0	5.6	6.1	4.7	4.4	4.2	4.3	4.4	6.7
Total Liabilities to Net Worth 37	2.2	•	4.7	2.0	2.9	1.5	2.7	2.9	2.5	1.5	2.3	1.2
Current Assets to Working Capital 38	3.6	•	2.5	3.1	4.2	4.5	4.4	4.3	17.9	2.3	5.9	4.1
Current Liabilities to Working Capital 39	2.6	•	1.5	2.1	3.2	3.5	3.4	3.3	16.9	1.3	4.9	3.1
Working Capital to Net Sales 40	0.1	•	0.0	0.1	0.1	0.1	0.1	0.1	0.0	0.2	0.1	0.1
Inventory to Working Capital 41	0.3	•	0.2	0.1	0.2	0.1	0.2	0.1	1.4	0.1	2.5	0.1
Total Receipts to Cash Flow 42	3.9	2.6	3.2	5.9	5.7	3.8	4.5	2.3	8.7	5.7	2.8	3.2
Cost of Goods to Cash Flow 43	1.2	0.4	0.6	2.6	2.8	1.1	2.1	0.5	3.1	2.6	0.9	0.5
Cash Flow to Total Debt 44	0.7	1.7	0.5	0.5	0.7	0.5	0.7	0.7	0.2	0.3	0.3	0.2

Selected Financial Factors (in Percentages)

Debt Ratio 45	69.2	82.4	67.1	74.5	60.7	73.3	72.7	71.6	59.9	69.8	55.1	•
Return on Total Assets 46	7.1	28.8	5.7	5.7	•	•	1.8	5.5	•	4.4		
Return on Equity Before Income Taxes 47	16.5	146.9	13.4	15.6	•	•	•	6.4	•	8.0		
Return on Equity After Income Taxes 48	14.2	145.0	12.2	11.0	•	•	•	3.9	•	8.0		
Profit Margin (Before Income Tax) 49	2.7	5.8	2.3	1.8	•	•	3.6	2.9	•	9.6		
Profit Margin (After Income Tax) 50	2.3	2.8	2.1	1.2	•	•	2.8	1.8	•	9.6		

351

Table II

Corporations with Net Income

OTHER PROFESSIONAL, SCIENTIFIC, AND TECHNICAL SERVICES

MONEY AMOUNTS AND SIZE OF ASSETS IN THOUSANDS OF DOLLARS

Item Description for Accounting Period 7/02 Through 6/03	Total	Zero Assets	Under 100	100 to 250	251 to 500	501 to 1,000	1,001 to 5,000	5,001 to 10,000	10,001 to 25,000	25,001 to 50,000	50,001 to 100,000	100,001 to 250,000	250,001 and over
Number of Enterprises 1	55094	4540	46588	1764	1803	219	104	34	18	0	0	0	0
Revenues ($ in Thousands)													
Net Sales 2	49369726	746148	21761870	2485792	10124472	2921192	3218484	1867729	1406044	0	0	0	0
Interest 3	83525	2132	31147	4366	12035	7459	6573	7556	3500	0	0	0	0
Rents 4	14499	531	2089	0	4691	39	2205	2554	157	0	0	0	0
Royalties 5	64390	0	32947	60	0	13	30853	289	0	0	0	0	0
Other Portfolio Income 6	239131	9977	32947	5981	22824	11338	14178	44134	11234	0	0	0	0
Other Receipts 7	1349423	20544	205769	198734	402270	25662	109896	78419	12091	0	0	0	0
Total Receipts 8	51120694	779332	22033822	2694933	10566292	2965703	3382189	2000681	1433026	0	0	0	0
Average Total Receipts 9	928	172	473	1528	5860	13542	32521	58844	79613	•	•	•	•
Operating Costs/Operating Income (%)													
Cost of Operations 10	30.5	22.5	17.5	42.4	49.6	32.8	45.3	18.4	46.9	•	•	•	•
Salaries and Wages 11	19.5	17.8	21.6	16.2	13.2	17.6	17.4	18.5	23.7	•	•	•	•
Taxes Paid 12	3.2	3.0	3.2	2.6	3.7	2.2	2.3	2.4	3.0	•	•	•	•
Interest Paid 13	0.8	0.9	0.6	0.9	0.5	0.2	0.9	1.0	1.0	•	•	•	•
Depreciation 14	1.6	1.1	1.3	1.4	1.7	1.0	1.7	2.1	2.7	•	•	•	•
Amortization and Depletion 15	0.4	0.5	0.2	0.4	0.2	0.2	0.3	0.5	1.0	•	•	•	•
Pensions and Other Deferred Comp. 16	1.1	1.0	1.3	1.3	0.6	0.5	0.5	0.5	0.8	•	•	•	•
Employee Benefits 17	1.6	1.8	1.0	1.0	1.5	4.1	1.5	1.9	2.4	•	•	•	•
Advertising 18	0.8	0.4	0.8	0.2	1.2	0.4	0.9	0.2	0.5	•	•	•	•
Other Expenses 19	26.1	23.3	30.5	19.4	18.7	28.1	23.7	51.0	14.0	•	•	•	•
Officers' Compensation 20	8.4	9.8	12.4	12.2	6.1	5.7	2.8	2.2	1.8	•	•	•	•
Operating Margin 21	6.1	18.0	9.5	2.0	3.1	7.0	2.7	1.2	2.2	•	•	•	•
Operating Margin Before Officers' Comp. 22	14.4	27.8	22.0	14.2	9.2	12.7	5.5	3.4	4.0	•	•	•	•

Selected Average Balance Sheet ($ in Thousands)

Net Receivables 23	72	0	7	118	564	1843	4985	10781	14357
Inventories 24	15	0	3	25	43	94	402	676	2845
Net Property, Plant and Equipment 25	66	0	23	115	542	798	1917	5505	9867
Total Assets 26	409	0	95	682	2092	7135	15824	35907	66368
Notes and Loans Payable 27	139	0	42	256	598	659	4130	8924	18483
All Other Liabilities 28	118	0	23	91	709	3250	7440	13889	18955
Net Worth 29	152	0	30	334	785	3226	4254	13094	28930

Selected Financial Ratios (Times to 1)

Current Ratio 30	1.5	•	1.7	2.2	1.5	1.3	1.3	1.4	1.3
Quick Ratio 31	1.2	•	1.4	1.8	1.3	1.1	1.0	1.0	0.8
Net Sales to Working Capital 32	14.8	•	23.8	7.4	13.3	11.7	12.0	9.8	11.4
Coverage Ratio 33	13.0	26.8	18.4	12.5	15.8	36.3	9.7	9.3	5.2
Total Asset Turnover 34	2.2	•	4.9	2.1	2.7	1.9	2.0	1.5	1.2
Inventory Turnover 35	18.2	•	24.6	23.5	65.0	46.5	34.9	14.9	12.9
Receivables Turnover 36	11.7	•	69.2	8.8	10.0	6.3	5.5	5.9	4.2
Total Liabilities to Net Worth 37	1.7	•	2.2	1.0	1.7	1.2	2.7	1.7	1.3
Current Assets to Working Capital 38	3.0	•	2.3	1.9	2.8	3.9	4.1	3.7	4.7
Current Liabilities to Working Capital 39	2.0	•	1.3	0.9	1.8	2.9	3.1	2.7	3.7
Working Capital to Net Sales 40	0.1	•	0.0	0.1	0.1	0.1	0.1	0.1	0.1
Inventory to Working Capital 41	0.1	•	0.2	0.1	0.1	0.1	0.1	0.1	0.5
Total Receipts to Cash Flow 42	3.3	2.7	2.9	4.2	4.8	3.0	3.6	1.8	7.7
Cost of Goods to Cash Flow 43	1.0	0.6	0.5	1.8	2.4	1.0	1.6	0.3	3.6
Cash Flow to Total Debt 44	1.0	•	2.5	1.0	0.9	1.1	0.7	1.3	0.3

Selected Financial Factors (in Percentages)

Debt Ratio 45	62.9	•	68.8	51.0	62.5	54.8	73.1	63.5	56.4
Return on Total Assets 46	22.8	•	56.3	23.5	21.3	16.3	17.0	14.2	6.3
Return on Equity Before Income Taxes 47	56.8	•	170.4	44.0	53.1	35.1	56.6	34.9	11.7
Return on Equity After Income Taxes 48	53.7	•	168.9	42.7	48.4	31.0	51.8	28.6	9.1
Profit Margin (Before Income Tax) 49	9.6	22.4	10.8	10.4	7.4	8.5	7.8	8.3	4.3
Profit Margin (After Income Tax) 50	9.1	20.8	10.7	10.1	6.8	7.5	7.1	6.8	3.4

Table I

Corporations with and without Net Income

OFFICES OF BANK HOLDING COMPANIES

MONEY AMOUNTS AND SIZE OF ASSETS IN THOUSANDS OF DOLLARS

Item Description for Accounting Period 7/02 Through 6/03	Total	Zero Assets	Under 500	500 to 1,000	1,000 to 5,000	5,000 to 10,000	10,000 to 25,000	25,000 to 50,000	50,000 to 100,000	100,000 to 250,000	250,000 to 500,000	500,000 to 2,500,000	2,500,000 and over
Number of Enterprises **1**	5347	76	419	•	28	62	299	705	1155	1429	581	446	147
Revenues ($ in Thousands)													
Net Sales **2**	168746628	354512	1303	•	493	11595	81488	394187	1439517	3162278	2409664	6050522	154841067
Interest **3**	355663880	1246260	12972	•	5604	9106	206740	878192	3131015	9420576	8912566	19920452	311920398
Rents **4**	33752395	62431	7	•	62	4	1667	2515	14007	50811	66149	266622	33288120
Royalties **5**	375514	0	0	•	0	0	3	44	70	99	212	316	374770
Other Portfolio Income **6**	33585320	482457	22297	•	1259	5643	18238	77272	240852	693002	705214	2088064	29251022
Other Receipts **7**	79391587	102436	91	•	290	8207	72282	409546	924915	2185183	1480653	3680157	70527829
Total Receipts **8**	671515324	2248096	36670	•	7708	34555	380418	1761756	5750376	15511949	13574458	32006133	600203206
Average Total Receipts **9**	125587	29580	88	•	275	557	1272	2499	4979	10855	23364	71763	4083015
Operating Costs/Operating Income (%)													
Cost of Operations **10**	6.3	•	•	•	•	•	0.2	0.0	1.0	0.0	0.1	0.1	6.9
Salaries and Wages **11**	55.9	79.2	128.9	•	217.8	27.5	53.0	52.5	48.7	64.8	85.9	80.2	54.4
Taxes Paid **12**	7.0	10.3	57.7	•	90.5	2.0	13.0	12.4	10.8	13.0	15.6	13.4	6.5
Interest Paid **13**	108.0	373.5	551.2	•	212.6	30.6	145.9	142.1	125.3	151.9	171.2	145.4	103.8
Depreciation **14**	27.4	8.4	16.9	•	30.0	2.1	13.0	14.2	13.5	16.8	20.1	20.8	28.2
Amortization and Depletion **15**	4.4	1.5	4.9	•	•	3.0	4.0	2.0	1.5	1.9	2.3	3.5	4.5
Pensions and Other Deferred Comp. **16**	5.7	9.1	2.7	•	11.2	0.0	4.2	3.7	4.3	4.3	5.3	5.5	5.8
Employee Benefits **17**	6.7	7.0	11.1	•	30.8	7.3	14.0	12.0	9.3	10.8	11.6	10.1	6.4
Advertising **18**	4.3	2.1	8.8	•	23.3	0.1	3.7	4.1	3.8	4.5	5.3	4.9	4.3
Other Expenses **19**	118.2	259.5	1631.9	•	1895.3	247.8	109.9	88.6	78.0	95.5	102.7	110.8	119.3
Officers' Compensation **20**	5.6	11.5	32.5	•	•	15.6	60.4	45.5	34.5	30.6	27.2	18.2	3.8
Operating Margin **21**	•	•	•	•	•	•	•	•	•	•	•	•	•
Operating Margin Before Officers' Comp. **22**	•	•	•	•	•	•	•	•	•	•	•	•	•

Selected Average Balance Sheet ($ in Thousands)

Net Receivables 23	733804	0	0	473	•	1131	10380	22122	44210	96810	209824	532097	22831563
Inventories 24	27	0	0	•	•	0	0	0	9	1	9	10	832
Net Property, Plant and Equipment 25	15805	0	0	23	•	60	274	672	1429	3179	6562	17221	450759
Total Assets 26	1750713	0	0	46	2273	7058	18598	37695	72848	158811	344773	965094	57051559
Notes and Loans Payable 27	265877	0	0	15	•	90	534	821	2922	6384	18019	69579	9298640
All Other Liabilities 28	1256525	0	0	390	•	1452	14856	32115	62347	136147	293138	807462	4098298
Net Worth 29	228311	0	46	1867	5515	4758	3208	7579	16281	33616	88053	7654621	

Selected Financial Ratios (Times to 1)

Current Ratio 30	0.8	•	•	64.9	2.5	1.0	1.1	1.0	1.0	1.0	1.0	0.9	0.8
Quick Ratio 31	0.7	•	2.5	63.9	1.9	1.0	1.0	1.0	0.9	1.0	0.9	0.9	0.7
Net Sales to Working Capital 32	•	2.5	1.7	0.0	0.1	0.3	0.8	2.7	1.5	1.6	•	•	1.4
Coverage Ratio 33	1.4	0.7	1.7	•	•	•	1.2	1.4	1.4	1.5	1.6	1.7	1.4
Total Asset Turnover 34	0.0	0.0	0.1	0.0	0.0	0.0	0.0	0.0	0.0	0.0	0.0	0.0	0.0
Inventory Turnover 35	74.2	•	•	•	•	1.4	7.3	1.4	0.7	0.4	1.3	87.3	
Receivables Turnover 36	0.0	•	•	0.1	0.1	0.0	0.0	0.0	0.0	0.0	0.0	0.0	0.0
Total Liabilities to Net Worth 37	6.7	•	0.0	0.2	0.3	4.8	6.9	8.6	8.8	9.3	10.0	6.5	
Current Assets to Working Capital 38	•	1.0	•	1.0	139.3	48.6	16.8	1.7	•	•	•	•	
Current Liabilities to Working Capital 39	•	•	0.0	138.3	47.6	15.8	0.7	•	•	•	•	•	
Working Capital to Net Sales 40	•	0.4	•	114.0	0.4	1.2	3.5	12.1	1.6	1.7	1.5	•	
Inventory to Working Capital 41	•	•	0.0	0.0	0.0	0.0	0.0	0.0	0.0	0.0	0.0	0.0	
Total Receipts to Cash Flow 42	0.7	1.0	•	0.1	0.5	0.7	0.7	0.7	0.6	0.5	0.5	0.7	
Cost of Goods to Cash Flow 43	0.0	•	•	•	0.0	0.0	0.0	0.0	0.0	0.0	0.0	0.0	
Cash Flow to Total Debt 44	0.0	135.8	•	0.2	0.0	0.0	0.0	0.0	0.0	0.0	0.0	0.0	

Selected Financial Factors (in Percentages)

Debt Ratio 45	87.0	•	1.0	17.8	21.9	82.7	87.4	89.6	89.7	90.2	90.9	86.6	
Return on Total Assets 46	2.8	•	61.8	•	2.6	2.9	3.1	3.2	3.2	3.5	2.7		
Return on Equity Before Income Taxes 47	6.4	•	24.9	•	2.8	6.6	9.2	10.9	12.1	16.0	5.9		
Return on Equity After Income Taxes 48	4.1	•	18.5	•	1.9	5.2	7.1	8.1	8.6	11.3	3.7		
Profit Margin (Before Income Tax) 49	46.4	•	366.3	•	33.2	56.0	55.9	80.5	97.8	103.6	42.9		
Profit Margin (After Income Tax) 50	29.7	•	271.7	•	22.0	44.5	43.3	59.6	69.8	73.5	27.1		

Table II

Corporations with Net Income

OFFICES OF BANK HOLDING COMPANIES

MONEY AMOUNTS AND SIZE OF ASSETS IN THOUSANDS OF DOLLARS

Item Description for Accounting Period 7/02 Through 6/03	Total	Zero Assets	Under 500	500 to 1,000	1,000 to 5,000	5,000 to 10,000	10,000 to 25,000	25,000 to 50,000	50,000 to 100,000	100,000 to 250,000	250,000 to 500,000	500,000 to 2,500,000	2,500,000 and over
Number of Enterprises **1**	4546	41	0	*	0	52	239	622	1060	1363	561	435	138
Revenues ($ in Thousands)													
Net Sales **2**	156886627	98127	0	*	0	7328	65732	356085	1270931	3035666	2320635	5981350	143750768
Interest **3**	314506928	435149	0	*	0	1011	165302	778094	2879267	9005647	8573075	19511084	273155820
Rents **4**	31292023	38016	0	*	0	4	483	2401	12679	45545	64295	253600	30875002
Royalties **5**	375512	0	0	*	0	0	3	42	70	99	212	316	374770
Other Portfolio Income **6**	30234598	69853	0	*	0	5350	16059	72132	222768	672368	675648	2065462	26415758
Other Receipts **7**	73593612	149782	0	*	0	179	62222	378301	869008	2122331	1453022	3550906	65008210
Total Receipts **8**	606889300	790927	0	*	0	13872	309801	1587055	5254723	14881656	13086887	31362718	539580328
Average Total Receipts **9**	133500	19291	*	*	*	267	1296	2552	4957	10918	23328	72098	3910002
Operating Costs/Operating Income (%)													
Cost of Operations **10**	6.8	*	*	*	*	*	0.2	0.0	0.6	0.0	0.0	0.1	7.4
Salaries and Wages **11**	52.8	118.9	*	*	*	10.4	46.0	50.2	49.3	63.8	84.9	79.3	51.0
Taxes Paid **12**	6.9	25.2	*	*	*	0.7	12.5	12.2	11.3	13.0	15.6	13.3	6.3
Interest Paid **13**	101.6	164.4	*	*	*	1.7	146.4	140.6	130.5	150.9	171.1	142.8	97.3
Depreciation **14**	26.3	24.5	*	*	*	0.0	10.9	13.3	13.8	16.3	20.0	20.3	27.0
Amortization and Depletion **15**	3.5	1.4	*	*	*	*	3.9	1.3	1.4	1.8	2.3	3.4	3.6
Pensions and Other Deferred Comp. **16**	5.5	10.3	*	*	*	0.1	3.8	3.8	3.9	4.4	5.3	5.4	5.5
Employee Benefits **17**	6.7	9.1	*	*	*	0.5	13.7	11.8	9.5	10.8	11.5	10.1	6.3
Advertising **18**	4.1	6.6	*	*	*	0.1	3.6	3.9	3.8	4.5	5.4	4.9	4.1
Other Expenses **19**	111.7	140.7	*	*	*	8.9	84.4	77.7	73.8	91.3	98.9	107.8	113.0
Officers' Compensation **20**	5.5	24.2	*	*	*	2.6	58.3	43.5	34.1	30.6	26.1	18.0	3.8
Operating Margin **21**	*	*	*	*	*	74.9	*	*	*	*	*	*	*
Operating Margin Before Officers' Comp. **22**	*	*	*	*	*	77.5	*	*	*	*	*	*	*

Selected Average Balance Sheet ($ in Thousands)

Item										
Net Receivables 23	770246	0	166	10725	22232	44617	96825	210123	536337	21410658
Inventories 24	32	0	0	0	0	9	1	9	10	887
Net Property, Plant and Equipment 25	16863	0	51	188	606	1407	3163	6534	17186	429618
Total Assets 26	1867780	0	6862	18837	37782	73055	159428	344864	968470	54731983
Notes and Loans Payable 27	305206	0	0	517	812	2423	6346	17819	68256	9680664
All Other Liabilities 28	1305868	0	254	15384	32350	62662	136647	293255	811378	37264697
Net Worth 29	256705	0	6608	2936	4620	7970	16435	33789	88836	7786621

Selected Financial Ratios (Times to 1)

Item										
Current Ratio 30	0.8	•	1.1	1.0	1.0	1.0	1.0	1.0	0.9	0.8
Quick Ratio 31	0.7	•	1.0	1.0	1.0	0.9	0.9	0.9	0.9	0.7
Net Sales to Working Capital 32	•	•	0.1	0.2	0.7	1.8	1.6	1.5	•	•
Coverage Ratio 33	1.5	2.7	1.5	1.5	1.5	1.6	1.6	1.6	1.7	1.5
Total Asset Turnover 34	0.0	•	0.0	0.0	0.0	0.0	0.0	0.0	0.0	0.0
Inventory Turnover 35	74.2	•	63.0	8.4	0.8	0.7	0.1	1.2	•	87.3
Receivables Turnover 36	0.0	•	0.0	0.0	0.0	0.0	0.0	0.0	0.0	0.0
Total Liabilities to Net Worth 37	6.3	•	5.4	7.2	8.2	8.7	9.2	9.2	9.9	6.0
Current Assets to Working Capital 38	•	•	1.1	14.4	40.1	94.7	•	•	•	•
Current Liabilities to Working Capital 39	•	•	0.1	13.4	39.1	93.7	•	•	•	•
Working Capital to Net Sales 40	•	•	19.7	4.2	1.5	0.6	•	•	•	•
Inventory to Working Capital 41	•	•	0.0	0.0	0.0	0.0	•	•	•	•
Total Receipts to Cash Flow 42	0.7	0.3	0.6	0.6	0.6	0.7	0.5	0.5	0.5	0.7
Cost of Goods to Cash Flow 43	0.0	0.0	0.0	0.0	0.0	0.0	0.0	0.0	0.0	0.1
Cash Flow to Total Debt 44	0.0	0.0	1.0	0.0	0.0	0.0	0.0	0.0	0.0	0.0

Selected Financial Factors (in Percentages)

Item										
Debt Ratio 45	86.3	•	3.7	84.4	87.8	89.1	89.7	90.2	90.8	85.8
Return on Total Assets 46	2.9	•	3.4	3.2	3.2	3.3	3.3	3.3	3.5	2.8
Return on Equity Before Income Taxes 47	7.2	•	3.5	7.0	9.1	10.2	11.8	12.8	16.5	6.6
Return on Equity After Income Taxes 48	4.8	•	2.7	5.7	7.5	8.1	8.8	9.2	11.8	4.3
Profit Margin (Before Income Tax) 49	53.2	273.6	164.0	74.5	73.0	67.8	86.8	104.6	106.4	49.1
Profit Margin (After Income Tax) 50	35.5	199.5	128.7	60.7	60.3	53.6	65.1	75.5	76.0	32.2

Table I

Corporations with and without Net Income

OFFICES OF OTHER HOLDING COMPANIES

MONEY AMOUNTS AND SIZE OF ASSETS IN THOUSANDS OF DOLLARS

Item Description for Accounting Period 7/02 Through 6/03	Total	Zero Assets	Under 500	500 to 1,000	1,000 to 5,000	5,000 to 10,000	10,000 to 25,000	25,000 to 50,000	50,000 to 100,000	100,000 to 250,000	250,000 to 500,000	500,000 to 2,500,000	2,500,000 and over
Number of Enterprises 1	42706	7284	25539	2211	4839	1115	821	360	193	155	80	83	26
Revenues ($ in Thousands)													
Net Sales 2	1767701	47560	13778	751	156894	23866	177508	37898	220541	260855	92503	186306	549240
Interest 3	6290487	314131	49229	27301	116149	50986	114382	109222	205549	251711	581232	1469488	3001105
Rents 4	225178	5549	4507	9939	32366	25498	23352	16855	21272	17479	27288	30969	10104
Royalties 5	215911	2256	293	0	1800	5428	9730	1279	45286	13044	74995	36651	25148
Other Portfolio Income 6	3768036	241967	159388	143473	286005	203043	326420	136375	159050	333068	426427	511321	841497
Other Receipts 7	6016829	141566	-197	72004	574225	725116	402262	213225	418038	657099	1176839	1069297	567360
Total Receipts 8	18284142	753029	226998	253468	1167439	1033937	1053654	514854	1069736	1553256	2379284	3304032	4994454
Average Total Receipts 9	428	103	9	115	241	927	1283	1430	5543	9892	29741	39808	192094
Operating Costs/Operating Income (%)													
Cost of Operations 10	21.1	64.2	*	6.4	7.9	29.2	37.1	13.6	45.2	12.6	14.2	13.2	14.8
Salaries and Wages 11	51.2	40.7	87.9	288.4	28.7	149.9	37.9	92.3	26.2	56.8	118.2	52.7	50.2
Taxes Paid 12	25.1	60.9	148.9	770.6	30.0	68.3	15.5	52.4	10.9	16.7	87.2	42.9	8.9
Interest Paid 13	242.6	587.4	190.8	1487.7	78.0	1005.2	78.8	347.8	84.2	84.1	383.1	548.7	283.3
Depreciation 14	12.1	24.6	45.7	205.6	7.3	47.1	9.6	24.0	11.9	8.4	28.5	20.3	6.1
Amortization and Depletion 15	11.5	15.3	8.2	14.4	8.8	7.0	8.1	16.7	6.0	7.3	20.5	53.7	1.3
Pensions and Other Deferred Comp. 16	3.2	0.2	50.6	58.9	4.9	55.4	1.2	3.1	1.4	0.8	5.4	1.2	2.3
Employee Benefits 17	10.4	1.7	103.9	313.6	3.6	11.8	3.3	10.1	5.2	6.2	5.6	48.5	4.5
Advertising 18	1.2	0.8	*	0.4	0.1	3.8	2.2	1.8	2.7	0.5	0.4	3.2	0.2
Other Expenses 19	309.1	1637.4	2465.2	19690.4	216.6	1695.7	243.3	970.5	154.6	216.3	461.9	250.1	155.6
Officers' Compensation 20	21.6	18.6	32.8	1590.8	32.1	104.3	20.6	50.4	17.1	12.9	101.2	24.3	2.8
Operating Margin 21	*	*	*	*	*	*	*	*	*	*	*	•	•
Operating Margin Before Officers' Comp. 22	*	*	*	*	*	*	*	*	*	*	*	•	•

Selected Average Balance Sheet ($ in Thousands)

Item													
Net Receivables **23**	439	0	2	55	78	448	628	1925	4024	10180	11721	111291	152569
Inventories **24**	19	0	0	0	21	17	33	61	339	2467	5940		320
Net Property, Plant and Equipment **25**	80	0	4	35	92	166	486	845	1628	3376	4171	6362	7885
Total Assets **26**	8855	0	129	747	2124	7108	15652	34618	70216	155874	353226	1048325	6796176
Notes and Loans Payable **27**	1316	0	41	84	508	1449	3604	8559	20094	26092	66984	159392	704514
All Other Liabilities **28**	1408	0	8	-4	365	906	1920	2895	6036	19674	37134	153299	1332157
Net Worth **29**	6131	0	79	666	1252	4753	10128	23163	44087	110108	249109	735634	4759505

Selected Financial Ratios (Times to 1)

Item												
Current Ratio **30**	1.5	•	4.2	1.8	2.3	1.8	2.5	1.8	1.8	2.4	1.5	1.3
Quick Ratio **31**	0.8	•	3.3	1.2	1.3	1.2	1.6	1.2	1.3	1.3	1.3	0.5
Net Sales to Working Capital **32**	0.1	•	0.0	0.1	0.0	0.1	0.0	0.2	0.1	0.0	0.0	0.0
Coverage Ratio **33**	2.5	•	6.9	5.2	2.2	3.0	0.2	2.4	3.4	4.8	2.5	2.5
Total Asset Turnover **34**	0.0	•	0.0	0.0	0.0	0.0	0.0	0.0	0.0	0.0	0.0	0.0
Inventory Turnover **35**	0.5	•	0.1	76.4	0.3	4.7	0.4	8.5	0.6	0.1	0.1	9.8
Receivables Turnover **36**	0.1	0.2	0.0	0.3	0.1	0.3	0.1	0.4	0.2	0.1	0.0	0.1
Total Liabilities to Net Worth **37**	0.4	•	0.1	0.7	0.5	0.5	0.5	0.6	0.4	0.4	0.4	0.4
Current Assets to Working Capital **38**	2.9	•	1.3	2.3	1.8	2.3	1.7	2.2	2.2	1.7	3.0	4.0
Current Liabilities to Working Capital **39**	1.9	•	0.3	1.3	0.8	1.3	0.7	1.2	1.2	0.7	2.0	3.0
Working Capital to Net Sales **40**	16.5	59.4	489.5	6.9	56.7	6.7	45.4	5.1	8.1	33.7	27.8	20.3
Inventory to Working Capital **41**	0.0	•	0.0	0.0	0.0	0.0	0.0	0.0	0.0	0.0	0.0	0.0
Total Receipts to Cash Flow **42**	0.2	0.3	0.0	0.2	0.0	0.3	0.2	0.4	0.3	0.1	0.1	0.2
Cost of Goods to Cash Flow **43**	0.0	0.2	0.0	0.0	0.0	0.1	0.0	0.2	0.0	0.0	0.0	0.0
Cash Flow to Total Debt **44**	0.1	•	0.6	0.2	0.2	0.1	0.7	0.1	0.1	0.1	0.1	0.1

Selected Financial Factors (in Percentages)

Item												
Debt Ratio **45**	30.8	38.5	10.7	41.1	33.1	35.3	33.1	37.2	29.4	29.5	29.8	30.0
Return on Total Assets **46**	2.8	•	4.7	6.2	6.7	3.3	0.3	3.2	3.0	6.0	2.9	2.2
Return on Equity Before Income Taxes **47**	2.4	•	4.5	8.5	5.5	3.3	•	3.0	3.0	6.7	2.5	1.9
Return on Equity After Income Taxes **48**	1.5	•	3.7	7.3	4.5	1.8	•	2.0	1.7	5.3	1.6	1.2
Profit Margin (Before Income Tax) **49**	358.5	•	8826.6	329.3	1229.3	156.5	•	115.3	197.9	1444.7	822.8	422.5
Profit Margin (After Income Tax) **50**	222.6	•	7282.3	280.7	1007.6	86.6	•	77.8	114.4	534.3	277.2	

Table II

Corporations with Net Income

OFFICES OF OTHER HOLDING COMPANIES

MONEY AMOUNTS AND SIZE OF ASSETS IN THOUSANDS OF DOLLARS

Item Description for Accounting Period 7/02 Through 6/03	Total	Zero Assets	Under 500	500 to 1,000	1,000 to 5,000	5,000 to 10,000	10,000 to 25,000	25,000 to 50,000	50,000 to 100,000	100,000 to 250,000	250,000 to 500,000	500,000 to 2,500,000	2,500,000 and over
Number of Enterprises **1**	16720	2426	0	1272	0	498	358	155	93	77	55	55	21
Revenues ($ in Thousands)													
Net Sales **2**	1031506	3603	0	690	0	15809	154566	18219	152300	122164	86844	48189	272207
Interest **3**	4357263	100313	0	22695	0	30576	48011	66745	159794	143513	510727	1140065	2037075
Rents **4**	165938	5076	0	9939	0	16957	16769	12052	8436	10405	25874	24003	9954
Royalties **5**	159763	1946	0	0	0	5420	7103	798	42102	5298	33231	36651	25148
Other Portfolio Income **6**	3299243	153290	0	137864	0	187403	296308	92204	141588	283646	410828	469561	734221
Other Receipts **7**	6816810	542378	0	114513	0	781544	472961	266049	398345	584208	1157917	1060879	532176
Total Receipts **8**	15830523	806606	0	285701	0	1037709	995718	456067	902565	1149234	2225421	2779348	3610781
Average Total Receipts **9**	947	332	·	225	·	2084	2781	2942	9705	14925	40462	50534	171942
Operating Costs/Operating Income (%)													
Cost of Operations **10**	25.7	·	·	·	·	21.1	39.3	4.6	48.3	25.9	13.1	4.6	29.9
Salaries and Wages **11**	33.7	52.3	·	173.2	·	82.1	27.0	62.6	18.5	14.6	29.4	134.3	43.3
Taxes Paid **12**	30.4	673.1	·	699.0	·	68.4	12.5	59.7	11.4	25.4	90.9	112.8	9.9
Interest Paid **13**	206.3	1124.0	·	1255.4	·	1324.8	32.9	287.5	47.0	70.1	277.0	1493.3	216.5
Depreciation **14**	9.4	102.7	·	214.1	·	21.7	3.3	28.6	4.4	5.5	24.2	23.2	8.1
Amortization and Depletion **15**	16.2	142.7	·	7.1	·	6.9	2.7	2.4	7.3	12.7	21.2	201.0	2.5
Pensions and Other Deferred Comp. **16**	2.7	0.1	·	63.2	·	6.1	0.7	1.8	1.9	0.6	3.9	1.4	4.4
Employee Benefits **17**	12.0	4.2	·	310.7	·	7.5	2.0	8.2	6.7	1.9	4.7	169.0	2.2
Advertising **18**	0.8	6.2	·	·	·	0.2	0.4	1.3	1.3	0.1	0.5	7.1	0.4
Other Expenses **19**	188.7	1587.8	·	14997.0	·	1701.0	71.4	512.8	82.8	90.9	352.3	421.0	118.0
Officers' Compensation **20**	15.3	3.1	·	577.7	·	84.7	10.9	41.1	8.5	5.8	28.5	53.6	3.9
Operating Margin **21**	·	·	·	·	·	·	·	·	·	·	·	·	·
Operating Margin Before Officers' Comp. **22**	·	·	·	·	·	·	·	·	·	·	·	·	·

Selected Average Balance Sheet ($ in Thousands)

Net Receivables 23	818	·	10	489	736	2118	4697	9053	15444	123017	188421
Inventories 24	36	0	0	1	22	71	201	673	256	8930	396
Net Property, Plant and Equipment 25	85	0	60	188	298	675	707	3409	4436	720	6570
Total Assets 26	14869	0	699	6891	15726	35058	70322	153124	355853	1007938	6354758
Notes and Loans Payable 27	1461	0	129	1558	2898	6755	14348	15618	72481	132018	294096
All Other Liabilities 28	1731	0	-52	724	2237	2933	4759	17827	35844	147653	680555
Net Worth 29	11677	0	622	4609	10590	25370	51216	119678	247529	728267	5380107

Selected Financial Ratios (Times to 1)

Current Ratio 30	2.1	·	4.1	3.9	1.6	3.7	2.0	2.6	1.8	2.0
Quick Ratio 31	1.5	·	2.5	2.2	1.2	2.4	1.5	1.4	1.5	1.5
Net Sales to Working Capital 32	0.0	·	0.0	0.0	0.4	0.0	0.1	0.0	0.0	0.0
Coverage Ratio 33	6.2	17.6	19.3	3.6	15.5	6.4	11.8	7.6	3.4	5.5
Total Asset Turnover 34	0.0	·	0.0	0.0	0.0	0.0	0.0	0.0	0.0	0.0
Inventory Turnover 35	0.4	·	·	12.0	7.7	3.9	0.6	0.8	0.0	9.8
Receivables Turnover 36	0.1	·	0.1	0.6	0.1	0.5	0.1	0.1	0.0	0.1
Total Liabilities to Net Worth 37	0.3	·	0.5	0.5	0.4	0.4	0.3	0.4	0.4	0.2
Current Assets to Working Capital 38	1.9	1.3	1.3	2.8	1.4	2.0	2.0	1.6	2.2	2.1
Current Liabilities to Working Capital 39	0.9	0.3	0.3	1.8	0.4	0.4	1.0	0.6	1.2	1.1
Working Capital to Net Sales 40	23.7	244.9	57.9	2.8	56.4	6.7	8.8	32.2	102.4	40.6
Inventory to Working Capital 41	0.0	·	0.0	0.0	0.0	0.0	0.0	0.0	0.0	0.0
Total Receipts to Cash Flow 42	0.1	0.0	0.0	0.2	0.1	0.3	0.1	0.1	0.0	0.1
Cost of Goods to Cash Flow 43	0.0	·	0.0	0.1	0.0	0.1	0.0	0.0	0.0	0.0
Cash Flow to Total Debt 44	0.2	1.7	0.6	0.4	0.2	0.3	0.3	0.2	0.1	0.1

Selected Financial Factors (in Percentages)

Debt Ratio 45	21.5	·	11.0	33.1	32.7	27.6	27.2	21.8	30.4	27.7	15.3
Return on Total Assets 46	5.3	·	18.8	21.8	14.0	6.1	9.4	8.6	9.3	4.4	2.4
Return on Equity Before Income Taxes 47	5.6	·	20.0	23.4	19.4	7.1	11.4	10.1	11.6	4.3	2.3
Return on Equity After Income Taxes 48	4.4	·	18.6	21.2	16.2	6.1	9.6	7.7	9.6	3.0	1.6
Profit Margin (Before Income Tax) 49	1065.5	18677.0	22940.9	3400.8	476.3	1541.6	355.3	760.3	1819.9	3586.8	975.0
Profit Margin (After Income Tax) 50	833.4	14705.7	21260.0	3081.7	396.2	1308.2	582.1	301.7	1497.5	2475.9	681.8

Table I

Corporations with and without Net Income

EMPLOYMENT SERVICES

MONEY AMOUNTS AND SIZE OF ASSETS IN THOUSANDS OF DOLLARS

Item Description for Accounting Period 7/02 Through 6/03	Total	Zero Assets	Under 500	500 to 1,000	1,000 to 5,000	5,000 to 10,000	10,000 to 25,000	25,000 to 50,000	50,000 to 100,000	100,000 to 250,000	250,000 to 500,000	500,000 to 2,500,000	2,500,000 and over
Number of Enterprises **1**	23272	1289	19643	1118	995	92	59	28	16	13	8	11	0
Revenues ($ in Thousands)													
Net Sales **2**	97062590	384242	16481862	9375916	11578315	5077936	6090155	4905768	4360516	4965665	15474402	18367813	0
Interest **3**	260923	1326	5373	2132	7176	937	1616	2950	11124	5617	8464	214207	0
Rents **4**	5175	0	0	0	313	45	119	294	1	0	932	3470	0
Royalties **5**	168799	0	0	0	0	0	0	0	8399	2692	633	157074	0
Other Portfolio Income **6**	124336	2463	2763	1283	20880	55	2266	7090	1274	399	842	85023	0
Other Receipts **7**	459279	295	71982	13966	47763	23225	17191	-44436	15765	26683	8843	278004	0
Total Receipts **8**	98081102	388326	16561980	9393297	11654447	5102198	6111347	4871666	4397079	5001056	15494116	19105591	0
Average Total Receipts **9**	4215	301	843	8402	11713	55459	103582	173988	274817	384697	1936764	1736872	*
Operating Costs/Operating Income (%)													
Cost of Operations **10**	52.7	39.3	34.4	40.2	68.7	67.0	64.2	50.2	63.1	50.9	62.7	48.3	*
Salaries and Wages **11**	25.2	43.1	33.3	41.7	13.2	17.7	21.7	30.1	18.8	27.5	19.1	24.5	*
Taxes Paid **12**	5.6	5.3	5.0	7.3	4.4	6.5	5.0	6.5	5.2	3.5	6.0	5.9	*
Interest Paid **13**	0.7	0.1	0.4	0.1	0.2	0.3	0.2	0.5	1.1	1.1	0.2	1.9	*
Depreciation **14**	0.6	1.0	0.5	0.3	0.3	0.4	0.3	0.4	0.6	0.9	0.6	0.9	*
Amortization and Depletion **15**	0.4	0.5	0.1	0.0	0.0	0.2	0.2	0.5	0.5	2.0	0.3	1.1	*
Pensions and Other Deferred Comp. **16**	0.2	0.0	0.8	0.0	0.1	0.0	0.1	0.1	0.1	0.2	0.1	0.2	*
Employee Benefits **17**	2.7	1.2	1.7	1.6	2.4	2.6	2.0	3.8	2.2	3.9	4.2	3.0	*
Advertising **18**	0.5	0.6	0.9	0.3	0.5	0.2	0.3	0.3	0.5	0.6	0.2	0.6	*
Other Expenses **19**	10.1	16.9	13.5	6.0	7.6	4.0	5.8	7.5	8.6	18.5	5.2	16.4	*
Officers' Compensation **20**	2.0	2.0	8.2	1.2	1.5	0.9	0.5	0.4	0.5	0.6	0.2	0.7	*
Operating Margin **21**	*	*	1.2	1.3	0.8	0.1	*	*	*	*	1.2	*	*
Operating Margin Before Officers' Comp. **22**	1.4	*	9.5	2.5	2.3	1.1	0.2	0.2	*	*	1.4	*	*

Selected Average Balance Sheet ($ in Thousands)

Net Receivables 23	329	0	24	333	752	2520	5667	10258	24414	55382	115874	287525
Inventories 24	2	0	0	0	2	20	81	59	32	175	3472	2107
Net Property, Plant and Equipment 25	72	0	13	66	134	396	1508	2315	3763	11083	36132	47869
Total Assets 26	1232	0	99	685	2028	6417	15584	35215	73529	164404	399508	1358834
Notes and Loans Payable 27	361	0	49	239	661	2883	4551	9353	23008	58644	34220	392385
All Other Liabilities 28	478	0	23	238	693	2511	5919	15329	33164	47815	178907	557632
Net Worth 29	393	0	27	207	675	1023	5114	10533	17357	57945	186382	408817

Selected Financial Ratios (Times to 1)

Current Ratio 30	1.4	•	1.6	1.6	1.5	1.4	1.5	1.1	1.5	1.9	1.6	1.3
Quick Ratio 31	1.2	•	1.2	1.4	1.3	1.0	1.1	0.9	1.1	1.6	1.1	1.1
Net Sales to Working Capital 32	21.0	•	33.4	39.5	28.3	39.2	33.1	72.3	21.9	9.6	23.7	10.6
Coverage Ratio 33	1.6	•	4.9	11.8	7.8	3.2	0.8	•	0.8	•	7.8	1.2
Total Asset Turnover 34	3.4	•	8.5	12.2	5.7	8.6	6.6	5.0	3.7	2.3	4.8	1.2
Inventory Turnover 35	1029.7	•	•	•	4950.6	1868.7	821.4	1493.6	5300.4	1111.1	349.3	382.6
Receivables Turnover 36	13.8	•	43.5	25.4	14.9	28.6	16.9	17.8	14.2	6.8	16.4	6.8
Total Liabilities to Net Worth 37	2.1	•	2.7	2.3	2.0	5.3	2.0	2.3	3.2	1.8	1.1	2.3
Current Assets to Working Capital 38	3.5	•	2.7	2.8	3.2	3.6	3.2	7.9	3.2	2.1	2.7	4.4
Current Liabilities to Working Capital 39	2.5	•	1.7	1.8	2.2	2.6	2.2	6.9	2.2	1.1	1.7	3.4
Working Capital to Net Sales 40	0.0	•	0.0	0.0	0.0	0.0	0.0	0.0	0.0	0.1	0.0	0.1
Inventory to Working Capital 41	0.0	•	•	0.0	0.0	0.0	0.0	0.0	0.0	0.0	0.0	0.0
Total Receipts to Cash Flow 42	11.5	18.4	8.1	15.3	13.0	25.4	20.7	18.5	15.2	13.6	20.9	6.7
Cost of Goods to Cash Flow 43	6.1	7.2	2.8	6.2	8.9	17.0	13.3	9.3	9.6	6.9	13.1	3.2
Cash Flow to Total Debt 44	0.4	1.4	1.1	0.7	0.4	0.4	0.5	0.4	0.3	0.3	0.4	0.3

Selected Financial Factors (in Percentages)

Debt Ratio 45	68.1	•	73.1	69.7	66.7	84.1	67.2	70.1	76.4	64.8	53.3	69.9
Return on Total Assets 46	3.5	•	18.3	19.3	9.7	7.7	1.3	3.2	•	•	7.4	3.0
Return on Equity Before Income Taxes 47	4.0	•	54.2	58.2	25.3	33.3	•	•	•	•	13.8	1.9
Return on Equity After Income Taxes 48	0.7	•	52.3	56.9	24.5	28.9	•	•	•	•	11.7	•
Profit Margin (Before Income Tax) 49	0.4	•	1.7	1.4	1.5	0.6	•	•	•	0.0	1.3	0.5
Profit Margin (After Income Tax) 50	0.1	•	1.7	1.4	1.4	0.5	•	•	•	•	1.1	•

Table II

Corporations with Net Income

EMPLOYMENT SERVICES

MONEY AMOUNTS AND SIZE OF ASSETS IN THOUSANDS OF DOLLARS

Item Description for Accounting Period 7/02 Through 6/03	Total	Zero Assets	Under 500	500 to 1,000	1,000 to 5,000	5,000 to 10,000	10,000 to 25,000	25,000 to 50,000	50,000 to 100,000	100,000 to 250,000	250,000 to 500,000	500,000 to 2,500,000	2,500,000 and over
Number of Enterprises 1	12117	403	10179	701	705	61	32	15	6	6	4	4	0
Revenues ($ in Thousands)													
Net Sales 2	54461212	126693	10569263	5903784	9158981	2388504	4446019	3756419	1558653	2120026	7453873	6978994	0
Interest 3	49490	0	1890	1849	5027	79	648	1979	5687	2643	3152	26535	0
Rents 4	872	0	0	0	39	21	117	294	1	0	0	399	0
Royalties 5	33572	0	0	0	0	0	0	0	7522	1822	0	24227	0
Other Portfolio Income 6	112926	2463	1586	1174	20416	55	667	6903	0	358	445	78861	0
Other Receipts 7	333868	33	45379	3444	44140	21899	15215	17658	2754	942	4264	178142	0
Total Receipts 8	54991940	129189	10618118	5910251	9228603	2410558	4462666	3783253	1574617	2125791	7461734	7287158	0
Average Total Receipts 9	4538	321	1043	8431	13090	39517	139458	252217	262436	354298	1865434	1821790	•
Operating Costs/Operating Income (%)													
Cost of Operations 10	43.7	•	29.7	11.4	66.5	69.9	66.0	42.3	37.5	17.1	40.9	53.6	•
Salaries and Wages 11	32.4	85.4	36.8	64.4	14.1	10.4	19.5	36.7	37.3	48.9	36.7	24.6	•
Taxes Paid 12	6.0	4.2	5.3	10.3	4.3	6.2	5.2	6.8	4.0	4.7	6.4	6.2	•
Interest Paid 13	0.3	•	0.2	0.1	0.2	0.1	0.2	0.3	0.4	0.7	0.3	1.0	•
Depreciation 14	0.4	0.0	0.4	0.4	0.3	0.3	0.2	0.3	0.4	1.1	0.5	0.8	•
Amortization and Depletion 15	0.2	•	0.1	0.0	0.0	0.0	0.2	0.1	0.3	0.9	0.4	0.3	•
Pensions and Other Deferred Comp. 16	0.2	0.0	0.5	0.0	0.1	0.0	0.1	0.1	0.4	0.4	0.1	0.3	•
Employee Benefits 17	2.3	0.1	1.7	1.1	2.5	2.6	2.1	4.0	1.7	8.0	2.7	1.0	•
Advertising 18	0.4	0.1	0.9	0.4	0.5	0.2	0.3	0.2	0.5	0.6	0.2	0.4	•
Other Expenses 19	8.7	7.8	12.5	7.4	8.1	4.7	5.2	7.7	14.2	13.1	7.9	6.9	•
Officers' Compensation 20	2.0	0.1	6.7	1.4	1.5	1.6	0.4	0.3	0.4	0.9	0.1	1.1	•
Operating Margin 21	3.2	2.3	5.3	3.1	1.9	4.0	0.6	1.2	2.8	3.5	3.7	3.8	•
Operating Margin Before Officers' Comp. 22	5.2	2.4	12.0	4.5	3.4	5.6	1.0	1.5	3.2	4.4	3.9	4.8	•

Selected Average Balance Sheet ($ in Thousands)

Net Receivables 23	314	0	36	304	705	3239	5986	11078	15522	58696	91340	339541	•
Inventories 24	2	0	0	0	0	7	54	104	74	154	44	5794	•
Net Property, Plant and Equipment 25	63	0	17	82	144	386	1584	2390	2066	14166	25250	29946	•
Total Assets 26	1310	0	141	710	2043	6289	16105	34713	74067	174832	370004	2025776	•
Notes and Loans Payable 27	268	0	32	276	577	1996	3634	7514	4546	26998	52925	393696	•
All Other Liabilities 28	552	0	30	164	683	1153	6405	21033	29624	54643	105867	1066753	•
Net Worth 29	490	0	80	270	783	3140	6066	6167	39897	93191	211212	565328	•

Selected Financial Ratios (Times to 1)

Current Ratio 30	1.4	•	2.0	1.8	1.6	2.0	1.5	1.0	1.7	2.0	2.5	1.2	•
Quick Ratio 31	1.2	•	1.6	1.8	1.4	1.8	1.2	0.9	1.1	1.8	1.3	1.1	•
Net Sales to Working Capital 32	18.3	•	21.0	31.9	24.3	15.9	40.6	383.9	16.6	7.5	13.8	9.7	•
Coverage Ratio 33	13.1	•	25.6	29.8	14.8	37.7	6.2	8.7	10.5	6.6	13.3	8.7	•
Total Asset Turnover 34	3.4	•	7.4	11.9	6.4	6.2	8.6	7.2	3.5	2.0	5.0	0.9	•
Inventory Turnover 35	831.4	•	•	•	20327.2	3826.9	1690.2	1021.0	1320.9	394.0	17512.0	161.4	•
Receivables Turnover 36	13.5	•	57.1	23.8	19.2	16.0	23.0	24.0	19.3	6.2	40.8	4.7	•
Total Liabilities to Net Worth 37	1.7	•	0.8	1.6	1.6	1.0	1.7	4.6	0.9	0.9	0.8	2.6	•
Current Assets to Working Capital 38	3.3	•	2.0	2.3	2.6	2.0	3.0	36.0	2.4	2.0	1.7	6.7	•
Current Liabilities to Working Capital 39	2.3	•	1.0	1.3	1.6	1.0	2.0	35.0	1.4	1.0	0.7	5.7	•
Working Capital to Net Sales 40	0.1	•	0.0	0.0	0.0	0.1	0.0	0.0	0.1	0.1	0.1	0.1	•
Inventory to Working Capital 41	0.0	•	•	0.0	0.0	0.0	0.0	0.3	0.0	•	0.0	0.0	•
Total Receipts to Cash Flow 42	9.1	8.3	6.5	10.6	10.7	11.5	18.2	11.4	6.2	6.6	11.1	7.6	•
Cost of Goods to Cash Flow 43	4.0	•	1.9	1.2	7.1	8.0	12.0	4.8	2.3	1.1	4.5	4.1	•
Cash Flow to Total Debt 44	0.6	•	2.6	1.8	1.0	1.1	0.8	0.8	1.2	0.7	1.1	0.2	•

Selected Financial Factors (in Percentages)

Debt Ratio 45	62.6	•	43.6	62.0	61.7	50.1	62.3	82.2	46.1	46.7	42.9	72.1	•
Return on Total Assets 46	15.5	•	44.0	39.7	18.4	31.6	9.8	15.9	14.8	9.0	20.8	7.8	•
Return on Equity Before Income Taxes 47	38.2	•	75.1	101.0	44.7	61.6	21.8	79.3	24.9	14.3	33.7	24.8	•
Return on Equity After Income Taxes 48	33.1	•	73.8	99.4	43.7	59.4	20.2	70.8	16.4	9.7	30.0	16.3	•
Profit Margin (Before Income Tax) 49	4.2	4.3	5.7	3.2	2.7	4.9	0.9	2.0	3.8	3.8	3.8	8.0	•
Profit Margin (After Income Tax) 50	3.6	4.3	5.7	3.2	2.6	4.8	0.9	1.7	2.5	2.6	3.4	5.3	•

ADMINISTRATIVE AND SUPPORT AND WASTE MANAGEMENT AND REMEDIATION SERVICES 561500

Table I

Corporations with and without Net Income

TRAVEL ARRANGEMENT AND RESERVATION SERVICES

MONEY AMOUNTS AND SIZE OF ASSETS IN THOUSANDS OF DOLLARS

Item Description for Accounting Period 7/02 Through 6/03	Total	Zero Assets	Under 500	500 to 1,000	1,000 to 5,000	5,000 to 10,000	10,000 to 25,000	25,000 to 50,000	50,000 to 100,000	100,000 to 250,000	250,000 to 500,000	500,000 to 2,500,000	2,500,000 and over
Number of Enterprises **1**	26231	3883	21337	300	469	115	53	25	19	13	10	6	0
Revenues ($ in Thousands)													
Net Sales **2**	36351536	587356	14753167	734732	2293944	1907378	2388446	1600969	2167722	1789523	3895740	4232559	0
Interest **3**	142630	1213	3368	1360	3357	3144	5124	6078	5337	10904	35616	67129	0
Rents **4**	42722	16	387	0	3118	1578	491	1766	2820	3292	4782	24474	0
Royalties **5**	25138	50	0	0	8	0	0	0	1	23275	0	1803	0
Other Portfolio Income **6**	255169	3434	5896	0	802	1401	4582	23288	6886	12659	24607	171611	0
Other Receipts **7**	947172	176025	116127	50650	10694	11674	117638	34760	52492	87446	278315	11353	0
Total Receipts **8**	37764367	768094	14878945	786742	2311923	1925175	2516281	1666861	2235258	1927099	4239060	4508929	0
Average Total Receipts **9**	1440	198	697	2622	4929	16741	47477	66674	117645	148238	423906	751488	•
Operating Costs/Operating Income (%)													
Cost of Operations **10**	61.3	58.7	77.7	81.3	39.4	47.4	74.9	70.1	55.1	40.6	61.6	19.3	•
Salaries and Wages **11**	14.8	31.5	7.8	6.8	27.8	26.3	11.4	11.3	16.5	25.7	17.6	21.6	•
Taxes Paid **12**	1.6	3.1	0.8	1.0	2.9	2.7	1.4	1.5	2.5	2.9	1.7	1.9	•
Interest Paid **13**	0.8	4.7	0.4	0.3	0.5	0.4	0.4	0.5	0.7	1.4	2.1	0.7	•
Depreciation **14**	1.2	0.7	0.4	1.0	1.2	2.7	0.9	1.7	2.1	2.7	1.4	2.2	•
Amortization and Depletion **15**	0.5	3.9	0.1	0.0	0.1	0.4	0.2	0.2	0.5	0.8	0.8	1.4	•
Pensions and Other Deferred Comp. **16**	0.5	•	0.1	0.1	0.1	0.2	0.3	0.3	0.6	0.3	1.0	1.8	•
Employee Benefits **17**	1.0	0.4	0.3	0.5	1.4	1.5	0.8	1.0	2.2	2.6	1.7	1.2	•
Advertising **18**	2.1	2.0	0.8	0.1	1.1	0.5	1.1	1.4	4.4	4.3	1.3	7.5	•
Other Expenses **19**	16.5	26.6	9.5	11.6	20.0	14.5	11.9	13.8	17.9	23.4	16.4	38.9	•
Officers' Compensation **20**	2.7	2.2	3.2	4.2	5.5	5.3	1.3	1.3	0.9	0.9	0.8	2.5	•
Operating Margin **21**	•	•	•	•	0.0	•	•	•	•	•	•	1.0	•
Operating Margin Before Officers' Comp. **22**	•	2.1	•	5.5	5.5	3.4	•	•	•	•	•	3.5	•

Selected Average Balance Sheet ($ in Thousands)

	C1	C2	C3	C4	C5	C6	C7	C8	C9	C10	C11	C12
Net Receivables 23	148	0	9	130	476	1946	3880	5260	7500	17834	59255	316854
Inventories 24	4	0	0	0	6	13	148	570	365	592	913	5383
Net Property, Plant and Equipment 25	93	0	14	171	412	1944	1615	6225	13243	23906	38909	79580
Total Assets 26	824	67	720	2200	6425	15052	36296	68002	161522	355529	1588061	
Notes and Loans Payable 27	186	39	99	741	1531	2016	5303	9180	25570	128631	242848	
All Other Liabilities 28	373	29	355	1350	2698	10563	18796	32760	80153	146295	657121	
Net Worth 29	265	-1	266	109	2196	2474	12198	26062	55798	80603	688092	

Selected Financial Ratios (Times to 1)

	C1	C2	C3	C4	C5	C6	C7	C8	C9	C10	C11
Current Ratio 30	1.0	1.4	0.8	0.9	1.3	1.0	1.2	1.0	0.9	0.7	1.1
Quick Ratio 31	0.7	1.2	0.7	0.7	1.1	0.8	0.8	0.7	0.6	0.5	0.7
Net Sales to Working Capital 32	58.1		18.3		21.6						12.9
Coverage Ratio 33	2.6	0.4	1.3	2.5		2.4	2.6	0.4	2.2	2.1	13.5
Total Asset Turnover 34	1.7	10.3	3.4	2.2	2.6	3.0	1.8	1.7	0.9	1.1	0.4
Inventory Turnover 35	240.8	1138.7	398441.3	320.1	627.6	228.5	78.8	172.5	94.5	262.8	25.3
Receivables Turnover 36	11.8	102.8	12.5	9.4	8.6	13.7	12.0	18.8	5.3	9.3	3.4
Total Liabilities to Net Worth 37	2.1		1.7	19.2	1.9	2.0	1.6	1.9	3.4		1.3
Current Assets to Working Capital 38		3.6		4.2		6.5					12.5
Current Liabilities to Working Capital 39		2.6		3.2		5.5					11.5
Working Capital to Net Sales 40		0.0		0.1		0.0					0.1
Inventory to Working Capital 41		0.0		0.0		0.2					0.1
Total Receipts to Cash Flow 42	6.9	14.5	10.1	5.9	9.1	9.6	8.0	6.9	4.6	6.6	2.5
Cost of Goods to Cash Flow 43	4.3	11.3	8.3	2.3	4.3	7.2	5.6	3.8	1.9	4.1	0.5
Cash Flow to Total Debt 44	0.4	0.7	0.5	0.4	0.4	0.4	0.3	0.4	0.3	0.2	0.3

Selected Financial Factors (in Percentages)

	C1	C2	C3	C4	C5	C6	C7	C8	C9	C10	C11
Debt Ratio 45	67.8	101.7	63.0	95.0	65.8	83.6	66.4	61.7	65.5	77.3	56.7
Return on Total Assets 46	3.3		1.3	2.9	2.8	2.5	0.5	2.7	4.8		4.0
Return on Equity Before Income Taxes 47	6.3	143.4	0.7	36.1	10.0	4.6	4.3	11.0			8.5
Return on Equity After Income Taxes 48	3.8	148.2		33.7	3.9	2.6	2.5	7.5			6.3
Profit Margin (Before Income Tax) 49	1.2		0.1	0.8	0.5	0.9	1.7	2.3			8.3
Profit Margin (After Income Tax) 50	0.7			0.8	0.2	0.5	1.0	1.6			6.1

Table II
Corporations with Net Income

TRAVEL ARRANGEMENT AND RESERVATION SERVICES

MONEY AMOUNTS AND SIZE OF ASSETS IN THOUSANDS OF DOLLARS

Item Description for Accounting Period 7/02 Through 6/03	Total	Zero Assets	Under 500	500 to 1,000	1,000 to 5,000	5,000 to 10,000	10,000 to 25,000	25,000 to 50,000	50,000 to 100,000	100,000 to 250,000	250,000 to 500,000	500,000 to 2,500,000	2,500,000 and over
Number of Enterprises 1	11463	786	10137	173	214	71	36	14	0	8	6	0	0
Revenues ($ in Thousands)													
Net Sales 2	22006357	132725	5480948	730332	1598572	1611928	1937476	941178	0	1277392	3121108	0	0
Interest 3	105955	757	1830	1358	2003	1477	3539	2217	0	6455	33605	0	0
Rents 4	36793	16	369	0	3118	203	491	803	0	2246	4782	0	0
Royalties 5	1803	0	0	0	0	0	0	0	0	0	0	0	0
Other Portfolio Income 6	229799	3434	5861	0	149	1282	1787	21788	0	6902	13646	0	0
Other Receipts 7	807642	172768	78399	50649	4442	8817	99875	14619	0	60090	262245	0	0
Total Receipts 8	23188349	309700	5567407	782339	1608284	1623707	2043168	980605	0	1353085	3435386	0	0
Average Total Receipts 9	2023	394	549	4522	7515	22869	56755	70043	•	169136	572564	•	•
Operating Costs/Operating Income (%)													
Cost of Operations 10	53.4	87.5	66.4	81.5	32.6	43.9	75.4	65.3	•	35.1	59.3	•	•
Salaries and Wages 11	17.1	29.4	12.3	6.6	32.7	28.4	11.2	10.9	•	28.1	18.9	•	•
Taxes Paid 12	1.8	4.5	1.0	0.9	3.4	2.9	1.5	1.6	•	3.3	2.0	•	•
Interest Paid 13	0.8	20.8	0.2	0.1	0.3	0.1	0.2	0.4	•	1.0	2.0	•	•
Depreciation 14	1.2	2.2	0.5	1.0	0.9	0.7	0.8	1.1	•	2.1	1.4	•	•
Amortization and Depletion 15	0.5	17.0	0.1	0.0	0.1	0.4	0.1	0.1	•	0.5	0.5	•	•
Pensions and Other Deferred Comp. 16	0.5	•	0.0	0.1	0.2	0.2	0.4	0.4	•	0.2	1.3	•	•
Employee Benefits 17	1.2	0.8	0.5	0.5	1.7	1.6	0.9	1.2	•	2.8	1.7	•	•
Advertising 18	1.8	1.5	1.2	0.1	1.2	0.3	0.7	1.6	•	4.2	0.7	•	•
Other Expenses 19	19.6	41.2	11.7	11.2	18.6	14.6	10.3	15.9	•	21.0	17.7	•	•
Officers' Compensation 20	2.6	9.5	4.2	4.1	5.7	5.7	1.3	1.3	•	0.9	0.6	•	•
Operating Margin 21	•	•	2.0	•	2.8	1.2	•	0.2	•	0.7	•	•	•
Operating Margin Before Officers' Comp. 22	2.1	•	6.1	•	8.5	6.9	•	1.6	•	1.6	•	•	•

Selected Average Balance Sheet ($ in Thousands)

Net Receivables 23	285	11	222	466	2435	3715	7647	•	24643	75297
Inventories 24	3	0	0	7	124	528	•	•	196	2049
Net Property, Plant and Equipment 25	117	10	64	264	672	1943	4706	•	17189	48092
Total Assets 26	1353	82	680	2630	5898	15608	38247	•	162260	367814
Notes and Loans Payable 27	243	25	14	333	618	1668	2947	•	21484	109797
All Other Liabilities 28	637	26	605	1655	3083	10325	19919	•	102414	160673
Net Worth 29	473	32	62	642	2197	3616	15381	•	38361	97344

Selected Financial Ratios (Times to 1)

Current Ratio 30	1.1	2.3	0.9	1.3	1.4	1.1	1.5	•	0.9	0.9
Quick Ratio 31	0.8	2.0	0.8	1.0	1.3	0.8	1.1	•	0.6	0.7
Net Sales to Working Capital 32	30.3	16.7	•	17.8	16.7	88.6	9.1	•	•	•
Coverage Ratio 33	7.6	1.9	16.0	19.9	13.2	14.2	12.5	14.7	6.9	3.1
Total Asset Turnover 34	1.4	•	6.6	6.2	2.8	3.8	3.4	1.8	1.0	1.4
Inventory Turnover 35	349.9	•	•	1246.9	1417.3	326.6	83.1	•	285.9	150.5
Receivables Turnover 36	9.3	79.1	13.4	12.6	8.7	16.7	8.9	•	6.0	6.4
Total Liabilities to Net Worth 37	1.9	1.6	10.0	3.1	1.7	3.3	1.5	•	3.2	2.8
Current Assets to Working Capital 38	10.5	1.8	•	4.7	3.3	17.7	3.1	•	•	•
Current Liabilities to Working Capital 39	9.5	0.8	•	3.7	2.3	16.7	2.1	•	•	•
Working Capital to Net Sales 40	0.0	0.1	•	0.1	0.1	0.0	0.1	•	•	•
Inventory to Working Capital 41	0.1	•	•	0.0	0.0	0.3	0.1	•	•	•
Total Receipts to Cash Flow 42	4.8	7.9	9.5	5.8	7.3	9.2	5.6	•	4.2	5.6
Cost of Goods to Cash Flow 43	2.5	5.2	7.7	1.9	3.2	6.9	3.7	•	1.5	3.3
Cash Flow to Total Debt 44	0.5	1.4	0.7	0.6	0.8	0.5	0.5	•	0.3	0.3

Selected Financial Factors (in Percentages)

Debt Ratio 45	65.0	61.6	90.9	75.6	62.7	76.8	59.8	•	76.4	73.5
Return on Total Assets 46	8.2	25.0	7.6	10.4	7.9	9.9	8.2	•	7.0	8.7
Return on Equity Before Income Taxes 47	20.4	61.0	79.2	39.2	19.7	39.9	18.8	•	25.5	22.1
Return on Equity After Income Taxes 48	17.3	60.7	64.5	38.4	16.4	33.7	15.9	•	21.4	17.4
Profit Margin (Before Income Tax) 49	5.0	18.9	3.6	1.2	3.4	1.9	2.7	4.3	6.1	4.1
Profit Margin (After Income Tax) 50	4.3	17.8	3.5	0.9	3.3	1.6	2.3	3.6	5.2	3.3

OTHER ADMINISTRATIVE AND SUPPORT SERVICES

Table I

Corporations with and without Net Income

MONEY AMOUNTS AND SIZE OF ASSETS IN THOUSANDS OF DOLLARS

Item Description for Accounting Period 7/02 Through 6/03	Total	Zero Assets	Under 500	500 to 1,000	1,000 to 5,000	5,000 to 10,000	10,000 to 25,000	25,000 to 50,000	50,000 to 100,000	100,000 to 250,000	250,000 to 500,000	500,000 to 2,500,000	2,500,000 and over
Number of Enterprises **1**	168415	23038	134976	5386	4053	442	267	108	61	35	22	21	5
Revenues ($ in Thousands)													
Net Sales **2**	158234104	3248261	48857430	11846292	23089198	6193163	8232307	6185224	6841789	5381921	6365186	18111677	13881657
Interest **3**	1008382	6074	36824	11227	16759	10980	11846	45113	54514	42319	83953	161437	527335
Rents **4**	93812	201	14994	5410	2232	1857	13288	6121	841	13080	2431	7920	25438
Royalties **5**	1175994	19441	112937	0	0	0	2627	42302	8719	8831	1227	67480	912430
Other Portfolio Income **6**	982652	10255	40158	12208	42044	53208	19401	18300	5096	24620	45844	26084	685434
Other Receipts **7**	4894206	64351	1396188	168043	109043	290236	500614	140504	275000	360550	160270	401672	1027735
Total Receipts **8**	166389150	3348583	50458531	12043180	23259276	6549444	8780083	6437564	7185959	5831321	6658911	18776270	17060029
Average Total Receipts **9**	988	145	374	2236	5739	14818	32884	59607	117803	166609	302678	894108	3412006
Operating Costs/Operating Income (%)													
Cost of Operations **10**	38.6	21.2	34.7	42.9	48.7	44.7	51.1	46.4	32.3	39.8	23.4	38.1	32.8
Salaries and Wages **11**	20.6	18.2	18.1	20.6	18.4	21.7	22.8	21.1	23.7	28.3	32.6	23.9	17.7
Taxes Paid **12**	3.4	2.9	3.4	3.8	3.5	4.5	3.6	3.5	3.7	4.1	4.2	3.6	1.9
Interest Paid **13**	1.8	1.4	0.7	0.7	0.9	1.0	1.4	2.2	2.1	3.5	2.5	2.7	6.6
Depreciation **14**	3.2	1.2	2.8	2.5	2.5	2.8	2.4	2.2	2.4	2.9	3.2	4.1	7.2
Amortization and Depletion **15**	1.2	0.3	0.1	0.1	0.2	0.4	1.2	0.9	1.2	3.2	2.3	1.4	6.7
Pensions and Other Deferred Comp. **16**	0.4	0.1	0.3	0.3	0.3	0.4	0.9	0.3	0.1	0.5	0.9	1.0	0.4
Employee Benefits **17**	1.8	3.0	1.0	1.5	1.6	1.4	2.5	2.3	2.2	2.4	3.3	2.6	1.8
Advertising **18**	1.2	1.3	1.3	1.5	0.7	0.4	0.5	1.1	0.6	2.0	0.9	0.8	2.7
Other Expenses **19**	26.7	28.2	20.7	20.7	17.5	22.3	18.6	22.3	32.8	24.8	28.4	21.6	49.7
Officers' Compensation **20**	4.0	5.2	7.8	5.1	3.7	3.5	2.1	1.4	1.2	1.7	0.7	0.8	0.2
Operating Margin **21**	*	*	1.7	0.4	2.1	*	*	*	*	*	*	*	*
Operating Margin Before Officers' Comp. **22**	1.0	2.8	9.5	5.5	5.8	0.5	*	*	*	*	*	*	0.2

Selected Average Balance Sheet ($ in Thousands)

Net Receivables 23	105	0	9	161	567	2035	4282	9458	15816	30230	55269	144581	780927
Inventories 24	10	0	2	44	91	122	419	1158	2056	3199	3904	7004	24614
Net Property, Plant and Equipment 25	112	0	25	204	504	1684	2664	5316	11205	20779	39580	168007	908851
Total Assets 26	819	0	67	706	1960	6906	15212	34208	70619	142596	349028	906733	14081347
Notes and Loans Payable 27	236	0	42	311	748	2619	6411	14916	26720	74507	99358	222835	2752858
All Other Liabilities 28	289	0	15	251	688	2423	6340	10676	22435	44495	146290	223582	5552771
Net Worth 29	294	0	10	144	524	1864	2461	8617	21464	23593	103379	460315	5775718

Selected Financial Ratios (Times to 1)

Current Ratio 30	0.9	•	1.3	1.4	1.3	1.3	1.2	1.3	1.1	1.2	1.1	1.4	0.5
Quick Ratio 31	0.7	•	1.1	1.0	1.0	1.1	0.9	1.0	0.9	0.9	0.8	1.0	0.3
Net Sales to Working Capital 32	•	•	49.9	19.9	21.6	14.8	20.0	12.5	29.6	14.8	21.4	12.3	•
Coverage Ratio 33	2.2	1.5	8.2	3.8	4.1	3.8	0.7	1.1	2.4	•	1.9	2.2	0.3
Total Asset Turnover 34	1.1	•	5.4	3.1	2.9	2.0	2.0	1.7	1.6	1.1	0.8	1.0	0.2
Inventory Turnover 35	34.9	•	64.3	21.6	30.5	51.3	37.6	23.0	17.6	19.1	17.3	47.0	37.0
Receivables Turnover 36	8.8	•	38.9	14.8	10.2	7.4	7.0	5.9	7.2	5.2	3.9	6.2	3.4
Total Liabilities to Net Worth 37	1.8	•	6.0	3.9	2.7	2.7	5.2	3.0	2.3	5.0	2.4	1.0	1.4
Current Assets to Working Capital 38	•	•	3.9	3.7	4.3	4.3	5.7	4.0	7.9	6.1	10.2	3.7	•
Current Liabilities to Working Capital 39	•	•	2.9	2.7	3.3	3.3	4.7	3.0	6.9	5.1	9.2	2.7	•
Working Capital to Net Sales 40	•	•	0.0	0.1	0.0	0.1	0.1	0.1	0.0	0.1	0.0	0.1	•
Inventory to Working Capital 41	•	•	0.3	0.4	0.3	0.2	0.3	0.3	0.5	0.3	0.2	0.1	•
Total Receipts to Cash Flow 42	4.2	2.3	3.5	6.0	6.2	4.9	7.1	5.8	3.1	8.1	3.8	5.1	2.6
Cost of Goods to Cash Flow 43	1.6	0.5	1.2	2.6	3.0	2.2	3.6	2.7	1.0	3.2	0.9	2.0	0.9
Cash Flow to Total Debt 44	0.4	•	1.8	0.7	0.6	0.6	0.3	0.4	0.7	0.2	0.3	0.4	0.1

Selected Financial Factors (in Percentages)

Debt Ratio 45	64.1	•	85.6	79.5	73.3	73.0	83.8	74.8	69.6	83.5	70.4	49.2	59.0
Return on Total Assets 46	4.6	•	30.6	8.6	10.8	7.6	2.1	4.2	7.7	•	4.0	5.5	0.4
Return on Equity Before Income Taxes 47	7.1	•	186.9	31.0	30.5	20.8	•	2.1	14.6	•	6.2	5.9	•
Return on Equity After Income Taxes 48	5.5	•	184.8	29.0	28.8	18.2	•	•	10.6	•	2.6	2.7	•
Profit Margin (Before Income Tax) 49	2.2	0.7	5.0	2.0	2.8	2.8	•	0.3	2.8	•	2.2	3.1	•
Profit Margin (After Income Tax) 50	1.7	0.0	4.9	1.9	2.6	2.4	•	•	2.0	•	0.9	1.4	•

Table II
Corporations with Net Income

OTHER ADMINISTRATIVE AND SUPPORT SERVICES

MONEY AMOUNTS AND SIZE OF ASSETS IN THOUSANDS OF DOLLARS

Item Description for Accounting Period 7/02 Through 6/03		Total	Zero Assets	Under 500	500 to 1,000	1,000 to 5,000	5,000 to 10,000	10,000 to 25,000	25,000 to 50,000	50,000 to 100,000	100,000 to 250,000	250,000 to 500,000	500,000 to 2,500,000	2,500,000 and over
Number of Enterprises	1	101512	10421	84103	3300	3064	314	169	61	0	17	14	0	0
Revenues ($ in Thousands)														
Net Sales	2	107298817	2144144	32456370	8270077	18900231	4935206	5845782	4929830	0	3446203	4188807	0	0
Interest	3	500860	5713	15820	4829	8563	6371	6601	8398	0	21454	49333	0	0
Rents	4	52800	201	9571	3738	956	524	12888	5304	0	11475	1860	0	0
Royalties	5	235934	4786	112937	0	0	0	0	34132	0	6605	1227	0	0
Other Portfolio Income	6	689788	9264	21125	9692	27975	52088	17163	3920	0	10055	20627	0	0
Other Receipts	7	2306155	82626	280341	67020	80557	239176	267015	91448	0	301744	154421	0	0
Total Receipts	8	111084354	2246734	32896164	8355356	19018282	5233365	6149449	5073032	0	3797536	4414275	0	0
Average Total Receipts	9	1094	216	391	2532	6207	16667	36387	83164	•	223384	315305	•	•
Operating Costs/Operating Income (%)														
Cost of Operations	10	40.3	15.9	33.3	48.8	49.2	45.5	52.2	48.7	•	43.1	21.9	•	•
Salaries and Wages	11	18.9	13.3	15.1	15.1	17.3	22.5	20.4	18.5	•	28.3	33.4	•	•
Taxes Paid	12	3.4	2.3	3.1	3.3	3.4	4.7	3.5	3.4	•	3.5	3.8	•	•
Interest Paid	13	1.2	1.1	0.6	0.6	0.7	0.8	0.7	1.0	•	2.1	1.9	•	•
Depreciation	14	2.5	1.0	2.4	2.0	2.2	2.6	2.0	1.8	•	2.8	2.7	•	•
Amortization and Depletion	15	0.5	0.3	0.1	0.1	0.1	0.3	0.2	0.4	•	0.3	2.2	•	•
Pensions and Other Deferred Comp.	16	0.5	0.1	0.3	0.2	0.3	0.3	0.7	0.3	•	0.6	1.3	•	•
Employee Benefits	17	1.7	3.7	0.9	1.2	1.6	1.2	1.9	2.3	•	2.9	2.3	•	•
Advertising	18	1.0	1.4	1.1	1.5	0.6	0.4	0.5	1.2	•	2.9	1.2	•	•
Other Expenses	19	22.1	46.3	27.2	16.6	15.9	17.8	14.8	18.1	•	18.8	26.7	•	•
Officers' Compensation	20	4.0	4.2	7.5	5.1	3.6	3.7	2.0	1.3	•	2.2	0.8	•	•
Operating Margin	21	4.0	10.4	8.4	5.4	5.2	0.1	1.0	3.0	•	•	1.9	•	•
Operating Margin Before Officers' Comp.	22	8.0	14.7	15.9	10.5	8.7	3.8	3.0	4.3	•	•	2.7	•	•

Selected Average Balance Sheet ($ in Thousands)

Net Receivables 23	115	13	159	550	1727	4617	11333	•	33575	67266
Inventories 24	13	0	61	87	149	507	1871	•	5132	4481
Net Property, Plant and Equipment 25	88	0	193	470	1678	2520	5543	•	25622	33412
Total Assets 26	700	0	686	1923	6605	14942	34612	•	146868	350097
Notes and Loans Payable 27	151	0	232	676	2218	4465	12115	•	53703	76491
All Other Liabilities 28	264	0	189	589	2163	5007	12443	•	48486	141899
Net Worth 29	284	0	265	658	2223	5471	10054	•	44680	131707

Selected Financial Ratios (Times to 1)

Current Ratio 30	1.0	•	1.6	1.9	1.5	1.4	1.2	•	1.1	1.3
Quick Ratio 31	0.7	•	1.3	1.4	1.2	1.1	1.0	•	0.8	0.9
Net Sales to Working Capital 32	•	•	33.5	12.0	15.1	14.3	21.9	•	29.9	7.6
Coverage Ratio 33	7.5	14.4	17.2	11.9	9.0	9.8	6.7	•	2.4	4.8
Total Asset Turnover 34	1.5	•	5.5	3.7	3.2	2.3	2.3	•	1.4	0.9
Inventory Turnover 35	32.4	•	63.4	20.2	34.8	48.1	21.0	•	17.0	14.6
Receivables Turnover 36	8.9	•	79.6	16.0	11.4	9.4	6.7	•	6.5	3.3
Total Liabilities to Net Worth 37	1.5	•	1.8	1.6	1.9	2.0	2.4	•	2.3	1.7
Current Assets to Working Capital 38	•	•	2.8	2.1	2.8	3.5	5.4	•	10.4	4.4
Current Liabilities to Working Capital 39	•	•	1.8	1.1	1.8	2.5	4.4	•	9.4	3.4
Working Capital to Net Sales 40	•	•	0.0	0.1	0.1	0.1	0.0	•	0.0	0.1
Inventory to Working Capital 41	•	•	0.2	0.3	0.2	0.2	0.5	•	0.8	0.1
Total Receipts to Cash Flow 42	4.0	1.7	3.1	5.5	5.5	5.6	4.9	•	5.8	3.4
Cost of Goods to Cash Flow 43	1.6	0.3	1.0	2.7	2.7	2.9	2.4	•	2.5	0.7
Cash Flow to Total Debt 44	0.6	•	2.8	1.1	0.9	0.7	0.7	•	0.3	0.4

Selected Financial Factors (in Percentages)

Debt Ratio 45	59.3	64.1	61.3	65.8	66.3	63.4	71.0	•	69.6	62.4
Return on Total Assets 46	13.1	56.5	25.8	21.0	16.5	16.0	16.2	•	6.8	7.8
Return on Equity Before Income Taxes 47	28.0	148.2	61.1	54.5	43.4	39.4	47.4	•	12.9	16.5
Return on Equity After Income Taxes 48	25.2	146.9	59.3	52.7	40.4	37.3	38.6	•	9.8	12.0
Profit Margin (Before Income Tax) 49	7.5	15.2	9.7	6.5	5.8	6.1	5.9	•	2.9	7.2
Profit Margin (After Income Tax) 50	6.8	14.2	9.6	6.3	5.6	5.7	4.8	•	2.2	5.3

Table I

Corporations with and without Net Income

OFFICES OF PHYSICIANS

MONEY AMOUNTS AND SIZE OF ASSETS IN THOUSANDS OF DOLLARS

Item Description for Accounting Period 7/02 Through 6/03	Total	Zero Assets	Under 500	500 to 1,000	1,000 to 5,000	5,000 to 10,000	10,000 to 25,000	25,000 to 50,000	50,000 to 100,000	100,000 to 250,000	250,000 to 500,000	500,000 to 2,500,000	2,500,000 and over
Number of Enterprises **1**	130935	11598	113537	3582	1802	247	119	32	10	3	4	0	0
Revenues ($ in Thousands)													
Net Sales **2**	176093351	2422581	112288987	16700352	21445066	7025741	4813912	3138257	1264646	556850	6436960	0	0
Interest **3**	125300	37	54001	9335	12302	6958	8484	3658	2251	2875	25399	0	0
Rents **4**	160586	334	83092	16066	2533	6037	12073	6318	4105	637	29392	0	0
Royalties **5**	1255	0	0	0	11	0	1244	0	0	0	0	0	0
Other Portfolio Income **6**	181780	16175	47585	19286	52400	8298	19470	4606	593	13	13355	0	0
Other Receipts **7**	4684809	-9495	2397984	196743	356138	125212	365016	77939	20954	601912	552403	0	0
Total Receipts **8**	181247081	2429632	114871649	16941782	21888450	7172246	5220199	3230778	1292549	1162287	7057509	0	0
Average Total Receipts **9**	1384	209	1012	4730	12136	29037	43867	100962	129255	387429	1764377	•	•
Operating Costs/Operating Income (%)													
Cost of Operations **10**	3.8	1.0	3.2	4.2	3.8	7.5	7.6	14.0	12.7	6.2	0.3	•	•
Salaries and Wages **11**	28.6	17.8	24.8	30.2	34.5	35.4	43.9	33.7	44.0	71.4	47.5	•	•
Taxes Paid **12**	3.2	3.0	3.1	3.5	3.0	2.6	2.9	2.2	3.8	3.5	4.2	•	•
Interest Paid **13**	0.5	0.3	0.3	0.4	0.4	0.6	0.8	0.9	0.7	4.6	3.3	•	•
Depreciation **14**	1.3	1.1	0.9	1.8	2.0	1.6	1.8	1.4	2.3	3.5	2.7	•	•
Amortization and Depletion **15**	0.1	0.2	0.0	0.1	0.1	0.3	0.3	0.2	0.2	1.1	0.9	•	•
Pensions and Other Deferred Comp. **16**	3.4	1.9	3.8	3.2	3.0	2.2	2.3	2.1	2.1	2.6	2.3	•	•
Employee Benefits **17**	2.1	1.6	1.8	1.9	1.8	2.3	3.2	5.3	3.9	2.6	5.2	•	•
Advertising **18**	0.5	1.3	0.4	0.6	0.6	0.5	0.3	0.5	0.3	0.2	0.1	•	•
Other Expenses **19**	31.2	39.2	29.1	25.7	32.4	40.8	42.8	41.4	35.0	111.4	43.1	•	•
Officers' Compensation **20**	25.0	28.9	30.4	26.5	18.2	7.9	3.1	0.8	0.5	0.2	0.8	•	•
Operating Margin **21**	0.5	3.8	2.1	1.8	0.2	•	•	•	•	•	•	•	•
Operating Margin Before Officers' Comp. **22**	25.4	32.7	32.5	28.3	18.4	6.3	•	•	•	•	•	•	•

Selected Average Balance Sheet ($ in Thousands)

Net Receivables 23	35	0	1	52	372	1819	4049	9933	9946	41523	541380
Inventories 24	1	0	0	1	21	42	144	208	1197	1042	1012
Net Property, Plant and Equipment 25	70	0	29	247	736	1935	4364	8722	27472	27645	526620
Total Assets 26	231	0	80	677	1939	6702	15223	31821	69762	168352	2410420
Notes and Loans Payable 27	101	0	42	394	980	3539	5049	10623	17779	52692	763076
All Other Liabilities 28	82	0	26	179	841	2653	8099	19905	33196	69113	691728
Net Worth 29	49	0	11	103	119	510	2076	1293	18787	46547	955616

Selected Financial Ratios (Times to 1)

Current Ratio 30	1.1	•	0.9	1.2	0.8	1.1	1.0	0.9	1.2	1.3	1.7
Quick Ratio 31	0.9	•	0.8	1.1	0.7	1.0	0.8	0.7	0.9	1.2	1.5
Net Sales to Working Capital 32	210.2	•	•	86.5	•	71.0	•	•	28.9	13.2	5.1
Coverage Ratio 33	8.3	15.5	18.0	8.6	6.1	1.7	0.2	1.4	•	1.3	0.7
Total Asset Turnover 34	5.8	•	12.4	6.9	6.1	4.2	2.7	3.1	1.8	1.1	0.7
Inventory Turnover 35	49.2	•	84.1	342.1	20.9	51.0	21.5	66.3	13.4	11.0	5.4
Receivables Turnover 36	44.1	•	468.8	87.3	32.1	17.2	10.0	11.3	11.2	3.7	5.9
Total Liabilities to Net Worth 37	3.7	•	6.2	5.6	15.3	12.1	6.3	23.6	2.7	2.6	1.5
Current Assets to Working Capital 38	14.5	•	•	5.3	•	8.8	•	•	5.7	3.9	2.4
Current Liabilities to Working Capital 39	13.5	•	•	4.3	•	7.8	•	•	4.7	2.9	1.4
Working Capital to Net Sales 40	0.0	•	•	0.0	•	0.0	•	•	0.0	0.1	0.2
Inventory to Working Capital 41	0.2	•	•	0.0	•	0.1	•	•	0.3	0.1	0.0
Total Receipts to Cash Flow 42	3.4	2.8	3.5	4.2	3.5	2.9	2.7	2.6	3.8	0.9	2.9
Cost of Goods to Cash Flow 43	0.1	0.0	0.1	0.2	0.1	0.2	0.2	0.4	0.5	0.1	0.0
Cash Flow to Total Debt 44	2.2	•	4.1	1.9	1.9	1.6	1.1	1.2	0.7	1.6	0.4

Selected Financial Factors (in Percentages)

Debt Ratio 45	78.9	•	86.1	84.7	93.9	92.4	86.4	95.9	73.1	72.4	60.4
Return on Total Assets 46	22.3	•	57.6	25.3	15.9	4.3	0.4	4.0	•	6.7	1.5
Return on Equity Before Income Taxes 47	92.6	•	392.0	146.3	217.1	23.9	•	30.2	•	•	5.8
Return on Equity After Income Taxes 48	90.4	•	386.7	141.7	213.0	19.1	•	15.5	•	•	•
Profit Margin (Before Income Tax) 49	3.4	4.1	4.4	3.2	2.2	0.4	•	0.4	•	1.5	•
Profit Margin (After Income Tax) 50	3.3	4.0	4.3	3.1	2.1	0.3	•	0.2	•	•	•

Table II

Corporations with Net Income

OFFICES OF PHYSICIANS

MONEY AMOUNTS AND SIZE OF ASSETS IN THOUSANDS OF DOLLARS

Item Description for Accounting Period 7/02 Through 6/03	Total	Zero Assets	Under 500	500 to 1,000	1,000 to 5,000	5,000 to 10,000	10,000 to 25,000	25,000 to 50,000	50,000 to 100,000	100,000 to 250,000	250,000 to 500,000	500,000 to 2,500,000	2,500,000 and over
Number of Enterprises **1**	76958	4750	68681	2318	1003	127	0	15	3	0	0	0	•
Revenues ($ in Thousands)													
Net Sales **2**	105425574	1758529	66193064	10864568	12460529	4604968	0	1912806	437132	0	0	0	•
Interest **3**	68313	7	30347	6547	4577	5336	0	2391	1023	0	0	0	•
Rents **4**	48356	227	30266	3416	1933	1826	0	1966	602	0	0	0	•
Royalties **5**	0	0	0	0	0	0	0	0	0	0	0	0	•
Other Portfolio Income **6**	127166	15603	19418	2769	49862	7237	0	3875	565	0	0	0	•
Other Receipts **7**	2869955	11519	1658738	149438	231677	90988	0	29322	257	0	0	0	•
Total Receipts **8**	108539364	1785885	67931833	11026738	12748578	4710355	0	1950360	439579	0	0	0	•
Average Total Receipts **9**	1410	376	989	4757	12710	37089	•	130024	146526	•	•	•	
Operating Costs/Operating Income (%)													
Cost of Operations **10**	3.2	1.2	2.1	5.5	3.2	6.6	•	19.2	14.5	•	•	•	•
Salaries and Wages **11**	26.2	22.2	21.7	29.0	33.3	33.7	•	29.0	49.7	•	•	•	•
Taxes Paid **12**	3.0	2.8	3.0	3.2	3.0	2.3	•	2.2	4.7	•	•	•	•
Interest Paid **13**	0.3	0.3	0.3	0.4	0.4	0.5	•	0.5	0.8	•	•	•	•
Depreciation **14**	1.1	1.1	1.0	1.3	1.9	1.3	•	0.8	2.6	•	•	•	•
Amortization and Depletion **15**	0.1	0.1	0.0	0.0	0.1	0.3	•	0.2	0.0	•	•	•	•
Pensions and Other Deferred Comp. **16**	3.0	0.7	3.0	3.8	3.1	2.0	•	2.3	3.8	•	•	•	•
Employee Benefits **17**	2.0	1.4	1.6	1.8	1.3	2.5	•	6.5	3.1	•	•	•	•
Advertising **18**	0.5	1.4	0.6	0.5	0.5	0.5	•	0.1	0.4	•	•	•	•
Other Expenses **19**	31.0	39.1	30.1	20.7	30.5	44.0	•	38.8	18.3	•	•	•	•
Officers' Compensation **20**	25.1	20.2	30.6	28.5	19.8	5.0	•	0.4	1.1	•	•	•	•
Operating Margin **21**	4.4	9.4	6.1	5.4	3.1	1.4	•	0.2	1.1	•	•	•	•
Operating Margin Before Officers' Comp. **22**	29.6	29.6	36.7	33.9	22.8	6.4	•	0.6	2.2	•	•	•	•

Selected Average Balance Sheet ($ in Thousands)

Net Receivables 23	17	0	1	44	310	1067	•	11341	10095
Inventories 24	1	0	0	0	29	49	•	96	1048
Net Property, Plant and Equipment 25	50	0	28	195	658	1746	•	7927	34391
Total Assets 26	180	0	84	685	1891	6923	•	32073	75377
Notes and Loans Payable 27	62	0	33	259	858	2335	•	8872	32781
All Other Liabilities 28	64	0	23	191	578	2933	•	15199	14804
Net Worth 29	54	0	28	235	455	1655	•	8003	27792

Selected Financial Ratios (Times to 1)

Current Ratio 30	1.2	•	1.2	1.3	1.2	1.2	•	1.1	2.1
Quick Ratio 31	1.0	•	1.0	1.2	1.0	0.9	•	0.9	1.8
Net Sales to Working Capital 32	115.1	•	169.4	60.3	91.1	74.7	•	59.3	10.0
Coverage Ratio 33	23.7	34.6	34.9	19.7	14.0	8.4	•	5.7	3.0
Total Asset Turnover 34	7.6	•	11.5	6.8	6.6	5.2	•	4.0	1.9
Inventory Turnover 35	41.6	•	43.2	3104.6	13.5	49.4	•	254.4	20.2
Receivables Turnover 36	58.6	•	428.0	101.4	37.1	26.4	•	22.5	24.8
Total Liabilities to Net Worth 37	2.3	•	2.0	1.9	3.2	3.2	•	3.0	1.7
Current Assets to Working Capital 38	6.7	•	6.5	3.9	6.6	7.5	•	9.1	1.9
Current Liabilities to Working Capital 39	5.7	•	5.5	2.9	5.6	6.5	•	8.1	0.9
Working Capital to Net Sales 40	0.0	•	0.0	0.0	0.0	0.0	•	0.0	0.1
Inventory to Working Capital 41	0.1	•	0.0	0.0	0.2	0.2	•	0.0	0.0
Total Receipts to Cash Flow 42	3.0	2.4	2.9	4.3	3.3	2.4	•	2.6	5.9
Cost of Goods to Cash Flow 43	0.1	0.0	0.1	0.2	0.1	0.2	•	0.5	0.9
Cash Flow to Total Debt 44	3.6	•	5.8	2.4	2.6	2.9	•	2.0	0.5

Selected Financial Factors (in Percentages)

Debt Ratio 45	69.9	•	67.0	65.7	75.9	76.1	•	75.0	63.1
Return on Total Assets 46	58.7	•	103.7	49.5	38.0	21.7	•	10.3	4.6
Return on Equity Before Income Taxes 47	186.8	•	305.5	136.7	146.5	80.1	•	33.9	8.4
Return on Equity After Income Taxes 48	183.3	•	302.0	133.6	144.5	77.3	•	28.8	7.4
Profit Margin (Before Income Tax) 49	7.4	11.0	8.7	6.9	5.4	3.7	•	2.1	1.6
Profit Margin (After Income Tax) 50	7.2	10.8	8.6	6.7	5.3	3.5	•	1.8	1.4

Table I

Corporations with and without Net Income

OFFICES OF DENTISTS

MONEY AMOUNTS AND SIZE OF ASSETS IN THOUSANDS OF DOLLARS

Item Description for Accounting Period 7/02 Through 6/03	Total	Zero Assets	Under 500	500 to 1,000	1,000 to 5,000	5,000 to 10,000	10,000 to 25,000	25,000 to 50,000	50,000 to 100,000	100,000 to 250,000	250,000 to 500,000	500,000 to 2,500,000	2,500,000 and over
Number of Enterprises **1**	59200	1607	55266	2096	216	0	8	5	0	3	•	•	•

Revenues ($ in Thousands)

Item Description for Accounting Period 7/02 Through 6/03	Total	Zero Assets	Under 500	500 to 1,000	1,000 to 5,000	5,000 to 10,000	10,000 to 25,000	25,000 to 50,000	50,000 to 100,000	100,000 to 250,000	250,000 to 500,000	500,000 to 2,500,000	2,500,000 and over
Net Sales **2**	45898535	462418	35656668	3977281	4627317	0	254822	457042	0	462987	•	•	•
Interest **3**	24623	56	23533	447	288	0	108	43	0	147	•	•	•
Rents **4**	10278	0	6660	32	3138	0	0	0	0	448	•	•	•
Royalties **5**	0	0	0	0	0	0	0	0	0	0	•	•	•
Other Portfolio Income **6**	197895	40322	157181	270	0	0	122	1	0	0	•	•	•
Other Receipts **7**	650274	271	595538	19095	6553	0	742	18891	0	9184	•	•	•
Total Receipts **8**	46781605	503067	36439580	3997125	4637296	0	255794	475977	0	472766	•	•	•
Average Total Receipts **9**	790	313	659	1907	21469	•	31974	95195	•	157589	•	•	•

Operating Costs/Operating Income (%)

Item Description for Accounting Period 7/02 Through 6/03	Total	Zero Assets	Under 500	500 to 1,000	1,000 to 5,000	5,000 to 10,000	10,000 to 25,000	25,000 to 50,000	50,000 to 100,000	100,000 to 250,000	250,000 to 500,000	500,000 to 2,500,000	2,500,000 and over
Cost of Operations **10**	5.5	1.9	5.1	9.2	5.8	•	10.8	2.6	•	10.7	•	•	•
Salaries and Wages **11**	23.4	26.1	22.4	25.5	24.2	•	30.0	42.4	•	46.1	•	•	•
Taxes Paid **12**	3.5	3.9	3.7	3.4	1.8	•	3.3	2.9	•	4.2	•	•	•
Interest Paid **13**	0.9	0.7	0.8	2.0	0.2	•	1.4	3.1	•	7.2	•	•	•
Depreciation **14**	2.0	0.9	2.1	3.8	0.5	•	2.9	2.6	•	2.5	•	•	•
Amortization and Depletion **15**	0.4	1.1	0.3	0.8	0.0	•	0.8	1.8	•	4.2	•	•	•
Pensions and Other Deferred Comp. **16**	2.4	5.0	2.7	2.3	0.4	•	2.1	0.0	•	0.1	•	•	•
Employee Benefits **17**	1.2	1.0	1.3	1.0	0.3	•	1.5	1.1	•	2.4	•	•	•
Advertising **18**	1.0	0.3	1.0	1.2	0.2	•	1.3	4.0	•	1.0	•	•	•
Other Expenses **19**	34.7	37.2	32.0	26.7	62.1	•	39.1	35.8	•	27.7	•	•	•
Officers' Compensation **20**	20.7	19.5	24.0	17.6	2.7	•	1.3	0.3	•	0.3	•	•	•
Operating Margin **21**	4.4	2.4	4.6	6.5	1.7	•	5.5	3.4	•	•	•	•	•
Operating Margin Before Officers' Comp. **22**	25.0	21.9	28.6	24.1	4.4	•	6.7	3.6	•	•	•	•	•

Selected Average Balance Sheet ($ in Thousands)

Net Receivables 23	6	•	3	16	28	3182	16669	10141
Inventories 24	0	•	0	0	3	30	694	2209
Net Property, Plant and Equipment 25	55	•	44	281	514	3397	8953	18499
Total Assets 26	145	•	111	690	1451	14270	41921	119521
Notes and Loans Payable 27	93	•	69	522	481	4222	36895	96669
All Other Liabilities 28	24	•	19	45	467	4208	7728	34012
Net Worth 29	28	•	23	124	503	5839	-2701	-11160

Selected Financial Ratios (Times to 1)

Current Ratio 30	1.1	•	1.3	1.3	1.8	1.2	0.6	0.2
Quick Ratio 31	1.0	•	1.1	1.1	1.0	1.1	0.5	0.2
Net Sales to Working Capital 32	164.6	•	89.4	65.0	55.2	28.1	•	•
Coverage Ratio 33	7.9	18.0	9.9	4.5	11.6	5.1	3.4	0.4
Total Asset Turnover 34	5.4	•	5.8	2.7	14.8	2.2	2.2	1.3
Inventory Turnover 35	108.5	•	131.9	•	430.6	116.7	3.4	7.4
Receivables Turnover 36	130.3	•	182.3	123.5	1396.7	15.9	7.6	30.4
Total Liabilities to Net Worth 37	4.2	•	3.8	4.6	1.9	1.4	•	•
Current Assets to Working Capital 38	9.4	•	4.8	4.5	2.3	5.3	•	•
Current Liabilities to Working Capital 39	8.4	•	3.8	3.5	1.3	4.3	•	•
Working Capital to Net Sales 40	0.0	•	0.0	0.0	0.0	0.0	•	•
Inventory to Working Capital 41	0.1	•	0.0	0.0	0.0	0.0	•	•
Total Receipts to Cash Flow 42	2.9	•	3.2	3.6	1.6	2.5	2.8	6.4
Cost of Goods to Cash Flow 43	0.2	•	0.2	0.3	0.1	0.3	0.1	0.7
Cash Flow to Total Debt 44	2.3	•	2.3	0.9	14.2	1.5	0.7	0.2

Selected Financial Factors (in Percentages)

Debt Ratio 45	80.9	•	79.2	82.1	65.4	59.1	106.4	109.3
Return on Total Assets 46	38.4	•	44.0	24.9	31.6	16.1	23.2	3.9
Return on Equity Before Income Taxes 47	175.5	•	190.7	108.0	83.5	31.6	•	58.5
Return on Equity After Income Taxes 48	174.2	•	189.4	107.5	83.5	29.1	•	63.2
Profit Margin (Before Income Tax) 49	6.3	11.2	6.8	7.0	2.0	5.8	7.5	7.5
Profit Margin (After Income Tax) 50	6.2	10.8	6.8	7.0	2.0	5.3	7.5	•

Table II

Corporations with Net Income

OFFICES OF DENTISTS

MONEY AMOUNTS AND SIZE OF ASSETS IN THOUSANDS OF DOLLARS

Item Description for Accounting Period 7/02 Through 6/03	Total	Zero Assets	Under 500	500 to 1,000	1,000 to 5,000	5,000 to 10,000	10,000 to 25,000	25,000 to 50,000	50,000 to 100,000	100,000 to 250,000	250,000 to 500,000	500,000 to 2,500,000	2,500,000 and over
Number of Enterprises 1	39988	1348	37020	1466	0	0	0	5	0	0	•	•	•
Revenues ($ in Thousands)													
Net Sales 2	30195346	422096	25774438	2547863	0	0	0	562591	0	0	•	•	•
Interest 3	11858	2	11105	406	0	0	0	48	0	0	•	•	•
Rents 4	5661	0	5240	0	0	0	0	421	0	0	•	•	•
Royalties 5	0	0	0	0	0	0	0	0	0	0	•	•	•
Other Portfolio Income 6	142594	40131	102069	270	0	0	0	1	0	0	•	•	•
Other Receipts 7	294100	0	268055	686	0	0	0	18066	0	0	•	•	•
Total Receipts 8	30649559	462229	26160907	2549225	0	0	0	581127	0	0	•	•	•
Average Total Receipts 9	766	343	707	1739	•	•	•	116225	0	0	•	•	•
Operating Costs/Operating Income (%)													
Cost of Operations 10	5.3	2.1	5.1	8.0	•	•	•	3.8	•	•	•	•	•
Salaries and Wages 11	23.2	24.3	22.1	26.7	•	•	•	42.4	•	•	•	•	•
Taxes Paid 12	3.5	4.0	3.5	3.4	•	•	•	3.5	•	•	•	•	•
Interest Paid 13	0.9	0.4	0.7	2.6	•	•	•	2.7	•	•	•	•	•
Depreciation 14	1.9	0.4	1.8	3.3	•	•	•	2.8	•	•	•	•	•
Amortization and Depletion 15	0.3	•	0.2	1.1	•	•	•	2.2	•	•	•	•	•
Pensions and Other Deferred Comp. 16	2.5	5.5	2.6	2.2	•	•	•	0.0	•	•	•	•	•
Employee Benefits 17	1.3	0.7	1.4	1.3	•	•	•	1.5	•	•	•	•	•
Advertising 18	1.1	0.2	1.1	1.4	•	•	•	2.8	•	•	•	•	•
Other Expenses 19	29.1	35.0	29.5	24.0	•	•	•	34.3	•	•	•	•	•
Officers' Compensation 20	21.8	21.2	23.3	14.1	•	•	•	0.2	•	•	•	•	•
Operating Margin 21	9.1	6.3	8.8	12.0	•	•	•	3.7	•	•	•	•	•
Operating Margin Before Officers' Comp. 22	30.8	27.5	32.1	26.1	•	•	•	4.0	•	•	•	•	•

Selected Average Balance Sheet ($ in Thousands)

Net Receivables 23	7	0	4	24	·	15639
Inventories 24	0	0	0	·	·	745
Net Property, Plant and Equipment 25	58	0	47	285	·	13325
Total Assets 26	151	0	118	742	·	61231
Notes and Loans Payable 27	85	0	61	557	·	43162
All Other Liabilities 28	20	0	17	45	·	7958
Net Worth 29	47	0	39	139	·	10111

Selected Financial Ratios (Times to 1)

Current Ratio 30	1.5	·	1.5	1.5	·	0.6
Quick Ratio 31	1.3	·	1.4	1.3	·	0.5
Net Sales to Working Capital 32	47.9	·	49.0	27.9	·	
Coverage Ratio 33	12.9	39.4	16.2	5.6	·	3.6
Total Asset Turnover 34	5.0	·	5.9	2.3	·	1.8
Inventory Turnover 35	93.9	·	106.8	·	·	5.8
Receivables Turnover 36	141.8	·	210.6	147.4	·	14.4
Total Liabilities to Net Worth 37	2.2	·	2.0	4.3	·	5.1
Current Assets to Working Capital 38	3.2	·	2.9	2.8	·	
Current Liabilities to Working Capital 39	2.2	·	1.9	1.8	·	
Working Capital to Net Sales 40	0.0	·	0.0	0.0	·	
Inventory to Working Capital 41	0.0	·	0.0	·	·	
Total Receipts to Cash Flow 42	3.0	3.1	3.0	3.3	·	3.1
Cost of Goods to Cash Flow 43	0.2	0.1	0.2	0.3	·	0.1
Cash Flow to Total Debt 44	2.4	·	2.9	0.9	·	0.7

Selected Financial Factors (in Percentages)

Debt Ratio 45	69.2	·	66.7	81.2	·	83.5
Return on Total Assets 46	57.2	·	65.1	34.3	·	17.9
Return on Equity Before Income Taxes 47	171.2	·	183.5	150.4	·	78.0
Return on Equity After Income Taxes 48	170.1	·	182.4	149.7	·	75.0
Profit Margin (Before Income Tax) 49	10.6	15.8	10.3	12.1	·	7.0
Profit Margin (After Income Tax) 50	10.5	15.4	10.3	12.0	·	6.7

Table I

Corporations with and without Net Income

OFFICES OF OTHER HEALTH PRACTITIONERS

MONEY AMOUNTS AND SIZE OF ASSETS IN THOUSANDS OF DOLLARS

Item Description for Accounting Period 7/02 Through 6/03	Total	Zero Assets	Under 500	500 to 1,000	1,000 to 5,000	5,000 to 10,000	10,000 to 25,000	25,000 to 50,000	50,000 to 100,000	100,000 to 250,000	250,000 to 500,000	500,000 to 2,500,000	2,500,000 and over
Number of Enterprises **1**	75490	8490	65287	1157	401	73	43	21	13	5	0	•	•
Revenues ($ in Thousands)													
Net Sales **2**	35180370	1230307	19879486	1353851	4688501	1595176	1385400	1084356	1335834	2627460	0	•	•
Interest **3**	57354	343	6318	1717	1378	3522	4154	6194	17822	15906	0	•	•
Rents **4**	18439	0	622	1340	3531	1428	3437	2289	5792	0	0	•	•
Royalties **5**	51	0	51	0	0	0	0	0	0	0	0	•	•
Other Portfolio Income **6**	120553	61252	39672	9285	759	518	1450	2626	826	4165	0	•	•
Other Receipts **7**	741830	24917	159544	12678	66678	-4865	90474	236922	144157	11325	0	•	•
Total Receipts **8**	36118597	1316819	20085693	1378871	4760847	1595779	1484915	1332387	1504431	2658856	0	•	•
Average Total Receipts **9**	478	155	308	1192	11872	21860	34533	63447	115725	531771	•	•	•
Operating Costs/Operating Income (%)													
Cost of Operations **10**	12.3	1.5	8.4	19.8	30.5	12.9	23.7	15.8	11.3	3.2	•	•	•
Salaries and Wages **11**	23.1	9.4	19.8	21.9	32.1	19.7	23.8	15.5	26.8	41.7	•	•	•
Taxes Paid **12**	3.0	2.2	3.5	4.7	3.1	2.3	1.6	1.8	2.0	1.6	•	•	•
Interest Paid **13**	0.8	0.1	0.5	1.1	0.4	1.1	0.7	1.3	2.4	2.1	•	•	•
Depreciation **14**	1.5	0.6	1.6	1.2	0.9	1.1	1.2	1.5	2.7	1.6	•	•	•
Amortization and Depletion **15**	0.3	0.1	0.1	0.4	0.2	0.5	1.4	0.8	0.7	1.1	•	•	•
Pensions and Other Deferred Comp. **16**	1.0	1.7	1.2	2.1	1.2	0.1	0.3	0.3	0.3	0.1	•	•	•
Employee Benefits **17**	1.6	0.3	1.1	1.5	1.2	1.2	6.8	1.4	2.0	3.3	•	•	•
Advertising **18**	1.6	1.0	2.0	2.0	1.2	3.0	0.3	0.9	0.1	0.4	•	•	•
Other Expenses **19**	39.3	58.2	35.6	26.6	25.7	56.7	48.5	81.8	64.0	43.9	•	•	•
Officers' Compensation **20**	11.5	18.0	17.2	13.9	3.4	1.7	0.9	0.8	0.9	0.4	•	•	•
Operating Margin **21**	3.9	7.0	8.9	4.7	0.0	•	•	•	•	0.6	•	•	•
Operating Margin Before Officers' Comp. **22**	15.5	25.0	26.1	18.6	3.4	1.4	•	•	•	1.0	•	•	•

Selected Average Balance Sheet ($ in Thousands)

Net Receivables 23	24	0	6	116	641	2116	4382	5696	11704	81120
Inventories 24	3	0	2	24	6	357	166	465	592	1420
Net Property, Plant and Equipment 25	28	0	16	145	697	1499	2181	5208	16811	26181
Total Assets 26	123	0	54	600	2505	7306	15570	36596	67748	230994
Notes and Loans Payable 27	53	0	27	302	1081	2808	3657	14487	21768	101033
All Other Liabilities 28	37	0	11	50	935	4699	7189	9367	28486	91465
Net Worth 29	32	0	17	249	489	-201	4724	12741	17494	38496

Selected Financial Ratios (Times to 1)

Current Ratio 30	1.4	•	2.0	2.3	1.2	0.8	1.1	0.9	0.9	1.2
Quick Ratio 31	1.1	•	1.7	2.0	1.0	0.7	0.9	0.7	0.8	1.1
Net Sales to Working Capital 32	27.8	•	20.9	6.6	59.5	•	33.9	•	•	26.6
Coverage Ratio 33	9.5	158.7	19.1	6.8	4.8	0.8	•	1.9	0.8	1.8
Total Asset Turnover 34	3.8	•	5.6	1.9	4.7	3.0	2.1	1.4	1.5	2.3
Inventory Turnover 35	18.9	•	11.8	9.8	593.3	7.9	46.1	17.5	19.6	11.9
Receivables Turnover 36	17.9	•	43.4	10.6	19.9	8.3	6.4	10.5	9.3	5.4
Total Liabilities to Net Worth 37	2.8	•	2.3	1.4	4.1	•	2.3	1.9	2.9	5.0
Current Assets to Working Capital 38	3.7	•	2.0	1.8	7.5	•	10.2	•	•	5.5
Current Liabilities to Working Capital 39	2.7	•	1.0	0.8	6.5	•	9.2	•	•	4.5
Working Capital to Net Sales 40	0.0	•	0.0	0.2	0.0	•	0.0	•	•	0.0
Inventory to Working Capital 41	0.2	•	0.2	0.1	0.0	•	0.2	•	•	0.1
Total Receipts to Cash Flow 42	2.5	1.5	2.7	3.8	4.2	1.9	2.3	1.3	1.7	2.2
Cost of Goods to Cash Flow 43	0.3	0.0	0.2	0.8	1.3	0.2	0.5	0.2	0.2	0.1
Cash Flow to Total Debt 44	2.0	•	3.0	0.9	1.4	1.5	1.3	1.7	1.2	1.2

Selected Financial Factors (in Percentages)

Debt Ratio 45	73.6	•	69.5	58.5	80.5	102.8	69.7	65.2	74.2	83.3
Return on Total Assets 46	28.0	•	58.5	15.0	9.1	2.6	•	3.3	2.9	8.9
Return on Equity Before Income Taxes 47	95.1	•	182.0	30.8	37.0	21.8	•	4.4	•	24.1
Return on Equity After Income Taxes 48	92.4	•	180.6	28.9	32.8	81.6	•	0.8	•	20.9
Profit Margin (Before Income Tax) 49	6.6	14.0	9.9	6.5	1.5	•	1.1	•	•	1.8
Profit Margin (After Income Tax) 50	6.4	13.7	9.8	6.1	1.4	•	0.2	•	•	1.5

Table II

Corporations with Net Income

OFFICES OF OTHER HEALTH PRACTITIONERS

MONEY AMOUNTS AND SIZE OF ASSETS IN THOUSANDS OF DOLLARS

Item Description for Accounting Period 7/02 Through 6/03	Total	Zero Assets	Under 500	500 to 1,000	1,000 to 5,000	5,000 to 10,000	10,000 to 25,000	25,000 to 50,000	50,000 to 100,000	100,000 to 250,000	250,000 to 500,000	500,000 to 2,500,000	2,500,000 and over
Number of Enterprises 1	53281	4306	47790	906	0	43	26	10	8	0	•	•	•
Revenues ($ in Thousands)													
Net Sales 2	23732092	855419	14153685	1074643	0	885449	1129218	491992	853424	0	•	•	•
Interest 3	22383	215	4059	493	0	2453	3683	4236	6111	0	•	•	•
Rents 4	8523	0	220	1340	0	1354	361	748	1170	0	•	•	•
Royalties 5	0	0	0	0	0	0	0	0	0	0			
Other Portfolio Income 6	115634	61252	38327	9285	0	46	1311	42	794	0	•	•	•
Other Receipts 7	303496	4655	99181	543	0	3141	24571	20261	73604	0	•	•	•
Total Receipts 8	24182128	921541	14295472	1086304	0	892443	1159144	517279	935103	0	•	•	•
Average Total Receipts 9	454	214	299	1199	•	20754	44582	51728	116888	•	•	•	•
Operating Costs/Operating Income (%)													
Cost of Operations 10	15.1	2.2	9.7	19.5	•	0.1	27.6	15.8	17.1	•	•	•	•
Salaries and Wages 11	18.9	10.8	18.0	16.9	•	14.7	17.0	17.0	16.4	•	•	•	•
Taxes Paid 12	2.9	2.0	3.2	4.9	•	1.4	1.4	1.6	1.5	•	•	•	•
Interest Paid 13	0.5	0.1	0.6	1.2	•	0.3	0.3	0.9	0.9	•	•	•	•
Depreciation 14	1.4	0.8	1.6	1.2	•	0.4	0.6	1.0	1.2	•	•	•	•
Amortization and Depletion 15	0.2	0.1	0.2	0.5	•	0.0	0.1	1.1	0.7	•	•	•	•
Pensions and Other Deferred Comp. 16	1.1	1.7	1.1	2.5	•	0.0	0.3	0.6	0.3	•	•	•	•
Employee Benefits 17	1.3	0.1	0.9	1.8	•	0.8	6.7	1.4	1.6	•	•	•	•
Advertising 18	1.5	1.5	2.2	1.7	•	0.2	0.2	0.2	0.1	•	•	•	•
Other Expenses 19	34.5	45.2	31.5	26.0	•	72.9	41.4	57.2	66.5	•	•	•	•
Officers' Compensation 20	11.7	18.7	16.4	15.2	•	1.8	0.8	1.1	0.6	•	•	•	•
Operating Margin 21	10.7	16.9	14.7	8.5	•	7.3	3.7	2.2	•	•	•	•	•
Operating Margin Before Officers' Comp. 22	22.4	35.6	31.1	23.7	•	9.1	4.5	3.2	•	•	•	•	•

Selected Average Balance Sheet ($ in Thousands)

Net Receivables 23	18	0	6	104	•	2670	5049	3182	11408
Inventories 24	3	0	3	17	•	26	137	294	303
Net Property, Plant and Equipment 25	23	0	14	173	•	429	1389	2126	9648
Total Assets 26	108	0	57	593	•	6581	15324	36844	64292
Notes and Loans Payable 27	36	0	23	298	•	1721	2001	12175	10800
All Other Liabilities 28	30	0	9	46	•	3571	8437	7359	32430
Net Worth 29	42	0	25	250	•	1289	4886	17310	21061

Selected Financial Ratios (Times to 1)

Current Ratio 30	1.6	•	3.1	1.7	•	1.2	1.1	0.9	0.9
Quick Ratio 31	1.4	•	2.5	1.5	•	1.1	0.9	0.8	0.8
Net Sales to Working Capital 32	21.0	•	14.1	10.3	•	29.0	63.4	•	•
Coverage Ratio 33	24.2	259.8	27.6	9.0	•	30.0	23.6	9.4	4.0
Total Asset Turnover 34	4.1	•	5.2	2.0	•	3.1	2.8	1.3	1.7
Inventory Turnover 35	24.5	•	11.3	13.5	•	1.0	87.2	26.5	60.1
Receivables Turnover 36	23.0	•	44.5	11.5	•	8.8	8.9	11.3	9.8
Total Liabilities to Net Worth 37	1.6	•	1.3	1.4	•	4.1	2.1	1.1	2.1
Current Assets to Working Capital 38	2.7	•	1.5	2.4	•	6.3	16.6	•	•
Current Liabilities to Working Capital 39	1.7	•	0.5	1.4	•	5.3	15.6	•	•
Working Capital to Net Sales 40	0.0	•	0.1	0.1	•	0.0	0.0	•	•
Inventory to Working Capital 41	0.1	•	0.1	0.0	•	0.0	0.2	•	•
Total Receipts to Cash Flow 42	2.5	1.5	2.6	3.4	•	1.3	2.2	1.6	1.5
Cost of Goods to Cash Flow 43	0.4	0.0	0.3	0.7	•	0.0	0.6	0.3	0.3
Cash Flow to Total Debt 44	2.7	•	3.6	1.0	•	3.1	1.9	1.6	1.7

Selected Financial Factors (in Percentages)

Debt Ratio 45	60.9	•	55.6	57.9	•	80.4	68.1	53.0	67.2
Return on Total Assets 46	54.1	•	85.1	21.6	•	26.2	18.7	10.9	6.1
Return on Equity Before Income Taxes 47	132.5	•	184.7	45.5	•	129.5	56.3	20.7	13.8
Return on Equity After Income Taxes 48	129.5	•	183.5	43.1	•	113.6	51.1	15.2	11.3
Profit Margin (Before Income Tax) 49	12.6	24.7	15.7	9.6	•	8.1	6.3	7.3	2.7
Profit Margin (After Income Tax) 50	12.3	24.2	15.6	9.1	•	7.1	5.8	5.3	2.2

Table I

Corporations with and without Net Income

OUTPATIENT CARE CENTERS

MONEY AMOUNTS AND SIZE OF ASSETS IN THOUSANDS OF DOLLARS

Item Description for Accounting Period 7/02 Through 6/03	Total	Zero Assets	Under 500	500 to 1,000	1,000 to 5,000	5,000 to 10,000	10,000 to 25,000	25,000 to 50,000	50,000 to 100,000	100,000 to 250,000	250,000 to 500,000	500,000 to 2,500,000	2,500,000 and over
Number of Enterprises **1**	5341	484	4262	107	361	37	41	19	5	11	3	10	0
Revenues ($ in Thousands)													
Net Sales **2**	37030673	715647	3254106	185772	1644561	939000	1196684	1327294	638047	4090934	267739	22770889	0
Interest **3**	160853	1775	921	0	738	645	4277	5172	6504	15892	6973	117955	0
Rents **4**	28143	0	24	0	109	0	979	1115	2043	14314	0	9558	0
Royalties **5**	292786	0	0	0	0	0	0	0	0	2618	0	290168	0
Other Portfolio Income **6**	72634	30663	785	10500	87	473	1632	1162	137	3517	228	23451	0
Other Receipts **7**	564721	20094	34100	6116	-10748	8423	51675	17348	7533	113691	81747	234743	0
Total Receipts **8**	38149810	768179	3289936	202388	1634747	948541	1255247	1352091	654264	4240966	356687	23446764	0
Average Total Receipts **9**	7143	1587	772	1891	4528	25636	30616	71163	130853	385542	118896	2344676	•
Operating Costs/Operating Income (%)													
Cost of Operations **10**	49.6	85.0	16.8	0.0	14.7	12.7	36.6	15.0	2.1	48.5	40.0	61.9	•
Salaries and Wages **11**	13.1	0.4	16.3	39.3	31.5	21.6	15.0	16.2	22.9	11.7	29.2	10.7	•
Taxes Paid **12**	2.0	0.1	3.0	5.4	3.7	0.8	1.5	1.5	2.1	0.8	1.0	2.1	•
Interest Paid **13**	2.0	0.1	0.7	0.2	0.9	0.4	1.2	0.7	1.9	0.3	10.6	2.7	•
Depreciation **14**	1.7	0.3	1.3	2.0	1.9	0.4	1.4	1.1	1.2	0.9	4.9	2.0	•
Amortization and Depletion **15**	0.8	0.2	0.1	0.0	0.3	0.1	0.1	0.4	0.7	0.4	11.5	1.1	•
Pensions and Other Deferred Comp. **16**	0.3	0.0	0.4	1.4	0.2	0.1	0.3	0.3	0.3	0.0	0.4	0.3	•
Employee Benefits **17**	3.9	0.1	1.0	0.3	2.8	5.8	16.5	19.4	2.9	7.2	0.6	2.4	•
Advertising **18**	0.3	0.0	0.8	0.5	0.3	0.7	0.3	0.3	0.4	0.4	1.0	0.2	•
Other Expenses **19**	25.2	21.6	41.7	45.2	34.4	58.7	32.5	45.6	66.3	29.3	34.6	17.1	•
Officers' Compensation **20**	1.6	0.7	12.6	0.1	2.3	0.8	1.0	0.7	0.4	0.7	4.6	0.3	•
Operating Margin **21**	•	•	5.3	5.6	7.2	•	•	•	•	•	•	•	•
Operating Margin Before Officers' Comp. **22**	1.1	•	17.9	5.6	9.5	•	•	•	•	0.5	•	•	•

Selected Average Balance Sheet ($ in Thousands)

Net Receivables 23	562	0	4	255	409	2732	3121	4113	10837	18152	17111	220033	•
Inventories 24	68	0	1	0	52	15	247	438	693	2103	3850	15342	•
Net Property, Plant and Equipment 25	529	0	44	176	656	748	3544	5377	14116	27172	10124	170564	•
Total Assets 26	4889	0	108	560	1969	7679	14915	32301	64248	142994	275716	2064974	•
Notes and Loans Payable 27	1733	0	107	211	1099	4532	5223	10189	22119	10623	121954	720915	•
All Other Liabilities 28	1444	0	27	384	632	5202	5876	17415	15405	42749	31607	592248	•
Net Worth 29	1713	0	-26	-35	238	-2055	3815	4697	26725	89623	122155	751811	•

Selected Financial Ratios (Times to 1)

Current Ratio 30	1.3	•	1.6	0.5	1.2	0.9	1.3	0.9	1.6	2.2	2.0	1.2	•
Quick Ratio 31	0.9	•	1.2	0.5	0.8	0.8	1.0	0.6	1.3	1.9	1.1	0.8	•
Net Sales to Working Capital 32	17.9	•	45.3	•	27.9	•	16.8	•	13.2	7.6	4.8	17.4	•
Coverage Ratio 33	2.3	•	10.8	67.0	8.7	•	•	2.3	1.7	13.9	0.5	1.8	•
Total Asset Turnover 34	1.4	•	7.0	3.1	2.3	3.3	2.0	2.2	2.0	2.6	0.3	1.1	•
Inventory Turnover 35	50.7	•	97.4	•	12.8	222.6	43.3	23.9	3.9	85.8	9.3	91.9	•
Receivables Turnover 36	13.2	•	117.0	13.6	9.9	6.1	8.7	11.2	7.1	19.1	4.7	16.1	•
Total Liabilities to Net Worth 37	1.9	•	•	•	7.3	•	2.9	5.9	1.4	0.6	1.3	1.7	•
Current Assets to Working Capital 38	4.5	•	2.6	•	7.6	•	4.6	•	2.8	1.8	2.0	5.1	•
Current Liabilities to Working Capital 39	3.5	•	1.6	•	6.6	•	3.6	•	1.8	0.8	1.0	4.1	•
Working Capital to Net Sales 40	0.1	•	0.0	•	0.0	0.1	0.1	•	0.1	0.1	0.2	0.1	•
Inventory to Working Capital 41	0.2	•	0.1	•	0.4	•	0.2	•	0.0	0.0	0.4	0.2	•
Total Receipts to Cash Flow 42	4.1	6.9	2.6	2.0	2.7	1.8	3.5	2.3	1.5	3.3	3.9	6.1	•
Cost of Goods to Cash Flow 43	2.1	5.8	0.4	0.0	0.4	0.2	1.3	0.3	0.0	1.6	1.6	3.8	•
Cash Flow to Total Debt 44	0.5	•	2.2	1.5	1.0	1.4	0.8	1.1	2.2	2.1	0.1	0.3	•

Selected Financial Factors (in Percentages)

Debt Ratio 45	65.0	•	123.6	106.3	87.9	126.8	74.4	85.5	58.4	37.3	55.7	63.6	•
Return on Total Assets 46	6.3	•	50.0	45.7	17.3	•	3.3	•	6.6	9.8	1.7	•	•
Return on Equity Before Income Taxes 47	10.1	•	•	•	126.9	14.6	•	12.8	6.6	14.4	•	6.2	•
Return on Equity After Income Taxes 48	7.9	•	•	•	121.2	14.6	5.9	•	4.0	10.9	•	4.5	•
Profit Margin (Before Income Tax) 49	2.5	•	6.4	14.5	6.6	•	0.9	1.4	1.4	3.5	•	2.1	•
Profit Margin (After Income Tax) 50	2.0	•	6.3	14.5	6.3	•	0.4	•	0.8	2.6	•	1.5	•

Table II

Corporations with Net Income

OUTPATIENT CARE CENTERS

MONEY AMOUNTS AND SIZE OF ASSETS IN THOUSANDS OF DOLLARS

Item Description for Accounting Period 7/02 Through 6/03	Total	Zero Assets	Under 500	500 to 1,000	1,000 to 5,000	5,000 to 10,000	10,000 to 25,000	25,000 to 50,000	50,000 to 100,000	100,000 to 250,000	250,000 to 500,000	500,000 to 2,500,000	2,500,000 and over
Number of Enterprises **1**	3273	74	2769	82	282	16	23	12	0	0	0	0	0
Revenues ($ in Thousands)													
Net Sales **2**	30951029	8824	2995756	183483	1275709	443184	647172	1581884	0	0	0	0	0
Interest **3**	128579	1765	881	0	525	419	2984	7323	0	0	0	0	0
Rents **4**	10176	0	24	0	84	0	359	1029	0	0	0	0	0
Royalties **5**	285846	0	0	0	0	0	0	0	0	0	0	0	0
Other Portfolio Income **6**	53634	30643	250	5	65	0	747	101	0	0	0	0	0
Other Receipts **7**	459680	19773	33899	5867	-18356	2287	46458	8641	0	0	0	0	0
Total Receipts **8**	31888944	61005	3030810	189355	1258027	445890	697720	1598978	0	0	0	0	0
Average Total Receipts **9**	9743	824	1095	2309	4461	27868	30336	133248	•	•	•	•	•
Operating Costs/Operating Income (%)													
Cost of Operations **10**	54.9	0.4	17.8	0.0	15.8	26.7	34.3	11.9	•	•	•	•	•
Salaries and Wages **11**	10.8	28.2	14.6	39.8	31.7	2.5	11.4	13.6	•	•	•	•	•
Taxes Paid **12**	2.0	7.9	3.0	4.6	3.8	0.2	1.7	1.2	•	•	•	•	•
Interest Paid **13**	1.8	4.3	0.2	0.2	1.0	0.1	1.1	0.6	•	•	•	•	•
Depreciation **14**	1.5	26.8	0.5	1.2	2.1	0.3	1.4	0.6	•	•	•	•	•
Amortization and Depletion **15**	0.7	5.8	0.0	0.0	0.2	0.0	0.2	0.3	•	•	•	•	•
Pensions and Other Deferred Comp. **16**	0.3	2.1	0.5	1.4	0.2	0.0	0.1	0.2	•	•	•	•	•
Employee Benefits **17**	3.9	4.4	0.8	0.3	2.5	10.7	19.3	15.1	•	•	•	•	•
Advertising **18**	0.3	0.0	0.8	0.5	0.3	0.1	0.3	0.3	•	•	•	•	•
Other Expenses **19**	20.7	131.7	38.3	30.9	27.1	55.4	30.4	53.3	•	•	•	•	•
Officers' Compensation **20**	1.7	59.7	13.4	0.1	1.6	0.6	1.2	0.5	•	•	•	•	•
Operating Margin **21**	1.5	•	10.1	20.9	13.8	3.5	•	2.4	•	•	•	•	•
Operating Margin Before Officers' Comp. **22**	3.2	•	23.5	21.0	15.4	4.1	•	2.9	•	•	•	•	•

Selected Average Balance Sheet ($ in Thousands)

Net Receivables **23**	705	0	6	333	387	560	2358	5798
Inventories **24**	82	0	2	0	67	38	131	165
Net Property, Plant and Equipment **25**	528	0	21	64	724	369	3081	6307
Total Assets **26**	6466		107	563	1857	7720	14943	38118
Notes and Loans Payable **27**	1903	0	78	173	588	3868	4451	9890
All Other Liabilities **28**	1948	0	8	77	381	4669	5960	18918
Net Worth **29**	2616	0	22	313	887	-817	4533	9310

Selected Financial Ratios (Times to 1)

Current Ratio **30**	1.3	•	2.2	1.7	1.9	1.0	1.3	1.0
Quick Ratio **31**	0.9	•	1.6	1.7	1.7	0.9	1.1	0.7
Net Sales to Working Capital **32**	17.4	•	34.2	14.4	9.1	•	15.8	15358.1
Coverage Ratio **33**	3.4	98.8	54.5	109.1	13.6	70.1	7.0	6.6
Total Asset Turnover **34**	1.5	•	10.1	4.0	2.4	3.6	1.9	3.5
Inventory Turnover **35**	63.3	•	101.8	•	10.7	197.0	74.0	95.3
Receivables Turnover **36**	15.2	•	111.8	13.4	12.3	98.9	11.6	20.3
Total Liabilities to Net Worth **37**	1.5	•	3.9	0.8	1.1	•	2.3	3.1
Current Assets to Working Capital **38**	4.4	•	1.8	2.5	2.1	•	4.1	2191.6
Current Liabilities to Working Capital **39**	3.4	•	0.8	1.5	1.1	•	3.1	2190.6
Working Capital to Net Sales **40**	0.1	•	0.0	0.1	0.1	•	0.1	0.0
Inventory to Working Capital **41**	0.1	•	0.1	•	0.2	•	0.0	20.1
Total Receipts to Cash Flow **42**	4.5	0.5	2.3	2.0	2.8	1.7	2.9	1.8
Cost of Goods to Cash Flow **43**	2.5	0.0	0.4	0.0	0.4	0.5	1.0	0.2
Cash Flow to Total Debt **44**	0.5	•	5.4	4.5	1.7	1.9	0.9	2.5

Selected Financial Factors (in Percentages)

Debt Ratio **45**	59.6	•	79.5	44.5	52.2	110.6	69.7	75.6
Return on Total Assets **46**	9.1	115.7	96.6	32.6	14.9	14.1	14.3	
Return on Equity Before Income Taxes **47**	16.0	553.2	172.5	63.2	•	•	39.9	49.8
Return on Equity After Income Taxes **48**	13.7	547.2	172.5	61.3	•	•	33.5	41.2
Profit Margin (Before Income Tax) **49**	4.4	420.0	11.3	24.1	12.4	4.1	6.4	3.5
Profit Margin (After Income Tax) **50**	3.8	413.3	11.1	24.1	12.0	4.1	5.4	2.9

Table I

Corporations with and without Net Income

MISC. HEALTH CARE AND SOCIAL ASSISTANCE

MONEY AMOUNTS AND SIZE OF ASSETS IN THOUSANDS OF DOLLARS

Item Description for Accounting Period 7/02 Through 6/03

	Total	Zero Assets	Under 500	500 to 1,000	1,000 to 5,000	5,000 to 10,000	10,000 to 25,000	25,000 to 50,000	50,000 to 100,000	100,000 to 250,000	250,000 to 500,000	500,000 to 2,500,000	2,500,000 and over
Number of Enterprises 1	47058	6518	36220	2010	1818	224	124	53	40	24	13	13	0
Revenues ($ in Thousands)													
Net Sales 2	66725457	834267	19153089	3666402	9336863	3735600	3617817	2460042	3285768	4032267	3743742	12859601	0
Interest 3	189550	2115	3338	2114	5033	7803	6152	12752	20209	27159	27061	75814	0
Rents 4	48084	28	31	65	4168	361	1526	2592	15012	4640	550	19112	0
Royalties 5	72279	0	0	0	112	853	15	9468	18977	15800	26333	721	0
Other Portfolio Income 6	347610	25540	6802	3524	37026	2206	7245	8378	4186	10272	203032	39400	0
Other Receipts 7	1608770	74697	340606	71419	174978	276078	67130	52398	155462	70892	183483	141626	0
Total Receipts 8	68991750	936647	19503866	3743524	9558180	4022901	3699885	2545630	3499614	4161030	4184201	13136274	0
Average Total Receipts 9	1466	144	538	1862	5258	17959	29838	48031	87490	173376	321862	1010483	•
Operating Costs/Operating Income (%)													
Cost of Operations 10	20.3	10.9	8.4	4.6	27.8	45.0	31.0	28.6	19.2	23.3	19.7	25.5	•
Salaries and Wages 11	31.3	33.2	35.0	42.3	28.0	23.4	28.5	33.0	30.8	32.4	33.0	26.7	•
Taxes Paid 12	3.8	5.5	4.3	4.7	3.9	2.5	3.9	3.6	4.0	4.2	3.0	2.9	•
Interest Paid 13	2.0	1.4	0.6	1.4	1.3	1.4	1.5	2.1	2.9	3.4	3.9	3.9	•
Depreciation 14	3.1	1.9	1.4	4.0	3.8	1.8	3.0	3.2	3.3	3.8	3.3	5.0	•
Amortization and Depletion 15	0.8	0.6	0.1	0.3	0.2	0.4	0.5	1.2	1.3	1.3	2.7	1.7	•
Pensions and Other Deferred Comp. 16	0.4	3.0	0.4	1.1	0.6	0.1	0.3	0.5	0.4	0.3	0.1	0.0	•
Employee Benefits 17	2.2	0.5	1.0	1.8	1.5	2.2	2.7	2.6	2.1	2.9	2.4	4.2	•
Advertising 18	0.7	1.5	0.8	1.1	0.5	0.7	0.5	0.5	0.9	0.4	0.3	0.6	•
Other Expenses 19	31.3	38.3	37.2	23.2	27.6	25.1	27.2	30.8	44.8	32.6	40.4	23.7	•
Officers' Compensation 20	5.3	16.5	8.7	13.9	5.8	4.9	3.6	1.7	1.9	1.2	0.6	1.7	•
Operating Margin 21	•	•	2.0	1.6	•	•	•	•	•	•	•	4.0	•
Operating Margin Before Officers' Comp. 22	4.2	3.1	10.7	15.5	5.0	1.0	•	•	•	•	•	5.7	•

Selected Average Balance Sheet ($ in Thousands)

Net Receivables **23**	163	0	4	117	555	2620	4704	7885	15498	33249	48441	201444
Inventories **24**	17	0	2	11	88	63	402	646	1031	4310	4534	20515
Net Property, Plant and Equipment **25**	199	0	38	301	681	1339	3800	7995	13209	37453	38727	233881
Total Assets **26**	841	0	75	706	2117	6723	15583	36130	70853	162930	330369	1170571
Notes and Loans Payable **27**	351	0	54	443	1001	3235	6214	12545	28425	53752	170771	386684
All Other Liabilities **28**	240	0	12	134	545	3011	5028	11974	22346	49449	63106	365060
Net Worth **29**	251	0	8	130	570	478	4342	11611	20082	59729	96491	418827

Selected Financial Ratios (Times to 1)

Current Ratio **30**	1.4	·	1.0	1.6	1.4	1.0	1.2	1.1	1.5	1.6	1.4	1.8
Quick Ratio **31**	1.0	·	0.8	1.3	1.1	0.9	1.0	0.9	1.1	1.2	0.9	1.1
Net Sales to Working Capital **32**	13.7	·	·	17.4	14.7	318.8	17.9	21.6	7.3	7.0	6.3	6.1
Coverage Ratio **33**	2.1	0.2	7.2	3.6	2.2	1.1	0.7	·	·	0.3	1.6	2.6
Total Asset Turnover **34**	1.7	·	7.1	2.6	2.4	2.5	1.9	1.3	1.2	1.0	0.9	0.8
Inventory Turnover **35**	16.6	·	24.3	7.6	16.2	119.2	22.5	20.5	15.3	9.1	12.5	12.3
Receivables Turnover **36**	8.5	·	81.5	17.3	8.0	5.7	6.8	5.8	6.1	5.6	5.9	4.6
Total Liabilities to Net Worth **37**	2.4	·	8.1	4.4	2.7	13.1	2.6	2.1	2.5	1.7	2.4	1.8
Current Assets to Working Capital **38**	3.3	·	·	2.8	3.4	83.3	5.1	8.2	3.0	2.7	3.3	2.3
Current Liabilities to Working Capital **39**	2.3	·	·	1.8	2.4	82.3	4.1	7.2	2.0	1.7	2.3	1.3
Working Capital to Net Sales **40**	0.1	·	·	0.1	0.1	0.0	0.1	0.0	0.1	0.1	0.2	0.2
Inventory to Working Capital **41**	0.2	·	·	0.1	0.2	1.2	0.3	0.3	0.1	0.2	0.1	0.1
Total Receipts to Cash Flow **42**	3.7	4.0	3.1	4.7	4.1	4.9	4.5	4.7	3.2	4.0	3.0	4.0
Cost of Goods to Cash Flow **43**	0.7	0.4	0.3	0.2	1.1	2.2	1.4	1.3	0.6	0.9	0.6	1.0
Cash Flow to Total Debt **44**	0.7	·	2.6	0.7	0.8	0.5	0.6	0.4	0.5	0.4	0.4	0.3

Selected Financial Factors (in Percentages)

Debt Ratio **45**	70.2	·	89.0	81.6	73.1	92.9	72.1	67.9	71.7	63.3	70.8	64.2
Return on Total Assets **46**	7.2	·	31.6	13.3	6.9	3.6	2.1	·	·	1.0	5.5	8.5
Return on Equity Before Income Taxes **47**	12.8	·	248.4	52.6	14.0	3.2	·	·	·	·	7.1	14.6
Return on Equity After Income Taxes **48**	9.0	·	243.2	49.0	10.9	·	·	·	·	·	5.0	9.8
Profit Margin (Before Income Tax) **49**	2.3	·	3.9	3.7	1.6	0.1	·	·	·	·	2.4	6.2
Profit Margin (After Income Tax) **50**	1.6	·	3.8	3.5	1.2	·	·	·	·	·	1.7	4.1

371

Table II

Corporations with Net Income

MISC. HEALTH CARE AND SOCIAL ASSISTANCE

MONEY AMOUNTS AND SIZE OF ASSETS IN THOUSANDS OF DOLLARS

Item Description for Accounting Period 7/02 Through 6/03	Total	Zero Assets	Under 500	500 to 1,000	1,000 to 5,000	5,000 to 10,000	10,000 to 25,000	25,000 to 50,000	50,000 to 100,000	100,000 to 250,000	250,000 to 500,000	500,000 to 2,500,000	2,500,000 and over
Number of Enterprises **1**	27341	2132	22186	1675	1100	114	0	23	15	12	6	0	0
Revenues ($ in Thousands)													
Net Sales **2**	46775011	393948	13983136	3161780	6407592	1747781	0	1435721	1177664	2702596	2391363	0	0
Interest **3**	107689	710	2416	1673	1943	929	0	3235	3175	11889	14740	0	0
Rents **4**	34495	28	0	0	412	2	0	4	12681	1515	0	0	0
Royalties **5**	45881	0	0	0	0	853	0	2896	0	15800	26333	0	0
Other Portfolio Income **6**	294232	2677	5589	409	35084	1084	0	261	757	2996	201589	0	0
Other Receipts **7**	1008821	63327	330620	71190	138223	86192	0	17743	63296	13193	109170	0	0
Total Receipts **8**	48266129	460690	14321761	3235052	6583254	1836841	0	1459860	1257573	2747989	2743195	0	0
Average Total Receipts **9**	1765	216	646	1931	5985	16113	•	63472	83838	228999	457199	•	•
Operating Costs/Operating Income (%)													
Cost of Operations **10**	18.1	18.9	8.2	1.2	22.1	21.4	•	18.7	25.7	16.8	20.6	•	•
Salaries and Wages **11**	30.9	20.3	32.5	45.5	30.9	28.2	•	38.7	27.0	34.0	31.3	•	•
Taxes Paid **12**	3.7	3.1	4.1	4.8	4.2	3.2	•	4.2	4.2	3.7	3.0	•	•
Interest Paid **13**	1.4	1.1	0.4	0.7	1.0	1.3	•	1.4	2.0	1.3	2.7	•	•
Depreciation **14**	2.6	1.7	1.2	2.6	3.9	1.8	•	2.1	3.0	1.7	2.2	•	•
Amortization and Depletion **15**	0.6	0.3	0.1	0.2	0.1	0.8	•	0.6	1.1	1.1	2.2	•	•
Pensions and Other Deferred Comp. **16**	0.4	0.1	0.5	1.2	0.6	0.2	•	0.7	0.6	0.3	0.1	•	•
Employee Benefits **17**	2.3	0.6	1.0	1.8	1.4	2.8	•	2.6	2.1	3.0	1.4	•	•
Advertising **18**	0.6	2.6	0.7	0.6	0.4	1.2	•	0.5	0.6	0.4	0.4	•	•
Other Expenses **19**	29.0	34.8	37.1	22.0	24.6	25.7	•	24.7	26.9	30.7	43.0	•	•
Officers' Compensation **20**	5.8	11.5	9.2	15.1	5.9	9.7	•	1.4	1.6	1.2	0.7	•	•
Operating Margin **21**	4.6	5.0	4.9	4.3	4.9	3.8	•	4.3	5.2	5.6	•	•	•
Operating Margin Before Officers' Comp. **22**	10.3	16.5	14.1	19.4	10.9	13.5	•	5.7	6.8	6.8	•	•	•

Selected Average Balance Sheet ($ in Thousands)

Net Receivables 23	192	0	5	130	522	3177	•	10515	15751	41455	56339
Inventories 24	20	0	1	10	114	75	•	719	1848	5594	5490
Net Property, Plant and Equipment 25	210	0	34	290	653	1351	•	8910	12766	25548	39855
Total Assets 26	880	0	72	708	2079	6173	•	36368	72589	160200	339266
Notes and Loans Payable 27	281	0	35	254	861	2607	•	12567	23251	32991	149916
All Other Liabilities 28	247	0	11	124	419	1972	•	9253	21732	45838	72943
Net Worth 29	352	0	26	330	799	1594	•	14548	27606	81371	116408

Selected Financial Ratios (Times to 1)

Current Ratio 30	1.8	•	1.3	2.4	2.0	1.2	•	1.5	1.3	2.0	2.3
Quick Ratio 31	1.3	•	1.1	2.2	1.4	1.1	•	1.2	1.0	1.7	1.9
Net Sales to Working Capital 32	10.9	•	102.4	10.5	9.5	19.1	•	10.8	11.2	6.2	4.5
Coverage Ratio 33	6.6	21.7	19.7	10.4	8.9	8.0	•	5.3	6.9	6.6	3.7
Total Asset Turnover 34	1.9	•	8.8	2.7	2.8	2.5	•	1.7	1.1	1.4	1.2
Inventory Turnover 35	15.1	•	60.5	2.4	11.3	44.0	•	16.2	10.9	6.8	14.9
Receivables Turnover 36	8.8	•	74.5	23.7	8.2	4.1	•	5.8	4.7	5.1	8.4
Total Liabilities to Net Worth 37	1.5	•	1.8	1.1	1.6	2.9	•	1.5	1.6	1.0	1.9
Current Assets to Working Capital 38	2.3	•	4.0	1.7	2.0	5.6	•	3.0	4.2	2.0	1.8
Current Liabilities to Working Capital 39	1.3	•	3.0	0.7	1.0	4.6	•	2.0	3.2	1.0	0.8
Working Capital to Net Sales 40	0.1	•	0.0	0.1	0.1	0.1	•	0.1	0.1	0.2	0.2
Inventory to Working Capital 41	0.1	•	0.0	0.1	0.2	0.1	•	0.1	0.3	0.1	0.1
Total Receipts to Cash Flow 42	3.2	2.2	2.7	4.2	3.5	3.4	•	3.7	2.9	2.9	2.5
Cost of Goods to Cash Flow 43	0.6	0.4	0.2	0.1	0.8	0.7	•	0.7	0.7	0.5	0.5
Cash Flow to Total Debt 44	1.0	•	5.0	1.2	1.3	1.0	•	0.8	0.6	1.0	0.7

Selected Financial Factors (in Percentages)

Debt Ratio 45	60.0	•	64.0	53.4	61.6	74.2	•	60.0	62.0	49.2	65.7
Return on Total Assets 46	17.8	•	67.4	19.4	24.2	25.4	•	12.7	15.1	12.3	11.7
Return on Equity Before Income Taxes 47	37.6	•	178.0	37.7	56.0	85.9	•	25.7	34.0	20.5	24.9
Return on Equity After Income Taxes 48	33.0	•	175.3	36.0	52.4	83.6	•	22.1	30.2	15.9	21.1
Profit Margin (Before Income Tax) 49	7.7	21.9	7.3	6.6	7.7	8.9	•	6.0	12.0	7.4	7.3
Profit Margin (After Income Tax) 50	6.8	21.3	7.2	6.3	7.2	8.7	•	5.2	10.6	5.8	6.2

HOSPITALS, NURSING, AND RESIDENTIAL CARE FACILITIES

Table I

Corporations with and without Net Income

MONEY AMOUNTS AND SIZE OF ASSETS IN THOUSANDS OF DOLLARS

Item Description for Accounting Period 7/02 Through 6/03	Total	Zero Assets	Under 500	500 to 1,000	1,000 to 5,000	5,000 to 10,000	10,000 to 25,000	25,000 to 50,000	50,000 to 100,000	100,000 to 250,000	250,000 to 500,000	500,000 to 2,500,000	2,500,000 and over
Number of Enterprises **1**	16281	1707	10639	1090	2193	283	198	60	44	33	11	15	7
Revenues ($ in Thousands)													
Net Sales **2**	87499581	239292	3990133	1755261	9317071	2957512	4178410	2958514	3647778	5396939	4678471	19119821	29260379
Interest **3**	762574	1036	11	1032	2732	834	5180	8812	16837	32781	73608	324112	295600
Rents **4**	281523	13	0	0	4669	1412	3670	5936	16652	15769	7952	53147	172303
Royalties **5**	0	0	0	0	0	0	0	0	0	0	0	0	0
Other Portfolio Income **6**	806428	112303	1699	2047	29676	5828	9977	3247	33712	21484	15663	413095	157697
Other Receipts **7**	2614579	6295	9964	38214	34365	31112	116745	43650	92067	229526	57741	357685	1597212
Total Receipts **8**	91964685	358939	4001807	1796554	9388513	2996698	4313982	3020159	3807046	5696499	4833435	20267860	31483191
Average Total Receipts **9**	5649	210	376	1648	4281	10589	21788	50336	86524	172621	439403	1351191	4497599
Operating Costs/Operating Income (%)													
Cost of Operations **10**	10.5	•	3.4	5.1	7.3	8.5	12.8	9.8	13.0	8.0	4.9	18.3	8.7
Salaries and Wages **11**	41.9	29.3	36.4	35.2	43.9	40.7	37.0	41.8	41.7	46.1	42.3	38.2	44.9
Taxes Paid **12**	5.3	6.4	6.0	4.5	5.5	5.1	5.7	5.5	4.8	5.4	5.0	5.4	5.1
Interest Paid **13**	3.3	1.5	1.3	2.9	2.2	3.7	3.0	2.5	2.9	4.9	4.0	4.0	3.3
Depreciation **14**	3.6	2.8	1.4	1.9	2.1	2.8	2.5	2.3	2.7	3.3	3.7	3.1	5.1
Amortization and Depletion **15**	0.8	26.9	0.0	0.3	0.1	0.2	0.2	0.2	0.4	1.2	1.3	1.2	0.7
Pensions and Other Deferred Comp. **16**	0.4	0.0	0.2	0.2	0.3	0.3	0.3	0.2	0.3	0.2	0.0	0.1	0.9
Employee Benefits **17**	4.4	2.9	2.7	1.9	3.0	3.5	3.9	4.0	4.7	4.5	4.8	4.4	5.4
Advertising **18**	0.3	0.5	0.3	0.7	0.4	0.5	0.4	0.3	0.3	0.3	0.2	0.3	0.2
Other Expenses **19**	30.1	75.5	40.0	48.4	32.2	32.8	34.6	33.2	32.1	31.8	42.2	29.5	23.4
Officers' Compensation **20**	0.9	5.6	5.9	2.6	1.6	1.2	1.2	0.8	1.1	0.7	0.4	0.2	0.3
Operating Margin **21**	•	•	•	•	1.4	0.9	•	•	•	•	•	•	2.1
Operating Margin Before Officers' Comp. **22**	•	•	8.4	•	3.0	2.1	•	0.2	•	•	•	•	2.4

Selected Average Balance Sheet ($ in Thousands)

Net Receivables 23	757	0	7	167	447	1364	2936	6827	12799	22240	64038	163211	752048
Inventories 24	19	0	1	0	10	25	104	128	340	845	2244	9420	7164
Net Property, Plant and Equipment 25	2204	0	52	345	1171	3981	7128	16413	32058	72869	149314	512309	2246654
Total Assets 26	6174	0	91	652	2201	6606	15552	34611	69735	151774	382969	1117999	8274173
Notes and Loans Payable 27	2675	0	85	743	1601	5656	9878	22002	40448	100946	169520	624063	2445017
All Other Liabilities 28	1623	0	30	183	611	1712	4466	8813	19142	43493	123205	341813	1986814
Net Worth 29	1876	0	-24	-273	-11	-761	1208	3797	10146	7335	90243	152123	3842342

Selected Financial Ratios (Times to 1)

Current Ratio 30	1.0	•	0.8	0.9	0.9	0.8	1.1	0.9	1.0	1.0	1.2	1.0	1.0
Quick Ratio 31	0.8	•	0.6	0.9	0.8	0.7	0.8	0.8	0.8	0.8	1.0	0.9	0.8
Net Sales to Working Capital 32	384.9	•	•	•	•	•	59.8	•	1537.2	•	16.1	240.2	143.5
Coverage Ratio 33	2.1	0.1	3.2	1.8	1.6	1.6	1.6	1.6	1.2	0.8	•	1.1	3.9
Total Asset Turnover 34	0.9	4.1	2.5	1.9	1.6	1.6	1.4	1.4	1.2	1.1	1.1	1.1	0.5
Inventory Turnover 35	30.2	•	11.7	1179.5	30.3	35.3	25.8	37.7	31.8	15.5	9.4	24.7	50.7
Receivables Turnover 36	7.2	•	26.9	9.0	9.9	7.7	7.5	6.8	7.9	7.4	8.4	6.0	6.4
Total Liabilities to Net Worth 37	2.3	•	•	•	•	•	11.9	8.1	5.9	19.7	3.2	6.3	1.2
Current Assets to Working Capital 38	90.5	•	•	•	•	•	15.5	•	464.3	•	5.8	50.0	38.2
Current Liabilities to Working Capital 39	89.5	•	•	•	•	•	14.5	•	463.3	•	4.8	49.0	37.2
Working Capital to Net Sales 40	0.0	•	•	•	•	•	0.0	•	0.0	•	0.1	0.0	0.0
Inventory to Working Capital 41	1.0	•	•	•	•	•	0.3	•	7.9	•	0.1	0.7	0.2
Total Receipts to Cash Flow 42	3.6	1.5	3.5	2.9	3.7	3.5	3.3	3.4	3.7	4.2	3.4	4.2	3.4
Cost of Goods to Cash Flow 43	0.4	•	0.1	0.1	0.3	0.3	0.4	0.3	0.5	0.3	0.2	0.8	0.3
Cash Flow to Total Debt 44	0.3	•	0.9	0.6	0.5	0.4	0.4	0.5	0.4	0.3	0.4	0.3	0.3

Selected Financial Factors (in Percentages)

Debt Ratio 45	69.6	•	125.8	141.9	100.5	111.5	92.2	89.0	85.5	95.2	76.4	86.4	53.6
Return on Total Assets 46	5.9	•	16.6	3.7	7.7	9.3	6.5	5.7	3.9	4.3	•	5.2	6.5
Return on Equity Before Income Taxes 47	10.0	•	•	•	8.3	•	31.6	19.0	3.7	•	•	4.2	10.4
Return on Equity After Income Taxes 48	6.2	•	•	•	8.5	•	26.8	15.2	1.3	•	•	•	6.8
Profit Margin (Before Income Tax) 49	3.5	•	2.8	•	1.8	2.2	1.8	1.5	0.5	•	•	0.5	9.5
Profit Margin (After Income Tax) 50	2.2	•	2.7	•	1.7	2.1	1.5	1.2	0.2	•	•	•	6.3

Table II

Corporations with Net Income

HOSPITALS, NURSING, AND RESIDENTIAL CARE FACILITIES

MONEY AMOUNTS AND SIZE OF ASSETS IN THOUSANDS OF DOLLARS

Item Description for Accounting Period 7/02 Through 6/03	Total	Zero Assets	Under 500	500 to 1,000	1,000 to 5,000	5,000 to 10,000	10,000 to 25,000	25,000 to 50,000	50,000 to 100,000	100,000 to 250,000	250,000 to 500,000	500,000 to 2,500,000	2,500,000 and over
Number of Enterprises **1**	8465	796	5648	349	1292	164	119	34	26	19	0	6	0
Revenues ($ in Thousands)													
Net Sales **2**	60235577	68686	1697448	443481	6148134	1746629	3016630	1628098	2919377	3251600	0	9980563	0
Interest **3**	369259	731	5	14	671	270	2375	6425	10715	17291	0	33592	0
Rents **4**	195800	13	0	0	682	70	1228	2288	11145	12288	0	26334	0
Royalties **5**	0	0	0	0	0	0	0	0	0	0	0	0	0
Other Portfolio Income **6**	627327	16758	650	1322	29076	3644	4087	3141	5522	18493	0	374848	0
Other Receipts **7**	2128997	9564	6393	37739	28901	11174	107961	31899	58424	154508	0	179672	0
Total Receipts **8**	63556960	95752	1704496	482556	6207464	1761787	3132281	1671851	3005183	3454180	0	10595009	0
Average Total Receipts **9**	7508	120	302	1383	4805	10743	26322	49172	115584	181799	•	1765835	•
Operating Costs/Operating Income (%)													
Cost of Operations **10**	11.6	•	7.4	15.7	8.2	8.8	14.6	13.8	14.6	8.9	•	21.4	•
Salaries and Wages **11**	40.1	27.3	28.5	11.8	43.9	39.6	34.2	39.5	41.1	46.2	•	31.3	•
Taxes Paid **12**	5.2	6.4	4.7	2.4	5.6	5.2	5.4	5.8	4.6	6.0	•	5.7	•
Interest Paid **13**	2.6	0.3	1.1	0.5	1.5	2.7	2.2	2.3	1.9	3.7	•	1.9	•
Depreciation **14**	3.7	4.6	1.4	1.2	1.8	2.8	2.2	2.3	2.2	2.9	•	4.0	•
Amortization and Depletion **15**	0.6	0.0	0.0	0.0	0.1	0.1	0.2	0.2	0.3	1.2	•	1.1	•
Pensions and Other Deferred Comp. **16**	0.5	0.0	0.5	1.0	0.4	0.4	0.3	0.3	0.3	0.3	•	0.1	•
Employee Benefits **17**	4.4	3.0	0.5	0.5	3.1	3.4	3.6	4.0	4.5	4.7	•	4.1	•
Advertising **18**	0.3	0.2	0.4	0.1	0.4	0.3	0.3	0.3	0.2	0.2	•	0.4	•
Other Expenses **19**	27.5	34.2	32.5	55.2	28.2	27.8	34.3	27.2	29.1	26.5	•	29.9	•
Officers' Compensation **20**	0.9	12.1	9.3	6.2	1.7	1.7	1.1	1.0	0.8	0.7	•	0.3	•
Operating Margin **21**	2.5	11.9	13.6	5.5	5.1	7.2	1.5	3.2	0.5	•	•	•	•
Operating Margin Before Officers' Comp. **22**	3.4	24.0	22.9	11.7	6.8	8.9	2.6	4.2	1.3	•	•	•	•

Selected Average Balance Sheet ($ in Thousands)

Net Receivables 23	1068	0	1	282	458	1154	3234	6757	17244	26384	·	223965
Inventories 24	15	0	2	0	7	24	120	128	326	922	·	4902
Net Property, Plant and Equipment 25	2903	0	36	104	996	3931	6762	16223	28248	68766	·	625264
Total Assets 26	8793	0	69	653	2107	6606	15525	34864	69279	153548	·	1332887
Notes and Loans Payable 27	3350	0	51	80	1151	4317	8444	19367	36191	93999	·	848864
All Other Liabilities 28	2307	0	6	123	530	1171	4493	8663	20534	32063	·	406388
Net Worth 29	3136	0	12	450	426	1119	2588	6835	12554	27485	·	77634

Selected Financial Ratios (Times to 1)

Current Ratio 30	1.0	·	3.4	2.8	1.3	1.3	1.3	1.1	1.1	1.2	·	0.8
Quick Ratio 31	0.8	·	2.0	2.7	1.1	1.1	1.0	1.0	0.9	1.0	·	0.7
Net Sales to Working Capital 32	91.0	·	20.2	5.7	22.6	26.7	20.9	52.3	35.2	20.0	·	·
Coverage Ratio 33	4.1	173.7	13.8	27.3	4.8	4.0	3.4	3.6	2.8	2.3	·	4.0
Total Asset Turnover 34	0.8	·	4.4	1.9	2.3	1.6	1.6	1.4	1.6	1.1	·	1.2
Inventory Turnover 35	53.8	·	10.9	6322.9	54.6	38.9	30.9	51.6	50.2	16.5	·	72.8
Receivables Turnover 36	7.3	·	20.1	4.0	11.5	8.9	9.0	6.0	8.4	8.0	·	3.0
Total Liabilities to Net Worth 37	1.8	·	4.8	0.5	3.9	4.9	5.0	4.1	4.5	4.6	·	16.2
Current Assets to Working Capital 38	22.0	·	1.4	1.6	3.9	4.9	4.8	11.9	9.7	6.3	·	·
Current Liabilities to Working Capital 39	21.0	·	0.4	0.6	2.9	3.9	3.8	10.9	8.7	5.3	·	·
Working Capital to Net Sales 40	0.0	·	0.0	0.2	0.0	0.0	0.0	0.0	0.0	0.0	·	·
Inventory to Working Capital 41	0.2	·	0.0	0.0	0.1	0.1	0.1	0.1	0.1	0.1	·	·
Total Receipts to Cash Flow 42	3.3	1.3	2.9	1.5	3.7	3.2	3.0	3.6	3.7	3.8	·	3.4
Cost of Goods to Cash Flow 43	0.4	·	0.2	0.2	0.3	0.4	0.5	0.5	0.5	0.3	·	0.7
Cash Flow to Total Debt 44	0.4	·	1.8	4.3	0.8	0.6	0.7	0.5	0.5	0.4	·	0.4

Selected Financial Factors (in Percentages)

Debt Ratio 45	64.3	·	82.9	31.1	79.8	83.1	83.3	80.4	81.9	82.1	·	94.2
Return on Total Assets 46	8.5	·	66.1	29.0	15.9	17.5	12.2	11.2	8.5	9.6	·	9.7
Return on Equity Before Income Taxes 47	17.9	·	358.1	40.6	62.5	77.1	51.9	41.4	30.2	30.9	·	124.1
Return on Equity After Income Taxes 48	13.5	·	356.0	40.3	60.9	74.9	48.1	37.6	26.9	23.7	·	95.6
Profit Margin (Before Income Tax) 49	7.9	51.3	14.0	14.4	5.6	8.1	5.3	5.9	3.4	5.0	·	5.8
Profit Margin (After Income Tax) 50	5.9	50.9	13.9	14.2	5.5	7.9	4.9	5.4	3.0	3.8	·	4.5

Table I

Corporations with and without Net Income

OTHER ARTS, ENTERTAINMENT, AND RECREATION

MONEY AMOUNTS AND SIZE OF ASSETS IN THOUSANDS OF DOLLARS

Item Description for Accounting Period 7/02 Through 6/03	Total	Zero Assets	Under 500	500 to 1,000	1,000 to 5,000	5,000 to 10,000	10,000 to 25,000	25,000 to 50,000	50,000 to 100,000	100,000 to 250,000	250,000 to 500,000	500,000 to 2,500,000	2,500,000 and over
Number of Enterprises 1	57739	11033	43959	1389	1041	126	93	38	19	31	5	5	0
Revenues ($ in Thousands)													
Net Sales 2	29171487	766041	8391080	2726928	3293221	1908164	1482720	1168491	1661879	3822725	1723330	2226907	0
Interest 3	127776	2380	4709	1045	7061	770	21223	5623	3415	33857	19979	27714	0
Rents 4	89441	2909	4555	1756	1601	0	3802	935	2718	27129	6937	37098	0
Royalties 5	83921	96	0	0	100	3668	409	20	4979	51113	19849	3687	0
Other Portfolio Income 6	304478	40532	2098	2829	50000	2289	9900	30703	38356	114308	9303	4161	0
Other Receipts 7	1249061	-107393	161210	37938	109828	118671	198006	120584	102749	434341	6426	66702	0
Total Receipts 8	31026164	704565	8563652	2770496	3461811	2033562	1716060	1326356	1814096	4483473	1785824	2366269	0
Average Total Receipts 9	537	64	195	1995	3325	16139	18452	34904	95479	144628	357165	473254	•
Operating Costs/Operating Income (%)													
Cost of Operations 10	17.3	4.0	13.8	17.2	17.1	9.5	36.3	23.2	10.2	22.0	22.3	19.6	•
Salaries and Wages 11	20.0	3.9	14.6	19.1	12.3	40.2	16.6	37.1	32.1	31.5	8.5	15.2	•
Taxes Paid 12	3.7	2.5	2.6	4.5	2.4	2.7	3.1	3.8	4.0	4.4	2.5	10.4	•
Interest Paid 13	1.6	2.7	0.5	0.3	0.6	1.3	1.5	1.4	2.2	2.6	2.0	6.5	•
Depreciation 14	4.0	4.9	1.9	2.8	4.1	3.0	3.6	3.6	3.8	4.0	5.5	13.0	•
Amortization and Depletion 15	1.4	0.3	0.0	0.0	0.3	2.7	6.6	0.7	0.6	4.2	0.3	2.5	•
Pensions and Other Deferred Comp. 16	1.2	3.5	2.0	0.7	0.7	0.0	0.4	1.1	0.6	1.7	0.8	0.4	•
Employee Benefits 17	1.0	0.4	0.7	0.4	0.6	0.2	0.9	1.1	1.2	2.3	1.1	1.3	•
Advertising 18	2.7	0.9	3.0	4.4	1.2	0.4	1.6	1.7	7.1	2.1	2.6	3.7	•
Other Expenses 19	36.5	61.6	43.1	29.5	21.1	37.4	35.8	34.9	35.1	34.1	55.2	26.4	•
Officers' Compensation 20	13.1	28.2	18.0	16.8	33.1	4.9	5.5	7.2	4.7	3.9	1.6	1.2	•
Operating Margin 21	•	•	•	4.3	6.5	•	•	•	•	•	•	•	•
Operating Margin Before Officers' Comp. 22	10.5	15.2	17.9	21.1	39.7	2.5	•	•	3.1	•	•	0.9	•

Selected Average Balance Sheet ($ in Thousands)

Net Receivables 23	31	0	2	23	109	506	3218	5851	12314	15360	31826	26944	•
Inventories 24	6	0	3	16	74	20	198	355	759	1726	422	3796	•
Net Property, Plant and Equipment 25	140	0	12	151	640	3293	3725	9640	16836	41541	208609	581056	•
Total Assets 26	384	0	50	712	2016	6894	15156	37339	78843	150355	418852	995813	•
Notes and Loans Payable 27	193	0	66	133	1476	5168	6945	12020	41394	55775	85183	364337	•
All Other Liabilities 28	130	0	24	120	371	3005	4545	15529	40509	49557	193393	247755	•
Net Worth 29	61	0	-41	459	169	-1279	3667	9790	-3060	45023	139676	383721	•

Selected Financial Ratios (Times to 1)

Current Ratio 30	1.1	•	1.7	2.3	1.6	0.6	1.4	1.5	1.0	1.0	0.8	0.8	•
Quick Ratio 31	0.8	•	1.1	1.5	1.2	0.5	1.0	1.0	0.7	0.6	0.8	0.6	•
Net Sales to Working Capital 32	29.9	•	15.0	9.4	12.0	•	8.4	5.4	134.1	188.0	•	•	•
Coverage Ratio 33	3.4	•	5.1	21.4	21.6	4.2	3.4	•	4.5	2.8	1.4	2.0	•
Total Asset Turnover 34	1.3	•	3.9	2.8	1.6	2.2	1.1	0.8	1.1	0.8	0.8	0.4	•
Inventory Turnover 35	13.7	•	8.0	20.7	7.3	73.7	29.3	20.1	11.7	15.7	182.5	23.0	•
Receivables Turnover 36	16.8	•	100.7	101.1	24.1	37.2	5.8	5.3	6.8	9.0	9.4	20.3	•
Total Liabilities to Net Worth 37	5.3	•	•	0.6	10.9	•	3.1	2.8	•	2.3	2.0	1.6	•
Current Assets to Working Capital 38	8.1	•	2.4	1.8	2.7	•	3.5	2.8	59.7	76.9	•	•	•
Current Liabilities to Working Capital 39	7.1	•	1.4	0.8	1.7	•	2.5	1.8	58.7	75.9	•	•	•
Working Capital to Net Sales 40	0.0	•	0.1	0.1	0.1	•	0.1	0.2	0.0	0.0	•	•	•
Inventory to Working Capital 41	0.4	•	0.3	0.1	0.3	•	0.1	0.1	1.7	3.6	•	•	•
Total Receipts to Cash Flow 42	2.8	3.1	2.5	3.3	3.4	2.5	2.9	3.5	3.1	3.2	1.9	3.5	•
Cost of Goods to Cash Flow 43	0.5	0.1	0.3	0.6	0.6	0.2	1.0	0.8	0.3	0.7	0.4	0.7	•
Cash Flow to Total Debt 44	0.6	•	0.9	2.3	0.5	0.7	0.5	0.3	0.3	0.4	0.7	0.2	•

Selected Financial Factors (in Percentages)

Debt Ratio 45	84.1	•	182.3	35.6	91.6	118.5	75.8	73.8	103.9	70.1	66.7	61.5	•
Return on Total Assets 46	7.1	•	9.4	17.1	19.1	12.0	5.5	•	10.8	5.9	2.4	5.7	•
Return on Equity Before Income Taxes 47	31.6	•	•	25.3	217.1	•	16.0	•	•	12.6	2.2	7.4	•
Return on Equity After Income Taxes 48	26.6	•	•	25.1	208.4	•	14.6	•	•	8.0	0.3	5.2	•
Profit Margin (Before Income Tax) 49	3.8	•	2.0	5.9	11.6	4.2	3.7	•	7.6	4.6	0.9	6.4	•
Profit Margin (After Income Tax) 50	3.2	•	1.8	5.9	11.1	4.2	3.4	•	7.6	2.9	0.1	4.4	•

Table II
Corporations with Net Income

OTHER ARTS, ENTERTAINMENT, AND RECREATION

MONEY AMOUNTS AND SIZE OF ASSETS IN THOUSANDS OF DOLLARS

Item Description for Accounting Period 7/02 Through 6/03	Total	Zero Assets	Under 500	500 to 1,000	1,000 to 5,000	5,000 to 10,000	10,000 to 25,000	25,000 to 50,000	50,000 to 100,000	100,000 to 250,000	250,000 to 500,000	500,000 to 2,500,000	2,500,000 and over
Number of Enterprises **1**	27375	5308	20409	880	0	65	47	20	9	20	0	5	0
Revenues ($ in Thousands)													
Net Sales **2**	21769459	605976	5144887	2383971	0	1702461	845514	885868	1164270	2643147	0	2226907	0
Interest **3**	91230	2152	2022	1039	0	353	2186	2574	1053	25512	0	27714	0
Rents **4**	83192	2909	3520	1756	0	0	1390	902	2718	26793	0	37098	0
Royalties **5**	52327	96	0	0	0	2943	409	20	4979	2045	0	3687	0
Other Portfolio Income **6**	217159	15641	2098	2038	0	200	8143	27951	32766	113384	0	4161	0
Other Receipts **7**	1261292	53638	106205	28540	0	110665	172940	138695	57137	424856	0	66702	0
Total Receipts **8**	23474659	680412	5258732	2417344	0	1816622	1030582	1056010	1262923	3253937	0	2366269	0
Average Total Receipts **9**	858	128	258	2747	.	27948	21927	52800	140325	162697	.	473254	.
Operating Costs/Operating Income (%)													
Cost of Operations **10**	14.4	4.5	8.6	15.1	.	9.6	34.4	23.8	13.2	17.6	.	19.6	.
Salaries and Wages **11**	19.3	2.3	14.7	18.9	.	41.6	20.9	25.1	18.2	35.8	.	15.2	.
Taxes Paid **12**	3.8	2.9	2.4	4.6	.	2.1	2.8	3.2	4.3	5.0	.	10.4	.
Interest Paid **13**	1.4	0.4	0.1	0.1	.	0.2	1.0	0.8	1.7	2.7	.	6.5	.
Depreciation **14**	3.4	1.2	1.3	1.6	.	1.2	4.9	2.7	3.4	3.7	.	13.0	.
Amortization and Depletion **15**	0.8	0.0	0.0	0.0	.	3.0	0.2	0.1	0.1	2.4	.	2.5	.
Pensions and Other Deferred Comp. **16**	1.2	4.4	1.7	0.9	.	0.0	0.5	1.2	0.6	2.4	.	0.4	.
Employee Benefits **17**	0.8	0.5	0.2	0.4	.	0.0	1.0	1.0	1.1	2.6	.	1.3	.
Advertising **18**	2.4	0.2	2.6	4.1	.	0.1	1.8	1.5	5.9	1.8	.	3.7	.
Other Expenses **19**	33.5	45.4	40.0	28.0	.	31.8	33.2	23.5	36.9	34.1	.	26.4	.
Officers' Compensation **20**	13.4	34.9	16.7	15.7	.	5.2	6.1	8.6	5.9	3.0	.	1.2	.
Operating Margin **21**	5.6	3.2	11.6	10.6	.	5.2	.	8.5	8.8	.	.	.	.
Operating Margin Before Officers' Comp. **22**	19.0	38.1	28.3	26.3	.	10.4	17.1	14.7	.	.	.	0.9	.

Selected Average Balance Sheet ($ in Thousands)

Line Item	1	2	3	4	5	6	7	8	9	10
Net Receivables 23	35	0	1	28	211	1602	4674	11261	14059	26944
Inventories 24	4	0	2	29	14	273	501	806	858	3796
Net Property, Plant and Equipment 25	199	0	11	121	1540	3644	9528	26637	40294	581056
Total Assets 26	536	54	712	6109	14545	36316	84146	144800	•	995813
Notes and Loans Payable 27	177	0	40	91	2633	4198	7845	42349	46128	364337
All Other Liabilities 28	176	•	18	160	2586	4644	13573	34477	55293	247755
Net Worth 29	183	-4	•	462	889	5704	14897	7320	43379	383721

Selected Financial Ratios (Times to 1)

Line Item	1	2	3	4	5	6	7	8	9	10
Current Ratio 30	1.2	•	2.1	2.8	1.3	1.4	1.6	1.0	1.0	0.8
Quick Ratio 31	0.9	•	1.3	1.9	•	1.1	0.8	1.0	0.8	0.6
Net Sales to Working Capital 32	22.4	•	13.8	8.8	37.3	10.9	7.3	106.7	•	•
Coverage Ratio 33	10.9	35.7	129.7	116.1	66.4	16.2	33.8	11.2	5.5	2.0
Total Asset Turnover 34	1.5	•	4.7	3.8	4.3	1.2	1.2	1.5	0.9	0.4
Inventory Turnover 35	26.4	•	14.0	14.3	181.2	21.1	22.6	21.1	27.1	23.0
Receivables Turnover 36	25.7	•	193.6	193.3	153.5	11.6	12.0	21.1	13.2	20.3
Total Liabilities to Net Worth 37	1.9	•	0.5	1.6	5.9	1.4	1.6	10.5	2.3	1.6
Current Assets to Working Capital 38	5.3	•	1.9	1.6	4.2	3.8	2.8	37.3	•	•
Current Liabilities to Working Capital 39	4.3	•	0.9	0.6	3.2	2.8	1.8	36.3	•	•
Working Capital to Net Sales 40	0.0	•	0.1	0.1	0.0	0.1	0.1	0.0	•	•
Inventory to Working Capital 41	0.2	•	0.1	0.1	0.0	0.2	0.1	0.1	1.2	•
Total Receipts to Cash Flow 42	2.3	1.8	2.0	2.8	2.3	2.1	2.4	•	2.6	3.5
Cost of Goods to Cash Flow 43	0.3	0.1	0.2	0.4	0.2	0.5	0.3	•	0.5	0.7
Cash Flow to Total Debt 44	1.0	•	2.2	3.8	2.1	0.9	1.0	0.7	0.5	0.2

Selected Financial Factors (in Percentages)

Line Item	1	2	3	4	5	6	7	8	9	10
Debt Ratio 45	65.9	•	107.9	35.2	85.4	60.8	59.0	91.3	70.0	61.5
Return on Total Assets 46	21.9	•	65.2	45.8	51.7	19.8	34.8	29.1	13.4	5.7
Return on Equity Before Income Taxes 47	58.3	•	•	70.1	350.0	47.3	82.4	304.9	36.4	7.4
Return on Equity After Income Taxes 48	54.8	•	•	69.8	349.8	45.5	78.6	304.5	29.2	5.2
Profit Margin (Before Income Tax) 49	13.4	15.5	13.8	12.0	11.9	15.0	27.7	17.3	12.0	6.4
Profit Margin (After Income Tax) 50	12.6	14.0	13.5	11.9	14.4	26.4	17.2	•	9.6	4.4

Table I

Corporations with and without Net Income

AMUSEMENT, GAMBLING, AND RECREATION INDUSTRIES

MONEY AMOUNTS AND SIZE OF ASSETS IN THOUSANDS OF DOLLARS

Item Description for Accounting Period 7/02 Through 6/03	Total	Zero Assets	Under 500	500 to 1,000	1,000 to 5,000	5,000 to 10,000	10,000 to 25,000	25,000 to 50,000	50,000 to 100,000	100,000 to 250,000	250,000 to 500,000	500,000 to 2,500,000	2,500,000 and over
Number of Enterprises **1**	52871	6811	36236	4344	4413	607	286	99	32	24	6	12	0
Revenues ($ in Thousands)													
Net Sales **2**	43502672	879126	8916664	3411836	7940718	4631029	2584210	1615336	1205696	2812462	1300957	8204637	0
Interest **3**	684032	1389	7199	6010	9247	10977	8031	5587	5507	19687	7168	603230	0
Rents **4**	110511	0	6605	3885	17880	19933	8920	10055	7505	7586	4389	23753	0
Royalties **5**	98626	0	0	0	1869	1310	29649	107	476	1360	6216	57639	0
Other Portfolio Income **6**	240193	22385	63352	27889	31531	23100	6775	3145	18756	3660	307	39294	0
Other Receipts **7**	3256234	692	168888	710289	350715	206746	166733	146576	273553	169966	97778	964298	0
Total Receipts **8**	47892268	903592	9162708	4159909	8351960	4893095	2804318	1780806	1511493	3014721	1416815	9892851	0
Average Total Receipts **9**	906	133	253	958	1893	8061	9805	17988	47234	125613	236136	824404	•
Operating Costs/Operating Income (%)													
Cost of Operations **10**	23.9	•	21.1	18.1	24.7	45.9	29.5	16.8	19.6	19.8	16.7	15.1	•
Salaries and Wages **11**	21.2	•	15.8	24.1	21.2	16.1	24.1	28.4	32.9	25.5	21.6	24.4	•
Taxes Paid **12**	7.1	•	4.8	6.6	6.7	5.2	6.5	7.5	11.2	9.8	5.3	10.6	•
Interest Paid **13**	5.7	•	1.7	3.3	4.5	2.3	4.1	3.7	3.5	5.2	4.6	16.0	•
Depreciation **14**	7.7	•	5.1	8.6	6.9	7.1	9.0	9.8	8.0	8.4	10.8	10.1	•
Amortization and Depletion **15**	0.7	•	0.1	1.3	0.4	0.3	0.8	0.4	1.2	1.4	0.9	1.4	•
Pensions and Other Deferred Comp. **16**	0.3	•	0.3	0.2	0.4	0.3	0.3	0.4	0.6	0.2	0.3	0.2	•
Employee Benefits **17**	1.3	•	2.6	0.5	1.1	1.1	2.1	2.4	1.6	2.5	1.1	2.0	•
Advertising **18**	2.5	•	1.0	2.2	1.7	1.9	2.8	2.2	4.8	3.0	3.3	3.4	•
Other Expenses **19**	36.8	•	42.8	49.0	32.6	22.7	29.5	35.4	39.6	34.9	35.2	40.5	•
Officers' Compensation **20**	3.4	•	7.7	4.6	4.6	1.7	2.1	1.8	1.1	0.9	1.2	0.8	•
Operating Margin **21**	•	•	•	•	•	•	•	•	•	•	•	•	•
Operating Margin Before Officers' Comp. **22**	•	5.3										0.1	•

Selected Average Balance Sheet ($ in Thousands)

Item	1	2	3	4	5	6	7	8	9	10	11	12
Net Receivables 23	67	0	4	38	102	415	664	1573	1850	8275	13988	152497
Inventories 24	25	0	7	16	58	410	349	485	1684	2920	6645	17644
Net Property, Plant and Equipment 25	565	0	58	484	1335	4099	9761	22463	38665	89256	160960	661840
Total Assets 26	1086	0	111	722	2014	7213	15447	34993	66126	160548	330091	1762056
Notes and Loans Payable 27	594	0	100	476	1294	3585	7384	12050	20941	73237	183356	914544
All Other Liabilities 28	195	0	19	74	271	1397	2560	7875	18456	42578	19601	333828
Net Worth 29	297	0	-8	172	449	2231	5504	15068	26729	44732	127134	513684

Selected Financial Ratios (Times to 1)

Item	1	2	3	4	5	6	7	8	9	10	11	12
Current Ratio 30	1.1	•	1.3	1.4	1.1	1.1	1.0	1.0	0.6	0.5	1.1	1.4
Quick Ratio 31	0.7	•	1.0	1.1	0.7	0.5	0.6	0.7	0.4	0.4	0.5	0.7
Net Sales to Working Capital 32	31.2	•	26.4	17.9	35.9	50.7	296.5	•	•	•	33.2	6.5
Coverage Ratio 33	0.9	•	1.2	2.1	1.1	1.5	0.5	1.4	1.3	0.2	2.7	0.8
Total Asset Turnover 34	0.8	•	2.2	1.1	0.9	1.1	0.6	0.5	0.6	0.7	0.7	0.4
Inventory Turnover 35	7.7	•	7.5	8.9	7.6	8.5	7.6	5.7	4.4	8.0	5.5	5.9
Receivables Turnover 36	13.0	•	70.3	24.0	17.2	22.4	12.7	9.3	15.9	12.4	16.8	5.0
Total Liabilities to Net Worth 37	2.7	•	•	•	3.2	2.2	1.8	1.3	1.5	2.6	1.6	2.4
Current Assets to Working Capital 38	9.1	•	3.9	3.8	8.6	13.6	93.2	•	•	•	11.3	3.7
Current Liabilities to Working Capital 39	8.1	•	2.9	2.8	7.6	12.6	92.2	•	•	•	10.3	2.7
Working Capital to Net Sales 40	0.0	•	0.0	0.1	0.0	0.0	0.0	•	•	•	0.0	0.2
Inventory to Working Capital 41	1.0	•	0.7	0.4	1.3	3.5	10.8	•	•	•	1.2	0.2
Total Receipts to Cash Flow 42	4.2	13.3	3.4	3.0	5.0	5.9	5.6	3.4	3.1	5.6	4.2	3.8
Cost of Goods to Cash Flow 43	1.0	8.1	0.7	0.5	1.2	2.7	1.6	0.6	0.6	1.1	0.7	0.6
Cash Flow to Total Debt 44	0.3	•	0.6	0.5	0.2	0.3	0.2	0.2	0.3	0.2	0.3	0.1

Selected Financial Factors (in Percentages)

Item	1	2	3	4	5	6	7	8	9	10	11	12
Debt Ratio 45	72.6	•	107.4	76.1	77.7	69.1	64.4	56.9	59.6	72.1	61.5	70.8
Return on Total Assets 46	3.9	•	4.7	7.4	4.5	3.7	1.1	2.5	2.6	0.6	8.1	4.7
Return on Equity Before Income Taxes 47	•	•	•	15.8	2.1	3.9	•	1.8	1.5	•	13.3	•
Return on Equity After Income Taxes 48	•	•	•	15.1	1.5	3.6	•	0.7	1.1	•	10.1	•
Profit Margin (Before Income Tax) 49	•	•	0.4	3.5	0.5	1.1	1.6	1.1	•	•	7.8	•
Profit Margin (After Income Tax) 50	•	•	0.2	3.3	0.4	1.0	0.7	0.8	•	•	5.9	•

377

Table II

Corporations with Net Income

AMUSEMENT, GAMBLING, AND RECREATION INDUSTRIES

MONEY AMOUNTS AND SIZE OF ASSETS IN THOUSANDS OF DOLLARS

Item Description for Accounting Period 7/02 Through 6/03	Total	Zero Assets	Under 500	500 to 1,000	1,000 to 5,000	5,000 to 10,000	10,000 to 25,000	25,000 to 50,000	50,000 to 100,000	100,000 to 250,000	250,000 to 500,000	500,000 to 2,500,000	2,500,000 and over
Number of Enterprises 1	26015	1573	18882	2694	0	281	103	41	9	6	0	4	0
Revenues ($ in Thousands)													
Net Sales 2	25553701	139462	6527302	2088869	0	2991531	1406675	989087	581256	725808	0	3176449	0
Interest 3	214953	315	4663	5058	0	1956	3708	3440	733	1605	0	180265	0
Rents 4	65676	0	2242	1979	0	14856	2957	7813	6796	0	0	9641	0
Royalties 5	94222	0	0	0	0	46	29642	105	0	831	0	57382	0
Other Portfolio Income 6	155645	2846	58158	27472	0	20729	3989	1450	1317	1187	0	14424	0
Other Receipts 7	1715317	448	61613	690682	0	101401	100905	92281	254338	45999	0	155272	0
Total Receipts 8	27779514	143071	6653978	2814060	0	3130519	1547876	1094176	844440	775430	0	3593433	0
Average Total Receipts 9	1068	91	352	1045	•	11141	15028	26687	93827	129238	•	898358	•
Operating Costs/Operating Income (%)													
Cost of Operations 10	25.2	12.2	21.2	20.4	•	48.1	33.5	13.5	28.8	36.9	•	19.2	•
Salaries and Wages 11	18.3	9.4	14.4	24.9	•	14.7	20.2	27.5	36.5	17.2	•	17.6	•
Taxes Paid 12	6.4	1.0	4.7	7.6	•	3.5	6.6	8.1	11.2	10.6	•	9.2	•
Interest Paid 13	3.0	0.5	1.1	2.2	•	1.4	2.4	2.1	0.9	2.6	•	10.5	•
Depreciation 14	6.0	6.4	4.2	5.9	•	5.7	6.0	7.6	4.7	8.1	•	9.4	•
Amortization and Depletion 15	0.5	0.2	0.1	0.4	•	0.2	0.5	0.3	0.2	0.4	•	2.0	•
Pensions and Other Deferred Comp. 16	0.3	•	0.4	0.3	•	0.3	0.3	0.3	0.9	0.2	•	0.1	•
Employee Benefits 17	1.1	12.9	0.4	0.8	•	1.0	1.7	1.7	1.0	2.3	•	1.5	•
Advertising 18	2.2	0.4	2.4	2.1	•	1.7	2.5	2.2	7.0	1.3	•	2.5	•
Other Expenses 19	32.0	49.3	36.0	51.5	•	17.2	23.8	30.8	31.8	18.7	•	33.0	•
Officers' Compensation 20	4.3	3.4	8.4	6.4	•	1.5	2.0	1.7	1.0	0.7	•	0.9	•
Operating Margin 21	0.7	4.4	6.9	•	•	4.8	0.4	4.2	•	0.8	•	•	•
Operating Margin Before Officers' Comp. 22	5.0	7.8	15.3	•	•	6.2	2.5	5.9	•	1.6	•	•	•

Selected Average Balance Sheet ($ in Thousands)

Net Receivables **23**	65	0	1	24	•	273	714	2262	2460	10881	205860
Inventories **24**	30	0	8	24	•	782	458	421	922	3417	14480
Net Property, Plant and Equipment **25**	438	0	57	397	•	3763	8884	20684	27070	62234	579138
Total Assets **26**	924	0	118	697	•	7283	15409	35897	60165	117266	1856281
Notes and Loans Payable **27**	445	0	66	309	•	3284	5550	8641	22749	40126	991237
All Other Liabilities **28**	139	0	13	87	•	1101	2523	6441	14924	25042	298832
Net Worth **29**	340	0	39	300	•	2897	7335	20815	22491	52098	566212

Selected Financial Ratios (Times to 1)

Current Ratio **30**	1.5	•	2.2	1.5	•	1.3	1.2	1.4	0.5	1.8	1.9
Quick Ratio **31**	1.0	•	1.6	1.2	•	0.5	0.8	1.1	0.4	1.4	1.4
Net Sales to Working Capital **32**	12.8	•	14.3	12.3	•	19.0	23.6	9.0	•	10.4	4.5
Coverage Ratio **33**	4.1	14.7	8.9	6.7	•	7.7	5.3	8.1	23.2	3.9	1.7
Total Asset Turnover **34**	1.1	•	2.9	1.1	•	1.5	0.9	0.7	1.1	1.0	0.4
Inventory Turnover **35**	8.2	•	9.1	6.5	•	6.6	10.0	7.8	20.2	13.1	10.5
Receivables Turnover **36**	14.3	•	206.9	65.9	•	32.5	17.8	9.0	14.7	6.0	3.9
Total Liabilities to Net Worth **37**	1.7	•	2.0	1.3	•	1.5	1.1	0.7	1.7	1.3	2.3
Current Assets to Working Capital **38**	3.1	•	1.9	3.1	•	4.5	5.9	3.4	•	2.3	2.1
Current Liabilities to Working Capital **39**	2.1	•	0.9	2.1	•	3.5	4.9	2.4	•	1.3	1.1
Working Capital to Net Sales **40**	0.1	•	0.1	0.1	•	0.1	0.0	0.1	•	0.1	0.2
Inventory to Working Capital **41**	0.4	•	0.3	0.4	•	1.9	0.6	0.1	•	0.3	0.1
Total Receipts to Cash Flow **42**	3.3	2.0	2.9	2.3	•	4.9	3.7	2.5	2.1	4.5	3.0
Cost of Goods to Cash Flow **43**	0.8	0.2	0.6	0.5	•	2.3	1.2	0.3	0.6	1.7	0.6
Cash Flow to Total Debt **44**	0.5	•	1.5	0.8	•	0.5	0.5	0.6	0.8	0.4	0.2

Selected Financial Factors (in Percentages)

Debt Ratio **45**	63.2	•	66.7	56.9	•	60.2	52.4	42.0	62.6	55.6	69.5
Return on Total Assets **46**	13.3	•	29.0	16.1	•	15.8	11.4	11.6	23.5	10.6	7.7
Return on Equity Before Income Taxes **47**	27.4	•	77.2	31.8	•	34.6	19.5	17.6	60.1	17.8	10.5
Return on Equity After Income Taxes **48**	25.5	•	74.8	31.2	•	34.0	18.7	15.7	58.4	14.3	7.4
Profit Margin (Before Income Tax) **49**	9.5	7.0	8.8	12.3	•	9.4	10.5	15.2	20.9	7.7	7.5
Profit Margin (After Income Tax) **50**	8.8	5.7	8.5	12.1	•	9.2	10.0	13.6	20.3	6.1	5.3

Table I

Corporations with and without Net Income

ACCOMMODATION

MONEY AMOUNTS AND SIZE OF ASSETS IN THOUSANDS OF DOLLARS

Item Description for Accounting Period 7/02 Through 6/03	Total	Zero Assets	Under 500	500 to 1,000	1,000 to 5,000	5,000 to 10,000	10,000 to 25,000	25,000 to 50,000	50,000 to 100,000	100,000 to 250,000	250,000 to 500,000	500,000 to 2,500,000	2,500,000 and over
Number of Enterprises 1	33996	3389	17944	3383	8036	615	351	100	62	49	28	27	11

Revenues ($ in Thousands)

Item Description for Accounting Period 7/02 Through 6/03	Total	Zero Assets	Under 500	500 to 1,000	1,000 to 5,000	5,000 to 10,000	10,000 to 25,000	25,000 to 50,000	50,000 to 100,000	100,000 to 250,000	250,000 to 500,000	500,000 to 2,500,000	2,500,000 and over
Net Sales 2	107999757	1312345	4033500	1472297	8698248	2216118	3392523	1814661	2245412	5392903	6217474	16799764	54404511
Interest 3	2245429	21853	5289	752	13243	5723	13959	22291	37356	60658	41295	474053	1548956
Rents 4	797126	51345	1902	5774	2745	4437	8139	7323	11375	58383	11011	111547	523146
Royalties 5	1455912	5484	0	0	1041	0	695	0	5	6975	141826	17293	1282594
Other Portfolio Income 6	1093164	433311	38154	52500	48071	2336	9780	25953	28175	78155	13370	53335	310027
Other Receipts 7	6799418	363022	113026	45821	166187	55328	122723	45571	108730	226664	81277	927582	4543485
Total Receipts 8	120390806	2187360	4191871	1577144	8929535	2283942	3547819	1915799	2431053	5823738	6506253	18383574	62612719
Average Total Receipts 9	3541	645	234	466	1111	3714	10108	19158	39211	118852	232366	680873	5692065

Operating Costs/Operating Income (%)

Item Description for Accounting Period 7/02 Through 6/03	Total	Zero Assets	Under 500	500 to 1,000	1,000 to 5,000	5,000 to 10,000	10,000 to 25,000	25,000 to 50,000	50,000 to 100,000	100,000 to 250,000	250,000 to 500,000	500,000 to 2,500,000	2,500,000 and over
Cost of Operations 10	43.2	14.0	28.5	7.5	16.4	20.0	22.6	18.9	26.1	23.6	46.6	44.5	55.2
Salaries and Wages 11	17.8	16.0	15.2	24.4	18.9	17.7	19.2	21.3	18.9	19.5	9.9	14.5	19.1
Taxes Paid 12	5.7	11.4	6.8	7.0	7.1	7.1	5.2	6.8	5.5	5.5	3.1	8.0	4.7
Interest Paid 13	6.5	10.3	2.3	6.6	10.2	7.8	5.7	7.4	5.2	5.4	3.3	7.2	6.5
Depreciation 14	5.4	6.8	4.2	7.5	8.9	7.7	7.7	9.6	8.9	6.4	4.4	7.1	3.9
Amortization and Depletion 15	0.6	0.4	0.2	0.7	0.5	0.6	0.4	0.4	1.1	0.5	0.9	0.9	0.5
Pensions and Other Deferred Comp. 16	0.4	0.1	0.1	0.5	0.1	0.1	0.1	0.2	0.3	0.3	0.4	0.1	0.7
Employee Benefits 17	1.8	0.8	0.6	0.4	0.8	1.3	1.6	3.0	2.2	2.2	1.1	1.7	2.1
Advertising 18	2.2	1.1	1.8	1.8	2.5	2.1	3.0	3.2	3.9	3.7	1.7	2.0	2.1
Other Expenses 19	25.8	87.7	43.3	45.4	33.7	35.6	41.3	40.0	40.7	40.7	32.5	22.1	17.8
Officers' Compensation 20	0.8	1.0	3.0	5.6	2.9	2.4	1.2	1.3	1.0	1.0	0.5	0.4	0.3
Operating Margin 21	•	•	•	•	0.7	•	•	•	•	•	•	•	•
Operating Margin Before Officers' Comp. 22	•	•	•	•	•	•	•	•	•	•	•	•	•

Selected Average Balance Sheet ($ in Thousands)

Net Receivables 23	227	0	4	19	43	204	832	1055	4084	11631	16401	37588	402044
Inventories 24	66	0	2	6	20	37	163	351	913	1555	1567	9813	133326
Net Property, Plant and Equipment 25	2471	0	80	529	1703	4822	9694	25664	41096	100527	150566	598386	2753950
Total Assets 26	5557	0	132	691	2202	6448	15097	35793	70263	165995	330821	1232224	8967808
Notes and Loans Payable 27	2679	0	107	600	1920	4869	9829	26344	37277	79961	146820	542080	3421637
All Other Liabilities 28	1146	0	20	68	129	522	2040	4086	13174	38790	68504	221001	2296997
Net Worth 29	1732	0	5	22	153	1058	3228	5363	19813	47244	115498	469143	3249174

Selected Financial Ratios (Times to 1)

Current Ratio 30	1.1	•	0.7	0.7	1.2	1.4	1.2	0.7	0.7	0.9	1.3	1.2	1.1
Quick Ratio 31	0.7	•	0.5	0.5	0.8	1.2	0.8	0.4	0.4	0.7	0.6	0.8	0.7
Net Sales to Working Capital 32	77.3	•	•	•	22.4	12.5	20.0	•	•	•	13.0	24.6	96.3
Coverage Ratio 33	1.2	2.6	0.1	1.0	1.1	1.1	0.4	0.1	•	0.9	1.1	1.1	1.4
Total Asset Turnover 34	0.6	•	1.7	0.6	0.6	0.6	0.6	0.5	0.5	0.7	0.7	0.5	0.6
Inventory Turnover 35	20.8	•	27.8	5.9	19.8	13.4	13.4	9.8	10.3	16.7	66.1	28.2	20.5
Receivables Turnover 36	13.9	•	59.0	25.3	16.0	24.8	11.2	21.3	7.2	10.5	11.1	14.0	13.0
Total Liabilities to Net Worth 37	2.2	•	27.1	29.9	13.4	5.1	3.7	5.7	2.5	2.5	1.9	1.6	1.8
Current Assets to Working Capital 38	17.7	•	•	•	5.2	3.3	5.9	•	•	•	5.0	6.8	18.2
Current Liabilities to Working Capital 39	16.7	•	•	•	4.2	2.3	4.9	•	•	•	4.0	5.8	17.2
Working Capital to Net Sales 40	0.0	•	•	•	0.0	0.1	0.1	•	•	•	0.1	0.0	0.0
Inventory to Working Capital 41	1.6	•	•	•	0.3	0.1	0.4	•	•	•	0.1	0.3	2.7
Total Receipts to Cash Flow 42	5.3	1.5	3.9	3.2	3.8	3.8	4.3	5.2	4.7	4.4	7.1	6.0	6.2
Cost of Goods to Cash Flow 43	2.3	0.2	1.1	0.2	0.6	0.8	1.0	1.0	1.2	1.0	3.3	2.7	3.4
Cash Flow to Total Debt 44	0.2	•	0.5	0.2	0.2	0.2	0.2	0.1	0.2	0.2	0.1	0.1	0.1

Selected Financial Factors (in Percentages)

Debt Ratio 45	68.8	•	96.4	96.8	93.1	83.6	78.6	85.0	71.8	71.5	65.1	61.9	63.8
Return on Total Assets 46	4.4	•	0.6	4.0	5.3	4.7	1.5	0.5	•	3.0	2.4	4.1	4.9
Return on Equity Before Income Taxes 47	2.1	•	•	3.3	1.8	•	•	•	•	•	0.6	1.1	3.6
Return on Equity After Income Taxes 48	0.6	•	•	2.5	0.8	•	•	•	•	•	•	0.3	1.9
Profit Margin (Before Income Tax) 49	1.1	16.8	•	0.5	0.5	0.5	•	•	•	•	0.3	0.8	2.3
Profit Margin (After Income Tax) 50	0.3	11.0	•	0.3	0.2	0.2	•	•	•	•	•	0.3	1.3

Table II

Corporations with Net Income

ACCOMMODATION

MONEY AMOUNTS AND SIZE OF ASSETS IN THOUSANDS OF DOLLARS

Item Description for Accounting Period 7/02 Through 6/03	Total	Zero Assets	Under 500	500 to 1,000	1,000 to 5,000	5,000 to 10,000	10,000 to 25,000	25,000 to 50,000	50,000 to 100,000	100,000 to 250,000	250,000 to 500,000	500,000 to 2,500,000	2,500,000 and over
Number of Enterprises **1**	17689	2468	8827	1581	4239	276	168	49	22	22	14	0	0
Revenues ($ in Thousands)													
Net Sales **2**	84947811	759405	2896479	429728	5227525	1014901	1602534	1011115	724522	2380992	5389094	0	0
Interest **3**	1602494	18838	4340	634	7917	4659	7312	11251	27681	24457	15316	0	0
Rents **4**	702289	51037	1587	5739	2089	1721	4249	4427	3776	45486	10503	0	0
Royalties **5**	1333438	5484	0	0	1041	0	693	0	5	3195	141826	0	0
Other Portfolio Income **6**	968162	433249	35639	52489	43244	1484	7485	24433	23157	47400	3510	0	0
Other Receipts **7**	5759153	366296	47367	37917	127486	36707	79510	31196	30982	146374	66400	0	0
Total Receipts **8**	95313347	1634309	2985412	526507	5409302	1059472	1701783	1082422	810123	2647904	5626649	0	0
Average Total Receipts **9**	5388	662	338	333	1276	3839	10130	22090	36824	120359	401904	•	•
Operating Costs/Operating Income (%)													
Cost of Operations **10**	49.5	21.7	31.6	3.6	15.0	10.5	21.1	16.0	26.7	25.9	50.3	•	•
Salaries and Wages **11**	17.2	24.9	11.6	25.0	18.5	17.8	22.0	22.7	18.8	25.3	7.7	•	•
Taxes Paid **12**	5.2	14.8	6.5	7.7	6.6	7.4	6.0	7.1	5.2	5.4	2.3	•	•
Interest Paid **13**	5.1	15.8	0.9	7.5	8.9	7.0	5.3	7.4	3.5	3.8	2.2	•	•
Depreciation **14**	4.6	10.7	2.4	8.0	7.6	7.4	7.7	8.1	8.7	7.5	2.6	•	•
Amortization and Depletion **15**	0.5	0.6	0.1	0.1	0.4	0.4	0.2	0.3	0.4	0.5	0.9	•	•
Pensions and Other Deferred Comp. **16**	0.5	0.1	0.1	1.0	0.1	0.2	0.2	0.2	0.2	0.6	0.4	•	•
Employee Benefits **17**	1.7	0.8	0.2	0.2	0.9	0.9	2.0	2.5	2.6	2.9	0.8	•	•
Advertising **18**	2.0	1.8	1.1	1.9	2.1	1.8	2.5	3.5	2.2	2.7	1.5	•	•
Other Expenses **19**	20.1	74.3	35.8	38.6	29.1	33.8	29.6	29.9	30.3	28.0	32.3	•	•
Officers' Compensation **20**	0.7	1.5	3.3	6.7	3.0	3.3	1.5	1.5	1.4	1.1	0.3	•	•
Operating Margin **21**	•	•	6.5	•	7.8	9.6	1.9	0.9	•	•	•	•	•
Operating Margin Before Officers' Comp. **22**	•	•	9.8	6.4	10.7	12.9	3.4	2.4	1.4	•	•	•	•

Selected Average Balance Sheet ($ in Thousands)

Net Receivables 23	187	0	3	37	40	197	814	1296	3408	5123	12633
Inventories 24	95	0	1	3	13	35	174	453	658	1788	2077
Net Property, Plant and Equipment 25	3115	0	59	424	1640	4656	9637	24138	34271	100886	146065
Total Assets 26	6996	0	118	676	2123	6466	15186	34991	69492	161133	318568
Notes and Loans Payable 27	2996	0	58	404	1633	4257	8679	22285	29960	65410	133946
All Other Liabilities 28	1561	0	10	40	90	502	1553	3382	6281	41840	85603
Net Worth 29	2439	0	50	231	399	1707	4955	9323	33251	53882	99019

Selected Financial Ratios (Times to 1)

Current Ratio 30	1.0	•	3.3	2.8	1.5	1.8	1.6	1.1	0.8	1.1	1.2
Quick Ratio 31	0.6	•	2.9	2.4	1.1	1.6	1.2	0.8	0.6	0.7	0.7
Net Sales to Working Capital 32	402.6	•	13.2	3.5	13.3	7.3	8.6	28.0	•	61.2	35.7
Coverage Ratio 33	2.0	4.0	12.0	4.0	2.3	3.0	2.5	2.1	4.4	2.9	2.4
Total Asset Turnover 34	0.7	•	2.8	0.4	0.6	0.6	0.6	0.6	0.5	0.7	1.2
Inventory Turnover 35	25.0	•	100.8	3.4	14.7	11.0	11.6	7.3	13.4	15.7	93.2
Receivables Turnover 36	21.8	•	195.2	10.2	28.8	15.6	10.0	19.6	6.3	19.4	20.8
Total Liabilities to Net Worth 37	1.9	•	1.3	1.9	4.3	2.8	2.1	2.8	1.1	2.0	2.2
Current Assets to Working Capital 38	67.5	•	1.4	1.6	2.9	2.2	2.8	7.7	•	17.5	6.7
Current Liabilities to Working Capital 39	66.5	•	0.4	0.6	1.9	1.2	1.8	6.7	•	16.5	5.7
Working Capital to Net Sales 40	0.0	•	0.1	0.3	0.1	0.1	0.1	0.0	•	0.0	0.0
Inventory to Working Capital 41	8.6	•	0.0	0.0	0.2	0.0	0.2	0.6	•	1.1	0.3
Total Receipts to Cash Flow 42	5.2	1.8	3.1	2.6	2.9	2.6	3.3	3.6	2.9	3.8	6.8
Cost of Goods to Cash Flow 43	2.6	0.4	1.0	0.1	0.4	0.3	0.7	0.6	0.8	1.0	3.4
Cash Flow to Total Debt 44	0.2	•	1.5	0.2	0.2	0.3	0.3	0.2	0.3	0.3	0.3

Selected Financial Factors (in Percentages)

Debt Ratio 45	65.1	•	57.4	65.8	81.2	73.6	67.4	73.4	52.2	66.6	68.9
Return on Total Assets 46	7.0	•	29.0	11.9	11.7	12.0	8.4	9.1	7.3	7.6	6.4
Return on Equity Before Income Taxes 47	10.0	•	62.5	26.1	34.8	30.2	15.5	17.6	11.7	15.0	12.2
Return on Equity After Income Taxes 48	7.9	4.0	60.7	24.9	34.2	28.9	14.2	16.2	10.2	10.8	10.2
Profit Margin (Before Income Tax) 49	5.1	47.8	9.6	22.2	11.3	14.0	8.0	11.8	10.2	7.5	3.1
Profit Margin (After Income Tax) 50	4.0	37.8	9.3	21.1	13.4	7.4	7.3	10.3	5.4		2.6

Table I

Corporations with and without Net Income

FOOD SERVICES AND DRINKING PLACES

MONEY AMOUNTS AND SIZE OF ASSETS IN THOUSANDS OF DOLLARS

Item Description for Accounting Period 7/02 Through 6/03	Total	Zero Assets	Under 500	500 to 1,000	1,000 to 5,000	5,000 to 10,000	10,000 to 25,000	25,000 to 50,000	50,000 to 100,000	100,000 to 250,000	250,000 to 500,000	500,000 to 2,500,000	2,500,000 and over
Number of Enterprises **1**	237531	25091	191904	12175	7011	748	344	103	53	46	20	23	12
Revenues ($ in Thousands)													
Net Sales **2**	264419096	3753328	86678789	23132550	27580013	9841126	9266428	6513337	6188104	11096797	9713304	23438191	47217129
Interest **3**	1589352	4797	19773	10625	11549	4490	9437	5338	6567	45758	121186	242908	1106924
Rents **4**	550867	2260	31577	11367	7212	9505	9296	10344	9743	53668	79355	215515	111024
Royalties **5**	3563991	8918	80	87	4102	2253	39056	41185	43371	227838	517936	687622	1991543
Other Portfolio Income **6**	944507	127177	150089	18391	46742	68665	22206	4287	3249	59490	13540	119819	310852
Other Receipts **7**	8328709	28326	569010	135055	493427	163345	204250	93778	49050	408080	59939	1018985	5105466
Total Receipts **8**	279396522	3924806	87449318	23308075	28143045	10089384	9550673	6668269	6300084	11891631	10505260	25723040	55842938
Average Total Receipts **9**	1176	156	456	1914	4014	13488	27764	64740	118870	258514	525263	1118393	4653578
Operating Costs/Operating Income (%)													
Cost of Operations **10**	40.0	52.6	41.8	39.5	40.8	37.3	41.8	45.3	38.9	41.0	38.2	35.6	37.2
Salaries and Wages **11**	20.8	10.0	18.0	19.5	19.2	23.6	19.8	17.3	20.0	22.4	22.8	26.2	25.1
Taxes Paid **12**	4.1	4.1	4.5	3.9	4.0	4.0	3.8	3.6	3.3	3.7	3.7	4.0	3.7
Interest Paid **13**	2.1	1.9	0.7	1.0	1.6	1.9	2.3	2.2	2.7	2.7	3.4	2.9	4.5
Depreciation **14**	3.4	1.8	2.2	2.8	3.1	3.2	3.7	3.6	4.0	4.8	4.4	5.9	4.5
Amortization and Depletion **15**	0.6	0.5	0.2	0.4	0.5	0.5	0.7	0.7	0.7	0.6	0.7	0.4	1.5
Pensions and Other Deferred Comp. **16**	0.2	0.0	0.1	0.1	0.1	0.3	0.1	0.2	0.1	0.2	0.2	0.2	0.7
Employee Benefits **17**	1.2	1.3	0.5	0.7	0.9	1.1	1.2	1.2	1.3	1.8	1.6	1.9	2.6
Advertising **18**	2.6	1.4	1.9	2.6	3.4	3.8	3.5	2.8	2.4	3.2	3.2	3.7	2.2
Other Expenses **19**	25.8	34.0	24.9	24.9	23.5	24.3	23.1	24.0	28.0	24.4	26.8	22.6	30.9
Officers' Compensation **20**	2.4	3.4	4.5	3.1	2.4	1.7	1.4	1.1	1.0	0.9	0.6	1.0	0.5
Operating Margin **21**	*	*	0.9	1.5	0.5	*	*	*	*	*	*	*	*
Operating Margin Before Officers' Comp. **22**	*	*	5.3	4.6	2.9	*	*	*	*	*	*	*	*

Selected Average Balance Sheet ($ in Thousands)

Net Receivables 23	45	0	4	30	96	235	727	2086	2979	6599	36054	50265	481218
Inventories 24	20	0	7	29	58	255	380	1125	2131	4618	11283	25782	88742
Net Property, Plant and Equipment 25	287	0	52	361	1032	3561	8262	18681	36949	83912	195563	445286	1597852
Total Assets 26	689	0	104	689	1828	6885	15025	34209	66705	152682	369693	902787	5837627
Notes and Loans Payable 27	302	0	76	417	1164	4114	8838	19028	37211	60562	191787	250319	1786488
All Other Liabilities 28	178	0	23	152	334	1860	3171	7752	15322	35185	68538	266608	1697767
Net Worth 29	210	0	5	120	330	912	3015	7430	14172	56935	109368	385860	2355372

Selected Financial Ratios (Times to 1)

Current Ratio 30	0.9	•	1.3	1.0	1.0	1.0	0.7	0.7	0.7	0.8	0.8	0.8	0.8
Quick Ratio 31	0.6	•	0.8	0.7	0.7	0.6	0.5	0.4	0.4	0.6	0.5	0.6	0.5
Net Sales to Working Capital 32	•	•	63.0	9150.5	•	•	•	•	•	•	•	•	•
Coverage Ratio 33	2.2	•	3.4	3.2	2.6	1.4	1.7	1.2	0.7	1.6	1.7	2.8	2.1
Total Asset Turnover 34	1.6	•	4.3	2.8	2.2	1.9	1.8	1.8	1.8	1.6	1.3	1.1	0.7
Inventory Turnover 35	22.4	•	27.7	26.2	27.6	19.3	29.6	25.4	21.3	21.4	16.4	14.1	16.5
Receivables Turnover 36	29.8	•	124.1	76.6	44.7	45.2	39.3	30.7	34.2	36.8	13.8	22.6	10.8
Total Liabilities to Net Worth 37	2.3	•	20.1	4.8	4.5	6.6	4.0	3.6	3.7	1.7	2.4	1.3	1.5
Current Assets to Working Capital 38	•	•	4.7	820.8	•	•	•	•	•	•	•	•	•
Current Liabilities to Working Capital 39	•	•	3.7	819.8	•	•	•	•	•	•	•	•	•
Working Capital to Net Sales 40	•	•	0.0	0.0	•	•	•	•	•	•	•	•	•
Inventory to Working Capital 41	•	•	0.9	137.0	•	•	•	•	•	•	•	•	•
Total Receipts to Cash Flow 42	5.2	7.9	6.0	5.7	5.8	5.9	6.0	6.4	5.1	5.7	4.4	5.4	3.5
Cost of Goods to Cash Flow 43	2.1	4.2	2.5	2.3	2.4	2.2	2.5	2.9	2.0	2.3	1.7	1.9	1.3
Cash Flow to Total Debt 44	0.4	•	0.8	0.6	0.5	0.4	0.4	0.4	0.4	0.4	0.4	0.4	0.3

Selected Financial Factors (in Percentages)

Debt Ratio 45	69.5	•	95.3	82.6	81.9	86.8	79.9	78.3	78.8	62.7	70.4	57.3	59.7
Return on Total Assets 46	7.5	•	10.8	8.9	8.8	5.1	7.1	4.9	3.5	6.6	7.8	9.1	6.6
Return on Equity Before Income Taxes 47	13.6	•	161.1	35.3	29.8	10.4	14.9	4.2	•	6.4	11.3	13.8	8.7
Return on Equity After Income Taxes 48	10.3	•	150.0	33.8	28.3	7.8	13.1	2.3	•	3.6	5.9	9.4	5.7
Profit Margin (Before Income Tax) 49	2.6	•	1.8	2.2	2.5	0.7	1.7	0.5	•	1.5	2.6	5.2	5.2
Profit Margin (After Income Tax) 50	1.9	•	1.6	2.1	2.4	0.5	1.5	0.3	•	0.9	1.3	3.6	3.4

Table II

Corporations with Net Income

FOOD SERVICES AND DRINKING PLACES

MONEY AMOUNTS AND SIZE OF ASSETS IN THOUSANDS OF DOLLARS

Item Description for Accounting Period 7/02 Through 6/03	Total	Zero Assets	Under 500	500 to 1,000	1,000 to 5,000	5,000 to 10,000	10,000 to 25,000	25,000 to 50,000	50,000 to 100,000	100,000 to 250,000	250,000 to 500,000	500,000 to 2,500,000	2,500,000 and over
Number of Enterprises 1	118738	8365	96994	7988	4512	494	213	64	27	33	16	0	0
Revenues ($ in Thousands)													
Net Sales 2	200044820	1585017	57992921	17507801	18990535	7275505	6110627	4280629	2996001	8101446	7853852	0	0
Interest 3	1517253	16	13400	8496	7123	4034	7050	3022	5383	19705	108417	0	0
Rents 4	438033	3	9041	3614	5361	9410	6523	7235	7322	41808	54962	0	0
Royalties 5	3315060	391	80	87	4101	1698	22240	9489	27680	158385	515933	0	0
Other Portfolio Income 6	818383	106167	119638	3989	44669	42043	16414	3262	2619	58282	9085	0	0
Other Receipts 7	7580086	25706	387631	83139	340328	119428	169431	63529	24102	206880	44918	0	0
Total Receipts 8	213713635	1717300	58522711	17607126	19392117	7452118	6332285	4367166	3063107	8586506	8587167	0	0
Average Total Receipts 9	1800	205	603	2204	4298	15085	29729	68237	113448	260197	536698	•	•
Operating Costs/Operating Income (%)													
Cost of Operations 10	39.1	41.4	40.6	37.9	42.0	37.8	42.3	46.5	35.5	43.0	39.4	•	•
Salaries and Wages 11	20.9	12.5	17.5	20.2	16.7	23.6	19.1	16.9	25.4	19.9	21.3	•	•
Taxes Paid 12	4.0	5.1	4.4	3.7	3.9	3.8	3.8	3.5	3.6	3.4	3.4	•	•
Interest Paid 13	2.1	0.6	0.6	0.8	1.4	1.3	1.8	1.8	1.7	1.9	3.3	•	•
Depreciation 14	3.3	1.3	1.5	2.1	2.6	2.9	3.5	3.4	4.4	4.7	4.0	•	•
Amortization and Depletion 15	0.6	0.3	0.2	0.4	0.4	0.3	0.4	0.5	0.6	0.5	0.8	•	•
Pensions and Other Deferred Comp. 16	0.3	0.0	0.0	0.1	0.1	0.2	0.1	0.2	0.2	0.3	0.2	•	•
Employee Benefits 17	1.3	0.3	0.5	0.6	0.8	1.0	1.3	1.3	1.4	1.6	1.5	•	•
Advertising 18	2.6	2.1	1.8	2.6	3.6	3.7	3.3	2.6	2.9	3.2	3.4	•	•
Other Expenses 19	24.7	28.8	22.7	23.3	22.3	21.1	21.8	21.0	22.6	22.1	26.4	•	•
Officers' Compensation 20	2.3	5.6	4.4	3.3	2.6	1.4	1.6	1.1	1.1	1.0	0.7	•	•
Operating Margin 21	•	1.8	5.7	5.0	3.6	2.9	1.0	1.4	0.7	•	•	•	•
Operating Margin Before Officers' Comp. 22	1.1	7.4	10.2	8.2	6.2	4.2	2.6	2.5	1.8	•	•	•	•

Selected Average Balance Sheet ($ in Thousands)

	•	•	•	•	•	•	•	•	•	•	•
Net Receivables 23	76	0	5	26	89	288	813	2465	3299	8116	31633
Inventories 24	30	0	8	32	61	305	417	1167	2401	4311	12873
Net Property, Plant and Equipment 25	436	0	51	326	960	3582	8139	19659	38642	86721	186099
Total Assets 26	1106	0	117	677	1815	6907	14999	34704	65815	154354	362499
Notes and Loans Payable 27	408	0	60	320	1005	3245	7472	17678	30721	52806	191119
All Other Liabilities 28	282	0	24	135	320	1208	3132	7070	15732	32462	59328
Net Worth 29	416	0	33	221	491	2454	4396	9955	19363	69086	112051

Selected Financial Ratios (Times to 1)

	•	•	•	•	•	•	•	•	•	•	•
Current Ratio 30	0.9	•	1.5	1.2	1.1	1.1	0.9	0.8	0.9	1.0	0.9
Quick Ratio 31	0.6	•	1.0	0.9	0.8	0.7	0.6	0.5	0.5	0.7	0.5
Net Sales to Working Capital 32	•	•	39.5	54.4	188.1	85.3	•	•	•	•	•
Coverage Ratio 33	3.7	16.7	13.0	8.2	5.0	4.9	3.5	2.9	2.7	3.2	2.5
Total Asset Turnover 34	1.5	•	5.1	3.2	2.3	2.1	1.9	1.9	1.7	1.6	1.4
Inventory Turnover 35	21.8	•	30.9	25.6	29.0	18.2	29.1	26.6	16.4	24.5	15.0
Receivables Turnover 36	27.2	•	243.6	96.1	45.2	41.7	37.5	29.5	29.6	33.3	17.1
Total Liabilities to Net Worth 37	1.7	•	2.6	2.1	2.7	1.8	2.4	2.5	2.4	1.2	2.2
Current Assets to Working Capital 38	•	•	2.9	5.2	20.7	10.3	•	•	•	•	•
Current Liabilities to Working Capital 39	•	•	1.9	4.2	19.7	9.3	•	•	•	•	•
Working Capital to Net Sales 40	•	•	0.0	0.0	0.0	0.0	•	•	•	•	•
Inventory to Working Capital 41	•	•	0.5	0.8	2.7	1.6	•	•	•	•	•
Total Receipts to Cash Flow 42	4.6	4.1	5.0	5.0	5.1	5.3	5.4	5.9	5.7	5.3	4.0
Cost of Goods to Cash Flow 43	1.8	1.7	2.0	1.9	2.1	2.0	2.3	2.7	2.0	2.3	1.6
Cash Flow to Total Debt 44	0.5	•	1.4	1.0	0.6	0.6	0.5	0.5	0.4	0.5	0.5

Selected Financial Factors (in Percentages)

	•	•	•	•	•	•	•	•	•	•	•
Debt Ratio 45	62.4	•	72.0	67.3	73.0	64.5	70.7	71.3	70.6	55.2	69.1
Return on Total Assets 46	11.9	•	36.8	20.4	16.5	14.1	12.3	10.1	7.9	9.8	11.1
Return on Equity Before Income Taxes 47	23.2	•	121.2	54.9	48.7	31.7	30.1	22.9	17.0	15.0	21.3
Return on Equity After Income Taxes 48	19.8	•	117.9	53.7	47.2	30.2	28.1	20.7	14.3	11.8	14.6
Profit Margin (Before Income Tax) 49	5.7	10.1	6.7	5.5	5.7	5.3	4.6	3.4	3.0	4.2	4.9
Profit Margin (After Income Tax) 50	4.9	10.0	6.5	5.4	5.5	5.0	4.3	3.1	2.5	3.3	3.3

Table I

Corporations with and without Net Income

AUTOMOTIVE REPAIR AND MAINTENANCE

MONEY AMOUNTS AND SIZE OF ASSETS IN THOUSANDS OF DOLLARS

Item Description for Accounting Period 7/02 Through 6/03	Total	Zero Assets	Under 500	500 to 1,000	1,000 to 5,000	5,000 to 10,000	10,000 to 25,000	25,000 to 50,000	50,000 to 100,000	100,000 to 250,000	250,000 to 500,000	500,000 to 2,500,000	2,500,000 and over
Number of Enterprises 1	102911	8748	86911	4626	2475	84	48	6	7	7	0	•	•
Revenues ($ in Thousands)													
Net Sales 2	59253293	1108755	37825447	7221382	8578719	793747	1126242	355492	739999	1503511	0	•	•
Interest 3	55464	358	7423	5454	6527	431	3583	838	462	30388	0	•	•
Rents 4	30257	0	9427	3489	8297	3674	3019	649	814	889	0	•	•
Royalties 5	14228	0	0	0	0	0	9064	3886	0	1278	0	•	•
Other Portfolio Income 6	273072	139843	93198	6193	15501	38	6381	11688	80	149	0	•	•
Other Receipts 7	292115	6474	172461	53421	30314	6191	10612	3361	5514	3766	0	•	•
Total Receipts 8	59918429	1255430	38107956	7289939	8639358	804081	1158901	375914	746869	1539981	0	•	•
Average Total Receipts 9	582	144	438	1576	3491	9572	24144	62652	106696	219997	•	•	•
Operating Costs/Operating Income (%)													
Cost of Operations 10	50.4	37.7	48.6	56.9	54.8	47.4	47.2	40.0	45.3	57.4	•	•	•
Salaries and Wages 11	12.5	12.4	12.2	11.3	13.3	15.0	15.4	18.9	24.0	9.2	•	•	•
Taxes Paid 12	3.5	4.2	3.5	3.6	3.7	3.5	3.6	3.6	3.0	2.4	•	•	•
Interest Paid 13	1.3	0.4	0.9	1.8	1.6	2.1	2.0	1.8	3.6	6.1	•	•	•
Depreciation 14	2.4	2.6	2.0	2.4	3.2	2.5	3.6	2.6	3.4	4.6	•	•	•
Amortization and Depletion 15	0.3	0.2	0.2	0.1	0.4	0.7	0.5	1.2	2.0	1.8	•	•	•
Pensions and Other Deferred Comp. 16	0.2	•	0.1	0.1	0.3	0.2	0.2	0.1	0.2	0.2	•	•	•
Employee Benefits 17	1.2	1.5	1.2	1.1	1.1	1.4	1.7	1.9	1.3	1.4	•	•	•
Advertising 18	1.5	2.5	1.3	1.6	1.7	3.5	2.8	2.0	2.0	1.4	•	•	•
Other Expenses 19	20.4	41.2	22.0	15.7	16.0	18.7	21.3	33.0	15.8	13.8	•	•	•
Officers' Compensation 20	6.3	6.7	7.6	3.9	5.0	1.7	2.2	0.8	0.6	0.9	•	•	•
Operating Margin 21	0.1	•	0.3	1.4	•	3.4	•	•	•	0.7	•	•	•
Operating Margin Before Officers' Comp. 22	6.3	7.9	7.9	5.4	4.0	5.1	1.9	•	•	1.7	•	•	•

Selected Average Balance Sheet ($ in Thousands)

Net Receivables 23	19	0	9	61	227	876	1736	3796	3986	11074
Inventories 24	22	0	13	80	208	909	1032	4483	6683	18296
Net Property, Plant and Equipment 25	87	0	43	350	894	3579	6560	5645	27644	79011
Total Assets 26	193	0	98	698	1797	7551	15193	37461	73858	222786
Notes and Loans Payable 27	116	0	63	423	1036	4293	6707	9733	43224	122550
All Other Liabilities 28	34	0	20	90	253	1301	3150	14072	15989	34264
Net Worth 29	44	0	16	185	509	1957	5335	13656	14645	65972

Selected Financial Ratios (Times to 1)

Current Ratio 30	1.5	•	1.5	1.9	1.5	1.4	1.3	1.2	1.2	1.0
Quick Ratio 31	0.9	•	1.0	1.1	1.0	0.8	0.8	0.6	0.4	0.4
Net Sales to Working Capital 32	24.9	•	31.3	13.6	16.6	13.2	22.9	30.6	38.7	•
Coverage Ratio 33	1.9	9.6	2.2	2.3	0.8	3.3	2.3	0.9	1.0	1.5
Total Asset Turnover 34	3.0	•	4.4	2.2	1.9	1.3	1.5	1.6	1.4	1.0
Inventory Turnover 35	13.0	•	16.9	11.2	9.1	4.9	10.7	5.3	7.2	6.7
Receivables Turnover 36	27.8	•	41.2	22.7	15.9	10.3	12.4	8.1	11.3	19.4
Total Liabilities to Net Worth 37	3.4	•	5.3	2.8	2.5	2.9	1.8	1.7	4.0	2.4
Current Assets to Working Capital 38	3.0	•	2.9	2.2	3.1	3.5	4.9	6.2	7.0	•
Current Liabilities to Working Capital 39	2.0	•	1.9	1.2	2.1	2.5	3.9	5.2	6.0	•
Working Capital to Net Sales 40	0.0	•	0.0	0.1	0.1	0.1	0.0	0.0	0.0	•
Inventory to Working Capital 41	0.9	•	0.9	0.7	1.0	1.2	1.0	1.1	2.5	•
Total Receipts to Cash Flow 42	6.8	2.8	6.4	7.5	10.3	6.4	7.0	4.5	9.2	9.2
Cost of Goods to Cash Flow 43	3.4	1.1	3.1	4.3	5.7	3.1	3.3	1.8	4.2	5.3
Cash Flow to Total Debt 44	0.6	•	0.8	0.4	0.3	0.3	0.3	0.5	0.2	0.1

Selected Financial Factors (in Percentages)

Debt Ratio 45	77.2		84.2	73.5	71.7	74.1	64.9	63.5	80.2	70.4
Return on Total Assets 46	7.4	•	8.6	9.5	2.5	8.5	7.0	2.6	4.9	8.9
Return on Equity Before Income Taxes 47	15.5		29.8	20.2	22.9	11.2	•	•	•	10.3
Return on Equity After Income Taxes 48	14.0		28.2	18.8	21.8	9.8	•	•	•	7.1
Profit Margin (Before Income Tax) 49	1.2	3.8	1.1	2.4	4.7	2.5	•	•	•	3.2
Profit Margin (After Income Tax) 50	1.1	3.8	1.0	2.2	4.5	2.2	•	•	•	2.2

Table II
Corporations with Net Income

AUTOMOTIVE REPAIR AND MAINTENANCE

MONEY AMOUNTS AND SIZE OF ASSETS IN THOUSANDS OF DOLLARS

Item Description for Accounting Period 7/02 Through 6/03	Total	Zero Assets	Under 500	500 to 1,000	1,000 to 5,000	5,000 to 10,000	10,000 to 25,000	25,000 to 50,000	50,000 to 100,000	100,000 to 250,000	250,000 to 500,000	500,000 to 2,500,000	2,500,000 and over
Number of Enterprises **1**	54581	3062	46464	3716	1271	0	27	0	0	0	0	0	•
Revenues ($ in Thousands)													
Net Sales **2**	37504504	477008	23460258	5695888	5199017	0	690094	0	0	0	0	0	•
Interest **3**	45144	0	5015	3049	6242	0	1136	0	0	0	0	0	•
Rents **4**	15819	0	2840	3489	6735	0	1042	0	0	0	0	0	•
Royalties **5**	8384	0	0	0	0	0	4443	0	0	0	0	0	•
Other Portfolio Income **6**	235641	139512	63349	2968	14278	0	3676	0	0	0	0	0	•
Other Receipts **7**	214702	5613	118470	52481	16708	0	6116	0	0	0	0	0	•
Total Receipts **8**	38024194	622133	23649932	5757875	5242980	0	706507	0	0	0	0	0	•
Average Total Receipts **9**	697	203	509	1549	4125	•	26167	•	•	•	•	•	•
Operating Costs/Operating Income (%)													
Cost of Operations **10**	49.6	25.6	47.7	56.8	53.1	•	44.4	•	•	•	•	•	•
Salaries and Wages **11**	11.6	8.9	10.9	12.2	14.5	•	13.1	•	•	•	•	•	•
Taxes Paid **12**	3.3	3.1	3.4	3.4	3.5	•	3.6	•	•	•	•	•	•
Interest Paid **13**	1.1	0.3	0.7	1.8	1.1	•	1.6	•	•	•	•	•	•
Depreciation **14**	2.0	4.1	1.6	2.3	2.3	•	3.1	•	•	•	•	•	•
Amortization and Depletion **15**	0.2	0.0	0.1	0.1	0.3	•	0.4	•	•	•	•	•	•
Pensions and Other Deferred Comp. **16**	0.2	•	0.1	0.1	0.4	•	0.2	•	•	•	•	•	•
Employee Benefits **17**	1.0	0.6	0.9	1.1	1.2	•	1.7	•	•	•	•	•	•
Advertising **18**	1.4	3.5	1.4	1.1	1.2	•	2.8	•	•	•	•	•	•
Other Expenses **19**	19.4	55.1	21.6	12.8	13.8	•	20.7	•	•	•	•	•	•
Officers' Compensation **20**	6.3	5.8	7.4	4.6	5.7	•	2.3	•	•	•	•	•	•
Operating Margin **21**	3.8	•	4.2	3.7	2.9	•	6.0	•	•	•	•	•	•
Operating Margin Before Officers' Comp. **22**	10.1	•	11.6	8.3	8.6	•	8.3	•	•	•	•	•	•

Selected Average Balance Sheet ($ in Thousands)

Net Receivables 23	21	0	10	70	224	1783
Inventories 24	25	0	13	82	226	1110
Net Property, Plant and Equipment 25	88	0	40	310	774	6873
Total Assets 26	217	0	106	686	1759	15075
Notes and Loans Payable 27	102	0	48	386	689	7258
All Other Liabilities 28	37	0	20	81	269	3287
Net Worth 29	78	0	39	219	801	4529

Selected Financial Ratios (Times to 1)

Current Ratio 30	1.8	•	1.8	2.2	1.9	1.3
Quick Ratio 31	1.2	•	1.3	1.4	1.3	0.8
Net Sales to Working Capital 32	18.4	•	23.8	10.3	12.1	24.2
Coverage Ratio 33	5.7	94.0	8.7	3.6	4.5	6.2
Total Asset Turnover 34	3.2	•	4.7	2.2	2.3	1.7
Inventory Turnover 35	13.8	•	17.9	10.6	9.6	10.2
Receivables Turnover 36	27.6	•	40.5	43.8	19.0	10.7
Total Liabilities to Net Worth 37	1.8	•	1.8	2.1	1.2	2.3
Current Assets to Working Capital 38	2.3	•	2.3	1.8	2.1	4.6
Current Liabilities to Working Capital 39	1.3	•	1.3	0.8	1.1	3.6
Working Capital to Net Sales 40	0.1	•	0.0	0.1	0.1	0.0
Inventory to Working Capital 41	0.7	•	0.6	0.6	0.6	0.8
Total Receipts to Cash Flow 42	5.5	1.4	5.1	7.3	8.1	5.4
Cost of Goods to Cash Flow 43	2.7	0.4	2.4	4.1	4.3	2.4
Cash Flow to Total Debt 44	0.9	•	1.5	0.5	0.5	0.5

Selected Financial Factors (in Percentages)

Debt Ratio 45	64.0	•	63.7	68.1	54.5	70.0
Return on Total Assets 46	20.0	•	26.9	14.8	11.2	17.0
Return on Equity Before Income Taxes 47	45.9	•	65.6	33.6	19.1	47.3
Return on Equity After Income Taxes 48	44.3	•	64.4	32.1	17.9	44.5
Profit Margin (Before Income Tax) 49	5.2	23.3	5.0	4.8	3.7	8.4
Profit Margin (After Income Tax) 50	5.0	23.3	4.9	4.6	3.5	7.9

Table I

Corporations with and without Net Income

OTHER REPAIR AND MAINTENANCE

MONEY AMOUNTS AND SIZE OF ASSETS IN THOUSANDS OF DOLLARS

Item Description for Accounting Period 7/02 Through 6/03	Total	Zero Assets	Under 500	500 to 1,000	1,000 to 5,000	5,000 to 10,000	10,000 to 25,000	25,000 to 50,000	50,000 to 100,000	100,000 to 250,000	250,000 to 500,000	500,000 to 2,500,000	2,500,000 and over
Number of Enterprises **1**	53716	7541	43103	1330	1548	100	64	12	8	6	4	0	•
Revenues ($ in Thousands)													
Net Sales **2**	28438700	909540	12287440	2222105	5660893	1280959	1846831	654111	776532	1424944	1375346	0	•
Interest **3**	38675	1180	7525	1139	6606	1651	1756	780	3871	7461	6704	0	•
Rents **4**	6643	0	780	180	959	3863	400	0	2	23	435	0	•
Royalties **5**	13218	0	0	0	1214	74	1	546	242	0	11140	0	•
Other Portfolio Income **6**	47458	815	5817	2712	11660	12418	1532	7221	20	2477	2784	0	•
Other Receipts **7**	280167	650	47536	3333	123961	3755	16161	8212	2164	9187	65214	0	•
Total Receipts **8**	28824861	912185	12349098	2229469	5805293	1302720	1866681	670870	782831	1444092	1461623	0	•
Average Total Receipts **9**	537	121	287	1676	3750	13027	29167	55906	97854	240682	365406	•	
Operating Costs/Operating Income (%)													
Cost of Operations **10**	49.6	44.0	41.0	27.6	55.2	57.2	65.7	73.1	73.1	66.5	72.7	•	•
Salaries and Wages **11**	14.3	6.9	15.1	28.8	13.6	12.0	11.6	8.4	7.1	11.0	8.3	•	•
Taxes Paid **12**	3.0	3.0	3.2	3.8	3.1	2.9	2.6	2.2	2.3	2.5	2.1	•	•
Interest Paid **13**	1.0	0.7	0.6	0.9	1.1	1.1	1.0	1.6	2.6	2.4	2.0	•	•
Depreciation **14**	2.4	2.3	2.4	3.0	2.4	3.2	3.1	2.5	1.1	2.2	1.2	•	•
Amortization and Depletion **15**	0.2	0.0	0.1	0.0	0.2	0.2	0.1	0.3	0.5	0.7	1.2	•	•
Pensions and Other Deferred Comp. **16**	0.5	0.1	0.3	0.4	0.9	0.7	0.9	0.5	0.1	0.1	•	•	•
Employee Benefits **17**	1.9	1.5	1.1	6.3	1.5	2.1	2.6	1.4	0.6	2.5	2.3	•	•
Advertising **18**	0.6	2.1	0.7	0.4	0.6	0.5	0.5	0.4	0.2	0.2	0.5	•	•
Other Expenses **19**	18.5	31.3	22.9	15.5	16.4	15.7	10.3	12.6	10.1	10.5	14.5	•	•
Officers' Compensation **20**	6.4	10.5	9.1	8.6	5.0	4.1	1.7	1.5	0.5	0.5	0.9	•	•
Operating Margin **21**	1.6	•	3.6	4.8	0.1	0.1	•	•	1.7	1.0	•	•	•
Operating Margin Before Officers' Comp. **22**	7.9	8.1	12.7	13.4	5.1	4.2	1.6	•	2.2	1.5	•	•	•

Selected Average Balance Sheet ($ in Thousands)

Net Receivables 23	62	0	10	223	475	2129	4364	10674	17127	39767	225921	•
Inventories 24	39	0	12	88	388	2041	3285	9839	8682	14183	44739	•
Net Property, Plant and Equipment 25	46	0	21	218	360	1396	3537	6179	4729	26403	20570	•
Total Assets 26	219	0	62	687	1822	6628	15045	33133	61755	174385	446770	•
Notes and Loans Payable 27	87	0	32	321	757	2398	4902	12412	11748	76641	107531	•
All Other Liabilities 28	73	0	14	141	581	1240	5294	13900	29599	52222	270477	•
Net Worth 29	59	0	16	225	484	2990	4850	6821	20408	45521	68762	•

Selected Financial Ratios (Times to 1)

Current Ratio 30	1.5	•	1.7	2.3	1.6	2.0	1.4	1.4	2.1	1.7	1.0	•
Quick Ratio 31	1.0	•	1.1	1.7	1.0	1.0	0.8	0.8	1.0	1.0	0.8	•
Net Sales to Working Capital 32	11.2	•	19.5	7.2	8.1	5.3	10.1	8.6	4.7	7.8	24.8	•
Coverage Ratio 33	3.9	•	7.8	7.0	3.4	2.7	2.0	•	2.0	2.0	1.3	•
Total Asset Turnover 34	2.4	•	4.6	2.4	2.0	1.9	1.9	1.6	1.6	1.4	0.8	•
Inventory Turnover 35	6.8	•	10.1	5.2	5.2	3.6	5.8	4.0	8.2	11.1	5.6	•
Receivables Turnover 36	9.3	•	24.9	7.8	8.0	6.2	6.3	5.0	5.6	8.5	2.2	•
Total Liabilities to Net Worth 37	2.7	•	2.8	2.1	2.8	1.2	2.1	3.9	2.0	2.8	5.5	•
Current Assets to Working Capital 38	2.9	•	2.5	1.7	2.6	2.0	3.3	3.5	1.9	2.4	24.0	•
Current Liabilities to Working Capital 39	1.9	•	1.5	0.7	1.6	1.0	2.3	2.5	0.9	1.4	23.0	•
Working Capital to Net Sales 40	0.1	•	0.1	0.1	0.1	0.2	0.1	0.1	0.2	0.1	0.0	•
Inventory to Working Capital 41	0.8	•	0.8	0.4	0.8	0.9	1.1	1.4	0.5	0.6	2.8	•
Total Receipts to Cash Flow 42	5.8	5.0	4.5	5.5	6.4	8.2	12.4	18.0	9.6	11.4	7.6	•
Cost of Goods to Cash Flow 43	2.9	2.2	1.8	1.5	3.6	4.7	8.1	13.1	7.0	7.6	5.5	•
Cash Flow to Total Debt 44	0.6	•	1.4	0.7	0.4	0.4	0.2	0.1	0.2	0.2	0.1	•

Selected Financial Factors (in Percentages)

Debt Ratio 45	73.2	•	73.8	67.3	73.4	54.9	67.8	79.4	67.0	73.9	84.6	•
Return on Total Assets 46	9.5	•	21.3	14.5	7.5	5.6	3.9	•	8.0	6.4	2.0	•
Return on Equity Before Income Taxes 47	26.4	•	70.8	37.9	20.0	7.8	6.0	•	12.1	12.1	2.9	•
Return on Equity After Income Taxes 48	23.4	•	68.9	37.4	16.8	5.0	3.3	•	6.8	8.1	•	•
Profit Margin (Before Income Tax) 49	2.9	•	4.1	5.1	2.6	1.8	1.0	•	2.5	2.3	0.6	•
Profit Margin (After Income Tax) 50	2.6	•	4.0	5.0	2.2	1.2	0.6	•	1.4	1.6	•	•

385

Table II
Corporations with Net Income

OTHER REPAIR AND MAINTENANCE

MONEY AMOUNTS AND SIZE OF ASSETS IN THOUSANDS OF DOLLARS

Item Description for Accounting Period 7/02 Through 6/03	Total	Zero Assets	Under 500	500 to 1,000	1,000 to 5,000	5,000 to 10,000	10,000 to 25,000	25,000 to 50,000	50,000 to 100,000	100,000 to 250,000	250,000 to 500,000	500,000 to 2,500,000	2,500,000 and over
Number of Enterprises **1**	30306	3010	25266	854	1038	82	41	0	0	0	0	•	•
Revenues ($ in Thousands)													
Net Sales **2**	18833999	573646	7952641	1719627	3980183	1062475	1307133	0	0	0	0	•	•
Interest **3**	24163	140	1926	637	5130	755	1066	0	0	0	0	•	•
Rents **4**	4595	0	0	180	959	3098	357	0	0	0	0	•	•
Royalties **5**	2650	0	0	0	0	0	1	0	0	0	0	•	•
Other Portfolio Income **6**	40421	6	5296	2712	9894	11985	1264	0	0	0	0	•	•
Other Receipts **7**	209926	532	42413	190	79249	3575	10441	0	0	0	0	•	•
Total Receipts **8**	19115754	574324	8002276	1722346	4075415	1081888	1320262	0	0	0	0	•	•
Average Total Receipts **9**	631	191	317	2018	3926	13194	32202	•	•	•	•	•	•
Operating Costs/Operating Income (%)													
Cost of Operations **10**	46.0	48.0	38.2	18.8	52.6	56.8	62.8	•	•	•	•	•	•
Salaries and Wages **11**	14.6	2.4	13.3	34.3	14.1	11.7	11.3	•	•	•	•	•	•
Taxes Paid **12**	2.8	2.8	2.9	3.8	2.8	3.0	2.6	•	•	•	•	•	•
Interest Paid **13**	0.7	0.6	0.4	0.6	1.0	0.7	0.8	•	•	•	•	•	•
Depreciation **14**	2.3	1.0	2.3	3.2	2.2	3.0	2.3	•	•	•	•	•	•
Amortization and Depletion **15**	0.1	0.1	0.0	0.0	0.2	0.0	0.1	•	•	•	•	•	•
Pensions and Other Deferred Comp. **16**	0.4	0.1	0.3	0.2	0.7	0.7	1.1	•	•	•	•	•	•
Employee Benefits **17**	1.9	1.0	0.9	8.0	1.2	2.1	2.7	•	•	•	•	•	•
Advertising **18**	0.5	2.6	0.4	0.3	0.7	0.4	0.4	•	•	•	•	•	•
Other Expenses **19**	17.9	27.7	22.4	15.4	15.4	15.4	9.5	•	•	•	•	•	•
Officers' Compensation **20**	6.6	9.5	9.5	8.1	5.3	4.1	1.9	•	•	•	•	•	•
Operating Margin **21**	6.1	4.2	9.4	7.3	3.8	2.2	4.4	•	•	•	•	•	•
Operating Margin Before Officers' Comp. **22**	12.7	13.7	18.9	15.4	9.1	6.3	6.3	•	•	•	•	•	•

Selected Average Balance Sheet ($ in Thousands)

Net Receivables 23	58	0	10	275	475	2107	4492
Inventories 24	44	0	9	58	449	2024	3616
Net Property, Plant and Equipment 25	49	0	18	206	356	1436	3520
Total Assets 26	225	0	60	693	1854	6591	15345
Notes and Loans Payable 27	71	0	20	293	707	1887	3925
All Other Liabilities 28	68	0	13	159	537	1307	4538
Net Worth 29	86	0	27	241	610	3397	6882

Selected Financial Ratios (Times to 1)

Current Ratio 30	1.8	·	1.9	2.3	1.9	2.0	1.8
Quick Ratio 31	1.1	·	1.3	1.8	1.1	1.0	1.1
Net Sales to Working Capital 32	9.9	·	17.6	8.5	6.7	5.6	7.0
Coverage Ratio 33	11.3	8.0	28.8	12.7	7.0	6.6	7.5
Total Asset Turnover 34	2.8	·	5.2	2.9	2.1	2.0	2.1
Inventory Turnover 35	6.5	·	13.4	6.5	4.5	3.6	5.5
Receivables Turnover 36	11.1	·	29.8	14.7	7.8	7.4	6.7
Total Liabilities to Net Worth 37	1.6	·	1.2	1.9	2.0	0.9	1.2
Current Assets to Working Capital 38	2.3	·	2.1	1.8	2.2	2.0	2.2
Current Liabilities to Working Capital 39	1.3	·	1.1	0.8	1.2	1.0	1.2
Working Capital to Net Sales 40	0.1	·	0.1	0.1	0.1	0.2	0.1
Inventory to Working Capital 41	0.6	·	0.5	0.2	0.7	1.0	0.7
Total Receipts to Cash Flow 42	4.6	4.2	3.6	4.7	5.6	7.4	8.0
Cost of Goods to Cash Flow 43	2.1	2.0	1.4	0.9	2.9	4.2	5.0
Cash Flow to Total Debt 44	1.0	·	2.7	0.9	0.6	0.5	0.5

Selected Financial Factors (in Percentages)

Debt Ratio 45	61.8	·	55.1	65.2	67.1	48.5	55.2
Return on Total Assets 46	23.1	·	54.3	23.8	14.9	9.2	12.9
Return on Equity Before Income Taxes 47	55.1	·	116.6	63.1	38.9	15.2	24.9
Return on Equity After Income Taxes 48	51.5	·	114.6	62.4	35.1	12.2	22.0
Profit Margin (Before Income Tax) 49	7.6	4.3	10.0	7.5	6.2	4.0	5.4
Profit Margin (After Income Tax) 50	7.1	4.2	9.9	7.5	5.6	3.2	4.7

Table I

Corporations with and without Net Income

PERSONAL AND LAUNDRY SERVICES

MONEY AMOUNTS AND SIZE OF ASSETS IN THOUSANDS OF DOLLARS

Item Description for Accounting Period 7/02 Through 6/03	Total	Zero Assets	Under 500	500 to 1,000	1,000 to 5,000	5,000 to 10,000	10,000 to 25,000	25,000 to 50,000	50,000 to 100,000	100,000 to 250,000	250,000 to 500,000	500,000 to 2,500,000	2,500,000 and over
Number of Enterprises 1	126917	17673	99732	5866	3225	211	116	42	21	13	5	10	3
Revenues ($ in Thousands)													
Net Sales 2	62133700	1487255	25350461	7113865	7687850	1727159	1898691	1401498	1989703	1743078	1432785	7634000	2667356
Interest 3	270597	990	13357	5432	14974	4865	8672	6681	7373	11366	8584	94858	93446
Rents 4	102860	0	4497	5125	2572	432	2991	1320	7302	7480	270	55122	15750
Royalties 5	45818	0	0	0	0	0	131	10504	8973	7522	1	18647	40
Other Portfolio Income 6	326143	48114	80887	28348	35187	8094	6474	3677	22823	481	7032	68590	16435
Other Receipts 7	939597	-29091	201812	53942	111958	23931	34573	191101	68107	38619	14174	157166	73303
Total Receipts 8	63818715	1507268	25651014	7206712	7852541	1764481	1951532	1614781	2104281	1808546	1462846	8028383	2866330
Average Total Receipts 9	503	85	257	1229	2435	8362	16824	38447	100204	139119	292569	802838	955443
Operating Costs/Operating Income (%)													
Cost of Operations 10	27.0	16.7	22.3	17.2	33.6	42.7	33.0	26.9	36.1	24.9	32.1	39.3	26.2
Salaries and Wages 11	22.8	20.3	22.2	28.9	22.6	15.6	19.3	24.8	16.8	23.5	30.9	19.1	30.7
Taxes Paid 12	4.1	3.2	4.0	5.2	4.0	3.5	3.8	3.9	2.5	3.1	3.9	3.9	5.3
Interest Paid 13	2.2	1.0	1.0	1.3	1.8	1.8	2.3	3.3	2.2	4.3	2.2	3.6	11.5
Depreciation 14	3.7	4.4	3.0	3.5	4.0	7.4	4.5	3.5	2.6	5.2	5.5	4.7	4.3
Amortization and Depletion 15	0.7	0.2	0.4	0.3	0.5	0.3	0.6	0.8	0.8	1.8	0.8	1.7	2.2
Pensions and Other Deferred Comp. 16	0.5	0.2	0.4	0.5	0.9	0.2	0.5	0.5	0.3	0.5	0.7	0.6	1.9
Employee Benefits 17	1.8	1.3	0.9	1.9	1.2	1.9	3.1	7.3	4.5	2.6	4.7	2.2	1.7
Advertising 18	2.0	2.2	2.1	1.9	1.8	2.0	1.8	3.0	2.5	4.5	0.7	0.8	2.3
Other Expenses 19	29.6	39.7	32.6	31.2	22.3	22.5	29.0	34.1	34.8	31.9	18.3	22.0	36.4
Officers' Compensation 20	6.2	12.6	9.2	8.4	6.5	3.4	3.2	3.6	1.3	1.3	0.5	0.4	0.5
Operating Margin 21	•	1.9	•	0.8	•	•	•	•	•	•	•	1.6	•
Operating Margin Before Officers' Comp. 22	5.7	10.8	11.1	8.2	7.3	1.9	2.1	•	•	•	•	0.2	2.1

Selected Average Balance Sheet ($ in Thousands)

Net Receivables 23	51	0	4	60	231	1097	2016	4033	10930	12210	43694	67474	995836
Inventories 24	18	0	3	24	63	255	953	1335	3750	7403	16510	82176	81395
Net Property, Plant and Equipment 25	133	0	34	330	791	2830	5324	11208	22376	36000	111668	217170	1229084
Total Assets 26	396	0	78	723	1866	6470	14358	35536	68769	133708	366629	909958	4550436
Notes and Loans Payable 27	176	0	55	315	826	3070	5322	14112	23523	63049	81771	242006	2085892
All Other Liabilities 28	115	0	11	109	402	1907	4894	11367	22644	46937	141611	255176	1925270
Net Worth 29	105	0	11	299	638	1493	4143	10057	22603	23721	143246	412776	539274

Selected Financial Ratios (Times to 1)

Current Ratio 30	1.5	•	1.7	2.3	1.5	1.4	1.2	1.6	1.6	0.7	1.3	1.3	1.6
Quick Ratio 31	1.1	•	1.3	1.7	1.2	1.2	0.7	1.1	1.0	0.4	0.9	0.6	1.3
Net Sales to Working Capital 32	12.7	•	26.2	8.7	12.2	11.4	19.9	7.6	10.3	•	12.5	15.1	1.9
Coverage Ratio 33	2.0	0.6	4.0	1.8	2.6	1.4	1.8	2.0	1.7	1.0	1.8	3.0	•
Total Asset Turnover 34	1.2	•	3.3	1.7	1.3	1.3	1.1	0.9	1.4	1.0	0.8	0.8	0.2
Inventory Turnover 35	7.5	•	16.9	8.7	12.7	13.7	5.7	6.7	9.1	4.5	5.6	3.7	2.9
Receivables Turnover 36	9.8	•	42.5	20.1	10.5	4.6	7.3	10.7	9.0	9.9	6.1	8.5	1.1
Total Liabilities to Net Worth 37	2.8	•	6.2	1.4	1.9	3.3	2.5	2.5	2.0	4.6	1.6	1.2	7.4
Current Assets to Working Capital 38	3.0	•	2.4	1.8	3.1	3.5	7.0	2.8	2.6	•	3.9	4.2	2.7
Current Liabilities to Working Capital 39	2.0	•	1.4	0.8	2.1	2.5	6.0	1.8	1.6	•	2.9	3.2	1.7
Working Capital to Net Sales 40	0.1	•	0.0	0.1	0.1	0.1	0.1	0.1	0.1	•	0.1	0.1	0.5
Inventory to Working Capital 41	0.4	•	0.3	0.2	0.3	0.4	1.1	0.4	0.4	•	0.4	1.5	0.2
Total Receipts to Cash Flow 42	4.8	4.2	4.2	6.2	5.7	5.7	4.8	3.2	3.5	6.9	6.2	4.7	8.8
Cost of Goods to Cash Flow 43	1.3	0.7	0.9	1.1	1.9	2.5	1.6	0.9	1.3	1.7	2.0	1.8	2.3
Cash Flow to Total Debt 44	0.4	•	0.9	0.5	0.3	0.3	0.4	0.4	0.6	0.2	0.2	0.3	0.0

Selected Financial Factors (in Percentages)

Debt Ratio 45	73.5	•	86.1	58.6	65.8	76.9	71.1	71.7	67.1	82.3	60.9	54.6	88.1
Return on Total Assets 46	5.4	•	13.6	4.0	5.9	3.1	4.5	6.3	5.3	4.4	3.1	8.9	•
Return on Equity Before Income Taxes 47	10.3	•	73.6	4.4	10.7	3.5	6.7	11.1	6.8	0.5	3.5	13.1	•
Return on Equity After Income Taxes 48	8.0	•	72.1	3.7	9.8	2.0	5.0	9.1	4.2	•	1.7	8.1	•
Profit Margin (Before Income Tax) 49	2.2	•	3.1	1.1	2.9	0.6	1.7	3.3	1.6	0.1	1.7	7.1	•
Profit Margin (After Income Tax) 50	1.7	•	3.1	0.9	2.6	0.4	1.3	2.8	1.0	•	0.8	4.4	•

Table II

Corporations with Net Income

PERSONAL AND LAUNDRY SERVICES

MONEY AMOUNTS AND SIZE OF ASSETS IN THOUSANDS OF DOLLARS

Item Description for Accounting Period 7/02 Through 6/03	Total	Zero Assets	Under 500	500 to 1,000	1,000 to 5,000	5,000 to 10,000	10,000 to 25,000	25,000 to 50,000	50,000 to 100,000	100,000 to 250,000	250,000 to 500,000	500,000 to 2,500,000	2,500,000 and over
Number of Enterprises **1**	66236	8341	52117	3425	2139	94	71	24	13	8	0	5	0
Revenues ($ in Thousands)													
Net Sales **2**	40563672	840188	16769389	5654255	5772077	787493	1276018	877479	1231277	1594729	0	5760767	0
Interest **3**	129731	789	10220	4484	8547	2289	5909	4192	2544	11655	0	79102	0
Rents **4**	66184	0	3611	264	1616	205	2898	503	6747	91	0	50249	0
Royalties **5**	40138	0	0	0	0	0	33	10504	8973	1980	0	18647	0
Other Portfolio Income **6**	227525	47599	35414	25914	27180	6141	5533	1436	22783	132	0	55395	0
Other Receipts **7**	648209	7497	172032	28736	46642	19741	22167	148457	47840	19370	0	135727	0
Total Receipts **8**	41675459	896073	16990666	5713653	5856062	815869	1312558	1042571	1320164	1627957	0	6099887	0
Average Total Receipts **9**	629	107	326	1668	2738	8679	18487	43440	101551	203495	·	1219977	·
Operating Costs/Operating Income (%)													
Cost of Operations **10**	26.1	9.2	22.1	17.4	30.9	38.2	33.0	15.3	45.7	23.4	·	38.8	·
Salaries and Wages **11**	24.1	22.3	23.9	30.0	24.3	16.1	20.4	26.3	14.8	26.7	·	21.6	·
Taxes Paid **12**	4.1	3.5	4.0	5.1	4.0	3.2	4.2	3.8	2.3	3.2	·	4.4	·
Interest Paid **13**	1.3	0.6	0.8	0.7	1.3	1.1	1.6	2.6	2.4	2.3	·	2.9	·
Depreciation **14**	3.0	1.6	2.4	2.4	2.8	6.4	3.8	3.3	3.1	6.7	·	4.2	·
Amortization and Depletion **15**	0.6	0.0	0.4	0.1	0.4	0.3	0.3	0.8	0.6	0.9	·	1.6	·
Pensions and Other Deferred Comp. **16**	0.6	0.3	0.5	0.6	0.9	0.2	0.7	0.7	0.4	0.7	·	0.7	·
Employee Benefits **17**	1.9	1.2	1.0	2.0	1.1	1.4	3.7	9.5	5.3	3.3	·	2.3	·
Advertising **18**	2.0	1.4	2.4	1.9	1.9	1.1	1.3	3.6	3.5	2.4	·	1.0	·
Other Expenses **19**	24.8	36.4	26.8	28.2	19.8	24.6	24.4	36.5	22.2	26.6	·	17.7	·
Officers' Compensation **20**	6.1	10.5	8.0	7.9	7.6	3.3	3.5	4.4	1.8	0.8	·	0.5	·
Operating Margin **21**	5.3	12.9	7.7	3.6	5.0	4.0	3.0	·	·	3.1	·	4.1	·
Operating Margin Before Officers' Comp. **22**	11.5	23.4	15.7	11.6	12.6	7.3	6.6	·	·	3.9	·	4.6	·

Selected Average Balance Sheet ($ in Thousands)

Net Receivables 23	33	0	6	78	223	1256	1923	3445	7416	20583	104526
Inventories 24	23	0	3	22	73	206	1071	1497	5206	9629	125437
Net Property, Plant and Equipment 25	111	0	34	294	655	1964	4695	8674	22826	71528	311153
Total Assets 26	324	0	85	734	1888	6556	14086	35871	67538	187123	1133618
Notes and Loans Payable 27	111	0	41	238	652	1753	3970	9409	24609	53890	311800
All Other Liabilities 28	60	0	11	96	421	2550	4341	11797	15490	37100	168050
Net Worth 29	154	0	33	400	815	2253	5776	14666	27439	96134	653769

Selected Financial Ratios (Times to 1)

Current Ratio 30	2.0	•	2.5	3.5	1.6	1.6	1.5	1.7	2.2	1.7	1.9
Quick Ratio 31	1.3	•	1.9	2.8	1.3	1.4	1.0	1.2	1.1	0.9	0.8
Net Sales to Working Capital 32	11.2	•	18.1	7.3	10.5	7.8	9.4	7.2	8.0	9.1	8.4
Coverage Ratio 33	7.1	33.3	12.1	8.0	6.0	7.9	4.8	5.6	3.2	3.3	4.6
Total Asset Turnover 34	1.9	•	3.8	2.2	1.4	1.3	1.3	1.0	1.4	1.1	1.0
Inventory Turnover 35	6.8	•	22.1	12.9	11.5	15.5	5.5	3.7	8.3	4.8	3.6
Receivables Turnover 36	14.3	•	110.9	22.1	11.7	7.7	8.8	12.2	10.6	10.8	22.0
Total Liabilities to Net Worth 37	1.1	•	1.6	0.8	1.3	1.9	1.4	1.4	1.5	0.9	0.7
Current Assets to Working Capital 38	2.0	•	1.7	1.4	2.6	2.7	3.1	2.5	1.8	2.4	2.1
Current Liabilities to Working Capital 39	1.0	•	0.7	0.4	1.6	1.7	2.1	1.5	0.8	1.4	1.1
Working Capital to Net Sales 40	0.1	•	0.1	0.1	0.1	0.1	0.1	0.1	0.1	0.1	0.1
Inventory to Working Capital 41	0.4	•	0.2	0.1	0.3	0.2	0.6	0.3	0.5	0.5	0.9
Total Receipts to Cash Flow 42	4.4	2.3	3.9	5.7	5.3	3.7	4.8	2.4	5.4	4.7	5.2
Cost of Goods to Cash Flow 43	1.1	0.2	0.9	1.0	1.6	1.4	1.6	0.4	2.5	1.1	2.0
Cash Flow to Total Debt 44	0.8	•	1.6	0.9	0.5	0.5	0.5	0.7	0.4	0.5	0.5

Selected Financial Factors (in Percentages)

Debt Ratio 45	52.6	•	61.5	45.5	56.8	65.6	59.0	59.1	59.4	48.6	42.3
Return on Total Assets 46	17.8	•	37.4	12.0	10.8	11.2	9.4	14.8	10.9	8.0	13.6
Return on Equity Before Income Taxes 47	32.4	•	89.2	19.3	20.8	28.5	18.2	29.8	18.5	10.8	18.4
Return on Equity After Income Taxes 48	29.3	•	88.3	18.5	19.8	26.2	16.1	27.5	15.0	8.6	12.0
Profit Margin (Before Income Tax) 49	8.1	19.5	9.0	4.7	6.3	7.7	5.8	12.0	5.4	5.2	10.4
Profit Margin (After Income Tax) 50	7.4	18.5	8.9	4.5	6.0	7.1	5.2	11.0	4.4	4.1	6.8

Table I

Corporations with and without Net Income

RELIGIOUS, GRANTMAKING, CIVIC AND PROFESSIONAL ORGANIZATIONS

MONEY AMOUNTS AND SIZE OF ASSETS IN THOUSANDS OF DOLLARS

Item Description for Accounting Period 7/02 Through 6/03	Total	Zero Assets	Under 500	500 to 1,000	1,000 to 5,000	5,000 to 10,000	10,000 to 25,000	25,000 to 50,000	50,000 to 100,000	100,000 to 250,000	250,000 to 500,000	500,000 to 2,500,000	2,500,000 and over
Number of Enterprises 1	37590	2738	31143	2083	1447	103	56	10	4	5	0	0	0
Revenues ($ in Thousands)													
Net Sales 2	9575588	77778	3614486	1083732	1993789	366211	848322	184605	699276	707388	0	0	0
Interest 3	157267	1722	50517	24475	40907	7768	8666	966	466	21780	0	0	0
Rents 4	30038	0	13122	4503	4726	703	699	333	0	5951	0	0	0
Royalties 5	4175	0	0	0	0	0	4175	0	0	0	0	0	0
Other Portfolio Income 6	32184	0	19312	1194	7415	455	1255	1482	0	1069	0	0	0
Other Receipts 7	1991810	348	528381	108189	265780	88603	77163	25096	16458	881797	0	0	0
Total Receipts 8	11791062	79848	4225818	1222093	2312617	463740	940280	212482	716200	1617985	0	0	0
Average Total Receipts 9	314	29	136	587	1598	4502	16791	21248	179050	323597	•	•	•
Operating Costs/Operating Income (%)													
Cost of Operations 10	31.5	•	25.8	21.7	20.2	7.8	57.0	5.8	81.9	50.1	•	•	•
Salaries and Wages 11	12.7	•	9.6	13.4	15.2	15.0	10.0	28.5	2.7	29.3	•	•	•
Taxes Paid 12	2.0	0.4	1.6	1.7	2.2	6.5	2.0	3.0	0.3	3.1	•	•	•
Interest Paid 13	0.6	7.9	0.3	0.3	1.0	1.9	1.1	0.4	0.1	0.2	•	•	•
Depreciation 14	1.9	•	0.8	1.2	2.6	5.2	2.6	7.0	1.9	3.1	•	•	•
Amortization and Depletion 15	0.1	•	0.0	0.0	0.2	0.1	0.0	0.3	•	1.2	•	•	•
Pensions and Other Deferred Comp. 16	0.3	•	0.2	0.4	0.1	0.2	0.4	1.2	•	1.7	•	•	•
Employee Benefits 17	2.1	•	0.4	1.0	1.4	2.2	12.4	2.5	0.6	4.2	•	•	•
Advertising 18	1.0	•	0.3	3.2	0.7	0.3	0.3	2.4	0.0	4.6	•	•	•
Other Expenses 19	67.2	104.8	72.8	62.0	70.7	87.3	23.6	62.5	14.5	127.3	•	•	•
Officers' Compensation 20	1.6	•	2.8	2.0	0.5	0.1	0.9	1.2	0.1	1.4	•	•	•
Operating Margin 21	•	•	•	•	•	•	•	•	•	•	•	•	•
Operating Margin Before Officers' Comp. 22	•	•	•	•	•	•	•	•	•	•	•	•	•

Selected Average Balance Sheet ($ in Thousands)

Net Receivables 23	22	0	4	42	128	305	1867	1250	28638	35666
Inventories 24	1	0	0	2	7	78	237	229	712	1868
Net Property, Plant and Equipment 25	74	0	7	64	710	3494	9013	27554	27554	39849
Total Assets 26	285	0	92	676	2030	7503	15566	35782	75967	240645
Notes and Loans Payable 27	29	0	5	121	214	997	2323	1522	21010	6921
All Other Liabilities 28	75	0	17	183	387	1157	3372	9004	24462	173059
Net Worth 29	181	0	70	372	1429	5349	9872	25256	30495	60665

Selected Financial Ratios (Times to 1)

Current Ratio 30	2.4	•	5.4	1.9	3.1	1.9	1.7	1.2	1.3	0.9
Quick Ratio 31	2.2	•	5.1	1.8	2.8	1.4	1.4	0.8	1.2	0.6
Net Sales to Working Capital 32	2.5	•	1.7	2.0	1.9	3.2	7.4	16.9	20.0	•
Coverage Ratio 33	4.2	•	9.2	24.6	2.2	1.1	1.5	0.4	3.6	12.1
Total Asset Turnover 34	0.9	•	1.3	0.8	0.7	0.5	1.0	0.5	2.3	0.6
Inventory Turnover 35	57.4	•	318.3	59.8	40.6	3.6	36.4	4.7	201.1	38.0
Receivables Turnover 36	11.8	•	30.1	15.2	10.8	10.1	10.0	6.1	5.7	4.5
Total Liabilities to Net Worth 37	0.6	•	0.3	0.8	0.4	0.4	0.6	0.4	1.5	3.0
Current Assets to Working Capital 38	1.7	•	1.2	2.1	1.5	2.1	2.4	7.3	4.3	•
Current Liabilities to Working Capital 39	0.7	•	0.2	1.1	0.5	1.1	1.4	6.3	3.3	•
Working Capital to Net Sales 40	0.4	•	0.6	0.5	0.5	0.3	0.1	0.1	0.0	•
Inventory to Working Capital 41	0.0	•	0.0	0.0	0.0	0.1	0.1	0.2	0.0	•
Total Receipts to Cash Flow 42	1.7	2.1	1.7	1.7	1.7	1.3	4.7	1.8	7.4	0.8
Cost of Goods to Cash Flow 43	0.6	•	0.5	0.4	0.3	0.1	2.7	0.1	6.0	0.4
Cash Flow to Total Debt 44	1.4	•	3.0	1.0	1.3	1.3	0.6	1.0	0.5	1.0

Selected Financial Factors (in Percentages)

Debt Ratio 45	36.6	•	23.9	45.0	29.6	28.7	36.6	29.4	59.9	74.8
Return on Total Assets 46	2.3	•	3.2	4.7	1.5	1.0	1.5	0.1	0.7	1.6
Return on Equity Before Income Taxes 47	2.7	•	3.7	8.2	1.2	0.1	0.7	•	1.2	5.8
Return on Equity After Income Taxes 48	2.1	•	2.9	7.7	0.8	0.1	0.2	•	0.8	3.5
Profit Margin (Before Income Tax) 49	1.9	•	2.2	5.9	1.3	0.2	0.5	•	0.2	2.5
Profit Margin (After Income Tax) 50	1.5	•	1.8	5.5	0.8	0.1	0.1	•	0.1	1.5

Table II
Corporations with Net Income

RELIGIOUS, GRANTMAKING, CIVIC AND PROFESSIONAL ORGANIZATIONS

MONEY AMOUNTS AND SIZE OF ASSETS IN THOUSANDS OF DOLLARS

Item Description for Accounting Period 7/02 Through 6/03	Total	Zero Assets	Under 500	500 to 1,000	1,000 to 5,000	5,000 to 10,000	10,000 to 25,000	25,000 to 50,000	50,000 to 100,000	100,000 to 250,000	250,000 to 500,000	500,000 to 2,500,000	2,500,000 and over
Number of Enterprises 1	22828	1736	18124	1735	1143	0	27	4	0	0	0	0	0
Revenues ($ in Thousands)													
Net Sales 2	6548299	57176	2647217	1024755	1358785	0	461587	134599	0	0	0	0	0
Interest 3	117525	1624	42946	22249	35489	0	7260	702	0	0	0	0	0
Rents 4	12105	0	4034	4503	2232	0	269	77	0	0	0	0	0
Royalties 5	0	0	0	0	0	0	0	0	0	0	0	0	0
Other Portfolio Income 6	28566	0	19312	0	6247	0	1179	1093	0	0	0	0	0
Other Receipts 7	707603	348	416534	59507	162495	0	34882	2753	0	0	0	0	0
Total Receipts 8	7414098	59148	3130043	1111014	1565248	0	505177	139224	0	0	0	0	0
Average Total Receipts 9	325	34	173	640	1369	•	18710	34806	•	•	•	•	•
Operating Costs/Operating Income (%)													
Cost of Operations 10	27.9	•	33.4	22.9	21.9	•	47.8	1.0	•	•	•	•	•
Salaries and Wages 11	12.7	•	9.2	9.7	18.6	•	9.0	20.4	•	•	•	•	•
Taxes Paid 12	1.9	0.4	1.4	1.1	2.4	•	1.7	2.6	•	•	•	•	•
Interest Paid 13	0.4	•	0.1	0.3	0.8	•	0.5	0.1	•	•	•	•	•
Depreciation 14	1.6	•	0.6	1.2	2.5	•	1.9	2.7	•	•	•	•	•
Amortization and Depletion 15	0.1	•	0.0	•	0.1	•	0.0	0.4	•	•	•	•	•
Pensions and Other Deferred Comp. 16	0.3	•	0.2	0.4	0.1	•	0.6	1.7	•	•	•	•	•
Employee Benefits 17	2.5	•	0.5	0.5	1.7	•	22.1	1.8	•	•	•	•	•
Advertising 18	1.1	•	0.3	3.3	0.4	•	0.3	3.0	•	•	•	•	•
Other Expenses 19	57.8	98.5	64.3	60.0	61.5	•	21.9	62.0	•	•	•	•	•
Officers' Compensation 20	2.3	•	3.8	2.1	0.7	•	0.9	1.5	•	•	•	•	•
Operating Margin 21	•	1.1	•	•	•	•	•	2.9	•	•	•	•	•
Operating Margin Before Officers' Comp. 22	•	1.1	0.5	•	•	•	•	4.4	•	•	•	•	•

Selected Average Balance Sheet ($ in Thousands)

Net Receivables 23	19	0	3	31	111	·	2736	2020
Inventories 24	1	0	0	2	4	·	385	793
Net Property, Plant and Equipment 25	70	0	5	77	665	·	8263	11024
Total Assets 26	308	0	112	665	2015	·	16889	33406
Notes and Loans Payable 27	18	0	3	22	129	·	1015	404
All Other Liabilities 28	68	0	18	174	348	·	4428	16431
Net Worth 29	222	0	92	470	1538	·	11446	16571

Selected Financial Ratios (Times to 1)

Current Ratio 30	3.7	·	7.9	3.0	3.8	·	1.8	1.1
Quick Ratio 31	3.4	·	7.5	2.8	3.3	·	1.6	0.8
Net Sales to Working Capital 32	1.9	·	1.6	1.6	1.5	·	5.2	30.3
Coverage Ratio 33	12.4	·	49.4	27.1	6.1	·	6.3	100.5
Total Asset Turnover 34	0.9	·	1.3	0.9	0.6	·	1.0	1.0
Inventory Turnover 35	56.2	·	·	87.2	74.0	·	21.2	0.4
Receivables Turnover 36	15.4	·	98.0	26.7	11.6	·	7.1	4.5
Total Liabilities to Net Worth 37	0.4	·	0.2	0.4	0.3	·	0.5	1.0
Current Assets to Working Capital 38	1.4	·	1.1	1.5	1.4	·	2.2	12.6
Current Liabilities to Working Capital 39	0.4	·	0.1	0.5	0.4	·	1.2	11.6
Working Capital to Net Sales 40	0.5	·	0.6	0.6	0.7	·	0.2	0.0
Inventory to Working Capital 41	0.0	·	·	0.0	0.0	·	0.0	0.1
Total Receipts to Cash Flow 42	2.0	1.8	2.0	1.7	2.0	·	4.7	1.6
Cost of Goods to Cash Flow 43	0.6	·	0.7	0.4	0.4	·	2.3	0.0
Cash Flow to Total Debt 44	1.7	·	3.6	1.8	1.3	·	0.7	1.3

Selected Financial Factors (in Percentages)

Debt Ratio 45	27.8	·	18.5	29.3	23.7	·	32.2	50.4
Return on Total Assets 46	4.5	·	5.6	6.3	3.1	·	3.0	5.8
Return on Equity Before Income Taxes 47	5.8	·	6.8	8.6	3.4	·	3.7	11.6
Return on Equity After Income Taxes 48	4.9	·	5.7	8.1	2.8	·	2.7	7.7
Profit Margin (Before Income Tax) 49	4.5	4.6	4.3	6.8	4.3	·	2.5	5.7
Profit Margin (After Income Tax) 50	3.8	3.9	3.6	6.4	3.6	·	1.8	3.8

Index

Index